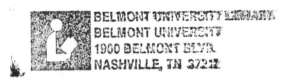

International Directory of
COMPANY HISTORIES

International Directory of COMPANY HISTORIES

VOLUME 61

Editor

Jay P. Pederson

ST. JAMES PRESS®

THOMSON GALE™

Detroit • New York • San Diego • San Francisco • Cleveland • New Haven, Conn. • Waterville, Maine • London • Munich

THOMSON
GALE

International Directory of Company Histories, Volume 61

Jay P. Pederson, Editor

Project Editor
Miranda H. Ferrara

Editorial
Erin Bealmear, Joann Cerrito, Jim Craddock, Stephen Cusack, Peter M. Gareffa, Kristin Hart, Melissa Hill, Margaret Mazurkiewicz, Carol A. Schwartz, Michael J. Tyrkus

Imaging and Multimedia
Randy Bassett, Lezlie Light

Manufacturing
Rhonda Williams

For more information contact
St. James Press
27500 Drake Rd.
Farmington Hills, MI 48331-3535
Or you can visit our Internet site at http://www.gale.com/stjames

LIBRARY OF CONGRESS CATALOG NUMBER 89-190943

ISBN: 1-55862-506-2

BRITISH LIBRARY CATALOGUING IN PUBLICATION DATA

International directory of company histories. Vol. 61
I. Jay P. Pederson
33.87409

Printed in the United States of America
10 9 8 7 6 5 4 3 2 1

CONTENTS

Company Histories

PREFACE

The St. James Press series *The International Directory of Company Histories (IDCH)* is intended for reference use by students, business people, librarians, historians, economists, investors, job candidates, and others who seek to learn more about the historical development of the world's most important companies. To date, *IDCH* has covered over 6,600 companies in 61 volumes.

Inclusion Criteria

Most companies chosen for inclusion in *IDCH* have achieved a minimum of US$25 million in annual sales and are leading influences in their industries or geographical locations. Companies may be publicly held, private, or nonprofit. State-owned companies that are important in their industries and that may operate much like public or private companies also are included. Wholly owned subsidiaries and divisions are profiled if they meet the requirements for inclusion. Entries on companies that have had major changes since they were last profiled may be selected for updating.

The *IDCH* series highlights 10% private and nonprofit companies, and features updated entries on approximately 45 companies per volume.

Entry Format

Each entry begins with the company's legal name, the address of its headquarters, its telephone, toll-free, and fax numbers, and its web site. A statement of public, private, state, or parent ownership follows. A company with a legal name in both English and the language of its headquarters country is listed by the English name, with the native-language name in parentheses.

The company's founding or earliest incorporation date, the number of employees, and the most recent available sales figures follow. Sales figures are given in local currencies with equivalents in U.S. dollars. For some private companies, sales figures are estimates and indicated by the abbreviation *est.* The entry lists the exchanges on which a company's stock is traded and its ticker symbol, as well as the company's NAIC codes.

Entries generally contain a *Company Perspectives* box which provides a short summary of the company's mission, goals, and ideals, a *Key Dates* box highlighting milestones in the company's history, lists of *Principal Subsidiaries, Principal Divisions, Principal Operating Units, Principal Competitors,* and articles for *Further Reading.*

American spelling is used throughout *IDCH*, and the word ''billion'' is used in its U.S. sense of one thousand million.

Sources

Entries have been compiled from publicly accessible sources both in print and on the Internet such as general and academic periodicals, books, annual reports, and material supplied by the companies themselves.

Cumulative Indexes

IDCH contains three indexes: the **Index to Companies**, which provides an alphabetical index to companies discussed in the text as well as to companies profiled, the **Index to Industries**, which allows researchers to locate companies by their principal industry, and the **Geographic Index**, which lists companies alphabetically by the country of their headquarters. The indexes are cumulative and specific instructions for using them are found immediately preceding each index.

Suggestions Welcome

Comments and suggestions from users of *IDCH* on any aspect of the product as well as suggestions for companies to be included or updated are cordially invited. Please write:

The Editor
International Directory of Company Histories
St. James Press
27500 Drake Rd.
Farmington Hills, Michigan 48331-3535

St. James Press does not endorse any of the companies or products mentioned in this series. Companies appearing in the *International Directory of Company Histories* were selected without reference to their wishes and have in no way endorsed their entries.

ABBREVIATIONS FOR FORMS OF COMPANY INCORPORATION

AB	Aktiebolag (Finland, Sweden)
AB Oy	Aktiebolag Osakeyhtiot (Finland)
A.E.	Anonimos Eteria (Greece)
AG	Aktiengesellschaft (Austria, Germany, Switzerland, Liechtenstein)
A.O.	Anonim Ortaklari/Ortakligi (Turkey)
ApS	Amparteselskab (Denmark)
A.Š.	Anonim Širketi (Turkey)
A/S	Aksjeselskap (Norway); Aktieselskab (Denmark, Sweden)
Ay	Avoinyhtio (Finland)
B.A.	Buttengewone Aansprakeiijkheid (The Netherlands)
Bhd.	Berhad (Malaysia, Brunei)
B.V.	Besloten Vennootschap (Belgium, The Netherlands)
C.A.	Compania Anonima (Ecuador, Venezuela)
C. de R.L.	Compania de Responsabilidad Limitada (Spain)
Co.	Company
Corp.	Corporation
CRL	Companhia a Responsabilidao Limitida (Portugal, Spain)
C.V.	Commanditaire Vennootschap (The Netherlands, Belgium)
G.I.E.	Groupement d'Interet Economique (France)
GmbH	Gesellschaft mit beschraenkter Haftung (Austria, Germany, Switzerland)
Inc.	Incorporated (United States, Canada)
I/S	Interessentselskab (Denmark); Interesentselskap (Norway)
KG/KGaA	Kommanditgesellschaft/Kommanditgesellschaft auf Aktien (Austria, Germany, Switzerland)
KK	Kabushiki Kaisha (Japan)
K/S	Kommanditselskab (Denmark); Kommandittselskap (Norway)
Lda.	Limitada (Spain)
L.L.C.	Limited Liability Company (United States)
Ltd.	Limited (Various)
Ltda.	Limitada (Brazil, Portugal)
Ltee.	Limitee (Canada, France)
mbH	mit beschraenkter Haftung (Austria, Germany)
N.V.	Naamloze Vennootschap (Belgium, The Netherlands)
OAO	Otkrytoe Aktsionernoe Obshchestve (Russia)
OOO	Obschestvo s Ogranichennoi Otvetstvennostiu (Russia)
Oy	Osakeyhtiö (Finland)
PLC	Public Limited Co. (United Kingdom, Ireland)
Pty.	Proprietary (Australia, South Africa, United Kingdom)
S.A.	Société Anonyme (Belgium, France, Greece, Luxembourg, Switzerland, Arab speaking countries); Sociedad Anónima (Latin America [except Brazil], Spain, Mexico); Sociedades Anônimas (Brazil, Portugal)
SAA	Societe Anonyme Arabienne
S.A.R.L.	Sociedade Anonima de Responsabilidade Limitada (Brazil, Portugal); Société à Responsabilité Limitée (France, Belgium, Luxembourg)
S.A.S.	Societá in Accomandita Semplice (Italy); Societe Anonyme Syrienne (Arab speaking countries)
Sdn. Bhd.	Sendirian Berhad (Malaysia)
S.p.A.	Società per Azioni (Italy)
Sp. z.o.o.	Spólka z ograniczona odpowiedzialnoscia (Poland)
S.R.L.	Società a Responsabilità Limitata (Italy); Sociedad de Responsabilidad Limitada (Spain, Mexico, Latin America [except Brazil])
S.R.O.	Spolecnost s Rucenim Omezenym (Czechoslovakia
Ste.	Societe (France, Belgium, Luxembourg, Switzerland)
VAG	Verein der Arbeitgeber (Austria, Germany)
YK	Yugen Kaisha (Japan)
ZAO	Zakrytoe Aktsionernoe Obshchestve (Russia)

ABBREVIATIONS FOR CURRENCY

$	United States dollar	KD	Kuwaiti dinar
£	United Kingdom pound	L	Italian lira
¥	Japanese yen	LuxFr	Luxembourgian franc
A$	Australian dollar	M$	Malaysian ringgit
AED	United Arab Emirates dirham	N	Nigerian naira
B	Thai baht	Nfl	Netherlands florin
B	Venezuelan bolivar	NIS	Israeli new shekel
BD	Bahraini dinar	NKr	Norwegian krone
BFr	Belgian franc	NT$	Taiwanese dollar
C$	Canadian dollar	NZ$	New Zealand dollar
CHF	Switzerland franc	P	Philippine peso
COL	Colombian peso	PLN	Polish zloty
Cr	Brazilian cruzado	PkR	Pakistan Rupee
CZK	Czech Republic koruny	Pta	Spanish peseta
DA	Algerian dinar	R	Brazilian real
Dfl	Netherlands florin	R	South African rand
DKr	Danish krone	RMB	Chinese renminbi
DM	German mark	RO	Omani rial
E£	Egyptian pound	Rp	Indonesian rupiah
Esc	Portuguese escudo	Rs	Indian rupee
EUR	Euro dollars	Ru	Russian ruble
FFr	French franc	S$	Singapore dollar
Fmk	Finnish markka	Sch	Austrian schilling
GRD	Greek drachma	SFr	Swiss franc
HK$	Hong Kong dollar	SKr	Swedish krona
HUF	Hungarian forint	SRls	Saudi Arabian riyal
IR£	Irish pound	TD	Tunisian dinar
ISK	Icelandic króna	TRL	Turkish lira
J$	Jamaican dollar	VND	Vietnamese dong
K	Zambian kwacha	W	Korean won

International Directory of

COMPANY HISTORIES

Aardman Animations Ltd.

Gasferry Rd.
Bristol BS1 6UN
United Kingdom
Telephone: +44-1179-848-485
Web site: http://www.aardman.co.uk

Private Company
Founded: 1976
NAIC: 512110 Motion Picture and Video Production; 512191 Teleproduction and Other Postproduction Services

Aardman Animations Ltd. is among the world's most celebrated film and video animation studios. Aardman has achieved widespread recognition for its stop-motion animation techniques—filming three-dimensional objects frame-by-frame—and especially its series of Wallace and Gromit short films, including the Oscar award-winning *The Wrong Trousers* and *A Close Shave.* Led by cofounders Peter Lord and David Sproxton, Aardman has branched out into feature films, including the 2001 success, *Chicken Run,* through a $150 million, four-film production agreement with DreamWorks. That agreement also includes the first full-length Wallace and Gromit film, expected to be released in 2005. Yet a primary source of the private company's revenues has long been its groundbreaking production for the advertising industry. Aardman is also a noted animator for the music video industry, particularly through its work for the 1980s hits ''Sledgehammer'' by Peter Gabriel and ''My Baby Just Cares For Me,'' by Nina Simone. The company continues to produce for the British television industry, as well as for other television markets, including the *Crackling Contraptions* series aired on BBC One in 2002 and streamed on the Internet, through AtomFilms, in 2003.

Kitchen Table Animators in the 1970s

Peter Lord and David Sproxton met in school in Woking, England, in the late 1960s and began making short animated films using Sproxton's father's 16mm camera. The pair were initially influenced by the animation techniques of Terry Gilliam for the acclaimed BBC series *Monty Python's Flying Circus.* Yet the clay-based animation techniques pioneered by the legendary Ray Harryhausen—whose work was featured in such film classics as *The Golden Voyage of Sinbad, One Million Years B.C.,* and *Jason and the Argonauts*—provided the strongest influence on Lord and Sproxton's own developing style.

Lord and Sproxton initially worked on the Lord family's kitchen table, using Lord's drawings and cutouts from magazines to produce their first film, titled *Trash,* after the Andy Warhol film of the same era. Sproxton's father then showed the film to an acquaintance, a producer at the BBC, who asked to see more of the boys' work. As Sproxton told the *Independent:* ''He said to us: 'Here's a roll of film, if we like what you do, we'll buy a sequence off you.' ''

Sproxton and Lord set to work developing the new film, and in 1972 created an ''idiotic superman'' called Aardman (supposedly an Afrikaans word meaning ''earth pig''). That film was subsequently purchased by the BBC and broadcast as part of a series of animated films. Sproxton and Lord then went off to university, with Sproxton studying geography in Durham, and Lord studying English in York. The pair met up again during the summers and continued making animated films.

Adopting the ''company'' name Aardman Animations, Lord and Sproxton began producing short films for *Vision On,* a television program for deaf children produced at the BBC Bristol station. It was during this time that Aardman began specializing in working with plasticine clay, in part because that medium had been largely ignored in English animation circles. The success of this early work led to a request from the station for a new animated character to act as a foil for the program.

In response, Lord and Sproxton created Morph in 1976, a small humanlike figure that, as its name suggested, could adopt a variety of forms—or none at all. The pair moved to Bristol to be closer to the BBC studios, officially launching Aardman Animations. The success of the Morph character led to the commissioning of a larger series of 26 five-minute episodes that aired between 1981 and 1983.

While Morph helped establish the Aardman name among the United Kingdom's top children's animators, Lord and Sproxton sought to attract a wider, and especially, adult audience. In

Key Dates:

1972: David Sproxton and Peter Lord complete their first film, *Aardman,* for BBC Bristol.
1976: Founding Aardman Animation, Sproxton and Lord create new character, Morph, for BBC's *Vision On.*
1978: Aardman receives commission for two Animated Conversation short films from BBC.
1982: Animated Conversation concept is developed into series of five "Conversation Pieces" for Channel Four.
1985: Nick Park joins Aardman.
1986: Aardman receives international acclaim for Peter Gabriel's "Sledgehammer" video.
1989: *A Grand Day Out,* the first film featuring Wallace and Gromit, directed by Nick Park, is released.
1993: The second Wallace and Gromit film, the Oscar-winning *The Wrong Trousers,* is released.
1995: Wallace and Gromit's third film, *A Close Shave,* also earns an Oscar.
1999: Aardman and DreamWorks sign 12-year, four-film deal for $150 million.
2000: The first Aardman feature film, *Chicken Run,* is released to critical and popular success.
2003: Filming begins on first full-length Wallace and Gromit film, with a proposed release date of summer 2005.

1978, the company received a new commission, again from BBC Bristol, for two short films to be aired in the late night segment. For that project, Aardman launched its Animated Conversations concept.

For these films, Aardman used recordings of actual conversations, and then created clay-based animated films to "act out" the dialogue—a radical departure from the standard animated films of the day. The company completed the two films, *Down and Out* and *Confessions of a Foyer Girl,* yet the films were ultimately rejected by the BBC. Instead, they came to the attention of Jeremy Isaacs, then in the process of launching the United Kingdom's first independent television station, Channel 4. The new station liked what it saw and Aardman received a new commission, now for a series of five "Conversation Pieces," which aired between 1982 and 1983.

Aardman's work for Channel 4 brought the company to the attention of a new and unexpected market: England's advertising community. As Lord told *Campaign:* "We never intended to get into advertising. I mean, if we had, I don't suppose we'd have ever set up the studio in Bristol for a start." Nonetheless, the Aardman group quickly learned to appreciate the income, as well as the technical challenges, brought by advertising campaigns for Enterprise Computers, in 1984, and for Scotch Videotape, Lurpak Butter, Domestos bleach, Perrier, and many others through the mid-1980s. With a new source of revenue, the company began investing in upgraded equipment and studios.

Joining Aardman at this time was a young animation student, Nick Park, who had been working on completing his thesis film, *A Grand Day Out,* featuring the man-and-dog team Wallace and Gromit. Park had been working with animation since childhood, and at the age of 13 had already seen his first film aired on the BBC. Impressed by Park's talent, and particularly his attention to sound (Park had spent most of the budget for his film in hiring a 22-piece brass band to perform the theme music), Lord and Sproxton brought Park in to help on their growing list of projects. In return, they agreed to help Park finish his own film.

The Right Trousers for the 1990s

With Park and a growing number of other animators on board, Aardman began accepting new and more diversified commissions. The growing market for music videos offered a natural outlet for the company's technical prowess. In 1986 the company broke new ground with its work on Peter Gabriel's "Sledgehammer" video. That effort was followed by a number of others, including Nina Simone's 1987 music video for "My Baby Just Cares for Me."

By 1989, Park and Aardman had completed *A Grand Day Out,* which went on to receive an Oscar nomination that year. Aardman had also begun work on a new project, the "Lip Synch" series of short subjects, featuring films from each of the group's animators. That series, completed in 1990, gave Aardman its first Oscar, for *Creature Comforts,* directed by Nick Park. The success of that film also inspired a number of television commercials, both in the United Kingdom and in the United States.

In the meantime, Aardman had begun work on a new Wallace and Gromit film. Competed in 1993, *The Wrong Trousers* earned Aardman a new Oscar—and international acclaim. The strong appeal of the Wallace and Gromit characters also spawned a new and steady source of product licensing revenues for the group.

If Wallace and Gromit became Aardman's signature characters, and Nick Park, the company's public face, during the 1990s, Aardman's growing staff of animators continued to produce a wide variety of films, including *Ident,* by Richard Goleszowski, produced in 1991 and launching a new character, Rex the Runt. Other films of the 1990s included Peter Lord's Academy Award-nominated *Adam* (1991) and *Wat's Pig* (1996); *Knobs in Space* (1994), by David Riddett and Luis Cook, as well as that duo's *Sam Fell's Pop* (1996); and *Stage-fright* (1997) by Steve Box.

In the meantime, Aardman went to work on the next Wallace and Gromit film, *A Close Shave.* Completed in 1995, the new film once again met with international acclaim, and earned the company a new Oscar. The success of Wallace and Gromit went beyond mere financial rewards. As Lord explained to *Billboard,* "It's proven to appeal to every audience. And that makes British people feel good about our own culture and says that we don't have to pretend to be something we're not to succeed in Europe or America."

Wallace and Gromit's success also encouraged the company to attempt a still riskier transition, from short subjects into full-length feature films. The company likened this decision to that of Walt Disney before them, who had met skepticism when he began work on his own first full-length film, *Snow White and the Seven Dwarfs.* Aardman began development of its first film in 1997, working with producer Jake Eberts, who had previously worked on *Dances with Wolves* and the animated film *James and the Giant Peach.*

Eberts then brought Aardman into contact with DreamWorks, and former Disney chief Jeffrey Katzenberg. The DreamWorks partnership quickly solidified into an agreement that promised Aardman $150 million in a four-film, 12-year contract signed near the end of 1999.

Big Plans for the Future

Aardman released its first feature film, *Chicken Run,* to critical and box office acclaim in 2000. Featuring a cast of chickens attempting to escape from a POW camp-styled chicken farm, the success of the film also proved that Aardman's appeal extended beyond Wallace and Gromit characters. The company's next project reached a snag in 2002, however, due to problems with the screenplay. That film, based on the ''Tortoise and the Hare'' fable, was put on hold indefinitely.

Nonetheless, Aardman continued to push ahead on a number of other fronts, including the development of a new *Creature Comforts* series. At the same time, the company began preproduction of the next Wallace and Gromit film, the first full-length film to feature the popular characters. Although that film was not slated for release until mid-2005, the company moved to slake its fans' thirsts at the end of 2002, with the release of *Cracking Contraptions.*

The first installment of the new series of ten short films aired on BBC One in October 2002, followed several hours later by a release on the Internet, through AtomFilms. By the beginning of 2003, the full series of *Cracking Contraptions*—each featuring one of Wallace's rather unusual inventions—was available for downloading and streaming through the paid AtomFilms service.

Aardman remained buoyant as filming began on the new and eagerly anticipated Wallace and Gromit feature in August 2003. At the same time, the company remained focused on the future, as Peter Lord started development of the next feature film to be produced within the DreamWorks agreement, *Flushed Away,* a story of two rats expected to begin shooting in 2005. Aardman Animations had molded a reputation as one of the world's top animation houses.

Principal Competitors

Warner Communications Inc.; Mediaset SpA; DreamWorks SKG; Carlton Communications PLC; Lucasfilm Ltd.; Pathe SAS; Maxell Europe Ltd.; Vox Film- und Fernseh-GmbH und Co. KG; Industrial Light and Magic Div.

Further Reading

''Aardman Gears up for PG Tips, Comforts and a Vegetable Plot,'' *Televisual*, February 2002, p. 7.

Corliss, Richard, ''Grin and Bear It,'' *Time International*, July 10, 2000, p. 52.

Dawtrey, Adam, ''Aardman Rolls 'Wallace and Gromit,' '' *Variety*, August 4, 2003, p. 9.

Fitzpatrick, Eileen, ''Animators Take Low-Tech Style Sky-High,'' *Billboard*, April 12, 1997, p. 51.

Gwyther, Matthew, ''Tinseltown Comes to Bristol,'' *Management Today,* May 2000, p. 73.

Lord, Peter, ''My 30 Years in Advertising,'' *Campaign*, September 18, 1998, p. S2.

Lord, Peter, and Brian Sibley, *Cracking Animation—The Aardman Book of Filmmaking*, London: Thames and Hudson, 1998.

Sproxton, David, and Peter Lord, ''Me and My Partner,'' *Independent*, December 6, 2000, p. 8.

''Wallace & Gromit Alive on the Web,'' *San Francisco Post*, January 2003, p. 8.

—M.L. Cohen

Adam Opel AG

Adam Opel Haus
D-65423 Rüsselsheim
Germany
Telephone: 49-6142-660
Fax: 49-6142-664-859
Web site: http://www.opel.com

Wholly Owned Subsidiary of General Motors Corporation
Incorporated: 1862
Employees: 34,103
Sales: EUR 14.88 billion ($15.97 billion) (2002)
NAIC: 336111 Automobile Manufacturing

Adam Opel AG ranks among Germany's largest automobile manufacturers, producing passenger cars, sport utility vehicles, and commercial vehicles at more than a dozen plants in Germany, Belgium, Hungary, Poland, Portugal, Spain, and other non-European countries. Wholly owned and operated by the American automotive giant General Motors Corporation, Opel was founded in the mid-19th century to make sewing machines. The company turned to the manufacture of automobiles in the earliest days of the industry, producing popular cars that were available to the common man. Opel survived the devastation of two world wars to prosper during the auto boom of the 1950s through 1970s, only to experience difficulties later as the market moved toward smaller, more economical cars. Rejuvenated in the early 1990s via factory upgrades and fresh new car designs, Opel became ''the centerpiece of General Motors' international strategy.'' But the internationalization of the Opel brand soon backfired as Opel lost ground in its base market of Europe because of a model lineup ill-suited to that market, and the company was hurt further by strained relations between the firm's German managers and employees and their bosses in the United States and by a deterioration in quality because of cost-cutting.

Mid-19th-Century Origins

The company was founded in 1862 by Adam Opel in Rüsselsheim-am-Main, Germany (which is near Mainz). Against the wishes of his father, a locksmith, the 25-year-old Opel formulated a plan to manufacture sewing machines. After working in Paris to learn his trade as a journeyman, he returned home to open a workshop in his uncle's cow stables. His first handcrafted machines sold quickly, and Opel's fledgling business flourished. By 1868 it had grown prosperous enough for him to build a new two-story sewing machine factory near the Rüsselsheim railroad station.

With the success of his business, Opel was able to turn his attention to starting a family, and he and his wife Sophie had five boys. As they grew, Opel's sons developed an avid interest in bicycling, and Opel purchased five of the machines for his family, over the objections of his wife. Observing his son's bicycles, Opel realized that the high, three-wheeled mechanisms could provide a new mode of transportation, as well as an additional source of revenue for his factory. The first bicycle left the Opel works in 1866 and before long the Opel factory was turning out 16,000 bicycles a year. The popularity of the Opel bike was enhanced by the fame of the five Opel sons, who won hundreds of bike races across Europe.

Second Generation Leading Firm into Auto Industry

Adam Opel died in 1895 as a consequence of typhoid infection, bringing to an end the first era of the Opel firm. Inheriting the business, his five sons looked to modernize, turning to new products in order to maintain the company's competitive edge. The men set their sights on the automobile, one of the latest products to be developed.

To obtain the expertise needed to convert their production line from bicycles to cars, the brothers hired Friedrich Lutzmann, a famous inventor and master metalworker previously employed by the court of Dessau, in 1894. Five years later, Lutzmann produced the first Opel automobile, a coach-like vehicle with a one-cylinder rear engine and a maximum speed of 20 kilometers per hour.

By the turn of the century, the Opel factory was producing six different auto bodies, all of which were labeled with ''Opel Patented Lutzmann Motor Wagon System.'' Lutzmann left the Opel firm in 1901, joining forces with the pioneering French

Company Perspectives:

Since its inception in 1862, Opel has set out to make technology affordable and widely available to a large segment of society. This vision has remained constant from its roots as a sewing machine manufacturer, its subsequent expansion to bicycles and today remains at the heart of all automotive product development.

Opel has a strong brand profile which rests on these four cornerstones: Versatility and interior flexibility; Driving dynamics; Contemporary, distinctive design; Modern infotainment system.

automobile firm, Darracq, and Opel and Darracq entered into cooperation. The French firm supplied engines, which were shipped to the Opel works in Rüsselsheim, while Opel manufactured auto bodies, combining them with the French parts for sale under the name Opel-Darracq.

The first car built entirely by the Opel brothers went on the market in 1902. The compact Tonneau had a two-cylinder engine that was upgraded to four cylinders within a year. During this time, Opel cars were winning races in Germany, France, Belgium, and the United States, bringing fame to the company name.

Because each car produced by the Opel factory at this time was extremely expensive, it was available to only a small segment of the population: in 1906 the company's top-of-the-line luxury touring vehicle was priced at DM 22,000. In an effort to broaden their customer base, the brothers decided to build a less expensive form of transportation. Soon motorized two-wheel bicycles were rolling out of the Opel factory. A line of more affordable cars was also introduced in 1908. Half the size of a larger four-seater, the 10/18 PS cost just DM 8,500. The following year, the company introduced what would become its famous "Doctor's Car." With a four-cylinder, eight horsepower engine, the car cost just DM 3,950. In addition to an autobody crafted by hand, the car featured standardized tire rims, which, for the first time, made it possible to change a punctured tire easily. Purchased by many lawyers and country doctors, the car was rugged enough to withstand poor rural roads, and the Opel factory received many letters of appreciation from satisfied new automobile owners.

The company continued to upgrade its product, introducing new, more aerodynamic, torpedo-shaped auto bodies. At the factory, division of labor was introduced as engines and auto bodies were mixed and matched according to size, and parts were standardized and made interchangeable. In 1911 the Opel brothers broadened the company's offerings further when they began to manufacture four-cylinder engines for airplanes as well as a four-cylinder, motorized agricultural plow.

In August 1911, the Opel factory was consumed by flames. In the wake of the fire, which struck in particular the portion of the plant where sewing machines were still being assembled from individual parts, the Opel company exited the sewing machine business, having produced more than a million of these devices. A newly rebuilt factory was completed in time for the company's 50th anniversary in 1912.

To commemorate its half century in business, Opel introduced a new flagship automobile, to succeed the Doctor's Car. With a four-cylinder engine, this car garnered even wider popularity, and was followed two years later by a new model that was given the nickname "*Puppchen,*" or little doll. With more than 3,000 cars manufactured in one year, Opel became the largest automaker in Germany.

World War I and Its Aftermath

Germany entered World War I in August 1914, and Opel's production was converted to provide material for the armed forces. The company manufactured trucks for the war effort, producing in particular a three-ton truck. For the first time, many parts were standardized, allowing them to be taken from one truck and used to fix another. Because 2,500 Opel men—a large part of the factory's workforce—were conscripted into the army and sent off to war, women and prisoners-of-war were used to operate the plant. As the war progressed, Opel experienced extreme shortages of resources, including rubber, and by 1915 the factory was turning out trucks with iron wheels.

The war affected the Opel family in ways that extended beyond the business. The youngest of the Opel brothers died in battle. In 1917 the surviving brothers were made knights, and the following year, the family was given the right to add the noble prefix "von" to their names.

In the wake of Germany's defeat, the Opel factory was occupied by French troops in December 1918, who surveyed production closely, controlling the plant's output. The country's strained economic circumstances increased demand for cheap transportation, and Opel began to build and sell more bikes and motorcycles. In 1919 the company began to market a bike with an accessory motor, which attached to its side. Production of automobiles resumed that year, though at a slowed pace given the low demand.

In the early 1920s Germany suffered hyperinflation, which quickly consumed the capital of the middle class. Under these conditions, Opel's cheapest car in 1922 sold for DM 225,000, an astronomical sum out of the reach of almost all consumers. In 1923 Opel was compelled to print its own emergency money with which to pay its worker's salaries, and finally, in August, the plant was forced to close.

Facing this crisis, two of the Opel sons traveled to the United States to learn about modernized car manufacturing methods, particularly the assembly line technique perfected by Henry Ford. They returned convinced that this was the key to rapid car manufacturing in the future, instead of the piecework method currently practiced in Germany. A 45-meter-long assembly line was installed in the Opel factory, and in the spring of 1924, the first car rolled off this line. Popularly called the "Tree Frog" because of its standard green color, this sturdy two-seater featured a directly operated transmission.

Opel sold more than 100,000 of the Tree Frogs throughout the 1920s. From 1924 to 1928, the company steadily reduced the prices of its products until the cost of the company's cheapest car had sunk below DM 2,000 at the end of the decade. In addition to possessing 37 percent of the German market, Opel was the country's largest exporter. Also in 1928, the firm be-

Key Dates:

1862: Adam Opel begins making sewing machines in Rüsselsheim, Germany.
1886: Production of bicycles starts at Opel's factory.
1895: The company founder dies, leaving the firm in the hands of his sons.
1899: With the help of newly hired engineer Friedrich Lutzmann, the firm produces the first Opel automobile.
1901: Opel begins jointly producing cars with the French automobile company, Darracq.
1902: The first car built entirely by the Opel brothers goes on the market.
1909: Opel introduces a low-priced car that becomes very popular, known as the "Doctor's Car."
1911: Large fire at the Opel factory leads the company to exit from the sewing machine business.
1914: Following the outbreak of World War I, production shifts to emphasize trucks for the armed forces.
1923: German economic crisis forces the closure of the Opel factory.
1924: After studying the car production methods of Henry Ford, the Opel brothers install an assembly line at the factory, which is reopened and begins producing the popular "Tree Frog" model.
1928: The firm becomes a stock corporation, Adam Opel AG.
1929: General Motors Corporation (GM) purchases 80 percent stake in Adam Opel.
1931: Opel becomes a wholly owned subsidiary of GM.
1937: Production of bicycles ends.
1939: After the beginning of World War II, the Rüsselsheim plant is converted to wartime use.
1945: More than half of Opel's main factory is destroyed by Allied bombing.
1947: Automobile production resumes.
1948: GM reassumes management control of the company.
1962: Second large factory complex opens in Bochum.
1982: Production of the new subcompact car called the Corsa begins at a new factory in Zaragoza, Spain.
1988: The Opel Vectra makes its debut.
1992: State-of-the-art plant opens in Eisenach in the former East Germany.
1998: Redesigned Opel Astra is launched and soon becomes GM's best-selling car in Europe.
2002: Company opens a new plant in Rüsselsheim.

came a stock corporation (a German Aktiengesellschaft), Adam Opel AG.

Acquisition by General Motors: 1929

In March 1929 Opel formalized its contacts with the U.S. automobile industry when General Motors (GM) purchased 80 percent of the company's stock for $26 million. Two years later GM acquired the remaining 20 percent of the company from the Opel family. In 1932 Opel increased its geographic reach when it opened manufacturing facilities in China, Japan, South America, and India.

The company also continued to expand its model lines. In 1931 Opel rolled out a new line of trucks, called Blitz, after a contest was conducted to find a name. Four years later, the company introduced its Olympia model at the Berlin car show. Using techniques developed for airplanes, this car had a detachable autobody, which could be separated from its engine block. Two other models added in the next few years, the Kadett and the Kapitan, designed for use on the newly constructed Autobahn, contained this feature.

In 1935 Opel opened a second factory, in Brandenburg, in eastern Germany. Two years later, the company, having stood for years as the world's largest manufacturer of bicycles, ended production of bikes; Opel had produced 2.6 million bicycles in just over 50 years. With Germany's launch of World War II, and Opel's main plant, in Rüsselsheim, which had produced over one million cars, was converted to wartime use, making cockpit covers and fuselages for fighter planes. During the war, Opel, as did many German factories, made use of slave labor to keep its production lines running. In August 1944, Allied bombers destroyed Opel's Brandenburg factory entirely. A year later the facility on the Main was targeted and more than half of it was destroyed. At war's end, Opel, along with the rest of the country, was in ruins.

By May 1945, Opel workers had begun to clear rubble from the factory, and within a brief period the first machines were running. The company soon learned, however, that its facility at Brandenburg would be demolished, not returned to use. In addition, Opel was compelled to sacrifice its entire Kadett production line to the Soviet Union as part of Germany's war reparations. Consequently, the Soviet model Moskwitsch 400 was a renamed 1947 Opel Kadett.

Because Germany needed trucks for reconstruction, Opel resurrected its old Blitz model, turning it out with the six-cylinder engine previously used for the prewar Kapitan luxury car. In December 1947, the company began automobile production once again. Opel's old partner, General Motors, resumed management of the firm the next year, as German currency reform stabilized the economy and enabled citizens to once again consider the purchase of a car. To take advantage of this new situation, Opel marketed the Kapitan, at a price of DM 10,000.

Return to Prosperity in Postwar Era

Germany's new federal republic prospered in the 1950s, and Opel marketed cars that reflected this new affluence in their design. Opel cars were loaded with chrome, their style heavily influenced by American automobiles. The 1952 Olympia Rekord featured a famous "shark mouth" grille, and the 1957 Rekord had "panorama" windows. Opel also adopted the practice of updating its models every year, as American car makers did, and the company began to export its cars to the United States. In 1956, the two-millionth car rolled off Opel's assembly lines.

In 1962, Opel's 100th anniversary, the company opened a second large factory complex, in Bochum, and also expanded its facilities at its flagship site in Rüsselsheim. In 1966 a testing center in Dudenhofer and a component manufacturing plant in Kaiserslautern were also opened.

Throughout the 1960s Opel continued to expand its model line, adding the Kadett A to compete with compact cars, and revamping older models. In 1970 the company introduced the Ascona and the Manta, both designed with a more sporty look. The Manta quickly gained a place in German popular culture as the workingman's dream car. By the end of 1972 Opel held the largest portion of the German car market with 20.4 percent.

In 1975 West Germany's automobile market entered a boom period, and Opel expanded its production capacity to keep pace with demand, adding 10,000 workers at its Rüsselsheim plant in just four years. The resultant crowding and pressure to produce created tensions between the plant's workers and its GM management.

In 1977 Opel added to its model line with the Senator, designed to appeal to Germany's ever-more-affluent middle class. Two years later the company added its first car with an engine over the front wheels, rather than behind the car. By this time, however, the German auto boom was over, as rising fuel costs made larger models unattractive. Opel's overly optimistic sales estimates caused it to suspend production at its main plant for ten days at the end of the year, in order to ease an oversupply of its larger cars.

In 1979 GM managers announced an ambitious $2.5 billion investment plan to revamp Opel facilities, build new factories in Spain and Austria, and introduce new models in the important compact and subcompact ranges. The company planned to produce a subcompact car called the Corsa at a plant in Zaragoza, Spain, and to start the production of a newly redesigned, aerodynamically sleek Kadett at Opel's Bochum works. These steps were part of an attempt to change Opel's image from that of a traditional, conservatively dependable car to a technologically sophisticated car.

Losses Mounting in 1980s

As Opel's slump continued into the 1980s, the company's financial problems began to foster dissent among its workers, and the company developed a reputation for the worst labor relations in Germany as it laid off 5,000 workers at its Rüsselsheim plant. Employees complained that they had no say in decisions being made about the company in GM's headquarters in Detroit, Michigan, and objected in particular to plans for producing cars in Spain. In the fall of 1980 GM replaced Opel's U.S. head and took steps to streamline the administration of its German subsidiary.

Opel's sales continued to lag in the early 1980s. Far from the days when it was known as GM's ''money machine,'' Opel—and its British affiliate—lost $426.7 million in 1981. By the start of the following year, however, the company's sales had started to pick up, spurred in part by its introduction of new, smaller, fuel-efficient models, such as a revamped Ascona and the Corsa, which began rolling off the new assembly in Spain. Opel's market share in Germany rose to 18.8 percent in 1982, led by sales of the Kadett and the Ascona, which trailed only Volkswagen's Golf.

This progress was stymied in part the next year, however, because of the company's continuing labor difficulties. A 50-day metalworkers' strike in mid-1983 cost Opel 13 percent of its annual production. Despite this setback, the company managed to retain 18.5 percent of the German market, turning a profit of $100 million.

By 1984, however, Opel was back in the red, with production down and losses totaling $227 million. In 1986 the company lost $372.1 million, as lowered prices and rising costs for advertising offset increases in sales. Facing a flat market for automobile sales, Opel managers looked to reduce its labor force further, increase automation, and overhaul inefficient systems. To this end, in 1988, the company announced a plan to cut 5,200 jobs. To further economize, the company began to purchase parts from other automakers, entering into an agreement with Isuzu Motors of Japan, in particular. Also in 1988, the Opel Vectra was introduced as a replacement for the popular Ascona.

Turnaround in the Early 1990s

Louis R. Hughes followed Dr. Horst Herke as chairman of Opel in 1989. Hughes told *Fortune*'s Richard S. Teitelbaum that the reunification of Germany that same year was ''the opportunity of the century.'' Opel moved quickly to take advantage of the changed situation, negotiating the purchase of an automobile plant in the East German town of Eisenach. Hughes set out to transform the Eisenach facility from a run-down plant filled with apathetic workers into a model of productivity, making Opel the former East Germany's market leader in the process. Hughes implemented modern management programs and invested DM 1 billion in automation. Production increased from about 60,000 Wartburgs under the communists to 160,000 Opel Corsas and Vectras by the mid-1990s. In 1995, the *New York Times* noted that ''Eisenach has been rated as the most efficient plant in Europe, with production of 59.3 cars a worker each year.''

Hughes was promoted to executive vice-president of General Motors (Europe) AG that year, later advancing to president of that division as well as president of GM's International Operations. The Opel chairmanship went to David Herman, a 15-year veteran of GM's European and South American operations.

After record-setting profits in 1991 and benchmark sales in 1992, Herman found himself faced with a recession-induced loss of $300 million in 1993, spurring a new phase of restructuring. By the spring of 1995, he had cut Opel's overall workforce by 19 percent, or 11,000 workers. New employee relations programs helped slash absenteeism by 18 percent, while wage and work rule concessions from labor unions helped free capital for multibillion-dollar capital improvements. Opel bounced back to a $198 million profit in 1994.

But the news at Opel was not all good. In the middle of 1995, a kickback scandal involving dozens of employees came to light. The scheme involved suppliers offering cash and gifts to Opel employees and executives in exchange for favorable consideration in contract negotiations. Three managers resigned amidst the investigation in 1995, and another may have committed suicide over the fraud. At the same time, Opel had accused its main German rival, Volkswagen AG, of industrial spying in a case centering on José Ignacio López de Arriortúa. López, famed as a cost-cutter while at GM/Opel, was accused of stealing secret corporate documents from Opel when he was lured away to Volkswagen in 1993. Without admitting guilt, Volkswagen settled with GM in 1997, when the former agreed to pay the latter $100 million cash and to purchase $1 billion in auto parts from General Motors by the year 2004.

In the meantime, Opel continued in its role as the spearhead of GM's international growth, pursuing European expansion and building assembly operations in Asia, South America, and Africa. In 1996 the company added the Cadillac Catera to its European lineup—which then included the Astra compact, the Omega large sedan, Vectra midsized sedan, and the award-winning Corsa subcompact. While not surpassing records set in 1992, sales rose from DM 25.9 billion in 1995 ($18 billion) to DM 28.3 billion ($18.4 billion) in 1996, while net slid from DM 363 million ($252.8 million) to DM 314 million ($203.9 million).

Return to Red Ink, Late 1990s and Early 2000s

Opel ran into serious and widespread problems in the late 1990s. One aspect of GM's global strategy was designing models that could be sold in both the United States and Europe, a strategy that sometimes backfired. For example, a team designing a new minivan for the two markets included only a small number of German engineers from Opel who felt they had little input into the final model design. The resulting Opel Sintra, introduced in 1997, was designed primarily for the U.S. market and was unable to stand up to the tougher crash tests conducted in Europe. German reviews of the car were highly critical of its safety, which contributed to a growing view among European car buyers that Opel models were of poor quality. Slow sales of Sintra forced the discontinuation of the minivan after just two years.

Meanwhile, production snafus delayed the launch of a new version of the Astra for six months, from late 1997 to early 1998. Although the Astra, which was eventually available in several styles, including a coupe and a convertible called the Astra Cabrio, soon became GM's best-selling car in Europe, its launch delay contributed to a net loss for Opel in 1997 of DM 228 million ($139.1 million). Opel posted an even larger loss in 1998, a year in which the company inaugurated a new plant in Gliwice, Poland, where production of Astras began.

The Sintra fiasco and other problems created the grounds for the rising frustration felt among Opel's German executives and engineers. GM further ruffled feathers at its German subsidiary through a series of changes at the top. In mid-1998 Herman, a popular leader, was sent off to Moscow to head up GM operations in Russia and the markets of the former Soviet Union. Replacing him as Opel chairman was Gary Cowger, who had led a turnaround effort at GM de Mexico. Just four months later, however, GM officials decided they needed Cowger in the United States to take over the firm's troubled North American labor relations. Robert Hendry, who was currently completing a turnaround of Saab Automobile AB, GM's Swedish affiliate, was then named to replace Cowger.

The Hendry era started off with high hopes, with Opel attempting to revitalize its brand with the introduction of several new models. During 1999 the company debuted the Zafira, a seven-seat minivan based on the Astra that became a hit with buyers. The following year the new plant in Poland began production of the Agila, a microvan based on the Suzuki Wagon R that was developed through an alliance with Suzuki Motor Corporation, a Japanese automaker affiliated with GM. The Agila was designed specifically for the European market, as was the Speedster, a two-seat roadster that also rolled off the assembly line for the first time in 2000. Unfortunately, Opel was hit hard by a prolonged decline in the German car market, and its domestic sales were even worse than the industry overall, resulting in a decline of the firm's German market share from 13.8 percent to 12.2 percent during 2000. That year, Opel posted an even larger operating loss of DM 982 million ($463 million).

Another key initiative of Hendry's was to replace Opel's aging flagship assembly plant at its home base in Rüsselsheim. Opel in 1999 began building a new state-of-the-art plant immediately adjacent to the old plant. It was conceived of as a ''lean production'' facility that would require 40 percent fewer workers to produce the same number of models annually. The plant opened in early 2002 with yearly production capacity of 270,000 vehicles. Hendry, however, was not on hand for the opening ceremonies. Early in 2001 Hendry resigned, having failed to deliver on his promises to return Opel to profitability by 2000 and to grow the company's domestic market share. Although Hendry had gained from GM a greater measure of independence for Opel, the supervisory board at the German automaker wanted even more freedom, leading to much infighting, some of which became public—further tarnishing the Opel image.

Adam Opel AG's new chairman was Carl-Peter Forster, a former production chief and board member at German luxury carmaker Bayerische Motoren Werke AG and a German who grew up in the United Kingdom. Forster launched a turnaround effort dubbed Project Olympia that emphasized profitability over market share and was expected to cost more than EUR 1 billion (the name was taken from the old Opel model). Opel cut its production capacity by 15 percent without closing any plants and made reductions in the workforce through attrition. To revitalize the brand and overcome the general perception that its models were boring and lacking in quality, plans were made to completely overhaul the product lineup between 2002 and 2006. Coming first off the assembly line in 2002 (at the brand new Rüsselsheim factory) was a redesigned version of the Vectra sedan. This was followed in the spring of 2003 by the Meriva, a small minivan, and the Signum, an upscale five-door hatchback, based on the Vectra, that featured flexible rear seating. Later in 2003 sales of a Vectra station wagon began. One of the key new products, slated to be introduced in 2004, was the latest redesign of the Astra, which ranked as Opel's top-selling car. Opel also planned to introduce the Tigra in 2004, a popular-priced two-passenger roadster that was based on the Corsa subcompact. Although a complete turnaround for Opel was likely to be years away, losses were narrowing and these new models showed early promise.

Principal Subsidiaries

Adam Opel Unterstuetzungskasse GmbH; Autohaus am Nordring GmbH; Carus Grundstucks-Vermietungsgesellschaft mbH & Co. Object Kuno 65 KG; Carus Grundstucks-Vermietungsgesellschaft mbH & Co. Object Leo 40 KG; GM Europe GmbH; GM Locomotive Group India Private Limited; General Motors CIS (Russia); General Motors GmbH & Co. OHG; General Motors Poland Spolka, zo.o.; GMAC Bank GmbH; GMAC Leasing GmbH; OPEL Guangzhou Precision Machining Co. Ltd (China); Opel Hellas, S.A. (Greece); Opel Hungary Consulting Service Limited Liability Company; Opel International GmbH (France); Opel Live GmbH; Opel Performance Center GmbH; Opel Polen GmbH; Opel Restrukturierungsgesellschaft mbH; Opel Southeast Europe Automotive Distribution Limited Liability Company (Hungary); Opel Special Vehicles GmbH; Opel Türkiye Limited Sirketi (Turkey).

Principal Competitors

Volkswagen AG; Ford Motor Company; PSA Peugeot Citroën S.A.; Renault S.A.; DaimlerChrysler AG.

Further Reading

Birch, Stuart, ''MAXX Effort from Opel,'' *Automotive Engineering,* July 1995, pp. 45–47.

Crate, James R. ''Scandal at Opel May Have Led to Suicide,'' *Automotive News,* July 10, 1995, pp. 1–2.

Culp, Eric, ''GM Puts a New Man at the Wheel,'' *European,* May 25, 1998, pp. 22+.

Geddes, John M., ''Ford and G.M. Cut Back at German Subsidiaries,'' *New York Times,* November 23, 1979.

''Getting into Gear,'' *Forbes,* April 10, 1995, p. 116.

Gooding, Kenneth, ''A German Gear Change for General Motors,'' *Financial Times,* November 18, 1980.

Haasen, Adolf, ''Opel Eisenach GmbH—Creating a High-Productivity Workplace,'' *Organizational Dynamics,* March 1, 1996, pp. 80–85.

Kranz, Rick, ''Opel to Replace Lineup by '06,'' *Automotive News,* October 6, 2003, p. 17.

Kurylko, Diana T., ''GM Seeks New Role for Harried Opel Unit,'' *Automotive News,* July 21, 1997, p. 1.

——, ''Hendry Oversees Opel's Rüsselsheim Rebirth,'' *Automotive News,* June 21, 1999, p. 24D.

——, ''Once-Grimy Eisenach Becomes Opel's Jewel,'' *Automotive News,* November 11, 1996, p. 42A.

——, ''Spirit of Daring Lives in Opel's Radical Maxx,'' *Automotive News,* March 25, 1996, p. 31.

Lewandowski, Jürgen, *Opel: Das Unternehmen, die Automobile, die Menschen,* Munich: Südwest Verlag, 1992.

Miller, Karen Lowry, ''GM's German Lessons,'' *Business Week,* December 20, 1993, pp. 67–68.

——, ''Something's Rotten in . . . Germany?'' *Business Week,* August 7, 1995, p. 44.

Miller, Scott, ''Car Wars: Opel Gets Its Act Together As Market Opens Up in Europe,'' *Wall Street Journal Europe,* September 13, 1999, p. 1.

——, ''GM's Opel Veers Off Course,'' *Wall Street Journal Europe,* June 13, 2000, p. 25.

——, ''How Opel Went from Wunderkind to Problem Child,'' *Wall Street Journal Europe,* March 28, 2001, p. 1.

——, ''Opel's Hendry Quits, Dealing Blow to GM,'' *Wall Street Journal Europe,* January 18, 2001, p. 1.

——, ''Opel Steers a New Course with 1 Billion Euro Restructuring,'' *Wall Street Journal Europe,* August 16, 2001, p. 1.

——, ''Opel to Speed Its Restructuring Plan, Slashing 2,500 Jobs Early This Year,'' *Wall Street Journal Europe,* January 17, 2002, p. 4.

Mitchener, Brandon, ''Driving Ambition: GM's Opel Subsidiary Frets Over Pitfalls of Globalization Push,'' *Wall Street Journal Europe,* February 26, 1998, p. 1.

——, ''GM's Opel Plans New Enterprise, More Cost Cuts,'' *Wall Street Journal,* February 7, 1997, p. A9B.

——, ''GM Takes a Gamble on Eastern Europe,'' *Wall Street Journal,* June 23, 1997, p. A10.

Mitchener, Brandon, and Rebecca Blumenstein, ''GM's Adam Opel Ranks Grow Skeptical As Unit Becomes Focus of Globalization,'' *Wall Street Journal,* June 18, 1997, p. A6.

Mullins, Peter J., ''GM Battles Back in Europe,'' *Automotive Industries,* November 1988, pp. 40–41.

Riedel, Manfred, *Friedrich Lutzmann: Ein Pionier des Automobilbaues,* Dessau, Germany: Anhaltische Verlagsgesellschaft, 1999.

Tagliabue, John, ''European Push by G.M., Ford,'' *New York Times,* October 19, 1982.

——, ''G.M.'s Sputtering Opel Unit,'' *New York Times,* June 24, 1986.

Teitelbaum, Richard S., ''GM's Man in New Germany,'' *Fortune,* October 22, 1990, p. 155.

Stationen: 125 Jahre Opel, Rüsselsheim, Germany: Adam Opel AG, 1987.

Welch, David, ''Has GM Pulled Opel Out of Its Skid?,'' *Business Week,* October 28, 2002, p. 52.

——, ''The Sexing-Up of Opel: GM's Dowdy Carmaker Is Doing Some Major Image Work,'' *Business Week,* October 1, 2001, p. 84.

White, Joseph B., ''Driver's Seat: Opel Shake-Up Tests GM Efforts to Unite World-Wide Units,'' *Wall Street Journal Europe,* October 26, 1998, p. 1.

Widman, Miriam, ''GM Thrives in Eastern Germany,'' *Journal of Commerce,* May 28, 1991.

Woodruff, David, ''Can Opel Deliver the ''World Cars' GM Needs?,'' *Business Week,* December 4, 1995, pp. 52–53.

Woodruff, David, and Kathleen Kerwin, ''Can GM Make a U-Turn in Europe?,'' *Business Week,* March 16, 1998, p. 31.

—Elizabeth Rourke
—updates: April Dougal Gasbarre, David E. Salamie

A C S®

Affiliated Computer Services, Inc.

2828 North Haskell
Building 1
Dallas, Texas 75204
U.S.A.
Telephone: (214) 841-6111
Fax: (214) 821-8315
Web site: http://www.acs-inc.com

Public Company
Incorporated: 1988 as Affiliated Computer Systems, Inc.
Employees: 40,000
Sales: $3.78 billion (2003)
Stock Exchanges: New York
Ticker Symbol: ACS
NAIC: 514210 Data Processing Services; 522320 Financial Transaction Processing, Reserve, and Clearinghouse Activities; 561499 All Other Business Support Services

Affiliated Computer Services, Inc. (ACS) has grown since it was founded in 1988 to become a *Fortune* 500 company providing business process outsourcing (BPO) services to commercial and governmental clients. The company has made more than 50 acquisitions and continually reinvents itself as new opportunities arise. ACS began by providing data processing and other services to banks and financial institutions. In the 1990s it operated an ATM network that was second only to that of Electronic Data Systems Corporation (EDS) among non-bank networks. Through acquisitions, ACS has grown from a regional provider based in Dallas to a national player in the outsourcing services field. After establishing itself as a major provider to federal, state, and local governments, ACS announced in August 2003 that it would sell its government solutions business to Lockheed Martin Corporation to focus on providing BPO services to commercial clients.

Providing Data Processing Services to Financial Institutions: 1988–90

Affiliated Computer Services, Inc. (ACS) was founded in Dallas, Texas, in 1988 by Darwin Deason and Charles M. Young. Deason became the company's chairman and CEO, while Young served as president and COO. ACS was originally called Affiliated Computer Systems, Inc., and began business as a financial data processing company. Deason and Young were both former executives of MTech Corporation, a bank technology outsourcing company. When MTech was put up for sale in 1988, Deason and other executives put in a bid of $245 million for a management buyout, only to lose to EDS's bid of $345 million. After Deason left MTech, he decided to build another financial data processing firm that would compete with EDS, and he took a substantial part of MTech's executive team with him.

From the start, ACS pursued an aggressive growth strategy. In its first two years, acquisitions accounted for an estimated 70 percent of the company's growth. Revenue in its first fiscal year ending June 30, 1989, was $74 million. Revenue for 1990 was in the $120 to $150 million range, and the firm's workforce grew to about 1,300 employees, 800 of whom worked in Dallas.

A key acquisition was completed in December 1989, when ACS acquired OBS Companies, Inc., of San Francisco. Located near Silicon Valley, OBS had a 55,000-square-foot data processing center in Santa Clara, California. OBS was a mature service company with a 20-year history, about 200 employees, and $25 million in annual revenue.

In addition to gaining new customers through acquisitions, ACS arranged to purchase mainframe computers from struggling savings and loan institutions, then provide them with data processing services. At the beginning of 1990 the company's data processing center was located near downtown Dallas and contained six IBM mainframes, each worth about $8 million if purchased new. ACS also pursued government clients. In association with the state of Maryland and technicians from IBM Corporation, Deason devised a system of using automated teller machines (ATMs) and bank cards to replace mailed food stamps and welfare checks. The system enabled ACS to beat out EDS for a five-year contract to computerize Los Angeles County's food stamp program.

Providing Services As a Private Company: 1990–94

ACS was well positioned to take advantage of changes in doing business that occurred in the 1990s. By utilizing tele-

Company Perspectives:

We're Affiliated Computer Services, Inc. (ACS), a premier provider of diversified business process and information technology outsourcing solutions to commercial and government clients worldwide. We are a Fortune *500 company comprised of more than 40,000 people in multiple locations around the world.*

It began in 1988 when Darwin Deason gathered together a group of extraordinary information technology professionals and formed a company dedicated to fulfilling client needs. From a single financial industry client, ACS expanded into the education, energy, financial, government, healthcare, retail, and transportation industries. Today, ACS delivers superior business process outsourcing, information technology outsourcing, and systems and integration services to hundreds of clients worldwide.

phone lines and computers, companies could eliminate paperwork through electronic data interchange (EDI) and achieve greater efficiencies. The role of ACS and its competitors was to operate mainframe computer hubs that connected to individual businesses, thereby providing an electronic network through which businesses could communicate.

Not all of ACS's acquisition attempts were successful. In 1991 the company tried to enter the mortgage banking business and buy BancPlus Mortgage Corporation. At the time BancPlus was under control of the Resolution Trust Corporation (RTC), which was accepting bids to take over the company. BancPlus was the largest mortgage company under government control, servicing more than $10 billion in loans. Ultimately, ACS lost out to a bid from BancPlus's management team, which was backed by the wealthy Bass family of Texas. ACS sought to have the RTC's decision overturned, but was denied in court.

In 1992 ACS expanded its business into the Northeast with the purchase of CIC/DISC, an outsourcing firm based in New York City. CIC/DISC specialized in the growing niche market of handling a financial institution's depository operations during a merger or liquidation. Among the clients gained by ACS through the acquisition were Manufacturers Hanover Corporation and State Street Bank.

During the first half of the 1990s ACS provided a range of computerized services to financial institutions, including outsourcing, facilities management, transaction processing, and data communication. The company also operated the MoneyMaker ATM network, signing up banks and other financial institutions. ACS then provided them with software and hardware systems for the ATMs as well as a range of support services, including transaction processing, card insurance, installation, monitoring, and maintenance. Most of MoneyMaker's clients were located in Texas, with others in Louisiana, Oklahoma, and other southwestern states.

In New Mexico one bank hooked up to the MoneyMaker network via satellite. ACS's satellite service allowed users either to purchase or lease a satellite dish. The company noted that it cost half as much to operate a satellite-based system than a land-based system. In addition to providing ATM service, ACS's MoneyMaker division also delivered electronic funds transfer (EFT) services.

By 1994 ACS's MoneyMaker network included about 2,200 ATMs, with 1,900 of them owned and operated by ACS. Most of the terminals were located in high-traffic locations, such as convenience stores, shopping malls, and sports venues. In 1994 ACS signed agreements with American Airlines and United Airlines to install ATMs in airport lounges in their terminals, including Chicago's O'Hare, Miami, and Los Angeles airports. Also in 1994 ACS signed an agreement with Wal-Mart to install MoneyMaker ATMs in its Supercenter Stores and Sam's Club Stores.

In April 1994 ACS re-entered the electronic benefits transfer (EBT) market by establishing a joint venture called Transfirst, Inc., with minority businessman Walter Patterson. Patterson was the director of the Arkansas Department of Human Services when Bill Clinton was governor of Arkansas. Whereas ACS had participated in early experiments to deliver welfare checks, food stamps, and other benefits electronically, the company did not pursue the market after determining there was not much demand for it. By 1994, however, many states were pursuing such initiatives, driven by federal cost-cutting mandates.

Continuing Aggressive Acquisitions Strategy As a Public Company: 1994–99

For its fiscal year ending June 30, 1994, ACS reported revenue of $271 million and net income of $12.3 million. On September 27, 1994, ACS went public as Affiliated Computer Services, Inc., offering 2.3 million shares of stock on the NASDAQ at $16 per share. Since its inception in 1988, ACS had acquired 13 data processing companies. At the time it went public, ACS's principal line of business was providing ATM services to banks. The company also provided a range of information processing services, including data processing services for retailers, wholesale distributors, hospitals, and transportation companies. Among ACS's subsidiaries, Dataplex Corporation specialized in document imaging and record storage and retrieval services. Following the initial public offering, Precept Business Products, Inc., another subsidiary, took control of the company's business support services, including business forms and products, a courier service, and some real estate operations previously controlled by ACS Properties, Inc.

During 1995 ACS announced plans to exit data processing for banks and focus on the electronic funds transfer (EFT) services market, as well as to expand its systems outsourcing business into industries other than banking. With 3,400 ATMs in its ATM network, ACS was second only to EDS's system of 5,300 ATMs among non-bank networks.

In an effort to expand its ATM network by installing them in retail grocery outlets, ACS offered a low-cost ATM called the Anycard ATM through an agreement with ATM manufacturer AnyCard International, Inc. These ATMs could be profitable at 400 to 500 transactions a month, compared with the 2,000 transactions a traditional ATM required to break even. ACS estimated it had deployed about 1,000 Anycard ATMs as of mid-1995. Toward the end of 1995 ACS created a new division, ACS Merchant Services, Inc., to market point-of-sale (POS) services to independent merchants, retail chains, and banks. The division also processed credit and debit bank card transactions for mer-

Key Dates:

1988: The company is founded in Dallas, Texas, as Affiliated Computer Systems, Inc.
1994: The company goes public as Affiliated Computer Services, Inc. (ACS), with an initial public offering on the NASDAQ.
1995: ACS reorganizes, plans to diversify, and leaves data processing for banks and financial institutions.
1996: ACS has more than 5,000 ATMs in its network.
1997: ACS moves its stock listing from the NASDAQ to the New York Stock Exchange and acquires Computer Data Systems for $350 million.
1998: The company acquires BRC Holdings, Inc. for $261 million.
1999: Jeffrey Rich replaces founder Darwin Deason as CEO.
2000: ACS sells its ATM unit for $180 million.
2001: ACS acquires IMS Corporation from Lockheed Martin Corporation for $825 million.
2003: ACS joins *Fortune* 500, ranked 488th; ACS announces a plan to sell its government solutions units to Lockheed Martin in exchange for a commercial business unit.

chant and agent banks. ACS also acquired a minority interest in Integrated Delivery Technologies, Inc., which was developing a new online financial transaction processing network geared toward supermarkets and other retail outlets. The Cartel Network, as it was called, debuted in November 1995. By mid-1996 ACS claimed to have more than 5,000 ATMs deployed.

ACS continued to acquire smaller companies in 1995 and 1996 and expand its presence nationally. Key investments and acquisitions included a 70 percent interest in systems integrator Systems Group Inc. of Dallas and Atlanta; a majority interest in LAN Co., a Philadelphia-based provider of network design and installation services and document management systems to law firms and other businesses; and the purchase of Pittsburgh-based Genix Group Inc.

To reduce the volatility of its stock price, ACS announced at the beginning of 1997 that it was moving its stock listing from NASDAQ to the New York Stock Exchange. In 1997 and 1998 ACS made two major acquisitions that gave it a strong presence serving state and local governments. In 1997 it acquired Computer Data Systems of Rockville, Maryland, a major systems integrator for federal agencies, for $373 million. In the second half of 1998 it acquired BRC Holdings Inc. for about $261 million. Founded in 1976 as Cronus Industries Inc., BRC Holdings was based in Dallas and specialized in providing automated record-keeping services to state and local governments. The acquisition of BRC Holdings added about 1,100 employees and increased ACS's workforce to more than 13,400 employees. The company had operations in North, South, and Central America as well as in Europe and the Middle East.

ACS also was making smaller targeted acquisitions. Toward the end of 1998 it acquired the unclaimed-property services division of State Street Corporation. The acquisitions added about 70 employees and was designed to enhance ACS's financial and securities services business.

In March 1999 company cofounder Darwin Deason stepped aside as CEO and was succeeded by Jeffrey A. Rich, who had been president of ACS since 1995. Deason, 58 years old and the largest individual shareholder in ACS, remained as chairman and planned to remain active in the company until he turned 65. For fiscal 1999, ACS reported revenue of $1.64 billion and net income of $86.2 million. About one-third of the company's revenue came from government clients.

Entering New Markets and Growth Through Acquisitions: 1999–2003

During 2000, ACS established a new division for BPO, gained new government clients, continued to make acquisitions, and divested its ATM business. The new BPO division consolidated a variety of outsourcing services, such as processing insurance claims, a task that was accomplished in part by 3,000 employees working in Guatemala and Mexico. ACS estimated that BPO would account for $950 million in fiscal 2000, or about half of the company's revenue. The BPO division also signed a $56 million contract with Ginnie Mae to support the government's mortgage-backed securities program over a three-year period.

Acquisitions completed in fiscal 2000 included Consultec LLC, a provider of administrative support services to the healthcare industry, for $105 million. The acquisition enabled ACS to compete better with other service providers for state government contracts to help them manage and administer their Medicaid and welfare programs and combat fraud and abuse. ACS also acquired Birch & Davis Holdings, Inc. of Silver Spring, Maryland, for $75 million. Birch & Davis specialized in providing healthcare management and consulting services, especially to state governments. The acquisition added more than 600 employees and strengthened ACS's position in the government healthcare services market, bolstering its ranking as a top systems integrator in the government information technology (IT) field. As a result of these acquisitions, ACS subsequently formed a new subsidiary, ACS Healthcare Solutions Inc.

At the end of fiscal 2000 ACS completed the acquisition of Intellisource Group Inc. of Vienna, Virginia. ACS gained 680 employees in the transaction and acquired a customer base that included the NASA Goddard Space Flight Center, the Federal Aviation Administration, the U.S. Air Force and Coast Guard, and the cities of Newark, New Jersey, and Philadelphia, Pennsylvania. ACS also sold off its ATM unit at the end of fiscal 2000, saying that it could no longer compete in that market. The unit was acquired by Genpass Inc., a subsidiary of the Chicago-based private equity firm of GTCR Golder Rauner, for $180 million.

Since its inception in 1988, ACS had completed more than 50 acquisitions through the end of fiscal 2000. To help ACS pursue acquisitions of IT and business process outsourcing companies, it hired merger and acquisition specialist Bill Deckelman as general counsel and executive vice-president in March 2000. For fiscal 2000 ACS reported revenue of $1.96 billion and net income of $109.3 million.

During fiscal 2001 ACS obtained a $450 million revolving credit facility from a consortium of financial institutions that included Wells Fargo Bank, Bank One, SunTrust Bank, and Bank of Tokyo-Mitsubishi. In June 2001 ACS agreed to acquire Global Government Solutions (GGS) from Systems & Computer Technology Corporation for $85 million in cash. GGS was based in Lexington, Kentucky, and provided IT solutions to state and local governments. The acquisition enhanced ACS's powerful market position in the government sector and made it the largest provider of local government IT solutions. For fiscal 2001 ACS reported revenue of $2.06 billion and net income of $134.3 million.

ACS began fiscal 2002 with an agreement with Lockheed Martin Corporation to purchase its IMS Corporation subsidiary for $825 million in cash. IMS specialized in providing a range of processing services to state and local governments, including child support payments collection, operation of welfare-to-work programs, and processing traffic violations. With 250 offices located in 44 states and Canada and 4,800 employees, IMS had estimated annual revenue of $700 million. Also in July 2001, ACS obtained a major defense contract worth up to $346 million over ten years from the Defense Finance and Accounting Service to provide data processing and payroll services for military retirees and annuitants. Another major acquisition was completed in June 2002, when ACS purchased AFSA Data Corporation for $410 million. AFSA had more than 3,500 employees and was the largest education services company in the United States, servicing 8.1 million student loans worth $85 billion. By the end of fiscal 2002 ACS was hiring new employees at the rate of 500 a month. For the year ACS reported revenue of $3.06 billion and net income of $229.6 million.

During fiscal 2003 ACS adopted an annual goal of increasing cash flow by 10 percent through internal growth and 10 percent through acquisitions. In September 2002 the company obtained an $875 million unsecured line of credit to consolidate its existing debt. It planned to seek out only one to three significantly large contracts a year. In December 2002 it obtained a ten-year, $650 million contract with Motorola Inc., to handle its human resources functions, including payroll and benefits administration. As part of the deal, ACS acquired parts of Motorola's human resources division, including 600 employees in 27 countries. An even larger contract, worth about $100 million a year, was signed in January 2003 with Texas's Medicaid system.

ACS became a member of the *Fortune* 500 in 2003, ranked 488th. For fiscal 2003 the company reported revenue of $3.79 billion and net income of $306.8 million. About two-thirds of the company's revenue came from BPO services. One key to ACS's success was its use of cheaper labor available outside the United States. The company opened its first foreign facility in 1997 in Mexico. Approximately 25 to 30 percent of the company's workforce of 40,000 employees worked outside the United States in 2003, including 5,000 employees in Mexico, 2,000 in Guatemala, and 1,000 in Ghana, among other locations.

Perhaps signaling a new direction for ACS, the company agreed in August 2003 to sell the majority of its federal government business to Lockheed Martin Corporation. ACS would retain its $150 million-a-year contract for loan servicing services with the U.S. Department of Education, which it has held since 1994. Some ACS operations would also continue to serve as subcontractors on portions of the transferred business. The deal, which was expected to close in 2004, called for Lockheed Martin to pay $658 million for ACS's government solutions business, while ACS would pay $107 million for Lockheed Martin's commercial IT outsourcing business. In addition to netting $551 million in cash, ACS would gain contracts worth about $240 million annually from new customers such as Nike Inc. and Simon & Schuster Inc., and existing customers such as General Motors Corporation and Goodyear Tire & Rubber Co. A spokesperson for ACS said the company decided to divest its government business because it did not have the resources to compete for the extremely large contracts common in the federal market. On the other hand, the company also felt it was too large to compete for some of the niche business. Following the deal ACS planned to focus on providing high-margin business process outsourcing (BPO) services to commercial clients.

Principal Subsidiaries

ACS Desktop Solutions, Inc.; ACS Healthcare Solutions, Inc.; CyberRep.

Principal Competitors

Computer Sciences Corporation; Electronic Data Systems Corporation; International Business Machines Corporation.

Further Reading

"ACS Acquires 70% of a Systems Integrator," *American Banker,* January 23, 1995, p. 11.

"ACS Consolidates Bridge Loan, Revolver in New Line," *Loan Market Week,* September 30, 2002, p. 7.

"ACS Offering Merchant Services," *Card News,* October 2, 1995, p. 7.

"ACS to Divest Government Solutions Arm," *Mergers & Acquisitions Report,* August 4, 2003.

"ACS Wins Ed. Contract Again," *Washington Technology,* May 26, 2003, p. 9.

"Affiliated Computer in Pact with AnyCard," *American Banker,* March 20, 1995, p. 26.

"Affiliated Computer Plans ATMs at Airports," *American Banker,* March 1, 1994, p. 2.

"Affiliated Computer Services," *Bank Loan Report,* November 27, 2000.

"Affiliated Computer Services' Quarterly Revenue Climbs 26 Percent," *Knight Ridder/Tribune Business News,* April 23, 2003.

"Affiliated Spreads Wings with ATMs at Airports," *American Banker,* March 3, 1994, p. 16.

Ante, Spencer E., "Solving Here-and-Now Problems Someplace Else," *Business Week,* June 23, 2003, p. 79.

Appin, Rick, "Corporate Policy: Affiliated Reaches into Its Past to Hire a New M&A Pro," *Mergers & Acquisitions Report,* March 20, 2000.

Barthel, Matt, "Affiliated Computer Acquires New York Outsourcing Firm," *American Banker,* February 11, 1992, p. 3.

Block, Valerie, "Wal-Mart to Install Affiliated's ATMs," *American Banker,* March 14, 1994, p. 7A.

Boney, Brian, "Common Cultures: Secrets of the Acquisition Game," *Dallas Business Journal,* August 29, 1997, p. B1.

Bridgeforth, Arthur, Jr., "Dallas Company Gets in Line to Buy MCN's Genix Group," *Crain's Detroit Business,* May 13, 1996, p. 3.

Churbuck, David, "Starting Over," *Forbes,* May 14, 1990, p. 128.

Crockett, Barton, ''B of A Extends First Gibraltar's Outsourcing Pact with ACS,'' *American Banker,* March 4, 1993, p. 3.

''Dallas-Based Computer Firm to Tackle Motorola's Human Resources Tasks,'' *Knight Ridder/Tribune Business News,* December 20, 2002.

''Dallas-Based Information Technology Firm Continually Recruits Talent,'' *Knight Ridder/Tribune Business News,* June 23, 2002.

''The Dallas Morning News Leverage Column,'' *Knight Ridder/Tribune Business News,* May 2, 2003.

''Defense Taps ACS for Outsourcing,'' *Washington Technology,* July 2, 2001, p. 8.

Fanelli, Christa, ''Live Deals,'' *Buyouts,* July 17, 2000.

Fisher, Daniel, ''The Human Factor,'' *Forbes,* February 7, 2000, p. 74.

Goldstein, Alan, ''Dallas-Based Data Services Firm to Make Acquisition,'' *Knight Ridder/Tribune Business News,* October 20, 1998.

Greenemeier, Larry, ''Health-Care Industry Turns Increasingly to IT,'' *InformationWeek,* October 11, 1999, p. 38.

Habal, Hala, ''Affiliated Computer Sells Business Units,'' *Dallas Business Journal,* July 7, 2000, p. 6.

''Inside the DBJ Index,'' *Dallas Business Journal,* June 29, 2001, p. 57.

''Integrator Acquired,'' *Computerworld,* October 6, 1997, p. 39.

''Intellisource Becomes Part of ACS,'' *Washington Technology,* July 3, 2000, p. 8.

Key, Peter, ''SCT Sells Gov't Software Line for $85M,'' *Philadelphia Business Journal,* July 6, 2001, p. 5.

LeSueur, Steve, ''Affiliated Computer Services Preps for Buffer Business,'' *Washington Technology,* March 20, 2000, p. 34.

''Lockheed Martin Completes Sale of IMS to ACS,'' *Defense Daily,* August 27, 2001.

''Lockheed Martin to Sell Interest in IMS Corporation for $825 Million,'' *Defense Daily,* July 20, 2001.

Marjanovic, Steven, ''ACS Leaving Nasdaq for NYSE Listing,'' *American Banker,* January 27, 1997, p. 18.

——, ''Founder of Affiliated, a Big Processing Firm, Passes the CEO Torch,'' *American Banker,* March 4, 1999.

''Matador Sees Red Over BRC Takeout,'' *Mergers & Acquisitions Report,* November 23, 1998.

''MoneyMaker ATM Net Lassos 7 Texas Clients,'' *American Banker,* January 4, 1993, p. 16A.

O'Leary, Chris, ''Retailer Payment Net Geared to Go On-line,'' *Supermarket News,* October 9, 1995, p. 23.

Piskora, Beth, ''ACS Adds Clout to Network for Supermarkets,'' *American Banker,* September 28, 1995, p. 14.

——, ''Affiliated Computer, Striving for No. 1, Adds 450 ATMs,'' *American Banker,* October 6, 1995, p. 12.

——, ''U.S. Banknote Drops Bid for Electronic Benefits Firm,'' *American Banker,* March 11, 1996, p. 15.

''Ready for Prime Time,'' *Washington Technology,* July 16, 2001, p. 4.

Roosevelt, Phil, ''Affiliated Computer, Loser in RTC Bidding, Cries Foul,'' *American Banker,* October 11, 1991, p. 11.

——, ''Judge Refuses to Bar RTC Sale,'' *American Banker,* October 18, 1991, p. 2.

——, ''Only Nonbanks in Last Lap of Race for BancPlus Unit,'' *American Banker,* June 7, 1991, p. 5.

Siemplenski, Janel, ''ACS Hits Market on High Note,'' *Dallas Business Journal,* September 30, 1994, p. 7.

——, ''Affiliated Computer Seeks $38 Million in Stock Issue,'' *Dallas Business Journal,* June 3, 1994, p. 1.

Smith, Frank, ''Reputation a Key Factor at Fledgling ACS,'' *Dallas Business Journal,* January 2, 1990, p. 1.

Strachman, Daniel, ''Ex-Clinton Aide in Venture with ATM Operator,'' *American Banker,* April 13, 1994, p. 15.

''Swap Meet: ACS and Lockheed Acquire Each Other's Practices,'' *InformationWeek,* August 1, 2003.

''Tech Bytes: State St. Selling Off Unclaimed Property Unit,'' *American Banker,* December 16, 1998.

''Tech Tip: Banks Find Savings in the Sky,'' *ABA Banking Journal,* July 1993, p. 73.

Tempkin, Adam M., ''Ginnie Outsources I.T. Responsibilities with ACS,'' *Mortgage-Backed Securities Letter,* July 26, 1999, p. 1.

''Thrift May Link with ATM Networks,'' *American Banker,* September 23, 1983, p. 2.

Tracey, Brian, ''ACS Tells Investors Diversification Will Keep Growth at 20%,'' *American Banker,* June 26, 1995, p. 20.

——, ''Affiliated Computer Services Inc. Gearing Up for More Acquisitions,'' *American Banker,* January 8, 1996, p. 14.

——, ''Affiliated Computer's Initial Stock Offering Proves a Big Draw,'' *American Banker,* November 7, 1994, p. 14.

Tucker, Tracy, ''Affiliated Focuses on Growing Fund Transfer Segment,'' *American Banker,* April 26, 1995, p. 16.

Welsh, William, ''ACS Extends Reach with Lockheed Unit Buy,'' *Washington Technology,* July 30, 2001, p. 1.

—David P. Bianco

Agere Systems Inc.

1110 American Parkway, Northeast
Allentown, Pennsylvania 18109
U.S.A.
Telephone: (610) 712-1000
Toll Free: (800) 372-2447
Fax: (610) 712-4106
Web site: http://www.agere.com

Public Company
Incorporated: 2000
Employees: 10,700
Sales: $1.83 billion (2003)
Stock Exchanges: New York
Ticker Symbol: AGR.A
NAIC: 334413 Semiconductor and Related Device Manufacturing; 334412 Printed Circuit Board Manufacturing; 334419 Other Electronic Component Manufacturing; 335999 All Other Miscellaneous Electrical Equipment and Component Manufacturing

Agere Systems Inc. designs and manufactures integrated circuits, which are made using semiconductor wafers imprinted with a network of electronic components. Integrated circuits perform several functions such as processing and storing data, controlling electronic system functions, and processing electronic signals. Agere ranks as the market leader in providing integrated circuits for the hard disk drive market, conducting its manufacturing activity in Orlando, Florida, and overseas, where the company owns facilities in Singapore and Thailand. The company divides its business according to the markets it serves, operating a client systems group and an infrastructure systems group. Through its client systems group, Agere caters to the computing and consumer communications market, marketing integrated circuits, software, and reference designs for various applications. Through its infrastructure systems group, the company serves the networking equipment market, selling integrated circuit solutions to network equipment customers. Agere's client systems group accounts for more than 70 percent of the company's total annual revenues. Roughly 80 percent of Agere's annual revenues are derived from sales outside the United States.

Origins

Agere was a spinoff of a spinoff, a company whose corporate roots were entwined in telecommunications giant AT&T Corp. In 1996, AT&T formed a separate company and sold it to the investing public, spinning off Lucent Technologies Inc. From its birth, Lucent towered as a leading designer, developer, and manufacturer of telecommunications systems and software products, employing more than 100,000 workers. Agere's future leader, John T. Dickson, made the move to Lucent following its spinoff, vacating his post as vice-president of AT&T's integrated circuit business unit—a position he had held for the previous three years—to become chief operating officer of Lucent's microelectronics group. In 1999, Dickson was named executive vice-president and chief executive officer of the microelectronics group, putting him in position to spearhead Agere's operations once it was freed from Lucent.

Agere was formed as a wholly owned subsidiary of Lucent on August 1, 2000. The former microelectronics group drew its name from an acquisition completed in the spring of 2000, when Lucent acquired a small microelectronics company based in Texas named Agere. Using some of the assets gained through the purchase of the Texas-based company, Lucent created a new company, a new Agere, whose business comprised communications semiconductors, including optoelectronics components and integrated circuits, which were considered to be the basic building blocks of electronic and photonic products and systems. Upon its formation, Agere had annual revenues of $4.7 billion, 16,500 employees, and facilities scattered throughout 22 countries. Dickson was named president and chief executive officer of the new company.

Lucent formed Agere for the express purpose of divorcing itself from its microelectronics business. The company announced its intention to spin off its microelectronics group in July 2000, one month before Agere was officially formed. By creating an operationally separate company, Lucent hoped Agere could have easier access to capital from investors and forge better relations with its customers, some of whom were

Company Perspectives:

We will become our customers' preferred silicon and software partner for personal broadband solutions by providing unparalleled value through technology, products, service and delivery.

direct competitors with Lucent, such as Cisco Systems and Nortel Networks.

The process of separating Agere from Lucent took longer than anticipated. On February 1, 2001, Lucent transferred its microelectronics assets and liabilities to Agere, but the initial public offering (IPO) of its stock was delayed. Agere filed for its IPO in December 2000, but market conditions were not favorable for the company's IPO. In early February 2001, the offering price range was set between $15 and $20 per share in anticipation of selling 370 million shares. With the economy in a recession and the technology sector in collapse, Lucent was forced to lower its offering price and reduce its stake in Agere two weeks later, when the price range was narrowed to between $16 and $19 per share and the number of shares offered raised to 500 million. Less than a week later, the price range was trimmed again, reduced to between $12 and $14 per share. By the end of March 2001, the offering price had been lowered to between $6 and $7 per share before being set at $6 per share. Agere's IPO was completed on April 2, 2001, when Lucent sold 600 million shares, raising $3.6 billion.

Independence in 2002

Agere's debut on the New York Stock Exchange did not translate to its independence from Lucent. The IPO, according to the March 18, 2002 issue of *EBN*, ''was supposed to herald [Agere's] freedom and ability to explore strategic business opportunities outside the Lucent group.'' The IPO, however, did not signal Agere's liberation from Lucent. Lucent retained a 58 percent interest in Agere following the IPO, making Agere a majority-owned subsidiary of Lucent. Lucent intended to complete the spinoff of Agere within months after the IPO, but its own financial problems delayed the separation. To free Agere, Lucent needed to post positive earnings for the fiscal quarter preceding the spinoff, something the troubled telecommunications and software company was having difficulty achieving. Lucent hoped to distribute Agere stock to its shareholders in September 2001, but the company pushed back the spinoff to negotiate new agreements with lenders after it realized it would incur as much as $9 billion in restructuring charges resulting from trimming its workforce by 49,000 employees. The distribution of Agere shares was rescheduled for March 2002, a target date that promised to pass without the spin off being completed after Lucent announced in October 2001 a greater than expected loss for its fiscal fourth quarter. The distribution of Agere stock to Lucent shareholders occurred, after several delays, on June 1, 2002, 14 months after the IPO.

While the process of separation dragged on, Agere contended with numerous difficulties. Following its IPO, Agere was saddled with $2.5 billion of bank debt, a burdensome inheritance from Lucent. The company also saw its primary markets weakened by anemic economic conditions, as its customers either went out of business or significantly reduced their expenditures. Consequently, the sale of Agere's optical and electronic components for communications networks and computing dropped alarmingly, making the company's first year after its IPO a trying period. Agere was forced to change its operating strategy to compensate for the decline in its core business, a move that gave the company a significantly altered profile.

Faced with mounting losses and waning sales, Dickson was forced to lay off employees, consolidate facilities, and sell assets. The divestitures raised much needed cash and reshaped the company's composition, giving it a new strategic focus. In December 2001, Agere sold its field-programmable gate arrays (FPGA) business to Lattice Semiconductor Corp., raising $250 million in cash. In June 2002, when the cord connecting Agere and Lucent was finally cut, Dickson sold the company's wireless LAN equipment business to Proxim Corp., gaining $65 million from the sale. The following month, Legerity Inc. agreed to pay $70 million to acquire Agere's analog linecard integrated circuit business. In August 2002, the company announced it intended to exit the optoelectronics business, one of its two principal businesses—the other being its integrated circuits business—in 2001. Agere's optoelectronics business, which comprised components that carried data and voice traffic over optical networks, generated approximately $1 billion in revenues.

The decision to exit the optoelectronics business coincided with the announcement of Agere's strategic focus for the future. The company announced it would concentrate on providing advanced integrated circuit solutions that accessed, moved, and stored network information. In an August 23, 2002 interview with *Fiber Optics Weekly Update*, Dickson explained, ''We are redefining Agere as a premier provider of integrated circuit solutions to target the communications and computing opportunities that present the best long-term potential.'' The change in perspective was dramatic. In 2001, roughly 70 percent of Agere's business was derived from the sale of infrastructure products—equipment that companies and telecommunication carriers used to carry voice and Internet traffic. When the sales of such products slowed, the company shifted to what it referred to as the ''client'' side of its business, focusing on chips used for disk drives, personal computer connectivity, wireless local-area networks, and cellular handsets. By the end of the three-month period ended in December 2002, Agere derived 69 percent of its revenue from the sale of client-side products, with the sales of storage chips accounting for one-third of the company's total sales.

By the spring of 2003, the sweeping restructuring efforts had created a smaller and refocused Agere. Manufacturing facilities had either been sold or consolidated, as the bulk of the company's production activity moved overseas. The divestitures, which shed businesses such as analog line cards, FPGA, wireless networking equipment, cable television components, and optoelectronics, stripped the company of more than half its annual revenue. Further, the sale and consolidation of facilities and businesses had drastically reduced the company's payroll, cutting Agere's workforce by approximately 60 percent. In its new guise, the company hoped to arrest its alarming pattern of losses, which totaled more than $6 billion since its IPO. In an

Key Dates:

2000: Agere is formed as a wholly owned subsidiary of Lucent Technologies Inc.
2001: Agere completes its initial public offering of stock.
2002: Lucent divests its 58 percent stake in Agere.
2003: Agere acquires Massana Ltd.

April 1, 2003 interview with *Electronic Business*, Dickson remarked, ''The two-year period after the IPO was very rough. It's been a bad period for the entire industry, but we've learned a lot in the process, and we're bringing a new Agere out of that, poised to prosper.''

Rebuilding in 2003

Set for its new course, Agere began to rebuild, taking steps to augment rather than reduce its operations for the first time in its existence. In September 2003, Agere announced it had acquired Massana Ltd., the first acquisition completed by the company since its IPO. The acquisition, valued at approximately $26 million, formed the basis of Agere's new Ethernet division. In November 2003, the company reported its first quarterly profit since gaining independence from Lucent, posting $11 million in net income, a celebratory occasion considering the company lost $885 million during the same quarter a year earlier.

As Agere plotted its future course, the company appeared to have put to rest questions regarding its financial viability. Its future success depended largely on the accomplishments achieved in its client systems group, which accounted for an increasing percentage of its revenue. In 2002, 65 percent of Agere's revenue was derived from its client systems group. In 2003, the client systems group generated 72 percent of the company's revenue. In the years ahead, Agere hoped to produce sustained profitability, a goal whose achievement depended on the company's ability to maintain its market leadership.

Principal Subsidiaries

Ortel Corp.

Principal Operating Units

Client Systems Group; Infrastructure Group.

Principal Competitors

Broadcom Corporation; Infineon Technologies AG.; Texas Instruments Incorporated.

Further Reading

''Agere Buys Ireland's Massana,'' *European Telecom,* September 2003, p. 12.

''Agere: Is a Little Good News Enough?,'' *Business Week Online,* May 29, 2002, p. 45.

''Agere Posts First Profit Since IPO,'' *EBN,* November 3, 2003, p. 8.

''Agere Quits Optoelectronics Biz,'' *Fiber Optics Weekly Update,* August 23, 2002, p. 1.

''Agere Systems Acquires TeraBlaze,'' *Wireless News,* January 2, 2004, p. 32.

Arensman, Russ, ''From Surviving to Thriving: Slimmed-Down Agere Systems Strives to Regain Profitability,'' *Electronic Business,* April 1, 2003, p. 20.

Cohen, Sara, ''Lucent Slump Threatens Agere Spin-Off,'' *Daily Deal,* October 23, 2001, p. 32.

Dunn, Darrell, ''Agere Continues Sell-Off, This Time to Legerity,'' *EBN,* July 1, 2002, p. 23.

——, ''Lucent Braves IPO for Agere; Conexant Spins Off Mindspeed,'' *EBN,* April 2, 2001, p. 14.

Gain, Bruce, ''Lucent Names Spinoff Chip Unit,'' *Electronic Buyers' News,* December 11, 2000, p. 20.

Gianatasio, David, ''Lucent Spinoff Selects Mullen,'' *ADWEEK New England Edition,* December 11, 2000, p. 5.

Lamb, Robin, ''Lucent Moving Ahead with Plans to Complete Spinoff of Agere,'' *EBN,* December 17, 2001, p. 10.

Ojo, Bolaji, ''Reduces Revenue Estimate—Lucent Still Unable to Give Agere Its Freedom,'' *EBN,* March 18, 2002, p. 14.

Smith, Aaron, ''What's in a Name?,'' *IPO Reporter,* December 18, 2000.

Souza, Crista, ''A Troubled Lucent Threatens Agere—Postpones Spinoff's IPO As Financial Concerns Mount,'' *EBN,* July 30, 2001, p. 1.

Wirbel, Loring, ''Agere Takes First Leap into Acquisition Waters,'' *EBN,* September 1, 2003, p. 8.

—Jeffrey L. Covell

Allen
Edmonds

Allen-Edmonds Shoe Corporation

201 E. Seven Hills Road
Port Washington, Wisconsin 53074-0998
U.S.A.
Telephone: (262) 235-6000
Fax: (262) 235-6255
Web site: http://www.allenedmonds.com

Private Company
Founded: 1922
Employees: 750
Sales: $82 million (2002 est.)
NAIC: 316213 Men's Footwear (Except Athletic) Manufacturing

Allen-Edmonds Shoe Corporation is a manufacturer of handmade, upscale men's shoes, which range in price from $200 to $415. The privately owned Port Washington, Wisconsin, company is one of the few remaining independent shoemakers in the United States. Although little known to the general public, Allen-Edmonds is well regarded by shoe aficionados around the world. Manufacturing is labor intensive, a process that includes more than 200 separate steps. Allen-Edmonds shoes have been worn by U.S. presidents and other prominent office holders, as well as Hollywood stars and other celebrities. Although the company offers a limited number of styles, embracing traditional looks, it provides an impressive range of widths and sizes, some 164 combinations in all—from sizes 5 to 16, and widths AAA to EEE. The company also offers a Recrafting service, restoring older Allen-Edmonds shoes to like-new condition. Allen-Edmonds shoes are sold at high-end department stores such as Nordstrom, Marshall Fields, and Saks Fifth Avenue, as well as 25 company-owned stores in the United States and two in Europe (Italy and Belgium). Furthermore, the company has a network of agents and distributors in 33 countries and also sells its wares via the Internet. In recent years Allen-Edmonds has expanded beyond men's shoes. Its Woodlore division offers shoe trees and other aromatic cedar products and wardrobe accessories. The company sells shoe care products, leather accessories such as belts and wallets, hosiery, and even cologne. Allen-Edmonds also maintains an affiliation with Elefanten, maker of premium children's shoes. In addition to its Port Washington location, the company operates manufacturing facilities in Lake Church, Wisconsin; Milwaukee, Wisconsin; and Lewiston, Maine.

Founding the Company in 1922

Allen-Edmonds was founded in 1922 by Elbert W. Allen, Sr., who was born and raised in the Cumberland River area of Tennessee. In his early 20s he moved to Texas to run a prison shoemaking operation. It was here that he envisioned a way to produce the most comfortable shoes possible, shoes that would flex in the same way that people walked, from heel to toe with each step. Colleagues in the shoemaking trade, however, were skeptical that such an approach was commercially viable. Allen continued to nurture his idea after relocating to Milwaukee, where for four years he served as general manager of the Ogden Shoe Company. He found a partner in Ralph Spiegel, a co-worker, and together they bought the Belgium Shoe Company, located in the small town of Belgium, Wisconsin. Here Allen was able to perfect his vision for making a new shoe. He relied on the Goodyear welt method, whereby tops and soles were each sewn into a strip of folded leather (the welt) that ran around the outside of the shoe. To increase flexibility and comfort, Allen found a way to remove the metal shank and nails that were normally used in the instep, and also added a cork heel. The partners sold the new shoe under the name ''Osteo-Path-Ik,'' promoting it as ''the shoe that needs no breaking in.'' Allen reduced his business philosophy to obtaining ''the best leather I can buy and the best craftspeople I can find.''

In the late 1920s Spiegel left the company, bought out by William Edmonds, who owned a Milwaukee company called Edmonds Foot Fitters. Edmond's trade name soon replaced the ''Osteo-Path-Ik'' moniker, and the company's expanding range of shoes now became known as Allen-Edmonds Footfitters. Despite the Great Depression of the 1930s, the company was able to expand sales nationally, due in large part to Edmonds's willingness to travel widely promoting the company's innovative shoes. Allen's sons also became involved in running the company. World War II proved to be a turning point. Not only

Company Perspectives:

At Allen-Edmonds, we do everything possible to make sure customers are completely satisfied. That means offering only the highest-quality products. It means going out of our way to deliver exceptional service. And it means treating customers with honesty and integrity at all times.

did Allen-Edmonds win contracts to make shoes for the Army and the Navy, the military personnel who wore the company's shoes were so impressed with the comfortable fit that they became customers after the war was over and they were discharged from the military.

Founder's Death in 1946

After Allen died in 1946, his eldest son, Elbert W. ''Bert'' Allen, took over management of the company, which continued to trade on the comfort of its shoes and quality of its craftsmanship. The company was so confident about the product that it offered a guarantee, promising to refund a customer's money if he believed that his Allen-Edmonds were not the most comfortable shoes he had ever worn. The company generally relied on word of mouth, helped to some extent by allowing retail clerks to buy the shoes at wholesale prices. In this way, clerks who normally would not be able to afford the product could provide personal testimony to their customers about the virtues of Allen-Edmonds shoes. Bert Allen also proved to be a tireless promoter of the product, traveling around the world extolling the virtues of Allen-Edmonds shoes.

In 1968 Bert's brother Boyd took over as president of the company. The 1970s was a difficult period for the company, as it was for the entire American shoe industry, which was adversely impacted by the increasing influx of cheap imports. It was in 1979 that Boyd Allen, needing help at a German trade show, enlisted the services of John J. Stollenwerk, a man who would transform the fortunes of Allen-Edmonds. Stollenwerk, a graduate of Milwaukee's Marquette University, had no experience in the shoe business. After college he worked in Latin America for a Catholic relief organization, the papal peace corps, became involved in the exporting of soybeans and animal feed, and later acquired an exporting consulting practice in Milwaukee, which accounted for Boyd Allen turning to him for help. Allen was so impressed with Stollenwerk during their trip to Germany that, according to Stollenwerk, he remarked over dinner one evening, ''You're so enthusiastic about this business, why don't you buy it?'' This comment planted a seed, Stollenwerk grew interested, and over the course of the next year he assembled the financing necessary to buy Allen-Edmonds. He took on partners Peter A. Fischer, head of Medalist Industries, and Ronald Creten, owner of RC Industries, and was also successful in securing support from Allen-Edmonds's bank, which believed that bringing in new management was in its best interest.

When Stollenwerk took charge of Allen-Edmonds in 1980 he faced some serious challenges. The company had just lost $400,000, after generating only $9.5 million in annual sales. Moreover, he had to contend immediately with rumors that he had merely bought the business in order to dress up the books and flip it for a quick profit. As a result, Stollenwerk had to devote a considerable amount of time visiting with customers to assure them that he was in the shoe business for the long haul. Stollenwerk also made a number of other changes to the way Allen-Edmonds conducted its business. According to a 1992 *Direct Marketing* profile, ''Stollenwerk carved out a marketing niche, cut out the middlemen and went directly to suppliers, modernized the plant, cross-trained co-workers and changed management philosophy to one of quality, integrity and service. He also reportedly concentrated on a high-end market niche and reoriented distribution to concentrate on upscale retail stores. . . . Importantly, he instilled a sense of direction and pride.'' Stollenwerk's fresh approach to the business was evident in other ways. For instance, as a way to sell shoes during the traditionally slow summer period, he decided to hold a tent sale as part of an event he wanted to call Belgium Days. When he tried to get the town of Belgium behind the idea, however, he was met with skeptics who could not fathom that anyone would want to make the trek to their backwoods town. Stollenwerk held the tent sale anyway and surprised his critics when around 2,000 people showed up looking for bargains. Belgium Days quickly became a summer tradition, each year producing a tidy profit for Allen-Edmonds, which benefited from the high margin on the sales, despite the discounting.

Another significant change that Stollenwerk brought to Allen-Edmonds was to view the world as the company's marketplace, a sales task to which he was well suited, given his experience in the export business. Allen-Edmonds had sold some shoes overseas but relied on a distributor system that greatly added to the price of its product. Stollenwerk cut out this link and established a warehouse in Holland and hired a French logistics firm to handle distribution. In order to expedite payments, the company opened bank accounts in each country, which allowed customers to pay in their native currency. Furthermore, Allen-Edmonds now took care to tailor product lines to match the tastes of individual countries, and even created advertisements in 15 foreign languages. Stollenwerk also attended 15 trade shows around the world to help promote Allen-Edmonds's shoes. The company made significant headway in the European market but found a great deal of resistance in Asia.

Overcoming Fire in 1984

After four years at the helm, Stollenwerk had achieved solid progress. The business was once again showing a profit and annual sales had grown to $17 million. But everything would be placed in jeopardy one January night in 1984 when the temperature was 25 degrees below, and a malfunctioning boiler in the headquarters plant started a fire that burned the entire structure—other than the chimney—to the ground. For about 30 minutes, Stollenwerk watched the blaze, which would destroy $14 million in equipment and some 50,000 pairs of shoes, then decided there was nothing he could do and went home to bed, knowing that he and his workers faced many long days in the weeks to come. The company was well insured, having just rewritten its fire and business-interruption insurance. In recent years, hundreds of U.S. shoe manufacturers had moved offshore, and the fire now presented Stollenwerk with an ideal

Key Dates:

1922: Elbert W. Allen and Ralph Spiegel found the company.
1946: Allen dies, and the firm is now headed by his eldest son.
1968: A second son, Boyd Allen, becomes president.
1980: John Stollenwerk leads a buyout of the company.
1988: Stollenwerk gains a 90 percent interest in the business.
1998: Allen-Edmonds begins producing leather belts.
2000: The company begins selling on the Internet.

opportunity to join the exodus to another country, or even move to another part of the United States where labor was cheaper. Development agencies from other states were quick to feel him out on the possibility of relocating the business. But Stollenwerk firmly believed that a major factor in the company's success was its skilled workforce, many of whom had worked their entire lives for Allen-Edmonds.

On the Monday following the fire, Stollenwerk spoke to his employees at a subsidiary factory in nearby Lake Church and assured them that Allen-Edmonds was going to stay in Wisconsin and that they were going to find a way to keep the business running. Luckily, the Lake Church facility housed the cut-and-sew operation, where 14,000 pairs of shoes were in the process of being completed. Of even greater importance, the crucial dies used to cut patterns of leather were kept in Lake Church. Quickly, makeshift arrangements were made. A former school became the company's new headquarters and its gymnasium was converted to serve as a warehouse for finished goods and inventory. Union workers at the Levernz Shoe Co. voted to permit Allen-Edmonds nonunion workers to use their company's New Holstein plant, located some 45 miles away, on Fridays, Saturdays, and Sundays for ten- to 12-hour shifts. This accommodation was of great help until Stollenwerk was able to arrange the rental of a 50,000-square-foot factory, the former home of the Badger Outerwear Co. Customers were also helpful, many returning unneeded goods to Allen-Edmonds to allow the company to assemble a reasonable level of inventory. Stollenwerk also made sure that relationships with employees and customers were maintained. Workers who could not be of use in the beginning were given two week vacations until temporary production arrangements were completed. Commissions to salesmen also were paid promptly, despite the delay in order completion. Further, Allen-Edmonds increased its advertising to emphasize management's commitment to the product. By June the company was able to meet pre-fire production levels.

According to a *Wall Street Journal* article, the fire was "a blessing of sorts. The factory Allen-Edmonds lost was old and inefficient. Because the company was well-insured and has been able to resume production in rented quarters, it has time, Mr. Stollenwerk says, 'to sit back and build a facility we really need . . . a year 2000 manufacturing facility.' " Two years later a 69,000-square-foot state-of-the-art shoe factory opened a few miles away in Port Washington. The company resumed its steady pattern of growth. In 1987 Allen-Edmonds launched a women's line of shoes, produced by a California manufacturer familiar with the different requirements in making women's shoes. In that same year, the company also decided to become involved in the production of shoe trees, establishing its Woodlore division. In 1988 Allen-Edmonds opened a dedicated plant for the business.

Overseas, Stollenwerk caused something of an international stir when he crashed a Tokyo trade fair, after enduring five frustrating years attempting to crack the Japanese market. Due to the publicity he generated, Allen-Edmonds achieved some success in exporting its wares to Japan and Taiwan, in order to avert negative publicity, also opened its markets somewhat. Nevertheless, Asia remained a difficult market in which to do business.

Allen-Edmonds was in line to top $30 million in revenues in 1988, but Stollenwerk's partners expressed a desire to cash in and sell the company to Timberland Co. Discussions took place, but in the end Stollenwerk put together a buyout deal, worth in excess of $10 million, working with the Wisconsin Investment Board and several banks. As a result he gained a 90 percent interest in the company and the employees held the remaining 10 percent.

In 1990 Allen-Edmonds attempted to employ a just-in-time manufacturing process but the plan proved to be counterproductive, resulting in a $1 million loss. The company returned to its more traditional approach and restored profitability. Allen-Edmonds's aggressive moves on other fronts, however, were more successful, as the company enjoyed annual sales growth in the 10 percent range. It steadily opened company-owned stores and established leased departments with retailers. With the advent of casual Fridays in the workplace in the early 1990s, the company added a line of "corporate casuals." It enlisted the services of Maine Shoe in Lewiston, Maine, to produce hand-sewn loafers. The demand for these shoes was so strong that in 1998 Allen-Edmonds bought the operation. One of the greatest challenges for the company during the decade was finding enough skilled workers. The children of longtime employees were now going to college and looking for other ways to make a living. Allen-Edmonds attempted to bus in workers from Milwaukee, but many left after they found employment closer to home. The company now decided to take the jobs to the workers, in 1998 opening a satellite state-of-the-art cut-and-sew plant in downtown Milwaukee.

The sale of Allen-Edmonds men's shoes was so strong in the late 1990s that the company suspended the women's line simply because it lacked the production capacity. In the meantime, the company branched out into accessories, adding belts in 1998, followed two years later by other high-end leather goods, such as wallets, organizers, and key chains. In 1999 Allen-Edmonds introduced hosiery and a line of $100 ties, and in 2001 tested the market for high-quality slippers.

With the start of a new century, Allen-Edmonds began selling its broadened line of wares on the Internet. Sales now reached the $95 million range, as the company prepared to build another new plant near Milwaukee. But when the economy took a downturn, especially in the aftermath of the terrorist attacks of September 11, 2001, the company held back on the start of construction. A dip in sales forced management to put some employees on a short leave until inventory levels were reduced. The workforce was also allowed to shrink by 10 percent due to attrition. Revenues recovered over the next two years, despite the poor economy, and Allen-Edmonds continued to open new retail stores in Dallas and southern California, while scouting for sites in Boston and Washington, D.C. Another challenge was a shortage of leather caused by the breakout of Mad Cow Disease in Europe. To maintain its place in a highly competitive marketplace, the company took steps in 2003 to change its production process, employing a cell system of manufacturing that called for workers to be trained to perform multiple tasks, and thereby achieve greater efficiency. Allen-Edmonds had considered sending work overseas, but in the end decided against the idea. Nevertheless, Stollenwerk would not foreclose on that option in the future. The economics of the shoe industry were such that the Wisconsin company might have little choice but to follow its competitors overseas. As Stollenwerk told Milwaukee's *Business Journal,* ''We can't be the last one operating here.''

Principal Subsidiaries

Woodlore Cedar Products.

Principal Competitors

Genesco Inc.; Gucci Group N.V.; Salvatore Ferragamo Italia S.p.A.

Further Reading

Fenn, Donna, ''Starting Over,'' *Inc.,* November 1985, p. 142.

Jacobs, Sanford L., ''Shoe Concern Turns Disaster into Means of Raising Quality,'' *Wall Street Journal,* April 16, 1984, p. 1.

Reiff, Rick, ''Party Crasher,'' *Forbes,* June 12, 1989, p. 128.

Siekman, Phillip, ''The Last of the Big Shoemakers,'' *Fortune,* April 30, 2001, p. 154B.

Strong, Wendy, ''Last Two Decades Hard on Shoe Manufacturers,'' *Business Journal* (Milwaukee), December 20, 2002, p. A6.

Svatko, James E., and Susan Palmer, ''The CEO's Role in a Successful Export Strategy,'' *Small Business Report,* May 1989, p. 28.

—Ed Dinger

Amscan Holdings, Inc.

80 Grasslands Road
Elmsford, New York 10523
U.S.A.
Telephone: (914) 345-2020
Toll Free: (800) 284-4333
Fax: (914) 345-2056
Web site: http://www.amscan.com

Private Company
Incorporated: 1996
Employees: 2,000
Sales: $385.6 million (2002)
NAIC: 422130 Industrial and Personal Service Paper Wholesalers

Based in Elmsford, New York, Amscan Holdings, Inc. designs, manufactures, and distributes a wide variety of party items. Party goods include tableware, centerpieces, candles, cutouts, crepe, flags and banners, party hats, piñatas, and latex balloons. Amscan's stationery items include invitations, notes, and stationery; decorative tissues; gift wrap, bows, and bags; ribbons; photograph albums; baby and wedding memory books; and stickers and confetti. The privately owned company offers close to 400 product ensembles, intended for seasonal events such as New Year's, Valentine's Day, St. Patrick's Day, Easter, Passover, Fourth of July, Halloween, Thanksgiving, Hanukkah, and Christmas, as well as everyday occasions such as birthdays, showers, christenings, graduations, anniversaries, retirements, first communions, bar mitzvahs, confirmations, summer picnics and barbecues, and theme parties such as Mardi Gras, Hawaiian luaus, and 1950s nostalgia. Each ensemble features from 30 to 150 coordinating items. In recent years the company has added home, baby, and wedding giftware, including plush toys, ceramic items, mugs, decorative candles, and picture frames. It manufactures more than 60 percent of its products, outsourcing labor-intensive items to other manufacturers, located mostly in Asia. Amscan sells to more than 20,000 retailers around the world, maintaining factories and distribution centers in the United States, Canada, Mexico, the United Kingdom, France, Germany, Spain, and Japan.

Company Started in 1947

Amscan was founded in 1947 by Elvera Svenningsen, the mother of the company's longtime chief executive officer and chairman, John A. Svenningsen. With just $1,000 and operating out of her family garage in Bronxville, New York, she began to import and distribute such party items as honeycomb decorations—expandable turkeys, clowns, and the like. In 1948 she incorporated the business as Amscan Inc. and within a few years was showing modest success, generating some $60,000 in annual sales. After graduating from Swarthmore College in 1953 John Svenningsen joined the company, eager to grow the business, confident that the party goods industry, dominated at the time by Dennison Manufacturing Company, held great potential. He became president and chief executive officer in 1958.

Under John Svenningsen's leadership, Amscan moved to a new 600-square-foot facility in Tuckahoe, New York, in 1960 and began to increase the variety of party goods the company had to offer. In just four years, Amscan outgrew this space, relocated to a larger facility in New Rochelle, New York, and then in 1968 moved yet again, this time to Harrison, New York. Over the next 20 years the company enjoyed steady growth, due in large part to the leadership of Svenningsen. A self-acclaimed amateur psychologist, he gave a great deal of credit for the company's success to the people he hired and nurtured. In a 1993 profile of Amscan by *Party & Paper Retailers,* he explained, ''I'm blessed with the ability to recognize people's strengths and place them in a job that will suit those strengths. Respect your employees—bring them in on decisions—and they will be stimulated to do a better job. Here, we run completely by committee—everybody can learn from everybody else.'' In addition, Svenningsen paid a great deal of attention to his customers, no matter how large. He said, ''I've always tried to put the customer's hat on and think like him. . . . We have a great synergy with our customers. We offer them quality, price, and we know what will sell for them.'' Over the years, many of those customers became large retailers dedicated solely to the sale of party goods. In 1986, for instance, Party City was founded as a single 4,000-square-foot store in New Jersey. Other Party City outlets would soon follow and other party goods retailing chains were also launched, looking to take

Company Perspectives:

With Amscan you can offer your customers a full array of coordinating products for entertaining and home decoration, then let them mix and match to their heart's content, as they add on and on and on.

advantage of a growing penchant of baby boomers' to attempt to outdo one another when it came to holding parties for their children and themselves. (Party City would ultimately emerge as Amscan's largest customer, accounting for approximately 10 percent of all sales.) The resulting increase in retail sales fueled the steady growth of Amscan, which saw revenues reach $64 million in 1989, $68.5 million in 1990, and $75.5 million in 1991. Also during the late 1980s, the company looked overseas. In 1987 Amscan began to test the market in the United Kingdom, bringing out tableware and plastic cutlery in specially selected colors. British consumers, like their American counterparts, were also becoming more affluent and increasingly engaged in hosting parties and barbecues.

In the early 1990s Amscan remained privately owned. Elvera Svenningsen passed away, leaving John Svenningsen as the last link to the founding of the company. He did not urge his children to become involved in the company, allowing them to pursue their own careers. Annual revenues topped the $100 million mark in 1993 ($108.9 million). The company enjoyed even stronger growth over the next two years, with revenues totaling $132 million in 1994 and $167.4 million in 1995. Moreover, net income jumped from nearly $10 million in 1994 to more than $17.4 million in 1995.

Svenningsen Diagnosed with Cancer in 1996

John Svenningsen was diagnosed with lymphoma in the first quarter of 1996. In April of that year Gerald C. Rittenberg was promoted to the position of president of the company. Svenningsen remained CEO and chairman and, as he underwent treatment for his condition, continued to play a major role in running the company. In truth, others in the organization had taken on an increasing level of responsibility. Rittenberg, for instance, was a key player. Trained as a printer, he headed product development since 1990. Another key executive was William S. Wilkey, senior vice-president in charge of sales.

In October 1996 Amscan Holdings Inc. was formed as a holding company for Amscan and subsidiaries in preparation for taking the business public. The initial public offering (IPO) was completed in December, underwritten by Goldman, Sachs & Co. and Alex. Brown & Sons Inc. Amscan sold four million shares priced at $14 apiece, netting the company $48 million, which was then used to pay down debt and allow some shareholders, such as Svenningsen, to cash in some of their equity. The stock then began trading on the NASDAQ. The company finished 1996 producing record levels of sales ($192.7 million), although net income dropped to $2.1 million. Amscan's tenure as a public company, however, would be short term. In May 1997, after a 15-month battle with cancer, John Svenningsen died at the age of 66. Rittenberg, the man who succeeded him as CEO (and filled in as chairman on an interim basis), commented at the time, "John was a true innovator and visionary for the party goods industry." By the end of 1997 Amscan was taken private again. GS Capital Partners II L.P., an investment fund managed by Goldman, Sachs & Co., formed Confetti Acquisition Inc. in order to acquire Amscan. Under terms of the $315 million transaction, shareholders were given their choice of tendering their stock for either $16.50 in cash or $9.33 plus a retained interest. At the end of the day, 83 percent of Amscan was now owned by Goldman, Sachs, the estate of John A. Svenningsen owned 10 percent, and the company's current management held a 7 percent stake. (A managing director of Goldman, Sachs, Terrence M. O'Toole, now took over as chairman of the board, while Rittenberg continued to maintain operational control.) Moreover, Amscan was infused with $75 million in capital in order to provide the financial clout the company needed to take advantage of the growing party goods industry, which was now responsible for around $3.5 billion in annual sales and was growing at a 10 percent clip each year. Superstores such as Party City not only continued to prosper, they promoted the celebration of an even larger number of occasions, which in turn greatly enhanced the prospects of Amscan with its well entrenched position in the marketplace. Rittenberg also maintained that the party supplies market was actually "understored." As a result, Amscan was well positioned to enjoy even greater growth in the years to come.

In September 1998 Amscan expanded via external means, paying approximately $87 million for Minneapolis-based Anagram International, Inc., manufacturer and distributor of metallic balloons and other products made from synthetic materials. Anagram was founded in 1977 by Garry Kieves and family members. At the time of the acquisition the company was generating annual revenues in the $70 million range. While Rittenberg portrayed the acquisition as representing "a unique opportunity for Amscan to leverage its distribution in the party superstores," others outside the company were less enthusiastic. As reported by the *Westchester County Business Journal,* " 'The outlook is negative,' according to a Standard & Poor's Rating Services report released six days after the deal was announced. S&P gave Amscan a single B plus corporate rating and single B minus subordinated debt rating. 'Ratings reflect Amscan's weak financial profile, stemming from its high debt leverage, and participation in the fragmented, highly competitive party goods industry,' wrote S&P analyst Nicole Delz Lynch."

With Anagram contributing to the balance sheet for an entire year, Amscan saw its revenues improve from $235.3 million in 1998 to nearly $305 million in 1999. Net income also increased from $6.7 million to $10.2 million. These strong numbers were also the result of some internal changes. The company created a specialty sales force in 1999, targeting card and gift stores and other independent retailers. In addition, Amscan launched a gift line geared towards independents as a way to offer a one-stop shopping possibility. Amscan's balance sheet continue to show improvement in 2000 and 2001, when the company recorded sales of $323.5 million and $345.2 million. The company posted net income of $8.1 million in 2000 and $11 million in 2001.

M&D Balloons Acquisition: 2002

Early in 2002, Amscan completed another acquisition, paying $27.5 million in cash and stock for M&D Balloons Inc. to

Key Dates:

1948: Amscan Inc. is formed by Elvera Svenningsen.
1958: John A. Svenningsen becomes CEO.
1997: John Svenningsen dies from cancer.
1998: Anagram International is acquired.
2002: M&D Balloons is acquired.

American Greetings Corporation. Based in Manteno, Illinois, M&D manufactured both metallic and plastic balloons. For American Greetings, the deal allowed it to continue a major cost-cutting effort, while retaining the ability to distribute Mylar balloons through its Balloon Zone subsidiary by way of a supply contract with Amscan. The addition of M&D complemented Amscan's prior acquisition of Anagram, which ranked as the largest metallized balloon manufacturer in the world, with some $75 million in annual sales. M&D was second with $25 million, and together they formed a dominant force in the nonlatex party balloon segment. M&D also brought with it a patented film technology, Dynafloat, which enhanced the longevity of metallic balloons. Moreover, M&D possessed an impressive portfolio of licenses, including popular Disney and Nickelodeon characters. Within months, Amscan closed M&D's balloon-making factory, transferring operations to Anagram's more automated plant in Eden Prairie, Minnesota. For years, M&D had been at a competitive disadvantage, relying on its workers to lift, stack, and pack balloons manually.

In June 2002 Amscan took steps to once again become a publicly traded company, filing a registration for a projected $180 million stock offering. The $150 million net was earmarked to pay down debt. The underwriters were Goldman, Sachs, William Blair & Co., CIBC World Markets Corp., and Stephens Inc. This time management planned on a New York Stock Exchange listing. Later in 2002, however, management dropped its plans for an offering, opting instead for a refinancing agreement with Goldman Sachs Credit Partners L.P., which extended the maturity of its senior debt facilities. But this deal did not come to fruition, making the IPO operative once again. Finally, in March 2003 the offering was shelved permanently when Amscan and Goldman Sachs Credit Partners negotiated $200 million in loans.

In 2002 Amscan recorded revenues of $385.6 million and net income of $16 million. Looking to the future, Amscan sought to maintain its leading position of supplier of party goods to superstore clients and other chains, while also making greater inroads into the independent retail distribution channel. Since adding a specialty sales force in 1999, the company saw sales in this segment increase from $15 million to $38 million in 2002. Amscan was also interested in growing international sales, which represented 14 percent of total revenues in 2002. Of special interest were the United Kingdom, Germany, and Australia. As was the case with the purchase of Anagram and M&D, Amscan was open to opportunistic acquisitions that could complement its business.

Principal Subsidiaries

Anagram International, Inc.; Ya Otta Pinata.

Principal Competitors

American Greetings Corporation; Hallmark Cards, Inc.; The SF Holdings Group, Inc.

Further Reading

''Amscan Is a Dominant Force in Party Supplies,'' *Chain Drug Review,* June 29, 1998, p. 16.

Drain, Trisha McMahon, ''Amscan-ning the Horizon,'' *Party & Paper Retailer,* January 1992, p. 68.

Phillippidis, Alex, '' 'Party People' Celebrate $48 Million Sale of Stock,'' *Westchester County Business Journal,* January 6, 1997, p. 3.

—Ed Dinger

APL Limited

1111 Broadway
Oakland, California 94607
U.S.A.
Telephone: (510) 272-8000
Toll Free: 800-999-7733
Fax: (510) 272-7941
Web site: http://www.apl.com

Wholly Owned Subsidiary of Neptune Orient Lines
Incorporated: 1983
Employees: 5,117
Sales: $3.42 billion (2002)
NAIC: 488320 Marine Cargo Handling; 484110 General Freight Trucking, Local; 483111 Deep Sea Freight Transportation; 483113 Coastal & Great Lakes Freight Transportation; 488390 Other Support Activities-Water Transportation; 488991 Packing & Crating; 488210 Support Activities for Rail Transportation; 551112 Offices of Other Holding Companies; 541613 Marketing Consulting Services

APL Limited, formerly called the American President Companies Ltd., operates container shipping services by container ships on Pacific and Indian Ocean trade lanes, conducts transportation services between major Asian and North American cities and commercial centers, and serves the transportation needs of North America with an intermodal transportation network that includes rail, trucking, and freight brokerage and consolidation services. The company is considered one of the most efficiently operated shipping companies in the world.

Early History of Oldest Continuously Operating U.S. Steamship Company

The Pacific Mail Steamship Company, predecessor of the American President Companies Ltd., was founded in 1848, two years before the transcontinental railroad was completed; its founding at this time provides American President Companies its claim as the oldest continuously operated steamship company in the United States. The Pacific Mail Steamship Company set out to carry mail from the Isthmus of Panama to the Oregon Territory. In 1867 it began the first regular shipping service between the United States and Asia, carrying passengers, cargo, and mail between the western United States, China, and Japan. The company's wooden ships, weighing 2,500 gross tons, used steam power to drive paddle wheels set amidships; the paddle wheels were augmented by twin square-rigged masts.

In 1921, the Pacific Mail Steamship Company was acquired by Dollar Steamship Lines, a company founded in the early 1900s by lumberman Robert Dollar, who established a fleet of steam schooners to carry his lumber from mills in northern California and Oregon to cities and railheads in southern and central California.

Dollar Steamship Lines established around-the-world shipping services in 1925 and expanded those services up until 1938 when, staggering under the combined effects of the Great Depression and debts incurred through building its fleet, the company was on the brink of bankruptcy. In 1938 the Federal Maritime Commission arranged a subsidy to keep the company solvent; later that year, the Commission released the company from its debt in return for 90 percent of the Dollar Steamship Lines' common stock. The services of the Dollar Steamship Lines were considered vital to the United States in light of the rise of fascism in Europe and the Sino-Japanese war in the Far East.

Wartime Government Contracts and Big Changes Through the 1980s

On November 1, 1938, Dollar Steamship Lines' new board of directors changed its name to American President Lines Ltd.; the name change was due in part to the company's practice of naming its ships after American presidents. American President Lines' fleet saw service activity during World War II, as several ships were sold to the U.S. Navy for troop transports and others operated as "Liberty Ships" to transport materiel for the war effort.

After the war the company was involved in a costly and bitter seven-year court battle that resulted in its acquisition in 1952 by Ralph K. Davies, a former executive of Standard Oil of California, who had begun buying shares in American President

Company Perspectives:

People are the engine at APL, one of the largest logistics and container transportation companies in the world—a company at the heart of international trade. APL's roots are in one of the most venerable economic activities transcending national and geographic borders: trading with those at a distance via commerce on the sea—literally, ''shipping.'' Indeed, even today, most of world trade travels over the water. While shipping continues to be an important business, it is also now a part of something larger. It is one link in global ''supply chains''—the complex movements of and demand for raw materials, parts, sub-assemblies and finished products. And so today, our business is assisting retailers, manufacturers and our other customers to manage their own supply chains in whole or to manage distinct and individual links of those supply chains, such as shipping.

Lines in 1944. By 1952, Davies owned 11 percent of the outstanding shares of the company, becoming its largest minority shareholder. On October 29, 1952, a group of investors led by Davies outbid two other investor groups, including one led by R. Stanley, a son of Robert Dollar, and paid $18.3 million for the Federal Maritime Commission's controlling interest in the company. Davies became chairman of American President Lines, a position he held until 1971, and he merged the APL Associates with Natomas Company, a gold-dredging firm that grew to become an oil and gas exploration company and, in 1965, the parent organization of American President Lines.

When Davies took control of the company, APL was a leader in providing cargo and passenger services between the Pacific Northwest of the United States and the Far East and offered around-the-world services for cargo and passengers. The company had recently launched its efforts in intermodal shipping, when it acquired more than 1,000 small shipping containers in 1951. In intermodal shipping, large containers are packed with cargo at its source and moved—by truck, train, or oceangoing vessel—to the cargo's destination without being unpacked. APL purchased its first partially containerized ships in 1961; 12 years later, fully containerized vessels were entering its fleet.

In a retrenchment in the mid-1970s, under the leadership of Chandler Ide—who became head of Natomas Company by succeeding Davies in 1971—APL discontinued its around-the-world freight services and passenger services to concentrate on its Pacific and Indian Ocean lines. But it also began to parlay its capabilities in containerization into a North American intermodal network. In 1979 the company introduced the first container train, with service between the West Coast and New York, under the trade name ''LinerTrain.''

While building that land-based intermodal network, APL constructed the ship President Lincoln, the first of three C9-class, diesel-powered container ships it would build through the 1980s. The President Lincoln entered APL's fleet in 1982, the same year the company introduced its 45-foot high-cube shipping container to the industry.

APL was spun off from Natomas as an independent, publicly held company on September 1, 1983, in part as a result of a hostile takeover attempt on the company by Diamond Shamrock. The spinning off of the company separated Natomas's real estate and oil and gas ventures, which led the companies in different directions through the 1970s in their own burgeoning growth. The growth of that company and American President Lines made them incompatible for future relations, so the companies went their separate ways. Consequently, APL became an independent company, coming full circle to the type of company it had been in the mid-1950s. Financial specialist W. Bruce Seaton, who was then president of APL, was named chairman and chief executive officer.

In 1984 and 1985 APL introduced innovations such as lightweight rail cars that could accommodate two shipping containers stacked one on top of the other; a ''double-stack'' system for its LinerTrain; 48-foot-long containers for use in North America; and high-cube, wide-bodied refrigerated containers. Also in that period APL acquired two new J9-class diesel-powered container ships and three freight brokerage firms in the United States that were managed by its new subsidiary, American President Domestic, later called APL Land Transport Services.

The company continued its growth with the launching of a $500 million capital expansion program in 1986 that included the purchases of five new C10-class container ships and new rail equipment, and provided enhancements for its shipping terminals and computer systems. A year later, in 1987, the company moved to double the size of its Oakland, California, port facilities.

In a move that expanded the range of its intermodal service, APL in 1988 launched a door-to-door truck load transportation service for domestic freight in the United States. The ''Red Eagle'' service was started to compete with over-the-road truckload carriers. These moves through the 1980s were directed by W. Bruce Seaton, who had come to the company through the Natomas organization.

Seaton was highly critical of APL and was considered an outsider in the shipping industry when he was named president of the company in August 1977; however, he was given the Admiral of the Ocean Sea Award by the United Seamen's Service—considered to be one of the industry's most prestigious ''insider'' awards—in 1989 for having established APL as a leader in the industry. The United Seamen's Service, a benevolent professional association for seafarers, sailors, and dock men, cited Seaton's emphasis on the Pacific and Indian Ocean trade routes, intermodal services, and electronic and information services as areas in which he extended his company's leading position in the industry. Seaton retired as chairman and chief executive officer of the corporation on January 2, 1992.

Costly Changes Through the 1990s

APL went through a restructuring in the second and third quarter of 1990 that resulted in the departure of Donald C. Orris, the president of American President Domestic; the move also forced the company both to consolidate and refocus several of its services. Orris was replaced by Timothy J. Rhein, formerly president and chief executive of American President Lines; the

Key Dates:

1848: Pacific Mail Steamship Company is founded; the company is given a ten-year government contract to deliver mail between Panama and Oregon; William Henry Aspinwall is elected president of the company.
1856: Aspinwall retires as president of the company.
1865: The company purchases its main rival, the Atlantic Mail Steamship Company.
1867: The company begins its trans-Pacific passenger service.
1875: The company begins service to Australia and New Zealand.
1915: Pacific Mail is restricted from using the Panama Canal; its parent company, the Southern Pacific Railroad, begins selling off Pacific Mail's fleet.
1923: The company begins its tradition of naming ships after U.S. presidents when it purchases seven president ships from the U.S. government.
1924: Dollar Steamship Lines acquires the Pacific Mail name.
1938: The U.S. government assumes control of Dollar Steamship Lines, renaming it American President Lines.
1950: Ralph K. Davies purchases American President Lines from the U.S. government for $18 million.
1973: APL makes its final trans-Pacific passenger voyage.
1980: APL stock goes public.
1990: The company begins service to Vietnam.
1997: APL merges with Neptune Orient Lines (NOL), keeping its name; the company enters into the New World Alliance agreement.
2001: APL is named Best Carrier in *Journal of Commerce*'s first annual award.

unit under Rhein's leadership was renamed APL Land Transport Services Inc. Robert Dahl, then the company's chief financial officer, left his position. The cost of the restructuring caused APL to report a $60 million loss for the year in 1990.

APL launched double-stack intermodal train services between the United States and Mexico in the 1980s to connect the Ford automobile plant in Hermosillo, automotive component manufacturers in Mexico, with Ford's automobile component suppliers in the United States. In 1991, in a move to capitalize on the possible free trade agreement between the United States and Mexico, APL established its double-stack train service from Mexico City to Chicago, Illinois, for general freight and auto supplies headed for Chrysler operations in Mexico. That move was seen as putting APL in the position to take advantage of an expected increase in trade between the United States and Mexico.

Also in 1991 APL spent $78 million to buy back 3.8 million shares of its stock from Itel Corporation, a transportation equipment leasing company based in Chicago that held nearly 21 percent of the company's stock. Itel Corporation was considered by some likely to take over APL from 1988 until that stock sale.

By 1992, APL was operating a fleet of 20 full container ships—each of which, clinging to corporate tradition, was named after an American president—and a network of foreign-flag feeder vessels that changed in number due to requirements in the trade. The company's ships sailed under the U.S. flag. The 20 ships had a nominal international transportation volume of more than 20,000 40-foot equivalent units (FEUs) and ranged in maximum speeds from 21.1 to 24 knots.

APL tracked its fleet of containers, chassis, and trains through its APL Information Services, Ltd. subsidiary, which used a system of mainframe and mini- and microcomputers linked through a telecommunications network with its ships and offices in North America, Asia, and the Middle East. Those computer systems booked cargo and generated bills; tracked and controlled rail cars and containers; pre-planned the loading of containers onto ships; and routed ship, rail, and truck movements, while providing customers the ability to access information on the location and status of their cargo via touch-tone telephones, personal computers, and facsimile machines.

APL's largest customer for its international transportation operations has been the government of the United States, which was responsible for approximately 8 percent of the company's 1991 consolidated revenues of $2.44 billion. The company reported that its 1991 revenues from the U.S. government were increased substantially because of increased shipping for the Persian Gulf War. The company bid competitively on its contracts for the U.S. government.

John M. Lillie succeeded Seaton as chairman and chief executive officer of APL in January 1992. Lillie, a former chief executive of Lucky Stores Inc., was considered even more of an outsider than was Seaton when he took the company's helm. Lillie took control while the company was redirecting its non-stacktrain business and while the economy was in a state of recession. For these reasons, APL's revenues from its North America transportation operations declined in 1992. At the same time, volumes in the company's North American stacktrain operations were down. Still, APL's sales exceeded $2.5 billion in 1992.

In 1993, APL's revenues and volumes from North American stacktrain operations improved. This was due in large part to increased stacktrain services to Mexico and Canada. Meanwhile, APL entered into a 30-year lease with the Port of Los Angeles to form a new terminal facility, at a cost of approximately $70 million.

In 1994, APL formed an agreement with Transportation Maritime Mexicana (TMM), a Mexican transportation company, which allowed each to equally charter vessel space for three years. APL also signed a lease with the Port of Seattle to improve and expand its existing terminal facility. The amended lease included an expansion from 83 acres to 160 acres. Meanwhile, APL's stacktrain volumes improved with the recovering U.S. economy. The company added 1,000 containers to its fleet and increased its Mexican and Canadian shipments, in particular, automotive shipments between the United States and Mexico. At the same time, a collision involving APL's vessel, the President Washington, cost the company $2 million. Another cost came when the company lost its position as primary carrier of U.S. military cargo.

APL entered into a Global Alliance Agreement in 1995 and began service to Europe and Latin America. The company also became the first global carrier to create a web site, offering online shipment transactions. In 1997, one year shy of the company's 150-year-anniversary, APL merged with Neptune Orient Lines (NOL), a shipping company from Singapore. The merger—which cost NOL $825 million, or $33.50 per share—created one of the world's largest global transportation companies. The following year, APL entered the New World Alliance agreement (with Hyundai Merchant Marine and Mitsui O.S.K. Lines), improving the company's coverage of world markets.

Staggering Losses Post-Millennium

APL sales increased to $3.8 billion in 2000. In the same year, APL expanded its container fleet with $100 million worth of new containers; bolstered its Asia-Australia service; and announced a new Mediterranean Atlantic Service. In the next few years, APL would receive a number of awards, including Best Intra-Asia Shipping Line by CargoNews Asia; Best Carrier in the *Journal of Commerce*; First Global Carrier Award from Philips Electronics; Sri Lanka's ICS awards (for both the east and westbound trade lanes); Wal-Mart's International Ocean Carrier of the Year; Asia Logistics Awards' top IT innovator; and ''Best Transpacific Shipping Line,'' at the Asian Freight & Supply Chain Awards.

Yet, the company's sales dropped to below $3.6 billion in 2001, while APL's parent company, NOL, reported a $57 million loss for the year. The loss was attributed to sluggish Asia-Europe trade markets and an overall poor economy. Specifically, for APL, trade volumes did not increase during a time when capacity increased more than 9 percent. At the same time, insurance costs, as well as those associated with new security requirements, skyrocketed.

In 2002, NOL suffered a staggering $330 million loss, while APL's sales dropped to $3.4 billion, with a $71 million loss in profits. In response, APL—led by acting CEO Ron Widdows—reduced costs and sped up decision making. For one, the position of COO, which was held by Ed Aldridge, was eliminated.

By 2003, business was improving for APL, which recorded first quarter earnings (before net interest expense and tax) of $87 million. For the same quarter, NOL reported a net profit of $88.7 million. APL expanded its capacity by upsizing vessels and partnership measures with other carriers. The company ended 2003 with a hopeful bilateral maritime agreement between the United States and China. China's market was thought to be one of the world's fastest-growing maritime trade zones.

Principal Subsidiaries

APL Logistics.

Principal Competitors

Alexander & Baldwin; A.P. Møller-Maersk; Bollore; Crowley Maritime; Evergreen Marine; NYK Line.

Further Reading

American President Lines Fact Book, Oakland, Calif.: American President Companies Ltd., 1987.

Armbruster, William, ''APC Dedicates Big Intermodal Facility in NJ,'' *Journal of Commerce and Commercial,* September 15, 1989.

''EBusiness Trademark Reports: APL Limited,'' *TrademarkBots.com, Inc.,* Business Reports, September 1, 2003.

''Freight Firm Launches Domestic Land Service,'' *Journal of Commerce and Commercial,* February 19, 1988.

Grabowicz, Paul, ''American President's Big Oakland Move,'' *Tribune* (Oakland, Calif.), July 22, 1987.

Levine, Daniel S., ''APC Buys Own Shares from Itel,'' *Tribune* (Oakland, Calif.), March 21, 1991.

''Lillie to Succeed Seaton at American President Cos.,'' *San Francisco Business Times,* December 14, 1990.

Magnier, Mark, ''APC's Inland Unit Realigns Operations,'' *Journal of Commerce and Commercial,* June 27, 1990.

——, ''Jury Still Out on Impact of Itel-Henley-APC Deal,'' *Journal of Commerce and Commercial,* August 1, 1991.

——, ''Layoffs Underway As APC Realigns,'' *Journal of Commerce and Commercial,* September 18, 1990.

——, ''Many on Street See American President As Ripe for Takeover,'' *Journal of Commerce and Commercial,* August 1, 1991.

——, ''Outsider Makes Mark in Shipping,'' *Journal of Commerce and Commercial,* October 18, 1989.

Niven, John, *The American President Lines and Its Forebears, 1848–1984: From Paddlewheelers to Containerships,* Newark: University of Delaware Press, 1987.

—update: Candice Mancini

Bauerly Companies

4787 Shadow Wood Dr. NE
Sauk Rapids, Minnesota 56379
U.S.A.
Telephone: (320) 251-9472
Fax: (320) 529-2716
Toll Free: (800) 450-9472
Web site: http://www.bauerly.com

Private Company
Incorporated: 1968 as Bauerly Brothers, Inc.
Employees: 750
Sales: $143 million (2003 est.)
NAIC: 327992 Ground or Treated Mineral and Earth Manufacturing; 237310 Highway, Street and Bridge Construction

Bauerly Companies, headquartered in Sauk Rapids, Minnesota, stands out as one of the largest producers of aggregate, asphalt, ready-mix, and concrete in the state. The company serves a primary market area consisting of approximately 30 counties in central Minnesota. Bauerly Companies maintains 22 ready-mix plants, five asphalt plants, 20 aggregate crushing and washing facilities, and five regional maintenance buildings.

Building a Better Life: 1950s–60s

In the early 1950s on the prairies of central Minnesota, family farms dotted the landscape. Leo Bauerly, his wife Agnes, and their young family of nine children operated such a farm near Sauk Rapids, Minnesota.

Hard work, dedication, and innovation were necessary to keep family farms afloat, but even with the best of care, circumstances often led farmers to look for alternative ways to supplement their limited income and increase their cash flow. A strong entrepreneurial spirit, and the incentive to support a growing family, inspired Leo Bauerly to create such a business. What began as a little side income evolved over the generations into a large private business known as Bauerly Companies.

The groundwork for the company was set in 1956 when Leo Bauerly invested some money in two single-axle dump trucks. Bauerly and his eldest sons began hauling materials for local construction projects. Two years later, impressed with the return from his previous purchase, Bauerly added two more dump trucks to his fleet and began leasing the trucks to area contractors.

By 1963, the Bauerlys had purchased a rock crusher and were manufacturing the construction materials themselves in addition to hauling construction supplies. With the purchase of the new crushing machine, the business was awarded a contract to crush gravel for Port Mille Lacs.

Leo's four oldest sons had grown up working for their father both on the farm and in his aggregate business. Summers and vacation time were spent hauling and helping out the family. Initially, Dave and Jerry Bauerly had gone off to college and had planned career paths outside the confines of the family business. Their brother, Brian, became the first of the brothers who began working part-time in the family enterprise in 1967.

In 1968, a tragic turn of events meant significant change for the family. Leo Bauerly was suddenly killed in a car accident. The two oldest of the Bauerly boys, Dave and Jerry, took over the responsibility of providing for the family. The brothers decided to build on the resources and reputation Leo had established and soon formally incorporated the business as Bauerly Brothers. The company continued its work of producing aggregates and hauling materials for construction.

In 1969, Mike and Mark Bauerly began working at the company and the partnership began to expand its operations. Bauerly Brothers bought Mille Lacs Sand and Gravel and increased its aggregate crushing. Through innovation and hard work the company took shape. To get the competitive edge the brothers would often buy and adapt equipment to suit specific needs. The long hours spent and the inventive spirit that the Bauerlys possessed helped the fledgling company make its mark in the local industry.

Throughout the 1970s all six brothers worked for the company. Brian and Jake Bauerly, the youngest of the clan, joined

Company Perspectives:

Bauerly Companies strives to be the preferred source of aggregate, asphalt, and concrete for customers in the regions we serve. We strive to continuously meet customer expectations, be a leader in the markets we serve, be a positive force in the communities in which we live and work, and provide growth opportunities for our employees while sustaining our profitability which guarantees our growth into the future.

Bauerly Companies is customer driven, provides superior quality and service, and builds strong relationships with its customers and suppliers. We strive to provide the safest work environment for our employees and those we serve. We invest in the development of productive employees through training and improvements in technology. We believe in an efficient process and a lean staff, the necessity of innovation to provide a competitive advantage, and the importance of people as individuals. We focus on what we know best to make a fair profit to meet our obligations and perpetuate our future growth. We encourage PRIDE (Personal Responsibility In Delivering Excellence).

the team in 1970. Agnes Bauerly, the family matriarch, always played an instrumental role at the office. Agnes maintained a constant presence at the company throughout its years, encouraging excellence and keeping an eye on daily happenings.

Togetherness paid off in 1971 when the family company received its first big crushing and hauling contract. The company was enlisted in Carlton County, Minnesota, to supply 150,000 cubic yards of aggregate for construction fill.

In 1972, with some capital behind them, the brothers purchased the company's first mobile concrete truck and began providing concrete in addition to aggregate. The company also bought its first asphalt plant in 1972 and added a Pioneer crusher to its equipment holdings.

By 1974, Bauerly Brothers was solidly poised to enter the concrete business and added two ready-mix plants to its assets. The first plant was in Foley, Minnesota. The Foley plant was soon followed by a second plant slightly farther east in the town of Milaca. The business had grown and in 1975 Jake and Mark Bauerly became full-time employees of the company.

The ready-mix plant in Foley was moved west to Sauk Rapids in 1976 where the company established its headquarters and several facilities. Towards the end of the decade the company continued to expand by buying ready-mix operations around the state, a trend that would continue throughout the 1980s and 1990s. Bauerly acquired its first such plant in 1979. That year, Bauerly bought out Economy Ready Mix with sites in Braham, Cambridge, and Mora, Minnesota, steadily adding to its regional influence and expanding its market share.

Throughout the decades, Bauerly Brothers built the company by combining a strong work ethic with many industry innovations, particularly those related to mechanical equipment. The company often adapted standard construction equipment to meet specialized needs or made improvements to equipment that allowed the company to be more efficient. Bauerly designed and built a Supertruck that could haul enormous loads. The company developed and operated eight Supertrucks for its construction hauling. In addition to its Supertrucks, the equipment division staff at Bauerly built signature crushers and screens for its aggregate crushing and washing division.

Over the years Bauerly Companies invested in industry-related technological advances to further develop its products. A state-of-the-art laboratory at its corporate headquarters allowed the company to meet technical requirements for asphalt and ready-mix production. Scientific laboratory precision in the design of products allowed the company to meet specifications at job sites. Bauerly Companies often set up portable labs on site to ensure that both quality and efficiency standards would be met.

The 1980s and 1990s: Crushing the Competition Through Expansion

The decade of the 1980s was characterized by rapid growth for Bauerly. The company bought out regional competitors through a series of acquisitions designed to broaden the company's geographic positioning. The business now operated east, west, north, and south of the hub city of St. Cloud, Minnesota.

In 1984, the company purchased Hanson Ready Mix in Princeton. The company's growth also created the need for larger administrative and maintenance work areas and Bauerly Brothers added on to its office building and shop spaces. The following year Bauerly built another drum mix plant to keep up with demand for its products.

The year 1987 proved the adage, "if you build it they will come," and the company put its plants to work. Bauerly Brothers had won the contract for a section of Interstate 35 and needed to produce, haul, and lay 350,000 tons of asphalt.

Expansion continued in 1988, when the company expanded its primary market to the south. Bauerly Brothers bought Rockite Ready Mix and Block with facilities in Hutchinson, Litchfield, South Haven, Glencoe, and Cosmos, Minnesota. In 1989, the company targeted the town of St. Joseph, Minnesota, and bought Borgert Block for an undisclosed price.

In 1993, Bauerly teamed up with the local Cold Spring Granite Company to recycle waste granite for use as a high-quality aggregate in its concrete and asphalt. The company maintained a commitment to the environment that could be seen through various company-sponsored programs.

The company recycled many of its own resources including oil, concrete, and asphalt. In addition to its commitment to recycling, Bauerly worked hard on the reclamation of its mining sites throughout the state. Many sites were transformed into wildlife habitat, wetlands, or developed into home subdivisions.

The next few years brought more growth through acquisition. In an area of isolated farming towns there were many independently run cement and block companies, and Bauerly Brothers bought them up one at a time, growing its identity and market share in a fairly short expanse of time.

Key Dates:

1956: Leo Bauerly purchases dump trucks to supplement farm income.
1958: Bauerly buys two more trucks and begins leasing them.
1968: Leo Bauerly is killed in car accident; Dave and Jerry Bauerly incorporate as Bauerly Brothers, Inc.
1984: Company acquires Hanson Ready Mix in Princeton, Minnesota; adds shop and office at headquarters in Sauk Rapids.
1987: Company paves Interstate 35.
1988: Bauerly purchases Rockite Ready Mix & Block.
1989: Company acquires Borgert Block.
1997–98: Bauerly Brothers reorganizes its management structure and consolidates its holdings.
1999: Regional offices are opened in Hutchinson, Minnesota.
2000: Company builds new ready-mix plants in Albertville, Isanti/Cambridge, and South Haven, Minnesota.
2001: Bauerly Companies merges with Knife River Corporation, a wholly owned subsidiary of MDU Resources, Incorporated.

By 1997, Bauerly Brothers had grown significantly and the company decided that it was time to work on its infrastructure. The brothers set up five divisional management teams. The five divisions included: asphalt, concrete, aggregates, equipment, and central services. Each of the brothers contributed to management of the divisions, with Jerry serving as president, Brian as head of the concrete division, Mike overseeing equipment, Dave leading engineering, Mark controlling aggregates and central services, and Jake managing finances and the company's asphalt operations. At the same time the company implemented a regional dispatching system for its concrete business.

With a new management structure in place the company began to look towards some consolidation and business revamping in 1998. It sold off its block company in St. Joseph and Hutchinson, moving the remainder of its St. Joseph operation to a new location. Bauerly consolidated its holdings in North Branch, Minnesota, and its BREMIX, BBI, and Economy Ready Mix facilities, forming one corporation.

In 1999, the newly named Bauerly Companies built a new regional office and ready-mix plant in Hutchinson, Minnesota. Three ready-mix plants were opened the following year. A plant opened in Albertville, Minnesota, followed by one in the Isanti/Cambridge area and one in South Haven, Minnesota.

Due to Bauerly Companies' strong belief in giving back to the communities in which it worked, the company established its Partners for Parks program. Partners for Parks provided cash and in-kind donations through grants for local public ''green space'' projects. The program provided significant resources to area cities and schools throughout its years. The company stated in its corporate newsletter that: ''environment, community, customers, and employees are the primary stakeholders at Bauerly Brothers. To recognize the value of these stakeholders, the Partners for Parks program was developed to collaborate with its stakeholders by building better communities.''

Bauerly Companies received many awards in recognition of its work. Some of the Associations that lauded the company were National Asphalt Paving Association, Minnesota Asphalt Paving, the Department of Transportation, Minnesota Association of Ready-Mix, and several National Sand and Gravel Awards. In 2001, Bauerly Companies was recognized as an outstanding business by the St. Cloud, Minnesota Area Chamber of Commerce when it received its 2001 Entrepreneur of the Year Award.

In June 2001, MDU Resources Inc., a publicly traded company on the New York Stock Exchange, signed an agreement to purchase Bauerly Brothers. The acquisition occurred through MDU's construction materials subsidiary, the Knife River Corporation. Knife River Corporation mined and marketed raw material and construction products and services in Alaska, California, Hawaii, Minnesota, Montana, Washington, and Wyoming.

Bauerly Companies, with its long history of successful growth and its commitment to giving back responsibly to the communities where it operated seemed poised to continue to be a industry leader in its market areas for years to come. The harsh environment in Minnesota and an insufficient roadway system to meet increased demand had put road construction on the list of state priorities. With many highways in the state of Minnesota slated for expansion, and existing highways in constant need of repair, the outlook for future markets appeared solid. Teaming up with Knife River Corporation gave the company resources for further development and expansion. With many years of leadership behind it, Bauerly was well-positioned for future growth.

Principal Competitors

AME Group; Gemstone Products Company; Aggregate Industries.

Further Reading

Bauerly Ink, May, August and December 2003 issues.
Dominik, John J., *St. Cloud: The Triplet City,* Sun Valley, Calif.: American Historical Press, 2002, p. 150.

—Susan B. Culligan

Blodgett Holdings, Inc.

44 Lakeside Avenue
Burlington, Vermont 05401-5242
U.S.A.
Telephone: (802) 860-3700
Toll Free: (800) 331-5842
Fax: (802) 864-0183
Web site: http://www.blodgett.com

Wholly Owned Subsidiary of The Middleby Corporation
Incorporated: 1854 as G.S. Blodgett & Company
Employees: 600
Sales: $125 million (2003 est.)
NAIC: 333319 Other Commercial and Service Industry Machinery Manufacturing

Blodgett Holdings, Inc., through G.S. Blodgett Corporation and other subsidiaries, is one of the world's leading manufacturers of specialized commercial cooking equipment. The product lines of Blodgett and its affiliates include Blodgett convection ovens, conveyor ovens, and ranges; Blodgett Combi combination convection oven/steamers; MagiKitch'n charbroilers and grills; and Pitco fryers. With the help of its parent company, The Middleby Corporation, Blodgett sells its products in more than 100 countries worldwide.

Early History

The company was started by Gardner S. Blodgett, an ambitious and imaginative plumber who ran his own store at 191 College Street in Burlington, Vermont. In 1848, when Blodgett was only 29 years old, he was approached by the owner of a nearby tavern, who told him that his oven was not heating food properly. Specifically, customers were complaining that the meat from the tavern was cooked on one side but not on the other. In response, Blodgett and his partner built a wood-burning stove that solved the tavern owner's problems. The success of Blodgett's creation spread quickly and soon tavern owners from the surrounding areas were requesting new and improved ovens. By 1854, the young entrepreneur patented his improved baking oven and incorporated his business as G.S. Blodgett & Company.

The company thrived during the mid- and late 1850s, but with the onset of the American Civil War in 1860, Blodgett joined the Union Army and his business came to a standstill. Blodgett attained the rank of assistant quartermaster of volunteers, helping to outfit all the members of the First Vermont Cavalry. He was also instrumental in acquiring and planning the United States National Cemetery in Arlington, Virginia.

When Blodgett returned to civilian life, he began to rebuild his company. In just a few years, Blodgett was again providing high-quality commercial ovens to tavern owners in Burlington, Vermont, and was also experimenting with other types of ovens as well. Blodgett was convinced that newer, more efficient types of ovens were needed by the commercial cooking and baking industry, and he began producing convection ovens, deck ovens, and conveyor ovens. With the addition of these products, the company's revenues climbed rapidly. Blodgett became a wealthy man by the 1880s.

During the 1890s, the company continued to increase its revenues and expand its customer base. More and more employees were hired, including a young man named John S. Patrick. Patrick, hired as the company's secretary and treasurer, soon became an indispensable part of Blodgett's management team. He learned quickly about the company's affairs, even the intricate details surrounding the manufacture of convection ovens. In 1892 Patrick decided to purchase Blodgett's interest in the company and assume control of the firm's operations. The new owner's acquisition signaled the beginning of three generations of Patrick family control and management over the company.

Establishment of Pitco Frialator and MagiKitch'n, Early 20th Century

Like his predecessor, John Patrick was determined to develop and expand the company's product line. In 1902 he began to develop ovens that used gas as their energy source. Then, following years of increasing sales and profits, Patrick decided to establish a new operating division outside Vermont. Located in Bow, New Hampshire, the new division was founded as Pitco Frialator in 1918. Specializing in the manufacture of commercial frying equipment, the new division was an immediate success. Restaurants from all over the country, especially on the

Company Perspectives:

Today, the Blodgett Oven Company is still one of the leading manufacturers of commercial ovens in the world. Restaurants, fast-food chains, hotels, hospitals, institutions, small businesses and large corporations alike rely on the Blodgett name. In fact, our ovens have been in demand overseas since the late 1880s—long before global markets and international trade became a focus of our modern world.

Despite widespread success—or maybe because of it—Blodgett has never strayed from its original goal. Or its roots. Our corporate headquarters are located in Burlington, Vermont—just 1 mile from where the company founder and namesake forged a cooking revolution in cast iron nearly 150 years ago.

And while the times and foodservice needs have changed since then, Blodgett's commitment to build the best remains the same.

eastern seaboard, began ordering Blodgett equipment, and sales continued to rise.

During the 1920s, the company took advantage of the expanding American economy and the plethora of new restaurants opening in major cities, including New York, Boston, Philadelphia, and Chicago. With the crash of the stock market in the fall of 1929 and the start of the Great Depression, however, people were forced to conserve their financial resources and, as a result, many restaurants were forced out of business because of a loss of customers. Although Blodgett felt the effects of the Depression, the company was able to remain competitive. In 1931 the firm was being managed so competently by the Patrick family that a new operating division was established in Quakertown, Pennsylvania. This division, called MagiKitch'n, a manufacturer of charbroilers for the commercial market, was another success story.

Having survived the Depression, Blodgett entered the 1940s poised to expand its market share in the burgeoning commercial foodservice industry. With the United States' entry into World War II, the U.S. government placed numerous contracts with Blodgett to supply ovens for cooking food near the front lines of battlefields. Former employees who were now soldiers would write back to company management describing how Blodgett ovens were able to cook food evenly in the most terrible weather conditions. When these same former employees were served food that was improperly cooked, they suggested to their quartermaster sergeants that Blodgett would be able to provide an efficient oven that would satisfy the battle-weary soldiers who needed a good hot meal. Surprisingly, it was in this way that Blodgett sold numerous ovens to the U.S. Army and Navy throughout the war years.

Continued Expansion in the Postwar Era

After World War II, and continuing through the 1950s, Blodgett built upon its previous success. Each passing year brought increased revenues, with more benefits accruing to the company's employees all the time. The Patrick family, still in control of the company's entire operations, built a tradition of excellent management-employee relations over the years. Not only rewarding its long-term workers with profit sharing and generous pension plans, the Patrick family never laid off a single worker during the time it ran the company. By 1958, Blodgett had grown large enough for management to consider expanding company operations overseas. Consequently, Blodgett International contracted its first foreign distributor in the same year. Another development in the 1950s was the introduction of a line of pizza deck ovens.

Growth continued apace from the 1960s into the 1980s. The company sold ovens to the entire spectrum of the foodservices industry, from such large fast-food restaurant chains as Pizza Hut and Taco Bell, to such small chains of three or four units as Zachary's Pizza in Burlington, Vermont. Blodgett also sold ovens to grade schools, high schools, universities, hospitals, bakeries, U.S. Army and Navy installations, sports complexes, gourmet restaurants, taverns, large-volume food manufacturers, and hotels. In the foreign arena, Blodgett contracted numerous distributors throughout Europe. The company in 1982 acquired Q Industries Food Equipment Company, a small manufacturer of conveyor ovens based in Chicago. In 1985 Blodgett purchased the intellectual property rights from a German manufacturer of multifunction steamer ovens. One year later, management created Blodgett Combi, a new division of the firm that produced both the multifunction steamer oven and the company's famous brand name Mastertherm conveyor ovens. Together, these two items quickly became the most popular of all Blodgett products.

Management-Led Buyout and Restructuring: Late 1980s and Early 1990s

During the mid-1980s, the Patrick family, who had remained in control of Blodgett over the years, began to contemplate how to raise liquidity for their shareholders. The three options the family considered included a merger with another company, a public offering of stock in the firm, and the sale of the company. Doug Johnson, hired as the president of Blodgett in 1985, reportedly contacted some of his friends on Wall Street and began to arrange for a leveraged buyout of Blodgett by the company's management. Along with Sam Hartwell, who joined Blodgett in 1988, the two men reached a deal with The First Boston Corporation and Metropolitan Life Insurance Company that accounted for approximately 85 percent of the capital needed for the buyout.

Johnson and Hartwell, acting as co-chairmen of the company, immediately analyzed Blodgett's financial condition and operational structure, and determined that certain changes were necessary. One year after the management buyout of Blodgett, Johnson and Hartwell either closed or sold three company divisions that were losing money or just breaking even. They relocated the conveyor oven business, which had previously been operating out of Chicago, to Burlington, Vermont. This relocation also signaled a more aggressive strategy for marketing the company's conveyor ovens, both domestically and internationally. Three production facilities were sold, including sites at Burlington and Philadelphia, and then leased back to Blodgett in order to raise more working capital. During these changes, Johnson and Hartwell also implemented strict cost-control measures, while at the same time reducing expenses and working capital.

In the early 1990s, under the new management, Blodgett made an aggressive move to expand its international image. The

Key Dates:

1848: Gardner S. Blodgett builds a wood-burning stove for a tavern owner in Burlington, Vermont.
1854: Blodgett patents his improved baking oven and incorporates his business as G.S. Blodgett & Company.
Post–Civil War Years: Blodgett rebuilds his business, expanding his line with such new products as deck ovens and conveyor ovens.
1892: John S. Patrick, the company's secretary and treasurer, purchases the company from the founder.
1902: Company begins developing ovens that use gas as their energy source.
1918: Pitco Frialator is established as a new division, based in Bow, New Hampshire, specializing in commercial frying equipment.
1931: A new operating division called MagiKitch'n is created; based in Quakertown, Pennsylvania, MagiKitch'n begins producing commercial charbroilers.
1958: G.S. Blodgett contracts its first foreign distributor.
1985: Blodgett gains the rights to a multifunction steamer oven from a German manufacturer.
1986: A new division called Blodgett Combi is created to produce the multifunction steamer oven.
1988: The Patrick family sells Blodgett through a management-led buyout.
1995: Blodgett International is established as an operating unit of G.S. Blodgett Corporation.
1997: Maytag Corporation acquires Blodgett for $96.4 million in cash and assumes $53.2 million in debt; Maytag sets up Blodgett Holdings, Inc. as a holding company for G.S. Blodgett Corp.
2001: Maytag sells Blodgett Holdings and subsidiaries to The Middleby Corporation in a $95 million deal.

company began to exhibit its products at trade shows in London, Prague, Singapore, and Sydney, Australia. As the firm's international revenues grew, management decided to open sales offices in Prague, Amsterdam, Singapore, and Toronto. Slowly, Blodgett began to successfully compete with other top companies in the highly specialized field of commercial cooking equipment, including Cidelcem of France, Fujimak of Japan, Zanussi of Italy, and Rational of Germany. In 1995 the company gave an even greater profile to overseas sales by establishing Blodgett International as an operating unit of G.S. Blodgett Corporation.

The reorganization of Blodgett after the leveraged management buyout started to reap rewards by the end of 1993. The term ''de-leveraging,'' used by Wall Street analysts to describe the paying off of debts after a leveraged buyout, was worked on assiduously by Johnson and Hartwell. Approximately 60 percent of all the company's senior debt was paid off during that year. At the same time, since 1988 Blodgett was able to increase its sales by an impressive 67 percent, up from $67 million to $110 million in just five years. More importantly, Blodgett snared nearly 12 percent of the entire market for products manufactured in the commercial cooking equipment industry, which has annual domestic sales greater than $1 billion. Of the 650 members that belonged to the National Association of Food Equipment Manufacturers, Blodgett was one of the top 50 companies with sales over the $25 million mark.

Blodgett management also made a commitment to research and development. Since the late 1980s, over $3 million per year was being devoted to developing new products, and by the mid-1990s over 50 percent of the company's offerings were new. The company manufactured ovens that could bake 300 to 400 pizzas in one hour; combined microwave and radio frequency technology with traditional methods of hot air and atmospheric steam; and was in the process of developing products that used voice activation to control oven temperatures, magnetic induction, and automatically programmed cooking cycles. In the early 1990s, the company's products cost anywhere from $500 to $20,000, and Blodgett engineers traveled as far away as Sao Paulo, Brazil, to investigate new ideas and search for new technology in order to improve and develop its products.

The Maytag Years: 1997 to 2001

By 1997 G.S. Blodgett Corp. was producing commercial ovens, fryers, and charbroilers at four manufacturing plants in Vermont and one each in New Hampshire and Pennsylvania. The company had 750 workers and annual revenues of about $135 million. In October 1997 Blodgett once again came under new ownership. As part of a push into the commercial appliance sector, home appliance giant Maytag Corporation acquired Blodgett for $96.4 million in cash and the assumption of $53.2 million in debt. Maytag set up Blodgett Holdings, Inc. as a holding company for G.S. Blodgett Corp. and its subsidiaries. In April 1998 Glenn B. Kelsey was named president of Blodgett, having previously served for 17 years in various executive positions at Oneida Ltd., a world leader in the manufacture of stainless-steel and silver-plated flatware.

Unfortunately, under Maytag, Blodgett changed from a thriving enterprise into a troubled, money-losing company by the early 2000s. John Briggs reported in the *Burlington Free Press* in early 2003 that according to Selim Bassoul, who later headed up Blodgett under new ownership, ''Blodgett had become 'bloated' under Maytag, driven off longtime customers with poor service, and made 'inadvisable product choices.' '' Maytag had intended to follow up its purchase of Blodgett with that of other commercial appliance makers, in order to gain a major presence in that market. But it was never able to complete another deal in that sector, most notably being a losing bidder in 1999 for Scotsman Industries, Inc., a leading producer of commercial refrigeration, ice-making, and food-storage products (the winner was Enodis plc with a $712 million offer). This left Blodgett in the position of comprising an extremely small part of Maytag's overall operations, its revenues accounting for only about 3 percent of Maytag's total sales of more than $4.2 billion. Another factor in Maytag's eventual decision to sell Blodgett was the lack of sufficient synergies between the firm's home-appliance and commercial-appliance operations.

In March 2001 Blodgett announced plans to build a new headquarters building and factory near its existing main office in Burlington. Just two months later, however, Maytag announced that it was exploring the sale of Blodgett in order to sharpen its focus on its core home appliances. An additional impetus for the divestiture came in June when Maytag agreed to buy the Amana line of refrigerators and microwave ovens.

Purchase by Middleby: 2001

Maytag thereupon agreed in August 2001 to sell Blodgett Holdings and subsidiaries to The Middleby Corporation. The deal closed in December of that year with Middleby paying $74 million in cash and $21 million in notes. Based in Elgin, Illinois, Middleby, like Blodgett, was a major manufacturer of commercial foodservice equipment, including Middleby Marshall conveyor ovens, Toastmaster toasters and sandwich grills, and Southbend ranges, ovens, broilers, steamers, and grills. Middleby had annual sales of about $127 million, so the purchase of Blodgett effectively doubled its revenues.

Following completion of the deal, Bassoul, the president and CEO of Middleby, was named acting president of Blodgett. He immediately concentrated on returning the firm to profitability: plans for the new headquarters/factory were shelved; two Blodgett factories in Williston and Shelburne, Vermont, were closed; and the workforce was cut by about 100 employees. During 2002, Blodgett turned a profit for the first time in several years. New product development was given a boost under the new ownership, with the introduction of the Blodgett Range, a premium, heavy-duty commercial range in late 2002 to further leverage the well-known Blodgett name. Another innovation was a new Blodgett Combi model that could steam without a boiler, simplifying cleaning and maintenance.

Blodgett appeared to have a bright future as a Middleby subsidiary, as it continued to be the market leader in both combination ovens and convention ovens, with Pitco holding onto the number two position in fryers. Although the U.S. fast-food industry was fairly saturated, limiting the potential for future sales in that core sector, Blodgett—and Middleby—were targeting two main opportunities for growth: the rapidly growing ''fast-casual'' restaurant sector and overseas sales, particularly based on the international expansion of major U.S. restaurant chains.

Principal Subsidiaries

Cloverleaf Properties, Inc.; Frialator International Limited (U.K.); G.S. Blodgett Corporation; G.S. Blodgett International, Ltd. (Barbados); MagiKitch'n Inc.; Pitco Frialator, Inc.

Principal Competitors

Enodis plc; Hobart Corporation; Vulcan-Hart Corporation; Wells Manufacturing Company; AB Electrolux; Ali Group.

Further Reading

Breskin, Ira, ''Maytag Caught in Buy-and-Sell Shuffle,'' *Daily Deal,* June 9, 2001.

Briggs, John, ''G.S. Blodgett in the Black,'' *Burlington (Vt.) Free Press,* March 12, 2003.

Guy, Sandra, ''Innovation Key Focus for Food-Service Equipment Company,'' *Chicago Sun-Times,* August 27, 2003, p. 70.

Johnson, Greg, ''Maytag Unloads G.S. Blodgett Unit,'' *Daily Deal,* September 1, 2001.

Johnson, J. Douglas, and Samuel A. Hartwell, *The Story of G.S. Blodgett Corporation: 145 Years of Success and Still Growing,* New York: Newcomen Society, 1993.

Kennedy, Kevin, ''Blodgett Makes Exporting Easy,'' *Vermont Business,* May 1987, p. 50.

—Thomas Derdak
—update: David E. Salamie

Blue Nile Inc.

705 Fifth Avenue South, Suite 900
Seattle, Washington 98104
U.S.A.
Telephone: (206) 336-6700
Fax: (206) 336-6750
Web site: http://www.bluenile.com

Private Company
Founded: 1999
Employees: 125
Sales: $120 million (2003 est.)
NAIC: 339911 Jewelry (Including Precious Metals) Manufacturing

Mark Vadon, founder of Blue Nile Inc., considered himself intelligent, discerning, and in complete control of his life. Yet when he began to shop for an engagement ring, he was in over his head. To the well-educated Vadon, the choices were endless and confusing, due in large part to the commission-based sales of local jewelry retailers. With thousands of dollars at stake, were salespersons truly being honest about the diamonds they were selling? Unwilling and unable to put his trust in traditional jewelry stores, Vadon made a critical decision and went home, where he turned to the Internet for help. What he found was the aptly named Internet Diamonds web site. The rest, as they say, is history. Internet Diamonds was reborn as Blue Nile Inc. in 1999 and in four short years became the Internet's largest online source for fine jewelry.

Dazzled and Confused: Late 1990s

Mark Vadon grew up in New Jersey as the middle of three children. His father was an M.D. and his mother sold real estate. An intelligent and adventurous soul, Vadon attended Harvard University, where he received undergraduate degrees in American history and European social theory, then went on to Stanford University for his M.B.A. During and after his higher education, Vadon backpacked around Europe and traveled throughout Asia and Africa. He then became a ''Bainie'' working in the San Francisco office of Bain & Company, the well known management consulting firm, in 1992. Vadon worked as a consumer products strategist, which proved invaluable in his later endeavors. He was still employed as a Bainie when he began looking for an engagement ring in 1998.

After giving up on traditional retail jewelers and disingenuous salespersons, Vadon started surfing the Web. He found an informative site called Internet Diamonds, which featured detailed descriptions of various diamonds and a toll free number to call for assistance. Vadon found what he considered an outstanding engagement ring at an excellent price. He was so impressed by the online experience—and its business potential—that he contacted the site's owner, Doug Williams, a diamond wholesaler based in Seattle, Washington. Vadon then flew to Seattle, met with Williams, and expressed an interest in buying the diamond web site if he could raise the necessary capital.

Vadon returned to San Francisco and met with a number of venture capitalists. By late spring in 1999 the 29-year-old Vadon had raised an initial $6 million in funds, selling his idea with relative ease in the dot.com boom. Vadon then lined up suppliers and distributors and turned Internet Diamonds into a full-service, user-friendly online store to sell baubles to bachelors.

After sealing the deal in May 1999, Vadon renamed the fledgling company ''Blue Nile,'' which he considered more in tune with his goals for the online jeweler. Within a few months Vadon had raised another infusion of capital for Blue Nile, this time $32 million, $10 million of which went into a major marketing thrust launched in November. The massive print and television campaign was created by the San Francisco office of Leagas Delaney, which had made a name for itself promoting a host of clients including Adidas, Goodyear, Harrods, Hyundai, and watchmaker Patek Phillipe. Most of the campaign went into television advertising and targeted sports-related events including ABC's *Monday Night Football* and ESPN programming. Whether it was the advertising blitz or word of mouth, sales for Blue Nile's maiden year reached $14 million, while online shopping as a whole racked up total retail sales of almost $26 billion for the same period, according to statistics published in *USA Today* (October 23, 2003).

Diamonds Are a Guy's Best Friend: 2000 to 2001

By 2000 the Internet's overcrowding began to thin as dot.coms, large and small, failed. Blue Nile, however, did not

Company Perspectives:

Our philosophy is simple: Offer high-quality diamonds and fine jewelry at outstanding prices.

stumble or fall—instead it flourished. Early in the year Vadon was again raising funds, and one investor of note was Microsoft cofounder Paul Allen's Vulcan Ventures Inc., who joined a host of well known firms willing to bank on Blue Nile's future. Part of the funding went into adding new products to Blue Nile's online store while remaining true to its status as a luxury jeweler. Sterling silver trinkets and classy watches (á la Swiss Army, Tag Heuer, Seiko, and Kenneth Cole) joined the web site's now famous diamonds. Blue Nile was cautious, however, not to expand into noncore items and stayed within the bounds of fine jewelry. The addition of the lower-priced sterling silver pieces helped attract customers who would not spend thousands for jewelry, and Vadon and his marketing staff also believed silver would attract more women to the Blue Nile site, which still catered primarily to men.

Much of the e-tailer's appeal was its no-nonsense approach to selling. The company web site was divided into simple categories for prospective buyers, with headings for engagement rings, jewelry, watches and accessories, or shopping by specific product (earrings, men's or women's items) or material (diamond, pearl, gold, platinum, etc.). Yet most impressive about the Blue Nile web shop was its emphasis on knowledge. An educated consumer was Blue Nile's best customer and a plethora of information was just a mouse-click away.

Presented in a straightforward manner under the link ''Education,'' Blue Nile provided online shoppers with subheadings about diamonds, pearls, gemstones, platinum, gold, silver, and even pewter, while its ''Buying Guide'' was broken down into categories such as engagement rings, necklaces, bracelets, watches, and other fine gifts. Since diamonds were Blue Nile's claim to fame, the diamonds link had anything and everything shoppers would want or need to know about purchasing the ultimate rock, especially under the ''Build Your Own Engagement Ring'' link and subsequent pages.

Blue Nile not only thoroughly covered the famed four Cs of diamond buying (color, clarity, cut, and carat weight) but threw in two additional all-important Cs as well—certification and care. Even the labyrinthine grading system of the Gemological Institute of America (GIA) and American Gem Society Laboratories (AGSL) were broken down into simple terms, since every Blue Nile diamond was certified by either the GIA or the AGSL (certificates were available for viewing online).

By the end of 2000 Blue Nile had gained a reputation for excellence and was lauded by business and lifestyle publications, including accolades from *Forbes* magazine as a ''*Forbes* Favorite'' among Internet retailers, and voted *Fortune* magazine's ''Best of the Web'' jewelry site. Blue Nile finished fiscal year 2000 with sales of $44.4 million.

In 2001 Blue Nile began researching a leap of faith—into actual retail stores bearing its name within the next several years. Despite being founded as the antithesis of traditional jewelry retailing, it was believed that Blue Nile's three largest markets (New York, San Francisco, and Seattle) might benefit from physical locations. The stores, however, would remain true to Blue Nile's basic business tenets, i.e. no commissioned sales staff, no hard sell, plenty of information and assistance. The pluses to the proposed storefronts included off-the-street impulse buyers, the opportunity to try on jewelry, and further branding of the Blue Nile name.

Blue Nile's sales and products continued to grow in the spring and summer of 2001. Then came the terrorist attacks of September 11th, and businesses throughout the United States and abroad suffered. Blue Nile was no exception; yet before the end of the year sales rebounded. Not only were sentimental favorites like engagement rings and engraved lockets in high demand, but Blue Nile's patriotic sterling silver bracelet—adorned with a flag—sold out several times over. While it was not possible to determine whether Blue Nile's sales would have reached the same levels for 2001 if September 11th had not happened, the firm's ongoing success was no fluke—sales for the online retailer reached $48.7 million for fiscal 2001.

All That Glitters Is Not Just Gold: 2002 and Beyond

More praise came in 2002 from *Time* magazine, when Blue Nile was called ''Best Indulgence'' from the periodical's ''Best Websites for Business'' roundup. Blue Nile had not only more than quintupled its sales in a mere three years (from $14 million in 1999 to a phenomenal $72 million for 2002), the firm had become the Internet's largest online jeweler with more than 30,000 independently certified diamonds to choose from and dozens of settings in gold, platinum, and sterling silver to dazzle even the most selective buyer. More significantly, at least to many, was the pricing—as much as 20 to 40 percent lower than traditional jewelers, along with free shipping, and a 30-day money back guarantee.

According to a *Time* magazine article in February 2003, online jewelry sales topped $1 billion for 2002 and Blue Nile had become the major player in the virtual jewelry trade. Many Internet shoppers came directly to Blue Nile through its ''anchor tenant'' agreements with AOL, MSN, and Yahoo. All shoppers had to do was click a jewelry tab on any of the three browsers to arrive at Blue Nile's home page. The simplicity and effectiveness of Blue Nile's browser links mirrored its matured approach to advertising—favoring less expensive online ads and direct mail over much more expensive ads for television, print, and radio.

In 2003 Blue Nile received a rare commendation from Bizrate.com, the Internet retailing rating service, by earning its ''Circle of Excellence'' Platinum Award. The Platinum Award, like its namesake, denoted the best of the best—in this case the top e-retailers who met a stringent set of criteria. Only 20 Internet retailers were so honored and Blue Nile was among them. Another online rating service, Internet Retailer, declared Blue Nile as its ''Best of the Web'' recipient in 2003, while Blue Nile also received mentions in a number of publications including the *Washington Post, USA Weekend, Time, InStyle, U.S. News & World Report, Newsweek, Fortune,* and *Forbes.* If sales for fiscal 2003 measured up to all the praise at a projected $120 million, it would be Blue Nile's best year ever.

Key Dates:

1998: Mark Vadon searches for the perfect engagement ring.
1999: Blue Nile Inc. is established in Seattle, Washington, as an online jewelry site.
2000: The firm adds sterling silver and upscale watches to its inventory.
2001: Blue Nile launches its ''Signature'' collection of top-rate diamonds.
2002: *Time* magazine names Blue Nile as a ''Best Indulgence'' in its ''Best Website for Business'' rankings.
2003: Blue Nile is one of only 20 Internet retailers to receive Bizrate.com's ''Circle of Excellence'' Platinum Award.

Mark Vadon believed Blue Nile's outstanding success was due in large part to bucking the usual retail trends. As he commented to *USA Today* in October 2003, ''Everything we do is heresy. Instead of marketing to women, we market to men. Instead of trying to push our gross margins as high as possible, we sell as cheap as we possibly can. Instead of hiding information, we're all about educating our consumer and making him feel comfortable.'' Obviously, many men did feel comfortable buying from Blue Nile's well-stocked virtual shelves and turned the relatively young e-tailer into a winner. Women, too, had begun shopping at Blue Nile and its client base continued to grow as did the company's headquarters. Blue Nile's 115 employees moved to new office space of more than 20,000-square feet in Seattle.

Buyers, investors, and sweethearts, as well as Wall Street, had become acutely aware of Blue Nile's status in the online jewelry trade. It seemed as if Blue Nile's future was sparkling as brightly as one of its flawless, colorless, large-carat Asscher-cut diamonds.

Principal Competitors

Ashford.com; Costco Wholesale; Diamonds.com; DirtCheap Diamonds.com; Tiffany & Co.; Zale Corporation.

Further Reading

Acohido, Byron, "He Turned Web Site in the Rough into Online Jewel,'' *USA Today,* October 20, 2003, p. 5B.
Andrews, Gregg, ''Blue Nile Looks to Add Stores,'' *National Jeweler,* October 1, 2001, p. 40.
Beres, Glen A., ''Online Jewelers Make Major Strides in Sales, Profit Growth,'' *Diamond Intelligence Briefs,* January 24, 3003.
''Blue Nile Announces Agreement with AOL,'' *Jewelers Circular Keystone,* January 2001, p. 216.
''Blue Nile Launches 'Signature' Line,'' *National Jeweler,* December 1, 2001, p. 20.
Foley, Michael F., and Thomas Melville, ''What Men Want,'' *Success,* April 2001, p. 20.
Hamilton, Anita, ''Click and Clink,'' *Time,* February 10, 2003.
Kim, Nancy J., ''Diamond E-Tailer Aims $10M Ad Blitz at Men,'' *Puget Sound Business Journal,* November 12, 1999, p. 10.
Lang Jones, Jeanne, ''Gold Rush: Blue Nile's Jewelry Sales Soared in Emotional Aftermath of Sept. 11,'' *Puget Sound Business Journal,* December 14, 2001, p. 1.
Mamer, Karl, ''Red Hot Blue Nile,'' *Luxury Magazine,* Spring 2002.
Markels, Alex, ''Baubels and Browsers,'' *U.S. News & World Report,* September 23, 2002.
Shin, Laura, ''These Jewelry Sites Are True Gems,'' *USA Weekend,* June 15, 2003.
Tice, Carol, ''Blue Nile Building Up Steady Current of Sales,'' *Puget Sound Business Journal,* august 25, 2000, p. 8.

—Nelson Rhodes

Bollinger Shipyards, Inc.

8365 Highway 308 South
Lockport, Louisiana 70374
U.S.A.
Telephone: (985) 532-2554
Fax: (985) 532-7225
Web site: http://www.bollingershipyards.com

Private Company
Incorporated: 1946
NAIC: 336611 Ship Building and Repairing

Based in the small town of Lockport, Louisiana, Bollinger Shipyards, Inc. is a leading builder of small and medium-sized offshore and inland vessels, serving the energy, commercial, and government marine markets. The privately owned company also provides repair and conversion services, operating out of 14 shipyards located along the Gulf of Mexico in southern Louisiana and Texas. All told, Bollinger has 42 dry docks at its disposal. Originally a repair shop, Bollinger has become a major player in the construction of certain specialized ships. The company supplies patrol craft to the U.S. Coast Guard and the U.S. Navy. These boats range in size from 87 feet to 170 feet and boast a range of specialized electronics and armament. Bollinger serves the energy industry by building supply vessels, tugboats, dredges, and lift boats to assist offshore drilling operations. In addition, the company builds a variety of barges and specialty vessels, including floating casinos.

Founding the Company in 1946

Bollinger Shipyards was founded by Donald G. Bollinger in 1946 in Lockport along the banks of the Bayou Lafourche, part of the complex of waterways that permeate southern Louisiana. As a result, boatbuilding was a natural occupation for the people of this region. Bollinger, a trained machinist, struck out on his own, with an investment of $17,353, much of which was drawn from a $10,000 inheritance he received from a former barge-building employer. He established a marine machine shop on 80 acres of land bordering Bayou Lafourche. He brought in his brothers, Ralph, a mechanic, and George, a welder, and Richard, an LSU graduate who became president. They also were joined by their father and a brother-in-law. Taking advantage of the oilfield boom in southern Louisiana, Bollinger began constructing barges and work boats. The company also built fishing vessels. During its first 25 years of existence, however, the company remained very much a small, local business. It was not until 1971, in fact, that Bollinger expanded beyond its original Lockport operation. Not until 1978 did the company open a second shipyard, located in nearby Larose, Louisiana.

Donald Bollinger's son, Donald Y. ''Boysie'' Bollinger, also joined the family business, after earning an undergraduate degree in business administration from the University of Southwestern Louisiana in 1971. He would prove instrumental in a deal in the later 1970s that marked a turning point in the fortunes of Bollinger Shipyards. Boysie was sent to Panama to negotiate a contract to build three tugboats for the Panama Canal Co., which he assumed was owned by the Panamanian government. Instead, he learned that the company was controlled by the U.S. government. Recounting the story to a group of business students at Louisiana State University, Boysie later recalled thinking, ''My father's gonna kill me. He told me never to work for the Government.'' But the elder Bollinger did not object to the contract, which was successfully completed. At the time, the company thrived on business with offshore oil and gas explorers, who were enjoying high times, but it would be government work that would save the company during the oil bust of 1984 and the resulting slump that proved to be the ruin of so many firms associated with the oil and gas industry. Bollinger took stock of the situation and elected to downplay its commercial work and to target government contracts.

In 1984 the company won its first U.S. government shipbuilding contract—but not until it overcame a legal challenge from a Seattle firm that submitted a lower bid. The $86 million deal called for Bollinger to deliver 13 110-foot-long Island Class cutters to the U.S. Coast Guard. The contract was subsequently increased to 16 vessels at a price of $99 million. The Coast Guard was so pleased with Bollinger's workmanship and its ability to deliver on time and under budget that it ultimately purchased 49 of these vessels by the early 1990s. Prior to this contract, Bollinger posted annual revenues in the $30 million

Company Perspectives:

Quality is long remembered after the price is forgotten.

range, but now sales grew to as much as $90 million a year. Moreover, because of the downturn in the oil and gas industry, there was little shipbuilding work to be found. Other Gulf Coast shipbuilders, totally dependent on the energy industry, were going under, leaving Bollinger in a highly advantageous position. The company began to expand externally, picking up the operations of distressed shipyards in southern Louisiana and southeastern Texas, in the process expanding its repair franchise to new industry segments and markets. Bollinger added a deepwater location on the Mississippi River in 1990, and in 1993 it acquired a major inland river business.

Change in Leadership in 1985

By now, Boysie Bollinger had taken over as chief executive, succeeding his father in 1985. The elder Bollinger had developed into a well-known man in the state, mostly due to his political activities. A Republican, he played a major role in the party's growth in the 1970s, which led to the 1979 election of Dave Treen, the first Republican governor in Louisiana since the Reconstruction era following the Civil War. Treen tabbed Bollinger to become the Secretary of the Louisiana Department of Public Safety and Corrections, a post he held during the early 1980s. Bollinger then served as chairman of the Louisiana Republican Party from 1984 to 1986. After giving up the CEO's role to his son, he retained the chairmanship of the company until his retirement in 1989.

When its Coast Guard work ran out in 1991, Bollinger was able to land a contract with the U.S. Navy to build 13 fast, shallow-water patrol boats. This business tied over the company until the oilfield business once again enjoyed an upturn. Now a much larger operation, Bollinger was again in a position to take advantage of economic conditions and began to build vessels needed to support the oilfield, such as supply boats, lift boats, tugboats, and dredges. These new commercial contracts overtaxed the company's five repair yards (located in Algiers, Harvey Canal, Fourchon, and Larose) and its main yard in Lockport. To bolster its operations, Bollinger in 1995 bought part of the McDermott Shipyard in Morgan City, Louisiana, taking over 20 of the facility's 100 acres, plus three floating dry docks, a machine shop, and other facilities. The reported price was in the $5 million to $6 million range, the same amount of business that Boysie Bollinger hoped to generate repairing oilfield vessels during the first year at the new operation. Older oilfield vessels were now prime candidates for refurbishment because few new boats had been built during the lean years endured by the oil and gas industry, and shipyards were not able to build enough new vessels to meet the current demand. In addition to buying facilities, Bollinger expanded its existing yards, such as the $3.5 million the company invested in its repair yard located at Algiers on the Mississippi River. A second dry dock was added and the wharf was extended from 165 feet to 465, thus allowing the yard to accommodate larger vessels. Before the extension, the yard was limited to work on tugboats, but it could now handle both the tugboats and the oceangoing barges they normally towed.

Not only did it desperately need these new facilities, Bollinger and other shipbuilders also had to contend with a severe shortage in skilled labor such as machinists, welders, and pipefitters. According to a 1995 *New Orleans Times-Picayune* article, ''Once it was true in Louisiana shipbuilding that 'when the daddy was a welder, the kid was a welder.' 'On the bayou (Lafourche), that quit happening 10 years ago,' said Marc Stanley, executive vice-president of Bollinger Shipyards Inc., of Lockport. 'This generation wound up playing Nintendo. We're the victim of blue-collar affluence.' '' Bollinger was in such need of workers that it offered cash bounties to employees who brought in successful job candidates. It even hired an employment agency, L'Homme Inc., in order to contract foreign workers from countries like Mexico, England, and India. To satisfy requirements of the U.S. Immigration & Naturalization Service, the company had to prove that there were not enough qualified U.S. citizens available to fill the job openings. Further, the foreign workers had to be paid at the same level as their American counterparts. Successful candidates were then able to work under a nine-month visa, which could then be renewed for a total of three years. To address its labor shortage, Bollinger also instituted an apprentice program for high school students, who received $8 an hour after school and during the summer while training under master craftsmen to become certified welders or pipefitters.

Considering an IPO in 1997

With the stock market soaring in late 1997 and Bollinger looking to fund further expansion, company officials explored the possibility of going public and making an initial public offering (IPO) of stock. Other firms, such as Bollinger's chief rival, Halter Marine Group Inc., and Friede Goldman, a rig platform builder, had completed successful offerings earlier in the year, and there was a consensus that Bollinger would be greeted with equal enthusiasm. But when drilling activity in the Gulf of Mexico began to dry up, Bollinger decided to scrap its plans to go public. In light of subsequent events the company's caution proved wise. Over the next two years, oil services companies saw their stock lose a considerable amount of value, forcing some, such as Friede Goldman, to lapse into bankruptcy. Bollinger, in the meantime, was able to respond to a drop in Gulf of Mexico exploration, quickly shift its business focus, and maintain its profit levels. The company also experienced no difficulty in securing the capital it needed from lenders to acquire a repair yard in Amelia, Louisiana. Moreover, management viewed the slowdown in building as a chance to repair and enhance its facilities in preparation for a resurgence in the market for offshore service vessels. In 1999 the company also introduced an integrated software package that was able to bring all of its facilities under a single business system, which could be shared by all locations via the Internet.

May 13, 2000 marked the passage of an era when Donald G. Bollinger succumbed to heart failure at the age of 85. The business he founded was still very much family run. In addition to Boysie Bollinger, other family members holding positions in the company included his brother Richard, Boysie's daughter Charlotte and son Chris, as well as Boysie's nephew Ben

Key Dates:

1946: Donald G. Bollinger founds the company.
1978: The second shipyard opens.
1984: Company wins a Coast Guard contract.
1985: Donald "Boysie" Bollinger succeeds his father as CEO.
1989: Donald G. Bollinger retires.
2000: Five repair yards are acquired from Friede Goldman Halter.

Bordelon. Several weeks after the death of his father, Boysie Bollinger engineered the most ambitious acquisition in the history of the company, paying $80 million in cash for five ship and offshore-platform repair yards from Friede Goldman. (Following its IPO, Friede Goldman merged with Halter Inc. in 1999, but the assumption of Halter's debt proved too onerous, forcing the company to file for bankruptcy in April 2000.) Previously, Bollinger had attempted to purchase the facilities on an additional basis. But now, in one stroke, the addition of the yards—Halter Gulf Repair, New Orleans; Gretna Machine & Iron Works, Gretna, Louisiana; Halter Calcasieu, Carlyss, Louisiana; Bludworth Bond-Houston, Houston, Texas; and Bludworth Bond-Texas City, Texas City, Texas—transformed Bollinger, with a total of 14 shipyards, into the largest vessel repair company in the Gulf of Mexico area, and one of the largest commercial ship repairers in the entire country. The acquisition doubled the number of dry docks Bollinger operated. Three of the new docks, in fact, were larger than any of the dry docks the company owned. As a result, Bollinger was now able to accommodate vessels up to 700 feet in length and could expand its customer base and move into bluewater ship repair. Despite the apparent advantages to the deal, it was a bold move for Bollinger, at a time when area shipyards struggled to find work during a slow period in the oil and gas industry. A number of people attempted to dissuade Boysie Bollinger from making the deal, but he believed it represented a ripe opportunity and carried it out. Although the new yards were in poorer shape than he had anticipated, and it required some time to integrate them into the Bollinger operation, the acquisition proved to be a success.

In 2002 Bollinger attempted to purchase additional assets from Friede Goldman Halter: the Halter Marine division and its seven southern Mississippi fabrication yards. After the rejection of an earlier offer, Bollinger appeared to submit a successful bid of $48 million, but another suitor, Singapore Technologies Engineering Ltd., stepped in. Its subsidiary Vision Technologies Kinetics became engaged in a fierce bidding war with Bollinger, and after 20 rounds succeeded in buying Halter Marine for $66.75 million. Despite losing out, Bollinger carried on as a thriving enterprise. In 2003 it delivered its 100th Coast Guard cutter, part of a lucrative contract that could be expanded from four to 13 cutters. The company looked to a new opportunity with the U.S. Navy, building "littoral combat ships," operating close to shore (an area known as the littoral zone), and featuring stealth technologies. Bollinger made the final cut among shipyards to land the Navy's business. Should Bollinger succeed, it had already lined up state money to build a new shipyard in Louisiana to handle the business. In addition to the Navy contract, Bollinger was also in the running to build a fleet of high-speed catamaran ferries for the Army and Navy, as well as to build tankers for private industry.

Principal Subsidiaries

Bollinger Shipyards Lockport, L.L.C.; Bollinger Algiers, L.L.C.; Bollinger Amelia Repair, L.L.C.; Bollinger Calcasieu, L.L.C.; Bollinger Fourchon, L.L.C.; Bollinger Gretna, L.L.C.; Bollinger Gulf Repair, L.L.C.; Bollinger Houston, L.L.C.; Bollinger Larose, L.L.C.; Bollinger Morgan City, L.L.C.; Bollinger Quick Repair, L.L.C.; Bollinger Texas City, L.L.C.

Principal Competitors

Vision Technologies Kinetics Inc.

Further Reading

"Bollinger Sparkles As Rapid Growth Is Consolidated," *Lloyd's List International,* June 6, 2001.

Darce, Keith, "Shipshape," *New Orleans Times-Picayune,* August 4, 2002, p. 1.

Hall, John, "Shipbuilders Vie for Labor Blue-Collar Trades Hit by Generation Gap," *New Orleans Times-Picayune,* December 2, 1995, p. C1.

Hocke, Ken, "Yard Sale," *Workboat,* October 2001, p. 30.

—Ed Dinger

C.I. Traders Limited

Traders House
1-3 L'Avenue Le Bas
Jersey
JE4 8NB
United Kingdom
Telephone: +44 01534 508200
Fax: +44 01534 768858
Web site: http://www.citraders.com

Public Company
Incorporated: 2002
Employees: 3,458
Sales: £268.9 million ($430 million) (2003)
Stock Exchanges: London (AIM)
Ticker Symbol: CIT
NAIC: 312120 Breweries; 452111 Department Stores (Except Discount Department Stores; 311811 Retail Bakeries; 312130 Wineries; 312229 Other Tobacco Product Manufacturing; 424470 Meat and Meat Product Merchant Wholesalers; 424810 Beer and Ale Merchant Wholesalers; 424820 Wine and Distilled Alcoholic Beverage Merchant Wholesalers; 424940 Tobacco and Tobacco Product Merchant Wholesalers; 441110 New Car Dealers; 452910 Warehouse Clubs and Superstores; 721110 Hotels (Except Casino Hotels) and Motels

C.I. Traders Limited, formed by the merger of Ann Street Group and Le Riche Group in 2002, is the largest company on the Channel Islands. The diversified group concentrates on four primary areas: Retail, Property, Food Services, and Hospitality. The company also operates a consumer finance business in support of its retail operations. Retail is the group's largest division, and stems from the Le Riche side of the business. C.I. Traders operates more than 40 grocery stores and related retail stores under the names Checkers, Le Riche's Stampers, Checkers Xpress, Le Riche Forecourts, and Island Shopper, making the group the leading retailer in Jersey, Guernsey, and Alderney. The company's retail holdings include two Checkers superstores, with the largest offering 52,000 square feet of sales space. In addition, the company operates two franchised Marks & Spencers stores in Guernsey and Jersey. While Retail attracts the Islands' consumers, the company's Food Services division meets the distribution needs of Channel Islands restaurants, hotels, bars, and related businesses, providing chilled and frozen food products through Trade Saver and Martin O'Meara, butcher meats through Russell Meats, and bakery and other goods through C.I. Bakeries and Warry's. Many of the Food Service Division's professional customers are, in fact, members of the C.I. Traders group, which operates more than 90 bars and pubs throughout the Channel Islands, as well as 13 restaurants under the Blubeckers and Edwinns names in the United Kingdom. The company also maintains the Ann Street Brewery operations, and manufactures and distributes soft drinks and other beverages under license. In addition, the company owns L'Abeille, the leading producer of private-label soft drinks for the French market. The company's Property Division is chiefly responsible for managing the Channel Islands real estate portfolio. With its dominant position on the Channel Islands, C.I. Traders has expressed interest in expanding further into England. C.I. Traders is led by Chairman Tom Scott and Chief Executive Michael Johnson. With annual sales of £269 million ($430 million), it is the third largest company listed on the London Stock Exchange's AIM index.

Island Grocer Origins in the 19th Century

C.I. Traders represented the coming together of two long-standing and complementary forces in the Channel Islands' business sector. The oldest of the two was the Le Riche Group, which originated as a grocery shop founded by the Le Riche family in 1818. Located in the Jersey capital town of St. Helier, the Le Riche grocery business grew into the most prominent retailer on the Channel Islands. In 1897, the business was incorporated formally as Le Riche's Stores Limited.

Le Riche expanded by opening new store locations across Jersey, Guernsey, and Alderney. Yet the company's retailing operations, and the necessity of bringing goods onshore from the English mainland, led it to extend its operations to include

Key Dates:

- **1818:** First Le Riche grocery shop opens in Jersey and begins business as a wine shipper as well.
- **1897:** Le Riche incorporates as Le Riche's Stores Limited.
- **1905:** The Ann Street Brewery is founded.
- **1952:** Ann Street extends into soft drinks with a Coca-Cola franchise for the Channel Islands.
- **1958:** Ann Street adds a distribution license for Bollinger champagne.
- **1960:** Le Riche takes over another prominent Channel Islands retailer, Orviss.
- **1967:** Le Riche acquires a Marks & Spencer franchise and opens the first store in Jersey.
- **1971:** Ian Steven becomes head of the Ann Street Brewery and leads its expansion as the Channel Islands' leading brewery and pubs group.
- **1980s:** Le Riche debuts the Stampers convenience store format.
- **1991:** Le Riche acquires C.I. Bakers, the leading commercial baker in Jersey.
- **1993:** Le Riche opens the first Checkers superstore in Jersey.
- **1995:** Le Riche débuts The Wine Warehouse retail format.
- **1998:** Le Riche acquires full control of Russell Meats.
- **1999:** Le Riche sells its automotive sales operation.
- **2000:** Ann Street acquires the Blubeckers restaurant group in southern England.
- **2001:** Le Riche opens a second Marks & Spencer store, acquires Warry's commercial baker, and opens a Checkers superstore—all in Guernsey.
- **2002:** Le Riche acquires Channel Rentals, Channel Publications, and TABS from ComProp Ltd.; Le Riche and Ann Street merge under privately held C.I. Traders, which then lists on the AIM market.
- **2003:** C.I. sells off the mainland England pubs portfolio in order to focus on retail growth.

grocery and beverage wholesale services. The company, given the Channel Islands' location between France and England, also became one of the islands' most important wine shippers, an activity begun in the group's early years. The company also later became involved in new and used automobile sales, and operated its own service stations.

By the late 1950s, Le Riche was one of the top two retailers on the Channel Islands. In 1960, the company claimed the top spot through its takeover of rival Orviss Ltd. That company had also been one of the oldest and largest grocers on the island. At mid-decade, Le Riche prepared to expand again, this time acquiring the franchise to operate Marks & Spencer stores on the Channel Islands. The first of these opened in 1967 in Jersey, but was later relocated to St. Helier's King Street in 1978.

While the Le Riche's grocery chain itself extended to six stores—two each on Jersey, Guernsey, and Alderney—the company began developing new retail formats in the 1980s. The first of these was launched under the name of Stampers. The small-scale, community convenience format catered not only to the islands' residents, but also to the growing numbers of tourists and day trippers. Featuring extended opening hours, on a seven days per week schedule, the Stampers format continued to grow into the 1990s, developing into a 12-store chain, including ten stores on Jersey and two on Guernsey.

Le Riche continued expanding in the 1990s. In 1991, the company moved into the wholesale bakery sector with its acquisition of C.I. Bakery Ltd., the islands' largest commercial baker, based in Jersey. On the retail front, Le Riche responded to the growing trend toward supermarket superstores in the United Kingdom and elsewhere by launching its own superstore format. Called Checkers, the company's first superstore was established in Jersey in 1993.

The company launched another successful retail formula at mid-decade, The Wine Warehouse. With an offer of guaranteed low prices, backed by a promotional campaign featuring a "gruff" Frenchman, Gaston Duplonk, Wine Warehouse opened in St. Martin's Guernsey. The success of the first store led the company to roll out two more self-standing stores, in New Era and Quennevais in Jersey, and as a boutique shop with the soon-to-début Guernsey Checkers.

After selling off its money-losing automotive business in 1999, Le Riche turned its attention to solidifying its hold on the Channel Islands' retail market, then under threat from the entry of U.K. supermarket giant Safeway and the plans to open a superstore by the Channel Islands Co-op retail group. The company began construction on a new Checkers superstore, which opened in Guernsey in 2001. At 52,000 square feet, the new store easily became the Channel Islands' largest. At the same time, the company began a renovation of the smaller Jersey-based Checkers.

Le Riche, which had changed its name to Le Riche Group in 1998, also had expanded its department store operation. In 2001, the company opened its second Marks & Spencer store, again under franchise, in Centre Point, St. Brelaide.

Merging for the New Century

Given the relatively small population of the Channel Islands—which stood at barely more than 87,000 at the end of the 20th century—a merger between Le Riche and the Ann Street Group, another leading Channel Islands business group, had been spoken about for years, with no result.

Ann Street had been founded as a brewery on St. Helier's Ann Street in 1905. The company had brewed ale originally, then switched to other beer types in the 1950s. At that time, the company had branched out into other beverage types, acquiring the license to manufacture and distribute Coca-Cola on the Channel Islands in 1952. In 1958, the company acquired the distribution license for Bollinger champagne for the Islands as well.

Ann Street remained a modest-sized business into the early 1970s. A turning point for the group came in 1971, when Ian Steven took over as the company's lead. Under Steven, Ann Street began developing its pub estate holdings, which grew to more than 100 across the Channel Islands. The company also entered the French market, acquiring L'Abeille, that country's leading supplier of private-label soft drinks for the French supermarket sector. Into the 1990s, Ann Street, which, like Le Riche, was listed on the London Stock Exchange's Main Board, began seeking an extension onto the English mainland, building up a pub estate in southern England. In 2000, the company moved into England with the acquisition of the Brubeckers restaurant chain.

This development came in part because of a steady decline in the tourism market on the Channel Islands, caused primarily by the opening of the tunnel across the English Channel connecting England to the European continent in the 1990s. The changing economic climate on the Islands encouraged both Ann Street and Le Riche to seek a means of increasing their scale at the end of the 20th century.

Le Riche launched an acquisition drive, starting with the purchase of full control of Russell Meats, a leading supplier of butchers meats on the Islands in 1998. In 2001, the company struck again, buying up LS Warry & Sons, the only commercial baker on Guernsey, cementing Le Riche's position as the leading commercial baker in the Channel Islands. In 2003, Le Riche paid Comprop Ltd. £1.75 million to acquire three more businesses, Channel Rentals, which provided videotape and DVD, as well as vending machine rentals on the islands; Channel Publications, which published two free Guernsey-based papers, *Finder* and *Home Finder,* and Channel Islands maps under the Perry's brand; and Trade Advisory Business Service, which was brought under Le Riche's finance department.

Ann Street in the meantime had come under the leadership of Tom Scott, an English expatriate who had relocated to the island to escape British taxes in the mid-1980s. Scott soon grew into a leading figure on the Channel Islands business scene, setting up a new business, C.I. Traders, which provided automotive financing, and acquiring a stake in Ann Street through another company. That shareholding gave Scott the executive chairman seat in the company.

In 2002, Scott led a three-way merger among Ann Street, Le Riche, and his own company, bringing the brewer and pub owner under the C.I. Traders banner. The newly enlarged company then transferred its listing to the London exchange's AIM market, where it became one of that market's top five companies. Under C.I. Traders, the company now shifted its emphasis onto its retail portfolio, selling off its mainland pub estate in order to step up its retail investments. Among the company's targets was an extension of its retail holdings into France—the company reportedly began seeking a franchise to open Marks & Spencer stores in that country, which the British group had exited nearly two years before. C.I. Traders hoped to expand beyond its dominance of the Channel Islands' business sector and become a mainland force in the new century.

Principal Subsidiaries

Ann Street Group Ltd.; C.I. Bakery; G. Orang & Co.; L'Abeille SA (France); Le Riche Group Ltd.; LR Trading; Russell Meats; Trade Saver Foods; Warry's Bakery.

Principal Competitors

Safeway Plc; Channel Islands Co-op.

Further Reading

Ann Street Brewery Co. Ltd. Jersey: The History, Tunbridge Wells, Kent: Martlet Publishing Company, 1993.

Blackwell, David, "C.I. Traders Has Expectations of Merger Benefits," *Financial Times,* April 17, 2003, p. 22.

Conway, Edmund, "C.I. Pulls Out of Eldridge Pope Deal," *Daily Telegraph,* September 18, 2003.

"Le Riche Gains Scale Through Merger," *Grocer,* July 13, 2002.

"Le Riche Trialing Express Format," *Grocer,* May 31, 2003.

"Le Riche's Riche Marques to Buy Rental, Publication, Credit Ops of Comprop," *AFX UK,* March 28, 2002.

Renault, Kenneth C., *Le Riches Story 175 Years of Progress,* Chichester, Sussex: Phillimore & Co. Ltd., 1993.

—M.L. Cohen

Canadian Imperial Bank of Commerce

Commerce Court
Toronto, Ontario M5L 1A2
Canada
Telephone: (416) 980-2211
Fax: (416) 980-5026
Web site: http://www.cibc.com

Public Company
Incorporated: 1961
Employees: 36,630
Total Assets: C$277.15 billion (US$210.04 billion) (2003)
Stock Exchanges: Toronto New York
Ticker Symbols: CM; BCM
NAIC: 551111 Offices of Bank Holding Companies; 522110 Commercial Banking; 522210 Credit Card Issuing; 522292 Real Estate Credit; 523110 Investment Banking and Securities Dealing; 523120 Securities Brokerage; 523130 Commodity Contracts Dealing; 523920 Portfolio Management; 523930 Investment Advice; 523991 Trust, Fiduciary, and Custody Activities; 525910 Open-End Investment Funds

The Canadian Imperial Bank of Commerce (CIBC) is Canada's third largest bank, trailing only Royal Bank of Canada and Bank of Nova Scotia. Based in Toronto, CIBC functions through three main operating units: CIBC Retail Markets, CIBC Wealth Management, and CIBC World Markets. CIBC Retail Markets serves more than nine million individual customers and nearly 470,000 small business customers in Canada through a network of about 1,100 branches and more than 4,400 automatic bank machines (ABMs), as well as four telephone banking centers and an Internet banking channel. The principal financial services offered by this unit include personal banking, small business banking, credit cards, and mortgages. CIBC Wealth Management maintains a network of 2,500 investment advisors responsible for C$193 billion in client assets under administration. The unit's services include investment advice, full-service and online discount brokerages, private banking, and trust services, and its three families of mutual funds—Renaissance, Talvest, and CIBC—make the bank the number four mutual fund provider in Canada, managing more than C$36 billion in assets. CIBC World Markets is a major investment bank operating throughout Canada and the United States, with a more modest presence in the United Kingdom and Asia. CIBC was formed through a 1961 merger between the Imperial Bank of Canada, which was founded in 1875, and the Canadian Bank of Commerce, which traces its origins back to 1867.

History of the Canadian Bank of Commerce

The older of CIBC's two predecessors, the Canadian Bank of Commerce, was founded in 1867, the same year as Canada's confederation. While Canadian statesmen discussed the advantages of uniting the British North American Colonies under one parliament, a prominent Toronto businessman, William McMaster, was busy acquiring a bank charter from a group of financiers who had been unable to raise the necessary capital to put it to use. They had been granted a charter for an institution to be called the Bank of Canada in 1858, but McMaster adopted the name Canadian Bank of Commerce, opening the new bank on May 15, 1867. Under his leadership, the bank grew at a tremendous rate. The bank's paid-up capital swelled from C$400,000 to C$6 million in its first seven years, and it soon had offices in New York and Montreal as well as throughout Ontario. Canada was in the midst of an industrial revolution at this time, and the Bank of Commerce was instrumental in financing a number of large capital projects. For its first 20 years, the bank's prosperity fluctuated with economic conditions, but in general it grew and was profitable.

In May 1893 the bank joined the Canadian push westward by establishing a branch in Winnipeg. In 1898 branches were established in Dawson City, Yukon Territory; Vancouver, British Columbia; and Skagway, Alaska. In 1901 the bank acquired the Bank of British Columbia, strengthening its position on the Pacific Coast. During the next ten years the Canadian Bank of Commerce acquired several other financial institutions, including Halifax Banking Company (1903), Merchants Bank of Prince Edward Island (1906), and Eastern Townships Bank (1912); by the start of World War I, it had 379 branches.

Company Perspectives:

At CIBC, we are in business to help our customers achieve what matters to them. We are focused on creating a winning culture for our employees, for our communities, and for our shareholders. A winning culture means a consistent drive to create more value for customers which, in turn, will contribute to achieving our objective to generate the best total return to shareholders.

To win—we must create value for all who have a stake in CIBC.

During the 1920s the bank nearly doubled its branch network by acquiring the Bank of Hamilton and later the Standard Bank of Canada. The general prosperity of the 1920s was reflected in the bank's growth. At the time of the stock market crash in 1929, the Canadian Bank of Commerce's assets were C$801 million. The Depression that followed, however, took a heavy toll on the bank, and its assets did not return to their pre-Depression high until 1940.

World War II finally brought economic recovery to Canada. The Canadian Bank of Commerce was active in the war effort, leading victory loan drives among other things. After the war, the bank grew steadily. By 1956, assets had reached C$2.5 billion, and by 1960, they had passed C$3 billion. Despite this success, however, the bank felt pressured by increasing competition and in 1961 agreed to a merger with the Imperial Bank of Canada.

History of the Imperial Bank of Canada

The Imperial Bank of Canada was established in Toronto in 1875. Its first president, Henry Stark Howland, had been the vice-president of the Canadian Bank of Commerce. The bank's first office actually had no vault—overnight deposits were stored at another bank—yet in its first year of operation, the Imperial Bank made a profit of C$103,637. Reluctant to open too many branches too soon, the Imperial Bank's growth was somewhat slower than that of the Bank of Commerce during the same period. By 1880, however, the Imperial Bank had frontier fever. That year it opened a branch in Winnipeg, and the next year it expanded to Brandon and Calgary. By 1900, the Imperial Bank had 32 branches spread across the continent. Between the turn of the century and World War I, Canada began to tap its mineral resources with amazing speed. The Imperial Bank of Canada earned the nickname the ''Mining Bank'' because of its ties to that industry.

After World War I, the bank opened about 50 branches within just a few years, but not all of them survived the volatile economic conditions that followed the war. In the 1920s, deposits reached record levels, but the stock market crash in 1929 caused severe problems for the bank. Many of its loans went bad, and a number of branches were closed. The bank struggled to recuperate during the late 1930s and by the end of the decade it was making headway once again.

During World War II costs of operation rose faster than earnings, leading to lower dividends during the war years. About one-third of the Imperial Bank's 1,800 employees enlisted in the various services, and 53 died.

After the war, Canada entered a period of widespread prosperity and the Imperial Bank grew rapidly. In 1956, it acquired Barclays Bank (Canada) and increased assets by nearly $40 million; by 1961, the Imperial Bank had assets of more than $1 billion and 343 branches.

Creation of Canadian Imperial Bank of Commerce: 1961

The amalgamation of the Canadian Bank of Commerce and the Imperial Bank of Canada in 1961 created the largest bank in Canada at the time, with total assets of C$4.6 billion. The new Canadian Imperial Bank of Commerce had at its helm L.S. Mackersy, of the Imperial Bank, as chairman and N.J. McKinnon, of the Bank of Commerce, as president and CEO. Altogether the new bank accounted for about one-quarter of the assets of all Canadian banks combined.

In 1962 McKinnon became chairman of CIBC's board of directors and steered the bank's course from that position until 1972. The 1960s were a prosperous time for Canada, and the nation's economy grew strongly. The Canadian Imperial Bank of Commerce's net earnings increased substantially each year throughout the decade. The bank also strengthened its foreign operations. At the end of the decade, Canada relaxed some of its restrictions on the banking industry. Notably, interest rates on loans were no longer limited to 6 percent. In this liberalized banking climate, Canadian banks did very well. In 1969 CIBC added 46 new branches while expanding its workforce by only 5 percent. That same year, CIBC also became the first Canadian bank to install 24-hour cash dispensers, which would evolve into ABMs. By 1970, annual profits had risen to C$43 million, more than twice what they had been at the time of amalgamation.

In the early 1970s, Canada began to invest heavily in energy development and agriculture, and the Canadian Imperial Bank of Commerce helped with the financing. Throughout the decade the bank had a close relationship with Canadian oil companies. That relationship would eventually cause the bank problems, but in the early 1970s, when oil prices were skyrocketing, investment in petroleum-related industries seemed like a gold mine.

In 1973 J.P. Wadsworth replaced McKinnon as chairman of CIBC, and remained in office until 1975. Late 1973 brought worldwide recession. Although Canadian domestic demand was adequate, overseas demand was low. This spelled trouble for Canada, whose economy was heavily dependent on exports. Nonetheless, CIBC continued to improve its earnings each year.

In 1976 Russell E. Harrison succeeded Wadsworth as chairman and CEO of CIBC. Harrison tended to run the bank in an autocratic manner. Top executives were not always given real power to make key decisions. In the late 1970s and early 1980s Canadian industry grew very quickly, and CIBC made large loans to many expanding firms. In 1980, however, this policy began to falter. Massey-Ferguson, the Canadian tractor manufacturer, was in danger of collapsing, and the Canadian Imperial Bank of Commerce was Massey's biggest lender. The Canadian government worked with Massey's creditors to try to bail the company out by allowing it to raise new capital, but it did not

Key Dates:

1858: Group of financiers are granted a charter for an institution to be called the Bank of Canada; they subsequently fail, however, to raise the capital needed to start up operations.
1867: After buying the Bank of Canada charter, William McMaster changes its name to the Canadian Bank of Commerce and opens for business in Toronto.
1875: Imperial Bank of Canada is established.
1961: The Canadian Bank of Commerce and the Imperial Bank of Canada merge to form Canadian Imperial Bank of Commerce (CIBC); it ranks as the largest bank in Canada, with total assets of C$4.6 billion.
1986: CIBC divides its operations into three units: the Individual Bank, the Corporate Bank, and the Investment Bank.
1988: A majority interest in Wood Gundy Corporation, a leading Canadian investment dealer, is acquired.
1997: CIBC acquires Oppenheimer & Co., Inc., a U.S. full-service securities firm; Oppenheimer is subsequently merged with CIBC Wood Gundy to form CIBC World Markets.
1998: CIBC's proposed merger with the Toronto-Dominion Bank is blocked by the Canadian government.
2003: The bank sells its Oppenheimer private client and asset management businesses in the United States.

work. Massey lost US$240 million in 1981, and US$413 million in 1982, leaving CIBC with a substantial amount of bad debt.

The Dome Petroleum Company was another of CIBC's large corporate debtors in deep trouble in the early 1980s. When oil prices dropped sharply in 1982, Dome lost more than C$100 million; CIBC had loaned Dome more than C$1 billion. The failing company was eventually bought by Amoco Canada, but again CIBC was left with a pile of bad debt. Between 1979 and 1984, CIBC had the lowest average return on assets of the five largest Canadian banks.

In May 1984 R. Donald Fullerton took over as CEO and set about restructuring the bank's operations. Fullerton eliminated branches to cut costs and service overlap and injected new blood into the bank's senior management. He also attacked the bank's bad debt, slowly eliminating bad loans from the bank's portfolio.

In 1985 a record number of farm failures caused mild concern among Canadian bankers. Canadian Imperial estimated that about 10 percent of its agricultural loans were in jeopardy. The problem was not nearly as severe in Canada as it was in the United States, however, where thousands of farmers defaulted on loans.

Restructuring and Diversification: Late 1980s

Under Fullerton's leadership, the bank bounced back from the troubles of the early 1980s to set a new earnings record in 1985. An aggressive new advertising campaign was launched in the United States as part of the bank's thrust internationally. In 1986 Fullerton announced that CIBC would split its operations into three separate units: the Individual Bank, the Corporate Bank, and the Investment Bank.

Each unit was to deal with a specific group of customers. The Individual Bank was CIBC's largest unit, employing three-quarters of the bank's workers to serve individuals and independent business people. The Corporate Bank was intended to provide standard financial services to a variety of Canadian and foreign companies. The Investment Bank was intended to take advantage of the upcoming liberalization of capital and other investment markets in Canada. It oversaw the operations of CIBC's brokerage firms and merchant banks overseas, and then domestically after June 1987, when Canada removed the regulations barring commercial banks from conducting investment banking activities. CIBC Securities Inc. was established in 1987 to offer stockbroker services. The bank also participated in a merchant bank, the Gordon Investment Corporation, with the Gordon Capital Corporation—each was an equal partner in the new bank. In Europe, CIBC operated CIBC Securities Europe Ltd. (formerly Grenfell and Colegrave Ltd., a U.K. firm acquired in 1986), and a stock brokerage for its overseas customers.

In 1987 Brazil announced that it would suspend interest payments on its foreign loans indefinitely. This action shocked the international banking community, which feared that other Third World countries would follow suit. In August 1987 the Canadian government issued a guideline that required banks to set aside a large sum to protect against possible losses on loans to Third World countries. CIBC set aside C$451 million, resulting in a net loss of C$63 million for 1987, though assets increased by almost C$8 billion.

Continuing its diversification in the newly deregulated environment, CIBC purchased a majority stake in the Wood Gundy Corporation, a leading Canadian investment dealer, for C$203.3 million in June 1988. The bank subsequently formed CIBC Wood Gundy, which offered asset management services for corporate and institutional clients. In 1989 CIBC gained an option to acquire Morgan Trust Company of Canada. When necessary revisions to the federal Bank Act went into effect in 1992, CIBC completed the acquisition, which formed the basis for CIBC Trust.

Worldwide deregulation, liberalization of financial markets, and information technology made banking more complex during the mid- and late 1980s. CIBC responded innovatively to a changing marketplace. The bank regained the lost ground of the early 1980s and made a greater effort to expand overseas than any other Canadian bank. But CIBC still held a significant portfolio of potential problem loans that it would have to correct if the bank was to thrive in the 1990s. To that end, CIBC management worked to improve its loan portfolio and to increase efficiency throughout its system during the late 1980s and early 1990s. It also shed employees in bloated divisions, while bolstering growing business segments.

1990s: New Business Ventures, Thwarted Mergers

Among the new business arenas targeted by CIBC were insurance and derivatives. CIBC's foray into insurance reflected ongoing bank-industry deregulation during the early and mid-1990s that was intended to give banks the opportunity to compete more effectively in evolving financial markets. CIBC was inundated with more than 50,000 inquiries when it began selling automobile insurance early in 1995. It subsequently began offering term life insurance. The company's efforts related to derivatives were the result of its intent to become a major player in the burgeoning derivatives market. CIBC hired a top-notch staff to compete in the risky investment niche, and was enjoying positive results in 1995. That same year, CIBC acquired Argosy Group, a junk bond dealer based in New York, and FirstLine Trust, a Toronto firm with a C$5 billion portfolio of residential mortgages.

Largely as a result of new business ventures, CIBC boosted its asset base to C$186.51 billion by 1995. Although sales remained relatively steady during the early 1990s, the bank posted a disappointing C$108 million loss in 1992, the same year that Al Flood took over as chairman and CEO. Net income surged to C$600 million in 1993, though, and then to a healthy C$890 million in 1994; one year later, CIBC saw its net income surpass the C$1 billion mark, becoming only the second Canadian bank—following Royal Bank of Canada (RBC)—to reach that level. Furthermore, CIBC's loan portfolio was much more secure by 1995 than it had been only a few years earlier. In addition, the organization continued to branch out globally, as evidenced by its 1994 listing on the Jamaica, Barbados, and Trinidad stock exchanges.

Mergers and acquisitions—some thwarted and some completed—dominated the news about Canadian Imperial Bank of Commerce in the late 1990s. Early in 1997 CIBC entered into talks with Imasco Limited to acquire Imasco's subsidiary CT Financial Services Inc., a Toronto-based financial services holding company operating under the name Canada Trust. Discussions ended, however, when the federal government told the parties that it would not approve the deal. (CT Financial was subsequently acquired in 2000 by the Toronto-Dominion Bank.)

In 1997 CIBC grabbed for a larger piece of the global securities markets by acquiring Oppenheimer & Co., Inc., a U.S. full-service securities firm, for US$525 million. Oppenheimer was subsequently merged with CIBC Wood Gundy to form CIBC World Markets, which was positioned as CIBC's international investment bank.

In January 1998 it appeared the banking megamerger wave that was roiling the U.S. banking and financial services sector was finally going to head north when RBC and Bank of Montreal, two of the top five Canadian banks, announced a merger that would create a new banking behemoth with total assets of nearly C$500 billion. Then, just three months later, the Toronto-Dominion Bank, the fifth largest Canadian bank, and CIBC followed suit by announcing a merger of their own to create what would have been the ninth largest bank in North America, with combined assets of C$466 billion. In December 1998, however, Canadian Finance Minister Paul Martin rejected both the proposed merger between Toronto-Dominion and CIBC and that of RBC and Bank of Montreal. Ignoring the banks' insistence that they needed to merge in order to compete in the increasingly globalized financial services market, Martin concluded that from the standpoint of Canadians the mergers would create two banks with too much power and would severely reduce competition.

There was other bad news at CIBC during 1998 as well. The CIBC World Markets unit suffered a net loss of C$186 million during the fourth quarter of fiscal 1998 as a result of pursuing the wrong markets during a period of international market turmoil. The poor performance at CIBC World Markets sent profits for Canadian Imperial Bank of Commerce tumbling by 32 percent for the full year. CIBC World Markets subsequently cut its staff by about 5 percent and pulled back from its global ambitions. It began refocusing primarily on the Canadian and U.S. markets, pursuing only some niches in the United Kingdom and the Asia Pacific region.

1999 and Beyond: Restructuring Under Hunkin

Given the troubles at CIBC World Markets it came as somewhat of a surprise when John S. Hunkin, the head of that unit, was named CIBC chairman and CEO, succeeding the retiring Flood. Soon after taking over in June 1999, Hunkin launched a reorganization aimed at flattening the bank's hierarchy and cutting costs. CIBC restructured into four operating units: electronic banking, retail and small-business banking, wealth management, and CIBC World Markets. Hunkin aimed to cut annual operating costs by C$500 million.

Searching for new ways to grow, CIBC in the late 1990s began partnering with major supermarket chains in both Canada and the United States to set up private-label electronic retail banks operating out of kiosks at the supermarkets' outlets. CIBC partnered with Loblaw Companies Limited to form President's Choice Financial in 1998. This was followed by the creation of Marketplace Bank in conjunction with the southern U.S. chain Winn-Dixie Stores, Inc. and Safeway Select Bank, which began operating in the western United States at supermarkets run by Safeway Inc. In 2000 these ventures were amalgamated under a new subsidiary called Amicus.

Canadian Imperial Bank of Commerce also sought to divest noncore operations during this period, aiming to focus more of its attention on its core banking business. In 1999 the bank exited from the life insurance and emergency travel insurance businesses. Then the following year, CIBC sold its home and auto insurance subsidiaries to Desjardins-Laurentian Financial Corp. for about C$330 million, leaving it virtually out of the insurance sector.

During 2001 and 2002, CIBC completed a series of acquisitions to build up its wealth management operations. The bank acquired the 34 percent of TAL Global Asset Management Inc. it did not already own and also bought Merrill Lynch Canada's private client and asset management businesses. As a result, CIBC created the largest full-service brokerage in Canada with more than 1,400 brokers. The bank also became Canada's fourth-largest provider of mutual funds. In another strategic move, CIBC in October 2002 merged its Caribbean banking operations with those of Barclays Bank PLC to create FirstCaribbean International Bank Limited. CIBC held an equity interest of about 43 percent in FirstCaribbean.

CIBC reacted almost immediately to the negative economic fallout from the events of September 11, 2001, by announcing that it would slash about 2,000 jobs from its workforce (a reduction of about 4 percent), increase its loan-loss provisions by nearly 60 percent, and sell off C$1 billion of unwanted loans and credit commitments. Fiscal 2002 turned even bleaker for CIBC as it was forced to set aside C$1.5 billion for bad corporate loans, including hundreds of millions it had loaned to two of the most famous victims of the now-burst stock market bubble: Enron Corporation and Global Crossing Ltd. At the same time, the ambitious Amicus venture continued to bleed red ink, losing C$871 million in both the United States and Canada between 2000 and 2002. Thus in October 2002 CIBC announced that it would shut down the U.S. operations of Amicus; the Canadian arm, which appeared to be on the road to profitability, would continue to operate. A restructuring charge of C$525 million—mostly related to the Amicus pullback—coupled with heavy loan-loss provisions, resulted in a fiscal 2002 fourth-quarter loss of C$100 million, CIBC's first quarterly loss since 1992.

One of the strategies for pursuing a turnaround adopted by CIBC management was to reallocate resources away from the riskier activities of CIBC World Markets and toward the more dependable operations of CIBC Retail Markets and CIBC Wealth Management. The goal was to have 70 percent of the bank's capital allocated to the latter two units, which would be a sizeable increase over the 50 percent figure of 2002. In January 2003 a major step was taken toward achieving this goal when CIBC sold its Oppenheimer private client and asset management businesses in the United States to New York-based Fahnestock Viner Holdings Inc. for C$354 million. CIBC succeeded in mounting a major comeback in fiscal 2003, reporting net income of C$2.06 billion.

While the outlook for Canadian Imperial Bank of Commerce certainly appeared to be brightening, the bank had to grapple with a number of legal issues related to some of the corporate scandals that grew out of the excesses of the 1990s. In December 2003 CIBC reached an agreement with the U.S. Securities and Exchange Commission to pay $80 million to settle civil charges that had been brought, alleging that the bank had helped Enron hide debt and inflate its profits by more than US$1 billion through intricate financial manipulations. CIBC also faced a number of civil suits that had been brought by Enron shareholders. The scandal involving illegal late-day trading in mutual funds ensnared CIBC in its widening web by early 2004 when it was reported that the bank was facing imminent regulatory action for making more than US$1 billion in financing available to investors who subsequently made illegal mutual fund trades.

Principal Subsidiaries

CIBC Asset Management Inc.; CIBC Mortgages Inc.; CIBC Trust Corporation; CIBC World Markets Inc.; Canadian Imperial Holdings Inc. (U.S.A.); CIBC World Markets Corp. (U.S.A.); TAL Global Asset Management Inc.; CIBC Holdings (Cayman) Limited; CIBC Offshore Banking Services Corporation (Barbados); CIBC Australia Limited; CIBC World Markets (Japan) Inc.; CIBC Asia Limited (Singapore); CIBC World Markets plc (U.K.).

Principal Operating Units

CIBC Retail Markets; CIBC Wealth Management; CIBC World Markets.

Principal Competitors

Royal Bank of Canada; Bank of Nova Scotia; The Toronto-Dominion Bank; Bank of Montreal.

Further Reading

Atlas, Riva D., ''Canada Bank Is Said to Face Legal Action by Regulators,'' *New York Times,* January 28, 2004, p. C1.

Barnes, Angela, ''Chairman of CIBC Places Emphasis on Teamwork,'' *Globe and Mail,* March 29, 1985, p. R7.

Blackwell, Richard. ''CIBC Widens Insurance Effort,'' *Financial Post,* February 24, 1995, sec. 1, p. 11.

——, ''New CIBC Boss Promises Shakeup,'' *Globe and Mail,* April 2, 1999, p. B1.

''Can Canada's No. 2 Bank Stop Its Slide?,'' *Business Week,* June 11, 1984, p. 57.

Craig, Susanne, ''Angry Bankers Face an Uncertain Future,'' *Globe and Mail,* December 15, 1998, p. A1.

Dalglish, Brenda, ''Banking on Change,'' *Maclean's,* November 2, 1992, pp. 46+.

Darroch, James L., *Canadian Banks and Global Competitiveness,* Montreal: McGill-Queen's University Press, 1994.

DeCloet, Derek, ''Banker with Attitude,'' *Canadian Business,* June 11, 1999, pp. 33–34, 36, 38.

——, ''King of the World,'' *Canadian Business,* July 10–July 24, 2000, pp. 56+.

Edinborough, Arnold, *A History of Canadian Imperial Bank of Commerce,* Volume IV: *1931–1973,* Toronto: Canadian Imperial Bank of Commerce, 1995.

Gibbon, Ann, ''CIBC, TAL Create Giant Funds Manager,'' *Globe and Mail,* January 20, 1994, p. B1.

Haliechuk, Rick, ''CIBC Grooms Staff for Play in Derivatives,'' *Toronto Star,* January 20, 1995, p. E8.

Heinzl, Mark, ''CIBC to Merge with Toronto Dominion,'' *Wall Street Journal,* April 20, 1998, p. A3.

Kalawsky, Keith, ''CIBC Goes Wal-Mart,'' *Financial Post,* September 13, 2003, p. FP7.

——, ''How Hunkin Put CIBC on Course,'' *Financial Post,* December 23, 2003, p. FP1.

Kraus, James R., ''Canadian Giant in Big Move Toward Investment Banking,'' *American Banker,* March 31, 1994, pp. 1+.

Milner, Brian, ''CIBC's Fullerton Stepping Down,'' *Globe and Mail,* December 7, 1991, p. B1.

Mittelstaedt, Martin, ''CIBC's Sweeping Austerity Plan Includes Layoffs, Salary Restraint,'' *Globe and Mail,* June 17, 1982, p. B4.

——, ''Harrison Resigns As CIBC Chairman,'' *Globe and Mail,* January 18, 1985, p. B1.

Noble, Kimberley, ''Bitterness on Bay Street: Ottawa Hands the Banks a Resounding Defeat,'' *Maclean's,* December 28, 1998, pp. 70–73.

——, ''How the Banks Blew It,'' *Maclean's,* December 7, 1998, pp. 26–30.

Partridge, John, ''CIBC Aims for Big Payoff: Forms Canada's First Integrated Global Investment Bank in Radical Reshaping,'' *Globe and Mail,* March 31, 1994, p. B3.

——, ''CIBC Chairman Sets Sights on First Place,'' *Globe and Mail,* January 15, 1996, p. B1.

——, ''CIBC Finally Pulls the Plug on U.S. Electronic Banking Unit,'' *Globe and Mail,* November 15, 2002, p. B1.

Ross, Victor, and Arthur St. L. Trigge, *A History of the Canadian Bank of Commerce,* 3 vols., Toronto: Oxford University Press, 1920–1934.

Stewart, Sinclair, ''CIBC Agrees to Settle over Enron Allegations,'' *Globe and Mail,* December 23, 2003, p. B1.

Stewart, Sinclair, and Andrew Willis, ''CIBC Sells U.S. Retail Broker,'' *Globe and Mail,* December 11, 2002, p. B1.

Stoffman, Daniel, ''Poor Little Rich Bank,'' *Canadian Business,* May 1, 1996, pp. 44+.

Wilson-Smith, Anthony, ''The Challengers,'' *Maclean's,* April 27, 1998, pp. 40–44.

—updates: Dave Mote, David E. Salamie

Cash America International, Inc.

1600 W. Seventh Street
Fort Worth, Texas 76102-2599
U.S.A.
Telephone: (817) 335-1100
Fax: (817) 570-1225
Web site: http://www.cashamericaonline.com

Public Company
Incorporated: 1984 as Cash America Investments, Inc.
Employees: 3,096
Sales: $387.8 million (2002)
Stock Exchanges: New York
Ticker Symbol: PWN
NAIC: 522298 All Other Nondepository Credit Intermediation; 522390 Other Activities Related to Credit Intermediation

Cash America International, Inc. is the world's largest international pawn company. In addition to providing secured nonrecourse loans (pawn loans) to individuals, the company provides check-cashing services through its Mr. Payroll Corporation subsidiary and short-term unsecured cash advances, known as payday advance loans, at Cash America pawnshops and through its Cashland subsidiary. As of September 2003, the company had 592 lending locations in the United States, Great Britain, and Sweden.

Getting Started: 1983–89

Jack Daugherty, the chairman and CEO of Cash America, opened his first pawnshop in Texas in the early 1970s and was so successful he moved into the oil business. When that industry went bust, he returned to pawnshops, founding the company in 1983, and incorporating it the following year as Cash America Investments, Inc. Daugherty took the company public in 1987, making it the first pawnshop company to be publicly owned. The initial offering raised $14.5 million, with five million shares sold. Using the money to expand, Cash America acquired the Big State chain of 47 pawnshops later that year. The company continued to grow, primarily through acquisitions. In 1988, five years after its founding, the chain opened its 100th location.

The stores in the Cash America chain did not fit the dark, dingy image of a storefront pawnshop. Daugherty's strategy was to provide big, well-lit stores, to computerize the inventory, and to centralize management. The company established a three-month training program for new employees that included classroom and on-the-job training in loans, layaways, merchandise, and general administration of store operations. More experienced workers received training in the fundamentals of management, and managers went through a year-long program that dealt with recruitment, merchandise control, income maximization, and cost efficiency. Each store had a unit manager who reported to a market manager responsible for about ten locations. The market manager in turn reported to a division vice-president.

''Cash America is bringing modern management to a backward industry,'' Prudential analyst John D. Morris told Ellen Stark of the *Wall Street Journal.* Investors, including some of the nation's largest banks according to Michael Hudson of the *Nation,* appeared to like it. In 1988, the company sold an additional 4.92 million shares, raising $24 million to finance its expansion.

Cash America used the term ''non-traditional borrowers'' to refer to its customers. These were people not willing or unable to use a credit card or get a bank loan to cover the cost of repairing their car, paying a utility bill, or other short-term need for cash. Many did not have a checking account and usually conducted their business on a cash basis.

Customers brought in items of personal value—wedding rings, silver tea sets, televisions, firearms, bicycles, radar detectors, weed whackers—to use as collateral for an immediate loan of money. Using sources such as catalogues, blue books, newspapers, previous similar pawn loan transactions, and his or her own experience, the Cash America employee determined the estimated value of the item and the amount to be financed.

The Cash America customer received a computerized pawn ticket that gave a detailed description of the collateral, amount loaned, and identifying information about the customer (ad-

Company Perspectives:

In last year's annual report, we discussed a return to our roots—a renewed focus on core lending activities. It was a strategy that had begun to show signs of success, and we made it our mission to continue these efforts throughout 2002.

We're proud to say that we're on the right course.

Our success is largely due to the people throughout Cash America. They are working hard to deliver the best service and products to our customers. The response has been very favorable and customer demand is unprecedented. Cash America is working to fill the short-term capital gap for thousands of people in America and Europe.

Our strategy has become our compass as we move forward. A compass is a tool that, in the right hands, can get people where they need to be. Guide them. Keep them moving in the right direction. This year we've reaffirmed that, in the hands of the right people, it will do the same for our Company.

dress, age, driver's license number). The average Cash America loan was for less than $100 and was outstanding for less than two months. The customer redeemed the item by paying the loan amount and service charge. About 70 percent of the company's loans were repaid. For those that were not, the collateral became the property of Cash America and could be sold.

The company's gross revenue was calculated by adding the amount received from the sales of unredeemed items plus the amount earned from service charges. Sales were generally around 70 percent of the gross revenue. But when the cost of the sales was subtracted, service charges accounted for at least half the net revenue each year.

The pawnshop industry has long been an extensively regulated activity. States determined the process to be followed in applying for a pawnshop license, what records had to be maintained and whether the local police could inspect them or whether transactions had to be reported to local law enforcement officials, how old a customer must be to be served, and what hours the business could be open. States also established the range of loan amounts and the maximum annual service charge for each range. In Texas, for example, in 1997, the most a pawnshop could charge was 240 percent per annum, and that only for loans of $1–$132. No pawn loan could be more than $11,000, for which the maximum annual rate was 12 percent. Oklahoma also had 240 percent as the maximum annual rate, but for loans of $1 to $150. Loans in that state could not exceed $25,000, with a maximum annual rate for that amount of 36 percent. Other states, including Florida and Georgia, allowed a maximum of 25 percent of the loan for each 30-day period of the transaction, with no breakdown by loan amount.

Rapid Expansion: 1990–95

By 1990, Cash America was operating 123 company-owned locations. That year the company was listed on the New York Stock Exchange and the stock split 3 for 2. In 1992, a 4.6 million stock offering raised $45 million, the stock split 2 for 1, and the company opened its 200th store, in Mission, Texas. It was at this point that Daugherty decided to take his company international. He acquired Harvey & Thompson, a U.K. chain with more than 100 years in the pawnshop business. Harvey & Thompson was based in London and had 26 locations in England and Scotland. The pawnshop business in the United Kingdom was essentially the same as that in the United States. Pawn loans, however, generally were secured only by jewelry and gold or silver items and the average loan was larger, approximately $120. In addition, for loans larger than about $40, unredeemed items were sold at auction. Finally, the Consumer Credit Act of 1974 prohibited pawnbrokers from entering into ''extortionate credit bargains'' with customers and Cash America charged a rate of around 6 percent per month.

The company continued to expand in the United States as well, opening more stores, buying the 18-store Express Cash chain and entering Alabama and Missouri in 1993. At the end of the year the chain operated 280 locations. In 1994, Cash America opened its 300th store and had more than 1,800 employees. That same year it bought shares in Mr. Payroll, a check-cashing franchise operation, and also acquired the ten-store Svensk Pantbelåning, one of the oldest operating pawnshop chains in Sweden. As in the United Kingdom, the pawnshops in Sweden handled primarily jewelry and precious metals, catering to a more affluent customer. Under a new pawnbroking act passed in 1996, loan terms were not to exceed one year, but the act set no maximum interest rates for pawn loans and did not authorize local boards to regulate those rates as the statute had in the past. Also as with Harvey & Thompson, unredeemed merchandise was sold at public auction, although pawnbrokers could sell items they purchased at auction to the public from their pawnshop. The average loan amount in Sweden was approximately $300. In both Sweden and the United Kingdom, loans generally were outstanding for 180 days or less and forfeiture rates were one-third less than in the United States. At the end of 1994, the company had gross revenues of $221.9 million and $15 million in net profits.

During 1995, the company faced increased competition in the United States. Several companies, including EZCorp, Inc. with 240 locations, and First Cash, Inc., with 50 operating units, completed initial public offerings and announced plans to expand through new locations and acquisitions. A number of smaller companies also entered the market.

The competition affected the company's Cash America VIP program, which offered discounts on unredeemed merchandise to frequent shoppers in an effort to attract bargain shoppers. Cash America turned to its proprietary loan and inventory tracking system to analyze the problems. The system linked all its U.S. stores to coordinate and manage thousands of loans and more than a million different items of inventory. Using information from that system, Daugherty found that inventory was too high, that unredeemed items were not being turned over quickly enough despite the discounts. He also decided that too much emphasis was being placed on retail to the detriment of the actual loan business.

The company established two goals for 1996: to reinforce U.S. operations on the importance of successful lending at the

Key Dates:

1983: Jack Daugherty founds Cash America.
1984: The company incorporates under the name Cash America Investments, Inc.
1987: Cash America becomes the first pawnshop company to go public, raising $14.5 million in its initial public offering of five million shares.
1992: Daugherty takes Cash America international, acquiring Harvey & Thompson, a London-based pawnshop chain with 26 locations in England and Scotland.
1994: Cash America acquires shares in Mr. Payroll, a check-cashing franchise operation; it also acquires Svensk Pantbelåning, one of the oldest operating pawnshop chains in Sweden.
1996: Mr. Payroll becomes a wholly owned subsidiary of Cash America.
2003: Cash America acquires Ohio-based Cashland for $51 million.

unit level and to sharpen the emphasis on cash-on-cash returns at every level of the organization, both domestic and foreign. Cash America also decided to slow its rate of growth, with a net gain of nine units during the year, for a total of 382.

Broad-Based Diversification in the Mid-1990s

The refocus did not stop Daugherty from moving into other alternative financial businesses. By December 1996, Cash America had purchased all the shares of Mr. Payroll, which then had about 160 locations in 21 states. Mr. Payroll was started by John Templer in 1988 as he lay in a hospital bed in High Plains, Texas, after battling Guillain-Barré, a rare neurological disease, for two years. Templer and his partner, Michael Stinson, began by cashing checks for nurses at the hospital, using an armored car. Running the armored car two days a week, they also cashed checks for workers at two nearby manufacturing plants.

Mr. Payroll expanded to Amarillo in 1989, putting check-cashing booths in eight Toot'n Totum Food Stores. People kept calling Templer, wanting to open booths in other towns, and he decided to franchise the concept. By the time it became a wholly owned subsidiary of Cash America, national companies such as Texaco, Circle K, and Diamond-Shamrock wanted to be franchisees. In Shreveport, Louisiana, for example, Mr. Payroll built eight locations for Circle K. ''They want it. It adds value to them. They take the cash out of the store and recycle it through checks they cash and the customers spend the money in the store. That's a big advantage to the stores,'' Templer explained to the *Amarillo Business Journal.* The acquisition was also advantageous to Cash America in its efforts to serve the non-banking segment of the population and become, to quote the 1996 annual report, ''a broader based, specialty financial services entity.'' Neither Mr. Payroll nor the company's affiliate, Express Rent-a-Tire, Ltd., contributed to earnings in 1996.

Cash America's income from its domestic operations increased in 1996 after dropping in 1995. Loan balances increased 23 percent while inventory levels dropped by 14 percent. The company ended the year with an all-time high average domestic loan balance of $190,000 per location and a year-end inventory level of $145,000 per location, the lowest in several years. Daugherty credited the company's ability to respond to a stronger than expected demand for loans, with the increase coming from more loans, not larger loans. This was evidence that the company was increasing its customer base and market penetration. For the first time in its history, Cash America had more than $100 million in outstanding loans.

In November, the company announced a ''Dutch Auction'' to buy back 4.5 million shares. Under that process, shareholders tendered shares at prices between $7.00 and $8.50 and Cash America then determined the single share price within that range that would allow it to purchase 4.5 million or fewer shares. In December the company purchased 4.5 million shares at $8.50 per share. In January 1997, the board of directors was authorized to repurchase up to one million shares on the open market. In May 1997, Cash America acquired Rothchilds Sales & Loans, the largest pawnshop chain in Utah with five locations in and around Salt Lake City. That same month, Mr. Payroll expected to have its first self-service check-cashing and automated teller machines up and running in three towns in Texas. With the TrueFace technology used in the machines, customers would be able to cash any check in less than a minute without showing any photo identification. Instead, the technology verified a customer's identity by recognizing the contour of his or her face.

The company's earnings continued to grow during 1997, with its loan balance standing at more than $100 million and its inventory down 12 percent at the end of the first quarter. While law enforcement officers remained concerned about customers pawning stolen property, the company stated that stolen property accounted for less than one half of 1 percent of property pawned with the chain.

In June, Daugherty announced a new franchise program: selected independent pawnshops would be franchised under the Cash America brand name starting later in 1997. ''By joining forces with hundreds of other quality and service-minded pawnbrokers, we will be able to reach markets beyond those served by our existing and planned company-owned stores,'' COO Daniel Feehan explained. According to Mike Rapoport, an analyst with Dabnehy/Resnick, in addition to Cash America's successful pawn business, the company was among the nation's largest gold producers. It sold gold melted down from unredeemed, unsold jewelry on the metals exchange as bullion. ''This thing makes money,'' Rapoport told the *Sun Sentinel.*

By 1998, however, with the explosive growth of Internet-related businesses and the U.S. economic boom taking a bite out of demand for short-term loans, Cash America began to second-guess its longstanding reliance on its core business activities. Jumping on the high-tech bandwagon, the company launched innoVentry, a strategic joint venture with Wells Fargo Bank aimed at providing a broad range of e-based financial products and services to a larger, more diverse, group of customers. Expanding on the idea of Mr. Payroll's automated check-cashing machine, innoVentry harnessed Internet and biometric technologies to create its own signature ''Rapid Payment Machine'' (RPM) cash management and information access machines, to be installed in retail outlets such as Albertson's, Kmart, Kroger, Circle K, and Wal-Mart. The investment seemed promising. Also in 1998, having tested the rent-to-own concept at four stores in the Dallas-Fort Worth area and believing there was great potential in adding to the range of services it offered to its traditional pawn customer, Cash America increased its ownership of its Rent-a-Tire subsidiary from 40 percent to 99 percent and launched an aggressive course of expansion into markets throughout Texas. Although Cash America saw little return on these investments during 1999, the company's management resolved to stay the course, promising shareholders that these new initiatives would yield positive results by the end of 2000.

In the last years of the decade, Cash America continued to grow its core business as well, keeping pace with four other publicly traded pawnshop companies, including First Cash, Inc., and EZCorp, Inc., which were vying for market share by grabbing up acquisitions. In 1998, Cash America acquired Doc Holliday's Pawnbrokers and Jewelers, Inc., an Austin, Texas-based company with 40 locations in six states, among the largest privately owned pawnshop chains in the United States. Chairman and CEO Jack Daugherty hailed the acquisition as key to building Cash America's presence in a variety of new and existing markets. Although Cash America did not disclose the terms of the acquisition, the purchase price of Doc Holliday's was estimated around $22 million. Roughly six times more than the total value of Doc Holliday's loans, the steep price was evidence of increasing competition in the rapidly consolidating industry.

Back to Basics for the 21st Century

Having attempted to play the odds with broad-based diversification, by the end of 2000 Cash America's management was forced to concede that its noncore investments were not going to pay off as expected. That year, the company reported a loss of $1.7 million, or 7 cents a share, a significant downturn, considering that it had reaped $3.9 million, or 15 cents a share, in 1999. In 2001 Dan Feehan, who had succeeded Jack Daugherty as chief executive in 1999, announced Cash America's decisive return to its core lending activities, along with the company's assured withdrawal from both its Rent-a-Tire and innoVentry business segments. While rededicating its resources to its pawnshop activities, the company would seek opportunities to bring in additional revenue through added fee-based financial services more compatible with its core competencies, such as money transfer, check cashing, bill payment, tax refund anticipation loans, and others. According to the new vision, Cash America would transform its image over time from a pawnshop operator to a neighborhood financial service center.

As luck would have it, Cash America's strategic retrenchment coincided beautifully with the long-anticipated downturn in the U.S. economy, and demand for short-term loans began to grow at a dramatic rate. Indeed, in 2002, Cash America's customers borrowed more than half a billion dollars, collectively, bringing loan volume to an unprecedented high for the first time in three years. The company also saw marked success with one of its newest services, the payday advance loan—a small, short-term loan designed to help customers solve cash flow problems until their next paycheck—which accounted for about 50 percent of the company's revenue growth in the first quarter of 2003. So promising was this service that in August 2003, Cash America spent $51 million to acquire Cashland, a check casher and payday loanmaker with 121 locations, mainly in Ohio. With the acquisition, Cash America now boasted 592 lending locations in 17 states and two foreign countries. With no reprieve in sight for the U.S. economy, the company appeared well positioned for continued robust growth and tidy profits well into the first decade of the 21st century.

Principal Subsidiaries

Mr. Payroll Corporation; Cashland.

Principal Competitors

Ace Cash Express, Inc.; EZCORP, Inc.; World Acceptance Corporation.

Further Reading

Bowser, David, ''Business Cashes in by Cashing Checks,'' *Amarillo Business Journal, Amarillo Globe-News Online,* February 12, 1997.

Falkner, R. Jerry, *Research Profile: Cash America International, Inc.,* Crested Butte, Colo.: RJ Falkner and Company, May/June 1997.

Foust, Dean, with David Lindorff in Philadelphia, Arthur Menke in Chicago, Mike McNamee in Washington, Heather Timmons in New York, and bureau reports, ''Easy Money,'' *Business Week,* April 24, 2000, p. 107.

Fuquay, Jim, ''Cash America Will Buy Payday Loan Maker for $53 Million in Cash, Stock,'' *Fort Worth Star-Telegram,* July 2, 2003.

——, ''Pawnbroker Seesaw: When Economy Goes Down, Pawn Business Booms,'' *Fort Worth Star-Telegram,* July 1, 2002.

Glover, Scott, and Evelyn Larrubia, ''Want a Piece of Shops? Try Wall Street,'' *Sun Sentinel,* November 25, 1996, http://www.sun-sentinel.com/news/1664.htm.

Hudson, Michael, ''Cashing in on Poverty: How Big Business Wins Every Time,'' *Nation,* May 5, 1996, http://www.thenation.com/issue/96520/0520huds.htm.

Jay, Sarah, ''A Clean, Well-Lighted Place for Loans; Pawnshop Chains Grow As They Remake Image,'' *New York Times,* August 19, 1997, p. D1.

LaHood, Lila, ''Cash America to Refocus on Pawnshop Financial Services,'' *Fort Worth Star-Telegram,* May 17, 2001.

Raghunathan, Anuradha, ''Pawnshops Benefit in Economic Hard Times,'' *Dallas Morning News,* October 6, 2002.

Stark, Ellen, ''You Can Hock the Silverware to Buy This Stock,'' *Time,* February 1995, p. 57.

Stickel, Amu I., ''Pawn Industry Is Ripe for Consolidation: Sector Analysts Foresee an M&A Wave Sweeping Over U.S. Pawn Shops,'' *Mergers and Acquisitions Report,* May 04, 1998.

Talmadge, Candace, ''Pawnshops Moving Upmarket: Large Chains Force Competitors to Address Image,'' *National Post (Canada),* December 14, 1998, p. C4.

—Ellen D. Wernick
—update: Erin Brown

Central European Media Enterprises Ltd.

PO Box HM66, Clarendon House
2, Church Street
Hamilton
Bermuda
HMCX
Telephone: (441) 296-1431
Web site: http://www.cetv-net.com

Public Company
Incorporated: 1994
Employees: 1,850
Sales: $92.6 million (2002)
Stock Exchanges: NASDAQ
Ticker Symbol: CETV
NAIC: 515120 Television Broadcasting

Central European Media Enterprises Ltd. (CME) was founded with the goal of bringing independent broadcast television to Eastern European countries eager for an alternative to state-run media. Company founder Ronald Lauder, heir to the Estée Lauder cosmetics fortune, also believed that CME would profit from growth in the developing economies of former Communist nations after the fall of the Iron Curtain. The company pairs its financial power and technological expertise with local entrepreneurs who hold broadcasting licenses in various Eastern European countries and operates television stations with programming calculated to appeal to popular tastes. Eastern Europe has been a difficult operating environment for CME, however, and the company has had to pull the plug on several of its ventures. The most notable dispute occurred when its partner in the Czech Republic, where CME established the enormously popular Nova TV, took his broadcast license away from the company. After traveling a very rough path, CME has emerged with six leading television stations in Slovakia, Slovenia, Romania, and the Ukraine. The company places importance on tailoring programming to local tastes, and its schedules are a mix of locally produced programs, Hollywood films, and top series from the United States.

Early Success in the Czech Republic: 1991–94

Ronald Lauder, founder of CME, left an executive position at the Estée Lauder cosmetics company in 1983 and took a foreign affairs position at the Pentagon. Later he was appointed ambassador to Austria, which gave him the chance to develop personal contacts and practical experience in Europe. The post also augmented his appreciation for his Eastern European heritage: his parents had come to the United States from Nazi-controlled Hungary in the 1930s. After the fall of the Iron Curtain in the early 1990s, Lauder's professional experience and personal heritage led him to pursue business opportunities in the countries newly liberated from Communist control. He teamed up with Mark Palmer, a former ambassador to Hungary, and founded Central European Development Corporation in 1991. The two focused on television broadcasting as an area with particular potential for growth. They believed that consumer spending was likely to continue growing in Eastern European countries and would soon generate a boom in the demand for television advertising space. Over the next few years, they explored the possibilities for partnerships in Eastern Europe and began amassing technical and programming capabilities.

Lauder and Palmer's first successes came in the Czech Republic. There they partnered with several Czech cultural figures and intellectuals, who formed the company CET 21. In 1993 CET 21 beat more than a dozen competitors to win a broadcasting license in the Czech Republic. According to Czech regulations, the license could not be owned by foreigners, so it remained in the hands of the Czech-controlled CET 21. CME provided financial backing, programming, and technology through its Czech subsidiary Ceska Nezavisla Televizni Spolecnost (CNTS), and CET 21 granted CNTS the exclusive right to use the license. The new station was launched in February 1994 under the name TV Nova.

Aside from its Czech operations, CME had acquired a broadcast license for Berlin in 1993. The company bought stakes in regional stations in Berlin and in the southern German city of Nuremberg in 1994. That June Central European Media Enterprises was incorporated in Bermuda to operate Nova and the other stations. John Severino was CEO. The company went

Company Perspectives:

Central European Media Enterprises operates the leading group of TV networks and stations across Central and Eastern Europe. Today, CME and its partners operate six stations in four countries, and are market leaders in every one of them, with news and information programming at the heart of each operation.

public on NASDAQ and raised $62 million. Secondary offerings over the next year brought in more capital for acquisitions. CME's prospectus acknowledged the risky nature of its operations and forecast losses for the first few years as the company focused on growth. Investors were encouraged to rely on the directors' expertise in Eastern Europe and on the potential for huge growth in advertising revenue.

The Czech station TV Nova turned out to be more successful than anyone had anticipated. It debuted in November 1994 with the film *Sophie's Choice*. After a year it had captured 68 percent of the Czech television audience and had already recouped its start-up investment. The station's success was due in large part to Vladimir Zelezny, a former journalist and television broadcaster who had been repressed under the Communists. Now in his 50s, he turned away from a more intellectual background producing documentaries and began producing lighter fare—soap operas and quiz shows—at Nova. Zelezny's low-brow style ran counter to the initial goal of the station. CME had partnered originally with a group of intellectuals with visions of language classes and international news programs. Zelezny first joined the company as a translator and lobbyist. His energy impressed the leadership of CME, who soon promoted him to station manager and allowed him to renovate the station's programming mix.

With relatively staid state-run television as the only competitor, Zelezny won viewers rapidly with a mix of popular U.S. series and sometimes racy Czech-produced shows. Although it aired sitcoms such as *Beverly Hills 90210* and *M.A.S.H.*, TV Nova retained a distinctively Czech flavor. The most popular show was a striptease version of the daily weather forecast, in which a naked male or female model dressed according to the next day's weather. The news program was also popular, because instead of showing dry meetings between heads of state, it aired graphic footage of car wrecks and murders. Critics referred to the programming as "tabloid television" and bemoaned the cultural degeneration of the nation. Zelezny told the *Wall Street Journal* in 1997, "The intellectuals believed Czechs were special, more sophisticated. We proved they were wrong. We showed that Czechs are like all other Europeans, whose first interest is soccer, with erotica a close second."

Launching Stations Throughout Eastern Europe: 1995–97

CEO Severino was replaced by Leonard Fertig, a former ABC executive and cable TV entrepreneur, in 1995. Fertig presided over several station launches across Eastern Europe. In late 1995 CME partnered with license holder Media Pro in Romania to form PRO TV. Adrian Sarbu was station director. A year later PRO TV reached 55 percent of Romania's population of 23 million and had captured 40 percent of television advertising revenues. Its programming combined U.S. films and series with locally produced shows such as a weekly quiz show, *Watch and Win.* Also in late 1995, POP TV was launched in Slovenia with local partners MMTV and Tele 59. The premiere movie, *Die Hard,* drew three quarters of the small country's population. After a year it had captured nearly half of the television advertising market and reached 80 percent of the population. A third station debut occurred in August 1996 in Slovakia, where CME established Markiza TV. By the end of the year the station had about 47 percent of the television advertising market.

CME had record revenues of $136 million in 1996, but its net loss, at $30 million, was also higher than ever. The company had yet to turn a profit. Still, its subsidiary stations seemed to be prospering and the company was doing well at delivering the programming that audiences wanted. Nova continued to be the star station, contributing 80 percent of revenue in 1996 and posting an operating income of $45 million. CME upped its stake in Nova from 66 percent to 88 percent that summer and moved to 99 percent in 1997. The German stations were the weakest part of the company's domain. CME had entered a joint venture with Time Warner to launch its Berlin and Brandenburg stations under the Puls brand name, but the German sector continued to be a cash drain.

CME also began moving into the Ukraine in 1996. The company already had the rights to sell advertising on the state-owned channel UT-2. That year CME managed to win a broadcasting license even though the Ukrainian Parliament had imposed a moratorium on new licenses. In initial meetings between CME executives and Oleksandr Volkov, a senior adviser to the president of the Ukraine, Volkov said the company had no chance of getting a license. Later, however, he suggested that CME team up with two wealthy and influential Ukrainians, Vadim Rabinovich and Boris Fuchsmann, who owned the broadcasting company Studio 1+1. CME acquired a share in Studio 1+1, managed to secure a license, and began broadcasting its usual mix of U.S. series such as *ER* and *Friends* and locally produced shows in January 1997. One popular program was an interview show called *Bez Tabu* (No Taboos). Viewers could call and ask questions about the allegedly sordid or violent lives of guests hidden behind a curtain. In 2001 the U.S. federal government began investigating CME for possibly bribing Ukrainian officials to obtain a license. Rabinovich and Fuchsmann also were accused of having ties to organized crime in Russia. CME issued a statement saying it was confident the investigations would clear Lauder of any wrongdoing.

With a profitable and popular television station in the Czech Republic as well as several successful stations in smaller East European markets, the future looked bright for CME through 1997. The company continued to expand its reach in the region that year: in October TVN Network was launched in Poland and TV-3 in Hungary. In Romania, where PRO TV had already cornered 60 percent of television advertising revenue, CME launched a second station in February 1998. Known as Acasa, the station was intended to appeal to female viewers and stave off the threat of rival stations that were appearing in the country.

Key Dates:

1991: Ronald Lauder and Mark Palmer launch a precursor to Central European Media Enterprises (CME).
1994: Nova TV, operated by CME, begins broadcasting in the Czech Republic.
1995–97: CME launches stations in Slovenia, Romania, Slovakia, and the Ukraine.
1998: Failed stations in Poland and Hungary contribute to a record net loss.
1999: CME loses control of TV Nova, its most profitable station.
2003: CME wins a $355 million settlement related to the loss of TV Nova.

Lost Stations and Legal Battles: 1998–2001

Early in 1998 Leonard Fertig resigned as CEO and was replaced by Michel Delloye. At this point, CME was the largest private broadcaster in Central and Eastern Europe. But its fortunes took a turn for the worse that year, heralding a difficult period that nearly wiped out the company over the next few years. First of all, CME closed down its German stations at the end of 1997, including interests in local stations in Berlin, Brandenburg, Leipzig, and Dresden. Next, both the Polish and the Hungarian stations ran into trouble. In Poland, CME underestimated the competition from existing stations and got mired in disputes with its local partner over the style of programming. TVN Network never caught on among Polish viewers, and CME was forced to refund money to advertisers who had been counting on a certain minimum audience. In late 1998, CME reluctantly left Poland, one of the biggest Eastern European markets, when it sold the station to its local partner and wrote off a loss of $44 million.

In Hungary, CME invested millions in developing an attractive programming schedule, only to have the broadcast license it expected to receive granted to a rival company. As a result, CME was able to air its program only over cable to limited audiences in Budapest. The station was finally abandoned two years later. By the end of 1998, numerous write-offs, as well as a drop in advertising revenues due to the August fiscal crisis in Russia, left CME with its biggest net loss ever of $125.3 million. From a high of $30, its share price plummeted to less than $5 late in the year. Ronald Lauder injected millions of dollars to keep the company going, buying stock at several times the trading price.

Despite these setbacks, CME's remaining stations were performing well for the time being. In 1999, CEO Fred Klinkhammer, who had replaced Delloye in March, began exploring a possible merger with SBS Broadcasting, a Luxembourg-based media company with stations in Scandinavia, Belgium, and The Netherlands. Klinkhammer described the merger as an ideal meeting of opposites: SBS was cautious yet reliable, while CME was a bold pioneer still smarting from recent failures. But before the deal could be clinched, it was blown apart by the sudden loss of TV Nova, CME's star broadcaster in the Czech Republic.

The conflict began when Klinkhammer accused station director Vladimir Zelezny of misappropriating funds through such activities as giving free advertising time to favored clients and guaranteeing his own company's debts with CME money. In April 1999 Klinkhammer fired Zelezny as CEO of CNTS, the CME subsidiary that operated Nova. Zelezny retaliated by refusing to let CNTS use the broadcasting license that he still controlled through CET 21. Zelezny set up broadcasting from his own makeshift offices, leaving CME with no outlet for its signal. CME had to shut down operations at CNTS and sought help from the international judicial system. Nova was by far CME's largest revenue generator, and its loss caused SBS to call off the proposed merger. CME's share price fell to less than $1 in the wake of these troubles and remained at abysmal levels through 2001. The company was delisted from the NASDAQ for about two years.

Emerging from Near Collapse: 2001–04

Observers were ready to pronounce CME dead, but the company continued its relatively successful operations at stations in Slovenia, Slovakia, Romania, and the Ukraine. But, with the exception of the Ukraine, these were small nations that could not generate enough advertising revenue to make up for the loss of TV Nova. Net revenue fell to $76.8 million in 2000 from a high of $182.4 million in 1998. Nevertheless, CME managed to acquire another station in October 2000 when it purchased Slovenia's Kanal A, a leading television broadcaster that had been in operation since 1991. The acquisition brought in about another 10 percent nationwide audience share in addition to the approximately 30 percent share CME already had in Slovenia through POP TV.

In 2001 international courts issued rulings on the TV Nova case. In February of that year an international arbitration tribunal in Paris ordered Zelezny to pay $27 million to CME. Zelezny handed over the sum the following year. Meanwhile, Lauder moved ahead with suits against the Czech government for allegedly encouraging Zelezny to deny CME its license. Early in 2001 two separate courts in London and Amsterdam ruled that Lauder could not claim compensation for his failed investment. Lauder filed a third suit via a Dutch subsidiary of CME and in September an international court in Stockholm found in Lauder's favor, ruling that the Czech government must pay Lauder the fair market value of TV Nova. The court determined that the Czech government had failed to protect Lauder's investment and that the Czech broadcasting council had actively conspired with Zelezny to push CME out. The amount of the settlement was to be determined later.

Net revenues rose to $92.6 million in 2002, and CME reported its first operating income, of $13.4 million, in four years. The company still had an overall net loss due to interest costs, but all four territories had posted profits. Studio 1 + 1 in the Ukraine was most impressive, with a 37 percent increase in revenues due to rapid development in the advertising market.

In 2003 CME put most of the problems related to TV Nova behind itself. In May the Stockholm panel ruled that the Czech Republic owed CME $355 million. The sum was staggering for a country that already had a nearly $5 billion deficit. Czech Prime Minister Vladimir Spidla lamented the size of the award and blamed the Czech broadcasting council for promoting Zelezny's efforts to oust CME. CME, for its part, planned to use the sum to retire much of the debt it had accumulated over years of net losses. The company also planned to seek an acquisition, perhaps to reenter the market in Poland or Hungary. In August Lauder filed a new claim against the company that was now running TV Nova. He asked for $275 million, but said he would hand over all but $72 million to the Czech treasury to shift some responsibility off the Czech taxpayer. Zelezny had been forced out of TV Nova earlier in the year and the station was now majority owned by the Czech financial concern PPF Group. CME sold CNTS, the subsidiary that once operated TV Nova, to the PPF Group in October for $53.2 million. In 2004 the company was left with six stations that were profitable market leaders, albeit in small markets: PRO TV and Acasa in Romania, Markiza TV in Slovakia, POP TV and Kanal A in Slovenia, and Studio 1 + 1 in the Ukraine.

Principal Subsidiaries

CME Development Corporation (Delaware); MKTV Rt (Hungary); Innova Film GmbH (Germany; 60%); Enterprise ''Inter-Media'' (Ukraine; 60%); Studio 1 + 1 (Ukraine; 18%); Kanal A (Slovenia; 97%); Pop TV (Slovenia; 97%); Media Pro S.R.L. (Romania; 44%); Pro TV S.R.L. (Romania; 49%); Media Vision (Romania; 70%); Media Pro International S.A. (Romania; 66%); Slovenska Televizna Spolocnost (Slovak Republic; 49%); Markiza s.r.o. (Slovak Republic; 8.5%).

Principal Competitors

TVR 1 (Romania); SLO 1 (Slovenia); STV1 (Slovak Republic); UT-1 (Ukraine); Inter (Ukraine).

Further Reading

Amdur, Meredith, and Debra Johnson, ''CME Brings Commercial Savvy to Central Europe,'' *Broadcasting & Cable,* January 22, 1996, p. 92.

Bauerova, Ladka, ''Post-Communist Media Deal Is Torn by Personal Dispute,'' *New York Times,* August 5, 1999, p. C4.

Bonner, Raymond, ''Lauder Media Company Faces a Federal Inquiry,'' *New York Times,* June 12, 2001, p. B1.

Done, Kevin, ''New Chief Quits Struggling CME,'' *Financial Times,* March 25, 1999, p. 18.

Drake, James, ''After Several Setbacks, Lauder Wins,'' *Daily Deal,* September 16, 2001.

''East European Television,'' *Economist,* May 1, 1999, p. 62.

Forrester, Chris, ''Europe's CME Hits Profitability,'' *Multichannel News,* December 15, 1997, p. 78.

Frank, Robert, ''Cultural Fare: A U.S.-Style Station Is Hit Among Czechs, And That's a Problem,'' *Wall Street Journal (Europe),* April 30, 1997, p. 1.

Green, Peter S., ''Czech Republic Pays $355 Million to Media Concern,'' *New York Times,* May 16, 2003, p. W1.

——, ''New Arbitration Claim in Battle Over Czech TV Station,'' *New York Times,* August 9, 2003, p. C3.

Gubernick, Lisa, ''Chip Off the Old Block,'' *Forbes,* February 24, 1997, p. 103.

Guyon, Janet, ''CME Taps Central, East Europe's Growth,'' *Wall Street Journal,* August 19, 1996, p. A7.

Jervis, Rick, ''Lauder-Zelezny Fight Moves to U.K.,'' *Wall Street Journal (Europe),* March 5, 2001, p. 27.

King, Neil, Jr., ''Czech TV Crusader Applies Shock Therapy, Live and in Color,'' *Wall Street Journal (Europe),* April 3, 1995, p. 26.

''Media: Is Lauder Tuning Out?,'' *Wall Street Journal (Europe),* October 26, 1998. p. 11.

Meils, Cathy, ''CME: Problems & Promises,'' *Variety,* May 24, 1999, p. S8.

Munk, Eva, ''Uncertain Station: A Bitter Feud Could Threaten the CME-SBS Merger,'' *Wall Street Journal (Europe),* May 31, 1999, p. 22.

Nadler, John, ''CME Finds Home on TV3,'' *Variety,* October 27, 1997, p. 30.

Reid, Alasdair, ''Can Lauder Increase His TV Strength in Eastern Europe?,'' *Campaign,* July 4, 1997, p. 20.

Rohwedder, Cacilie, ''CME, Backed by Lauder, Plans IPO to Aid Push into Eastern European Media Markets,'' *Wall Street Journal (Europe),* October 3, 1994, p. 5.

—Sarah Ruth Lorenz

Cheltenham & Gloucester PLC

Barnett Way
Gloucester
GL4 3RL
United Kingdom
Telephone: +44 1452 372372
Fax: (+44) 1452 373955
Web site: http://www.cheltglos.co.uk

Wholly Owned Subsidiary of Lloyds TSB Plc
Incorporated: 1850
Employees: 4,500
Total Assets: £52.2 billion ($87.7 billion) (2002)
NAIC: 522292 Real Estate Credit; 522120 Savings Institutions

Cheltenham & Gloucester PLC (C&G) is the third largest mortgage bank in the United Kingdom and represents the home mortgage arm of parent company U.K. banking giant Lloyds TSB. As such, C&G sells its mortgage products through the more than 2,300 branches of the Lloyds TSB banking network. Yet C&G also has established its own independent sales channels, including its C&G Mortgage Direct telephone sales division; C&G Invest Direct, which offers investment products in the postal and telecommunications sectors; and, since the mid-1990s, an active Internet sales operation. C&G is itself a symbol of the transformation of the U.K. building society sector, sparked by the Building Society Act of 1986. Formed more than 150 years ago, C&G has seen its assets leap from slightly more than £7 billion ($14 billion at the time) in the early 1990s to more than £52 billion ($87 billion) in 2002. The company is also one of the most recognized branded names in the U.K. mortgage sector.

Building a Building Society in the 1850s

The building society movement responded to the upsurge in demand for new urban housing amid the Industrial Revolution of the United Kingdom in the 19th century. Early forms of lending, or mutual aid, societies had already been in existence since the late 18th century, where members pooled resources and took turns building their homes or businesses. These pools, known as "terminating societies," generally disbanded after the last member had used his share.

While the early mutual aid societies catered to the more affluent artisan and middle classes, the surging urban working class population and the need to provide new housing inspired the emergence of a different type of mutual aid society. The idea for a "permanent" building society was first proposed in 1845, and that year saw the founding of the first of the new generation of building societies.

The new society began providing loans to its members, rather than direct payments provided by terminating societies. With members expected to repay their loans, the new building societies could then begin building up a more solid asset base, from which they could pay interest on members' accounts. This in turn led the building societies to develop savings accounts and services, taking on aspects of traditional banks. The building societies were able to counter the lower wealth of their working class member base with larger and fast-growing numbers.

The idea caught on quickly. By 1860, the United Kingdom boasted more than 2,700 building societies. Whereas London itself accounted for nearly a third of this total, the building society movement had spread quickly throughout the entire country. Many of the new building societies were focused exclusively on a local and regional level. Such was the case with the Cheltenham & Gloucester Permanent Mutual Benefit Building Society and Investment Association (C&G), which was created in 1850 in Cheltenham.

Despite its name, the new society's offices remained based in Cheltenham, operating out of that town's Belle Vue Hotel. In 1896, however, C&G made good on its name, opening a branch office in Gloucester. Three years later, the building society, which remained quite tiny, opened its first permanent office, on Cheltenham's Clarence Street. Over the next half-century, Cheltenham & Gloucester added new branch offices to serve its region.

Progressive legislation, including the Building Society Acts of 1874 and 1894, had by then codified the building society movement, providing a solid base for the industry while putting

Company Perspectives:

While remaining focused on its core business of mortgages and investments, C&G, now the UK's third-largest mortgage lender, has massively expanded its customer base and become a key component of one of the world's best-known financial services providers.

into place a number of safeguards to protect society members. As a result, the numbers of building societies dropped back to just 1,700 on the eve of World War I. At the same time, and despite its importance in the construction of new homes for much of the British population, the building society movement remained relatively modest. At the outbreak of World War I, total assets among all building societies reached just £76 million.

Postwar Survivor

The transformation of the building society movement began especially in the years following World War II. With the passage of the Building Society Act of 1939, building societies were required to establish more stringent mortgage guarantee standards. At the same time, building societies remained limited in the range of services they were allowed to offer. In the aftermath of the war and the necessity of reconstruction, the societies faced new competition from the nation's large, wealthy banks, which began competing heavily for the new mortgage market. Rising interest rates demanded by the British government in the early 1950s also cut into the building societies' margin of movement.

Yet Cheltenham & Gloucester's relatively large size—with five branches and nearly £15 million in assets—at the beginning of the 1950s enabled it to resist the new government-imposed rate hike. By maintaining its mortgage rates, C&G was able to position itself as a low-cost alternative. This gave the company an edge during the decade, as the United Kingdom underwent a building boom—with new construction topping more than 300,000 homes per year. As a result, C&G embarked on a new era of growth.

By the middle of the decade, the society's membership had swelled to more than 55,000 shareholders and depositors, of which some 27,000 were borrowing members. C&G's asset base also expanded strongly, leaping from £22 million in 1954 to more than £36 million in 1960. By then, the society also had expanded its branch network, to a total of seven.

The passage of a new Building Societies Act in 1960 restricted the size of loans, especially to corporate customers, in an effort to ensure liquidity of assets. Two years later, that act was replaced by a new Building Societies Act, which consolidated all previous legislation, further restricting the sector. As a result, the building society sector moved toward its own consolidation.

C&G, which remained among the top 20 building societies at the time, became an early participant in the first wave of consolidation, taking over two smaller societies, Yeovil and South Somerset Mutual Building Society and Vale of Evesham Permanent Building Society, that year. Other acquisitions followed, and by the beginning of the next decade, C&G had been transformed into a society with assets of more than £150 million and more than 45 branches—including new branch office openings that year in Manchester, Leeds, Glasgow, Devizes, and Cardigan—operating through much of the United Kingdom. C&G also boasted lowered management costs with the addition of its first computer system in 1969.

The early 1970s marked a new wave of industry consolidation, as the total number of building societies shrunk back to just 450. At the same time, a small number of more powerful societies had been emerging, and by the mid-1970s, the top 30 societies accounted for more than 85 percent of the total market. Cheltenham & Gloucester remained a primary player in the consolidation of the building society sector, adding such acquisitions as those of Smethwick Building Society and Tewkesbury and District Building Society in 1973.

By 1974, the society's assets had nearly doubled, and by 1977, C&G boasted assets of more than £500 million. The company opened its 100th branch office in Pershore two years later. Meanwhile, C&G also distinguished itself as an aggressive creator of new banking products, such as the launch of new investment vehicles in the early 1970s and the creation of its own ''Paddington Bear'' children's savings account at the end of the decade.

In 1981, C&G had a new hit product with the launch of a groundbreaking, high-interest Gold account. Interest in the new type of account proved so strong that, just six months after its launch, the bank was forced to suspend new accounts for some two months. The new inflow of capital provided by the Gold product enabled the company to step up its mortgage lending wing, and by the end of the decade, C&G emerged as one of the nation's top ten building societies.

C&G's rapidly growing market strength also gave it an edge in the developing consolidation of the building society sector in the 1980s. The society now embarked on an aggressive acquisition campaign, which lasted more than a decade. Among the group's additions were smaller groups Cotswold Building Society in 1983 and Waltham Abbey Society in 1985. C&G also attempted to merge with a large rival, Alliance, in 1984, but that deal fell through. Nonetheless, by then C&G's total assets had reached £1.5 billion and its number of total branches neared 175 by the decade's end.

The field of building societies continued to shrink through the 1980s, dropping from slightly less than 200 at mid-decade, to only 100 at the start of the 1990s. Part of the reason for this was the passage of the new Building Societies Act of 1986, which ushered in a new era of British banking history. Under the new act, building societies were at last allowed to extend the range of products beyond their traditional mortgage and savings products to include a larger array of financial services. Building societies also were given the right to convert their status to full bank status, sparking a wave of public offerings in the 1990s.

Joining a Banking Empire for the New Century

C&G at first joined in the fray, stepping up its acquisition program in the late 1980s, with acquisitions including the Bolton Building Society, and, between 1989 and 1991, the Guardian

Key Dates:

1850: The Cheltenham & Gloucester Permanent Mutual Benefit Building Society and Investment Association (C&G) is founded in Cheltenham.
1896: C&G opens its first branch office in Gloucester.
1899: C&G opens its first permanent head office in Cheltenham.
1962: C&G acquires Yeovil and South Somerset Mutual Building Society and Vale of Evesham Permanent Building Society.
1969: The company introduces its first computer system, enabling significant management cost savings.
1981: The company launches the groundbreaking, higher-interest Gold account.
1983: The Cotswold Building Society is acquired.
1985: The Waltham Abbey Building Society is acquired.
1989: Continuing its aggressive acquisition program, the company acquires the Bolton Building Society, the Guardian Building Society, and building societies in Peckham, Walthamstow, Bedford, and Portsmouth.
1995: The company converts to PLC status and is acquired by Lloyds Bank Group, which acquires TSB Bank that year to become Lloyds TSB.
1997: The company absorbs TSB's home mortgage business, becoming the dedicated home mortgage division of Lloyds TSB.
2003: The company launches the first C&G credit card.

Building Society, and societies in Peckham, Walthamstow, Bedford, and Portsmouth. C&G's asset base rose accordingly, topping £7 billion at the start of the decade, and climbing past £16 billion before the middle of the 1990s. C&G also had taken advantage of the loosened rules, adding new products such as brokerage services and unit trust dealing services.

Abbey Life became the first building society to take advantage of the right to convert its status, becoming a full-fledged, publicly held bank in 1989. C&G began preparing its own conversion—with a difference. At the end of 1993, C&G let it be known that it was interested in becoming part of a larger group. By early 1994, the society announced that it had agreed to be purchased by the Lloyds Bank Group.

Founded in 1765, that banking group had expanded through the first half of the 20th century into a worldwide banking operation. By the early 1970s, Lloyds was present in more than 40 countries worldwide. During that decade, Lloyds joined the ''bancassurance'' movement, combining banking and insurance operations, then adding other financial services, including home mortgages, real estate agency operations, and merchant banking through the 1980s. Yet the bank's exposure abroad, particularly in South America, led it to begin a restructuring effort, refocusing itself on its core U.K. market in the 1990s. The acquisition of C&G played an important part in the drive to become a more purely British financial services leader.

Cheltenham & Gloucester formally converted its status to PLC in 1995, and became a Lloyds subsidiary that same year. The move marked the first time one of the United Kingdom's building societies had used the provisions of the 1986 legislation to allow itself to be acquired by a banking corporation outside the building society sector. After Lloyds completed its next acquisition, of the TSB Bank network, becoming Lloyds TSB in December 1995, Cheltenham & Gloucester found itself as part of one of the United Kingdom's leading financial empires.

Under Lloyds TSB, C&G gained access to the group's more than 2,300 branch offices. C&G now became the number three home mortgage provider in the United Kingdom. In 1997, C&G took on greater weight in the market when it absorbed TSB's home mortgage operation as well. By the beginning of the new century, C&G's support network included more than 4,500 employees and three regional administration centers, in Gloucestershire, Hampshire, and Warwickshire, as well as its own branded network of branch offices.

C&G continued to offer new products at the dawn of the 21st century. The company joined a movement among mortgage lenders to offer a restricted, two-tier, cut-price mortgage product—a move that led C&G, as well as its rivals, into trouble with the Financial Ombudsman Service, which insisted that the lower-priced mortgages be rolled out to all customers. In 2003, C&G launched a more promising—and less controversial—product, its own credit card, the C&G Platinum. After more than 150 years in operation and with total assets topping £50 billion, Cheltenham & Gloucester had claimed a solid position among the United Kingdom's home mortgage leaders.

Principal Subsidiaries

C&G Mortgage Direct; C&G Invest Direct.

Principal Competitors

Royal Bank of Scotland Group PLC; Nationwide Building Society; Northern Rock PLC; Bradford and Bingley PLC; Britannia Building Society; Bristol and West PLC; Yorkshire Building Society; Portman Building Society; Yorkshire Bank PLC; Coventry Building Society; Coutts and Co.; Chelsea Building Society.

Further Reading

Inman, Phillip, ''Lenders Told to Pay Out,'' *Guardian,* June 22, 2002.
McConnell, Sara, ''C&G Savers Win Taxation Fight,'' *Times,* February 5, 1997, p. 23.
Merrell, Caroline, ''C&G Savers Celebrate Revenue Climb Down,'' *Times,* March 28, 1997, p. 26.
Nugent, Helen, and Caroline Merrell, ''C&G Forced to Drop Cut-Price Loans,'' *Times,* September 11, 2001.

—M.L. Cohen

CLARCOR Inc.

2323 S. 6th Street
Rockford, Illinois 61104-7117
U.S.A.
Telephone: (815) 962-8867
Fax: (815) 962-0417
Web site: http://www.clarcor.com

Public Company
Incorporated: 1904 as J.L. Clark Manufacturing Company
Employees: 4,594
Sales: $715.6 million (2002)
Stock Exchanges: New York
Ticker Symbol: CLC
NAIC: 333411 Air Purification Equipment Manufacturing; 333999 All Other Miscellaneous General Purpose Machinery Manufacturing; 336399 All Other Motor Vehicle Parts Manufacturing; 332431 Metal Can Manufacturing; 326199 All Other Plastics Product Manufacturing

CLARCOR Inc. is a leading manufacturer of engine, industrial, and environmental filtration products and a major producer of specialty packaging products. Despite CLARCOR's long history and strong reputation as a maker of top-quality packaging for such consumer goods as battery shells, razor blade containers, and bandage boxes, filtration products account for the largest portion of the company's sales. CLARCOR's filtration operations, which include a number of operating subsidiaries in North America, Western Europe, and Asia, contributed more than 90 percent of the company's 2002 sales and 94 percent of its operating profit for that year. Altogether, the firm's filtration subsidiaries produce thousands of filtration products, including aftermarket and OEM mobile heavy-duty filters, locomotive engine filters, gas turbine filters, and environmental and industrial filtration systems, giving CLARCOR the broadest product line in that market.

J.L. Clark, Inc., the operating subsidiary responsible for CLARCOR's consumer division, based at the company's original headquarters in Rockford, Illinois, commands a strong position in such niche markets as metal spice packaging, specialty plastic closures, decorative promotional metal packaging, and film canisters. Although metalworking has traditionally formed the core of CLARCOR's consumer division, since the mid-1980s the company has expanded into plastic and combination metal/plastic packaging. Consumer products formed almost 10 percent of CLARCOR's $715.6 million in 2002 sales. Given the relatively mature domestic markets for both the company's filtration and consumer products, CLARCOR has moved to expand its international presence; its main overseas subsidiaries can be found in Australia, Belgium, Canada, China, France, Germany, Italy, Malaysia, Mexico, The Netherlands, Singapore, South Africa, Spain, Venezuela, and the United Kingdom. In 2002, 16 percent of the company's revenues originated outside the United States.

An Early 20th-Century Flue Stopper

John Lewis Clark was born in Vermont in 1845, but moved with his family to Rockford, Illinois, in 1857. After graduating from high school, Clark joined the Union Navy, serving under Farragut during the Civil War. When that war ended, Clark, then 20 years old, returned to Rockford and obtained an apprenticeship as a tinsmith with a local hardware store. Throughout his apprenticeship, Clark dreamed of opening his own hardware store, which he accomplished in 1874 when he and a friend opened the Robinson & Clark Hardware store in Rockford. This partnership lasted for ten years. The partners eventually sold the store; Clark planned to move west and become a cattle rancher. The day before he intended to leave, however, the new owners begged Clark to buy back the store. Clark did.

The store, especially its tinsmith shop, prospered. In 1889 Clark formed a new partnership and opened a larger store. This partnership, the Clark & McKenney Hardware Co., also lasted ten years, until Clark bought out his partner and brought in his son, Lewis Harold Clark, as a partner. The store was renamed the J.L. Clark Hardware Company in 1899. With the elder Clark's tinsmithing expertise and the younger Clark's Cornell University education, the pair set out to develop a product and move into manufacturing.

Company Perspectives:

For nearly 100 years, through both good times and bad, CLARCOR has focused on profitable growth markets with above-average opportunities and on continual improvement in each of our businesses. This is our core strategy. It was put in place many years ago and is still the foundation of CLARCOR. We believe there is tremendous value in consistency—both in strategy and in execution. These principles guide our company today as they have in the past.

One year later, Clark received a patent for an improved flue stopper. These round disks were needed to plug the holes left in walls when oil and coal stoves were dismantled for the summer. Clark sold 271 gross of his Gem Flue Stoppers that first year, primarily to local hardware dealers. It cost the store $70 for the dies and punch press needed to start large-scale production of the flue stopper. Originally a flat blank disk, the Gem Flue Stopper was soon available in three styles, with raised and embossed blanks featuring attractive lithographed designs. In 1901, sales of the stoppers grew to 500 gross. Through a small network of hardware sidemen, jobbers, advertisements, and direct mailings, sales of the Gem Flue Stopper jumped to nearly 2,400 gross in 1903. The early Gem Flue Stoppers were priced generally higher than competing flue stoppers; the company added a fourth, lower-priced stopper design to the Gem line in 1902.

Clark was not yet satisfied with his relatively inefficient operation. The volume of Gem Flue Stopper sales was not high enough to keep the punch press working full-time. In addition, cutting the blanks for the stoppers left a great deal of scrap metal. To improve efficiency, Clark added a new product line, the Gem Ointment Boxes, cut from the leftover material. In 1903, Clark added two more products, a Crispy Toaster for the stovetop and the Gem Flour Sifter. By the end of that year, the Clarks decided to move fully into manufacturing, and they sold their hardware store.

Renamed the J.L. Clark Manufacturing Company in 1904, the company began operations in a 7,000-square-foot facility in Rockford's Water Power District. With a $25,000 investment, Clark installed a complete line of punch presses, seamers, beading machines, and shears. The company also added a metal lithographing press and baking ovens. Its first lithographing order was for the decoration of fire extinguishers. By then, the company had 13 employees. One of its early major customers was Rockford-based W.T. Rawleigh, then a worldwide distributor of household and pharmaceutical products. As Rawleigh's product line grew, Clark's production expanded into a broad range of containers for products such as cosmetics and spices. In its first year of operation, Clark Manufacturing produced more than 500,000 pieces, including nearly 400,000 Gem Flue Stoppers. By 1905, the number of company employees increased to 41. Four years later, when Clark added a company-designed and -produced bodymaker, employment rose to 89.

Production continued to increase and by 1911 the company had outgrown its Water Power District facility, which by then had reached nearly 20,000 square feet. The company purchased a 15-acre tract on the edge of town and designed and built a modern 55,000-square-foot plant, including storage space and corporate offices, which was considered among the most up-to-date in the country. By then, Clark customers included many leading manufacturers, such as Milton Bradley and others. Sales of the Gem Flue Stopper continued to rise, topping 500,000. But Clark's other products also contributed to its growth. According to an early newspaper article on the company, Clark's total production volume reached 50 million pieces per year by 1911.

Growth Between the Wars and Beyond

Clark's growth slowed somewhat during World War I (in 1919, the year founder John Clark died, the company posted the first of only two unprofitable years in its history). But with Harold Clark leading the company, Clark regained its momentum in the decade that followed. Photographic lithography processes were added to the production line, and this, coupled with the addition of a rotary printing press in 1925, allowed the company not only to speed up production but also to improve quality, establishing Clark's long-held reputation for excellence. Between 1918 and 1928, sales tripled, from $408,000 to nearly $1.4 million. In 1924, an addition to the plant doubled its production area.

Clark's growth enabled it to survive the Great Depression of the 1930s. Despite declining sales, down to $800,000 in 1933, in part due to a cutback to a four-day workweek, the number of the company's employees actually grew. The drop in consumer spending during the Depression encouraged companies to turn to quality packaging, which improved the durability of their products and were more attractive to consumers. At this time, 3M, among others, became a longtime Clark customer. This trend helped raise Clark's revenues, to $1.1 million in 1936 and to $1.4 million in 1937. The next year, however, Clark posted its second annual loss. But Clark received a new boost to revenues when the company designed the first metal battery jacket, later to become an industry standard, for Ray-O-Vac. The company also invested heavily in capital improvements, raising the quality and efficiency of production.

The outbreak of World War II stimulated Clark's growth, as production was converted to wartime orders, and the company established three branch plants to continue filling consumer orders. The company added a new major customer, Gillette, in the 1940s, designing and producing the packaging for that company's razor blades. At the same time, Clark began producing Band-Aid boxes, baby powder cans, and tape dispensers for Johnson & Johnson, which soon became the company's largest customer. By 1946, the company was able to add a new addition to its Rockford plant; two years later, the plant expanded again, and in 1950, Clark doubled its lithograph facility. Then, in 1951, Clark completed a 31,000-square-foot expansion of the Rockford plant.

In 1952, longtime employee Ralph Rosecrance replaced Harold Clark, who died the following year, as president of the company. Under Rosecrance, the company made its first acquisition, buying the Liberty Can and Sign Company of Lancaster, Pennsylvania, in 1955 for $2 million. The acquisition gave the company increased access to the important East Coast market. Clark's sales, which had reached $10.7 million in 1954, rose to nearly $15 million in 1956.

Key Dates:

1904: John Lewis Clark, co-owner of J.L. Clark Hardware Company, sells his hardware store to concentrate on manufacturing metal products, such as the Gem Flue Stopper; the company is renamed the J.L. Clark Manufacturing Company.
1955: The first acquisition, that of Liberty Can and Sign Company of Lancaster, Pennsylvania, is completed.
1959: The acquisition of G. Felsenthal & Sons of Chicago brings Clark into plastics for the first time.
1964: The company goes public.
1981: The company enters the filter field via the purchase of J.A. Baldwin Manufacturing Company of Kearney, Nebraska.
1987: To emphasize its diversified status, the firm changes its name to CLARCOR Inc.
1993: CLARCOR acquires Louisville, Kentucky–based Airguard Industries, Inc., maker of commercial environmental control systems.
1997: United Air Specialists, Inc., a Cincinnati producer of commercial and industrial air filtration systems, is acquired.
1999: CLARCOR pays Mark IV Industries, Inc. $141 million for three filtration businesses, including Purolator Products Air Filtration Company.
2000: The one-stop-shopping Total Filtration Program is launched.

The Liberty acquisition proved to be the first in a series, as the company moved to expand its product offerings. Significant among these was the 1959 acquisition of G. Felsenthal & Sons of Chicago, which brought Clark into plastics for the first time. The following year, Clark developed a plastic spice can closure to replace the traditional sliding metal closures, which were prone to rust, tended to stick, and were generally difficult to use. A second spice can closure was designed, with lift-tops for a shaker and for spooning, which attracted the attention of McCormick & Company, then the country's largest spice supplier. When Clark was awarded a contract to supply all of McCormick's spice cans, Clark built a 40,000-square-foot plant in California to satisfy the growing demand there. By the mid-1960s, Clark's customers included other major spice companies, including Durkee, French, and A&P. At the same time, Clark added another 41,000 square feet to its Rockford lithographing operations. By 1964, when the company made its initial public offering, sales had reached $23 million, with earnings of $1.2 million.

The newly public company next embarked on a string of acquisitions that not only raised its revenues to $82 million by 1976 but also allowed the company to diversify into a wide range of packaging materials. One of Clark's most important acquisitions was that of Maryland-based Stone Container Corporation, which gave Clark a technological and market lead in the manufacture of composite cans. Other acquisitions increased the company's plastic molding capabilities. As then President William Nelson told *Forbes* in 1979, Clark's diversification efforts were made because ''[t]here's always a possibility that metal containers will become too expensive for some uses. Today there's no other firm that can offer such versatility in materials.''

By the end of the 1970s, Clark posted net earnings of $12 million on sales of nearly $105 million. The company's diversification efforts were succeeding, bringing revenues to $124.5 million in 1981, despite the national slide into a recession. But it was in that year that diversification would take on a new meaning for the company.

Becoming a Filtration Giant in the 1980s

Clark had succeeded by pursuing niche markets, avoiding head-on competition with industry giants such as American Can Co., Crown Cork & Seal Co., and Continental Group. In 1981, however, Clark made its largest acquisition to date, that of the J.A. Baldwin Manufacturing Company in Kearney, Nebraska, bringing Clark into a new market altogether. Baldwin was a maker of premium quality heavy-duty filters, with a product line of more than 2,100 filters for oil, fuel, air, coolants, hydraulic, and transmission applications. With a base of 2,500 distributors, Baldwin was a national brand name.

The Baldwin acquisition helped boost revenues to $174 million and net earnings of $16 million by 1984. In addition, filtration was soon to become more important to the company's bottom line. Sales in Clark's packaging division began to slip in the second half of the 1980s as customers turned to other materials or to manufacturing their own packaging. The company began to invest more heavily in its filtration business, acquiring in 1986 Dahl Manufacturing, Inc. of California and that company's line of marine filters, diesel engine fuel/water separators, and related products. The company further enhanced its nonpackaging business with the acquisition of Michigan Spring Company, adding close-tolerance spring and wire forms to the company's product line and increasing its molded plastics capabilities. Clark began producing its first all-plastic packages, containers for Colgate Palmolive Co.'s Curad bandages.

In 1987 Clark changed its name to CLARCOR Inc. to emphasize its diversified status. Nelson, by then chairman and CEO, retired and was replaced by Larry Gloyd, former company president. Under Gloyd, the company managed to reverse the slide in its packaging revenues. Yet that market was increasingly seen as too mature for further domestic growth. Accordingly, the company moved to boost its filtration business, acquiring HEFCO of New Jersey, which enabled CLARCOR to enter the industrial filtration market. At the same time, the company attempted to move beyond manufacturing and into the services market, with the acquisition of the Furst Group, an executive placement firm, leading to the establishment of a short-lived Services Group. Sales by the end of the 1980s had topped $202 million.

As the 1990s began, CLARCOR's filtration business already represented more than half of the company's total revenues. The recession of these years, however, placed pressure on the company's earnings. The company undertook a series of divestitures, exiting all but its filtration and consumer packaging businesses. In 1991 the company entered its first overseas partnership, purchasing a 20 percent stake in GUD Holdings,

Ltd., the largest filtration products maker in Australia. The following year, CLARCOR expanded its locomotive filter capacity with the acquisition of M&J Diesel Locomotive Filter Co. of Chicago and made plans to move into other transportation markets, including heavy equipment and boating, as well as nontransportation industries such as generators.

The sale of CLARCOR's precision products subsidiaries enabled the company, in 1993, to purchase with cash Airguard Industries, Inc., a Louisville, Kentucky-based maker of commercial environmental control systems, allowing the company to take advantage of business generated by the passage of the Clean Air Act. The company also purchased Eurofilter Airfilters Ltd. of England, giving the company access to the European market and expanding its product line to include gas turbine filters. At the same time, CLARCOR entered a joint venture agreement with Filtros Continental in Mexico City, forming Filtros Baldwin de Mexico. The following year, CLARCOR acquired Filtros Continental, the second largest filter maker in Mexico, changing its name to Fibamex.

These acquisitions helped fuel a growth in revenues, with a 20 percent rise both in 1993 and 1994. The 1995 purchase of Hastings Manufacturing Company of Michigan, which added filtration products for the automotive and light truck markets, helped boost CLARCOR's sales that year to $290 million and net earnings to $22 million. By 1996, CLARCOR was present in nearly every filtration market, with a dominant position in many of the market segments. A joint venture with Weifang Power Machine Fittings Ltd. in China, closed at the end of 1995, continued CLARCOR's international expansion. Also in 1995 Norman E. Johnson was promoted to president and chief operating officer, with Gloyd remaining chairman and CEO.

Expanding Air Filtration Operations in the Late 1990s

The 1993 acquisition of Airguard Industries had marked CLARCOR's first substantial move into the market for air filters for industrial and commercial customers—the firm having previously focused primarily on fluid filters. Air filtration was believed to have better growth prospects in part because of stricter U.S. Environmental Protection Agency regulations. Through a number of strategic ventures in the late 1990s CLARCOR made further inroads into the air filtration sector. In early 1996 the company took a 70 percent interest in Baldwin-Unifil S.A., a South African joint venture that simultaneously acquired Unifil (Pty.) Ltd., maker of air filters for heavy-duty transportation equipment and automobiles. In February 1997 CLARCOR paid $28 million in stock for United Air Specialists, Inc. (UAS), a Cincinnati-based producer of commercial and industrial air filtration systems. UAS had 1996 revenues of $40.8 million. The following month CLARCOR gained a Southeast Asian base for its industrial and environmental filter production by purchasing Airklean Engineering Pte. Ltd., a distributor of air filtration products headquartered in Singapore. Early in 1998 CLARCOR completed a minor though strategic acquisition, that of Air Technologies, Inc. (ATI) of Ottawa, Kansas, principally a producer of air filtration products to clean the air exiting out of painting operations. CLARCOR now had a full range of air filtration products for painting applications as it had previously purchased producers of filters that cleaned air coming into painting facilities and those that filtered the air within such facilities.

By 1999 revenues had reached $477.9 million, with just 13 percent of the total coming from the company's founding consumer packaging operations. About 37 percent of revenues was already attributable to the nascent industrial and environmental filtration business. Half of sales derived from the engine filtration segment, which was by far the most profitable CLARCOR unit, generated more than three-quarters of operating profits. In September 1999, however, the corporation completed a major acquisition that substantially increased the industrial/environmental filtration segment. That month CLARCOR paid Mark IV Industries, Inc. about $141 million for three filtration businesses: Purolator Products Air Filtration Company, a Henderson, North Carolina–based producer of a wide variety of air filters used in heating, ventilation, and air conditioning systems; Torino, Italy–based Facet International, a maker of industrial process filters and filtration systems used in aviation refueling and general industry; and Purolator-Facet Filter Products, which was headquartered in Greensboro, North Carolina, and focused on specialty filtration products for aerospace, fluid processing, and hydraulic systems. The deal did not include the well-known Purolator brand of automotive filters (which Mark IV sold earlier in 1999 to Arvin Industries, Inc.).

A huge jump in revenues, to $652.1 million in 2000, resulted from this major acquisition. Industrial/environmental filtration was now the firm's largest segment, responsible for nearly 50 percent of revenues. In March 2000, meantime, Gloyd retired and Johnson was appointed chairman, president, and CEO.

Total Filtration Program in the Early 2000s

The economic travails of the early 2000s certainly affected CLARCOR, but the company remained solidly profitable. This was principally because the bulk of its revenues—about 80 percent—were of the recurring kind, composed of aftermarket filters that were necessary for the continuing operation of various equipment. One of the corporation's major initiatives during this period was the launch of the Total Filtration Program in 2000. Through this program, CLARCOR began offering its customers the opportunity to use one company for all of its filter needs, including the supply, installation, and service of a full range of filtration products. Some companies were buying such products from as many as 50 different vendors, so the new program had the potential to significantly reduce these companies' purchasing and sourcing costs.

CLARCOR strengthened its Total Filtration Program through additional acquisitions. In June 2001 CLARCOR spent about $29 million for several filtration management companies that together made up one of the leading distributors of filtration products to some of the largest firms in North America. The acquired companies were combined into one company called Total Filtration Services, Inc. (TFS), which was based in Rochester Hills, Michigan. TFS became the linchpin for the Total Filtration Program. Three smaller acquisitions were completed in 2002, including Locker Filtration Limited, a U.K.-based producer of heavy-duty air filters, gas turbine filters, and specialty bag filters.

Through 2002, CLARCOR had recorded 16 consecutive years of revenue growth and had increased its dividends for 19 straight years—stellar achievements. The company had a number of strategies in place as it aimed to continue these trends, including: getting more nonautomotive customers into the Total Filtration Program; increasing revenues from filter services, which were generally more profitable than the sale of filter products themselves; expanding the use of the Purolator and Facet brand names—two of CLARCOR's better known trademarks; increasing operations in China; and seeking additional acquisitions. The filter industry remained highly fragmented, with no firm holding more than an 8 percent market share, so there appeared to be ample opportunity for CLARCOR to bolster its already impressive position.

Principal Subsidiaries

CLARCOR Consumer Products, Inc.; J.L. Clark, Inc.; Clark Europe, Inc.; CLARCOR Filtration Products, Inc.; Airguard Industries, Inc.; Airklean Engineering Pte. Ltd. (Singapore); Airguard Asia Sdn. Bhd. (Malaysia); Airguard de Venezuela, S.A. (70%); Purolator Products Air Filtration Company; Baldwin Filters, Inc.; Baldwin Filters N.V. (Belgium); Baldwin Filters Limited (U.K.); Baldwin South Africa, Inc.; Baldwin-Unifil S.A. (South Africa; 80%); Hastings Filters Ltd. Canada; Baldwin Filters (Aust.) Pty. Limited (Australia); CLARCOR UK Limited; Clark Filter, Inc.; Filtros Baldwin de Mexico (90%); Purolator Facet, Inc.; Facet FCE S.A.R.L. (France); Facet Iberica S.A. (Spain); Facet Industrial B.V. (Netherlands); Facet Industrial U.K. Limited; Facet Italiana, S.p.A. (Italy); Facet USA Inc.; Filter Products, Inc.; GS Costa Mesa, Inc.; Locker Filtration Limited (U.K.); FilterSource; Purolator Filter GmbH (Germany); Total Filtration Services, Inc.; Total Filtration Services LLC of VC (Mexico); Total Filter Technology, Inc.; United Air Specialists, Inc.; CLARCOR International, Inc.; Baldwin-Weifang Filters Ltd. (China, 75%), CLARCOR Foreign Sales Corporation (Barbados); CLARCOR Trading Company.

Principal Competitors

Donaldson Company, Inc.; Cummins, Inc.; Flanders Corporation; AAF-McQuay Inc.; Pall Corporation; CUNO Incorporated.

Further Reading

Berman, Phyllis, "Virtue Well Rewarded," *Forbes,* August 20, 1979, p. 120.

Clarcor Inc., *From Hardware Store to . . . Clarcor, 1904–1989,* Rockford, Ill.: CLARCOR Inc., 1989.

"Company Interview: CLARCOR Inc.," *Wall Street Transcript,* August 25, 2003.

Liebowitz, David S., "Playing with the Big Boys," *Financial World,* June 8, 1993, p. 88.

Murphy, H. Lee, "Acquisitions Fueling Expansion at Clarcor," *Crain's Chicago Business,* April 18, 1994, p. 28.

——, "Aftermarket Sales Bolster Clarcor Results," *Crain's Chicago Business,* April 7, 2003, p. 18.

——, "Air Filtration Acquisitions Vital to Clarcor Expansion Effort," *Crain's Chicago Business,* March 30, 1998, p. 20.

——, "As Core Biz Lags, Clarcor Shifts to Air Filters to Pump Up Sales," *Crain's Chicago Business,* April 7, 1997, p. 28.

——, "Clarcor Repackage Tied to Expansion," *Crain's Chicago Business,* April 18, 1988, p. 40.

——, "Clarcor Set to Add Overseas Plant to Support Global Push at Home," *Crain's Chicago Business,* April 10, 1995, p. 49.

—M. L. Cohen
—update: David E. Salamie

COBE Cardiovascular, Inc.

14401 West 65th Way
Arvada, Colorado 80004-3599
U.S.A.
Telephone: (303) 425-5508
Toll Free: (800) 221-7943
Fax: (303) 467-6525
Web site: http://www.cobecv.com

Wholly Owned Subsidiary of Sorin S.p.A.
Incorporated: 1990
Employees: 793
Sales: $100 million (2003 est.)
NAIC: 334510 Electromedical and Electrotherapeutic Apparatus Manufacturing; 339112 Surgical and Medical Instrument Manufacturing; 339113 Surgical Appliance and Supplies Manufacturing

COBE Cardiovascular, Inc. is a leading producer and distributor of medical devices and systems used in cardiac surgery. COBE's cardiopulmonary products, which include oxygenators, heart-lung tubing packs, autotransfusion systems, and heart-lung machines, help sustain the functions of the heart and lungs while a patient undergoes open-heart surgery. COBE Cardiovascular evolved out of COBE Laboratories, Inc., a firm founded in 1964 focusing initially on custom heart-lung tubing packs. COBE Laboratories gradually developed a broader product line centering on medical devices and systems for handling blood outside the body, with three major areas of focus: renal care, cardiovascular products, and blood component technology. The Swedish medical technology company Gambro AB acquired COBE Laboratories in 1990, at which time COBE's cardiovascular division was transformed into COBE Cardiovascular, Inc. Early in 1999 Gambro sold COBE Cardiovascular to Sorin Biomedica S.p.A., an Italian medical technology firm affiliated with SNIA S.p.A., which at the time was a conglomerate with interests in medical technology, chemicals, and real estate. Early in 2004 SNIA spun off its medical technology business into a separate, publicly traded firm called Sorin S.p.A.

Early History of COBE Labs

COBE Laboratories was founded in 1964 by Robert Collins and Randall Bellows, both of whom had worked at a major hospital supplier near San Francisco called Pharmaseal. COBE's name was derived from the first two letters of the founders' last names. Working out of a garage in Los Angeles, the two men made custom heart-lung tubing packs used to connect patients to heart-lung machines. In 1965 COBE merged with Medical Marketing, a Seattle firm owned by Collins's and Bellows's friend Ted Dale, who had persuaded the Seattle Artificial Kidney Center to use COBE's custom tubing packs. The merger increased the young company's ability to market its products and initiated its venture into the dialysis industry, which would eventually become the core of its business.

Dialysis products introduced in the company's first five years included hemodialysis blood tubing sets and the Kiil dialyzer (a dialyzer is an artificial kidney—essentially a specialized filter—used in dialysis to cleanse the patient's blood). In 1967 Collins and Bellows relocated the company to Lakewood, Colorado, a suburb of Denver, in part because they felt they needed a more centralized location for distribution purposes.

During the early 1970s, COBE expanded its presence in the dialysis market. COBE replaced the Kiil dialyzer (weighing 75 pounds) with a less bulky one called the Mini-D. It also developed the Centry dialysis monitoring system, at 78 pounds also more portable than earlier models. Together, these introductions began to make home dialysis more practical—a boon for the patient in terms of improved chances of rehabilitation, the elimination of thrice-weekly trips to the hospital, and much lower costs. The Centry system also had some advantages over existing systems: it was compatible with elements of dialysis machinery manufactured by other firms and used tap water in its mixture of cleansing solution. Added to the COBE line in 1971 was an Automated Peritoneal Dialysis unit for patients not able to tolerate hemodialysis, a system designed to complement the Centry system.

Such product introductions, particularly those involving COBE's dialysis products, were bolstered in 1972 when Medicare was expanded to cover end-stage renal disease. As a result,

Company Perspectives:

To exceed the expectations of our worldwide customers by fostering a work environment where highly-motivated, action-oriented employees work together to continuously create and deliver high-quality, innovative products and services.

many more people could be supported with dialysis treatments and the market for dialysis equipment grew. That same year, COBE became a public company.

Very early in its history, COBE executives recognized the international market as a key to the company's growth. In 1967 the company's first international distributor, AMCO, Inc., was appointed in Japan. The company established its first international subsidiary in Brussels, Belgium, in 1973, followed by additional subsidiaries in West Germany, Canada, France, and the United Kingdom over the next four years.

Domestic sales efforts were facilitated through the establishment of three regional distribution centers covering the West (Fremont, California), Midwest (Chicago), and East (Glen Burnie, Maryland). COBE's new product development and marketing efforts resulted in sales of $16.8 million by its tenth anniversary in 1974 and its first $10 million sales quarter in 1977.

In 1975, with the introduction of its next dialysis machine—the Centry 2—COBE could offer a complete dialysis system, the first in the industry, and one designed for portability and ideal for home use. The system was also attractive to hospitals and dialysis centers because the dialysis process was faster than in older models, cutting costs by allowing staff to handle more patients in the same amount of time. The Centry 2 controlled the complete dialysis process, which involved transporting blood through tubing to an artificial kidney (dialyzer) which cleansed the blood and removed excess fluid. A monitor kept track of the complete process. COBE manufactured all components of the system, including dialyzers, blood tubing, chemicals, and other supplies necessary to the hemodialysis process. This first application of a system approach to renal care helped COBE become a market leader in the United States over the next several years. By 1978, renal care accounted for 76 percent of the company's revenues, and COBE posted a one-year increase of 49 percent in renal care sales from $32.1 million in 1977 to $47.7 million in 1978.

Securing Market Leadership Position in Cardiovascular Field

COBE also secured a place in the cardiovascular field with the acquisition of Galen Laboratories in 1973. The key product acquired thereby was the Optiflo Oxygenator. During heart surgery when blood flow to the heart and lungs was halted, the function of the lungs was replaced by the oxygenator, which supplied the patient's blood with oxygen as the lung normally would, while the blood-pumping function of the heart was replaced by an artificial pump. Having thus entered the oxygenator market, COBE introduced the second-generation Optiflo II Oxygenator in 1978. With the development of the COBE Stöckert Perfusion Pump, the company could offer a complete life-support system for the increasingly common open-heart surgery procedures of the time. Further innovation occurred in 1982 with the development of the COBE Membrane Lung (CML) Oxygenator. This membrane oxygenator significantly advanced the safety of cardiovascular surgery; virtually made obsolete the commonly used bubble oxygenator; and propelled COBE to a market leadership position in the cardiovascular field, eventually to a 20 percent worldwide market share by the end of the 1980s.

After more than a dozen years of healthy growth (net sales more than doubled in a four-year span alone from $45.6 million in 1977 to $92.6 million in 1980), COBE experienced some difficult years in the early 1980s. Net sales growth in 1981 slowed to less than 5 percent over 1980, while in 1982 it only improved to 8.5 percent. Although the sales increases were higher during the next three years (due in part to several acquisitions), profits fell from $6 million in 1982 to $5.6 million in 1983 and to $3.2 million in 1984, again due in part to acquisitions, notably that of IBM Biomedical Systems, but also attributable to the failure of a new product, a hollow fiber dialyzer.

Moreover, separate sales figures for the Medical Systems Division (primarily the renal care products) indicated that during the first five years of the 1980s that concern had grown only 11 percent, while the Cardiovascular Division grew by an impressive 126 percent. Indeed, the dialysis market had stagnated because of increased competition initiated by cost-containment efforts by doctors and hospitals affected by changes in government-sponsored health coverage. The company sought to offset these troubles by renewing its emphasis on new product development, aggressively pursuing strategic acquisitions, and broadening its product line with the expansion into a third major product area: blood component technology.

During this time, COBE's Centry dialysis systems held about 40 percent of the U.S. market in single-patient machines. In 1981 the company introduced two new renal care products to the Centry line. The Centry 2 Rx system was designed to provide patients with prescription hemodialysis by allowing a doctor to vary the amount of sodium and sodium bicarbonate delivered to the patient during dialysis depending on individual needs. The Centry 2000 was a more sophisticated microprocessor, with additional safety features, giving a doctor greater control over the dialysis process. The company's commitment in the 1980s to new product development was particularly evident in its introduction of the Centrysystem 3 in 1986, its first new dialysis system in 11 years. In designing its third-generation system, COBE kept firmly in mind the increasing cost-consciousness of physicians and hospitals. The major advantage of the Centrysystem 3 was its ability to safely cut the treatment time for a dialysis session in half, thus allowing hospitals and dialysis centers to handle twice as many patients in the same amount of time. The company promised further cost savings from the system's ease of use and lower maintenance costs because of its increased reliability. Complementing this new product development activity was the acquisition also in 1989 of Secon GmbH, a German medical technology company that manufactured a compact hollow fiber dialyzer that worked perfectly with the Centrysystem 3 and could be readily marketed with it.

With the goal of decreasing the company's reliance on its renal care products, COBE expanded into its third major area of

Key Dates:

1964: Working out of a garage in Los Angeles, Robert Collins and Randall Bellows establish COBE Laboratories, Inc. to produce custom heart-lung tubing packs; the company soon makes its first foray into the dialysis market.
1967: Collins and Bellows relocate their business to Lakewood, Colorado, a Denver suburb.
1972: COBE becomes a public company.
1973: Acquisition of Galen Laboratories brings the Optiflo Oxygenator into the fold, laying the foundation for the cardiovascular division.
1982: The COBE Membrane Lung (CML) Oxygenator is introduced, propelling the company to a leadership position in the cardiovascular field.
1988: Cardiovascular division expands into blood processing with the acquisition of the BRAT system.
1990: Sweden's Gambro AB acquires COBE Laboratories for about $253 million; the operations of COBE are divided into several subsidiaries, with the cardiovascular division transformed into COBE Cardiovascular, Inc.
1998: COBE Cardiovascular introduces cardiopulmonary bypass circuits featuring the SMARxT biocompatible surface; a Gambro restructuring essentially eliminates COBE Laboratories as a subsidiary and transforms the subsidiaries of COBE Laboratories into three units, one of which is Arvada, Colorado-based COBE CV, the former COBE Cardiovascular.
1999: Gambro sells COBE CV to Italy's Sorin Biomedica S.p.A., a company majority owned by SNIA S.p.A.; the acquired company once again assumes the name COBE Cardiovascular, Inc.
2004: COBE Cardiovascular becomes a subsidiary of Sorin S.p.A., the firm that results from the spinoff of SNIA's medical technology division.

research and development in the early 1980s by introducing the Therapeutic Plasma Exchange System, or Centry TPE System. Blood component technology had become increasingly important during this period for the treatment of cancer and immune system diseases. Treatments for these ailments involved transfusions of individual blood components, such as platelets, stem cells, bone marrow, and plasma. In some treatments certain components were extracted from the patient's blood, treated, and then reinfused. After Centry TPE was introduced in 1981, COBE delved further into this area with its 1984 acquisition of IBM's Biomedical Systems division. The acquisition brought products that became known as the COBE 2991 Cell Processor and the COBE 2997 Blood Cell Separator, both used for blood component therapy. It also led to the development and 1988 introduction of the COBE Spectra Apheresis System used to collect from donors very pure blood components (such as platelets) primarily for cancer therapy treatments. That same year a related acquisition of Kardiothor brought the BRAT Intraoperative Blood Salvage System to the COBE cardiovascular line. The BRAT system was used during surgery to clean and recycle the patient's blood for reinfusion, reducing the need for transfusions from donors. All of these blood banking technologies became increasingly important as the purity of the world's blood supply came into question with the discovery of the HIV virus and AIDS.

By 1989 COBE had grown to net sales of $237.9 million with a profit of $9.8 million, up from sales of $92.6 million in 1980. Besides its overall growth and profitability, the company successfully diversified its product line and eliminated its overreliance on the inconsistent dialysis market. At the end of the decade, sales were almost evenly divided between the Medical Systems Division (51.6 percent) and the Cardiovascular Division (48.4 percent). Significant too was the company's impressive increase in sales outside the United States. Since establishing an International Division in 1985 for marketing its products overseas, COBE increased its foreign sales from $39.5 million to $82.1 million, a 108 percent increase. Further, the International Division accounted in 1989 for 45 percent of the company's sales, compared to only 26 percent in 1985. Particularly given COBE's increasing success outside the United States, many observers were surprised to learn in 1990 that COBE was to be acquired by Sweden-based Gambro AB. Having fended off several hostile takeover bids over the course of the 1980s, however, COBE officials agreed to sell the company to Gambro.

The 1990s: COBE's Gambro Decade

The terms of the sale were an offer to buy all outstanding shares of COBE stock for $37 per share, or a total of approximately $253 million. The deal was announced in March and consummated in June after a detailed antitrust examination by the U.S. Federal Trade Commission. At the time of the acquisition, Gambro was based in Lund, Sweden, was partly owned by the Swedish automobile manufacturer Volvo, and had sales of about $500 million (or twice that of COBE). The two companies were both leaders in the renal care field, and in the year of the acquisition renal care sales accounted for 74 percent of Gambro's sales. Although they were competitors, their dialysis products and marketing efforts were considered complementary. For instance, while COBE's dialysis machines were considered market leaders, the company lacked certain components of dialysis systems that Gambro excelled in, particularly dialysis membranes. In terms of marketing, Gambro could take advantage of COBE's dominant presence in the U.S. market, while COBE products could now be more easily sold worldwide. The acquisition also significantly diversified Gambro, which had been limited to the renal care and intensive care/anesthesia fields. It now gained a significant foothold in the cardiovascular and blood component technology fields. The primary reason given by COBE's cofounders for the sale was to "assist COBE in expanding the marketing of its products in countries outside the U.S."

Following the acquisition, COBE's operations were divided into several subsidiaries under COBE Laboratories, Inc. The dialysis products were organized as COBE Renal Care, Inc.; the cardiovascular products as COBE Cardiovascular, Inc.; the international marketing division as COBE International Division; and the blood component technology products as COBE BCT, Inc. (separated for the first time). Robert Collins and Randall Bellows, the company founders, both retired following the sale, but continued to be involved in the operations as members of COBE's board of directors. Observers estimated that Collins's share of the sale amounted to $30 million, while Bellows reaped $10.1 million. Gambro then brought in Mats Wahlström to become the new president of COBE.

The benefits to COBE from the merger became readily apparent over the next two years as the company began to get involved in major acquisitions it would have been unable to afford on its own. The largest involved a series of 1991 and 1992 investments (the final one totaling $53.6 million) in REN Corporation-USA, Inc., giving COBE a majority interest in the company and control of its board. Based in Nashville, Tennessee, REN owned the fourth largest chain of dialysis clinics in the United States, with 51 clinics, about 4,000 patients, and potential for growth based on the increasing privatization of healthcare services. The acquisition of REN not only moved the company into the field of healthcare services for the first time but also changed its renal care activities into a more vertically integrated operation. In 1994 the COBE Renal Care subsidiary acquired the Florida-based Dial Medical for an undisclosed sum. This deal further broadened COBE's renal care assets by giving it a much stronger presence in the market for dialysis concentrates, which Dial Medical produced and distributed.

Meanwhile, COBE BCT was busy making alliances with other medical firms. In September 1993 an agreement was reached between the subsidiary and Cryopharm Corporation of Pasadena, California. Under the terms, COBE invested $4.6 million over two years for the development and marketing of a cryogenic preservation technology patented by Cryopharm. While blood components stored at room temperature were viable for only five days, using the new freezing method meant that platelets, red blood cells, bone marrow, and blood stem cells could be successfully stored in freezers for several months. The agreement called for the companies to co-develop the technology and for COBE to market it, having obtained worldwide rights. Two months later a second alliance was announced between COBE BCT and Aastrom Biosciences, Inc., based in Ann Arbor, Michigan. COBE invested $20 million in Aastrom's Stem Cell Expansion System, which used a bioreactor to multiply stem cells 75 to 100 times. The technology would allow many more patients to receive cancer treatment at reduced costs. COBE gained worldwide rights to the bioreactor technology for such treatments using stem cells.

COBE Cardiovascular, meantime, rolled out a series of new products and new versions of older products under the new ownership scheme. These included the CMS oxygenator family (1990), the CML Duo Flat Sheet oxygenator (1994), the Optima Hollow Fiber oxygenator and the BRAT 2 Autotransfusion System (both 1995), and the COBE Century heart-lung system (1997). In 1998 COBE Cardiovascular introduced cardiopulmonary bypass circuits that featured the SMARxT biocompatible surface. This innovation reduced the chance of platelets adhering to the bypass circuit, an occurrence that can compromise the blood returning to the patient's body, potentially leading to postoperative complications.

Late in 1995 COBE Laboratories acquired full control of REN Corporation, which was integrated into COBE Renal Care early the following year. COBE Renal was renamed Gambro Healthcare, while REN took on the new name Gambro Healthcare Patient Services. A Gambro restructuring in mid-1998 essentially eliminated COBE Laboratories as a subsidiary and transformed the subsidiaries of COBE Laboratories into three Colorado-based units: Gambro Healthcare, responsible for operating dialysis clinics and marketing and sales of dialysis products (with worldwide development and production of dialysis products taken over by an Italian unit called Gambro Renal Products); COBE BCT, covering blood component technology products; and COBE CV, producer of cardiovascular surgery products. This set the stage for COBE CV's exit from the Gambro group, which aimed to increase its focus on its renal care activities.

Beginning of Sorin Era for COBE Cardiovascular: 1999

In November 1998 Sorin Biomedica S.p.A., the largest medical technology company in Italy, reached an agreement to buy COBE CV from Gambro for $267 million. (The acquisition technically also included COBE Laboratories and other assets, but COBE CV was at the heart of the deal.) Sorin was affiliated with SNIA S.p.A., which at the time was a conglomerate with interests in medical technology, chemicals, and real estate. COBE CV was seen to be a perfect fit with Sorin, which already had a strong presence in the cardiac surgery sector through its ownership of Dideco S.p.A., an Italian producer of products for extracorporeal blood circulation and blood reinfusion; and the German firm Stöckert Instrumente GmbH, one of the world's leading producers of heart-lung machines. Other related products produced by Sorin companies included cardiovascular implantable devices, such as valves and stents (tiny devices placed into diseased arteries to prop them open), and cardiac rhythm management equipment, such as pacemakers and implantable defibrillators. Sorin also had a smaller presence in renal-care products, which, following the acquisition of COBE CV, accounted for 20 percent of sales.

Sorin completed its purchase of COBE CV in May 1999. In granting its approval of the deal, however, the U.S. Federal Trade Commission ordered Sorin to divest the COBE Century heart-lung machine business because of Sorin's overlapping heart-lung business. Also in May 1999, then, Sorin sold COBE Century to Baxter International Inc.

COBE CV was set up as a subsidiary of Sorin Biomedica, reassuming the name COBE Cardiovascular, Inc. At the time of the transaction, COBE had annual sales of about $146 million, and it employed about 840 people at its Arvada headquarters and approximately 950 worldwide. Sorin consolidated its U.S. operations in Arvada, closing down a manufacturing plant in Orange County, California, it had acquired in 1992. Later restructuring moves affected COBE's two non-U.S. plants. The company's manufacturing subsidiary in Gloucester, England, was absorbed into Sorin Biomedica (UK) Ltd., while its Melbourne, Australia, plant was shut down. The sales organizations of COBE, Dideco, and Sorin were also streamlined. (Gambro, meantime, in early 2000 eliminated its last usage of the COBE name when it gave COBE BCT the new name Gambro BCT.)

Sorin Biomedica had been a publicly traded company, controlled by SNIA through a 75 percent ownership interest. In 2000, however, Sorin was merged into and absorbed by SNIA, which restructured its holdings into business units. COBE Cardiovascular became part of the Medical Technology unit.

COBE gained several sister companies in the United States during the early 2000s. In 2001 SNIA acquired Ela Medical Inc. from Sanofi-Synthélabo. Based in Minneapolis, Ela Medical was a producer of pacemakers and implantable defibrillators. In January 2003 SNIA purchased CarboMedics Inc., an Austin, Texas-based maker of mechanical and tissue heart valves. COBE, meantime, was gaining additional traction from cooperative product developments projects undertaken with Dideco and Stöckert. For example, in 2002 COBE introduced its Revolution centrifugal pump which was integrated with Stöckert's SCP drive unit.

In January 2004 SNIA spun off its Medical Technology unit as Sorin S.p.A., which was listed on the Borsa Italiana. Boding well for COBE Cardiovascular's future were Sorin's plans to increase the U.S. share of its revenues from 25 percent to 34 percent by 2008, as well as the Italian parent company's focus on cardiovascular products.

Principal Competitors

Medtronic, Inc.; Terumo Corporation; Baxter International Inc.; C.R. Bard, Inc.; Minntech Corporation; United States Surgical Corporation.

Further Reading

Bettelheim, Andriel, ''Swedish Company Buys Cobe Labs,'' *Denver Post,* March 17, 1990, pp. 1C, 6C.

Bulman, Philip, ''Cobe Pumps Profits into Pioneering Blood Research,'' *Denver Post,* October 6, 1986, p. 3D.

''COBE Seeks Higher Share of Cardiovascular Market,'' *Rocky Mountain News,* June 30, 1976, pp. 74, 77.

Day, Janet, ''Merger, Acquisition Beef Up Medical Equipment Industry,'' *Denver Post,* July 8, 1992, p. 2C.

Gonzalez, Erika, ''COBE CV Target of Buyout Proposal,'' *Denver Rocky Mountain News,* November 25, 1998, p. 4B.

Kaplan, Howard M., ''While Waiting for a Kidney . . . : A Fast-Growing Colorado Firm Builds—and Exports to Scores of Countries—the Remarkable Dialyzers That Save Lives,'' *Denver Post Empire Magazine,* June 25, 1972, pp. 16–20.

Margolin, Morton L., ''Cobe Labs a Star in Chamber Campaign,'' *Rocky Mountain News,* August 22, 1977, pp. 69, 71.

Printz, Carrie, ''COBE Hopes Merger Will Inject New Blood into Its Foreign Sales,'' *Denver Business Journal,* May 28, 1990, p. 20.

Weber, Joe, ''COBE Chiefs' Business Savvy Pays Off in Product Success,'' *Rocky Mountain News,* July 13, 1986, pp. 76–77.

—David E. Salamie

Devon Energy Corporation

20 N. Broadway
Oklahoma City, Oklahoma 73102-8260
U.S.A.
Telephone: (405) 235-3611
Fax: (405) 552-4550
Web site: http://www.devonenergy.com

Public Company
Incorporated: 1969
Employees: 3,436
Sales: $4.3 billion (2002)
Stock Exchanges: American
Ticker Symbol: DVN
NAIC: 211111 Crude Petroleum and Natural Gas Extraction

With its headquarters in Oklahoma City, Oklahoma, publicly traded Devon Energy Corporation is the largest independent oil and gas producer based in the United States. It is also a leading North American independent processor of natural gas and natural gas liquids. Devon is ranked as one of the world's 50 largest oil companies. While most of its proved reserves are located in Colorado, New Mexico, Texas, and Wyoming, Devon also has exploration and production assets in Canada, South America, west Africa, the Caspian Sea, and China. Approximately 60 percent of these reserves are in the form of natural gas.

Company Founded in 1971

Devon was founded in Oklahoma City in 1971 by John W. Nichols and his son J. Larry Nichols. The elder Nichols was raised in Ardmore, Oklahoma, and graduated from the University of Oklahoma with a degree in accounting in 1936. He then became a certified public accountant in Oklahoma City, where he learned the oil business by auditing the books of area oil companies. He became so knowledgeable about how the tax laws impacted the oil industry that in 1950 he was credited with creating the first public oil and gas drilling fund to be registered with the Securities and Exchange Commission. His partner was Oklahoma oilman F.G. "Blackie" Blackwood. Over the next two decades their company, Blackwood & Nichols Co., grew into one of the area's leading oil and gas companies. In 1969 he and his son incorporated Devon Energy Corporation in Oklahoma, but the company dates its history to 1971 when Larry Nichols was able to actively participate in the privately held business—after taking an unusual sidetrack for an oilman. Nichols earned a geology degree from Princeton University, followed by a law degree from the University of Michigan, and then moved to Washington in 1968 to spend a year clerking for Justice Tom Clark and Chief Justice of the Supreme Court, Earl Warren. Nichols then spent another three years in Washington working for assistant U.S. Attorney General William Rehnquist, who would also later become chief justice. Urged by his father, Larry Nichols then returned to Oklahoma City to help run Devon. A director and vice-president from the outset, he became executive vice-president and general counsel in 1973, president of the company in 1976, and chief executive officer in 1980. His father retained the chairmanship, and although he supposedly retired from the day-to-day running of the business during the 1980s, he remained actively involved in the business. It was not until 2000, when he was 85 years old, that he relinquished the chairmanship to his son.

In a 2003 *Oil & Gas Journal* profile Larry Nichols recalled the early days at Devon: "We started this company with my father, myself, an accountant, and a couple of clerical staff." Over the years, Devon would grow through acquisitions, essentially completing a significant purchase each year, then parlaying its size to go after even larger targets. Because the major oil companies were looking overseas for exploration opportunities during the 1970s, Devon focused on already producing North American properties, hoping to emerge as one of the dominant players among the 400 publicly traded independents working the same field. The company looked to apply modern technology to already exploited properties that could be bought at reasonable prices. The focus was on natural gas, which at the time was a surplus commodity, but the Nicholses believed that the industry would soon experience a change in the cycle and natural gas would emerge as a scarce commodity and rise in price. Because the same situation prevailed in Canada, Devon soon set its sight north of the border as well. In general, it was a conservatively run organization, but a key to the company's success over the years

Company Perspectives:

Devon is well positioned to continue its extraordinary path of growth and value creation for its shareholders.

had been its willingness to buck traditional thinking. An example of this tendency to go against the grain came in 1981 when Devon acquired its first interest in the San Juan Basin of New Mexico, an area that within a few years became one of the top natural gas providers in the lower 48 states. For funding, Devon in the first decade of operation relied on innovative partnerships it created for European investors.

The Nicholses preferred to acquire properties when most of the competition was not in the market. In June 1982, Devon acquired the U.S. oil and gas interests from the Canadian firm of Cominco for $31 million, but it was at this point that the Nicholses and their management team became aware of a sea change: Contraction in the industry was resulting in a lot of attractive properties going on the market but too much cash was chasing them. Adhering to its conservative approach, Devon had targeted properties that could realize a 20 to 25 percent rate of return. Now, prices were such that returns would average less than 15 percent. In order to participate and maintain its pattern of growth, management felt that it had to change strategy.

Master Limited Partnership Launched in 1985

After being on the sidelines for more than a year, in January 1984 Devon decided to create a master limited partnership in order to attract investors and return to pursuing acquisitions. Units in an MLP were registered and traded like stock, thus offering liquidity to investors, who were generally trapped in other forms of oil and gas partnerships. Investors were to receive quarterly cash distributions based on net cash flow, as opposed to dividends. In addition to tapping new sources of funding, Devon, acting as general partner, would also be able to use the units to acquire properties. In short, an MLP could combine the favorable tax benefits of limited partnerships with the liquidity and operating ability of a corporation. Devon spent 18 months studying MLPs already in operation, then in July 1985 launched Devon Resource Investors, trading on the Devon name while offering investors the benefits of an MLP. The company rolled in some $42 million in property, with an 85 to 15 percent mix of gas to oil. Unlike most general partners of MLPs, Devon acquired a stake, buying a 38 percent interest, or a 25 percent share of the total assets. To assure investors that Devon had a long-term interest in Devon Resource, the company entered into an agreement not to sell its interest without the permission of its underwriter, Paine Webber. The goal of the MLP was to make quarterly cash distributions equal to half of its net cash flow.

Oil prices collapsed in the mid-1980s, which forced many independents out of business and adversely impacted the fortunes of Devon and its MLP. Commodity prices dropped and the cost of managing the partnership rose. Moreover, changes in tax laws in 1986 also made the investment less attractive. As a result, Devon Resource posted a string of eight losing quarters, and management reassessed its strategy. Rather than return to the simplified structure of a private company, Devon Energy elected to go public, after concluding that bank funding was likely to dry up for independents for a number of reasons. Thus, in April 1988 Devon Energy merged with Devon Resource, along with a privately held fund, Devon-Smedvig 1973 Oil & Gas Program Ltd., to form a larger, publicly traded version of Devon Energy. When energy stocks tanked in mid-1988, Devon's shares lost over a third of their value within a matter of weeks, but as would be the case throughout its history, Devon was able to prosper by operating out of sequence with the rest of the industry. Assets acquired years earlier in the San Juan Basin now became quite attractive, due to advances in technology that allowed exploiters to tap into gas trapped in coal seams previously ignored by drillers because of water problems. Not only did Devon extract this gas, it received attractive federal tax credits to do so. In 1989, Devon returned to profitability. Its annual revenues at this stage totaled less than $30 million, but the company was poised for an impressive run during the 1990s, when it aggressively acquired producing properties.

Devon made several small deals in 1990 and 1991 before completing its first major acquisition as a public company in July 1992: the $122 million purchase of Hondo Oil and Gas Company of Roswell, New Mexico. Devon picked up some 2,700 properties and 5,300 producing oil and gas wells spread across 13 states, but situated mostly in Texas, Oklahoma, New Mexico, and Wyoming. Furthermore, Devon added 180,000 to 200,000 net acres of undeveloped leases and 3,200 miles of seismic information related to both the producing and undeveloped sites. Another major acquisition followed a year later when Devon paid $54 million to oil and gas properties in the San Juan Basin. As would be the case with all of Devon's acquisitions, these properties complemented the company's current holdings, and in many cases set up the next acquisition. At this stage, Devon did not carry much debt and as a result was able to prosper whether commodity prices were high or low. While low prices hurt highly leveraged competitors, Devon was able to hold back on drilling and take advantage of acquisition possibilities. During periods of high prices, the company could realize greater revenues and have even more funds to earmark for new properties. In fiscal 1993 Devon posted record results in terms of production, revenues, profits, and shareholders' equity. Revenues totaled $98.8 million for the year, a significant increase over the previous year's $71.6 million. Net income grew from $14.6 million in 1992 to $20.5 million in 1993.

Alta Energy Acquired in 1994

During several years of low energy prices in the 1990s, Devon bought a large number of properties. In March 1994 the company completed its next significant purchase, paying $66 million for Denver-based Alta Energy Corporation. Devon's total proved oil and gas reserves increased by 37 percent. Of particular importance was the Grayburg-Jackson Field located in southeast New Mexico, which fit nicely with Devon's other holdings in the area. During the final weeks of 1995, the company supplemented another core area of operation, Wyoming, where Devon had enjoyed success in drilling for coalbed methane. It spent $50.3 million to acquire oil and gas properties and a gas processing plant in the region. The pickups in New Mexico and Wyoming were not without risk, however. According to *Oil*

Key Dates:

1969: "Old" Devon Energy Corporation is formed.
1971: "New" Devon Energy begins operations when J. Larry Nichols joins father, John W. Nichols.
1980: Larry Nichols becomes CEO.
1988: Devon becomes a public company.
1992: Hondo Oil & Gas Company becomes first major acquisition.
1999: Acquisition of PennzEnergy makes Devon a top ten independent.
2003: Ocean Energy Acquisition makes Devon largest U.S.-based independent.

& Gas Investor, "Devon has seemingly been in the wrong places at the wrong times—holding natural gas properties in the Rocky Mountains and the San Juan Basin during the miserable early months of 1996, for example—only to come out smelling like a rose when pipeline extensions came on line."

In December 1996, Devon completed its largest acquisition to that point, trading more than $250 million in stock for the North American onshore oil and gas properties of Kerr-McGee Corporation, which received 31 percent of Devon's stock as well as three seats on its board. The deal boosted Devon's reserves by 46 percent, bolstered its Wyoming presence, and also added some interests in Canada. Devon's next big deal added to the company's Canadian holdings. In 1998 it used another $750 million in stock to acquire Northstar Energy Corp. to achieve critical mass in Canada, adding 550 billion cubic feet of natural gas and 36 million barrels of oil and natural-gas liquids located in Alberta and British Columbia. As a result of this transaction, Devon became a $2 billion company in market capitalization and one of the top 15 U.S.-based independents. In a lesser deal in 1998, Devon paid $57.5 million to acquire natural gas properties in Alberta from a subsidiary of Canadian Occidental Petroleum Ltd.

Devon's penchant for completing ever larger acquisitions on an annual basis continued in 1999, when Devon acquired PennzEnergy, the oil and gas business of Pennzoil Co., in a stock swap. Once again, Larry Nichols's ability to shun conventional thinking paid off. According to *Forbes,* "In 1997 oil was going for as much as $26 a barrel and many producers borrowed money and bought each other out. At the height of the frenzy, Pennzoil got a $6.4 billion offer (including assumed debt) from Union Pacific Resources—and rejected it. Nichols went the other way. He used profits from selling oil to pay down debt and prepare for the inevitable crash. The next year oil prices dipped to $10. That's when he started talking to Pennzoil about selling some assets. Devon wound up buying Pennzoil's oil and gas exploration and production operations for a measly $2.6 billion, a bargain that appeared even cheaper after Nichol's eliminated $50 million a year in operating costs. Thrown in essentially free: a 5% interest in a 4-billion-barrel oilfield in Azerbaijan." Doubled in size as a result, Devon now cracked the top 10 of U.S.-based independent oil and gas companies. For 1999 Devon topped $1 billion in revenues for the first time, increasing from $604 million in 1998 to $1.14 billion. With the Pennzoil assets available for the full year, in 2000 Devon's revenues approached $2.6 billion and the company posted net earnings of $730 million.

With the dawn of the new century, Devon continued its pattern of growth through opportunistic acquisitions. In 2000 Devon paid $3.5 billion in cash and the assumption of debt to add Houston-based Santa Fe Snyder Corp. In addition to supplementing Devon's holding in the Rocky Mountains, Permian Basin, and Gulf of Mexico, the deal also included assets in South America, southeast Asia, and west Africa. Devon now became a top five independent. In 2001 Devon engineered a $3.5 billion takeover of Mitchell Energy & Development Corp. (completed in 2002), a deal that increased its reserve base by 38 percent. In particular, it greatly enhanced the company's presence in the important Fort Worth Basin. Devon then completed the $4.6 billion acquisition of Anderson Exploration Ltd., which solidified Devon's position in Canada, as it now became the country's third largest gas producer. Revenues in fiscal 2002 exceeded $4.3 billion, making Devon the 47th largest oil company in the world, according to *Petroleum Intelligence Weekly.* Devon struck next in 2003 when in a $3.5 billion stock deal, plus the assumption of $1.8 billion in debt, it acquired Houston-based Ocean Energy. This acquisition elevated Devon to the top spot among U.S. independent producers of oil and gas, with the ability to produce 2.4 billion cubic feet of natural gas and 250,000 barrels of oil and gas liquids per day. In addition, Devon became the largest independent deepwater Gulf of Mexico leaseholder with over 500 deepwater blocks, and also held 29 million net undeveloped acres around the world. Annual revenues were projected to approach $6 billion. Some analysts were concerned that Devon had taken on too much debt, but management took steps to sell off some $1.5 billion in assets picked up in the Anderson and Mitchell acquisitions, freeing itself of a large portion of debt. Nevertheless, interest payments for 2003 were an estimated $550 million. For a company that for decades had been cautious about taking on debt, it was a significant departure. But given Devon's track record, there was every reason to believe that the company would find a way to maintain its pattern of ongoing prosperity.

Principal Subsidiaries

Devon Energy Corporation; Devon Energy Production Company, L.P.; Devon Canada Corporation; Devon Gas Services, L.P.

Principal Competitors

BP p.l.c.; Burlington Resources Inc.; Royal Dutch/Shell Group of Companies.

Further Reading

Danker, Jessica, "Devon Success Strategy Not Tied to Market," *Journal Record,* May 27, 1994.

Duey, Rhonda, "Deal of the Century," *Oil & Gas Investor,* April 1997, p. 55.

Egan, John, "Beyond the Law," *FW,* January 9, 1990, p. 34.

Fisher, Daniel, "Odd Man In," *Forbes,* September 3, 2001, p. 66.

Fletcher, Sam, "Devon Energy Puts Early Focus on Long-Term Strategy," *Oil & Gas Journal,* September 22, 2003, p. 38.

Gold, Russell, "Devon Looks Good, But Could Stumble If Gas Prices Drop," *Wall Street Journal,* July 16, 2003, p. C1.

—Ed Dinger

DS Smith Plc

4-16 Artillery Row
London
SW1P 1RZ
United Kingdom
Telephone: 44 20 7932 5000
Fax: 44 20 7932 5003
Web site: http://www.dssmith.uk.com

Public Company
Incorporated: 1940
Employees: 10,879
Sales: £1.48 billion ($2.51 billion) (2003)
Stock Exchanges: London
Ticker Symbol: SMDS
NAIC: 424120 Stationery and Office Supplies Merchant Wholesalers; 322121 Paper (Except Newsprint) Mills; 322130 Paperboard Mills; 322211 Corrugated and Solid Fiber Box Manufacturing; 551112 Offices of Other Holding Companies

DS Smith Plc has wrapped up leading European positions in its two primary lines of business: packaging (paper-based and plastics) and wholesale office supplies and products. Packaging is the London-based company's largest division, representing 64 percent of its nearly £1.5 billion in 2003 revenues. Corrugated and paper production alone accounted for more than half of the group's total sales. The company operates six paper mills in the United Kingdom, two mills in France, and a mill in Turkey; three-quarters of DS Smith's production is of the corrugated case type, complemented by a range of specialty papers for the packaging and other markets. DS Smith is the leading producer of corrugated packaging in the United Kingdom and France, while subsidiary St. Regis is the leading U.K. producer of recycled paper. A vertically integrated group, DS Smith also produces transit packaging, decorative and point-of-sale packaging, and industrial and heavy duty packaging products. At the other end of the spectrum, the company is also the United Kingdom's largest collector and recycler of commercial waste paper, used as raw product for much of the group's production. DS Smith's Plastics division is one of the world's leading producers of "bag-in-box" packaging, as well as thermoformed transit packaging. Representing 13 percent of total group sales, the plastics division operates worldwide from sites in the United Kingdom, France, the United States, Germany, Spain, Italy, Belgium, Poland, the Dominican Republic, Israel, Australia, and New Zealand. Since the 1990s, DS Smith has moved to reduce its reliance on the highly cyclical paper sector by expanding into the wholesale office supply market. The group is Europe's leading supplier of wholesale office products, through its Spicers Ltd. subsidiary, which operates 20 distribution centers in the United Kingdom, France, Germany, Ireland, and Spain, as well as the Plein Ciel wholesale office supply store chain in France. DS Smith is listed on the London Stock Exchange.

Cigarette Carton Maker in the 1940s

DS Smith was founded in London by David Solomon Smith in 1940. Known as David S. Smith Ltd. for most of its history, the company has specialized from the start in providing packaging services to a number of clients, including Creamola Food Products, Cerebos, Helena Rubenstein, and other consumer products producers. Yet the company was to become most closely identified as a producer of cigarette cartons, notably for British-American Tobacco and Imperial Tobacco. In 1949, the group's growing operations enabled it to build a new plant in Neath, Glamorganshire, South Wales. That plant was expanded in 1969, at which time it became one of England's most modern packaging plants.

In 1960, the company, by then joined by Smith's son, also named David Smith, made its first public offering. The group remained quite tiny however, and at the end of the 1970s sales remained under £8.5 million per year. By the beginning of the 1980s, the company had begun to feel the worst effects of the recession that gripped the United Kingdom, and sales quickly slumped—slipping under £5 million in the early years of the decade.

Smith's difficulties—and its plummeting share price—brought it to the attention of Richard Brewster, then finance

Company Perspectives:

DS Smith Plc is an international Group focused on two major activities—Packaging and Office Products.

We hold strong positions in many of the markets in which we operate: the leading UK producer of recycled paper board; the largest UK collector and merchant of recovered paper; a leading manufacturer of corrugated packaging in the UK and France; a leading worldwide supplier of bag-in-box packaging; the leading European wholesaler of office supplies; the largest UK manufacturer of envelopes, books and pads.

director at Giltspur, which itself had been recently acquired by Unigate. Putting up his own savings, and arranging additional bank financing, Brewster bought up a 10 percent stake in David S. Smith in 1983. At the same time, Brewster orchestrated the buyout of another 20 percent in the company by an investor group. Brewster then took over as company CEO and began steering the group on a new course.

Brewster immediately recognized that David S. Smith's future lay in gaining scale. The company went shopping, and in 1984 found its first acquisition target, Western Board Mills, also located in South Wales. In November 1984, that group's chairman agreed to sell his stake of more than 51 percent to Smith; by the beginning of 1985, David S. Smith had completed the acquisition. The purchase not only extended the company's production by adding Western's specialty as a maker of boxes for ladies' shoes, but also added nearly £2 million in annual sales and at the same time bringing a treasury of some £6 million.

Smith quickly became more attractive to banks, which agreed to back its continued acquisition drive. In 1985, the company completed its next important acquisition, Abbey Corrugated, paying more than £15 million. The purchase of Abbey Corrugated in particular enabled the group to enter the corrugated paper manufacturing sector. By the end of that year, the company's sales had once again topped £8 million.

Yet Smith's growth spurt had only just begun. In 1986, the company paid £83 million for the St. Regis Paper Company. Originally part of the U.S.-based St. Regis paper group, the U.K. operation had been spun off at its parent's hostile takeover by Champion Consolidated in 1984. The addition of St. Regis extended Davis S. Smith's operations into the paper sector, while making it a major player in the United Kingdom's packaging sector. St. Regis also brought Smith into the heavy duty corrugated case market, through its stake in the Tri-Wall Europe partnership set up with Weyerhauser in the 1960s.

Two years later, the company confirmed its intention of becoming the United Kingdom's leading packaging player through its acquisition of Kemsley Paper mill in 1988. That purchase, for £11 million, also enabled the company to shift toward developing a vertically integrated business.

Acquisitions had formed part of Brewster's successful strategy in the 1980s, while the company continued to invest in its organic growth as well. Yet the company attributed a large part of its success to its hands-off management style, allowing existing management of its acquired subsidiaries to continue acting more or less autonomously.

As Brewster himself described his philosophy in *Packaging Week:* ''We have grown by improving our existing businesses and by acquiring companies which complement our strategy. We always look for companies with something special to offer, such as technological supremacy, the potential for greater capacity or specialist products. In addition, we try to identify good quality management.'' Brewster continued: ''All our acquisitions have been on a friendly rather than a hostile basis. This usually results in skilled management and staff remaining with the group and encourages a future workforce to be both loyal and enthusiastic.''

Diversified in the 1990s

Smith bought out full control of Tri-Wall Europe in 1990, paying Weyerhauser $12 million. The purchase also gave the group control of Tri-Wall's brands, including the Tri-Wall and Uni-Pak trademarks. While Tri-Wall remained close to the group's hereditary core, Brewster had already begun to lead the company into a new era of diversification.

In 1989, the company acquired Waddington & Duval, a plastics-based packaging group with a specialty in so-called ''bag-in-box'' tap technologies. That acquisition cost the company £2 million, but was followed by a larger entry into the plastics packaging market, when the company paid £12 million to acquire Corrugated Products, and its subsidiary, CP Plastics, which also focused on the bag-in-box packaging sector. Rounding out the group's range of plastics acquisitions was the purchase of British Sisalkraft, which specialized in plastic film wrap.

Brewster left the group in the early 1990s to pursue new challenges. Following his departure, the company embarked on a new phase in its expansion, taking a two-pronged approach: on the one hand the group targeted growth on the European continent and elsewhere, and on the other continued diversification in an effort to reduce its reliance on the cyclical paper and packaging markets.

Smith's first foreign move came in 1991 with the £170 million acquisition of French packaging group Kaysersberg, which was especially strong in heavy duty corrugated packaging, but also gave the company a foothold in the European plastic packaging sector. The Kaysersberg group gave the company three manufacturing plants in France, and a sales presence in Germany as well.

Smith quickly reinforced both its French operations—through the acquisition of Paris-based Cartonnerie Chouanard, merged into Kaysersberg—and its new position in Germany, with the purchase of Sieger Plastics. That company, with manufacturing plants in Im Grossen Tal and Duren, helped extend Smith's bag-in-box capacity onto the European continent.

Throughout the 1990s, David S. Smith continued building up its international operations, establishing a manufacturing presence in the United States, Spain, Italy, Belgium, Poland, the

Key Dates:

1940: David Solomon Smith launches a business providing lithographed cartons.
1949: Company opens factory in Neath, Glamorgan, South Wales.
1960: David S. Smith Ltd. is incorporated.
1969: Company completes expansion of Neath plant, making it one of most modern packaging plants in the country.
1983: Richard Brewster buys stake in company and becomes CEO.
1984: Company acquires Western Board Mills, which specializes in boxes for ladies' shoes.
1985: Company acquires Abbey Corrugated, entering heavy duty corrugated sector.
1986: Company acquires St. Regis Paper, adding papermaking facilities.
1988: Company acquires Kemsley Paper Mill.
1989: Plastics packaging sector is entered with acquisition of Waddington & Duval and Corrugated Products.
1991: Expansion onto European continent occurs with acquisitions of Kaysersberg Packaging and Cartonneri Chouanard in France and Siegers in Germany.
1993: Company diversifies into office supplies market with acquisition of Spicers wholesale office supply group.
1996: Company enters office supplies manufacturing with acquisition of John Dickinson in the United Kingdom.
2000: Company acquires U.S.-based Packaging Systems LLC and its Rapak trademark.
2001: Company forms Rapak Asia joint venture with AEP in Australia and New Zealand; acquires Plein Ciel wholesale office supplies network in France; changes name to DS Smith Plc.
2002: Germany's Zewathener is acquired.
2003: Company acquires northern England-based manufacturing operations of MacFarlane Group.

Dominican Republic, Israel, Australia, and New Zealand by the beginning of the 2000s. Yet the company had also put into place the second prong of its expansion strategy.

In 1993, Smith moved into new territory with the purchase of U.K.-based Spicers wholesale office products group. Paying £93 million, Smith instantly became a leader in that market in the United Kingdom, before extending its operations onto the European continent through a network of distribution facilities in Germany, Spain, France, and elsewhere. In 1996, the company strengthened its position in the office supplies market by adding a manufacturing component as well, in the form of John Dickinson. For £17 million, Smith now became one of the U.K. leaders in the production of envelopes, notebooks, and pads.

In addition to its external expansion, Smith also invested in its organic growth. These efforts included spending some £110 million in upgrading its main paper production facility at Kemsley, completed in 1996, building a new corrugated production plant in Fordham in 1998, and expanding its Tri-Wall factory in Monmouth. The company also expanded its continental European operations, opening facilities in Poland and Italy.

Like much of the packaging sector, David S. Smith weathered some difficult years at the end of the 1990s, in part because of the strength of the pound against European currencies. In order to provide a buffer for itself, the company, which had already acquired Formative Engineering in the United States, returned to that country, paying £17million to acquire Packaging Systems LLC, which used the trade name Papak, in 2000.

By then, as signs of an upturn in the European economy firmed, the company announced its interest in spending as much as £200 million on a new round of acquisitions. That process began in 2001 when the company spent £21 million buying up part of food giant Danisco's corrugated packaging operations. That year, also, Smith, through Spicers, took a major position in the French wholesale office supplies market when it bought that country's leading Plein Ciel, giving it a national network of cash-and-carry stores as well.

Smith paused to change its name, to DS Smith Plc, in 2001. The company then continued its expansion, forming an Australasian 50–50 joint venture with that region's AEP, called Rapak Asia Pacific. The company took full control of the joint venture at mid-2003, however. By then, Smith had already paid £17.5 million to acquire Germany's Zewathener GmbH in 2002, a bag-in-box specialist. In 2002, also, Smith opened its first Spicers distribution center in Spain, in Barcelona, in 2002.

By the end of 2003, Smith had grown into a global leader, posting annual sales of nearly £1.5 billion with operations worldwide. The company showed no immediate sign of slowing down its growth. In October 2003, for example, Smith purchased the northern England-based manufacturing operations of MacFarlane Group for some £900,000. DS Smith appeared prepared to package more growth in the future.

Principal Subsidiaries

AA Griggs & Co. Ltd; Cartón Plástico s.a. (Spain); Çopikas AS (Turkey); David S. Smith America Inc. (U.S.A.); Demes Logistics GmbH & Co KG (Germany); DS Smith (UK) Limited; DS Smith Packaging; DS Smith Packaging Poland SA; DS Smith Plastics; DSS Rapak Inc. (U.S.A.); Ducaplast SAS (France); DW Plastics NV (Belgium); John Dickinson Stationery Ltd.; Kaysersberg Packaging SAS (France); Kaysersberg Packaging SA; Rapak Asia Pacific (Aust) Pty Ltd (Australia; 50%); Spicers Ltd.; St Regis Paper Company Ltd; StePac L.A. Ltd (Israel; 55%); Toscana Ondulati SpA (Italy; 65%); Zewathener GmbH (Germany).

Principal Competitors

REXAM PLC; Linpac Group Ltd.; Cinram UK Ltd.; S.C.A. Packaging Ltd.; CarnaudMetalbox PLC; British Polythene Industries PLC; Surface Specialties PLC; Autobar Group Ltd.; Avon Rubber PLC; Lawson Mardon; MY Holdings PLC; Field Group PLC.

Further Reading

''DS Smith Suffers Poor Market,'' *Print Week*, December 18, 2003, p. 7.

Duckers, John, ''It's a Wrap As Rival in US Bagged,'' *Birmingham Post*, June 29, 2000, p. 26.

Gimbel, Florian, ''DS Smith May Spend £100m on Acquisitions,'' *Financial Times*, December 6, 2001, p. 28.

Grimond, Magnus, ''European Rivals Muscle in on Smith,'' *Independent*, July 17, 1997, p. 24.

Kipphoff, John, ''Strong Action' by DS Smith Fails to Offset Fall in Demand,'' *Financial Times*, June 28, 2002, p. 24.

Murphy, Mary, ''Perfect Marriage,'' *Packaging Week*, January 31, 1990, p. S12.

''Smith Sets Its Sights on the Continent,'' *Packaging Week*, January 8, 1992, p. 15.

—M.L. Cohen

Decide with Confidence

The Dun & Bradstreet Corporation

103 JFK Parkway
Short Hills, New Jersey 07078
U.S.A.
Telephone: (973) 921-5500
Fax: (908) 665-5524
Web site: http://www.dnb.com

Public Company
Incorporated: 1933 as R.G. Dun-Bradstreet Corporation
Employees: 6,600
Sales: $1.3 billion (2002)
Stock Exchanges: New York London Tokyo Geneva Zurich Basel
Ticker Symbol: DNB
NAIC: 511140 Database and Directory Publishers; 523999 Miscellaneous Financial Investment Activities; 561450 Credit Bureaus

The Dun & Bradstreet Corporation (D&B) is the leading provider of business information worldwide, priding itself on its indispensability as a facilitator of business-to-business commerce for 160 years. Derived from a global database of 79 million companies, D&B's integrated array of products and services includes D&B Risk Management Solutions for minimizing credit exposure, D&B Sales & Marketing Solutions for identifying profitable customers, D&B Supply Management Solutions for efficient management of suppliers, and D&B E-Business Solutions for fast, Web-based access to reliable business information. In 2001 the company launched a new branding initiative, officially changing its name to D&B, the already familiar acronym, and creating a new logo along with the tagline, ''Decide with Confidence.''

Company Origins

Dun & Bradstreet traces its origin to Lewis Tappan, who in 1841 left Arthur Tappan & Company (a New York silk trading firm that he ran with his elder brother) to found a credit information bureau called the Mercantile Agency. Tappan had long been aware of the need for better credit reporting. As the borders of the United States expanded westward, traders were moving beyond the easy view of the East Coast merchants and bankers who kept them supplied and capitalized. Information on the creditworthiness of these far-flung businesses was collected by individual trading houses and banks in a scattershot fashion, and Tappan saw that centralizing the process of collecting information would result in greater efficiency. Accordingly, he took out an advertisement in the *New York Commercial Advertiser* on July 20, 1841, and opened shop 11 days later on the corner of Hanover and Exchange streets in Manhattan.

The Mercantile Agency operated by gathering information through a network of correspondents and selling it to subscribers. The agents were attorneys, cashiers of banks, merchants, and other competent persons—anyone who might have an impartial familiarity with local merchants through business or civic affairs. Over the years people as famous as U.S. presidents Abraham Lincoln, Ulysses S. Grant, Grover Cleveland, and William McKinley, as well as presidential candidate Wendell Willkie, would serve as agents for the company that Tappan founded.

The Mercantile Agency opened branch offices in Boston in 1843 and Philadelphia in 1845. In 1846 Benjamin Douglass, a young New York businessman with connections in the southern cotton trade, joined the firm. When Lewis Tappan retired in 1849, Douglass and Tappan's brother, Arthur, ran it as partners until 1854, when the elder Tappan sold out to Douglass. Then, in 1859, Douglass sold out to Robert Graham Dun, who immediately changed the firm's name to R.G. Dun & Company. That year the company published its first reference book of credit information, the *Dun Book.*

As the nation grew and commerce boomed in the decades following the Civil War, Dun had to keep up with it by establishing new branch offices. The firm expanded into the South, west to California, and north into Canada. An office in San Francisco opened in 1869. In 1891 there were 126 Dun branch offices. Robert Dun Douglass, who was Benjamin Douglass's son and Robert Graham Dun's nephew, became general manager of the firm in 1896. After his uncle died in 1900, the company operated as a common-law trust with Douglass in charge as executive trustee. He retired as general manager in 1909 and was succeeded by Archibald Ferguson.

Company Perspectives:

D&B has undergone a period of restructuring in recent years, designed to make D&B a smaller, more tightly focused company. A.C. Nielsen, Cognizant, R.H. Donnelley and Moody's Corporation were all spun off to allow each company to pursue focused strategies for its specific business. And in October 2000, D&B launched an ambitious new plan called the Blueprint for Growth—a strategy designed to transform itself into a growth company with an important presence on the Web.

We're creating a whole new generation of products and services that give customers exciting opportunities to manage business information more efficiently. We are constantly expanding the size and improving the quality of our global database, which now covers more than 75 million businesses worldwide. And we're working hard to continuously improve the high-quality service that is our hallmark.

We're a company poised to meet the new century. But we will always have a fundamental legacy to define us, a legacy that ties us to our past and supports us as we venture into the next millennium.

R.G. Dun also began to expand overseas at about this time. The firm opened its first office in London in 1857, and added five more foreign offices—in Glasgow, Paris, Melbourne, Mexico City, and Hamburg—by the end of the century. From 1901 to 1928 R.G. Dun opened 41 overseas branches, scattered across Europe, South Africa, and Latin America.

Growth and Acquisitions: 1930s–80s

In 1931 R.G. Dun acquired National Credit Office (NCO), a credit-reporting service. The firm then reorganized into a holding company called R.G. Dun Corporation, which assumed control of the assets of both NCO and the original R.G. Dun & Company. NCO President and former owner Arthur Dare Whiteside became president of the new entity.

In 1933, at the nadir of the Great Depression, R.G. Dun merged with one of its main competitors, the Bradstreet Company. Since the two companies overlapped each other in many activities and resources, an amalgamation at that time made sense. Bradstreet was founded in Cincinnati, Ohio, in 1849 by John Bradstreet, a lawyer and merchant whose ancestors included Simon Bradstreet, a colonial governor of Massachusetts, and the prominent colonial American poet Anne Bradstreet. A large file of credit information had come into John Bradstreet's possession as he was overseeing the liquidation of an estate, and he decided to enter the same business in which Lewis Tappan had pioneered eight years earlier. In 1855 Bradstreet packed up and moved to New York, where he challenged the Mercantile Agency directly. Two years later the firm started publishing a semiannual reference book that offered more extensive coverage than the early *Dun Book*.

John Bradstreet died in 1863 and was succeeded by his son, Henry, who ran the firm until it incorporated in 1876 under the name the Bradstreet Company. A group headed by Charles F. Clark then ran the company until 1904, when Clark died and was succeeded by Henry Dunn. Dunn retired in 1927 and gave way to Clark's son, Charles M. Clark. The younger Clark was still chief executive when Bradstreet merged with Dun in 1933. The new company changed its name to R.G. Dun-Bradstreet Corporation and then to Dun & Bradstreet, Inc., in 1939.

Business remained slow for Dun & Bradstreet through the 1930s and during World War II and then picked up again after the war ended. In 1942 the company acquired Credit Clearing House, a credit-reporting agency that specialized in the clothing industry. In 1962 Arthur Dare Whiteside retired and was succeeded by J. Wilson Newman, who headed Dun & Bradstreet as president until 1960 and then as chairman and chief executive until 1968. Under Newman, Dun & Bradstreet embarked on a course of expansion and technological improvement. In 1958 the company began operating its own private wire network, which linked 79 of its major offices. This allowed credit information to be handled more expeditiously.

In 1961 Dun & Bradstreet acquired R.H. Donnelley Corporation. Donnelley, best known for publishing the Yellow Pages telephone directories, was founded in Chicago in 1874 and also published trade magazines. The next year Dun & Bradstreet acquired Official Airline Guides and added it to the Donnelley division. The company also acquired Moody's Investors Service, which provided financial data for investors on publicly owned corporations through its series of Moody's manuals.

In 1966 Dun & Bradstreet acquired Fantus Company, which specialized in area development surveys. In 1968 it bought book publisher Thomas Y. Crowell. When Newman retired that year, he was succeeded by former University of Delaware president John Perkins, who served as chairman for one year.

In 1971 Dun & Bradstreet acquired Corinthian Broadcasting, which owned five CBS television affiliates and publisher Funk & Wagnalls. In 1973 the company changed its name to the Dun & Bradstreet Companies Inc. It had acquired some 40 businesses since J. Wilson Newman inaugurated this expansion in 1960 and had seen its annual sales rise from $81 million in 1960 to $450 million in 1973. In 1973 the Dun & Bradstreet Corporation was formed to become the parent company.

In 1978 Dun & Bradstreet acquired Technical Publishing, a trade and professional magazine publisher. The next year it acquired National CSS, an information-processing technology company. In 1983 it diversified into computer software when it acquired McCormack & Dodge, which published systems software for mainframe computers. The next year it cut back a bit on diversification when it spun off Funk & Wagnalls and sold most of its Corinthian Broadcasting television assets to A.H. Belo. The company, however, acquired Datastream, a British business information company, and the market research firm A.C. Nielsen. Nielsen, famous for its television rating service, was founded in Chicago in 1923 by Arthur C. Nielsen, Sr. Harrington Drake, chief executive officer of Dun & Bradstreet, was a longtime friend of the Nielsen family, and the two companies had been discussing a merger on and off since 1969.

Divestiture and Acquisitions: 1990s

Dun & Bradstreet continued restructuring itself through divestiture and acquisitions from the late 1980s and into the 1990s.

Key Dates:

1841: Lewis Tappan founds a credit information bureau called the Mercantile Agency.
1849: Another credit information bureau, the Bradstreet Company, is founded in Cincinnati, Ohio, by John Bradstreet, a lawyer and merchant.
1855: Bradstreet moves to New York, placing itself in direct competition with the Mercantile Agency.
1859: The Mercantile Agency is sold to Robert Graham Dun, who changes the company's name to R.G. Dun & Company; the company publishes its first reference book of credit information, the *Dun Book.*
1876: The Bradstreet Company incorporates under the leadership of Henry Bradstreet, the founder's son.
1931: The firm reorganizes into a holding company called R.G. Dun Corporation, controlling the assets of its newly acquired credit-reporting service, National Credit Office (NCO), and the original R.G. Dun & Company.
1933: R.G. Dun & Company merges with the Bradstreet Company, becoming R.G. Dun-Bradstreet Corporation.
1939: The merged company changes its name to Dun and Bradstreet, Inc.
1942: The company acquires Credit Clearing House, a credit-reporting agency that specializes in the clothing industry.
1958: The company begins operating its own private wire network, linking 79 of its major offices and allowing credit information to be handled more expeditiously.
1961: Dun & Bradstreet acquires R.H. Donnelley Corporation, a company founded in Chicago in 1874 and best known for publishing the Yellow Pages telephone directories.
1962: The company acquires Moody's Investors Service, a provider of financial data for investors on publicly owned corporations through its series of Moody's manuals.
1973: Having acquired some 40 businesses since the launch of its expansion program in 1960, the company changes its name to the Dun & Bradstreet Companies Inc.; the Dun & Bradstreet Corporation is formed to serve as the parent company.
1996: Dun & Bradstreet divides itself into three new publicly traded corporations: Cognizant Corporation, The Dun & Bradstreet Corporation, and A.C Nielsen.
1998: Dun & Bradstreet restructures again, spinning off the R.H. Donnelley Corporation.
2000: The Dun & Bradstreet Corporation splits into two companies, spinning off Moody's Investors Service.
2001: Dun & Bradstreet changes its name to D&B as part of a new corporate branding effort.
2003: D&B acquires Hoover's, Inc.

It sold Official Airline Guides to Propwix, an affiliate of British Maxwell Communications, in 1988 and Zytron, Petroleum Information, and Neodata in 1990. Also in 1990 the company announced its intention to sell two divisions of Dun & Bradstreet Software: Datastream International, Ltd., and Information Associates, Inc. The company sold Donnelley Marketing, the IMS communications unit, and Carol Write Sales in 1991.

By 1993, however, Dun & Bradstreet began shifting gears and entering a phase of acquisitions. Through the various divisions of Dun & Bradstreet, the company focused on acquiring smaller, primarily information-based companies. For example, it acquired a majority interest in Gartner Group Inc., an international market research firm, on April 8, 1993. Dun & Bradstreet Information Services acquired Solidited, a Swedish company that provided commercial-credit information for Scandinavian businesses, on May 12, 1993. Also in 1993 the company formed HealthCare Information Inc. to conduct research in the healthcare industry, and on February 17, 1994, HealthCare Information acquired Lexecon Health Service Inc.

Acquisitions continued in 1994. A.C. Nielsen acquired two companies: IPSA S.A. (Argentina) and Survey Research Group, Hong Kong. IMS America acquired Emron Inc. and Amfac Chemdata (Australia), and Dun and Bradstreet Information Services purchased Orefro L'Informazione (Italy), S&W (France), and Novinform A.G. (Switzerland) and formed an alliance with Tokyo Shoko Research (Japan). The Dun & Bradstreet Corporation acquired Pilot software, an online software company. Also in 1994 Dun & Bradstreet announced that it would be getting out of the magazine publishing business and in the process ceasing publication of D & B Reports.

On January 9, 1996, Dun & Bradstreet announced plans to divide itself into three new publicly traded corporations: Cognizant Corporation, which consisted of IMS International, the Gartner Group, Nielsen Media Research, Pilot Software, and Erisco; the Dun & Bradstreet Corporation, made up of Dun & Bradstreet Information Services, Moody's Investors Service, and R.H. Donnelley; and A.C. Nielsen. The Cognizant Corporation was created to focus on such high-growth business segments as healthcare and media markets. The Dun & Bradstreet Corporation was to continue its historically successful financial information services. A.C. Nielsen was to focus on marketing research in the consumer packaged-goods industry, where it was already the global leader. As part of the reorganization, several Dun & Bradstreet divisions, including Dun & Bradstreet Software Services, Inc. and American Credit Indemnity, were scheduled to be sold.

In 1997 Dun & Bradstreet announced the release of two coding systems designed to simplify the process of making purchases on the Internet. The first was the Data Universal Numbering System (DUNS), which employed nine-digit company identification tags. Until then the DUNS system had been used only internally by Dun & Bradstreet. The second release was an Internet database of the Standard Products and Service Code (SPSC). This database provided 11-digit codes that identified product types. With the help of the codes, Internet users could more easily find companies that provided particular products or services. Although the Internet was a new medium for Dun & Bradstreet, its Internet products were in line with its traditional mission of providing information and information services.

Continued Restructuring and a Blueprint for Growth in the 21st Century

Having successfully implemented a major restructuring in 1996, Dun & Bradstreet sought to further streamline its corporate structure in 1998 by spinning off R.H. Donnelley. According to the new structure, the Dun & Bradstreet Corporation would retain its two main financial information businesses, Moody's Investors Service and the Dun & Bradstreet (D&B) operating company, while Donnelley, the top independent seller of yellow pages advertising in the United States, would become a fully independent, publicly traded company. The split was designed to enable both companies to better focus on their core competencies and more accurately allocate resources toward the realization of their strategic and financial objectives. Another benefit of the spinoff was improved financial flexibility for Dun & Bradstreet, as about $450 million of the corporation's existing debt was assumed by Donnelley. Ultimately, with net income of $280.1 million in 1998, the Dun & Bradstreet Corporation achieved its second consecutive year of double-digit earnings growth, surpassing its own financial objectives by year's end.

In 1999, the D&B operating company established strategic alliances to integrate D&B information into business systems and processes. Through new partnerships with such enterprise software companies as SAP AG of Germany, SAS Institute, Siebel Systems, and Oracle Corporation, D&B sought opportunities to embed its data into customers' system software and position itself amid the rising current of e-commerce. Also in 1999, D&B launched a new Internet business, eccelerate.com, designed to leverage D&B's worldwide database of 57 million companies for online business-to-business transactions. A subsequent alliance between eccelerate.com and VeriSign, Inc., the preeminent provider of Internet trust services around the world, further strengthened D&B's online position by providing its customers with optimum information security on the Web. D&B's strides into e-commerce paid off, as revenue from Internet-related business reached $100 million in 1999, a 150 percent increase from the preceding year. By comparison with 1998, however, 1999 was a disappointing year for the Dun & Bradstreet Corporation. While Moody's continued to produce phenomenal results, boasting a fourth consecutive year of double-digit revenue growth, the D&B operating company underperformed, causing the parent company to fall short of its earnings goals.

In 2000, then, the Dun & Bradstreet Corporation split in two again, spinning off Moody's Investors Service as an independent, publicly traded company. It was then incumbent on the D&B operating company to spearhead improved earnings, particularly through the aggressive expansion of its Internet presence. To transform the company and meet its strategic goals for the coming three years—which included a 10 percent increase in earnings per share—D&B created a ''Blueprint for Growth'' that focused on five major objectives: leveraging the D&B brand as the most trusted source of business information; creating financial flexibility by improving efficiency at all levels of operation, thereby freeing up $100 million for investment in B2B e-commerce and other ventures; enhancing its current business by creating deeper and broader market penetration among its current base of multinational customers, among small businesses, and on the Web; becoming a key player in B2B e-commerce with the aim of deriving 80 percent of its total revenue from Internet-related business by 2004; building a winning culture by honing company objectives, increasing individual and team accountability; and improving corporate leadership.

During 2001, as the Blueprint for Growth came into full swing, the company acquired Harris InfoSource International, Inc., a privately held company noted for its national database of in-depth manufacturer profiles. As a wholly owned subsidiary of Dun & Bradstreet, Harris InfoSource would significantly strengthen D&B's portfolio of sales and marketing products and services. Also that year, toward the goal of better leveraging the Dun & Bradstreet brand, the company officially changed its name to D&B, the already familiar acronym, launching a new logo along with the tagline, ''Decide with Confidence.'' As a result of these and other initiatives, the company achieved earnings per share (EPS) growth of 16.7 percent for the year, well above its stated goal. Further, its revenue from Internet business reached 33 percent, up from 17 percent in 2000.

D&B's performance only improved in 2002, as the company continued to expand the range of its value-added products, investing in signature tools and services including ''Global DecisionMaker,'' ''Portfolio Management Solutions,'' and ''Data Integration Toolkit.'' In 2002, D&B delivered EPS growth of 26 percent, while the company's revenue from Internet business soared to 65 percent. In February 2003, the company further strengthened its complement of products with the $119 million acquisition of Hoover's, a prominent provider of information on private and publicly traded companies through its website, Hoovers.com. Having increased its worldwide database from 60 to 79 million companies in the course of just two years, D&B's Blueprint for Growth promised to yield gratifying results for the company and its shareholders for the foreseeable future.

Principal Subsidiaries

Hoover's, Inc.; Harris InfoSource International, Inc.

Principal Competitors

Acxiom Corporation; Equifax Inc.; infoUSA Inc.

Further Reading

Abrahams, Paul, ''Dun & Bradstreet Opts for Divorce,'' *Financial Times,* November 1, 1996, p. 26.

Bharadwaj-Chand, Swati, ''Dun and Bradstreet Identifies Web As Major Focus Area,'' *Times of India,* February 17, 2001.

Bowen, Ted Smalley, ''Dun & Bradstreet Agrees to Acquire Pilot Software,'' *PC Week,* July 25, 1994, pp. 105–06.

Byrne, John A., ''Why D&B Is Glued to the Ticker: Wall Street Greets a Breakup Plan with Deafening Silence,'' *Business Week,* February 19, 1996, pp. 58–59.

Doescher, William F., ''A Final Word,'' *D & B Reports,* March-April 1994, pp. 6–7.

Dun & Bradstreet: A Chronology of Progress, New York: Dun and Bradstreet, Inc., 1974.

Dun & Bradstreet: The Story of an Idea, New York: Dun and Bradstreet, Inc., 1966.

Gilpin, Kenneth N., ''New Dun and Bradstreet Split Planned If the I.R.S. Agrees,'' *New York Times,* December 19, 1997, p. D2.

Greenberg, Ilan, ''Dun & Bradstreet Finds Its Strength in Data Management,'' *San Jose Mercury News,* August 18, 1999.

King, Julia, ''D&B Software Users Cheer Sell-Off Plan,'' *Computerworld,* January 15, 1996, p. 4.

Moeller, Michael, and Jim Kerstetter, ''E-Commerce Grows Up with Aid of D&B, Actra,'' *PC Week,* March 10, 1997, pp. 1–2.

Pine, Michael, ''Dun's Do-Over: Two of Dun & Bradstreet's Three Parts Are Worth More Than the Whole,'' *Financial World,* July 8, 1996, pp. 44–45.

—Claire Badaracco and Douglas Sun
—updates: Terry Bain, Erin Brown

EILEEN FISHER

Eileen Fisher Inc.

2 Bridge Street
Irvington, New York 10533-1527
U.S.A.
Telephone: (914) 591-5700
Toll Free: (866) 512-5197
Fax: (914) 591-8824
Web site: http://www.eileenfisher.com

Private Company
Incorporated: 1986
Employees: 200
Sales: $143 million (2002 est.)
NAIC: 315232 Women's and Girls' Cut and Sew Blouse & Shirt Manufacturing; 315233 Women's and Girls' Cut and Sew Dress Manufacturing; 315234 Women's and Girls' Suit, Coat, Tailored Jacket, and Skirt Manufacturing; 448120 Women's Clothing Stores

Eileen Fisher Inc. makes women's business and casual clothing, specializing in loose-fitting garments that change only slightly from year to year. Suitable for most body shapes, the company's easy-to-wear, easy-to-wash styles have been described as ''sophisticated suburban.'' Comfortable knit pants and boxy jackets in neutral colors are considered easy to mix and match. Eileen Fisher's customer base consists of women aged 35 to 55.

Getting Started: 1984–92

Eileen Fisher grew up in a suburb of Chicago, creating outfits that her mother translated into patterns and sewed into clothes. She later recalled that when she found something she really liked, she would try to go back to buy the same thing, only to find that the store had replaced its merchandise with newer goods. Interviewed in 1994 by Julie Szabo for *Working Woman,* she said, ''I felt angry about all the time and energy spent fussing. It isn't fair to me that men can wear a suit for five years without feeling out of fashion, but women—it seems like every year shapes change, colors change, fabrics change. God, it makes me crazy! Especially when you've found something that works for you.''

Her attention to fashion waned, however, while attending the University of Illinois in the countercultural 1960s, a period in which college students all seemed to be wearing jeans. She received a degree in home economics and moved in 1973 to New York City, where she became an interior and graphics designer. Interviewed by Merri Rosenberg for the *New York Times,* she recalled, ''Just dressing in the morning was overwhelming. Shopping would turn my stomach. I felt a longing for my [parochial] school uniform, a tweed jacket and textured skirt—even though I hated it because my uniform didn't make me feel special.'' In retrospect, she described the tale of her company as ''a school uniform story. . . . What we do is keep what's good about the school uniform, but not that limited.''

Fisher's dormant interest in designing clothes was revived in 1984, when a friend asked her to take over a booth he had rented at the New York Fashion and Boutique Show. She bought a dozen yards of linen and got a friend to help pattern and sew four articles of clothing: a vest, boxy top, sleeveless blouse, and flowing crop pants. ''If I had really known what it meant to start a business, I probably would have been too scared to go ahead,'' she recalled in a 1994 *Forbes* article. She received $3,000 worth of orders and advice to try another type of fabric instead. Opting for a softer knit material, she returned several months later with a new dress, jacket, skirt, and trousers and won another $40,000 in trade.

Eileen Fisher was now in business, with two part-time helpers. With no capital other than loans from friends, she had to confine production to actual orders. ''I put the pieces together one day at a time, one step at a time,'' she later told Donna Fenn for *Executive Female.* ''I still find that's an important way to do things.'' Her company doubled its first $50,000 in annual revenue during the second year, then doubled its revenue again in the third. Then, in 1987, its textile supplier delivered a knit fabric lighter in weight than in the past. Pressed for time and money, Eileen Fisher felt she had to accept this material. Deliveries of the revamped designs were late, and orders were canceled. But the experience ultimately proved a blessing, because Fisher decided it proved that her product line had to be diversified. Soon the company was winning an entirely new customer by producing the same basic styles in dressier fabrics such as silk and wool jersey.

Company Perspectives:

Our Mission. Purpose: To inspire women to celebrate who they are. Product: To create products that simplify life and nurture the spirit. To design clothes that work together, guided by these principles: Simplicity. Beauty. Comfort. Ease. Function. Versatility. To invite every woman to express her own style. To produce only what we love. Practice: To work as a reflection of how our clothing works. Simply, and in connection. Individual Growth and Well-Being. Collaboration and Teamwork. Joyful Atmosphere. Social Consciousness.

Revenues reached $1.3 million in 1988. That year Eileen Fisher married David Zwiebel, a client who stocked her garments in his Ithaca, New York, boutique. He became vice-president and convinced her to open her own stores. By 1991 the company had more than $7 million in annual sales. The following year it owned three stores in Manhattan and one in Chicago and was also selling in numerous other retail stores in the United States. Eileen Fisher now was also receiving orders from department-store chains for the first time, among them Marshall Field, Saks, and Nordstrom. That year Fisher, who now had two children, moved her company from Manhattan to Irvington, New York, in suburban Westchester County.

Expanding Its Foothold: 1992–97

Eileen Fisher boosted its sales to about $25 million in 1993. The company continued to create simple, fluid separates in silk, linen, cotton, rayon, and various knits. Boxy tops, tunic tops, crop pants, long wrap skirts, and short skirts continued to be the staples, with styles varying only slightly from season to season. "We've found there's a customer out there who doesn't follow fashion in a traditional way," Eileen Fisher told *WWD's* Janet Ozzard. "She's a therapist, a teacher, an art director. She's busy, she doesn't have time to deal with fashion, yet she wants to look good and pulled together." For the first time her company had an advertising budget and marketing plans beyond the mailers it had been sending its customers.

The rapid expansion of Eileen Fisher's business resulted in its second setback. Because it had to double its production run with little margin for time, the company ordered $1 million worth of a wool tweed even before it made a garment. These items bombed in the marketplace, and as a result Eileen Fisher had to sell about 20 percent of its line at a loss. Chastened, Eileen Fisher's founder brought in key buyers early the next season to show them samples and get their opinions on what would sell. She also sent a staff member to the factory for preproduction sampling in order to reduce approval time on fabric quality. Sales passed $50 million in 1995, when about 750,000 units were shipped, about 40 percent from China and Hong Kong rather than domestic manufacturers. The company's number of stores rose to 12, and it opened boutiques in a few department stores, including Seibu in Tokyo. By the fall of 1996, it was operating 28 in-store shops.

Eileen Fisher moved its shipping and distribution center from Irvington to a larger, upgraded Secaucus, New Jersey, facility in 1996. The company also installed a CAD system to make style adjustments easier. Eileen Fisher's four designers were receiving regular input from the merchandising team with the purpose of assuring that customer favorites remained in the product line from season to season, even while new colors and fabrics were introduced. "The customer wants to feel it's the same," Fisher explained to Staci Bonner of *Apparel Industry*. "A wrap skirt might be offered in three new fabrics, but consistency has to be maintained. The fabric may drape differently or have a different weight, so you can't just use the same pattern—your specs have to be different." The CAD system made it easier for the company's designers to make subtle adjustments in a style when changing the fabric. It also made it easier to issue the petite line introduced in the fall of 1995 and the large-size line added in the fall of 1996.

Eileen Fisher Inc. was in many ways a model employer. When its founder, who promoted from within and knew everybody by name, decided to move to the suburbs, she selected a site convenient to public transportation. The company paid for the commute, and only a few staffers quit. Employees received 10 percent of the profits in the form of year-end cash bonuses. They were also provided with $4,000 ergonomic chairs. When a fabrics cutter developed carpal tunnel syndrome, the boss paid for physical therapy out of her own pocket because the firm's health-insurance plan did not cover it. Fisher also encouraged community involvement. Even some employees who continued to live in Manhattan joined the Irvington volunteer ambulance corps, interrupting work to go out on calls. The company donated 3 percent of its pretax profits to charitable organizations, many of them based in Westchester County. Fisher herself promoted the county as a desirable business location in television commercials. Eileen Fisher hired a manager of social accountability in 1998 to address human-rights issues in the factories of its suppliers, including the ten plants in south China. The company committed itself to meeting the guidelines developed by Social Accountability International for child labor, compensation, working hours, and health and safety. Fisher offered aid to her suppliers in meeting the SAI's certification standards.

Higher-Priced Goods: 1998–2003

During the fall of 1996 Eileen Fisher introduced a limited line of gift-oriented menswear in the form of a Merino wool polo shirt and a silk herringbone classic shirt. For the spring 1998 season it unveiled a higher-priced "bridge" line—the name given in the industry for goods priced just below designer level—featuring sweaters, sweater dresses, and jackets in doubleface wools from Italy, cashmeres, and silks, with a color emphasis on berry, burgundy, and purple. The items wholesaled from between $100 to $400 and were shipped to upper-end department stores and some of the company's own stores. At the same time Eileen Fisher introduced a more structured knitwear look for the standard line. "People are just beginning to understand the possibility of knitwear, the washability, the comfort of it all," she told Anne D'Innocenzio of *WWD*. "What's driving the trend is the relaxed dress code in the workplace. . . . You can pack five knitwear pieces in a suitcase, and you don't have to worry about them wrinkling."

In an article published in the *Toronto Star* on the first day of 2002, Fisher offered some style tips for the women her

Key Dates:

1984: Eileen Fisher designs and sells her first articles of clothing.
1992: The company now has four stores and is selling in many other retail stores.
1995: Annual sales have exceeded $50 million, and the company has 12 stores in operation.
1998: Sales volume reaches the $100 million mark as Eileen Fisher unveils a higher-priced line.
1999: All of Eileen Fisher's production is now in its higher-priced bridge line.
2002: The number of Eileen Fisher company-owned stores reaches 26.

company typically served. She said that for relaxing at-home wear she started with a pair of slim pants with stretch fibers, almost always in black. Then, she said, she usually added a turtleneck sweater on top. She recommended soft merino wool because it is not ''itchy'' and lets the skin breathe. ''When you're trying on clothes,'' she recommended, ''dance in the dressing room. Sit. Walk. Stretch. Make sure they move.'' She added that a sweater coat or duster, fleece pants, and the layered look successfully blend style and comfort and can conceal a few extra pounds gained during the year-end holidays. In this respect she recommended Lycra as ''our friend during the holidays because it's forgiving. It's not too tight, it adjusts to your shape and it requires little maintenance.'' She also recommended well-concealed elastic waistbands. However, she warned readers not to wear any of these styles too big. ''Baggy will make you look heavier,'' she said. ''A good option is a thick-gauge ribbed turtleneck because its clings enough.''

Eileen Fisher's expansion raised 1998 sales volume to about $100 million. Some $77 million came from sales to about 360 department stores and about 600 specialty stores. The retail division, which was operating 15 stores, accounted for the remainder. About a quarter of sales came from petite and large sizes. For the fall of 1999 Eileen Fisher moved its entire production into the higher-priced bridge line, which was wholesaling at between $38 to $188 as opposed to between $20 and $78 for the signature, or contemporary, collection. The new bridge collection featured textured sweaters, structured mandarin jackets, and Italian wool jackets, with about 40 percent in knitwear. As always, the clothes featured simple shapes such as kimono jackets, sleeveless shells, loose tunics, elastic-waist skirts, drawstring pants, and empire-waist sun dresses. Fabrics included Irish linen, silk crepe, and velvets.

Eileen Fisher's sales increased 11 percent in 2002, to $143 million. An advertising campaign for the spring of 2003 featured 15 women ranging in age from 24 to 72, including a choreographer and contemporary dancer; an obstetrician-gynecologist who had founded the African Women's Health Center; a charter school principal in New York City's borough of the Bronx; a civil rights lawyer; a producer of documentary films; a professor of architecture; and a professional boxing judge. The company now owned 26 Eileen Fisher stores and was planning to open two more in 2003: one in Manhattan's AOL Time Warner Center in Columbus Circle, and the other in Walnut Creek, California. Fisher owned more than 80 percent of the company in 2000.

Principal Competitors

AnnTaylor Inc.; Donna Karan International Inc.; Jones Apparel Group Inc.; The Leslie Fay Company, Inc.; The Talbots, Inc.

Further Reading

''Be Chic, Not Shabby, Around the House,'' *Toronto Star,* January 1, 2002, p. E2.
Bonner, Staci, ''Profit of Unconventional Wisdom,'' *Apparel Industry,* September 1996, pp. 48, 50–51.
Curan, Catherine, ''Eileen Fisher Grows Up,'' *Crain's New York Business,* March 8, 1999, pp. 3, 31.
D'Innocenzio, Anne, ''Eileen Fisher Sees Room for Growth,'' *WWD/Women's Wear Daily,* February 26, 1997, p. 17.
——, ''Eileen Fisher Shifting Entire Line to Bridge,'' *WWD/Women's Wear Daily,* February 10, 1999, p. 4.
——, ''Eileen Fisher 'Tests the Waters' for a Future IPO Move,'' *WWD/Women's Wear Daily,* September 18, 1996, p. 23.
Fenn, Donna, ''The Just Do It Strategy for Success,'' *Executive Female,* January-February 1996, pp. 41+.
Gubernick, Lisa, ''Out of Adversity, Enlightenment,'' *Forbes,* November 21, 1994, pp. 182–84.
Lockwood, Lisa, ''Eileen Fisher's 15 Real Women,'' *WWD/Women's Wear Daily,* February 7, 2003, p. 11.
Mikus, Kim, *Arlington Heights Daily Herald,* June 9, 2001, p. 1.
Ozzard, Janet, ''Fisher's Forward Roll,'' *WWD/Women's Wear Daily,* March 30, 1994, p. 9.
Rosenberg, Merri, ''A Designer Who Lives Like Her Clients,'' *New York Times,* September 10, 2000, Sec. 14 (Westchester), p. 8.
''SAI Helps Companies Be Responsible,'' *Work & Family Newsbrief,* June 2001, p. 6.
Szabo, Julia, ''The Cutting Edge of Non-Fashion,'' *Working Woman,* February 1995, pp. 38–39, 74.

—Robert Halasz

Elvis Presley Enterprises, Inc.

P.O. Box 16508
3737 Elvis Presley Boulevard
Memphis, Tennessee 38186-0508
U.S.A.
Telephone: (901) 332-3322
Toll Free: (800) 238-2000
Fax: (901) 345-8511
Web site: http://www.elvis.com

Private Company
Incorporated: 1981
Employees: 500
Sales: $50 million (2003 est.)
NAIC: 711410 Agents and Managers for Artists, Athletes, Entertainers, and Other Public Figures; 712110 Museums; 712120 Historical Sites

Elvis Presley Enterprises, Inc. (EPE) manages Graceland and other assets of the Elvis Presley Trust, which is owned by Elvis Presley's daughter, Lisa Marie. EPE owns the rights to Elvis's name and likeness, and some music publishing. RCA Records, now a unit of Bertelsmann Music Group (BMG), acquired rights to his recordings before 1973. There were 110 official licensees producing 700 Elvis-related items in 2002. Elvis Presley was the largest-selling recording artist of all time and continued to be BMG's biggest star 25 years after his death. From the beginning of his recording career in 1954 to 2002, Elvis Presley sold one billion records around the world; he had 131 gold and platinum albums in the United States; he also made more than 30 movies.

EPE also manages his estate's real estate holdings, centered around that most evocative address, Graceland. With 650,000 visitors a year, Graceland, Presley's Memphis mansion, is second only to the White House among the most visited residences in the United States. EPE does not release financial information, and estimates of annual revenues vary from $25 million to $250 million, with $50 million a likely number. With an economic impact of up to $400 million a year for Memphis, and charitable programs reminiscent of Presley's legendary generosity, EPE is one of that city's prized corporate citizens.

Origins

Elvis Presley Enterprises, Inc. was formed in 1981 to take care of business, the business of managing the estate of the most influential popular singer of all time. Elvis Presley died on August 16, 1977. He had been legendary for giving away such items as Cadillacs (as many as 14 in one day), and he left assets valued at $4.5 million to $10 million—a relatively small fortune, considering Elvis's stature.

Elvis's father, Vernon Presley, was made executor of his estate, but he too died two years later, in 1979. By this time, reported Britain's *Daily Mirror,* royalty revenues had fallen to $1 million a year, with little left over after the upkeep of Graceland. Worse, the estate owed the Internal Revenue Service $13 million in inheritance tax.

It was then left to Elvis's ex-wife, Priscilla Beaulieu Presley, to look after the estate, as stipulated in Vernon Presley's will. She had two co-executors, the National Bank of Commerce of Memphis, and Elvis Presley's former accountant, Joseph A. Hanks.

A for-profit company, Elvis Presley Enterprises, Inc. (EPE), was set up in 1981 to manage the assets of the estate. Jack Soden, a former stockbroker, was brought in as executive director. Priscilla Presley had been a client of his through Kansas City, Mo.-based Strategic Financial Services. According to the *New York Times,* Soden was able to impress upon Mrs. Presley the importance of guarding the integrity of Elvis's brand identity.

The first order of business was to take care of Graceland. The 23-room mansion was reportedly costing $500,000 a year to maintain. Both the City of Memphis and the Grand Ole Opry declined to operate it as a public attraction, so Soden was placed in charge of this iconic landscape at the tender age of 35. He modeled the operation after that of the Hearst Castle in San Simeon, California.

Graceland had been built in 1939 on the site of a farm owned by a wealthy Memphis family. The surrounding area was eventu-

Company Perspectives:

Elvis Presley Enterprises, Inc. (EPE) is the corporate entity that was created by the trust to conduct business and manage its assets. EPE is wholly owned by the Elvis Presley Trust. The Graceland operation in Memphis is a major source of revenue for EPE and is the home base. EPE also has an office in Los Angeles.

EPE's business extends far beyond the Graceland operation. It includes worldwide licensing of Elvis-related products and ventures, the development of Elvis-related music, film, video, television and stage productions, the ongoing development of EPE's Internet presence, the management of significant music publishing assets and more.

ally developed into a suburb called Whitehaven. Presley bought the mansion in 1957 for $102,500. He was only 22 years old at the time, and would live there throughout his adult life. Graceland was also a gift to his parents and grandparents, who lived there until he died. It was the opposite of the Mississippi shotgun shack Elvis's father had built by hand during the Depression.

Over the course of two decades of redecorating, it had come to be filled with stylistic excesses of the 1970s, including red and gold walls and elaborately carved oversized furniture. Some of the affected rooms were tastefully returned to their 1950s charm prior to Graceland's opening to the public.

Presley's estate spent $550,000 to ready the mansion for public tours. Graceland—at least the main floor—was opened to public tours on June 7, 1982. Some of Elvis Presley's relatives continued to live on upper levels, and he himself was buried on the grounds.

By the mid-1980s, Graceland was drawing 500,000 visitors a year. Attractions on the 32-acre complex included Elvis's tour bus, two private planes (the "Lisa Marie" Convair airliner and the "Hound Dog II" Lockheed Jet Star corporate aircraft), and eight gift shops.

Taking Care of Business in the 1980s

Two developments cemented EPE's role as custodian of Elvis's name and likeness. In 1983, Presley's controversial former manager, Colonel Tom Parker gave up all rights to Elvis's name and likeness for $2 million, an EPE spokesman told the *Chicago Sun-Times.* EPE lobbied for a law passing rights to deceased celebrities' images to their heirs, resulting in Tennessee's Personal Rights Protection Act of 1984.

Another area was also being tidied. In November 1983, the estate and a pair of Kansas City investors acquired an adjacent strip mall of souvenir shops for $2.5 million. A reported $1 million was then spent to upgrade its façade and landscaping; the site was relaunched as "Graceland Crossing" in 1987. It featured a retro diner as well as gift stores.

Debbie Johnson became general manager of EPE in 1987. Revenues that year were estimated at around $9 million. Graceland then employed 70 full-time and 300 seasonal workers.

Though Elvis's early generations of fans were aging, over half of Graceland visitors were younger than 35, reported the *Boston Globe.* There were more than 300 fan clubs around the world. Graceland was a kind of Mecca for rock stars of the day: Paul Simon wrote songs about it; Bruce Springsteen was said to have jumped the fence one night while Elvis was still in the building.

Presley had supported 50 local charities while he was alive. This legacy continued on May 14, 1985, as EPE formed the Elvis Presley Memorial Foundation, Inc., later called the Elvis Presley Charitable Foundation (EPCF).

Still Making History in the 1990s

Graceland was added to the National Register of Historic Places in November 1991. A widowed aunt, Delta Biggs, was the last of Elvis's relatives to live at Graceland; she died in 1993. In the early 1990s, Graceland increased its attention on special events such as family reunions and corporate meetings.

The U.S. Postal Service issued an Elvis stamp in January 1993. With 500 million printed, it had by far the largest circulation of any commemorative stamp until then.

Lisa Marie was scheduled to inherit the estate when she turned 25 in 1993. She chose to form a new trust, the Elvis Presley Trust, retaining the three executors. Priscilla Presley handed the trust over to Lisa Marie in 1998. In the 20 years she had been responsible for it, it had gone from being nearly insolvent to being worth an estimated $200 million.

Graceland had a record 750,000 visitors in 1995. It employed 500 people at the peak season surrounding the anniversary of Elvis Presley's death—Elvis Week. This culminated in a candlelight vigil on August 15 that drew thousands of fans.

A Virtual Graceland CD-ROM was released in the summer of 1996. By this time, EPE's corporate headquarters had moved to a two-story building next to the grounds. The Sincerely Elvis Museum showcased Presley's considerable collection of memorabilia.

A restaurant and nightclub, Elvis Presley's Memphis, opened on historic Beale Street in 1997. The menu featured Southern cooking, including Elvis's favorite dishes. Opened at a cost of $5.3 million, it was shut down in October 2003 after six years in business.

At the 20th anniversary of Elvis Presley's death in 1997, there were more than 100 companies manufacturing more than 500 licensed products, noted the *Boston Herald.* International Creative Management Inc. had been hired to explore licensing possibilities. In 1998, EPE produced a live show in conjunction with SEG Events, featuring members of the Taking Care of Business Band performing live along with a video projection of archived clips of Elvis himself.

The privately owned company did not release sales figures, and revenue estimates varied wildly, from $35 million to $500 million a year. Graceland's revenues alone were estimated at $20 million to $25 million based on an adult ticket price of $18.50 in 1998.

EPE acquired a nearby Wilson World hotel for $3.2 million and spent another $3 million to transform it into the Heartbreak

Key Dates:

1977: Elvis Presley dies at Graceland.
1981: Elvis Presley Enterprises (EPE) is formed.
1982: Graceland opens for public tours.
1983: Col. Tom Parker sells EPE rights to Presley's name and likeness.
1984: Personal Rights Protection Act is passed.
1985: Elvis Presley Memorial Foundation formed.
1987: Adjacent strip mall relaunched as Graceland Crossing.
1991: Graceland is added to National Register of Historic Places.
1993: U.S. Postal Service issues Elvis postal stamp.
1995: Graceland greets a record 750,000 visitors.
1999: Heartbreak Hotel opens next to Graceland.
2001: Presley Place transitional housing opens.
2002: A remix of "A Little Less Conversation" tops charts worldwide.

Hotel, which opened in 1999. Its modern, eclectic furnishings were much more luxurious than might be suggested by the famous song that gave the inn its name. Four of the suites were modeled after rooms at Graceland. Others included the Hollywood Suite, a nod to Elvis's 1950s film career, and the "Burning Love" honeymoon suite. There were 128 rooms in all.

Elvis's family had once lived in public housing, and Lisa Marie Presley displayed an interest in the concerns of homelessness. Through the EPCF, she funded Presley Place, a 12-unit transitional housing development in Memphis. It opened in 2001. Interestingly, its laundry building was styled after Graceland, reported the *Commercial Appeal.*

Thriving After 25 Years

Fifty employees were laid off at Graceland in the lull in tourism that followed the September 11, 2001 terrorist attacks on the United States. However, the business soon recovered. Soden told the *New York Times* there were no plans to take the company public. Lisa Marie Presley remained the sole shareholder.

A number of record-setting events accompanied the 25th anniversary of Elvis's death. The Disney film *Lilo & Stitch* incorporated a half-dozen Elvis songs in its soundtrack. A dance club remix of "A Little Less Conversation" topped the charts worldwide after first appearing in a Nike ad. Presley also had a chart-topping album, *30 No. 1 Hits,* that sold nine million copies around the world. Forty percent of Elvis's record sales were abroad; foreign visitors accounted for up to one-third of revenues at Graceland.

There were 110 official licensees producing 700 Elvis-related items in 2002. Merchandise included Graceland-inspired furniture produced by Vaughan-Bassett, and a special edition of the Monopoly board game. The web site was getting 45 million hits a month. Exposure from the 25th anniversary carried over into increased sales in 2003.

Elvis Presley remained one of the most enduring icons of American pop culture. According to EPE spokesperson Todd Morgan, "The way we say it at Graceland is, if music is the universal language, Elvis Presley spoke it fluently. And when he opened his mouth to sing, the whole world listened and understood and sang along."

Principal Divisions

Elvis Presley Charitable Foundation; Graceland; Heartbreak Hotel, LLC.

Principal Competitors

Apple Corps Limited; CMG Worldwide Inc.; Signature Network Inc.

Further Reading

Brettman, Allan, "Presley Estate and Memphis Find the King Is Worth More Dead Than Alive," *Chicago Sun-Times,* Fin. Sec., August 16, 1987, p. 1.

Carr, Coeli, "Keeper of the Blue Suede Shoes," *New York Times,* August 4, 2002.

Cnuschke, John E., "Elvis Is Still Big Business in Memphis," *Business Perspectives,* Summer 2002, pp. 2+.

Edwards, David, "The Elvis Dynasty; How Priscilla Keeps the King at No. 1 Two Decades After He Died," *Daily Mirror,* June 18, 2002, p. 18.

Feeny, Mark, "Guardians, Marketers of Elvis See Strong Financial Future in King's Legacy," *Boston Globe,* March 12, 2003.

Finnigan, David, "Brand Builders," *Brandweek,* August 13, 2001, p. 18.

Goff, Leslie, "What It's Like to Work On ... www.elvis-presley.com," *Computerworld,* August 14, 2000, p. 38.

Haight, Kathy, "King of Rock Is Still Big Business; Graceland Empire Is Flourishing," *The Record,* August 19, 1986, p. B9.

Honey, Jean N., "The Evolution of Elvis Presley Enterprises," *Business Perspectives,* Summer 2002, pp. 9+.

Laurence, Charles, "Elvis Lives," *Sunday Telegraph* (London), August 11, 2002, p. 16.

Lollar, Michael, "Elvis's Empire As Strong As Ever," *Commercial Appeal* (Memphis), August 10, 2003, p. A1.

——, "Graceland-Modeled Hotel Says Welcome to the King's World," *Commercial Appeal* (Memphis), August 7, 1999, p. A1.

——, "A Mission for Lisa Marie; Graceland-Funded Transitional Homes Are Where Her Heart Is," *Commercial Appeal* (Memphis), July 10, 2001, p. A1.

Margolis, Lynne, "The Once and Future King," *Christian Science Monitor,* August 9, 2002, p. 13.

Orwall, Bruce, "The King Lives: Presley Estate Signs ICM to Expand Commercial Potential," *Wall Street Journal,* May 12, 1997, p. B6.

"The Other Jubilee," *Economist,* May 25, 2002.

Perigard, Mark A., "Family Preserves Presley Image," *Boston Herald,* August 6, 1997, p. 40.

Romine, Linda, "Taking Care of Business: Elvis Presley Enterprises Turns Estate into One-Man, $250 Million Industry," *Memphis Business Journal,* June 12, 1998, p. 1A.

Semien, John, "All the King's Workers Assemble Elvis Week; Team Graceland Knows What Becomes Its Legend," *Commercial Appeal* (Memphis), August 11, 1996, p. 1B.

Snow, Donnie, "Graceland Changes Tune on Impersonators," *Commercial Appeal* (Memphis), November 24, 2002, p. A1.

—Frederick C. Ingram

Finnair Oyj

Tietotie 11
Helsinki-Vantaa Airport
P.O. Box 15
01053 Helsinki
Finland
Telephone: +358 9 818 81
Fax: +358 9 818 4401
Web site: http://www.finnair.com

State-Controlled Public Company
Incorporated: 1923 as Aero O/Y
Employees: 9,956
Sales: Fmk 1.64 billion ($1.78 billion) (2002)
Stock Exchanges: Helsinki London
Ticker Symbol: FIA
NAIC: 481111 Scheduled Passenger Air Transportation; 481112 Scheduled Freight Air Transportation; 481211 Nonscheduled Chartered Passenger Air Transportation; 481212 Nonscheduled Chartered Freight Air Transportation; 488190 Other Support Activities for Air Transportation; 561510 Travel Agencies; 561520 Tour Operators; 561599 All Other Travel Arrangement and Reservation Services

Based in Helsinki, Finnair Oyj is the national airline of Finland and the fifth oldest airline in the world. Operating passenger and air freight services throughout Finland and the Baltic region, Finnair also provides regular and seasonal service to Europe, North America, and Asia. The airline's route network for scheduled air traffic includes 16 domestic and 50 international destinations. Long-haul routes fly to cities such as New York, Miami, Tokyo, Osaka, Singapore, Bangkok, Hong Kong, Beijing, and Shanghai. Finnair services additional destinations through its membership in the global oneworld alliance, which includes American Airlines, British Airways, and several other airline partners. The charter operations of Finnair reach more than 60 destinations, mainly consisting of vacation spots in the Mediterranean, the Canary Islands, southeast Asia, and the Caribbean. During 2002, Finnair's fleet of 60 aircraft carried more than seven million passengers and cargo weighing in excess of 82,000 metric tons. Other operations of the corporation include technical, ground-handling, and catering services; travel agencies; and travel information and reservation services. Although its stock is publicly traded, Finnair is controlled by the government of Finland, which holds a 58.4 percent stake.

An Early Start

Finnair was established in Helsinki in 1923 as Aero O/Y. The company was the creation of a small circle of financiers, including Gustav Snellman, Fritiof Ahman, and Bruno Otto Lucander, formerly a Belgian vice-consul. Lucander became involved in aviation in 1918 as the general manager of Finland Spedition, a managerial group that oversaw the Finnish operations of an airline based in Tallinn, Estonia, known as Aeronaut.

At that time, the local aviation industry was dominated by German interests, including the aircraft manufacturer Junkers, a company experienced with aircraft designs that were capable of enduring the extreme physical demands of northern European weather. Aero purchased several seaplanes from Junkers, inaugurating airmail service between Helsinki and Tallinn on March 30, 1924, with a single-engine, four-passenger model F-13. In exchange for the aircraft and technical advisors, Junkers was given a 50 percent financial interest in Aero. The airline operated out of a seaplane ramp in the Katajanokka district of Helsinki. The company's aircraft were fitted with water floats in the summer and skis in the winter.

Aero began services to Stockholm on June 2, 1924, in conjunction with the airline Swedish ABA. With rail connections from Tallinn and Stockholm, travelers were afforded quick passage to Copenhagen, Konigsberg, and Berlin. While the route system remained small, Aero launched a campaign to promote air travel. In 1925 alone, it operated 833 sightseeing tours.

Also in 1925, Junkers amalgamated its Nord Europa Union and Trans Europa Union air transport subsidiaries into a single company consisting of 16 airlines in nine countries. This new company, Europa Union, was then combined with another German airline interest, Aero Lloyd, to form Deutsche Luft Hansa (later Deutsche Lufthansa).

Company Perspectives:

Finnair is committed in its business operations to profitable, value-creating growth. Operational efficiency and product quality are at the highest level among European airlines. This provides a good foundation to continue the good start that has been made on increasing traffic in strongly growing markets.

Aero remained outside this consortium, but received less support from Junkers, which gave priority to the new German air consortium. Aero turned to the Finnish government for financial assistance to acquire new aircraft, and in 1926 the airline took delivery of its first Junkers G 24, a three-engine, nine-passenger seaplane.

Aero was reluctant to switch to land-based aircraft. In a country with more than 60,000 lakes, the trouble and expense of building runways remained prohibitive as long as Aero continued to operate seaplanes. In addition, Aero could establish new destinations virtually anywhere there was a lake. With the 1929 death of Lucander, Aero appointed Gunnar Ståhle, who was trained as an engineer, general manager. Aero also ended its financial relationship with Junkers in 1929, when Finnish investors completed a buyout of the German company's interest. In 1930 Aero began to establish a closer relationship with other Scandinavian airlines. The company ran night airmail services in cooperation with Swedish, Danish, and later, Dutch airline companies. Junkers, however, remained the company's aircraft supplier, providing five 14-passenger Ju 52s during the decade.

With the opening of an airport at Turku in 1935 (Finland's first civil airport) and Stockholm in 1936, pressure mounted to establish a landing strip in Helsinki. Land operations began at Malmi airport later that year, although the airport remained officially closed until May 1938. Aero converted its aircraft to wheel landing gear and operated its last seaplane service on December 15, 1936.

In 1937 Aero took delivery of its first non-Junkers aircraft, two twin-engine DH 89A Dragon Rapides. These planes were operated on domestic routes to northern Finland. The following year, the Tallinn route was extended to Berlin, via Riga, Latvia, and Kaunas, Lithuania. In anticipation of increased air traffic for the 1940 Helsinki Olympic Games, Aero ordered two 26-passenger Condor aircraft from Focke-Wulf.

World War II

Because of a complex history of financial and cultural ties with Germany, Finland at this time was politically allied with the fascist Nazi-installed government in Germany. German Chancellor Adolf Hitler made one of his few international trips to Finland to lend support to the Finnish government, which by 1939 had fallen into acrimonious relations with the government of Hitler's archenemy, Joseph Stalin.

Tensions between Finland and the Soviet Union mounted. In October 1939 all civilian aviation was placed under Finnish military control. On November 30 hostilities broke out. Finnish troops held off Soviet advances for several months. Aero ceased operation from Helsinki but continued to operate to Stockholm from Vaasa and Turku, despite sporadic air attacks. Of the 3,900 passengers it ferried to Sweden, 1,500 were children who were being evacuated to safety. The Helsinki Olympics were canceled, and Aero never took delivery of the Condors it had ordered.

By the following spring the Soviets had achieved a hard-won victory in Finland. As part of its peace treaty with Stalin, Finland was forced to cede land in its eastern Karelian sector to the Soviet Union. Aero, however, was free to reestablish air services, and in April 1940 resumed flights to Tallinn and Stockholm. On the domestic front, the company began a ''Lapland Express'' to the northern city of Petsamo, in addition to more than a dozen other destinations.

As a result of the Molotov-Ribbentrop pact, in which Germany and the Soviet Union partitioned Poland and occupied Latvia, Lithuania, and Estonia, Finland was afforded an opportunity to reestablish stronger links with Germany. In 1941 Aero acquired two Douglas DC-2s from Lufthansa. The aircraft had been seized from Czechoslovakia when Germany invaded the country two years earlier.

On June 25 of the previous year, the war between Germany and Britain and France broke out. This war, which Finns call the ''Continuation War,'' forced the Finnish government to once again place civilian air resources under government control. Aero ceased its operations from Helsinki and Turku and relocated temporarily to the city of Pori. Even after the United States and the Soviet Union became involved in hostilities during the Continuation War, and in spite of fuel shortages, Aero continued to operate air services to Rovaniemi, Stockholm, and even Berlin.

For Finland, a nominal German ally, the Continuation War ended on September 19, 1944, after Soviet troops had again overrun Helsinki. Malmi airport was placed under Allied military control. Aero, however, was allowed to resume operations to Turku, Maarianhamina, and Stockholm from Hyvinkaa.

The Allies banned all commercial aviation from March to August 1945, when Aero was permitted to resume only domestic schedules. Gunnar Ståhle, however, was forced to resign by order of the Allied Control Commission, which cited the director's sympathies to Nazi Germany during the war. Ståhle was replaced by C.J. Ehrnrooth, who shortly afterward was succeeded by Uolevi Raade. The company also was reorganized during this period, and a board of directors was established.

Postwar Expansion

Finnish investment capital was scarce after the war, and Aero was forced to turn to the government to fund new equipment. In return for its backing, the Finnish government was allowed to acquire 70 percent of Aero's shares in 1946. The remainder were held by banks, other companies, and private citizens.

Through the Finnish Ministry of Supply, Aero purchased several surplus American C-47s and commissioned the Dutch aircraft company Fokker to convert them to their civilian equivalent, the DC-3. These aircraft entered service in May 1947,

Key Dates:

1923: Aero O/Y is established in Helsinki.
1924: Aero makes its first flight, carrying mail from Helsinki to Tallinn, Estonia; the initial fleet consists of seaplanes, some of which can be converted to snow landings via skis.
1935: The opening of Finland's first civil airport at Turku provides the first impetus for Aero's conversion to land-based aircraft.
1936: Aero operates its final seaplane service.
1939: Just prior to the inauguration of hostilities between Finland and the Soviet Union late in the year, all civilian aviation is placed under Finnish military control.
1946: The Finnish government acquires a 70 percent stake in Aero.
1947: Aero places several DC-3s into service, emblazoned with the title Finnish Air Lines and featuring Aero's first flight attendants.
1953: The company introduces the name Finnair in its advertising and on its aircraft.
1963: Aero acquires a 27 percent interest in another Finnish airline, Karair.
1968: Aero officially adopts Finnair Oy as its new corporate name.
1979: A subsidiary called Finnaviation is created to handle domestic charter operations and general aviation maintenance and repair services.
1989: Finnair shares are first listed on the Helsinki Stock Exchange.
1996: Karair and Finnaviation are merged into Finnair.
1999: Finnair joins the oneworld alliance, a global airline alliance led by American Airlines and British Airways.
2002: Estonia-based Aero Airlines, 49 percent owned by Finnair, begins flying between Helsinki and Tallinn.
2003: The company acquires an 85 percent stake in Nordic Airlink, a Swedish discount carrier.

emblazoned with the title Finnish Air Lines and featuring Aero's first flight attendants.

The following year, Aero resumed international services and by 1949 had retired all of its DC-2s, Rapides, and Junkers aircraft. In preparation for the Helsinki Olympic Games, which were rescheduled for 1952, Aero reconfigured its DC-3s and designed the new Helsinki Airport near Seutula. After transporting more than 100,000 passengers in 1952, Aero began to investigate a need for larger, more modern aircraft and decided on the Convair 340, a 44-passenger aircraft with a pressurized cabin, and the more advanced Convair 440 Metropolitan.

In 1953 the company introduced the name Finnair in its advertising materials and on its aircraft, partly out of concern that the name Aero had become outdated and generic. The company's official name, however, did not change. By 1957 Finnair operated one of the densest domestic route structures in Europe. The short-term nature of this structure led the company to plan for a new generation of aircraft to replace its Convairs and DC-3s on long-distance flights. Aero chose the 73-passenger Sud Aviation Caravelle twin jet, which entered the fleet in 1960.

The Caravelles were later deployed on winter charter flights to Majorca, the Canary Islands, and Rimini. At the time, International Air Traffic Association (IATA) regulations prevented Aero from directly operating charter and student flights. Instead, the company created a subsidiary, Polar Air, to handle this business. In 1963, however, Aero acquired a 27 percent interest in another Finnish airline, Karair, which took over Polar Air's operations.

In 1960, after 13 years of leadership under Leonard Grandell, an economist named Gunnar Korhonen was appointed managing director of Aero O/Y. Several changes occurred under Korhonen's leadership. In addition to introducing the Caravelles, Aero opened its Finnair Aviation College to train pilots who could be recruited out of the Finnish air force. The company's route structure continued to expand, adding flights to Leningrad, Athens, Dubrovnik, and Brussels.

Early in 1968 the company officially adopted Finnair Oy as its new corporate name and laid plans to expand into the hotel and travel agency businesses as part of an effort to achieve greater control over all aspects of the tourism industry. The company took delivery of its first 189-passenger DC-8 the following year, placing it into service on a new route to New York. Two years later, continuing its association with Douglas Aircraft, Finnair added somewhat smaller DC-9 aircraft to its fleet and opened new routes to Lisbon and East Berlin.

In 1975 Finnair began operating wide-body DC-10 aircraft, opening routes to Bangkok and numerous destinations in the Middle East. Four years later the airline created a subsidiary called Finnaviation (60 percent owned by Finnair) to handle domestic charter operations and general aviation maintenance and repair services. In 1982 Finnair revived the Aero Oy name for another subsidiary handling technical services and aircraft leasing and sales activities. Forced to close both its service to Baghdad, because of the war between Iran and Iraq, and its Amman route, because of low demand, Finnair opened routes to Seattle and Los Angeles in 1981 and to Tokyo via the North Pole in 1983.

Like many other Finnish businesses, Finnair benefited greatly from its government's unusual relationship with the former Soviet Union. Finland shared many parallel interests with the Soviet government. As an agent of the Finnish government, and because of its proximity, Finnair was afforded greater access to Eastern Bloc cities and airspace than Western airline companies, and it succeeded in using this as a corporate asset.

One result of this relationship was a growth in air freight, which compelled the company to invest heavily in a new air cargo facility at Helsinki Vantaa Airport in 1986. Political changes in the Soviet Union after 1986 opened Eastern Europe to more Western airlines and shifted Soviet business alliances to Germany, where greater investment capital was available. In addition, Finnair was faced with high cost structures, which led the company's chairman, Antti Potila, to undertake a series of cost-cutting moves and reduce the number of employees by 10 percent beginning in 1990.

Also in 1990 Karair and Finnaviation were reorganized as independent subsidiaries and made responsible for their own productivity. Finnair, however, managed to retain its position as the gateway airline to the Soviet Union and the Baltic states. This position was strengthened in 1989 after Finnair backed the opening of Strand Inter-Continental in Helsinki and the Savoy Hotel in Moscow. Also maintaining its close relationship with aircraft manufacturer McDonnell-Douglas, Finnair added advanced MD-11, Airbus A-300, and ATR planes to its fleet.

Finnair shares were first listed on the Helsinki Stock Exchange in May 1989. By this time the carrier was flying about five million passengers per year.

Finding a Place in the New World Order

In the early 1990s Finnair teamed with Scandinavian Airlines System (SAS), Austrian Airlines, and Swissair to pool financial resources for future aircraft purchases. The European Quality Alliance collapsed, however, as Chairman Antti Potila felt Finnair was losing its independence. Finnair then concentrated on an alliance with Lufthansa beginning in 1991.

After the Soviet Baltic states gained their independence from Moscow in 1990, Finnair stepped in to help establish an Estonian airline company. The airline soon had distinguished service and air safety records, and maintained one of the most modern air fleets in Europe. It existed under the majority control of the government of Finland, with the remaining share in the hands of banks and other institutional investment interests.

Finnair launched some cost-cutting measures in 1991. It pulled back flights from the Mediterranean in response to the Persian Gulf crisis, but found that Portugal increased in popularity as a tourist destination.

The onset of glasnost not only opened up new routes with Russia but also allowed more direct flights to the Far East. The airline, however, also had to deal with an economic recession during this time, accumulating losses of Fmk 576 million between 1991 and 1993. A recovery came in 1994, both within the Finnish economy and in regard to business traffic in particular. Still, the company continued to reduce its workforce as a means of remaining profitable.

Another part of the company's strategy in the mid-1990s was to reduce the number of aircraft types it operated. Finnair began replacing its DC-9s with used McDonnell Douglas MD-80 aircraft. A stock offering in January 1995 helped fund the purchases. This offering received much attention from European investment institutions and raised foreign ownership of the company from 5 to 16 percent. In another streamlining move, both Karair and Finnaviation were merged into Finnair during 1996.

In 1997 Finnair's board voted to replace the MD-80 airliners on its European routes with Airbus aircraft, the order to be worth Fmk 2 billion. Finnair still operated a dozen DC-9 aircraft and in June 1998 announced that it was retrofitting them with newly available noise-reduction hush kits. The company also leased several Boeing 757s.

Finnair completed expansion work on its cargo terminal late in 1997. The company carried approximately 80,000 tons of mail and cargo, providing about Fmk 900 million, or 13 percent, of the company's total turnover. The Far East accounted for 30 percent of its business.

Finnair terminated its partnership with Lufthansa after the German carrier teamed with SAS in 1997. Finnair then installed a second hub in Stockholm—the site of SAS's headquarters but not its operating center, which was Copenhagen. Finnair fed the hub via code shares with other Scandinavian carriers and declared itself Stockholm's official airline. It also teamed with Maersk Air to compete on one of SAS's most lucrative routes, Copenhagen–Stockholm, after SAS began flying from Frankfurt into Maersk's home base of Billund, Denmark. Meanwhile, competitors were slowly taking away from Finnair's domestic market share.

Early in 1998, Finnair and SAS rival British Airways announced a new alliance, which offered travelers the prospect of reduced fares. The cooperation was intended to help both carriers cope with competing alliances such as the Star Alliance created in 1997 of SAS, Lufthansa, United, Thai International, Varig, and Air Canada. Code-sharing agreements with Delta, Braathens, Swissair, Austrian Airlines, Sabena, and Maersk Air were in force as well. Flights outside of Europe remained a low priority for the carrier; but the company planned to triple its flights to Russia.

In 1998 Finnair celebrated its 75th anniversary. Demand increased in all sectors, with passenger numbers increasing 4.5 percent for the fiscal year ending in March 1999, reaching 7.4 million. The carrier was hurt that year, however, by increased operational costs, heightened competition, the Russian economic crisis of summer 1998, and a five-week strike by Finnish air traffic controllers in early 1999; these combined to lead to a sharp decline in profits. At the end of 1998 Potila retired as president and CEO and was replaced by industrialist Keijo Suila. In September of that year, Finnair agreed to join the oneworld alliance, a new global airline alliance whose other initial partners included American Airlines, British Airways, Canadian Airlines, Hong Kong's Cathay Pacific Airways, Australia's Qantas Airways, and Spain's Iberia. Finnair began officially participating in the alliance in September 1999; two other members joined in 2000: the Irish airline Aer Lingus and Linea Aerea Nacional de Chile (LanChile). Among the partners' cooperative ventures were agreements to link their frequent-flier programs and give each other access to their airport lounge facilities. as well as some code-sharing arrangements. In examples of the latter, both initiated in June 2000, Finnair began to code-share with Iberia on flights between Finland and Spain and with Qantas on flights between Finland and Australia. For Finnair, oneworld provided it with new international partners in the wake of Lufthansa's teaming up with SAS as well as Maersk joining forces with SAS in the autumn of 1998.

The Turbulent Times of the Early 2000s

To cut operating costs Finnair shed a number of noncore assets during 1999. In April 1999 the company sold its remaining 40 percent interest in Nordic Hotel Oy to Scandic Hotels. It sold tour operator Finntours to Thomson Travel Group in November and its 60 percent stake in Finnair Gateway Restaurants to GourmetNova in December. To further improve operational efficiency, Finnair announced a major restructuring in late 2000 whereby a centralized hierarchy would be replaced by a decentralized structure encompassing six mostly autonomous operating divisions: scheduled passenger traffic, leisure traffic, cargo, aviation services, travel services, and support services. At the same time, Finnair altered its flight network to place additional emphasis on routes to and from Asia, its highest growth region. Unprofitable routes to such destinations as Toronto and San Francisco were dropped in favor of increasing the frequency of flights to Beijing, Bangkok, and Singapore and adding the new destination of Hong Kong. Finnair also joined with local partners in setting up a new affiliated carrier based in Estonia to offer regional service within Scandinavia and the Baltic region. Finnair took a 49 percent stake in the new airline, which was given the historically fitting name Aero Airlines. Appropriately enough, Aero's first flight, which took place on March 31, 2002, was on the Helsinki–Tallinn route—the same route flown on the first flight of the original Aero.

The events of September 11, 2001, coupled with the global economic downturn, crippled airlines throughout the world, with some forced into bankruptcy or needing government subsidies to stay afloat. Finnair managed—barely—to stay in the black during 2001 thanks to an aggressive program to cut costs by Fmk 115 million. Despite the difficult times, the airline continued to overhaul its fleet, one-third of which by the end of 2002 consisted of new Airbus models—the A319, the A320, and the A321. Finnair and other carriers were deeply affected by a double blow in early 2003: the launching of the Iraq war by the United States and the sudden acute respiratory syndrome (SARS) epidemic; the latter particularly affected Finnair's growing Asian traffic given that the epidemic was centered in that region. Also in 2003 Finnair acquired an 85 percent stake in Nordic Airlink, a Swedish discount airline. In September, with the SARS crisis over, Finnair added Shanghai to its growing list of Asian destinations.

Principal Subsidiaries

Kiinteistö Oy Aerolan A-talot; Kiinteistö Oy Aerolan B-talot; Amadeus Finland Oy (95%); Matkatoimisto Oy Area; Area Baltica Reisiburoo AS (Estonia); A/S Estravel Ltd. (Estonia; 72%); Oy Aurinkomatkat—Suntours Ltd. Ab (99.1%); Finnair Travel Services Oy; Finnair Catering Oy; Finnair Facilities Management Oy; SkyCellar Oy; Finnair Cargo Oy; Aero Airlines (Estonia; 49%); Finncatering Oy; Norvista Travel Ltd. (Canada); Norvista Ltd. (U.S.A.); Karair Ab (Sweden); Mikkelin Matkatoimisto Oy (51%); Norvista B.V. (Netherlands); Suomen Matkatoimisto Oy; Nordic Airlink (Sweden; 85%).

Principal Operating Units

Scheduled Passenger Traffic; Leisure Traffic; Cargo; Aviation Services; Travel Services; Support Services.

Principal Competitors

SAS AB; Deutsche Lufthansa AG; KLM Royal Dutch Airlines.

Further Reading

The Art of Flying Since 1923, Finland: Finnair Oy, 1983.

Burt, Tim, "Finnair: Trying to Keep Up with the Neighbours," *Financial Times,* July 9, 1998, p. 7.

Elliot, Tom, "In Pole Position," *Airfinance Journal,* April 1995, pp. 36–38.

"The European Skies," *New York Times,* June 7, 1992.

Feldman, Joan M., "The Nordic Airline War," *Air Transport World,* November, 1997, pp. 85–89.

Finnair 1923–1986: Blue-White Wings—Over Sixty Years of Operation, Finland: Finnair Oy, November 26, 1986.

Haapavaara, Heikki, *Time Flies: Finnair 75,* Helsinki: Finnair, 1999.

"Helsinki to Miami," *Aviation Week and Space Technology,* June 29, 1992.

Hill, Leonard, "Flying Finns," *Air Transport World,* June 1998, pp. 63–65.

——, "Nordic Fast-Tracker," *Air Transport World,* September 2001, pp. 65, 69–70.

Lefer, Henry, "Small Is Beautiful," *Air Transport World,* December 1991, pp. 30–35.

Malkin, Richard, "Air Cargo: Looking for a Niche in the World," *Distribution,* March 1994, p. 62.

Marray, Michael, "From Start to Finnish," *Airfinance Journal,* June 2001, p. 34.

O'Dwyer, Gerard, "Finnish Privatisation Train Stays on Course," *European,* May 19, 1995, p. 17.

Shifrin, Carole A., "Finnair's MD-80 Plan Reflects Stronger Traffic, Finances," *Aviation Week and Space Technology,* December 12–29, 1994, p. 39.

"Small Is Beautiful," *Air Transport World,* December 1991.

—John Simley
—updates: Frederick C. Ingram, David E. Salamie

Fisher Controls International, LLC

205 S. Center Street
Marshalltown, Iowa 50158
U.S.A.
Telephone: (641) 754-3011
Fax: (641) 754-3081
Web site: http://www.fisher.com

Wholly Owned Subsidiary of Emerson Electric Company
Incorporated: 1888 as Fisher Governor Company
Employees: 2,000
Sales: $3.4 billion (2002)
NAIC: 332912 Fluid Power Valve and Hose Fitting Manufacturing (pt); 334513 Instruments and Related Product Manufacturing for Measuring, Displaying, and Controlling Industrial Process Variables

A global designer, manufacturer, and supplier of control valves and regulators, Fisher Controls International, LLC is one of the largest and oldest process control companies. Fisher's Type 1 pump governor was invented by the founder in 1880 and remains—virtually unchanged—part of the company's product line today. In addition to valves and regulators, Fisher also designed and implemented final control systems. Fisher's products are used in a number of industries, including chemical, refining, power, and pulp and paper. Fisher is a subsidiary of Emerson Process Management, an operating division of Emerson Electric Company.

Entrepreneurial Beginnings in the Late 1800s

Those unfamiliar with the work of control valves and regulators might dismiss them as simple hardware store items, but they are more vital than their modest names imply. They help to maintain steady pressure in the pipes that carry gases, fluids, or steam to keep those pipes from exploding.

Company founder William Fisher was first inspired to create a control device after he and others spent hours trying to keep a city from being engulfed in flames. Fisher had moved to the United States from England at the age of 14. Upon reaching the United States, his family settled in Iowa. Working in a small engine shop, Fisher became well-versed in the major power source of the era: steam. After he helped to install new water facilities in two other Iowa cities, Fisher was invited to apply his knowledge of water and steam to the waterworks system in a third city.

As a fire raged all night in Marshalltown, Iowa, Fisher throttled the city's steam-driven pumps by hand in order to keep the pressure in the city's mains steady. It seemed to him that a device could be made that would control the pumps and maintain them at a constant pressure. After months of experiments, the young man designed the Fisher Type 1 constant pressure pump governor.

Joining with a town machinist, Fisher pooled $600 to buy a manufacturing building. The pumps were in production in 1880, although Fisher did not receive a patent for another four years. To keep the company afloat, Fisher also repaired machines and sold bicycles and Kodak cameras. In fact, Fisher was an exclusive sales representative for Eastman Kodak cameras and supplies in 1898.

The company scraped together $30,000 by 1888 and was incorporated as the Fisher Governor Company. Fisher spread the gospel of his new invention through his membership in the power plant engineering association and, soon enough, word of mouth kicked in. Company sales reached $44,000 by 1905. Only two years later, Fisher's invention was laboring away in power plants throughout the United States, Canada, and Great Britain.

As demand for the product increased, so did the need for variations of the pump. A vertical-type reducing valve became the first of a series of controls that were added to the Type 1. Not long afterward, lever valves, exhaust relief valves, back pressure valves, and steam trap valves were added.

Increasing Sales in the Early 1900s

Business boomed, but the company lost its founder in 1905. His widow, Martha, took Fisher's place as president, while their son Jasper traveled the country as a cigar salesman. Jasper Fisher came home and took the company's reins in 1912, when annual sales were about $60,000. At that time the company had nine machinists and assemblers and five office employees.

Company Perspectives:

Fisher Controls International LLC is now a member of the Emerson Process Management family of companies which is a division of Emerson. Becoming part of this new corporation is the latest in the long history of growth and change for the control valve manufacturing company founded as the Fisher Governor Company in 1880.

Knowledgeable about sales, Jasper Fisher knew that quality products were not always enough to be successful. A sales agency was established in 1913, and Fisher traveled the continent himself as the company launched its first nationwide advertising campaign. As World War I unfolded, demand for Fisher's products in various industries rose dramatically, particularly in the petroleum industry. The company soon employed 60 workers. By the end of World War I, Fisher was on more solid financial ground. It also had developed new technologies and products.

Fisher enjoyed substantial profits from the growth in the steel, petroleum, power, and gas industries in the early 1920s. The company's automated valves were indispensable in each of these burgeoning industries, so Fisher grew with them. This was fortunate, because the Great Depression of the early 1930s devastated the nation's economy. Half of the factories in the United States were forced to close their doors during the Great Depression, but Fisher managed to stay open. Sales were limp and production was minimal, but the plants stayed alive. As soon as business began to grow stronger in the late 1930s, Fisher updated machinery and added new products to its line. The company even finished an addition to its manufacturing plant in 1940.

During this time, the company lost another helmsman. Jasper Fisher died in 1938. Like his father, he was well-loved by employees and colleagues. Jasper's son, J.W. ''Bill'' Fisher, joined the company's finance department in 1940. Jasper's widow, Edna, became president and her son Bill became vice-president in 1944. Although this succession seemed a continuance of Fisher tradition, the company had in fact shifted its management style. A strong board now led Fisher. The two Fishers were elected to their positions.

Unprecedented Growth in the 1940s

Although the company had enjoyed growth spurts earlier in its history, nothing in its past matched the surge of growth experienced by the company during World War II. The demand for the company's automatic control valve equipment was substantial, as valves were used in the production of ships, planes, tanks, and guns. Fisher also supplied valves that were used in the manufacturing of life-saving drugs, as well as valves used in oil refineries and gas production, and chemical and synthetic rubber manufacturing.

Despite a shortage of materials and men, the company built new plants and machines and operated 24 hours a day to meet demand. The shortage of manpower put a premium on automation, and any ideas that reduced labor were lauded. In light of its wartime achievements, the company received an Army-Navy ''E'' flag in 1943, given in recognition of ''superior production achievements of vital war materials.''

The technological advances spawned by World War II continued after the conclusion of the conflict. Although Fisher was faced with labor problems, a new manufacturing addition was installed in 1948 to help meet rising sales. Edna Fisher retired in May 1954 and was succeeded by her son, Bill. At this point, Fisher was alert to expanding markets in Europe, but international growth was set back by currency exchanges and export fees.

Global Expansion and Innovation in the 1950s and 1960s

Fisher addressed this dilemma by entering into a licensing agreement with Elliott Automation of the United Kingdom in 1950. Under the terms of the agreement, the two companies would jointly manufacture Fisher valves and controllers. In 1955 Fisher opened a factory in Ontario, Canada, to meet ''the demands of that country's expanding oil and natural gas'' industries.

By the late 1950s, Fisher's expansion was swift. The company moved into a new office building designed to house its research, engineering, sales, and administrative departments, which had been cramped because of the growing need for factory space. In 1957 Fisher purchased the Pennsylvania-based Continental Equipment Company. Continental was known for its superior butterfly control valves, which were used by process industries. In the late 1950s process industries, like so many other industries, were being revolutionized by electronics. Fisher, which was determined to flow with the changes, established electronic design and assembly departments. Assemblers acquired a new technical language and tool skills in these departments, and soon they were generating new products such as electronic level controllers and transducers.

This emphasis on new products and technologies remained throughout the 1960s. Overseas growth continued at the same time. Fisher entered into a new licensing agreement to manufacture in Japan in 1960. This allowed the company to use manufacturing facilities in Japan to produce all Fisher products sold in that market. The following year, Fisher opened a temporary factory in Monterrey, Mexico, until a permanent plant was opened near Mexico City in 1965. In order to be closer to its LP-gas customers, the gas regulator division of Fisher moved to Texas that same year. Manufacturing capacity continued to explode in 1967, when Fisher enlarged two more plants and opened a new eight-acre facility in Marshalltown, birthplace of the founder's inspiration. A joint venture named Nippon-Fisher was launched in 1969, whereby Fisher manufactured and sold its products in Japan and the Far East.

Fisher also merged with Monsanto Company, the country's fourth largest chemical company. Monsanto purchased 67 percent of Fisher in 1969; the remaining 33 percent was purchased in 1983. At that time, Monsanto was determined to diversify. Upon joining the company, Fisher began manufacturing a line of electronic instrumentation that Monsanto had developed. Fisher's name, to reflect its own diversification, was changed to Fisher Controls Company. Bill Fisher resigned as president in 1969, but stayed on as chairman of the board until 1974. Tom Shive became Fisher's president in 1969.

Key Dates:

1880: William Fisher invents the Fisher Type 1 constant pressure pump governor and founds the company.
1884: Fisher obtains a patent for the Fisher Type 1.
1888: The company incorporates as Fisher Governor Company.
1905: Founder Fisher dies.
1912: Jasper Fisher, the founder's son, assumes control of the company.
1938: Jasper Fisher dies.
1940: Edna, Jasper Fisher's widow, becomes president.
1955: The company opens a manufacturing plant in Ontario, Canada.
1957: Fisher acquires Continental Equipment Company of Pennsylvania.
1969: Fisher merges with Monsanto Company and changes its name to Fisher Controls Company.
1975: Fisher acquires Marshall Die Casting.
1979: Fisher and segments of the General Electric Company of the United Kingdom merge to form Fisher Controls Corporation.
1981: The company changes its name to Fisher Controls International.
1985: Fisher buys Posi-Seal International.
1992: Monsanto sells Fisher to Emerson Electric Company for $1.4 billion.
1993: Fisher and Rosemount Incorporated merge to form Fisher-Rosemount.
2001: Fisher-Rosemount is renamed Emerson Process Management.

Diversification and Growth Through Mergers: 1970s–90s

Electronic instrumentation was Fisher's theme for the 1970s. The line of analog instrumentation developed by Monsanto for process control was the progenitor of the PROVOX distributed control system, which Fisher introduced in 1980. The company invested heavily in product development and the buildings needed to make them. Fisher opened its first European manufacturing facility in 1970, in Cornwall, England. The plant made electronic instrumentation. Two years later, the company's engineering team moved to a new facility large enough to accommodate its expanding needs. Repair facilities were added to the company's services in the early 1970s and proved popular enough to be quickly expanded, with representatives in Louisiana, Texas, New Jersey, Ohio, and Alberta, Canada. These facilities repaired control valves and instruments.

Marshall Die Casting joined Fisher in 1975, after supplying aluminum and zinc die castings to the company for more than 30 years. A new line of rotary-shaft valves was unveiled in the 1970s. The product line was immediately successful, and a new plant was opened in 1976 just to manufacture this popular line. Fisher Brazil, a facility that produced both control valve and instrumentation products for South American countries, opened its doors in 1977. Two years later, portions of the General Electric Company of the United Kingdom united with Fisher to form Fisher Controls Corporation of Delaware, a manufacturing, sales, and service system poised to install Fisher's products worldwide.

In 1981 Fisher's sales reached $650 million. North and South American customers made up 60 percent of those sales. New service centers were opened in the United Kingdom, followed by a new valve manufacturing plant in Medway, England. Fisher also acquired Posi-Seal in 1985.

Fisher's place within Monsanto began to chafe both companies, however. Monsanto, which had decided to focus its operations on agricultural products, pharmaceuticals, chemicals, and food ingredients, sold Fisher to Emerson Electric Company in 1992 for $1.28 billion. Fisher experienced an increase in its 1991 operating income when Monsanto decided to sell it, but sales for that year were $928 million. The wedding to Emerson seemed to be a sensible one. Emerson produced electrical, electronic, and other products for consumer, commercial, and industrial markets. Its sales for 1991 were $7.4 billion. The purchase made Emerson the largest provider of process control equipment. Fisher also entered into a joint venture with Tianjin Fourth Automation Instrumentation Factory in China in 1992. The arrangement was made to produce control valves for Asian markets.

Emerson orchestrated the blending of Fisher's strengths with those of Rosemount Incorporated, a much younger company with innovative products used in the aeronautics and space industries, as well as control and instrumentation product lines and temperature and pressure transmitters. The Fisher-Rosemount family of companies dominated the global market of process management in the early 1990s. It offered the widest line of process automation products, including process management systems, control valves, regulators, transmitters, and analyzers. The combined companies had operations—including sales, service, and manufacturing—in more than 80 countries and served a range of process industries. Few industries were not touched by Fisher: Fisher-Rosemount supplied companies in diverse areas such as chemical processing, plastics, glass, refining, oil and gas production, natural gas distribution, power, pulp and paper, food and beverages, pharmaceuticals, and metals and mining.

Adapting to New Management and Economic Shifts: 1990s–2000s

With the acquisition of Fisher, Emerson created a new division—Emerson Process Management. In the early 1990s Emerson Process Management's family of companies included eight separate operating divisions: Fisher-Rosemount Systems, Fisher-Gulde Valves, Fisher Regulators, Xomox, Rosemount Measurement, Rosemount Analytical, Micro Motion, and Brooks Instruments. Sales for the division as a whole in 1993 reached $2.3 billion.

The sale of Fisher to Emerson increased Fisher's potential for growth, but it also meant Fisher had to adhere to the business strategies of new management. Emerson planned to increase profits and become more competitive in a global marketplace, and this meant a bit of housecleaning for Fisher, namely cutting costs by moving production to cheaper markets, modernizing and refurbishing some existing plants, and streamlining operations to improve efficiency.

Unfortunately for some of Fisher's workers, Fisher's new plans did not include them. At the end of 1993 Fisher announced it would close down Marshalltown's Center Street plant and move those operations to plants in Texas, Mexico, and Asia, where labor costs were cheaper. Fisher reported that its employees in Marshalltown earned above-average wages for the industry—an average of $26.50 hourly in wages and benefits. Employees in Mexico, in contrast, would earn about $3 per hour. The Center Street plant was one of two Marshalltown plants run by Fisher, and the closure meant more than 300 employees would be laid off.

Fisher continued to add to its now extensive product line by designing and constructing innovative new products and technologies. The FIELDVUE DVC was a digitally based valve controller first introduced in 1993. In 1994 the company created the Y693 gas tank regulator and Design SC, a cryogenic valve. Two years later Fisher introduced PlantWeb digital plant architecture, which tied together open communication standards, software, and new technologies to automate and ensure smooth plant operations. Many of the company's products and technologies in the late 1990s and early 2000s were components of PlantWeb and offered a total system solution to clients.

Also in 1996 Fisher made a contribution to the energy sector with the introduction of the Snug Meter, a natural gas meter designed for multi-dwelling buildings. Marking Fisher's first product in the meter industry, the Snug Meter was significantly more compact than existing models. Fisher reported that it designed the product at the behest of gas utility companies, which felt that compact and portable equipment was mandatory to remain competitive in the energy market.

Acquisitions also helped Fisher grow and diversify, and in 1994 Fisher purchased Con-Tek, Inc., a producer of steam conditioning equipment, and Francel, a manufacturer of natural gas pressure reducing regulators in France. The following year Fisher acquired H.D. Baumann Associates, a control valve producer.

After 80 years in operation, the Center Street plant was officially closed in 1997, the same year Fisher shut down the Woodstock plant. The Woodstock plant, located in Woodstock, Ontario, Canada, had been in operation for 42 years. At the same time North American plants were being closed, foreign expansion continued. Fisher announced plans to construct new plants in Hungary and Brazil, and in 1999 a new plant in Malaysia began operation. Also in 1999 Fisher shut down the Medway plant in the United Kingdom and moved its operations to Cernay, France.

In the late 1990s Fisher made a breakthrough in the Japanese market with the introduction of the DeltaV scalable process control system, a comprehensive package of hardware, software, and peripherals. The system was designed to help manufacturers design and operate process control applications. Fisher sold more than 1,000 systems from late 1997, when DeltaV was initially introduced, to March 1999. Few had been sold in Japan, where Fisher's market share was low, but in 1999 the company launched a Japanese language version to attract more customers. Fisher hoped to sell about 100 units in the first year with its sights on grabbing 10 percent of the Japanese process control systems business by the mid-2000s. One of the Japanese companies to buy the system was Coca-Cola Holdings West Japan Co., Ltd., which planned to use the system in a bottling plant.

Fisher continued its international growth in the early 2000s. It opened a cutting-edge valve performance diagnostics laboratory at its Cernay, France, plant in 2002, and in 2003 the operation of a PlantWeb dynamic performance laboratory in Marshalltown began. The Marshalltown lab was Fisher's fifth PlantWeb lab and was designed for dynamic flow testing of control valve performance.

Despite expansion, the sagging economy affected Fisher's operations, and in the spring of 2003 the company announced plans to lay off 75 employees at the Marshalltown plant. Several months later, in July, Fisher said it would close the Posi-Seal plant in North Stonington, Connecticut, by early 2004. The shutdown would result in the layoff of 130 workers.

Fisher had come a long way since its beginnings as a valve and regulator manufacturer in the late 1800s. The company had evolved into a technological innovator and offered total management solutions that combined digital communications, open systems, and intelligent field devices. Fisher planned to remain a leader in the process control industry and to continue to increase its presence worldwide.

Principal Subsidiaries

Fisher-Rosemount Japan Co., Ltd.

Principal Competitors

Honeywell International Inc.; Eaton Corporation; Tyco International Ltd.; American Standard Companies Inc.

Further Reading

"Advanced Control Systems," *Pulp & Paper*, February 1992, p. 101.

" 'Cascaded' Pilot Regulators Help Reduce LPG Loss in Hot Weather," *Oil and Gas Journal,* August 8, 1994, p. 63.

"Emerson to Buy Monsanto Subsidiary," *Journal of Commerce and Commercial,* August 5, 1992, p. 7A.

Feder, Barnaby, "Emerson to Buy Fisher for Nearly $1.28 Billion," *New York Times,* August 5, 1992, p. D3.

"Fisher Controls Flow with Software," *Design News,* July 19, 1993, p. 34.

"Fisher Controls International," *Oil and Gas Journal,* February 10, 1992, p. 67.

"Fisher Controls International Inc.," *Prepared Foods,* August 1992, p. 146.

"Fisher Controls International, Inc.," *Pulp & Paper,* September 1992, p. 195.

Milligan, Valerie, "Cutbacks at Fisher Controls Not Pessimistic, Says Leader," *Times Republican,* February 16, 1994.

"Monsanto Surprises with Fisher Sell-Off," *ECN-European Chemical News,* August 10, 1992, p. 8.

Mullin, Rick, "Computers and Process Control," *Chemical Week,* November 25, 1992, p. 30.

Share, Jeff, "Fisher Controls Introduces Snug Meter to Gas Industry," *Pipeline & Gas Journal,* April 1, 1996, p. 47.

Storck, William, "Monsanto to Sell Fisher Controls Subsidiary," *Chemical & Engineering News,* August 10, 1992, p. 5.

—Carol I. Keeley
—update: Mariko Fujinaka

Fred Weber, Inc.

2320 Creve Coeur Mill Road
Maryland Heights, Missouri 63043
U.S.A.
Telephone: (314) 344-0070
Fax: (314) 344-0970
Web site: http://www.fredweberinc.com

Private Company
Incorporated: 1972
Employees: 564
Sales: $218 million (2002 est.)
NAIC: 324121 Asphalt Paving Mixture and Block Manufacturing

Based in the St. Louis suburb of Maryland Heights, Missouri, Fred Weber, Inc. is an employee-owned company that through ten subsidiaries is involved in three service areas. Fred Weber's construction services, acting as a general contractor, offers a full range of roadwork, including heavy grading, concrete and asphalt paving, sewers, and all aspects of bridge building. Fred Weber also makes its own material through its material services division, which owns nine quarries and provides materials to most of the builders and contractors in the St. Louis metropolitan area. In addition, Fred Weber takes advantage of a depleted quarry to operate a sanitary landfill. The natural gases that are a byproduct of the landfill are then used to heat a concrete ready mix plant boiler, an asphalt plant burner, a number of greenhouses, as well as a local high school. Fred Weber is also looking into ways to use methane gas from the landfill to run mini-turbines and produce electricity for the local market. Finally, Fred Weber offers transportation services, operating as many as 350 trucks each day, hauling materials from company quarries to production facilities, transporting construction materials from third parties to production facilities, and providing internal hauling of cement and asphalt from company plants. In addition, the company operates a helicopter charter service through subsidiary Adeletom Aviation L.L.C.

Company Formally Launched in 1928

The man behind the eponymous company was Fred Weber, Sr., born in St. Louis in 1899, known for years by his employees as ''Old Man Weber.'' When he was just a teenager he went to work for his father after World War I, delivering ice and coal with a horse-drawn wagon. He soon revealed his ambitious nature, renting a truck in order to deliver even greater volumes. In 1920 he was able to buy the vehicle, a five-ton dumpster. Because the truck was better suited for hauling construction materials, Weber left the ice and coal business. Operating out of his home in South St. Louis, he began transporting materials from area quarries to construction sites. He was successful enough by 1926 to buy more trucks and hire his first employees: foreman Fritz Saur, and drivers Johnny Rathouse and Red O'Connell. At this stage, Weber was still driving a truck himself. A key moment in his business career came in 1928 when he won his first road contract, which involved the excavation and pipe work for a stretch of road in St. Louis County. According to the company, this contract marked the start of Fred Weber, Inc.

Because of the excavation needs of this first road contract, Fred Weber bought its first heavy equipment: a gas shovel and a ''Skimmer Scoop'' (which featured a large bucket with a hinged bottom on a boom that allowed its operator to move and dump a load of dirt and rock dug up by the gas shovel). Despite the advent of the Great Depression in the 1930s, Fred Weber secured enough business to warrant the purchase of a second shovel. In addition to hauling and subgrading, the company, starting in 1930, also began to build brick sewers. Another important source of revenues during these lean years was the excavation work Fred Weber did on several major building sites in St. Louis. The business prospered enough that the owner was able to move the company's headquarters out of his own home, in 1939 paying $4,500 for an old ice warehouse. This site would serve as Fred Weber's base of operations for the next 50 years. It was also in 1939 that a second generation became involved in the business, as Fred ''Freddie'' Raymond Weber joined his father. His first taste of the work came when he was 14 and hired to fetch water for the construction workers.

Because of restrictions caused by World War II, Fred Weber had to find other sources of income to make up for the lack of

Company Perspectives:

The "We" in Weber truly makes the difference.

road construction during the early 1940s. Thus, in 1941 the company established a rock crushing business, which helped to do its part in the war effort. The company now supplied materials needed for area military bases, such as Fort Leonard, for roads and other construction needs. One achievement of note during this period in the company's road construction efforts was the work done by Fred Weber on the "Devil's Elbow" section of U.S. Route 66. Crews completed the largest vertical rock cut in Missouri, some 118 feet, accounting for nearly 1.2 million cubic yards of material.

Postwar Boom Leading to Growth

In 1945, as the war was winding down, Fred Weber achieved another milestone, landing its first major concrete job to enclose Cold Water Creek at St. Louis Lambert Airport, the erstwhile balloon launch site, today known as Lambert-St. Louis International Airport. A year later, when Lambert began an expansion program, Fred Weber was awarded its first airport contract to build a new runway—measuring 4,100 feet in length and 200 feet wide—as well as necessary taxiways. Two years later the company won a contract to do work at the airport serving the state capital, Jefferson City Memorial Municipal Airport. Rapid economic growth in the postwar years also led to robust building in the St. Louis area and Jefferson County. As was the case around the county, war veterans and their families flocked to the suburbs, requiring the construction of many new roads to serve the shift in population. A pair of milestones also marked the second half of the 1940s. In 1947 the company was incorporated as Fred Weber Contractor, Inc., and in 1949 a second son, John R. Weber, came to work for the family business on a full-time basis.

Because of the increasing need for construction materials, Fred Weber became involved in the quarry business. Through auction it purchased 340 acres of land on Creve Coeur Mill Road. This operation was incorporated in 1952 as Vigus Quarries, Inc. Now known as the North Quarry, it represented the launch of Fred Weber's present-day material services division. During its first two years, all the crushed limestone produced by Vigus was entirely devoted to the runway work being performed at Lambert. In the meantime, Fred Weber, Sr., suffered a stroke in 1953 and as a consequence was partially paralyzed on his right side. Nevertheless, he stayed active in the business and continued to visit job sites. A major development for the company during the 1950s was the passage of the Federal Aid Highway Act of 1956, which led to the U.S. Interstate Highway System. Fred Weber holds the distinction of being awarded the program's first contract.

Also of note during this period, Fred Weber, Jr., was named president of the company in 1959. Just four years later, on September 13, 1963, Old Man Weber died. He left behind a flourishing business. During the 1960s the company won numerous roadwork contracts, the result of ongoing expansion in the federal highway system as well as local development. In 1966 Fred Weber established the Heavy & Highway Division to accommodate the increase in highway construction business. For its work for the state, Fred Weber was named by the Missouri State Highway Commission as the "Contractor of the Year" for 1963, the first such honor to be awarded by the commission. During the period 1964 to 1969, Fred Weber was ranked by the U.S. Federal Highway Administration as the 14th largest road contractor in the nation based on dollar volume.

The decade of the 1960s also brought with it the introduction of Fred Weber's current chief executive and chairman to the company, Thomas P. Dunne. Dunne's father was a friend of Old Man Weber, who encouraged the young man to study civil engineering at college, promising to provide him a summer job as long as he kept his major. Although Dunne's dream was to one day play professional football, he studied civil engineering at Washington University. Old Man Weber passed away, but Dunne continued his studies, graduating in 1965. He went to work for Fred Weber as a field engineer, involved in the building of culverts and bridges. At this point, the company was only doing about $5 million in work each year, a far cry from the $200 million turnover of today.

Fred Weber Inc.: Result of 1972 Merger

Fred Weber underwent a number of changes during the decade of the 1970s. In 1972 Fred Weber, Inc. was created out of the merger of Fred Weber, Contractor, Inc. and Vigus Quarries, Inc. A year later a second quarry and asphalt plant was opened in O'Fallon, Missouri. In 1972 Fred Weber found a use for depleted sections of the first quarry when area voters rejected an incinerator project and the company was able to secure state permits to convert 90 acres of the quarry into a sanitary landfill. Because of the limestone and hard shale that lined the 200-foot-deep pit, which was also well below the water table, the landfill was not a danger to local water supplies. It started operation in 1974. Over the years, the landfill business was a perfect complement to Fred Weber's quarry activities and a profitable sideline. It was also in 1974 that Fred Weber, Jr., decided to retire and John R. Weber succeeded him as president and chairman of the board. In 1978 the company celebrated its 50th anniversary. It continued to win a large number of roadbuilding contracts in the St. Louis area.

Dunne was named Fred Weber's president in 1980. Also in that year, the company created the Building and Industrial Division, part of an effort to diversify. Projects included the construction of the School of Business at Washington University and a parking garage on the grounds of St. Louis's Gateway Arch. In 1981 the company formed subsidiary Webcom Systems to develop computer systems for asphalt and concrete plants. In 1986 Fred reached a major turning point when the Weber family elected to sell the business to its employees and management team. As a result, Dunne now became chief executive officer and chairman of the board. The company then underwent further reorganization when management elected to merge the Heavy and Highway Division with the Building and Industrial Divisions, creating Fred Weber's Construction Division. Two years later, in 1988, the company moved into its current Maryland Heights headquarters facility after spending half a century in a converted icehouse.

Fred Weber continued to prosper in the 1990s. Early in the decade it added another quarry, the New Melle quarry, which it

Key Dates:

1899: Fred Weber, Sr., is born in St. Louis.
1928: Weber launches company with first road contract.
1952: Vigus Quarries, Inc. is established.
1963: Fred Weber, Sr., dies.
1972: Fred Weber, Inc. is created out of merger of Fred Weber, Contractor, Inc. and Vigus Quarries, Inc.
1986: Weber family sells company to its employees and management.
1988: Company moves to its Maryland Heights location.
2003: Company lays off 450 employees due to transportation spending cuts.

began to mine as an open pit operation. But the bulk of Fred Weber's revenues still came from its construction services. By the end of the decade the company was generating an estimated $139 million in annual sales, at which point Fred Weber experienced a major bump in business, with sales growing to nearly $150 million in 2000. The company then won several large contracts at the close of the year, including a $48 million interchange at Interstate 70 and Flourissant Road and a $39 million project at Interstate 55 and 141. These deals helped to create the biggest backlog of work in the company's history and led to a major increase in revenues for 2001, when Fred Weber recorded $218.9 million. Because the company was so heavily dependent on Missouri transportation projects, the company was hard pressed to reproduce those results when the state began to cut back on the kind of infrastructure projects that were the life blood of the company.

Fred Weber managed to generate revenues of $218 million in 2002, just $1 million less than the year before, but because Missouri voters rejected a highway funding proposition, resulting in transportation spending cuts in the state, the company was forced to lay off some 450 workers in January 2003. In the meantime, Fred Weber also took steps to diversify, looking across the Mississippi River to the state of Illinois, where there was a well funded road program, part of an Illinois First initiative that earmarked several billions of dollars in the upcoming years for roads in southern Illinois. As a first step, Fred Weber spent $2 million to acquire Quality Sand Co. near Collinsville, Illinois, and later added the Bluff City Minerals quarry and sand plant in Alton, Illinois, in order to secure a necessary supply of materials in the area. Dunne explained to the *St. Louis Business Journal,* "We haven't really done work in Illinois. In our type of work, if you don't have materials, you have a hard time keeping control of your work." Only time would tell whether Fred Weber was about to embark on a new era in its history, expanding beyond its traditional areas of operation.

Principal Subsidiaries

Bluff City Minerals; EZ Street Cold Asphalt; Iron Mountain Trap Rock Company; Jotori Dredging, Inc.; Quality Sand, Inc.; Adeletom Aviation L.L.C.

Principal Competitors

F.A. Wilhelm Construction Company, Inc.; J.E. Dunn Construction Company; Nooter Corporation.

Further Reading

Brown, Bob, "Filling a Void," *Waste News,* March 9, 1998, p. 1.
Droog, Pam, "Building Roads, Bridges and a 35-Year Career in Infrastructure," *St. Louis Commerce Magazine,* May 1, 2000, p. 88.
Jackson, Margaret, "Impact of Prop B Defeat: Fred Weber Cuts 450," *St. Louis Business Journal,* December 13, 2002, p. 1.
A Walk Through Time With Fred Weber, Inc., Maryland Heights, Mo.: Fred Weber, Inc., 1998, 24 p.

—Ed Dinger

Frequency Electronics, Inc.

55 Charles Lindbergh Blvd.
Mitchel Field, New York 11553
U.S.A.
Telephone (516) 794-4500
Fax: (516) 794-4340
Web site: http://www.frequencyelectronics.com

Public Company
Incorporated: 1961
Employees: 340
Sales: $31.5 million (2003)
Stock Exchanges: American
Ticker Symbol: FEI
NAIC: 334515 Instrument Manufacturing for Measuring and Testing Electricity and Electrical Signals

Based in Mitchel Field, New York, Frequency Electronics, Inc. (FEI) is a leading research and development company devoted to the advanced control of time and frequency. Precise timing is key to proper synchronization in communications and data transfer for spacecraft systems, military applications, and telecommunications networks. FEI makes such timing products as oscillators and distribution amplifiers based on quartz, rubidium, and cesium technology. For most of its history, FEI has served the government sector but in recent years has taken steps to apply its products to wireless communications systems. Because there is a growing demand for cellular service in the world, but a limited amount of bandwidth, precise timing becomes a crucial factor in the synchronization of voice and data transfer. To serve this market, FEI manufactures a Rubidium Atomic Standard, an atomic clock, and temperature stable quartz crystal oscillators. FEI also provides synchronization products for wireline systems such as fiber optic networks. Further, FEI manufactures several products used by satellites involved in communications, navigation, weather forecasting, and video and data transfer. They include master clocks, made from quartz, rubidium, or cesium; DC-DC power converters for instrumentation power control; hybrid assemblies used for onboard spacecraft command, control, and power distribution; and oven-controlled crystal oscillators, needed for satellite transmission and GPS systems. In addition to its main facility and headquarters on Long Island, New York, publicly traded FEI operates plants in Belgium, France, and China.

Company Started in 1961

FEI was founded and incorporated in New York in 1961 by Martin Bloch. A City College of NY graduate, he worked for seven years during the 1950s for watchmaker Bulova, where as chief electronics engineer he was heavily involved in the development of the Accutron, the world's first electronic watch. Early in the decade the first battery-powered watches came onto the market, but they still relied on a balance-wheel movement and were no more accurate than traditional spring-wound watches. Bulova researchers developed a tuning fork movement that was a revolutionary departure from previous methods and resulted in the first timing devices capable of providing the accuracy required by the emerging space program. Bulova launched the Accutron wristwatch in 1961, the same year that Bloch left to found his own company to apply new timing technologies to spacecraft.

During the first 20 years of its history, FEI, operating out of a facility in New Hyde Park, Long Island, concentrated on the development of timing devices to be used by the space programs of the National Aeronautics and Space Administration, including the Apollo moon landings, all of which required pinpoint precision for navigation in space. In 1968 FEI reincorporated in Delaware and went public. A year later the company took a major step when it acquired the Atomichron product line from National Radio Company for $733,000 in cash and notes. National Radio had been in the electronics business since 1914, when it started out in the early days of radio producing shortwave and amateur receivers. During the 1950s National Radio joined the quest to develop the atomic clock and its pioneering efforts in quantum mechanics and nuclear theory led to the 1956 introduction of the Atomichron, the world's first commercial atomic clock. It was accurate to within one billionth of a second, and was the direct ancestor of today's cesium beam clocks found on GPS satellites.

The market for FEI's high-tech products was small, but by 1980 new customers emerged in the form of the military, which

Company Perspectives:

With the ongoing worldwide expansion of telecommunications capabilities, Frequency Electronics is well positioned to meet the demands of this rapidly expanding marketplace.

needed the company's timing and frequency control devices for navigational purposes, guidance systems, and encryption needs. FEI was involved in three major military programs. Navstar was a military navigation system developed for use by non-Communist countries. Another program, named The Tiger, provided secure digital transmission of data for use by satellites and other military applications. Finally, FEI's quart crystal oscillators were incorporated into the radar warning systems of fighter aircraft. As a result of these defense contracts, FEI saw its annual revenues increase to $9.3 million in 1980 and $14.2 million a year later. Net income grew from $784,000 to $2.2 million in 1981. Moreover, FEI caught the attention of investors who bid up the company's stock. In anticipation of even greater growth, the company began to construct its present-day Mitchel Field facility, a 131,000-square-foot site that boasted a shipping capacity of $125 million a year. FEI moved to Mitchel Field in December 1981. The land was leased from Nassau County, New York, and was partially built and equipped with the proceeds of a $5 million bond from the county. In 1988 FEI opened a contiguous 90,000-square-foot facility, financed by another $3.5 million bond arranged by the Nassau County Industrial Development Agency.

During the 1980s FEI established an alliance with TRW, Inc., acting as a subcontractor on satellites built for the U.S. government. In 1987 FEI bought a TRW unit, TRW Microwave, paying approximately $16.7 million. This acquisition was the start of a shift away from dependence on business from the Department of Defense and an effort to fill the need for private-sector satellite hardware as well as ground-based communications systems. Also of note during this transitional phase was the establishment in late 1989 of an Employee Stock Ownership Plan, which gave employees a 10 percent stake in the company.

Company Indicted in 1993

The costs associated with moving into the commercial sector led in 1991 to FEI reporting its first loss (nearly $6.4 million) since 1979. Annual revenues at this stage topped $56.5 million, but business did not pick up after fiscal 1991, dipping to $53.2 million in 1992 and $43.2 million in 1993. To make matters worse, FEI would soon be saddled with legal bills, which would average over $1 million a year over the next several years. In December 1993 the company was indicted by a federal grand jury for allegedly conspiring to defraud the government in connection with its subcontracting for TRW. In a separate action, Bloch and three other executives faced similar charges. The underlying point of contention was the 1988 termination by TRW of three of the six subcontracts on highly classified government space satellites it had with FEI. As part of the process, FEI submitted statements that laid out in detail the costs the company had incurred on these contracts and for which it was eligible for reimbursement. The FBI began looking into the matter in 1990, sealed indictments were then made in a complaint dated December 1992 and finally became known to FEI in November 1993. The government maintained that the company's officers agreed to defraud the government, submitted false bills, and destroyed records related to FEI's actual costs on the terminated contracts. The company vehemently denied the charges, which were soon matched by a civil suit by the government seeking damages, as well as a shareholder suit that sought reimbursement from the company's officers for the financial damage caused to FEI by their alleged actions. As soon as the government charges were made public, FEI's stock plummeted. In an attempt to maintain its government business, the company rearranged its top rank of officers. For his part, Block resigned as chairman and chief executive officer, and took a leave of absence as president, but he stayed on to serve as FEI's chief scientist. Replacing him as chairman and CEO was board member Joseph P. Franklin, a retired Army Major General who since his retirement in 1987 had been running a Spanish business consulting firm in Madrid, Spain. Despite the changes, a few weeks later FEI was banned from contracting with or acting as subcontractor with any agency of the U.S. government. Moreover, defense spending was already trending downward in the wake of the collapse of Communism.

Revenues fell to $43.2 million in 1993, $27.5 million in 1994, and bottomed out at $24 million in 1995. The company also posted net losses of $8 million, $4.6 million, and $3.8 million during these years. As a cost-cutting measure, the company closed a California plant, moving its operations to the Long Island facility. Business began to pick up in 1995 as sales topped $25 million and net earnings totaled more than $2.8 million, representing FEI's first profitable year since 1992. But legal problems continued to haunt the company. It was not until June 1998 that FEI was able to settle its outstanding criminal and civil cases. In the end, the company pleaded guilty to one count of filing a false statement. It also agreed to pay a $400,000 fine, $1.1 million for investigation costs, and another $6.5 million to settle the government's civil suits. Bloch was able to regain his role as the company's CEO, although Franklin stayed on as chairman of the board.

By this point, FEI was already well on its way to making the transition away from a dependence on defense contracting in favor of commercial work. In keeping with this focus, the company established two new divisions. The intention of FEI Space was to produce off-the-shelf products, as opposed to its traditional custom-designed government projects, suitable for the satellite communications industry. FEI Communications targeted the cellular and personal communications services markets. The company's shifting emphasis away from government contracting was evident in the steadily decline in sales to the public sector. FEI recorded net sales to the U.S. government of nearly $18 million in 1995, but by 1998 that amount dropped to $5.6 million.

Late 1990s Focus on Commercial Customers

Over the final years of the 1990s and into the new century, FEI continued in its efforts to recast itself as a provider of timing and frequency solutions to a range of commercial customers. In September 2000 (fiscal 2001), FEI strengthened its telecommunications business with the acquisition of Gilliam S.A., a Bel-

Key Dates:

1961: Company is founded by Martin Bloch.
1968: Company goes public.
1969: Atomichron atomic clock line is acquired.
1993: Company is indicted for alleged government fraud.
1998: Company pleads guilty to one count in fraud case.

gium company, in a cash and stock deal worth in excess of $12 million. Gilliam was involved in four main areas: the management of timing and interconnectivity for wireline networks; remote network monitoring systems; equipment to connect isolated, primarily rural, customers to telephone networks via satellites; and power supply products for telecom service providers.

FEI integrated Gilliam into its structure and took steps to introduce its wireline synchronization products in the U.S. market. In 2002 the company launched an Asian subsidiary, which began to manufacture components in China. It also invested in Morion, Inc., a Russian maker of high-quality quartz products. FEI also established a German subsidiary to act as a sales and marketing platform in Europe. Moreover, the company established FEI Government Systems, Inc. to handle FEI's renewed interest in government contracts. Sales to the U.S. government bottomed out at $3.7 million in 2001 but began to reverse course, growing to $4.5 million in 2002 and $8.9 million in 2003. In May 2003 FEI completed another acquisition, paying $2.7 million to acquire Anaheim, California-based Zyfer, Inc., a subsidiary of Odetics, Inc. Zyfer offered cutting edge, proprietary global positioning systems (GPS) technology.

Although it was adversely impacted by a lack of investment in telecommunications infrastructure during difficult economic conditions, FEI continued to look forward to what appeared to be a promising future. A large number of satellites were reaching the end of their design life and in need of replacement. There was an opportunity for FEI to transfer its quartz oscillator technology—with a strong track record on space probes to Jupiter and Venus—for use in heavy industry to monitor processes under extreme conditions. Defense contracting also offered strong potential, especially with programs involving secure radio and pilotless vehicles, both of which required sophisticated timing systems. In addition, the high demand in the world for greater telecommunications services, for greater voice, video, and data service, whether it be wireless or wireline, also played to the strengths of FEI.

Principal Subsidiaries

Gilliam-FEI (Belgium); Satel FEI (France); FEI Asia (China); FEI-Zyfer; FEI Europe (Germany); Morion, Inc. (Russia).

Principal Competitors

Agilent Technologies, Inc.; Iteris Holdings Inc.; Symmetricom, inc.

Further Reading

''Frequency Electronics Reshuffles Managers to Keep Defense Jobs,'' *Wall Street Journal,* December 8, 1993, p. 6.

Larson, Lisa, ''Frequency Electronics Settles Litigation After 7+ Years,'' *Radio Communications Report,* June 29, 1998, p. 23.

''Martin Bloch: On the Right Frequency,'' *Long Island Business,* February 28, 1994, p. S9.

Metz, Robert, ''Technology and High P/E's,'' *New York Times,* June 12, 1981, p. D6.

—Ed Dinger

GEORG FISCHER +GF+

Georg Fischer AG Schaffhausen

Amsler-Laffon-Strasse 9
Schaffhausen
CH-8201
Switzerland
Telephone: 41 52 631 11 11
Fax: 41 52 631 28 3741 52 631 2856
Web site: http://www.georgfischer.com

Public Company
Founded: 1802
Employees: 2,903
Sales: SFr 3.48 billion ($2.56 billion) (2002)
Stock Exchanges: Swiss
Ticker Symbol: GF
NAIC: 333512 Machine Tool (Metal Cutting Types) Manufacturing; 326122 Plastics Pipe and Pipe Fitting Manufacturing; 331210 Iron and Steel Pipes and Tubes Manufacturing from Purchased Steel; 331511 Iron Foundries; 331512 Steel Investment Foundries; 331513 Steel Foundries (Except Investment); 333513 Machine Tool (Metal Forming Types) Manufacturing; 333514 Special Die and Tool, Die Set, Jig, and Fixture Manufacturing; 333515 Cutting Tool and Machine Tool Accessory Manufacturing; 333518 Other Metalworking Machinery Manufacturing; 336399 All Other Motor Vehicle Parts Manufacturing; 551112 Offices of Other Holding Companies

Switzerland's Georg Fischer AG Schaffhausen is a world-leading industrial engineering group engaged in four primary areas of operation. Piping Systems is one of the company's oldest activities, stemming from the early period of its more than 200-year history. Georg Fischer manufactures a wide range of pipes, fittings, and piping systems for the industrial, construction, and residential markets. The Automotive Products Group, the company's largest division at some 40 percent of sales, represents the continuation of another historic core business, that of cast iron forged products, now concentrated on producing cast iron and aluminum components and systems for the automotive industry. Manufacturing Technology is conducted through the company's Agie Charmilles subsidiary, and is a world leader in electric discharge machining (EDM) manufacturing systems. Last, Georg Fischer's Plant Engineering Group, created from the merger of Buss and Waeschle and Werner & Pfleiderer in 2000, is a provider of turnkey production plants and processes, and related services. Georg Fischer is a globally operating company, with subsidiaries in some 30 countries. Switzerland itself represents just 5 percent of the group's sales of nearly SFr 3.5 billion ($2.5 billion). Germany is the group's largest single market, accounting for 40 percent of sales, while the rest of Europe adds a further 32 percent to annual revenues.

Swiss Industrial Pioneer in the 19th Century

Georg Fischer's origins lay in the earliest years of the Industrial Revolution. In 1802, Johann Conrad Fischer, then 29 years old, bought a mill near Schaffhausen, in Switzerland on the German border. Fischer converted the water-driven mill into a copper melting plant and began researching new alloy types for steel production. By 1805, Fischer had successfully developed a process for producing cast steel, marking a first on the European continent, and breaking the monopoly on cast steel held until then by England's Huntsman.

Fischer's work put Switzerland on the industrial map, and established the Schaffhausen region as the heart of the country's industrial development. Over the next decades, Fischer continued to develop new alloys and production processes. Among Fischer's most significant patents was that for the production of malleable cast iron, developed in 1827. In 1845, Fischer successfully developed a new method for producing cast steel, although the industrial scale use of the process by the company did not begin until some 30 years later.

Joined by son Georg Fischer I, the elder Fischer began expanding the company, opening two new steelworks in Austria, in Hainfeld in 1827 and in Traisen in 1833. Another of Fischer's sons, Berthold, took over direction of the Traisen site. Yet it was under Fischer's grandson, Georg Fischer II, that the company turned to an area that was to become a company specialty for much of the next century.

Company Perspectives:

Our Mission—Create value through industrial leadership. Our Vision—We want to: provide innovative industrial systems solutions enabling customers to improve their products and contributing to the quality of life; grow profitably by working towards value-oriented goals; achieve competitiveness, excellence and sustainability through industrial leadership.

The gathering momentum of the Industrial Revolution at the mid-19th century had brought about dramatic population increases in the world's cities. These in turn were faced with developing new public infrastructures to handle the growing population demand, installing sewer and water systems, and, later, gas transmission systems for lighting and heating utilities. Fischer turned its production of malleable cast iron to this sector in 1864, launching a range of pipe fittings. The company quickly became a prominent specialist in the area, which grew steadily through the end of the century.

Commercially Oriented Public Company in the 20th Century

Fischer launched industrial production of cast steel in 1877, becoming one of Switzerland's leading producers. Rising competition from Germany, as well as stiff import duties, in the later years of the century led Fischer to open a sister plant in Singen, over the border from Schaffhausen in 1895. The investment forced the company, by then headed by Georg Fischer III, to turn to the public market for backing, a move completed in 1896. At this time the company took on the name of Aktiengesellschaft der Eisen- und Stahlwerke von Georg Fischer.

Although initially the majority shares were acquired by Fischer's family, by the turn of the century a significant proportion had come under control of banks and other institutional investors. When Fischer ran into financial difficulties in 1902, its bank shareholders insisted that Georg Fischer step down from management control, marking the last time a member of the Fischer family was to exert operational control of the company. The company now transformed itself from a family-run organization to a professionally managed, commercially oriented corporation.

Georg Fischer III, in the meantime, founded a competing steelworks in Schaffhausen, remaining in business until near the end of World War I, when he sold that business to Georg Fischer. The company continued to look for new acquisitions in the interwar years, acquiring another Schaffhausen-based company, Maschinenfabrik Rauschenbach. That purchase introduced the company to the industrial engineering and gray cast iron markets. At the same time, the company had continued to expand its product lines, adding a variety of items, such as automated weaving loom machinery in 1926, mass lathe production in 1938, and others, including cast iron pots and other kitchenware and cookware. Another product, the Trilex truck wheel system launched in 1933, became an important source of company revenues, accounting at one point for more than 10 percent of its total sales.

The company's operations had remained focused on the Schaffhausen region into the 1930s. In 1933, however, the company made its first major international acquisition, buying up England's Britannia Iron and Steel Works Ltd. That purchase enabled the company to begin production of malleable cast iron products for the U.K. market as well. The company's holdings in both the United Kingdom and Germany during World War II, however, placed the group into an extremely difficult position—the company later commissioned a noted historian to produce a report on its conduct in Germany during World War II, including addressing allegations that the company had used slave labor in its facilities.

Following the war, Fischer simplified its name to Georg Fischer AG. In the 1950s, the company targeted new growth opportunities. In 1952, the company developed new fully automatic molding and casting systems as part of its Engineering Machinery component. Although that market remained close to the group's cast iron and steel core, Georg Fischer had by now started to look beyond that market. In 1952, the company began developing new pipe fittings and pipe systems production methods using a new material: plastic, in the form of PVC.

Expansion in the 1970s and 1980s

By 1957, the company had succeeded in rolling out full-scale industrial production of plastic pipe fittings. The company's early entrance into the category enabled it not only to capture a leading share of the plastic pipes market, but to bolster its status as a world-leading producer of pipe fittings in general. The company backed up its plastic fittings production with the development of a special PVC adhesive, called Tangit, launched in 1964. This new product, which solved a key problem in plastic fittings, brought about a surge in demand for plastic fittings in the 1960s. The company responded by expanding production, opening a new facility in England in 1966 and a second plant in Seewis, Switzerland, in 1971.

The move into plastics was also a key factor in the company's shifting geographic focus—by the mid-1960s, more than half of Georg Fischer's sales came from outside of Switzerland. By the beginning of the 1970s, those sales had topped SFr 1 billion for the first time. The company's research and development efforts, meanwhile, turned toward its cast iron production. In 1971, the company patented a new magnesium converter process that made possible the mass production of cast iron-based automotive components. This category became a key product group in the company's Automotive division.

The 1970s represented the start of an important period of expansion for the company, which developed from a limited manufacturing presence in Switzerland, Germany, and the United Kingdom, to a globally operating group with subsidiaries in some 30 countries. Acquisitions formed an important part of the group's growth, starting with the purchase of Waeschle, based in Ravensburg, Germany, in 1972. That purchase marked the start of the group's later Plant Engineering Group, solidified by the 1979 purchase of Swiss company Buss, based in Basel. That year, also, the company acquired a 50 percent stake in a foundry in Lincoln, England, later acquiring full control of the plant.

The company moved into the United States at mid-decade, setting up a sales subsidiary, Georg Fischer Inc., in California, which

Key Dates:

1802: Johann Fischer buys a water mill near Schaffhausen, Switzerland, and converts it to a copper melting plant.
1805: Fischer develops a method for producing cast steel, a first on the European continent.
1827: Fischer acquires the first of two steel works in Austria.
1864: Production of malleable cast iron fittings begins.
1877: Industrial production of cast steel begins.
1895: A plant is built in Singen, Germany.
1896: The company goes public.
1902: The Fischer family loses control of the company.
1921: The company acquires Maschinenfabrik Rauschenbach in Schaffhausen and begins production of industrial machinery.
1933: The company acquires Britannia Iron and Steel Works in England.
1936: The company launches the Trilex wheel system.
1957: The company launches the first PVC fittings.
1966: A new plastics plant is built in England.
1972: The company acquires Waeschle as a basis of the Plant Engineering division.
1976: A sales subsidiary is established in California for entry into the North, Central, and South American markets.
1979: The company acquires Buss, which is merged with Waeschle.
1983: The company acquires Ateliers des Charmilles, entering the EDM market.
1991: The company completes the restructuring of the Schaffhausen and Singen manufacturing plants; the steel foundry at Schaffhausen is shut down.
1995: The company acquires the automotive components maker Schubert & Salzer Eisenguss in Germany.
1996: The company acquires Agie of Switzerland, which is merged with Charmilles to form Agie Charmilles, a world-leading EDM group; the company acquires R&G Sloane Manufacturing Co. in the United States to establish plastics production there.
1998: Agie Charmilles forms two joint ventures in China.
2000: The company acquires Krupp Werner & Pfleiderer from Krupp Thyssen, which is merged into Buss and Waeschle to form Coperion Holding.
2002: Georg Fischer celebrates its 200th anniversary.
2003: With sales slipping, the company announces its restructuring and plans to shed 1,000 jobs.

provided oversight for the company's expansion into the North, Central, and South American markets. In 1979, Fischer targeted expansion into the rapidly developing Middle East markets, forming a manufacturing operation in Riyadh, Saudi Arabia, that year.

Expansion continued through the 1980s. In 1983, the company purchased a 51 percent stake in Ateliers des Charmilles, based in Geneva, which became known as Charmilles Technologies after its full acquisition in 1988. That company had been a pioneer in electric discharge machining (EDM) manufacturing techniques, and formed the basis of the group's Manufacturing Technology business group.

Fischer began restructuring at the end of the decade, spending some SFr 250 million between 1987 and 1991 on a redevelopment of its Schaffhausen and Singen plants. At the same time, the company set up a new Piping Systems distribution center, plastics production plant, and testing laboratory in Schaffhausen. In 1990, the company restructured its corporate organization as well, setting up Georg Fischer AG as a holding company for its primary business groups. These were now reorganized as separate, autonomously operating businesses.

As part of its restructuring effort, the company shut down its steel foundry at its Schaffhausen site, converting the plant to automotive components production in 1991. Two years later, Georg Fischer shut down its Worms, Germany steel foundry as well. Then in 1994, the company began spinning off a number of noncore operations, such as a real estate business, and logistics and accounting businesses.

Four-Pronged Focus for the New Century

The company's restructuring led the way to a focus on four core business areas at the approach of the 21st century. The Automotive Products division was boosted in 1995 with the purchase of Schubert & Salzer Eisenguss, based in Leipzig, Germany, which produced components for trucks and other heavy industrial vehicles and construction equipment. The following year, the group boosted its EDM branch to world-leading status with the purchase of Switzerland's Agie SA. That company was merged into the group's existing Manufacturing Technology operation, which was renamed Agie Charmilles. Fischer next turned to its fittings business, buying up R&G Sloane Manufacturing Company in Little Rock, Arkansas, establishing the company as a plastic fittings and pipe manufacturing presence in North America.

The company's other core businesses grew as well into the next century. Agie Charmilles led the company into China, establishing two joint ventures to manufacture EDM machinery in 1998, and launching its first products on the Chinese market by 1999. The company also moved into the Latin American market that year, buying the manufacturing rights to EDM equipment developed by Brazil's Engemaq.

By the end of the decade, Fischer's Automotive Components segment had become its largest business group, a position solidified by the company's acquisition of mb-Guss and Mössner, both based in Germany. These purchases, made in 1999, raised the company's aluminum components casting capacity by more than four times.

Fischer's acquisition drive continued into the new century, as the company joined in the purchase of Krupp Wermer & Pfleiderer, in Stuttgart, part of the Thyssen Krupp group and a leader in the German plastics processing market. That company was then merged with Fischer's Buss and Waeschle, and the entire operation was renamed as Coperion Holding GmbH.

Fischer's share of Coperion stood at 50.1 percent, against the 49.9 percent stake held by acquisition partners Westdeutsche Landsbank and West Private Equity of London. At the time of the establishment of Coperion, Fischer announced its intention to spin off the company early in the new century.

Even as it celebrated its 200th year anniversary, Georg Fischer was hit hard by a depressed industrial climate. By the end of 2002, the group's sales had shrunk by some 11 percent from the previous year, to slightly less than SFr 3.5 billion. In response, Georg Fischer announced a companywide restructuring effort at the end of 2003, cutting some 1,000 jobs in an effort to boost operating profits. Despite these difficulties, Georg Fischer remained a world-leading industrial engineering group.

Principal Subsidiaries

Georg Fischer has subsidiaries in Australia; Austria; Belgium; Bermudas; Brazil; China; Czech Republic; Denmark; England; France; Germany; Hungary; India; Israel; Italy; Japan; Korea; Netherlands; Norway; Poland; Saudi Arabia; Singapore; Spain; Sweden; Switzerland; Taiwan; Turkey; U.S.A.

Principal Competitors

Renault S.A; S.C. Automobile Dacia; Mondragon Corporacion Cooperativa; ThyssenKrupp Technologies AG; Giddings and Lewis L.L.C.; NKMZ; J Lauritzen A/S; Liebherr-International AG; Benteler AG; Kurgan Engineering Plant Joint Stock Co.

Further Reading

Hall, William, ''Georg Fischer Health Restored,'' *Financial Times,* March 4, 1998, p. 26.

——, ''Plastics Deal for Fischer,'' *Financial Times,* October 16, 2000, p. 26.

Simonian, Haig, ''Georg Fischer to Cut 1,000 Jobs,'' *Financial Times,* October 8, 2003, p. 22.

Wrigley, Al, ''Swiss Auto Components Firm Weighs US Die-Cast Sites,'' *American Metal Market,* October 26, 2001, p. 1.

—M.L. Cohen

Georgia Gulf Corporation

400 Perimeter Center Terrace
Suite 595
Atlanta, Georgia 30346-1232
U.S.A.
Telephone: (770) 395-4500
Fax: (770) 395-4529
Web site: http://www.ggc.com

Public Company
Incorporated: 1985
Employees: 1,216
Sales: $1.23 billion (2002)
Stock Exchanges: New York
Ticker Symbol: GGC
NAIC: 325181 Alkalies and Chlorine Manufacturing; 325211 Plastics Material and Resin Manufacturing; 325110 Petrochemical Manufacturing; 325191 Gum and Wood Chemical Manufacturing; 325192 Cyclic Crude and Intermediate Manufacturing

Georgia Gulf Corporation is a major manufacturer of two highly integrated product lines, chlorovinyls and aromatic chemicals. The company is the third largest producer of both vinyl chloride monomer and vinyl suspension resins in North America, as well as the continent's number two producer of vinyl compounds; it is among the largest North American manufacturers of both cumene and phenol and also produces caustic soda, chlorine, and acetone. Manufacturing plants are operated in nine U.S. cities, mainly in the Southeast. Export sales generated about 12 percent of 2002 revenues, with the company serving markets in Canada, Mexico, Latin America, Europe, and Asia. Established in 1984 as a leveraged buyout of Georgia-Pacific Corporation, a large forest products manufacturer, Georgia Gulf began as an extremely successful corporation and was able to take advantage of increases in the demand for salt and petrochemical products.

Development of the Georgia-Pacific Chemicals Business in the 1970s

The assets that form Georgia Gulf Corporation today were built up by Georgia-Pacific Corporation over a period of 14 years. In 1971 Georgia-Pacific established the first of several chemical plants, phenol/acetone and methanol manufacturing facilities at Plaquemine, Louisiana. Both products are used to make plywood and a wide variety of granulate, wood fiber boards.

Georgia-Pacific added a caustic/chlorine plant at Plaquemine in 1975. There salt mined from large salt domes located nearby was converted into salt brine. Electricity passed through the solution and chlorine, caustic soda, and hydrogen were formed. Chlorine was used in pulp and paper manufacturing and to make vinyl chloride monomer (VCM), an intermediate to vinyl or plastic resins. Caustic soda, the coproduct of chlorine, was key to the manufacture of aluminum and pulp and paper as well as being a key element in the production of other chemicals.

Later that year a polyvinyl chloride (PVC) resin plant was completed at the site. This facility converted purchased VCM into vinyl resins. These resins are one of the most widely used plastics today and can be found in pipe, window frames, siding, flooring, shower curtains, bottles, medical tubing, and many other end-use products. The vinyl resin facility positioned Georgia-Pacific to eventually produce value-added vinyl compounds.

In 1978 Georgia-Pacific added an ammonia plant adjacent to the methanol plant. This enabled the company to use excess hydrogen, a byproduct of the methanol and chlorine manufacturing processes, in the production of ammonia, a key ingredient in the manufacture of fertilizers.

The company built a cumene facility in Pasadena, Texas, in 1979. Cumene, a petroleum product made from benzene and propylene, is used to make phenol and acetone. In addition to resin adhesives, phenol is also a precursor to high-performance plastics used in automobiles, household appliances, electronics, and protective coating applications. Acetone is a precursor to methyl methacrylate, which is used to produce acrylic sheeting and in surface coating resins for automotive and architectural

Company Perspectives:

Georgia Gulf's mission is to continue to be an efficient, integrated manufacturer and marketer of quality chemical and plastic products to users worldwide and to grow responsibly in present and closely related businesses. We are dedicated to continuous improvement of the processes, products and services required to meet our customers' changing needs. We will strive to earn a superior long-term return for our shareholders while providing meaningful work for our employees and always operating with the highest regard for environmental protection, safety and overall well-being in the communities where we live and work.

markets. It is also an intermediate for the production of engineering plastics and several major industrial solvents.

Georgia-Pacific again expanded the Plaquemine complex in 1979 to include sodium chlorate production. Along with chlorine, the uses for sodium chlorate are primarily industrial. It has major applications in the bleaching process for pulp and paper, and it is also an ingredient in blasting agents, explosives, and solid rocket fuels. In 1980 the Plaquemine facility began producing its own VCM, which integrated the company from raw material to finished vinyl resins.

The company's chemical operations were extended to the northeastern United States in 1981, when Georgia-Pacific purchased a phenol/acetone facility in Bound Brook, New Jersey. Two years later, the company added three resin compounding facilities producing specialty resins. The addition of these plants, in Tennessee, Mississippi, and Delaware, further integrated Georgia-Pacific's vinyl resins into value-added products.

Creation of Georgia Gulf Through Management-Led Leveraged Buyout in 1984

Many companies, spurred on by growth in chemical markets, simply overbuilt capacity, and the limits of this expansion were not discovered until recessionary pressures had already shrunk the market. Companies were left with massive production facilities, but few sales. Georgia-Pacific was no different. After several years of consideration, the company decided to spin off the chemical operations and return its focus to core businesses in the paper and lumber industries.

The first group to organize a plan to take over Georgia-Pacific's chemical interests consisted of five senior executives of the operation, led by James R. Kuse, a senior vice-president of Georgia-Pacific who had been in charge of the division for several years.

Kuse and his associates risked long and successful careers with Georgia-Pacific, and set out to raise the necessary capital. Together, the group managed to collect the asking price of $275 million, representing about 20 percent of the asset value. These assets included some of the most technically advanced and efficient plants in the industry.

Having succeeded in making the deal, the owners needed a name for the new company. Locating its headquarters in Atlanta, the name Georgia was linked with Gulf, which represented the company's substantial assets in Louisiana and Texas.

Georgia Gulf came into existence as a privately owned company on December 31, 1984. The first priority of Kuse and his team was to lower costs and increase sales. Already in possession of a viable, integrated chemical enterprise, Kuse only needed a recovery in his company's markets.

This began only months after Georgia Gulf came into existence. The recession ended and demand made its way back through the production cycle to the products manufactured by Georgia Gulf. In fact, demand was so strong that the company's plants operated at more than 90 percent of capacity.

Very strong sales provided an unforecasted increase in available funds, almost all of which were devoted to paying down the company's substantial debt. The debt, which was a result of the leveraged buyout, was not planned to be eliminated until about 1992, but the strength of sales growth virtually eliminated the debt four years later.

This placed the company in an excellent position to go public. The initial offering of eight million shares on the NASDAQ went off successfully in December 1986. The following April, a secondary offering of an additional 4.8 million shares was completed. In November 1987 Georgia Gulf gained a listing on the New York Stock Exchange and was listed on the *Fortune* 500. During 1987, Georgia Gulf shares recorded a 183 percent return.

Through this period of economic growth, Georgia Gulf captured market share as it was one of the low-cost producers because of the efficiency of its operations. In addition, falling oil and natural gas prices helped to further strengthen Georgia Gulf's financial position. Georgia Gulf closed its Bound Brook facility in 1987, later relocating the plant to Pasadena, Texas, where it was closer to raw materials.

With the debt nearly eliminated, Georgia Gulf began to expand by acquiring Freeman Chemical Corporation from H.H. Robertson Co. for about $67.2 million. Headquartered in Port Washington, Wisconsin, and operating six plants, Freeman added a new line of polyurethane specialty resins and brought revenues up to $1 billion. Also that year, Georgia Gulf purchased the Great River Oil and Gas Corporation, a Louisiana-based petroleum company. Great River provided Georgia Gulf with a potential source for hedging future supplies of natural gas. Georgia Gulf also diverted significant operating income toward the repurchase of shares. The repurchase program was initiated in 1987 and continued for three years.

In 1989 Jerry Satrum, a team member of Kuse's 1985 purchase of the Georgia-Pacific assets, succeeded Kuse as president of the company. Kuse remained chairman and CEO until 1990, when Satrum took over as CEO.

Blocking a Takeover Attempt via Recapitalization in the Early 1990s

The year 1990 was an extremely difficult one for Georgia Gulf. Although the company had virtually no debt and was well positioned to weather the anticipated economic downturn, the

Key Dates:

1971: Georgia-Pacific Corporation establishes phenol/acetone and methanol manufacturing facilities in Plaquemine, Louisiana.
1975: The Plaquemine site is expanded to include the manufacture of caustic soda, chlorine, and polyvinyl chloride.
1979: Georgia-Pacific builds a cumene plant in Pasadena, Texas.
1980: The Plaquemine complex begins producing its own vinyl chloride monomer (VCM), further integrating the product lines.
1984: Georgia-Pacific spins off its chemical operations through a management-led leveraged buyout; the executives call their new company Georgia Gulf Corporation.
1986: Georgia Gulf is taken public with a listing on the NASDAQ.
1987: Company stock begins trading on the New York Stock Exchange.
1990: A hostile takeover attempt is blocked via a plan of recapitalization, which saddles the firm with debt of $746 million.
1998: North American Plastics, Inc. is acquired for approximately $100 million.
1999: Georgia Gulf spends about $270 million to acquire the vinyls business of CONDEA Vista Company; it exits from the methanol business to focus exclusively on chlorovinyls and aromatics.
2000: The company achieves net income of $64.2 million on record sales of $1.58 billion.
2001: An economic downturn results in a 24 percent decline in sales and a net loss of $12 million, necessitating cost-cutting measures; company cofounder James R. Kuse dies and President and CEO Edward A. Schmitt becomes company chairman.
2002: The company returns to profitability.

company was forced to defend itself from a hostile takeover. The takeover attempt by billionaire corporate raider Harold C. Simmons, which began in July 1989, was brought to a resolution through a plan of recapitalization, which the stockholders approved in April 1990. The recapitalization plan was a combination of cash distributions, senior subordinated notes, and a new issue of common stock. The company borrowed approximately $746 million and used $65 million from the sale of Freeman Chemical to fund the recapitalization.

The emphasis, therefore, necessarily shifted to sales growth and cost reduction. Already one of the most efficient companies in the chemical industry, there were few costs to cut. While lean, Georgia Gulf still managed to trim nearly 300 jobs.

On the other side of the equation, sales growth was tied directly to the economy, which continued to languish through 1991 and, when recovery seemed imminent, ''double-dipped'' in 1992. Sales, which hit an all-time high of $1.1 billion in 1989, decreased, with the sale of Freeman, to $932 million in 1990, $838 million in 1991, and $779 million in 1992.

While sales were depressed, Georgia Gulf continued to operate efficiently, maximizing opportunities. By all accounts the company succeeded in preserving itself through the recession, although it was saddled with substantial debt. The company was nevertheless able to service its debt obligations and maintain profitability. The company made significant progress in this direction in 1992, reducing its debt to $444 million in 1992.

In an attempt to de-emphasize the sharp effects of the American markets on its business, Georgia Gulf intensified an effort to boost export sales in 1992. This was made more difficult by lingering weaknesses in the world economy. Still, the company managed to make significant sales in European and Asian markets.

In early 1993, demand had begun to recover in the key vinyl resins market. In addition, the provisions of the federal Clean Air Act came into force, dictating the use of cleaner fuels that increased demand for methanol, which was used as an oxygenate for gasoline.

Expansion Program and Acquisitions in the Mid- to Late 1990s

During the mid-1990s, between 1994 and mid-1997, Georgia Gulf undertook a $360 million capital program designed to modernize and increase the capacity of its production facilities, cut costs, and improve compliance with environmental standards. Capacity was expanded in the production of phenol, acetone, alpha-methylstyrene (AMS), cumene, VCM, and PVC. An improved financial position enabled the firm to undertake this major expansion; Georgia Gulf had had a negative net worth since the recapitalization thanks to the hefty debt load, but by the end of 1994 total debt had been reduced to $314.1 million and the company returned to positive net worth territory. At the same time, the resurgent economy helped drive the company's revenues back over the $1 billion mark by 1995, with net income reaching a record $186.5 million that year. The next two years were not nearly as strong, but Georgia Gulf remained solidly profitable.

Late in 1997, Edward A. Schmitt, who had helped spearhead the expansion program as vice-president of operations, was named president and chief operating officer. Schmitt was promoted to president and CEO in April 1998, with the retiring Satrum retaining a seat on the board of directors; company cofounder Kuse remained board chairman. Also in 1997, Georgia Gulf sold Great River Oil and Gas, thereby exiting from the oil and gas exploration sector.

Revenues and profits declined in both 1998 and 1999 as commodity chemicals suffered from another downturn in the industry cycle, with a key contributing factor being the economic difficulties in Asia and elsewhere. Georgia Gulf took advantage of the downturn, however, by making two significant acquisitions at bargain prices. In May 1998 the corporation expanded its downstream pipeline by purchasing North American Plastics, Inc. for about $100 million. North American Plastics was a $90 million per year manufacturer of flexible PVC compounds for such products as wire and cable coatings, automotive interiors, and vinyl sheeting. It had compounding facilities in Aberdeen and Madison, Mississippi. Georgia Gulf next spent approximately $270 million to acquire the vinyls business of CONDEA Vista Company, the U.S. chemicals arm of Germany's RWE-DEA. The acquired assets included a VCM plant, two PVC resin plants, three PVC compounding facilities, and a 50 percent stake in PHH Monomers, L.L.C., a VCM manufacturing joint venture with PPG Industries, Inc. The deal made Georgia Gulf the third largest North American maker of both PVC and VCM. Together, these two acquisitions significantly expanded the firm's presence in the more highly profitable and less cyclical downstream side of the business. Georgia Gulf simultaneously focused more tightly on its two core chemical lines—chlorovinyls and aromatics—by closing down its methanol business late in 1999.

Struggles in the Early 2000s

After achieving net income of $64.2 million on record sales of $1.58 billion in 2000, Georgia Gulf suffered the full effects of the economic downturn of the following year, experiencing a 24 percent decline in sales and recording a net loss of $12 million. Poor demand for the company's products domestically was coupled with high energy costs that left it at a competitive disadvantage compared with overseas rivals. Cost-cutting efforts were undertaken, including the closure of two of the vinyl compounding facilities acquired via the CONDEA Vista deal. Georgia Gulf also strived to improve productivity through such efforts as a 50 million pound expansion of its Oklahoma City resin plant. Also that year, Kuse died and Schmitt took over as company chairman.

Georgia Gulf returned to profitability in 2002, although revenues were flat. Its aromatics business, which had been operating at a loss for some time, continued to suffer, leading to a temporary shutdown of the phenol and acetone production plant in Pasadena, Texas. Higher sales prices during 2003 helped turn the aromatics segment profitable for the first nine months of 2003. The chlorovinyls operations, meantime, were reporting a drop in profits thanks to significantly higher raw materials and natural gas costs and a fall in demand.

Principal Subsidiaries

GG Terminal Management Corporation; Georgia Gulf Europe, ApS (Denmark); Georgia Gulf Chemicals & Vinyls, L.L.C.; Georgia Gulf Lake Charles, L.L.C.; Great River Oil and Gas Corporation; GGRC Corporation.

Principal Competitors

OxyVinyls, LP; Shintech, Inc.; Formosa Plastics Corporation; PolyOne Corporation; The Dow Chemical Company.

Further Reading

Adams, Jarret, ''Georgia Gulf Buys Condea Vista Vinyl Operations,'' *Chemical Week,* September 8, 1999, p. 9.

Coleman, Zach, ''Georgia Gulf Ready to Settle Chemical Suits,'' *Atlanta Business Chronicle,* June 7, 1999.

Finotti, John, ''The Gold Mine Georgia-Pacific Gave Away,'' *Business Week,* May 9, 1988, p. 106D.

''Georgia Gulf Corp.,'' *Wall Street Transcript,* May 9, 1988, pp. 89, 390.

''Georgia Gulf Corp. +182.1%,'' *Institutional Investor,* March 1988, pp. 79–80.

Hunter, David, ''Georgia Gulf Bets on Chlorovinyls,'' *Chemical Week,* August 23–August 30, 2000, pp. 52–53.

Jenks, Alan, ''A Secure Georgia Gulf Roars into a New Decade,'' *Atlanta Business Chronicle,* July 2, 1990, pp. 4A+.

McCosh, John, ''Solo Success Story at Georgia Gulf,'' *Atlanta Business Chronicle,* April 13, 1987, p. 3A.

Mullin, Rick, ''Bucking the Trends: Georgia Gulf Keys on Domestic Operations,'' *Chemical Week,* September 30, 1992, pp. 38+.

Research: Ideas for Today's Investors—Georgia Gulf, San Francisco: Research Magazine, Inc., 1989.

Richards, Don, ''EPA Proposes Fines Against Condea Vista and Georgia Gulf,'' *Chemical Market Reporter,* September 4, 2000, pp. 5, 37.

Sweitzer, Letitia, ''Rave Reviews for Georgia Gulf,'' *Business Atlanta,* December 1988, pp. 40–41.

Tullo, Alex, ''PVC Market Tightens As Georgia Gulf Buys Condea's Operations,'' *Chemical Market Reporter,* September 13, 1999, pp. 3, 34.

Willoughby, Jack, ''Pipe Dreams at Georgia Gulf,'' *Financial World,* June 25, 1991, pp. 18, 20.

—John Simley
—update: David E. Salamie

Giant Industries, Inc.

23733 North Scottsdale Road
Scottsdale, Arizona 85255-3410
U.S.A.
Telephone: (480) 585-8888
Toll Free: (800) 937-4937
Fax: (480) 585-8948
Web site: http://www.giant.com

Public Company
Incorporated: 1969
Employees: 2,465
Sales: $1.29 billion (2002)
Stock Exchanges: New York
Ticker Symbol: GI
NAIC: 324110 Petroleum Refineries; 422710 Petroleum Bulk Stations and Terminals; 422720 Petroleum and Petroleum Products Wholesalers (Except Bulk Stations and Terminals); 447110 Gasoline Stations with Convenience Stores; 454311 Heating Oil Dealers; 454319 Other Fuel Dealers

Giant Industries, Inc. is a refiner and marketer of petroleum products based in Scottsdale, Arizona. Most of the company's operations are in the southwestern portion of the United States, centering on the Four Corners area—where Utah, Colorado, New Mexico, and Arizona converge. These include two crude oil refineries located in New Mexico, near Gallup and Farmington; a crude oil gathering operation based in Farmington with approximately 239 miles of pipeline; two distribution terminals for finished petroleum products in Flagstaff, Arizona, and Albuquerque, New Mexico; a transportation company with 32 trucks that carry crude and finished petroleum products to its own service stations in the Four Corners area; and 127 service stations that include either convenience stores or kiosks, which are located in New Mexico, Arizona, and Colorado. The vast majority of the service stations are branded under one of three names: Giant, Mustang, or Conoco—the former two are company-owned monikers, while the latter is used under a licensing agreement with oil giant ConocoPhillips. In addition, Giant owns Phoenix Fuel Co., Inc., an industrial/commercial wholesale distributor of petroleum products, including diesel fuel, gasoline, jet fuel, kerosene, and motor oil; Phoenix Fuel is primarily active in Arizona but also serves customers in Nevada, New Mexico, and Texas. During 2002 Giant Industries gained a foothold on the East Coast—and more than doubled its refinery capacity—through the acquisition of a crude oil refinery in Yorktown, Virginia, from BP p.l.c.

Early History

The founder of Giant Industries, Inc. has become one of the living legends in the Southwest. James E. Acridge started his rise to prominence in 1961 when, at the tender age of 21, he leased a small gasoline station in Glendale, Arizona, from Richfield Oil (later to change its name to Atlantic Richfield). Four years later, the ambitious young man leased another station in the southern part of Phoenix, Arizona. This time he operated it under his own sign, Giant, while still holding onto his first station in Glendale. The new station was a much larger, three-island, nine-pump gas station, supplied by Shell Oil Company. Within one year, Acridge had his new Giant gas station pumping more than 60,000 gallons per month. When the owner of the property on which his Giant station was situated demanded 1.5 cents per gallon instead of a flat rent fee, Acridge moved into another station where he put up his Giant shingle and was soon pumping 50,000 gallons per month.

It was not until 1968, however, that Acridge jumped into the big league of gas station operators. He purchased a small two-island station, an old Signal Oil gas station in Phoenix, and put up the first self-serve sign in the region. Almost overnight the volume jumped to 150,000 gallons per month. The next step was a natural one. Acridge purchased a plot of land near Mesa, Arizona, borrowed $30,000 from a bank to begin operations, leased all the necessary equipment, and built his own multipump gas station. This station was pumping 150,000 gallons of gas by its third month in operation. Acridge incorporated his company in 1969, and from that time on he was the undisputed king of self-serve gas stations in Arizona.

Expansion and Growth in the 1970s

Fully aware that he was 15 years ahead of the market, Acridge built his second self-serve unit in 1970. The design of this unit was the forerunner of all subsequent self-serve gas

Company Perspectives:

Core Values. Do your best. Do what's right. Treat others the way you would like to be treated.

stations. Under the world's largest gas station canopy up to that time, Acridge wanted to make it a pleasant experience for his customers to pump gas, so he piped in soft, soothing music under the canopies, constructed high retaining walls so that people would not be embarrassed if their friends saw them at a self-service station, and provided ample space between all the gas pumps for customers to pump their own gas without any significant delay. Within a short time, the two self-serve stations were pumping between 250,000 and 300,000 gallons of gas per month. By 1973, Giant Industries had expanded to include 12 self-serve gas stations and was pumping more than one million gallons of gasoline per month.

Acridge was confident that the full service gas stations were not able to compete with his innovative units. Soon major oil companies began to court the rapidly growing company, and Acridge decided to switch from his traditional independent supply sources to Phillips Petroleum Company. But almost as soon as the ink had dried on the contract, Phillips informed Acridge that the company was pulling out of the Phoenix market and cutting off Giant's supply of gasoline. When Acridge discovered that most independents like Giant had been cut off by the larger oil companies, he went into federal court and procured an injunction requiring Phillips to continue supplying his company. After a meeting of more than 60 independents in Phoenix, the group devised a strategy to lobby Washington and the Federal Energy Office to enact new rules that would allow for a more equitable sharing of oil supplies. Before the regulation went into effect, however, Giant was forced to close all but four of its gas stations.

When the oil embargo by OPEC exacerbated an already existing supply crisis, Acridge decided to enter into the refinery business to ensure a steady supply for his own stations. He purchased a small gas processing facility located in Carthage, Texas, had it completely dismantled, and transported the entire plant to Farmington, New Mexico, where it was reassembled and put in working order. As the worry about supply subsided, Acridge focused on reopening his closed units and constructing new ones. As his operation grew, he also decided to develop tie-in businesses that augmented his self-serve stations. His first idea involved what he called a "C-Store," a huge store situated in back of his gas stations that sold a large line of groceries, including such items as sporting goods and automotive parts, and included an on-site dry cleaners. The customers did not come, sales were almost nonexistent, and Acridge was forced to close the stores within a few months. Other misguided tie-in developments included a tire business and a fast food restaurant called "Fast Eddie's."

One of the tie-in businesses that did work was a scaled-down version of the C-Store concept, which Acridge named Giant's "Goodies C-Store." Designed as a small kiosk of approximately 1,000 square feet, situated in the middle of a gas station between the pump islands, it allowed customers to pay at a window for their gas or to enter the store and purchase an item. The stores carried about 400 to 450 products, mostly such things as cigarettes, beer, soft drinks, pre-made sandwiches, snacks, candies, and picnic-type supplies. The per-store average sales figure quickly climbed to $10,000 per month, and some were even averaging sales as high as $25,000 per month. With this income, Acridge was able to reopen most of his stores that were forced to close during the early 1970s. By the end of 1979, Giant was operating 23 gas stations and pumping more than four million gallons of gasoline per month.

Consolidation and Profitability During the 1980s

The 1980s were years of dramatic change for the company. In 1981 the major oil companies initiated a strategic campaign to squeeze out independent gas station entrepreneurs such as Acridge and reestablish themselves in markets from which they had long been absent. During the middle and late 1970s, independents had captured 55 percent of the gas station market in Phoenix. But after companies such as Shell and Texaco increased their presence, most independents were soon pushed out of the market. Giant, however, was one of the few that remained, and at some cost. Acridge was forced to scale back his operations dramatically, and he closed all of his stations in the Phoenix metropolitan area. Branching out into smaller towns, Giant found a more stable, and lucrative, market.

In 1982 Giant acquired the Ciniza refinery from Shell, a more sophisticated and modern facility, and closed down the refinery it had built in Farmington, New Mexico. Acridge decided to close the New Mexico refining operation because the regional demand for residual fuel began to subside. At Ciniza, located near Gallup, New Mexico, Giant added a $12 million, state-of-the-art 5,000 barrels-per-day (b/d) isomerization unit to enhance the facility's ability to produce unleaded gasoline. By the mid-1980s, Ciniza was producing approximately 25,000 barrels per day and supplying motor fuels to more than 100 different customers throughout Arizona and New Mexico. Almost 25 percent of the company's annual production was sold through its own retail outlets, service stations, and two super retail centers.

Heartened by the success of his Goodies C-Stores during the early and mid-1980s, Acridge decided to open what became known as a "highway extravaganza," an enormous combination truck stop/gas station/retail store close to the Ciniza refinery, about 20 miles east of Gallup, New Mexico, on Interstate 40. Opened in 1987 and covering about 35 acres of property, the Giant Travel Center complex included a Truck Center; a fueling center for truckers with its own C-Store; a travelers' fueling center for passenger cars and recreational vehicles, separate from the Truck Center; and a 29,000-square-foot shopping mall with six retail stores, a restaurant, and a movie theater.

The first one of its kind, the Giant Travel Center went against one of the principles upon which Acridge built his independent business. The Truck Center itself had 18 fully attended pumping islands that provided diesel fuel—at self-serve prices, of course. The decision to have attendants was based on the fact that Giant had to get certain information from truckers who paid their fuel bills with credit cards or vouchers. The Truck Center also included a service center, where truckers could have repairs done by a staff of certified mechanics and

Key Dates:

1961: James E. Acridge leases a small gasoline station in Glendale, Arizona, from Richfield Oil.
1965: Acridge leases a second station in Phoenix, operating it under his own brand, Giant.
1969: Acridge builds his own multipump self-serve gas station near Mesa, Arizona; he incorporates his company as Giant Industries, Inc.
1973–74: A supply squeeze—engendered both by larger oil companies and the OPEC oil embargo—forces Giant to close all but four of its gas stations; company soon responds by building its own refinery in Farmington, New Mexico, using equipment purchased from a Texas gas processing facility; Giant begins reopening closed gas stations and opening new ones, some of which start to feature kiosks.
1979: Giant is operating 23 gas stations, pumping more than four million gallons of gas per month.
Early 1980s: Competition from the oil majors forces Acridge to close all his stations in the Phoenix metro area and to shift the focus of his retail operations to smaller towns.
1982: Company acquires the Ciniza refinery, located near Gallup, New Mexico, from Shell; the Farmington refinery is shut down.
1987: The Giant Travel Center, an enormous combination truck stop/gas station/retail store, is opened on Interstate 40 near Gallup.
1989: Company goes public with a listing on the New York Stock Exchange.
1995: Giant acquires a crude oil gathering operation based in Farmington that includes about 340 miles of pipeline.
1996: Company acquires its second refinery, located in Bloomfield, New Mexico.
1997: Giant acquires 96 service stations in Arizona, New Mexico, Colorado, and Utah from Thriftway Marketing Corp.; wholesale distributor Phoenix Fuel Co., Inc. is acquired; Giant enters into an alliance that enables it to begin using the Conoco brand on some of its service stations.
1998: About 50 of Giant's service stations adopt a new company-owned name, Mustang; Giant agrees to a merger with Holly Corporation, operator of refineries in New Mexico and Montana, but the deal falls apart later in the year.
2002: Acridge is ousted from his position as CEO and president; Giant acquires a refinery in Yorktown, Virginia, from BP p.l.c. for about $195 million.
2003: The Giant Travel Center is sold to Pilot Travel Centers LLC.

service technicians. Oil changes, grease jobs, and tire replacements were the most common types of maintenance required by truckers, and Giant began to garner a reputation for its efficiency and competence. In addition, the service center had the only truck wash between Barstow, California, and Oklahoma City, Oklahoma, and, as word of the facilities at the Travel Center spread, truckers would sometimes drive 350 miles out of their way just to get their rig washed.

Although tourists and local customers were always welcomed at the Giant Travel Center, it was the intention of Acridge to cater to and treat the truckers as if they were royalty. Truckers were spending an average of between $100 to $150 on fuel alone, not to mention all the other purchases they made at the retail stores and restaurant. So Acridge arranged for a van to carry truckers back and forth from their rigs in the vast parking lot of the Travel Center, built 26 shower stalls of hotel-like quality for truckers who wanted to clean up between rides, installed laundry facilities, and a shoe shine. Perhaps most important of all, a trucker could order a 16-ounce T-bone steak for $10.95, have it cooked to order, and call home from the telephone situated on his table. As business boomed and more truckers began to arrive at the Travel Center, Acridge expanded his operation to include more retail stores and a new restaurant whose staff included a head chef trained at the highly respected Culinary Institute of America.

Acridge took Giant Industries public in 1989 with a listing on the New York Stock Exchange. That year also saw the company enter the oil and gas exploration business through the acquisition of Hixon Development Co., which was renamed Giant Exploration & Production Co. Giant also constructed a new headquarters building in Scottsdale.

Acquisition-Fueled Growth in the 1990s

During the early 1990s, Giant Industries continued its rapid growth. In 1993 the Travel Center alone reported that it pumped more than 20 million gallons of fuel. Over the years, the company had built up its transportation operation to include a fleet of 90 trucks that carried crude and finished petroleum products not only to its own facilities but also to a growing number of customers in the Four Corners region. In 1995 Acridge made another investment by acquiring a crude oil gathering operation located in San Juan County (where Farmington was located) that included approximately 340 miles of pipeline.

By 1996, Giant Industries was one of the most successful petroleum products companies in the southwestern part of the United States. Having found its niche in the Four Corners area, the company increased its revenues from $301 million in 1992 to $499 million by the end of fiscal 1996. Giant Industries purchased its second refinery in 1996, located in Bloomfield, New Mexico, from the Gary-Williams Energy Corporation, for $55 million. This acquisition helped the company to consolidate some of its refining operations, lower transportation costs, and improve production. With the Ciniza and Bloomfield refineries working at full capacity, the company increased the number of barrels sold per day from 27,000 to 39,000 in less than one year. Because of the growing demand for more of its products, Giant decided to initiate a capital project to increase the number of barrels produced per day at both the Ciniza and Bloomfield refineries.

Also during 1996, Giant made a major purchase involving Diamond Shamrock, Inc. For $5.4 million the company acquired seven gasoline stations operated by Shamrock in northwestern New Mexico. This acquisition brought the total number of Giant-run gas stations to 56, largest of all the independents in the Four Corners region. The company also built two new combination service stations/convenience stores in Albuquerque, New Mexico; and Sedona, Arizona, and initiated a major campaign to remodel 28 of its existing service stations/convenience stores. There was also a significant divestment completed in 1996: Giant sold nearly all of its oil and gas exploration and production assets for $25.5 million.

Growth remained high on Giant's agenda in 1997. The company's refineries had excess capacity, and Giant attempted to remedy this situation through a large expansion of its retailing operations. In May 1997 Giant acquired, through a mix of buying and leasing, 96 service stations and convenience stores in Arizona, New Mexico, Colorado, and Utah from Thriftway Marketing Corp. Giant also acquired 22 truck transports as part of this deal. Later in 1997 the company acquired Ever-Ready Oil Co., an Albuquerque-based wholesaler and retailer that owned and operated 27 retail outlets, most of which were located in the Albuquerque area. Meanwhile, in June 1997, the company further diversified and secured another outlet for the products from its refineries by acquiring Phoenix Fuel Co., Inc. for $30 million in cash. Phoenix, an industrial/commercial distributor of petroleum products, had fuel sales of about 16,000 b/d.

The next year began with the acquisition of DeGuelle Oil Company, owner of seven Conoco brand gasoline stations in southwestern Colorado. The stations remained Conoco outlets under Giant ownership as Giant and Conoco had entered into a branding alliance in 1997 whereby Giant would begin using the oil giant's name at some of its stations. By the end of 1998, 49 of Giant's outlets, along with the Giant Travel Center, began sporting the Conoco name. Also during 1998, around 50 of the company's service stations adopted a new, company-owned name, Mustang. Giant acquired another 32 Arizona service stations from Kaibab Industries Inc., most of which were located in the Phoenix and Tucson areas. This deal brought the company's retail outlet count to 170.

In April 1998 Giant Industries agreed to a $350 million merger with Holly Corporation, a Dallas-based firm with refineries in southern New Mexico and Montana. But the two companies called off the merger in September of that year, apparently for two main reasons: a $1 billion lawsuit that was brought against Holly in late August and conditions on the merger that were demanded by the Federal Trade Commission, which was particularly concerned about the merger's impact on competition in the Four Corners area. For Giant, 1998 ended on a sour note as well: The company reported a net loss of $2.2 million (on revenues of $642.5 million) because of falling crude oil and finished product prices.

The company returned to profitability in 1999, a year in which Giant also built a new gasoline and diesel fuel terminal near Flagstaff, Arizona, with a capacity of 78,000 b/d. Giant also announced plans that year to sell about 25 of its service station/convenience stores in eastern Arizona, southern Colorado, and northern Arizona that were seen as noncore operations.

Adding a Third Refinery in the Early 2000s

Production of crude oil in the Four Corners region began declining in 1997, making it difficult for Giant to operate its two refineries at full capacity in a cost-efficient manner. The company therefore began seeking to acquire one or more refineries outside of its core area of operation. The abandoned merger with Holly was part of this effort, as were two other deals that failed to materialize in 2001. A joint venture with Western Refining to run a Chevron refinery in El Paso and one other refinery collapsed, and Giant also unsuccessfully bid for a refinery in Mandan, North Dakota, owned by BP p.l.c. Giant finally achieved its goal in May 2002 when it acquired another BP refinery, this one located in Yorktown, Virginia, for about $195 million. The refinery, the only one in Virginia, had crude oil capacity of 62,000 b/d, more than doubling Giant's total refining capacity.

Ironically, Acridge, the person who had guided Giant Industries since its founding, was ousted from his position as CEO and president in March 2002, before the Yorktown deal closed. The firing was evidently related to a $5.4 million insider loan to Acridge, which the company wrote down during the fourth quarter of 2001. Acridge remained on the board of directors but was replaced as chairman by Fred L. Holliger, who was named CEO as well. Holliger had previously served as chief operating officer.

Giant substantially increased its debt load in order to complete the Yorktown refinery purchase. Its long-term debt jumped from $256.7 million at the end of 2001 to $398.1 million one year later. The increased burden in servicing this debt contributed to the company's $9.3 million net loss for 2002, while revenues that year increased 35 percent, reaching $1.29 billion, as a direct result of the addition of the Yorktown facility. Giant embarked on a program of debt reduction that chiefly involved the divestment of noncore retailing assets. Eleven service stations were sold off during 2002, and by late 2003 the station count was down to 127. The company was particularly concentrating on selling off money-losing outlets in the Phoenix and Tucson areas. In addition, Giant sold its Travel Center near Gallup to Pilot Travel Centers LLC for $6.3 million in June 2003; sold its corporate headquarters building in Scottsdale, leasing back a portion of the building; and sold about 132 miles of its Farmington-based pipeline system. Through these and other moves, Giant Industries reduced its debt by about $83 million by late 2003. The company was committed to further trimming its debt load, thereby enhancing its profitability and placing it in position to seek further avenues of growth.

Principal Subsidiaries

Giant Industries Arizona, Inc.; Giant Four Corners, Inc.; Giant Mid-Continent, Inc.; Phoenix Fuel Co., Inc.; DeGuelle Oil Company; Ciniza Production Company; Giant Stop-N-Go of New Mexico, Inc.; San Juan Refining Company; Giant Pipeline Company; Giant Yorktown, Inc.; Giant Yorktown Holding Company.

Principal Competitors

Exxon Mobil Corporation; ConocoPhillips; Valero Energy Corporation; Tesoro Petroleum Corporation; Marathon Ashland Petroleum LLC; Holly Corporation.

Further Reading

Barrett, William P., "The Mother of All Truck Stops," *Forbes,* April 12, 1993, pp. 116–18.

Byrne, Harlan S., "Giant Industries," *Barron's,* May 13, 1991, pp. 31–32.

"CEO of Giant Ousted, Move Said to Be Linked to Personal Loan," *Oil Express,* April 8, 2002, p. 5.

Emond, Mark, "Giant Expands in Its Primary Market," *National Petroleum News,* June 1997, p. 21.

——, "Giant Industries Expands in Far Southwest," *National Petroleum News,* October 1995, p. 28.

Evans, Beth, "U.S. Refiners Giant, Holly Merge to Create Niche Player," *Platt's Oilgram News,* April 16, 1998, p. 1.

"Giant Buys Seven Stations," *Oil Daily,* June 3, 1996, p. SW2.

"Giant's Profits Grow with Refining Sector," *Oil Daily,* May 14, 1996, p. 4.

"Giant to Sell Retail Assets, Postpone Refinery Upgrade, to Boost Bleak Bottom Line," *Oil Express,* August 12, 2002, p. 7.

Kiernan, Peter, "Tiny Giant More Than Doubles with Purchase of BP's Yorktown Refinery," *Oil Daily,* February 13, 2002.

Kovski, Alan, "Giant to Buy, Lease 96 Thriftway Outlets," *Oil Daily,* April 24, 1997.

——, "Plant Purchases Help Giant Increase Profits," *Oil Daily,* March 5, 1996, p. 3.

Luebke, Cathy, "Giant Industries Inc. Files for Initial Public Offering," *Business Journal of Phoenix,* October 23, 1989, pp. 1+.

"Mapco, Giant Industries Beat Segment Trend," *Oil Daily,* October 31, 1996, p. 2.

McDonald, Michele, "Think Big: Giant Shops for Refinery," *Scottsdale (Ariz.) Progress,* June 7, 1994, p. 5.

Murphy, Marvin, "Phoenix-Based Giant Industries Details Major Expansion Program," *Oil Daily,* August 2, 1990, p. 5.

Norman, James, "Giant Branches Out, Buying BP Refinery," *Platt's Oilgram News,* February 13, 2002, p. 3.

Reid, Marvin, "Flying High in Tough but Tempting Phoenix," *National Petroleum News,* September 1980, pp. 60–66.

Share, Jeff, "Successful Southwest Refiner Faces New Competition from Diamond Shamrock," *Oil Daily,* April 7, 1994, pp. 2+.

Tyson, Ray, "Merger of U.S. Refiners Giant, Holly Falls Apart," *Platt's Oilgram News,* September 3, 1998, p. 1.

Vandeveire, Mary, "Arizona Market Ripe for Giant Expansion," *Business Journal of Phoenix,* October 20, 1997.

Victoria, Frank, "How Giant's "Travel Center' Shatters Old Truck Stop Image," *National Petroleum News,* March 1988, pp. 32–38.

—Thomas Derdak
—update: David E. Salamie

Granite Construction Incorporated

585 W. Beach Street
Watsonville, California 95076
U.S.A.
Telephone: (831) 724-1011
Fax: (831) 722-9657
Web site: http://www.graniteconstruction.com

Public Company
Incorporated: 1922 as Granite Construction Company
Employees: 5,017
Sales: $1.76 billion (2002)
Stock Exchanges: New York
Ticker Symbol: GVA
NAIC: 237310 Highway, Street, and Bridge Construction

Granite Construction Incorporated is one of the leading heavy civil contractors in the United States, operating primarily through its Granite Construction Company subsidiary. The Watsonville, California-based company is publicly traded, with employees owning 21 percent. The business of Granite Construction Company is divided into two divisions. The Branch Division serves local markets in California, Arizona, Nevada, and Utah, concentrating on highways, bridges, pipelines, and large and small local site projects valued at less than $50 million. Granite's Heavy Construction Division operates on a national level. While it occasionally accepts small local projects, it generally takes on such major public and private projects as highways, dams, rapid-transit bridges, tunnels, pipelines, and canals—generally valued in excess of $50 million. The division maintains estimating offices in Florida, Georgia, New York, and Texas. The Branch Division is also able to take advantage of the resources possessed by the Heavy Construction Division, which are normally not available to local firms, to gain a competitive advantage. In some cases the two divisions may collaborate on a project that is beyond the capabilities of a local branch. To achieve a competitive edge, Granite produces its own sand, gravel, and aggregate-based construction materials, which it also sells to other companies. Granite owns or leases strategically located reserves of aggregate materials, as well as 158 processing plants for rock, asphalt, and concrete. In addition, it operates one of the largest contractor equipment fleets in the country.

Granite's Founder Buys Quarry in 1900

Granite's founder was Arthur Roberts Wilson, better known as A.R. Wilson. Born in San Francisco in 1866, he was the nephew of the only Hispanic to ever serve as governor of California, Romualdo Pachero, who played an influential role in the young man's life after the early death of his father. Wilson was sent East for his education, earning a degree in engineering from the Massachusetts Institute of Technology in 1890. He then returned to the Bay area to become a construction engineer, serving a term as City Civil Engineer for Oakland and running the local quarry. Following this stint, he sought a source for high quality aggregate materials. He would find it in a small quarry located near Watsonville, alerted to the opportunity by Warren Porter, the son of an area banker. A major deposit of granite formed 200 million years ago had been pushed to the surface and made accessible by the actions of the San Andreas Fault. The granite would not be discovered until 1871 when the Southern Pacific Railroad was laying a coastal line and ran into it near Watsonville. The railroad took advantage of the deposit, mining the rock for ballast—which formed a bed for the tracks, providing drainage and support for heavy loads. Porter enlisted Wilson and four other investors to purchase the quarry. To raise his share of the money, Wilson borrowed $10,000 from a cousin, backed by a life insurance policy. He then moved his family to Watsonville, and on February 14th, 1900—Valentine's Day—the partners incorporated Granite Rock Company.

San Francisco Earthquake of 1906 a Turning Point

The Great Earthquake of 1906, which caused tremendous fires and leveled San Francisco, propelled Granite Rock into the construction business. In the aftermath of the quake, the company had contracted to build the Gilroy City Hall and a Wells Fargo building in San Francisco, as well as structures in the Monterey Bay area. In 1907 Granite Rock landed its first road construction job, paving the streets of Watsonville. As the automobile became more commonplace and the need for paved

Company Perspectives:

Granite's participation in both the public and private sectors and its diverse mix of project types and sizes have contributed to the Company's revenue growth and profitability in changing economic environments.

roads increased, California in 1915 passed legislation to modernize streets, what wags called the ''Get Out of the Mud Act.'' Granite Rock was especially aggressive in drumming up paving business from local communities. The state's economy was also booming, providing ample construction jobs for Granite Rock. In 1922 the company underwent a number of changes. First, Porter had suffered heavy losses on an outside investment with Java Coconut Oil Company, which acquired his interest in Granite Rock. Wilson purchased the stock to become majority shareholder as well as president. Also in 1922 he established Granite Construction Company, a separate entity, becoming its president as well. Two years later a Salinas branch was opened. In addition, Wilson formed Central Supply Company, a materials distributor, thus allowing the family of businesses to offer a full range of service, from materials to construction. Wilson ran these three companies until just ten days before the stock crash of 1929. Driving home from the quarry one day he suffered a heart attack and died.

Wilson's wife Anna took over as president of the Granite companies and son Jeff Wilson served as general manager. The stock crash ushered in the Great Depression of the 1930s, and with the industries that it served suffering, the Granite companies struggled as well. Finding it too difficult to keep three businesses operating during this difficult period, the Wilson family decided in 1936 to sell Granite Construction Company to businessmen Walter Wilkinson, Sr., and Bert Scott. As a result, Granite Rock and Granite Construction now followed their own destinies.

Granite managed to survive the 1930s. During World War II, with Bert Scott serving as president, the company did some work for military installations, including Watsonville Naval Air Station. But it was during the postwar economic boom that Granite really began to grow. In 1946 it opened branches in Santa Cruz and Monterey. A year later Granite launched its Engineering Construction Department. It was also during this period, in 1945, that longtime CEO and Chairman Richard C. Solari began working for the company.

Granite remained very much a California contractor over the next 30 years. In 1955 it opened a Sacramento branch, and also during the 1950s acquired American Sand & Gravel Company. The company completed no significant acquisitions during the 1960s, then in 1971 bought E.H. Haskell Company to establish a branch in Santa Barbara. A Bakersville branch was established in 1976 through the acquisition of Owl-Folsom. In addition, Granite opened a branch in Stockton in 1978 when it acquired McGaw Company. It was also during the 1970s that Granite took on major projects outside of California. It completed a number of jobs related to the Washington Metropolitan Area Transit Authority, including several train stations in the District of Columbia and nearby Maryland. In Washington state, Granite worked on the Chief Joseph Powerhouse and the Rock Island Powerhouse, both on the Columbia River. Other jobs of note during the 1970s included Travis Air Force Base in California, Skitook Dam in Oklahoma, Kayenta Mines in Arizona, Aberdeen Lock & Dam in Missouri, and Spinney Mountain Dam in Colorado, and the Howard Street to Wilmette Tunnel in Chicago, Illinois. Granite closed the decade with Richard Solari succeeding Bert Scott as president.

The 1990s: Bringing Robust Growth

Solari oversaw a period of tremendous growth for Granite during the 1990s. The decade started with the creation in January 1990 of holding company Granite Construction Inc., which subsequently acquired Granite Construction Company as well as affiliate Wilcott Corporation. Granite was then taken public in April 1990, and its shares began trading on the NASDAQ. A secondary offer was held a year later. The company solidified its California base of operations during the early 1990s. A Palm Springs branch was opened in 1992, as was a San Diego branch. Also during the early 1990s, Granite expanded into Georgia and Texas. In 1995 Granite moved into the Utah market by acquiring Salt Lake-based Gibbons Co. for $42.8 million. Gibbons Co. was a holding company for several subsidiaries: Gibbons & Reed Co., a heavy civil contractor doing business in a number of Western states; Concrete Products Co., producers of concrete, asphalt, sand, and gravel; Garco Testing Laboratories, which conducted tests on materials used in the civil contracting industry; Inter-Mountain Flurry Seal, which made emulsions used in the maintenance and rejuvenation of asphalt; and Bear River Contractors, a construction and materials processing company. Tallied together, the Gibbons' companies generated annual revenues in the $90 million range. Granite completed another significant acquisition in 1997, bolstering its business in the Southeast by buying the highway and heavy civil construction divisions of Hardaway Co., a major construction company based in Columbus, Georgia, which sold the assets in order to concentrate on more profitable lines of business.

With the economy soaring in the second half of the 1990s and the construction industry further stimulated by new government spending on highway projects, Granite enjoyed strong growth. Revenues in 1995 totaled nearly $895,000, with net income of $28.5 million. In 1997 the company topped the $1 billion mark in revenues and continued to climb. The company also moved to the New York Stock Exchange in 1997. A major problem facing Granite and the entire industry at this point was its ability to find enough skilled operators of heavy construction equipment. The company began to recruit in high schools, and in Florida it turned to prisons, where convicts doing road work in conjunction with Granite would have a job once their sentences were completed.

Annual revenues reached $1.23 billion in 1998 and $1.33 billion in 1999, with net income growing from $46.5 million to nearly $53 million. A major portion of these revenues were projects paid for or partially funded by the Federal Highway Administration, as well as work that resulted from damage caused by El Niño. Also of note, the company created a land development business, Granite Construction, which grew out of an effort to convert a former gravel mine into a major Sacramento park. Because the company donated the land for the

Key Dates:

1900: Granite Rock Company is incorporated.
1922: Granite Construction Company is formed as Granite Rock subsidiary.
1936: Granite Construction is sold.
1985: Employees gain ownership stake.
1987: David Watts is named CEO.
1990: Company is taken public.
2001: Halmar Builders of New York is acquired.

public park, Granite, in partnership with area developers, was permitted to build a business park within the confines. Private development fees then paid for the park's facilities. Over the next three years Granite Land became involved in other projects, including a shopping center in Antioch, California, and an industrial park in Dallas, Texas.

In May 1999, after working 54 years at Granite, Richard Solari retired as chairman, assuming the title of chairman emeritus. He was succeeded by Watts, who continued to act as the company's president and chief executive officer, leading Granite into a new century. The company continued to expand its reach and acquire assets. In 2000 it bought some operations of Wilder Construction Company, a Lubbock, Texas-based heavy civil contractor. A more significant transaction took place a year later with the $19 million purchase of Halmar Builders of New York, Inc., a heavy construction contractor located in Mt. Vernon, New York, with annual revenues of approximately $200 million. The move allowed Granite to participate in the highly attractive New York City market, which spent $6 billion each year on heavy construction. Prior to this point, Granite had only been involved in one major project in New Jersey. Rather than start up a New York operation, Granite elected to buy in, taking over Halmar's backlog of work worth close to $200 million. It was also an advantageous deal for Halmar, which was undergoing a transition in leadership among its four partners. The two older partners were able to cash out, and the two younger partners were able to maintain their management group and carry on the business as a subsidiary of Granite.

With Halmar in the fold, Granite saw its revenues rise to $1.55 billion in 2001 and $1.76 billion in 2002, along with net income of $50.5 million in 2001 and $49.3 billion in 2002. Revenues through the third quarter of 2003 were flat compared to the previous year, but net income was ahead of the pace of 2002 by close to $2.8 million. While the year-end results were being tallied, in January 2004, Watts turned over the CEO position to William G. Dorey, who had been named president in February 2003. Watts continued on as chairman. The 59-year-old Dorey had been with the company for more than 30 years, holding a number of executive positions and serving in key roles during Granite's impressive run of growth since going public in 1990.

Principal Subsidiaries

Granite Construction Company; Wilcott Corporation; Granite Land Company; Granite Halmar Construction.

Principal Competitors

Bechtel Group, Inc.; Peter Kiewit Sons', Inc.; Washington Group International, Inc.

Further Reading

Akasie, Jay, ''Make Just One Thing; Make It Cheaply,'' *Forbes,* January 11, 1999, p. 154.
Korman, Richard, ''Granite Grabs Halmar Builders,'' *ENR,* May 28, 2001, p. 16.
Philippidis, Alex, ''Granite to Build on Halmar's Project Base,'' *Westchester County Business Journal,* August 27, 2001, p. 6.
Rattle, Barbara, ''Salt-Lake-Based Gibbons Co. Sold to Calif. Firm for $42 Million,'' *Enterprise,* May 15, 1995, p. 1.

—Ed Dinger

Harlem Globetrotters International, Inc.

400 East Van Buren Street, Suite 300
Phoenix, Arizona 85004
U.S.A.
Telephone: (602) 258-0000
Fax: (602) 258-5925
Web site: http://www.harlemglobetrotters.com

Private Company
Incorporated: 1927
Employees: 67
Sales: $85 million (2003 est.)
NAIC: 711211 Sports Teams and Clubs

Harlem Globetrotters International, Inc. is the company behind the world-renowned Harlem Globetrotters basketball team. Multiple teams, each wearing the distinctive red, white, and blue uniforms of the Globetrotters, tour throughout the world, playing nearly 300 games annually. The company is owned and led by Mannie Jackson, a former Harlem Globetrotters player who purchased the team in 1993. During its history, the Globetrotters have played more than 20,000 games in 117 countries.

Origins

The nucleus of the first Harlem Globetrotters team was drawn from a basketball team named ''Savoy Big Five,'' formed by Abe Saperstein in 1926. Saperstein, the principal personality behind the singular success of the Harlem Globetrotters for nearly a half-century, organized the Savoy Big Five when he was 24 years old, naming the team after Chicago's Savoy Ballroom. Located above a movie theater, the dance hall featured many of the prominent big bands of the era, patterning itself after the New York establishment of the same name. When the Chicago version of the Savoy began to suffer a decline in business, the owners decided to schedule basketball games in the facility, hoping the attraction would invigorate business. Accordingly, the Savoy's owners agreed to sponsor Saperstein's team. The arrangement lasted for only a short while. The spectacle of a basketball game failed to lure dancers to the Savoy, ending the agreement between Saperstein and the Savoy's owners, but the initial failure did not end Saperstein's involvement in managing and promoting a basketball team. Saperstein began forming a team he intended to take on tour. Several members of the disbanded Savoy Big Five agreed to join Saperstein's new touring team, which made its debut on January 7, 1927, in Hinckley, Illinois, marking the first game of what would become known as the Harlem Globetrotters.

At the inaugural game in Hinckley, a crowd of 300 spectators gathered, generating a gate receipt of $75. Saperstein's squad competed against a locally formed team, the first of its matches against any foes willing to challenge the touring team. For the first game, Saperstein's players wore uniforms that advertised the team name as ''New York.'' Saperstein later added his own name to the uniforms, creating ''Saperstein's New York Globetrotters.'' After the game in Hinckley, the players loaded up in Saperstein's Model ''T'' Ford and began touring in several Midwest states.

For roughly its first decade of existence, Saperstein's Globetrotters played its games conventionally, without the antics and orchestrated comedy routines that became the organization's signature style. The team, which became known as the ''Harlem New York Globetrotters'' in 1930, toured throughout Wisconsin, Minnesota, and Iowa by the beginning of the 1930s, compiling an impressive record against locally organized adversaries. The team played in small markets until it made its debut in its first major city in 1932, when the five-year-old team played in Detroit. The following year, the Globetrotters expanded its touring schedule by moving westward, adding venues in Montana, North Dakota, South Dakota, and Idaho. In 1934, the organization played its 1,000th game, finishing the year with 152 wins and two losses, typical of the dominance of Saperstein's squad.

At the end of the 1930s, the Globetrotters reached a turning point in their history. Expansion of the team's playing schedule had extended the geographic reach of the organization to the Pacific Northwest by 1936. In 1939, the team played in its first professional basketball championship tournament, which resulted in a rare loss to the New York Rens. The year also marked perhaps the most defining moment in the Globetrotters' history. During one game in the 1939 season, Saperstein's team

Company Perspectives:

The Harlem Globetrotters introduced most of the world to the game and continue to lead basketball's popularity globally. Much of what fans enjoy about the game today began with the Harlem Globetrotters. The team's message, flair, and appeal knows no boundaries and crosses barriers between cultures, societies, and people. The Harlem Globetrotters are the true champions and pioneers of basketball around the globe.

exhibited its considerable dominance over an opponent, assuming a 112–5 lead. With no risk of losing the game, the Globetrotters broke free from the conventions of team play and began to show off their skills, titillating the crowd with clownish antics and improvised comedy routines. The audience loved the display, leading Saperstein to inform his players that their extracurricular behavior was permissible, if not encouraged, once they had established a comfortable lead over their opponent. From that night forward, the team gradually developed the entertaining, choreographed routines that became the centerpiece of a Globetrotters show.

The Globetrotters organization flowered during the 1940s, becoming a nationally recognized phenomenon whose lure transcended the attraction of a sports team. The squad played its 2,000th game in 1940, finishing the year with a 159–8 record for the season. The team played in the World Professional Basketball tournament during the year as well, beating the New York Rens in the semifinals and the Chicago Bruins in the finals to capture its first World Basketball Championship. In 1942, the team signed Reece ''Goose'' Tatum, who would distinguish himself as the organization's first ''basketball comedian,'' originating many of the routines that formed the core of the Globetrotters' portfolio of antics. Other luminaries who would follow in his wake included Meadowlark Lemon and Fred ''Curly'' Neal. In 1946, a year in which the Globetrotters were featured in *LIFE* magazine, the team played its 3,000th game and its first game overseas, playing in front of U.S. soldiers in the U.S. Territory of Hawaii.

International Expansion in the 1950s

During the 1950s, the Globetrotters established themselves as the world ambassadors of basketball, becoming a genuine global attraction. In 1950, Saperstein organized his first European tour, scheduling games in Portugal, Switzerland, England, Belgium, France, Germany, and Italy. In 1951, during the team's 25th anniversary, the Globetrotters embarked on a tour of South America, playing before more than 50,000 spectators in Rio de Janeiro, Brazil. The team returned to Europe as well, drawing an impressive 75,000 fans in Berlin's Olympic Stadium, which stood in sharp contrast to a game played in Italy during the same tour that was organized for only one spectator, Pope Pius XII. The following year, the Globetrotters embarked on the team's first around-the-world tour, playing a 108-game schedule.

The demands of travel and an ever expanding playing schedule forced Saperstein to increase the size of the Globetrotters organization. Annual tours throughout Europe, a demanding North American schedule, and trips to other parts of the world, such as the Soviet Union in 1959, required the formation of additional Globetrotters squads. By the mid-1950s, there were four separate teams on tour, each wearing the distinctive red, white, and blue colors of the Globetrotters organization. On any given day, somewhere in the world, a Globetrotters team was playing in front of an audience, stirring an irrepressible level of excitement and fascination. Increased exposure of the team came not only from its on-court contact with fans worldwide, but also from television, films, and press attention. In 1953, the Globetrotters appeared on national television for the first time, when an estimated 77 percent of U.S. households watched the team on the *Ed Sullivan Show*. The first film featuring the Globetrotters, produced by Columbia Pictures, was released in 1951, followed by a second film, produced by United Artists, that was shown in more than 11,000 movie theaters in 1953.

The 1950s represented a pivotal decade in many respects, both on the court and off the court. One of the hallmarks of the Globetrotters organization, its official theme song, ''Sweet Georgia Brown,'' achieved such status in 1952. The following year, another signature trait of the Globetrotters organization was adopted, its genesis stemming from the popularity and the prowess of the team. By the early 1950s, it was becoming increasingly difficult to find opponents for the Globetrotters. In 1953, Saperstein turned to a respected name in basketball circles, Louis ''Red'' Klotz, to organize and coach teams to play against the Globetrotters. Although the Globetrotters would continue to play in tournaments against college all-stars and other teams, the majority of its games would be played against Klotz's teams, which were variously known as the Washington Generals, Boston Shamrocks, Baltimore Rockets, New York Nationals, Atlantic City Seagulls, and New Jersey Reds.

After a decade of progressive change, the Globetrotters entered the 1960s, a decade of transition for the organization. The team celebrated its 40th anniversary in 1966, returning to Hinckley, Illinois, for a game to mark the occasion. After four decades of existence, the team had played 8,945 games, 8,615 of which resulted in a Globetrotters victory. The Globetrotters had played in more than 1,200 cities, visiting 82 countries. The team's 40th anniversary also marked the end of an era. In March, Saperstein died at age 63, leaving the Globetrotters without its founder and owner. Ownership of the team remained held by Saperstein's estate until the following year when a trio of sports figures—Potter Palmer IV, George Gillett, Jr., and John O'Neil—purchased the team.

The change in ownership caused no disruption to the Globetrotters' unwavering success. The organization entered the 1970s drawing record crowds, having attracted more than two million spectators for the first time during its North American tour the year after the new owners acquired the team. In 1970, when the team played its 10,000th game, the Globetrotters recorded another first for a sports team—the debut of its own network television series. *The Harlem Globetrotters Show* first aired in September 1970, a cartoon series that earned the highest ratings in the history of Saturday morning television and, through syndication, reached audiences in more than 30 countries.

The 1970s saw the Globetrotters' vision of basketball entertainment reach several new locations. In 1978, the team made

Key Dates:

1927: The Globetrotters play their first game in Hinckley, Illinois.
1939: The Globetrotters begin to develop routines to highlight the players' skills.
1950: The Globetrotters embark on their first European tour.
1976: Macromedia, Inc. acquires the Globetrotters.
1986: International Broadcasting Corporation acquires the Globetrotters.
1993: Mannie Jackson acquires the Globetrotters for $6 million.
2003: The Globetrotters win their 21,000th game.

its first trip to west Africa, playing in Senegal, Ivory Coast, and Gabon, which raised the tally of foreign countries visited to 97. The following year, Deng-Hsiao Ping, the Premier of the People's Republic of China, visited the United States, and requested to meet the Globetrotters. The team fulfilled his request and played an exhibition game, which was broadcast by satellite and watched by 900 million viewers in China. By this point, ownership of the team had changed hands again, an event that occurred in 1976, when Macromedia, Inc., the owner of television and radio stations, billboard advertising properties, and the Ice Capades, acquired the Globetrotters organization.

The 1980s saw the Globetrotters honored with several distinctions. In 1982, the team became the first sports organization to earn a place along Hollywood's ''Walk of Fame.'' In 1985, the year the organization signed its first female player—Olympic Gold Medalist Lynette Woodard—the Smithsonian Institution's National Museum of American Social History erected a permanent display dedicated to the Globetrotters, referring to the team as ''An Important Part of American Social History.'' In 1986, ownership of the team changed hands again when Macromedia sold the team to International Broadcasting Corporation.

New Ownership for the 21st Century

For the Globetrotters, the union with International Broadcasting proved to be ill-fated. The team was not being marketed effectively, perhaps because International Broadcasting was distracted by its own financial problems. In 1993, International Broadcasting declared bankruptcy, putting the Globetrotters organization in an untenable position. At this point, the team found its savior, a corporate executive from Honeywell Inc. named Mannie Jackson. A former collegiate, professional, and Globetrotters player, Jackson made his reputation in the corporate world at Honeywell, the massive industrial control systems company. Jackson was serving as Honeywell's senior vice-president when he formed an investment group and purchased the Globetrotters for $6 million in 1993. Jackson became the Globetrotters' new owner, chairman, and president.

Under Jackson's stewardship, the Globetrotters benefited from an invigorated approach to marketing. In an August 21, 1995 interview with the *Los Angeles Business Journal,* Jackson explained his reaction upon taking the helm. ''Because this is probably the best-known name in sports anywhere in the world,'' he said, ''the groundwork is there. What has to be done is it has to be sold. When I came in there were a lot of problems. It wasn't being marketed.''

Jackson presided over the Globetrotters' resurgence. In 1996, the company forged sponsorship agreements with Walt Disney Inc., Walt Disney World of Sports, and Reebok International Ltd. The following year, in November, Jackson's focus on marketing was embodied in the formation of Globetrotters Properties, the parent company's new licensing and merchandising subsidiary responsible for managing the production and marketing of the Globetrotters branded merchandise.

The Globetrotters entered the 21st century as a thriving organization, its status as a sports icon serving the team and its parent company well. In 2001, during the team's 75th anniversary, the Globetrotters played more than 260 games in its North America tour alone. In 2003, ten years after Jackson acquired the Globetrotters, the team registered its 21,000th victory. Further victories were guaranteed in the years ahead, as the itinerant Globetrotters organization looked to spread its blend of basketball and showmanship to audiences throughout the world.

Principal Subsidiaries

Globetrotters Properties.

Principal Competitors

National Basketball Association; National Football League Inc.; World Wrestling Entertainment, Inc.

Further Reading

Deady, Tim, ''Making a Three-Point Play,'' *Los Angeles Business Journal,* August 21, 1995, p. 19.

Emmons. Natasha, ''Globetrotters to Go Head-to-Head Against College Squads This Fall,'' *Amusement Business,* March 27, 2000, p. 18.

''Globetrotters Tickets Hold Steady for '99,'' *Amusement Business,* June 29, 1998, p. 4.

—Jeffrey L. Covell

Ho-Chunk Inc.

1 Mission Drive
Winnebago, Nebraska 68071
U.S.A.
Telephone: (402) 878-2809
Toll Free: (800) 439-7008
Fax: (402) 878-2560
Web site: http://www.hochunkinc.com

Private Company
Incorporated: 1994
Employees: 350
Sales: $95 million (2003 est.)
NAIC: 447110 Gasoline Stations with Convenience Stores; 484220 Specialized Freight (Except Used Goods) Trucking, Local; 514191 On-Line Information Services; 334119 Other Computer Peripheral Equipment Manufacturing

Ho-Chunk Inc. is the business arm of the Winnebago tribe of Nebraska. The corporation was founded in 1994 to provide long-term economic growth to the perpetually impoverished Indian nation. Ho-Chunk Inc. operates eight divisions in several business sectors. It runs Dynamic Homes, a Minnesota company that manufactures modular housing, as well as HCI Construction, a residential and commercial building company. Ho-Chunk Inc. runs the Heritage Express chain of convenience stores. It also operates HCI Distribution Company, which sells gas and tobacco products blended on the Winnebago reservation. Ho-Chunk has two e-commerce divisions, AllNative.com, which sells Native American goods, and Indianz.com, a news outlet. All Native Systems is Ho-Chunk's voice and data communications division. Ho-Chunk also operates a nonprofit subsidiary, Ho-Chunk Community Development, which manages fundraising and development of projects on the reservation. Ho-Chunk Community Development in 2003 began to build an entire new town on Winnebago reservation land. Ho-Chunk Inc. began with seed money derived from the tribe's casino and developed a thriving, diversified business that has served as a model of reservation economic development. The corporation is run separately from Winnebago tribal government, though the Winnebago Tribal Council does appoint Ho-Chunk's board of directors.

Winnebago History

The Winnebago tribe initially lived in the area around Green Bay in Wisconsin. A substantial number of Winnebago still inhabit that area, but their tribal governance and business ventures are separate from the Nebraska Winnebago. The early Winnebago lived in villages near Green Bay, Lake Winnebago, and along the Wisconsin, Rock, and Fox Rivers. Their early relations with French fur trappers and missionaries were amicable. Around 1670 the Winnebago came into conflict with the Illinois tribe. The Illinois almost eradicated the Winnebago in this war. Gradually the Winnebago population recovered. In 1760 the British government took over French interests in the area. The Winnebago allied themselves with the British, and fought for the King in the American Revolution. They also took the British side in the war of 1812. In 1816, the U.S. government signed its first peace treaty with the tribe. A series of treaties in ensuing years meant the Winnebago gave up their original territory and were pushed westward. An estimated one-quarter of the Winnebago population died of smallpox in 1836. In 1837, the Winnebago gave up all their land east of the Mississippi, which amounted to some seven million acres of prime forest and farm land. The Winnebago moved or were forcibly relocated several times over the next decade. In 1852 the tribe was held on a reservation in Minnesota. Total Winnebago population had dwindled to approximately 2,500. In 1862, the United States was at war with the Sioux tribe, and the people of Minnesota demanded that the Winnebago leave the state. In 1863, soldiers forced the Winnebago out of Minnesota and resettled them on a reservation in northeastern Nebraska. Almost half the tribe died in this final resettlement.

The Winnebago lived on 30,000 acres of reservation land in Nebraska. Over the next hundred years, little changed in terms of economic development for the tribe. The area offered little or no business opportunities, and the people suffered high unemployment. By the late 1980s, unemployment on the Winnebago reservation was around 70 percent. People who did make enough money not to qualify for government-subsidized hous-

Company Perspectives:

The Winnebago Tribal Council understands that the Winnebago Tribe of Nebraska (''Tribe'') is entering into a new phase of economic development. Tribal business operations are growing in sophistication and in the amount of attention they require. In order to allow Tribal business enterprises to be developed and operated more efficiently, the Tribal Council has established Ho-Chunk Inc., a Tribally-chartered corporation which is wholly owned by the tribe. Ho-Chunk Inc. was established so that Tribal business operations would be free from political influence and outside of the bureaucratic process of the government.

Ho-Chunk Inc.'s immediate mission is a simple one—to use the Tribe's various economic and legal advantages to develop and operate successfully Tribally-owned business enterprises, and to provide jobs and opportunities for Tribal members. Such businesses will be developed both on and off the Winnebago reservation.

ing usually had to leave the reservation, as there was no other affordable housing.

Gambling As the First Business Opportunity in the Early 1990s

In 1988, U.S. law made it possible for Native American tribes to operate casinos. Arcane laws governing gambling had often led to odd strictures on casinos, which had to ply offshore waters, for example. The 1988 law took advantage of the sovereign nation status of Native American tribes, and this at last provided a unique opportunity for the tribes to get into business for themselves. The Winnebago opened a casino, the WinneVegas, on tribal land near Sloan, Iowa, in 1992. The casino was a success, and quickly generated much welcome revenue for the Winnebago tribe.

But in 1994, the Iowa government decided to revise its strictures on gambling. The state already had riverboat gambling, though these floating casinos were restricted by rules about loss limits and how much could be wagered. The state government lifted these rules in 1994, and thus put its casinos in competition with the Winnebago's casino. Revenue from WinneVegas slumped as soon as the regulations were lifted from the state's other gambling operations.

The Winnebago, however, had a gifted leader, John Blackhawk, and he took unprecedented steps to safeguard the tribe's new financial independence. First, Blackhawk went to Washington, D.C. and hired a public relations firm to counter negative press perceptions of the Winnebago people. He hired McCarthy Communications in 1993, and the agency came to Nebraska and helped tribal representatives figure out how to get better stories in the local media. Then in 1994, Blackhawk tracked down a tribe member, Lance Morgan, who had just graduated from Harvard Law School. Blackhawk convinced Morgan to leave a lucrative position at a Minneapolis law firm and come back to the reservation. His job was to build up some kind of financial entity that would lift the tribe out of its endemic poverty. Morgan's seed money was 20 percent of the casino's earnings over two years. In 1994 the tribe incorporated Ho-Chunk Inc. with Morgan as chief executive.

Lance Morgan's father was a roofer of Czech descent and his mother was a full-blooded Winnebago. Morgan's family left the reservation for Omaha, but they remained involved in tribal affairs. As a child, Morgan ran his own business selling snow cones at Winnebago gatherings. He also helped his father on roofing jobs from the age of six on. Morgan told *Fortune Small Business* (December 2003/January 2004) that his ambition as a child was very simple: ''I wanted to quit being poor.'' He traced his desire to become a lawyer to watching television shows such as *L.A. Law*. He studied economics as an undergraduate at the University of Nebraska. Then he went on to Harvard Law School in 1990. After getting his law degree, he took a post at a prestigious Minneapolis firm. Although he never claimed to be particularly interested in Native American legal issues, his first case involved his own Winnebago tribe. He was only 26 when Blackhawk approached him in 1994, but Morgan already had some expertise in tribal law. He took the job as CEO of Ho-Chunk Inc., determined to get the tribe out of gambling and into a less fragile industry.

Ho-Chunk Inc. immediately differed from other existing tribal business plans. Its aim was not to give a quick turnaround of profits to individual tribal members. It operated independently of tribal government, so it was not subject to the whims of elected leaders. It set out to make an economic impact on the future of the tribe, even if members in the present might not benefit. In its first year, Ho-Chunk Inc. basically was Lance Morgan, who worked alone out of his apartment. The company first invested in hotels. By 1997 it owned three, one in Sloan, Iowa, and one each in Lincoln and Omaha, Nebraska.

Diversifying the Company in the Late 1990s

Owning motels and real estate were passive investments for Ho-Chunk Inc. They offered monetary returns without requiring much manpower. But as revenue from the casino dried up, Ho-Chunk realized it had to look harder for an industry in which it could grow. Morgan told the *South Dakota Business Review* (March 2003) that the young company reached a ''make or break'' point when funds from the gaming operation disappeared. Although this was a difficult time, he told the *Business Review,* ''The experience was extremely beneficial because it forced Ho-Chunk Inc. to be an innovative and aggressive entity.'' The company began to move in several different directions. It began buying up convenience stores on reservation land. Eventually it owned ten. Then in 1999 Ho-Chunk Inc. began a new business, HCI Distribution, which distributed gasoline and tobacco products to other Native American businesses. In 2001, the company finessed the leveraged buyout of Dynamic Homes, a publicly traded Minnesota company that was one of the nation's leading purveyors of modular housing. Dynamic Homes was founded in 1970, and had its best years in the late 1970s, when there was high demand for its prefabricated houses. The company had fallen on hard times in the 1980s, and then recovered in the early 1990s, with sales of around $12 million. Ho-Chunk Inc. was interested in the company because it knew people in its area had a high need for good, cheap housing. Ho-Chunk Inc. bought 10 percent of Dy-

Key Dates:

1863: The Winnebago tribe is forcibly resettled to Nebraska.
1988: Indian gaming is legalized.
1992: The Winnebago open a casino in Sloan, Iowa.
1994: Ho-Chunk Inc. is founded with seed money from the casino.
1999: HCI Distribution division is begun.
2001: Ho-Chunk buys out Dynamic Homes.
2003: The nonprofit division breaks ground on a new reservation housing development.

namic's stock, and Lance Morgan took a seat on the board. Morgan and two other Dynamic directors then formed a management group that took the company private in a leveraged buyout. This was one of the first business deals of its kind by an Indian tribe.

Shortly after buying Dynamic Homes in 2001, Ho-Chunk Inc. founded a construction business, HCI Construction. Ho-Chunk moved out of owning real estate and into construction and prefabricated houses. Ho-Chunk also began to develop some information technology businesses. It established its All-Native Systems division in 1999, which manufactured computers for major vendors including Dell. Soon Ho-Chunk Inc. was running two e-commerce businesses as well. One was a news clearinghouse for Native American matters. The other, run by Lance Morgan's wife Erin, sold all kinds of Native American products and crafts on line.

Setbacks and Success in the 2000s

By 2001, annual revenue at Ho-Chunk Inc. had risen to more than $50 million. The company had reinvested all profit over its first five years, but now was able to pay out a small dividend to the Winnebago. Unemployment had dropped on the reservation, from 65 percent when Ho-Chunk Inc. incorporated to 10 percent. The company had close to 300 employees by 2001. Ho-Chunk's success also helped other tribes in the region. It built a call center on the Lakota tribe's Pine Ridge Indian Reservation in South Dakota in 2001, financing the construction of the building in exchange for equity in the business. Ho-Chunk's gas and tobacco distribution business, HCI Distribution, sold its goods to other area tribes, including the Fox, Sac, Iowa, and Kickapoo.

Ho-Chunk's success did not go unnoticed, and the company garnered both awards and unwelcome legal action. The Winnebago operated as a sovereign nation inside the United States. This gave the tribe's businesses a tax status different from that of other non-Indian area businesses. Gas prices on the reservation were lower, for example, because of the different tax structure. The issue was extremely complicated, and Ho-Chunk Inc. worked hard to negotiate with state governments to come up with a fair taxation plan. At its convenience stores, no gas tax was required on sales to Native American customers. Although 90 percent of its customers were Indian, the stores were bound to pay the state taxes on all of its customers. The company then applied for a refund of 90 percent. Lance Morgan eventually decided this system was unfair, and offered instead to remit the 10 percent the company owed, avoiding the refund process. Native American taxation issues were slowly hashed out in the affected states' legislatures, while Kansas unsuccessfully sued to collect taxes on inter-tribal gas sales. Then in April 2002, the Kansas Department of Revenue stopped two HCI Distribution gas trucks, arrested the drivers, confiscated the vehicles, and issued arrest warrants for tribal leader John Blackhawk, Ho-Chunk CEO Lance Morgan, and Morgan's wife Erin. The state claimed Ho-Chunk owed it $1.25 million in motor fuel taxes, and it threatened to sell off personal property of the Morgans and Blackhawk in order to recoup the money.

This crisis set off more negotiations. In 2003 a U.S. district court ordered the state of Kansas to cease its attempts to collect delinquent taxes from the company. The state continued to press its case in appeal. The irony of the criminal charges filed in 2002 was that just a few months earlier, Ho-Chunk Inc. had been awarded the prestigious Innovation in American Government award from Harvard University. The company won $100,000 in tribute to its innovative business plan, and its transformation of the bleak reservation into a viable financial entity. Ho-Chunk Inc.'s rapid success made it a model for other tribes. It had found a new way for tribal nations to parlay their special circumstances into economic power.

In 2001 Ho-Chunk Inc. founded a new division, the nonprofit Ho-Chunk Community Development Corporation. This division worked to secure grants and funding for housing and business projects in and around the Winnebago reservation. In 2003 the Community Development Corporation broke ground for a large new development on the reservation, Healthy Village. The $20 million project was to be a mixture of houses, government buildings, and businesses, replacing the derelict and dilapidated structures that had been all the reservation had to offer earlier. In 2003 the nonprofit arm also set up a small business incubator to help smaller ventures, such as an office supply store, get a start.

By 2004, Ho-Chunk Inc. employed around 350 people and was bringing in close to $100 million in sales. The distribution business alone brought in some $40 million. The company had clearly done what it set out to do, bringing financial independence to the Winnebago. Ho-Chunk Inc., first launched with casino money, had evolved into a complex and sophisticated business that seemed sure to last.

Principal Divisions

HCI Distribution Company; Heritage Express; AllNative.com; Indianz.com; All-Native Systems; Dynamic Homes; HCI Construction; Ho-Chunk Community Development.

Principal Competitors

Davies Oil Company, Inc.; Kugler Company; Arctic Slope Regional Corporation.

Further Reading

''Better Life for Winnebagoes,'' *Indian Life,* March 2002, p. 11.
Fields-Meyer, Thomas, ''Native Son,'' *People Weekly,* April 8, 2002, p. 183.

Humphrey, Kay, ''Winnebago on a Roll to a Financial Empire,'' *Indian Country Today,* January 3, 2001.

Jones, J.A., *Winnebago Indians,* New York & London: Garland Publishing, 1974.

''Kansas Charges Tribe Chairman for Failure to Pay Gas Taxes,'' *Knight Ridder/Tribune Business News,* April 15, 2002.

''Kansas Threatens Winnebagos with Extradition from Nebraska Over Untaxed Oil,'' *Knight Ridder/Tribune Business News,* April 19, 2002.

McCarthy, Colman, ''Self-Reliance Takes Winnebago Nation Far in 10 Years,'' *National Catholic Reporter,* February 8, 2002, p. 17.

Newman, Gary, ''Winnebago Tribe Opens Carter Lake, Iowa's First Motel,'' *Knight Ridder/Tribune Business News,* September 19, 1997.

''Profile: McCarthy Is Native Americans' PR Rainmaker,'' *PR Week,* March 17, 2002, p. 13.

Spragins, Ellyn, et al., ''The New Color of Money,'' *Fortune Small Business,* December 2003/January 2004, p. 74.

Waara, Clint, ''Ho-Chunk, Inc.: A National Model in Reservation Economic Development,'' *South Dakota Business Review,* March 2003, p. 1.

—A. Woodward

Independent News & Media PLC

Independent News & Media PLC

Independent House
2023 Bianconi Avenue
Citywest Business Campus
Naas Road
Dublin 24
Ireland
Telephone: +353 1 466 3200
Fax: +353 1 466 3222
Web site: http://www.independentnewsmedia.com

Public Company
Incorporated: 1904
Employees: 11,700
Sales: EUR 1.5 billion (2003)
Stock Exchanges: London Irish New Zealand
Ticker Symbol: INWS
NAIC: 511110 Newspaper Publishers

Independent News & Media PLC is one of the leading newspaper groups in the English-speaking world. Independent publishes more than 200 national and regional publications in Ireland, Australia, New Zealand, the United Kingdom, and South Africa.

Australasia accounted for 44 percent of 2002 sales. Ireland, with 28 percent of sales, was the next largest segment, followed by the United Kingdom (18 percent) and South Africa (10 percent). According to Chairman Sir Anthony O'Reilly, a fall-off in the economy of one region was usually offset by growth in another. O'Reilly, former CEO of food giant H.J. Heinz Co., is believed to be Ireland's wealthiest individual.

Origins

William Martin Murphy, an Irish businessman who had made a fortune installing Dublin's streetcar system, acquired a number of newspapers in the 1890s. One of these, the *Daily Independent and Nation,* was relaunched as the *Irish Independent* in 1904, forming the basis for what would become the Independent Newspapers publishing group.

Independent Newspapers remained family owned for several decades. The *Irish Independent* was a morning paper; in the 1950s and 1960s more evening, Sunday, and regional publications were added.

International Expansion in the 1970s

Dr. Anthony J.F. (John Francis) O'Reilly was a top-scoring rugby star of the 1950s. After graduating from Dublin's University College, he was appointed chief executive of Bord Bainne, the Irish milk board, at the tender age of 25. There, he developed the tremendously successful Kerrygold brand of butter.

He then headed the Irish Sugar Company and in 1968 went to work for H.J. Heinz Co. In 1979 O'Reilly was the first non-family member to become CEO of the American food giant, a position he held for 20 years.

As one source later told the *Sunday Telegraph,* "Newspapers are much more fascinating than ketchup and beans." O'Reilly began his association with Independent Newspapers on St. Patrick's Day, 1973, through his Columbia investment company.

At the time, Independent employed 1,000 people; its activities were limited to Ireland. O'Reilly already had a vision for expanding the newspaper group into new media and new geographic territories.

Sales reached IR£43.6 million in 1980, producing a pretax profit of IR£3 million. In the 1980s, Independent acquired some British newspapers and took holdings in outdoor advertising companies in Europe and Australia.

The biggest boost to Independent's international stature came in 1988, when Independent acquired a holding in Australia's APN News & Media, then called Provincial Newspapers (Queensland) Ltd. (PNQ). The investment was made possible by the Aussie citizenship of O'Reilly's children (O'Reilly's first wife was Australian)—a new joint venture, Haswell Pty. Ltd., was formed between Independent and a trust fund for the children for the acquisition. Haswell paid News Ltd. A$130 million for its 48 percent stake in PNQ, which it had been mandated to sell by the government.

Company Perspectives:

"We rise at dawn in Auckland with the New Zealand Herald *and continue the day through Australia and the* Queensland Times *and our 14 other regional titles, our four million radio listeners at nine stations in Australia, through to the* Cape Times *and South Africa's largest paper, the* Star *in Johannesburg, through London and finally to Belfast and Dublin—a rolling news room, that through the miracle of the internet and the satellite, allows us to share more than 1,200 articles every week. From the America's Cup in Auckland to the Cricket World Cup in Cape Town, the dynamic and controversial Robert Fisk on the Middle East situation at the* Independent *in London, or the insightful Maurice Hayes and David McKittrick on the complexities of the ever changing Irish political scene, we are attempting—and I hope succeeding—in focusing world-class resources on making our products more appealing and relevant everywhere.*

In all of this, and in the 15 million newspapers and magazines that we publish each and every week, we attempt to underline the impartial, to entertain and to inform, to expose corruption and praise achievement. Mostly we get it right; occasionally we get it wrong; but at all times, we endeavour to be fair, reasonable and independent."

—Sir Anthony O'Reilly, executive chairman

Diversifying in the 1990s

Independent Newspapers achieved pretax profits of IR£12.5 million on revenues of IR£154.9 million ($256.1 million) in 1990. O'Reilly's vision of expanding Independent into new markets and new media worldwide did not really begin to take shape until the appointment of Liam Healy as chief executive in January 1991. Healy had joined Independent's staff in 1963. O'Reilly had appointed him head of Independent's international division in 1981, where he oversaw the acquisition of APN (Australian Provincial Newspapers).

Independent then focused on diversifying into different media and markets, including outdoor and radio. Down under, APN branched out into radio in a joint venture with Clear Channel Communications. APN also acquired an outdoor advertising business.

There were also a number of high-visibility acquisition offers that did not go through. Independent tried unsuccessfully to acquire Australia's Fairfax newspaper group in 1991 and Britain's *Daily* and *Sunday Express* publisher United Newspapers in 1993. United's market capitalization of £1.3 billion was more than four times that of Independent.

In 1994, Independent acquired a 24.99 percent stake in Newspaper Publishing, publisher of a London newspaper also called the *Independent.* Within a couple of years it had built up its holding to 47 percent, and in 1998 bought out the shares of the Mirror Group, Spanish publisher Prisa, and five dozen other shareholders. Andreas Whittam-Smith had founded the *Independent* as an up-market paper in 1986. It had yet to turn a sustainable profit, but O'Reilly admitted its value as a prestige asset—it was a well-respected, national publication in Britain—while professing plans to make it profitable.

Key Dates:

1904: *Irish Independent* is launched in Dublin by William Martin Murphy.
1973: Anthony O'Reilly invests in Independent Newspapers.
1988: Independent Newspapers and Anthony O'Reilly acquire PNQ—Queensland's largest provincial newspaper group.
1992: PNQ—renamed APN News & Media Pty.—is listed on the Australian Stock Exchange.
1991: Liam Healy is appointed chief executive.
1994: Independent acquires control of the Argus Group—South Africa's largest publishing group.
1997: Independent acquires control of Wilson & Horton—New Zealand's largest publishing group.
1998: Full control of London's the *Independent* is acquired.
1999: Group is renamed Independent News & Media PLC (INM).
2000: Anthony O'Reilly is appointed executive chairman; INM acquires Belfast Telegraph, Northern Ireland's largest publisher.
2001: INM restructures New Zealand operations into APN News & Media, creating a major Australasian media conglomerate (APN is owned 40.7 percent by INM).
2003: INM restructures worldwide operations and recapitalises balance sheet via noncore asset divestments, layoffs, and a focus on being the "low cost operator."

Independent expanded its holdings into South Africa and Portugal in 1994. It acquired Argus Newspaper Group, the largest newspaper group in South Africa, later renaming it Independent Newspapers Holdings. (O'Reilly had struck up a friendship with future South African President Nelson Mandela while touring the country with the British Lions rugby team.) Independent acquired a 19 percent holding in Jornalgeste, later called Lusomundo Media. The company also acquired a regional newspaper operation around London. A 28 percent stake in New Zealand's largest newspaper, Wilson & Horton, was acquired in 1995. Independent gradually built up its holdings in W&H, achieving full control in 1996.

O'Reilly retired as chief executive of H.J. Heinz Co. in April 1998. He continued to have interests outside Independent Newspapers, having acquired control of venerable crystal and ceramic maker Waterford Wedgwood.

Renamed Independent News & Media PLC in 1999

The name Independent News & Media PLC (INM) was adopted in 1999 to reflect the group's expanding focus. During the year, INM bought a share of iTouch, a wireless portal. O'Reilly was knighted in 2000 for his work relating to Northern Ireland. The *Belfast Telegraph,* Northern Ireland's leading newspaper, was acquired from Trinity Mirror during the year for UK£295 million.

By this time, INM had global turnover of more than UK£1 billion. It owned the leading papers in Ireland, South Africa, and New Zealand.

In 2001, INM increased its shareholding in the Australian media group APN from 40 to 45 percent by selling it Wilson & Horton, the New Zealand-based publisher and radio broadcaster, for $410 million. This nearly doubled APN's size.

Reducing Debt in 2003

Following a period of significant investment and acquisition, INM set about to restructure and recapitalise its balance sheet. The group disposed of its 19.1 percent holding in Portugal's Lusomundo Media for EUR 24 million (UK£17 million) in October 2003, leaving INM to concentrate on English-language titles. INM's regional London papers were sold off a couple of months later for EUR 89 million.

INM ended 2003 with news of a major restructuring, designed to reduce by 5 percent the group's 12,000-strong workforce, and position the group as the ''low cost operator'' in the industry. The group had spent EUR 1.6 billion on international expansion and upgrading all of its production facilities in the previous decade and was eager to reduce its EUR 1.2 billion (£850 million) debt.

Principal Subsidiaries

APN News & Media (Australia; 43.7%); Independent Magazines (U.K.); Independent Newspapers (Pty) Limited (South Africa); Independent News and Media Limited (U.K.); Independent Newspapers (Ireland) Limited; Independent Newspapers (Finance) Plc (U.K.); iTouch plc (U.K.; 51.77%); News & Media NZ Limited (27.43%); Newspread Limited; Princes Holdings (50%); Sunday Newspapers Limited; Tribune Newspapers Plc (29.99%).

Principal Competitors

Associated Newspapers Ltd.; Hollinger International Inc.; News International Ltd.; Trinity Mirror Plc.

Further Reading

Brown, John Murray, ''Friends Put Money on O'Reilly's Judgment: The Irish Entrepreneur Has Made Some Spectacular Investments,'' *Financial Times* (London), October 26, 2002, p. 15.

——, ''Independent's Rights Issue Delivers a Reality Check,'' *Financial Times* (London), March 28, 2003, p. 28.

——, ''Murdoch and O'Reilly Rivalry Hots Up,'' *Financial Times* (London), January 31, 2002, p. 24.

Byrne, Ciar, ''Connery Raises Indy's Profile,'' *Guardian* (Manchester), March 20, 2003, p. 23.

Cassy, John, ''O'Reilly Props Up Independent Group,'' *Guardian* (Manchester), March 27, 2003, p. 23.

Gapper, John, ''Independent's Hopes Rest with an Irish Solution,'' *Financial Times* (London), March 12, 1998, p. 8.

Greenslade, Roy, ''A Man of Indie Means,'' *Guardian* (Manchester), March 9, 1998, p. 106.

——, ''Still Full of Beans,'' *Guardian* (Manchester), September 11, 2000, p. 8.

Hobson, Rodney, ''Independent News Sells Portuguese Stake for EUR 24M,'' *Independent* (London), Bus. Sec., October 14, 2003, p. 22.

''Independent Head Cements Long Aust. Ties,'' *Sydney Morning Herald,* June 13, 1988, p. 27.

Jury, Louise, ''Connery Joins Board of Independent,'' *Independent,* March 20, 2003.

Mac Carthaigh, Sean, ''The Quiet Man Behind Success,'' *Irish Times,* June 14, 1997, p. 9.

McGrath, Brendan, ''Independent May Buy O'Reilly Trust Holding in APN,'' *Irish Times,* June 26, 1996, p. 16.

——, ''Independent Raises W&H Stake to 44%,'' *Irish Times,* December 1, 1995.

Majendie, Paul, ''Heinz's O'Reilly Eyes Media in Britain, Australia,'' *Reuters News,* April 23, 1993.

Murdoch, Bill, ''O'Reilly Welcomed Aboard,'' *Irish Times,* February 4, 1995, p. 16.

O'Toole, Fintan, ''A Baron of Beanz,'' *Observer,* March 8, 1998, p. 20.

''Press Baron O'Reilly Makes Breakthrough,'' *Times* (London), Bus. Sec., February 6, 1994.

Price, Christopher, ''INL Seeking to Spend Up to £200m on Purchases,'' *Financial Times* (London), September 11, 1997, p. 34.

Rees, Jon, ''Ireland Newspaper Group's Chairman Looks to Bid Anew for Australian Publisher,'' *Sunday Business* (London), November 18, 2001.

——, ''Son of Dublin-Based Media Firm's Chair Wants to Be Judged by Work, Not Dad,'' *Daily Mail,* February 23, 2003.

Ruddock, Alan, ''O'Reilly Fights on for Place Among World's Press Barons,'' *Times* (London), November 28, 1993.

''Rugby Star Played to Win,'' *Times* (London), February 21, 2003.

Siklos, Richard, '' 'I Want More of Everything',' *Business Week,* December 20, 1999, pp. 158+.

Smith, Andreas Whittam, ''A Newspaper Is No Ordinary Business, It Is a Trophy Asset; The Founder of the 'Independent' Says the Dream May Be Over but the Future Remains Bright,'' *Independent* (London), March 17, 1998, p. 21.

Snoddy, Raymond, ''Fighting to Put the Indy Back on Track,'' *Times* (London), Bus. Sec., February 21, 2003, p. 32.

Steiner, Rupert, ''O'Reilly Steps Out from Father's Shadow,'' *Sunday Times* (London), Bus. Sec., April 21, 2002, p. 9.

Stewart, Andrew, ''Queensland's New Boy Press Baronet,'' *Business Review Weekly* (Australia), November 25, 1988, p. 44.

Warner, Jeremy, ''O'Reilly Agrees to Split Chairman and Chief Executive Roles at Independent News & Media,'' *Independent,* June 7, 2003.

Weever, Patrick, ''The Life of O'Reilly,'' *Sunday Telegraph* (London), July 28, 1996, p. 3.

Weir, James, ''Radio Jewel Glitters for British, Irish,'' *Dominion* (Wellington, New Zealand), March 6, 1996, p. 21.

—Frederick C. Ingram

Inter Link Foods PLC

Sett End Rd.
Blackburn
Lancashire BB1 2PT
United Kingdom
Telephone: (+44) 1254-554-95
Fax: (+44) 1254-663-602
Web site: http://www.interlinkfoods.co.uk

Public Company
Incorporated: 1994
Employees: 729
Sales: £51.4 million ($82.24 million) (2003)
Stock Exchanges: London (AIM)
Ticker Symbol: ITF
NAIC: 311812 Commercial Bakeries; 424490 Other Grocery and Related Product Merchant Wholesalers; 551112 Offices of Other Holding Companies

Inter Link Foods PLC is the rising star of the British baking industry. Since its formation in 1994, the company has grown through acquisitions and organically to take a place in the United Kingdom's top five industrial bakers, with the objective of claiming the number two spot in the market (number one, Mr Kipling, a subsidiary of Tomkins, holds a more than 50 percent share of the market). Inter Link itself is composed of a number of smaller bakery businesses, including Crossfield, Lisa, Hepworth & Whittles (Newton House), William Lusty, Maid Marian, Nicholas & Harris, The Creative Cake Company, Cakes for the Connoisseur, and, since February 2003, Soreen. This gathering of companies has enabled Inter Link to build a strong portfolio spanning most of the major cake and pastry categories, including sponge cakes, fruit pies, celebration cakes, low-fat loaf cakes, cherry bakewell tarts, chocolate mini rolls, swiss rolls, and malt cakes. The company also has a thriving business in licensed cakes, holding the licenses to create cakes in the image of such popular characters as Bob the Builder and Harry Potter. Most of Inter Link Foods' production goes toward private label and third-party branded items, and Inter Link counts nearly all of the major multiple supermarket groups among its customers. With the acquisition of Soreen, however, Inter Link has gained controlled of that brand's malt cakes, U.K. leader in its category. Inter Link has traded on London's Alternative Investment Market (AIM) since 1998, and has seen its revenues shoot up from just £1.5 million to more than £51 million since it was founded. The company is led by founder and CEO Alwin Thompson, and Managing Director Paul Griffiths.

Spotting a Market in the 1990s

The son of a Stockport newsagent, Alwin Thompson started his professional career at the age of 16. Over the years, he worked in a variety of jobs, beginning in the packing room of the drapery company James Stewart and Sons. That experience was to help Thompson later when he set up his own business, giving him an insight into his workers' needs.

Thompson moved into James Stewart's accounting department, then left for a sales job at cake and confectionery company Cadbury's, and later stints at Gallaghers and ADT Security Systems. In 1986, Thompson set out to run his own business, and founded Country Fitness Foods. After successfully launching that business, Thompson sold out, to Northumbrian Fine Foods, and instead joined that company on its board of directors.

In the meantime, Thompson kept an eye out for a new business opportunity. In the early 1990s, the diversified Yorkshire Food Group had begun preparing a public offering to support its push to focus itself as a specialist in the dried fruit and nuts market. Yorkshire sought to sell a number of non-core units, including a money-losing bakery operation, called Crossfield Foods. In the meantime, Thompson had recognized a new opportunity in the baking market, which by then had become dominated by Tomkins and its Mr Kipling, Cadburys, and Lyons brands. Thompson recognized that the major supermarket groups, eager to launch their own private label cakes, pastries, and other baked goods, including packaged and fresh products, would welcome a company willing to supply their needs.

In 1994, Thompson joined with ex-Asda and Tesco executive John Cummings and approached venture capital group 3i with a plan to create a new company, Inter Link Foods, in order

Company Perspectives:

Chairman's Statement: Our continued objective is to grow the business both organically and by selective acquisition and in the medium term become the number two supplier of high quality cakes and pastries in the UK.

to buy Crossfield Foods from Yorkshire Group. Yorkshire was on the brink of shutting down Crossfield, based in Blackburn, which at the time had been posting losses of £350,000 per year on sales of just £1.4 million.

Thompson and Cummings quickly reorganized the company. A major part of that effort went towards streamlining Crossfield's production. Previously, the bakery had produced more than 20 different products, most of which had to be fashioned by hand, or through antiquated equipment. Under Inter Link, the Crossfield site narrowed its product focus to just four low-cost, high-volume lines, cherry bakewells, sponge cakes, fruit pies, and mini-rolls. In support of its new product focus, the company installed new, highly automated equipment.

By the end of its first year, Inter Link had succeeded in turning around the Crossfield site, posting a profit of £35,000, while maintaining its sales volume despite the drastic reduction in product assortment. By the late 1990s, the Crossfield site alone generated more than £5 million in sales each year.

Flush with that success, Thompson and Cummings went in search of their next acquisition target. In 1995, the company turned to Lancashire Enterprises Venture Funds to acquire another small, family-owned bakery threatened for its survival. The addition of that company, Lisa Bakery, enabled Inter Link to expand its product range to include swiss rolls and sponge cakes. At the time of its acquisition, Lisa Bakery posted sales of less than £2 million per year. Within three years, Inter Link succeeded in nearly doubling that figure.

The acquisition of Lisa Bakery also enabled the company to cross-sell its expanding list of products among Crossfield's and Lisa's major supermarket customers. In 1996, Inter Link added another important product line to the Lisa site, that of packaged mini-rolls, which quickly became one of its strongest selling products. The company by then featured three of the United Kingdom's largest supermarket groups, Asda, Tesco, and Morrisons, among its customers.

AIMing High for the New Century

By 1998, the company's sales had climbed past £8 million, with profits topping £450,000. Inter Link now sought to accelerate its expansion, in particular by investing in new production lines and equipment. In order to raise funding for this new effort, the company decided to enter the stock market, and in April 1998 the company listed its shares on London's Alternative Index Market, or AIM, which specialized in listing small-scale companies. With the more than £2 million raised from the offering, Inter Link carried out its capital investment program, spending more than £600,000 on new equipment at both the Lisa and Crossfield sites. The increased production capacity in turn enabled it to attract a broader customer base, adding such key U.K. supermarket players as Aldi and Somerfield.

Until 1999, Thompson and Cummings had served as co-managing directors. After Cummings left in September of that year, to take up a senior executive position at Asda, Thompson took on a new position, as Inter Link's CEO.

Having proved its operating model, Inter Link now prepared to step up its growth. The company began identifying new acquisition targets to increase the scope of its product lines and enhance its penetration of the U.K. bakery market. In 1999, the company reached an agreement with the Bank of Scotland to assist in rebuilding the William Lusty Bakery, then in receivership. In return, Inter Link was given an option to purchase that company.

Yet the company's first new acquisition was in Nottingham, where Inter Link bought Maid Marian, a specialist in celebration, as well as novelty, cakes. The purchase also enabled the company to enter the fast-growing market for licensed cake products. Following the acquisition, Inter Link transferred Maid Marian's production to its main Blackburn site. In support of its growing range of products, the company commissioned a new production facility in Shadworth. Offering some 32,000 square feet of production space, the new facility was inaugurated at the beginning of 2001.

That year Inter Link confirmed its status as one of the fastest-growing U.K. bakery groups, in part through a series of strategic acquisitions, starting with Hepworth & Whittles, which operated under the trade name of Newton House Bakery. The addition of that company added a number of small cake specialties, such as cup cakes and vienna whirls, for a cost of £4 million. Inter Link quickly linked the customer pool of its new acquisition into its existing pool, enabling the company to introduce its full range of products into the expanded customer base.

Acquisitions remained at the heart of Inter Link's growth strategy that year, although its next purchase, of Cakes for the Connoisseur (CFTC), represented its first non-bakery acquisition. Instead, CFTC, bought from bankrupt NFF for £2.7 million, enabled the company to gain access for its products to a wider distribution market, including the large numbers of small-scale independent retailers, as well as other catering outlets, such as train station and airport concessions.

The company returned to bakery expansion with its next acquisition, however, that of the celebration cake division of Nicholas & Harris Ltd., which was then renamed Creative Cake Company. The new division boosted Inter Link's position in the licensed baked goods segment, with licenses including Bob the Builder, Pokémon, and Harry Potter. The latter license was bought by the company for £50,000 in October 2001, ahead of the launch of the latest in the hugely successful book and film series. Later that year, Inter Link completed its £12 million acquisition drive with the purchase of the William Lusty Bakery, for £400,000.

By the end of 2001, Inter Link had transformed itself into one of the U.K. baking industry's top five companies. Although the company remained far behind longtime leader Mr Kipling, Inter Link's rapid growth was set to push its sales past £40 million, and earned it the title of AIM Company of the Year in 2001.

Key Dates:

1986: Alwin Thompson founds Country Fitness Foods, which he then sells to Northumbrian Fine Foods, where he becomes a company director.
1994: Thompson, joined by John Cummings, founds Inter Link Foods and buys failing Crossfield Bakery from Yorkshire Food Group.
1998: Company lists on AIM market.
2000: Company acquires Nottingham-based Maid Marian, a specialist in celebration, novelty, and licensed cakes.
2001: Company acquires Hepworth & Whittles (Newton House); Cakes for the Connoisseur; Creative Cake Company; and William Lusty; opens new 32,000-square-foot production facility.
2003: Inter Link acquires Soreen Bakery, a leading producer of malt loaves.

Inter Link took the year off from acquisitions in order to integrate new operations and pursue organic growth as well. By the end of the year, the company had succeeded in gaining more than 50 product listings (that is, space on supermarket shelves) from all of the country's major supermarket groups, with the exception of Marks & Spencer. Inter Link had also continued to pursue its growing licensing operation, grabbing the lucrative Spiderman and the children's television characters The Fimbles that year.

With sales topping £50 million, Inter Link returned to acquisitions in 2003, buying Trafford Park's Soreen Bakery, the leading producer of malt loaves in the United Kingdom. That purchase also represented another first for Inter Link, in that it gave the company its first branded product line. Nonetheless, Inter Link remained committed to its more lucrative—and less costly—business of producing for private and third-party brands. The company also remained committed to growth, scouting for new acquisitions with the intention of doubling its sales and claiming the number two bakery products spot in the new century.

Principal Subsidiaries

Crossfield Foods Limited; Inter Link Food Group Limited; William Lusty Limited; Lisa Bakery Limited; Soreen Bakery Limited.

Principal Competitors

Tomkins PLC; Allied Bakeries; British Bakeries Ltd.; Jacob's Bakery Ltd.; Fletchers Bakeries Ltd.; Kears Group Ltd.; Hibernia Foods Bakeries Ltd.

Further Reading

''Baker's Joy,'' *Daily Post*, September 16, 2003, p. 25.
''Bigger Slice of Cake,'' *Birmingham Evening Mail*, July 9, 2003, p. 34.
Blackwell, David, ''Inter Link Aims to Be UK's Number 2,'' *Financial Times*, July 9, 2003, p. 24.
Gregory, Helen, ''Let Them Eat Cake,'' *Grocer*, May 4, 2002, p. 44.
Jones, Shiela, ''Inter Link Acquires Malt Bread Business,'' *Financial Times*, January 23, 2003, p. 23.
''Magic Moment . . . ,'' *Daily Telegraph*, July 9, 2003.
''Soreen a Tasty Morsel for Inter Link,'' *Evening Standard*, January 22, 2003.
Stone, Laurie, ''Piece of Cake,'' *Sun*, October 23, 2001, p. 5.

—M.L. Cohen

InterDigital Communications Corporation

781 3rd Avenue
King of Prussia, Pennsylvania 19406-1409
U.S.A.
Telephone: (610) 878-7800
Fax: (610) 992-9432
Web site: http://www.interdigital.com

Public Company
Incorporated: 1972 as International Mobile Machines Corporation
Employees: 312
Sales: $87.9 million (2002)
Stock Exchanges: NASDAQ
Ticker Symbol: IDCC
NAIC: 533110 Lessors of Nonfinancial Intangible Assets (Except Copyrighted Works)

InterDigital Communications Corporation has been a pioneer in wireless telecommunications technology for more than 30 years. The publicly traded company is based in King of Prussia, Pennsylvania, a suburb of Philadelphia. InterDigital's inventions, technology, and systems can be found in cell phones, personal digital assistants (PDAs), mobile computing devices, and other wireless devices—as well as base stations and other infrastructure equipment. A leader in the development of the first two generations of wireless technology, InterDigital is now concentrating on the development of intellectual property for the third generation of wireless communications, or 3G, and the WCDMA (wideband code division multiple access) air-interface protocol. The company focused on two different ways to achieve two-way communication, known as duplexing. Frequency Division Duplexing (FDD) splits the channels into separate frequencies. Time Division Duplexing (TDD) creates time slots to split a single channel. In addition to its King of Prussia facility, InterDigital also maintains operations in Canada, the United Kingdom, and Germany.

Company Is Incorporated in 1972

The visionary behind the creation of InterDigital was Sherwin Seligsohn, a high school dropout who made a fortune in the stock market during the 1960s when he was still in his 20s. His interest in wireless technology dated back to 1968, when one day while in Atlantic City he longed for a way to keep up with the stock market without leaving his spot on the beach. According to some accounts, he wanted to receive stock quotations by way of a portable data machine, and others say he simply wanted to talk to his stockbroker on the phone. Whatever the details of his inspiration, Seligsohn began to pursue the development of a portable wireless telephone. He worked on the idea for three years and in 1971 presented a prototype of the world's first wireless handheld analog telephone. In 1972 he launched a company to exploit the idea, incorporating International Mobile Machines Corporation (IMM). The first product the company developed was a portable analog radio system in the 450 Mhz band, capable of connecting to the public switched network. During the bicentennial celebrations held in Philadelphia in 1976, IMM demonstrated its wireless telephone in Franklin Park, the same place 100 years earlier that Alexander Graham Bell made his first demonstration of the telephone.

While IMM worked to perfect a commercially viable radio telephone, which it hoped to sell to the rural market as well as to developing nations which could not afford the costs of establishing a wired infrastructure for a telephone system, the company's scientists began to explore the analog cellular technology that was emerging in the 1970s. Because computer chips were getting smaller and cheaper while gaining greater processing power, it was apparent that a pocket telephone would become an eventuality. But the IMM scientists identified a number of drawbacks to the analog approach, including poor voice quality and high power consumption. Instead, IMM elected to go digital, turning to a well established technology called Time Division Multiple Access (TDMA), used by the military and some commercial wire-line system. Under this method, the frequency spectrum was split into time slots and individual users were assigned a slot. What IMM did was to apply TDMA to create a wireless cell phone system.

In the meantime, IMM also worked on telephone calling security and screening technology, forming a subsidiary, Telephone Access Control Technology. In 1981 the business was sold off when IMM decided to concentrate its efforts on the portable digital telephone. In that same year, IMM went public,

Company Perspectives:

For more than 20 years, InterDigital Communications Corporation has been a recognized pioneer in the architecture, design, and delivery of advanced wireless technology platforms.

making an initial offering of stock. Over the next five years the company made a total of three offerings, raising $32 million. The company opted not to become a cell phone manufacturer. Rather, it would patent its cellular hardware and software technology and license those patents to other companies interested in making handsets. IMM began filing patents around the world, ''in places,'' in the words of an InterDigital executive, ''that during the '80s, a rational person might not have filed.'' These efforts, however, would pay off years later.

UltraPhone Rolled Out in 1986

While IMM worked on cellular technology and filed patents in the 1980s, it continued to pursue its founder's original rural radio-telephone idea, which had evolved into the digital UltraPhone system. Rather than being mobile, it provided ''fixed wireless access,'' a ''last mile'' device to provide local telephone service to areas that were either too remote to be wired by copper into a telephone system or developing countries where the cost of establishing a wire infrastructure was out of reach. The system's central network station had the ability, depending on the terrain, to serve customers within a 40-mile radius. The first UltraPhone System was installed in the mountainous area of Glendo, Wyoming, in 1986, purchased by Mountain Bell, a subsidiary of US West Inc. The system was set up to serve ten houses at a cost of $100,000. If copper wired had been used, the cost would have been an estimated $40,000 per house. By the end of 1988 the UltraPhone system was operating in ten communities in North America, including Kodiak, Alaska. Despite all of IMM's promise, whether it be its cellular technology or the UltraPhone system, the company posted modest revenues and a string of losses throughout the 1980s. Although sales of the UltraPhone system grew steadily from 1987 to 1992, so too did IMM's losses. In 1991, for instance, IMM recorded revenues of $33.6 million and a loss of $7.7 million. A year later revenues improved to $39.7 million, yet the company lost nearly $23 million. (It was also during this period, in June 1990, that Seligsohn relinquished the chairmanship of IMM, becoming chairman emeritus. He went on to launch another company, Universal Display Corp.)

In October 1992 IMM made a major course correction. It used stock to acquire long Island-based SCS Mobilecom, Inc. and SCS Telecom, Inc. SCS and IMM had a working relationship for several years, and by now merging their technologies the combined company was in a strong position to benefit from changes that were about to emerge in the wireless field—which was ready to move from first generation analog technology to second generation (2G) digital technology and ultimately broadband digital 3G technology. IMM brought to the table its leadership position in Time Division Multiple Access (TDMA) digital radio technology, while SCS had some 30 patents either granted or pending related to its Broadband-Code Division Multiple Access (B-CDMA) digital wireless telecommunications technology. SCS had been working on B-CDMA for 20 years and now had a prototype system in operation. It offered a number of advantages over rival Narrowband-CDMA in replacing or supplementing first and second generation wireless technology. It was fully compatible with both analog cellular and TDMA digital cellular, and unlike Narrowband-CDMA it operated effectively inside buildings and in congested urban areas. In conjunction with the SCS acquisition, IMM changed its name to InterDigital Communications Corporation. The name was meant to connote the intermeshing of the companies' two digital technologies. The combined company also brought in a new chief executive officer, cellular industry veteran William Erdman.

InterDigital continued to produce and market the UltraPhone system as well as such products as wireless PBX and cordless telephones, but the company was less concerned with short-term profits than it was in pursuing 3G technology and positioning itself for even greater paydays in the future. It was also determined to protect its intellectual property and to earn some licensing fees. InterDigital's approach to arranging royalty payments from manufacturers it believed were using its proprietary technology was somewhat ham-fisted, however. Rather than working with these companies—who were in effect their customers—during product development, InterDigital opted to wait until the products were on the market. At this point, it demanded royalties and as a consequence created an acrimonious relationship with manufacturers, which led to a series of long-running patent infringement lawsuits against such heavyweights as Motorola and Ericsson. In 1994 InterDigital was successful in working out a royalty deal with AT&T, the first time the company would be paid for its technology without having to sue. A year later, it sued Motorola for patent infringement and, to the surprise of many, InterDigital lost. It was almost a devastating blow to the company, which was now severely weakened in its ability to enforce its patents around the world and coming close to ruin.

While InterDigital's attorneys sought to reverse many of the jury decisions in the Motorola case and pursued other patent infringement cases through the legal system, the company's researchers in the 1990s forged good working alliances with other companies. In 1994 InterDigital established a marketing and technology alliance with German electronics giant Siemens AG, a major producer of digital switches. In 1996 InterDigital entered into an alliance with Korea's Samsung Electronics Co. Ltd., the world's 14th largest corporation in the world. Another technology partner was found in the French electronics firm Alcatel. InterDigital received both cash and engineering help from its partners, focusing on applying wideband CDMA technology to fixed wireless systems (suitable, say, for a fixed location wireless fax machine). During this period, from 1994 to 1999, the partners did not see much of a need, hence market, for mobile broadband technology. Cell phones were thought to simply transmit voice and nothing more. But with the rise of the Internet, coupled with the explosive popularity of the cell phone, that thinking would change. Now InterDigital, which held exclusive patents in wideband wireless, and its alliance partners came to realize that far from developing a niche product, they were on the verge of a technological breakthrough. Wideband technology applied to mobile wireless would permit the transmission of voice and data (i.e. the Internet) at essentially the same cost as fixed location service.

Key Dates:

1972: Company is incorporated as International Mobile Machines Corporation.
1981: Company goes public.
1992: Name is changed to InterDigital Communications Corp.
1998: Alliance with Nokia is established.
2003: Patent infringement suit is settled with Ericsson.

Nokia Alliance Forged in 1998

Finland's Nokia Corporation, today the world's top cellphone maker, became aware of InterDigital's patent position in wideband and in 1998 forged a four-year $70 million contract with InterDigital to develop 3G cell phones. The cell phones would be manufactured under the Nokia name, but InterDigital would own the technology. This positive development was offset somewhat by the announcement by Siemens and Alcatel that they were pulling their support from InterDigital's fixed wireless products. From their perspective, there was little reason to provide funding and expertise to a company that in partnership with rival Nokia might very well make their fixed wireless telecommunications products outdated. For its part, InterDigital pulled back from fixed location wireless and chose to concentrate on the far more promising mobile wireless field. Starting in 1999 InterDigital adjusted its business plan. No longer would it develop fixed wireless telecommunications systems or act as a manufacturer/distributor of these systems. The company recast itself as a think tank for next generation wireless communication, offering its technology and engineering expertise to the entire industry.

One of the major challenges InterDigital faced in the early years of the new century was finding enough qualified engineers to hire. The company began to recruit in Canada and Europe. A design office was opened in Canada to accelerate its hiring effort. While InterDigital pushed forward on the development of the next generation of wireless technology, litigation with Ericsson over the previous generation of wireless technology was finally coming to a head in a U.S. District Court. The two sides began their patent infringement suit in February 2003, but in March they reached a settlement that was a major victory in InterDigital's quest to receive royalties on its 2G wireless patents. The company estimated it could receive $100 million in royalty payments over the next four years from Ericsson Inc. and Sony Ericsson Mobile Communications AB. Moreover, InterDigital, its position validated, was poised to strike deals with other licensees, making it possible that the company was on the verge of receiving a windfall of hundreds of millions of dollars in the near term. InterDigital estimated that it could be in line for $360 million to $430 million in damages, retroactive fees, and advanced payments. These positive developments for the company centered on its 2G technology. Given its strong position in 3G technology, it was very likely that InterDigital, a 30-year overnight success, was on the verge of even greater prosperity.

Principal Subsidiaries

Digital Cellular Corporation; InterDigital Mobilecom, Inc.; InterDigital Communications (Europe) Ltd.; InterDigital Germany GmbH.

Principal Competitors

Lucent Technologies Inc.; Motorola, Inc.; QUALCOMM Incorporated.

Further Reading

Abelson, Reed, ''Ultra Faith,'' *Philadelphia Business Journal,* February 10, 1986, p. 1.

Kay, Peter, ''For InterDigital, R&D May Finally Pay Off,'' *Philadelphia Business Journal,* January 17, 2003, p. 1.

''The Rise of InterDigital Communications,'' *America's Network,* February 15, 1997, p. S20.

Tanaka, Wendy, ''Pennsylvania Cell Phone Software Firm Set to Reap Benefits of Technology,'' *Philadelphia Inquirer,* June 30, 2003.

Wilen, John, ''InterDigital Up-and-Down Saga Over Its Wireless Systems Patents,'' *Philadelphia Business Journal,* December 6, 1996, p. 10.

—Ed Dinger

Itoham Foods Inc.

4-27, Takahata-cho
Nishinomiya City
Hyogo 663
Japan
Telephone: (0798) 66-1231
Fax: (0798) 64-1140

Public Company
Incorporated: 1948 as Ito Ham Company, Ltd.
Employees: 6,242
Sales: ¥473 billion ($3.94 billion) (2003)
Ticker Symbol: 2284
Stock Exchanges: Tokyo Osaka Nagoya
Ticker Symbol: 2284
NAIC: 311611 Animal (Except Poultry) Slaughtering; 311119 Other Animal Food Manufacturing; 311612 Meat Processed from Carcasses; 311615 Poultry Processing; 422470 Meat and Meat Product Merchant Wholesalers

Japanese company Itoham Foods Inc. produces and markets fresh meat and processed meat and sausage products. The company also manufactures and distributes other food products, including edible oils, dairy products, wine, and frozen foods. Itoham has subsidiaries in the United States as well as Europe and Australia and has ventures in biotechnology and restaurant services.

Shaky Beginnings: 1920s–40s

Denzo Ito established meat-processing firm Ito Processed Food Company in Osaka, Japan, in 1928. Two years later this company went bankrupt in response to the worldwide Depression, but it was re-formed in 1932 as Ito Meat Processing Company, in Kobe, Japan. A year later the company first marketed what was called the Pole Wiener, a sausage wrapped in cellophane, a popular base from which the company's product line was to grow in later years.

In 1943 Ito Meat's factory was closed as a result of the emergency conditions brought about by World War II, but Ito Meat's investors were quick to reestablish their company soon after the war. In 1946, the factory in Kobe returned to production, this time as the Ito Food Processing Company. Pressed ham, or yose ham, was one of the first products on-line at the Kobe factory. Two years later, the company was reorganized again as the Ito Ham Company Limited, with ¥3 million in capital.

Growth and Joint Ventures: 1950s–80s

In 1957 Ito Ham Company developed a method of producing hams and sausages that used mutton as well as pork, which was still scarce in Japan. Finding this method a worthwhile money-saver, the company imported 3,000 tons of mutton that year. The company also expanded its production capacity, building a plant in Tokyo in 1959 and one in Nishinomiya the next year.

The business was renamed Ito Ham Provisions Company, Limited, in 1961, and its stock was listed for the first time on the Tokyo and Osaka stock exchanges. The following year Ito Ham built another plant, in Toyohashi. By 1965 Ito Ham was attracting foreign interest. Three years later Ito Ham launched its first ship, to import raw materials from Australia and New Zealand. In 1967 the company opened yet another plant, this time in Kyushu, and began to produce dairy products, its first nonmeat food products.

Several foreign delegations visited Ito Ham's plants throughout Japan. These included economic delegations from New Zealand, Great Britain, Denmark, Australia, and China. In 1973, Ito Ham began business relations with the United States as the exclusive distributor of Armour Food Company's products in Japan. Then, in 1974, Ito Ham acquired Cariani Sausage Company, a sausage maker in San Francisco, California.

Nine years later Ito Ham was again involved with an American company, this time in a joint endeavor with the Carnation Company. In March 1983 Ito Ham and Carnation agreed to jointly produce cooking oils, chilled foods, sauces and seasoning, milk products, and soft drinks through a venture called Ito Carnation Company. This plan gave Carnation the footing in Japanese manufacturing that it had been seeking and expanded Ito Ham's product range at a time when meat consumption in Japan was slowing.

Company Perspectives:

The Itoham Group strives to contribute to the health and culinary enjoyment of customers with sincere service and high-quality products.

In September 1985 Ito Ham entered into an agreement with a French cheese company, Fromageries Bel. Ito Ham agreed to sell three of Bel's natural cheeses in supermarkets throughout Japan, promising initial sales of at least ¥600 million. The companies agreed that when sales of the cheeses exceeded ¥2 billion, Ito Ham would begin to produce the cheese in Japan using Bel's production technology.

Ito Ham again dealt with French food manufacturers in May 1984, this time hammering out an agreement with Tour d'Argent, a prestigious French restaurant. According to the agreement Ito Ham would distribute the restaurant's specialty food products like tea, coffee, and mustard in department stores and boutiques around Japan.

To ensure long-term growth and stability, Ito Ham decided to develop its interest in biotechnology. In August 1984 it announced plans to commercialize its method of extracting valuable chemical elements from pig blood, particularly an amino acid used for flavoring. The company began building a new laboratory for this and other biotechnical research in December 1988, and it was during this period that the name Itoham Foods Inc. was adopted.

Diversification and New Challenges: 1990s–2000s

Itoham Foods entered the 1990s in a strong position as a leading meat processor and an increasingly integrated food business. Kenichi Ito, Itoham's president, cited Japan's abundant food supply and the resulting stiff competition in the domestic food market as two of the difficult conditions Itoham faced. A third and more threatening difficult condition Itoham would battle was the deep recession the Japanese economy suffered throughout the 1990s.

As consumers tightened their wallets, Itoham sought to maximize market share and cut expenses by introducing a number of new products, including Houjyun ham products in 1991, Arabiki Frank wieners in 1993, and Alt Bayern wieners in 1998. At the same time, Itoham dropped unprofitable product lines and focused on core products. In the late 1990s the company implemented ambitious plans to reduce its product lineup in its Ham and Sausage Division by half, from about 1,500 items in the spring of 1999 to 750 by the end of 2000. Itoham also made efforts to accommodate consumer preferences by introducing lower-priced products in the Fresh Meat Division and moving away from expensive, luxury items. In addition, to elevate sales more efficiently, Itoham chose to focus on corporate, large-volume clients, such as major supermarket chains.

The company's efforts to streamline its product offerings and increase sales paid off by the end of the decade. Itoham's net sales for the fiscal year ending March 31, 2000, reached ¥470 billion, with net income at ¥6.3 billion, a significant increase over the ¥2.4 billion reported the previous year and higher than net income reported through the 1990s. Itoham's net income hit a low of ¥973 million in fiscal 1997.

As Itoham entered the new millennium, the company anticipated it would continue to face new demands, primarily increased competition and a weak market for meat consumption as a result of the poor economy. In addition, perpetually changing trends in consumer spending and strides toward globalization presented challenges. In order to best prepare itself Itoham adopted a three-year Medium-term Management Plan in April 2001. The strategy was to concentrate on core products, reduce costs by increasing efficiency and phasing out unprofitable operations, restructure and consolidate the supply and sales system, and increase marketing efforts.

Unfortunately for Itoham, an unexpected problem arose in the fall of 2001 with the first case in Japan of bovine spongiform encephalopathy (BSE), commonly referred to as mad cow disease. Although the tainted beef was not from Itoham, overall beef sales throughout the nation plummeted as consumers boycotted beef. Itoham's sales sagged, and for the fiscal year ending March 31, 2002, the company posted net sales of ¥465 billion, down from ¥475 billion the previous fiscal year. Itoham also posted a net loss of ¥707 million, a significant change from fiscal 2000's net income of ¥6.3 billion and even fiscal 2001's net income of ¥1.7 billion.

Problems within the meat industry continued through the following year, but they worked to Itoham's advantage. Two of Itoham's competitors, industry leader Nippon Meat Packers Inc. and Snow Brand Food Co., which ranked fifth in 2001, were guilty of mislabeling imported beef as domestic in 2002. The scandal resulted in the liquidation of Snow Brand and a boycott of Nippon Meat products by a number of supermarket chains. The boycott led Nippon Meat's ham and sausage sales to drop nearly 30 percent. Taking advantage of the absence of Nippon Meat products, Itoham stepped up production by nearly 30 percent. Itoham's efforts helped reverse fiscal 2002's net loss, and the company posted a net income of ¥312 million in fiscal 2003 on sales of ¥473,891 million. Although Nippon Meat managed to remain the industry leader with 21.6 percent of the ham and sausage market, Itoham succeeded in upping its market share 1.7 points to 20.4 percent.

Masami Ito became Itoham's new president on October 1, 2002, and Kenichi Ito remained with Itoham as chairman. The company continued to streamline production while also concentrating on diversification and innovation. To that end Itoham formed Ito Life Science Co., Ltd., a new subsidiary that would consolidate the company's pharmaceutical operations, in May 2003. Itoham planned to transfer the operations of its Health Science Division as well as U.S.-based subsidiary American Peptide Co., Inc., to Itoham Life Science.

In the summer of 2003 Itoham formed a partnership with Jiangsu Yurun Food Industry Group Co. and Mitsui & Co., Ltd. and began producing and selling ham and sausages in China, thus becoming the first Japanese company to manufacture and sell meat products in Beijing and other major metropolitan areas in China.

Sales of fresh meat and other meat products appeared to be on an upward trend in 2003, but the growth was slow and the

Key Dates:

1928: Denzo Ito establishes the Ito Processed Food Company in Osaka, Japan.
1932: The Ito Processed Food Company reorganizes as Ito Meat Processing Company in Kobe, Japan.
1933: Ito Meat Processing introduces the Pole Wiener.
1946: Ito Meat re-emerges from World War II as Ito Food Processing Company.
1948: Ito Food Processing reorganizes again as Ito Ham Company Limited.
1959: Ito Ham expands and establishes a plant in Tokyo.
1961: The company is listed on the Tokyo and Osaka stock exchanges and changes its name to Ito Ham Provisions Company, Limited.
1967: Ito Ham begins production of dairy products, its first foray into nonmeat products.
1973: The company forms its first venture with a U.S. company, becoming the exclusive distributor of Armour Food Company in Japan.
1983: Ito Ham forms Ito Carnation Company, a joint venture with Carnation Company.
1988: The company adopts the name Itoham Foods Inc., and ventures into biotechnology.
1990: The Itoham Central Research Institute is founded.
1997: The Alt-Ito Building is opened as the company's new Tokyo base.
1998: Itoham launches the Alt Bayem wiener line.
2001: The first case of bovine spongiform encephalopathy (BSE), or mad cow disease, is documented in Japan, causing consumers to boycott beef and Itoham's sales to decline.
2002: Masami Ito becomes Itoham's new president.
2003: A new subsidiary, Ito Life Science Co., Ltd., is formed to consolidate the company's pharmaceutical operations; a partnership is formed with Jiangsu Yurun Food Industry Group Co. and Mitsui & Co., Ltd. to produce and sell ham and sausages in China.

market still relatively stagnant. Although Itoham's net sales for the interim period from April 1, 2003 to September 30, 2003, reached ¥239 billion, up from ¥229 billion for the same period in 2002, net income dropped, from ¥308 million in 2002 to ¥242 million. The company revised its earnings forecasts downward for fiscal 2004 but remained confident that its commitment to providing safe and innovative products to the public, coupled with its vigilance in emphasizing efficiency, would lead Itoham to great financial success and stability in years to come.

Principal Subsidiaries

Sankyo Meat Co., Ltd.; Rockdale Beef Pty. Ltd. (Australia); Five Star Beef Ltd. (New Zealand); Tohoku Fresh Pack Co., Ltd.; Kanto Fresh Pack Co., Ltd.; Chubu Fresh Pack Co., Ltd.; Kansai Fresh Pack Co., Ltd.; Kyushu Fresh Pack Co., Ltd.; Okinawa Fresh Pack Co., Ltd.; Itoham Kanto Meat Sales Inc.; Itoham Chubu Meat Sales Inc.; Itoham Kansai Meat Sales Inc.; Itoham Kyushu Meat Sales Inc.; Itoham Foods (Australia) Pty. Ltd.; Itoham Daily Inc.; Itoham Shokuhin Inc.; HW Delicatessen Inc.; Asakusa Ham Inc.; Ito Cariani Sausage Company, Inc. (U.S.A.); Itoham Kanto Sales Inc.; Itoham Chubu Sales Inc.; Itoham Kansai Sales Inc.; Itoham Food Solutions Co., Ltd.; Okinawa Itoham Inc.; Kikusui Inc.; Dairyu Inc.; Ito Fresh Salad Co., Ltd; World Kitchen Co., Ltd.; IH Food Service Co., Ltd.; Hong Kong Garden Co., Ltd.; Hoei Bussan Co., Ltd.; American Peptide Company, Inc. (U.S.A.); Daily Distribution Co., Ltd.; IH Distribution Services Co., Ltd.; Itoham Distribution Co., Ltd.; S.A.R.L. Domaine de la Lauzade Kinu-Ito (France); Toei Techno Services Inc.; Itoham Marketing Institute Co., Ltd.; Ito Life Science Co., Ltd.

Principal Competitors

Nippon Meat Packers Inc.; Marudai Food Co.; Prima Meat Packers.

Further Reading

''Itoham Expects 25% Fall in Beef Sales,'' *Japan Today,* November 22, 2001.
''Japan Itoham Foods to Produce, Sell Ham, Sausages in China,'' *Japanese News Digest,* July 22, 2003.
''Nippon Meat Shares Plummet As Beef Scandal Widens,'' *CNN.com,* August 13, 2002.

—update: Mariko Fujinaka

J. & W. Seligman & Co. Inc.

100 Park Avenue
New York, New York 10017
U.S.A.
Telephone: (212) 850-1864
Toll Free: (800) 221-2783
Fax: (212) 922-5726
Web site: http://www.seligman.com

Private Company
Incorporated: 1980
Employees: 500
Total Assets: $17 billion (2003 est.)
NAIC: 52392 Portfolio Management

Bearer of an illustrious name and a distinguished past, J. & W. Seligman & Co. Inc. is now only one of many investment firms located in New York City albeit one of the few that remains independent in an increasingly concentrated industry. Although no longer what it once was—a potent force in the rise of the United States to world prominence—the Seligman name still stands for sound investment strategy. The firm manages nearly $20 billion in assets for its clients, mainly in equity mutual funds. The Seligman group of funds offers clients more than 60 investment options, including fixed income, growth and income, growth, and value equity portfolios.

"American Rothschilds": 1837–1937

Joseph Seligman, a German-born Jew, arrived in the United States in 1837 at the age of 17 and worked as an itinerant peddler in Pennsylvania. By 1840 two of his seven brothers had joined him and were working in the dry goods store he had opened in Lancaster, Pennsylvania. By the time J. Seligman & Brothers was founded in New York City in 1846, all seven were under his direction. While opening a store in Watertown, New York, Joseph made a useful connection—an army officer named Ulysses S. Grant. Brothers Jesse and Leopold followed the gold rush out to San Francisco, developed a thriving trade, bought gold bullion with the profits, and shipped the metal back East, making the Seligmans bankers in the process.

By 1857 the eight Seligman brothers had accumulated $500,000 in capital. With the opening of the Civil War in 1861, Joseph told his brothers to put everything in clothing, particularly uniforms, and the Seligmans became purveyors to the Union Army. However, the beleaguered government paid in bonds that Joseph felt the firm could only convert to cash in Europe. With the British and French governments discouraging such sales in the hope that the Confederate cause would be successful, the Seligmans concentrated on the German and Dutch financial markets and by the end of 1863 had placed nearly $125 million in bonds. Based on the model established earlier by the Rothschilds, the Seligmans established branches of their business—now J. & W. Seligman & Co. Inc.—in London, Paris, and Frankfurt, as well as New Orleans and San Francisco.

During the Grant administration (1869–77) Joseph Seligman was so important a financial figure that at one point he was offered the position of secretary of the treasury, which he declined. The firm became fiscal agent for the conversion of existing war bonds to new ones and acted for years as fiscal agents for the Department of State and Department of the Navy. The Seligmans invested heavily in railroads and acted as broker for lucrative transactions engineered by Jay Gould. In New York, the firm invested in the development of the city's elevated railroads.

The eight Seligman brothers fathered no less than 36 sons, but only Isaac Newton Seligman—Joseph's second son—assumed a position of leadership, becoming head of the firm on his uncle Jesse's death in 1894. (Joseph had died in 1880.) During the following years the firm backed the construction of the Panama Canal. Albert and Frederick Strauss became the first non-family managing partners of the firm in 1901. Under their direction J. & W. Seligman underwrote the securities of a variety of companies. Correspondence books for the period are rich in details on the firm's participation in syndicates for underwriting stock and bond issues in the railroad and steel and wire industries, investments in Russia and Peru, the Standard Oil Company, and shipbuilding, bridges, bicycles, mining, and a variety of other industries. In 1910 William Durant of the fledgling General Motors Corporation gave the Seligmans control of his company's board in return for underwriting $15 million worth of corporate notes.

Company Perspectives:

Seligman offers a wide selection of core options, including fixed income, growth and income, growth, and value equity portfolios. These portfolios have a history of solid, long-term performance—a strong foundation for any investment strategy—and have helped investors reach their financial goals for many generations.

The New Orleans and San Francisco branches of J. & W. Seligman had closed by 1897, when a family liquidation agreement separated the foreign firms from the New York branch. There were still three Seligmans among the nine J. & W. partners in 1928, but the last one resigned in 1937. J. & W. Seligman broke new ground in 1929 when it organized the Tri-Continental Corporation, a diversified closed-end investment company that remains the largest of its kind listed on the New York Stock Exchange. The following year the firm began managing its first mutual fund, Broad Street Investing Co., which later became the Seligman Common Stock Fund. Other early Seligman mutual funds included the Whitehall Fund, National Investor's, and the Seligman Growth Fund.

Wall Street Investment Manager: 1938–89

New Deal legislation in 1934 forced J. & W. Seligman to choose between its banking and underwriting activities, and it chose the latter. But it withdrew from the underwriting of securities in 1938, when Union Securities Corp., an affiliate of Tri-Continental, was established for this purpose, and henceforth confined its activities to investment management, including that of Tri-Continental. Francis Fitz Randolph, a well-connected Yale graduate, was the firm's senior partner in the ensuing years. Oklahoma-born Fred E. Brown was named a general partner in 1955 and managing partner ten years later. Reviewing Seligman's performance in *Forbes* in 1983, when it was managing six mutual funds with about $4.6 billion in assets, Barbara Rudolph wrote, "The firm was late into money market funds, slow to bring out new mutual funds, cautious in investment policy and little known to the public."

But, as Rudolph noted, Seligman was in the process of change. The firm, long owned by its employees, was incorporated, its antiquated fee structure was revised to raise more capital and offer money managers competitive compensation, and it introduced its first major advertising campaign ever with the headline, "J. & W. Who?" Seligman benefited from the bull market of the 1980s, ending the decade with about $6.7 billion in total assets under management. In 1989 the 43 employees—past and present—who had invested $3.3 million to incorporate the firm were rewarded with $52.6 million in cash and notes from a leveraged buyout group of Seligman directors headed by William C. Morris and financed by insurance company lenders.

Struggling to Survive: 1990–2002

Morris, who succeeded Brown as chairman and chief executive officer of Seligman, invested in marketing the firm and added international equities to its roster of stock mutual funds. Clients were offered the option of paying their mutual fund load fees over time, instead of all at once. The firm's assets under management increased to over $11 billion during the next three years from a combination of open-end mutual funds and pension and individual accounts. Nevertheless Seligman ranked only 128th among U.S. money managers in 1992 in terms of total assets under management. Its 30 or so funds included 19 in the stodgy field of tax-exempt municipal bonds, which Seligman first entered in 1983. The venerable firm moved to Park Avenue in 1993, leaving behind its longtime quarters on Wall Street.

Seligman decided to concentrate on institutional investors in 1995, when it sold the accounts it was managing for wealthy individuals and families to U.S. Trust Corp. The transaction paid Seligman cash for the $900 million in assets that it shed. As part of the agreement, U.S. Trust also bought Seligman's trust bank, which meant the firm would no longer be trustee for the 6,000 individual retirement accounts and 1,500 retirement plans that it was managing. Seligman continued to manage $6.5 billion in mutual funds and $3.5 billion in institutional accounts and to sell its mutual funds through wholesalers to stockbrokers, who in turn offered them to their investment clients.

Seligman's star at this time was Phil Wick, the 32-year-old manager of Seligman Communications & Information Fund, which at midyear was the biggest technology fund in the United States. This fund was the best performing one over the past 12 months and five years, having climbed 289 percent since mid-year 1974 and 860 percent for the decade, according to one count. About half the fund was invested in stocks related to the semiconductor industry, including companies such as Oracle, Compaq Computer, Hewlett-Packard, and Seagate Technology. So popular was this fund—which had only $40 million in assets when Wick assumed its management at the end of 1989—that it closed its doors to new investors in mid-1995. (After technology stocks dropped in price in the first half of 1996, the fund became available for customers of the retail brokerage Charles Schwab & Co.)

Tri-Continental, by contrast, was delivering mediocre performance by the standards of the bull market, with an annual average return of only 10.03 percent over the ten years ended in April 1997. Writing in *Forbes,* Thomas Easton contended, "Customers are locked in because that's the way closed-end funds work. The sponsor does not redeem shares. . . . So if . . . you want out, you have to auction them on the New York Stock Exchange. Given the weak results at the fund. . . . They trade at an 18% discount to their net asset value." Easton maintained that Seligman was "well paid" for its "unsuccessful efforts to beat the market" and added that by the terms of a rights offering made in 1992, existing shareholders could buy a certain number of new shares at a discount. This meant, he argued, that those declining to do so would experience dilution of net asset value to their shares. Seligman, however, gained a bigger asset base ($2.7 billion in 1997) from which to draw management fees.

As a new millennium began to dawn, Seligman was seen as being in a perilous position by one consultant, who told *Bond Buyer* that the firm was "too large to be called a boutique, but too small to have the marketing infrastructure and resources to compete" with major mutual fund firms such as Putnam Investments Inc. "They're caught in a very, very difficult position in terms of

Key Dates:

1837: Joseph Seligman arrives in the United States and finds work as an itinerant peddler.
1864: J. & W. Seligman is a banking house with offices in Europe as well as the United States.
1897: A family liquidation agreement separates the foreign branches from New York.
1929: J. & W. Seligman enters the mutual fund business.
1938: The firm has left banking and underwriting and is wholly in investment management.
1980: Seligman changes from a partnership to a corporate structure.
1989: A leveraged buyout puts the firm in the hands of some of its directors.
1995: Seligman's technology mutual fund has become the largest of its kind in the United States.

building market share,'' he added. In 1997 the firm began offering mutual funds to foreign investors with the introduction of Seligman Global Horizon Funds, a Luxembourg-based investment company available exclusively to investors not citizens or residents of the United States. To better serve its clients Seligman introduced, in late 1998, a computer program that it distributed free to financial planners. Once the user entered its clients' financial data and goals, the program recommended suitable Seligman investments for both long- and short-term needs.

A few months later, Seligman sought to capitalize on Wick's success by launching Seligman New Technologies Fund, a diversified open-end fund to be co-managed by its technology-stock wizard. In 2000 the firm introduced a closed-end fund by the same name. The plan for this fund involved placing as much as 35 percent of its assets in private equity, investing directly in venture capital companies as well as in private funds investing in those companies. It was described by a Seligman officer as a cross between a specialty technology fund and a private equity fund. In addition to being difficult to dispose of, the fund required a minimum initial investment of $10,000, a 3 percent upfront sales charge, and what Patrick McGeehan of the *Wall Street Journal* described as an ''especially steep'' annual expense ratio of 3 percent, including a 2 percent management fee.

Although Wick's reputation lost some of its luster during the fall from favor of technology stocks, which lasted through 1998, Marion Schultheis, a Seligman managing director, won attention for her performance as manager of the Seligman Capital Fund. As of mid-September 2000, this growth fund was in the top 3 percent of all 8,040 equity funds for the year. Schultheis, who also was head of the growth investment team at Seligman, was said to rely on her staff for involved mathematical analysis of a company's stock while employing intuition and a vision of the future as well as studying both the underlying fundamentals of a firm and industry and economic trends.

The bear market of the early years of the new century wrought havoc with J. & W. Seligman. The firm's Communication & Information Fund retained only about half of the $6.5 billion in its coffers in 1999, and Wick, who acknowledged to Ian McDonald of the *Wall Street Journal* that the 2000–02 free-fall of technology stocks had been ''incredibly depressing,'' said he was now gravitating to companies engaged in medical technology. By the fall of 2003 Seligman was engaged in the third round of layoffs since 2000, its assets having dropped from $40 billion to only $17 billion. *Institutional Investor* reported that the firm was nearly sold to New York Life Insurance Co. during the year, but that an agreement broke down over Morris's insistence that Seligman's partners retain a controlling interest. The firm was said to be worth as much as $200 million in any acquisition.

Principal Subsidiaries

Seligman Capital Fund, Inc.; Seligman Common Stock Fund, Inc.; Seligman Data Corp.; Seligman Frontier Fund, Inc.; Seligman Growth Fund, Inc.; Seligman Henderson Global Fund Series, Inc.; Seligman Income Fund, Inc.; Seligman Municipal Fund Series, Inc.; Seligman New Technologies Fund, Inc.; Seligman Portfolios, Inc.; Seligman Time Horizon/Harvest Series, Inc.; Seligman Value Fund Series, Inc.; Tri-Continental Corp.

Principal Competitors

INVESCO Capital Management Inc.; Janus Capital Group Inc.; John Nuveen Co.; Putnam Investments Inc.

Further Reading

Birmingham, Stephen, *''Our Crowd'': The Great Jewish Families of New York,* New York: Harper & Row, 1967.

Callan, Sara, '' 'Hello, Mr. Chips': One Fund Takes Honors for Three Periods,'' *Wall Street Journal,* July 7, 1995, p. R3.

Easton, Thomas, ''Prisoners of Poor Performance,'' *Forbes,* April 21, 1997, pp. 368, 370.

Gould, Carole, ''Tri-Continental Directors Turn Deaf Ear on Wake-Up Call,'' *New York Times,* May 18, 1997, Sec. 3, p. 7.

Halverson, Guy, ''One Manager Making a Name for Herself,'' *Christian Science Monitor,* September 25, 2000, p. 15.

Hellman, Geoffrey T., ''Sorting Out the Seligmans,'' *New Yorker,* October 30, 1954, pp. 34–40, 42, 44, 46–48, 51–65.

McDonald, Ian, ''Tech-Fund Manager Wary of Sector,'' *Wall Street Journal,* July 2, 2003, p. D7.

McGeehan, Patrick, ''Seligman Plans an Unusual Tech Fund,'' *Wall Street Journal,* July 1, 1999, p. C27.

Merrill, Cristina, ''U.S. Trust Buys Units from J&W Seligman,'' *American Banker,* May 12, 1995, p. 11.

Phalon, Richard, ''New Broom at Seligman,'' *Forbes,* February 20, 1989, p. 140.

Rudolph, Barbara, ''Seligman Wakes Up,'' *Forbes,* August 15, 1983, p. 116.

''Seligman Reopens a Technology Fund,'' *Wall Street Journal,* January 31, 1996, p. B5.

''Seligman's Strategy,'' *Bond Buyer,* April 16, 1999, pp. 1, 8.

''Will Seligman Sell?'' *Institutional Investor,* October 2003, p. 12.

Willis, Gerri, ''Market Rouses Wall St. Sleeper,'' *Crain's New York Business,* September 6, 1993, p. 5.

Wren, Daniel A., ''The J. and W. Seligman Archives at the Harry W. Bass Business History Collection,'' *Business History Review,* Spring 2000, pp. 113–17.

Wyatt, Edward, ''Market Place,'' *New York Times,* July 25, 1995, p. D10.

—Robert Halasz

Jersey European Airways (UK) Ltd.

Exeter International Airport
Exeter, Devon EX5 2BD
United Kingdom
Telephone: +44-1392-366-669
Fax: +44-1392-366-6151
Web site: http://www.flybe.com

Private Company
Incorporated: 1979
Employees: 1,500
Sales: £236 million (2004 est.)
NAIC: 481111 Scheduled Passenger Air Transportation

Jersey European Airways (UK) Ltd. is the third largest airline in the United Kingdom. The company, which began marketing itself under the name ''FlyBE'' in 2002, calls itself the largest independently owned regional airline in Europe. FlyBE flys about four million passengers a year to 17 domestic and 25 international destinations. About 80 percent of its bookings were made online. Due to its evolution as a regional carrier, FlyBE is unique in maintaining a headquarters and hub in relatively rural Exeter. However, this has helped the airline carve its own niche. As company Managing Director Jim French put it, ''We are enabling the population living outside London and the southeast to enjoy the same benefits of low-fare travel as the city dwellers.''

Jersey Origins

The growth of the Channel Islands as a tourist destination in the 1950s and 1960s led to the formation of a number of small airlines to compete with ferryboats. One of these, Intra Airways, was established in Jersey in 1969 to operate war surplus DC-3 aircraft.

Intra merged with Express Air Services (EAS) ten years later to form Jersey European Airways (JEA). EAS soon left the partnership, however. JEA replaced its DC-3s with a variety of smaller, newer island-hopping commuter aircraft.

Walker Aviation Group of Lancashire then acquired JEA in 1983. Walker also owned a small airline, Spacegrand, which flew routes from Northern England (Blackpool) to Ireland and the Isle of Man. Jack Walker, founder of Walkersteel, had established a base in Jersey for tax reasons. He had originally founded Spacegrand in 1980 as an air taxi for Walkersteel executives; in 1982 it had contracted with JEA's sister maintenance unit.

Exeter, a city of 100,000 people in rural southwest England, became the hub linking the two route networks and became the company's headquarters when JEA and Spacegrand were amalgamated in 1985. The next year, JEA expanded its capacity with three Shorts SD360 aircraft. JEA carried 160,000 passengers in 1985; its annual revenues were less than £9 million.

In 1989, the ten-year-old maintenance operation, JEA (Engineering) Ltd., was moved to Exeter, where it acquired Westcountry Aviation Services. The unit, JEA's sister company under Walker Aviation ownership, was then renamed Jersey European Technical Services. It had 180 workers in 1991 and grew to employ 450 people by 2001.

JEA, the airline, had 200 employees at the start of the 1990s. Passenger count rose 40 percent in 1990 to 460,000. The growing airline started the 1990s with a new corporate livery. JEA began flying to London in 1991 from Guernsey and Jersey.

David McCulloch was JEA managing director from the end of 1991 to May 1992. He was replaced for a time by Walker Aviation Managing Director Trefor Jones. Then in September 1992 JEA hired Barry Perrott, a British Airways alumnus, as chief executive.

Jets Acquired 1993

In 1993, JEA added three BAe 146 ''Whisper Jets'' to its fleet, which then consisted primarily of Fokker F-27 turboprops. A fourth BAe 146 was soon added to connect Belfast and Birmingham. Business Class service was introduced around this time. The Exeter hub was being supplemented by connections at London and Birmingham.

JEA posted pretax profits of £1.8 million on turnover of £51.7 million in fiscal 1995. The airline was again in expansion mode. The previous year, the airline had lost £3.7 million; it had

Company Perspectives:

The new millennium has seen a period of evolution for the airline. Following a change of brand to British European, the next stage of the development came on 18th July 2002, with the launch of a new airline name, FlyBE. Along with the new image came a raft of fundamental changes to the business, with new deals for both the customer and the travel trade. FlyBE has blended the innovative style of the new breed of airlines yet retained the service values customers have a right to expect.

returned one of its leased BAe 146s and trimmed 40 employees from its workforce.

In the mid-1990s, JEA leased a full-size airliner to fly to Amsterdam. JEA acquired its seventh BAe 146 in 1995. A code-share arrangement with Air Inter allowed JEA to offer London (Stansted) and Marseilles. In October 1996 the airline began operating routes from London to Lyons and Toulouse on behalf of Air France. A Birmingham-Paris route soon followed. However, a promising stock offering planned for November 1998 was canceled when the market for airline stocks collapsed. The airline had been expected to be valued at £100 million.

New Names in 2000, 2002

Five more BAe 146s were acquired in 1997. Another series of route extensions followed the April 1999 order for 11 Dash 8 turboprops and four Canadair Regional Jets (both aircraft produced by Canada's Bombardier). The order was worth £160 million ($250 million). The new capacity allowed the route network to expand to Dublin and Edinburgh.

JEA was the leading carrier at both London City and Belfast City, in spite of recent incursions into the Northern Ireland market from budget carriers easyJet and Ryanair. JEA's schedules were more oriented towards business travelers than those of these two upstarts.

In June 2000, a change of name to British European was effected to reflect the carrier's international work with Air France and the extension of the network into Scotland. (There was no relation to the former British European Airways Corporation.)

By 2001, BE was flying to several major cities in the British Isles and France; Air France contracted for Glasgow-Paris service. BE, which had 1,200 employees, operated 1,100 flights per week, including some charters. Revenues were £162 million in fiscal 2000; sister company British European Aviation Services took in £14 million. Walker Aviation's aircraft leasing business accounted for another £8 million.

The Regional Jets were dropped from the fleet in 2001, though the carrier continued to operate BAe 146 jets, which could take off from shorter runways. BE had planned to be the launch customer for the BAe 146's replacement, the RJX, but BAe canceled that program.

BE was able to pick up routes from Gill Airways and Sabena when they were grounded. A July 2001 marketing agreement with Delta Air Lines gave BE a share of its traffic beyond London. BE signed another codeshare agreement with Continental Airlines in September 2002.

Key Dates:

1969: Intra Airways is formed in Jersey.
1979: Intra merges with Express Air Services to form Jersey European Airways (JEA).
1980: Spacegrand is established as air-taxi service in Blackpool.
1985: JEA joins Spacegrand; headquarters are relocated to Exeter.
1989: Maintenance operations are moved to Exeter.
1991: JEA enters London-Guernsey, London-Jersey markets.
1993: BAe 146 jets are added to the fleet.
2000: The company is renamed British European.
2002: The business is rebranded as FlyBE.

BE then faced a number of serious challenges that resulted in £30 million in losses in just two years. The 9/11 terrorist attacks on the United States and Britain's mad cow crisis both conspired to cut traffic.

Barry Perrott, British European's CEO for the previous nine years, resigned in June 2001 to be replaced by Jim French. French had begun working for Jersey European in 1989 following positions with Air UK and others.

JEA was relaunched on July 18, 2002, as a budget, Internet-based, consumer-oriented airline under the brand name ''FlyBE.'' Within a year the carrier would be able to announce that 80 percent of its bookings were being made online. FlyBe celebrated this achievement by offering special fares, as low as £12 between Belfast and Birmingham.

Turnover reached £213 million in fiscal 2003, though the company struggled to regain profitability. Revenues were expected to climb to £236 million in fiscal 2004.

A significant route expansion was announced in 2003, including the addition of hubs at Bristol and Southampton. One testament to FlyBE's influence was British Airways' abandonment of the Southampton-Jersey and Southampton-Belfast markets in the summer of 2003.

FlyBE was launching more services to France and one to Spain in March 2004. Up to 11 more European routes were in the works for 2005. The airline was discussing options for larger short-haul aircraft along the lines of the Boeing 737 or Airbus A319 used by other low-cost carriers. These were to replace the company's fleet of smaller BAe 146s.

After losing £28 million in two years of transition to a low-cost business model, FlyBE was beginning to post profits again. With FlyBE flying high and boosting market share, observers were anticipating a public stock offering for the airline by 2006.

Principal Competitors

Aer Lingus Group Plc; Aurigny Air Services Limited; British Airways Plc; easyJet Airline Co. Ltd.; Ryanair Holdings plc; ScotAirways.

Further Reading

''Birmingham Is Hub of Success,'' *Birmingham Post,* February 16, 1998, p. 29.

''British European Hit by Surprise Departure of Chief Executive Officer,'' *Airclaims Airline News,* June 29, 2001.

Buyck, Cathy, ''The Niche Player,'' *Air Transport World,* June 1, 2001, p. 73.

Crump, Eryl, and Chris Penny, ''Flybe: The United Kingdom's Major Regional Airline,'' *Regional Airliners,* Key Classic Aircraft Series No. 16, 2003.

Dey, Iain, ''French Speaks Language of Aviation Success,'' *Scotsman,* May 16, 2003, p. 21.

Done, Kevin, ''FlyBE Negotiates to Join the Big League,'' *Financial Times,* December 10, 2003, p. 30.

——, ''FlyBE to Set Up Base in South,'' *Financial Times* (London), December 19, 2002, p. 24.

Elliott, Harvey, ''Ex-Steel Chief Aims to Be an Airline Leader,'' *Times,* Bus. Sec., October 18, 1990.

''Flybe Whispers of Huge Growth,'' *Western Daily Press,* August 16, 2003, p. 64.

Halstead, Ian, ''Jersey European Heading for Sky-High Success,'' *Birmingham Post,* June 30, 1999, p. 25.

Jersey European Airways (UK) Ltd., ''History of FlyBE.,'' http://www.flybe.com/history/, 2004.

''Jersey European Cuts BAe 146 Fleet, Reduces Workforce,'' *Commuter/Regional Airline News International,* January 17, 1994.

''Jersey European Goes International, Changes Name,'' *Commuter/Regional Airline News,* May 22, 2000.

Lea, Robert, ''FlyBE Steps Up Challenge with Regional Rollout,'' *Evening Standard* (London), December 1, 2003, p. A32.

''Leading the Charge,'' *Western Morning News,* July 3, 2003, p. 14.

Lewis, Paul Richfield Arnold, ''Most Unusual Order,'' *Business & Commercial Aviation,* May 1, 1999, p. 56.

Lynn, Matthew, ''Walker Is on Course for Twin Floats,'' *Sunday Times,* Bus. Sec., August 16, 1998.

McGill, Adrienne, ''Jersey European Is Spreading Its Wings,'' *Belfast News Letter,* June 8, 1999, p. 27.

——, ''New-Look Airline to 'Tear Up the Rule Book','' *Belfast News Letter,* July 19, 2002, p. 17.

''One-on-One with Jersey European's Barry Perrott,'' *Commuter/Regional Airline News,* August 14, 2000.

Reed, Arthur, ''Standing Pat in England,'' *Air Transport World,* March 1, 1991, p. 92.

Schofield, Adrian, ''Flexibility Helps British European Seize New Growth Opportunities,'' *Commuter/Regional Airline News,* March 4, 2002.

Wain, Ron, ''Flybe Downs BA Jersey Service,'' *This Is Hampshire,* August 22, 2003.

Woodhouse, Tania, ''Wwwonderful; FlyBE Reveals 80% of Bookings Made on Net,'' *Mirror,* July 26, 2003, p. 37.

—Frederick C. Ingram

Klement's Sausage Company

207 E. Lincoln Avenue
Milwaukee, Wisconsin 53207
U.S.A.
Telephone: (414) 744-2330
Toll Free: (800) 553-6368
Fax: (414) 744-2438
Web site: http://www.klements.com

Private Company
Incorporated: 1958
Employees: 420
Sales: $120 million (2002 est.)
NAIC: 311612 Meat Processed from Carcasses

Klement's Sausage Company produces more than 700 varieties of sausage and meat products at its two plants on the south side of Milwaukee. Its processing activities are split into three distinct ''kitchens'' based on the type of product produced: a Pre-Rigor Pork (Fresh Sausage) Kitchen, a Cooked and Smoked Sausage Kitchen, and a Summer Sausage Kitchen. The company emphasizes the production of sausages using traditional European recipes to create the distinct flavors of Italian, German, or Polish sausages. In addition to its processing, distribution, and warehouse operations, Klement's facilities also encompass a hog slaughtering plant and a USDA certified lab that regulates product safety.

Klement's sausages are sold mainly in Wisconsin and the surrounding area, although the company's products can be found at special venues in all 50 states. Aside from the products sold under its own brand, Klement's supplies meat products for private-label contracts, for restaurants and caterers, and for institutions such as schools, theme parks, hotels, casinos, and correctional facilities. The company also has exclusive agreements to sell its sausages at a number of sports venues. It is particularly well known for sponsoring the ''sausage races'' at Miller Park, home of the Milwaukee Brewers. The company is family-owned and is still led by members of the Klement family.

An Old-Style European Sausage Kitchen: Founding the Company in 1956

Klement's Sausage Company was founded in 1956 when three brothers, John, George, and Ronald Klement, bought the Badger Sausage Company at Lincoln Avenue on Milwaukee's south side. They had learned the art of sausage making from their father Frank, who was part owner of the Milwaukee Sausage Company. The brothers used recipes that ''Grandpa'' Frank had brought from Europe to open a small sausage kitchen that catered to the tastes of area residents. The south side district where their shop was located had a strong European heritage, and many of the Klement brothers' earliest customers were descendants of Polish or German immigrants who appreciated sausage with the distinct flavors of the old world. The shop was ensured a steady supply of fresh meat thanks to its location in the midst of Wisconsin's thriving pork and cattle industry.

The company was renamed Klement's Sausage Company in 1958. At first, the sausage shop had only six employees and all products were made in a small kitchen. But the company grew as each brother brought his own particular talent to the enterprise. Ron was known as a good salesman, George was an expert sausage maker, and John (or ''Jack'') had a gift for administration. His son John told the *Milwaukee Journal Sentinel* in 2002, ''He could bring an organization together so it could work like a finely tuned machine. He was able to get the personnel and put them in the right positions to make the company grow.'' Klement's expanded its meat processing facilities at the original Lincoln Avenue site into a full-scale factory in the 1960s.

Expanding Visibility in the 1980s

Klement's increased its public visibility with the institution of the ''sausage races'' in the early 1980s. The promotion got its start from a popular crowd diversion at Milwaukee Brewers baseball games, where a group of cartoon sausages would race across the scoreboard. Fans liked the sausage entertainment enough that Brewers executives decided to make it a live event with real humans wearing large sausage costumes. Klement's became the event sponsor. By the mid-1980s, at every home Brewers game, the Hot Dog, the Bratwurst, Stash the Polish,

Company Perspectives:

Mission Statement: To continue to improve our leadership in the production of the finest quality meat products for all of our valued customers at an affordable price in a very safe and efficient working environment.

and Guido the Italian would race each other to home plate as spectators made bets on who would win.

In 1985 Klement's built a hog butchering facility at its main Lincoln Avenue plant to provide a reliable source of fresh meat for its processing operation. With the onsite slaughterhouse, an animal could be turned into sausage within an hour after being eviscerated. Three years later the company expanded again when it built an 85,000-square-foot distribution center and warehouse on Chase Avenue, a few blocks away from the existing plant. Klement's also had acquired a 32,000-square-foot sausage plant, formerly known as the Uncle August Sausage Co., in the northeast part of Milwaukee. Production of summer sausage and beef sticks was transferred there for several years. The Chase Avenue facility served as the distribution hub for both plants.

Product Diversification in the Early 1990s

Klement's Sausage's association with the Milwaukee Brewers became official in 1992 when the company won a contract to supply all the bratwurst at the team's home County Stadium. Over the next few years the company built connections with other sports teams as well. Klement's sausages became available in the home venues of the Minnesota Twins, the Minnesota Vikings, the Kansas City Chiefs, and the Green Bay Packers. The sausage races, however, remained unique to County Stadium. But by the early 1990s the sausage characters were venturing out of the stadium to mingle with the public at events including grand openings, parades, the Wisconsin State Fair, and the Polish Fest. Klement's even developed sausage-race jackets that grocery stores could give away in customer drawings. Now, even those who were not sports fans might bump into the 8-foot tall sausage characters over the meat cooler at the grocery store. ''Klement's realized that if we were going to continue to be successful, we would have to connect with our target consumers on a different level,'' said Daniel Lipke, senior vice-president, to the *Milwaukee Journal Sentinel* in 1998. Klement's also launched a web site in 1995 to sell gift packages over the Internet—and the web site included a sausage race game.

By the mid-1990s Klement's product line had diversified into more than a hundred different products. A light line was introduced in the early 1990s in response to consumer demand for low-fat products. By the middle of the decade, the light line, which included light bratwurst; bologna; and Italian, smoked, and summer sausage, accounted for about 10 percent of sales. Turkey bratwurst was introduced near the end of the decade as another light option. Another growing product category was ready-to-eat meats, including pre-sliced deli-style meats such as ham, corned beef, and bologna. The category grew about 20 percent a year through the early 1990s. Finally, sales of non-refrigerated meat snacks such as ham and beef sticks also were rising rapidly. Klement's promoted them as a high-protein, low-fat snack and worked to place the products in more convenience stores as well as grocery stores. In general, according to the company's market research, consumers were looking for more conveniently packaged products in smaller portions with lower fat so long as flavor was not sacrificed. Klement's developed a wider array of products each year as it worked to address those demands. Still, the company's largest sellers overall continued to be traditional products such as bratwurst, liver sausage, and summer sausage. Private-label contracts, in which Klement's produced products to be sold under another company's name, also contributed to sales. The company became a supplier for Sysco Food Services Inc., Reinhart Institutional Foods Inc., and Saz's Barbecue Products.

Klement's celebrated its 40th anniversary in August 1996 with an employee party at the Milwaukee Zoo. The company now had more than 350 employees at the main Lincoln Avenue plant and the Chase Avenue distribution center. After four decades in business, Klement's was still making sausages with strong ethnic flavors. ''We use natural spices for higher and more intense flavor profiles,'' James Klement told the *National Provisioner* in 1996. ''We put garlic in Polish sausage because people want to taste it. They would rather have more than less.''

Building Capacity for the New Millennium

By the mid-1990s, the Lincoln Avenue plant was getting to be too small for the company's increased production, so Klement's embarked on a $5 million project to add 60,000 square feet to the Chase Avenue facility. The facility had been used previously only as a distribution center, but most of the addition was devoted to processing activities. Several employees were moved there once it was completed in 1998 and five to ten more workers were hired. The Uncle August factory on the northeast side was sold within the next few years and all production was focused at the two south side plants.

George Klement, one of the founding brothers, died in 1996. He had been vice-president and production supervisor. John ''Jack'' Klement was now the only brother still at the plant; he acted as president. Several second-generation members of the family were involved in the company. John's sons James and Jeffrey both held high management positions, and James had even earned a Ph.D. in food science. George's son Roger was vice-president of finance. Over the years, the company had received offers to move out of Wisconsin, but Klement's stayed where it was. Jeff Klement told Milwaukee's *Business Journal* in 1996, ''We're very committed to Milwaukee. My dad always says he's keeping the business here because Milwaukee's where the sausage eaters are.''

Aside from making sausages, Klement's was involved in some real estate dealings, mainly managing some commercial and residential property in the neighborhood around its facilities. In 1996 the company bought a 75,000-square-foot office building in the Town of Pewaukee west of Milwaukee. Three years later the company bought a 160-unit apartment building in the southern part of Milwaukee. Jeffrey Klement eventually started an independent company to pursue real estate development.

Key Dates:

1956: The Klement brothers buy the Badger Sausage Factory in Milwaukee.
1958: Badger Sausage is renamed Klement's Sausage Company.
1980s: Klement's Racing Sausages become popular at Milwaukee Brewers games.
1985: Klement's adds a hog butchering facility at its main plant.
1988: The Chase Avenue distribution center is opened.
1998: A processing addition opens at the Chase Avenue site.
2000: Klement's hires 45 workers to support increased production of meat snacks.

In 1998 Klement's profited from historically low hog prices. Prices were low due to overproduction and the closing of several slaughterhouses, so that there was more pork than could be processed. Retail prices at grocery stores, however, dropped only slightly and pork consumption by consumers remained steady. Klement's operating profit rose in 1998 due to the lower raw material costs and wider profit margin.

Klement's announced a new partnership with the Milwaukee Brewers in 1999. The team was moving to a new stadium, Miller Park, and Klement's would be the official provider of hot dogs, Polish sausages, and bratwurst at the new venue. The company opened its own ''Sausage Haus'' building adjacent to the stadium as a place for fans to gather over beer and brats. Klement's also would be promoted with signs at the stadium and ads during game telecasts. The sausage races continued at the new stadium. The sausage characters branched out into other sports as well: in 2001 they arranged to play basketball at a Milwaukee Bucks game. That year Klement's became the exclusive supplier of sausages for Bucks games as well as any other event that was held at the team's Bradley Center.

Yet baseball and hot dogs would always be first and foremost. In a bizarre occurrence during the 2003 Brewers season, the team played host to the Pittsburgh Pirates. When the sausage race was underway during the seventh-inning stretch, Pirates first baseman Randall Simon took a playful whack at the Italian sausage with his bat. The sausage went down, and the hot dog also tumbled to the ground. The incident drew considerable media and legal attention, but in the end, with no injuries reported, Simon paid a fine of $432 for disorderly conduct and all was forgiven.

A growth in the sales of jerky and other meat snacks helped fuel an 11 percent increase in growth at Klement's in 1999. The company spent $2 million that year on additional processing equipment for meat snacks and hired more sales representatives to market the products in as many convenience locations as possible. In 2000 Klement's announced plans to hire 45 new workers by March of that year, the largest single addition in the company's history. Even though meat snacks accounted for only about 3 percent of sales, Klement's anticipated growth in the sector. Nationwide meat snack consumption had grown in the late 1990s. Jeff Klement told the *Milwaukee Journal Sentinel* in 2000, ''We're finding growth is harder to get in certain lines. So we're making commitments to segments that will give us growth in the long haul.''

Founder and CEO John Klement died in 2002 at the age of 84. He had continued to guide the company even in the last years of his life. Now the cousins Dr. James Klement and Roger Klement became co-presidents of the company. Klement's came up with new products and promotions to keep its sales strong in the new millennium. The Bella Delina brand was introduced as a high-end line of gourmet deli products that used particularly high-quality meats and ingredients. The company also started the ''Patio Daddio'' King of the Grill promotion. The campaign's slogan was ''Who's Your Patio-Daddio?'' Consumers got a free T-shirt and the chance to win a wooden deck or a Weber grill if they sent in four Klement's UPCs along with a picture of their favorite cook grilling Klement's products.

Principal Divisions

Pre-Rigor Pork Meat Kitchen; Cooked and Smoked Sausage Kitchen; Summer Sausage Kitchen.

Principal Competitors

Johnsonville Sausage, LLC; Fred Usinger Inc.

Further Reading

Behm, Don, ''Klement Was an Owner of Sausage Firm,'' *Milwaukee Journal Sentinel,* January 28, 1996, p. 7.

Bergquist, Lee, ''Crisis Forces Farmers to Give Up,'' *Milwaukee Journal Sentinel,* January 17, 1999, p. 1.

Causey, James E., ''Klement's Sausage Will Celebrate 40 Years,'' *Milwaukee Journal Sentinel,* July 8, 1996, p. 6.

——, ''Klement Wins Miller Park Sausage Race,'' *Milwaukee Journal Sentinel,* April 7, 1999, p. 7.

Daykin, Tom, ''Klement More Than a Sausage Company,'' *Milwaukee Journal Sentinel,* April 16, 1999, p. 1.

——, ''Lower Hog Prices Hurt Farmer, Help Processors,'' *Milwaukee Journal Sentinel,* December 18, 1998, p. 1.

——, ''Milwaukee-Based Sausage Maker Hiring 45 More Workers to Make Snacks,'' *Milwaukee Journal Sentinel,* January 17, 2000.

——, ''Sausage Company Enters Sponsorship Deal to Supply Products at Milwaukee Arena,'' *Milwaukee Journal Sentinel,* March 15, 2001.

Dries, Mike, ''Klement Sausage Building $5 Million Addition,'' *Business Journal-Milwaukee,* August 10, 1996, p. 7.

Flanigan, Kathy, ''Klement's Dogs Have Their Own Case to Make,'' *Milwaukee Journal Sentinel,* August 9, 1998, p. 4.

Jones, Meg, ''Klement Led Sausage Company into Big Time,'' *Milwaukee Journal Sentinel,* January 8, 2002, p. 5B.

Quigley, Kelly, ''Developing an Icon,'' *Business Journal-Milwaukee,* April 7, 2000, p. 3.

Young-Huguenin, Barbara, ''Sausage Sizzle,'' *National Provisioner,* July 1996.

—Sarah Ruth Lorenz

Krispy Kreme Doughnuts, Inc.

370 Knollwood St., Suite 500
Winston-Salem, North Carolina 27103-1880
U.S.A.
Telephone: (336) 725-2981
Toll Free: (800) 457-4779
Fax: (336) 733-3791
Web site: http://www.krispykreme.com

Public Company
Incorporated: 1937
Employees: 3,913
Sales: $491.5 million (2003)
Stock Exchanges: New York
Ticker Symbol: KKD
NAIC: 722213 Snack and Nonalcoholic Beverage Bars; 311811 Retail Bakeries; 311812 Commercial Bakeries; 533110 Lessors of Nonfinancial Intangible Assets (Except Copyrighted Works)

Krispy Kreme Doughnuts, Inc. makes what some would argue are one of the highlights of life on this planet: yeast-raised doughnuts. Sweet and impossibly fluffy, the Original Glazed earned a zealous following throughout the southern United States—and then beyond once expansion outside the South began in the mid-1990s. By late 2003, the company was operating more than 300 doughnut shops in 42 states; Ontario, Canada; Sydney, Australia; and the United Kingdom. It was producing 7.5 million doughnuts per day, adding up to 2.7 billion per year. The company's shops sell more than doughnuts, however, offering snack food, fruit pies, cinnamon buns, and beverages, including coffee, espresso, and frozen drinks. In addition to sales to customers entering its stores or using its drive-through windows, Krispy Kreme also uses its outlets as factories that additionally distribute fresh doughnuts for sale at convenience stores and supermarkets. The company also owns Montana Mills Bread Co., Inc., operator of about two dozen upscale bread stores located in the northeastern and midwestern United States.

Sweet Success in the 1930s

Sometime before the Great Depression, a French chef from New Orleans named Joe LeBeau developed the recipe for yeast-raised doughnuts—possibly the first of its kind in the United States—that would later form the basis of the Krispy Kreme empire. Eventually LeBeau established a doughnut shop in Paducah, Kentucky, which he sold in 1933, along with the secret recipe (speculated to contain vanilla and potato flour).

Vernon Rudolph and his uncle were the buyers. They moved the operation to Nashville, Tennessee, in 1935 and, through other family members, opened stores in Charleston, West Virginia, and Atlanta, Georgia. These stores sold their products wholesale to grocery stores.

Rudolph decided to strike out on his own. He brought with him two men, some equipment, and the secret recipe and eventually settled on booming Winston-Salem, North Carolina, as a location (some say a pack of Camel cigarettes sold him on the town). He lacked capital but was able to rent a building and obtain ingredients on credit. The first doughnuts from this new shop—called Krispy Kreme Doughnuts—were made on July 13, 1937. Such was their success that eager customers soon began requesting hot doughnuts directly from the doughnut shop, initiating the company's retail trade. Five cents bought two doughnuts, and a dozen cost a quarter. The company established its national headquarters in Winston-Salem in 1941.

Cold War Standardization

Krispy Kreme initiated an expansion program in 1946 that included producing the mix at a central plant in Winston-Salem to ensure consistency. In 1948 it opened the plant, which also produced equipment for the stores, and relocated its headquarters to the site (Ivy Avenue). During the 1950s mechanization brought an end to hand-cut doughnuts as the company gradually automated the entire doughnut-making process. By the end of the decade, 29 Krispy Kreme shops in 12 states each had the capacity to produce 500 dozen doughnuts per hour via specialized doughnut-making machines.

The distinctive Krispy Kreme decor was standardized in 1960. The shops (which by then populated 12 states) were

Company Perspectives:

Strategic Philosophy: All products we make in our stores will have a taste and quality that are second to none. The starting point in controlling product quality is controlling the quality and freshness of the ingredients. We will be thoroughly prepared to execute growth initiatives when they become needed. We view quality, service, and innovation as keys to creating and maintaining a competitive advantage. We view our company as a set of capabilities, not just a product or brand. We view our growth and success as a company as a natural result of the growth and success of our people.

sheltered by a green roof and red-glazed brick exterior. Inside, a large viewing window revealed doughnuts in production on an overhead conveyor belt—the first incarnation of the ''doughnut-making theater'' that Krispy Kreme would adopt as the centerpiece of all of its stores. In 1962 the company began to use air pressure to form almost perfectly symmetrical doughnuts. That same year, Krispy Kreme opened two new factories in Charlotte, North Carolina, and one in Richmond, Virginia.

Company founder Vernon Rudolph died in 1973. In 1974 the chain had 94 stores and 25 franchisees. Beatrice Foods Company bought Krispy Kreme two years later. Beatrice, according to one Krispy Kreme official, valued short-term profits at the expense of quality, even changing the traditional formula. To maximize sales, some stores began selling sandwiches. Development capital disappeared, stifling the company's long-term plans, and the company stopped selling franchises. Nevertheless, the company grew to 116 stores by 1980.

After Krispy Kreme was bought back from Beatrice, that growth disappeared to help repay debts of approximately five times the company's equity. Joseph A. McAleer, Sr., led the group of investors who bought the company in 1982 in a $22 million leveraged buyout. McAleer had been one of the chain's most successful franchisees. After grooming his son, Mac, for the CEO position, Joseph McAleer, Sr., retired in 1988. Another son, Jack, served as vice-president of sales and marketing. Scott Livengood, a Winston-Salem native who had joined the company during the Beatrice years, served as president.

Soon afterward, market research convinced the company to focus on the retail market, particularly hot doughnuts. The company reintroduced glowing red ''Hot Doughnuts Now'' signs, lit when new doughnuts were ready (which was most hours of the day), and guaranteeing a virtually Pavlovian response. The company tried expanding with drive-through only ''Express'' stores, which were less expensive to build than traditional stores (which cost about $1 million to open), but found customers missed the seating areas. The compact stores also lacked space for wholesale operations.

Northern Expansion in the Mid-1990s

In 1995 Krispy Kreme moved its headquarters and 230 corporate employees to 370 Knollwood Street in Winston-Salem. The headquarters also housed Doughnut University, a training center. New management talent had been drafted in the early 1990s to prepare the chain for its most ambitious expansion yet attempted. Jack and Mac McAleer and Scott Livengood retained the top positions at Krispy Kreme, but other conservative Winston-Salem businessmen were brought in to advise the company. To leverage its growth, Krispy Kreme would rely heavily on franchising: only 100 of 500 new stores would be company owned. Its first venture into northern territory was a shop in Indianapolis. The opening, which stopped traffic for blocks, was a sign of things to come.

The man who would introduce Krispy Kreme to New York, Mel Lev, a garment manufacturer, discovered the doughnuts while visiting friends and relations in Jackson, Mississippi. ''Why do we need four dozen doughnuts?'' were his reported last words before changing career paths. In June 1996 Lev opened the first store in Manhattan, at 265 West 23rd Street, near the historic Chelsea Hotel. The enterprise was named Harem, not in reference to the decadence of its products, but after the initials of family members. The family planned to open at least 30 stores in New York and New Jersey by 2005.

Reception was superlative. In the style column of the *New York Times Magazine,* Southern humorist Roy Blount, Jr., said, ''When Krispy Kremes are hot, they are to other doughnuts what angels are to people.'' He had hurried to the store opening and eaten five Original Glazed. New York being the capital of the publishing industry, many other odes by displaced Southerners were published on the hottest snack in town. Television also caught the buzz: Rosie O'Donnell had her own doughnut machine installed on her talk show, complete with conveyor belt and ''Hot Doughnuts Now'' sign. Late actress Jessica Tandy had already seen to it that the doughnuts had their moment on the silver screen, in such movies as *Driving Miss Daisy* and *Fried Green Tomatoes.*

The company's introduction to New York mirrored the sensation caused by the world's first doughnut-making machine, unveiled by Adolph Levitt in Harlem in 1921. Lev would open the second of the New York stores in Harlem, across from the Apollo Theater. Not everyone was delighted with the new stores, however. Some neighbors complained of fryer fumes, which resulted in Lev incurring fines from municipal environmental monitors.

Aside from pleasing transplanted Southerners in the Big Apple, the openings also suited Krispy Kreme's strategic plans. New York's only national doughnut chain was Dunkin' Donuts. Owned by British conglomerate Allied-Lyons plc (later known as Allied Domecq PLC), Dunkin' Donuts, with 115 stores in New York City, had led the market for years and had recently bought its closest competition, Mr. Donut, a West Coast chain. It also sold a range of sandwiches, soups, and muffins; doughnuts accounted for only half of the chain's sales. Krispy Kreme's supporters, though, believed the uniqueness of the yeast-raised products would ensure its success.

Stores in Scranton, Pennsylvania; Wilmington, Delaware; and Indianapolis figured into the company's assault on the North. The Indianapolis store overcame a mere 2 percent name recognition factor to set a first day sales record. Louisville, Kentucky, had previously had the northernmost store. Sweet Traditions LLC, a partnership of Canadian expatriate Eric

Key Dates:

1933: Vernon Rudolph and his uncle buy a doughnut shop in Paducah, Kentucky, from a French chef from New Orleans who had developed a secret recipe for yeast-raised doughnuts.
1935: The partners move the operation to Nashville, Tennessee; their initial focus is selling doughnuts wholesale to grocery stores.
1937: Rudolph leaves Nashville to open his own doughnut shop in Winston-Salem, North Carolina, called Krispy Kreme Doughnuts; after first concentrating on wholesaling, the new operation soon begins retail operations in response to demand from the public.
Late 1950s: There are 29 Krispy Kreme shops in 12 states.
1973: Company founder Rudolph dies.
1976: Beatrice Foods Company purchases Krispy Kreme.
1982: Group of investors led by franchisee Joseph A. McAleer, Sr., buy Krispy Kreme in a $22 million leveraged buyout.
1995: First shop outside the South opens in Indianapolis.
1996: The first New York City Krispy Kreme outlet makes its debut.
1999: First West Coast store opens in La Habra, California.
2000: With 141 stores in 27 states, the firm goes public as Krispy Kreme Doughnuts, Inc., raising net proceeds of $63 million on the NASDAQ.
2001: Krispy Kreme's stock is shifted to the New York Stock Exchange; first store outside the United States opens near Toronto, Canada.
2003: Montana Mills Bread Co., Inc. is acquired for about $40 million in stock.

Sigurdson and Chicago native Ken Marino, announced plans to open five St. Louis stores by the end of the decade.

Late 1990s: A New Brew, Going Coast to Coast

Coffee bars had been a feature of Krispy Kreme stores at least since the 1960s. In 1996 Krispy Kreme introduced its proprietary blend, titled ''America's Cup of Coffee.'' One and a half years of extensive research (assisted by 1,200 customers) preceded the introduction. ''Americans are drinking more coffee and becoming more knowledgeable about coffee,'' explained Jack McAleer. The beans were sold by the bag as well.

Convenience stores sold a variety of Krispy Kreme pastries, particularly single-serve items such as fruit pies, Krispy Knibbles (doughnut ''holes''), and cinnamon rolls. In 1995 the company tested a cobranding concept with Kroger grocery stores, whereby the doughnuts would be shipped fresh daily and placed in the bakery section, rather than the bread shelves. The Krispy Kreme stores themselves offered 15 varieties of doughnuts; some stores test-marketed bagels. Lowe's hardware superstores began hosting Krispy Kreme shops in 1996 in what turned out to be a short-lived experiment. Reviving a concept tried in the Beatrice days, the outlets also sold sandwiches supplied by an outside source.

Fund-raising traditionally accounted for around 10 percent of the company's sales and brought in more than $12 million in 1995. Half of the trade was wholesale. Before the company placed a new emphasis on retail sales in 1989, they had accounted for only a quarter of sales.

Expansion continued with the opening of new Krispy Kreme shops in Omaha, Nebraska; Las Vegas, Nevada; and the Kansas City area. By the end of 1997 there were 130 stores in 17 states, nearly half of which were franchised outlets. That year, the Smithsonian Institution confirmed Krispy Kreme's place in the American culinary pantheon by honoring it on its 60th anniversary. Artifacts from the company were contributed to the Smithsonian's National Museum of American History.

Remarkably, Krispy Kreme's successful expansion into new markets was accomplished entirely without a traditional media advertising budget. The company found that it could get more effective advertising for next to nothing by giving its doughnuts away; upon entering a new market, Krispy Kreme provided free doughnuts to local television and radio outlets and newspapers, which typically obliged by running puff pieces. From that point, word-of-mouth advertising had proved sufficiently effective to maintain the brand's cult status.

During the final two years of the decade, the chain entered several more major markets, including Houston, Dallas, and Chicago. Perhaps most importantly, the first West Coast store opened in La Habra, California, near Los Angeles, in January 1999. The company announced plans to open more than 40 franchise outlets in southern California over a four- to six-year period. Now operating coast to coast, Krispy Kreme ended the decade with 144 shops (86 franchised) in 27 states, making more than three million doughnuts daily and 1.3 billion per year. Revenues reached $220.2 million for the fiscal year ending in January 2000, a 40 percent increase over the figure from two years earlier. Livengood was named president and CEO in 1998 and then became chairman as well the following year.

Early 2000s: Raising Dough via IPO, Venturing into Foreign Territory

Leveraging its growing cult status to fund further expansion and the remodeling and relocating of some older units, the company went public as Krispy Kreme Doughnuts, Inc. on April 5, 2000. The offering of 3.45 million shares was priced at $21 per share, generating net proceeds of $63 million. In that first day of trading, the stock rose 76 percent, finishing at $37 a share, which placed the market capitalization of the company at nearly $462 million. With the bursting of the technology stock bubble around this time, Krispy Kreme became one of the hottest stocks around, and another 10.4 million shares were sold in a secondary offering in February 2001. A few months later, trading in the stock was transferred to the more prestigious New York Stock Exchange.

Krispy Kreme had long been vertically integrated on the doughnut side, producing its own doughnut mixes and manufacturing its own doughnut-making machinery, in addition to making, retailing, and wholesaling the finished product. During the early 2000s, the firm began adopting a vertical integration model for its beverage offerings. In February 2001 the company acquired Digital Java, Inc., a Chicago-based sourcer and microroaster of premium-quality coffee and producer of a wide line of coffee-based and non-coffee-based beverages. The assets and operation of the acquired firm were subsequently relocated to a brand-new coffee-roasting plant built in Winston-Salem. During 2002 and 2003 Krispy Kreme began rolling out a new beverage program featuring drip coffee, espresso, and frozen beverages. The overall goal was to increase the amount of sales deriving from beverages from 10 percent to about 20 percent by around 2008.

Another new initiative was the late 2001 launch of a new test concept called the ''doughnut and coffee shop.'' These stores aimed to provide customers with the hot doughnut experience that they had come to expect from Krispy Kreme, but in smaller locations—as small as 900 square feet—such as in a food court at a mall, in a downtown area, or at an airport. These outlets featured a new machine called the ''Hot Doughnut Machine,'' which took cooked but unglazed doughnuts that had been prepared at one of the company's ''factory'' stores, reheated them, and then glazed them. (Krispy Kreme considered each of its standard stores to be a ''doughnut factory''; capacity of these ''factories'' ranged from 4,000 dozen to 10,000 dozen doughnuts per day.) By early 2003 there were five of these outlets, which also offered a full line of coffee and other beverages. During 2003 Krispy Kreme also began experimenting with satellite outlets, which did not make their own doughnuts at all but rather were supplied with fresh—but cold—doughnuts from a nearby factory store. Yet another experiment, harkening back to the failed outlets that had opened in the late 1990s in some Lowe's stores, saw Krispy Kreme testing out stores located within Wal-Mart Stores, Inc. supercenters.

On the expansion front, Krispy Kreme by late 2003 had stores in 42 states, including its first outlets in New England, a stronghold of archrival Dunkin' Donuts, which was based in Randolph, Massachusetts. Among the newer Krispy Kreme franchisees were two celebrities: singer Jimmy Buffett acquired the rights to build outlets in Palm Beach County, Florida, in 2000; and Hank Aaron, baseball's all-time home-run hitter, reached an agreement in mid-2002 to begin opening franchises in the West End of Atlanta, Georgia. Expansion outside the United States began as well, with the first foreign outlet opening near Toronto, Canada, in December 2001. Through a joint venture with a franchise group, the corporation said that it planned to open 32 shops in eastern Canada over a six-year period. Here too, Krispy Kreme was venturing into territory dominated by a major doughnut player, namely Tim Hortons, a ubiquitous Canadian chain owned by Wendy's International, Inc. (Fittingly, Tim Hortons was simultaneously expanding into the U.S. market.) In June 2002 the company announced that it had entered into a joint venture to open 30 Krispy Kreme stores over a five-year period in Australia and New Zealand. Later that year, yet another joint venture was formed with two partnership groups, one of which included legendary television personality Dick Clark, to open 25 stores in the United Kingdom and the Republic of Ireland. In May 2003 the firm formed a joint venture with Grupo AXO to open 20 units in Mexico by 2009. Other markets under consideration for expansion included Japan, South Korea, and Spain.

Early in 2003 Krispy Kreme acquired Montana Mills Bread Co., Inc. for about $40 million in stock. Founded in 1996 and based in Rochester, New York, Montana Mills operated about two dozen upscale bakeries in the Northeast and Midwest that were modeled after old fashioned neighborhood bakeries. They offered nearly 100 varieties of bread, muffins, cookies, and scones, as well as sandwiches, soups, salads, and specialty coffees. The two chains had some notable similarities, particularly Montana Mills' ''bread-baking theater'' concept, which was akin to Krispy Kreme's doughnut-making theater. Workers at Montana Mills ground their own wheat every day, and the bakers worked in full view of the customers, mixing and kneading dough on large tables and then placing the loaves into huge ovens that were also visible to customers. By contrast, of course, Montana Mills was at a much earlier stage of development, and Krispy Kreme executives said that they would take a couple of years to refine the concept before beginning to expand it further.

Fiscal 2003 revenues reached $491.5 million, while systemwide sales hit $778.6 million, a 28 percent jump over the previous year. Net income that year totaled $39.1 million, up 51.6 percent over the 2002 level. Systemwide sales were expected to surpass the $1 billion mark during fiscal 2004, a year in which the corporation planned to open 77 new stores, most of them franchise outlets. Krispy Kreme still had plenty of expansion opportunities in the Unites States, through both its traditional formats and its experimental concepts, as well as in wholesaling to convenience and grocery stores, in addition to the great potential for overseas growth. In Montana Mills, it now also had the possibility of seeking growth through a second chain. Although it seemed likely that the stellar growth that Krispy Kreme had been enjoying was bound to taper off, the company and its doughnuts certainly seemed hotter than ever.

Principal Subsidiaries

Krispy Kreme Doughnut Corporation; Krispy Kreme Distributing Company, Inc.; Krispy Kreme Coffee Company, LLC; Krispy Kreme Mobile Store Company; HD Capital Corporation; HDN Development Corporation; Montana Mills Bread Co., Inc.; Panhandle Doughnuts, LLC; Oliver Acquisition Corp.; Krispy Kreme International Ltd. (Switzerland); Hot Doughnuts Now International Ltd. (Switzerland); Krispy Kreme Europe Limited (U.K.).

Principal Competitors

Allied Domecq Quick Service Restaurants; Starbucks Corporation; Winchell's Donut Houses Operating Company, L.P.; The TDL Group, Ltd.; Cinnabon.

Further Reading

Blount, Roy, Jr., ''Southern Comfort,'' *New York Times Magazine,* September 8, 1996.

Coleman, Zach, ''Doughnuts Hot Now,'' *Winston-Salem Journal,* September 23, 1996, p. B1.

Cook, Karla, ''The South Rises Again As Dixie Doughnuts Arrive in N.Y.,'' *Newark Star-Ledger,* August 7, 1996.

Ephron, Nora, ''Sugar Babies,'' *New Yorker,* February 1997.

Foderaro, Lisa W., ''What's Round, Fried, and Inspirational?,'' *New York Times,* April 25, 1997, p. B1.

Gardiner, Beth, ''Old Southern Delicacy Putting New Yorkers in Sweeter Mood,'' *Columbia (S.C.) State,* April 13, 1997, p. G1.

Greene, Kelly, "Krispy Kreme Has Holes, Skeptics Say," *Wall Street Journal* (Southeast Journal), April 12, 2000, p. S1.

Hagerty, James R., "Krispy Kreme at a Krossroads," *Wall Street Journal,* February 24, 2000, p. B1.

Haire, Kevlin C., "Krispy Kreme to Open Doughnut Franchises in Area," *Baltimore Business Journal,* April 1, 1994, p. 11.

Hill, Sheridan, "The Dough Boys," *Business North Carolina,* August 1994, pp. 50–56.

Joyner, Amy, "Krispy Kreme Buying Bakery," *Greensboro (N.C.) News and Record,* January 25, 2003, p. B9.

——, "Turning Doughnuts into Dough," *Greensboro (N.C.) News and Record,* March 5, 2000, p. E1.

Kazanjian, Kirk, and Amy Joyner, *Making Dough: The 12 Secret Ingredients of Krispy Kreme's Sweet Success,* Hoboken, N.J.: Wiley, 2004.

Klara, Robert, "Sweet Surrender: New York's Newest Craze Is a 60-Year-Old Southern Donut Concept," *Restaurant Business,* March 15, 1997.

"Krispy Kreme and the Cult of Fat," *Forbes,* December 16, 1996.

Kuntzman, Gersh, "A Hole New Taste Treat for New Yorkers," *New York Post,* June 12, 1996, p. 37.

Maremont, Mark, "Krispy Kreme Sales Seem to Show Signs of a Sugar Crash," *Wall Street Journal,* September 16, 2003, p. C1.

Mattingly, Rick, "Hot Krispy-Kreme Doughnuts on a Cold Day—Almost Heaven," *Louisville Courier-Journal,* November 27, 1993.

McCormack, Scott, "Sweet Success," *Forbes,* September 7, 1998, pp. 90–91.

Parker, Akweli, "Glazing New Trails," *Norfolk (Va.) Virginian-Pilot,* January 14, 1997, p. D1.

Peters, James, "Krispy Kreme Brews New Drink Slate As Doughnut Field Booms," *Nation's Restaurant News,* June 9, 2003, pp. 4, 137.

——, "Krispy Paradox?: Weekly, Same-Store Rates at Odds," *Nation's Restaurant News,* September 29, 2003, pp. 1, 6, 11.

——, "Sugar Rush: Krispy Kreme Rises, Challenges Segment," *Nation's Restaurant News,* July 9, 2001, pp. 4, 89.

Reynolds, Annette Fuller, "Yeast of Eden," *Indianapolis Star,* July 30, 1994, p. E1.

Rublin, Lauren R., "Dollars to Doughnuts," *Barron's,* July 10, 2000, pp. 21–22.

Sagon, Candy, "In Search of the Krispy Kreme Dream," *Washington Post,* October 6, 1993.

Serwer, Andy, "The Hole Story: How Krispy Kreme Became the Hottest Brand in America," *Fortune,* July 7, 2003, pp. 52–56, 60, 62.

Silver, Deborah, "Dollars to Doughnuts," *Restaurants and Institutions,* May 15, 2000, pp. 165–66+.

Smith, Samantha Thompson, "Hot Doughnut Wars Now: Dunkin' Donuts and Krispy Kreme Have Big Expansion Plans," *Raleigh (N.C.) News and Observer,* November 15, 2001, p. D1.

——, "Krispy Kreme Certainly Making a Lot of Dough," *Raleigh (N.C.) News and Observer,* April 7, 2001, p. D1.

Stone, Ann, "Holey Rollers," *Restaurants and Institutions,* October 1, 1997, pp. 40–41+.

Strauss, Karyn, "Looking to Raise Dough . . . the Public Way: Krispy Kreme Goes for IPO," *Nation's Restaurant News,* January 3, 2000, p. 26.

Tucci, Linda, " 'Hot Doughnuts Now': Krispy Kreme to Open Five Stores Here," *St. Louis Business Journal,* November 18, 1996, p. 20A.

—Frederick C. Ingram
—update: David E. Salamie

L.D.C. SA

ZI Saint-Laurent
72302 Sablé-sur-Sarthe Cedex
France
Telephone: (+33) 2 43 62 70 00
Fax: (+33) 2 43 92 34 18
Web site: http://www.ldc.fr

Public Company
Incorporated: 1968
Employees: 9,460
Sales: EUR 1.51 billion (2002)
Stock Exchanges: Euronext Paris
Ticker Symbol: LOUP
NAIC: 311615 Poultry Processing

L.D.C. S.A. (also Groupe LDC or LDC) is France's leading poultry processor, and one of the European top three. L.D.C. produces fresh poultry products—primarily chicken, turkey, duck, but also goose and pheasant—under the Fermiers de Loué, Poulet de Bresse, Poulet d'Ardeche, and Le Gascogne brand names. The company also sells unlabeled poultry and poultry cuts. At the same time, L.D.C. is also a leading producer of poultry-based processed foods, primarily under the Le Gaulois brand name. In a move toward vertical integration, L.D.C. acquired control of Huttepain, a leading producer of poultry and poultry feed and related products. Since the 1990s the company has also diversified into the catering and restaurant sector, producing a line of fresh and prepared foods under the La Toque Angevine and other brand names, and is one of the leading French producers of Asian-style prepared foods through its Chiplong brand. Listed on the Euronext Paris stock exchange, L.D.C. remains controlled by the founding Lambert (42 percent) and Chancereul (18.5 percent) families. In 2002, L.D.C.'s revenues topped EUR 1.5 billion.

Artisan Poultry Production in the 1960s

L.D.C. was formed in 1968 when two small poultry slaughterers, Lambert, in the Sarthe region, and Dodard Chancereul, based in the Mayenne region, decided to combine their businesses, thereby covering a wider geographic area. The resulting company, L.D.C., remained largely artisan in nature, and, like the French poultry sector in general, limited to the slaughtering of fresh chickens, which were then delivered more or less unprocessed—complete with head and fcct—to thc company's customers.

L.D.C. also restricted itself to processing poultry—leaving the raising of livestock to others. One of the company's primary partners became poultry cooperative Les Fermiers de Loué. Also based in the Sarthe region, the Loué cooperative had been formed in the late 1950s and grew to include more than 1,000 small poultry farmers. Rejecting the industrialized techniques of modern poultry groups, the Loué cooperative instead focused on high-quality, free-range poultry, and established itself as the French leader in that segment.

Soon after its creation, L.D.C. moved to centralize processing, building a dedicated slaughtering facility in the Lambert home of Sablé sur Sarthe. The new plant enabled the company to reach the respectable level of 40,000 birds slaughtered each week.

The shift in French consumer shopping away from smaller stores and markets and toward the growing number of large-scale supermarkets and hypermarkets offered new growth opportunities for L.D.C. In response the company began to emphasize the Loué brand, launching a new abattoir in Loué itself. The new subsidiary, called Cavol, was dedicated to the slaughtering and processing of Loué-branded poultry. At the same time, L.D.C. met the demand for new and innovative poultry products, such as filets and other fresh poultry parts, creating its own brand, Le Gaulois, which later came to represent an extensive line of breaded chicken parts and other prepared poultry-based foods. Launched in 1981, Le Gaulois quickly became one of France's leading poultry foods brands.

National Growth in the 1980s

The 1980s marked a period of strong growth for L.D.C. as the convenience of store-bought chicken and other poultry parts stimulated demand. The company began expanding geographically, beyond its core Sarthe region to other major poultry-breeding centers of France. For this, the company launched a long series of acquisitions which were to continue through the 1990s.

Company Perspectives:

Demanding innovation, quality and safety, reinforcing our core business by enriching our product range, exploiting our brand capital, building new channels for growth in the catering sector and internationally: these are the challenges that will ensure a solid development of growth and profitability.

L.D.C. began its external expansion in 1984 with the purchase of the Mathey poultry processor and slaughterhouse, based in Louhans, in the Saône et Loire department of the Bourgogne region. That operation, which added processing facilities for chicken and turkey, was renamed L.D.C. Bourgogne. In 1988, L.D.C. turned northwest, adding chicken specialist Serandour, in Lanfains, in the Brittany region. L.D.C.'s original share of that company stood at 35 percent; by the end of the 1990s, however, L.D.C. had acquired full control and changed the unit's name to L.D.C. Bretagne.

The acquisition of Guillet, in Daumeray, in Maine et Loire, allowed L.D.C. to expand beyond poultry, adding slaughtering of rabbit, duck, and pheasant, as well as chicken. In exchange, the Guillet family joined the ranks of L.D.C. shareholders. By then, too, L.D.C. had opened its capital to outside investors, placing a number of shares with institutional investors in 1987 in order to fuel its further expansion. In 1995, the company went public, listing its shares on the Euronext Paris exchange. Nonetheless, the Lambert family remained the dominant shareholder, seconded by the Chancereul family.

L.D.C.'s national expansion continued into the 1990s, with the purchase of Bidou, based in Bazas, in the Gironde, which was renamed L.D.C. Acquitaine. In 1991, the company added further diversified meat production with the purchase of Palmid'or, specialist in ducks, rabbits, and lamb, based in Trambly, in Saône et Loire. By 1991, L.D.C. had succeeded in extending its distribution throughout much of France. In support of its growing operation, therefore, the company founded a new subsidiary, CEPA, for Centre d'Expédition de Produits Alimentaire, which took over as the company's centralized distribution facility.

Diversification in the 1990s

Part of L.D.C.'s success lay in the company's willingness to invest in expanding and extending its business, despite the difficult economic climate of the early 1990s. Among the company's projects was the continued expansion of its core Sablé sur Sarthe facility, which combined both slaughtering and processing operations, and reached a capacity of more than 230,000 chickens and 135,000 turkeys each week, as well as 80,000 ducks and 80,000 rabbits. The company also began developing its own livestock production, founding SA Bressane de Production, launching a new Bresse branded line.

Meanwhile, L.D.C. sought new value-added outlets, including packaged fresh parts, and, especially, the addition in the early 1990s of production equipment and facilities to develop and produce new lines of breaded and fried products under the Le Gaulois brand. In another move to diversify its processed offerings, the company took a 24.5 percent stake in a joint venture called Foie Gras du Maine, which began producing poultry-based pâtés. L.D.C. raised its holding in that company to 75 percent in 1997.

In the meantime, diversification became a company focus through the early 1990s, partly in response to two fast-developing consumer trends: the adoption of ready-to-eat prepared foods as a time-saving option, and an increasing tendency toward snacking—both in-between meals, and as a meal replacement. As a response, L.D.C. decided to extend its operations into a new category altogether, that of the catering segment. In 1994, the company acquired LA Toque Angevine, located in the Maine et Loire region and specializing in the production of cold cuts and, especially, fresh pizzas.

L.D.C.'s growing focus on the prepared and deli foods sectors led it to seek new acquisitions in the late 1990s. In 1998, the company formed Atlantic Traiteur Innovation (ATI), and acquired Soprat, the number two leading producer of Asiatic-style prepared foods in France. ATI also represented L.D.C.'s investment in the in-house development of new prepared food types. In 2000, L.D.C.'s catering operation added Européenne de Plats Cuisinés, based in Roëze, in the Sarthe region, which produced a range of fresh, precooked dishes and sauces.

Despite its interest in prepared food, L.D.C. was no less dedicated to building its traditional poultry business, which remained its largest segment by far, accounting for more than 80 percent of sales at the beginning of the new century. In 1997, the company acquired the Fléchard poultry group, based in the Orne region, changing its name to Société Normande de Volaille (SNC). L.D.C. maintained the Fléchard brand name into the next century; in 2003, however, it dropped Fléchard in favor of a new and more elaborate branded line of processed fresh poultry foods, under the more "feminine" brand name Autour de Lise.

International Foods Leader for the New Century

By then, L.D.C. had weathered a new crisis affecting the poultry industry, after a dioxin scandal, coupled with the outbreak of mad cow disease elsewhere, caused poultry sales to drop off sharply in France. In response, L.D.C. shifted its production to include only animals fed with 100 percent vegetables, vitamins, and minerals in 2000. The company also launched new tracing and sourcing initiatives, guaranteeing that its products came from France and met high quality standards. Also as part of that effort, in 1999, the company bought up Barou, in the Ardeche region, a specialist in organic, free range poultry and poultry cuts.

Another direct result of the crisis in the poultry and meats sectors for L.D.C. was its 2001 acquisition of Huttepain, a leading producer of poultry feed, livestock, and related products. The addition of Huttepain gave L.D.C. a specialized business in the breeding and raising of livestock for the first time, and also direct control of some 40 percent of its livestock supply needs.

Yet L.D.C. had also been putting into place another element of its growth strategy. In 1995, the group took its first step

Key Dates:

1968: Lambert and Dodard Chancereul families combine their poultry slaughtering businesses, forming L.D.C., and begin processing livestock supplied by Les Fermiers de Loué, among others.
1970: Company opens new dedicated poultry slaughtering and processing facility in Sablé-sur-Sarthe.
1980: Company constructs new facility dedicated to processing of Les Fermiers de Loué livestock.
1981: The brand name Le Gaulois is launched.
1984: Company completes its first acquisition, of Mathey, in the Bourgogne region.
1987: Company sells stake to institutional investors.
1991: A central distribution facility, CEPA, is formed.
1994: Company diversifies into catering through acquisition of La Toque Angevine.
1995: L.D.C. goes public on Paris stock exchange; completes first international acquisition, of Hermanos Saiz in Spain.
2000: Company acquires Drosed, leading poultry producer in Poland.
2001: Company acquires Huttepain, a leading poultry feed and livestock producer.
2003: Company acquires Avilaves, in Spain; acquires Regalette, producer of crepes.

beyond France when it acquired Hermanos Saiz, based in Madrid, Spain. The company originally acquired 40 percent of this Spanish poultry producer, before raising its stake to 98 percent in 1999. The company then stepped up its position in the Spanish market with the acquisition of Avilaves, based in Avila, adding both livestock production and slaughtering operations in 2003.

Two years later, L.D.C. identified another highly promising market, and formed a joint venture in China, in the Shandong province. L.D.C.'s stake in that company, called Shandong Fengxiang L.D.C., remained fixed at 35 percent. At the same time, however, L.D.C. formed a second joint venture, Sandong L.D.C., in which L.D.C. initially took a 65 percent position (since reduced to 45 percent).

Closer to home, L.D.C. began scouting an entry into the Eastern European market, targeting the politically stable Polish market. In 2000, the company bought Polish group Drosed, the leading poultry producer in the country. L.D.C.'s stake in Drosed later reached 97 percent.

By 2003, L.D.C. had grown into the number one poultry group in France and the number three in all of Europe, with sales topping EUR 1.5 billion. While poultry remained the primary source of group revenues, catering had become an important motor for growth. Already in the top five in the sector in France, L.D.C. reaffirmed its intention to develop into a European prepared foods leader in 2003 with the acquisition of Regalette, a specialist maker of crepes and similar food products based in the Morbihan region of Brittany. L.D.C. prepared to carry on its history of quality and innovation in the years to come.

Principal Subsidiaries

Alimab; Ardevol; Atlantic Traiteur Innovation; Aves Ldc Espana (Spain); Bellavol; Cabri Production; Cepa; Drosed (Poland); Européenne de Plats Cuisinés; Foie Gras Du Maine; Guillet; Huttepain Aliments; Huttepain Bouix; Jeusselin; L.D.C. Aquitaine; L.D.C. Bourgogne; L.D.C. Bretagne; L.D.C. Cavol; L.D.C. Sablé; La Gamme (Poland); La Toque Angevine; Les Fermiers De L'ardeche; Oufs Sovopa-Sacofel; Palmid'or; Regalette; Richard; Saiz (Spain); Servol; Shandong Fengxiang L.D.C. (China); Societe Bressanne De Production; Societe Normande De Volaille; Stam/Chantovol; Tom'pain; Volabraye.

Principal Competitors

Doux SA; Gastronome SA; Arrivé SA; Unicopa SA; Glon Volaille SA; Loeul et Piriot SA.

Further Reading

"Le bon choix avec Huttepain pour Le Gaulois," *Filières Avicoles,* January 2003, p. 6.
"LDC confirme son ambition au traiteur," *Linéaires*, July/August 2003, p. 64.
"LDC poursuit son essor malgré la crise," *RIA*, July/August 2003, p. 13.
"Le sandwich nourrit aussi l'emploi," *Ouest-France*, April 11, 2003, p. 6.
Tigale, Claude, "LDC résiste," *Le Télégramme,* June 4, 2003,
——, "LDC tire son épingle sur un marché au ralenti," *Le Telegramme,* December 9, 1999

—M.L. Cohen

Lacks Enterprises Inc.

5460 Cascade Road, S.E.
Grand Rapids, Michigan 49546
U.S.A.
Telephone: (616) 949-6570
Fax: (616) 285-2367
Web site: http://www.lacksenterprises.com

Private Company
Incorporated: 1972 as Lacks Industries Inc.
Sales: $286.8 million (2003 est.)
NAIC: 332813 Electroplating, Plating, Polishing, Anodizing, and Coloring

Lacks Enterprises Inc. is a privately owned company based in Grand Rapids, Michigan, which produces molded, painted, or plated plastic products (in lieu of die-cast and stainless steel) for three separate business segments. Subsidiary Lacks Wheel Trim Systems, Inc. manufactures automotive wheel covers. The automotive trim sector of the Lacks business is handled by Lacks Trim Systems, Inc., which makes trim for both the interior and exterior of vehicles. Products include grills, molding, and rocker panels. Although most of the unit's facilities are located in western Michigan, Lacks Trim also operates plants in Fountain Inn, South Carolina, and Germany, as well as a sales and engineering office in Sweden. Lacks's third business area involves consumer electronics, primarily the production of cell phone covers, which is the province of subsidiary Plastic-Plate, Inc. Lacks also maintains a research and development facility, which has been successful in developing important proprietary technologies, such as the high-impact plated plastic (HIPP) process, Chromtec Wheels, Platinum Chrome, and Spinelle Metal Finishes. As a result of these advances, Lacks is able to offer products that are lighter and less expensive than older materials, as well as being more resistant to dents and rust.

Father and Son Launching the Business in 1961

The elder of the father-and-son duo that founded Lacks Enterprises was John P. Lacks, who emigrated with his family from Germany in 1910 when he was just five years old. Although he never graduated from college, he harbored a dream to own his own business. In the meantime he worked as a truck driver, and also spent time in the decorative hardware industry and tool and die making. He was in his mid-20s in 1941 when he moved to western Michigan and became involved in the zinc cast business in both manufacturing and sales. In his late 50s, he was working as a sales representative for the Dutch zinc die-casting firm, REM Die Casting, when he convinced his son, Richard Lacks, Sr., who was a paint salesman, to form their own business. They started out acting as sales representatives for REM, and then in 1961 formed Metalac Corp. to provide basic machining for REM products. They eventually became involved in manufacturing their own die cast products for the automotive industry. The father focused on the manufacturing side of the business, while the son, with a more aggressive personality, handled the sales responsibilities. Over the next three years, Metalac added other metal finishing companies: Ace Plating and Dec-o-lac.

In 1972 the Lacks family incorporated their growing business, forming Lacks Industries. At this stage, the company was generating $6 million in annual sales. The following year a third generation of the family became involved when Richard Lacks, Jr., joined the business. His inclination, however, was not to carry on the Lacks tradition. Having graduated from Western Michigan University as a marketing major, he accepted a position with an auto manufacturer because Lacks was simply not yet large enough to justify having a marketing department. In a 2003 article published by the *Grand Rapids Press,* he recalled, "My father sent some of his business associates to convince me I had a better alternative. He kept sending them. Ultimately, I broke." He was soon joined by his younger brother, Kurt. "Each generation brought its own unique skill levels," he also told the *Press.* "My grandfather was an entrepreneur, my father was an entrepreneur and a salesman. I fit more the mold of a pure business strategist."

The three generations of the Lacks family steadily grew their business, by nature both visionary and conservative. Early on, the Lackses recognized that plastic components would eventually supersede die cast, and in the 1970s began to transform the company into a maker of plastic parts and assemblies. Richard

Company Perspectives:

We know our future lies in listening—and responding—to our customers' needs and expectations, and our success depends entirely on the people we hire.

Lacks, Jr., outlined the family's cautious side in a 1994 article that appeared in the *Grand Rapids Business Journal:* "The thing I learned from both my father and grandfather is that if you can't pay for it, don't buy it or build it. . . . Don't ever overextend yourself or go out on a limb where you can't pay a debt back. The other thing is that they expect total loyalty from the people that work for them, and they give it back tenfold in return. There's a real loyalty here, and that's made this company successful, too."

Accelerating Growth in the Mid-1980s

Because of Lacks's conservative business approach it remained profitable despite lean times in the highly cyclical auto industry. During difficult economic conditions in the late 1970s, early 1980s, the late 1980s, and again in the early 1990s, Lacks was in a position to grow. While competitors were forced to cut back and wait for better days ahead, Lacks cut back and remained profitable. Those profits were then invested in property and buildings, so that when the economy and the auto industry recovered, Lacks was able to carve out an ever increasing market share. It was in the mid-1980s that the company began an accelerated pattern of growth that made it a $200 million company by the early 1990s. A good deal of this growth was attributed to a growing amount of business Lacks did with foreign automakers who had begun constructing manufacturing plants in the United States. For the auto model year 1990, Lacks attributed 2 percent of its sales to these so-called transplants. Two years later that amount topped 10 percent, as Lacks furnished an increasing number of front-end grills, wheel covers, and body side moldings to Mazda, Toyota, Nissan, and Subaru. Lacks also achieved some diversification by fashioning products for other industries, such as appliances, plumbing, and computers. To accommodate the growing demand for its products, Lacks built several factories, all located within a five-mile area in Grand Rapids. But even during good economic times in the 1990s, when other companies were constructing massive factories, Lacks coupled caution with a desire for expansion. The company built small plants, none larger than 150 employees, linked together by underground tunnels. This modular approach afforded Lacks, should it ever need to downsize because of tough economic times or the loss of a major customer, the ability to sell off plants piecemeal.

Lacks received some adverse publicity during the mid-1980s and into the early 1990s because of air pollution caused by its painting plants and environmental concerns regarding sludge lagoons in Cascade County that were part of the electroplating process. Although the lagoon system had a state permit, the company was pressed by Michigan to clean up the lagoons that were contaminating area groundwater and residential wells. Early in 1989, Michigan's Department of Natural Resources filed a lawsuit against the company, charging that it had violated environmental laws, only days after Lacks had offered a $5.5 million cleanup plan. The company maintained that the state had needlessly delayed the work by filing the suit, but state officials insisted that litigation was necessary because the company had been "continually dragging [its] feet." According to the state's attorney general's office, Lacks had been aware of the problems at the Cascade plant since 1968, yet had made no effort to address the problem. In the end the two parties settled on a $7.5 million cleanup program.

During the 1990s the company made a concerted effort to improve its reputation regarding the environment and went beyond mere compliance and ultimately achieved an excellent reputation in both environmental and ergonomic matters. Sludge from its plating operations, for instance, was now dried and sold to a recycler. Lacks became the first automotive supplier, and one of a select number of U.S. manufacturers, to receive certification in the ISO 14001 environmental management standard and the Occupational Health and Safety Assessment Series (OHSAS) 1800a specification.

Although the Lacks family was very devoted to the Grand Rapids area, starting in the 1980s it began to look for opportunities to open plants in the Sunbelt states. In 1988 it considered expanding into Florida, sending a team to scout the cities of Gainesville, Jacksonville, Lake City, Orlando, and Tallahassee. The site group concluded that there was no major advantage to doing business in Florida, and the company ultimately backed away. Five years later, however, Lacks established a six-person group, eschewing the help of outside consultants, to look at sites in Kentucky, North Carolina, South Carolina, and Tennessee. A major factor in this effort was the belief that Michigan was taking Lacks for granted and was unwilling to offer the same financial incentives it made to much smaller concerns officials were ardently courting to relocate to the state. Eventually the site group settled on two promising communities—Lexington, Kentucky, and Greenville/Spartanburg, South Carolina—both of which offered economic incentives and met other criteria important to Lacks. Nevertheless, it was a difficult decision for the company to open a plant hundreds of miles away from its headquarters, especially for John P. Lacks, now almost 90 years old yet very active in the business. In mid-1994 the board of directors voted to expand in Greenville, land was bought, and construction was begun on a 60,000-square-foot plastic-injection molding plant. For its part, South Carolina offered help in finding an appropriate industrial site, and with the screening and hiring of employees. It also issued tax credits for newly created jobs and $400,000 in grant money. Two years later, when Lacks was once again ready to expand as part of a $40 million capital investment program, the state of Michigan stepped in with an economic incentive package that Richard Lacks, Jr., called "hard to resist."

A major factor in Lacks's growth during the 1990s was the result of the company's strong investment in research and development. In 1992 it opened a 25,000-square-foot Research & Development Center to pursue plastics product innovations and processes. One of the unit's early successes was the development of HIPP-140, a high-impact, high-temperature plastic, able to withstand 14 footpounds of impact and hold its shape to temperatures in excess of 230 degrees Fahrenheit. The material was specially treated to be chrome-plated. HIPP-140 was intro-

Key Dates:

1961: John P. Lacks and Richard Lacks, Sr., found Metalac Corp.
1972: Lacks Industries Inc. is created.
1973: The second generation of the Lacks family joins the business.
1999: The founders die within one month of each other.

duced as the world's first flexible chrome grill with the 1994 Chrysler New Yorker. The HIPP name was then copyrighted and the process applied to a larger number of auto trim products, replacing stainless steel, die cast, and glass-filled materials. The process held other advantages for automakers. The copper-nickel chrome-plating process was able to reach into difficult-to-reach crevices, through providing greater protection from corrosion and an extended part life. The parts were lighter, helping to create more fuel-efficient cars. HIPP-140 also allowed for the creation of more complex shapes, offering greater freedom to car designers. Moreover, such items as snap tabs and fasteners could be molded into parts using the process, allowing automakers to reduce inventories. Eventually all of Lacks's trim products incorporated the HIPP-140 process. Lacks's R&D efforts also led to the creation of its Chromtec process. Instead of bonding plate to plastic, it bonded plate to aluminum and steel wheel, resulting in the so-called chrome-clad wheel.

Deaths of Founders: 1999

By the mid-1990s the Lacks family business was composed of two divisions, Lacks Industries, which was entirely devoted to the automotive industry, and Plastic-Plate, which did 85 percent of its business with automakers and the remainder with the appliance, computer, plumbing, and, more recently, the telecommunications industries (in particular the cell phone enclosure business). Both divisions were now under the umbrella corporation, Lacks Enterprises. The company continued to be run by three generations of the Lacks family, a situation that Kurt Lacks described as ''four cooks in the kitchen.'' Because the company structure was becoming too unwieldy, the Lackses reorganized the business in early 1999, creating the company's current three business units. According to Richard Lacks, Jr., ''We were becoming way too bureaucratic. . . . We were at a crossroads. We lacked strategic focus and we couldn't keep a hand on the business.''

Other changes were also soon at hand. Richard Lacks, Sr., was diagnosed with a rampant form of cancer, news that proved hard on his father. On April 14, 1999, at the age of 94, John P. Lacks died. Just one month later, on May 13, 1999, Richard Lacks, Sr., also died, leaving the running of Lacks Enterprises in the hands of Richard Lacks, Jr., and Kurt Lacks.

Lacks continued to grow into the new century. By the close of 2003 it was generating sales in the neighborhood of $300 million. The company was looking to increase its cell phone business as well as taking steps to forge a joint venture in China as part of an effort to make Lacks more competitive in the world marketplace. In addition, a fourth generation of the Lacks family was on the verge of becoming involved in the business. Both Richard and Kurt Lacks had sons majoring in business at the University of Indiana. According to the *Grand Rapids Press,* ''Dick and Kurt agreed they will try to get out of their heirs' way sooner than their grandfather did—but it won't be easy. 'It's pretty hard to give up the ship,' Dick said. 'My grandfather kept control until he was 94. I'm never going to do that to my kids.' He sets age 70 as his deadline for stepping aside, assuming the fourth generation is on board with the culture of the business—and they aren't spending too much money.''

Principal Subsidiaries

Lacks Trim Systems, Inc.; Lacks Wheel Trim Systems, Inc.; Plastic-Plate, Inc.

Principal Competitors

Lund International Holdings, Inc.; Siegel-Robert Inc.; Venture Industries.

Further Reading

Bauer, Julia, ''Sparkling Success,'' *Grand Rapids Press,* September 28, 2003, p. E1.

Czurak, David, ''Lacks Enterprises Inc. Is HIPP to Plastics,'' *Grand Rapids Business Journal,* April 29, 2002, p. B4.

Ghering, Mike, ''Lacks' Growth Pattern Molds High Expectations,'' *Grand Rapids Business Journal,* October 21, 1996, p. B1.

VanderVeen, Don, ''Succession Puts Lacks in Line for Continued Expansion,'' *Grand Rapids Business Journal,* October 24, 1994, p. B1.

—Ed Dinger

LaCrosse Footwear, Inc.

18550 N.E. Riverside Parkway
Portland, Oregon 97230-4975
U.S.A.
Telephone: (503) 766-1010
Toll Free: (800) 323-2668
Fax: (503) 766-1015
Web site: http://www.lacrossefootwearinc.com

Public Company
Incorporated: 1983 as La Crosse Rubber Mills, Inc.
Employees: 400
Sales: $97.8 million (2002)
Stock Exchanges: NASDAQ
Ticker Symbol: BOOT
NAIC: 316211 Rubber and Plastics Footwear Manufacturing; 316213 Men's Footwear (Except Athletic) Manufacturing; 316214 Women's Footwear (Except Athletic) Manufacturing

Named after its former hometown of La Crosse, Wisconsin, but now headquartered in Portland, Oregon, LaCrosse Footwear, Inc. is a leading designer, manufacturer, and marketer of rubber, leather, and vinyl footwear. It specializes in premium-quality protective footwear for the sporting, occupational, and recreational markets. It has three major brands: the original LaCrosse brand; the Danner brand, established in 1932 and acquired by LaCrosse in 1994; and the Rainfair brand, originally marketed through a joint venture established in 1996 between LaCrosse Footwear and Rainfair, Inc., of Racine, Wisconsin, before becoming wholly owned by LaCrosse in 1998. The product line of Rainfair, which now operates as the LaCrosse Safety & Industrial division, includes rainwear, footwear, and other protective clothing for occupational markets. Historically, LaCrosse Footwear manufactured most of its products at its own manufacturing plants in the United States. In the early 2000s, however, the company began shifting to outsourcing. By 2002, 70 percent of the products sold by LaCrosse were manufactured by third parties, most of them located in the Asia-Pacific region. LaCrosse continues to operate two U.S. factories, located in Portland and in Claremont, New Hampshire. Sales of the company's products are made through more than 4,300 accounts in the United States, including sporting goods and outdoor retailers, shoe stores, general merchandise stores, wholesalers, catalog merchants, and the U.S. government. Two factory outlet stores can be found in Portland and La Crosse. Less than 3 percent of the company's net sales originate overseas, principally from Japan. More than 44 percent of LaCrosse's common stock is owned by members of the family of George W. Schneider, through the Schneider Family Voting Trust; Schneider was the main investor and driving force behind the management-led group that bought the company in 1982 from the heirs of the founders.

Establishment in Late 1890s

The company was first established in 1897 as La Crosse Rubber Mills Company, a manufacturer of rubber horseshoes, by a group of local citizens in La Crosse, Wisconsin. Led by Albert Hirshheimer, Michael Funk, and George Zeisler, the company started with 25 employees working on 160 steam-powered sewing machines. It originally planned to manufacture rubber goods of every description, with the notable exception of footwear. It soon switched from producing horseshoes to making rubber-coated fabrics and raincoats. From the beginning, La Crosse stressed "quality goods, workmanship, and honest values."

Business was good for La Crosse Rubber Mills in the late 1890s, and by the beginning of the 20th century the company had expanded its facilities and increased its workforce to 400 people. It was producing about 850 rubber-coated garments a day. To reduce the risk of fire, it installed the city's first sprinkler system in its factory, which was reportedly located on land once owned by Buffalo Bill Cody. In 1898 the opening of a new addition was celebrated by a "rubber ball" for employees, complete with orchestral music. In 1899 Albert Hirshheimer took over as president of the Rubber Mills, as it was known locally.

Capitalizing on the popularity of a nonrubber rain garment called Laxette, the La Crosse Rubber Mills launched a national magazine advertising campaign in 1904 to market its clothing under the "Indian Hill Brand." Just two years later, however,

Company Perspectives:

LaCrosse stands for the highest quality rugged footwear you can find, built so people who work and play outdoors can do it without worrying about their feet. It's a reputation we're proud of because we earned it the hard way, by holding ourselves accountable for the performance of each and every boot we make.

After 100 years we're still protecting feet in adverse conditions—building tough, hard-working boots for people who need to get out earlier, go deeper and stay longer than the rest. Because if you can't stay out all day, you might as well stay inside.

the company discontinued making rubber-coated fabrics and raincoats and started producing canvas and rubber footwear. Its workforce was reduced to 150 employees, who could produce about 1,200 pairs of footwear a day. It adopted a new slogan, "Everything in Rubber Footwear," in 1908 and produced a line of 1,000 different styles of shoes. Among its most popular offerings were the Red Fibre Heel Brand of rubbers and overshoes built for long-lasting wear and the first buckle overshoes ever made. Showrooms were opened in a leased building on South Front Street in La Crosse, showing the company's line of clothing as well as its popular footwear.

In 1912 two of the company's founders, Michael Funk and Albert Hirshheimer, purchased controlling interest in the La Crosse Rubber Mills. They put Michael Funk's two sons, Albert P. Funk and Arthur S. Funk, in charge of management and operations. Arthur S. Funk had recently returned to La Crosse from studying at the University of Notre Dame in South Bend, Indiana, where he had pioneered the development of synthetic rubber, also known as neoprene.

Construction of New Concrete Facility in 1913

Until 1913 the company's manufacturing operations were housed in a wooden structure. That year the first of several concrete buildings was constructed on St. Andrew Street, directly north of the old facility. Originally three stories high and later expanded to four, the new building had twice as much space devoted to manufacturing, and the 350-member workforce began to produce 6,000 pairs of footwear a day. In 1916 a second concrete building was built, adding 75,000 square feet and doubling capacity yet again. The workforce grew to about 1,000 employees and was producing about 15,000 pairs of footwear a day. The company started its own bus line to transport workers, who had difficulty getting to work because of inadequate roads and too-short streetcar lines. With business booming, another "rubber ball" was held, with attendance reaching 5,000 people.

By 1921 production had leveled off to about 13,000 pairs per day, with a "rush" capacity of about 20,000 pairs. In the early 1920s the Funk family bought out Albert Hirshheimer, who retired as president in 1922. He was succeeded by Albert P. Funk. Soon the company started an aggressive building campaign, adding a one-story fireproof warehouse and cafeteria as well as research and test facilities. In 1923 a third four-story concrete building, plus powerhouse, warehouse, and laboratory buildings, added another 75,000 square feet. In 1927 a single-story building with a new mill room and storage areas added another 85,000 square feet. By this time the company was truly national, with a retail presence in every state. It also did a healthy export business under the direction of a New York City-based export manager.

Still growing in 1929, the company announced a 100,000-square-foot expansion that would add factory and office space as well as a new machine shop and vulcanizing area. Company President Albert P. Funk said at the time, "We are undoubtedly facing one of the brightest years in our history, with every department operating at full capacity." He noted that sales in tennis footwear were an especially bright spot for the company. With 2,000 employees on the payroll, La Crosse Rubber Mills was named the largest employer in La Crosse in 1930.

Awarding of First Army Contract in 1941

The company weathered the economic depression of the 1930s, and at the end of the decade it installed the latest conveyorized assembly-line equipment and shoe-making machinery. In 1941 it received a contract from the U.S. Army to produce 43,200 pairs of Arctic, rubbertop overshoes. It was the first of several government contracts that La Crosse Rubber Mills would fulfill over the coming years. During World War II it produced jungle rubber footwear, hip boots, four-buckle overshoes, tennis shoes, and rubbers for use by military personnel. When the war ended in 1945, the company promised all returning veterans who had worked for the company that they would either get their old jobs back or be hired for even better ones. The company also streamlined its manufacturing and fabricating processes by eliminating all bench work. Albert P. Funk died in 1945, and his brother, Arthur S. Funk, succeeded him as president of the company.

La Crosse Rubber Mills began the 1950s marketing a full line of rubber footwear, including sporting boots, tennis and basketball shoes, and novelty shoes. In 1951 it introduced the Big Chief hip boot and the Duluth work overshoe. In 1954 Albert P. Funk, Jr., became the company president, and annual sales totaled $4.5 million. Under a newly negotiated pension plan with the United Rubber Workers-CIO, 65-year-old workers with at least 25 years of service were given full payments. As the 1950s drew to a close, La Crosse Rubber Mills was offering 192 different products in eight product groups: insulated footwear, sporting boots and pacs, industrial and general business boots, farm and work overshoes, family fashion overshoes, rubber-soled canvas shoes, and vinyl plastic protective boots.

La Crosse Rubber Mills continued to grow steadily during the 1960s and 1970s at a rate of about 10 percent annually. The modern "Burly" knee-high rubber boot was introduced in 1963 and featured an innovative ankle-gripping design. During the mid-1960s the company maintained a production capacity of 20,000 pairs of footwear a day at its 350,000-square-foot facility in La Crosse and a workforce of 700 to 750 people. It advertised 31 styles of canvas shoes. By 1972 sales reached $10.5 million. The company's workforce grew to an average of 850 during the 1970s. In 1978 Frank J. Uhler, Jr., became

Key Dates:

1897: Albert Hirshheimer, Michael Funk, and George Zeisler found La Crosse Rubber Mills Company in La Crosse, Wisconsin, as a manufacturer of rubber horseshoes; company soon switches from producing horseshoes to making rubber-coated fabrics and raincoats.
1906: Company switches to the production of canvas and rubber footwear.
1912: Funk and Hirshheimer purchase controlling interest in La Crosse Rubber Mills.
Early 1920s: The Funk family buys out Hirshheimer.
1930: Following several expansions, La Crosse Rubber Mills is the largest employer in La Crosse, with 2,000 workers.
1941: Company receives its first footwear contract from the U.S. Army.
1978: With shift away from athletic footwear, boots become an even more important core line.
1982: To fend off a hostile takeover bid by Endicott Johnson Co., a management buyout is engineered and led by George W. Schneider, husband of Virginia Funk, granddaughter of one of the cofounders.
1983: Company is incorporated as La Crosse Rubber Mills, Inc.; an injection-molding plant in Claremont, New Hampshire, is purchased for the production of low-priced boots.
1985: Company is renamed LaCrosse Footwear, Inc.
1994: Danner Shoe Manufacturing Company, a Portland, Oregon-based producer of high-quality leather footwear, is acquired; LaCrosse Footwear goes public through an IPO.
1996: Red Ball, Inc., maker of outdoor sporting and protective footwear, is purchased; LaCrosse establishes a joint venture with Racine, Wisconsin-based Rainfair, Inc., leading producer of protective clothing and footwear for the safety, industrial, and uniform markets.
1998: LaCrosse takes full control of the Rainfair venture.
2001: Company announces that it will shift from a manufacturing and distribution model toward one focusing on product development and marketing—with production increasingly outsourced; plant in La Crosse is shut down and production shifted to Asia; headquarters are moved from La Crosse to Portland, Oregon.
2002: Rainfair factory in Racine is shut down; the Rainfair division, now operating out of Portland, is renamed LaCrosse Safety & Industrial.

president, and the company stopped manufacturing and started importing athletic footwear. At the same time, even more of the company's resources were channeled into boots, La Crosse's core line. By the end of the decade sales reached the $20 million mark, with 80 percent of sales from rubber footwear and 20 percent from canvas footwear.

Sale to New Owners Ended Hostile Takeover Bid in 1982

In 1980 sales of canvas footwear decreased to 10 percent of sales, with 90 percent attributed to rubber footwear. With 800 employees, La Crosse Rubber Mills was the third largest employer in La Crosse. In 1982 the company had to fight off a hostile takeover bid from Endicott Johnson Co., of Endicott, New York. To avoid a takeover, George W. Schneider and President and COO Frank J. Uhler, Jr., purchased the company from the heirs of the founding family and other shareholders in a leveraged buyout. Schneider was a member of the company's board of directors and husband of Virginia Funk, granddaughter of founder Michael Funk. He became chairman and Uhler remained president.

In 1983 the company acquired an injection-molding plant in Claremont, New Hampshire, that allowed it to produce low-priced boots to complement its higher-priced products made in La Crosse. Annual sales rose that year to $27 million, and the company was producing about 8,800 pairs of footwear per day, or 2.2 million pairs annually. The next year sales rose more than 10 percent to $30 million, and company employees enjoyed their first checks under a new profit-sharing plan. La Crosse also introduced the first waterproof boot with a removable liner for kids in 1984.

Adopting New Corporate Name for 1986

On December 26, 1985, the company adopted a new name, LaCrosse Footwear, Inc., eliminating the space between ''La'' and ''Crosse'' in its new logo. Under its LaCrosse label the company introduced the Iceman boot, which pioneered the use of double-insulation construction in rubber footwear. The popular Iceman boot would be worn by Iditarod dogsled winners and be used on an expedition in China that explored the frigid upper reaches of the Yangtze River. Five years later the company expanded the line with the Ice King, a triple-insulated boot rated to −100 degrees Fahrenheit. That was later followed by the LaCrosse Footwear ''boot system,'' a line of rubber bottom performance footwear with interchangeable liners that was designed for use in hunting, fishing, and other rugged outdoor activities.

Toward the end of the decade LaCrosse stopped importing athletic shoes from the Far East. Sales continued to grow steadily and by 1989 had reached $50 million, boosted in part by a $4.7 million contract—the company's largest ever—with the U.S. government to produce more than 682,000 vinyl overshoes for U.S. military personnel. The company's 300-item product line reflected a shift in marketing strategy, as LaCrosse sought to offer products less dependent on weather conditions. Mild winters usually had a negative effect on LaCrosse's sales. As a result, the company tried to place greater emphasis on its industrial and sporting footwear as it entered the 1990s.

As the 1990s began, LaCrosse continued to enjoy good relations with the U.S. military. In 1990 it received a $3 million defense contract to manufacture 300,000 pairs of mustard gas-proof boots for the Persian Gulf War. A second defense contract was awarded in 1991 to produce an additional 700,000 pairs of the mustard gas-proof boots. As a result of its new marketing focus, LaCrosse achieved a leadership position in the sporting goods apparel industry by 1993. It had 1,465 full-time employees, who were producing 21,000 pairs of footwear a day. Sales reached $85 million, and the company was manufacturing more than 400 types of boots and rubber footwear from 170 compound formulas.

Acquisition of Danner in 1994

In March 1994 LaCrosse acquired the Danner Shoe Manufacturing Company, located in Portland, Oregon, which specialized in high-end leather footwear for hiking, hunting, fishing, and cross-training (the LaCrosse line was aimed more at the middle of the market). Danner was originally founded in 1932 in Chippewa Falls, Wisconsin, by Charles Danner and his father-in-law, William Weyenberg, as a small family factory that handcrafted work shoes. After Weyenberg passed away in 1933, Danner relocated his family and business to Portland in 1936. By the end of World War II, Danner had become established as a high-quality manufacturer of popular logger-style work boots. During the 1960s Danner produced leather hiking boots that were light and flexible, yet sturdy and comfortable. In the 1970s Danner designed and patented a unique way of making a waterproof boot using the first free-hanging Gore-Tex inner bootie.

LaCrosse acquired Danner for $13.5 million in cash, 277,778 shares of common stock ($13 per share market value), and the assumption of approximately $4.4 million in liabilities. In April LaCrosse completed its initial public offering (IPO), resulting in net proceeds to the company of $17.6 million, plus an additional $2.7 million the next month in connection with the exercise of an over-allotment option granted to the underwriters. LaCrosse used the proceeds from the IPO to reduce short-term debt taken on to finance the Danner acquisition, pay off $3.4 million of long-term debt, and plow into working capital. Sales for 1994 reached an all-time high of $108.3 million. New product introductions included the Firetech line, firefighting footwear that fit like a shoe and had a patented steel arch guard that offered greater protection against punctures. Frank J. Uhler, Jr., retired as president and CEO and was succeeded by Patrick K. Gantert.

Sales for 1995 were down about 9 percent to $98.6 million. Even though LaCrosse had been focusing on making its products less weather-dependent, sales were affected by the mild winter weather during the first quarter of the year. Sales were also affected by softening in the retail market during the fourth quarter of 1995. However, the harsher winter weather had a favorable impact on first quarter earnings in 1996. It had the effect of helping to clear retailers' shelves, resulting in larger advance orders for the fall.

String of Acquisitions: 1996–98

LaCrosse made two major acquisitions in the first half of 1996. The first was the acquisition of Louisville, Kentucky-headquartered Red Ball, Inc., a leading designer, manufacturer, and marketer of branded outdoor sporting and protective footwear used in hunting, fishing, and other outdoor activities. Red Ball, with 1995 revenues of $5.8 million, had been operating under the protection of Chapter 11 of the federal bankruptcy code since February 1996. The acquisition of Red Ball for approximately $5 million in cash provided LaCrosse with the opportunity to expand the distribution of the Red Ball brand to mass merchants as well as to introduce new products to the LaCrosse line. In July LaCrosse began manufacturing Red Ball products at its Claremont, New Hampshire, facility.

The second major acquisition involved establishing a joint venture in May 1996 with Racine, Wisconsin-based Rainfair, Inc., a leading designer, manufacturer, and marketer of protective clothing and footwear for the safety, industrial, and uniform markets. The company was established in 1879 as Chicago Rubber Co. and then moved to Racine in 1886; it changed its name to Rainfair in 1943. The joint venture between the two companies assumed the old Rainfair name and purchased the assets of the old Rainfair, Inc. Rainfair's owner and CEO, Craig L. Leipold, continued as CEO of the joint venture and gained a seat on LaCrosse's board of directors. The joint venture brought together complementary product lines and brand names, providing significant cross-selling opportunities, especially in the industrial market.

When LaCrosse celebrated its 100th anniversary in 1997, it occupied a leadership position in its established markets. The acquisitions of the previous few years had increased its product offerings and provided it with an even stronger position in the sporting and outdoor, farm and general utility, and occupational and children's markets for rubber, leather, and vinyl footwear and rainwear. By retiring all of its preferred stock in 1996 to lower its borrowing costs, LaCrosse had also enhanced its already excellent financial condition.

LaCrosse continued its acquisitive ways during its centenary year by acquiring Pro-Trak Corporation in July. Pro-Trak owned the Lake of the Woods brand, a line of leather boots for the outdoor and recreational markets. Over the next two years, the Lake of the Woods product line was merged into the LaCrosse line, expanding the company's flagship line to include leather boots. The acquisition spree ended in January 1998 with the purchase of the 50 percent interest in Rainfair not already owned, for about $2.4 million. Meantime, LaCrosse posted its best results ever in 1997: profits of $6.8 million on revenues of $145.5 million.

Shifting Production Overseas to Stem Losses: Late 1990s and Early 2000s

Sales slumped in the late 1990s because of mild and dry winters as well as increased competition from rivals importing into the United States less-expensive boots made in lower-cost countries. Sales and profits dropped in 1998, and then the following year LaCrosse suffered a net loss of $2.6 million. In addition to phasing out the Lake of the Woods brand, the company also significantly reduced its Red Ball line as it shifted its mix of products more toward leather boots, the sales of which are not tied to the weather as much as rubber and vinyl boots are. LaCrosse began to trim its workforce as well.

In August 2000, in the midst of another year in the red, Gantert resigned from his position as president and CEO. He was succeeded by George Schneider's son Joseph, who had most recently headed up the Danner subsidiary. During the remaining months of that year, LaCrosse eliminated about 350 jobs at its headquarters and factory in its hometown, shifting part of its production to a third-party manufacturer in China. The company earlier in the year had ended production at a plant in Clintonville, Wisconsin, and moved that work to Mexico.

Early in 2001 LaCrosse officially announced that it would follow the trend among U.S. footwear companies by shifting from a manufacturing and distribution model toward one focusing on product development and marketing—with the actual production of its products increasingly outsourced. Soon thereafter, in June 2001, another 140 manufacturing jobs were cut when the company took the historic move of closing down its plant in La Crosse, taking a $4.4 million charge to do so. Once again, production was shifted to contractors in the Far East. A smaller boot factory in Hillsboro, Wisconsin, was closed later in 2001. A further shift out of Wisconsin came in late 2001 when the company moved its headquarters to Portland, Oregon, ending more than 100 years as a La Crosse firm. Warehouse space, a distribution facility, and an outlet store remained located in the company's namesake town, which now had only 70 LaCrosse Footwear employees. The head office shift was made mainly for efficiency's sake, as it eliminated the need for separate offices for the LaCrosse and Danner brands. Company officials also cited two other advantages: the proximity to several other outdoor footwear brands as well as to the contract manufacturers in Asia. For 2001, LaCrosse Footwear reported a net loss of $7.9 million, with the poor economy now added to the company's woes.

LaCrosse remained in the red during 2002, and sales plunged 22 percent, to $97.8 million as a result of the weak economy and the elimination of several lower-margin product lines, such as children's insulated footwear. That year also saw the name of the Danner Shoe Manufacturing subsidiary changed to simply Danner, Inc. The most important event that year, however, involved the Rainfair division. In August, the 123-year-old Rainfair factory in Racine—LaCrosse's last Wisconsin plant—was shut down; all of Rainfair's products would now be made overseas, and the Rainfair division would be operated out of Portland. Craig Leipold, who had sold Rainfair to LaCrosse, resigned from the LaCrosse board of directors in protest over the decision to shut down the Racine plant. Later in 2002, the Rainfair division was renamed LaCrosse Safety & Industrial, although this unit continued to market its rainwear and other protective clothing under both the Rainfair and LaCrosse brands. This closure left LaCrosse Footwear with just two U.S. factories—in Portland and in Claremont, New Hampshire; 70 percent of its products were now produced by third-party manufacturers. Between 1997 and 2002, LaCrosse had slashed its workforce from 1,520 to 400—the bulk of the lost jobs coming on the manufacturing side.

Through the first nine months of 2003 LaCrosse Footwear posted net income of $1.5 million, compared to a net loss of $5.9 million for the same period in 2002. Revenues were down slightly, but LaCrosse was heartened by strong sales of the newly introduced Alpha line of rubber-clad neoprene sporting and occupational boots. LaCrosse hoped to maintain this forward momentum by continuing to focus on creating innovative new products and on using bold marketing strategies to sell them.

Principal Subsidiaries

Danner, Inc.

Principal Divisions

LaCrosse Safety & Industrial.

Principal Competitors

The Timberland Company; Wolverine World Wide, Inc.; C&J Clark International Ltd.; R. Griggs Limited; Red Wing Shoe Company, Inc.; L.L. Bean, Inc.; Columbia Sportswear Company; Rocky Shoes & Boots, Inc.

Further Reading

Abel, Katie, "LaCrosse to Relocate Rainfair Div.," *Footwear News,* July 22, 2002, p. 6.

Bergquist, Lee, "LaCrosse Footwear Cutting 200 Jobs, Moving Work to China," *Milwaukee Journal Sentinel,* October 21, 2000, p. 1D.

Cahalan, Steve, "Footwear CEO Remains Upbeat Despite El Niño," *La Crosse (Wisc.) Tribune,* May 15, 1998, p. B1.

——, "Footwear Plant Closing June 29," *La Crosse (Wisc.) Tribune,* May 12, 2001, p. A1.

——, "Footwear Property Sold," *La Crosse (Wisc.) Tribune,* August 2, 2001, p. A1.

Hajewski, Doris, "Acquisitions Helping Expand Product Lines," *Milwaukee Journal Sentinel,* June 29, 1997.

——, "LaCrosse Footwear Is Moving Its Headquarters," *Milwaukee Journal Sentinel,* August 2, 2001, p. 3D.

——, "Sunnier Skies: Rainfair Thrives Despite Parent Company's Losses," *Milwaukee Journal Sentinel,* July 5, 2001, p. 1D.

Hill, Jim, "Danner Shoe to Merge with Wisconsin Bootmaker," *Portland Oregonian,* January 25, 1994, p. B16.

Lenetz, Dana, "LaCrosse to Close Rubber Boots Plant in Wisconsin," *Footwear News,* May 21, 2001, p. 2.

Magney, Reid, "Sole Man: LaCrosse Footwear's New CEO Is Man with a Mission," *La Crosse (Wisc.) Tribune,* January 23, 1995, p. B1.

Parlin, Geri, "Steps of Success," *La Crosse (Wisc.) Tribune,* March 29, 1997, p. E12.

Renner, Maxene, "Footwear to Buy Red Ball," *La Crosse (Wisc.) Tribune,* April 18, 1996, p. A1.

Rovito, Rich, "Rainfair Turns Foul: Leipold Quits Board in Protest of Plant Closing," *Business Journal of Milwaukee,* August 19, 2002.

Tripp, Julie, "Best Boot Forward," *Portland Oregonian,* March 29, 2003, p. E1.

—David P. Bianco
—update: David E. Salamie

The Lamson & Sessions Co.

25701 Science Park Drive
Cleveland, Ohio 44122-7313
U.S.A.
Telephone: (216) 464-3400
Fax: (216) 464-1455
Web site: http://www.lamson-sessions.com

Public Company
Incorporated: 1883
Employees: 1,116
Sales: $314.5 million (2002)
Stock Exchanges: New York Pacific
Ticker Symbol: LMS
NAIC: 326199 All Other Plastics Product Manufacturing; 335129 Other Lighting Equipment Manufacturing; 335931 Current-Carrying Wiring Device Manufacturing; 335932 Noncurrent-Carrying Wiring Device Manufacturing; 335999 All Other Miscellaneous Electrical Equipment and Component Manufacturing

For the vast majority of its over 135 years in business, The Lamson & Sessions Co. was a top manufacturer of industrial fasteners—including nuts, bolts, screws, and some exclusive parts—for original equipment manufacturers. But after inexpensive imports infiltrated the company's traditional markets beginning in the late 1960s, Lamson & Sessions made an ill-advised diversification into the manufacture of railroad freight cars. The utter collapse of that market in the early 1980s nearly caused the company's demise. After a series of debt restructurings, divestments, and strategic acquisitions, the reformed company was primarily involved in the production of thermoplastic products. By the early 2000s, Lamson & Sessions was headed by its Carlon division, producer of electrical and telecommunications conduit systems, enclosures, electrical outlet boxes, and fittings. Among the customers served by Carlon are electrical contractors and distributors, original equipment manufacturers, electrical power utilities, and cable television and telecommunications firms. Serving the consumer market is Lamson Home Products, producer of electrical conduit and outlet boxes, lighting controls, and door chimes. The company's PVC Pipe unit produces polyvinyl chloride conduit for electrical, power, utility, and telecommunications markets, as well as large-diameter thermoplastic pipe used in wastewater management systems. Lamson & Sessions operates 11 manufacturing facilities in California, Florida, Georgia, Iowa, Missouri, Ohio, Oklahoma, Pennsylvania, and Texas. Only about 3 percent of the firm's revenues are generated outside the United States, with the bulk coming from Canada.

Concentrating on Fasteners for First 100 Years

Lamson & Sessions was founded in 1866 as a partnership among three men—brothers Thomas H. and Isaac P. Lamson, and Samuel W. Sessions. Their Connecticut business hand-forged nuts and bolts for carriages and wheels using a technique developed during the Civil War. Each of the partners contributed his own expertise to the company: Sam was the office manager, Isaac managed the seven employees on the shop floor, and Thomas was in charge of packing and shipping. The company's 30-product line generated $20,000 in annual sales by 1867.

Growing markets, little competition, and plentiful sources of raw materials, fuel, labor, and transportation drew the company to the banks of northeast Ohio's Cuyahoga River in 1869. The company moved to a larger plant in 1882 and was incorporated in Cleveland in 1883 as The Lamson & Sessions Co. By the turn of the century, the company had begun producing standardized fasteners for the automotive industry. Production for the U.S. effort in World War I drove sales over the $1 million mark in 1916 and past the $2 million level in 1918.

Under a plan devised by George S. Case, Jr., and Roy Smith in the 1920s, the company grew through acquisition and internal expansion to become a leading producer of industrial fasteners. Lamson & Sessions acquired Falls Rivet Company in 1921, merged with the Kirk-Latty Manufacturing Company five years later, and added Foster Nut & Bolt Company, Lake Erie Bolt & Nut Company, and American Bolt Company in 1929. A new plant was constructed in Birmingham, Alabama, during this period as well. These additions not only expanded Lamson & Sessions' geographic reach but also broadened its line of fas-

Company Perspectives:

We are a diversified company and a leader in providing innovative products and services to sustainable growth markets. Our growth comes from expanding our expertise in manufacturing technology, distribution, and the strategic acquisition of complementary products and services.

We provide leadership, resources, information, and a learning environment to enable all associates to be creative and innovative in their pursuit of continuous improvement. Our associates understand that taking care of our customers is number one.

We believe our final responsibility is to ensure that all our stakeholders are enthusiastic about our success.

teners to include parts for the railroad and auto industries, among others. The company made an initial public stock offering of 20,000 shares and earned a listing on the Cleveland Stock Exchange in 1928. Having achieved a successful expansion, George Case, Jr., was elected president of Lamson & Sessions in 1929.

In spite of the stock market crash in 1929 and the ensuing Depression that gripped the economy, Lamson & Sessions boasted eight plants and $11 million in annual revenues by 1930. But as the economic crisis deepened, the company's cash flow dried up. A $750,000 Reconstruction Finance Corporation loan kept the company afloat in 1935. Following the company's emergence from the Great Depression, Case added chairman of the board to his title. He would serve in that capacity through the late 1960s, overseeing an eightfold increase in annual revenues, from $11 million in 1930 to $89 million in 1969.

World War II-driven demand helped fuel another upturn at Lamson & Sessions in the 1940s, and the company was able to resume its growth through acquisition in the 1950s. The purchase of Stoker Locknut and Machinery Corporation (Pennsylvania) in 1954 was followed by Lamson & Sessions' first foray outside the fastener industry with its 1955 acquisition of Kent Machine Company, a job machine shop. The firm constructed new plants in Chicago and Cleveland and consolidated several operations in those cities over the course of the next two years. Lamson & Sessions closed the decade with the 1959 acquisition of a majority interest in Industria de Parafasos Mapri, S.A., a Brazilian company that ranked as South America's preeminent producer of nuts and bolts. The corporation ventured across the Atlantic Ocean to acquire a controlling interest in a West German fastener maker, Fastenrath-Lamson & Sessions GmbH, in 1964.

Beginning of Diversification: Mid- to Late 1960s

The growing company undertook a more deliberate diversification in the mid- to late 1960s. In 1966, the firm acquired Angell Manufacturing Company (Kentucky), manufacturer of decorative metal trim and brand identification plates for appliances. Lamson & Sessions also established a Canadian subsidiary that year, in Toronto, to make and distribute all its products in that country. The purchase two years later of Standard Mirror Company (New York) added a leading producer of automotive mirrors to Lamson & Sessions' roster of businesses. Seeking a high-margin niche in the fastener industry, Lamson & Sessions acquired Valley Bolt Corporation, a California manufacturer of specialized fasteners for the aerospace and aircraft industries, in the mid-1960s. Lamson & Sessions bought Todeco, Inc., another California producer of bearings and other engineered machine components for the same field, and merged the two as the Valley-Todeco, Inc. subsidiary. The 1970 purchase of Expert, Inc. (Michigan) expanded machining operations to include manufacture of machinery for automated assembly systems.

Harold F. Nunn succeeded George Case as president and CEO in 1968. When Nunn was sidelined just two years later with an illness, the board selected George Grabner to lead Lamson & Sessions. Although the company sold its Brazilian fastener subsidiary to U.S. Steel in 1970, it bolstered its domestic fastener business with the acquisition of Zimmer Manufacturing Industries, Inc. (Michigan) and American Screw Products Company (Ohio) in 1973 and 1974, respectively. But when cheap imports began to infiltrate the industry in the 1960s and competition intensified in the 1970s, the firm's management began to question their dedication to the fastener industry.

Ill-Timed Venture into Railroad Freight Cars: Late 1970s

In the late 1970s, Lamson & Sessions began a new program of diversification that focused on transportation. Specifically, the company acquired Youngstown Steel Door Company, the leading manufacturer of railroad freight cars and components in the United States, in 1976, and added Itel Railcar, Inc. (subsequently renamed United-American Car Co.), another company in that field, in 1979. Lamson & Sessions merged with Midsco, Incorporated in 1979 as well. Midsco's lead company was Midland Steel Products Co., the country's preeminent producer of midsized truck frames.

The entry into railcar manufacture could not have been more poorly timed. Lamson's two primary businesses, industrial fasteners and railcars, were in swift and irreversible decline. Worse, a recession bruised the company's truck frame business. Lamson & Sessions suffered a $15.5 million loss that year.

Grabner brought in Russel B. Every, who had been chairman and president of Midsco, to be president of Lamson & Sessions in 1980. The two men struggled mightily to stop the company's downward spiral. From 1981 through 1985, they divested the fastener interests (the bulk of which was sold to Russell, Burdsall & Ward Corporation in April 1981 for $20 million), sold several losing divisions, and shut down foundry and die-casting operations. The divestments and layoffs slashed employment by 78 percent, from 6,000 to 1,300. The company also reduced its selling and administrative expenses by more than half, from $31 million in 1980 to $14 million by 1986, and cut its debt from $100 million to $52 million through belt-tightening measures. Nonetheless, Lamson & Sessions' losses continued to mount, while annual revenues dropped. Sales declined from $216 million in 1981 to $130 million in 1982, while losses increased from $9 million to $18.8 million during the same period. The company's net worth plummeted from nearly $88 million in 1979 to just $300,000 in 1983, when net losses peaked at $44 million. Investors balked after Lamson & Ses-

Key Dates:

1866: Three men—brothers Thomas H. and Isaac P. Lamson, and Samuel W. Sessions—form a partnership in Connecticut, producing hand-forged nuts and bolts for carriages and wheels.
1869: Company relocates to Cleveland.
1883: Partnership is incorporated in Cleveland as The Lamson & Sessions Co.
1921: Acquisitions begin with the purchase of Falls Rivet Company.
1928: Company goes public with a listing on the Cleveland Stock Exchange.
1935: A $750,000 Reconstruction Finance Corporation loan keeps the company afloat during the Great Depression.
Mid- to Late 1960s: Diversification outside fastener sector begins.
1976: Ill-timed venture into railroad freight cars begins with acquisition of Youngstown Steel Door Company.
1979: Company acquires Itel Railcar, Inc. (later renamed United-American Car Co.).
1981: Bulk of industrial fastener business is sold off.
1984: United-American Car is divested.
1986: Company acquires Carlon, entering the thermoplastics industry.
1988: Youngstown Steel Door is divested.
1994: Lamson & Sessions exits from the truck-frame sector, selling Midland Steel Products.
1995: Company completes exit from metalworking with the sale of its Valley-Todeco aerospace fastener unit.
2000: Pyramid Industries, Inc. and Ameriduct Worldwide, Inc. are acquired.

sions eliminated its dividend, depreciating the stock from $19 in 1980 to $1.75 per share in 1983.

According to an April 1983 article in the *Cleveland Plain Dealer,* Grabner continued to express confidence in the doomed railcar industry, asserting that the market ''may be dormant right now, but demand for railroad cars and trucks will return.'' Unfortunately, he was wrong. Railroad car orders overall plummeted from 119,000 in 1979 to only 6,300 in 1982 and boxcar orders plunged from 4,200 to 250 over the same period.

In 1987 Russel B. Every told the Cleveland chapter of the Association for Corporate Growth, in a speech reprinted in the *Journal of Corporate Growth,* that ''the sale of United-American Car in early 1984 saved Lamson & Sessions.'' That February, Emery and Grabner cut a handwritten, midnight deal for the divestment of United-American Car, thereby bringing in $10 million cash. According to Every, ''That sale gave Lamson & Sessions the cash infusion we needed to make our massive debt restructuring program viable.''

The executives had started bargaining with the company's 24 debt-holders, mostly insurance companies and banks, to restructure Lamson & Sessions' debt in 1983. Early in 1984, they used $15 million borrowed from Congress Financial Corp. to retire about $13 million of its $54 million debt. New, two-year notes for the remaining $41 million of the obligations were issued as interim financing. That July, Lamson & Sessions exchanged $12 million of the short-term notes for $12 million in newly created preferred stock that could be converted into about one-third of Lamson's common shares. The company completed the first phase of its financial restructuring by converting the remaining $29 million debt into low- and no-interest notes. These efforts helped lower annual debt service, free up operating capital, and thereby allowed the company to avoid Chapter 11 bankruptcy.

Every succeeded Grabner as CEO that same year and was elected chairman early in 1985 upon his predecessor's retirement. Every soon realized that Lamson & Sessions' contraction had positioned it primarily in ''mature and possibly shrinking markets,'' as he noted in the *Journal of Corporate Growth.* The new CEO was convinced that his company would not be able to achieve ''real health without a major acquisition of a company serving a growing market.'' The firm's creditors, however, had made strictures against the company assuming more debt as part of their restructuring agreement, and they were extremely reluctant to abandon that safety valve. Over six months of what Every called ''lengthy and very difficult negotiations,'' Lamson & Sessions talked its creditors into taking $17.5 million in cash (part of which was again borrowed from Congress Financial) in exchange for the $31.4 million in securities and interest owed them. The lenders also surrendered part of their preferred stock in exchange for warrants to purchase 500,000 common shares. The restructuring gave Lamson & Sessions an extraordinary gain of $13.3 million and made possible the financing of a sizable acquisition.

Moving into Thermoplastics via Mid-1980s Acquisition of Carlon

Although Lamson & Sessions thought it had the wherewithal to make a major purchase, some industry observers disagreed. In 1986, the company targeted the Carlon division of TBG Inc. (New York), which ranked as a top American manufacturer of thermoplastic accessories for electrical applications. But neither Carlon's European owners (the Thyssen-Bornemisza Group) nor their financiers, Salomon Brothers, believed that Lamson & Sessions would be able to garner the financing commitments necessary to acquire Carlon. According to December 1987 coverage in the *Cleveland Plain Dealer,* Carlon was over twice the size of Lamson & Sessions. Every, however, had earned the confidence of Congress Financial Corp., which increased the company's $20 million credit line more than fivefold, to $110 million, in order to enable Lamson & Sessions to make the purchase. At the time, it was Congress Financial's largest ever acquisition line of credit. The company completed its $85 million leveraged buyout of Carlon late in 1986.

Transformed over the space of a few years from a company with 78 percent of its sales in the railroad and fastener businesses to one with 62 percent of its annual revenues in industrial construction, Lamson & Sessions was reorganized around its new subsidiary. It even moved its headquarters to the east Cleveland suburb of Beachwood, where Carlon was based. After the 1988 divestments of the Youngstown Steel Door

Company (spun off to a management group) and a couple of other unrelated businesses, Lamson & Sessions was reorganized around its two remaining businesses. Midland Steel Products Co. and Valley-Todeco were organized as the Transportation Equipment Products division, while Carlon formed the Industrial/Construction Products division.

As it turned out, the Carlon acquisition was infinitely better timed than Lamson & Sessions' railroad fiasco. The division, which contributed 65 percent of the parent's 1987 sales of $340.4 million, prospered in the burgeoning construction environment of the late 1980s, posting a record-high net income of $9.4 million in fiscal 1988. Lamson & Sessions quickly became a darling of Wall Street investors. A 1987 stock offering raised about $58 million for debt reduction, and from January to October 1988 the shares appreciated 243.3 percent to almost $19. By mid-1988, Lamson & Sessions' net worth had rebounded to $56 million.

Although he had barely served a year with Lamson & Sessions, president and chief operating officer John B. Schulze was selected to succeed Russel B. Every as chief executive officer in January 1989. Schulze, formerly a longtime executive at appliance maker White Consolidated Industries Inc., advanced to chairman upon Every's retirement one year later.

Unfortunately, the early 1990s brought a recession that hit Lamson & Sessions' chief markets, construction and trucking, especially hard. The company's annual sales declined slightly in 1991 and continued to slip in 1992. Although revenues started to climb in 1993 and 1994, the company was unable to record a profit in any of these fiscal years. Losses totaled over $70 million and the stock dropped to just under $5 in early 1994.

It was around that time that Lamson & Sessions elected to exit the truck business. Midland Steel Products was sold to a subsidiary of Iochpe-Maxion S.A., a Brazilian firm, in mid-1994. The proceeds of the divestment were used to lower the company's debt service. In a seeming vindication of the decision, Lamson & Sessions reported that the year's fourth quarter was the company's first profitable quarter in five years. Although Carlon was also characterized as a cyclical business, CEO Schulze hoped that expanding its markets to include the consumer "do-it-yourself" segment would help to smooth the ups and downs. By 1994, that segment contributed 17 percent of annual revenues.

Late in 1995 Lamson & Sessions completed its exit from metalworking with the sale of its Valley-Todeco aerospace fastener unit to a subsidiary of the U.K. firm McKechnie PLC. Now focused exclusively on thermoplastic products, Lamson & Sessions for the first time in several years posted a full-year net profit in 1995—a total of $12.1 million on revenues of $299.2 million. In October of the following year, the company gained a greater presence in the retail home improvement sector with the acquisition of Brighton, Michigan-based Dimango Products Corporation, maker of wireless door chimes, home security devices, and other wireless products.

Ups and Downs in the Late 1990s and Early 2000s

Unfortunately, an April 1997 fire destroyed the Dimango Products plant, and a spike in resin prices contributed greatly to a third-quarter loss that year. In addition, the company ran into problems installing a new management information system, which led to customer service snafus and the loss of business. Lamson & Sessions consequently posted a net loss of $9.7 million for 1997, which included an extraordinary charge of $4 million for complying with an accounting change. Revenues fell 6 percent to $271.8 million.

Seeking to reduce debt and focus on its higher-margin product lines, Lamson & Sessions reached an agreement in December 1998 to sell its PVC pipe business to Eagle Pacific Industries Inc. for $58 million. Lamson & Sessions was at a competitive disadvantage in this commodity-like business as its rivals were vertically integrated, also being producers of PVC resin. In April 1999, however, Eagle Pacific backed out of the deal, and subsequent efforts by Lamson & Sessions to offload the business went for nought. This setback soon turned positive as the company's PVC pipe business experienced a boom in 1999 and 2000 partly because of a burgeoning construction market but particularly because of the explosive growth in telecommunications infrastructure. Lamson & Sessions then gained further capacity in this sector through a pair of 2000 acquisitions: the September buyout of Pyramid Industries, Inc. of Erie, Pennsylvania, for $51.9 million and the December purchase of Ameriduct Worldwide, Inc. of Fort Myers, Florida, for $63.8 million plus assumed debt of $3.9 million. Both of these firms produced high-density polyethylene (HDPE) conduit for telecommunications and utility infrastructure. For 2000, Lamson & Sessions turned in a particularly strong performance: profits of $21.4 million on revenues of $348.7 million.

The company's fortunes soon took another turn as one of the most noteworthy aspects of the severe economic downturn that began in 2001 was the dramatic collapse of the telecommunications market. Lamson & Sessions was forced into restructuring mode late in the year. It shut down one plant and also reduced its HDPE capacity by 15 percent by disposing of a number of excess extrusion lines. A $7.7 million restructuring charge led to a net loss for the year of $3.8 million.

Continued weakness in the construction and telecommunications markets in 2002 led to an 11 percent drop in revenues, to $314.5 million. The company reported a net loss of $41.2 million as a result of a $46.3 million after-tax goodwill impairment loss taken because of a change in accounting principles. Lamson & Sessions' stock fell to as low as $2.30 per share that year. This brought the firm's total market capitalization below the New York Stock Exchange's (NYSE) minimum of $50 million. Warned that it might be delisted, Lamson & Sessions developed an 18-month business plan for returning to compliance with NYSE criteria that was accepted by the stock exchange in January 2003. Through the first nine months of 2003, Lamson & Sessions recorded a 9.2 percent increase in net sales, and although the firm's shareholders' equity was on the increase, at $40.2 million it was still well below the required NYSE level.

Principal Subsidiaries

Carlon Chimes Co.; Lamson & Sessions Ltd. (Canada); LMS Asia Limited (Hong Kong); Dimango Products Corporation; Pyramid Industries II, Inc.

Principal Operating Units

Carlon; Lamson Home Products; PVC Pipe.

Principal Competitors

Compagnie de Saint-Gobain; Thomas & Betts Corporation; Hughes Supply, Inc.; AMSTED Industries Incorporated; Channell Commercial Corporation.

Further Reading

Barker, Robert, "Nothing but Blue Skies? The Dark Clouds Are Lifting Over Lamson & Sessions," *Barron's,* September 2, 1985, p. 15.

Case, George B., *Lamson & Sessions: Starting a Second Century of Industrial Fastener Development and Production,* New York: Newcomen Society in North America, 1965.

DeRosa, Angie, "Lamson & Sessions Grows in Compounding," *Plastics News,* May 12, 2003, p. 36.

"Drive to Upgrade Its Operations to Pay Off for Lamson & Sessions," *Barron's,* August 10, 1964, p. 20.

Every, Russel B., "The Rebuilding of Lamson & Sessions: An American Success Story," *Journal for Corporate Growth,* June 1988, pp. 99–105.

Gerdel, Thomas W., "Divesting the Past: Lamson & Sessions Adds Markets As It Casts Off Metalworking Holdings," *Cleveland Plain Dealer,* January 2, 1996, p. 1C.

——, "Lamson & Sessions Co. to Sell PVC Pipe Unit to Eagle Pacific," *Cleveland Plain Dealer,* December 15, 1998, p. 2C.

——, "Lamson Revamps Debt Structure, Looks to Future," *Cleveland Plain Dealer,* March 31, 1984, p. C1.

——, "NYSE May Delist Lamson," *Cleveland Plain Dealer,* November 1, 2002, p. C1.

Gleisser, Marcus, "Lamson & Sessions Chief Is Optimistic," *Cleveland Plain Dealer,* April 23, 1983, p. C7.

Henle, Faye, "Nuts and Bolts," *Barron's,* October 29, 1956, p. 5.

History of the Lamson & Sessions Co., Cleveland: Lamson & Sessions Co., 1975.

Karle, Delinda, "Lamson & Sessions Continues Growth," *Cleveland Plain Dealer,* December 10, 1987, p. F9.

——, "Lamson Rebounds from Deep Plunge," *Cleveland Plain Dealer,* July 25, 1988, p. C9.

"Lamson Buys Back All Its Debt at a Discount," *Cleveland Plain Dealer,* June 7, 1985, p. B18.

Ledson, Shannon, "Eagle Pacific Dumps Deals for Resin, Pipe," *Plastics News,* April 26, 1999, p. 1.

——, "Failed Lamson PVC Pipe Deal Becomes Stroke of Good Luck," *Plastics News,* May 8, 2000, p. 8.

Prizinsky, David, "Lamson's Recent Good Fortune Tied to Booming Telecom Field," *Crain's Cleveland Business,* September 18, 2000, p. 36.

——, "Software Snafus Snag Sales Efforts at Lamson," *Crain's Cleveland Business,* September 22, 1997, p. 2.

Rose, William Ganson, *Cleveland: The Making of a City,* Cleveland: World Publishing Co., 1950.

Sabath, Donald, "Lamson Meeting Hears Good News," *Cleveland Plain Dealer,* June 29, 1984, p. C8.

——, "Weakness in Two Markets Leads to Loss at Lamson," *Cleveland Plain Dealer,* April 27, 1991, p. D3.

Urey, Craig, "Lamson & Sessions May Sell Vylon Business," *Plastics News,* May 4, 1998, p. 4.

——, "Lamson Seeks Offers for Five Pipe Facilities," *Plastics News,* January 26, 1998, p. 1.

Van Tassel, David D., and John J. Grabowski, *The Encyclopedia of Cleveland History,* Bloomington: Indiana University Press, 1987.

Waterman, Phil, "Recovery Appears in the Works This Year for Lamson & Sessions," *Barron's,* October 2, 1972, p. 25.

—April D. Gasbarre
—update: David E. Salamie

Lancaster Colony Corporation

37 W. Broad Street
Columbus, Ohio 43215
U.S.A.
Telephone: (614) 224-7141
Toll Free: (800) 264-6826
Fax: (614) 469-8219
Web site: http://www.lancastercolony.com

Public Company
Incorporated: 1961
Employees: 5,500
Sales: $1.1 billion (2003)
Stock Exchanges: NASDAQ
Ticker Symbol: LANC
NAIC: 422420 Packaged Frozen Food Merchant Wholesalers; 311999 All Other Miscellaneous Food Manufacturing; 311421 Fruit and Vegetable Canning; 551112 Offices of Other Holding Companies; 541613 Marketing Consulting Services; 541330 Engineering Services

Lancaster Colony Corporation's subsidiaries manufacture a wide variety of products, including automotive floor mats, aromatherapy candles, and salad dressings. These products are sold to such steady retail and food industry customers as Albertson's, Ford Motor Company, and the fast-food chain Arby's. The company consists of three largely autonomous divisions: Specialty Foods, Glassware & Candles, and Automotive Accessories.

Early History

The corporation was founded in 1961, when Ohio entrepreneur John B. Gerlach decided to organize the companies in which he was a major stockholder. He chose to incorporate them in Delaware as subsidiaries under a central holding company he called Lancaster Colony Corporation.

Individually well-established, profitable companies, the new subsidiaries together represented a hodgepodge of manufactured items. Indiana Glass in Dunkirk, Indiana, specialized in decorative gifts and stemware, and Jackson Corporation was an Ohio-based producer of injection-molded plastic housewares. Lancaster Glass Corporation, an industrial supplier concentrating on components for televisions and scientific instruments, was also part of the lineup, as were National Glove, a source of work gloves, and Pretty Products, which turned out "Rubber Queen" kitchen and bath accessories and industrial components.

Although Lancaster Colony had no readily apparent focus, Gerlach, an experienced investor, had deliberately assembled this collection of manufacturers according to a personal maxim: all of his companies operated with common production techniques and distribution channels. This pragmatic principle also brought Pitman-Dreitzer & Company into the fold in the early 1960s. A manufacturer and importer of gift items and decorative glassware, Pitman-Dreitzer fitted the Gerlach strategy perfectly and offered merchandise suitable for giftware departments of retail outlets and boutiques.

Variations on Gerlach's corporate theme came in 1966, when the string of Lancaster Colony subsidiaries was expanded by two. The newcomers, both targeting retail chain outlets, were Enterprise Aluminum, a manufacturer of cookware, and Barr, Inc., which produced balls and other sporting equipment. Both settled comfortably into their designated market slots, as did August Barr, acquired in 1969.

Finely honed market and production strategy was only half of the 1960s success story for Lancaster Colony's consumer products. Just as important were cutting-edge production techniques, state-of-the-art facilities, and creative design, all of which kept the company's glassware and bath accessories competitive in a market whose products rapidly became obsolete due to the trendy tastes of home decorators.

Other segments of the company inventory were constantly updated to keep pace with scientific advances. Glass envelopes for small television sets, cathode ray tubes, and parts for oceanographic equipment, lighting systems, and other industrial components with secure market niches made up a healthy 30 percent of company inventory by the end of the decade. Net sales figures for all these, plus housewares (contributing 60 percent of

Company Perspectives:

Lancaster Colony Corporation is a diversified manufacturer and marketer of consumer products including Specialty Foods for the retail and foodservice markets; Glassware and Candles for the retail, industrial, floral and foodservice markets; and Automotive products for the original equipment market and aftermarket. These groups operate autonomously, allowing each to focus on their specific customer base and market opportunities.

company inventory) and recreational equipment (about 7 percent) rose steadily through the 1960s, soaring from $24.2 million in fiscal 1963 to $63.5 million by 1969. This success prompted Lancaster Colony to go public on May 7, 1969, and by the end of the fiscal year, the corporation boasted about 1,250 shareholders.

Enormous Growth in the 1970s

In 1970 the company finalized a $4.6 million purchase of the T. Marzetti Company, a Columbus-based salad dressings manufacturer. Encouraged by the increase in public demand for salad bars, the new Marzetti owners soon broadened their range with seven new flavors and spent $1 million on a line called Frenchette, previously the property of the Carter-Wallace Company. The two moves added 26 percent to sales by 1972.

In other new marketing ventures, Tiara Exclusives, launched in 1970, began selling Lancaster Colony glassware through a party-plan marketing strategy that provided part-time jobs for homemakers. Along with several other similar businesses, such as Avon and Tupperware, Tiara enjoyed an undisputed success, employing 750 active party-plan counselors by 1972.

Candles also were added to the growing string of Lancaster Colony products during this period. Candle-Lite Inc., costing 87,550 adjusted shares, was added to Lancaster Colony's holdings in 1972, while Christian & Company came aboard the following year. Between them, the two companies were equipped to supply a full range of tapers as well as scented and hand-decorated candles, all of which were eagerly snapped up by longtime wholesale customers such as florists' supply houses and retail outlets.

Loma Housewares, a company based in Fort Worth, Texas, and a division of Vistron Corporation, was purchased for $6.2 million, a price Lancaster Colony gladly paid in order to open up the lucrative new Texas market area to established Lancaster Colony houseware lines.

Automotive products also hit the spotlight during the early 1970s. Splash guards and heavy-duty bumpers for trucks now came from newly acquired Koneta Rubber, a leading manufacturer in the industry. Also in the automotive line, management chose to enhance their aftermarket accessories sales at the same time, by offering Pretty Products' ''Rubber Queen'' line of auto mats on new hanging racks that made selection easier for shoppers.

All new products received the in-house support of a huge new warehousing facility in Georgia, from which merchandise was issued nationwide. Slowed only slightly by a nine-week strike at Barr, Inc. in addition to higher prices for raw materials at the Marzetti subsidiary, the net earnings for 1973 reached $130.7 million.

As the decade progressed, Lancaster Colony began to pay close attention to its food-producing subsidiaries. In 1977, in accordance with its custom of acquisitions offering products saleable in existing markets, the corporation bought Quality Bakery Company, whose annual turnover of $5.5 million made its price of 210,000 common shares worthwhile. The following year the addition of New York Frozen Foods fleshed out the food division along with Frozen Specialty Bakers and Bakery Equipment Leasing Company.

Not all of Lancaster Colony's acquisitions were successful. One effort doomed to failure was a 1977 attempt to buttress glass-manufacturing operations through the $45 million purchase of the Columbus-based Federal Glass Division of the Federal Paper Board Company. The deal fell under the scrutiny of the Federal Trade Commission (FTC), which regarded the purchase as providing Lancaster Colony with an unfair competitive advantage. The FTC eventually allowed the purchase to proceed on the grounds that it would provide hundreds of needed jobs for the community. Still, the company faced further difficulties. The subject of wages for unskilled workers brought an impasse, as the American Flint Glass Workers Union insisted on the wages equal to those paid by the previous owners. Lancaster Colony concluded that it could not pay the same wage and still make a profit and, on this sour note, the deal was finally scrapped in 1979.

Further Internal Growth and More Acquisitions in the 1980s

Although sales figures for many of Lancaster Colony's products dipped due to an economic recession in the early 1980s, its automotive products division actually benefited during this period. Nearly 30 percent of the division's 1982 inventory was shipped to Ford, General Motors, and Chrysler, even though the market for new automobile equipment was declining. On the other hand, the automotive ''aftermarket'' grew, as many drivers passed up new cars, choosing instead to refurbish their older vehicles with relatively inexpensive accessories, of which car mats were a prime example. Both channels were an important earning force for the company, bringing in $105 million in sales for 1982 alone.

The specialty foods division also maintained profitability. By the end of 1982, 11.5 percent of company profits came from frozen pies, partially baked frozen breads, noodles (courtesy of Inn Maid Products, acquired in 1981), and salad dressings. Lancaster Colony continued to look for ways to expand in the food market. Just as it had opened new vistas in Texas by buying Loma Housewares, it now chose to enter the Atlantic seaboard area by acquiring a local manufacturer. In 1983 New York-based Pfeiffer salad dressing operations, previously a subsidiary of Hunt-Wesson Foods, joined the Lancaster Colony lineup.

Key Dates:

1961: Lancaster Colony Corporation is formed.
1966: The company purchases Enterprise Aluminum and Barr, Inc.
1969: Lancaster Colony goes public; it purchases T. Marzetti Company and August Barr.
1972: The company purchases Candle-Lite, a small candle business.
1977: The company purchases Quality Bakery Company.
1983: The company buys Pfeiffer salad dressing operations.
1986: The company buys LRV Corporation and A-Mar Inc.
1992: Lancaster Colony is incorporated in Ohio.
1997: John G. Gerlach, founder of Lancaster Colony, dies; the company acquires Chatham Village Croutons.
1998: The company's sales exceed $1 billion.
2001: The company acquires Mamma Bella Frozen Breads.
2003: Lancaster Colony acquires Warren Frozen Foods, Inc.; it celebrates its 41st consecutive year of cash dividend increases, becoming one of only 23 American companies to do this.

While most products were finding ready markets, cookware, which had comprised 12 percent of houseware sales and 10 percent of profits in 1982, began to lose steam in the mid-1980s. In 1985, the housewares division lost $3.05 million on sales of 1986, to allow for the closing of several facilities, and the consolidation of Housewares and Candles into a single unit under a single team.

Furthermore, due to overseas competition, the company closed the Fosteria Glass plant in West Virginia but kept the name to be used on products from other facilities. By the end of March, production had ceased at National Glove Inc. in Mount Sterling, Ohio. The Loma Housewares plant in Texas was the next to go, along with the Barr, Inc. unit at Sandusky, Ohio, where inflatable plastic balls, rubber bumper parts, and automobile components had been produced. Such products remained lucrative, however, and their production was moved to other manufacturing facilities, the automotive parts now coming from the plant in Coshocton, Ohio, where rubber housewares had been made originally. The Nelson McCoy Pottery Company, a 1974 acquisition, was sold to a Columbus-based group headed by Intercoastal Investments Corporation.

Lancaster Colony now focused attention on the profitable automotive and food specialty divisions. By the end of 1986 the company had purchased LRV Corporation of Elkhart, Indiana, in exchange for 700,000 shares of stock. With affiliates in Utah and Canada, LRV broadened the Lancaster Colony line of truck accessories with bed liners sold under the Protecta and Line-A-Bed names, and tool boxes, also for trucks. The same year Lancaster Colony bought a second auto accessories company called A-Mar, Inc., changing the subsidiary's name to Dee Zee. It proved to be a profitable acquisition, adding aluminum running boards, side rails, kick plates, and tailgate protectors, all of which were soon on display in custom auto stores.

These two acquisitions enhanced sales considerably. Reflecting the plant closings and sales, 1987 net sales were $429.6 million, sinking slightly from the 1986 total of $456.8 million, but by 1988 the figures had begun to rise again, reaching $453.4 million.

By the late 1980s, corporation President John Gerlach, Jr., had become concerned over the possibility of a hostile takeover attempt by Newell Company, an Illinois-based home furnishings company to which Lancaster Colony had sold its aluminum cookware division in 1986. Newell, with a 5.6 percent share of the company, wanted more, and in 1990 it challenged federal antitrust legislation to seek as much as a 15 percent stake in Lancaster Colony, by combining its own consumer glassware operations with Lancaster Colony's $100 million operations. Although at least one quarter of Lancaster Colony stock was controlled by management, who would not part with it easily, caution was exercised since Newell had recently been successful in acquiring the Anchor Hocking glass company after a hostile takeover bid. As a precautionary measure the company's Employee Stock Ownership Trust borrowed $10 million to increase its ownership. Newell was undeterred, but Gerlach did not lose heart.

Gerlach speculated that the solution might lie in shifting incorporation from Delaware to Ohio. The State of Ohio had passed antitakeover laws in the wake of British financier Sir James Goldsmith's attempted hostile takeover of Goodyear Tire and Rubber and had given their antitakeover law protective shields, in the form of two tough statutes. The first of these required that a hostile acquirer wait three years before an actual merger could be documented. The second allowed for backup support for any threatened company, demanding board or stockholder approval before 20 percent of company stock could be acquired. The 10,000 or more Lancaster Colony stockholders could certainly provide such a bulwark of support, in the unlikely event of a problem.

Reaching Billion-Dollar Sales in the 1990s; Maintaining After the Millennium

Although Newell had evidently lost hope for a takeover by March 1991, reducing its stake to less than 5 percent, Gerlach did not drop the idea of shifting incorporation. At the stockholders' meeting in November 1991, he requested approval for this move, pointing out that it would bring the company an annual tax savings of between $30,000 and $40,000. The move was approved, and Lancaster Colony was incorporated in Ohio on January 2, 1992.

By 1994, Lancaster Colony's sales exceeded $700 million and continued to grow steadily. In 1998, the company, for the first time, celebrated billion-dollar sales. The overall sales increase of $85 million was attributed mostly to the company's Specialty Foods division, which contributed more than $60 million to this amount. A large factor in this growth was the division's 1997 acquisition of Chatham Village Product Lines, a maker of croutons. Other factors included Lancaster Colony's cash-flow strategies for growth, including internal investing and repurchasing common shares.

In the same year, Glassware & Candles' sales increased by more than $27 million. The division had recently added upscale

Lancaster Colony Candles to its product line. The Candle-Lite product, the largest line of candles and potpourri available through mass merchants, was the division's main source of growth. Alternatively, Lancaster Colony's Automotive division, in 1998, suffered a loss in sales exceeding $2 million. A General Motors strike was to blame, in part, for the loss.

For the next two years, Lancaster Colony's sales continued to rise steadily: to $1.04 billion in 1999 and $1.09 billion in 2000. During this time, the company introduced a number of new products, including cream-cheese fruit dips for Marzetti. It also acquired, in 2000, Sister Schubert's Homemade Rolls, Inc.

In 2001, Lancaster Colony's sales barely increased and earnings dropped to $89.2 million (from the previous year's $99.3 million). The company blamed the figures on a slowing economy and high energy costs. Still, having recently acquired Sister Schubert's, as well as Mamma Bella Frozen Breads, Specialty Foods experienced strong growth for the year. Overall the division's sales increased to $464 million, from $420 million in 2000.

In 2002 more challenges surfaced for Lancaster Colony, particularly for its Glassware & Candles division. For one, Kmart Corporation—to which the company sold candles—filed for bankruptcy, costing Lancaster Colony $8.8 million. Overall, Glassware & Candles lost more than $20 million for the year. Alternatively, Specialty Foods experienced another solid year, increasing sales $60 million from the previous year. Sales from Automotive decreased slightly, though the division won two awards for its service: Kia's Most Valued Partner Award and Toyota's Most Improved Supplier Award.

The 2003 fiscal year ended with a sales decrease of 2 percent to $1.1 billion; however, the company set a record net income of $113 million (increased from $92 million in 2002) and concluded the year with no debt. Lancaster Colony also celebrated its 41st consecutive year of cash dividend increases, being one of only 23 companies to have done this. The year 2003 also marked the 33rd consecutive year in which Specialty Foods increased its own sales. Its 2003 fiscal sales were $610 million, a 5.2 percent gain over 2002.

Glassware & Candles, in 2003, closed down its glass manufacturing operations in Dunkirk, Indiana, to consolidate its manufacturing operations in its consumer glassware business. Automotive experienced a positive year for sales, increasing its operating income by 12 percent. This was attributed, in large part, to increased sales in aluminum light truck accessories.

Lancaster Colony ended 2003 by acquiring Warren Frozen Foods, Inc., a privately owned producer of frozen noodle and pasta products. With annual sales exceeding $18 million, Warren's products were expected to enhance Lancaster Colony's already lucrative Special Foods Division. Glassware & Candles also looked ahead, with plans to introduce a new line of aromatherapy candle products, as well as new seasonal items. Automotive's plans included the introduction of new products for a fast-growing import car market. Growth within all three divisions of Lancaster Colony reflected its belief in thorough market research, as well as a concentration on internal growth.

Principal Subsidiaries

Candle-Lite Inc.; Chatham Village Foods Inc.; Colony Printing and Labeling Inc.; Dee Zee Inc.; Fostoria Factory Outlet Co.; Koneta/LRV; La Grange Molded Products Inc.; Lancaster Colony Corporation Automotive and Truck Group; Lancaster Glass Corporation; T. Marzetti Company; Warren Frozen Foods, Inc.; Waycross Molded Products.

Principal Divisions

Specialty Foods; Glassware and Candles; Automotive.

Principal Competitors

Blyth Industries, Inc.; Collins & Aikman Corporation; Kraft Foods, Inc.

Further Reading

"Barr Inc. Plant Shot," *Columbus Dispatch,* June 4, 1986, p. 1H.

Bowden, William D., "Lancaster Colony Expects to Show Continued Operating Improvements," *Investment Dealer's Digest,* November 10, 1981, p. 21.

——, "Lancaster Colony Gains Markets and Profits Through Acquisitions," *Investment Dealer's Digest,* February 15, 1972, p. 25.

Buchanan, Doug, "Stagnant Sales, Kmart Hurt Lancaster Colony Profit," *Columbus Business First,* February 1, 2002.

"Glass Firm Attracted to Ohio Laws," *Columbus Dispatch,* November 18, 1991, p. Q1E.

"Lancaster Colony Bid for Glass Firm Ends, Apparently for Good," *Wall Street Journal,* April 3, 1979, p. 14.

"Lancaster Colony Buys Pickup Truck Accessory Company," *Columbus Dispatch,* December 24, 1986, p. 12D.

"Lancaster Colony Corporation," *Wall Street Journal Transcripts,* December 13, 1982, p. 68032.

"Lancaster Colony Drops Plans to Buy Federal Paper Unit," *Wall Street Journal,* July 22, 1977, p. 5.

"Lancaster Colony Products Aimed at Home, Industry, Leisure Time," *Investment Dealer's Digest,* January 20, 1970, p. 30.

"Lancaster Colony Purchase Plan," *Wall Street Journal,* February 1, 1977.

"Lancaster Colony's Annual Profit Falls 10%," *Columbus Business First,* August 22, 2001.

"Lancaster Colony Sets Closing of Glove Factory," *Columbus Dispatch,* March 6, 1986, p. 2G.

"Lancaster Colony to Sell Gift Art Pottery Subsidiary," *Columbus Dispatch,* May 3, 1986, p. 10C.

"Lancaster Colony Wants Ohio Incorporation," *Business First of Columbus* (Ohio), November 4, 1991.

"Lancaster Colony Will Close Fostoria Glass Plant in West Virginia," *Columbus Dispatch,* February 26, 1986, p. 2H.

"Lancaster Sells Unit to Newell," *Wall Street Journal,* September 15, 1990, p. 33.

Sample, Ann, "Lancaster Colony Reports Income Dip," *HFN The Weekly Newspaper for the Home Furnishings Network,* May 10, 1999, p. 32.

—Gillian Wolf
—update: Candice Mancini

Lojas Arapua S.A.

Rua Sergipe, 475
9 Andar
Sao Paulo SP 01243-912
Brazil
Telephone: +55 (11) 5503-1787
Fax: +55 (11) 5503-1764

Public Company
Incorporated: 1957
Employees: 1,300
Sales: R$350 million (2002)
Stock Exchanges: Sao Paulo Rio de Janeiro
NAIC: 443111 Household Appliance Stores; 443112 Radio, Television, & Other Electronics Stores (pt)

Once the largest retailer of household appliances and electronics in Brazil with 16 percent of the market for durable consumer goods, Lojas Arapua S.A. plunged from success to bankruptcy in the late 1990s due to mounting debt. The company decreased in size from 265 stores in 1997 to 88 stores in 2003. It operates stores in the northeast region of Brazil, selling consumer electronics and affordable furniture.

Mid-20th-Century Origins

The Arapua saga is a rags-to-riches tale that reflects the upward mobility of a nation as well as a family. It opens in the 1940s with the Jacobs, a family of second-generation immigrants who had moved from the Middle Eastern nation of Lebanon to South America's Brazil in the early 20th century. They ran a textiles shop in the small town of Lins, about 200 miles inland from the city of Sao Paulo. Tragedy befell the family when both parents died in 1950, leaving the business to 16-year-old Jorge Wilson Simeira Jacob. Although as a minor he was banned from many legal functions, Jacob continued to operate the shop.

At this time, Brazil was entering a period of democratization, modernization, and rapid industrial growth. The virtual dictatorship of Getzlio Vargas was supplanted by democratic elections after 1945. Under the presidency of Juscelino Kubitschek de Oliveira from 1956 to 1961, Brazil's gross national product mounted by more than 6 percent each year as the government made large investments in infrastructure. The 23-year-old Jacob was not one to be left behind in this era of growth. In 1957, he diversified into household appliances, as well as toys, furniture, and clothing—virtually anything an upwardly mobile Brazilian might want. It was at this time that he changed the store's name to Lojas Arapua, the ''lively bird shop.'' That same year Jacobs established the company's second retail outlet in the city of Aracatuba, about 50 miles inland from Lins.

There was an important caveat, however, to this period of rapid economic expansion; government spending was financed in large part through borrowing. During the Kubitschek administration the nation's foreign debt doubled and the cost of living tripled, yet most people's standard of living worsened. Perhaps most important, the government's policies set off rampant inflation, ranging as high as 2,000 percent per year at its worst. Ironically, high inflation had an important effect on consumerism as it related to Arapua. It discouraged saving and encouraged spending; instead of watching their money lose value on a daily basis in a savings account, Brazilians hurried to ''invest'' their earnings in affordable items that had intrinsic value. Appliances fit the bill perfectly.

Pioneering Consumer Credit in the 1960s

Jacob's timing proved prescient when Brazil came under military rule in 1964, ushering in an era of economic planning dubbed ''the Brazilian miracle.'' Under the administration of Castelo Branco from 1964 to 1966, the country enjoyed rising standards of living, low inflation, and economic expansion. This economic trend endured a series of political crises into the early 1970s. With increased real incomes came demand for modern conveniences, and Lojas Arapua was there to fulfill this need.

For the many whose expectations were higher than their incomes, Jacob pioneered consumer credit in 1967. That year, he acquired Fenicia S.A. and was authorized by the Central Bank of Brazil to finance purchases in his stores. The move

Company Perspectives:

Lojas Arapua S.A. is the only specialty retailer of household appliances and consumer electronics in Brazil and one of the largest in terms of sales. Arapua's sales mix is divided into ten main lines: televisions, refrigerators, audio equipment, VCRs, stoves, freezers, washing machines, microwaves, portable appliances and home office products, including personal computers and printing machines.

heralded a new era for Arapua and its customers. Jacob tailored his financing programs to fit the needs of Brazil's working poor, offering lengthy payoff periods of up to two-and-a-half years and correspondingly low monthly payments. He made it even easier in the mid-1990s, revising the credit policy so that the monthly payment did not amount to more than one-fifth of a client's monthly net earnings. At that time, most of Arapua's customers made less than Cr 500 per month. Of course, Jacob was not motivated entirely by magnanimity to his clients; interest on their debts averaged 72 percent annually in 1996, adding a second layer of profit to Arapua's margin.

A majority of Arapua's customers took advantage of the credit program, and the finance operation soon gained precedence over the appliance chain. Jacob eventually reorganized his company, with Fenicia as the parent company and Lojas Arapua its key subsidiary. Over the years, Fenicia invested in food processing, construction, and other interests, but Lojas Arapua continued to account for most of the group's sales and profits. The chain boasted more than 50 stores by 1974. An expansion into Brazil's northwest region brought the store count to nearly 140 by 1980. Acquisitions added stores in Rio de Janeiro and other southern states by mid-decade.

Evolution into High-Tech Niche Marketer in the 1990s

Jacob's success did not bring complacency, however. In the late 1980s, he made a pilgrimage to that holy land of consumerism, the United States. Seeking enlightenment, he visited Circuit City and Best Buy. Within days Jacob had embraced the tenets of niche marketing, and he hurried home to spread the gospel. With his nephew and heir-apparent Ricardo Jacob, Arapua's CEO, the chairman set a reorganization in motion in 1989, stripping his stores of about one-fourth of their product lines, leaving only appliances and electronics. The Jacobs also dumped more than 85 percent of their suppliers, thereby streamlining procurement. Jorge Jacob told *Forbes* magazine's Kerry A. Dolan that his competitors thought his changes were ''crazy.''

In keeping with the Arapua slogan, ''Tuned in on you,'' consumer electronics, including televisions, VCRs, and audio equipment, generated more than 40 percent of Arapua's sales volume in the mid-1990s. These were followed by white goods—refrigerators, stoves, and washing machines—which contributed about one-third of revenues. The company's own Lotus brand of such small appliances as hair dryers, blenders, and steam irons added 22 percent of sales. Launched in 200 stores by the end of 1996, personal computers and peripherals accounted for less than 5 percent of sales that year. The chain hoped to market PCs in all its stores by the end of 1997.

The chain was privately held until 1995, when Jacob sold about Cr 80 million worth of equity on the Sao Paulo and Rio de Janeiro stock markets. Arapua invested some of the proceeds in a computer automation program dubbed the ''Paper Free Sales System,'' which upgraded point-of-sale cashier stations with barcode scanners. In 1996 Arapua joined forces with two key suppliers to develop an electronic data interchange (EDI) system to manage inventory and distribution. The company also embarked on a chainwide remodeling effort and opened dozens of new stores. Arapua even had to recruit a new sales staff, supplanting computer-phobic older sales reps with better educated, and often younger, workers.

Arapua enjoyed rising sales volume in the early 1990s, with annual revenues increasing from about Cr 750 million in 1990 to nearly Cr 1.7 billion by the end of 1996. Net profits topped Cr 116 million, giving the chain a net margin of almost 7 percent of gross sales. (In order to provide a basis of comparison from year to year, the company used the Full Monetary Correction Method to account for inflation. Previous years' financial results, therefore, are restated each year to reflect the inflationary climate.) With an estimated 16 percent of the Brazilian market for durable consumer goods, Lojas Arapua S.A. was the nation's largest retailer of household appliances and electronics. The company ended 1996 with more than 260 stores and six distribution centers throughout Brazil. In fact, the chain had units in all but four of Brazil's 26 states.

Instability and Uncertainty in the Late 1990s and into the Early 2000s

Although Arapua's accelerated growth had driven the chain to the top of its market, the company faced several challenges as it headed toward the end of the millennium. Brazilian President Fernando Henrique Cardoso's currency stabilization strategies had succeeded in slashing annual inflation rates from nearly 1,800 percent in 1989 to less than 10 percent in 1997, but a recession and high unemployment began to cut into Arapua's sales. In January 1997, the company started setting aside 6.7 percent of each financed sale to allow for bad debts. As inflation fell, Arapua's financing programs became less attractive to consumers, forcing the company to compete on cash prices. From 1996 to 1997 television prices dropped by about one-fourth, VCRs sold for nearly one-third less, and white goods dropped 10 percent.

Arapua fought to lure and retain customers by sweetening consumer credit deals. Despite the rising interest rates and falling demand for durable goods, Arapua forged ahead, offering payment plans that lasted up to three years, a duration unheard of in Brazil's retail market. In addition, Arapua offered these credit deals with no down payment required. As a result, defaults on consumer credit accounts skyrocketed. The defaults, in combination with an industrywide drop in sales and high interest rates, severely impacted Arapua's bottom line, and the company reported a net loss of R$183 million ($164 million) in 1997, a significant contrast to its 1996 reported net income of R$124 million ($111 million). Half of that total loss occurred during the fourth quarter. Sales dropped 28.6 percent from 1996

Key Dates:

1950: Jorge Wilson Simeira Jacob begins running the family textile shop in Lins, Brazil.
1957: The shop begins carrying household appliances and is renamed Lojas Arapua; a second retail shop is opened in Aracatuba.
1967: Lojas Arapua acquires Fenicia S.A. and begins offering credit to consumers.
1989: Lojas Arapua reorganizes and begins selling only electronics and appliances.
1995: The company goes public and begins selling shares on the Sao Paulo and Rio de Janeiro exchanges.
1996: The chain begins selling personal computers.
1998: Lojas Arapua files for bankruptcy protection.
2001: The company begins selling MDF furniture, an inexpensive furniture line.
2003: Lojas Arapua emerges from the bankruptcy reorganization process with 88 stores remaining; the company offers insurance to customers who opt to purchase on credit, gaining some R$150,000 per month via insurance premiums.

to $1.1 billion. Financial analysts attributed the majority of Arapua's problems to the credit default rate, which was twice as high as competitors' default rates. Retail analyst David Wheeling of Bear Stearns Investments told *Latin Trade,* ''Arapua's aggressive sales policy would have been O.K. if the economy had kept clipping along, . . . but in Brazil the market can turn on a dime and that's what happened.''

Unable to lift itself out of the financial quagmire, Arapua filed for bankruptcy protection in 1998. The company was estimated to have outstanding debts of about R$800 million ($720 million). Sales of Arapua shares were suspended following the announcement. Arapua had been in negotiations with its primary suppliers for several months in an attempt to reschedule payments, but the inability to reach agreements left the company with no alternative but to seek help from the government. Arapua agreed to repay some R$550 million ($495 million) of its debt over the following two years at a yearly interest rate of 4 percent. Among Arapua's suppliers were Philips Electronics NV, Samsung Electronics, Sony Corporation, Matsushita Electric Industrial Co. Ltd., and Sharp SA Equipamentos.

Speculation arose that a competing retailer might acquire the beleaguered chain. The likely buyer was business magnate Ricardo Mansur, owner of the Mappin department store chain. Mansur also purchased Brazilian bankrupt retailer Mesbla in 1997. The acquisition of Arapua would give Mansur a leading edge in the consumer electronics market in Brazil.

In May 1999 Arapua transferred all of its business operations to subsidiary Arapua Comercial. The company also succeeded in renegotiating 66 percent of its debts with creditors by agreeing to pay its debts with new debentures that would mature in ten years. By the end of July, Sony, to which Arapua owed about R$25 million, accepted the compromise, but major creditor Evadin, a maker of consumer electronics, refused the new terms. Arapua owed Evadin about R$100 million. Arapua ended 1999 with a net loss of R$270.53 million.

Arapua continued its decline into the new millennium. The Comissao de Valores Mobiliarios launched an investigation into Arapua's financial operations in August 2000. Arapua reported a net loss of R$204.8 million and debts of R$1.2 billion at the close of 2000. Controller Arapua Comercial's net income of R$492.4 million helped to offset Arapua's operating loss, which decreased from R$267 million in 1999 to R$197 million in 2000.

Financial hardship continued to plague Arapua, and bankruptcy seemed imminent. Arapua proved unable to pay either of the two installments it had agreed to pay when it sought bankruptcy protection in June 1998. The company missed its first installment of an estimated R$260 million in June 1999. Over the course of the next few years, Arapua tightened its operations, closing 167 stores and laying off 4,700 employees. Arapua finally managed to emerge from the bankruptcy reorganization process in mid-2003.

Amid the chaos of bankruptcy, Arapua moved ahead as best it could, seeking to elevate sales by meeting consumer demand. In 2001 the stores began selling MDF furniture, an inexpensive furniture line targeted to lower-income customers. That year Arapua invested some R$30 million on furniture. Sales of the furniture rose quickly, accounting for 15 percent of sales during the first nine months of 2002. In 2003, after closing 30 stores, which resulted in the exit of Arapua from the south and central west regions of Brazil, the company focused on the northeast region and furniture sales. Although consumer electronics still accounted for the majority of Arapua's sales at 70 percent, furniture sales continued to climb, and Arapua expected furniture transactions to account for 50 percent of total sales in 2003.

In 2003 the company turned a profit by offering insurance to its customers who made purchases based on installment plans. The financial protection insurance, made through Assurant Seguradora, helped protect consumers in case of death or unemployment. Of Arapua's 1.2 million customers who opted for the credit plan, 720,000, or 60 percent, purchased the insurance. Insurance premiums amounted to some R$150,000 per month for Arapua.

Nearly obliterated by its financial decline in the late 1990s, Arapua managed to beat the odds and emerge from disaster in the early 2000s. Although the company had decreased in size from 265 stores in 1997 to 88 stores in 2003, it began to show some signs of growth and profit, helped in large part by its attention to consumer needs and desires.

Principal Subsidiaries

Arapua Importacao e Comercio S.A. (69.5%).

Principal Competitors

Ponto Frio S.A.; Telelok; Casas Bahia S.A.; Mappin.

Further Reading

''Arapua: Revenues Could Reach R$850 Mil in 1991 Vs. R$750 Mil in 1990,'' *Jornal do Brasil,* October 8, 1991, p. 10.

''Arapua Will Invest US$3 Mil to Informatize 350 Shops,'' *Gazeta Mercantil,* February 18, 1994, p. 8.

''Brazil's Maybe Miracle Man,'' *Economist,* February 12, 1994, p. 37.

''Casas Buri: Ponto Frio Bonzao Buys This Electronic Household Appliances Retailer,'' *Exame,* May 1992, p. 50.

Dolan, Kerry A., ''A Lively Bird That Gets the Worm,'' *Forbes,* November 3, 1997, pp. 338–39.

Dyer, Geoff, ''Brazil Retailer Seeks Protection—Lojas Arapua,'' *Financial Times,* June 24, 1998, p. 16.

''Furniture Is Solution for Arapua,'' *Gazeta Mercantil,* April 2, 2003.

Stevens, James R., ''Appliance Market Grows in South America,'' *Appliance Manufacturer,* September 1994, p. 8.

Stinson, Douglass, ''When the Economy Is Rolling Along, It Is Easy to Be a Financial Whiz. Brazilian Appliance Retailer Lojas Arapua Found Out the Hard Way What Can Happen When Things Go Bad,'' *Latin Trade,* September 1998.

Taylor, Robert, ''Cardoso's Next Battle,'' *Banker,* January 1997, pp. 59–60.

—April Dougal Gasbarre
—update: Mariko Fujinaka

Mack Trucks, Inc.

2100 Mack Boulevard
Allentown, Pennsylvania 18105
U.S.A.
Telephone: (610) 709-3011
Fax: (610) 709-3308
Web site: http://www.macktrucks.com

Wholly Owned Subsidiary of AB Volvo
Incorporated: 1901 as Mack Brothers Company
Employees: 4,314
NAIC: 336111 Automobile Manufacturing; 336112 Light Truck and Utility Vehicle Manufacturing; 336120 Heavy Duty Truck Manufacturing; 336211 Motor Vehicle Body Manufacturing

A prominent fixture in the U.S. truck industry, Mack Trucks, Inc. is one of North America's largest producers of heavy-duty trucks and major product components. In 2000 Mack became a wholly owned subsidiary of AB Volvo, a publicly held company headquartered in Gothenburg, Sweden, with annual sales of approximately $20 billion. In addition to its widely recognized line of heavy-duty trucks, Mack produces a line of medium-duty diesel trucks throughout North America. As of 2002, Mack trucks were sold and serviced in more than 45 countries worldwide.

Early 20th-Century Origins

It was by hauling heavy artillery pieces through the mud of World War I battlefields that Mack trucks first earned their famous nickname. Legend has it that a British officer, trying to free an artillery piece that was mired in mud, coined the name ''bulldog'' when he called out to a Mack driver, ''Bring that bulldog over here.'' Management liked the term. In 1932 Mack began putting the bulldog emblem on the front of all trucks and in the 1960s, to raise company morale, Mack produced bulldog pins, carpets, flags, T-shirts, and other items. The square-shouldered grimly determined bulldog was an appropriate symbol. Mack, a quality-conscious, pioneering truck manufacturer, had a history of cash flow problems and near collapses.

The youngest of five brothers, 14-year-old Jack Mack ran away from his Pennsylvania home in 1878 to join the Teamsters and work as a mechanic. In 1893 Jack, with his brother Augustus, purchased a small carriage- and wagon-building firm in Brooklyn, New York. The firm was ruined by the financial panics of the 1890s, and the two brothers were forced to enter the business of maintaining and repairing engines, rather than manufacturing them.

During this time they began to experiment with new types of self-propelled vehicles. The Macks had exacting standards, and both an electric car and a steam-powered wagon were dumped into the East River for having too many mechanical flaws. But in 1900, after eight years of testing, the brothers finally produced a vehicle that satisfied them. ''Old Number One,'' the first successful bus built in the United States, was a chain-driven vehicle that featured a Mack-built four-cylinder engine, a cone-type clutch, and a three-speed transmission. It conveyed 20 sightseers at a time through Brooklyn's Prospect Park. The vehicle, which was converted into a truck in 1908 and finally retired in 1917, was the first Mack ''million-miler.''

Orders for more buses came rapidly, and Jack and Augustus, joined by their other brothers, incorporated Mack Brothers Company in New York with a capitalization of $35,000. In addition to manufacturing buses, the young company pioneered the design of custom-built, heavy-duty trucks. This ran against the prevailing wisdom on such matters. Automakers at that time considered trucks a poor relation to the automobile, and manufactured them from surplus or obsolete auto parts. They made trucks in order to keep their shops busy during periods of slow business. Jack Mack, however, anticipating that the days of the horse and wagon were numbered, decided to make trucks with a capacity of one to seven tons. He introduced the ''seat-over-engine'' truck, made a seven-ton, five-cubic-yard dump truck for the construction of the New York City subway, and began manufacturing rail cars and engine-driven fire trucks. By 1911 the Mack Brothers Company, manufacturers of ''The Leading Gasoline Truck in America,'' had 825 employees producing about 600 units a year.

Due to depressed market conditions the demand for trucks slowly diminished and the company, which had relocated to Allentown, Pennsylvania, merged first with the Saurer Motor

Company Perspectives:

Mack Trucks, Inc. is dedicated to providing customers worldwide with heavy-duty trucks and components that provide total satisfaction.

Company and then the Hewitt Motor Company. The new management did not meet the approval of Jack and three of his brothers, and they left the company. Although regrettable, their departure did not end Mack innovation. The new chief engineer, Edward R. Hewitt, designed a medium-duty Mack truck that was the mainstay of the market from 1914 until 1936. The AB Mack featured a four-cylinder engine with a three-speed transmission, a worm drive rear axle, and two large inspection ports that allowed a quick inspection of the crankshaft and rod bearings. Hewitt's successor, Alfred F. Masury, designed the Mack AC, a heavy-duty, chain-driven truck that featured clutch brakes to prevent its gears from clashing. This was the truck that hauled artillery pieces in Europe during World War I. Its performance there gave rise to the phrase, ''Built like a Mack truck.''

With improved roads and an increased demand for point-to-point delivery, the truck industry prospered in the 1920s. For Mack, which was producing more than 7,000 units by 1927, sales rose from $22 million in 1919 to $55 million in 1927. The company added improved cooling systems, four-speed transmissions, dual-reduction drive, and the Mack Rubber Shock Insulator (the first major breakthrough in vibration dampening since automobiles were introduced) to the AB and AC models.

At the end of the decade Mack launched a line of high-speed, six-cylinder trucks. These models, designated the BJ, BM, BX, and BQ, marked the beginning of the transition from slow, four-cylinder trucks to high-speed transports. Mack also manufactured the country's first practical off-highway dumper designated the AP. It was used in the construction of the Hoover Dam.

The Depression had a devastating effect on Mack. In addition to the drop in demand, light-duty trucks introduced by other manufacturers created competition for Mack's large models. Mack sales dropped 75 percent between 1929 and 1932. But the company fought back. Instead of reducing production Mack offered a new line of small trucks, and introduced the CH and CJ cab-over-engine models. The cab-over-engine design, the best way of getting a distribution by weight on the front and rear axles, was necessitated by laws restricting axle loading, gross vehicle weights, and overall lengths. Despite the Depression, Mack's new line was successful. Those manufacturers in financial distress, needing more efficient ways of transporting goods, turned to the transportation that offered the lowest cost per ton per mile, namely, the truck. Furthermore, the urban demand for public transit ensured a strong bus market.

Mack's leadership of the industry continued in 1938 with the introduction of the Mack Diesel, the first diesel engine made by a truck manufacturer. In 1940 Mack sales hit $44 million on domestic deliveries of 7,754 units, with a net profit of $1.8 million. By making heavy-duty trucks, small delivery trucks, dump units, buses, and fire trucks, Mack offered the most comprehensive product line of any truck manufacturer.

World War II and Postwar Years

As early as 1940 Mack began producing the NR military six-wheeler, a tank transporter that would be used for British General Montgomery's North African campaign. After Pearl Harbor, Mack produced virtually nothing but military equipment, including power trains for tanks, military trucks, torpedo bombers, and the ''MO,'' which pulled 150 mm field guns. Since it suspended civilian truck production for the duration of the war, Mack set up an extensive maintenance network that enabled those trucks to remain in running condition. Its contribution to the war effort won the company numerous government awards.

But that contribution meant little in the post-World War II environment. Strikes and new taxes resulted in a loss of profits for the company in 1946, while contract renegotiations and a soft market made the late 1940s a financially difficult period in general for Mack. In 1952 the manufacturer again reversed its fortunes by introducing the best-selling ''B'' series. These trucks featured a widened chassis frame in front for easier maintenance, a wider front axle for improved maneuverability, and rounded fenders with a sleek hood and cab. This appearance was a significant change from earlier long-nosed and box-shaped trucks. By the time the ''B'' series was discontinued in 1966 approximately 127,000 models had been sold.

Another major innovation was the END 673 ''Thermodyne'' diesel engine, which was introduced in 1953 and featured direct fuel injection, allowing for greater power (170 horsepower) and reliability. Close to 80 percent of the heavy-duty ''B'' trucks were sold with Thermodyne engines.

These innovations notwithstanding, Mack's financial condition declined drastically in the 1950s and early 1960s. Finance-oriented executives, with no experience in truck manufacturing, deferred maintenance and allowed facilities to deteriorate in order to maintain a strong cash flow. Corporate offices were moved to Montvale, New Jersey, effectively isolating management from union employees. This management style, in conjunction with repeated work stoppages and strikes, left the company with reduced sales. From 1959 to 1964 earnings fell from $15.8 million to $3.4 million. A proposed merger with Chrysler Corporation, which might have saved the company, was not approved by the Justice Department.

In 1965 a dispirited management offered the presidency to career trucking executive Zenon C.R. Hansen. He eagerly accepted the challenge. ''Many well-informed individuals advised me that I was taking over a sinking ship . . . that Mack was too far gone to save . . . that Mack would either go under or be absorbed by one of our competitors,'' Hansen said later. ''But I thought they were wrong. Mack still had a great name, a great product, and above all it had the people.''

Hansen assured employees that there would be internal promotions and a cessation to the firings, and he distributed bulldog flags, jewelry, rugs, and other items to boost morale. He set up an accelerated program to improve all the previously deferred maintenance. Corporate offices were moved back to Allentown, and a new assembly plant was built on the West Coast. He also approved manufacture of the ''Maxidyne'' diesel engine, which produced constant horsepower over a wide operating range. It

Key Dates:

1900: After eight years of testing, brothers Jack and Augustus Mack produce ''Old Number One,'' a chain-driven vehicle that features a Mack-built four-cylinder engine, a cone-type clutch, and a three-speed transmission.
1901: The Mack Brothers Company incorporates in New York with a capitalization of $35,000.
1938: The company introduces the Mack Diesel, the first diesel engine made by a truck manufacturer.
1952: The company introduces its best-selling ''B'' series.
1967: Mack agrees to become an affiliate of Signal Oil & Gas Company, on the condition it will retain complete autonomy.
1983: French auto manufacturer Renault purchases 41 percent of Mack from Signal for $228 million; Mack goes public.
1990: Renault gains full control of Mack.
2000: Volvo buys Mack from Renault for $1.71 billion in shares.

featured a simple five-speed transmission, compared with earlier transmissions that had 10, 13, or 15 speeds.

These reforms helped Mack improve its financial situation by 1967. But the company remained plagued by a lack of capital. It was forced to stockpile millions of dollars of parts to ensure production of enough trucks during high demand periods, while at the same time advancing millions of dollars in loans to customers. To ease this crisis, Mack agreed to become an affiliate of Signal Oil & Gas Company in 1967 on the condition it was guaranteed complete autonomy.

Mack did not, however, stay abreast with the industry innovations during the 1970s. Because profits went back to the parent company, Mack could not modernize its plants. It did introduce an air-to-air intercooled diesel engine in 1973, the ENDT 676 ''Maxidyne,'' which featured 285 horsepower, 1,080 pound/feet of torque. But industry deregulation and foreign competition drained Mack's profits, and those of other American truck manufacturers as well.

1980s Malaise

To cope with these problems the new president, John Curcio, persuaded the French auto manufacturer Renault to purchase 41 percent of Mack from Signal for $228 million in 1983. Renault not only contributed new capital, but also helped to distribute the Mack light trucks. In 1983 the company went public, although it was unable to pay dividends. Cost-cutting measures by Curcio, which reduced expenses $160 million in four years, returned the truck manufacturer to a sound financial condition in 1984 for the first time since 1980. Sales increased by 73 percent to $2.1 billion. But a write-off on the antiquated Allentown plant led to $58 million in losses during 1985.

Early in 1986 Mack announced that it was moving its main production plant from Allentown to an $80 million computerized facility in Winsboro, South Carolina. The Allentown plant, built in 1926, was so old that trucks were still spray-painted by hand. Parts had to be moved by forklifts since there was no robotic technology. Furthermore, in Pennsylvania unionized labor cost close to $23 an hour including benefits, compared with labor costs of about $12 an hour in the South.

In 1986 Curcio told *Forbes* magazine that truck transportation had become more efficient, causing the demand for trucks to drop to 125,000 a year. The country's seven largest manufacturers had a combined production capacity of 230,000 trucks a year. ''In the next five years, we expect a major skirmish, if not a major war,'' he said.

Curcio's words were prophetic, for Mack did indeed find itself embattled as the 1980s progressed, but the company's fight for survival was an introspective one rather than a war raged against competitors. Mack was beset by myriad problems during the 1980s, problems that stemmed from its relationship with Renault and precluded the smooth operation of the trucking company's activities. Renault officials had mistakenly thought they could direct Mack's operation from Renault headquarters near Paris, and were slow to recognize their mistake. Quality control slipped as a result. Under the stewardship of Renault, Mack failed to keep pace with its competitors in centralizing purchasing and trimming costs incurred from design and production processes. Renault also failed to expand Mack's distribution network, leaving the truck manufacturer with dealers and service centers situated primarily in the East, far removed from the majority of long-haul truckers who were Western-based. The impact on Mack was decisive and devastating. Executives in France may not have realized what was happening, but Mack's customers did, and they demonstrated their recognition by taking their business elsewhere. Mack's market share, which had stood as high as 20 percent in the late 1970s, was cut in half during the 1980s. By the end of the decade, the situation had become grave enough to set off alarms in Paris.

Mack entered the 1990s losing $20 million a month, part way through a five-year period when the truck manufacturer racked up a staggering $900 million loss. The company was teetering on the brink of bankruptcy. Its trucks broke down at an alarming rate and its distributors frequently were too far away to provide expedient assistance. Employee morale was depressingly low. To begin curing Mack's numerous problems, Renault officials made two important decisions in 1990. First, pressing financial concerns were given a reprieve when Renault V.I., the commercial vehicle division of the Renault Group, acquired the remaining 55 percent of Mack it did not already own. Second, and perhaps most important, Elios Pascual was dispatched from Renault's truck division to Mack's headquarters in Allentown. To Pascual, who assumed the title of chief executive officer of Mack, fell the task of arresting the truck manufacturer's deleterious financial slide and turning the venerable company around.

Turnaround Beginning in 1990

Pascual immediately set about cutting costs, improving manufacturing quality and efficiency, and instilling a sense of pride among Mack employees. A plant was closed in Ontario, Canada, the number of Mack suppliers was sharply reduced, and the company's finance division was sold. Pascual ordered a redesign of Mack trucks, which greatly increased productivity. In 1991, 2.5 trucks were produced each year per employee; by 1994, four trucks were produced each year per employee. As these productivity figures rose, Mack's payroll shrank, making the turnaround more dramatic. From more than 13,000 employees during the mid-1980s, the number of workers was reduced to roughly 7,000 by the early 1990s, with the sharpest reductions coming from the salaried ranks.

Although Pascual orchestrated sweeping changes throughout Mack's operations, the impact of these changes did not materialize immediately. The company continued to languish throughout the early years of the 1990s, making little ground in the face of mounting competition. In 1993, when Mack lost $64 million on revenues of $1.7 billion, the U.S. heavy-duty truck industry recorded its greatest sales volume in the previous 15 years, engendering sizable profit totals for many of the industry's largest players. Mack was excluded from the celebrations. Progress was being made, however, and the supporting evidence was readily discernible by the mid-1990s.

By the end of 1995, Mack had improved its market share for the third year in a row after four consecutive years of decline. The changes implemented in 1990 were showing their effect at last. After recording financial losses every year during the 1990s, Mack moved back into the black in 1995, returning to profitability after a long absence. The market for Class 8 trucks was in a slump in 1995, declining more than 15 percent, but Mack held its own and gained some ground. The company's market share rose during the year, up to 12.1 percent, making 1995 the fourth consecutive year in which Mack increased its share of the market. Further, Mack was one of only two manufacturers to increase its market share in a declining market. On this bright note, the company celebrated its 95th anniversary with renewed optimism and charted its course for the future, intent on bringing the unique Mack mystique into the 21st century.

Consolidating Gains for the New Millennium

In 1996, Mack's leadership was faced with the challenge of shoring up the company's tentative recovery. An essential aspect of this task was to find ways of insulating Mack from the cyclical volatility of the U.S. heavy truck market. Although by 1995 demand had more than doubled from its nadir in 1991, the forecast for 1996 was dismal, with demand expected to decline 30 percent. To escape the impact of this downturn, then, Mack would have to improve its margins enough to remain profitable from the sale of only 14,000 vehicles—6,000 vehicles fewer than its bottom line for 1995. Other means of bolstering Mack against the precarious domestic market included improving Mack's presence in markets outside its stronghold in the Northeast and expanding sales overseas. In October 1996, responsibility for these initiatives fell squarely on the shoulders of the company's new president and chief executive, Michel Gigou, who had been with Renault for 24 years.

Luckily, the market was revitalized after 1996, and by March of 1998 Mack was boasting its fourth consecutive year of profitability, along with its fifth consecutive year of increased market share. The company reported overall sales of $2.45 billion for 1997, a marked increase from sales of $2.14 billion in 1996. While the company held fast to its position as the third leading U.S. brand, it also managed to increase its overseas sales by 54 percent, capturing 22.5 percent of market share and moving into the number two spot among U.S. truck exporters. Indeed, the company appeared poised to enter the new millennium—and celebrate its own centennial—on solid footing.

Still, the new century brought with it more change, and by the end of 2000, Mack had come under new ownership. That year Renault sold Mack to Volvo for $1.71 billion in shares. With the acquisition of Mack, Volvo expected to develop several key manufacturing efficiencies and become the number two truck manufacturer in the world, capturing 28 percent of the European market for heavy trucks and 24 percent of the U.S. market. According to the terms of the deal, Renault would become Volvo's largest shareholder, with a 20 percent stake in the Swedish company. All three companies retained their own brand names, as well as their manufacturing plants and employees.

No sooner had Volvo closed the deal on its new subsidiary than it was faced with serious challenges posed by the dramatic downturn in the U.S. economy—and nowhere was the downturn felt more acutely than in the trucking industry. The total U.S. market for heavy trucks declined from its high level of about 309,000 units in 1999 to an approximate volume of only 170,000 units by the end of 2001. Mack responded to the weakened market by scaling back production, with manufacturing plants in Pennsylvania, New River Valley, Virginia, and Winnsboro, South Carolina, operating at only about 30 percent of capacity. By September 2001, Volvo announced that it would close the Winnsboro plant altogether, and implement restructuring measures to maximize efficiencies between its Mack Trucks and Volvo Trucks North America subsidiaries.

While pursuing aggressive cost-cutting measures in 2001, Mack also sought to improve its product offering. In June of that year, the company unveiled a new line of trucks, the Granite Series, designed to further secure its position as North America's leading supplier of heavy-duty vocational vehicles. Well received by industry experts, the trucks proved immediately popular with Mack customers as well, and by early 2002 the company was increasing production of the Granite series to meet growing demand—even while the overall market for heavy trucks remained weak. Still, Mack's truck deliveries remained weak through the end of 2003, with the company reporting a 23 percent decline at the end of October over the same period for the previous year. Well seasoned in the art of riding out cyclical downturns, Mack could only hope to maintain the sound reputation of its brand, as well as a focus on stringent cost-cutting, while the economy fought its way to recovery in 2004.

Principal Subsidiaries

Mack Americus, Inc.; Mack Canada, Inc.; Mack Properties, Inc.; Mack Truck Worldwide Ltd.; Mack Truck Australia Pty., Ltd.

Principal Competitors

DaimlerChrysler AG; Navistar International Corporation; PACCAR Inc.

Further Reading

Berss, Marcia, "Mack Malaise," *Forbes,* April 11, 1994, p. 73.

Griffiths, John, "US Trucks Role for Gigou," *Financial Times (London),* October 30, 1996, p. 18.

Hannon, Kerry, "Missed Turn," *Forbes,* August 7, 1989, p. 10.

Hansen, Zenon C.R., *The Legend of the Bulldog,* New York: Newcomen Society, 1974.

Jocou, Pierre, "Beyond Buzzwords: TQM at Mack Trucks," *Chief Executive,* September 1996, p. 54.

Sawyer, Christopher A., "Mack Under Attack," *Automotive Industries,* February 1992, p. 111.

Simonian, Haig, "Europeans Find US Market Tough to Colonise: Truck Groups Have Encountered a String of Obstacles Since They Crossed the Atlantic in the 1980s," *Financial Times (London),* August 22, 1996, p. 24.

——, "Recovering Its Faded Image As the Bulldog Breed," *Financial Times (London),* March 12, 1996, p. 32.

——, "Volvo GM Has Eye on the Ball," *Financial Times (London),* November 22, 1996, p. 28.

Southall, Brooke, "Mack Trucks Inc. Posts Solid Gains," *Daily Record,* March 30, 1998, p.1.

Sternberg, Ernest R., *A History of Motor Truck Development,* Warrendale, Pa.: Society of Automotive Engineers, 1981.

Tillier, Alan, and Hendrik Lundin, "Volvo to Buy Renault Truck Unit," *Daily Deal,* April 25, 2000.

—updates: Jeffrey L. Covell, Erin Brown

Manitoba Telecom Services, Inc.

333 Main Street
Winnipeg, Manitoba R3C 3V6
Canada
Telephone: (204) 941-8244
Toll Free: (800) 565-1936
Fax: (204) 777-6391
Web site: http://www.mts.mb.ca

Public Company
Incorporated: 1908 as Manitoba Government Telephones
Employees: 3,566
Sales: $588.1 million (2002)
Stock Exchanges: Toronto
Ticker Symbol: MBT
NAIC: 513310 Wired Telecommunications Carriers; 513322 Cellular and Other Wireless Telecommunications

Manitoba Telecom Services, Inc. (MTS) is the leading telecommunications company in the Canadian province of Manitoba. The company handles local telephone service throughout Manitoba, and also offers cellular communication, paging, and group communication networks. The company also offers long-distance service throughout the province. The company's MTS Media subsidiary produces advertising and information directories, especially through the Internet. Another subsidiary, Qunara, Inc., is a leading information technology company. It provides consulting services on information security, web management, and information management. Its clients are primarily businesses in the financial services, information, healthcare, and energy industries, and it has many government clients as well. MTS also owns a 40 percent share in Bell West Inc., a local and long-distance communications carrier. MTS was formerly known as the Manitoba Telephone System, a public utility owned and managed by the province of Manitoba. The utility became a public for-profit company in 1996.

Early Years in Canada with Bell

The Manitoba Telephone System emerged out of a patchwork of private telephone systems that spread across Canada soon after the invention of the telephone. Alexander Graham Bell, the inventor of the telephone, was of Scottish descent and eventually became a citizen of the United States. But his family lived in Canada, and Bell did much of his seminal work in his parents' home in Brantford, Ontario. Bell moved to Boston in 1871 to work as a teacher for the deaf. In his spare time, he tinkered in an electrical shop, and in 1875 he made his first workable "harmonic telegraph," the device that became the telephone. Bell patented his telephone in the United States in 1876 and in Canada in 1877. It was several years before Bell did anything but lose money on his invention. He assigned Canadian rights to the telephone to his father, Alexander Melville Bell, and the elder Bell did much to promote the new device. Melville Bell tried to sell a percentage of his patent rights to several businesses, including the *Toronto Globe* and the Toronto Dominion Telegraph Company. Yet no one was interested in what seemed at the time to be only an expensive and curious toy.

In 1880 Bell's backers hired Charles Fleetford Sise, an insurance executive and retired sea captain, to put together a business that would sell telephones and telephone service across Canada. Sise organized the Bell Telephone Company of Canada. The telephone was beginning to catch on as a communications device, and already Bell Canada faced a flurry of small regional competitors. Bell bought them out in many cases. The telephone industry had made it as far west as Winnipeg by 1878, when an agent for the territory managed to sell one pair of phones. In 1881 Winnipeg received its first switchboard, which was operated by a boy with a powerful voice. According to E.B. Ogle's history of the telephone industry in Canada, *Long Distance Please*, the young Winnipeg switchboard operator "... kept the window in the exchange open, presumably so that he could reach his customers with a good shout if any of his connections failed." By 1882, the Winnipeg telephone exchange had 110 customers.

However, Manitoba and its neighboring Prairie provinces Alberta and Saskatchewan resisted the encroachment of Bell Canada. The predominant phone company was trying to link up the entire country, but the sparsely populated Prairie regions presented difficulties. It was not entirely economical to run telephone wires out to scattered farms in the rural West. By the late 1880s, Bell Canada had grown into a powerful entity, at

Company Perspectives:

MTS is Manitoba's preeminent, full-service telecommunications company. Seamlessly blending innovative solutions and world class technology, MTS connects its customers to the world.

times resented for the way it handled right-of-way issues when stringing wires. Though Bell had a significant operation in Winnipeg by the early 1900s, local sentiment turned toward a publicly owned phone company. Manitoba held a referendum in 1906, and the majority voted to form a government-owned telephone utility. Manitoba's premier then began negotiating with Charles Sise to buy out Bell Canada. Eventually the provincial government bought out Bell's interest for $3.3 million and formed Manitoba Government Telephones. The new utility, founded in 1908, already had 17,000 subscribers and 700 employees. The other Prairie provinces came to similar arrangements with Bell, forming Alberta Government Telephones and Saskatchewan Government Telephones.

Public Utility Through the 1970s

The new Manitoba Government Telephones kept on most of the people who had previously worked for the Bell company in the area. The company quickly set about expanding service, stringing almost 1,500 miles of new long-distance line in its first year. Immigration was swelling the population, and by 1912 the number of subscribers in Manitoba had more than doubled, to 40,000. The company as a whole subsidized the cost of building rural lines. In 1912 Manitoba swallowed the territory previously called Rupert's Land, giving it many more square miles to cover. Bringing the telephone to rural areas was part of the mandate of the new government company, and Manitoba Government Telephones did this regardless of the cost. As a result, the utility lost a spectacular amount of money in its first few years. In 1912 the government initiated a Public Utility Commission to regulate rates, weed out government corruption and influence, and hold the company to its mission. The company worked to balance the needs of rural customers for efficient service and of urban customers for livable rates.

The company seemed to do well in the 1920s, a time of booming economic and technological expansion across Canada. The company changed its name in 1921 to Manitoba Telephone System (MTS). At that time, the company was still run as a department of the provincial government. MTS made Winnipeg one of the first Canadian cities with a totally automatic dial service (eliminating the need to ask the operator for a line) in 1926. The company improved its long-distance service to Saskatchewan and Alberta, though calls to the East and West coasts still had to go through other exchanges. The Depression years of the 1930s brought a vast slow-down to MTS, which began losing money again and was forced to lay off workers. In 1933 the utility changed its governance, as required by the passage of the Manitoba Telephone Act of 1933. After that point, MTS was no longer a department of the provincial government. The law asked for up to three commissioners to run the telephone utility. This regulation was revised several times, providing for the appointment of five and then up to seven commissioners.

During the Depression, many Manitoba customers gave up their telephone service. It was not until 1938 that the utility again began installing more phones than it removed. The years of World War II were also difficult for MTS, as much of the labor force went off to war. But the postwar years saw a boom in telephone installation. The number of phones installed in the years between 1945 and 1955 exceeded the number installed in all the company's preceding years put together. MTS flourished, despite some obstacles. In the spring of 1950, flooding along Manitoba's Red River reached record highs. Yet MTS telephone operators reported to work, in one instance climbing over sandbag barricades to enter the exchange building through a window. Flood waters stood ten feet deep in the town of Morris, and MTS workers had to be evacuated by boat. At the worst point in the flooding, one-tenth of Winnipeg was under water, and 8,500 customers temporarily lost their phone service.

While MTS had a government mandate to extend phone service to all parts of the province, some areas nevertheless ran their own independent telephone exchanges. Small groups of rural customers got together to provide neighbor-to-neighbor phone service. These independent telephone services were usually not even legally incorporated. Informal telephone exchanges dotted Manitoba during MTS's early years. By 1969, the last of these municipal phone companies had closed, and Manitoba Telephone provided service in all corners of its large territory.

Changing Competitive Environment in the 1980s and 1990s

Manitoba Telephone continued to provide convenient phone service across Manitoba through the 1970s. The company was considered a technological leader, keeping pace with developments in communications equipment in Canada and the rest of the world. In the 1980s, though, the telecommunications industry in North America went through upheavals that left MTS rethinking its strategy. In 1984, a court order in the United States demanded the breakup of the monopoly phone company Alexander Graham Bell and his backers had founded in the 19th century. The huge company colloquially known as ''Ma Bell'' was broken into regional ''Baby Bells.'' New companies also entered the telecommunications industry.

In Canada, telephone service had not been controlled by a monolithic corporation but instead regulated by a hodgepodge of government entities. The three Prairie provinces ran their own phone companies, the Maritime provinces had a similar set-up, and the federal government in Ottawa controlled phone utilities in Ontario, Quebec, the Northwest Territories, and British Columbia. The rapid development of new technologies, such as digital and data transmission, made it expensive for telephone utilities to keep up. In 1989, a new communications bill transferred authority over Canadian telecommunications to the federal government, with the expectation that unified regulation would make the industry more adaptable. However, the 1989 ruling exempted the Prairie provinces.

Nevertheless, Alberta's phone company, Alberta Government Telephones, announced in 1990 that it would become a private company. It restructured and broke into several interrelated subsidiaries. Saskatchewan's phone utility, then called SaskTel, declared at the same time that it had no intention of changing its governance, though the prevailing wisdom was

Key Dates:

1877: Bell patents telephone in Canada.
1908: Provincial government buys out Bell, founds Manitoba Government Telephones.
1921: Name is changed to Manitoba Telephone System (MTS).
1950: MTS continues operating despite record floods.
1969: Last of small regional phone companies closes in Manitoba.
1991: MTS comes under regulatory power of federal Radio-Television and Telecommunications Commission.
1996: Company converts to public for-profit status.
1997: Name is changed to Manitoba Telecom Services, Inc.

that privatizing would make the Prairie companies more competitive. Caught between these two, MTS announced in 1990 that it was considering following Alberta's route. Government ministers felt that Manitoba businesses were being held back from investments in data processing and other communications industries by the current regulatory restrictions. MTS began to move slowly toward privatization.

In 1991 Manitoba's Public Utility Board gave up its control of MTS, ceding its regulatory power to the federal Canadian Radio-Television and Telecommunications Commission. This put Manitoba in line with the other provinces that had come under federal control as a result of the 1989 regulation. Yet changes in the competitive landscape threatened the economic health of MTS in the early 1990s. Revenue for 1991 was $560 million. The company finished 1992 with $800 million in debt. During 1993, the company saw its net income drop by half. Not only was the Canadian economy in a slump, but MTS lost out on long-distance fees that were going to new competitors.

Business began to pick up the next year, but MTS was still in trouble. By 1995, the company had run through three chief executives in five years. Bill Fraser, who took over the top job in 1995, protested to *Manitoba Business* (October 1995) that ". . . We're not a dying industry; we're a growth industry." But it was difficult to turn the company around. Fraser hoped to cut down the enormous debt, now 80 percent of equity, and to lay off employees in order to get MTS back into shape. Critics sniped that Fraser should simply put a "For Sale" sign on the company. In 1996 MTS did become officially for sale, with its high debt and the need to invest $500 million in new equipment cited as the pressing reason.

The transition came with much political bickering and contradictory sets of statistics. One poll showed that 70 to 80 percent of Manitobans opposed the privatization. Despite much turmoil, MTS became a publicly-owned for-profit company in late 1996. In 1997 the company was renamed Manitoba Telecom Services.

New Ventures in the Late 1990s and Early 2000s

The new company moved quickly to form joint ventures and to invest in new markets. In 1999 MTS entered a joint venture with the larger telecommunications firm BCE to expand into the business services market in Calgary, Edmonton, and Vancouver. In 2000, MTS began spending some $300 million on high-speed Internet technology, deploying thousands of kilometers of new fiber optic cable to carry the advanced connection. The company hoped to put 85 percent of Manitobans within reach of high-speed Internet access. The company already held 60 percent of the Internet access market in Manitoba, with the great bulk of customers using the slower dial-up service. MTS hoped to lay the groundwork for other broadband services, such as video on demand, over the next few years. MTS applied to the federal telecommunications governing board in 2001 for a residential phone rate increase, as the company now had to pay income tax since it had become a for-profit company. The increase still gave Manitoba customers relatively low phone rates compared to the rest of the country. In addition, MTS was upgrading and improving its services. The company had also cut costs, reducing staff by over 40 percent between 1990 and 2000, and reorganizing some of its marketing ventures to gain efficiency.

By 2003, the company had emerged on much sounder financial footing than in its last years as a public utility. Though the telecommunications industry in Canada was in something of a doldrums in the early 2000s, Manitoba Telecom stood out. According to *Canadian Business* (June 9, 2003), MTS was ". . . the belle of the telco ball." MTS did well in part because, though it was now a for-profit, competitive company, it still had much of Manitoba to itself. It still provided 98 percent of local phone service in the province, and 77 percent of long-distance service. Though wireless and Internet services were new markets for it, MTS also controlled close to 70 percent of the Manitoba wireless market by 2003, and almost 60 percent of the Internet services sector. With a strong stance in its traditional market area, the company also risked expanding into new projects. It began offering a digital television product, MTS-TV, in 2003. This service, which was first available only in portions of Winnipeg, gave customers access to 200 television channels, plus radio, and an interactive feature that let users search for information. While MTS President Bill Fraser characterized the company as conservative and "sticking to its knitting," MTS had nevertheless reached out for new technology and market sectors, so far very successfully.

Principal Subsidiaries

AAA Alarm Systems Ltd.; MTS Media Inc.; Qunara, Inc.; Bell West Inc. (40%).

Principal Competitors

Shaw Communications, Inc.; Allstream Inc.; Rogers Wireless Communications Inc.

Further Reading

Black, Errol, "The Privatisation of the Manitoba Telephone System," *Canadian Dimension*, March/April 1997, p. 11.
"CRTC Hears Arguments on MTS Rate Increase," *Market News Publishing*, June 8, 2001.
Kirbyson, Geoff, "Tops in Telco: Manitoba Telecom Shines Brightly in a Dim Sector," *Canadian Business*, June 9, 2003, p. 47.
Love, Myron, "Debt Pushes MTS onto Selling Block," *Computing Canada*, June 20, 1996, p. 33.

Macleod, Kirsteen, ''Static Should Drop Between Ottawa and Prairie Provinces,'' *Financial Post* (Toronto), March 5, 1990, p. 43.

''Manitoba Telephone Laying Off 200 Workers,'' *Financial Post* (Toronto), May 4, 1994, p. 47.

''Manitoba Telephone Set to Come Under Federal Regulation,'' *Computing Canada*, March 1, 1991, p. 37.

Morrison, Scott, ''BCE Continues Expansion Drive,'' *Financial Times*, January 29, 1999, p. 25.

''MTS Breaks the Internet Speed Limit in Manitoba,'' *Canadian Corporate News*, September 25, 2000.

Ogle, E.B., *Long Distance Please: The Story of the TransCanada Telephone System*, Toronto: Collins Publishers, 1979.

Sale, Tim, ''MTS Sale Nets Big Bucks for Brokers,'' *Canadian Dimension*, March/April 1997, p. 13.

Stulberg, Linda Gregg, ''Prairie Provinces Cast Fresh Eye on Phone Service,'' *Financial Post* (Toronto), November 14, 1990, p. 26.

Trans-Canada Telephone System, *History of Regulation and Current Regulatory Setting (Telecommission Study 1 (b))*, Ottawa: Trans-Canada Telephone System, 1970.

Waytiuk, Judy, ''On the Party Line,'' *Manitoba Business,* October 1995, p. 5.

—A. Woodward

Maple Leaf Sports & Entertainment Ltd.

Air Canada Centre, 40 Bay St., Ste. 400
Toronto, Ontario M5J 2X2
Canada
Telephone: (416) 815-5500
Fax: (416) 359-9330
Web site: http://www.theaircanadacentre.com

Private Company
Incorporated: 1998
Employees: 500
Total Assets: $1 billion (2003 est.)
NAIC: 711211 Sports Teams and Clubs; 711310 Promoters of Performing Arts, Sports, and Similar Events with Facilities

Maple Leaf Sports & Entertainment Ltd. (MLSE) owns the National Hockey League's Toronto Maple Leafs, the National Basketball Association's Toronto Raptors, and the $265 million Air Canada Centre, as well as Leafs TV and Raptors NBA TV. MLSE, which brought the two professional sports teams under one new roof, has established a reputation as one of the best-run sports franchises in North America. Fans pack the arena paying the highest ticket prices in Canada.

Conflict on and off the Ice: 1927–91

The Maple Leaf hockey tradition dates back to 1927. The founder, Conn Smythe, created a public company to finance an arena for the team. Maple Leaf Gardens—erected in six months—was completed in 1931. Workers on the project received company shares as part of their pay.

The Maple Leafs won their first Stanley Cup during the 1931–32 season. Then in the 1940s, despite the loss of players to combat in World War II, the team won five more. The 1950s produced only one championship. However, the 1960s was another stellar decade. The Leafs put their name on the Cup four more times.

In 1961, Smythe had passed on leadership of the team to his son Stafford, Harold Ballard—a friend of Stafford's—and John Bassett, the owner of the *Toronto Telegraph.* A conflict among the partners resulted when Bassett tried to gain control. Ballard aligned with Smythe. In September 1971, Bassett sold out to the pair. Smythe died a month later, giving Ballard access to his shares. Maple Leaf Gardens, Limited, a public company owned by the Ballard family holding company, held majority interest in the hockey team and arena for the next two decades.

Although ownership was established, things remained unsettled for the Leafs. In 1972 Ballard was sent to prison for defrauding Maple Leaf Gardens (MLG). His son Bill stepped in to fill the gap but was pushed aside when his father returned. The younger Ballard moved into concert promotion and made him a name for himself in that venue, booking rock concerts and other entertainment at the Gardens and elsewhere in Toronto. On the ice the Leafs languished. Salaries were kept low and Ballard pulled out a lion's share of dividends.

During the 1980s, though, Ballard was in financial trouble. He had received funding from Toronto Dominion Bank (TD) to buy out his partners in the early 1970s. A combination of high inflation, rising interest rates, and inadequate dividend income left him in danger of losing the Gardens. Beer company Molson bailed him out on the TD loan and received an option to buy 19.9 percent of the outstanding shares. As the 1980s progressed, a battle heated up among Ballard and his children—particularly Bill—over control of the enterprise.

Ballard owned more than 80 percent of MLG when he died in 1990, but the estate was weighed down by millions in debt and familial lawsuits. Gardens Director and Secretary-Treasurer Donald Crump, Gardens Chairman and CEO Donald Giffin, and Steve Stavro, Harold Ballard's longtime friend and president of Knob Hill Farms Ltd. grocery chain, were named executors of the troubled estate. Over the years, Giffin had tried and failed to gain more of a toehold in the Gardens, and when Stavro and Crump formed an alliance he again was thwarted.

Stavro wanted control. He bailed out the estate when the loan from Molson came due and received a five-year option to buy 60.3 percent of the Gardens from the estate and the interest held by Molson Cos. Ltd.

1992–97: Reviving the Leafs

Stavro took over as chair and CEO of the Gardens in 1991. Over the next few years, he pumped $2 million into arena

Company Perspectives:

Air Canada Centre is Toronto's theatre of sport and entertainment. Our challenge is to deliver the very best in these two mediums by holding fast our corporate vision and values that support this stated intention.

In order to deliver championship service, we first cultivate ''champions'' within our organization, and the sense of civic pride that accompanies this as its natural extension. This determination comes with a view to exciting our fans, inspiring our employees and by bringing pride to our community When we deliver, our fans believe it.

renovations, double the annual salary budget, and bring the team back into contention. In 1994, Stavro exercised the Molson option. Harold Ballard's son Bill continued to try to check Stavro's moves, but Stavro had powerful backers. The Ontario Teachers' Pension Plan (OTPP), a $34.7 billion fund, supported Stavro to a tune of $44.4 million. Toronto Dominion Bank chipped in another $12.5 million in an indirect investment. The acquiring company, MLG Ventures, made a bid of $34 per share according to the *Financial Post*. Since Ballard's death the stock price had been volatile, fluctuating between $22.75 and $44.25 a share. The deal ended the Leafs history of public ownership, which included hockey fans who passed stock down from one generation to the next.

Under Stavro, revenue for the club increased from $37.5 million in 1991 to $56.2 million in 1993. Profits, though, declined between the two years, from $7.5 million to $5.3 million, because of the increase in player salaries. Likely means to boost revenues included increases in promotion, events, and broadcasting.

Persistent legal battles stemming from Harold Ballard's dealings, prevented Stavro from bringing on construction executive Larry Tanenbaum as an investor until 1996. Tanenbaum's failed bid for an NBA franchise in 1993 had included a joint use facility with the Leafs.

Tanenbaum's $21 million gave him a 25 percent share in MLG Holdings. Toronto Dominion held 20 percent and Stavro 55 percent. In turn, MLG Holdings held 51 percent of MLG Ventures, which owned 100 percent of Maple Leaf Gardens. OTPP held the remaining 49 percent of MLG Ventures. The ownership structure gave Stavro a majority position even though he was not the largest shareholder.

Tanenbaum, in addition to bringing in an infusion of fresh money, was viewed as a possible conduit between Stavro and the owners of the NBA franchise the Toronto Raptors in negotiations for a possible joint use facility.

Son of a leading Canadian foodservice family, John I. Bitove and Allan Slaight, head of Standard Broadcasting Ltd., had led the successful bid to bring professional basketball to Toronto. The arena plan they put forth helped them beat out the two other contenders, including Tanenbaum's group. The league's 28th team went for a record franchise expansion fee of $125 million.

Once the franchise was awarded, the work to start building the team began. In 1994, former Detroit Pistons star Isiah Thomas was introduced as the team's vice-president of basketball operations. The arena site was switched to a larger location to accommodate a hockey rink. By year's end, 50 percent of the seats for the first season were held by deposits.

The franchise became official in 1995, with the SkyDome serving as home court. Pro basketball had been absent from Toronto since the mid-1940s, when the Toronto Huskies operated as a charter member of the forerunner to the NBA, the Basketball Association of America. The team hosted the league's inaugural game in 1946 but folded after its first season.

Bitove sold out to Slaight in 1996. Construction on the new arena would begin without Leaf involvement, and later than anticipated. In addition to delays caused by negotiations with the Leafs, economic and political conditions slowed the progress toward construction of the arena, which would take the name of its primary corporate sponsor.

Slaight looked to a former competitor to fulfill his vision for the team. Richard Peddie had been among the players in Tanenbaum's losing bid for the franchise. ''Richard, you're the only guy in the country who has general manager, packaged goods and facility and broadcast experience. Come run the Raptors for me,'' *Canadian Business* recounted.

A New Venue in Toronto: 1998–2001

A few years down the road, Slaight was ready to part with the team, and MLG Ltd. bought the Toronto Raptors in 1998. The Raptors were bleeding red ink, and the Leafs, who needed a new building, were unlikely to get outside financing. Furthermore, the OTPP was dissatisfied with the return on its Leafs investment.

The total price tag for Stavro, OTPP, TD, and Tanenbaum for their combined venture was estimated by the *Financial Post* to be $600 million: $175 million for the Leafs; $400 million for the Raptors and Air Canada Centre (ACC); and $25 million for additional luxury boxes at the ACC.

Peddie was named CEO and president of the combined operations and continued as president of the Raptors. Air Canada Centre opened its doors in February 1999.

After four losing season, the NBA team finally turned around and made it to the playoffs in 2000 and 2001. Thanks to Peddie's marketing savvy, the team's economic outlook improved. Corporate sponsors, for example, seeking a tie-in with the ever popular Leafs, had to sign on with the Raptors as well. To build connections with fans Peddie relaunched web sites and obtained licenses to operate two digital TV specialty stations.

Meanwhile, Stavro's fortunes took a slide when his Knob Hill Farms chain faltered in 2000. Woodbridge Co., controlled by the Thomson family—Canada's wealthiest—stepped in to help. Stavro's real estate properties would be redeveloped and the ten Knob Hill outlets would be closed.

On the ice, Stavro's beloved Leafs' three-decade drought continued. The last Stanley Cup was brought home in 1967. However, fans remained loyal and filled the ACC to overflowing each home game.

Ticket sales, the main source of revenue for MLSE, matched player salaries nearly one-to-one for both clubs. Profits came

Key Dates:

1994: Ontario Teachers' Pension Plan (OTPP) buys into NHL team the Toronto Maple Leafs.
1995: Toronto Raptors take the court as NBA team.
1998: Maple Leafs buy the Raptors.
1999: Air Canada Centre opens.
2002: Maple Leafs mark their 75th anniversary.
2003: OTPP becomes majority owner of Maple Leaf Sports & Entertainment.

from secondary sources: advertising sponsorships, corporate partnerships, broadcast rights, merchandise, concessions, and event rental.

Valuable Commodity: 2002–03

The Leafs marked their 75th anniversary in 2002 as part of Canada's largest sports and entertainment enterprise. MLSE's estimated value was about $1 billion. Battles on the ice and on the court, however, paled in comparison to the action in the boardroom. Stavro's debt to Woodbridge was coming due and his only significant asset was his controlling interest in MLSE, to which he also had financial obligations. Moreover, Stavro had alienated fellow investors in MLSE through his dealings with Woodbridge that conflicted with his previous agreements. Additionally, Stavro's management style was frustrating, especially to OTPP, which was known for its strong stance on good corporate governance.

''Apparently, there are no proper procedures at the executive level; no committee structures; informal agendas that allow items to be added without any notification; and Mr. Stavro is said to make decisions on behalf of directors and management, often without their prior consent,'' the *National Post* reported.

The issues were resolved in 2003 when Stavro sold his shares and a new ownership structure was formed. The private equity arm of OTPP, Ontario Merchant Bank, acquired a majority holding of 58 percent. Bell Globemedia—a BCE Inc. and Thomson family business concern—came aboard with a 15 percent stake. TD Capital Group and Tanenbaum's Kilmer Sports Inc. held 14 percent and 13 percent, respectively. Three seats on the board would go to the pension fund, which would leave the handling of the teams to the sports management team. The addition of Bell Globemedia, owner of print and broadcast concerns, provided a variety of media opportunities for MLSE.

No one disputed the value of the franchise: profitability was another matter. ''According to Forbes, the Leafs alone bring in $24.2 million in profits,'' wrote Andy Holloway for *Canadian Business*. ''MLSE president Richard Peddie vehemently disputes that figure, saying it doesn't include taxes or the interest and amortization costs of carrying the $265-million ACC. Peddie does say MLSE is 'very modestly profitable' and has been almost every year, even in its previous life as publicly traded Maple Leaf Gardens Ltd. 'Sports is a very sexy business, but it's a business,' says Peddie. 'You have to run it like a *Fortune* 500 Company.' ''

As 2004 began, the ACC had seen over 15 million guests. The longtime home of the Maple Leafs was still looking for a new owner. The Toronto Maple Leafs ranked as the top hockey brand in the world. Moreover, the Raptors were better at getting season seat renewals than any one else in the NBA. Yet, Toronto's sports fans were still waiting for their teams to bring home championships.

Principal Subsidiaries

Toronto Maple Leafs; Toronto Raptors; Air Canada Centre.

Principal Competitors

Madison Square Garden, L.P.; Club de Hockey Canadien, Inc.; Calgary Flames Limited Partnership.

Further Reading

''Canada's Top 75 Companies of All Time,'' *Canadian Business*, February 17, 2003.
Feinberg, Phyllis, ''Sweat Equity: Portraits in Diversification,'' *Pensions & Investments*, March 3, 2003, p. 8.
Gibson, Will, ''A Real Mug's Came,'' *Canadian Business*, March 17, 2003.
Holloway, Andy, ''How the Game Is Played,'' *Canadian Business*, April 2, 2001, pp. 26+.
Johnson, Arthur, ''The Maple Leaf Follies,'' *Financial Post*, September 28, 1991, pp. S26+.
''Loblaw to Buy Maple Leaf Gardens,'' *CBC .CA News*, October 21, 2003.
MacFadyen, ''Teachers' Merchant Bank Corners Sports Market,'' *Buyouts*. March 3, 2003.
Noble, Kimberley, ''A Breakaway Deal,'' *Maclean's*, February 23, 1998, p. 49.
McQueen. Rod, ''A Funny Thing Happened on the Way to the Gardens.'' *Financial Post*, August 31, 1996, p. 6.
——, ''Stavro Aims for Top in the Big Leagues,'' *Financial Post*, April 16. 1994, pp. S26+.
——. ''Two into One Will Go,'' *Financial Post*, February 14, 1998, p. 16.
Muret. Don, ''Raptors May Not Be Only Inhabitants of Toronto's New Air Canada Centre,'' *Amusement Business*, October 27, 1997, p. 13.
Tedesco. Theresa, ''The Backroom Battle for Maple Leaf Sports,'' *National Post*, November 16. 2002, pp. FP1+.
——. ''Control of Struggling Leafs Could Soon Be Up for Grabs,'' *National Post*, November 16. 2202, pp. A1+.
Weber, Terry, ''Loblaw Ices Gardens Plan,'' *globeandmail.com*, December 23. 2003.

—Kathleen Peippo

Marcolin S.p.A.

32913 Longarone (BL)
Località Villanova, 4
Italy
Telephone: +39 437 777111
Fax: +39 437 777282
Web site: http://www.marcolin.com

Public Company
Incorporated: 1961
Employees: 1,200
Sales: $174.9 million (2002)
Stock Exchanges: Milan
Ticker Symbol: MCL
NAIC: 339115 Ophthalmic Goods Manufacturing

Marcolin S.p.A. manufactures more than six million fashion sunglasses and optical frames a year at two factories in Italy. In addition, it produces ski goggles and sports eyewear through its subsidiary Cébé at two plants in France. For the first several decades of its existence, the company produced optical frames only. But with the emergence of sunglasses as a popular fashion accessory in the 1990s, Marcolin began making sunglasses for leading international fashion houses. The company now has licenses to produce frames under more than a dozen different brand names, including Dolce & Gabbana, Roberto Cavalli, Montblanc, Mossimo, and North Face. Marcolin's designers work with each fashion house to retain the distinctive look and individual identity of the brand. In addition, Marcolin produces and markets sunglasses and optical frames under its own house brand. The company has several subsidiaries that handle distribution in Europe, as well as a U.S. subsidiary and branches in Brazil and Hong Kong. Members of the Marcolin family are executives at the company and the largest shareholders.

Producing Optical Frames: 1961–88

In 1961 Giovanni Marcolin Coffen began producing optical frames at his "Fabbrica Artigiana Giovanni Coffen Marcolin," or "Artisan Workshop of Giovanni Coffen Marcolin," in the small Italian town of Vallesella di Cadore. The town is located in the northeastern part of the country not far from the Swiss and Austrian borders. His specialty was frames for glasses in rolled gold. Six years later he opened a full-scale factory in the same city and presented his first line of products. His distinctive designs caught on not only in Italy, but in greater Europe as well. The first foreign branch opened in France in 1976. Branches in Switzerland and Germany followed soon afterward. The firm was incorporated officially as Marcolin S.p.A. around 1980 and took direct control of the distribution of its products.

Marcolin entered the U.S. market in 1982 with a joint venture to distribute its brands. By 1985 the second generation of the Marcolin family was involved in the firm: that year Cirillo Marcolin started working for the company at the French branch. A year later he was called back to Italy and rose through positions as an administrative manager, manager of production at three plants, sales manager, and eventually an executive director.

In 1988 Marcolin moved its management and administrative offices about a dozen miles south from Vallesella to the slightly larger city of Longarone. There the company established a second factory for the production of acetate frames, expanding its line beyond the metal-only frames it had been producing up to that point. Distributor branches in Portugal and the United Kingdom also were opened in the late 1980s.

Making Sunglasses for Fashion Brands in the 1990s

The perception of eyewear was changing gradually in the late 1980s and into the early 1990s. Glasses came to be seen not just as a tool for sight correction, but as a fashion accessory that reflected the wearer's individual style. Sunglasses, too, began to be valued more for their role in creating a stylish image than for their function as eye protection. Fashion trendsetters were seen ever more frequently wearing sunglasses at night or indoors, as part of a look that had nothing to do with shielding the eyes from bright light.

Gucci became the first major fashion house, in 1989, to introduce a line of sunglasses. Many other big names in the fashion industry jumped on the bandwagon in the following years, licensing their brands to manufacturers of traditional eyewear for the production of sunglasses. The trend allowed the

Company Perspectives:

Marcolin is a creative space where eyewear is created that can interpret a modern way of life, conforming to the wishes and suggestions of designers. It is a place where stylistic proposals and precise formal requirements are rationalized and industrialized to create accessories that are perfectly in line with the collections they belong to, but at the same time they are unmistakably characterized by their quality and refinement.

more exclusive fashion names to achieve a degree of mass distribution for their brands. Sunglasses were a slightly less expensive ''point of entry'' into higher-end brand names, allowing the consumer to acquire the style of the season with a simple accessory.

Marcolin's first step toward becoming a major licensee for high-fashion brand names came in 1993 when Calvin Klein met with the company and soon after set up a partnership that gave Marcolin the exclusive right to distribute Calvin Klein eyewear in Europe. In 1994 Maurizio Marcolin, son of the company's founder, joined the family business. He eventually became a leader in the company's marketing and licensing activities and presided over the development of partnerships with an array of fashion houses over the next several years. He told the *Financial Times* in 2000, ''We found that consumers were looking at eyewear increasingly as a lifestyle expression by the mid-1990s.'' Marcolin's first major agreement was signed in December 1995 with the Italian fashion company Dolce & Gabbana. Marcolin acquired the exclusive right for the worldwide production and distribution of Dolce & Gabbana eyewear, including both sunglasses and prescription frames. Designers Stefano Gabbana and Domenice Dolce captured the prevailing attitude in fashion circles when they referred to sunglasses as ''dressing for the face.'' This was the first foray into sunglasses production for both Marcolin and Dolce & Gabbana. Marcolin was easily able to adapt its production capabilities to include sunglasses as well as optical frames.

Marcolin's sales increased as its products gained wider fashion appeal. Sales rose from L 100 billion in 1995 to L 125 billion in 1996 and L 160 billion in 1998. The company strengthened its U.S. presence in 1997 by opening a fully owned distribution subsidiary in New Jersey. Meanwhile, the company added more brand names to its portfolio. In 1997 the company signed an agreement with the Fashion Box Group of Treviso, Italy, to produce sunglasses and reading glasses for men and women under the designer label Replay Eyes. This product line appealed to a younger, more casual market than Dolce & Gabbana. It was available in Italy by the end of 1998 and abroad in 1999. More licensing agreements were signed in 1998, with the designer label Romeo Gigli and with the fashion house Chloé, part of the international Vendome group. The Chloé collection, known as Chloé Lunettes, would include sunglasses and corrective eyewear for women only, and was characterized by large shapes with an elegant 1950s-inspired style. Also in 1998, Marcolin expanded its partnership with Dolce & Gabbana by introducing the line of D & G Eyewear for the youth market.

By 1998 Marcolin was making about 2.5 million frames a year, and sunglasses already accounted for half. The company was planning for aggressive growth by the new millennium. Its goals included a public offering, a license with an American designer, and a 40 percent increase in sales. But Maurizio Marcolin also stressed that the company wanted to be circumspect in its expansion. ''We don't want to act like a supermarket of eyewear brands but like a boutique,'' he told *WWD* in 1998. ''Our approach is one of a partnership with the designers. Our structure still has room for new labels, and now that we've consolidated our European portfolio, we can go overseas.''

Growth Through Acquisitions and Licensing Agreements: 1999–2004

Marcolin forged ahead with its expansion plans in 1999. The company was listed on the Milan stock exchange that July in an offering that raised about L 8 billion. The proceeds helped finance the acquisition that July of Cébé, a French company that designed and manufactured ski goggles and other sports eyewear. The acquisition brought about 200 new employees into the Marcolin group and also, for the first time, gave Marcolin the technological ability to make injection-molded plastic eyewear. Cébé was a well-known brand that had been produced for more than 100 years. Marcolin continued producing goods under the Cébé brand name at the company's two factories in the French cities of Morez and Frasne. Marcolin also acquired Cébé's distribution subsidiaries in Sweden, Japan, the United Kingdom, Switzerland, Spain, and Italy. In addition, Marcolin opened a new subsidiary for its own products in Hong Kong that year, to oversee distribution in the Far East as well as Australia and New Zealand.

In 1999 Marcolin also found the American brand it had been seeking when it signed a licensing agreement that summer with the Los Angeles-based casual fashion brand Mossimo Inc. The Mossimo Vision collection was launched in 2000 and included eyewear for both men and women. The company acquired more licensing agreements with European designers that year as well. In May Marcolin partnered with Roberto Cavalli, the Florentine fashion designer, to inaugurate the Roberto Cavalli eyewear collection. Cavalli's icon was the snake, and snake motifs and curvy lines were incorporated into a collection of sunglasses for women. The collection debuted internationally in 2000. In September Marcolin acquired a license to produce sunglasses and optical frames with the Fornarina Vision Up! brand name. The partnership was discontinued at the end of 2003, however. Finally, in 1999 Marcolin renewed its license for the Dolce & Gabbana brand name until 2005. Dolce & Gabbana continued to be one of the company's strongest brand names, accounting for about half of total turnover.

As a result of the acquisition of Cébé, Marcolin's sales rose more than 25 percent in 2000 to L 236 billion. Overall sales were more than double what they had been five years earlier. That October Marcolin added the Miss Sixty brand name to its portfolio, signing an agreement with the Italian fashion firm Sixty S.p.A. The line was targeted at a younger market and would include sunglasses and optical frames for women only. The Miss Sixty line was scheduled to debut in Europe in November 2001, followed by international distribution.

Key Dates:

1961: Giovanni Marcolin Coffen begins producing eyeglass frames in rolled gold in northeast Italy.
1967: The first factory opens in Vallesella.
1976: A French distribution subsidiary opens, followed by branches in Switzerland and Germany.
1982: A joint venture opens for distribution in the United States.
1988: Company headquarters moves to Longarone, where a second factory is built.
1995: Marcolin begins making sunglasses after signing a licensing agreement with Dolce & Gabbana.
1999: Cébé, a French manufacturer of sports eyewear, is acquired; Marcolin lists on the Milan exchange and establishes licensing arrangements with more fashion brands.
2001: Creative Optics, an eyewear distributor in the United States, is acquired.

Marcolin grew substantially again in 2001, thanks to the acquisition of a subsidiary in the United States. In February that year Marcolin paid $13 million for Creative Optics Inc., a distributor of eyewear with headquarters in Miami and a distribution center in Scottsdale, Arizona. As a result, Marcolin closed its New Jersey subsidiary and reorganized its North American operations around the new acquisition. Creative Optics was an attractive acquisition for Marcolin because most of its sales were made through mass distribution channels, a sector where Marcolin had only a small share. The acquisition added several ''all-American'' brands to Marcolin's lineup: Essence, Unionbay, Bob Mackie, NBA Eyewear, and FAO Schwarz. These brands had $28.7 million in net sales the previous year.

Marcolin also signed several more licensing agreements in 2001. In January it partnered with the U.S. sportswear company North Face to introduce a line of technically sophisticated sports eyewear. The agreement enhanced Marcolin's presence in the sports eyewear market and built on the existing sportswear expertise of its subsidiary Cébé. The North Face line would be available starting in 2003. In March 2001 Marcolin signed an agreement with E.C. S.p.A. to make optical frames and sunglasses for men and women under the Costume National brand name. This was a higher-end line, produced in partnership with the designer Ennio Capasa and characterized by large sizes and enveloping shapes. In July that year Marcolin acquired the right to produce eyewear for Montblanc International, the maker of luxury products such as pens, watches, and jewelry. The Montblanc line would be for men only and would emphasize a classic, restrained style. Finally, in September Marcolin signed an agreement with Procter & Gamble to make optical frames and sunglasses under the Cover Girl brand in North America. Marcolin also opened its tenth distribution branch in 2001 in Brazil near Sao Paulo. This was its first location in South America.

By the first years of the new millennium, technology was beginning to rival style as one of the deciding factors in attracting buyers of sunglasses. Maurizio Marcolin told the *Financial Times* in 2003, ''In fashion brands, style is still the number one consideration, but technology now comes a very close second. The consumer demands innovation now, even though the technology already available is far in advance of anything most consumers need. Emphasizing the technology creates a feeling that the sunglasses are both very current and of a certain quality.'' Marcolin kept pace with this trend by adding technological flair to its product descriptions. For example, the new lines for Costume National and Montblanc featured ''mat ruthenium polychromic'' or ''injected polycarbonate decentered'' lenses. In 2002 Marcolin even made an enhanced version of one of its sports sunglasses for a yacht racing team, fitting them with technology that allowed real-time information to be displayed wirelessly on the individual lenses of each team member.

Despite the economic downturn in late 2001 and 2002, Marcolin's sales remained strong, particularly in the Roberto Cavalli and Dolce & Gabbana lines. The company expanded its facilities in October 2002 when it opened a new design location just outside the city of Treviso. The site was housed in an 18th-century Venetian villa. The company planned to hire more staff, including some foreigners, to meet the design needs of its numerous fashion and sports lines. In July 2003 Marcolin started a renovation of its headquarters in Longarone. Warehouse operations were to be transferred to a new building near the existing plant, and the space that was freed up would be used to enlarge the eyeglass production area. Later that year Marcolin added more brand names to its portfolio when it signed licensing agreements with Kenneth Cole and The Timberland Company. In 2004 Marcolin had grown to be the world's third largest eyewear manufacturer, and its reach was likely to increase as new lines were introduced to fulfill the licensing agreements signed in the preceding years.

Principal Subsidiaries

Marcolin International B.V.; CEBE S.A. (France); Marcolin USA, Inc. (85.4%); Marcolin Asia Ltd. (Hong Kong); Marcolin & Co. S.p.A. (Italy); Marcolin Iberica SA (Spain); Marcolin Portugal; Marcolin Benelux (Belgium); Marcolin UK; Marcolin France; Marcolin Deutschland (Germany); Marcolin GmbH (Switzerland); Marcolin do Brasil.

Principal Competitors

Luxottica S.p.A.; De Rigo; Safilo.

Further Reading

Comstock, Mireilia, ''Italy's Coolest Shades: Maurizio Marcolin,'' *Women's Wear Daily Italy Supplement,* January 1997.

Friedman, Vanessa, ''How to Spend It: The Eyes Have It,'' *Financial Times,* June 3, 2000, p. 13.

Ilari, Alessandra, ''Marcolin Eyes IPO, Expanding U.S. Focus,'' *WWD,* December 7, 1998, p. 9.

——, ''Sunglasses Keep Their Cool at Mido,'' *WWD,* June 4, 2001, p. 9.

Johnson, Greg, ''From Around the Americas,'' *Daily Deal,* February 23, 2001.

Kaiser, Amanda, and Melanie Kletter, ''Marcolin Signs Deal with Kenneth Cole,'' *WWD,* August 6, 2003, p. 3.

''La Dolce Vita,'' *WWD,* May 18, 1995, p. 14.

''Listing for Spectacles Manufacturer Marcolin in 1999,'' *Il Sole 24 Ore,* May 7, 1999.
''Marcolin Applies for Listing on Stock Exchange,'' *Wall Street Journal (Europe),* May 20, 1999, p. 16.
''Marcolin Gets Chloé License for Eyewear,'' *WWD,* April 28, 1998, p. 2.
''Marcolin Shows Good Growth,'' *Optician,* March 28, 2003, p. 2.
Sims, Josh, ''The Future's Bright—Wear Your Shades,'' *Financial Times,* April 12, 2003, p. 10.

—Sarah Ruth Lorenz

Martin-Baker Aircraft Company Limited

Higher Denham, Near Uxbridge
Middlesex UB9 5AJ
United Kingdom
Telephone: +44 (0) 1895 832214
Fax: +44 (0) 1895 832587
Web site: http://www.martin-baker.com

Wholly Owned Subsidiary of Martin-Baker (Engineering) Ltd.
Incorporated: 1934
Employees: 750
Sales: $90 million (2003 est.)
NAIC: 332912 Fluid Power Valve and Hose Fitting Manufacturing; 336413 Other Aircraft Parts and Auxiliary Equipment Manufacturing; 541710 Research and Development in the Physical, Engineering, and Life Sciences; 551112 Offices of Other Holding Companies

Martin-Baker Aircraft Company Limited is the world's leading producer of ejection seats. With 70,000 seats produced and 7,000 lives saved as of 2003, no one in the industry has more experience. Seats cost up to $150,000 each; they are made with the knowledge that one in ten of them will be used. The firm also supplies related safety equipment, such as life rafts.

Martin-Baker has remained family-owned throughout its existence. The company's main facilities are located in the English countryside; some of its World War II-vintage buildings once housed captured German aviators. Martin-Baker still flies a 1950s-era Meteor jet as a test bed.

Martin-Baker controls between 70 and 75 percent of the market for ejection seats for Western-made military aircraft. The U.S. Navy traditionally has been its single largest customer; in 2000 the company opened two plants in Pennsylvania.

Origins

James Martin was born in 1893 in County Down, Ireland, the son of a farmer. A self-taught engineer, he established Martin Aircraft in 1929. In 1934 he was joined by a pilot friend, Captain Valentine Baker, in forming Martin-Baker Aircraft Co. Ltd. in Denham, England. Although Martin's engineering skills were admired, none of the firm's aircraft designs achieved commercial success. Baker was killed testing a prototype in 1942; this event set the course of the company's future focus on aircraft safety products.

James Martin is credited with a number of innovations in armament systems during World War II. His firm began developing its first ejection seat toward the end of the war. According to *Reuters,* it took some doing for Martin to convince the British government of the value of saving pilots with his invention. The high speeds of jet aircraft gave pilots no time to pop open the canopy and bail out conventionally.

The essence of Martin-Baker's ejection seat design would remain unchanged for decades: an aluminum seat shot from the plane via explosive charges. Germany had earlier developed a cruder, catapult-like system for their Messerschmitt 262 fighter; Sweden also had a primitive ejection seat.

The seat began trials in 1946 in a Gloster Meteor (Britain's first operational jet fighter). After the first live test on July 24, the Irish test pilot, Bernard Lynch, was able to walk to a nearby pub for a well-deserved pint.

The new ejection seat was soon being installed in the first generation of British and American jet aircraft. The company's first life was saved on May 30, 1949, when test pilot ''Jo'' Lancaster ejected from the experimental Armstrong Whitworth AW52 Flying Wing Jet near Bitteswell Aerodrome.

Supersonic in the 1950s and 1960s

After a decade of involvement with the company, the U.S. Navy became a virtually exclusive user of Martin-Baker ejection seats in 1957. A remarkable ejection demonstrating Martin-Baker's developments geared toward supersonic flight came two years later, when English Electric test pilot John Squier successfully ejected from a Lightning fighter at a speed of 1,250 m.p.h. and an altitude of 40,000 feet.

An important milestone—1,000 lives saved—was passed in 1965. James Martin was knighted the same year. During the

Company Perspectives:

Martin-Baker is the world's longest established and most experienced manufacturer of ejection seats and related equipment to safeguard the aviator throughout the escape, survival, location and recovery phases.

It is the only company that can offer a fully integrated escape system that satisfies the very latest in pilot operational capability and safety standards offering a complete "end-to-end service" from helping the customer to establish operational safety and escape requirements, design, development and qualification, to ongoing support throughout the entire service life of the aircraft.

With headquarters at its original site in Denham, Buckinghamshire, locations in France, Italy and the United States, and representatives all over the world, Martin-Baker has established an extensive range of facilities and engineering capabilities to support ejection seat work, insuring that these products are of the highest quality and reliability, and will perform as designed—the first time. The Company continues as a successfully family run business headed by the Chairman who is the cousin of the late founder, Sir James Martin and his twin sons as joint Managing Directors. The directors, like their father, are engineers. They are great enthusiasts for the product and actively run the Company, day-to-day together with an extremely loyal and skillful workforce.

Martin-Baker appreciates fully that this equipment may represent the crew members' last chance to survive and that there can be no compromise. Every facet of the safety system from initiation, escape path clearance, ejection sequencing, stabilization, life support, parachute descent to final rescue, must work perfectly to safeguard a precious life. The aircrew member must also reach the ground uninjured, especially in a hostile environment, if they are to have the best possible chance of survival.

It is because of this understanding, backed by 55 years of continuous ejection seat manufacture that only Martin-Baker can offer a fully integrated escape system that satisfies the very latest safety standards. Only Martin-Baker has saved over 7,000 lives in more than 90 Air Forces.

1960s, ejection seat technology made the switch from explosive charges to rocket motors.

The legal precursor to Martin-Baker Aircraft Co. Ltd., Stravale Trading Co. Ltd., was incorporated on January 3, 1966. Its name changed to Martin-Baker Aircraft Co. Ltd. on April 26, 1967. On April 5, 1993, it became a subsidiary of Martin-Baker (Engineering) Ltd., which transferred its manufacturing capacity to the company.

According to *Aviation Week & Space Technology,* Martin-Baker seats performed 700 successful ejections during the Vietnam War. Later, the company won a unique contract to retrofit Soviet-made MiG-19 fighters for the Pakistani air force.

In the 1970s, the company was developing its Mk. 10 seat to cope with a variety of difficult ejection scenarios, including zero-zero (airspeed and altitude), inverted, high-g, and underwater. Martin-Baker had escaped nationalization into British Aerospace Corp., noted *Aviation Week & Space Technology.* Much of the company's spirit of independence was attributed to founder Sir James Martin, who continued to come to work bright and early throughout the 1970s (he died in January 1981). In keeping with its self-reliant attitude and concern over quality control, Martin-Baker produced every component it could onsite. It did outsource parachutes (from GQ, Ltd.) and rocket propellant.

New Seats, New Techniques in the 1980s and 1990s

Martin-Baker had three main development programs entering the 1980s: retrofits of the Mk. 10; an ultra-lightweight seat for trainers and helicopters; and an advanced seat for the next generation of aircraft. With robust defense spending, production reached 100 seats per month by the middle of the decade.

The Mk. 14 Naval Aircrew Common Escape System (NACES) seat, first delivered to the U.S. Navy in 1989, was both high-tech and practical. It was the first naval ejection seat to incorporate an electronic sequencer (supplied by Teledyne-McCormack-Selph) allowing it to adjust for altitude and speed. Its modular design made it possible to switch units between different types of aircraft using a common set of tools and spare parts. Martin-Baker's production methods also were becoming more sophisticated as the firm invested in automation.

Martin-Baker formed an airline seat venture with Aircraft Interior Components (AIC) in September 1990. After studies on the danger of passenger and crew seating collapsing during crashes, the airline industry was looking for a crashworthy seat.

Ejection seats cost between £50,000 and £100,000 at the time. Martin-Baker had a 75 percent share of the market among aircraft made in the West. Employment had been scaled back to 1,000 workers as the company made increasing use of automation and defense contracts dwindled. By early 1992, Martin-Baker had claimed 6,000 lives saved. The company presented ejection survivors with exclusive Gieves and Hawkes ties.

Company founder James Martin's twin sons, John and James, became managing directors of the firm in June 1995. At the same time, their cousin, Dennis J. Burrell, was appointed chairman.

Revenue was £65 million in the fiscal year ending March 1997, reported London's *Financial Times.* Martin-Baker's main customer was the U.S. Navy; the U.S. Air Force preferred competitor McDonnell Douglas. Martin-Baker was able, however, to obtain a contract for supplying up to 1,422 seats for the joint services trainer. In the late 1990s, the company also was designing a three-man seat for the European spacecraft Hermes.

Opening a U.S. Transplant in 2000

In February 2000, the company announced plans to build two facilities in Pennsylvania. The first of these opened in June 2000 in Johnstown. Martin Baker's experience with the state dated back to 1946, when it constructed a test tower in the Philadelphia Navy Yard.

This gave Martin-Baker a new ally—the Pennsylvania legislature—against the federal protectionism that had been brewing for decades. Martin-Baker's sole competitor in the United States was B.F. Goodrich Corporation, which had since 1986 built up its

Key Dates:

1934: Company is formed in Denham, England.
1946: The first ejection seat is demonstrated.
1949: The Martin-Baker seat is credited for the first time with saving a life.
1957: The U.S. Navy becomes an exclusive user of Martin-Baker seats.
1965: The 1,000th life is saved.
1989: An electronically-sequenced Mk. 14 NACES seat is delivered to the U.S. Navy.
1991: The first female military pilot is saved by a Martin-Baker seat.
2000: Martin-Baker opens a pair of plants in Pennsylvania.
2003: The 7,000th life is saved.

Evacuation Division through acquiring related businesses such as Universal Propulsion Co. The only other supplier of ejection seats for military aircraft was Russia's Zvezda Design Bureau.

The lucrative U.S. Air Force/Navy Joint Ejection Seat Program (JESP), which had been the focus of intense competition, faced a severe drop-off in funding in the federal budget for 2003. Sales of existing seats and retrofits of 1,500 older fighters and trainers for the U.S. Navy, however, kept Martin-Baker busy. The seats on these latter planes were being modified to accept a wider range of body weights to accommodate more female pilots in the fleet (the first female life saved by Martin-Baker was a U.S. Navy lieutenant who bailed from an A-6 in 1991).

Saving the 7,000th Life in 2003

Martin-Baker logged its 7,000th life saved with the bail-out of a Royal Navy pilot from a Sea Harrier on June 11, 2003. In fact, this was the second successful ejection for Lt. Commander Robert Schwab, who had bailed out of a Hawk trainer nine years earlier after its landing gear failed.

By this time, Martin-Baker had produced about 70,000 ejection seats in all. In a somewhat ironic development for a company whose existence was dedicated to saving human lives, Martin-Baker also was developing ejection systems for unmanned aircraft, to protect their valuable reconnaissance cargoes.

All of the seats the company had ever made were kept in production in order to support older aircraft still in service, such as the 1950s-era Canberra jets used by the Royal Air Force. According to *Professional Engineering,* Martin-Baker still employed Meteor jets, first used in World War II, as test aircraft.

Principal Subsidiaries

J. Martin Armaments Ltd.; Martin-Baker America Inc. (U.S.A.); Società Italiana Costruzioni Aeronautiche Martin-Baker (SICAMB); Société d'Exploitation des Matériels Martin-Baker (SEMMB) (France).

Principal Competitors

B.F. Goodrich Corporation; Zvezda Design Bureau.

Further Reading

''Bitteswell Flight Made Ejection Seat History,'' *Leicester Mercury,* June 18, 1999, p. 10.

Brown, David A., ''Navy Aircraft Will Receive Seats That Adjust Ejection to Speed, Altitude,'' *Aviation Week & Space Technology,* September 12, 1988, p. 58.

——, ''New Ejection System Being Developed,'' *Aviation Week & Space Technology,* December 8, 1980, p. 52.

Campbell, Christy, ''Alive—By the Seat of Their Pants,'' *Sunday Telegraph* (London), July 14, 1996, p. 15.

——, ''Flying in the Hot Seat,'' *Sunday Star-Times* (Wellington, New Zealand), July 28, 1996, p. A13.

Elgood, Giles, ''Ejector Seat Maker Marks 50 Explosive Years,'' *Reuters News,* August 4, 1996.

Fisher, Paul, ''Ejector Seats Getting Off to a Flying Start,'' *Guardian* (London), January 30, 1992, p. 33.

Lewis, Paul, ''Ejection-Seat Companies Face New-Product Famine; With Funding for Developments Withdrawn, Manufacturers Are Looking at Upgrades,'' *Flight International,* July 2, 2002, p. 18.

Lowe, Christian, ''Pa. Lawmakers Blast Pentagon, Force Contest,'' *Navy News Week,* June 19, 2000.

''Martin-Baker Joins Airline Market,'' *Flight International,* September 12, 1990.

''Martin-Baker to Build Navy Common Ejection Seat,'' *Aviation Week & Space Technology,* May 13, 1985, p. 26.

''Martin-Baker to Retain Independence,'' *Aviation Week & Space Technology,* September 6, 1976, p. 135.

Michaels, Daniel, ''To Help Aviators Eject, U.K. Company Doesn't Fly by the Seat of Its Pants,'' *Wall Street Journal Europe,* August 7, 2003, p. A1.

——, ''When Pilots Are in Trouble, They Need a First-Class Seat; One That Ejects, That Is,'' *Wall Street Journal* (Eastern ed.), August 7, 2003, p. A1.

Miller, Charles, ''Ties Await New Members of Ejection Seat Club,'' *Press Association,* January 26, 1991.

Morrocco, John D., ''Martin-Baker to Set Up Assembly Site in U.S.,'' *Aviation Week & Space Technology,* October 4, 1999, p. 38.

Muradian, Vago, ''Commerce Survey May Help Eject U.K. Firm from U.S. Seat Market,'' *Defense Daily,* September 25, 1996.

North, David M., ''Navy Drafts New Ejection Seat Plan,'' *Aviation Week & Space Technology,* January 10, 1983, p. 24.

Oakham, Martin, ''Hold Onto Your Seat,'' *Metalworking Production,* March 1, 2000, p. 28.

Phillips, Don, ''Blasting Pilots Out of Harm's Way; Modern Ejection Seats Prove Selves in Battle,'' *Washington Post,* January 24, 1991, p. A26.

Pope, Chris, ''Safe Seats,'' *Professional Engineering,* June 13, 2003, p. 34.

''Seat of Learning,'' *Flight International,* December 16, 1992.

Sharman, Sarah, *Sir James Martin: The Authorised Biography of the Martin-Baker Ejection Seat Pioneer,* Sparkford, Nr. Yeovil, Somerset, England: Patrick Stephens Ltd., 1996.

''Sir James Martin: Designer of the Martin-Baker Ejector Seat,'' *Times* (London), Obituaries, January 6, 1981, p. 14.

Swann, Christopher, ''No Escape from Success: Ejector Seat-Maker Records Strong Performance in the Face of Unpromising Market Conditions,'' *Financial Times* (London), April 23, 2001, p. 7.

Wagstyl, Stefan, ''The Sky's the Limit: A Family-Owned Company Dominates the World Market for Ejection Seats,'' *Financial Times* (London), April 21, 1997, p. 7.

Winn, Allan, ''Fast Exit,'' *Flight International,* June 18, 1997, p. 56.

—Frederick C. Ingram

Mattel, Inc.

333 Continental Boulevard
El Segundo, California 90245-5012
U.S.A.
Telephone: (310) 252-2000
Fax: (310) 252-2180
Web site: http://www.mattel.com

Public Company
Incorporated: 1948
Employees: 25,000
Sales: $4.89 billion (2002)
Stock Exchanges: New York Pacific
Ticker Symbol: MAT
NAIC: 339931 Doll and Stuffed Toy Manufacturing; 339932 Game, Toy, and Children's Vehicle Manufacturing

The world's largest toy company, Mattel, Inc. designs, manufactures, markets, and distributes a wide variety of toy products in 150 countries. The company's products include a number of core toy lines, including Barbie dolls, clothing, and accessories; Hot Wheels toy die-cast vehicles; Warner Bros. merchandise, including Harry Potter, Batman, Superman, and Looney Tunes products; the American Girls Collection of books, dolls, clothing, and accessories; Fisher-Price infant and preschool toys, including Little People figures and playsets and toys based on various licensed characters from sources such as Disney and Sesame Street; and games such as Scrabble and UNO. The company's toys are produced in company-owned manufacturing facilities in China, Indonesia, Malaysia, Mexico, and Thailand, as well as through independent contractors located in the United States, Europe, Mexico, the Far East, and Australia. Approximately 36 percent of 2002 revenues was generated outside the United States, with 60 percent of international sales originating in Europe. During 2002, about half of Mattel's revenues was derived through three main retail customers: Wal-Mart Stores, Inc., Toys 'R' Us, Inc., and Target Corporation. Mattel's toys have delighted generations of children throughout the world.

From Picture Frames to Toys: 1945–49

Mattel was founded in 1945 by Elliot and Ruth Handler. The youngest of ten children of Polish immigrants, Ruth was a secretary for Paramount Pictures in Los Angeles when she married Elliot Handler, an industrial engineer. Handler started out designing light fixtures but soon began making furniture to sell out of his garage. The business attracted four partners and quickly rose to become a $2 million enterprise making giftware and costume jewelry. By 1945 Elliot Handler grew restless and wanted a new business approach to remain competitive in the fast-changing postwar world. Handler's plans led to a dispute with his partners and he sold his interest in the company at a loss. Meanwhile, also in 1945, Ruth hooked up with an old friend, Harold ''Matt'' Matson, and they started Mattel Creations, with Elliot designing products. The name Mattel was formed by combining Matson's last name with Handler's first name. Ill health soon forced Matson to sell out.

Mattel first entered the picture frame business using scrap plastic and wood. With the leftover wood slats and plastic, Elliot Handler designed dollhouse furniture. Ruth Handler formed a simple sales organization, and the company was off to a winning start. In its first year the company pulled in $100,000, netting $30,000.

The Handlers had little business experience and even less capital, but the demographics of a baby boom plus a virtual toyless marketplace immediately after World War II gave them a unique opportunity to make their mark. Even so, it took a couple of years to see profits. In 1946 another low-cost line of molded furniture with meticulous detail put the Handlers out of the doll furniture business. Because of their introduction of a ''birdy bank'' and a ''make-believe makeup set,'' however, they managed to break even, and in the following year the Handlers introduced the first in a long string of hits in the toy industry. The ''Uke-A-Doodle,'' a miniature plastic ukelele, was an immediate success and drew large orders. In 1948 the Handlers introduced another hit—a new all-plastic piano with raised black keys. Although a winner, the company lost ten cents for each piano it sold because of quality problems relating to the die-cast sound mechanism breaking loose from the plastic.

Company Perspectives:

Mattel's management has articulated its overall company vision: The World's Premier Toy Brands—Today and Tomorrow. Management set five key company strategies: (i) improve execution of the existing toy business; (ii) globalize the brands; (iii) extend the brands; (iv) catch new trends; and (v) develop people.

These early business experiences taught the Handlers some poignant lessons in avoiding obsolescent products, ruinous price competition, poor cost control, and product quality problems. They realized that a successful business had to produce unique and original products of superior quality and strength that could not be copied easily by competitors.

The company incorporated in the state of California in 1948. At the same time the Handlers and an outside inventor began developing a music box employing a unique mechanism. A shortage of capital and the refusal of banks to gamble on the struggling young firm put the project on hold. With a $20,000 loan from Ruth Handler's brother-in-law, however, Mattel completed the project and produced another winner. As Elliot Handler later recalled, ''Our music box had a patented mechanism which had continuous play value because it operated only when the child turned the crank. It was different, it was well-made, and because we were able to mass-produce it, the price was lower than the imports.'' By taking an Old World idea and adapting it to modern production techniques, the Handlers beat out their Swiss competition, which up to then had dominated the domestic market for music boxes.

The success of the music box taught the Handlers a few other lessons. First, they discovered that child participation was essential for any quality toy; children should be able to interact with a toy and want to play with it often and for extended periods of time. Second, the Handlers recognized that a toy with lasting appeal is preferable to short-lived faddish products and can serve as a basis for other toys to follow.

Innovation, Diversification, and Success: 1950–69

Mattel reached several important firsts in 1955. Sales climbed to $5 million; the company introduced another hit, Burp Guns; and the Handlers decided to take a gamble that would change the toy business forever. In what seemed a risky venture, the Handlers agreed to sponsor a 15-minute segment of Walt Disney's *Mickey Mouse Club* on the ABC television network. The Handlers signed for 52 weeks at a cost of $500,000, equal to Mattel's net worth at the time. Up until this time, toy manufacturers relied primarily on retailers to show and sell their products and advertising occurred only during the holiday season; never before had a toy company spent money on advertising year-round. With television, however, toys could be marketed directly to children throughout the country. Thus with the slogan, ''You can tell it's Mattel, it's swell,'' the Handlers began a marketing revolution in the toy industry that produced an immediate payoff. The company sold many toy Burp Guns and made the Mattel brand name well known among the viewing audience.

In 1957 the company, exploiting the popularity of television westerns, introduced toy replicas of classic western guns and holsters. From the basic Burp Gun mechanism, Mattel developed the ''Fanner 50'' western pistol and a toy version of the Winchester rifle, complete with ejecting bullets. Mattel's sales reached $9 million and the following year hit $14 million. Then in 1959 Mattel made toy industry history with the introduction of the Barbie doll, the best-selling toy of all time. The idea for the doll originated with Ruth Handler, who had observed that their daughter favored adult-looking paper dolls over baby dolls. So the Handlers set to work designing a teenage fashion model doll and, despite a cool reception at the 1959 New York Toy Fair, the result was a smash hit, propelling Mattel into the national spotlight. Barbie, the famed doll named after the nickname of the Handlers' own daughter Barbara, soon prompted the founding of official fan clubs across the United States, which by 1968 had a total membership of about 1.5 million. Mattel marketed Barbie as an insatiable consumer of clothes and accessories, which were sold separately. In 1961 the company provided her with a boyfriend, the Ken doll.

After the phenomenal success of Barbie, Mattel entered the competitive large doll market in 1960 with another winner, Chatty Cathy, the first talking doll. That year Mattel made its first public stock offering, and by 1963 its common stock was listed on the New York Stock Exchange (NYSE). Mattel's sales skyrocketed from $26 million in 1963 to more than $100 million in 1965, due in part to the expansion of the Barbie line with Ken (named after the Handlers' son), Midge, and Skipper; Christie, an African American doll, debuted in 1968.

Throughout the 1960s the company continued to introduce popular toys: Baby First Step (the first doll to walk by itself), live-action dolls with moving eyes and mouths, See 'N Say talking educational toys, the Vac-U-Form machine, and an entire line of Thingmaker activity toys, including Creepy Crawlers, Fun Flowers, Fright Factory, and Incredible Edibles. Another spectacular hit, Hot Wheels miniature model cars, was introduced in 1968, which proved to be a pivotal year for Mattel as a host of its products dominated the market, including its original toy music boxes, which had sold more than 50 million. The company reincorporated in Delaware, and by the end of the decade it was the world's number one toy maker.

During the 1960s the company began aggressively diversifying its operations into a worldwide enterprise with a host of acquisitions: Dee & Cee Toy Co. Ltd. (1962); Standard Plastic Products, Inc., Hong Kong Industrial Co., Ltd., and Precision Moulds, Ltd. (1966); Rosebud Dolls Ltd. (1967); Monogram Models, Inc. and A&A Die Casting Company (1968); Ratti Vallensasca, Mebetoys, Ebiex S.A., H&H Plastics Co., Inc., and Metaframe Corp. (1969).

Stretched Too Thin: 1970s Through Mid-1980s

At the dawn of the 1970s, Mattel still was gobbling up other companies, such as Ringling Bros., Barnum & Bailey Circus and others. But the good times soon soured. In 1970 Mattel's plant in Mexico was destroyed by fire, and the following year a shipyard strike in the Far East cut off its toy supplies. To maintain the appearance of corporate growth, Seymour Rosenberg, executive vice-president and chief financial officer, fixed the books by reporting orders as sales, although many of the orders had been canceled and shipments had not been made. For two years Mattel issued false and misleading financial reports,

Key Dates:

1945: Ruth and Elliot Handler and Harold ''Matt'' Matson form a partnership called Mattel Creations, making and selling first picture frames and later dollhouse furniture; Matson is soon forced to sell out because of ill health.
1947: The ''Uke-A-Doodle'' becomes the first of many hit Mattel toys.
1948: The company is incorporated in California.
1955: In a revolutionary move, Mattel becomes a year-round sponsor of the Walt Disney television program *Mickey Mouse Club.*
1959: Mattel introduces the Barbie doll, which will eventually become the best-selling toy ever.
1960: Mattel goes public.
1963: The company gains a listing on the New York Stock Exchange.
1968: Hot Wheels miniature model cars, another spectacular hit, are introduced.
1974: The Handlers are ousted from the company after investigators find that the company issued false and misleading financial reports.
1983: The company verges on bankruptcy with a $394 million loss after an ill-advised venture into video games.
1987: John W. Amerman, who has been named chairman, revitalizes the company through an emphasis on core brands.
1988: Mattel revives its collaboration with Disney.
1993: Fisher-Price Inc., the world leader in infant and preschool toys, is acquired.
1997: Mattel buys out Tyco Toys, Inc., the third largest U.S. toy maker.
1998: Pleasant Company, maker of the American Girl brand, is acquired.
1999: The Learning Co., a major player in computer games and educational software, is acquired for $3.5 billion.
2000: Mattel sells off Learning Co. at a huge loss; the company reports a net loss for the year of $430.9 million.

until 1973, when the company reported a $32 million loss just three weeks after stockholders had been assured that the company was in sound financial condition. Mattel's stock plummeted and the Security and Exchange Commission (SEC) stepped in to investigate. Before Judge Robert Takasugi of the federal district court in Los Angeles, Ruth Handler and Rosenberg pleaded no contest to the SEC charges.

In 1974 Rosenberg was fired, the banks pressured the Handlers to resign, and the court ordered Mattel to restructure its board so that its majority would be company outsiders. In addition, the court fined Ruth Handler and Rosenberg each $57,000 and gave them 41-year sentences, which were suspended on the condition that they both performed 500 hours of charitable work annually for five years. Finally, in 1980 the Handlers cashed in most of their Mattel stock, ending their involvement in the company they had founded. Comprising approximately 12 percent of the company, the stock was worth about $18.5 million. Ruth Handler then went on to start Nearly Me, a company producing prosthetic breasts for mastectomy patients.

A new management team under Arthur S. Spear, a Mattel vice-president, replaced the Handlers in 1975 and by 1977 the company had returned to profitability. By 1980 Mattel was running a slew of other businesses, including the Ringling Bros., Barnum & Bailey Circus; Shipstad & Johnson's Ice Follies; Western Publishing, the largest publisher of children's books; and an entire line of electronic toys, most notably Intellivision video games.

Yet, unfortunately, Mattel stumbled badly for much of the 1980s. Many of the company's business acquisitions turned out to be unprofitable and had to be sold. Further, a big slump in video game sales in the early 1980s drove Mattel out of the video game business with a $394 million loss for 1983, putting the company on the edge of bankruptcy. Mattel might have gone under if the New York venture capital firms E.M. Warburg, Pincus & Co., and Drexel Burnham Lambert had not stepped in with $231 million in 1984 to save the company from the video game debacle. Still, in 1985 the company fell behind Hasbro, Inc. as the world's largest toymaker.

A New Direction: 1987–92

By 1987 Mattel suffered a $113 million loss when the market for its Masters of the Universe toy line for boys evaporated. As a result of Mattel's troubles, its stock plummeted from 1982's peak of $30 per share to just $10 per share in 1987. But the company's fortunes took a dramatic upswing when John W. Amerman, who had joined the company in 1980 as head of the international division, was named chairman. Under his direction the division's sales had quadrupled, far outpacing the profitability of Mattel's domestic operations. In his new role, Amerman moved quickly to cut Mattel's overhead by closing 40 percent of the company's manufacturing capacity, including plants in California, Taiwan, and the Philippines. He slashed the payroll by 150 at Mattel's corporate headquarters in California, saving an estimated $30 million annually. Mattel also refinanced high-cost debt and curbed advertising costs.

Amerman turned the company around by focusing on core brand names with staying power, such as Barbie and Hot Wheels, and by making selective investments in the development of new toys. One such selection was the re-emergence of Disney toys, due to a chance meeting in Tokyo, which, starting in 1988, gave Mattel licensing rights for a new line of infant and preschool plush toys. Renewing its collaboration with Disney proved more than serendipitous for Mattel, as their union in the 1990s would prove far more advantageous than Amerman ever imagined.

Despite a lackluster economy and generally flat sales in the toy industry, Amerman's strategy paid off big for Mattel. The Barbie line was bolstered and expanded to include approximately 50 different dolls per year and about 250 accessory items, including everything from shoes and clothing to linens, backpacks, furniture, and a cosmetics line. A promotional campaign in honor of Barbie's 30th birthday in 1989 propelled her onto the cover of *Smithsonian Magazine,* confirming her status as a true American icon. In 1990 Mattel moved from the Handlers' original offices to new headquarters in El Segundo, propelled in large part by Barbie's continuing popularity. By the next year the company estimated that 95 percent of all girls in the United States aged 3 to 11 owned several Barbie dolls; in fact, Barbie was so good for Mattel that between 1987 and 1992 sales shot up from $430 million to nearly $1 billion, accounting for about half of the company's $1.85 billion in sales. As a result of this phenomenal growth, Mattel opened a new state-of-the-art Barbie manufacturing plant in 1992 just outside Jakarta, Indonesia.

Mattel's emphasis on other core brands, including Hot Wheels die-cast vehicles, large dolls, Disney products, and See 'N Say educational preschool toys, provided a string of continuous hits. Mattel also pushed aggressively into other areas of the toy business, including plush toys, games, boys' action figures, and activity toys, which comprised 46 percent of the total toy market. By entering these areas, Mattel increased its participation in the total industry from 34 percent to approximately 80 percent, becoming a full-line toy company. The company made a particularly strong move into the toys for boys market, where it had been weak traditionally, with a range of new products, including the following: Bruno the Bad Dog (a monster truck that changed into a ferocious dog); action figures based on Arnold Schwarzenegger movies; and Nickelodeon's gooey Gak, a stretchy, oozing substance.

A strengthened strategic alliance with the Walt Disney Company allowed Mattel to sponsor attractions and to develop and sell toys at three Disney theme parks. The agreement gave Mattel unparalleled exposure to millions of children and adults who visited the parks each year. Mattel also negotiated the exclusive rights to sell dolls, stuffed characters, and preschool toys based on Disney movie characters, such as those from *Cinderella, Beauty and the Beast,* and *Aladdin.* The agreement was a boon for Mattel, and Amerman predicted that sales for the Disney line would top $500 million by 1995. Beyond Disney, Mattel also had reached an agreement with Hanna-Barbera to market toys based on the cartoon characters Yogi Bear, Boo-Boo, Cindy Bear, and the Flintstones; another agreement with Turner Broadcasting allowed Mattel to develop and sell Tom and Jerry products. A push into the game market led Mattel to acquire International Games, Inc. in 1992, the producer of such profitable core franchises as the UNO and Skip-Bo card games.

Mattel executives believed that the company's best growth opportunities for the mid-1990s were overseas markets, and sales for its international division exploded from $135 million in 1982 to $1.7 billion in 1992, with much of the sales through retail giants Toys 'R' Us and Wal-Mart. Overall net sales of Mattel products reached $2.6 billion, and Jill Barad, who had joined the company in 1981 as a product manager and had been most recently president of Mattel's U.S. operations, was promoted to president and COO of the company.

Bigger and Better Than Ever: 1993–98

In 1993 the company embarked on the landmark acquisition of venerable toy producer Fisher-Price Inc., the world's leading maker of toys for infants and preschoolers. The stock-for-stock deal, valued at $1.19 billion, bought Fisher-Price from the Quaker Oats Company and further cemented Mattel's unrivaled position in the toy industry. Year-end net sales hit $3.4 billion, and although Fisher-Price products contributed $750 million to the pie, Mattel had an extraordinary year—business was up a whopping 27 percent, aided by the sturdy dollar overseas. The distribution of sales relied heavily on Mattel's old standby, Barbie, with 35 percent or $1 billion, with Hot Wheels (5 percent or $150 million) and Disney (10 percent or $330 million) bringing in healthy shares, while other popular products like the Polly Pocket line, Mighty Max toys, and UNO card games brought in the rest. Mattel also doubled the capacity of its Indonesia plant; opened offices in Austria, Scandinavia, and New Zealand; and had hopes of adding others the next year in Portugal, as well as Argentina and Venezuela, in an effort to tap into Latin America's market of 120 million children. Latin America's child population was second only to Asia's at 800 million in 1993, far beyond the United States' 40 million and Europe's 70 million.

Mattel made two strategic acquisitions in 1994—those of J.W. Spear & Sons PLC, a British company that owned the international rights to the popular Scrabble games, and Kransco, whose Power Wheels and Wham-O (which included Frisbee and Hula Hoop) brands complemented its ever-growing products list. The next year Mattel became the new licensee of the Cabbage Patch Kids dolls, a top-notch addition to the company's large dolls line. Both 1994 and 1995 were record years for the company, with net sales of $4 billion and $4.4 billion, respectively, and net income of $225 million in 1994 and $338 million in 1995. The company also was looking to the future; it initiated a $72 million restructuring program in 1994 to consolidate manufacturing operations and slash unnecessary corporate expenses.

Also in 1995, Mattel approached Hasbro about a possible merger of the two largest toy companies in the world. Negotiations took place in secret over the course of several months until the Hasbro board early in 1996 unanimously turned down a $5.2 billion merger proposal that would have given Hasbro stockholders a 73 percent premium over the then current selling price. Hasbro officials expressed doubts that the merger could pass antitrust challenges and wanted a large upfront payment to help the company's performance during what would have likely been a lengthy antitrust review and to protect itself against the possibility that the merger would collapse. Mattel officials believed the merger would have had little difficulty gaining approval, but backed away—and did not initiate a hostile takeover—when Hasbro waged a vigorous media campaign emphasizing the possible negative ramifications of such a megamerger.

In 1996 sales grew to $4.5 billion, with income topping $372 million. The 38-year-old Barbie was once again the backbone of Mattel's net sales, hauling in $1.7 billion, up by 20 percent from the previous year. Hot Wheels sales also increased by nearly 20 percent, and Disney products were up 8 percent, surpassing the $500 million mark. International sales, however, were relatively flat—complicated by a strengthened dollar. At the end of the year Mattel initiated the acquisition of another major player in the toy industry, Tyco Toys, Inc., the third largest toy manufacturer in the United States. The merger of Tyco into Mattel's lineup, completed in March 1997, made the latter the unparalleled leader of the industry, far beyond any of its other competitors. Tyco's successful products, such as Sesame Street brand toys and its radio-controlled and electric race cars, bolstered Mattel's infant and preschool as well as boys' toy lines.

As the decade was coming to a close, a changing of the guard was imminent. John Amerman, who had turned Mattel away from slumping sales and mismanagement, retired as Mattel's chairman of the board after 17 years, tossing the reins to

Barad, who had been promoted to CEO earlier in the year. At the time of her appointment as chairman in 1997, Barad was one of only two women running a *Fortune* 500 company.

Never one to rest on her laurels, Barad moved forward with new Barbie innovations and aggressive expansion. International sales climbed a cautious 3 percent (in local currency), with net sales at $1.2 billion for Canada and Europe and $2.1 billion in net sales from Asia and Latin America, representing a 35 percent jump for Latin America and the emergence of a market in Japan. Stateside, sales grew by 14 percent, with Barbie bringing in $1.9 billion, especially in the burgeoning interactive market, where Barbie-brand CD-ROMs quadrupled sales to $20 million. Even the adult collector market in Barbies had reached $200 million, with new Oscar de la Renta and Vera Wang designs slated to debut. Infant and preschool toys, meanwhile, were close on Barbie's heels, bringing in $1.8 billion in net sales despite a slump in Fisher-Price. Winnie the Pooh and Sesame Street more than took up the slack, generating $175 million and $350 million, respectively. During 1998 the Fisher-Price unit was given control of Mattel's complete lines of infant and preschool toys.

In early 1998 Mattel celebrated Barbie's 39th birthday. Continuing its interactive success, a new web site was introduced (Barbie.com), as well as new dolls, including one with an official WNBA uniform. The year also marked the 30th anniversary of Hot Wheels, with booming sales, as well as the 15th anniversary of Cabbage Patch Kids dolls. Barbie remained the bigger news, however, as the centerpiece of PBS's *P.O.V.,* which dedicated an hour-long program to her evolution, entitled ''Barbie Nation: An Unauthorized Tour.'' Although the program provided publicity, its content was sometimes controversial—dealing with the good, the bad, and the ugly, including some Barbie-inspired obsessions. Ruth Handler, extensively interviewed for the piece, vehemently supported her creation.

Still on the prowl for acquisitions, Mattel in July 1998 completed a $715 million purchase of Pleasant Company, the Wisconsin-based maker and direct marketer of the popular American Girl brand composed of books, dolls, clothing, accessories, and the *American Girl* magazine. Pleasant's founder and president, Pleasant Rowland, became Mattel's vice-chairman. The company also was gaining a reputation as an excellent employer, named one of the ''100 Best Companies To Work For'' by *Forbes* magazine, and similarly lauded by *Working Mother* for the fifth consecutive year. With a state-of-the-art in-house daycare center, health and fitness facility, half-day Fridays, and generous vacation days, which included shutting down operations the week between Christmas and New Year's, the toymaker seemed to provide employees with almost as much fun as consumers.

The Learning Company Debacle and Its Aftermath: 1999 and Beyond

Although Mattel's acquisition of Pleasant Company, which brought together the world's two largest girls' toy brands—Barbie and American Girl—proved highly successful, the company's next acquisition turned into a disaster. In May 1999 Mattel took over the Learning Company in a $3.5 billion deal. Based in Cambridge, Massachusetts, the Learning Co. was a major player in computer games and educational software, producing such ''edutainment'' titles as ''Reader Rabbit'' and ''Carmen Sandiego.'' This acquisition was intended to broaden Mattel's product line and help Mattel sell more products that appeal to boys, but the Learning Co. began reporting unexpected losses before the deal was even completed. In October, Mattel announced that its earnings would fall well below expectations, prompting the departure one month later of Learning Co.'s two founders. For the year, Mattel reported a net loss of $82.4 million on sales of $5.52 billion, which reflected a $345 million charge stemming from a restructuring that involved some 3,000 job cuts as well as a fourth quarter Learning Co. loss of $183 million. The latter loss led to the abrupt resignation of Barad in February 2000, by which time Mattel's stock had plunged below $10 per share, after trading for more than $45 in 1998.

Robert A. Eckert was named chairman and CEO in May 2000. He had been the head of Philip Morris Companies Inc.'s Kraft Foods unit. In the meantime, Mattel in July 1999 had entered into a global marketing alliance with Bandai Co., Ltd., Japan's largest toy maker and best known at the time for its line of Power Rangers action figures and the Tamagotchi electronic virtual pets. Initially, the alliance involved Bandai marketing Mattel's toys in Japan and Mattel doing likewise for Bandai in Latin America. In February 2000 Mattel reached a deal with Warner Bros., making Mattel the master toy licensee for the best-selling Harry Potter book series and for the first two Harry Potter feature films. Mattel that same year gained the multiyear licensing rights to characters owned by the popular Nickelodeon children's cable television channel.

In October 2000, soon after Eckert came onboard, the Learning Co. was sold to Gores Technology Group, a corporate turnaround firm, for no cash and an unspecified share of future Learning Co. earnings. Mattel agreed to pay off $500 million in Learning Co. debt, and losses from the sale led to a net loss for 2000 of $430.9 million. The consequences of this disastrous acquisition—widely regarded as one of the biggest corporate blunders ever—were not over yet. Numerous lawsuits were filed by shareholders in 1999 and 2000 alleging mismanagement and breach of fiduciary duty by company executives and the board of directors. In November 2002 Mattel agreed to pay $122 million to settle these actions.

Eckert took a conservative approach to running Mattel, concentrating more on returning the firm to profitability than on seeking huge new blockbuster toys that would greatly increase revenues. As a result, revenues were relatively flat during his first two years at the helm (2001 and 2002), but net income figures were decent: $298.9 million and $230.1 million, respectively. Among the successes during this period were the Harry Potter products, a line of products derived from the Nickelodeon hit *Sponge Bob Square Pants,* and a line of big-eyed talking dolls called Diva Starz. As part of Eckert's strategy of expanding Mattel's core brands into additional product categories, the company in October 2001 released the first Barbie video, *Barbie in the Nutcracker,* which sold quite well. Overall, however, sales of the Barbie line were on the decline under pressure from new competitive dolls, particularly MGA Entertainment's hip Bratz dolls, which debuted in 2001. In the computer games sector, Mattel took a new partnership-oriented approach, entering into license agreements with computer games makers Vivendi Universal and T-HQ Inc. in 2001 for the development of interactive software games based on such Mattel brands as Barbie, American Girl, Hot Wheels, and Fisher-Price. On the licensing side, Mattel gave up licenses for toys based on new Disney movies, which tended to be hit-or-miss propositions, but kept the rights to established Disney characters such as Mickey and Minnie Mouse. Other early Eckert initiatives included cutting costs, speeding up toy production turnaround time, overhauling the supply chain, and placing additional emphasis on international sales.

In early 2003 Mattel streamlined its operations, consolidating its Boys/Entertainment and Girls divisions into a new business unit known as Mattel Brands. The Pleasant Company was separated from the Girls division and placed into a new unit called American Girl Brands. The firm's third unit, Fisher-Price Brands, remained unchanged. Meantime, while Mattel's doll lines were contending with the upstart Bratz dolls, Fisher-Price was under pressure from another upstart, LeapFrog Enterprises, Inc., which quickly became a leader in electronic learning toys after its founding in the mid-1990s. Fisher-Price responded in August 2003 with the launch of the PowerTouch system, through which youngsters could play—and learn—on interactive-learning books. PowerTouch competed directly with LeapFrog's popular LeapPad system, and LeapFrog was troubled enough by similarities between the two products to file a patent-infringement lawsuit against Fisher-Price in October.

Although some analysts were disappointed with the lack of revenue growth at Mattel, particularly the flat to declining sales in the United States, Eckert remained committed to improving bottom-line profits rather than the top line. International sales were growing at a double-digit percentage pace, enabling Mattel to expand its overall sales in the mid-single-digit range, which was actually a little better than the industry norm. Perhaps in the first decade of the 21st century the more measured approach of Eckert would serve Mattel better than the approaches of the leaders of the three previous decades—particularly because each of these decades included a major crisis that called into question the company's future.

Principal Subsidiaries

Fisher-Price Inc.; Mattel Factoring, Inc.; Mattel International Holdings B.V. (Netherlands); Mattel Investment, Inc.; Mattel Overseas, Inc.; Mattel Sales Corporation; Pleasant Company.

Principal Operating Units

Mattel Brands; Fisher-Price Brands; American Girl Brands.

Principal Competitors

Hasbro, Inc.; JAKKS Pacific, Inc.; LEGO Company; LeapFrog Enterprises, Inc.; Bandai Co., Ltd.; MGA Entertainment; TOMY Company, Ltd.

Further Reading

Bannon, Lisa, "New Playbook: Taking Cues from GE, Mattel's CEO Wants Toy Maker to Grow Up," *Wall Street Journal*, November 14, 2001, pp. A1+.

Bannon, Lisa, and Joann S. Lublin, "Jill Barad Abruptly Quits the Top Job at Mattel," *Wall Street Journal*, February 4, 2000, p. B1.

Beauchamp, Marc, "Barbie at 30," *Forbes*, November 14, 1988, pp. 248+.

Deutsch, Stefanie, *Barbie, The First 30 Years, 1959 Through 1989 and Beyond: Identification and Value Guide*, 2nd ed., Paducah, Ky.: Collector, 2003.

Donahue, Ann, and Nola Sarkisian-Miller, "How Mattel's Brass Ring Turned to Lead," *Los Angeles Business Journal*, February 14, 2000, p. 1.

Donlon, J.P., "A Doll's House," *Chief Executive* (U.S.), September 1997, pp. 32+.

Grant, Linda, "Mattel Gets All Dolled Up: Buying Fisher-Price Will Make the Toy Giant Less Reliant on Barbie," *U.S. News and World Report*, December 13, 1993, pp. 74+.

Handler, Elliot, *The Impossible Is Really Possible: The Story of Mattel*, New York: Newcomen Society in North America, 1968.

Handler, Ruth, with Jacqueline Shannon, *Dream Doll: The Ruth Handler Story*, Stamford, Conn.: Longmeadow Press, 1994.

Kim, Queena Sook, "Mattel's Babes in Toyland Struggle to Gain Market Share," *Wall Street Journal*, November 21, 2003, pp. C1, C3.

"Looking for a Few Good Boy Toys," *Business Week*, February 17, 1992.

Lublin, Joann S., and Lisa Bannon, "Mattel Taps Kraft Chief Robert Eckert to Succeed Jill Barad As CEO," *Wall Street Journal*, May 17, 2000, p. B1.

"Mattel Has to Play Harder Than Ever," *Business Week*, May 25, 1987.

Morgenson, Gretchen, "Barbie Does Budapest," *Forbes*, January 7, 1991, pp. 66+.

Morris, Kathleen, "The Rise of Jill Barad," *Business Week*, May 25, 1998, pp. 112+.

——, "Searching for Turnaround Barbie," *Business Week*, September 6, 1999, pp. 80, 82–83.

Palmeri, Christopher, "Mattel: Up the Hill Minus Jill," *Business Week*, April 9, 2001, pp. 53–54.

——, "Mattel's New Toy Story," *Business Week*, November 18, 2002, pp. 72, 74.

"Playing Favorites," *Marketing and Media Decisions*, March 1990.

Quirt, John, "Putting Barbie Back Together Again," *Fortune*, September 8, 1980, pp. 84+.

Stevens, Tim, "Playing to Win," *Industry Week*, November 3, 1997, pp. 18+.

"The Story of Mattel, Inc.: Fifty Years of Innovation," Newcomen Address, 1995.

—Bruce P. Montgomery
—updates: Taryn Benbow-Pfalzgraf, David E. Salamie

Medline Industries, Inc.

1 Medline Place
Mundelein, Illinois 60060
U.S.A.
Telephone: (847) 949-5500
Toll Free: (800) 633-5463
Fax: (800) 351-1512
Web site: http://www.medline.com

Private Company
Incorporated: 1966
Employees: 3,500
Sales: $1.5 billion (2003 est.)
NAIC: 339112 Surgical and Medical Instrument Manufacturing; 325412 Pharmaceutical Preparation Manufacturing; 339113 Surgical Appliance and Supplies Manufacturing

Based in Mundelein, Illinois, Medline Industries, Inc. is the largest privately held manufacturer and distributor of medical supplies and equipment in the United States. More than 500 sales representatives support its cost management services and product line of 100,000 items, 70 percent of which it manufactures at its five facilities in North America. Medline distributes products to hospitals, extended care facilities, surgery centers, hospital laundries, home care providers, and agencies from its 27 distribution centers.

The Early Years of Medline's Predecessor: 1910–61

In 1910, A.L. Mills founded Northwestern Garment Factory, a business that sold garments for meat cutters to wear in Chicago's meat packing houses. Looking for a way to expand sales for his company, Mills branched out into nurses' uniforms in 1912 and changed the name of his company to Mills Hospital Supply. In 1918, Irving Mills, then 12 years of age, joined his father's business; six years later, at age 18, Irving Mills took over as head of the company.

A.L. Mills left Chicago for his native Arkansas in 1930, leaving the business to his son and his wife, Jennie Mills. Irving Mills attended Northwestern University at night while running the family company and graduated in 1939 with a degree in business. During World War II textiles became hard to get, and industry employees stopped wearing uniforms. As a result, Mills shifted the focus of the company to concentrate on manufacturing and marketing textiles for hospitals.

In 1946, one of the company's sales representatives, working with a group of hospitals in Colorado, came up with the idea of consignment shipping. According to Jon Mills in a 2003 *Chicago Tribune* article, "You couldn't ship into Durango, Colorado in winter because the roads were dirt. So we would ship the supplies [before the winter] and then bill them the next spring or summer [for what they actually used]." Consignment shipping helped Mills Hospital Supply grow beyond its midwestern roots, and by the time Irving Mills sold the company in 1961 to Cenco Scientific, it had branches in Houston, Texas; Norfolk, Virginia; and Columbus and Toledo, Ohio.

The Early Years of Medline Industries, Inc.: 1966 to the Mid-1980s

Five years later, in 1966, Irving Mills helped his sons found Medline Industries, Inc., a hospital supply company. Jon Mills and Jim Mills became company president and chief executive, respectively. First year revenues reached $1 million. With this auspicious start, the company began evolving from a distributor to both a manufacturer *and* distributor.

Medline went public in 1972, and then, in 1977, became a private enterprise again. Over the years, as it grew its manufacturing capabilities, Medline developed a reputation for offering inexpensive products. This reputation proved something of a double-edged sword. While some hospital materials departments appreciated the fact that Medline would reveal its costs to customers, others perceived Medline's products as being substandard because of their lower price. In an effort to make the point that Medline sold high-quality goods and to increase customer familiarity with its products, Medline came out with a glitzy and unconventional catalogue in 1979. The catalogue, which cost the company $300,000 (about a third of its profits in 1978), was reminiscent of the glossy ad pages of a popular and

Company Perspectives:

Medline's primary mission is to provide quality products and cost containment solutions to health care providers while enhancing the quality of patient care.

upscale magazine and featured doctors and orderlies in uniform in such venues as a law library, jazz nightclub, disco, and Old West saloon. There was a Betsy Ross figure sewing surgical drapes and winged laparotomy sheets; a magician secured by postsurgical restraints and bindings; a young man playing tug-of-war with a white-uniformed nurse who was tugging on his sheet; and belly dancers veiled by surgical masks.

Although the approach offended some people, Medline's textile sales increased by 40 percent the following year, and it was not until 1985 that the company retired its unique catalogue. The new catalogue of that year, the size of a telephone book, featured black and white photographs except in the textiles section and focused on providing technical information about Medline products.

Medline—by then the second largest national distributor of healthcare products—had about $120 million in revenues for 1984. Although this figure represented a 225 percent increase over 1980 revenues of $53 million, the company still only generated half the profits of the nation's largest healthcare products distributor. Confident of its status with customers, however, Medline opened a 435,000-square-foot combined headquarters, distributing facility, and manufacturing plant in Mundelein, Illinois, in late 1984.

Continued Growth: Mid-1980s to Mid-1990s

Beginning in the mid-1980s, healthcare professionals began taking greater steps to protect themselves against the risks of exposure to disease, such as AIDS. This move was backed by federal and state health agencies that mandated more safety measures. The emphasis on protection spelled increased sales for Medline; so did increased concern for the environment and the increasing cost of infectious waste disposal. In January 1990, Medline formed a sterile pack division to take advantage of the growing move toward reusable prepackaged, sterile linen surgical gowns, drapes, and incontinence products.

By the early 1990s, Medline had four manufacturing facilities in the United States, an assembly plant in Mexico, and 14 distribution facilities. In 1990, it added to its capacity on the East Coast with a new 100,000-square-foot distribution facility in Allentown, Pennsylvania. In 1993, it began a five-year contract to supply Veterans' Administration hospitals. In 1995, Medline, then the largest privately owned medical supplies manufacturer, added a new 130,000-square-foot production facility for surgical and medical trays in Waukegan, Illinois. In the early 1990s, Medline also formalized its inventory consignment program under the name ACCESS. ACCESS allowed customers to have Medline-supplied products on the shelves of their warehouses, which they paid for only after using them.

The year 1996 saw some unfortunate publicity for Medline. The company's former vice-president for international sales brought suit against Medline under the False Claims Act, stating that Medline had bilked Department of Veterans Affairs by selling it foreign-made, inferior products, breaking a contract that required that it sell domestically manufactured goods to the government. Medline paid the United States $6.4 million in settlement, but the company was not deterred in its growth.

The following year, the company's leadership changed with Andy Mills, Jon Mills's son, assuming the role of president and Charlie Mills, Jim Mills's son, becoming chief executive. The company purchased land in Orlando, Florida, and soon built a 163,000-square-foot distribution center, the twin of another distribution center it had recently completed in Dallas. In 1999, in a move to expand its online presence into the physician offices marketplace, it purchased the latex exam glove business Kendall Healthcare Company (a division of Tyco International, Inc.) and began listing and selling products on Neoforma.com.

The emphasis by the end of the 20th century on cost-cutting throughout the medical industry provided further opportunities for Medline, which by 2000, was earning revenues of $1 billion. According to Mills in a 1999 *Chicago Tribune* article, "The more hospitals are squeezed to cut costs, the more receptive they are to products that can help solve their problems." In a shift to provide those products and take advantage of some of the growth opportunities technology introduced, Medline added several higher-tech items to its traditional line of low-tech goods. Rather than investing in research and development to come up with new product ideas, however, Medline tapped into its longstanding customer relationships. Most of its new offerings were in the area of advanced wound care, such as a product with controlled-release silver to fight antibiotic-resistant bacteria and a new wet-therapy dressing that both rinsed and debrided chronic wounds.

Despite attempts on the part of Wisconsin and Iowa to entice Medline to relocate to their state, the company made a firm decision to stay in Illinois and broke ground in 2000 for a $14 million, 124,000-square-foot corporate headquarters. The decision was in part the result of Illinois's "Economic Development for a Growing Economy," whereby the company received 3 percent of the income taxes its employees paid to the state.

Expansion continued at Medline's facilities as well. It purchased Sun Healthcare Group in 2000, one of the nation's largest nursing home operators, which had fallen into bankruptcy. To meet its ever growing manufacturing and distribution needs, Medline also purchased a 225,000-square-foot building in Monroeville, Alabama, for cutting and embroidery operations and warehousing. The company increased its number of employees as well, adding a call center in Dubuque and absorbing Carrington Laboratories sales reps after signing a five-year distribution licensing agreement in 2000 with Carrington that awarded it exclusive rights to sell and market Carrington's wound care and skin products.

The September 11, 2001 collapse of the World Trade Center in New York afforded Medline other opportunities for growth as well. Sales of rubber gloves, safety masks, and other protective medical clothing soared in the wake of the terrorist attack. The company went from a few calls a day to hundreds as schools, fire departments, police departments, and the everyday

Key Dates:

1910: A.L. Mills founds Northwestern Garment Factory.
1912: Mills shifts the focus of his business and changes its name to Mills Hospital Supply.
1924: Irving Mills takes over management of his father's business.
1961: Cenco Scientific buys Mills Hospital Supply.
1966: Irving Mills founds Medline with sons, Jon, who becomes president, and Jim, who becomes chief executive.
1972: Medline holds its initial public offering.
1977: Medline once again becomes a private company.
1984: The company moves from Northbrook to Mundelein, Illinois.
1997: Andy Mills, son of Jon, becomes company president; Charlie Mills, son of Jim, becomes CEO.
1999: Medline purchases Kendall Healthcare Company's latex exam glove business.
2000: The company breaks ground for a new 124,000-square-foot corporate headquarters; purchases a 225,000-square-foot building in Monroeville, Alabama; and increases its workforce.
2001: Sales of rubber gloves, safety masks, and other protective medical clothing soar in the wake of the September 11 terrorist attacks.
2002: Medline signs a distribution agreement with A & A Medical Supply; healthcare apparel business of Angelica Corporation is acquired; new distribution facilities open in Illinois, Maryland, and Texas.

consumer sought precautions against anthrax and other feared biological weapons. Medline saw a 40 percent increase in the sale of medical exam gloves between September 11th and mid-November 2001. Other ''hot'' items included high-filtration masks and a personal protection kit that included a pair of exam gloves and mask.

In 2001, Medline posted sales of $1.2 billion and opened a 276,000-square-foot distribution center in Lathrop, California. It also signed an agreement with Ascension Health, the nation's largest nonprofit healthcare network of almost 80 Roman Catholic facilities in the United States, to supply medical and surgical products and act as distributor for products it did not manufacture.

In 2002, Medline signed a distribution agreement with A & A Medical Supply to distribute Medline's line of medical and surgical products to physician offices throughout the United States, thus furthering the company's move into the physician offices marketplace. Medline also acquired the healthcare apparel business of Angelica Corporation, a business that had provided uniforms for healthcare workers since the 1800s. Despite the national economic slowdown, the company was in so strong a financial position that it self-financed the building of a 145,000-square-foot manufacturing and distribution facility in Waukegan, Illinois, a 400,000-square-foot distribution facility in Baltimore, Maryland, and a 290,000-square-foot warehouse in San Antonio, Texas. Company estimates put projected annual sales at $2 billion by the year 2005.

Principal Competitors

Allegiance; American Hospital Supply Corporation; Owens & Minor, Inc.; Tyco Healthcare.

Further Reading

Hwa-shu, Long, ''Medline on the Move: Self-Financed Expansion Projects Include New Waukegan Plant,'' *News Sun,* July 27, 2002, p. C1.

Japsen, Bruce, ''Medical Apparel Sales Jump As Firms, Public Seek Cover,'' *Chicago Tribune,* November 4, 2001, p. 2.

Morris, Steven, ''The Line on Medline: It's Making Inroads As Medical Supply Provider,'' *Chicago Tribune,* June 22, 1984, p. 1.

Van, Jon, ''Medline's High-Tech Pulse: Hospital Products Add Complexity,'' *Chicago Tribune,* December 4, 1999, p. 1.

Werner, Curt, ''White Sale: Medline Sews Up Rare Acquisition in Hospital Uniform Segment,'' *Healthcare Purchasing News,* July 2002, p. 16.

—Carrie Rothburd

Mega Bloks, Inc.

4505 Hickmore
Montreal H4T 1K4
Canada
Telephone: (514) 333-5555
Fax: (514) 333-4470
Web site: http://www.megabloks.com

Public Company
Incorporated: 1967 as Ritvik Holdings
Employees: 1,000
Sales: $188.8 million (2002)
Stock Exchanges: Toronto
Ticker Symbol: MB
NAIC: 339932 Game, Toy, and Children's Vehicle Manufacturing

Mega Bloks, Inc. is Canada's largest toy company. It is the world's second biggest manufacturer of construction toys, and one of the fastest-growing toy brands in the world. Based in Montreal, Canada, the company sells its plastic interlocking toys in more than 100 countries worldwide and has offices or manufacturing operations in 11 countries. The company's principal product is sets of plastic building blocks. It markets to two main categories: children under the age of five, and children five and older. Its toys in the preschool category are mainly large blocks that are easy for young children to hold and manipulate. The blocks designed for older children are smaller, and indeed are the same size as the blocks of Mega Bloks' key competitor, Lego. Mega Bloks successfully challenged Lego's dominance in the interlocking building blocks category, winning patent infringement cases brought against it in various courts. Although Lego is the market leader in this category, Mega Bloks showed that there was room for more. The company's sales grew precipitously in the late 1990s, and Mega Bloks, formerly Ritvik Holdings, went public in 2002. The company is run by the sons of the founders, Rita and Victor Bertrand.

Early Immersion in the Toy Industry

Victor Bertrand had his first job in the toy industry at the age of 17. He was born in 1943, and while still a teenager he worked to support his parents, going to school in the evenings. By the age of 20, Bertrand was already very knowledgeable about the toy industry, plastics, and injection molding. In 1967, he was confident enough of his ability to start his own toy distribution company. He named it Ritvik Holdings, taking the name from the combination of his first name with his wife's, Rita.

Ritvik Holdings was a distribution business, making sales in Canada for toys manufactured elsewhere. Ritvik also negotiated contracts with Canadian manufacturers to make toys for foreign brands. Ritvik Holdings grew to become a vertically integrated company. It owned plastic injection molding operations, design operations, tooling manufacturers, and marketing services. By the early 1980s, Ritvik Holdings controlled a leading share in the Canadian market for plastic injection molded toys.

At this point, Victor Bertrand set his sights on expanding the business beyond Canada. He was interested in construction block sets, and believed there was room in this market for growth. Construction sets had been toy industry staples since the early years of the 20th century. Batima Blocks came out in Belgium in 1905, and the American construction sets Tinkertoys and Lincoln Logs dated back to 1916. Erector Set, another leading brand, came on the market in 1913. These kinds of toys tended to be perennial. They appealed to a wide range of children, from early school-age kids to teenagers. The world's leading brand of construction toy was Lego. Lego was a Danish firm founded in 1932. It came out with its signature interlocking plastic bricks in the mid-1950s. By the early 1970s, Lego had sales of $50 million, and the brand was known around the world. In Canada, Lego sets were manufactured by contract with the Samsonite Corporation.

Victor Bertrand's friends apparently tried to dissuade him from making a plastic interlocking construction kit like Lego. But Bertrand thought he had two competitive advantages. One was that he aimed to make plastic bricks much like Lego, but in a jumbo size suitable for very young children. Traditional Lego bricks were too small for little children to handle, but Ritvik's Mega Bloks would be large and sturdy enough for toddlers to play with. Ritvik's second advantage was price. With Bertrand's extensive knowledge of the injection molding business, he knew he could design and manufacture plastic bricks that

Company Perspectives:

Our vision: To be the most dynamic and innovative toy company, building quality products that are expandable and universal.

retailed for less than Lego. Sure of himself despite contrary opinions from his advisors, Bertrand went ahead with his plans.

New Product Line in the 1980s

Ritvik Holdings first showed its line of Mega Bloks construction sets at trade shows in the United States and Canada in 1984. Mega Bloks caught on instantly. The company made substantial sales in Canada, and also got into the leading U.S. toy chain, Toys 'R Us, with an order worth $1 million. Mega Bloks were available at retailers across the United States and Canada in 1985.

As soon as Ritvik showed its new line in 1984, bigger toy companies came calling. Bertrand told *Canadian Business* (November 1993) that several multinational companies asked to either buy the distribution rights to Mega Bloks or to buy Ritvik Holdings outright. Bertrand told the magazine, "We've turned down some very rich proposals in various markets because we did not believe they were long-term formulas for success." Ritvik Holdings, at that point 100 percent owned by Bertrand and his family, was financially sound and did not need quick cash. Mega Bloks was not meant as an instant sensation but was the cornerstone of a long-range plan to bring the company into wider markets.

By the late 1980s, Ritvik was distributing Mega Bloks in 30 countries. Mega Bloks became popular in the United States, Canada, and Europe. The company found that consumers were very loyal to the Lego brand. But initially Mega Bloks could compete by appealing to children who were too young for the more intricate Lego sets. The company developed 30 different play sets, all designed for children under the age of six. In 1988 Ritvik also brought out some preschool toys, such as a piano with Mega Bloks keys that could be integrated into other Mega Bloks construction sets. In 1989 Ritvik Holdings divested itself of all its other toy and plastics lines. Its business was now solely centered on Mega Bloks.

Head to Head with Lego in the 1990s

Mega Bloks sold well from the start, and Ritvik was growing. Bertrand gambled on the continued success of the line by selling off the company's other toy lines in 1989. Bertrand claimed that marketing the jumbo plastic bricks was easy because they immediately impressed mothers. He told *Marketing Magazine* (September 29, 2003) that Mega Bloks had been an instant hit because "Moms identified with it immediately as being a 'wow.' " After five years of selling blocks intended for very young children, the company was ready to move on to construction sets geared for older children. In 1991 Ritvik brought out its "Micro" line of Mega Bloks. These blocks were the same size and shape as Legos, and were essentially interchangeable with the older brand's sets. Mega Bloks had so far avoided trampling on Lego's toes by pitching its toys to kids too young for the Danish company's products. But now Ritvik was offering something that looked like Lego, made for kids aged 8 to 14. Lego Canada eventually brought a suit against Ritvik for unfair competition.

Lego's Canadian operations had been contracted to Samsonite between 1961 and 1988. After that time, Lego took over manufacturing operations for itself. Lego's patent on the shape of its brick had expired, and the Canadian lawsuit hinged on the claim that Ritvik had caused confusion between its Micro Mega Bloks and Legos. The case was not decided for years, during which time sales of Mega Bloks continued to grow around the world. But the Canadian court found in favor of Ritvik, saying that the company had done what it could to distinguish its brand from its venerable competitor's. European and U.S. courts came to a similar conclusion in other cases brought by Lego.

Ritvik had great success with both its toddler lines and the smaller Micro lines of Mega Bloks throughout the 1990s. Sales grew by an average of 70 percent a year through the mid-1990s. In 1996, the company got financial backing from the New York investment firm the Blackstone Group. The Blackstone Group, founded in 1985, grew to be one of the top U.S. private investment firms. It bought a 27 percent share of Ritvik. Rita Bertrand, who had been instrumental to the company since its inception, retired in 1996, along with her daughter Chantal. Two other Bertrand children, Marc and Victor, Jr., were active in the company's management.

Worldwide Competitor in the 2000s

Ritvik pushed into more international markets in the late 1990s. It established a Latin American subsidiary, Mega Bloks Latinoamerica S.A. de C.V., in 1997. The next year it opened a European subsidiary, Mega Bloks Europe N.V., to promote sales to European retailers. During the 1990s, international sales grew to about 30 percent of revenue. Canada and the United States accounted for the remainder. Ritvik depended heavily on sales to four major chains: Toys 'R Us, Wal-Mart, Target, and Kmart. These retailers accounted for almost 60 percent of Ritvik's sales. This situation was typical of the toy industry, however, which had become increasingly consolidated in North America, both among manufacturers and retailers.

Ritvik followed some other industry trends in the late 1990s. It began licensing characters for use on its toys in 1998. Many toy companies had jumped on this bandwagon, tying their products to movies or cartoon characters. Ritvik signed licensing agreements in 1998 with *Teletubbies,* the British television show aimed at toddlers, and with toy company Fisher Price for its Sesame Street characters. Ritvik also signed stock car race drivers Jeff Gordon, Dale Earnhardt, and Mark Martin for a new Nascar-Mega Bloks product line. Ritvik also added new features to its play sets in 2000, in line with similar moves by Lego and the budding U.S. construction kit brand K'Nex. Ritvik added building sets that could transform into vehicles, and made an electronic kit with a remote control called the Mega Bloks RO Action Builder. Also in 2000, Ritvik began advertising Mega Bloks on television for the first time. The company initiated a $2 million campaign with a Cincinnati, Ohio agency that specialized in advertising children's products. By 2002, the

Key Dates:

1967: Victor Bertrand founds Ritvik Holdings.
1984: Ritvik shows Mega Bloks at trade shows.
1989: The company divests all other product lines.
1991: Mega Bloks micro line is unveiled.
1996: Blackstone Group invests in Ritvik.
2002: The company goes public as Mega Bloks, Inc.

company was spending almost $30 million annually on advertising, marketing, and research and development.

Ritvik's sales continued on a steep upward swing through the late 1990s into the 2000s. Between 1999 and 2003, sales doubled, and the company's international sales expanded to more than 35 percent of revenue. With things going so well, Ritvik decided to sell stock to the public. It held its initial public offering on the Toronto exchange in May 2002. At that time the company changed its name to Mega Bloks, Inc. Marc Bertrand became president and chief operating officer, while his brother Victor, Jr., became chief operating officer. Founder Victor Bertrand remained chairman of the board.

Mega Bloks, Inc. advanced its sales in Asia by forming a joint venture with the Japanese toy company Bandai in 2003. Bandai held licenses for a slew of Japanese cartoon characters. It agreed to market Mega Bloks sets featuring some of these characters, for sale in Japan, Hong Kong, Taiwan, and South Korea. Mega Bloks also kept up with the trend toward fantasy, stimulated by the worldwide success of J.K. Rowling's Harry Potter books and the hit *Lord of the Rings* movies. In 2003 Mega Bloks came out with a Dragons series of construction sets, with bricks colored to look like castle walls and fortresses. The sets included helmets, shields, chain mail, and axes. The company also put out huge new sets called Mega Play! Mega Play! featured jumbo-sized blocks that kids could put together to make a structure they could fit inside.

By the early 2000s, Mega Bloks was one the fastest-growing toy brands in the world, and the company held down the number two spot in the construction toy market, second to Lego. Mega Bloks did well even when industry trends worked against it. The toy market was in a downturn in 2002 and 2003, with the construction toy segment dropping in the United States by some 10 to 15 percent. Nevertheless, Mega Bloks' sales were up. It did well in international markets, but it continued to expand its grip on North America even as the toy market slumped. By 2003, the company had seen 17 straight years of growth. Mega Bloks seemed poised to continue its rise as it developed new products and moved into new markets.

Principal Subsidiaries

Mega Bloks Latinoamerica S.A. de C.V.; Mega Bloks Europe N.V.

Principal Competitors

Lego A/S; K'Nex Industries, Inc.; Mattel, Inc.

Further Reading

Delean, Paul, "Mega Bloks Builds 22% Hike in Profit," *Montreal Gazette,* October 31, 2003.
Eisenberg, Bart, "Toy Story," *Product Design & Development,* November 2001, p. 36.
"Fantasy Blocks," *DSN Retailing Today,* July 21, 2003, p. 19.
"Focus '89," *Playthings,* March 1989, p. 48.
Frazier, Mya, "WonderGroup Nabs $2M Toy Branding Contract," *Business Courier Serving Cincinnati,* May 12, 2000, p. 2.
"Japanese Toy Maker Partners with Canadian Firm to Enter Toy Block Market," *Knight Ridder/Tribune Business News,* June 9, 2003.
Kucharsky, Danny, "Mega Marketing," *Marketing Magazine,* September 29, 2003.
"Lego One Brick Short of a Case in Toronto," *Marketinglaw.co.uk,* August 28, 2002.
"Mega Bloks," *Discount Store News,* November 8, 1999, p. 48.
"Mega Bloks Expands with Added Features," *Playthings,* April 2000, p. 61.
"Ritvik Holdings Inc.," *DSN Retailing Today,* February 5, 2001, p. 51.
"Ritvik Toys Inc.," *Canadian Business,* November 1993, p. S6.
"Swiss Court Declares Lego Shape Marks Void," *Monday Business Briefing,* February 26, 2003.

—A. Woodward

Metromedia Company

1 Meadowlands Plaza
East Rutherford, New Jersey 07073
U.S.A.
Telephone: (201) 531-8000
Fax: (201) 531-2804

Private Company
Incorporated: 1955 as Metropolitan Broadcasting Corp.
Employees: 29,500
Sales: $1.45 billion (2002)
NAIC: 722110 Full-Service Restaurants; 513210 Cable Networks; 513322 Cellular and Other Wireless Telecommunications; 513310 Wired Telecommunications Carriers; 513111 Radio Networks; 513330 Telecommunications Resellers; 518111 Internet Service Providers

Founded by venture capitalist John Kluge, Metromedia Company is a private holding company for AboveNet, Inc. (formerly Metromedia Fiber Network), Metromedia International Group, Inc., and Metromedia Restaurant Group. AboveNet is a leading provider of fiber-optic network infrastructures enabling high-speed information exchange in 12 key markets along the East and West Coast corridors of the United States as well as in four key European markets. Metromedia International Group provides telecommunications, cable television, broadband networks, Internet access, and other subscriber-based voice, data, and video services to emerging markets in Eastern Europe, the former Soviet Republic, and China. Metromedia Restaurant Group owns and operates nearly a thousand restaurant franchises under the names Bennigan's, Steak and Ale, Ponderosa Steakhouse, and Bonanza Steakhouse, serving more than 160 million guests a year in the United States and abroad.

The Early Business Ventures of John Warner Kluge: 1940s–50s

Chairman John Warner Kluge was the driving force behind Metromedia's formation and growth. Kluge (which means ''smart'' in German) earned a reputation for identifying promising businesses in their infancy, a knack he has modestly attributed to luck. The independent television stations he accumulated in the 1960s and 1970s formed the nucleus of the country's fourth major broadcasting network—Rupert Murdoch's Fox holdings in the early 1980s quickly grew into a multibillion-dollar stake. But in the early 1990s, media attention focused on his apparent loss of ''the Midas touch,'' as his investments in budget steakhouses and film wallowed.

Kluge (pronounced ''Kloo-gy'') was born in Germany in 1914 and immigrated to the United States with his family in 1922. He fostered his moneymaking skills while on scholarship at Columbia University, both in the classroom and at the poker table. By the time he graduated in 1937 with an economics degree, Kluge's combination of skill and luck helped him accumulate about $7,000 in winnings. (He has since gratefully bestowed more than $100 million on his alma mater.) Upon graduation, Kluge went to work at Otten Brothers Co., a small paper company in Detroit. Within four years, he had doubled the firm's sales, earning a 30 percent share of the company as well as its presidency.

After serving in the Army during World War II, Kluge began investing his hoard, purchasing Silver Spring, Maryland's WGAY radio station in 1946 with a partner. Over the next decade, Kluge honed his business skills with a series of wide-ranging ventures. First, he was attracted to businesses with high cash food brokerage. Essentially a manufacturers' representative, he sold goods to supermarkets on a flat 3 percent commission. His brokerage eventually became the largest in the Baltimore-Washington, D.C., metropolitan area, and Kluge maintained a 25 percent interest in the highly profitable business through the early 1980s.

Another hallmark of Kluge's business strategy was his liberal use of debt. Metromedia routinely maintained a higher than average debt-to-equity ratio. Although this tactic was criticized, sometimes strongly, Kluge never got burned. He used leverage in many crafty ways, often as a means to another favorite end, tax avoidance. According to a 1984 *Forbes* article by Allan Sloan, examples of his anti-tax shuffles included ''a complicated sale-leaseback of most of the company's outdoor advertising division and the purchase of depreciating rights to 100 million of New

Key Dates:

1955: Metropolitan Broadcasting Corp. is established.
1959: Venture capitalist John Kluge and a group of investors buy Paramount Pictures' 24 percent interest in Metropolitan for $4 million.
1961: Having assumed leadership of Metropolitan Broadcasting Corp. and taken it public, Kluge renames the company Metromedia, Inc.
1984: Kluge and a group of investors take Metromedia private in a $1.6 billion deal.
1988: Kluge buys the Ponderosa Steak House chain, the first of two major acquisitions that would become Metromedia Steakhouses Inc.; Kluge also invests $78 million in Orion Picture Corp., gaining a 70 percent interest in the company by the end of the year.
1990: Kluge enters into an Eastern European cable television business venture called International Telcell; he also re-enters the outdoor advertising segment with Metromedia Technologies, the world's only computerized billboard-painting company.
1993: Metromedia Communications Corp. merges with Atlanta's Resurgens Communications Group Inc. and LDDS Communications Inc., moving the resulting company—which, in 1995, would become WorldCom Inc.—into the top tier of long-distance providers.
1999: Metromedia Fiber Network acquires San Jose, California-based AboveNet Communications.
2002: Metromedia Fiber Network files for Chapter 11 bankruptcy protection in May; John Kluge resigns from the Metromedia board of directors.
2003: Metromedia Fiber Network emerges from Chapter 11 under the new name, AboveNet, Inc.

York City buses and subway cars.'' Kluge even moved Metromedia's headquarters from New York City to Seacaucus, New Jersey, to avoid the former metropolis's high taxes.

Examples of Kluge's strong contrarian bent have cropped up throughout his career. For example, whereas other venture capitalists shunned the hotel industry in the early 1990s, Kluge sunk at least $150 million in an aging Manhattan hotel. The most significant aspect of Kluge's contrarianism was that it was more often successful than not.

A final noteworthy facet of Kluge's strategy was his passion for cost-cutting. Although he spared no expense on his own lavish lifestyle, strict on-the-job cost controls were sometimes criticized as cheap. In her captious 1988 book, *Too Old, Too Ugly and Not Deferential to Men,* Christine Craft, an anchorwoman at one of Metromedia's midwestern television stations, attributed a general lack of upkeep to corporate stinginess. Notwithstanding such criticism, Kluge's combination of strategies served him well.

The Emergence of the Metromedia Empire: 1960s to Early 1980s

The budding entrepreneur laid the foundation of what would become a billion-dollar media empire in 1959, when he and a group of investors bought Paramount Pictures' 24 percent interest in Metropolitan Broadcasting Corp. for $4 million. The company's interests included independent television stations in New York and Washington, D.C. (two of the country's leading markets), as well as four radio stations.

After assuming leadership of the company, which had been spun off from Allen B. DuMont Laboratories in 1955, Kluge took it public, retaining a 12 percent stake. At the time, Metropolitan was generating about $12.4 million in annual revenues, but its profits were practically nil.

Renamed Metromedia, Inc., in 1961, the company specialized in independent television stations, those not affiliated with one of the three national broadcasting networks. Although some observers judged several of his purchases overpriced (especially since independent television was widely construed as a dead end), the stations were bargains in comparison with their network-affiliated counterparts. Once Metromedia accumulated the FCC-mandated limit of seven television stations, Kluge started ''trading up'' to stations in ever larger and more influential markets.

But Metromedia's upward climb was not uninterrupted. The company struggled through the 1960s, when many of Kluge's ideas proved too far ahead of their time to suit shareholders and analysts. Hoping to build a multimedia empire, he bought a magazine, bus and subway poster concessions, and attempted to form a fourth television network. (His concept, in fact, came to pass in the form of Rupert Murdoch's News years that started in 1969. When, in 1971, one reporter snidely wrote that he had turned ''a helluva company into a shelluva company,'' Kluge launched a rarely suspended personal press blackout.) A mid-1970s recession took Metromedia to its 1974 nadir, when the company's stock sank to $4.25 a share. Kluge tightened cost controls and shed the magazine and other extraneous holdings.

His notoriously good luck combined with Metromedia's retrenchment to pull the company out of its slump shortly thereafter. In 1976, advertisers loosened their purse strings to the benefit of independent as well as network television stations. Metromedia's revenues grew by one-fourth that year, and its profits doubled. By 1980, the company's $450 million annual revenues were generating $55 million in profits.

Kluge the contrarian eschewed the hoopla surrounding cable television and focused instead on programming in the late 1970s and early 1980s. Although his own production efforts proved less than successful, Kluge was good at picking off top shows going into syndication. He even applied his contradictory logic to programming, employing ''counter-programming,'' instead of going head-to-head with network schedules, Metromedia stations slated something different, such as putting a sitcom against the evening news. During this period, the company acquired the rights to perennially popular syndicated shows including *All in the Family* and *M*A*S*H,* as well as such first-run syndicated programs as *Thicke of the Night* and *Too Close for Comfort.* Metromedia's success was reflected in its stock price, which skyrocketed from $4.50 in 1974 to more than $500 by 1983.

By the early 1980s, Metromedia had stations in seven of the top ten markets: New York; Washington, D.C.; Los Angeles; Boston; Houston; Minneapolis-St. Paul; and Cincinnati. His stable of stations was outranked only by network holdings. The company also held the legal limit of 14 radio stations, the Foster & Kleiser billboard company (which had 42,000 billboards by 1982), the Harlem Globetrotters exhibition basketball team, and the Ice Capades figure skating show.

Kluge and a group of investors took Metromedia private late in 1984 with a $1.6 billion deal. The leveraged buyout (LBO) team borrowed the vast majority of the money needed to pay off shareholders, pledging future cash flow and projected asset sales to retire the accumulated debt. The terms of the transaction offered public stockholders about $40 per share ($30 in cash and $10 in debt): an 80 percent premium over its normal trade. Although the deal went through, Kluge found himself in a difficult position, as he was expected to begin liquidating Metromedia's holdings in order to meet the terms of his heavy debt load. He was faced with a stagnant market, however, where low prices for his prime media properties compelled him to sit tight. With the help of famed (and later discredited) junk bond wizard Michael Milken, Kluge bought some time with a "more favorable" debt refinancing.

The Metromedia "garage sale" started in 1985, after Capital Cities Communications' acquisition of the American Broadcasting Corporation heated up the media market. The company raised $2 billion with the sale of six television stations to Rupert Murdoch and the seventh to the Hearst Corporation. In 1986, Metromedia added more than $1 billion more to its coffers with the sale of the billboard subsidiary, nine radio stations, the Globetrotters, and the Ice Capades.

Kluge's contrariety helped boost that already massive payoff by billions. Against a prevailing opinion that gauged a ten-year payoff period for car phone investments, he had guided Metromedia's expansion into cellular telephony with a $300 million investment in 1983. Writing for *Forbes* in 1990, Vicki Contavespi called it "one of Kluge's best bets." He sold most of those properties to Southwestern Bell for $1.65 billion and divested the rest for $3 billion in 1990. Within less than two years, the LBO and subsequent sell-offs transformed Kluge's 25 percent, $250 million interest in the publicly owned Metromedia into a multibillion personal fortune and made him the second richest American.

Wide-Ranging Diversification in the Late 1980s and Early 1990s

Kluge began using the proceeds of his media sell-off to amass a restaurant empire. In 1988, Metromedia bought the Ponderosa Steak House chain from Asher Edelman. Edelman had bought the 20-year-old business barely a year before, but bailed out to relieve himself of the hefty debt incurred during the LBO. Kluge then bought Dallas-based USA Cafes, operators of Bonanza steakhouses, from the founding Wyly brothers for $83 million in 1989. These two chains formed Metromedia Steakhouses Inc.

The steak segment's top two chains were very different. Ponderosa was concentrated in the Midwest and was dominated by company-owned units. Bonanza's stronghold was in the Southwest, and the chain had operated as a "pure franchiser," with only two company-owned locations. After an initial period of criticism, both from Bonanza franchisees and restaurant industry observers, several major Bonanza franchise owners converted to the Ponderosa format. There did not, however, appear to be a concerted effort to compel a wholesale changeover. Metromedia also added S&A Restaurant Corp., franchisers of the Steak and Ale and Bennigan's chains, to his stable of steak shops. These more upscale steak restaurants were operated separately from the budget chains, as S&A Corp.

Although Kluge was said to have invested more than $1 billion in the 1,000 units, they lost more than $190 million from 1989 to 1994. To top it off, by 1993 Ponderosa had slipped from number one to number two, and Bonanza dropped to sixth place in annual sales. Industry analysts blamed the problems on everything from high competition to scanty capital improvements, but no one seemed to know how to turn them around.

Kluge entered a completely different milieu in 1988, when Orion Pictures Corporation was threatened with a hostile takeover from Sumner Redstone's National Amusement Corp. Orion was then headed by Arthur Krim, who called on friend Kluge to act as a "white knight." Kluge's investment of $78 million not only staved off the threat, but also gave him a 70 percent interest in the company by the end of the year. But in spite of producing award-winning films including *Platoon, Silence of the Lambs,* and *Dances with Wolves,* Orion ran into trouble in the late 1980s. A string of "box office bombs" combined with Orion's heavy debt load ($500 million debt to $485 million in annual sales) to drive the company into bankruptcy by the end of 1991. Orion emerged from bankruptcy in 1992, but lost $250 million from 1990 to 1994.

In an effort to maintain the studio's viability, Kluge took the unusual step of merging it with Actava Group, maker of Snapper lawn mowers, and Metromedia Inc., the group's investment arm, to form Metromedia International Marketing Inc. in 1994. This company expanded into Eastern European radio with the early 1995 acquisition of stations in Moscow and Bucharest.

Notwithstanding his apparent missteps into steakhouses and moviemaking, Kluge had his fingers in other, perhaps more promising "pies" as well. In 1990, he bought into a venture called International Telcell, an Eastern European cable television business. He also re-entered the outdoor advertising segment with Metromedia Technologies, the world's only computerized billboard-painting company.

Having acquired International Telephone & Telegraph Corporation's long-distance service division in 1989, Kluge used it as the basis of a strike into the long-distance telephone industry. The September 1993 merger of Metromedia Communications Corp. with Atlanta's Resurgens Communications Group Inc. and LDDS Communications Inc. moved the resulting company into the top tier of long-distance providers, behind American Telephone & Telegraph Company, Sprint Communications Company L.P., and MCI Communications Corporation. With Kluge as chairman, the publicly held company (of which Metromedia Companies retained a significant stake) changed its name to WorldCom Inc. in mid-1995.

Some analysts speculated that Kluge would need to rid himself of the troubled restaurant and movie businesses to concentrate on the long-distance interests. But Joseph Weber of *Business Week* noted, "Metromedia's chief has often been quoted as saying he would be bored with just one business to worry about.'' There was no question that Kluge had the patience to wait out lean times; he juggled independent television stations that others derided as ''dogs'' for more than two decades before cashing in. Whether the octogenarian still had the stamina to see these projects to profitability was another question entirely.

Although Kluge retained control of Metromedia into the mid-1990s (and the company had no mandatory retirement rule), his general partner and Executive Vice-President Stuart Subotnick emerged as a likely candidate for succession. Subotnick, who was nearly three decades younger than Kluge, had been with Metromedia since 1967. Thrust into the position of chief financial officer upon his superior's untimely death, Subotnick came to the fore in the early 1980s, when Kluge made him a member of his ''office of the president'' troika. In the late 1980s he had been one of the participants in Kluge's failed LBO venture. Some sources said that he had been a chief (albeit behind-the-scenes) negotiator since the early 1980s. His status as a trusted personal tax advisor to John Kluge, as well as his survival of several upper management purges, appeared to clinch his role as successor.

Rapid Expansion for Fiber-Optics in the Late 1990s

Under increasing pressure from investors to exit the entertainment business, in mid-1997 Metromedia sold off its 2,200-title film and television library and other film assets to Metro-Goldwyn-Mayer for $573 million in cash. Throughout the remaining years of the decade, the company honed its focus on the rapid expansion of its fiber-optic division, Metromedia Fiber Network.

On the domestic front, a key area for this expansion was the Northeast corridor, where Metromedia began to develop a single fiber-optic infrastructure connecting Chicago, Philadelphia, Washington, D.C, New York, and Boston. Using state-of-the-art technology, Metromedia pioneered a new concept in network infrastructure called dedicated dark fiber infrastructure, which offered customers many advantages over the customary, leased capacity service. Indeed, many hailed dedicated dark fiber as a revolution in the broadband market: its dense, meshed network ''trunks'' gave customers the ability to increase their capacity, or bandwidth, according to business demands, without any increase in service cost. That is, with dedicated dark fiber, Metromedia could offer its customers unmetered—and virtually unlimited—bandwidth at a set cost. As such, Metromedia established itself among a new breed of fiber-optic provider, the ''carrier's carrier,'' selling its services primarily to corporate, carrier, and government customers.

To this end, in 1998 the company signed major agreements with Northeast carriers, including a $6.1 million contract with Hyperion Telecommunications and a $33.2 million contract with Internet service provider PSINet. That year Metromedia also formed a joint venture with the United Kingdom's Racal Telecom to create a fiber-optic infrastructure between the United States and Britain, and announced plans to extend its dark fiber network infrastructure to a strategic West Coast corridor including the San Francisco Bay area and Silicon Valley. Industry experts lauded Metromedia's strategy, even when the company reported continued losses for 1997, insisting that it was positioning itself well for an anticipated boom in customer demand. With the company boasting an 875 percent increase in sales—to $11.7 million—for the third quarter of 1998, these predictions appeared to be accurate.

Continuing to bolster its fiber-optics capabilities, in 1999 Metromedia Fiber Network acquired San Jose, California-based AboveNet Communications in a deal estimated to be worth $1.55 billion. AboveNet, the designer and owner of the ''AboveNet Global One-Hop Network,'' became a wholly owned subsidiary of Metromedia. Together, the companies planned to develop an unmatched optical platform for Internet connectivity in the 21st century.

On the international front, in late 1999 Metromedia announced plans to bring its dark fiber networks to 11 new European markets: Paris, Brussels, Hamburg, Dusseldorf, Munich, Berlin, Hanover, Vienna, Zurich, Geneva, and Milan. The addition of these major corporate, financial, and government hubs would bring Metromedia's infrastructure to a total of 16 key European markets—and pave the way for penetration of the entire continent.

An Inauspicious Entry into the 21st Century

Despite its strategic successes, however, trouble was brewing for Metromedia by mid-2000. Investors had become increasingly impatient with the Metromedia International Group's faltering stock price—which had plummeted 400 percent since the spring of 1998—and its less-than-transparent management practices. Under scrutiny by Lens Investment Management, a Maine-based shareholder activist firm, the company was called upon to turn over its books for inspection and sell or spin off various noncore assets, especially Snapper Inc. By November 2001, under continued pressure from investors, Metromedia International Group announced a sweeping reorganization of its senior management, including the resignation of President and CEO Stuart Subotnick, who was replaced by Carl C. Brazell, Jr. The Snapper unit was finally sold in 2003 to Simplicity Manufacturing, in a deal valued at $73 million.

The situation had turned equally sour for Metromedia Fiber Network, which entered the 21st century staggering under the weight of a massive debt and scrambling to secure a $150 million credit facility necessary to avoid a bankruptcy filing. Even after receiving a $611 million funding package led by Citicorp USA in October 2001, however, the company, which had never reached profitability, found itself filing for Chapter 11 bankruptcy protection in May 2002. Matters continued to spiral downward in 2002: in November the company alerted the Justice Department and the SEC to possible misconduct by its executives in their eastern European dealings, and in December John Kluge resigned from the company's board of directors. After 16 months in bankruptcy, Metromedia Fiber Network emerged from Chapter 11 in September 2003, having assumed the name of its subsidiary, AboveNet. It remained to be seen whether, and how, this company, and Metromedia as a whole, would regain its once prominent stature.

Principal Subsidiaries

AboveNet, Inc.; Metromedia International Group, Inc.; Metromedia Restaurant Group.

Principal Competitors

Deutsche Telekom AG; Level 3 Communications, Inc.; Outback Steakhouse, Inc.

Further Reading

Baldo, Anthony, "Orion: Is Kluge Dancing with Wolves?," *FW,* December 11, 1990, p. 14.

Benjamin, Jeff, "Metromedia Under the Lens," *Investment News,* November 6, 2000, p. 45.

Benjamin, Matthew, "Metromedia Fiber Network Inc.," *Investor's Business Daily,* December 29, 1998.

Bernstein, Charles, "Conglomerate Menace Stalks Chains," *Nation's Restaurant News,* August 14, 1989, p. 3F.

"Billion-Dollars-Plus Buyback at Metromedia," *Broadcasting,* December 12, 1983, p. 2.

Brooks, Steve, "Round Up: Can an East Coast Billionaire Corral a Herd of Restaurants into One Rugged Team?," *Restaurant Business,* October 10, 1992, p. 86.

Carlino, Bill, "Ponderosa Ropes Bonanza," *Nation's Restaurant News,* September 11, 1989, p. 1.

——, "Wild Ride May Not Be Over for Metromedia and Its Steak Chains," *Nation's Restaurant News,* February 25, 1991, p. 8.

Cecil, Mark, "Will Metromedia 'Snap' Out of It?," *Mergers and Acquisitions Report,* June 12, 2000.

Cohen, Laurie P., "The Man with the Midas Touch Meets His Match in the Nation's Steakhouses," *Wall Street Journal,* January 3, 1994, p. 9.

Colodny, Mark M., "Jack Kluge's Other Divorce," *Fortune,* June 4, 1990, p. 265.

Contavespi, Vicki, "Tips from Winners in the Game of Wealth," *Forbes,* October 22, 1990, p. 32.

Craft, Christine, *Too Old, Too Ugly, and Not Deferential to Men,* Prima Publishing & Communications, 1988.

Denitto, Emily, "Investors Access Rising Stock of Growing Fiber-Optic Company," *Crain's New York Business,* March 30, 1998, p. 4.

Heuton, Cheryl, "Kluge's Return to Radio," *MEDIAWEEK,* April 3, 1995, p. 14.

Lazaroff, Leon, "Desperate Metromedia Caves in to Bondholders," *Daily Deal,* August 29, 2001.

——, "Metromedia Sinking Again," *Daily Deal,* March 18, 2002.

"Metromedia on a Roller Coaster," *Newsweek,* August 22, 1983, p. 48.

Noer, Michael, "Stu Is Running the Show," *Forbes,* October 24, 1994, p. 284.

Reed, Julia, "The Billionaire Who Just Won't Quit," *U.S. News & World Report,* June 28, 1988, p. 41.

Romero, Simon, "Metromedia Fiber Files for Bankruptcy," *New York Times,* May 21, 2002, p. C2.

Rudnitsky, Howard, "The Play's the Thing," *Forbes,* June 8, 1981, p. 71.

Sloan, Allan, "The Magician," *Forbes,* April 23, 1984, p. 32.

——, "Metromedia Revisited," *Forbes,* December 17, 1984, p. 32.

——, "Two Paths Diverged: Warren Buffett and John Kluge Investment Activities," *Forbes,* June 3, 1985, p. 40.

Sherman, Strat, "Why Metromedia's Stock Went from $4.25 to $175," *Fortune,* April 5, 1982, p. 96.

Weber, Joseph, "The Millstones at Metromedia," *Business Week,* March 1, 1993, p. 68.

—April Dougal Gasbarre
—update: Erin Brown

Mitsubishi Estate Company, Limited

Otemachi Building
6-1, Otemachi 1-chome
Chiyoda-ku, Tokyo 100-8133
Japan
Telephone: (03) 3287-5100
Fax: (03) 3212-3757
Web site: http://www.mec.co.jp

Public Company
Incorporated: 1937
Sales: $4.76 billion (2002)
Stock Exchanges: Tokyo Osaka Nagoya Kyoto Hiroshima Fukuoka Sapporo Niigata
NAIC: 531110 Lessors of Residential Buildings and Dwellings; 531120 Lessors of Nonresidential Buildings (Except Miniwarehouses); 531190 Lessors of Other Real Estate Property; 531210 Offices of Real Estate Agents and Brokers; 531320 Offices of Real Estate Appraisers; 531311 Residential Property Managers; 531312 Nonresidential Property Managers; 233320 Commercial and Institutional Building Construction

A unit of the Mitsubishi Group, Mitsubishi Estate Company, Limited (MEC) is one of the foremost real estate management, leasing, sales, and development firms in Japan. MEC is the largest holder of office space in Tokyo, much of it centered in the Marunouchi district. The company has undertaken urban development programs in Tokyo and residential projects throughout Japan and has pursued real estate investments internationally. MEC constructs and owns a vast array of real estate, including office buildings, shopping centers, golf courses, hotels, and residential projects. It also offers architectural and civil engineering services as well as a real estate brokerage.

Building a Modern Tokyo: Late 1800s–Early 1900s

Although MEC was incorporated in 1937, its history of operations began in 1890. In March of that year, during the Meiji era, the Mitsubishi *zaibatsu* acquired 353,000 square meters of land owned by the Department of War at Marunouchi, Tokyo. Investing in land was seen as an innovative move for a company that up to that time was concerned primarily with shipping. Of the ¥2.4 million the company invested in the late 1880s and early 1890s, almost ¥2 million was spent on land in Tokyo.

The most notable purchase, the Marunouchi district, was a vast area that consisted of a grass plain and military drill field running from the moat outside the Imperial Palace east toward the merchants' district. It also contained military barracks and some government offices. In the late 1880s the army decided to sell the land. Yanosuke Iwasaki, then leader of Mitsubishi and younger brother of Mitsubishi's founder Yataro Iwasaki, was strongly urged to buy the land by two of his managers who had recently spent time in London. They envisioned building a modern office center in Tokyo for Mitsubishi, similar to those they had seen in England. The company was abetted in this aim by the government, which wanted to sell the Marunouchi land to a single buyer, making the price prohibitive for many. Mitsubishi was able to acquire the property in March 1890 for ¥1.28 million.

Construction planning for the office center began soon after the purchase in the Marunouchi district. Marunouchi Design Office of Mitsubishi Company, the predecessor of today's architectural division of Mitsubishi Estate, was founded that same year. In 1892, Mitsubishi began construction on Marunouchi's modern, Western-style, red brick business avenue, still the heart of Mitsubishi operations. After the development was completed, the government agreed to locate Tokyo's central railroad in the district, placing Mitsubishi squarely at the core of the Tokyo business district.

In 1893, Yanosuke Iwasaki initiated a reorganization of Mitsubishi in line with its diversification from shipping, changing its name to Mitsubishi Goshi Kaisha, Ltd. One year later, Mitsubishi's first building at Marunouchi was completed. It was Japan's first office rental building. Also in 1894, the office building division established its first office. By this time, real estate constituted 38.8 percent of Mitsubishi's company assets. In 1895, Mitsubishi's second building was completed. Building number three, finished in 1896, housed the head office of Nippon Yusen Kaisha (NYK), a leading shipping enterprise,

Company Perspectives:

We will strive to create a truly meaningful society through the development of a secure, safe, comfortable, and appealing urban environment in each of our locations, acting as representatives of the people who live, work, and seek leisure there.

created through the merger of Mitsubishi Shokai and its leading competitor, Kyodo Unyu Kaisha (Cooperative Transport Company), in 1885.

Mitsubishi set up its first real estate section in 1906. The company's accelerated growth began about 1917 when business divisions were incorporated and Mitsubishi Goshi Kaisha began to act as holding company and controller. The company continued to build in the Marunouchi district through World War I and the depression of the 1920s while pursuing its activities in mining, shipping, and trading. The Marunouchi Building was completed in 1923. In 1929, the Marunouchi Garage Building, the first parking structure in Japan, was completed. Mitsubishi's real estate and architectural design and supervision activities were consolidated when Mitsubishi Estate Company, Limited was established on May 7, 1937.

Continued Growth and International Expansion: Mid-1900s

After World War II the four largest *zaibatsu,* including Mitsubishi, held almost one-third of the paid-in capital in heavy industry in Japan. During the postwar occupation, the *zaibatsu* were disbanded under American-style antimonopoly laws. Mitsubishi was divided into 139 independent companies. These strictures were eased by 1950, and MEC reestablished ties with other Mitsubishi firms by 1954. Group cohesiveness was further strengthened in 1970 when Mitsubishi Development Corporation was formed. Its primary mission was to undertake long-term housing, city and regional development plans for which no single member of the group had the resources. It was capitalized by 33 group companies. The company's president was also president of Mitsubishi Corporation and its chairman, the chairman of MEC.

MEC's influence in Japan and its longstanding ties with government were demonstrated in the mid-1950s. The governor of Tokyo, Seiichiro Yasui, asked Minoru Higuchi, retired president of MEC, for his advice on easing congestion in Tokyo's business district. Higuchi recommended that the governor allow private industry to build a roadway over income-producing properties, which would help pay for its construction and maintenance. Higuchi and 38 prominent members of the business community contributed $333,000 and formed the Tokyo Express Highway Co., Ltd. Higuchi was elected president. Construction of the seven-eighths of a mile roadway began April 1, 1953. Eventually the roadway ran from the financial district to the Ginza.

In 1959, the office building division set up the Marunouchi Reconstruction Program, a plan for the renewal of the Marunouchi district, often referred to as Mitsubishi Village due to the concentration of Mitsubishi firms headquartered there. Under the program, the Marunouchi Park Center was established in 1960, and a number of new buildings were built between 1965 and 1973. This renewal process continues. Through the 1980s, rents from these and other buildings in Tokyo accounted for about 70 percent of MEC's income.

In the 1960s, while MEC was rapidly increasing its holdings in Japan, it also began expanding overseas. Since 1962 MEC has invested in real estate operations in Houston, Atlanta, Detroit, Florida, Oregon, and New York in the United States and in London, England. By the 1970s, MEC began to establish local affiliates. In 1971 MEC founded MEC Hawaii Corporation. In 1972, the company established Mitsubishi Estate New York Inc. Also in 1972, MEC and Morgan Stanley & Co., an investment banking firm, formed Morgan Mitsubishi Development, a New York-based partnership to develop real estate in the United States. MEC USA, Inc. followed in 1983, and in 1984 MEC built the Pacwest Center Building in Portland, Oregon. In 1985, MEC acquired Atlas House in London and established MEC UK Ltd. in 1986. Until the late 1980s, however, MEC's presence in the United States was comparatively small, standing at $24 million in September 1983.

MEC has been active in residential development since the 1970s, with developments in the Sapporo, Sendai, Tokyo, Yokohama, Osaka, and Hiroshima areas. Its Izumi Park Town in Miyagi-ken, the largest private-sector development project in Japan, contains 12,000 homes on 1,030 hectares with a population estimated at 48,000. Construction on the first stage of this project began in 1972. By 1983 revenues from house sales accounted for 20 percent of MEC's income. In 1988, MEC began construction of the Park Town Tamagawa condominium project in Tokyo.

Diversification in the 1980s–Early 1990s

In 1983 MEC diversified into the hotel business by opening the Nagoya Dai-ichi Hotel. Three years later, it opened the Atsugi Royal Park Hotel near Tokyo and then ventured into resort operations, opening the resort park Hotel Onikobe in 1987. In 1989, MEC and an affiliated company opened the Royal Park Hotel adjoining the Tokyo City Air Terminal. The company also operated ski slopes, hotels, and resort villas on the Onikobe Highlands and golf courses at the foot of Mount Fuji. The resort park Izu Atagawa's country houses, under development in 1990, were equipped with hot springs.

In the 1980s land prices skyrocketed in Tokyo and other major cities in Japan. Between 1986 and 1988 alone, speculation in real estate helped double the price of Tokyo property. MEC's holdings similarly increased in value. In terms of assets, MEC was the largest real estate firm in Japan. By the end of the 1980s, under the direction of leaders like Chairman Otakazu Nakada, in office through 1987, President Tatsuji Ito, in office through 1988, and his successor, Jotaro Takagi, MEC became a world competitor.

Beginning in 1987, MEC worked jointly with local developers to build 2,500 homes outside Los Angeles. In 1988 MEC began construction of the 53-story 777 Tower in Los Angeles and expanded residential and resort facilities in Palm Desert, California.

Key Dates:

1890: Mitsubishi acquires land in the Marunouchi district of Tokyo.
1892: Mitsubishi starts construction in the Marunouchi district.
1906: Mitsubishi establishes its first real estate unit.
1937: Mitsubishi Estate Company, Limited is founded.
1970: Mitsubishi Development Corporation is established.
1971: Mitsubishi Estate Company founds MEC Hawaii Corporation.
1972: The company sets up Mitsubishi Estate New York Inc. and forms Morgan Mitsubishi Development with Morgan Stanley & Co.
1983: MEC USA, Inc. is formed, and Nagoya Dai-ichi Hotel opens.
1986: Mitsubishi Estate Company establishes MEC UK Ltd.
1989: The company buys a controlling interest in the Rockefeller Group.
1995: MEC gives up its stake in Rockefeller Center.
1996: The company posts a net loss for the first time in its history.
2002: The Marunouchi Building is completed.

In 1989 MEC made a major acquisition, a controlling interest in the Rockefeller Group Inc. (RGI), owner and manager of 14 buildings in New York City, including Rockefeller Center, Radio City Music Hall, the General Electric—formerly the RCA—Building, and the Warner Communications Building. The financial arrangements were complex. MEC's price of $846 million in cash bought 51 percent of the group, or 627,000 shares of Rockefeller common stock held by trusts established by John D. Rockefeller in 1934. In 1985, the RGI had sold a mortgage on Rockefeller Center to a real estate investment trust, Rockefeller Center Properties, Inc. The trust's holdings could be converted at its option to a 71.5 percent interest in the group in the year 2000, which would leave MEC with 51 percent of the remaining 28.5 percent of the group. MEC considered the investment a long-term proposition, and acquired an additional 6.6 percent stake for $110 million in July 1990.

The sale set off considerable controversy. It followed pleas by the Japanese government and leading business organizations for companies to refrain from purchasing highly visible properties in the United States, for fear of public resentment. For MEC, the purchase placed it in the forefront of Japanese real estate investors overseas.

In 1990, MEC celebrated its 100th anniversary, as well as the 14th consecutive year of significant growth in both revenue from operations and net income. Full occupancy in its buildings contributed to a 14.8 percent increase in revenue over 1989. The office building division contributed 55.1 percent of MEC's total revenue.

In February 1990, MEC participated in the redevelopment of Paternoster Square next to St. Paul's Cathedral in London in partnership with U.S. and British developers. In March 1990, construction began on what would be Japan's tallest building, the 70-story Landmark Tower, in the Block 25 district at the Minato Mirai 21 development in Yokohama, Japan's largest port and second largest city. MEC planned to open an international hotel on the upper floors of Landmark Tower by the spring of 1993. MEC was the largest private-sector landowner to participate in the redevelopment of Yokohama's coastal region.

Hard Times and Financial Woes: Mid 1990s–Early 2000s

Rapid construction continued in the mid-1990s. In 1993 Akasaka Park Building and Yokohama's Landmark Tower were completed. The following year marked the completion of Hamamatsu Act Tower, and the Osaka Amenity Park (OAP) began operations in early 1996. MEC announced plans to rebuild the historic Marunouchi Building in 1995.

Although MEC continued to expand, it faced major growing pains, the worst from its stake in the Rockefeller Center. After acquiring a majority interest in the building, the New York property market fell, which led to the lowering of commercial rents and a decline in property values. The difference between MEC's mortgage payments and its rental income grew to a staggering $460 million by late 1994. In May 1995 MEC's losses had climbed to $600 million. Unable to make its mortgage payments, MEC filed for bankruptcy protection. The company's initial hope was that it would be allowed to renegotiate terms for its $1.3 billion loan. In September, however, MEC gave up its ownership to Rockefeller Center Properties, the real estate investment trust, which then made a $250 million deal with an investment group that included real estate executive Sam Zell, Merrill Lynch & Co., Walt Disney Company, General Electric Company, and later Goldman, Sachs & Co.

For the fiscal year ended March 31, 1996, for the first time in its history MEC reported an annual loss: ¥99.5 billion ($934 million). The company took a special charge because of its investment in the Rockefeller Center, and that reduced MEC's earnings by some $1.4 billion.

Despite the Rockefeller Center fiasco, MEC maintained confidence in its RGI unit, and in February 1997 MEC made RGI a wholly owned subsidiary by acquiring the remaining 20 percent interest. RGI owned New York City's Time & Life Building as well as a 55 percent stake in the McGraw-Hill Building.

MEC faced another crisis in late 1997 when the company was raided by the police and accused of making illegal payments to a corporate racketeer. The racketeer in question was what is known as a ''*sokaiya,*'' someone who purchases a certain number of shares in a company and then threatens to shame the company and its executives by attending shareholder meetings and making a scene. Corporate executives often pay off the *sokaiya* in order to avoid embarrassment. Although such payoffs had been made illegal since the early 1980s, the practice continued. Two MEC executives were arrested, and Chairman Jotaro Takagi, who had been chairman since 1994, resigned.

In 1998 MEC restructured its overseas subsidiaries. In the United States the company made MEC U.S.A. Inc. a subsidiary of RGI. The strategy appeared to work, as MEC reported an increase in its group pretax profit for the fiscal year ended

March 31, 1999. Its pretax profit was helped greatly by a strong performance by RGI. MEC's sales increased 3 percent to ¥565.26 billion, up from ¥548.73 billion the previous year.

In the domestic condominium market MEC had in the past concentrated on low-rise units of about three or four stories. Heading into the 21st century, however, MEC said it would change its focus to high-rise condominiums. The company hoped to cash in on the rising demand for condominiums in the metropolitan Tokyo area and planned to triple the number of units offered in the early 2000s. By the end of March 2001 MEC had about 2,400 condominiums on the market, the highest number the company had ever offered.

MEC also planned to expand aggressively in the hope of increasing group operating profit by 55 percent between 2002 and 2005. To reach that goal, however, MEC had to reorganize and clean up some past decisions. For the fiscal year ended March 31, 2002, MEC took a special loss of ¥176.8 billion to reflect declining property values and inventory losses. This resulted in a net loss of ¥71.06 billion ($572 million). During the previous fiscal year, MEC reported a net profit of ¥19.8 billion. Despite the loss, MEC believed it was poised to return to profitability by the following fiscal year.

The rebuilding of the Marunouchi Building that began in April 1999 was completed in September 2002 with much fanfare. The 37-story building housed numerous restaurants, offices, and shops and proved to be a winner for MEC. Sales from the Marunouchi Building were better than anticipated, contributing some ¥6 billion to MEC's revenues for the fiscal year ended March 31, 2003. MEC managed to report a net income of ¥36.04 billion that year with sales of ¥681.73 billion. The company's strategy of building more condominiums also had paid off, and its housing development sector saw sales rise 15.4 percent.

MEC suffered through some difficult times in the 1990s, but it proved it was a survivor. Determined to continue its success well into the 21st century, the company planned to continue expansion while shedding unprofitable properties. MEC also planned to listen to consumer demand and to perhaps take more risks—its innovative Marunouchi Building was more successful and popular than expected. Shigeru Takagi, president of MEC since 2001, believed an open mind was just what MEC needed and told *Nikkei Weekly,* "Discarding this idea that we are 'king of the hill' and rekindling 'the mind of a developer' are absolutely essential."

Principal Subsidiaries

Marunouchi Direct Access Limited; Jyoni Shoji Co., Ltd.; IMS Co., Ltd.; Aqua City Co., Ltd.; Yokohama Sky Building Co., Ltd.; Keiyo Tochi Kaihatsu Co., Ltd.; Tokyo Kotsu Kaikan Co., Ltd.; Chelsea Japan Co., Ltd.; Act City Corporation; Mitsubishi Estate Building Management Co., Ltd.; Ryoei Building Management Co., Ltd.; MEC Building Management Co., Ltd.; MEC Building Facilities Co., Ltd.; Marunouchi Tatemono Kanri Co., Ltd.; Chiyoda Tatemono Kanri Co., Ltd.; Hokuryo City Service Co., Ltd.; Hibiya City Co., Ltd.; Yuden Building Kanri Co., Ltd; O.A.P. Management Co., Ltd.; Marunouchi Parking Co., Ltd.; Grand Parking Center Co., Ltd.; Hibiya City Parking Co., Ltd.; Tokyo Garage Co., Ltd.; Marunouchi Heat Supply Co., Ltd.; O.A.P.D.H.C. Supply Co., Ltd.; Minato Mirai 21 D.H.C. Co., Ltd.; Mitsubishi Jisho Sekkei Inc.; MEC Design International Corporation; Ascott International Management Japan Co., Ltd.; Royal Park Hotels and Resorts Co., Ltd.; Ryoei Kanko Development Co., Ltd.; Royal Park Inn Nagoya Co., Ltd.; Tohoku Royal Park Hotel Co., Ltd.; Yokohama Royal Park Hotel Co., Ltd.; Royal Park Hotel Co., Ltd.; Okayama International Hotel Co., Ltd.; Higashinihon Kaihatsu Co., Ltd.; MEC Urban Resort Tohoku Co., Ltd.; Liv Sports Co., Ltd.; Kume Country Club, Co., Ltd.; Fuji International Speedway Co., Ltd.; Mitsubishi Estate Home Co., Ltd.; Mitsubishi Estate Housing Component Co., Ltd.; Kanto Gang-Nail Truss Co., Ltd.; Mitsubishi Jisho Investment Advisors, Inc.; Japan Real Estate Asset Management Co., Ltd.; Rockefeller Group, Inc.; MEC Finance Co., Ltd.; MEC Information Development Co., Ltd.; MEC Human Resources, Inc.; Tsunagu Network Communications, Inc.; Super Regional, Inc.; Ryoei Life Service Co., Ltd.; Mitsubishi Real Estate Services Co., Ltd.; Otaru Toshi Kaihatsu Kosha Co., Ltd.; Izumi Park Town Service Co., Ltd.; Daiya Community Co., Ltd.

Principal Competitors

Daikyo Incorporated; Mitsui Fudosan Co., Ltd.; Tokyu Corporation; Sumitomo Realty & Development Co. Ltd.

Further Reading

Cole, Robert J., "Japanese Buy New York Cachet with Deal for Rockefeller Center," *New York Times,* October 31, 1989.

Halverson, Guy, "Japan's Investments in U.S. Lose Jewel-Like Lustre," *Christian Science Monitor,* May 15, 1995, p. 3.

Kennard, Mary, "The Beginning of a Marunouchi Renaissance," *Daily Yomiuri,* September 12, 2002, p. 17.

"Mighty Mitsubishi," *Business Week,* September 24, 1990.

"Mitsubishi Estate Gets Dose of Fresh Thinking," *Nikkei Weekly,* November 25, 2002.

Pitman, Joanna, "Mitsubishi Shaken to Its Foundations," *Times,* November 25, 1994.

Rubenfein, Elisabeth, "Investor in Rockefeller Center Took Risk," *Wall Street Journal,* November 1, 1989.

Usborne, David, "Mitsubishi Misfortune Signals End of Great Japanese Spree," *Independent—London,* May 15, 1995, p. 29.

—Lynn M. Kalanik
—update: Mariko Fujinaka

Molinos Río de la Plata S.A.

Uruguay 4075 (B1644HKG)
Victoria, Buenos Aires
Argentina
Telephone: (54) (11) 4340-1100
Fax: (54) (11) 4340-1413
Web site: http://www.molinos.com.ar

Public Company
Incorporated: 1931
Employees: 2,150
Sales: 2.01 billion pesos ($601.8 million) (2002)
Stock Exchanges: Buenos Aires; OTC
Ticker Symbols: MOLI; MOPL F
NAIC: 311211 Flour Milling; 311212 Rice Milling; 311222 Soybean Processing; 311223 Other Soilseed Processing; 311225 Fats and Oils Refining and Blending; 311411 Frozen Fruit, Juice and Vegetable Processing; 311423 Dried and Dehydrated Food Manufacturing; 311611 Animal (Except Poultry) Slaughtering; 311612 Meat Processed from Carcasses; 311615 Poultry Processing; 311822 Flour Mixes and Dough Manufacturing from Purchased Flour; 311823 Pasta Manufacturing; 311920 Coffee and Tea Manufacturing; 311941 Mayonnaise, Dressing and Other Prepared Sauce Manufacturing

Now a century old, Molinos Río de la Plata S.A. is one of Argentina's largest food companies. Its products have long been staples in Argentine household kitchens, and it is the market leader for a number of food products, including flour, cooking oils, pasta, and sausages. It is also the leading Argentine exporter of branded food products, with a presence in 45 countries worldwide. Molinos leads the world in the manufacture of sunflower oil and is the leading exporter of refined and bottled sunflower oil.

Undisputed Argentine Food Products Leader: 1902–79

Molinos Río de la Plata was, until the very last years of the 20th century, the most important Argentine holding of the Bunge multinational business empire. This enterprise was established in Amsterdam in 1818 as Bunge & Cia. and moved its headquarters to Antwerp in 1850. The firm imported tropical products from Africa and southeast Asia. The Argentine branch of this enterprise had its origins in 1876, when Ernesto Bunge moved there from Belgium. Four years later he founded a bank whose objective was to finance Argentine wheat farmers who would sell their harvests to the firm for export to Europe. Jorge Born, Ernesto's brother-in-law, soon joined him, and Ernesto Bunge y Jorge Born S.A. was founded in 1884. This firm and two other foreign-owned ones controlled 80 percent of Argentina's wheat exports in 1910.

Bunge & Born exported the wheat to Belgium for processing until 1897, when it established its first flour mill in Argentina. The second was founded in 1902, the year a presidential decree gave the firm the exclusive right to build a mill and grain elevator in the port of Buenos Aires. A Belgian-chartered company, Río de la Plata Flour Mills and Grain Elevators, was established that year to store and mill the grain in the port. (It was incorporated in Argentina under its present name in 1931.) The company grew rapidly. In 1910 it acquired three of the biggest flour mills in Argentina and installed others in Brazil and Uruguay. A former employee told a congressional investigatory commission in 1919 that Molinos paid high prices for wheat and sold the flour cheap in order to ruin local millers. Profits rose from 173,223 gold pesos in 1909 to 2.17 million in 1917.

Molinos started to mill Argentina's cotton crop for cottonseed oils in 1925 and soon added sunflower, peanut, and flax oils, contributing to the development of northern Argentina. In 1940 it produced tung oil for the first time anywhere in the world at a plant in Puerto Vilelas, Chaco. By then it had added a rice mill (1933) in Tucumán and one for olive oil (1936) in Mendoza.

Jorge Born was in charge of Bunge & Born's Argentine operations until his death in 1920. Ernesto Bunge succeeded him, serving until 1927, when he returned to Belgium. Under Alfredo Hirsch, who succeeded Bunge and served as Bunge & Born's president until his death in 1956, Molinos's array of products came to include pasta and yerba maté tea (1942), enriched feed for cattle and fowl (1951, at Mendoza), vitamin-fortified semolina flour (1955, at Labouleye, Córdoba), self-rising flour (1956, Buenos Aires), cake premixes (1959, Buenos

Company Perspectives:

Molinos Río de la Plata is a consumer-focused company based on three main pillars: leadership by continuous improvement in costs and productivity; brand leadership by innovation and quality; and leadership by excellence in performance.

The key to our Company's success is the undertaking, identification and loyalty to our values and principles.

Aires). Margarine (1960, at Avellanada, Buenos Aires), soybean oil (1962, Puerto Vilelas), and hydrogenated fishmeal (1966, Mar de la Plata, Buenos Aires), followed in the next decade. Mayonnaise and other sauces were added by a 1968 acquisition.

With 27 factories and 4,600 workers in 1968, Molinos was undisputedly the biggest food company in Argentina, its flours and oils meeting one-quarter of the nation's consumption. It was completing the largest grain elevator in South America that year in Buenos Aires. Subsidiaries marketed its products in Brazil, Uruguay, and Peru, while another Bunge & Born company still exported as much as one-third of Argentina's grain harvest to Europe. Eight years later, Molinos still accounted for 23 percent of all cooking oils sold in Argentina; 21 percent of all flour; 20 percent of all rice; 19 percent of all yerba maté tea; and 15 percent of all enriched cattle feed.

Bunge & Born was the largest private enterprise in Argentina as late as 1974, when Jorge Born III and his brother Juan were kidnaped by leftist urban guerrillas. Jorge was freed two months later but Juan was held for almost a year, until the firm met their demand of $60 million in ransom, distributing of food and clothing to the nation's most needy, the publication of a manifesto in major world newspapers, and the placement of busts of Juan and Eva Perón in all buildings of the group. In the wake of this incident Jorge Born II, who had succeeded Hirsch as president of the firm, decided to leave Argentina, moving company headquarters to Brazil. But as late as 1979—following acquisition of Matarazzo, S.A. the previous year, thereby adding pasta to the company's range of products—Molinos was the ninth largest company in Argentina, its sales accounting for 40 percent of Bunge & Born's Argentine total.

Growing Competition in the 1980s and 1990s

Beginning in the 1980s, food companies—both national and international—began to provide growing competition for Molinos, modernizing their existing plants and building new ones to augment their productive capacity. Liberalized trade laws now allowed foreign flour, pasta, and oils—previously denied admission—to be exported to Argentina. Although the company's commodities—its raw materials—still accounted for 40 percent of its sales and 72 percent of its exports in 1997, these were giving ground to new lines of added-value products. Between 1992 and 1997 Molinos invested $210 million in productive capacity while reducing employment from 6,000 to 4,300. Annual revenues rose from $765 million to $1.26 billion in this period, and the company's participation abroad grew from 17 to 43 countries.

Molinos extended its range to meat products in 1990, when it acquired the Frigorifico Tres Cruces slaughterhouse. That year the company added regular and stuffed fresh pasta, pizza breads, and pie and pastry shells under the Matarazzo brand name. Matarazzo frozen ready-to-eat pasta dishes and pizza were introduced in 1995, the year Molinos acquired Pindapoy, importer of refrigerated fruit juices from Brazil. In 1997 the company entered the frozen food market by acquiring the Granja del Sol lines of hamburgers, breaded chicken, vegetables, and fish.

Some 250 products were introduced to the market by Molinos during the early and mid-1990s, and by the end of 1997 Molinos enjoyed 40 percent of the national market for frozen foods. Conversely, in that year the company withdrew from soybeans, even though it had become Argentina's main farm export and accounted for $150 million of Molinos's annual exports. The judgment was that the company could make a much larger profit by devoting its soybean-processing facilities to the production of bottled sunflower oil. At the same time Molinos decided that its 26 categories of products should be placed into four groups—flours, oils, dry foods, and refrigerated and frozen products—in the interests of assuring greater efficiency and profit. The company was seeking to raise its average profit margin from about 3 percent to 5 percent, which was about the industry average. In 1998 Molinos began marketing ready-to-eat bakery products under the Exquisita Bakery name.

By 1999 traditional commodities accounted for less than 20 percent of company revenues, compared to 47 percent in 1996. Exports accounted for 43 percent of total revenue in 1997, nearly triple the level in 1993. The year 1998 was not a good one, however, for Molinos. Following five consecutive years of profits, the company lost almost $40 million as a result of increased competition, falling prices for its commodities, and recessions in Russia and Brazil, two of its largest export markets. At the beginning of 1999 Bunge International sold its controlling interest in Molinos Río de la Plata to the Pérez Companc family, whose holding company had been previously concentrated in the energy sector. Through a company based in the Cayman Islands, Pérez Companc paid almost $400 million to purchase 60 percent of Molinos. The purchaser also assumed $364 million in debt, of which about $200 million was long-term, in the form of bonds and other loan instruments. In 2001 an affiliate of this company owned 40 percent of Molinos' common stock; J. Gregorio Pérez Companc, now head of Molinos and believed to be the richest man in Argentina, owned another 24 percent.

Molinos in the 21st Century

Competition continued to challenge Molinos' effort in the following years to increase market share and profit margins. The growth of supermarket chains made it easier for these powerful retailers to pick and choose among their suppliers and to buy cheaper products from Molinos' competitors abroad, or even to issue their own private-label food products. Responding in 1999 to changing conditions, Molinos formed a strategic alliance with Cargill S.A.C.I. in the industrial flour market, taking 35 percent of the subsequent joint venture, Trigalia, S.A., and acquired Cargill pasta and household-flour brands. The company closed its deficit-ridden subsidiaries in Chile and

Key Dates:

1902: Molinos wins the right to erect the first grain mill and elevator in Buenos Aires.
1925: The company's mills begin producing a variety of vegetable cooking oils.
1951: Rice, pasta, and enriched cattle feed have been added to Molinos's products by this time.
1968: Molinos Río de la Plata has 27 factories and 4,600 employees.
1979: Molinos has added pasta and is Argentina's ninth largest company in terms of sales volume.
1990: Molinos adds prepared meats to its product line.
1997: The company adds frozen foods by acquiring the Granja del Sol line.
1999: The Pérez Companc Family Group buys the majority stake in the firm.

Uruguay and entered distribution agreements with Empresas Carozzi and Carrau & Cia., respectively, instead. The dressings and seasonings brands first introduced in 1985 were sold, but the company enhanced its market leadership in premixes by acquiring the Betty Crocker license.

Molinos entered agreements with two new Brazilian distributors and launched several new products: flavored yerba maté tea, a balsamic vinegar, a cake margarine, and a new pasta in four varieties. The company also sold its Buenos Aires headquarters building and moved to Victoria in the province of Buenos Aires, where it already had a distribution center.

In 2000 Molinos acquired Fagnani Hnos S.A., the company manufacturing and marketing Don Vicente pasta products. This made Molinos the leader in premium dry pastas. The company introduced yerba maté in collectible cans, a ricotta pasta line, a homemade pizza bread mix, and an aromatic olive oil. Molinos also launched an Internet shopping service during the year to reach retailers directly. In 2001 the company purchased the Lucchetti brand of dry pasta and introduced 11 new products: a gnocchi mix, Lira-brand olives and vinegars, two more yerba maté brands, Vitina baby food and oats, new varieties of Matarazzo, Don Vicente, and Favorita pastas, and Granja del Sol Milanese (superfrozen breaded meat). In 2002—its centennial year—Molinos introduced new quick-preparation cake mixes, Cocinero vinegar, lemon juice, all-soy oil, Granja del Sol soy Milanese, and stone-hearth Granja del Sol pizza. Also in 2002, the company acquired Molfino Hnos. S.A., the third-largest dairy company in Argentina, with two plants and annual sales of $120 million. The following year, however, it sold Molfino to the Canadian firm Saputo Inc. for $68 million.

During the year 2002, Molinos was the market leader in Argentina in traditional and special oils; flours, including premixed flour; dry pastas; premixed cakes; batter; sausages; and semolinas. It ranked second in baby food; yerba maté, rice, margarine, premixed desserts, and hamburger. The company owned ten industrial processing plants in Argentina and six distribution centers. But the financial collapse of Argentina in 2002 affected even companies such as Molinos that were engaged in the sale of basic products. It sustained a loss of 80.24 million pesos ($24.02 million) on sales of 2.01 billion pesos ($601.8 million). The company earned a small profit during the first nine months of 2003, however.

The company's main brands for oils at this time were Cocinero, Lira, Patito, Ideal, La Patrona, Gallo, Fritolim, and Reno. Among dry pasta, the brands were Matarazzo, Lucchetti, Favorita, La Bella, Regio, Olimpico, and Don Vicente. For fresh pasta, the main brands were Matarazzo and Favorita. For pizza mix it was Favorita, for semolina, Vitina, and for prefried foods and frozen vegetables and fish, Granja del Sol. The main brands of yerba maté tea were Nobelza Gaucha, Chamigo, and Pico de Oro. For hamburgers, brands included Good Mark, Granja del Sol, and Wilson, and for frankfurters, Vienissima, Wilson, and Hamond. For flour the main brands were Blancaflor, Favorita, and Letizia, and for margarine, Manty, Delicia, and Blancaflor. For tapas the main brands were Blancaflor and Favorita, for breadings, Preferido and Favorita, for rice, Maximo and Condor, and for biscuits, Exquisita and Favorita. For premixes Blancaflor was foremost, and for cold cuts, Tres Cruces.

Principal Operating Units

Commodities Trading; Distribution and Logistics; Industrial Management; International Business; Marketing; National Sales.

Principal Subsidiaries

Alimentaria, S.A.; Bodegas Nieto Senetiner S.A. (60%); Congelados del Plata, S.A.; Molinos International S.A.

Principal Competitors

Arcor S.A.I.C.; Cargill, S.A.C.I.; Socma Alimentos S.A.

Further Reading

"A la busqueda del valor agregado," *Mercado,* January 1998, pp. 52–53.
Green, Raul, and Catherine Laurent, *El poder de Bunge & Born,* Buenos Aires: Editorial Legusa, 1988.
"Las vueltas de Molino," *Mercado,* February 1999, pp. 67–69.
Majul, Luis, *Los dueños de la Argentina,* Buenos Aires: Editorial Sudamerica, 5th ed., 1995, pp. 255–310.
Rubinstein, Beth, "Losing Brand," *Latin Trade,* August 1999, p. 26.
"Saputo to Acquire Argentinean Processor," *Dairy Foods,* November 2003, p. 10.
Schvarzer, Jorge, *Bunge & Born,* Buenos Aires: Grupo Editor Latinoamericano, 1989.
Sguiglia, Eduardo, *El club de los poderosos,* Buenos Aires: Planeta, 1991.

—Robert Halasz

Morinaga & Co. Ltd.

33-1, Shiba 5-chome, Minato-ku
Tokyo 108-8403
Japan
Telephone: +81-3-3456-0134
Fax: +81-3-3456-1809
Web site: http://www.morinaga.co.jp

Public Company
Incorporated: 1899 as Morinaga Western Candy Confectionery
Employees: 3,210
Sales: ¥173.35 billion ($1.44 billion) (2003)
Stock Exchanges: Tokyo
NAIC: 311330 Confectionery Manufacturing from Purchased Chocolate; 311411 Frozen Fruit, Juice, and Vegetable Processing; 311520 Ice Cream and Frozen Dessert Manufacturing; 311821 Cookie and Cracker Manufacturing

One of Japan's leading candy and confectionery manufacturers, Morinaga & Co. Ltd. is also credited with introducing Western-style treats to Japan at the dawn of the 20th century. After more than 100 years, Morinaga has remained at the top of the Japanese candy industry, producing a strong line of candies, chocolates, frozen desserts and snacks, and nutritional products. Entering the new century, Morinaga has developed a new "power brand" strategy emphasizing its core product lines, which include Milk Cocoa, Hotcake Mix, Amazake drinks, frozen desserts, and Weider in Jelly, a line of drinkable, gelatin-like drinks marketed under license from the United States' Weider Nutrition International Inc. The company also produces a number of other licensed candy products, including Pez and Werther's Original. Morinaga operates five manufacturing facilities in the Tokyo region; the company also has launched a manufacturing subsidiary in Taiwan and has begun construction on a new plant in Shanghai, China, expected to be operational by 2004. The company also operates sales subsidiaries in Europe and North America, and sells its products in more than 26 countries. Listed on the Tokyo Stock Exchange, Morinaga is led by Gota Morinaga, grandson of the company's founder.

Candy Missionary in the 20th Century

Born in Kyushu, in the north of Japan, in 1863, Taichiro Morinaga went to work for his uncle, a potter, in exchange for room and board after his father's death when Morinaga was just seven. Morinaga, who had no formal education, became the bookkeeper of the pottery business, and then, at the age of 18, was sent to Tokyo as the company's sales representative. Morinaga later went to work for a wholesale company, rising to become manager of a branch office in Yokohama. Yet, after extending too much credit to customers, the office went into debt. In order to repay his employer, Morinaga decided to try his luck in California.

Morinaga moved to San Francisco in 1887 and opened a hardware store, trading in high-quality, high-priced goods—in a working class neighborhood. The business, which suffered equally from the pervasive anti-Oriental sentiment of the era, soon failed and forced Morinaga to look elsewhere for a livelihood.

Yet Morinaga's stay in the United States led him to an important discovery: candy. Japan had remained closed to outside influences for more than 250 years, finally opening its borders to foreigners only in the late 19th century. If the country's elite class had access to sweets—typically based on boiled beans—the majority of the population had limited access to confectionery products, and sugar consumption in general remained low. Milk and milk products were also absent from the Japanese diet. The opening of the country's borders stimulated interest in all things foreign, and the country's growing foreign population encouraged the import of Western-style confectionery and candy.

Morinaga recognized that the growing foreign influence in Japan, and the country's readiness to adopt attributes of Western culture, would inevitably extend to the country's eating habits. Morinaga became determined to learn the art of candy making, in order to introduce new confectionery products to the Japanese market. Despite the anti-Asian prejudice, Morinaga found a job as a janitor at a candy factory, and there learned how to make candy.

Company Perspectives:

Established in 1899 by Taichiro Morinaga, who had a pioneer spirit and the dream of ''offering nutritious and good-tasting confectionery to Japanese children,'' Morinaga & Co. Ltd. was the first Western-style confectionery manufacturer in Japan.

During the past 100 years, Morinaga has carried out its corporate operations guided by the vision, ''We Offer Good Health with Delight & Taste.'' We now aim to extend our vision to encompass people all over the world.

By the end of the century, Morinaga was ready to return to Japan and start his own candy company. Before leaving, Morinaga performed his own bit of market research, questioning members of San Francisco's Japanese community and other Japanese visitors to the city on their candy preferences. Morinaga discovered that the sweet most preferred by the people he questioned was marshmallows, at the time also known as ''angel food.'' The fluffy, egg white-and-sugar-based candy also resembled existing Japanese confections, making it a natural first product.

Morinaga founded his business with partner Hanzaburo Matsuzaki in 1899, opening a small shop in the Akasaka neighborhood of Tokyo. The business, called Morinaga Western Candy Confectionery, developed quickly as the country eagerly greeted the new candy type. Morinaga himself acted as salesman, pushing a cart from which he sold marshmallows, and other Western-styled cakes and candies. Among these were caramels. This product represented even more of a novelty in Japan in that it contained butter—at a time when dairy products still had not penetrated the Japanese diet. Morinaga's caramel sales were at first limited to his foreign customers, as the Japanese shied away from the strange product. In addition, the country's climate made it difficult to produce—and to eat—caramel, which tended to melt and become too sticky to hold in the heat and humidity.

Morinaga set out to develop a new caramel recipe for the Japanese market, and by 1914 had perfected a recipe that both appealed to the Japanese palate and also offered a longer shelf life. The new product debuted in 1914, and was packaged in a pocket-sized yellow box. Known as Hi-Chew, the product became a company flagship and one of its core products into the next century. In the meantime, the company's strong marshmallow sales inspired the adoption of a logo, an angel, in 1905—the angel logo also fit in with Morinaga's work as a Christian missionary. The company adopted the name Morinaga Confectionery Inc. in 1912.

The success of Hi-Chew led Morinaga to seek its own source of dairy products, and in 1917 the company set up a dairy operation, which became Morinaga Dairy Industries. A year later, the company launched a new candy line, becoming the first to introduce the chocolate bar to Japan. Meanwhile, the company began extending its dairy product line, launching its first powdered baby formula in 1920. That launch marked the start of the company's involvement in the nutritional products category as well.

Hitting the Sweet Spot in the 1960s

By the 1920s, Morinaga's sales had been growing steadily. To meet the rising demand, the company installed its first production machinery—previously, production had been by hand—and launched mass production in 1925. Over the next decades, the company continued to add to its production capacity, opening four more plants, and adopting increasingly sophisticated, modernized production techniques. By the 1980s, the company manufacturing operations had become fully automated.

In the meantime, the company continued developing new product lines. Among these were baby biscuits, called Morinaga Manna, which the company began producing in 1930. In 1935, Hanzaburo Matsuzaki became company president. The company took a leaf from its Western counterparts in the 1930s, promoting holidays—such as Mother's Day starting in 1937—as a means of stimulating candy and confectionery sales.

During World War II, Morinaga turned part of its resources toward the production of penicillin, saving a good number of lives. Following the war, the company, now led by Taihei Morinaga, decided to split up its operations, separating its dairy business into a separate company, which became known as Morinaga Dairy Industries in 1949. That company then developed into one of Japan's major dairy groups. The two companies nonetheless remained closely linked, sharing the angel logo and developing common products and marketing campaigns.

The 1950s saw new expansion for the company. In 1954, its production capacity expanded with a new band oven—the first to be brought into Japan. Two years later, Morinaga extended its dessert offerings with the production of ice cream, which quickly developed into one of the company's key product lines. Another strong seller for the company came in 1957, when it introduced its popular Hotcake Mix. That line also became one of Morinaga's flagship brands.

Attempts to introduce Valentine's Day celebrations—and linking that holiday with chocolate—had been made since the 1930s by various Japanese companies. At the beginning of the 1960s, however, Morinaga at last succeeded, launching a ''Chocolate for St. Valentine's Day'' marketing campaign. The company had other hit products during the decade, such as Hi-Crown Chocolate, launched in 1964, and a new soft, milk-based caramel, Hi Soft, launched in 1969. At the beginning of the 1970s, the company added a new line of Twiggy chocolates as well.

''Power Brand'' Focus for the New Century

The early 1980s nearly spelled disaster for the company, however. At the beginning of the decade, a mysterious group that called itself ''The Man with 21 Faces'' after a popular Japanese character, launched a series of attacks against the Japanese food industry. The crime wave started with the kidnapping of the president of a rival company, Ezaki Glico, in 1984, followed by a demand for ¥1 billion and 100 kilograms of gold bullion—and a threat that the band would place poison in Glico products on supermarket shelves. Ezaki Glico's stock plummeted in the aftermath.

Yet, after Glico refused to give in to the ransom demands (and after the kidnapped Ezaki had escaped), the band an-

Key Dates:

1899: Taichiro Morinaga returns from San Francisco and founds a candy and confectionery company with partner Hanzaburo Matsuzaki, becoming the first to introduce Western-style snacks to Japan.
1914: After years of research, Morinaga launches a caramel candy, Hi-chew, designed to appeal to the Japanese market.
1917: Morinaga founds a dairy operation.
1918: Morinaga becomes the first company to market chocolate bars in Japan.
1920: The company begins production of powdered baby formula.
1925: The company installs machinery and begins mass production of candies and confectionery.
1949: The dairy operation is spun off as a separate company, Morinaga Dairy Industries.
1956: Morinaga begins production of ice cream.
1964: The company has a new hit product with the launch of Hi-Crown Chocolate.
1983: The company launches a nutritional foods division and begins a product development and marketing agreement with Weider, of the United States.
1995: The highly popular Weider in Jelly product line is launched.
2000: The company launches a new corporate ''power brand'' strategy focusing on core brands and product lines.
2004: A new manufacturing facility is expected to be completed in Shanghai in order to supply the market in mainland China.

nounced that it had declared a truce on Glico. Instead, the group turned its interests toward Morinaga, threatening to poison the company's products. Once again, the threat spread panic among Japanese consumers, and a large number of stores pulled Morinaga's products from their shelves. Morinaga's sales collapsed, as did its share price—which only climbed back after the gang's announcement, more than a year later, that it would no longer target the company. The perpetrators—who had made good on their threat, placing boxes of Morinaga candy laced with cyanide, but clearly labeled as poisoned, on grocery shelves—were never to be caught. After the detective in charge of the investigation committed suicide, the gang announced that it was abandoning its career of crime, stating that it had never had the intention of hurting anyone. Indeed, observers later suspected that the gang's chief purpose was to profit through speculating on the food companies' stock.

With the poisoning scare over, Morinaga's sales rose once again, nearing the equivalent of $1 billion by the end of the decade. The company by then had opened its fifth manufacturing facility and had continued to extend its product range, launching, for example, its brand of Ottoto crackers. The company also had expanded beyond candies and confectionery to some extent, adding production of alcoholic beverages. That business, operated under the name of Fukutokucho, produced primarily sake and shochu.

Closer to the group's core was its drive into the health and nutritional foods market. The company's entry into the sector began in the early 1980s, and a 1983 licensing agreement with the United States' Weider Nutrition International to develop and market Weider-branded products for the Japanese market. The company also entered the soft drinks market, launching a rice-based health drink, Amazake, which became one of its key brands. Tofu represented another fast-growing nutritional product for the company, and formed a strong part of the group's international growth. By the end of the 1980s, the company had entered some 32 countries, backed by sales and marketing subsidiaries in the United States and The Netherlands.

Morinaga's product development continued through the 1990s. Among the most successful company products launched during the decade were its Sold Dazen chocolates, introduced in 1993. The following year marked the debut of a new product line, developed under Morinaga's partnership with Weider. The new snack, called Weider in Jelly, was the first in a range of drinkable, jelly-like snacks touted by the company as nutritional foods. The Weider line, fully launched in 1995, was credited with creating an entirely new product category. The first variations included Weider Energy In, which claimed to provide a sustained, quick energy boost; and Weider Vitamin In, which claimed to provide a full spectrum of vitamins provided by a balanced meal. Targeting a young male market, the Weider line grew steadily into the next decade, and by 2002 represented nearly 20 percent of the company's total sales.

The sustained Japanese recession into the 2000s slowed the confectionery market as well. In response, Morinaga, now led by Gota Morinaga, developed a new ''Power Brand'' strategy for the new century, with a focus on a limited range of key brands. As part of that effort, the company sold off its liquor operation in 2000. The company then began stepping up development of new products, to be launched under its array of ''power'' brands—including Milk Cocoa, Weider in Jelly, Hotcake Mix, and Amazake. Meanwhile, the company continued to manufacture and market a number of products under license, such as the popular Pez candies and, since 2002, European favorite Werther's Original.

The 100-year-old company also had begun to look beyond the Japanese market, which remained its chief source of revenues. At the beginning of the 21st century, Morinaga established a manufacturing subsidiary in Taiwan, in an attempt to conquer a share of the island's market. Morinaga also targeted Hong Kong for sales. Yet its main interest lay in the huge potential of the Chinese mainland, with its consumer market of more than 1.2 billion people. The company launched construction of a manufacturing facility in Shanghai, which was expected to be operational by the end of 2004. After more than a century of appealing to the sweet tooth at home, Morinaga's angel looked forward to spreading its wings even further.

Principal Subsidiaries

Angel Food Systems Co., Ltd.; Morinaga Angel Dessert Co., Ltd.; Morinaga Dessert Co., Ltd.; Morinaga Finance Co., Ltd.; Morinaga Food Service Co., Ltd.; Morinaga Institute of Biological Science; Morinaga Restaurant Dessert Co., Ltd.; Morinaga

Service Co., Ltd.; Morinaga Shoji Co., Ltd.; Morinaga Snack Co., Ltd.; Shanghai Morinaga Co., Ltd.; Sunrise Co., Ltd.; Taiwan Morinaga Co., Ltd.

Principal Competitors

Central Group of Cos.; Meiji Seika Kaisha Ltd.; Taiwan Sugar Corporation; Tiger Brands Ltd.; Ezaki Glico Company Ltd.; Katokichi Company Ltd.

Further Reading

Carpenter, Susan, ''The Candy Man Can,'' *Inside/Outside Japan,* August 1993.

''Morinaga Lowers 1st-Half Net Profit Estimate,'' *Jiji,* October 21, 2003.

''Morinaga to Retail Werther's Original Candy,'' *New Food Products in Japan,* November 25, 2002.

100 Years with Morinaga, Tokyo: Morinaga & Co. Ltd., 2000.

—M.L. Cohen

Nagase & Co., Ltd.

5-1 Nihonbashi
Kobunacho, Chuo-ku
Tokyo 103-8355
Japan
Telephone: (03) 3665-3021
Fax: (03) 3665-3030
Web site: http://www.nagase.co.jp/english

Public Company
Incorporated: 1917 as Nagase Shoten Company
Employees: 829
Sales: $4.2 billion (2003)
Stock Exchanges: Tokyo Osaka
NAIC: 422690 Other Chemical and Allied Products Wholesalers; 422950 Paint, Varnish, and Supplies Wholesalers

Originally a wholesaler and trader of dyestuffs, Nagase & Co., Ltd. is Japan's foremost chemical products trading company. Nagase's four main divisions focus on chemicals, synthetic resins, electronic materials, and healthcare. The company develops, produces, and markets chemical products as well as plastics, semiconductor manufacturing materials and equipment, pharmaceuticals, enzymes, medical and dairy farming equipment, abrasives, and cosmetics. With operations worldwide, Nagase runs an extensive network of subsidiaries and branch offices. It also has business alliances with major companies, including Eastman Kodak Company.

Early Years As a Trader of Dyestuffs: Late 1800s and Early 1900s

Like many other venerable Japanese companies, Nagase traces its history back more than 160 years. The company was originally established as a small family trading enterprise, dealing mainly in dyestuffs that were used to color fabric. Even then Nagase did not function as a manufacturer of commodities, but as a wholesaler/retailer. Although little is known about the founding family, the company was established in Osaka in 1832 at a time when Japan was closed to international relations. Osaka, one of Japan's major pre-industrial centers of commerce, provided an excellent market for Nagase. Many of the area's industries were based in the production and finishing of textiles. As these industries prospered, so did Nagase's small business.

Decades later, when Japan opened its doors to international commerce, Nagase became acquainted with foreign dyes that contained unusual pigments, derived mostly from unique plants and other organic sources along the trade routes of the Middle East, India, southeast Asia, and the United States. At the time of the Meiji Restoration in the 1860s, when Japan embraced an effort to modernize and industrialize along Western models, Nagase experienced another period of expansion. As Japanese textile manufacturers adopted more efficient Western production methods, their output increased. This resulted in increased demand for silk and other fabrics and the dyes to color them. The growth of Japan's production capacity enabled the country to export a wide variety of products. One of the most lucrative at the beginning of Japan's industrial period was textile products. The fine quality of the silk, careful construction, and beautiful pure dyes made Japanese fabrics and clothing extremely valuable in trading.

As the production capacity of resource-poor Japan increased, the economy became increasingly mercantilist. Japanese manufacturers now imported the majority of the resources needed to make a product, and then finished the goods and sold them at a value-added premium. The same situation existed for Nagase, which in 1900 established business ties with the Chemical Industry of Basle, A.G., now known as Ciba-Geigy Ltd. Nagase imported a variety of products from Ciba, but virtually all were chemicals limited to industrial applications. Ciba, meanwhile, had become involved in manufacturing pharmaceuticals, a few of which Nagase later handled.

By 1917 Nagase had outgrown its heritage as a family company. In order to expand, the company required massive sums of money that could not be satisfied through conventional investment loans. In December of that year the company was formally incorporated. The majority of shares remained in family hands or were purchased by banks and other large corporations.

Company Perspectives:

The Nagase Group is a member of the world society. As such, it is our duty to maintain good and fair business practices and, through continued growth and development, provide society with the goods and services needed while improving the welfare of our employees.

To establish better ties with emerging chemical industries in the United States, Nagase had set up a sales office in New York City in 1915. From this office, Nagase could better observe developments in the American chemical industry and quickly establish purchase orders and sales agreements for new products. The office marked a major success in 1923 when Nagase established an important trading relationship with Eastman Kodak Company, a manufacturer of chemicals and photographic materials. The importance of Nagase's agency business grew dramatically in 1930 when the company reached an agreement with the Union Carbide Corporation to market that company's products in Japan. A few months later Nagase established a similar agreement with the Swedish chemical concern Aktiebolaget Separator, now known as Alfa Laval AB.

Surviving the War Years: Mid-1900s

Japanese industry continued to grow at an enormous pace through much of the 1930s as Japanese industrial companies began to exploit the massive natural resources of neighboring countries, such as Korea and Taiwan, which were occupied by Japan. By 1937, however, Japan turned toward military adventurism, by invading China and, ultimately, the rest of Asia. With Japan on a war footing, called the ''quasi-war economy,'' many of Japan's principal industries came under direct government control. Nagase, a major company in the chemicals industry, also was committed to war production. The primary nature of its business, however, was in trading. A trade embargo from the United States cut off Nagase's supply of American products, and the war in Europe virtually eliminated business with Ciba and other firms located in England and Germany.

But Nagase did manufacture a small quantity of products under license agreements. As long as raw materials were available, the company could remain in production. It managed to stay in business through much of the war, manufacturing coloring agents for military uniforms, flags, camouflage, and clothing. By the end of the war, Nagase was less devastated by bombing than by the complete unavailability of raw materials. The firm was effectively closed even before the armistice was concluded.

The managerial leadership of many companies, primarily the *zaibatsu* conglomerates, were subject to review by war tribunals. Many lost their positions, but few were imprisoned. Nagase, for its small and mostly involuntary role in the Japanese war effort, was spared from these investigations. Faced with rebuilding the Japanese economy, many industries picked up where they left off. Once again, the textile industry emerged as an engine of growth for the economy because its factories survived the war and there was both strong domestic and foreign demand for the products. With trade restrictions eliminated, Nagase was able to resume its import agreements with numerous manufacturers. Nagase also rebuilt its non-dye operations, providing crucial chemicals and chemical technologies to a variety of industries, including ferrous and nonferrous metals manufacturing, paint, and other compound manufacturing. The company's position in this area was strengthened in 1952 when it expanded its agreement with Eastman to include trading contracts with Eastman Chemical Products.

The 1950s was a period of strong growth for Japan's basic heavy industries. Companies in these fields laid the foundation for many new industries, including ship and vehicle manufacturing, electronics, and chemicals. Nagase's role in this period was primarily that of supplier, providing the necessary ingredients for paints and other treatments that finished large machinery. As volume increased, so did the demand for specially engineered products with unusual qualities and tolerances. This gave rise to additional contracts with foreign companies, bringing high-technology compounds and processes to Japan and firmly establishing Nagase's position as a market leader in high-tech chemicals.

Nagase gained a listing on the Osaka stock exchange index in 1964, enabling a wider variety of primarily local private investors to become owners of the company. Five years later Nagase was listed on the larger Tokyo index, and shares in the company were traded nationally and internationally.

Building Strategic Partnerships: 1960s–Early 1990s

In 1968 Nagase concluded an exclusive distributorship with General Electric Company of the United States, handling a variety of that company's products in Japan. Three years later, General Electric and Nagase established a plastics manufacturing joint venture called Engineering Plastics, Ltd. This important agreement was followed by the formation of a special joint venture with Ciba-Geigy in 1970. Nagase re-established its relationship with Ciba-Geigy immediately after World War II, when the Swiss company was divested from the German pharmaceutical combine IG Farben. Ciba remained one of the world's leading chemical engineering companies, and was a major supplier and licenser of Nagase. Nagase established a third joint venture company in 1974, called Landauer-Nagase Ltd. Nagase's partner in the venture was the American company Technical Operations, Inc. (later called Landauer, Inc.).

During the 1970s, Nagase strengthened its position in the international market as a supplier of proprietary engineered compounds and processes. Foreign offices were no longer established with the single aim of gaining distribution of production rights. Instead, Nagase was now competing in foreign markets as a supplier. The company set up two subsidiaries in 1971, Nagase (Hong Kong) Ltd. and the Nagase America Corporation. The company established another subsidiary, Nagase Singapore (Pte) Ltd., in 1975. In 1980 the company opened an operation in Germany, Nagase Europa GmbH, and a second office in Singapore called Chang Fong Overseas Enterprises (Pte) Ltd. Rounding out its expansion into southeast Asia, the company established Nagase (Malaysia) Sdn. Bhd. in 1982. Nagase subsequently opened new offices in the United States, Taiwan, Korea, England, Holland, Thailand, Canada, India, and Indonesia.

Key Dates:

1832: Nagase is established as a trader of dyestuffs for textiles.
1900: The company begins importing products manufactured by Chemical Industry of Basle, A.G. (later Ciba-Geigy Ltd.).
1915: A New York City sales office is opened.
1917: Nagase incorporates as Nagase Shoten Company.
1923: Nagase establishes a trading relationship with Eastman Kodak Company.
1943: The company name is changed to Nagase & Co., Ltd.
1964: Nagase is listed on the Osaka stock exchange.
1968: The company becomes the exclusive Japanese distributor for General Electric Company.
1969: Nagase is listed on the Tokyo stock exchange.
1990: Nagase builds a plastics manufacturing operation in Taiwan called Nagase Wah Lee Plastics.
1992: Five new subsidiary companies—Nagase Electronic Chemicals, Teikoku Chemical Industries, Nagase Chemicals, Nagase Biochemicals, and Nagase Fine Chemical—are established to pioneer biochemicals and organic compounds.
1997: The company expands into east Asia, establishing Nagase Philippines Corp. and Shanghai Nagase Trading Co., Ltd.
1998: P.T. Nagase Impor-Ekspor Indonesia is founded.
2000: The company strikes a deal with British chemical manufacturer Laporte PLC to purchase pharmaceutical and agrochemical raw materials for the Japanese market.
2001: The company forms a joint venture in China, called Guangzhou Kurabo Chemicals Co. Ltd., with Japanese company Kurabo Industries Ltd., to manufacture urethane products for use in the automobile manufacturing industry.
2002: The company plans its eighth production facility in China, expands its U.S. holdings, and sets up a representative office in Hungary.

In 1988 Nagase received an award from the Ministry of International Trade and Industry, Japan's government agency charged with industrial coordination. Nagase was awarded for its contributions to international trade through import promotion. This was an unusual and important commendation in light of Japan's much larger and often maligned export industries.

In 1989 the bulk of Nagase's business was still in the distribution of other company's products, leading to a decision to establish a new Science and Technology Foundation and a Research and Development center at Kobe. These research institutes were dedicated to testing existing processes for improvement and developing new biotechnologies and organically engineered chemicals. This marked an important turn in Nagase's mission; the company was no longer interested in merely handling another company's products. The lead time required to yield such technological breakthroughs was long. In addition, it took many years to assemble a qualified staff that could properly channel the group's energies toward a successful discovery. The primary focus of the group was the development of organic chemical products.

In 1990 Nagase set up a plastics manufacturing operation in Taiwan called Nagase Wah Lee Plastics. This facility manufactured plastic compounds for several manufacturers in Taiwan that produced computer and electrical appliance casings and other products. In April 1992 Nagase reintroduced itself to the chemical industry as a ''technical information trader,'' promoting a new group of five subsidiary companies: Nagase Electronic Chemicals, Teikoku Chemical Industries, Nagase Chemicals, Nagase Biochemicals, and Nagase Fine Chemical. These companies formed the crux of Nagase's effort to pioneer biochemicals and organic compounds.

Amidst all these changes, Nagase remained under the control of the founding family. Shozo Nagase, who oversaw much of the company's expansion during the 1960s and 1970s, served as chairman. Hideo Nagase, another descendant of the company's founder, was president. Over the course of more than 160 years, Nagase had grown into one of Japan's largest chemical companies. Dyes and pigments for fabric, paper, and detergents comprised 10 percent of the company's sales volume, while fine and industrial chemicals—including pharmaceuticals, cosmetics, and biochemicals—comprised 38 percent. A further 42 percent of Nagase's sales were derived from plastics used in the automotive and electronics industries. The remainder of Nagase's sales came from electronics, machinery, medical systems, and cosmetics.

Nagase was one of the first Japanese companies to make the foray into biochemicals. With the practical experience of its manufacturing affiliates and sales operations and the strength of its research institute, Nagase was a leader in these technologies. The company had been successful in laying the foundation for diversification and indigenously developed chemical technologies. It was hoped that, in the future, this would enable the company to distance itself from lower-margin license production agreements with other companies and to develop its own more profitable patented products and processes.

Continued International Expansion and Diversification: Mid-1990s–2000s

With the decline of the Japanese economy in the 1990s, Nagase looked toward international investments to boost its bottom line. It planned to expand aggressively in China and southeast Asia and to introduce innovative and desirable new products. In the late 1990s Nagase changed its corporate structure to reflect four core businesses: dyes and chemicals, synthetic resins, electronic materials, and healthcare. It folded its beauty product and medical system divisions into healthcare and streamlined its chemical division. No longer content to be viewed simply as a trading company, Nagase decided to promote itself as a marketing company—a company that was not only involved in trading but also in research and development, manufacturing, and marketing.

Foreign expansion, particularly in east Asia, kept Nagase busy. In 1997 the company established Nagase Philippines Corp. and Shanghai Nagase Trading Co., Ltd., and the following year it founded P.T. Nagase Impor-Ekspor Indonesia. Nagase planned to push its chemical products, as demand was expected to increase in the Asian market.

For the fiscal year ended March 31, 1999, Nagase reported sales of ¥490 billion, down from ¥538 billion in 1998. In 2000 Nagase's sales rose to some ¥568 billion.

In 2000 Nagase struck a deal with British chemical manufacturer Laporte PLC to purchase pharmaceutical and agrochemical raw materials for the Japanese market. It was anticipated that the Japanese pharmaceutical market would look increasingly to foreign suppliers for raw materials, and Nagase's agreement with Laporte put it ahead of the game. The company hoped to attain sales of ¥3 billion annually from the deal beginning about 2005.

Nagase continued to work on self-improvement and reorganization, and in early 2001 the company underwent additional restructuring to boost productivity and profitability. In addition to continued overseas expansion, Nagase planned to invest more heavily in electronics and healthcare. The company consolidated several divisions to streamline operations, including combining production companies Teikoku Chemical, Nagase Biochemicals, Nagase Chemicals, and Nagase Chemtex into one company—Nagase ChemteX Corp. Nagase also pushed for joint ventures.

Fine chemicals, such as pharmaceutical chemicals and synthetic dyestuffs, was another area in which Nagase hoped to expand. It set out to push fine chemicals aggressively in the Asian market, and in 2001 Nagase formed Nagase Finechem Singapore (Pte) Ltd. The company divided its Asia sales areas into two regions: Greater China, which encompassed China, Hong Kong, and Taiwan, and the ASEAN zone, which included Singapore and surrounding areas. Sales in the combined zones totaled some ¥60 billion per year in the early 2000s, but the company's goal was to reach about ¥150 billion per year in the Greater China region and ¥100 billion in the ASEAN sector by the mid-2000s.

In other Asian news, Nagase founded a new business in China to produce synthetic resin trays. The trays, which were used to move electronic parts, would be sold to Japanese companies with manufacturing plants in China. Nagase planned to launch operations in March 2002 and to produce some 1,500 tons of resin sheet per year. Nagase hoped for sales of ¥1 billion in 2004.

In 2001 Nagase formed a joint venture in China with Japanese company Kurabo Industries Ltd. The venture, called Guangzhou Kurabo Chemicals Co. Ltd., manufactured urethane products for use in the automobile manufacturing industry. The venture planned to sell its products to Japanese car makers doing business in China beginning in October 2002.

In healthcare, Nagase formed a company with Fujikura Kasei and UMA known as Nippon U.N.F. The companies planned to establish a joint venture with a Chinese producer of analytical chemicals and reagents with the purpose of manufacturing biochemical diagnostics for the Chinese market, which was estimated to grow greatly. The venture, Shanghai Shesuo UNF Medical Diagnostic Reagents Co., marketed its products to hospitals and aimed for sales of ¥500 million within the first few years of operation.

In September 2002 Nagase announced plans for its eighth production facility in China—an adhesives and electronics materials production company to be called Nagase ChemteX (Wuxi) Corp. Also that year Nagase expanded its U.S. holdings by establishing Nagase America Corp. and Nagase Plastics America Corp., a designer of autoparts, such as airbags, instrument panels, and dashboards. In addition, Nagase set up a representative office in Hungary.

Nagase proved it was flexible enough to change with the times. It had transformed itself from a dyestuffs trader to a full-service chemical and electronic products company. Although chemicals and plastics accounted for 70 percent of sales in 2003, healthcare and electronics products were growing rapidly. Still run by the Nagase family, the company understood what was necessary to remain successful. Sales for the fiscal year ended March 31, 2003, reached $4.2 billion, an increase of 13.6 percent compared with the previous year.

Principal Subsidiaries

Nagase ChemteX Corporation; Grelan Pharmaceutical Co., Ltd.; Nagase Medicals Co., Ltd.; Honshu Rheem Co., Ltd.; Totaku Industries, Inc.; Kyusyu Totaku Industries, Inc.; Thermo Co., Ltd.; Gigatec Inc.; Idea System Co., Ltd.; Nagase Alphametics Co., Ltd.; Nagase Cosmetics Co., Ltd.; Kotobuki Kasei Corporation; Setsunan Kasei Co., Ltd.; Kyoraku Co., Ltd.; Alpha Bumping Technology Co., Ltd.; Delta Twenty-One Corp.; Design & Die Co., Ltd.; Nagase Electronic Equipment Service Co., Ltd.; Nagase CMS Technology Co., Ltd.; Nagase Landauer, Ltd.; NCC Engineering Co., Ltd.; MEDICANET Co., Ltd.; Nagase Logistics Co., Ltd.; Nagase General Service Co., Ltd.; Nagase Information Development, Ltd.; Nippon Vopak Co., Ltd.; Nagase Business Support Corporation; Nagase Trade Management Co., Ltd.; Choko Co., Ltd.; Nagase Colors & Chemicals Co., Ltd.; Nagase Chemical Co., Ltd.; Kyushu Nagase Co., Ltd.; Nishinihon Nagase Co., Ltd.; Shizuoka Nagase Co., Ltd.; Nagase Bio-Chemical Sale Co., Ltd.; Nagase Chemspec Co., Ltd.; Nagase Agritech KK; Griffin Nagase KK; Nagase Plastics Co., Ltd.; Nagase Elex Co., Ltd.; Hoei Sangyo Co., Ltd.; Nagase Barre Finishing Systems Co., Ltd.; Shinshu Nagase Denzai Co., Ltd.; OnFine Co., Ltd.; Nagase Beauty Care Co., Ltd.; Herbal Care Co., Ltd.; Nagase Medix Co., Ltd.; Nagase America Holdings Inc. (U.S.A.); Nagase America Corporation (U.S.A.); Nagase Plastics America Corporation (U.S.A.); Nagase California Corporation (U.S.A.); Sofix Corporation (U.S.A.); Canada Mold Technology Inc.; Nagase (Europa) GmbH (Germany); Nagase & Co., Ltd., London Branch (U.K.); Shanghai Nagase Trading Co., Ltd. (China); Nagase ChemteX (Wuxi) Corporation (China); Nagase (Hong Kong) Ltd. (China); Nagase Precision Plastics Shanghai Co., Ltd. (China); Shanghai Hua Chang Trading Co., Ltd. (China); Guangzhou Nagase Trading Ltd. (China); NCC Shanghai Techno Center Co., Ltd. (China); Nagase (Taiwan) Co., Ltd. (Taiwan); Nagase Wah Lee Plastics Corporation (Taiwan); Nagase Korea Corporation; Nagase Engineering Service Korea Co., Ltd.; Nagase (Thailand) Co., Ltd.; Advanced Mold Technology Co., Ltd. (Thailand); Sanko Gosei Technology (Thailand) Ltd.; Nagase (Malaysia) Sdn. Bhd.; Nagase Singapore

(Pte) Ltd.; Chang Fong Overseas Enterprises (Pte) Ltd. (Singapore); Nagase Finechem Singapore (Pte) Ltd.; P.T. Nagase Impor-Ekspor Indonesia; Nagase Philippines Corporation.

Principal Competitors

Dow Chemical Company; Ube Industries, Ltd.; Kanematsu Corporation.

Further Reading

"China—Nagase to Build Production Base for Adhesives and Electronics Materials," *Japan Chemical Week,* September 19, 2002.

"Nagase & Co.—Healthcare As New Core Business," *Japan Chemical Week,* June 15, 1999, p. 4.

"Nagase & Co., Ltd.," *Diamond's Japan Business Directory 1991,* p. 1030.

"Nagase & Co., Ltd.: Financial Data," Osaka: Nagase & Company, 1992.

"Nagase & Company, Ltd.—Aiming to Be a Company That Creates/Moves the Market," *Japan Chemical Week,* February 2, 1998, p. 4.

"Nagase Builds Up Relation with Laporte," *Japan Chemical Week,* November 16, 2000.

"Nagase to Double China Business by Promoting Fine Chemicals," *Japan Chemical Week,* April 26, 2001.

"Technical Info Trader Adopted As Catchword," *Japan Chemical Week,* July 9, 1992.

—John Simley
—update: Mariko Fujinaka

Nam Tai Electronics, Inc.

15/F., China Merchants Tower
Shun Tak Centre
168-200 Connaught Road Central
Hong Kong
Telephone: (852) 2341-0273
Fax: (852) 2263-1223
Web site: http://www.namtai.com

Public Company
Incorporated: 1975
Employees: 4,274
Sales: $406.3 million (2003)
Stock Exchanges: New York
Ticker Symbol: NTE
NAIC: 334412 Printed Circuit Board Manufacturing; 334111 Electronic Computer Manufacturing; 334419 Other Electronic Component Manufacturing

From its early days as a simple calculator manufacturer, Nam Tai Electronics, Inc. has developed into a supplier of components for a variety of large electronics companies. Since its founding in 1975, the company's business has grown as more and more manufacturers have begun outsourcing parts of the production process. Nam Tai's major customers, so-called ''original equipment manufacturers'' (OEMs) like Epson Precision, Texas Instruments, Canon, and Hitachi, retain responsibility for brand name promotion, product design, and marketing, while Nam Tai supplies components and subassemblies from its plant in Shenzhen, China. The company's major products include liquid crystal display monitors (LCDs) and radio-frequency modules for mobile phones, as well as LCD panels for a variety of other electronic products, flexible printed circuit assemblies, and finished products such as calculators, personal digital assistants, and electronic dictionaries. Although the company's manufacturing activities take place in southern China, Nam Tai was founded in Hong Kong, is incorporated in the British Virgin Islands, is traded on the New York Stock Exchange, has affiliated administrative offices in Vancouver, and counts many transplants from the Japanese electronics industry among its top executives.

Making Calculators for Hong Kong and China: 1975–87

Nam Tai got its start in Hong Kong in 1975, when M.K. Koo founded a trading company that marketed calculators and other consumer goods from Taiwan, South Korea, and Japan to Hong Kong customers. A successor company, Nam Tai Electronics Company Limited, was founded in 1978. Calculator sales proved successful, so Koo took steps to ensure the quality, supply, and cost of his product by starting his own manufacturing facilities in Hong Kong. From the beginning, Koo recruited executives from the Japanese electronics industry to take advantage of their experience with the precision and efficiency of Japanese manufacturing methods.

Manufacturing soon became the company's focus. In 1980 production moved to the People's Republic of China to take advantage of lower labor and material costs and was established subsequently in Shenzhen in southern China. Sales of calculators and other consumer products in Hong Kong and China grew substantially in the early 1980s. Nam Tai also began exporting calculators to Europe, Canada, and eventually to the United States. In November 1983 the company went through a reorganization. Nam Tai Management Services Limited, or NT Management, was formed under Hong Kong law as a holding company for various operating subsidiaries. The company's sales volume grew dramatically to $53 million in 1985, helped along by China's ''open door'' economic policy. In 1986, however, China suddenly restricted imports because of a shortage of foreign currency reserves. Nam Tai was hit hard: sales fell by 50 percent, pushing the company to find ways to lessen its dependence on the Chinese market. Before 1985, calculators accounted for nearly all of Nam Tai's sales volume, but by the fiscal year ending March 1987 calculator sales were down to 81 percent of total sales. The company was diversifying into products such as digital thermometers, electronic blood pressure meters, electronic scales, and typewriters.

Another major restructuring occurred in August 1987 when Nam Tai Electronics, Inc. was incorporated in the British Virgin Islands as a holding company for Hong Kong-based NT Management, the previous parent company for Nam Tai. The Virgin Islands was chosen to facilitate share trading, since it did not tax share transfers, income, or dividends between parent companies

Company Perspectives:

For over 10 years, our vision has been to become the world's leading China-based contract manufacturer of sophisticated handheld communication/computing devices and their key components. This vision has been a consistent, long-term strategic goal, executed upon in carefully planned stages.

and subsidiaries. The following year Nam Tai went public on the NASDAQ, after unsuccessful attempts to gain a listing on the Hong Kong stock market.

Sales Growth and Product Expansions in the Early 1990s

Nam Tai's sales grew steadily through the early 1990s, from $70.8 million in 1993 to $121.2 million in 1995. Calculators remained the company's main product through most of the decade. Hand-held consumer electronics such as personal organizers, electronic dictionaries, and spell checkers also accounted for a portion of sales. The company developed a supply relationship with large-volume original equipment manufacturers such as Texas Instruments and Sharp Corporation.

In 1992 Nam Tai established a second plant, Zastron Plastic & Metal Products Ltd., in Shenzhen. The Zastron factory made metal and plastic parts for Nam Tai's use as well as for other customers. At the same time, Nam Tai was exploring the possibilities for an international manufacturing base. In 1993 the company opened a plant in Vancouver to make blood pressure monitors. During the early 1990s, many people from Hong Kong and Taiwan were moving to Canada, partly in anticipation of the 1997 transfer of Hong Kong from Britain to China. Nam Tai founder Koo lived in Vancouver for several years and established administrative offices there. After the Vancouver plant was up and running, employing about 50 people, Koo considered expanding into Mexico as well. The company, however, failed to reach agreement with a minority shareholder over a planned share offering and the plans were abandoned. The Vancouver factory was wound up after a few years as well; the Canadian subsidiary was sold to management in 1999 and continued to provide investor relations services to Nam Tai as a separate company. Subsequent manufacturing expansions remained focused in China.

In 1994 the first of a series of leadership changes occurred at Nam Tai. Tadao Murakami took over the president's job from Koo and became CEO a year later; Koo remained chairman. The company further expanded its product line and technological capabilities in the mid-1990s. Nam Tai reached an agreement with Sharp Corporation in 1994 to make a personal organizer with address book, schedule, and calculator functions. The introduction of the advanced product caused some losses as employees adjusted to new manufacturing techniques. Nam Tai was working to stay on the cutting edge of manufacturing technology by introducing new surface mount technologies such as "tape automated bonding" and "outer lead bonding." In 1996 Nam Tai opened a new facility in Shenzhen, doubling total manufacturing capacity. That year the company also set up a research and development subsidiary known as Shenzhen Namtek Co., Ltd. Namtek's role was to develop software for consumer electronics and help Nam Tai keep pace with ever more sophisticated product designs. The subsidiary employed a few dozen software engineers and posted its first profit in 1998.

A Bumpier Ride in the Late 1990s

The late 1990s brought some conflicts, missteps, and more leadership changes. A struggling Chinese company known as Tele-Art owed Nam Tai about $800,000 and Nam Tai filed to have it liquidated in 1997. A British Virgin Islands court awarded Nam Tai $34 million in damages in 2002. According to Nam Tai allegations, however, the Bank of China colluded with the auditing firm PriceWaterhouseCoopers to fabricate debts and artificially strip Tele-Art of assets before any funds could be paid out to creditors such as Nam Tai. Nam Tai filed suit against the Bank of China and PriceWaterhouseCoopers in 2003.

In 1998 Shigeru Takizawa replaced Murakami as president and CEO. Takizawa was a former senior fellow at the Japanese firm Toshiba and had had an advisory relationship with Nam Tai for more than 20 years. Murakami became chairman and Koo remained on the board and in an executive position. That year Nam Tai also made its first move into the telecommunications market when it paid $16 million for a 20 percent share in Group Sense Ltd. of Hong Kong. The company produced telecommunications products as well as educational electronics such as Chinese dictionaries and translators. Nam Tai sold the stake in 2000.

The Asian economic crisis also hit in 1998. Nam Tai's customers slowed their orders and put pressure on for lower prices, but the company rode out the crisis as the trend toward outsourcing at electronics companies continued. The company's sales zigzagged from a high of $132.9 million in 1997 to $101.6 million in 1998 to $145.1 million in 1999. In the fall of 1998 Nam Tai made an ill-fated acquisition when it bought a majority stake in Albatronics, a struggling electronics group. About five months later serious debt problems were uncovered at the company; Albatronics posted a $700 million loss for 1999 after profits of $10 million to $20 million in previous years. Serious cash flow problems and a dearth of orders did not inspire much hope, so Nam Tai closed the company and wrote it off at the end of 1999 after attempts at debt restructuring fell through.

Expansion Through Additions and Acquisitions in the New Millennium

In 1999 Nam Tai took steps that further distanced itself from its reliance on calculator sales. Early in the year it bought a Korean maker of cordless telephones, which brought with it a research and development facility and several licenses for mobile phone service in Europe. On that basis, Nam Tai established Nam Tai Telecom Co. Ltd. in August 1999. The new subsidiary set up production lines in Shenzhen to address the growing demand for mobile phone components such as LCD modules. It also manufactured end products such as cordless phones and family radio systems. Other new product developments in 1999 included an agreement to make palm-sized computers for Legend, China's largest PC maker, and a joint venture with Toshiba Battery Co. to design and manufacture rechargeable lithium battery packs for mobile phones.

Key Dates:

1975: M.K. Koo founds a calculator trading company in Hong Kong.
1980: Manufacturing commences in China.
1985: Dramatic sales growth is achieved due to calculator sales in China.
1986: Restricting of trade with China pushes Nam Tai to diversify.
1988: Nam Tai goes public on the NASDAQ.
1992: Zastron Plastic & Metal Products is established in Shenzhen.
1996: A new factory is completed in Shenzhen, doubling capacity.
1999: Nam Tai Telecom is established to make cell phone components.
2000: The company acquires J.I.C. Group, manufacturer of LCD panels.
2002: The company completes expansion incorporating the latest manufacturing technology.

As electronic products grew more complex, Nam Tai implemented advanced manufacturing techniques necessary to meet the demands of the latest product designs. One such technology was chip on glass, or COG, a process that connected integrated circuit chips directly to LCD display panels without the usual wire bonding. The COG technique made for lighter, more efficient products. The company experienced higher defect rates when the unfamiliar COG process was first introduced in 1999. But by late 2000 the difficulties were surmounted, for the most part, and the company was planning expansion to make room for more COG production lines.

By the time the new millennium arrived, electronic components for communication devices—in particular LCD modules for cell phones, PDAs, and digital cameras—had surpassed calculators as the leading revenue generators for Nam Tai. In 1998, calculators still accounted for 61 percent of sales, but by 2000 calculators accounted for significantly less than half of sales, and were grouped in with other finished consumer goods produced by Nam Tai such as digital camera accessories for cell phones. A pair of acquisitions in the fall of 2000 broadened Nam Tai's involvement in the manufacture of consumer electronics. First, the company acquired a 5 percent stake in TCL Mobile, a branch of the Chinese state-controlled phone company involved in the manufacture and distribution of cell phones on the digital standard. Second, Nam Tai bought the J.I.C. Group (BVI) Limited for $32.8 million in cash and shares. J.I.C. had been making transformers and LCD panels since 1983. The acquisition added 2,400 employees to Nam Tai and pushed the company's net revenue to $234 million in 2001.

Nam Tai added another 180,000 square feet of manufacturing space to its existing 310,000 feet in 2000. Construction also was underway on a 138,000-square-foot expansion, finished in 2002, which included two floors of clean rooms for COG production technology. The year 2001 brought another management shuffle: president and CEO Takizawa became chairman of the board, the former chairman Murakami moved to an executive position, and Toshiaki Ogi, who like Takizawa came from Toshiba, became CEO. Joseph Li became president; he was a cofounder of J.I.C., Nam Tai's newest subsidiary. The following year Li also took over the CEO position and Murakami was put back in the post of chairman. In other developments in 2002, Nam Tai listed J.I.C. Technology on the Hong Kong stock exchange by way of a reverse merger into the failed Albatronics subsidiary. Nam Tai retained 94 percent control of J.I.C.

Nam Tai moved its primary listing from the NASDAQ to the New York Stock Exchange in January 2003. A secondary offering was planned for that spring but was postponed due to repercussions of an outbreak of the SARS respiratory illness, which hit the area around Nam Tai's Shenzhen factories particularly hard. Later in the year, however, the company announced plans to spin off three major subsidiaries—Zastron Electronic, Namtai Electronic, and Shenzhen Namtek—on the Hong Kong exchange. ''The aim of the listings is more of enhancing corporate governance and brand recognition in the mainland than raising funds,'' founder M.K. Koo told the *South China Morning Post.*

Production continued to expand and advance in 2003. That fall the company began construction of a $40 million five-story facility to meet demand for high-end telecommunications products. Nam Tai had a new agreement to provide LCD modules and radio frequency modules to JCT Wireless Technology Company, a Hong Kong-based maker of wireless application software for cell phones. The agreement came after Nam Tai paid $10 million to acquire 25 percent of JCT's parent company earlier in the year. Nam Tai also invested $4.2 million in a new assembly line to make flexible printed circuits, which it had formerly purchased from other companies for use in LCDs. With strong technological capabilities and broadening manufacturing expertise, Nam Tai was beginning to make cell phones and other products in ''semiknockdown'' form: this meant that Nam Tai took care of all but the last few steps in making a product for an original equipment manufacturer. The product was shipped in an incomplete state in order to take advantage of lower tax rates for unfinished products. As it looked into 2004 and beyond, Nam Tai planned to apply its well-developed production capabilities and a proactive acquisition strategy to capture more market share in electronic components manufacturing and begin to tap China's cell phone market and other developing markets.

Principal Subsidiaries

J.I.C. Technology Company Limited (94%); Nam Tai Group Management Limited; Nam Tai Telecom (Hong Kong) Company Limited; Namtai Electronic (Shenzhen) Co., Ltd.; Shenzhen Namtek Company Limited; Zastron Electronic (Shenzhen) Co. Ltd.

Principal Competitors

Celestica, Inc.; Flextronics International Ltd.; Hon Hai Precision Industry Co., Ltd.; Jabil Circuit, Inc.; Sanmina-SCI Corporation; Solectron Corporation; Kinpo Electronics, Inc.; Inventec Co. Ltd.

Further Reading

Austin, Scott, ''AOL Case Shows How Far-Flung Courts Can Cooperate Over Dot-Com Issues,'' *Miami Daily Business Review,* December 4, 2002.

Dunn, Darrell, ''Nam Tai Names New Chief Exec,'' *Electronic Buyers' News,* September 14, 1998, p. 90.

Gold, John, ''Electronics Firm Plans New Plant,'' *South China Morning Post,* May 7, 1993.

McKeefry, Hailey Lynne, ''Nam Tai Ramping Capacity to Boost Telecom Revenue,'' *Electronic Buyers' News,* January 22, 2001, p. 68.

''Newcomers: Twenty Chinese Immigrants Who Reflect a Community That Mainstreamers Might Do Well to Get to Know,'' *Canadian Business and Current Affairs,* September 1994, pp. 24–34.

Ng, Eric, ''Albatronics Faces Voluntary Wind-Up; Biggest Shareholder's Talks with Creditors Fail,'' *South China Morning Post,* June 19, 1999.

Reeves, Amy, ''Nam Tai Electronics Inc., Blue-Chip Clients Give Outsourcer an Edge,'' *Investor's Business Daily,* June 27, 2003.

Scouras, Ismini, ''Nam Tai's Plan to Double Sales Hits Snags,'' *Electronic Buyers' News,* November 29, 1999, p. 66.

Serant, Claire, ''Nam Tai Carefully Calibrates New Focus,'' *Electronic Buyers' News,* September 18, 2000, p. 90.

Yau, Winston, ''BOC, PWC Face Fraud Charges; Nam Tai Accuses China's Biggest Bank,'' *South China Morning Post,* April 28, 2003.

——, ''Nam Tai Eyes $2b in Hong Kong Spin-Offs,'' *South China Morning Post,* November 10, 2003.

—Sarah Ruth Lorenz

National Iranian Oil Company

Hafez Crossing, Taleghani Avenue
Tehran
Iran
Telephone: 98-21-615-4975
Fax: 98-21-615-4977
Web site: http://www.nioc.com

State-Owned Company
Incorporated: 1951
Sales: $16 billion (2002 est.)
NAIC: 211111 Crude Petroleum and Natural Gas Extraction; 211112 Natural Gas Liquid Extraction; 213111 Drilling Oil and Gas Wells

The second largest producer of oil among Organization of the Petroleum Exporting Countries (OPEC) companies in 2003, state-owned National Iranian Oil Company (NIOC) boasts about 7 percent of the world's total oil reserves. Its natural gas reserves are the second largest in the world, totaling about 812 trillion cubic feet in the early 2000s. NIOC produces some 3.8 million barrels of oil daily, and it provides nearly half of the Iranian government's revenues. Earnings from oil exports account for about 80 percent of the country's total export revenues. The company hopes to step up its exploration efforts in the early 21st century.

Nationalizing the Oil Industry: 1940s–50s

NIOC was formed as a result of tensions between the British-owned Anglo-Persian Oil Company—renamed Anglo-Iranian Oil Company in 1935 and British Petroleum Company in 1954—and the Persian and then Iranian government, which came to a head after World War II. The British oil company had found oil in southwest Iran in 1908 and, on the basis of this discovery and the support of the British government, which acquired a 51 percent shareholding in it in 1914, it had grown to become one of the world's largest international oil companies by the 1930s. There was resentment within Iran, however, at the privileged position held by Anglo-Iranian, and its close association with the British government, whose imperialist ambitions were feared. The British invaded and occupied Iran in alliance with the Soviet Union in 1941, which did nothing to reduce suspicion of the oil company. There was particular resentment at the low amount of royalties paid to the government by Anglo-Iranian. In 1948 negotiations began to improve the share of oil income retained by Iran, but these were unsuccessful, and in 1951 the strongly nationalist prime minister, Dr. Muhammad Mussadegh, nationalized the oil industry. The resulting conflict became one of the great causes célèbres in the history of oil-company-host-government relationships in the 20th century.

NIOC was incorporated by the Iranian government on April 30, 1951, as the corporate instrument of the government's nationalization policy. Initially it took over all the employees and physical assets of Anglo-Iranian within Iran, with instructions to set aside 25 percent of its profits to meet compensation claims by the British company. NIOC's attempts to take control of the industry were gravely weakened, however, because the main international oil companies boycotted Iranian oil exports to demonstrate their support for the British company. Iranian production collapsed, as the oil majors replaced Iranian oil with expanded production from Kuwait and Saudi Arabia. In 1953 Mussadegh was overthrown in a coup. In the following year agreement was reached between the conflicting parties. The result was a new role for NIOC.

In September 1954 an eight-member consortium called the Iranian Oil Participants (IOP) was formed. The arrangement was similar to others in operation in much of the rest of the Middle East. The shareholding was in the hands of the major Western oil majors. British Petroleum Company (BP) held 40 percent, Shell 14 percent, Chevron 8 percent, Exxon 8 percent, Gulf 8 percent, Mobil 8 percent, Texaco 8 percent, and Compagnie Française de Pétroles 6 percent. NIOC was recognized as the owner of Iran's oil deposits and of all installed assets of the Iranian oil industry, but actual control over the industry was placed firmly in the hands of the consortium members. NIOC lacked influence over the production, refining, and export of Iranian crude oil and products. Two companies owned by IOP—the Iranian Oil Exploration and Producing Company and the Iranian Oil Refining Company—operated the assets formally owned by NIOC, to whom they were officially appointed as contractors. They produced oil for NIOC, which was then sold to IOP member companies that were responsible

Company Perspectives:

Now in its 24th year of self-reliance, the national petroleum industry is moving on with full strength and confidence utilizing up-to-date technology, powerful and innovative management, highly skilled and creative manpower resources, and a futuristic approach to planning development projects.

for export marketing. An additional secret agreement between the IOP companies, which did not become public until the early 1970s, established the aggregate programmed quantity formula, which effectively gave those member companies with the lowest reliance on Iranian oil the greatest influence over how much should be produced. The upshot was that Iran's oil production grew comparatively slowly over the following decade.

Despite these constraints, NIOC was able, during the second half of the 1950s, to develop its role as an independent oil company. A law in 1957 empowered it to enter into joint ventures with foreign oil companies to explore areas other than those leased to IOP. The first joint venture agreement was signed by the Italian oil company Agip SpA. This was a subsidiary of the state energy corporation ENI and was led by the entrepreneurial Enrico Mattei, who was searching for a source of cheap oil not controlled by the oil majors. In August 1957 the Société Irano-Italienne des Pétroles (Sirip) was formed, owned 50 percent by NIOC and 50 percent by Agip. In June 1958 a similar joint venture agreement was signed with Standard Oil Company of Indiana, which formed a company jointly owned with NIOC called the Iran Pan American Oil Company (Ipac). By 1961 both ventures were producing crude oil, with Ipac enjoying particular success.

Seeking Independence and Strength Through Joint Ventures: 1960s–70s

The joint venture strategy was developed in the 1960s. In 1965 six new joint venture agreements were signed, followed by three more, including one with a Japanese group, in 1971. In December 1966 the Iranian government, having discovered the existence of the aggregate programmed quantity formula, forced IOP to increase production to give up 25 percent of the area in which it had exploration rights, and to supply NIOC with 1.47 billion barrels of crude oil for export over the following five years. As a result of the joint venture arrangements and the December 1966 agreement NIOC began to have its own supply of crude oil, although it still controlled only a tiny proportion of total Iranian crude exports. In 1960 the consortium accounted for 99.9 percent of Iranian crude oil exports. By 1973 its share had fallen to 89.2 percent. NIOC accounted for 5.8 percent and the varying joint ventures accounted for the remaining 5 percent by that date.

During the second half of the 1960s NIOC heightened its exploration efforts within Iran through the use of service contracts. Service contracts differed from joint ventures in that the foreign operator had no ownership rights in Iran at all, but was only a contractor working for NIOC and was remunerated for its services with crude oil. In August 1966 NIOC concluded a 25-year service contract with the French state oil company ERAP, which created a new Iranian-registered subsidiary, Sofiran, to explore for oil. NIOC made all policy decisions in respect to Sofiran's operations within Iran, while Sofiran had functional management responsibility. During 1969 two further service contracts were awarded to a group of European oil companies and of U.S. independents.

During the 1960s NIOC had sufficient crude to begin international marketing. Initially, attention was focused on Eastern Europe, Asia, and Africa. In Eastern Europe NIOC reached a number of barter agreements, under which it would exchange oil for manufactured goods. NIOC also sought to establish a presence in overseas refining. In 1969 NIOC and Standard Oil Company of Indiana each took a 13 percent stake in an Indian refinery at Madras that was supplied with Iranian crude by Ipac. In 1971 NIOC took a 17.5 percent interest in a new South African refinery, again signing a long-term supply contract. In the same year, a 24.5 percent stake was taken in the Madras Fertilizer Plant. A tanker fleet was developed by a NIOC subsidiary, the National Iranian Oil Tanker Company. By 1974 the fleet had four oceangoing tankers. In 1965 NIOC established another subsidiary, the National Petrochemical Company (NPC), which launched a series of wholly owned and joint venture chemicals and fertilizer plants within Iran. By the early 1970s NIOC had become a medium-sized international oil company, ranked alongside ENI and U.S. independents such as Atlantic Richfield Company and Occidental. In terms of share of world crude oil production, it controlled slightly less than 1 percent at this time, which made it about the 19th largest oil company in the world by this measure.

The Iranian government was a prominent player in the events in the early 1970s that led to the end of the consortium system in the Middle East, and the huge price rises of 1973 and 1974. Because the 1951 nationalization of the Iranian oil industry had never been canceled, however, there was no formal transfer of assets of the kind seen almost everywhere in the Arab world. In July 1973 negotiations between IOP and the Iranian government led to a new agreement, which replaced that signed in 1954. NIOC assumed sole responsibility over the former consortium area. The IOP member companies agreed to provide part of the future capital investment in production operations by NIOC in the form of annual prepayments against their future crude oil purchases. The IOP companies also were given preferential oil-purchase rights in Iran for a period of 20 years. Subsequently, there were endless disputes between the oil company, the Iranian government, and NIOC about these arrangements, which continued right up to February 1979, when the shah and his government were swept away by the Islamic revolution.

Throughout its existence in the shah's Iran, NIOC had been an instrument of the government. Nominally it was a public company and not a state-owned corporation, although all its shares were government owned. In practice NIOC operated under the close scrutiny of the government. The prices of its four main products—gasoline, kerosene, gas oil, and fuel oil—could not be changed without the approval of the Iranian Cabinet. In 1962 Dr. Eqbal, a former prime minister, was appointed chairman and managing director, and government control was further exercised through a body called the Shareholders's Representatives, which consisted of seven ministers headed by the contemporary prime minister. Oil was the driving force behind the shah's flawed attempt to modernize Iran, hence NIOC was of key strategic importance to the regime. Oil provided 90 percent of Iran's foreign-exchange earnings in the last years of the shah's

Key Dates:

1951: The Iranian oil industry is nationalized, and National Iranian Oil Company (NIOC) is founded.
1954: The Iranian Oil Participants (IOP), an eight-member consortium, is established.
1957: NIOC begins forming joint ventures with foreign companies.
1979: NIOC comes under the control of the newly formed Ministry of Petroleum.
1995: The United States places economic sanctions against Iran.
1999: NIOC discovers Azadegan, the largest oilfield discovery in 30 years.

rule. Given the atmosphere of corruption that pervaded most aspects of Iranian life by the 1970s, it was remarkable that NIOC was able to develop and function as a modern integrated oil company, but the enterprise was not immune to the intense personal and political rivalries that afflicted the ruling elite.

Struggling to Survive Under Political Upheaval: 1980s

NIOC was placed under the direct control of a newly created Ministry of Petroleum in September 1979. The Islamic government immediately ended the purchasing privileges enjoyed by IOP, and the 1973 agreement with IOP was abrogated by Iran in 1981. In 1980 all NIOC's joint venture and service contract agreements with foreign oil companies were terminated. The joint venture companies were wound up and regrouped under the Iranian Offshore Oil Company of the Islamic Republic. Names of oil fields with imperial connotations were changed. From 1980, for example, Cyrus became Sorush, and Feridun became Foroozan. The investment in the South African refinery was abandoned, although NIOC retained its holding in India's Madras refinery. There was a period of considerable confusion in the first years after the revolution, with NIOC losing strategic direction. The first postrevolutionary chairman, Hassan Nazeh, caught on the wrong side in this period of rapid political change, resigned along with the rest of the board of directors six months after his appointment, and fled to France. The influence of the workers' committees that sprang up in this period was a prime reason for management instability, but NIOC seems to have been able to retain some professional managers by hiring them on advisory contracts.

The following years were bleak ones for the company. Oil production fell 75 percent between 1979 and 1981. The disruption caused by the revolution was followed by the imposition of trade sanctions by the United States and other industrial countries during the period of the U.S.-Iranian hostage crisis between November 1979 and January 1981. The outbreak of war with Iraq in September 1980 was followed by physical damage to oil installations. The large Abadan refinery was badly damaged by Iraqi attacks in 1980 and 1982. Iran's main crude oil export terminal at Kharg Island was damaged repeatedly by Iraqi air attacks, and in August 1986 NIOC's Sirri Island terminal was wrecked by Iraqi bombers. NIOC had to switch to a temporary loading point at Larak Island, in the Strait of Hormuz, which could be better protected but raised costs. The revolutionary government was committed to reducing Iran's dependence on oil, and had a stated policy of restricting output to less than three million barrels per day. In practice, the disastrous war with Iraq, combined with the deterioration in the world market for crude after 1981 and OPEC export quotas, left NIOC in no position to expand production even if it had so wanted.

NIOC's situation when the Iranian cease-fire with Iraq was arranged in August 1988 was difficult. Many oil installations were destroyed. By 1990 crude oil production had risen to 2.3 million barrels per day from two million in 1988 with exports averaging 1.7 million barrels per day, but refining capacity was still down, and NIOC had to import some petroleum products from overseas refineries that processed Iranian crude.

NIOC displayed considerable resilience in these circumstances. Its oil engineers were able to repair war damage and increase production during 1989, which grew to 2.85 million barrels per day. During 1989 several new medium and large oil fields were discovered. Plans were made to construct additional refinery capacity of 450,000 barrels per day, mostly at Bandar Abbas and Arak, by the end of 1993. At the end of 1990 a contract was awarded to ETPM Entrêpose of France to rebuild the Kharg oil export terminal.

In 1991 NIOC remained as dependent as ever on the political conditions in its home economy and region, which had been thrown into uncertainty yet again by Iraq's invasion of Kuwait in August 1990. Leaving aside these fundamental uncertainties, the company controlled a considerable amount of crude oil production. In 1990 it was announced that it would join with Malaysian and Indonesian interests in a new refinery project in Keddah state, Malaysia. NIOC also claimed to operate, through its subsidiary the National Iranian Oil Tanker Company, the world's third largest tanker fleet of 5.55 million tons. The company owned 28 oil tankers and 32 other vessels and had on charter 35 oil tankers and 34 other vessels. NIOC was also one of the largest employers in Iran, where it was engaged on a large scale in the provision of housing and medical care for its workers alongside more conventional activities. Arguably the rehabilitation and further development of the Iranian oil industry would be best achieved by re-establishing contracts with Western oil majors who could provide technology and expertise, but that—like so much in NIOC's history—would be a political decision on which NIOC's management was unlikely to have the final word.

Continued Struggles Amid Sanctions in the 1990s–2000s

As NIOC headed into the 1990s, it worked to rebuild itself and regain strength lost during the war against Iraq. NIOC planned to build five new refineries with an aim to have 11 operational plans in the mid-1990s. In addition, the company expressed an interest in working with Western countries to develop oil and gas projects in Iran. In the early 1990s Mobil Corporation and Coastal Corporation began purchasing Iranian crude oil, and NIOC claimed it was in negotiations to sell crude to additional U.S. companies.

NIOC's attempts to establish ties with U.S. investors came to a halt in 1995 when U.S. President Clinton imposed sanctions against Iran. The sanctions prohibited U.S. companies and any foreign subsidiaries from engaging in business activities with

Iran or providing financing for energy exploration or development. President Bush extended the sanctions in March 2003. In addition, to further discourage business dealings with Iran, in 1996 the U.S. Iran-Libya Sanctions Act was enacted. It imposed sanctions on non-U.S. businesses that invested more than $20 million per year in Iranian oil or natural gas markets. The Act was extended for an additional five years in July 2001.

In October 1999 Iran made what it believed to be its largest oil discovery in 30 years: an onshore field known as Azadegan, located near the Iraq border in the southwestern province of Khuzestan. Estimated to hold in-place oil reserves of 26 to 70 billion barrels, Azadegan had the potential to produce some 300,000 to 400,000 barrels per day over 20 years. On November 1, 2000, Japan earned exclusive negotiating rights to develop Azadegan in exchange for a $3 billion loan to Iran. Japan negotiated the agreement for a consortium of Japanese firms that included Japex, Inpex, and Japan National Oil Corp. Negotiations dragged on, however, and by early 2003 no final agreement had yet been reached. In addition, the United States placed pressure on Japan to delay any finalization of the agreement until Iran agreed to allow more thorough inspections of its nuclear plants. In September 2003 Iran indicated it would open negotiations regarding Azadegan to other countries, and in November Iran announced that it was in talks with France's TOTAL S.A. and Norway's Statoil.

Another significant oil discovery NIOC made since 1995 was the Darkhovin onshore oilfield. The field was estimated to have reserves of three to five billion barrels. NIOC made a deal with ENI of Italy in 2001 to develop Darkhovin. Production output was expected to reach 160,000 barrels per day. In February 2001 NIOC discovered a large offshore oilfield known as Dasht-e Abadan.

All of NIOC's agreements with foreign companies fell under the regulations of Iran's 1987 Petroleum Law. The law allowed for contracts with outside companies under a buyback system, meaning the foreign company provided all financial investments and at the end of the contract gave up all operating rights to the state company. In return, the foreign company received a share of the production at a set price. Buyback contracts generally were for short periods of time, which often was a disadvantage to the foreign company. NIOC's risk was that oil prices could drop below the fixed compensation rate.

Despite the somewhat unattractive nature of buyback contracts, many foreign companies signed agreements with NIOC to develop oil fields. The first under the agreement came onstream in October 1998 and was the offshore Sirri A field operated by TOTAL and Petronas of Malaysia. The following year Iran signed contracts with France's Elf Aquitaine and Italy's ENI/Agip to implement an oil recovery program at the Doroud oil and natural gas field. Iran also agreed to allow Bow Valley Energy of Canada and TOTAL to develop the Balal field, an offshore oil field with 80 million barrels of reserves. In 2000 Iran signed a development deal with Statoil that allowed Statoil to begin exploration of the Strait of Hormuz region as well as to develop a processing plant for four onshore fields.

The industrywide plunge in oil prices in the late 1990s adversely affected NIOC's revenues, but by the early 2000s Iran was able to establish an oil stabilization fund thanks to high oil export revenues. The fund included the earnings that were above budget and by about 2003 totaled about $8 billion.

The Iranian government remained confident its economy would stabilize, and in keeping with this belief it established a five-year economic plan in 2000 that called for the privatization of a number of Iran's major industries, including parts of the oil and natural gas markets. The government hoped to boost GDP and create hundreds of thousands of new jobs, but political opposition slowed the restructuring process.

Despite its worn, out-of-date oil industry, NIOC moved ahead with goals to increase foreign investment and oil output. Increased earnings meant NIOC might be able to modernize its oil industry and invest in improved technology. The company hoped to boost oil production to seven million barrels per day by 2015, and to accomplish this it would need foreign investments of as much as $5 billion annually. In late 2003 Iran boasted 32 producing oil fields and net exports of about 2.6 million barrels per day. Iran exported oil to a number of customers, including Japan, China, South Korea, Taiwan, and Europe. Iran was the largest heavy fuel oil exporter in the Middle East.

Principal Subsidiaries

National Iranian South Oil Company; National Iranian Offshore Oil Company; National Iranian Central Oil Fields Co.; Khazar Exploration & Production Co.; Petroleum Engineering & Development Co.; Pars Oil and Gas Company; Pars Special Economic Energy Zone Co.; National Iranian Oil Terminals Company; National Iranian Drilling Company; Petroiran Development Company; Fuel Consumption Optimization Org.; Kala Naft London Ltd.; Kala Naft Canada Ltd.

Principal Competitors

Petróleos de Venezuela S.A.; Petróleos Mexicanos; Saudi Arabian Oil Company (Saudi Aramco).

Further Reading

Evans, John, *OPEC: Its Member States and the World Energy Market,* London: Longman, 1986.

Fesharaki, Fereidun, *Development of the Iranian Oil Industry,* New York: Praeger, 1976.

"Iran Finds Onshore Buybacks an Uphill Struggle," *International Petroleum Finance,* October 8, 2003.

"Iran's Buyback Deals Proving Hard Sell," *Petroleum Intelligence Weekly,* March 4, 2002, p. 2.

"Iran's New Oil Streams Boost Crude Quality," *Petroleum Intelligence Weekly,* January 21, 2002, p. 1.

Stocking, George W., *Middle East Oil,* London: Allen Lane, 1970.

"U.S. Pressure Stalls Japan's Iran Plans," *Petroleum Intelligence Weekly,* June 30, 2003.

"Western Firms Look to Iran's New Buy Back Chief," *Energy Compass,* January 18, 2002.

—Geoffrey Jones
—update: Mariko Fujinaka

The New York Times Company

229 West 43rd Street
New York, New York 10036
U.S.A.
Telephone: (212) 556-1234
Fax: (212) 556-7389
Web site: http://www.nytco.com

Public Company
Incorporated: 1851 as Raymond, Jones & Company
Employees: 12,150
Sales: $3.1 billion (2002)
Stock Exchanges: American
Ticker Symbol: NYT
NAIC: 511110 Publishers, Newspaper, Combined with Printing; 516110 Internet Publishing and Broadcasting; 519110 News Syndicates; 513112 Radio Broadcasting Stations; 513120 Television Broadcasting Stations

The New York Times Company (NYTC) is a diversified media company including newspapers, magazines, television and radio stations, electronic information services, and electronic publishing. The company publishes three major daily newspapers, the *New York Times* (the *Times*), the *International Herald Tribune,* and the *Boston Globe,* and 16 regional newspapers. The company operates eight network-affiliated television stations and two New York City radio stations. The Times Syndicate sells columns, magazine and book excerpts, and feature packages to more than 2,000 newspapers and other media to clients in more than 50 countries. It is the largest syndicate in the world specializing in text, photos, graphics, and other non-cartoon features. As part of an aggressive expansion campaign the New York Times increased its U.S. distribution from 62 markets in 1997 to 235 in 2002.

19th-Century Founding

The principal founders of the *New York Times* were Henry Jarvis Raymond, a sometime politician, reporter, and editor who learned his trade working for Horace Greeley on the *New York Tribune,* and George Jones, an Albany, New York, banker who had also once worked for Greeley as a business manager on the *Tribune.* Raymond proposed a newspaper that would present the news in a conservative and objective fashion, in contrast to the yellow journalism of the day, which emphasized crime, scandal, and radical politics. They raised $70,000 to establish Raymond, Jones & Company, in large part by selling stock to wealthy upstate New York investors, and set up their editorial offices in a dilapidated six-story brownstone on Nassau Street in downtown New York City. The first issue of the *New York Daily Times* (the word ''Daily'' was dropped from the title in 1857) was dated September 18, 1851, and it announced an editorial policy that would emphasize accurate reporting and moderation of opinion and expression.

Jones handled the company's business affairs, and Raymond, as editor, provided journalistic leadership. Under their management, helped by booming population growth in New York City, the *Times* grew rapidly, reaching 10,000 circulation within ten days and 24,000 by the end of its first year. In 1858 the paper moved into a new five-story building containing the most modern printing equipment. As the *Times* prospered, Raymond established and continually encouraged the high standards of journalism that prevail to this day. It also became a newspaper of record. For example, it carried the entire text of Lincoln's ''Gettysburg Address'' on the front page on November 20, 1863. Among other journalistic successes, the *Times* provided outstanding coverage of the U.S. Civil War, with Raymond himself reporting on the Battle of Bull Run.

Raymond was active in Republican politics throughout the war. He was present at the creation of the party in Pittsburgh in 1856 and wrote its first statement of principles. He wrote most of the party platform in 1864. Between political activity and journalism, Raymond was chronically overworked for years, and his health suffered. On June 19, 1869, at the age of 49, he died. George Jones assumed the editorial leadership of the *Times.*

By the time of Raymond's death, each of the 100 shares of stock in the company had increased in value from the original $1,000 to about $11,000, with 34 shares held by Raymond and 30 by Jones. In 1871, after a series of *Times* articles on the misdeeds of corrupt New York City politicians headed by William Marcy (Boss) Tweed, an attempt was made by Tweed interests to buy Raymond's 34 shares from his widow. Jones

Company Perspectives:

The core purpose of The New York Times Company is to enhance society by creating, collecting and distributing high quality news, information and entertainment.

quickly arranged to have the shares purchased by one of his associates, thus establishing his control of the newspaper. In 1884 Jones chose to oppose the nomination by the Republican party of James G. Blaine for president, thus losing the much needed support of Republican readers and advertisers. The paper's profits fell steadily until Jones's death in 1891. His heirs had little aptitude for the newspaper business, and the panic and depression of 1893 brought the *Times* close to failure.

In 1893 the *Times*'s editor-in-chief, Charles Ransom Miller, bought control of the paper from Jones's heirs with $1 million raised from Wall Street interests. Miller, a fine editor, had no business aptitude and was unable to maintain the newspaper's capital requirements. Staff reductions and declining journalistic quality brought the *Times* to its historic low point, and by 1896 it was on the verge of bankruptcy and dissolution. During this critical year salvation came in a dramatic fashion. A group of Wall Street investors in what was then called the New York Times Publishing Company arranged to save the firm—and their investments—by placing it in receivership and recapitalizing it as a new company, The New York Times Company. The new capitalization was 10,000 shares with 2,000 being paid out in exchange for the original *Times* stock. A large stock position with contractual assurance of eventual majority stock ownership was purchased with borrowed money by a then little known but respected newspaper editor and publisher from Chattanooga, Tennessee, Adolph Simon Ochs.

Ochs, the son of German immigrants, had received little formal schooling, but had learned the newspaper business from the ground up as newsboy, printer's devil, journeyman printer, business manager, and reporter. He was hard-working and ambitious. In 1878, at the age of 20, he borrowed $250 to buy the controlling interest in a failing Tennessee newspaper, the *Chattanooga Times,* thus beginning his career as a newspaper publisher before he was old enough to vote. He promoted high standards of journalism in the Chattanooga paper and soon brought it back to financial health. In 1896, looking for new challenges, he heard about the *New York Times*'s troubles. Ochs offered to take over as publisher in return for a contract that would give him a majority of the paper's stock if he succeeded in making it profitable for three consecutive years. One of his early acts after becoming publisher of the *Times* on August 18, 1896, was to add the slogan, ''All the News That's Fit To Print,'' thus serving notice that the *Times* would continue to avoid sensationalism and follow high editorial standards.

Arrival of Adolph Ochs at the End of the 19th Century

Ochs's first two years with the *Times* were a continual struggle to carry on operations and improve the paper with inadequate capital. The expenses of covering the Spanish-American War in 1898 came close to ruining the paper, which sold then for three cents a copy. Some *Times* executives advised raising the price, but Ochs made the brilliant and daring decision to reduce the price to one cent. Within a year paid circulation trebled from 26,000 to 76,000. Advertising linage increased by nearly 40 percent, and the paper was profitable. Despite subsequent price increases, this was the beginning of a long upward trend in circulation and profitability. On August 14, 1900, Ochs received the NYTC stock certificates that established his control over the paper and the company, a controlling interest that was still held by his descendants in 1991.

The *Times*'s success under Ochs was due to much more than price-cutting. He improved financial and Wall Street coverage, added a Sunday magazine supplement, and a Saturday book review section, which was later moved to Sunday. With a brilliant managing editor, Carr Van Anda, the *Times* carried out numerous journalistic coups. It scooped the world on the Japanese-Russian naval battle in 1904 by sending the first wireless dispatches from a war area. It again scooped the world on the *Titanic* shipwreck in 1912 and outdid all competition in reporting the events of World War I. The paper warned of the excesses of the 1920s, but was well equipped financially to survive the Great Depression thanks to Ochs's conservative policy of plowing back into the paper a major portion of its profits.

Under Ochs, the NYTC followed a general policy of avoiding diversification, although Ochs himself continued as the personal owner and publisher of the *Chattanooga Times* and had a private investment in a Philadelphia paper between 1901 and 1913. In 1926, however, the NYTC did take part ownership, along with Kimberly & Clark Company, in a Canadian paper mill, the Spruce Falls Power and Paper Company, to assure its supplies of newsprint.

The *Times* did relatively well during the Great Depression, with daily circulation holding in the 450,000 to 500,000 range. Ochs's health declined during the early 1930s, and he died on April 8, 1935. On May 7, 1935, the company's directors elected as president and publisher Ochs's son-in-law, Arthur Hays Sulzberger, who had married Ochs's daughter Iphigene in 1917 and subsequently worked his way up through the executive ranks of the newspaper.

New Leadership in the Postwar Period

Under Sulzberger the *Times* improved steadily in news coverage, financial strength, and technical progress. In a diversification move in 1944 the NYTC purchased New York City radio stations WQXR and WQXR-FM. Sulzberger opposed without success the unionization of *Times* employees. The company's first published financial statement in 1958 showed 60 consecutive years of increasing profits. In 1957 a recapitalization split the common stock into A and B common stock, with the B shares, mostly held by the Ochs trust, having voting control over the company. Sulzberger's health began to fail in the late 1950s. He retired in 1961. His successor as president and publisher was his son-in-law, Orvil E. Dryfoos. Dryfoos died in 1963. On June 20, 1963, he was succeeded in turn as president and publisher by Arthur Hays Sulzberger's son, Arthur Ochs Sulzberger, who continued in 1991 to lead the NYTC as chairman and chief executive officer.

Key Dates:

1851: The *New York Daily Times* is founded by Henry Jarvis Raymond and George Jones, with the first issue appearing on September 18.
1857: The newspaper changes its name to the *New York Times.*
1869: Upon Henry Jarvis Raymond's death, George Jones assumes control of the newspaper.
1896: With the newspaper close to bankruptcy, a group of Wall Street investors arranges to save the firm—and their investments—by placing it in receivership and recapitalizing it as a new company, The New York Times Company; the paper's new publisher, Adolph Simon Ochs, adopts the slogan, ''All the News That's Fit To Print.''
1935: Following Ochs's death, his son-in-law, Arthur Hays Sulzberger, is elected president and publisher of the NYTC.
1963: Arthur Hays Sulzberger's son, Arthur Ochs Sulzberger, becomes president and publisher of the NYTC.
1965: The company embarks on its first major program of diversification, expanding its interests to include new newspaper, magazine, television, and book properties.
1995: The company enters cyberspace by joining with eight other newspaper companies in an online news service, New Century Network, and by creating The New York Times Electronic Media Company as a wholly owned subsidiary to develop new electronic products and distribution channels for the *Times.*
1997: The *New York Times* introduces color printing to its front page.
1999: Revenues reach an unprecedented $3.1 billion; the company invests $15 million in TheStreet.com, a top Internet provider of financial information and investment news and commentary.
2000: The company sells its Magazine Group to Advance Publications, Inc.
2001: The company is awarded six Pulitzer Prizes for the *New York Times*'s coverage of the events of 9/11.

Although Sulzberger made some administrative changes and broadened the scope of the *Times* news coverage, the company continued to earn a relatively low profit margin on revenues, partly because of his policy of spending freely for thorough reporting, even to the extent of throwing out advertisements to make room for news. A second bitter strike against the paper in 1965 unsettled the management, and a decision was made to undertake a significant program of diversification. In 1967 the company's book and educational division was enlarged, and in 1968 the *Times* purchased a 51 percent interest in Arno Press. In 1969 the A common stock was given the vote for three members of the nine-member board. This action together with a public offering qualified the A stock for listing on the American Stock Exchange. The B stock, which controlled the company, continued to be held mostly by the Ochs family trust. In 1971 the NYTC paid Cowles Communications Company 2.6 million shares of class A stock to purchase substantial newspaper, magazine, television, and book properties, including *Family Circle* and other magazines; a Florida newspaper chain; a Memphis, Tennessee, TV station; and a textbook publisher.

During the 1970s the newspaper's profit margins continued to be under pressure because of competition, especially in New York City suburban areas. The former Cowles properties helped buoy earnings despite the 1976 sale of some medical magazines acquired from Cowles. In 1980 the NYTC paid about $100 million for a southern New Jersey cable television operation, its largest acquisition since the Cowles deal. In 1984 the book publishing operation was sold to Random House, but in 1985 the NYTC, flush with record profits, spent about $400 million on the purchase of five regional newspapers and two TV stations. In 1986 yet another recapitalization converted every ten shares of B stock into nine shares of A and one share of B, with the B stock still controlling the company. Since more than 80 percent of the B stock was held by the Ochs trust, this move gave the trustees more liquidity without sacrificing control of the company. The years 1989 and 1990 continued to be profitable. In 1989 the NYTC, admitting it was not making progress with cable, sold all of its cable TV properties to a consortium of Pennsylvania cable companies for $420 million. Also in 1989 the company acquired *McCall's* magazine, which, together with the acquisitions in 1988 of *Golf World* and *Sailing World,* substantially strengthened the NYTC's magazine group. The company's large new automated printing and distribution facility in Edison, New Jersey, which had been under construction for several years, was scheduled to become operational in late 1990.

Diversification in the 1990s

Throughout the 1990s, the company would buy and sell properties in the areas of print, cable broadcasting, and electronic media because the decline in newspaper readership in the United States was continuing. In 1993, NYTC bought Affiliated Publications, which owned the *Boston Globe* and specialty magazines published by its division, BPI Communications. In 1994, the company sold its one-third interest in BPI, along with a group of women's magazines, including *Family Circle* and *McCall's,* to Germany's Bertelsmann AG. Also in 1994, NYTC began construction on a state-of-the-art printing plant that would allow adding more color to newspapers and allow for later deadlines.

In 1995, the purchase of a majority interest in Video News International, a video newsgathering company, was made. A return to cable was made when the company bought a minority stake in the cable arts network Ovation and launched two cable news channels in Arkansas. Also in 1995, the company entered cyberspace in two ways. One was by joining with eight other newspaper companies in an online news service, New Century Network. The other was creating The New York Times Electronic Media Company as a wholly owned subsidiary that would develop new products and distribution channels for the *Times,* such as on the Web, America Online (AOL), and The New York Times Index.

Two years later, in 1997, a new, expanded version of the AOL site debuted with a new design, improved navigation and functionality, new content areas, and expanded advertising opportunities, such as allowing advertisers to target ads to readers of particular sections. The new content, available only to AOL members who made the *Times* site one of the service's most popular since its debut in 1994, included People in the News area, enhancements to Science Times, live crosswords and news chats, a weekly news quiz, a Topic of the Day message board for discussions based on Page One articles, monthly Times retrospectives, free access to Times crossword puzzles and the bridge and chess columns, a themed monthly crossword puzzle, and The New York Times Magazine.

The New York Times Syndicate launched a weekly column written by the Duchess of York in 1997. The Duchess, who was the former Sarah Ferguson and former wife of Prince Andrew, the second son of Great Britain's Queen Elizabeth, wrote about current events and social issues that interested her.

The New York Times Company had come a long way from the small brownstone on Nassau Street where Henry Raymond published the first issue of the *New York Times* in 1851. Company success resulted not only from strong business leadership during much of its history but also from a series of capable publishers, editors, and reporters who built and continued to operate one of the world's great newspapers, in print and online.

Ambitious Expansion Efforts for the 21st Century

In 1997, the New York Times Company embarked on an ambitious program of expansion focused on transforming its flagship product, the *New York Times* newspaper, from a regional to a national publication. Integral to the goal of building widespread brand recognition was a new, $20 million advertising campaign featuring the slogan, ''Expect the World.'' That year, the newspaper also implemented the most extensive changes to its operations and format since the 1970s. With more advanced production equipment, the paper was able to included later-breaking news and sports scores, as well as new sections and features. On October 16, the paper introduced color printing to its front page.

Further, as 1997 marked the culmination of a ten-year, $1 billion program of capital investments to shore up the paper's strengths, its print facilities, and its customer base, the company enjoyed a dramatic increase in cash flow, which it began to allocate toward two long-term goals, both aimed at increasing shareholder value. First, the company launched an aggressive share repurchasing initiative—starting with three million shares valued at $145.6 million that year, the initiative grew every year with the company allocating $623.7 million for the repurchase of 15 million shares in 2001—in order to improve its overall leverage and increase stock dividends. Second, the company sought strategic acquisitions to expand its portfolio of products and services, enter new markets, and facilitate distribution by opening new print sites around the country.

The company continued to flourish. Among other efforts to increase the appeal of its nationally distributed newspaper, the *New York Times* added new features such as Circuits, a weekly technology section introduced in 1998, which was soon generating about $1 million per month in advertising revenue. In 1999, with the economic boom of the 1990s still holding, the company enjoyed earnings per share growth of 20.5 percent, its fifth consecutive year of double-digit growth. Moreover, revenues for 1999 reached an unprecedented $3.1 billion, while total costs increases were comparatively modest. Indeed, even while the company focused on expansion, it continued to keep a firm grasp on its expenses, and to hone its focus on core businesses. In 1997 the Magazine Group sold off six of its smaller, low-margin publications in order to channel more resources into its high-margin golf publications, especially the award-winning *Golf World.* Although the golf magazines remained popular and profitable, they contributed only about 3 percent to the company's overall revenue, and by 2000 the company moved to sell off its Magazine Group entirely to Advance Publications, Inc.

To keep pace with the growing Internet economy, in 1999 the company established New York Times Digital, an independent business unit, to oversee the operations of NYTimes.com, then boasting more than ten million registered users. The company adopted what it called a ''click and brick'' business model, by which it sought to establish synergies between its traditional print media and its electronic offerings, as well as to maximize the revenue potential of the Internet. To this end, in 1999 the NYTC invested $15 million in TheStreet.com, one of the top Internet providers of financial information and investment news and commentary, a digital publication with whom the *Times* shared a key customer base. The New York Times Digital unit reached profitability in 2002.

The year 2001 proved turbulent for the NYTC, as the dot-com bubble burst, the economic slowdown bloomed into a full recession, and as New York City weathered the terrorist attacks of September 11. Still, the company managed to perform well in the midst of chaos, with earnings per share growth of 8 percent in a year when the S&P 500 dropped by 13 percent, and an impressive six Pulitzer prizes to show for the *New York Times*'s coverage of 9/11. Staying the course with its national expansion program, the company had increased its distribution from 62 markets in 1997 to 235 in 2002. Even as the national program enjoyed overwhelming success, the company also continued to invest in its regional media properties, especially through its ownership of the *Boston Globe,* and to lay the groundwork for penetration of international markets through the introduction of branded pages into respected foreign newspapers such as France's *Le Monde.*

The *New York Times* newspaper was beset by an internal crisis in the spring of 2003 when news emerged that one of its reporters had written numerous fraudulent and even plagiarized stories that had gone undetected by his supervisors. The scandal resulted in the resignation of two of the paper's top editors, Howell Raines and Gerald M. Boyd, and a serious blemish on the record of the otherwise revered paper. Despite this unfortunate episode, however, most agreed that the paper's image would soon be restored. Overall the New York Times Company appeared exceptionally well-positioned for continued success into the first decade of the 21st century.

Principal Subsidiaries

NYT Capital, Inc.; NYT Holdings Inc.; The New York Times Syndication Sales Corporation; The New York Times Distribution Corporation; The New York Times Electronic Media Company; The New York Times Sales Company; The New York Times Syndication Sales Corporation.

Principal Competitors

Dow Jones & Company, Inc.; Gannett Co., Inc.; The News Corporation Limited.

Further Reading

Berger, Meyer, *The Story of the New York Times, 1851–1951,* New York: Simon and Schuster, 1951.

Goulden, Joseph C., *Fit to Print,* Secaucus, N.J.: Lyle Stuart Inc., 1988.

''Keeping the Gray Lady Spry: CEO Russell Lewis Explains How Constant Investment, Even in Bad Times, Ensures New York Times Co.'s Long-Term Health,'' *Business Week Online,* November 8, 2002.

Salisbury, Harrison E., *Without Fear or Favor,* New York: Times Books, 1980.

Steinberg, Jacques, ''Changes at the Times: The Overview,'' *New York Times,* June 6, 2003, p. 1.

Talese, Gay, *The Kingdom and the Power,* New York: World Publishing Company, 1969.

White, Christina, ''A French Beau for the New York Times: The Paper's New English-Language Supplement in *Le Monde* Could Be a Long-Sought Short-Cut into Europe's Mainstream Readership,'' *Business Week Online,* April 12, 2002.

Wyatt, Edward, ''New York Times to Invest $15 Million in TheStreet.com,'' *New York Times,* February 23, 1999, p. C8.

—Bernard A. Block
—updates: Dorothy Kroll, Erin Brown

NEXTmedia

Next Media Ltd.

8 Chun Ying Street
Tseung Kwan O I
New Territories
Hong Kong
Telephone: 852 2896 8688
Fax: 852 2247 4154
Web site: http://www.nextmedia.com

Public Company
Incorporated: 1999
Employees: 2,037
Sales: HK$2.5 billion ($277.20 million) (2003)
Stock Exchanges: Hong Kong
Ticker Symbol: 0282
NAIC: 551112 Offices of Other Holding Companies; 323110 Commercial Lithographic Printing; 511120 Periodical Publishers; 541820 Public Relations Services

One of Hong Kong's leading newspaper and magazine publishers, Next Media Ltd. has been making a push into the highly competitive Taiwan market in the early 2000s. The company, headed by controversial founder and Chairman Jimmy Lai, publishes *Next Magazine,* Hong Kong's leading weekly magazine with a circulation of more than 450,000, and *Apple Daily,* the city's second largest selling daily newspaper. The company also produces a number of other titles in Hong Kong, including the ''bundled'' magazines *Sudden Weekly* and *Eat & Travel Weekly,* and the youth-oriented *Easy Finder,* which became bundled with a special teen edition of *Eat & Travel Weekly* in 2003. Taiwan's population, more than four times the size of Hong Kong, offers a potentially major market for Next Media, which began publishing a Taiwanese edition of *Next Magazine* in 2001. Faced with more than 6,000 magazine and newspaper competitors, and difficult entry into the island's distribution market, Next has managed to install itself as a new force in that market, a position underscored by the launch of a Taiwanese edition of *Apple Daily* in 2003. Next Media also has its own printing operations and a limited Internet presence. The company is listed on the Hong Kong stock exchange, and posted HK$2.15 billion ($277 million) in revenues in 2003.

From Rags to Riches in the 1980s

The formation of Next Media at the end of the 1990s represented a new chapter in a true rags to riches story. Lai Chee Ying, known as Jimmy Lai, was born into poverty in mainland China's Guangdong province during the early years of the Cultural Revolution. Lai started working when he was just nine years old, carrying bags for passengers at the Guangdong railway station. Lai also began selling goods on the black market, telling *Success:* ''It was a good education. I learned about human nature and how to anticipate people's reactions.''

Lai also learned about the world outside of Guangdong and, especially, Hong Kong. One of Lai's first contacts with the British-controlled city came when he was given a piece of imported chocolate, a rarity amid Chinese austerity of the time. Working at the train station also brought Lai in contact with wealthy Hong Kong residents visiting the mainland. By the time he was 12, Lai had become determined to flee to Hong Kong.

Lai's family put together the smuggler's fee, the equivalent of nearly $500, and Lai made the crossing hidden in the bottom of a boat. In Hong Kong, Lai's uncle helped him find a job as a laborer in a textile factory earning less than $10 per month. Yet Lai had no intention of remaining a simple laborer. Recognizing that success in Hong Kong required the ability to speak English, Lai, who had no formal education, began teaching himself the language, using money he had managed to save from his wages to buy an English dictionary and textbook.

Lai already displayed the character traits that enabled him to become one of Hong Kong's most successful businessmen by the late 1980s. As he explained to *Success:* ''I spoke lousy English to other people, and eventually, they would correct me. I was never bashful. I always reveal my shortcomings to others. I let them criticize me, and then I eliminate the errors.''

At the age of 20, Lai had fought his way to the factory's general manager position. Lai continued building up his savings, while focusing his ambitions on new areas. Lai decided to

Company Perspectives:

In its corporate culture, Next Media strives for: A simple hierarchy. Direct communication, and a high degree of transparency. A challenging working environment where employees are encouraged to tackle challenges through trial and error, as well as assume responsibility for their actions. Flexible working practices that provide room for creativity and the development of individual capabilities. An attitude that "This is My Company," and the sharing of profits among employees. Encouragement to stay abreast of changes and run ahead of the media.

gamble his savings, padded by his first year-end bonus as general manager, on the Hong Kong stock exchange. Lai's speculations soon paid off, and by mid-decade, Lai had built up enough capital to start his own business. According to *Success,* Lai had parlayed his initial $3,000 investment into a fortune worth $750,000.

In 1975, Lai bought out the owners of a bankrupt garment factory, Comitex, and began producing sweaters. The company was a quick success, selling to J.C. Penney, Montgomery Ward, and others. As part of that business, Lai made a number of trips to the United States, where he was exposed to Western-style retail formats. By the beginning of the 1980s, restless for a new challenge, Lai decided to go into the retail market himself.

Then in the early 1980s, Lai formed a new business, Giordano's, named after a favorite New York restaurant, and began opening stores in Hong Kong. Over the next several years, Lai opened a number of stores in the city, attempting to target an upscale market. Yet, as Lai himself admitted: "The more stores we built, the worse we did. I was trying to show the world how great I was, instead of showing the customer how great our goods were."

Faced with shutting down the business, Lai instead decided to transform it, turning to other successful retailers for inspiration. As he told *Forbes:* "I gave up thinking I knew what the retailing business should be. I went out and picked the best in the market and stole what they had learned by trial and error."

Eventually, Lai settled on a new formula. As he described it to *Success:* "McDonald's was doing the best. It has a very basic menu, so I concluded that simplicity should be the core value of Giordano. But simple becomes boring very quickly. So I looked at Benetton. It gives items a fresh look by extending the colors, which costs nothing. From Marks and Spencer, I learned you can sell high-quality goods at a reasonable price." Other retailers also contributed to Lai's new retail visions, including The Gap and The Limited and their use of computerized ordering and production techniques. The changes at Giordano's also involved the company's staff, who were instructed to emphasize customer service—and who received motivation through a doubling of their salaries. By the beginning of the 1990s, Giordano's was one of Hong Kong's leading clothing retailers and had spread its network to more than 200 stores, including its first stores in mainland China.

Media Magnate in the 1990s

The 1989 massacre on Beijing's Tiananmen Square inspired Lai's next career move. By then, Lai had become restless for a new business venture, saying of Giordano's: "Everything was on track. I no longer felt motivated." In the face of the Tiananmen Square massacre, Lai discovered new motivation, and became determined to add his voice to the pro-democracy movement—by entering the publishing arena. Watching the Chinese government's actions at Tiananmen had, as Lai told the *Washington Times,* "made me realize information was the core of freedom. Just making money no longer motivated me. But if I could deliver information, which is freedom, and still make money at the same time. . . ."

In 1990, Lai launched his first magazine, *Next Weekly.* The title immediately became a success on the market, in part due to its outspoken opposition to the Communist mainland government. In addition, the weekly became noted for its hard-hitting investigative journalism. Yet the magazine also shrewdly blended in a more lurid mix of true crime, celebrity gossip, and sex, wooing increasing numbers of readers and advertisers. By 1993, the magazine had captured some 15 percent of Hong Kong's adult readers.

Lai's media wing, Next Media International, launched three more magazine titles, *Sudden Weekly, Eat & Travel Weekly,* and the youth-oriented *Easy Finder,* through the 1990s. The company also began preparations to enter the newspaper market in the early 1990s, seeking backers for the launch of a daily newspaper, to be called *Apple Daily.*

In the meantime, however, Lai had continued his outspoken criticism of the Chinese government. In 1993, he published a column in which he labeled Chinese Premier Li Peng, who had been responsible for the Tiananmen Square massacre, "the son of a turtle's egg"—one of the worst insults in China. The Chinese government retaliated by placing pressure on Giordano's. By then, Taiwan had become the chain's major market, while also growing into Singapore. Yet the fast-evolving Chinese mainland remained the single largest potential market for the chain. Some weeks after the Lai column, the government shut down its main branch in Guangdong. Soon after, Lai agreed to sell his shares of Giordano, including his control of its mainland subsidiary.

Lai's difficulties with Chinese authorities, in the face of the coming handover of Hong Kong to the Communist government, prompted investors to balk on the launch of *Apple Daily.* Lai was forced to put up $100 million of his own funds for the establishment of the newspaper.

First released in the summer of 1995, *Apple Daily* was a quick success. Despite entering a market crowded with some 60 newspapers for a population of just six million, *Apple Daily* soon climbed to the top of the pack, reaching a circulation of 300,000 before the end of the year. Part of the paper's success could be attributed to Lai's willingness to learn from others' successes, and, in the case of *Apple Daily,* the success of *USA Today* in particular. Featuring a similar reliance on graphics and shortened, highlighted text, *Apple Daily* also provided a strong lifestyles and gossip quotient to appeal to Hong Kong readers. By 1997, the paper had become the second leading newspaper in Hong Kong, with a circulation of 400,000.

Key Dates:

1975: Lai Chee Ying (Jimmy Lai) buys a bankrupt garment producer and redevelops it into a successful manufacturer of sweaters for department store customers.
1981: Lai enters retail, setting up Giordano's clothing chain.
1989: After the Tiananmen Square massacre, Lai decides to enter the media sector.
1990: *Next Weekly,* which grows into Hong Kong's leading weekly magazine, is established.
1995: Lai sells the stake in Giordano's and launches *Apple Daily,* which becomes Hong Kong's second largest daily newspaper.
1999: Lai acquires the publicly listed Paramount Publishing Group, which is renamed Next Media.
2000: After an attempt to enter the Internet retail market, Lai moves to Taiwan to set up media titles there; Lai transfers ownership of *Next Weekly* and *Apple Daily* to Next Media.
2001: A Taiwan edition of *Next Weekly* is launched.
2002: The "bundled" magazine concept is launched, combining *Sudden Weekly* and *Eat & Travel Weekly,* for the Hong Kong market.
2003: The second bundled magazine, *EasyFinder/Eat & Travel Weekly,* is launched; the Taiwan edition of *Apple Daily* is launched.
2004: The Taiwan *Apple Daily* circulation tops 435,000, placing it among the island's top five daily newspapers.

Lai hoped to bring his newly focused media group to the Hong Kong stock exchange in the second half of the decade. Yet Lai's apparent vulnerability in the face of the 1997 handover caused bankers to back off from a listing. Even Lai recognized his vulnerability, admitting to the *Washington Times* in 1997: "If we survive the next two or three years, we can survive forever." Nonetheless, Lai remained defiant, stating: "As the free market expands, their power will erode—time is on our side."

Unable to find backing for an initial public offering, Lai made it to the market through the back door in 1999, acquiring Paramount Publishing Group in October of that year. Lai added the magazine title *Easyfinder* and other holdings to Paramount and the company name was changed to Next Media. For the time being, Lai kept both of his major titles, *Next Weekly* and *Apple Daily,* private and separate from the publicly listed company. Yet Next Media became the vessel for Lai's latest business interest, the Internet, including the company's own Internet provider service, nextmedia.com, as well as an online travel service.

Swept up in the hype surrounding the new Internet and high-technology markets, Lai decided to take on Hong Kong's retailing elite, Hutchison Whampoa and Jardine Matheson, which controlled most of the colony's retail sector. Lai determined to attack these leaders by setting up an online grocery and home delivery service, Admart. That business quickly expanded its range of offerings far beyond grocery. Yet distributors proved unwilling to supply Admart for fear of offending Hutchison Whampoa and Jardine Matheson, and Admart was forced to buy goods, often of inferior quality, on the gray market, in order to meet customer orders.

Admart started out losing money and its losses only deepened through its first year. By 2000, after just 15 months in business, Admart's—and Lai's—losses had topped $120 million. Lai pulled the plug on Admart, and drastically scaled back his other Internet ventures.

New Horizons for the New Century

Lai's Internet failure forced him to leave Hong Kong. As he told *Time International:* "Hong Kong has no place for me." Lai transferred control of *Next Weekly* and *Apple Daily* to Next Media and turned toward a new horizon: Taiwan. With a population of nearly 30 million, Taiwan offered new opportunity for growth for the company. In 2001, Lai teamed with local partner PC Home Publishing to launch a Taiwanese edition of *Next Weekly.* Despite intense competition from some 6,000 magazines and newspapers on the island, and despite the company's inability to enter the market's distribution channels beyond newsstand sales, *Next Weekly* successfully found a market among Taiwan readers. By 2002, Taiwan Next had already begun to turn a profit.

Buoyed by this first success, Lai and Next Media began preparing for the launch of a Taiwanese edition of *Apple Daily* as well. Back in Hong Kong, in the meantime, the company had been developing a new "bundling" concept of combining complementary magazine titles into a single format. In January 2002, the company debuted its first bundle, combining *Sudden Weekly* and *Eat & Travel Weekly.* By March of that year, circulation for the new concept had already topped 200,000. In April 2003, Next Media launched a second bundled magazine for the Hong Kong market, adding a specially edited teenager version of *Eat & Travel Weekly* to the youth-oriented *Easyfinder* magazine.

Next Media debuted the Taiwanese edition of *Apple Daily* in May 2003, backed by a strong promotional campaign and a low introductory sales price. The launch of *Apple Daily* sparked a price war among Taiwan's newspaper leaders, yet by the beginning of 2004, Lai had once again revealed his magic touch. With a circulation of some 435,000, *Apple Daily* had claimed a spot among the island's top five newspapers. Jimmy Lai promised to remain a force in the region's media market in the new century.

Principal Subsidiaries

Apple Daily Limited; Apple Daily Online Limited; Apple Daily Printing Limited; Cameron Printing Company Limited; Database Gateway Limited; Easy Finder Limited; Easy Finder Hong Kong Marketing Limited; Easy Media Limited; Eat and Travel Weekly Company Limited; Next Magazine Advertising Limited; Next Magazine Publishing Limited; Next Media Group Management Limited; Next Media Hong Kong/Publication Publishing Limited; Paramount Printing Company Limited; Rainbow Graphic & Printing Company Limited; Sudden Weekly Limited.

Principal Competitors

Oriental Press Group Ltd.; Ming Pao Enterprise Corporation Ltd.; Global China Group Holdings Ltd.; Dai Nippon Printing Company Hong Kong Ltd.; Midas International Holdings Ltd.; Culturecom Holdings Ltd.; Jessica Publications Ltd.; Sino United Electronic Publishing Ltd.; Asia Magic Hong Kong Ltd.

Further Reading

Balfour, Frederik, ''A Thorn in China's Side,'' *Business Week,* July 28, 2003.

Barnathan, Joyce, ''Readers Take a Shine to Hong Kong's Apple Daily,'' *BusinessWeek,* October 2, 1995.

Clifford, Mark, ''The Humbling of Jimmy Lai,'' *Business Week,* October 23, 2000.

Jacob, Rahul, and Swee Lin Ho, ''A Talent for Shock Tactics,'' *Financial Times,* February 25, 2000, p. 12.

Meredith, Robyn, ''At It Again,'' *Forbes,* January 12, 2004.

Stein, Tom, Katherine C. Allan, Drusilla Menaker, and Christopher Brown-Humes, ''The King of Hong Kong,'' *Success,* June 1996, p. 34.

''Taipei's Next,'' *Time International,* January 22, 2001, p. 26.

Tanzer, Andrew, ''Studying at the Feet of Masters,'' *Forbes,* May 10, 1993, p. 43.

Witter, Willis, ''Hong Kong Paper Not Easing Up on Tiananmen Attack,'' *Washington Times,* June 13, 1997, p. 17.

—M.L. Cohen

Nippon Shinpan Co., Ltd.

33-5, 3-chome
Hongo, Bunkyo-ku
Tokyo 113-8411
Japan
Telephone: 81-3-3811-3111
Fax: 81-3-3817-8775
Web site: http://www.nicos.co.jp

Public Company
Incorporated: 1951 as Nippon Shinyo Hanbai Company
Employees: 4,954
Sales: $2.54 billion (2003)
Stock Exchanges: Tokyo Osaka Nagoya Frankfurt Paris
NAIC: 522210 Credit Card Issuing; 522291 Consumer Lending; 561450 Credit Bureaus

One of Japan's leading consumer lending companies, Nippon Shinpan Co., Ltd. deals not only in consumer credit cards but also in loan guarantees, loans, and bill collection. More than 14.5 million of its NICOS credit cards have been issued. The company also offers loans for automobiles and other durable goods and has some 200 branches throughout Japan. Nippon Shinpan hopes to boost e-commerce in Japan in the 21st century.

Arrival of Consumer Credit in Japan: 1950s

When Mitsunari Yamada convinced four Japanese department stores to accept coupons in lieu of cash in 1951, he started what would become Japan's first and largest consumer credit company, one that today handles credit cards, loans, credit guarantees, real estate, financing, and leasing. Yamada pioneered Japan's credit industry during a time of high consumer prices and economic uncertainty. In the years following World War II, Japan faced not only rampant inflation, but a shortage of resources amid a boom in population. This economic plight was ripe ground for Yamada's credit services. With the founding of Nippon Shinpan's forerunner, Nippon Shinyo Hanbai Company, in Tokyo in 1951, Yamada offered consumers a chance to pay for goods on installment. Yamada had negotiated an agreement with four major department stores to accept Nippon Shinyo Hanbai's coupons as payment for goods. In the years to follow, the company, which soon changed its name to Nippon Shinpan, gradually added stores to its network, to make credit payment more convenient and appealing to consumers.

Just five years after launching its credit business, Nippon Shinpan moved into another industry, real estate, marketing Japan's first luxury condominium in 1956. The successful endeavor led to handling mortgages and selling homes and home sites.

Nippon Shinpan's housing business would prove vital after the Ministry of International Trade and Industry (MITI) in 1959 set restrictive guidelines on credit services. Designed to help small retailers, the MITI guidelines limited coupon use geographically, severely curtailing Nippon Shinpan's credit business.

Growth and Diversification: 1960s

The company responded to the stringent MITI guidelines by stepping up its housing-related activities. In 1960, Nippon Shinpan became the first company to offer housing loans, with more housing and condominium development to follow. Taking a bold step, the company also began to guarantee unsecured cash loans made by other financial lenders. The move brought new opportunities to consumers and, according to the company, the service grew ''phenomenally'' after it was initiated.

By 1963, Nippon Shinpan had found a way to sidestep MITI guidelines by offering ''shopping loans.'' These loans involved no coupons and as a result were not covered by the MITI rules. Under the procedure, consumers would apply for credit at member stores. Once credit was approved, Nippon Shinpan would pay the purchase price for goods and consumers would pay the loan back in installments.

Nippon Shinpan began issuing credit cards in 1966, launching what would turn into its largest business. Also during this time, the company made plans for an extended network of offices and branched into loans backed by securities.

International Expansion: 1970s–80s

The 1970s marked Nippon Shinpan's first ventures abroad. In December 1969, the company struck an agreement with MasterCard International (then Interbank Card Association) to

Company Perspectives:

Today, continuously valuing its relationship with consumers highly, Nippon Shinpan aspires to be a ''Dream-Network Company'' that contributes to the creation of a more prosperous society by striving to deliver products and services that match individual lifestyles and life stages.

make the Nippon Shinpan card accepted internationally. By June 1973, Nippon Shinpan was issuing MasterCards overseas.

Its ventures overseas prompted the company to establish liaisons with retailers and banks in Hong Kong and Hawaii, two popular Japanese tourist destinations. Leisure had already become an important sideline for Nippon Shinpan. In 1971, the company opened its exclusive U-Topy tennis club in the resort area of Karuizawa.

Foreign bonds became company business in the late 1970s; Nippon Shinpan issued Swiss franc bonds in 1976 and deutsche mark bonds in 1978.

In 1981, Nippon Shinpan entered a joint venture with the BankAmerica Group to set up the International Factoring Corporation, a financing concern targeting small and medium-sized companies. The newly formed company focused on purchasing debt and servicing accounts. Japan's sluggish loan business prompted BankAmerica to pursue the partnership, according to the *Financial Times*.

Although continuing to expand both its financial and real estate businesses, growth in the credit card arena was Nippon Shinpan's signature for the 1980s. During a four-year period between 1984 and 1988, card circulation grew from ten million to nearly 18 million. Member stores in Japan hit 334,000 in 1988. The company also entered joint card agreements with Japan's Postal Savings system, a major savings organization, as well as MasterCard and Visa International.

The Visa deal, in 1987, put the Visa logo on the 13 million cards Nippon Shinpan had in circulation in Japan at the time. Most of the cards were private-label cards for such companies as Shell Oil and Shiseido, a cosmetics retailer. The remaining cards Nippon Shinpan issued itself.

In 1988, the company established the International Credit Card Business Association, an organization with a goal of promoting MasterCard and Visa credit cards, ensuring that credit cards would continue to be the backbone of Nippon Shinpan's business well into the next decade.

New Challenges in the 1990s–2000s

Continuing to diversify, Nippon Shinpan acquired a 50 percent interest in Equitable Life Insurance Co., a subsidiary of U.S.-based Equitable Life Assurance Society, in 1991. The purchase was Nippon Shinpan's inaugural foray into life insurance. The company hoped the addition of life insurance would complement its existing services.

In 1996 Nippon Shinpan adopted a medium-term business plan that called for developing its consumer credit business into a core operation. The credit card business would remain the primary unit, but the company believed bulking up its consumer credit business would increase profitability. Nippon Shinpan hoped to increase the balance of consumer credits from about ¥230 billion in 1996 to some ¥400 billion by the end of the decade. It also aimed to boost the credit card business from ¥1.62 trillion to ¥2.2 trillion.

In order to meet its goals, Nippon Shinpan was forced to do some reorganization. Some of the company's affiliates, namely Rotary Service Co., credit association Nippon Shinpan Shinyo Kumiai, and lender International Factoring Corp., had amassed considerable debt, and Nippon Shinpan chose to write off these bad loans, which eventually totaled some ¥107.6 billion. This extraordinary loss affected Nippon Shinpan's bottom line, and for the first time since it had been listed on the Tokyo Stock Exchange, it reported a net loss. The loss amounted to ¥65.1 billion for the fiscal year ended March 31, 1997.

Reacting to increasing debt and a poor Japanese economy, Nippon Shinpan focused on strengthening core businesses and shedding poorly performing units. In 1998 the company announced plans to liquidate a number of subsidiaries, including Nippon Shinpan Finance (U.K.) PLC and Nippon Shinpan Finance (U.S.A.) Co. Nippon Shinpan also shut down its U.S.-based resort development unit Monarch Bay Resort Inc. after selling its assets, which included golf courses, to Capital Pacific Holdings Inc. of the United States.

In addition, in the late 1990s, Nippon Shinpan decided to exit the mortgage loan market and, in reaction to lower demand for new automobiles, to shrink its automobile loan business. In 2000 the company said it would be out of the real estate business completely within a year or two. The value of real estate in Japan had declined considerably during the 1990s, which hurt Nippon Shinpan's bottom line—the real estate division posted a loss of about ¥300 million in the fiscal year ended March 31, 1999. At the time of the announcement, Nippon Shinpan held some ¥80 billion worth of available real estate in Japan, as well as ¥50 billion worth of real estate abroad. It also had about ¥50 billion in mortgage loan credits. Nippon Shinpan was expected to lose about ¥40 billion in its divestment plan.

Nippon Shinpan ran into additional problems with affiliates in the early 2000s with the bankruptcy of Inter-Lease Corporation, a leasing unit that had been established in 1974. Inter-Lease had some ¥300 billion in outstanding loans in the early 1990s, and its debt only climbed. Nippon Shinpan, with an 8.8 percent stake in Inter-Lease, was its biggest shareholder. In 1997 Nippon Shinpan launched a ten-year restructuring plan for Inter-Lease, but by 2000 it was clear Inter-Lease could not be revived. Inter-Lease had about ¥800 billion in liabilities. Nippon Shinpan's investment amounted to ¥45 billion, and it also had guaranteed about ¥27 billion worth of Inter-Lease's loans.

As a result of its financial struggles in the late 1990s and early 2000s, Nippon Shinpan underwent a restructuring and implemented a four-year plan that focused on streamlining operations, divesting noncore businesses, and cutting personnel. The plan, known as the NicoS V Plan, aimed to lower liabilities from ¥2.6 trillion in 2000 to ¥900 billion in fiscal 2004. The plan called for shedding 41 percent of its workforce, about

Key Dates:

1951: Nippon Shinyo Hanbai Company is founded in Tokyo.
1956: The company enters the real estate industry.
1960: Nippon Shinpan begins offering housing loans.
1966: The company begins offering credit cards.
1969: Nippon Shinpan and MasterCard International launch a business relationship.
1970: The company is listed on the Tokyo Stock Exchange.
1981: Nippon Shinpan and BankAmerica Group establish a joint venture known as International Factoring Corporation.
1988: The company founds the International Credit Card Business Association to promote MasterCard and Visa credit cards.
2000: Subsidiary Inter-Lease collapses.
2003: UFJ Bank announces plans to acquire a controlling stake in Nippon Shinpan.

3,700 jobs, by the end of 2004, as well as the reduction of its affiliates from 36 to 18.

Nippon Shinpan seemed to be on the road to recovery when it was slammed with a scandal. In November 2002 a number of its top officials were arrested by the police for allegedly making illegal payments to a corporate racketeer, known as a ''sokaiya.'' The officials were accused of paying about ¥28 million to the racketeer between November 1999 and September 2002. Although President Yoji Yamada was not among the accused, he tendered his resignation to accept blame for the scandal.

Net income for the fiscal year ended March 31, 2003, was ¥896 million ($7.5 million), a drop of 71.2 percent compared with the previous year. Sales reached $2.54 billion, down 1.5 percent. The company sustained an extraordinary loss of ¥20.82 billion. Its workforce decreased by 7 percent, to total 6,184.

Although things were bleak for Nippon Shinpan, it was still among the largest credit card and consumer credit companies in Japan. In late 2003 UFJ Bank, which owned 7.69 percent of Nippon Shinpan, announced that it would gain a majority interest in Nippon Shinpan by March 2005 and make it an operating subsidiary. UFJ Bank sought to expand its credit card business, and the combination of UFJ and Nippon Shinpan would increase its cardholders to some 23 million.

Principal Subsidiaries

Aomori Nippon Shinpan Co., Ltd.; Akita Nippon Shinpan Co., Ltd.; Yamagata Nippon Shinpan Co., Ltd.; Nippon Shinpan Gifu Co., Ltd.; Kinki Nippon Shinpan Co., Ltd.; Nishi Nippon Shinpan Co., Ltd.; Seibu Nippon Shinpan Co., Ltd.; Minami Nippon Shinpan Co., Ltd.; NS Australia Pty. Ltd.

Principal Competitors

Mitsubishi Tokyo Financial Group, Inc.; Pocket Card Co., Ltd.; UFJ Holdings, Inc.

Further Reading

Cameron, Doug, and David Ibison, ''Inter-Lease Could Face Bankruptcy,'' *Financial Times,* October 13, 2000.
''Japanese Firms Buy 70% of Equitable Unit,'' *Asian Wall Street Journal,* July 22, 1991, p. 4.
Mollet, Andrew, ''UFJ Buying Nippon Shinpan, May Combine Cards,'' *Cards International,* December 16, 2003, p. 5.
Nakamoto, Michiyo, ''Emergency Loans Provide Relief to Nippon Shinpan,'' *Financial Times,* October 19, 2000.
——, ''Nippon Shinpan to Withdraw from Leasing,'' *Financial Times,* November 9, 2000.
''Nippon Shinpan Changes Outlook, Expects Net Losses,'' *Asian Wall Street Journal,* April 26, 2000, p. 14.
''Nippon Shinpan to Launch Mobile Payments,'' *Electronic Payments International,* March 30, 2000, p. 6.
''Racketeer 'Wined, Dined' by Nippon Shinpan,'' *Daily Yomiuri,* November 17, 2002.
''Scandal Casts Pall Over Nippon Shinpan Recovery Drive,'' *Asahi Shimbun,* November 19, 2002.
''UFJ Bank to Make Nippon Shinpan Subsidiary by March 2005,'' *Japan Weekly Monitor,* November 24, 2003.

—Angel Abcede
—update: Mariko Fujinaka

Nooter Corporation

1400 S. 3rd Street
St. Louis, Missouri 63104-4430
U.S.A.
Telephone: (314) 421-7200
Fax: (314) 425-7807
Web site: http://www.nooter.com

Private Company
Incorporated: 1998
Sales: $660 million (2001 est.)
NAIC: 541330 Engineering Services

Nooter Corporation is a St. Louis, Missouri-based holding company for a family of subsidiaries, located in both the United States and Austria, involved in providing engineering solutions and other services to a broad range of industrial customers. Nooter owns two companies involved in fabrication. Scholler Bleckman Nooter, operating out of Ternitz, Austria, supplies high-performance, multi-layer tanks and containers for industrial and agricultural uses. Optimum Engineering Solutions (Openso) is a Glen Carbon, Illinois, consulting engineering company, primarily serving process petrochemical plants and related industries. Openso holds a worldwide license on Nooter's proprietary methods of fabricating equipment from such metals as titanium and zirconium. Nooter has two companies involved in field construction. With its home office located in St. Louis and a field office in Philadelphia, Pennsylvania, Nooter Construction is involved in all phases of field construction, primarily serving the chemical, paper, petrochemical, refining, and utility industries. Houston-based Wyatt Field Service Company concentrates on the refining and petrochemical industry, offering field fabrication, maintenance, and emergency repair services. Nooter's St. Louis Metallizing Company is a major thermal spray and finishing shop, offering metal and ceramic coatings that minimize wear and corrosion to parts and machine components. Nooter's Pressline Service, Inc. subsidiary is devoted to the needs of newspaper pressrooms, including press overhauls, retrofits, and color unit additions. The company also maintains a parts division and provides maintenance and engineering support. Finally, Nooter also owns Superior Corporate Travel, Inc., providing greater diversity to the company's business mix. Superior offers corporate travel services for air, train, and ship. About one-third of the workforce owns stock in the private company.

Humble Beginnings: 1880s–90s

The man behind the Nooter name was John Nooter, Dutch by birth and seaman by trade. An expert in the rigging of sailing ships he was able to find work in St. Louis as a rigger in the early 1880s for the John O'Brien Boiler Works. In 1896 he struck out on his own in St. Louis. His first major contract was painting trolley poles for the Lindell Railway Line. From the proceeds he acquired a sheet-metal bending roll and a small hand punch, which allowed him to set up shop as a stack fabricator in his backyard and put to use the knowledge he gained during his time at John O'Brien. He named his business the John Nooter Boiler Works Company.

1904 St. Louis World's Fair Provides Boost

Nooter enjoyed a major boost from the work he received in preparation for the 1904 St. Louis World's Fair (officially known as the Louisiana Purchase Exposition, intended to mark the 100th anniversary of the Louisiana Purchase in 1803, but the fair was pushed back a year when it became apparent that the organizers needed more time). The event was planned on an epic scale, taking place on more than 1,200 acres with 62 nations and 43 states participating, not to mention the Olympic games that were also held in St. Louis during the run of the fair. Preparations for the fair were further complicated by an 1899 cyclone that caused severe damage to the city and placed an even greater premium on construction services, and in turn benefited the John Nooter Boiler Works, which continued to work out of the founder's backyard. An important contract of this early period was the construction of a stack for the Lindell Hotel. It was also during this time that Nooter took on a partner, his neighbor Tom Ryan. As the young company grew, it took on another partner in John Eschmann, Sr., one of Nooter's former coworkers at John O'Brien and who now became shop foreman. Ryan was key to Nooter's ongoing success. Tragedy struck in 1910 when Ryan fell off a smokestack and was killed, leaving

Company Perspectives:

Vision Statement: To be our customers' preferred choice.

Nooter and Eschmann to carry on the business by themselves. By 1911 they had laid a strong enough foundation that the company was finally able to graduate from Nooter's backyard and purchase a plot of land in order to erect its first building on the site of Nooter's present-day factory.

John Nooter Boiler Works during the second decade of the 20th century was mostly involved in the making of horizontal return tubular boilers. It also continued to erect riveted smokestacks and did some tank work. In the 1920s Nooter kept pace with the rise of new metals and such new tools and technologies as acetylene welding, electric welding, and the air hammer. In the middle of the decade the company began to weld vessels in carbon steel. By the end of the decade, Nooter was regarded as an expert in the electric welding industry. The company also reached a crossroads in its history. Instead of mass producing a line of products, Nooter elected to focus its attention on making higher-end, custom-fabricated metal plate products.

In the early 1940s Nooter first began producing stainless steel vessels, but like most companies its normal work was disrupted by the United States' entry into World War II. Not only did many skilled workers leave for military service, but Nooter also shifted its focus to serving military-related industries. For its part in the war effort, Nooter produced process vessels needed for the manufacture of explosives, gasoline, synthetic rubber, and penicillin. During the postwar years of the 1940s, Nooter took advantage of new materials, such as InConel, Incoloy, Carpenter 20, and Hastelloy B and C. Nooter soon gained expertise, making it a highly sought fabricator of these materials. The company also benefited greatly by the postwar economic boom that drove industries to employ new equipment that relied on Nooter's advanced metalworking abilities.

Nooter's major customers in the 1950s were oil and chemical companies. Early in the decade Nooter began to work with zirconium in order to fabricate heat exchangers and reactor vessels for chemical processors. A notable achievement of the decade was the construction of the vessels used to manufacture the new polio vaccine developed by Dr. Jonas Salk, which would eradicate a disease that had plagued generations of children. During the 1950s Nooter also expanded on its welding expertise, adding such technologies as submerged arc, tungsten inert gas shielded arc, and consumable electrode inert gas. Because of the company's growing diversity, it was decided in the 1950s that "Boiler Works" was no longer suitable, and the company shortened its name to Nooter Corporation.

Nooter continued to make technological advances in the 1960s, fabricating with solid titanium, followed by solid zirconium, and solid tantalum. In 1963 Nooter became the first company in the world to use these materials in reactive metal clad welding, which led to the construction of reactive metal clad pressure vessels and heat exchangers that were sold around the world. Until this point the company had done no business outside of the United States. It was also during this period that Nooter developed a number of other technologies, including multilayer vessels, inner bore tube welding, hot gas cycle testing, and plasma arc weld overlay. In addition, during the space race of the 1960s, Nooter used its expertise to help in the bid to send men to the moon.

Nooter's export business began to accelerate in the 1970s, primarily selling to England and Germany. Nooter achieved a notable distinction early in the 1970s when it constructed a 109-foot-long zirconium column for use with sulfuric acid. At the time, it was the largest zirconium column ever built. In keeping with its tradition of staying on the cutting edge of technology, Nooter also became an early user of Computer-Aided Design/Computer-Aided Manufacture (CAD-CAM), which in the 1980s the company began to rely on increasingly in the design of vessel components. But because so many of its products were custom made, encompassing too many variables, becoming completely robotic was not viable for Nooter. The company's only standardized product was a giant kettle—measuring 13 feet across, over six feet deep, and weighing in excess of 100 tons. Nooter produced as many as 40 of the kettles a year for the lead smelting industry.

Company Veterans Taking Turns at the Top: 1990s

In truth, Nooter was still very much dependent on its human capital. A major factor in the success of the company was its ability to retain skilled people at all levels and maintain continuity in the business. This trait was evident by the changes in top management during the 1990s, as one longtime executive after another retired and was replaced from within the ranks of the company. In January 1995 George Hays retired as chairman of the board and chief executive officer at the age of 65. He began his tenure with the company in 1955 as a sales engineer. Hays was replaced by Gene R. Smith, who started as a sales engineer with Nooter in 1956. He retired two years later, replaced by 62-year-old George P. Bouckaert, who had been working for the company since 1960. In 1999 he retired, succeeded by 63-year-old Frank Martin, who started out in 1959 as a sales engineer for a Nooter division, Missouri Boiler and Tank Co.

By the middle of the 1990s Nooter was posting annual sales in the $350 million range, a significant increase over the estimated $20 million turnover of the mid-1950s. Much of this growth could be attributed to a steady climb in export sales, which now accounted for half of Nooter's business. Rather than remain complacent, the company's string of leaders bordering on retirement age took steps to diversify the business mix. Pressline Services, for instance was established in 1995 as a subsidiary of St. Louis Metallizing Company, growing out of a two-year press overhaul project Nooter had taken on for the *St. Louis Post-Dispatch* in 1992. The company rebuilt six massive presses, with St. Louis Metallizing restoring components by use of thermal-spray coatings. The project was so successful that three of the top people involved—St. Louis Metallizing's project manager, the *Post-Dispatch* rebuild project manager, and the technical support representative from the press manufacturer—approached Nooter about launching a field service company to the newspaper press market.

Either through acquisition or by starting greenfield operations, Nooter diversified into such areas as corporate travel, so

Key Dates:

1896: John Nooter starts his own St. Louis business.
1911: John Nooter Boiler Works purchases its first commercial site.
1998: Nooter Corporation becomes holding company.
2001: Nooter discontinues fabrication business after more than 100 years in operation.

that by 1998 management decided to reorganize the business. For decades Nooter Corporation was linked to the company's century-old fabrication business, which was now renamed Nooter Fabricators. The Nooter Corporation name was then applied to a new holding company that would oversee all of the operating units. Ties to the company's traditional business were short-lived, however. In 2001 Nooter Fabricators was closed, the business unable to compete with Japanese and Korean competitors and crippled by diminishing domestic demand. Nevertheless, Nooter was a thriving company in the areas that it chose to participate. Revenues grew from $535 million in 2001 to $660 million in 2001. In 2002 Frank Martin retired as chairman and CEO, replaced by yet another company veteran, Russ Osiek, who started out with Nooter as a sales engineer. There was every reason to believe that he would maintain the company's long history of success.

Principal Subsidiaries

Scholler Bleckman Nooter; Optimum Engineering Solutions; Nooter Construction; Wyatt Field Service Company; Nooter's Pressline Service, Inc.; Superior Corporate Travel, Inc.

Principal Competitors

Tyco International Ltd.; Emerson Electric Co.; Armstrong World Industries, Inc.

Further Reading

Flannery, William, ''Nooter Is Making Its Mark Making Weighty Products,'' *St. Louis Post-Dispatch,* May 6, 1996, p. 10.
''Nooter Corp.,'' *St. Louis Business Journal,* March 27, 2000, p. A44.
Stamborski, Al, ''Nooter Corp. Transforms Itself,'' *St. Louis Post-Dispatch,* January 1, 1998, p. B1.

—Ed Dinger

North Pacific Group, Inc.

815 NE Davis Street
Portland, Oregon 97232
U.S.A.
Telephone: (503) 231-1166
Toll Free: (800) 547-8440
Fax: (503) 238-2641
Web site: http://www.northpacific.com

Private Company
Incorporated: 1948 as North Pacific Lumber Company
Employees: 900
Sales: $1.1 billion (2002)
NAIC: 421310 Lumber, Plywood, Millwork and Wood Panel Wholesalers; 321113 Sawmills; 422910 Farm Supplies Wholesalers; 421390 Other Construction Material Wholesalers

North Pacific Group, Inc. (NOR PAC) is one of the nation's largest wholesale distributors of building materials, distributing wood, steel, agricultural, and food products through more than 30 separate business units and subsidiaries and more than 175 inventory locations. Its eight business units are decentralized by product areas and regions and include: Burns Lumber, a market leader in the distribution of construction-grade forest products; Hardwoods Business Unit, a major manufacturer, distributor, and trading company of quality hardwoods nationally and internationally; Landmark Business Products, supplier of products used in the industrial, furniture/cabinet, and retail lumber yard markets; Saxonville USA, distributor of building materials in the Northeast; Schultz, Snyder & Steele, supplier of building products in the upper Midwest; Softwoods Business Unit, worldwide distributor of OSB, plywood, MDF, particle board, and softwood lumber; Southern Business Unit, wholesaler of lumber, building materials, and specialty products in the southern United States; and Specialty Products Business Unit, supplier of treated wood poles and pilings, composite products, steel pipes, tubing and coils, and various food and agricultural products. NOR PAC's customers include furniture makers, building products retailers, power companies, and farm supply retailers. The company has been employee-owned since 1986 when its founder retired. It is the second largest privately held company headquartered in Oregon.

Steady Growth and Diversification: 1948 to the 1960s

Doug David and Herman Tenzler founded North Pacific Lumber Co. in November 1948 with an initial investment of $15,000 and 12 employees in three trading departments. David, born in 1916, grew up in Tennessee and came to Oregon in 1934 to work in its sawmills. He was graduated from the University of Oregon in 1942, having worked his way through school. David went on to earn a master's degree in business administration from the University of Washington and then served stateside in the U.S. Army during World War II.

Described as a survivor, according to a 1983 *Oregon Business* article, David was ''adept at steering an intuitive course through the wood products industry's many minefields.'' After World War II, the timber industry cut its way west, and full-scale logging began in the Pacific Northwest. Throughout the 1940s and 1950s, the lumber industry sold its goods primarily through wholesale companies in the Midwest or through commissioned salesman scattered throughout the rest of the country. David built NOR PAC into a highly diversified forest products manufacturer-wholesaler-distributor that prided itself on benefiting suppliers with prompt payment and customers with flexible payment terms, ample inventories, and on-time shipments.

In the 1950s, NOR PAC formed its plywood division when it entered into trading plywood and panel products. It also formed its hardwoods division. By mid-decade, the company had formed specific trading divisions to focus on hardwoods, inland species, plywood, import, export, and specialty products. It moved its corporate office from Vaughn Street to Gideon Street in Portland in 1955.

By the early 1960s, the company was handling more than 124 forest products, including 45 exotic species of wood and all domestic species and plywood. It shipped 25,000 carloads of forest products annually, via rail, truck, ship, and barge to customers in the United States, Canada, Europe, Australia, Japan, Hong Kong, and Korea. It also was importing wood from

Company Perspectives:

We are a billion dollar company offering the economies of scale that come from being big. But, in reality, we operate like several dozen small companies, each with their own independent decision makers with the power to solve your problems quickly and efficiently.

North Pacific Group, Inc. is committed to being the ''Supplier of Choice'' through product and service excellence. Our emphasis is on being a responsible, innovative business partner providing value-added services to customers and suppliers worldwide. Employees remain our most important asset. Through training in all areas with an emphasis on technology, service and ingenuity will be enhanced, promoting our long-held tradition of commitment to service, ethical business practices, financial strength, and flexibility.

sources worldwide. In a company brochure from 1963, NOR PAC boasted that ''[i]f all the lumber and plywood sold annually by North Pacific were laid end to end, [it] would form a path 12 inches wide that would encircle the earth at the equator more than eight times.''

The 1960s saw several changes designed to increase the efficiency of NOR PAC's operations. In 1961, the company introduced telephone sales and WATS (wide area telephone service) lines. The WATS lines enabled the company's traders to be in much closer contact with buyers, and the company boasted weekly—or even daily—calls to check on prices for customers. NOR PAC's traders also began to focus by region with the debut of the Western Sales Division, which sold products only in 11 western states (and later Hawaii and Alaska). In 1966, NOR PAC also added its trucking department to facilitate the shipping of its products to all the western states.

In addition, NOR PAC diversified its business to include two new realms. In 1962, it formed North Pacific Trading Co. to trade agricultural products and various items produced by or used by farmers and ranchers, which included peas, beans, lentils, grains, feed, fertilizers, and chemicals, and by the later 1970s twine, wire, steel, nails, fiberglass items, and salt. In 1968, it moved into mill operations with the purchase of a mill in Waynesboro, Missouri. This purchase marked the debut of NOR PAC's Southern Sales Division, which joined its Western Sales and Canadian Divisions that same year. By the late 1960s, its advertising and printing department was producing its owns price lists, catalogs, and educational materials.

Expansion Followed by Curtailment: 1970s and 1980s

Although NOR PAC's core business continued to be distribution, growth in the 1970s came in the area of production with special emphasis on hardwoods, southern pine, western red cedar, and cedar specialty items, such as fencing. The company went into lumber production in the West with the purchase of the San Poil Company in Republic, Washington, in 1969. Its construction lumber division developed a program geared to the manufacturers of mobile homes that included notched and dadoed lumber of all sizes. The plywood division branched out in the areas of mixed car shipments, cut-to-size plywood, and treated products. The company also began to serve the mobile home and recreational vehicle market with shipments of prefinished paneling, mouldings, particle board, and hardwood plywood. With annual consolidated sales greater than $100 million in the early part of the decade, NOR PAC added a 40-acre distribution facility in Portland and an office in British Columbia, Canada, which went by the name of Cascade Imperial Mills. Ownership of NOR PAC shifted when Doug David and employee stockholders bought out Herman Tenzler. David became the majority stockholder of the solely employee-owned company with operations in Oregon, Mississippi, and British Columbia.

With production came an emphasis on scientific forest management for NOR PAC: planting vigorous fast-growing trees, controlling insect damage and fires, utilizing harvested trees as efficiently as possible, according to a booklet published by the company in the mid-1970s, ''[b]ecause trees are a renewable crop and forests can be harvested and regenerated, a more complete utilization of this resource is realized. Now, it is to each of us to help preserve this heritage for future generations, and enjoy the maximum benefits of our forests—trees are for people!''

In the late 1970s, NOR PAC went through a difficult spell when it faced litigation over noncompetition agreements with former employees. The company was accused of barring Les Oliver, former assistant manager of its hardwood division, from taking employment in similar work for two years after he left NOR PAC and of encouraging hardwood traders to make money on claims by settling with mills for a greater amount than customers had agreed to accept in settlement. Despite such bad press, in 1979, NOR PAC achieved its peak volume of business. The company had 1,179 employees, including 290 traders, and did business through 13 specialized profit centers, several subsidiaries, two lumber mills, its trucking company, and storage and distribution facilities.

The economic challenges of the 1980s led to cutbacks at NOR PAC. It shut down storage yards and warehouses in northeast Portland and sold all of its mills (including San Poil Lumber in 1981), trucks, planes, and distribution facilities. Leo Gibbons, who had joined the firm as a trader in 1969, became president and chief operating officer in 1982, and under his leadership, the company undertook extensive restructuring to refocus once again as a trading company. The Western Sales Division closed, and the company liquidated its inventories. Yet despite the 60 percent cutback in personnel—the company scaled down to about 200 traders and slightly fewer than 1,000 employees by 1980—NOR PAC served more than 20,000 customers and producers that year. Its 1983 sales volume of greater than $450 million equaled its 1979 peak.

Another development of the late 1980s that affected NOR PAC had to do with supply. In the face of timber shortages in the West and environmental restrictions in the Northwest, the leading timber companies began to seek new sources of supply to keep their mills running. Many North American timber interests moved to South America, where there were more trees and

Key Dates:

1948: Doug David and Herman Tenzler found and incorporate North Pacific Lumber Company (NOR PAC).
1955: NOR PAC moves to larger facilities.
1961: The company installs WATS (wide area telephone service) lines.
1962: The company forms North Pacific Trading to trade agricultural and other products.
1966: Company adds its trucking department.
1968: The company debuts its Southern Division to support sales from its new lumber mill in Mississippi.
1969: The company buys the San Poil Lumber Co. in Washington state.
1981: NOR PAC sells the San Poil Lumber Co.
1982: Leo Gibbons succeeds Doug David as president and chief operating officer.
1986: Doug David sells his company to his employees; Gibbons becomes board chair and chief executive officer; Tom Tomjack succeeds Gibbons as president and chief operating officer.
1989: Tomjack becomes board chair and chief executive officer.
1991: NOR PAC acquires Saxonville USA.
1994: Company acquires and merges with Schultz, Snyder & Steele.
1996: NOR PAC moves its headquarters to Portland, Oregon; the company acquires Moore Co., an electronics wholesaler.
1997: Company changes its name to North Pacific Group, Inc.
2000: The company acquires Burns Lumber.
2002: Jay Ross becomes president and chief operating officer; the company acquires Wasatch Technologies, which becomes North Pacific Composites.
2003: The company sells both North Pacific Composites and its steel department; Ross becomes chief executive officer.

fewer rules, in their search for additional sources of wood. NOR PAC began importing radiata pine from Chile in 1989.

In 1986, the company also underwent a change in management. David sold the company to a group of nine employee-stockholders. Gibbons became board chair and chief executive officer, and Tom Tomjack replaced Gibbons as president and chief operating officer. Gibbons' term was brief, and, in 1989, Tomjack moved on to become chief executive and board chair. NOR PAC now had operations in Oregon, Mississippi, British Columbia, and Missouri and boasted of being one of the only distributors to maintain inventories throughout the United States with the effect that it could offer lower prices through economies of scale.

Leadership in a Changing Market: The 1990s to the Early 2000s

By the early 1990s, NOR PAC had annual sales in excess of $500 million and a staff of nearly 400 people. North Pacific Trading Co. had branched out into worldwide sourcing and distribution of everything from frozen seafood to exotic birdseeds, dried edible foodstuffs, processed oils, grass seeds, fertilizer, and hardware. In the mid-1990s, NOR PAC was the third largest privately held company in the state of Oregon, according to a new listing by *Oregon Business* magazine of Oregon's 150 biggest private firms. With $950 million in sales, NOR PAC was also the nation's fourth largest building materials wholesaler. In 1991, it had purchased Saxonville USA, a leading distributor in the northeast of building materials sold to professional lumber dealers and manufacturers. In 1994, it acquired and merged with Schultz, Snyder & Steele Lumber Co. of Lansing, Michigan, which would operate as a wholly owned subsidiary of NOR PAC.

These two purchases allowed NOR PAC to grow and respond to changing market conditions and industry consolidation by developing as a full-line distributor. By 1994, Saxonville had grown 74 percent to $96 million in sales, doubling its distribution centers to six and extending its territory in the Northeast. It also became more involved in remanufactured products, such as cedar fencing and siding. With the addition of Schultz, Snyder & Steele Lumber Co., NOR PAC became one of several large building materials distributors to put more emphasis on distribution by purchasing regional companies that could respond to customer requests within 24 hours.

As NOR PAC moved further away from its wholesaler role, a change came about in its corporate culture; it moved from fulfilling customer requests to anticipating them. Beginning in 1992, it initiated a training program for its traders, teaching them sales skills, improving their market knowledge, and widening their computer skills. As a result, the average order per trader per day began to rise. The company also moved into other markets, as, in 1996, when it acquired Moore Co., an electronics wholesaler.

In 1997, the company changed its name to North Pacific Group, Inc., and began "whole-tailing," selling directly to end-users to accommodate a dealer base that wanted more products less expensively and more quickly. The year was a good one for lumber shippers in the Pacific Northwest as there was continued demand for new houses and relatively high lumber prices. Three years later, the company acquired Burns Lumber, a market leader in the distribution of construction-grade forest products.

Management changed again in 2002. Jay Ross became president, replacing Tomjack, who continued as chief executive officer and chair of the board. The company purchased Wasatch Technologies Inc., with which it had collaborated in 2000 on a project to develop a fiberglass wrap for wood poles, and changed the name of its newest venture to North Pacific Composites. NOR PAC ranked once again as one of the largest privately held companies in Oregon in 2002, according to *Oregon Business,* moving up to second place.

Principal Subsidiaries

Burns Lumber Company, Inc.; Cascade Imperial Mills, Ltd.; Comercial Norte Pacifico de Chile; Landmark Building Products, Inc.; Roberts Pacific LLC; Saxonville USA; Schultz, Snyder & Steele Lumber Company.

Principal Competitors

Georgia-Pacific Company; Louisiana-Pacific; Weyerhaeuser Company.

Further Reading

Brent, Elizabeth, ''Acquisitions Help Growth Through Diversification,'' *National Home Center News,* September 11, 1995, p. PD14.

Carter, Steven, ''NOR PAC Stock Fight Settled,'' *Oregonian,* April 23, 1977, p. B7.

——, ''President of Lumber Company Sues Board for 'Illegal Scheme,' '' *Oregonian,* December 22, 1976, p. C4.

Fisher, Lionel L., ''NOR PAC Packs a Quiet Wallop,'' *Oregon Business,* November 1983, p. 28.

''Judge Finds Corporation's Employment Limit Unenforceable,'' *Oregonian,* December 16, 1976, p. B8.

Meeker, Richard, ''N. Pacific's Dirty Hands,'' *Willamette Week,* December 20, 1976, p.1.

Sleeth, Peter, ''Logging to the Ends of the Earth,'' *Oregonian,* October 2, 1994, p. A1.

—Carrie Rothburd

Northern Foods plc

Beverley House
St. Stephen's Square
Hull HU1 3XG
United Kingdom
Telephone: (01482) 325432
Fax: (01482) 226136
Web site: http://www.northern-foods.co.uk

Public Company
Incorporated: 1949 as Northern Dairies Ltd.
Employees: 22,011
Sales: £1.42 billion ($2.24 billion) (2003)
Stock Exchanges: London
Ticker Symbol: NFDS
NAIC: 551112 Offices of Other Holding Companies; 311412 Frozen Specialty Food Manufacturing; 311421 Fruit and Vegetable Canning; 311511 Fluid Milk Manufacturing; 311520 Ice Cream and Frozen Dessert Manufacturing; 311612 Meat Processed from Carcasses; 311812 Commercial Bakeries; 311813 Frozen Cakes, Pies, and Other Pastries Manufacturing; 311821 Cookie and Cracker Manufacturing; 311991 Perishable Prepared Food Manufacturing; 422410 General Line Grocery Wholesalers

Northern Foods plc is one of the United Kingdom's leading manufacturers of high-quality fresh foods, supplying the country's preeminent retail outlets with both private-label and branded products. Nearly three-quarters of its revenues are derived from private-label deals with five big U.K. food retailers: Marks and Spencer p.l.c., J Sainsbury plc, Safeway plc, Tesco PLC, and ASDA Group Limited. Northern Foods specializes particularly in fresh-chilled prepared foods, including a wide variety of ethnic entree dishes, quiches, sandwiches, pizza, and dairy products. Other food products produced by its 17 mostly independently run operating companies include desserts, baked goods, cookies, baked beans, canned vegetables, and frozen pizza. The NFT Distribution Limited subsidiary distributes nationally the chilled food products of Northern Foods and other food makers. Northern Foods has the reputation of being one of the most adventurous, idiosyncratic, and successful companies in the United Kingdom, with a track record of steady, respectable growth.

Establishing a Retail Dairy Business: Mid-20th Century

In 1932 Alec Horsley joined his father's condensed milk business, Pape and Co., Ltd., a small Hull-based concern importing Dutch condensed milk for wholesale. From the beginning, however, Horsley was convinced that strength lay in size; he was eager to expand and saw his opportunity in 1936. Amid the growing threat of war and rumors that new import duties might affect their business, Horsley, with his father's support, determined to change the focus of the business to production of their own supply. To that end he convened a meeting with six other small dairy firms in Hull, suggesting that they should merge for their mutual benefit. Only one of the six proved interested: Southwick's Dairies, a wholesale and manufacturing concern. The two entered into a partnership with the object of building their own condensery. Foreshadowing the energy and determination that were to characterize the growth of Northern Foods, Horsley and his partner managed to choose the site, prepare the plant, and build the factory in only four and a half months. By October 1937 the new factory at Holme-on-Spalding-Moor was up and running.

The onset of the war radically altered the face of the dairy trade in Britain. The need to change to meet wartime conditions proved fatal to many small dairies, but Horsley, a reformer at heart and quick to see opportunity in adversity, eagerly adapted to and profited from the altered circumstances. Because of wartime shortages, the Ministry of Food discouraged the use of cans and sugar—necessary in the making of condensed milk—and supported the sale of liquid milk. Horsley, therefore, saw the need to move into retail, a shift he had long wanted to make but that had been resisted by his partner George Southwick.

The prewar system of doorstep delivery had been haphazard and circuitous. A dozen small dairies might service different

Company Perspectives:

Northern Foods is a leading U.K. food producer. We operate in eight core product areas which benefit from long term demographic and lifestyle trends favouring high quality foods that are convenient to eat.

Our focus is on serving the leading retailers and we have strong market positions in the supply of high quality chilled foods under their retail names. We also have successful brands in biscuits, frozen food and savoury products.

addresses on the same street, then each travel separately to another neighborhood to make more deliveries. The wartime shortages of labor and material, particularly gasoline, made this complicated network of delivery routes unacceptable. The government suspended free competition and insisted upon ''rationalization'' of dairy delivery. Established routes were disrupted, sometimes drastically altered; in many cases small dairies were forced to completely swap their customers with other businesses.

Recognizing that the time of the small dairyman was over, Horsley embarked upon an energetic and ambitious campaign of expansion, acquiring other dairies one by one. The larger the business grew, the more attractive it became to small firms beset by the bombing (Hull was very hard hit during the war), the chronic shortages, and the difficulties of adapting to rationalization. As the firm expanded it actually became more efficient with each new addition, as Horsley chose the best dairies and plants when consolidating operations. By 1942 Horsley controlled a considerable network of retail and wholesale businesses scattered throughout Humberside and Yorkshire, and the retail end of the company was renamed Northern Dairies to reflect this (although the wholesale operations continued to be known by their individual names).

As the war progressed, Northern Dairies found itself in the enviable position of having to decline to take over several businesses because of the sheer volume of the requests for amalgamation. Horsley and his associates decreed that three of four conditions must be met before they could consider acquiring a business: (1) the town in which it was situated must be flat for ease of delivery; (2) the proposed firm had to be near enough to another of Northern Dairies' depots to allow for convenient exchange of plant or vehicles, or to act as a shadow dairy in areas where bombing was a problem; (3) there was to be no other sizable dairy in the area with the exception of the Co-operative; and (4) there had to be the possibility of future expansion in the area.

The wartime strategies that had proved so advantageous to Northern Dairies were equally successful after the war. Indeed, to a considerable extent the exigencies of wartime business provided the bedrock of the company's future corporate philosophy, particularly the importance of acquisition as well as organic growth and the significance of the concept of rationalization. Horsley established principles of rationalization with other large dairy concerns—in 1950 alone, for example, Northern Dairies sold its Sutherland trade to Craven Dairies in part exchange for its Middlesborough trade, struck a deal to avoid overlapping trade in County Durham, and exchanged Huddersfield and Barnsley for Mansfield in an agreement with Express Dairies. Northern Dairies' amalgamation with the Hull- and Bridlington-based Riley/Granger dairy group also happened in 1950.

Ironically, Riley/Granger, then two separate entities, had attended Horsley's meeting in 1936, when they had both declined to merge with Pape and Co. Riley's had at that time been the market leader in Hull. When it finally joined Northern Dairies in 1950 it was half the size of the company it had once rejected. This amalgamation, significant to Northern Dairies because of the size of the parties involved, was also important in that it brought the center of the company's operations, grown rather dispersed, back to its origins in Hull.

Expansion of product line was a natural corollary of Northern Dairies' growth; in 1946 it had entered the ice cream market through the acquisition of Kingston Ices and Harmers Ices, and soon expanded into cheese, curd, whey, and chocolate crumb. Nevertheless, the firm's original product of condensed milk was not neglected. As soon as the government allowed it after the war, Northern Dairies moved back into milk processing, expanding its condensing operations at Holme-on-Spalding-Moor, and in 1950 established another, more modern plant, able to condense 20,000 gallons per day as compared with the original plant's 8,000.

Northern Dairies had been registered as a private company in 1949, and then it became a public company in 1956. Its expansion continued, making its name a misnomer as the company moved into the Midlands and Northern Ireland. Northern Dairies expanded throughout the dairy trade, and its profits surpassed the one million mark by 1970. In that year Horsley retired as chairman and was succeeded by his son Nicholas. Under second-generation leadership, Northern Dairies began its rapid expansion into new and lucrative fields of business. Cream cakes, yogurts, desserts, sandwiches, recipe dishes, pizza, pasta, meat, fish, soups, hors d'oeuvres, cheeses, fresh produce: throughout the 1970s and 1980s the product line continually expanded.

Development of Relationship with Marks and Spencer: 1970s

The year 1970 was a watershed for Northern Dairies in another highly significant way: a chance meeting sent the company onto a new and phenomenally successful path. Christopher Haskins—Alec Horsley's son-in-law, later to become chairman of Northern Foods after Nicholas Horsley stepped down—found himself sitting next to an executive from Marks and Spencer (the ubiquitous and well-respected department store with a high-quality, upmarket grocery division) on a plane; from their chat was built a successful and mutually rewarding business relationship.

Throughout the 1970s the relationship with Marks and Spencer was a major focus for the company, which was renamed Northern Foods plc in 1972 to reflect the expanding nature of its business. From its relatively humble beginnings as manufacturer of the St. Michael (Marks and Spencer's own brand) trifle, Northern Foods grew to become Marks and Spencer's biggest supplier, employing its typical enthusiastic

Key Dates:

1937: Alex Horsley spearheads the establishment of a milk condensing plant at Holme-on-Spalding Moor, England.
1942: Consolidation during the war enables Horsley to control a large network of retail and wholesale dairy businesses throughout Humberside and Yorkshire; the retail side of the operation is registered as Northern Dairies.
1949: Northern Dairies Ltd. is registered as a private company.
1956: The company goes public.
1970: Northern Dairies begins an important relationship, supplying Marks and Spencer with food products.
1972: Park Cakes is acquired; the company changes its name to Northern Foods plc to reflect the expanding nature of the product line.
1977: Fox's Biscuits is acquired.
1985: The company acquires Bowyers and Elkes Biscuits.
1986: Batchelors is acquired.
1992: Eden Vale is acquired.
1995: Restructuring, mainly of the dairy operations, includes the elimination of 3,450 jobs.
1998: The company's dairy operations are spun off to shareholders as Express Dairies plc.
1999: Northern Foods gains full ownership of Fletchers Bakeries.
2002: The Ski and Munch Bunch brands are divested.
2003: The company acquires full control of Solway Foods; it announces that it will divest several noncore operations.

blend of acquisition and innovation. As part of this two-pronged approach, Northern Foods set out on a policy of acquiring existing suppliers to Marks and Spencer wherever it could (witness, for example, its purchase of Park Cakes in 1972 and Fox's Biscuits in 1977). Equally, the company concentrated on creating new products for its favored customer: by 1988 Northern Foods was producing a range of 250 products for Marks and Spencer. Key acquisitions in the 1980s included Bowyers, maker of meat products (1985); Elkes Biscuits, a private-label producer (1985); Batchelors, producer of baked beans, canned vegetables, and fruit juices (1986); and Evesham Foods, maker of hot and cold pies and sausage rolls (1987).

Northern Foods' unique business relationship with Marks and Spencer is best illustrated in the construction of the sophisticated Fenland Foods factory in 1986. As a gesture of its goodwill and enthusiasm, Northern Foods built this Marks and Spencer dedicated plant—at a cost of £8 million—before it had yet been established what products were to be made there. Echoing Alec Horsley's 1937 achievement with his first milk processing plant, Fenland Foods, which was hailed as Europe's most advanced food factory, was built in 40 weeks—and was selling to Marks and Spencer three weeks later.

Northern Foods' rise was not uniformly smooth; it had its share of well publicized (and ruefully admitted) fiascoes. Some of its forays into new lines of business proved unwise. Its move into consumer finance with the purchase of British Credit Trust was initially profitable (at one point it accounted for 40 percent of the company's profits), but in the banking crisis of the mid-1970s it lost all its deposits and nearly went under, which came as "a bloody shock," according to Chairman Chris Haskins. The company sold the British Credit Trust in 1978. A failed attempt to move into the brewing industry in 1972 strengthened the firm's subsequent resolve to stay within its bounds as a food company.

Particularly embarrassing, however, was Northern Foods' attempt to enter the American market with the acquisition of Bluebird Inc. and Keystone Foods Corporation in 1980 and 1982, respectively. Legal problems with the former and philosophical differences with the latter prompted Northern Foods to withdraw from the U.S. market quickly. With characteristic forthrightness, Chris Haskins referred to the experience as Northern Foods' "American cock-up." A sortie into the chicken market with the 1986 acquisition of Mayhew Foods was equally unfortunate, preceding the first recorded falling-off of chicken consumption in the United Kingdom. The venture, Haskins admitted, "has been a disaster. . . . We will probably have to get rid of it." Northern Foods finally completed its exit from the poultry sector in 1994.

Continued Growth in the Early to Mid-1990s

Northern Foods continued its dual policy of aggressive acquisition and organic growth into the 1990s, concentrating on its four main areas: dairy, convenience foods, meat products, and groceries. In a clear sign that it meant to stay true to its roots, the company acquired the dairy company Express in 1992, consolidating its position as the United Kingdom's leading liquid milk company, and holding 24 percent of the market in England and Wales. Doorstep delivery, although an anachronism in the modern world, remained a staple with Northern Foods, which served some three million households throughout the country. Hedging its bets, the company was also the leading supplier of milk to U.K. supermarkets. Also acquired in 1992 was Eden Vale, producer of fresh-chilled dairy products for both Marks and Spencer and Safeway.

Rationalization remained a priority for Northern Foods in the 1990s, as the company sought to simplify and consolidate wherever possible, concentrating on the aggressive rationalization policies that made its fortune in the first place. The company invested heavily in new facilities and technologies, and as a sideline of its main business Northern Foods—through its NFT Distribution subsidiary—operated its own chilled distribution service, for itself and for other food manufacturers, including a dedicated transport operation for Sainsbury's. Bread products were one new focus for the future, as the company made several acquisitions in this area in the early 1990s: Kara Foods, Grain D'Or Bakeries, and Fletchers Bakeries (a 24 percent interest in the latter, which became wholly owned in 1999). Through these businesses, Northern Foods began producing fresh and frozen buns, baguettes, doughnuts, muffins, and other specialty baked goods.

Governmental deregulation of the milk market in 1994, coupled with the steady shift from home delivery of milk to consumer purchasing at supermarkets, roiled Northern Foods' dairy operations. In March 1995 the company launched a £91 million restructuring that entailed slashing 3,450 jobs from the workforce of about 27,000. Plant closures reduced dairy bottling capacity by 40 percent. On the prepared foods side, the increasing dominance of supermarkets led to a 75 percent cut in the firm's fleet of vans that supplied small shops. Meantime, in June 1995 the company gained majority control of Green Isle, an Irish producer of branded and private-label frozen foods, including pizzas, pastries, and fish products.

After a couple of years of declining profits, Northern Foods returned to profit growth during the second half of the 1996 fiscal year, but it then had a bit of a setback stemming from the crisis in British agriculture over worries about bovine spongiform encephalopathy (BSE) in cattle and its link to so-called mad cow disease in humans who eat beef from infected cows. Sales of prepared foods that contained beef fell, and Northern Foods moved quickly to produce for its supermarket customers a large number of new nonbeef entrees, such as lamb curry and chicken chow mein.

Late 1990s and Beyond: Focusing Solely on Prepared Foods

The dairy side of the company continued to suffer as the industry continued to be wracked by overcapacity. To give that business a freer hand in participating in an anticipated industry-wide consolidation drive, Northern Foods in 1998 engineered a demerger. The dairy and prepared foods businesses had been run separately since 1994, and the 1998 demerger formalized this split. The company's entire dairy business, except for the Eden Vale fresh-chilled dairy product unit, was spun off to shareholders as Express Dairies plc in March 1998. At that time, Haskins became nonexecutive chairman of Northern Foods, which was now fully focused on value-added prepared and convenience foods. The head of the prepared foods operations, Jo Stewart, was named company chief executive. Also in 1998, Northern Foods completed two acquisitions, adding Cavaghan and Gray, producer of a wide range of chilled foods for both Marks and Spencer and Safeway; and the confectionary brands of James Finlay, consisting of Poppets and Just Brazils, as well as the Lift instant tea business. The latter marked Northern Foods' entrance into the confectionery market and was seen as an extension of its biscuits and cakes operation.

During 1999, in addition to taking full ownership of Fletchers Bakeries, Northern Foods announced that it would join a growing number of U.K. food producers and distributors and stop using genetically modified ingredients in its products. Late in the year, the company announced a restructuring of its pizza and quiche operations involving the closure of two plants in Rotherham and Carlisle. Early the following year, Northern Foods bought a 40 percent stake in Solway Foods for £16 million; Solway, which had factories in Northamptonshire and Nottinghamshire, supplied Tesco with chilled foods, including sandwiches, sushi, and salads. Later in 2000, Irish subsidiary Green Isle divested its foodservice and frozen food distribution unit in order to concentrate on its frozen foods brands. Green Isle acquired Lacemont Ltd., producer of frozen pizza and breads, during 2001.

Continuing to adjust its product portfolio, Northern Foods acquired from Nestlé UK Limited the Fox's confectionery business, which included Fox's Glacier Mints and Fruits sweets as well as XXX Mints. On the divestment side, the Lift tea brand was divested in 2001, and then in early 2002, in a £145 million deal, Northern Foods sold its Ski yogurt and Munch Bunch *fromage frais* brands as well as a yogurt factory in Cuddington, Cheshire, to Nestlé UK. The latter deal, which helped the company slash its heavy debt load, left Northern Foods with just one dairy-related operation, that of dairy dessert maker Eden Vale. In February 2002, four decades after joining the firm, Haskins retired. Taking over as chairman was Peter Blackburn, who until June 2001 was the head of Nestlé UK.

In mid-2003 Northern Foods acquired the 60 percent of Solway Foods it did not already own for £26.7 million. Early in September of that year, Stewart was ousted from his position as chief executive after the company for the third time in 18 months had to issue a warning that its profits would fall below expectations. Blackburn took over on an interim basis while a search for an outside replacement was conducted. Shortly after this development, Northern Foods sold its Fox's Confectionery business to a management buyout group; included were the Fox's Glacier Mints and Fruits, Paynes Poppets, Just Brazils, and XXX Mints brands.

This marked the beginning of a new divestment program as the company was now ready to follow the advice that analysts had been promulgating for some time: the firm needed to make large cuts in a product portfolio that had grown too large and unwieldy. Northern Foods aimed to overhaul its portfolio to concentrate on the fastest growing food sectors. This meant focusing on such company specialties as cakes, puddings, bread, frozen foods, biscuits, and recipe dishes. Late in 2003 Northern Foods announced that it planned to divest three non-core businesses: the NFT Distribution operation, Smiths Flour Mills, and the Batchelors canning unit in Ireland. In a cost-saving move, the company reorganized its biscuit business by merging its Fox's and Elkes biscuit operations.

Principal Subsidiaries

Convenience Foods Limited; F W Farnsworth Limited; Fletchers Bakeries Limited; Northern Foods Grocery Group Limited; NFT Distribution Limited; Batchelors Limited (Ireland); Green Isle Food Group Limited (Ireland); Cavaghan & Gray Group Limited; Cavaghan & Gray Limited.

Principal Competitors

United Biscuits Finance plc; Uniq plc; Geest PLC; Brake Bros plc; Nestlé S.A.; Unilever; Kraft Foods International, Inc.

Further Reading

Able, Leslie, "Now's the Time to Go, Says Lord Haskins," *Yorkshire Post,* November 13, 2001.

Caulkin, Simon, "Christopher Haskins," *Management Today,* June 1994, pp. 58–60.

——, "Northern Foods' Changing Recipe," *Management Today,* February 1988, pp. 48–52.

"Champion Who Bats Well for the North," *Yorkshire Post,* February 21, 1994, p. 12.

''Dedicated Foe of Fashion: The Northern Foods Chairman Insists He Does Not Set Out to Make Trouble,'' *Financial Times,* October 2, 1997, p. 17.

Forrest, Tracy, ''Northern Lights,'' *Super Marketing,* November 22, 1991, pp. 52+.

Hamilton, Sally, ''Food's Clean Bill of Health,'' *Business,* March 1991, pp. 105–08.

Horsley, Alec, *The Story of Northern Dairies,* Hull: Northern Dairies, 1953.

Maitland, Alison, ''Express Milk Shake from Northern Foods,'' *Financial Times,* January 27, 1998, p. 24.

Moore, Sheryl, ''Northern Foods' £145m Deal Will Help Slash Debt,'' *Yorkshire Post,* February 1, 2002.

''Northern Ready for the Sales,'' *Yorkshire Post,* November 11, 2003.

''Northern's Chief Leaves As Profits Fall,'' *Yorkshire Post,* September 4, 2003.

Smith, Alison, ''Northern Foods to Narrow Activities,'' *Financial Times,* November 12, 2003, p. 29.

Watson, Elaine, ''Northern's Frontiers,'' *Grocer,* September 13, 2003.

''Wicklow's Big Bite,'' *Business and Finance,* June 3, 1993.

—Robin DuBlanc
—update: David E. Salamie

Novo Nordisk A/S

Novo Allé, 2880 Bagsvaerd
Denmark
Telephone: +45 4444 8888
Fax: +45 4449 0555
Web site: http://www.novonordisk.com

Public Company
Incorporated: 1940
Employees: 18,664
Sales: DKr 25.18 million ($4.0 billion) (2002)
Stock Exchanges: Copenhagen London New York
Ticker Symbol: NVO
NAIC: 325412 Pharmaceutical Preparation Manufacturing

Novo Nordisk A/S is one of the world's leading suppliers of insulin and industrial enzymes. Although the Danish company is engaged in a variety of pharmaceutical and chemical activities, the production of insulin and enzymes remains the core of Novo Group's diverse enterprises. The company's current international stature evolved out of refining long-established skills and acquiring expertise within these specific fields. Novo Nordisk also produces the antidepressant Seroxat (Paxil in the United States), the NovoSeven clotting drug, Norditropin growth hormone therapy, and hormone replacement therapy treatments. The Novo Nordisk Foundation owns a controlling interest in Novo Nordisk A/S.

Origins

August Krogh, a Danish physiologist and Nobel Prize recipient, informed his colleagues of innovative drug research taking place in Toronto. There, scientists were using pancreas extracts as a treatment for diabetes. Inspired by Krogh's enthusiasm, a number of Danes engaged in further investigation of this "revolutionary" hormone called insulin. Among these early converts were Harald Pedersen, a mechanical engineer, and his brother Thorvald, a pharmacist. Together they established a rudimentary production facility in the basement of Harald's home in Copenhagen. In 1925, just four years after the discovery of insulin, the Pedersen brothers were producing a stable, commercially viable, solution called "Insulin Novo."

By 1931 production demands required the Pedersens to leave their cellar and rent space in a former dairy factory. Eventually the brothers purchased the building along with property surrounding the plant. Growing in just ten years from a fledgling basement operation into a large-scale enterprise, the company sold insulin in 40 countries. Pancreas from oxen, calves, and swine were procured from slaughterhouses across Europe and were transported to Novo first by refrigerated car, then by railway van, and finally by lorries. To satisfy Novo's growing need for space Arne Jacobsen, the renowned Danish architect, was contracted to design modern factories.

Research and development remained a priority from the very beginning of the company's history. Profits from insulin sales were reinvested to fund the company's laboratories. Novo opened the Hvidore Hospital for the exclusive treatment of diabetic patients and as an additional facility for investigating the uses of insulin. Yet it was not until Knud Hallas-Moller joined Novo in 1937, immediately after graduating in pharmacy, that the company's research activities accelerated. As head of a new research team comprised mostly of former classmates, Hallas's first project involved investigating methods of improving insulin yields and prolonging its effectiveness.

The result of Hallas's years of study became the foundation for Novo's Lente series of insulins. Based on his discovery that auxiliary substances were not necessary to produce sustained effects, at present the Lente series remains one of the most widely used insulin preparations around the world. Hallas's research garnered him a doctorate from the University of Copenhagen. Later, Hallas received an honorary doctorate from the University of Toronto where insulin was first discovered. In 1977 he received the H.C. Orsted Gold Medal for his significant scientific contribution and in 1981, the year he retired as president to become chairman of the board, Hallas was elevated to the First Class of the order of Knights of the Dannebrog. Hallas met his wife, Gudrun Hallas-Moller (daughter of founder Harald Pedersen), while still working as a researcher.

An additional product line was added to Novo's operations in 1938, thus expanding the company's activities outside the exclusive task of manufacturing insulin. Sterilizing and autoclaving sheep guts produced a versatile surgical thread called Catgut. The popularity of this product kept Novo Facilities

Company Perspectives:

Our Vision. We will be the world's leading diabetes care company. Our aspiration is to defeat diabetes by finding better methods of diabetes prevention, detection and treatment. We will work actively to promote collaboration between all parties in the healthcare system in order to achieve our common goals.

We will offer products and services in other areas where we can make a difference. Our research will lead to the discovery of new, innovative products outside diabetes. We will develop and market such products ourselves whenever we can do it as well as or better than others.

We will achieve competitive business results. Our focus is our strength. We will stay independent and form alliances whenever they serve our business purpose and the cause we stand for.

A job here is never just a job. We are committed to being there for our customers whenever they need us. We will be innovative and effective in everything we do. We will attract and retain the best people by making our company a challenging place to work.

Our values are expressed in all our actions. Decency is what counts. Every day we strive to find the right balance between compassion and competitiveness, the short and the long term, self and commitment to colleagues and society, work and family life.

Our history tells us, it can be done.

occupied over the course of many years; however, in the 1950s, when new methods of suturing wounds supplanted the need for Catgut, production was abandoned.

Producing Trypsin in World War II

Novo introduced another product during this time that marked a significant step in the direction of developing biochemicals. When the company began competing with the tanning industry for animal glands during World War II, Novo decided to extract both insulin and trypsin, an enzyme necessary for batting hides. The combined manufacture of these two products complemented each other well; once insulin was extracted, trypsin could be produced from the gland residues. From the first production of trypsin in the dark cellar of the insulin factory, Novo proceeded to manufacture a wide range of enzymes, which eventually led to its becoming one of the world's leading manufacturers of enzymes.

At the same time Novo pursued this early enzyme production, the company possessed basic knowledge of fermentation techniques. This knowledge soon proved useful both for the future manufacture of enzymes and the immediate need for penicillin. During World War II there was increased pressure on the scientific community to produce mass quantities of the recently isolated bacterial combatant. Novo, eager to contribute, ordered its employees to examine anything from old ski boots to jam jars in order to find the correct fungi. While yields varied as Novo attempted to improve its technology, it was not until Hallas's postwar visit to the United States that the company finally perfected production.

Observing the superior qualities of crystalline penicillin developed at Cornell University, Hallas encouraged Novo to develop its own method of crystallization. By 1947 Novo researchers obtained the desired results and the company became one of the first to commercially produce this stable form of penicillin. With this success Novo proceeded to extend its operations to include the manufacture of second generation antibiotics. Today these pharmaceuticals remain indispensable for the treatment of patients with penicillin allergies and for fighting bacteria resistant to penicillin.

The following decade saw the introduction of Heparin Novo, a notable drug used in the treatment of blood clots. As trypsin is a necessary ingredient in the manufacture of this new product, heparin fit well with Novo's established activities. Using organ tissue from oxen or pigs as raw materials, Novo packaged heparin in small disposable syringes enabling doctors to closely monitor the dosage.

Restructuring in the 1950s

In addition to the manufacture of heparin, the 1950s brought significant structural changes to the growing company. Under Hallas's encouragement, the Pedersen brothers created the Novo Foundation as a receptacle for all Novo's non-negotiable shares. Prior to this decision, control of the company remained in the hands of the founding family. As the Pedersens neared retirement, a solution was sought to protect Novo's future as an independent company. By establishing a foundation with a voting majority, the company acquired an important defense against hostile takeovers as well as a source for contributing to humanitarian projects.

By acquiring expertise in fermentation technology through the manufacture of penicillin, Novo stood well prepared to initiate enzyme production by fermentation of microorganisms. The first product of this technology was amylase, an industrial enzyme used in the manufacture of textiles. Over the next 15 years a number of enzymes emerged from Novo's laboratories that no longer required animal organs for raw materials. The most successful of these products was Alcalase, an enzyme used in detergents. In the mid-1960s these types of enzymes became popular around the world and propelled Novo to the forefront of the industry.

A major setback in 1970, however, caused enzyme sales to drop precipitously. A campaign in the United States to expose alleged health hazards for users of enzymes brought Novo under harsh criticism. After just having completed three new fermentation plants, the company was forced to lay off 400 workers as millions of kroner were lost in sales. Only when the National Academy of Sciences dismissed evidence of health risks did enzyme sales in the United States regain some of their lost momentum. In 1979 Novo completed an enzyme factory in North Carolina for the production of fructose sugar. Increasing demand for this product resulted in expansion of this facility.

In 1955 Novo purchased a piece of land in Bagsvaerd, an area north of Copenhagen. Over the course of the next several years Novo built an array of facilities on this site and Bagsvaerd became the center of administrative and production activities. Also during this period several new lines of pharmaceuticals

Key Dates:

1925: Commercially available Insulin Novo is produced.
1938: Catgut surgical thread is added to product line-up.
1947: Novo becomes early producer of crystalline penicillin.
1979: North Carolina enzyme plant is built.
1982: First commercially produced human insulin is marketed.
1989: Novo Industri merges with Nordisk Gentofte.
1992: Antidepressant Seroxat (Paxil) is introduced.
1995: Epilepsy treatment Gabitril and NovoSeven clotting drug are introduced.
2000: Novo Nordisk restructures.
2002: ZymoGenetics is spun off.

augmented Novo's traditional businesses. These included steroid products for gynecological applications and Glucagon, a diagnostic aid.

Despite these successful additions, the improvement of insulin products remained a company priority. In a major scientific breakthrough, Novo introduced Monocomponent insulins, the purest preparation of insulin available. For the first time in the treatment of diabetes insulin could be administered without the presence of contaminants found in other preparations. Other improvements included the basal/bolus concept of treatment whereby a diabetic could simulate the natural patterns of short- and long-acting insulin. The compact NovoPen, an injection device based on this concept, allows diabetics more freedom in their lifestyles.

First Commercially Produced Human Insulin in 1982

Novo's innovation in insulin products included the 1982 introduction of the first commercially produced human insulin. Aware that porcine insulin differs from human insulin by only one amino acid, Novo discovered a chemical process to transform porcine insulin into an identical copy of that found in the human body. Novo's industry competitors had successfully developed human insulin produced through genetic engineering. In response to this and other technological developments in the industry, Novo organized its own genetic laboratory to manufacture both enzymes and hormones.

The need for capital to support Novo's growth over the past years resulted in the company's stock being listed first on the Copenhagen and later on the London and New York exchanges. In 1975, to celebrate Novo's 50th anniversary, company employees were allowed the opportunity to become co-owners through the purchase of stock at nominal value. Some 90 percent of Novo's employees were shareholders. While Novo's stock was an attractive investment, fluctuations in exchange rates caused earnings per share to decline between 1984 and 1986. Nevertheless, sales for human insulin more than doubled during the same time period.

Novo factories then operated in the United States, Japan, France, South Africa, and Switzerland with plans underway to construct new facilities around the world. In 1981 a jointly owned company was initiated with the large U.S. pharmaceutical concern Squibb. Research and development, always a company priority, was funded through the annual reinvestment of an average 10 percent of sales. In addition to insulin research, the company was engaged in developing a broad range of innovative applications for enzymes. These applications included such diverse areas as pollution control, fuel alcohol projects, and food protein sources.

Creation of Novo Nordisk: 1989

In 1989, Novo Industri A/S merged with Nordisk Gentofte A/S to create Novo Nordisk A/S. Nordisk Gentofte, a leader in blood factors and growth hormones (Norditropin brand), was also a force in the world insulin market, though it was only a fifth the size of Novo. While Nordisk was much smaller, it was respected for its research capacities and was then planning to build an advanced insulin production plant in Ireland. Novo was considered the best-managed company in Denmark, reported Britain's *Financial Times.*

The combined company had annual revenues of more than DKr 6 billion ($835 million) and 7,350 employees. It was estimated to control up to half of the market for insulin in the Western world.

While Novo Nordisk had a market share of 75 percent in Europe, in the United States it only controlled 20 percent. Towards the end of 1989, the company formed a U.S. subsidiary, Novo Nordisk Pharmaceuticals Inc., to replace the marketing joint venture set up with Squibb in 1982.

Innovation in the 1990s

Novo Nordisk introduced a number of innovations after the merger, including NovoLet pre-filled insulin syringes. The Novopen insulin ''pen'' was another convenience. Novo researchers were also studying Alzheimer's disease and other central nervous system disorders.

Novo rolled out a depression drug, Seroxat—known as Paxil in the United States—in 1992. Gabitril, for epilepsy, was introduced in 1995, as was the clotting drug NovoSeven, used to treat hemophilia. In the same year, Novo teamed with leading blood glucose monitor manufacturer LifeScan (owned by Johnson & Johnson) in a marketing alliance.

The company was also a leader in industrial enzymes, particularly for detergents. It had a 50 percent market share in the early 1990s. In 1992 Novo spent $100 million expanding its enzyme manufacturing facilities in North Carolina. The company also spent $50 million opening a nearby insulin plant, which employed about 150 people. In 1994, the U.S. sales office was relocated from Connecticut to North Carolina.

Novo Nordisk stepped up its attack on the U.S. insulin market, dominated by Eli Lilly, by forming another alliance with Schering-Plough Corp. in 1998. The pact was formed to market a recently approved, oral non-insulin drug called Prandin (Novonorm outside the United States) for treatment of adult-onset diabetes.

NovoLog, a fast-acting insulin product to challenge Lilly's Humalog, was introduced in the United States in 2000. Novo continued to increase market share in other areas. Novoseven, a hemophilia treatment, was introduced in the United States in 1999 and in Japan in 2000. This helped maintain momentum for the drug, whose sales grew 40 percent a year between 1996 and 2001.

Restructuring for the New Millennium

Novo Group underwent some restructuring between 1999 and 2002. A holding company, Novo A/S, was established in September 1999. New brand identities were unveiled for Novo A/S, Novo Nordisk A/S, and the newly formed Novozyme A/S during a demerger in 2000. U.S.-based ZymoGenetics Inc. was spun off in 2002, with Novo Nordisk retaining a 40 percent stake.

In 2000, Novo had begun building up a portfolio of promising biotech stocks in Denmark and the United States. These included a 25 percent holding in BioImage, a promising Danish biotechnology company.

Novo was also looking at new uses for existing products. Novoseven, a treatment for hemophilia, was being developed as a hemostatic drug to treat cerebral hemorrhage and other conditions.

Novo Nordisk was planning to build a $200 million insulin plant in Montes Claros, Brazil. It was to become operational in 2007. Emerging markets in India, China, and Latin America were expected to provide ample demand for growth. The company was planning to employ 36,000 people globally by 2010, reported *Workforce.*

Principal Subsidiaries

FeF Chemicals A/S; Hermedico B.V. (Netherlands); Hermedico GmbH (Germany); Home Care Srl. (Italy); Nippon Novo Ltd. (Japan); Novo Investment Pte. Ltd. (Singapore); Novo Nordisk Asia Pacific Pte. Ltd. (Singapore); Novo Nordisk Canada Inc.; Novo Nordisk Comercio Produtos Farmaceuticos, Lda. (Portugal); Novo Nordisk Engineering A/S; Novo Nordisk Engineering Tianjin Co. (China); Novo Nordisk Europe N.V. (Belgium); Novo Nordisk Farma B.V. (Netherlands); Novo Nordisk Farma OY (Finland); Novo Nordisk Farmaceutica do Brasil Ltda. (Brazil); Novo Nordisk Farmaceutici SpA (Italy); Novo Nordisk Farmaka A/S; Novo Nordisk Health Care AG (Switzerland); Novo Nordisk Hellas Ltd. (Greece); Novo Nordisk Holding Ltd. (U.K.); Novo Nordisk Hungaria Kft. (Hungary); Novo Nordisk Pharmaceuticals Ltd. (U.K.); Novo Nordisk Invest 1 A/S; Novo Nordisk IT A/S; Novo Nordisk Limited (Ireland); Novo Nordisk Ltd. (Israel); Novo Nordisk of North America, Inc. (U.S.A.); Novo Nordisk Pharma AG (Switzerland); Novo Nordisk Pharma Argentina S.A.; Novo Nordisk Pharma AS (Norway); Novo Nordisk Pharma AS (Spain); Novo Nordisk Pharma GmbH (Austria); Novo Nordisk Pharma GmbH (Germany); Novo Nordisk Pharma India Ltd; Novo Nordisk Pharma Korea Ltd.; Novo Nordisk Pharma Ltd. (Japan); Novo Nordisk Pharma (Malaysia) Sdn. Bhd.; Novo Nordisk Pharma (Singapore) Pte. Ltd.; Novo Nordisk Pharma Sp.Zoo. (Poland); Novo Nordisk Pharma (Taiwan) Ltd.; Novo Nordisk Pharma (Thailand) Ltd.; Novo Nordisk Pharmaceutical, Inc. (U.S.A.); Novo Nordisk Pharmaceutical Industries, Inc. (U.S.A.); Novo Nordisk Pharmaceuticals A/S; Novo Nordisk Pharmaceuticals Ltd. (New Zealand); Novo Nordisk Pharmaceuticals (Philippines) Inc.; Novo Nordisk Pharmaceuticals Pty. Ltd. (Australia); Novo Nordisk Pharmaceutique SA (France); Novo Nordisk (Pty) Ltd. (South Africa); Novo Nordisk Saglik Urunleri Ticaret Ltd. Sti. (Turkey); Novo Nordisk Scandinavia AB (Sweden); Novo Nordisk Servicepartner A/S; Novo Nordisk Servicepartner Sikring A/S; Novo Nordisk s.r.o. (Czech Republic); Novo Nordisk Tianjin Biotechnology Co. Ltd. (China); S.A. Novo Nordisk Pharma N.V. (Belgium); S.A.V.P.O. (France; 50%).

Principal Divisions

Diabetes Care; Haemostasis Management; Growth Hormone Therapy; Hormone Replacement Therapy.

Principal Competitors

Aventis; Eli Lilly & Co.; Pfizer Inc.; Wyeth.

Further Reading

Barnes, Hilary, ''Drug Rivals Increase Firepower by Mixing Their Staff,'' *Financial Times* (London), Sec. I, April 18, 1990, p. 32.

——, ''An Injection of Co-Operative Spirit,'' *Financial Times* (London), Sec. I, January 19, 1989, p. 40.

——, ''Novo Nordisk Plans Shake-Up,'' *Financial Times* (London), June 20, 1996, p. 25.

Barnett, Jim, ''Novo Nordisk Expansion, New Plant to Bring 250 Jobs,'' *News & Observer* (Raleigh, N.C.), Bus. Sec., May 3, 1992.

''Borsen: BioImage Expected to Turn Over Billions in the Future,'' *Financial Times World Media Abstracts,* September 5, 2001, p. 11.

Forman, Craig, '' 'Pen' Makes Injections Easier for Diabetics,'' *Wall Street Journal,* July 20, 1990, p. B1.

Fountain, Henry, ''An Enzyme to Challenge Rogue Colors in the Washer,'' *New York Times,* April 13, 1999, p. F5.

Lachnit, Carroll, ''A People Strategy That Spans the Globe,'' *Workforce,* June 2003, p. 76.

Leff, Marni, ''Seattle Biotech to Go Public; ZymoGenetics Could Raise As Much As $180 Million Through IPO,'' *Seattle Post-Intelligencer,* September 11, 2001, p. E1.

Lindberg, Ole, ''Drugs Keep Novo in the Pink,'' *International Management,* June 1993, pp. 58+.

MacCarthy, Clare, ''A Focus for Biotech Ventures: The Flow of Funds into Biotech Companies in the Region Is Gathering Speed,'' *Financial Times* (London), Survey—Denmark, May 25, 2001, p. 4.

Marshall, Kyle, ''Plant Part of Insulin Strategy,'' *News & Observer* (Raleigh, N.C.), July 26, 1997, p. D1.

''Mr. Ovlisen's Outlook on Management,'' *New York Times,* January 27, 1991, p. 36.

Moore, Stephen D., ''Novo Nordisk Hopes New Drug Helps It Gain Ground in U.S. Diabetes Market,'' *Wall Street Journal,* April 7, 1998, p. 1.

''Morgenavisen Jyllands-Posten: Novo Nordisk Focuses on New Market Worth Billions of Danish Kroner,'' *Financial Times World Media Abstracts,* May 28, 2001, p. 7.

''Novo, Nordisk Merger Creates Major World Biotechnology Group,'' *Pharmaceutical Business News,* January 20, 1989.

Pederson, Alfred, ''Spawning a New Biotech Giant,'' *Chemical Week,* January 25, 1989, pp. 10+.

Shenker, Israel, ''Novo-Nordisk Rides the Enzyme Tide,'' *New York Times,* January 27, 1991, p. 36.

Starr, Cynthia, ''Novo Hot on the Trail of Alzheimer's, Other Woes,'' *Drug Topics,* December 12, 1988, pp. 30+.

—update: Frederick C. Ingram

NRT Incorporated

339 Jefferson Road
Parsippany, New Jersey 07054-0259
U.S.A.
Telephone: (973) 240-5000
Fax: (973) 240-5271
Web site: http://www.nrtinc.com

Wholly Owned Subsidiary of Cendant Corporation
Incorporated: 1997
Employees: 52,801
Sales: $4 billion (2002 est.)
NAIC: 531210 Offices of Real Estate Agents and Brokers

Based in Parsippany, New Jersey, NRT Incorporated is the world's leading residential real estate brokerage firm, serving 30 major U.S. markets and boasting more than 900 offices and some 52,000 sales associates. Only in existence since 1997, NRT has been an aggressive consolidator in the highly fragmented world of real estate brokers. Once acquired, realty firms are converted to one of three brands—Century 21, Coldwell Banker, or ERA—owned by NRT's parent company, Cendant Corporation. Other NRT brands, gained through acquisitions, are The Corcoran Group and the Sunshine Group. In 2002 NRT generated $149 billion in closed sales volume and posted revenues in excess of $4 billion.

Events Leading to Launching of NRT in 1997

NRT was formed in April 1997 (and incorporated in August of that year) as a joint venture between Hospitality Franchise Systems Inc. (HFS) and Apollo Management LP, a New York City real estate investment firm. HFS was organized in 1990 by Blackstone Capital Partners LP to purchase the franchise systems of Ramada and Howard Johnson. Two years later it added the Days Inns franchise system, followed by the acquisition of Super 8 Motels and the hotel franchise systems of Park Inn and Villager Lodge. Although HFS was viewed by outsiders as a hotel business, the company regarded itself as a franchiser and moved aggressively into new areas in the mid-1990s. It become involved in casino development and bought the Avis car rental business. HFS also turned its attention to real estate. In August 1995 it paid $200 million in cash to Metropolitan Life Insurance Co. for Century 21 Real Estate Corp., the world's largest franchiser of residential real estate brokerage offices, numbering more than 6,000. In February 1996 it paid approximately $36.8 million to acquire ERA Franchise Systems. ERA was formed in 1972 as Electronic Realty Associates, a pioneer in the use of the fax machine in the real estate business. By the time of the HFS acquisition, ERA had grown to be the fourth largest residential real estate brokerage franchise system, numbering more than 2,500 independently owned operations. Finally, in May 1996 HFS paid $640 million in cash and repaid an additional $105 million in debt to purchase Coldwell Banker Corporation. Coldwell Banker boasted a long history, founded by Colbert Coldwell in 1906 in San Francisco in the aftermath of the great San Francisco earthquake that essentially leveled the city. He soon joined forces with Benjamin Arthur Banker, which led to the Coldwell Banker franchise system, which at the time it was acquired by HFS ranked as the second largest real estate brokerage network, with some 2,600 independently owned operations.

Coldwell Banker also owned 370 brokerage offices. In order to remain a pure franchiser, HFS elected to package these assets into an independent trust it named National Realty Trust, established in May 1996. A year later, NRT Incorporated was formed in conjunction with Apollo Management to purchase National Realty as a roll-up vehicle that would then be able to convert purchases to one of the three HFS real estate brands. For its part in the joint venture HFS contributed $157 million to buy senior and convertible preferred stock shares, while Apollo paid $75 million for NRT's common and junior preferred stock. In addition, HFS received an option to buy the common stock from Apollo for $20 million, with NRT required to pay Apollo an additional $166 million. NRT-acquired brokerages would also pay royalty fees to HFS for one of its three real estate franchise brands. Moreover, HFS would be able to boost the fortunes of PPH Inc., a mortgage subsidiary which became the sole mortgage provider for NRT acquisitions.

Robert Becker Heading Coldwell Banker in 1994

A month after NRT was created, veteran real estate executive Robert Becker was named chief executive officer. Despite

Company Perspectives:

NRT is a family of companies dedicated to creating exceptional real estate experiences for our customers and communities through the passionate delivery of truly remarkable service.

his extensive experience in real estate, he maintained that he drifted into the business to assist his mother. She had become involved in real estate as a part-time associate and went on to own with her husband a Mountain Lakes, New Jersey, agency named Klintrup Realtors. When he was 19 he earned his real estate license in order to help her during the summers. In an interview with the *Star-Ledger,* Becker recalled, "Funny thing was, as I started to get involved, listing and selling real estate in my spare time, I found that I really loved it." Becker eventually bought the agency from his parents and built it into a two-office business, increasing the number of sales agents from three to four dozen. In 1980 he sold it to Coldwell Banker, became a manager, and began working his way up through the ranks of the organization. He became a regional vice-president, general sales manager, and senior vice-president before being named president and CEO of the firm in 1994. When HFS acquired the company he became president and CEO of Coldwell Banker Real Estate Corp., a position he held until asked to head NRT.

Becker and NRT wasted no time in pursuing the plan to roll up independent brokerages and become a major player in the consolidation trend taking place in the real estate industry. Not only did a booming real estate market make brokerages an attractive investment, many independents were owned by older individuals with no children interested in carrying on the business, and they were thus looking to cash in. In September 1997 the company acquired the nation's third and tenth largest residential real estate agencies, both operating in the California market. They were Cornish & Carey Residential Inc. of San Mateo, involved in annual sales transactions of $3.3 billion, and Jon Douglas Co. of Beverly Hills, California's largest independent real estate brokerage, handling more than $10.5 billion in annual sales transactions. It was also Prudential Real Estate Affiliate Inc.'s largest franchisee, but along with Cornish & Carey it would now become a Coldwell Banker franchisee. When the National Realty assets were combined with these two acquisitions, NRT accounted for $22.6 billion in transaction volume in the previous year, while posting $1.2 billion in revenues.

NRT's aggressive move into the West Coast, in particular the San Francisco area, was not free of controversy, however. According to an October 1997 *Business Journal-Portland* article, "Owners and agents of residential real estate companies in the path of NRT Inc.'s West Coast buying spree are telling some sordid stories about the tactics of the New Jersey-based company. There are tales of threats to company executives who refuse to sell, the hiring of private detectives to follow agents thinking about leaving companies already bought by NRT, and promises of retribution for agents that do leave." The article also reported that 130 Jon Douglas agents working in the Bay area were so disgruntled about the sale to NRT that they left en masse to join a rival brokerage. NRT was further alleged to have hired private detectives to take pictures of dissidents and threaten to have commissions withheld. NRT officials categorically denied all such charges.

Several months later, *Business News New Jersey* addressed concerns about NRT, but took a more positive slant: "NRT's steamrolling approach to growth caused substantial anxiety both industry-wide and in some of the brokerages that it acquired. Local firms feared losing their independence. . . . But the experience of NRT's acquisitions seems to have eased that concern. Burgdorff Realtors, whose 31 offices joined NRT under the ERA umbrella, initially with some skepticism, is now doing business much the way it always has, and has had little problem integrating new improvements." Furthermore, Becker, who knew the real estate brokerage business at every level, was adamant about not micromanaging, telling *Business News New Jersey,* "Real estate is a local business, and must be representative of the way in which business is conducted in its locale." Because of its sheer size and ability to achieve economies of scale, NRT was able to offer valuable support to the brokerages it acquired. In particular, the buying power of the parent corporation could significantly lower capital expenditures, a major factor in the profitability of midsize businesses. In addition to saving money, NRT could improve the technology capabilities of its affiliates, primarily through an Internet-based data-sharing platform that was robust as well as inexpensive. Savings were also reinvested to provide salespeople with marketing-oriented technology as well as advanced training.

NRT made great strides by the end of 1997. In addition to scores of smaller deals, the company completed six of the year's 13 most significant acquisitions, according to REAL Trends, an industry newsletter. Another significant occurrence in 1997 involved NRT's co-owner. In December HFS merged with Stamford, Connecticut-based CUC International Inc. in a $14 billion deal. CUC, a direct marketing firm, was best known for its NetMarket online superstore, Entertainment coupon books, and direct-markets club memberships. The resulting combination was named Cendant. The rationale for the merger was summarized by *Mortgage Banking* in a December 1997 profile: "The idea behind the merger was to combine CUC's marketing expertise with HFS's products and cross-sell everything from real estate, mortgages and home security systems to pizzas and rental cars. . . . It's a story Wall Street seems ready to buy. [Robertson, Stevens & Co. analyst Keith E.] Benjamin says Cendant has the capacity to dominate the entire homebuying process. 'We envision a corporate employee being transferred across the country, securing a preapproved mortgage through PHH, being shown a variety of homes by a Century 21 real estate agent while having the whole process managed by [HFS Mobility Services]. We also imagine this individual renting an Avis car and potentially residing in a Days Inn while in the homebuying process,' Benjamin says. And remember, every step along the way, Cendant will be collecting information about the buying habits of that corporate employee for its $5.5 million data warehouse."

IPO Cancellation: 1999

NRT continued to acquire independent real estate brokerages at a steady clip. By early 1999 it was ready to conduct an initial public offering of stock; taking NRT public had been part

Key Dates:

1996: National Realty Trust is formed.
1997: NRT Incorporated is formed to acquire National Realty and roll up independent real estate brokerages.
1999: Planned public offering is canceled.
2002: Cendant Corporation buys out Apollo Management to become sole owner of NRT.

of the plan since the creation of the company. The goal was to sell a 41 percent stake and raise $225 million, of which $84.5 million was earmarked to redeem Apollo's Series C preferred shares, carrying an interest rate of 18 percent. Because 1998 had been a record year for new home sales, it appeared that the timing for an offering was ideal. By June, however, market conditions deteriorated to the point that the company called off the stock sale. In a prepared statement, Becker explained, "Thanks to the continuing, long-term commitment of our current investors, we are well positioned to await a more favorable IPO markct. Mcanwhile, we are fortunate to have access to the resources necessary to continue acquiring brokerages and enhancing our existing operations." Just two months later, and less than two years since being incorporated, NRT completed the acquisition of its 100th company, buying Boston-area's Papagno Real Estate. As a result, NRT maintained more than 340 offices and was involved in annual sales volume in the range of $94 billion.

NRT's acquisition spree continued during the balance of 1999 and into 2000. By October 2000, when NRT announced the addition of three large real estate brokerage firms located in California, Illinois, and Massachusetts, the number of companies acquired by NRT since its inception totaled 157. By the end of the year NRT completed one of its most important deals, buying Los Angeles-based Fred Sands Realtors, the largest independent residential broker in California, operating 23 offices and generating in excess of $5 billion in sales volume for 1999. Founded in 1969 by Fred C. Sands, the brokerage developed into a high-end realtor, boasting numerous film, music, and sports celebrity clients.

In 2001 NRT continued to add to its brokerage empire. It bought major firms in Sacramento; Lake Tahoe; Dallas/Ft. Worth; Denver; Columbus, Ohio; St. Louis; New York City; San Diego; and Atlanta. In April 2002 NRT's ownership arrangement changed shape. Cendant exercised its option to buy out Apollo in a $224 million stock deal in which Cendant paid the $166 million that NRT was slated to pay Apollo as part of the original joint venture agreement. Clearly, Cendant was pleased with NRT, which in 2001 contributed $220 million in royalty fees. NRT acquisitions mounted throughout 2002 and into 2003, despite the effects of a poor economy. Precisely when market conditions would show enough improvement to justify a public offering of stock, one of the company's original goals, remained uncertain.

Principal Operating Units

Century 21; Coldwell Banker; ERA.

Principal Competitors

HomeServices of America, Inc.; Prudential Financial, Inc.; RE/MAX International, Inc.

Further Reading

DeZube, Dona, "Putting It All Together," *Mortgage Banking,* December 1997, p. 12.
Feyder, Susan, "Deal Part of NRT's Rapid Growth Plan," *Star Tribune,* February 18, 1998, p. 1D.
Haigney, Karen R., "The Star-Ledger Profiles Bob Becker," *Star-Ledger,* May 12, 2000.
Jacobs, Charles, "NRT Builds Muscle," *Business News New Jersey,* May 18, 1998, p. 7.
Miller, Brian K., "Agents Decry Real Estate Giant's Tactics," *Business Journal-Portland,* October 31, 1997, p. 1.
Rich, Motoko, "Cendant Exercises Its Option to Acquire NRT Common Stock," *Wall Street Journal,* April 18, 2002, p. D6.
Taylor, Iris, "HFS Cuts a Deal to Grow," *Star-Ledger,* August 13, 1997, p. 33.
Timmons, Heather, "HFS Eyes Originations Push by Buying Brokerages," *American Banker,* August 14, 1997. p. 15.

—Ed Dinger

Old Mutual PLC

Old Mutual Pl., 2 Lambeth Hill
London
EC4V 4GG
United Kingdom
Telephone: 44 20 7002 7000
Fax: 44 20 7002 7200
Web site: http://www.oldmutual.com

Public Company
Incorporated:
Employees: 46,462
Total Assets: £37 billion (2003)
Stock Exchanges: Johannesburg London Frankfurt
Ticker Symbol: OML.L
NAIC: 522110 Commercial Banking; 524113 Direct Life Insurance Carriers; 524114 Direct Health and Medical Insurance Carriers; 551112 Offices of Other Holding Companies

Old Mutual PLC has shrugged off nearly 150 years as an almost exclusively South African financial services business, emerging as a major up-and-comer on the international market. Demutualized in 1999, Old Mutual has switched its headquarters to London in order to be able to join the FTSE 100—the company is valued at more than £5 billion ($8 billion) and has more than £134 billion ($214 billion) in assets under its management. In less than five years, Old Mutual has successfully shifted its geographic mix—by 2003 just 60 percent of the group's business came from South Africa, while the United States contributed 30 percent, and the United Kingdom 10 percent. The company intends to continue to re-balance its operations so that its business is divided equally among these three primary markets. Concurrent with its geographic expansion, Old Mutual also has moved to reinvent itself as a major assets gathering and assets management group. In South Africa, the group's operations are based around a core of Old Mutual (South Africa), the largest provider of financial services, including insurance products, in the country; a majority shareholding in the country's leading domestic bank, Nedcor; and Mutual & Federal, a leading South African general insurer. In the United States, the company has gained a position among the industry's top ten by building a multistyle asset management operation through an aggressive, multibillion-dollar acquisition drive. The group's main U.S. operations include US Asset Management, a grouping of 23 affiliated asset management companies; and US Life, which generates more than $4 billion in new business each year. The company's holdings in the United Kingdom, which included Gerrard, a leading private client broking business until its sale in December 2003, are focused around Old Mutual Financial Services, a major U.K. assets management firm. Old Mutual expects to continue its international acquisition campaign into the middle of the decade as it refines the scope and scale of its operation. The company is listed on the London, Johannesburg, and Frankfurt stock exchanges. Old Mutual is led by Chairman Mike Levett and CEO Jim Sutcliffe.

Mutually Exclusive in South Africa in the 19th Century

Old Mutual's origins trace back to the mid-19th century, and the beginnings of the mutual aid movement that had helped transform the British housing market in the United Kingdom. In 1845, a Scotsman, John Fairburn, led a group of 166 members in the formation of South Africa's first mutual aid society, Mutual Life Assurance Society of the Cape of Good Hope. The society's members were also its first customers—and their premiums represented the group's sole capital.

Yet the group grew strongly through the end of the century, already claiming a position as a leader in South Africa's financial services market. In 1885, the company changed its name, to South Africa Mutual Life Assurance Society, to reflect its status as an insurance provider for the entire South African colony. Faced with a growing number of competing mutual groups—many of whom began introducing themselves to customers as "the mutual"—the company began referring to itself as the "old" Mutual, emphasizing its status as the colony's first mutual society. The name caught on, and the group eventually formally adopted the corporate name of Old Mutual.

Where South Africa's economy had been based, in large part, on agriculture, the discovery of gold in the Transvaal

Company Perspectives:

Strategy: Old Mutual is on a path to internationalization of the company. Founded over 150 years ago in Cape Town, South Africa, today Old Mutual is an expanding financial services organization with operations in the USA, UK, India, and other territories, plus the largest and best-known financial services group in the whole of Southern Africa. Recently we have been bedding down acquisitions in SA, Namibia, USA and UK prior to the next step forward in the Old Mutual Strategy.

region in 1870, and the discovery and exploitation of the region's vast mineral resources, including diamonds, helped transform the colony into a regional economic leader. The rising wealth of the colony transformed into a rising number of policyholders for Old Mutual, and growing economic and political influence for the society.

Old Mutual's importance for the colony was confirmed after South Africa was granted its independence in 1910, and Chairman John X. Merriman was elected as the new British commonwealth's first premier. Over the next several decades Old Mutual became one of South Africa's most dominant institutions, capturing as much as a one-third share of the country's insurance market. In the face of the government's strict exchange controls, Old Mutual, like many South African companies, focused its energies primarily on its domestic market. Similarly, the society's investment portfolio reflected the increasing ostracism of the apartheid state; unable to invest in corporations outside of South Africa, Old Mutual became a major shareholder in a number of South African institutions, such as the future Nedcor bank, Richemont, the diversified Rembrandt group, Standard Bank, industrial group Barlow, mining group Anglo American, and others.

Despite its focus on South Africa, Old Mutual nonetheless established operations elsewhere on the African continent. The early 1900s saw the group extend into then-Rhodesia, and into German South West Africa. In 1927, Old Mutual set up sales operations in Zimbabwe, in Salisbury (later the capital city of Harare). Soon after, the company added Kenya to its scope, and in 1930 set up a new office in Nairobi. Into the 1950s, the society continued to follow the region's rapidly expanding mining sectors into Tanzania, Zambia, and elsewhere.

By 1954, the company had issued its one millionth policy. Old Mutual also continued to expand its range of financial services, and in 1966 set up a new subsidiary, South African Mutual Unit Trust Company, which took over the society's mutual fund and unit trust products. By the beginning of the 1970s, Old Mutual income from premiums had topped R 100 million per year. By the beginning of the 1990s, the company's yearly premium totals topped R 1 billion for the first time. By then, the group had achieved the ranking as number 38 among the world's top insurance companies.

Throughout its history, the company had actively recruited South Africa's black population into its membership, in part by actively promoting group memberships and group-based insurance and other financial products—one popular Old Mutual product was that of advance-sale funerals. By the late 1990s, more than half of the society's member-customers, which by then numbered more than three million, were black South Africans.

Run-Up to ''Demutualization'' in the 1990s

With international pressure to abolish South Africa's apartheid policies mounting in the mid-1980s, Old Mutual made its first moves to test the international waters. In 1986, the mutual bought Providence Capital, based in the United Kingdom, which later formed the foundation of the group's Old Mutual International subsidiary. The end of apartheid and the creation of a new South African government led by Nelson Mandela in 1994, signaled the start of a new era for the country and for its leading financial services group.

Old Mutual began preparations for its ''demutualization'' and conversion to a public limited company. Faced with impending new competition at home, as trade embargoes against South Africa were lifted on the one hand, and the country's exchange restrictions were abolished on the other, Old Mutual began preparing its full-scale foray into the global market. In 1993 the company created a new subsidiary, OMAM (for Old Mutual Assets Managers), which acted as an umbrella for the grouping of affiliated assets managers. In 1995, the group set up a new business in Boston, Massachusetts, Old Mutual Investment Advisors. That same year, Old Mutual opened offices in Hong Kong and Guernsey.

Old Mutual launched its international expansion in earnest in 1997, when it acquired Capel-Cure Myers, based in the United Kingdom and that country's leading private client stockbroker and investment management firm. The following year, as the group prepared its demutualization, the company struck again, acquiring U.K. stockbroking firm Alfred E. Sharp for more than £40 million. That operation was then merged with Capel-Cure Myers, forming Capel-Cure Sharp. The new company was immediately one of the leading assets groups in the United Kingdom, with more than £10 billion in assets under its control.

Old Mutual faced criticism for its plans to shift its headquarters to London, in order to list its share on that city's stock exchange—and satisfy the requirements for listing its shares in the FTSE 100. Nonetheless, the windfall, represented by the group's public offering, handed out to the group's three million policyholders in the form of shares in the group—and that represented more than a year's earnings for many of the participants in the offering, as well as the group's promise not to eliminate South African jobs—allowed the offering to go through in 1999. The company transferred its headquarters to London, then listed its stock on the London, Johannesburg, and Frankfurt exchanges, as well as in Zimbabwe and Malawi to satisfy mutual members in those markets.

With the proceeds from its public offering, Old Mutual launched an ambitious acquisition drive to propel itself among the ranks of international financial services groups. Yet the group, which maintained its insurance operation in South Africa, also sought to redefine itself, at least internationally, as an assets ''gathering'' and assets management group.

Key Dates:

1845: John Fairburn leads a group of 166 members in the founding of the Mutual Life Assurance Society of the Cape of Good Hope.
1885: The company changes its name to South Africa Mutual Life Assurance Society, but becomes known as Old Mutual.
1927: A branch is opened in Zimbabwe.
1930: A Kenya branch is opened.
1954: The one millionth policy is issued.
1966: The company sets up a new subsidiary, South African Mutual Unit Trust Company, which takes over the society's mutual fund and unit trust products.
1986: The company makes its first entry into the U.K. market with the purchase of Providence Capital.
1993: The company sets up OMAM (Old Mutual Assets Managers).
1995: The company establishes Old Mutual Investment Advisors in Boston, Massachusetts, as its first entry into the United States; offices in Hong Kong and Malawi are opened.
1997: Capel-Cure Myers in the United Kingdom is acquired.
1998: The company acquires Alfred E. Sharp, which is merged with Capel-Cure Myers to form Capel-Cure Sharp.
1999: Old Mutual demutualizes, moves its headquarters to London, and takes a listing on the London, Johannesburg, Frankfurt, Zimbabwe, and Malawi stock exchanges.
2000: The company acquires the Gerrard Group in the United Kingdom for £525 million; the company acquires United Assets Management Corporation of the United States for $2.2 billion.
2001: The company acquires Unified Life Insurance Company of the United States; the company acquires Fidelity & Guaranty Life Insurance for $635 million.
2003: Gerrard Management Services is sold to Barclays.
2004: The company acquires full control of publicly listed South African insurance subsidiary Mutual & Federal, which is delisted.

International Assets Management Group in the New Century

That process got underway when Old Mutual sold off its existing U.K. insurance operations. Instead, the newly public company put up £525 million to acquire the Gerrard Group, a prominent fund manager in the United Kingdom. The Gerrard acquisition led the company to restructure its Capel-Cure Sharp holding under the Gerrard brand, which now asserted itself as one of the United Kingdom's leading private client wealth managers in that market.

Soon after the Gerrard purchase, Old Mutual struck again, this time in the United States, where it agreed to pay $2.2 billion to buy up United Asset Management Corporation (UAM, later renamed as Old Mutual Assets Management US). That acquisition catapulted the company not only into the top ranks of U.S. assets groups, but also made it a world player.

The UAM acquisition set the stage for Old Mutual's entry into the U.S. insurance market as well. In March 2001, the company paid $45 million to acquire Kansas's Unified Life Insurance Co. Although a relatively small company, Unified Life (renamed as Americom) brought with it licenses authorizing Old Mutual to operate in 43 states across the country. The Unified Life acquisition provided the springboard for Old Mutual's next purchase: the $635 million acquisition of Baltimore's Fidelity & Guaranty Life Insurance Co. (F&G). That year, in addition, the company created a U.S. branch of OMAM.

By 2003, Old Mutual's expansion phase had evolved into a consolidation of its operations. The group began refocusing its holdings, shedding nearly half of the affiliated companies added in its acquisitions. By the end of 2003, Old Mutual's affiliated company list had been whittled down to less than 25. Among the companies sold off were Gerrard Management Services, bought by Barclays in December 2003. Old Mutual nonetheless remained committed to providing a full range of asset management styles and products, while maintaining its insurance wing as a means of providing equity income. In January 2004, the company strengthened its South African insurance holdings when it agreed to buy out the minority shareholders of its publicly listed Mutual & Federal subsidiary. After nearly 160 years in business, Old Mutual had proved capable of renewing itself for a new century.

Principal Subsidiaries

Old Mutual South Africa; Fairbairn Capital; OMAM (South Africa); Nedcor; Mutual & Federal; Old Mutual Asset Management (U.S.A.); Old Mutual Financial Network (U.S.A.); Palladyne Asset Management; Old Mutual Asset Managers; OMAM Bermuda; Bright Capital; Selestia; Old Mutual International; Old Mutual Namibia; OM Kotak Mahindra.

Principal Competitors

BANKFIRST N.A.; HSBC Holdings PLC; J.P. Morgan Chase and Co.; Barclays PLC London; Bank of America Corporation; HBOS PLC; Abbey National PLC.

Further Reading

"Further Phase in Its US Strategy," *Market News Publishing,* May 21, 2001.

Kovaleski, Dave, "Quiet Evolution," *Pensions & Investments,* February 17, 2003, p. 31.

Miller, Rick, "Old Mutual Goes on Safari to Build US Business," *Investment News,* May 14, 2001, p. 20.

Moore, James, "Old Mutual Delists Insurer," *Daily Telegraph,* January 21, 2004, p. 29.

"Old Mutual's Yield Powers Asian Rocket," *Euroweek,* May 16, 2003, p. 6.

—M.L. Cohen

Ontario Teachers' Pension Plan

5650 Yonge Street
Toronto, Ontario M2M 4H5
Canada
Telephone: (416) 226-2700
Toll Free: (800) 668-0105
Fax: (416) 730-7807
Web site: http://www.otpp.com

Nonprofit Company
Incorporated: 1989
Employees: 500
Total Assets: $68.2 billion (2003)
NAIC: 525110 Pension Funds

The Ontario Teachers' Pension Plan (OTPP) evolved into one of the most powerful institutional investors in Canada during the 1990s. The plan serves teachers in elementary and secondary schools, pensioners, and their survivors. Forced to change to meet a rising tide of benefits, the plan has been retooled to allow for more creative investment of the teachers' retirement contributions.

Old Plan, New Design: 1917–93

A pension plan for Ontario teachers was created in 1917 and for the next 70-odd years acted as a government agency. As required by law, contributions from the teachers and matching funds from the government were put into nonnegotiable provincial bonds. The system came under stress in 1975, following the indexing of benefits to the cost of living. The level of government and teacher contributions and rate of return on nonmarketable Ontario debentures could not keep pace with inflation. The plan was running a multibillion-dollar deficit by the end of the 1980s.

An outcry for change rose up, and a committee representing the province and the Ontario Teachers Federation was formed to address the problem. They determined the best route was to convert the plan to a nonprofit private corporation and allow for flexibility in its investment options. In addition, the government would boost its level of contributions to the reconstituted organization. The Ontario Teachers' Pension Plan Board was established on December 31, 1989, replacing the Ontario Teachers' Superannuation Fund.

Chairman of the nine-member board, Gerald Bouey, asked Claude Lamoureux, former CEO of Metropolitan Life's Canadian operations, to lead the change. Trained as an actuary, Lamoureux knew how to manage benefits, but to build the assets needed to pay out future claims, he would need a team of investment specialists. He tapped Robert Bertram as chief investment officer.

The pair inherited a staff of 256 employees who primarily dispersed pension checks, according to *Institutional Investor Americas.* The benefits administration system was in dire need of repair and sorely lacking on the customer service end. A $10 million upgrade of information technology was set in motion. The economy in the 1990s would cooperate as well, by cooling inflation and lessening pressure on the plan's resources.

With its diversification plan in motion, the fund ventured into Canadian real estate. Given the depressed market, OTPP was on the lookout for bargains on income-producing property. In 1991 OTPP paid about $180 million for a 50 percent stake in three Cadillac Fairview Corporation Ltd. shopping centers, according to the *Financial Post.* The overall plan was to create a real estate portfolio totaling 5 percent to 15 percent of assets and consisting of industrial and office properties. Geographic expansion was also on tap.

As of March 31, 1991, the OTPP held $21 billion in assets: 81 percent in Ontario debentures; 5 percent in marketable bonds; and 4 percent in money market assets. An additional 10 percent of assets were evenly split between Canadian and U.S. stocks, but the pension plan had much more ambitious goals for its equity investments.

Whirlwind Ride: 1994–98

When Lamoureux and Bertram began their quest to rebuild the plan, they envisioned two-thirds of investments in equities

Company Perspectives:

This is a defined benefit plan co-sponsored by the Ontario government through the Ministry of Education, and the plan members, represented by the Ontario Teachers' Federation. The co-sponsors are equally responsible for plan gains and losses. A six-member Partners' Committee is responsible for changing benefits in the plan.

The Ontario Teachers' Pension Plan has the fiduciary duty to administer the plan and manage the investment fund in the best interests of present and future plan members and their survivors. This duty is vested in a nine-member board of directors appointed equally by the partners. Day-to-day management is delegated by the directors to a chief executive officer and his staff.

The Pension Benefits Act (Ontario) defines the fiduciary duties of all pension plan administrators in Ontario and obliges them to administer the plan and invest assets with the same prudence expected of a person dealing with another's property. The standards of conduct expected of a fiduciary are also set out in common law.

by 1997. By early 1994, the figure had reached 44 percent and climbed to 63 percent by early 1995.

In slightly more than four years, the country's largest single pension fund had put together a staff of 45 investment professionals and plowed almost $10 million into Canadian equities. Bertram asserted, "I would argue that with $6 billion-plus in equity index funds, we probably represent over half of all index funds in Canada. Just guessing." "A change in the fund's strategy can alter the shape of an industry," wrote Gord Mclaughlin for the *Financial Post.*

The formerly low-profile pension fund further boosted its name recognition when it got involved in some volatile corporate power struggles. OTPP backed one brother over another for the control of McCain Food Groups Inc., in 1993. Entry into the arena of professional sports, through its investment in Maple Leaf Gardens in 1994, would involve more intrigue.

Internal workings caused public recognition of another kind. In December 1995, Lamoureux noted that the technology upgrade and related consolidation of data had revealed a shocking error rate in entitlements. Two-thirds of recipients had been either underpaid or overpaid. Small errors made over a period of decades caused part of the problem, but of greater consequence were periodic regulatory and labor related shifts. Mandates on methods and types of data collected changed over the years. In addition, plan implementation itself was subject to interpretation. To rectify the problem OTPP established an entitlement review. More than $450 million went toward compensation. Underpaid pensioners received lost benefits. Those being overpaid were not penalized with cuts. An additional $22 million was spent on the review process, according to *Ivey Business Quarterly.*

Lamoureux's commitment to public disclosure was evident in the handling of the entitlement crisis. More was revealed about him by the way he got to work each day. Even though OTPP's capital pool totaled $54.5 billion in March 1998, placing it among the most powerful of Canadian financial institutions, the fund's top executive rode the subway to work. Raised next to a pipe-organ factory in his hometown of Cap-de-la-Madeleine, Québec, and educated at the Université de Montreal and Laval University in Quebec, his lifestyle appeared in sharp contrast to his peers in the financial industry.

"While Lamoureux doesn't act like a Bay Street power broker, the numbers say he is," wrote Sandra Rubin for the *Financial Post.* "With just a third of its capital, Ontario Teachers' owns about 1.5% of the $1.17 trillion in shares listed on the Toronto Stock Exchange. It's among the biggest single shareholders of BCE Inc., Royal Bank of Canada, Maple Leaf Foods, Canadian Imperial Bank of Commerce, and Bank of Montreal, with investments of more than $500 million in each."

With the plan in such solid state, the government ceased its special payments to the fund in 1998 and returned to its normal contribution level.

Power Plays: 1999–2001

The companies in which OTPP invested could expect to have Lamoureux keeping an eye on more than the bottom line. Issues of corporate governance and executive compensation topped his list of concerns. A U.S. counterpart, the California Public Employees Retirement System (Calpers), held companies to open accountability, while Lamoureux had used more low-key tactics to voice his concerns.

Corporate executives had reason to listen when Lamoureux spoke. OTPP was among a new breed of institutional power brokers. Large pension plans—such as OTPP, Caisée de depot et placement du Québec, and the Ontario Municipal Employees Retirement Board—plus an array of mutual fund managers, as a group, controlled more than half the equity value of Canada's publicly traded companies, according to *Maclean's.* While the new concentration of power worried some, Ontario's current and former teachers, retired teachers, and beneficiaries could rest more easily about their financial futures.

Lamoureux, Bertram, and the OTPP investment team had moved the seriously underfunded plan into a position of overfunding during the 1990s. The legacy of conservatism had been replaced by forays into private equity, emerging markets, quantitative investing, junk bonds, commodities, and real estate. In addition, Bertram, with help from Goldman, Sachs & Co., devised an end run around a government-set 20 percent limit on its foreign investment, according to Barry Rehfeld, writing for *Institutional Investor Americas* in 1999. "Its foreign holdings are funded for the most part through a combination of interest rate and equity swaps. Ontario Teachers first swaps the fixed coupon on its provincial nonmarketable bonds for the floating-rate interest on foreign debt; it then swaps the floating coupon for the returns of foreign indexes. Because the fund doesn't actually own the underlying foreign assets, it technically meets government guidelines." Bertram was lobbying to have the 20 percent restriction on foreign investment lifted.

Although no more government debentures had been issued after 1998, the OTPP's last was not set to expire until 2012. The return on these assets and other fixed-income investments had yields below what was needed in relation to liabilities. To

Key Dates:

1917: A pension plan is created for Ontario teachers.
1975: Ontario teachers' benefits are linked to inflation.
1989: The Ontario Teachers' Pension Plan Board is created by the Ontario government.
1990: A new investment strategy for teachers' pension contributions is implemented.
1991: Teachers' Merchant Bank for private equity investments is created.
1995: Widespread error in entitlement distribution is revealed.
1999: Volatile markets lead to more active management of the public equity portfolio.
2002: Corporate governance is in the spotlight.

compensate for this, OTPP started buying Canadian bonds indexed to inflation, known as real bonds. On the other hand, the plan's return on its private equity investments at times was stellar. OTPP invested $9 million in Canada's Westjet Airlines in 1996. Following its public offering in 1999, the shares were worth $60 million.

Due to concerns over high-tech stocks, OTPP moved to lessen its exposure to equity holdings late in 1999. A percentage of its U.S. equities, held mainly though a Standard & Poor's 500 index fund, were the first to go, according to *Pensions & Investments.* Then in early 2000, OTPP moved to limit its exposure to Canada's Nortel Networks Corporation, a big player on the Toronto Stock Exchange 300 index—not a popular position at the time. Non-North American international stocks, also in index funds, hit the chopping block as well. By year-end 2000, the wisdom of the move was evident by the tumble taken by the market. In keeping with its more active investment strategy, OTPP went looking for bargains in U.S. stocks, following the September 11, 2001, market slide. Funds once earmarked for indexes also were going into private equity and infrastructure investments.

Securing the Future: 2002 and Beyond

OTPP's level of equity investments remained high and so did Lamoureux's obsession with good corporate governance. He gained some allies when he and Stephen Jarislowsky, CEO of an investment counsel managing $33 billion, established the Canadian Coalition for Good Governance. "I want this (coalition) to do what the OSC (Ontario Securities Commission) and government with its laws have not been able to do," Jarislowsky told *Pensions & Investments* in August 2002. "We want these companies to understand if they don't have good governance, they'll have trouble with us. If they fake figures, the accountants will have trouble with us. If companies give too many stock options, they will have trouble with us."

The need to keep on top of its investments was no less crucial in 2002 than it had been in 1990. The number of teachers contributing to the plan in relation to the number of pensioners had dropped dramatically over the past three decades. OTPP needed to maintain sufficient return to pay out future pension benefits. In addition, the public equity market of the early 21st century continued to be uncertain.

The Teachers' Merchant Bank, created in 1991 to handle private equity deals, was expected to double in size by mid-decade. It participated in the largest leveraged buyout in Canadian history in 2002, teaming with Kohlberg Kravis Roberts & Co., New York, for BCE Inc.'s telephone directory business. As of mid-year 2003, the merchant bank had invested in more than 100 companies and 25 private equity funds. The rate of return exceeded 25 percent per annum.

Investments in retail and office property were concentrated in North America—plans for entry into South America, Asia, and Europe had been scratched. The $11.5 billion real estate portfolio was in the hands of Cadillac Fairview Corporation Ltd., a wholly owned subsidiary since 2000.

Overall returns moved to the positive side for the first time in two years, during the first half of 2003. Net assets climbed $2 billion to $68.2 billion during the period. Asset distribution included: 50 percent in equities; 20 percent in fixed-income securities; and 30 percent in inflation-sensitive investments.

Principal Subsidiaries

Cadillac Fairview Corporation Ltd.

Further Reading

Feinberg, Phyllis, "Creating a Code," *Pension & Investments,* August 5, 2002, p. 14.
——, "Doubling in Size," *Pensions & Investments,* October 14, 2002, p. 14.
——, "Goodbye to Indexing," *Pensions & Investments,* June 24, 2002.
——, "Prescient Move," *Pensions & Investments,* December 11, 2000, p. 3.
Gray, John, "Shareholder No. 1," *Canadian Business,* August 4, 2003.
Hayes, Victor, "A Legacy of Confusion," *Ivey Business Quarterly,* Autumn 1998, p. 42.
Horvitch, Sonita, "Teachers' Fund Diversifies by Buying into Malls," *Financial Post,* September 28, 1991, p. 23.
MacFadyen, Ken, "The Ontario Teachers' Pension Plan Looks to Be More Direct," *Buyouts,* August 11, 2003.
Mclaughlin, Gord, "Teachers' Fund Dared to Be Great," *Financial Post,* March 4, 1995, p. 4.
McMurdy, Deirdre, "Walk Softly, Carry $73 Billion," *Canadian Business,* June 25, 2001.
"Ontario Teachers' Pension Plan Reports Results for 2002," *Canadian Corporate News,* March 10, 2003.
Rehfeld, Barry, "Second City, First Rate," *Institutional Investor Americas,* October 1999, pp. 75+.
Rubin, Sandra, "Walk Softly, Carry a Big Stick," *Financial Post,* March 21, 1998, p. 8.
"The $60-Billion Investor: Claude Lamoureux," *Maclean's,* November 2, 1998, p. 58.
Verburg, Peter, "We Don't Need No Regulation," *Canadian Business,* August, 5, 2002.

—Kathleen Peippo

Orbitz, Inc.

200 South Wacker Drive, Suite 1900
Chicago, Illinois 60606
U.S.A.
Telephone: (312) 894-5000
Toll Free: (888) 656-4546
Fax: (312) 894-5010
Web site: http://www.orbitz.com

Public Company
Incorporated: 2000 as DUNC, LLC
Employees: 306
Sales: $175.5 million (2002)
Stock Exchanges: NASDAQ
Ticker Symbol: ORBZ
NAIC: 561510 Travel Agencies

Orbitz, Inc. operates a top three online travel agency. Orbitz.com has more than 19 million registered users, who can search among more than two billion fares on 455 airlines. This includes the largest selection of web-only airfares. Orbitz also offers deals on lodging (among 39,000 properties), rental cars (from 25 companies), vacation packages (30 providers), and cruises (18 lines). Airline ticket sales account for an estimated 70 percent of revenues. Other offerings include Orbitz for Business, aimed at corporate travelers, and Supplier Link Technology, an airline ticket distribution system. Orbitz was founded by United, American, Continental, Delta, and Northwest.

Origins

Five airlines—United Airlines Inc., Delta Air Lines Inc., Continental Airlines Inc., Northwest Airlines Corp., and, later, AMR Corp. (American Airlines)—teamed to create a new online travel service. (American became an equity partner in March 2000; total start-up funding was around $100 million.) Together, the five founding partners controlled 90 percent of seats on domestic commercial flights. Existing computer reservations systems such as SABRE did not present competing fares in an unbiased way, said company officials.

The venture was known to the media as ''T2'' when it was announced in November 1999. In fact, the partnership was incorporated as ''DUNC, LLC'' on February 24, 2000; ''DUNC, Inc.'' was incorporated on May 4, 2000. These entities were officially named Orbitz, LLC and Orbitz, Inc. in July 2000. By this time, 30 affiliate airlines had signed up. Users could still buy tickets from 450 other airlines on the site.

Orbitz hired consumer advocate Cornish Hitchcock as an adviser at the time of its launch, when it had a total of 12 employees. By this time, six other airlines—Hawaiian, Midway, Midwest Express, Spirit, US Airways, and Vanguard—had agreed to sponsor the service. The total investment was $50 million.

The next month, Orbitz landed Jeffrey Katz, former CEO of Swissair AG, who left the airline to head the Internet start-up. Katz, an American native, would then commute from Los Angeles to Chicago in true airline exec fashion. Katz had once been an executive for the SABRE computer reservation system, owner of the Travelocity online ticket site.

Orbitz ended 2000 with 125 employees and no sales as it ramped up for a four-month beta test to begin the next February. The company's first hire was Chief Technology Officer Alex Zoghlin. Nara Schoenberg's profile of him in the *Chicago Tribune* painted him as an irrepressible, ponytail-wearing prankster and unlikely Navy vet with a strong entrepreneurial upbringing. He was also a computer whiz who had pioneered web browsers at the University of Illinois with Netscape cofounder Marc Andreessen (who would join the Orbitz board in 2003). Zoghlin left the firm in April 2003.

Traditional travel agents and competing travel sites protested Orbitz' cozy relationship with airlines, including its ability to sell cut-rate Internet specials not available through such traditional computer reservation systems as SABRE, Worldspan, and Galileo. Orbitz was also enabling the airlines to save on the fees they had been paying to have their flights listed on these databases by setting up its own ''Supplier Link'' distribution system.

However, Orbitz was able to successfully clear antitrust investigations, beginning with that of the Department of Transportation, in April 2001. (However, in June 2002, the Transportation

Company Perspectives:

Orbitz was designed for you—to make your travel planning experience easier and more affordable.

Department reported it was conceivable that Orbitz might be able to undercut other web sites because of its close alliance with the airlines, reducing competition in the long run.) A Justice Department probe was finally completed in August 2003.

There were a number of rivals online. The oldest, Priceline, used a formula that required customers to essentially bid for tickets, rather than pick among listed fares themselves. Another group of airlines was launching a service called Hotwire that operated on a similar concept. There was also software designed to sort through fare offerings on individual airlines' web sites.

Launching the Site: 2001

Orbitz.com officially opened for business in June 2001. It claimed to have more web-only bargain fares than any other site. Orbitz also boasted the ability to inform customers of flight cancellations and changes through their pagers and mobile phones. The site also made it easy to search nearby airports for better fares. Orbitz.com sold $3.3 million on its first full day; it signed up 5,000 new customers in a single Sunday.

The Orbitz site had been billed as being powered by the fastest search engine in the world, custom designed at MIT. However, users experienced a number of technical glitches, particularly relating to international flights. There were also compatibility problems with older web browsers and with AOL, and complaints of inadequate customer service. An Orbitz spokesperson accused competitors of a ''smear campaign.''

Southwest Airlines sued Orbitz, complaining that the site listed its fare and flight information in a misleading way. Orbitz did not actually sell Southwest tickets. Vanguard Airlines, one of Orbitz's own partners, also had a troublesome relationship with the company.

A number of factors affected the travel industry after Orbitz started business. These included a weak global economy and the 9/11 terrorist attacks on the United States. This resulted in a weak reception on the stock market for another couple of years.

Orbitz began charging a $5 per ticket fee in December 2001. The company reported $43.4 million in operating revenue for the year. Orbitz's estimated $2.5 billion in bookings in 2002 more than tripled the previous year's result. The company lost $17.9 million for the year on revenues of $175.5 million.

In July 2002, Orbitz launched Supplier Link, billed as the first new airline ticket distribution system in more than 30 years. Around the same time, the company unveiled a special service to help corporate users save money on business travel. Savings of up to 75 percent on transaction fees were touted, since it only charged a $5–$6 per ticket fee. Specialized cost reporting and itinerary management tools were part of the service. The business unit originally targeted smaller businesses with annual travel budgets between $1 million and $10 million; Orbitz landed its first account with a major corporation, McDonald's, in October 2003.

Key Dates:

1999: Five major airlines announce new online travel agency.
2001: Orbitz.com is launched.
2003: Orbitz, Inc. goes public.

Public in 2003

An initial public offering was scheduled for 2002, but postponed due to weakness in the stock market and other conditions. While the online travel market was competitive, Orbitz's prospectus suggested a successful future by leveraging the site's pull on seekers of airline tickets to pitch higher margin services. The company began reselling hotel rooms online in the spring of 2003. According to *Business Week,* Orbitz actually listed rooms available on Travelweb.com in exchange for commissions.

Orbitz gained by the postponement of its initial public offering (IPO). The IPO had originally been expected to take in $125 million when set for May 2002. In the next year and a half, the company's numbers grew and it was coming closer to profitability. Skeptics blasted Orbitz's lack of consistent profits, and noted that the commission rates the airlines paid were scheduled to drop to 37 percent of their value by 2006.

When the IPO was rescheduled in November 2003, the company said it expected to reap up to $303.6 million. Orbitz, Inc. began trading on December 16 at $26 a share, and the company raised $317 million in the IPO. The five founding airlines sold some stock but retained an ownership stake.

Orbitz increased its offerings of rooms at 100 independent hotels in March 2003. The company already had an association with TravelWeb, a consortium made up of Marriott International Inc., Hilton Hotels Corp., Hyatt Corp., and others. Orbitz sold 2.3 million room nights in 2002, one-fifth that of Expedia, Inc., owned by USA Interactive.

Principal Divisions

Booking Engine Services; Orbitz for Business; Supplier Link.

Principal Competitors

Hotels.com; Priceline.com; Sabre Holdings Corp. (Travelocity.com); USA Interactive (Expedia Inc.).

Further Reading

Bly, Laura, ''Katz Orbits the Web World,'' *USA Today,* December 29, 2000, p. 1D.

Chandler, Susan, ''Antitrust Ruling Clears Path for Orbitz Takeoff,'' *Chicago Tribune,* Bus. Sec., August 22, 2003, p. 1.

Chase, Tammy, ''Orbitz Down About 4% in First Day of Trading,'' *Chicago Sun-Times,* Fin. Sec., December 18, 2003, p. 76.

——, ''Orbitz Expects an IPO to Bring Up to $303.6 Mil.,'' *Chicago Sun-Times,* Fin. Sec., November 27, 2003, p. 71.

——, ''Orbitz Not Hurting Airline Competition or Causing Fares to Rise, U.S. Says,'' *Chicago Sun-Times,* August 1, 2003, p. 61.

——, ''Orbitz Raises $317 Million in IPO,'' *Chicago Sun-Times,* December 17, 2003, p. 93.

——, ''Orbitz Working to Gain As Firms Look to Cut Travel Costs,'' *Chicago Sun-Times,* Fin. Sec., October 29, 2003, p. 69.

Claburn, Thomas, ''Turbulence at Takeoff,'' *Ziff Davis Smart Business for the New Economy,* November 1, 2000, p. 38.

Clark, Jayne, ''In New TV Commercial, Orbitz Has Gay Travelers in Its Sights,'' *USA Today,* August 1, 2003, p. D1.

Compart, Andrew, ''Orbitz-Vanguard Skirmish Gets Ugly,'' *Travel Weekly,* July 30, 2001, p. 1.

——, ''Vanguard Steers Away from Orbitz,'' *Travel Weekly,* July 26, 2001, p. 1.

Costello, Jane, ''Technical Glitches Still Plague Online Travel Service Orbitz,'' *Wall Street Journal,* August 27, 2001, p. B4.

DiSabatino, Jennifer, ''Southwest Airlines Pulls Flight Information to Hinder Orbitz,'' *Computerworld,* July 16, 2001, p. 15.

Foss, Brad, ''Orbitz Latest to Start Booking Tool Aimed at Corporate Fliers,'' *Chicago Sun-Times,* July 16, 2002, p. 54.

Garfield, Bob, ''Creepiness Dwarfs the Upside in Orbitz's Marionette Show,'' *Advertising Age,* April 14, 2003, p. 49.

Grimes, Paul, ''Orbitz Entry Gives Some Help in an Already Confusing Web World,'' *Chicago Tribune,* Travel Sec., July 29, 2001, p. 17.

Hamilton, Anita, ''The Orbitz Blitz; Consumers Are Curious—and Rivals, Furious—About the Website Created by the Major Airlines,'' *Time,* July 30, 2001, p. Y15.

''Katz in Orbitz,'' *Air Transport World,* August 2000, p. 11.

Kopytoff, Verne, ''Rivals Air Reservations About Orbitz Practices,'' *Chicago Sun-Times,* August 5, 2002, p. 49.

Maddox, Kate, ''Internet Travel Firm Flies into Biz Orbit,'' *Crain's Chicago Business,* September 30, 2002, p. 8.

Maroney, Tyler, ''An Air Battle Comes to the Web,'' *Fortune,* June 26, 2000, pp. 315+.

Mullaney, Timothy J., ''Orbitz' Heavy Baggage; Why It's Unprofitable—And Why the IPO May Have to Wait,'' *Business Week,* July 8, 2002, p. 64.

——, ''Sky-High Pay for Orbitz' Chief,'' *Business Week,* November 10, 2003, p. 13.

——, ''This IPO Doesn't Deserve to Fly,'' *Business Week,* September 29, 2003, p. 110.

Mullins, Robert, ''Travel Site Orbitz.com Feeling Scorn from Competition,'' *Silicon Valley/San Jose Business Journal,* June 22, 2001, p. 18.

Nairn, Geoffrey, ''Turning Lookers into Bookers,'' *Financial Times* (London), May 2, 2001.

O'Donnell, Jayne, ''Big Airlines Officially Open Online Outlet; Critics Fear Orbitz Fare Site Will Be Unfair,'' *USA Today,* June 4, 2001, p. B1.

Power, Stephen, and Melanie Trottman, ''U.S. Report Gives Mixed Review on Effect of Orbitz on Competitors,'' *Wall Street Journal,* June 28, 2002, p. B2.

Rich, Motoko, ''Orbitz, Expanding Inn Offerings, to List More Independent Hotels,'' *Wall Street Journal,* March 13, 2003, p. D3.

Rose, Barbara, ''Orbitz Sets $125 Million Stock Offering,'' *Chicago Tribune,* May 21, 2002, p. 1.

——, ''Tech Visionary Sights Maturity in Orbitz Orbit,'' *Chicago Tribune,* Bus. Sec., June 7, 2001, p. 1.

Schmeltzer, John, ''Airlines' New On-Line Travel Service Hires In-House Critic,'' *Chicago Tribune,* Bus. Sec., June 16, 2000, p. 3.

Schoenberg, Nara, ''The Bad Boy of Travel,'' *Chicago Tribune,* November 10, 2002, p. Q1.

Shapiro, Michael, ''Orbitz's Rude Awakening; A First-Week Report on the Airlines' New Site,'' *Washington Post,* June 10, 2001, p. E1.

Stewart, Janet, ''Swissair's Katz Takes Flight into New Orbitz,'' *Chicago Tribune,* Bus. Sec., July 6, 2000, p. 1.

Stroud, Toni, ''Much Ado About Orbitz,'' *Chicago Tribune,* Travel Sec., April 22, 2001, p. 21.

Sweeny, Phil, ''Cambridge Company Helps Get Orbitz Web Site Airborne,'' *Boston Business Journal,* June 15, 2001, p. 29.

Tedeschi, Bob, ''Orbitz Takes Off, in the Spotlight,'' *New York Times,* June 17, 2001.

Trottman, Melanie, ''Dropping the Corporate Travel Office; McDonald's Makes Employees Book Trips Through Orbitz,'' *Wall Street Journal,* October 28, 2003, p. D1.

Tsuruoka, Doug, ''Orbitz Is Flying High, But Regulators Still Have Questions,'' *Investor's Business Daily,* April 4, 2002, p. A8.

Van, Jon, ''Orbitz Tech Guru Takes Leave of Online Travel Firm,'' *Chicago Tribune,* Bus. Sec., January 29, 2003, p. 1.

Williamson, Tammy, ''Giant Airlines' Internet Travel Site Launched—And the Boss Is Confident,'' *Chicago Sun-Times,* June 5, 2001, p. 47.

—Frederick C. Ingram

Parlex Corporation

1 Parlex Place
Methuen, Massachusetts 01844
U.S.A.
Telephone: (978) 685-4341
Fax: (978) 685-8809
Web site: http://www.parlex.com

Public Company
Incorporated: 1970
Employees: 507
Sales: $82.8 million (2003)
Stock Exchanges: NASDAQ
Ticker Symbol: PRLX
NAIC: 331491 Nonferrous Metal (Except Copper and Aluminum) Rolling, Drawing, and Extruding; 334412 Printed Circuit Board Manufacturing; 334413 Semiconducting and Related Device Manufacturing; 335931 Current-Carrying Wiring Device Manufacturing

Parlex Corporation is a world leader in the flexible circuitry and laminated cable assemblies used throughout the computer and electronics markets. Based in Massachusetts, the company has manufacturing facilities in Rhode Island, Mexico, China, and the United Kingdom. While few have heard of Parlex and even fewer have ever seen one of the firm's flexible interconnects, most people probably interact with them every day. Parlex components are used in cars, SUVs, planes, computers, printers, cellular phones, handheld electronics, medical equipment, and more. As an industry leader with stringent quality control, Parlex has met industry standards for ISO and QS certification, as well a number of other compliance qualifications.

Flexibility Is the Key: 1970–97

Parlex Corporation was founded in 1970 and began operations at a 125,000-square-foot facility in Methuen, Massachusetts. Parlex's primary production centered on flexible circuits used in a number of electronics products. Parlex's three-dimensional flexible printable circuit boards, used in computers, phones, and other products, were thin, lightweight, bendable, and compact; their predecessors, however, were two-dimensional, rigid, heavier, less reliable, and prone to breakage. Parlex also made laminated cable, which produced higher-speed, sturdier interconnects for electronics (computers, disk drives, printers), automotive (stereo systems, vehicle sensors), medical (scanning devices, electronic scales), and military (night vision systems, aircraft ID systems) industries.

By the end of its first decade, Parlex had grown slowly but steadily with sales close to $10 million. In the 1980s the company had reached its capacity at its Methuen plant and went shopping for additional space. In 1986 Parlex began leasing a 46,000-square-foot manufacturing facility for its laminated cable production, situated in nearby Salem, New Hampshire. The new plant was a stone's throw (nine miles) from Parlex's headquarters and flexible circuitry operations. Two years later, in 1988, Parlex bought Cirtec Nevada, Inc. and formed a new subsidiary called Parlex Nevada, Inc. The Nevada venture, however, did not work out as planned; by 1990 certain operations were dissolved and the remainder of the subsidiary was sold in 1992.

Despite its Nevada snafu, Parlex's flexible circuit boards and laminated cables were selling well. By 1993 sales for the fiscal year (ending in June) reached $31.3 million and in the following year Parlex had earned ISO 9002 certification for its products. Sales rose to $34.9 million for 1994. Revenues continued to climb for the next several years; in 1995 sales topped $40.2 million, and in 1996 sales reached $47.3 million.

Part of what drove sales in the middle of the decade was a 1995 joint venture with the People's Republic of China to create Parlex (Shanghai) Circuit Company Ltd. The new operation acquired a 35,000-square-foot plant in downtown Shanghai to serve Parlex's growing Asian market in flexible printed circuit boards. Parlex's workforce grew from 1995's 450 to 475 in 1997, and sales for 1997 hit $55.1 million.

Innovations: 1998 to 2000

As demand for Parlex's products grew, the company spent more and more on research and development (R&D) not only to stay ahead of its competitors but to improve its flexible circuits

Company Perspectives:

At Parlex, we continue to develop cost-effective technology solutions to improve the performance and reliability of our customers' products. As a global leader in developing flexible interconnect technology, Parlex leads the industry in new product introduction. Our application-driven engineering teams design products that support our OEM (original equipment manufacturers) partners' aggressive time-to-market and cost requirements. Supporting the front-end engineering effort is a global manufacturing footprint. The Company has manufacturing operations in Asia, North America, and Europe.

and laminated cables. By the late 1990s Parlex was an established leader in the electronic interconnects market; its increased R&D spending had paid off with several new developments, including PALFlex, Spray Mask, and other patented technology. PALFlex was a new ''plate to film'' technique that allowed the company to shave several steps from its manufacturing process, while Spray Mask eliminated a soldering step from its circuit panel production, and expected to save as much as $1 for every panel manufactured using the new technology.

As Parlex prepared to switch its facilities over to the new money-saving processes (to be completed by early 1998), the company opened a new manufacturing plant in Empalmé, Mexico, and received lucrative contracts with Iomega Corporation and Samsung Electronics Company Ltd. Iomega, located in San Diego, California, was known for its computer components, such as portable zip disk drives, while the Seoul, South Korea-based Samsung Electronics Company, Ltd. was known throughout the world for its consumer electronics products including televisions, radios, cameras, computer monitors, memory drives, and printers. In addition, Parlex had secured QS 9000 certification for both its cable and circuit operations, and major clients Motorola and Siemens had increased their production demands.

By the end of the decade, Parlex had expanded its headquarters and nearby manufacturing facility and bought a 55 percent stake in Dynaflex, a printed circuit board producer based in New Hampshire. Parlex paid Hadco Corporation, the parent company of Dynaflex, $2.7 million for the majority stake with an opportunity to purchase the remainder of the business in the future. Dynaflex's manufacturing facility in San Jose, California, mainly used for small orders needing a fast turnaround, became a Parlex entity once the dust settled. Parlex ended the century with revenues totaling $67 million and a workforce of more than 1,000 employees worldwide.

In 2000 Parlex continued to lead the electronic interconnects market; the firm was also in an enviable position with no debt, a multitude of patents protecting its proprietary technology, and a vastly untapped market in Europe to pursue. After having little or no sales in Europe for the last several years, by the early 2000s Parlex had $15 million in sales with every expectation of more. Further, Parlex was not as dependent on any one particular market for the majority of its revenues, as sales for its five business segments (automotive, aerospace/military, industrial/medical, electronic, and telecom/datacom) were more evenly spread than in past years.

A new international purchase bolstered the flexible circuits division, when Parlex paid just under $20 million to the Cookson Group PLC for its two Poly-Flex Circuits subsidiaries. With the U.S. subsidiary located in Cranston, Rhode Island, and the other based in Newport, Isle of Wight, Parlex hoped the British-based subsidiary would open a larger gateway to the United Kingdom's electronic interconnects market. Fiscal sales for 2000 reached $101.8 million and Parlex's workforce numbered 1,500.

Highs and Lows: 2001 and Beyond

In 2001 Parlex was named as one of *Forbes* magazine's best 200 small companies in the United States, and made the *Boston Globe*'s ''Globe 100'' list of Massachusetts companies for the third year in a row. Other highlights of the year included increasing technological breakthroughs in electronic identification, such as RFID (radio frequency identification) and ''Smart Card'' applications. With the RFID market poised for takeoff, Parlex segued into the design and production of tiny chips for low cost antennas (which then transferred data across radio waves) as well as Smart Cards that placed tiny chips in credit cards, airline tickets, and passports for instant identification. Parlex also had a number of new and pending patents for its constantly evolving technology. Sales for fiscal 2001, which ended June 30th, reached $103.6 million; yet the brunt of the economic downturn that occurred after September 11th showed up in Parlex's 2002 revenues as sales fell to $87.1 million.

Near the end of 2001 (but in Parlex's fiscal 2002 year), the company took measures to shore up its performance by slashing its workforce and closing its Salem, New Hampshire plant (operations were transferred to the Shanghai facility). Despite the firm's difficulties, however, there were a number of highlights in 2002, including a second Chinese joint venture called Parlex Shanghai Interconnect Products, the acquisition of another 40 percent ownership in its original Chinese partnership, and two prestigious awards: making Samsung Electronic's ''Outstanding Supplier'' list, one of only 10 suppliers to receive such a commendation in 2002; and Johnson Controls Inc.'s ''Gold Supplier'' award for outstanding performance as a flexible circuits supplier.

In 2003 Parlex banked on its growing RFID product development by forming a partnership with the New Hampshire-based Nashua Corporation to design and manufacture flexible circuitry for use in the cellular, automotive, and radio frequency markets. Despite its new partnership with Nashua and other innovations, Parlex experienced another year of disappointing sales and was forced to transfer more of its production to its plants in China. To make up for losses in the telecom market, Parlex concentrated on its medical and military applications for the coming years. Revenues for 2003 were slightly lower than the previous year's $87.1 million, at $82.3 million.

Aside from two years operating at a loss, Parlex remained a world leader in the flexible interconnects marketplace. In just over three decades Parlex parlayed its way from a relatively unknown electronics designer and manufacturer into a techno-

Key Dates:

1970: Parlex Corporation is founded in Methuen, Massachusetts.
1986: Parlex leases a manufacturing facility in Salem, New Hampshire, for its laminated cable production.
1988: The company acquires Cirtec Nevada, Inc.
1995: Parlex forms a joint venture with the People's Republic of China, and opens a manufacturing plant in Mexico.
1991: Parlex buys a controlling stake in Dynaflex and gains a California subsidiary.
1997: Parlex inks deals with Iomega Corporation and Samsung Electronics Company Ltd.
1998: A new addition is built to Parlex's laminated cable manufacturing facility in New Hampshire.
2000: The Cookson Group's Poly-Flex subsidiaries are bought for just under $19.7 million.
2002: Parlex establishes a second joint venture with China.
2003: Parlex acquires the remaining shares of Dynaflex and begins a joint venture with Nashua Corporation.

logical trailblazer servicing *Fortune* 500 companies including Johnson Controls, Lockheed Martin, Raytheon, Delco, Motorola, Siemens, Whirlpool, Dell, Iomega, Nortel, Hewlett-Packard, and Pitney-Bowes. With applications in the automotive, aerospace, telecommunications/networking, home appliance, computer, military, and medical fields, Parlex continued to set the standard for flexible circuitry and laminated cable interconnects. Never content to rest on its laurels, Parlex continually sought ways to upgrade its technology and remain a step ahead of its competitors.

Principal Subsidiaries

Parlex Asia Pacific Ltd.; Parlex Acquisition Corporation; Parlex (Shanghai) Circuit Company, Ltd. (China); Parlex Dynaflex Corporation; Parlex International Corporation.

Principal Competitors

ADFlex Solutions, Inc.; Amphenol Corporation; Fujikura Ltd.; Innovex, Inc.; Molex Incorporated; Nippon Mektron; Sheldahl Company.

Further Reading

"Cookson Companies Bought by Methuen Firm," *Providence Business News,* March 20, 2000, p. 16.
"Cookson Cuts Circuits," *Chemical Week,* February 2, 2000, p. 35.
"Corporate Album: Profile," *Boston Business Journal,* November 2, 2001, p. 31.
"Hadco, Parlex Eye Joint PC Board Output," *Electronic News,* January 11, 1999, p. 35.
Lacoursiere, Catherine, "Flexible Strategy," *Investor's Business Daily,* July 20, 2000, p. A12.
"Nashua, Parlex Sign Agreement," *CircuiTree,* May 2003, p. 19.
"Parlex Completes Plant Expansion," *Electronic Materials Update,* July 1999.
"Parlex Corporation," Investment Report, Advest, Inc., December 22, 1997, pp. 1–8.
"Parlex Praised by *Forbes,*" *CircuiTree,* January 2001, p. 58.
"Parlex Receives Gold Supplier Award," *CircuiTree,* August 2002, p. 18.
"Parlex Takes Dynaflex into Its Fold," *Electronic Buyers' News,* May 24, 1999, p. 38.
Richtmyer, Richard, "Parlex Takes 55% Stake in Hadco Subsidiary," *Electronic Buyers' News,* January 11, 1999, p. 8.

—Nelson Rhodes

Pediatrix Medical Group, Inc.

1301 Concord Terrace
Fort Lauderdale, Florida 33323
U.S.A.
Telephone: (954) 384-0175
Toll Free: (800) 243-0175
Fax: (954) 233-3202
Web site: http://www.pediatrix.com

Public Company
Incorporated: 1979 as South Florida Neonatology Associates
Employees: 2,291
Sales: $465.5 million (2002)
Stock Exchanges: New York
Ticker Symbol: PDX
NAIC: 621111 Offices of Physicians (Except Mental Health Specialists)

Pediatrix Medical Group, Inc. is the largest national practice group of neonatal physicians, providing hospital-based care for ill newborns, including premature babies with low birth weight or medical complications. Pediatrix employs over 630 neonatologists, including sub-specialists in maternal-fetal (perinatal) medicine for women with high-risk pregnancies and pediatric cardiology. Through direct ownership or contract Pediatrix manages more than 200 neonatal intensive care units (NICUs) in 30 states and Puerto Rico. Regional networks operate in Phoenix-Tucson, Denver-Colorado Springs, Seattle-Tacoma, southern California, Las Vegas, Kansas City, Des Moines, San Antonio, and Dallas/Ft. Worth. Also, Pediatrix manages newborn nurseries for healthy babies during their stay in the hospital after birth. Pediatrix operates as a physician practice management group, handling the billing, collections, and other daily administrative responsibilities of NICUs so that doctors can direct their energies to caring for babies. Pediatrix provides physicians with several means of learning and improving medical skills, such as the Research Data System which collects and organizes the outcomes of patient care to ascertain the best approaches to treatment.

Slow Start Yielding to Rapid Growth in Early 1990s

Founded in 1979, South Florida Neonatology Associates preceded Pediatrix Medical Group. Neonatologists Roger Medel and Greg Melnick created the company to manage and staff hospital-based neonatal intensive care units, offering hospitals a means of cost containment. Medel and Melnick took responsibility for hiring physician specialists for the critical care unit itself, and for administration of the unit, including billing and collections. Such outsourcing contracts were unusual at that time, so the company handled few contracts in its early years.

The organization's first contracts served Memorial Hospital and Broward General Medical Center, both in the Fort Lauderdale area. The contracts renewed every three years. Broward General expanded to 63 beds at the time of the first contract renewal in 1983. Seven doctors and three nurse practitioners staffed the NICU, providing 24-hour care. A lower bid from another practice group resulted in a loss of the contract when it expired in 1986, but South Florida Neonatology returned to Broward General in 1992 when the North Broward Hospital District awarded a five-year, $9 million contract to the company without a formal bid process. The contract involved care for premature babies as well as for ill newborns.

As the potential benefits of professional management became accepted during the 1980s, Medel found hospital administrators more receptive to the idea of an outside contractor managing a sector of hospital operations. Also, demand for neonatology increased as new technology helped doctors to save more lives of ill newborns. After several years of marketing Medel obtained contracts with Coral Springs Medical Center, Boca Raton Community Hospital, Westside Regional Medical Center in Plantation, and Bethesda Memorial Hospital in Boynton Beach. The company's first contract outside of Florida involved a hospital in Charleston, West Virginia, initiated in 1991. The company grew quickly in the early 1990s and, by the end of 1994, managed 22 NICUs, five pediatric intensive care units (PICUs), and one pediatric department in 12 states and Puerto Rico. That year the company generated $32.8 million in net patient service revenue and earned $5.4 million in net income.

Company Perspectives:

Pediatrix Medical Group provides quality, cost-effective care to all of our patients through a team approach to health care delivery and management, and a total commitment to honesty, quality, professionalism and the highest level of moral and ethical responsiveness to our patients, clients, shareholders and the community at large.

Funding from 1995 IPO Accelerating Growth

In 1995 South Florida Neonatology shifted to a strategy of growth through acquisition in response to consolidation in the healthcare industry as physician practice management (PPM) groups proliferated. Allowing a national practice group to acquire their small practices became an attractive option to doctors because South Florida Neonatology relieved them of increasingly complex coding and billing issues and improved their negotiation power with payers, allowing doctors to focus on patient care. In August the company completed its first acquisition of a physician practice group, located in Orange County, California. The company added 16 units through acquisition or contract in 1995, primarily in California and Ohio.

South Florida Neonatology Associates adopted the name Pediatrix Medical Group in preparation for an initial public offering (IPO) of stock which took place in September 1995. At the time of the IPO, Pediatrix provided physician management services to 37 NICUs and five PICUs, as well as two pediatric departments, employing or contracting 116 physicians in 12 states and Puerto Rico. Proceeds of $88 million funded acquisitions and expansion through internal growth. A secondary offering of stock in August 1996 raised an additional $59 million for acquisitions.

In 1996 Pediatrix acquired ten neonatal physician practice groups. Pediatrix entered the Colorado market with three acquisitions, Pediatric and Newborn Consultants PC, Colorado Neonatal Associates PC, and Rocky Mountain Neonatology PC for a total of $12.2 million cash. The company expanded its Phoenix network with the acquisition of Neonatal Specialists, Ltd. for $6 million. In El Paso Pediatrix acquired the West Texas Neonatal Associates for $5.25 million cash. For $6 million Pediatrix acquired certain assets of Infant Care Specialists Medical Group, the largest neonatology practice in southern California, and one of the largest in the country, with ten NICUs. Other acquisitions included locations in West Palm Beach, for a total of 29 practices in Florida, as well as Reno and Houston.

In 1996 Pediatrix bought 36 NICUs, four PICUs, and two pediatric departments under its management, including three obtained by hospital contract, adding a total of 78,000 NICU patient days. By the end of 1996 Pediatrix managed 68 NICUs, eight PICUs, and three hospital pediatric departments in 17 states and Puerto Rico. The company employed 195 physicians and handled 185,702 NICU patient days in 1996. Net patient service revenue reached $80.8 million and net income reached $13.1 million.

Pediatrix's strategy involved developing regional and statewide networks, then obtaining exclusive contracts with managed care companies, serving all of the customers in need of neonatology pediatric physicians for a capitated rate. At the end of 1996 Pediatrix operated under four contracts with independent practice associations, three in California and one in Texas, and under one contract with a health management organization (HMO), Cigna HealthCare in Phoenix. Acquisitions in Denver provided the network for a possible managed care contract in that area.

During 1997 Pediatrix acquired ten physician group practices, bringing 28 NICUs under management. The company entered new markets with acquisitions in Dallas and Albuquerque. Other acquisition locations involved practices in San Jose and Pasadena, California; Columbia, South Carolina; Fort Worth; Pensacola, Florida; and Colorado Springs. Pediatrix obtained new contracts for NICUs in Las Vegas, Nevada; Harrisburg, Pennsylvania; and Roanoke, Virginia, covering an aggregate of 10,000 patient days.

In March 1998 Pediatrix formed a new subsidiary, Obstetrix Medical Group, to manage the company's growing portfolio of perinatology group practices handling high-risk pregnancies. Through expansion in perinatology Pediatrix hoped to gain referrals to neonatologists and hospitals where the company's practices were located. At this time perinatologists charged on a fee-for-service basis, but Pediatrix considered providing a single rate for a high-risk pregnancy and care of the infant through the release from the hospital.

During 1998 Pediatrix completed several acquisitions of perinatal practices, including Perinatal Consultants in Kansas City; Rocky Mountain Perinatal Associates in Denver; Texas Maternal Fetal Medicine in Fort Worth; and an undisclosed practice in Las Vegas. Also, in 1997 the company formed a perinatology practice for an existing client, Intracoastal Health Care Systems in West Palm Beach. Perinatal practice acquisitions in late 1998 were located in San Jose, California, and Reno, Nevada.

Pediatrix continued to acquire neonatal practices, including locations in Augusta, Little Rock, El Paso, West Palm Beach, Oklahoma City, and Wichita. The company completed eight acquisitions in 1998, adding 18 NICUs. Internal growth occurred through several new contracts, two in Cheverly and Baltimore, Maryland, another in Las Vegas, two in San Cristobal and Ponce, Puerto Rico, and one in Overland Park, Kansas.

Pediatrix sought an integration of neonatal and perinatal specialization at its facilities. In March 1999 the company acquired Perinatal-Neonatal Associates in Seattle, involving 12 neonatologists and six perinatalogists serving ten area hospitals; the practice group recorded 20,000 NICU patient days in 1998. Obstetrix purchased a perinatal physician group in Tacoma, near Seattle, further developing a network of company services in that area. Obstetrix acquired a perinatal practice in Phoenix, with ten physicians serving seven hospitals, including many where Pediatrix operated, and one in Harrisburg, Pennsylvania, with two physicians at two hospitals where Pediatrix managed NICUs.

Billing Investigations Hinder Earnings, Not Growth: Late 1990s to Early 2000s

In April 1999 attorneys general in Arizona, Colorado, and Florida began investigations into billing practices at Pediatrix managed centers, questioning whether their states paid too

Key Dates:

- **1979:** South Florida Neonatology Associates is founded; operations commence through contracts with two hospitals in Broward County, Florida.
- **1991:** First out-of-state contract provides impetus for growth in other states.
- **1995:** Company initiates acquisition strategy, takes the name Pediatrix, and goes public.
- **1996:** Pediatrix completes ten acquisitions.
- **1998:** Obstetrix Medical Group is formed as company expands in perinatology.
- **2000:** Pediatrix launches NATAL U online university for the continuing education of neonatal physicians.
- **2003:** Pediatrix acquires Neo Gen Screening, including proprietary processes for genetic screening of newborns.

much for services for Medicaid patients. While Medel expressed confidence that the company's billing guidelines met legal requirements, announcement of the investigations resulted in a 36 percent decline in the company's stock value, to slightly over $17 per share. The company's share value had already suffered after the Securities and Exchange Commission (SEC) demanded an audit of 1998 financial statements which were deemed fairly stated. The investigations impacted earnings as physicians began to ''downcode,'' applying lower-paying hospital care codes, in fear of overcharging. Though revenues continued to rise, from $185.4 million in 1998 to $243.1 million in 2000, net income declined from $29.1 million to $11 million in those same years, respectively. Pediatrix stock value declined to a low of $8 per share in March 2000, compared to $64 per share in January 1999, before the SEC audit.

The investigations into Pediatrix's billing practices did not sway physicians from joining the company. Pediatrix acquired neonatologist practice groups in Greenville, South Carolina; Topeka, Kansas; Yakima, Washington; and Colorado Springs in the summer of 1999. During 1999 Pediatrix added 29 NICUs and Obstetrix added 25 perinatal physicians through acquisition and internal growth. In early 2000 Pediatrix acquired practices in Melbourne and Sarasota, Florida. The company also acquired Mercy Neonatology in St. Louis which provided 18,000 NICU patient days annually.

The attorneys general in Florida and Arizona concluded their investigations of Pediatrix during the summer of 2000, citing a lack of clarity in the relevant billing codes, but no fraud. In June Pediatrix settled with the State of Florida for $40,000 for possible Medicaid overpayments since January 1, 1997. The company reached a $220,000 settlement with the State of Arizona in August for possible overpayments since January 1, 1990. Pediatrix installed a new electronic billing and coding system to assist doctors with questionable situations. The software reviewed physician case notes, then automatically recommended a billing code.

Pediatrix developed a range of activities to improve neonatal care. In July 2000 the company signed a clinical trial agreement with Forest Laboratories to direct research in the effectiveness of two surfactant drugs to treat Respiratory Distress Syndrome, a common condition among premature babies. Pediatrix received $2.5 million to direct the two-year project involving enrollment of 4,000 patients.

In August Pediatrix launched NATAL U, an online university, or forum, for neonatal and perinatal physicians to share information about treatments and medical discoveries. The virtual campus provided several places where physicians could learn and interact. These included a library of links to medical literature and other informative sites. The Differential Diagnosis (DDx) Lounge provided a chat room for discussion of unique cases and the Grand Rounds Amphitheater provided a place for physicians to present material on a specific, evidence-based topic and allowed for discussion of the topic. In addition to other rooms, NATAL U provided opportunities for physicians to earn Continuing Medical Education credits.

Pediatrix attained its first university-based NICU in January 2001, through a contract with Texas Tech University Health Sciences Center. Located at University Medical Center Hospital in Lubbock, Pediatrix physicians performed as faculty to residents and students while attending to ill newborns.

In February 2001 Pediatrix announced an agreement to merge with Magella Healthcare Corporation, the company's only large competitor. Magella reported $79.4 million in net patient revenue and $9 million in net income in 2000, compared to $243.1 million revenue and $11 million net income at Pediatrix. Together Pediatrix and Magella held a 17 percent share of the hospital neonatology market, managing 185 hospital-based NICUs in 27 states and carrying a staff of 90 perinatologists. The $173.6 million acquisition involved payment of $25 million in bank debt, the assumption of $23.5 million in subordinated notes convertible to common stock, and a stock exchange. The board of directors expanded to nine to accommodate Magella's CEO, chief medical officer, and a board director.

In 2001 Pediatrix continued to expand in existing markets. Acquisitions included Maternal Fetal Medicine at Seattle hospitals served by Pediatrix neonatologists. Another new neonatal contract in southern California further solidified Pediatrix's presence in that market. Acquisition of three central Florida practice groups included an eight-physician practice in Orlando which covered 30,000 NICU patient days in 2000. Also, Pediatrix entered the Atlanta market.

Federal Investigations Accompanying Continued Growth: Early 2000s

Through the merger with Magella Healthcare and improvements to its billing collection, Pediatrix reported a 43 percent increase in profit to $30.4 million in 2001, while net patient revenues increased 68 percent to $354.6 million. Acquisitions and new contracts accounted for $86.5 million in revenues. Pediatrix employed a staff of 250 bill collectors, an unusually large number; however, the staff effectively lowered the time payers took to remit invoices. Pediatrix received payments within 60 days in 2001, compared to 125 days during the previous two years. Regional organization of managed care coding facilitated billing and collections as well. Contracted managed care providers accounted for 49 percent of revenues, government programs accounted for 23 percent, other third party payers for 27 percent, and private pay patients for 1 percent.

Pediatrix settled billing investigations in late 2001 and early 2002. In April 2001 the State of Nevada began to investigate Pediatrix billing practices. Two separate billing investigations were resolved in the late fall of 2001, with Pediatrix paying $145,000 for possible overpayments; however, no violations of regulations were found. The investigation in Colorado was resolved in April 2002, with Pediatrix paying $1.3 million. Pediatrix agreed to retain an independent third party to review billing on an annual basis.

Just as Pediatrix concluded billing investigations, the Federal Trade Commission (FTC) began an investigation into the merger with Magella Healthcare. The FTC examined the structure of the company, particularly in three markets where facilities operated by the two companies overlapped, in Dallas, Austin, and Las Vegas. Announcement of the investigation in June 2002 troubled investors and the stock price dropped nearly $12 per share to $26.20, down from a high of $48.60 on May 1.

Pediatrix continued to expand through acquisition and internal growth. Group practices acquired were located in Memphis; Fort Worth; Lexington, Kentucky; Charlotte, North Carolina; and Florence and Columbia, South Carolina. The Columbia acquisition involved an eight-physician practice serving two hospital NICUs and covering 19,000 patient days annually. The company obtained NICU contracts for hospitals in San Angelo, Texas, to operate in conjunction with a Pediatrix site in San Antonio, as well as at Driscoll Children's Hospital in Corpus Christi.

Acquisitions in 2003 involved a large neonatal practice in Knoxville, with six physicians serving ill and well babies at five hospitals, as well as a large perinatal practice in Chicago, with seven physicians serving three hospitals. Pediatrix entered the Tampa market with the acquisition of a seven-physician practice serving two hospitals. Pediatrix obtained a contract with HCA, Inc. to manage NICUs at two hospitals in Kansas City. The company also acquired a neonatal practice in West Palm Beach specializing in pediatric cardiology.

In an effort to continue improving the care Pediatrix provided, in May 2003 the company acquired Neo Gen Screening, Inc. of Pittsburgh for $34 million. The largest independent laboratory specializing in screening newborn metabolic health in the United States, Neo Gen utilized patented proprietary processes for determining if an infant had any genetic disorders. Using blood samples taken from an infant within days of birth, the company screened for more than 50 genetic conditions that early detection could make manageable throughout the infant's life. Pediatrix already operated the country's largest newborn hearing screening program, developed internally. The company formed a subsidiary, Pediatrix Screening, to combine Neo Gen Screening with Newborn Hearing Screening.

In June 2003 the U.S. Attorney's Office began an investigation into Pediatrix's Medicaid billing practices nationwide. A shareholder lawsuit followed.

Principal Subsidiaries

Magella Healthcare Corporation; Newborn Hearing Screening, Inc.; Obstetrix Medical Group, Inc.

Principal Competitors

Per-se Technologies, Inc.; PhyAmerica Physician Group, Inc.; Sheridan Healthcare, Inc.

Further Reading

Carrns, Ann, "Pediatrix Medical Billing Information Is Sought by 2 State Attorneys General," *Wall Street Journal,* April 6, 1999, p. 1.

Chandler, Michele, "More Physicians Let Pediatrix Take Care of Their Business," *Knight Ridder/Tribune Business News,* September 16, 1996.

"District OKs $9 Million Medical Contract," *Miami Herald,* April 25, 1991.

"Investigation Prompts Stock Price Fall for Sunrise, Fla.-Based Medical Group," *Knight Ridder/Tribune Business News,* June 11, 2002.

Jacklevic, Mary Chris, "Branching into High Risk; Vivra, Pediatrix Tap Units to Buy Perinatology Practice," *Modern Healthcare,* May 11, 1998, p. 44.

Miller, Susan R., "Pediatrix Sees Big Growth Spurt," *South Florida Business Journal,* February 9, 1996, p. 1A.

"Pediatrix Gets OK to Repurchase Stock, Completes Acquisition of Physician Group," *Daily Business News,* April 22, 2003, p. A3.

"Pediatrix Medical Group Inc./Sunrise, Fla. Looking to Add Clout? Gobble Up a Big Rival," *Investor's Business Daily,* May 16, 2002, p. A11.

"Pediatrix Medical Group Inc./Sunrise, Florida Neonatal Care Provider Really Delivers Results," *Investor's Business Daily,* October 15, 2001, p. A10.

"Pediatrix Medical Group Inc./Sunrise, Florida Premature Baby Boom Breeds Comeback Here," *Investor's Business Daily,* March 22, 2001, p. A10.

Tschida, Molly, "Spreading the Blame; Pediatrix Points to Billing by Doctors for Poor Earnings," *Modern Physician,* November 1999, p. 16.

——, "Too Soon to Tell," *Modern Physician,* March 2000, p. 12.

—Mary Tradii

Phoenix Mecano AG

Hofwisenstrasse 6
CH-8260 Stein am Rhein
Switzerland
Telephone: +41 (0)43 255 4 255
Fax: +41 (0)43 255 4 256
Web site: http://www.phoenix-mecano.com

Public Company
Incorporated: 1975 as Phoenix Maschinentechnik AG
Employees: 3,935
Sales: SFr 319.84 million ($371.84 million) (2002)
Stock Exchanges: Zurich
Ticker Symbol: PM
NAIC: 326199 All Other Plastics Product Manufacturing; 332116 Metal Stamping; 334413 Semiconductor and Related Device Manufacturing; 334419 Other Electronic Component Manufacturing; 335931 Current-Carrying Wiring Device Manufacturing

Phoenix Mecano AG produces a variety of electrotechnical and mechanical components. The company has divisions producing Enclosures, or housings, for electronic devices (fabricated from plastic, aluminum, and fiberglass); Electromechanical Components (including terminals and connector systems); Mechanical Components (sensors, industrial clamps, mechanical parts); and Electronic Contract Manufacturing (of telecommunication and medical technology devices). Mechanical Components, with 39 percent of 2002 revenues, is the largest division. The company prides itself on paying attention to the oft-neglected design of commonplace components. Customers include producers of machinery, electronics, and medical equipment. Most sales come from Europe, with Germany accounting for more than 40 percent. The family of Dr. H. Christian Goldkamp holds a 29 percent stake in the company.

Origins

The company's history can be traced back to 1975, with the formation of Phoenix Maschinentechnik AG. Its first line of business was producing welding gases. Company leaders soon spotted an opportunity in producing welding torches as well.

Phoenix Mecano, which was based in Stein am Rhein, Switzerland, soon bought Rose Elektrotechnik GmbH und Co KG, a West German manufacturing company. It would make more than a dozen acquisitions in the next 15 years, including Alexander Binzel und Co., a producer of industrial gases.

In the 1980s, the company specialized in manufacturing metal containers, and supplying welding and technical gases. Annual turnover in the middle of the decade (1986) was SFr 111.8 million, producing a net profit of SFr 5.5 million.

Public in 1988

To reflect its wider focus, the company was renamed Phoenix Mecano AG in 1986. The Zurich stock market began listing the company's shares in September 1988. The Goldkamp family, including Chairman Hermann Goldkamp, owned 30 percent of the company.

During the year, Phoenix had acquired a controlling interest in RK Rose + Krieger, a maker of terminal components, assembly systems, and other mechanical components. In 1989, PTR, a producer of plug connectors and terminal clamps, was acquired.

Turnover rose 19 percent to SFr 203 million in fiscal 1990. While the casing technology division accounted for about 70 percent of sales; the electromechanical and mechanical components division reported the strongest growth, up 70 percent. During the year, Phoenix Mecano had sold off welding technology units in North America, reducing the importance of that sector. The company employed more than 900 people in 14 subsidiaries; the holding company had a staff of just three.

Kundisch, a SFr 9 million producer of keyboards, was acquired in 1991. The next year the company bought Dewert, which made linear drives and had sales of SFr 50 million a year.

Strategic Acquisitions in the 1990s

Apart from an office furniture venture started in the early 1990s, the company had chosen a path that would suit it well throughout the decade. It was acquiring manufacturers of com-

Company Perspectives:

Market leadership: Phoenix Mecano AG has gained a leading position worldwide with its innovative products. Phoenix Mecano aims to maintain and extend the lead already attained.

Growth: Phoenix Mecano AG is committed to steady growth while maintaining a solid financial foundation.

Scope: Phoenix Mecano AG operates at the interface between man and machinery. It has a reputation for distinctive solutions acknowledged by the market to set new trends.

Initiative: It has a decentralized structure which facilitates quick decisions. It responds to market requirements, market changes and market opportunities before the competition. It strives to prevail over its rivals and over complacency within its own ranks.

Key Dates:

1975: Phoenix Maschinentechnik AG is founded.
1985: Hartmann is acquired.
1986: The company is renamed Phoenix Mecano AG.
1988: Shares begin trading on the Zurich Stock Exchange.
1993: Production commences in Hungary.
1998: The purchase of GU Hartmann expands Phoenix into Tunisia.
1999: Phoenix invests in a Romanian tool and molds business.
2002: Phoenix records its first annual loss in company history.
2003: The company reaps the benefits of its restructuring program.

ponents that larger companies overlooked, at the same time devoting its attention to adding value and innovation.

By this time, Phoenix had acquired Bopla Gehäuse Systeme GmbH, a maker of enclosures to complement its Rose Elektrotechnik GmbH und Co KG subsidiary, which was bought in the mid-1970s. It also had bought a company called Hartmann, which produced coding switches; this subsidiary's sales reached SFr 15.4 million in 1992.

Longtime director Peter E. Rued was appointed to the newly created position of president in October 1992. Phoenix Mecano acquired Budapest's PTR Magyar Kft in August 1992. A manufacturing plant was established in Hungary the next year. This would become Phoenix Mecano's most important production facility. Located southeast of Budapest at Kecskemet, it employed 670 people by 1999. A variety of components, including plastic casings and electric motors, were assembled there.

By 1995, turnover had reached SFr 316 million, which produced a SFr 30 million net profit. The Casings division accounted for a little less than half of sales; next largest was mechanical components, followed by electromechanical, both of which were increasing in importance.

A German inductive components producer, Bauelemente Götz-Udo Hartmann Group, was acquired in 1998. GU Hartmann, which had a factory in Tunisia, had sales of more than DM 15 million a year.

Phoenix Mecano acquired the remaining shares (26 percent) of RK Rose + Krieger toward the end of 1998. By this time the unit, which produced mechanical modules, had annual sales of SFr 50 million, making it one of Phoenix Mecano's biggest units.

The company's U.S. unit, Phoenix Mecano Inc., acquired a former Kinney Shoe plant in West Virginia in 1999, reconfiguring it to produce electrical components. Phoenix Mecano acquired an 80 percent interest in a Romanian tool and molds business in December of that year. The business was a part of the state-owned company Flaro of Hermannstadt (Sibio). It had 70 employees. Phoenix Mecano aimed to benefit from Romania's much lower labor costs; the group had a total of 700 employees in Hungary. The Flaro unit was renamed Phoenix Mecano Mould after the purchase.

Telecom Investments in 2000

Phoenix Mecano management then perceived a growing need for electronics enclosures in the telecommunications industry. OMP Officina Meccanica di Precisione S.R.L., an Italian manufacturer of casings for telecom infrastructure, was acquired in July 2000. OMP had 200 employees at the time; 1999 turnover was SFr 50 million.

In October 2000, the company acquired France's Twinbay S.A., which had 42 employees. Consolidated sales rose more than 22 percent in 2000.

Phoenix Mecano acquired a 30 percent interest in Hartmann Elektronik GmbH in January 2001. Hartmann Elektronik produced backplanes, or circuit boards for rack-mounted electronics. It had 26 employees and sales of EUR 5.7 million. Phoenix Mecano acquired the remaining 70 percent of Hartmann Elektronik shares in April 2002.

Phoenix Mecano posted a EUR 5.0 million (SFr 8 million) profit on consolidated gross turnover of EUR 342 million in 2001. Phoenix Mecano cut 400 jobs during the year. The company then had 4,000 employees; 1,400 were located in Germany. Hungary and Romania accounted for another 900.

Phoenix was by far the European market leader in standard aluminum, plastic, and fiberglass casings; machine control panels and suspension arm systems; clamping components; and coding switches. Phoenix also dominated the world market for twin linear drives for beds and slatted bed frames.

After nine years as managing director, Peter E. Rued resigned in October 2001 due to disagreements over the company's strategic direction. He was replaced by Benedikt Goldkamp, son of Chairman H. Christian Goldkamp, who was guiding a restructuring of the company. The electronic contract manufacturing arm was most affected. The restructuring program cost EUR 9 million (SFr 13 million).

Posting Its First Loss in 2002

Phoenix Mecano opened a new HUF 1.5 billion facility in central Hungary in March 2002. The Hungarian subsidiary, which had annual sales of HUF 17 billion, then employed 820 people; the new site added another 100 jobs. By this time,

Phoenix Mecano also had begun to tap Asia's low-cost labor market as well, setting up a facility in Shanghai to produce electrotechnical components for southeast Asian markets.

Phoenix Mecano posted the first annual loss in its history in 2002, as consolidated turnover fell 5.3 percent to EUR 324 million. This resulted in a net loss of EUR 38.3 million (SFr 56 million) versus a EUR 5 million profit the previous year. Turnover was down in all four divisions: Enclosures, Electrotechnical Components, Mechanical Components, and Electronics Contract Manufacturing. Management attributed the loss to terrible global economic conditions and the writing off of goodwill.

Management's optimism for 2003 appeared justified by the end of the first nine months of the year. Continued positive results were anticipated for 2004.

Principal Subsidiaries

Bopla Gehäuse Systeme GmbH (Germany); Dewert GmbH + Co. KG (Germany); Götz-Udo Hartmann GmbH + Co. KG; Hartmann Elektronik GmbH (Germany); IPES Industria de Produtos e Equipamentos de Solda Ltda. (Brazil); Kundisch Electronic GmbH + Co. KG; OMP Officina Meccanica di Precisione S.R.L. (Italy); Phoenix Mecano Digital Elektronik GmbH (Germany); Phoenix Mecano Electronic GmbH (Germany); Phoenix Mecano Finance Ltd. (U.K.); Phoenix Mecano Management AG; Phoenix Mecano Trading AG; PTR Messtechnik GmbH + Co. KG (Germany); RK Rose + Krieger GmbH + Co. KG (Germany); Rose Gehäusetechnik GmbH (Germany); Rose Systemtechnik GmbH + Co. KG (Germany).

Principal Divisions

Enclosures; Electrotechnical Components; Mechanical Components; Electronics Contract Manufacturing.

Principal Competitors

Elma Electronic AG.

Further Reading

''Boitiers et composants: Phoenix Mecano dans le rouge en 2002,'' *SDA—Service de base français,* March 17, 2003.

''Desmond Harvey Quits Phoenix Mecano to Join AB Abtech,'' *Electronics Times,* November 7, 1991, p. 2.

''Developpement Composants et boitiers; Nette progression du benefice pour Phoenix Mecano sur neuf mois,'' *SDA—Service de base français,* November 6, 2003.

''FAZ Profiles Phoenix Mecano AG,'' *Frankfurter Allgemeine Zeitung,* September 8, 1990, p. 14.

''Nouvelle strategie de croissance pour Phoenix Mecano; Acquisition imminente dans le secteur des telecommunications,'' *SDA—Service de base français,* May 15, 2000.

''Phoenix Mecano acquiert une entreprise roumaine,'' *SDA—Service de base français,* December 21, 1999.

''Phoenix Mecano AG Plans to Go Public Some Time in 1988,'' *Neue Zuercher Zeitung,* June 18, 1988, p. 18.

''Phoenix Mecano Creates Conditions for Better 2003,'' *Hugin,* March 17, 2003.

''Phoenix Mecano Expands,'' *Neue Zuercher Zeitung,* July 28, 2000, p. 12.

''Phoenix Mecano in Romanian Tools, Moulds Deal,'' *Reuters News,* December 21, 1999.

''Phoenix Mecano on Course for Success (Phoenix Mecano auf Erfolgskurs),'' *Neue Zurcher Zeitung,* p. 14.

''Phoenix Mecano Opens Plant in Kecskemet,'' *Hungarian News Agency (MTI),* March 21, 2002.

''Phoenix Mecano Takes Over German Subsidiary Completely (Phoenix Mecano Ubernimmt Deutsche Tochter Ganz),'' *Neue Zurcher Zeitung,* January 26, 1999, p. 14.

''Phoenix Mecano 2002: First Posted Loss Since the Company Was Founded—Prospects for 2003 Remain Intact,'' *Hugin,* April 30, 2003.

Richenberger, Hans, ''Phoenix Mecano mit ungebrochener Dynamik; Konsequente Produktionsverlagerungen und Marktausweitungen,'' *Neue Zuercher Zeitung,* Mai 14, 1996.

''Swiss Phoenix Mecano Plant Proves Successful,'' *Neue Zuercher Zeitung,* October 27, 1999, p. 12.

''Tough Times for Phoenix Mecano (Phoenix Mecano traverse la phase la plus delicate de son histoire),'' *L'Agefi Suisse,* October 30, 2001, p. 15.

—Frederick C. Ingram

Placer Dome Inc.

Suite 1600, Bentall IV
1055 Dunsmuir Street
Vancouver, British Columbia
V7X 1P1
Canada
Telephone: (604) 682-7082
Fax: (604) 682-7092
Web site: http://www.placerdome.com

Public Company
Incorporated: 1987
Employees: 11,950
Sales: $1.25 billion (2002)
Stock Exchanges: New York Toronto Montreal Paris Australia Swiss
Ticker Symbol: PDG
NAIC: 212221 Gold Ore Mining; 212222 Silver Ore Mining; 212234 Copper Ore and Nickel Ore Mining; 541360 Geophysical Surveying and Mapping Services

Placer Dome Inc., the fifth largest gold mining company in the world, produces approximately 3.5 million ounces of gold annually. Based in Vancouver, British Columbia, the company also mines silver and copper and has interests in 18 mines, many outside of Canada, in countries including South Africa, Australia, the United States, and Papua New Guinea. A leader in mine exploration, Placer Dome spent about $60 million in 2003 on exploration.

The Creation of a New Company

Placer Dome Inc. was formed in 1987 by the amalgamation of three Canadian mining companies, creating the largest gold producer in North America with an annual output of more than 800,000 ounces of gold. Dome Mines Limited, the oldest of the three predecessors and one of Canada's most venerable gold producers, was incorporated in 1910, following the discovery of the Dome Mine, a hard-rock mine in northern Ontario, which was still producing gold in 1997. The mine and the company got their name from the shape of the gold-studded rock structure a band of prospectors literally stumbled over in 1909.

Placer Development Limited was incorporated in British Columbia in 1926 and made its first earnings during the 1930s, dredging gold from the gravel of a river in Papua New Guinea, then under Australian mandate. "Placer," which was Spanish for shoal, referred to water-borne deposits of sand or gravel containing particles of gold or silver. Mining that deposit was no easy task. Because there were no roads over the mountains from the coast to the interior, the dredges had to be disassembled and then flown in. This, according to the company, resulted in what was at that point the greatest peacetime airlift ever undertaken. The Bulolo project produced gold until 1965. Between then and 1984, when its next mine was developed, the company invested in coal mining, cattle ranching, timber production, and fishing. It even established a cattle company in Papua New Guinea to provide Bulolo workers with fresh meat. By the early 1980s, Placer Development had sold off most of these interests and was focused on developing the Kidston Mine in Queensland, Australia.

The third company, Campbell Red Lake Mines Limited, was incorporated in 1944 in Ontario, and eventually became a subsidiary of Dome Mines. Its Campbell Mine, one of the highest-grade and lowest-cost gold mines in the world, has produced continuously since 1949.

The merger itself came about because both Placer and Dome Mines were threatened with hostile takeovers by Australian-based companies. Placer arranged the merger to protect itself, raising its market value from $700 million to $4.3 billion.

Separate Managements: 1987–92

The type of gold mining done by the companies was not their only difference. Dome Mines and Campbell Red Lake were considered conservative operations. They concentrated on their long-term operations and did not increase their output or acquire new mines despite rising gold prices and lower production costs. Placer, on the other hand, continued to bring new mines on-stream, increasing its gold production from 45,000 ounces in 1982 to 331,000 ounces in 1986, the year before the merger.

Company Perspectives:

Placer Dome is one of the world's largest gold mining companies, operating 18 mines on five continents. Our shares trade on five stock exchanges and we employ more than 13,000 people around the world.

Placer Dome is committed to long-term profitable growth through focused exploration; disciplined acquisitions; and investments in research and technology. We believe in integrating the efficient extraction of mineral resources with responsible environmental stewardship and providing a safe and healthy workplace for our employees.

During its first five years, Placer Dome kept the separate managements of the original companies in place, along with their conflicting business philosophies. The company did expand through acquisitions. Between 1988 and 1991, the company sold its Canadian and U.S. oil and gas operations as well as various mines, developed and constructed six new mines, and acquired several other mining properties. These acquisitions included shares in Consolidated TVX Mining Corporation, which owned the La Coipa gold/silver property in Chile and the Kiena Gold Mines Limited and Sigma Mines in Canada. In 1989, Placer Dome acquired a 50 percent interest in the La Coipa gold/silver property in Chile as well as 50 percent of the shares of a newly formed Chilean company that bought the La Coipa property from the TVX Group. In addition, the company expanded its interest in the 23-year-old Cortez Gold Mine joint venture in Nevada following the discovery of the Pipeline gold deposit in 1991, and in 1992, purchased 50 percent of Compania Minera Zladivar, the owner of the Zladivar copper property in Chile.

To finance its gold mines, Placer Dome often used a relatively new form of financing called a ''gold loan.'' As the mine developer, the company borrowed actual gold deposits from its financing institutions, not their cash. The company sold the gold to pay for building the mine and then repaid the loan in gold from production. Because the gold deposits earned little or no interest, Placer Dome was usually able to negotiate a lower, more favorable rate than if it had borrowed cash. If the rates were too high, however, Placer Dome or another developer could incorporate a new company to hold the property and the mine when it was built, then sell shares to raise the money to develop the property.

Among its other activities during this period, the company and its partners were trying to come up with an acceptable feasibility plan for extracting the gold deposits along the shore of Lake Opapimiskan in northern Ontario. The problem was that the gold was collected within a convoluted iron foundation. The debate had been going on since the Musselwhite brothers discovered the gold in 1962. One thing that was finalized, even before the project was approved for mining, was an agreement between Placer Dome and the leaders of the four First Nations (aboriginal) communities in the area. The company agreed to hire one-quarter of the mine's workforce from the local communities, to provide other economic benefits, such as education, healthcare, communication, and transportation to the area during the life of the mine, and to respect both the land and the First Nations' culture.

The issue of complex community conditions was not limited to Canada. At the Porgera mine in Papua New Guinea, the joint venture was spending approximately $10 million a year on infrastructure improvements in the region. In 1991, to help the national government channel tax and royalty revenues from the mining back into the community, Placer Dome proposed a Tax Credit Infrastructure Scheme, under which the mine held back some of the taxes owed and directly invested that amount in local improvements.

During this period, sales revenues increased from $624 million in 1987 to $1.02 billion in 1992. Earnings, however, fluctuated, and the company ended 1992 with earnings of $105 million.

Creating a Common Goal: 1993–94

In 1993, John M. Willson joined Placer Dome as president and CEO. Willson came to the mining industry ''genetically''—his father was a mining engineer. Born in Sheffield, England, Willson graduated from the Royal School of Mines at the University of London in 1962 and immediately went to work at the Nsuta manganese mine in Ghana. Two years later he moved to the United States, where he took a job in Butte, Montana, at Anaconda's copper mine and learned ''how mining should not be done,'' as he related in the Placer Dome company magazine. He moved on after two and a half years to Cominco Limited's Sullivan zinc-lead mine in Canada, ''the first mine I worked at where they knew what they were doing.'' Four years later, in 1971, Cominco made Willson project manager for construction and operation of its Black Angel zinc-lead mine in Greenland. When that job was completed he left the mining industry for seven years, returning to Cominco in 1981. In 1989 he was appointed president and CEO of Pegasus Gold Inc. of Spokane, Washington, a middle-rank gold producer. He held that position until Placer Dome selected him to replace retiring Tony Petrina.

Willson set about uniting the Placer Dome companies into a single unit with a common goal: higher productivity and lower costs. His aim was to have the company produce 2.5 million ounces of gold by the year 2000 (an increase of nearly 40 percent) while cutting costs by a third.

He began by starting a companywide debate about how to meld the organization's three disparate cultures. The debate produced two strategic changes: concentrate on mining gold, reducing earnings from the company's other minerals to 25 percent of revenues; and decentralize management into four regional units, each responsible for the mining activities in its own area. It also reinforced the importance of the company's tradition of corporate responsibility and high ethical values.

The management reorganization established four subsidiaries: wholly owned Placer Dome Canada, Placer Dome U.S. Inc., Placer Dome Latin America, and publicly owned Placer Pacific Limited, with the corporate headquarters in Vancouver overseeing strategic growth. Internally, the company flattened its structure and introduced team-building, career development, and succession planning and extended its stock option plan to retain its employees in a highly competitive industry. The concentration on gold saw the continued purchase of shares in gold

Key Dates:

1910: Dome Mines Limited, a gold producer, is established.
1926: Placer Development Limited forms in British Columbia and begins gold mining activities in Papua New Guinea.
1944: Ontario-based Campbell Red Lake Mines Limited is incorporated.
1987: Dome Mines Limited, Placer Development Limited, and Campbell Red Lake Mines Limited merge to create Placer Dome Inc.
2002: Placer Dome acquires AurionGold Limited, an Australian mining company.

companies, including all the shares of Sulphurets Gold Corporation and Continental Gold Corporation. It also led to an increase in exploration costs, which by 1994 were around $100 million.

Continued Expansion: Mid-1990s

In 1995, the company completed construction of two more mines, the Zaldivar copper mine in Chile and the Osbourne gold mine in Australia, and had 85 exploration projects in 28 countries.

The year 1996 began well. The price of gold hit a six-year high of $414.80 per ounce during the first quarter. In March, construction began on two new gold mines, the underground and open pit Musselwhite mine at Opap Lake, the first mine to be approved under Canada's stringent Environmental Assessment Act, and the Pipeline project in Nevada.

But that same month, in the Philippines, there was an accidental discharge of four million tons of mill tailing, or waste, at the Marcopper Mine, and that mine was closed. Although Placer Dome owned only 40 percent of the corporation operating the mine, neither the joint venture nor the major shareholder had the resources or interest to contribute to the cleanup. Placer Dome assumed 100 percent of the financial responsibility. Cleanup involved re-sealing a drainage tunnel that had failed and clearing the spill itself and resulted in a $43 million after-tax charge to earnings.

As if that were not trouble enough, the price of gold declined for the rest of the year. Contributing factors included the strength of the U.S. dollar, movement toward a single European currency (and the fear of sales from reserves by European central banks), and gains in stock markets around the world. The main problem was that with low inflation, people put their money in investments other than gold. On the other hand, demand for gold jewelry set a new record in 1996.

To reach its long-term corporate goals, the company decided it needed to focus its development and mining activities on a smaller number of larger, sustainable mines. During the year, Placer Dome acquired properties in Africa, Australia, Brazil, Canada, Ecuador, Mexico, the Philippines, and Russia for investigation. Mineral systems had been identified on these and additional work was planned to confirm known gold resources while searching for more. Total exploration expenditures for 1996 came to $117 million and was expected to increase slightly to $120 million in 1997.

In December the company announced it was selling the relatively small Sigma and Kiena gold mines in Quebec as well as the Enkado molybdenum mine in British Columbia. The company ended the year with revenues at an all-time high of $1.2 billion, but with an earnings loss of $65 million arising from the after-tax charges reflecting the mine sales and the Marcopper cleanup.

The environmental accident at Marcopper caused the company to reevaluate its participation in joint ventures. As Willson stated in a 1997 speech, "In joint ventures, the rewards of success are shared in proportion to equity interest; but unless our partners share our principles of corporate responsibility and are willing to act accordingly, we will end up bearing the full cost of any untoward event. . . . It has made us more determined not to take on a minority partnership in the future, and to be more selective about the partners that we team up with."

In line with that thinking, the company initiated takeovers of Highlands Gold Limited, a Papua New Guinea company that owned 29 percent of the Porgera Mine, and the 24.8 percent publicly owned interest of Placer Pacific Limited. By early 1997, Placer Dome owned 50 percent of the Porgera Mine and all of Placer Pacific Limited. The company hoped this would simplify its holdings in the Asia Pacific region and give it a greater share of the exploration potential of the area. Placer Dome also announced plans to combine two of its wholly owned subsidiaries, Placer Dome Canada and Placer Dome U.S. Inc., to form Placer Dome North America.

In January 1997, the company bid $6.2 billion for Bre-X Minerals Ltd. of Calgary, which owned 90 percent of the Busang gold deposit in Indonesia, "the richest gold find on earth," according to *Maclean's,* with an estimated holding of 100 million ounces of gold. The company withdrew its bid the following month, however. Investigators later reported evidence that gold had been salted at the deposit.

On March 6, 1997, the first gold doré bar was poured at the Pipeline plant, three months ahead of schedule and $70 million under budget. Four days later, the first bar was poured at the Musselwhite mine, one day less than a year after construction of the mine began. Placer Dome's Project Development Division had built two gold mines concurrently, one in Canada and one in the United States, in a 12-month period. Production at the two mines began in April. Annual gold production at Musselwhite was expected to be 200,000 ounces, and 400,000 ounces at Pipeline.

But the year was not without controversy: there was a question of rightful ownership of the Las Cristinas mine in Venezuela. Crystallex International Corporation, a small, Vancouver-based mining company, claimed it had the rights, based on its claim to two of the deposit's richest blocks. According to the Venezuelan mining ministry, that ownership had expired in 1989, and belonged to Venezuela. That had certainly been Placer Dome's understanding when it formed a joint venture with a government agency earlier in the decade to develop the site. In July, the Venezuelan supreme court allowed Crystallex's copper rights to be reviewed by the court, but prohibited a trial regarding the gold rights. While Crystallex appealed, Placer Dome took the court's action as acknowledgment of its rights to the gold and began construction of the $576 million project in August, the 15th mine construction or expansion project since the company was formed ten years earlier.

Whatever the legal outcome, Las Cristinas has been the site of innovative approaches to problems arising when a huge mining operation comes into an isolated, undeveloped area. At Las Cristinas the local population was a mixture of aboriginal communities and migrating, small-scale miners of mixed race and nationality. In 1995, the company instituted a program to help a group of the miners form a collective and work on a part of the project's construction concessions under controlled conditions. The World Bank recognized that effort as a new model for reducing problems between huge mining operations and small miners. In addition, Placer Dome was exploring new ways to create "sustainable development" of the region around the mine. In a joint venture with the Industrial Co-operation Branch of the Canadian International Development Agency, the company was attempting to involve nongovernmental and for-profit organizations in both Canada and Venezuela in community development projects, such as municipal water and sewer systems and agricultural diversification, at Las Cristinas.

While the technology of gold exploration and mining has changed dramatically since the Dome Mine began operating in 1910, the high level of risk involved has not. Placer Dome appeared to be able to move quickly, selling off older, less productive mines and taking advantage of low gold prices to acquire high-quality properties. Furthermore, its new mines were exceeding production expectations. In 1997 the company's gold production increased 34 percent, and its ore reserves rose to 31 million ounces, the seventh consecutive year of growth. In addition, Placer Dome was able to cut production costs significantly; in 1996 gold production costs were $235 per ounce, and the following year they were $202 per ounce.

Despite increases in production, Placer Dome faced a net loss of $264 million for fiscal 1997. The net loss was primarily due to write-downs of mining interests. Net sales increased to $1.09 billion compared with 1996 sales of $1.06 billion.

Increased Production and Cost Cutting: Late 1990s and into the New Millennium

Although the price of gold continued to slump in the late 1990s, Placer Dome remained committed to gold as its primary focus. The company's strategy was to lower operating and production costs as much as possible while boosting exploration and seeking strategic acquisitions of high-yield, high-quality mines. Placer Dome allotted approximately $115 million to fund exploration in 1998 alone, making the company the industry leader.

Placer Dome wasted no time putting the exploration monies to work, and in February 1998 the company acquired a 51 percent interest in Chile's Aldebaran gold-copper property in a deal with Bema Gold and Arizona Star. The following year Placer Dome increased its holdings in Africa when it established a joint venture with Western Areas Ltd. of South Africa to develop the Western Areas gold mine, which included the South Deep region, the country's largest undeveloped deposit. The transaction marked the first major foreign investment in South Africa's mining industry since the African National Congress assumed governmental power in 1994. Placer Dome anticipated that following development of South Deep by 2003, the joint venture would produce about 750,000 ounces of gold annually. It was estimated that the Western Areas holdings included a reserve of 59 million ounces of gold, with 52 million ounces at South Deep.

At the close of 1998 Placer Dome acquired the Getchell Gold Corporation of Nevada. Getchell Gold operated Nevada's Getchell and Turquoise Ridge underground gold mines and estimates placed its gold reserves at 14.8 million ounces. Placer Dome planned to implement an aggressive exploration and development strategy in hopes of increasing gold inventory to 20 million ounces by the end of 1999. The Getchell acquisition and the Western Areas joint venture cost Placer Dome more than $1.3 billion.

To stay competitive in a climate that remained unfriendly to gold, Placer Dome faced a few bumps. In the summer of 1999 the company halted development at its Las Cristinas mine in Venezuela and also closed down production at Nevada's Turquoise Ridge for a year. The money saved from these cost-cutting measures could now be channeled to further exploration or development of new acquisitions if necessary.

Placer Dome's financials improved considerably in the late 1990s. Net earnings for 1998 reached $50 million on net sales of $1.12 billion, a marked improvement compared with the net loss of $264 million in 1997. Although net earnings dropped to $35 million in 1999, net sales rose to $1.16 billion. In addition, Placer Dome's gold output in 1999 reached 3.15 million ounces, and its gold reserves were estimated at 66 million ounces, with the South Deep mine accounting for nearly half of that total.

As Placer Dome headed into the new millennium, the company faced new challenges and changes. John Willson retired at the end of 1999, and Jay K. Taylor became president and CEO. Taylor outlined his goals for Placer Dome in his letter to shareholders in the 1999 annual report, noting that the company would continue with a disciplined financial approach and seek high-yield acquisitions.

Sales increased to a record $1.4 billion in 2000, but Placer Dome reported a net loss of $92 million; the company adjusted its asset values to take into account low gold prices, and it was hit with a $116 million charge for writing off its investment in the Las Cristinas mine. In August 2001, the year Las Cristinas was originally slated to begin production, Placer Dome decided to sell its 70 percent stake.

Although Placer Dome reported a net loss of $133 million on sales of $1.22 billion in 2001, the company maintained a positive outlook on its performance, noting that both cash flow from operations and mine operating earnings were strong. In addition, were it not for the write-down of mining interests, the company's net earnings would have been $133 million. Many of Placer Dome's mines produced favorable results as well: the Granny Smith joint venture in Australia began operation ahead of schedule; and the Cortez joint venture in Nevada produced more than one million ounces of gold at some of the lowest costs in the industry.

Placer Dome made waves across the mining industry in 2002 with the acquisition of Australia's AurionGold Limited. The deal, which made the company the fifth largest gold producer in the world, included full ownership of the Granny Smith mine, 75 percent ownership of the Porgera mine, and the Kanowna Belle, Henty, and Kalgoorlie West mines. The acquisition was estimated to boost Placer Dome's yearly gold production an additional one million ounces for a decade.

Also in 2002 Placer Dome entered into a joint venture with Kinross Gold Corporation. The resulting Porcupine Joint Venture involved the underground and surface exploration of the Pamour pit in Canada. Help from the Granny Smith mine, which boosted production 57 percent, and the Cortez mine, which produced more than one million ounces of gold for the fifth straight year, led to total gold production of 2.8 million ounces in 2002. Sales reached $1.2 billion, and net earnings totaled $116 million.

Placer Dome had a welcome surprise in 2003 with the discovery of a new mineral deposit through the Cortez joint venture in Nevada. Exploration estimates set the gold resources at the new Cortez Hills site at 4.5 million ounces. Excitement brewed as well with the acquisition of East African Gold Mines Limited, an Australian company. The sale included the North Mara mine in Tanzania, with reserves estimated at 4.25 million ounces.

The company reported record gold production of more than one million ounces during the third quarter of 2003. CEO Taylor announced in a press release, ''Consistent with our strategy of optimizing assets, our operations performed well this quarter, and we remain on track to achieve the highest annual production in our history.'' For the first nine months of 2003, sales were $1.27 billion, compared with $854 million for the same period of 2002, and gold production reached 2.8 million ounces, compared with 1.9 million ounces in 2002. Placer Dome's focused efforts to reduce costs and boost assets to create a leaner and stronger company appeared to be paying off, and the company had no plans to change its strategy.

Principal Subsidiaries

Placer Dome Latin America (Chile); Placer Dome U.S. Inc.; Placer Dome North America; Placer Dome Asia Pacific Limited (Australia); Placer Dome Exploration, Inc.; Placer Dome (CLA) Limited; Placer Dome America Holding Corporation; Getchell Gold Corporation.

Principal Competitors

AngloGold; Barrick Gold Corporation; Kinross Gold Corporation.

Further Reading

Atlas, Riva, ''All That Glitters . . . ,'' *Forbes,* July 29, 1996, p. 96.

''Brawling for Busang Gold,'' *Maclean's,* January 27, 1997, p. 55.

Crespo, Mariana, ''All That Glitters,'' *Financial World,* September 13, 1994, p. 58.

Gibbon, Ann, ''Firms Dig in for Battle Over Venezuelan Gold,'' *Globe and Mail,* July 25, 1997.

''Highlands Set to Sell Porgera Mine Stake,'' *American Metal Market,* January 9, 1997, p. 5.

Jenish, D'Arcy, and Ann Shortwell, ''Defence of a Gold Mine,'' *Maclean's,* August 17, 1987, p. 32.

Leggatt, Hugh, ''Deep Roots Down Under,'' *Placer Dome Inc. Prospect,* March 1997, p. 2.

——, ''Executive Profile: John M. Willson,'' *Placer Dome Inc. Prospect,* June 1997, p. 13.

McMurdy, Deirdre, ''Chile's Copper Rush,'' *Maclean's,* November 1, 1993, p. 45.

''The Mine Development Process,'' Vancouver: Placer Dome Inc., 1995.

Nikiforuk, Andrew, ''Still a Fine Mess,'' *Canadian Business,* March 4, 2002, p. 14.

''Placer Dome Inc. and Getchell Gold Corp. Agreed to a Merger,'' *Engineering and Mining Journal,* February 1999, p. 38.

''Placer Dome's View on Gold—It's Here to Stay,'' *Engineering and Mining Journal,* June 1998, pp. 9–10.

Rathbone, John Paul, ''Las Cristinas Mine Bogged Down in Legal War,'' *Focus,* July 18, 1997.

Ross, Priscilla, ''Placer Dome Injects Confidence,'' *African Business,* January 1999, p. 14.

Terry, Edith, ''Placer Dome: Will It Pan Out?,'' *Business Week,* September 7, 1987.

Werniuk, Jane, ''Miracle at Opap Lake,'' *Placer Dome Inc. Prospect,* June 1997, p. 8.

——, ''Pipeline to the 21st Century,'' *Placer Dome Inc. Prospect,* June 1997, p. 2.

—Ellen D. Wernick
—update: Mariko Fujinaka

Planar Systems, Inc.

1195 NW Compton Drive
Beaverton, Oregon 97006
U.S.A.
Telephone: (503) 748-1100
Toll Free: (866) 475-2627
Fax: (503) 748-1541
Web site: http://www.planar.com

Public Company
Incorporated: 1983
Employees: 460
Sales: $251.9 million (2003)
Stock Exchanges: NASDAQ
Ticker Symbol: PLNR
NAIC: 334419 Other Electronic Component Manufacturing; 339112 Surgical & Medical Instrument Manufacturing; 541613 Marketing Consulting Services

Planar Systems, Inc. is a leading developer, manufacturer, and marketer of high-performance electronic display systems. Its products, which range from display components to stand-alone systems built for specific market applications, rely upon different technologies, including active matrix liquid crystal displays (LCDs), passive matrix LCDs, plasma display panels, and Planar's proprietary electroluminescent flat-panel displays. Planar has a diversified customer base in the medical, industrial control, test and measurement, avionics, and computer industries. Major operations also are located near Boston, Massachusetts, and Helsinki, Finland.

Early Pioneer and Leader in Electroluminescence in the 1980s

In 1983, Jim Hurd, a researcher and manager since 1980 of Tektronix's solid-state research laboratory at Oregon-based Tektronix, founded Planar Systems, Inc. Hurd was a native of Spokane, Washington, with a degree in physics from Lewis and Clark College in Portland, Oregon. He had gone to work for Tektronix in 1968 immediately after college and rose through its ranks to eventually head up a team working on electroluminescent flat-panel display manufacturing.

Along with Chris King and John Laney, Hurd raised $6 million and entered into a venture capital partnership with Tektronix that allowed Tektronix to protect its potential electroluminescent market while allowing the new spinoff to take on the risk of development and production of flat computer screens. The new company employed 14 former Tek employees and acquired the rights from Tektronix to the company's solid-state flat panel display technology. Planar Systems moved into the Oregon Graduate Center Science Park in Beaverton, Oregon, in late 1983 and began high-volume production at the site in February 1984. Tektronix remained a strong supporter of Planar throughout its early years, making some of its research facilities available to the new firm and holding a 31 percent interest in Planar.

Planar introduced its alternative to the boxy, cathode ray tube display screen, its flat (three-quarter-inch thick) monochrome computer screen in early 1984. Potential customers—computer, auto, medical, and military manufacturers—welcomed the flat panels as a replacement for the cathode ray tube, despite the fact that they cost significantly more, about $275, in the mid-1980s. Planar's amber-on-black monochrome screens were easier on the eye than the standard monochrome green, and the flat screen eliminated defocus or elongation of images in the corners. The company's higher-volume customers included Hewlett-Packard and Grid Systems Corporation, which produced a portable business computer. The new company's sales reached $12 million its second year.

At the time, three technologies were being explored in the flat-panel market—electroluminescence, liquid crystal display—both passive (light reflecting) and active (light emitting)—and plasma. All employed microprocessors called ''drivers'' that sprayed electrical impulses through or between thin panels that, when sandwiched together, formed the screen. In an LCD panel, the active ingredient was an organic liquid; in a gas plasma screen, argon or neon gas; in an electroluminescent screen, it was a metal film. Liquid crystal and plasma displays each took up about 40 percent of the market in the late 1980s, with electroluminescent displays at about 20 percent.

Company Perspectives:

We provide innovative solutions to connect people with information.

Notwithstanding its lesser percentage, electroluminescence was considered one of the more promising display technologies since its screen image could be read from nearly every angle and in any room light. Its main drawback was that it required almost six times the power of a backlit LCD screen and was thus more susceptible to burnout. Planar's electroluminescent screens, however, offered a 50 percent increase in brightness and a 30 percent reduction in the amount of power needed to drive them. Its screens were scrupulously tested for two days before being shipped to customers. While others were cautious, uncertain that electroluminescent technology would take off, Planar invested $20 million in German-made production line equipment over a period of 14 months in the mid-1980s, increasing capacity from 60,000 units a year to almost 500,000 and doubling its production line employees.

As fast growth became inevitable for Planar, founder Jim Hurd invested in a new manufacturing plant in 1986. Hurd's chief desire was to make Planar profitable in the short run, and in order to do so, he had to enable Planar to meet the needs of a bigger market than he, Chris King, and John Laney had ever dreamed of. ''Our biggest single problem is product availability,'' he announced in a 1986 *Portland Business Journal* article. In 1988, Planar, which had been working with the army's Electronic Display and Devices Laboratory, broke new ground in the electroluminescent market when it introduced the first full-color, flat-panel display. By 1989, Planar shipped 25,000 units each year to 60 to 70 production customers, which it claimed represented 40 percent of the electroluminescent market. With production increasing 50 percent annually, Planar employed more than 130 people. It could not recruit enough highly trained people within Oregon, however.

Acquisition As a Strategy for Quelling Competition in the 1990s

Planar broke into the computer workstation market in 1990 when it began producing computer monitors for Digital Equipment Corporation (DEC). The year was a banner one for the company, marked by revenues of $25 million; a $1 million two-year contract with the U.S. Defense Department that included Planar in the Defense Advanced Research Projects Agency and solidified its position at the cutting edge of the high-definition display market; and the acquisition of its major European competitor, the Finlux division of Lohja Corporation of Helsinki, Finland. The purchase of Finlux had many advantages: it doubled Planar's market share and sales and made it the largest company of its kind in the world. It increased Planar's production capacity. Finally, it gave Planar a strong presence in Europe and put it in a more competitive position with Japanese manufacturers, who had a lock on the color flat display market and were investing heavily in LCD technology.

The year 1991 also was marked by a bitter international trade dispute between domestic flat-panel display makers and the Japanese companies that were selling their products on the U.S. market. Hurd led a band of domestic manufacturers against the industry's free trade advocates, arguing that Japanese competitors were violating U.S. trade law by ''dumping'' their products at well below cost in U.S. markets.

Notwithstanding these challenges, Planar enjoyed another outstanding year in 1991. The company's sales reached an all-time high of about $55 million, and the Defense Department awarded it a $2.5 million grant to build a new manufacturing line after Planar introduced its first multicolor display screen mid-year. The new screens offered red, yellow, green, and black, a big step forward from the former amber-on-black color scheme; lacking until 1993 was the color blue. Electroluminescence was then still the smallest, but fastest-growing of the three flat display technologies. The Department of Commerce awarded another $7.6 million federal contract to Planar, Tektronix, and eight other domestic makers of flat-panel displays in 1991 to conduct five years of research into advanced manufacturing of flat-panel displays.

It was not until 1992, however, that Planar finished a year in the black. Sales grew to $45.7 million with $6 million in profits, up from $38.1 million the year before. The company's workforce tallied close to 400. Despite its accumulated ten-year losses of $16.1 million, however, Planar maintained a strong balance sheet, and, in 1993, it held its initial public offering. That same year, Jim Hurd was chosen as the High Technology Executive of the Year of the Cascade Pacific Council of Boy Scouts of America, and the company, poised for growth, purchased its neighboring building in order to expand its manufacturing operations.

The expansion cost Planar more than $10 million beginning in 1994 and accommodated the company's need for a new manufacturing line for its full-color displays. Planar also branched out in another new direction in 1994, acquiring Tektronix's avionics display unit, and began to market small numbers of small active matrix LCDs to the military and avionics industry for use in cockpits. In 1996, it landed a contract with the government to design flat-panel military avionics displays, which it began shipping in 1999. In 1997, it expanded its customer base for active matrix displays to the consumer computer market, and the company went into full production of active matrix displays. This move came in response to the 1995 push by Asian flat-panel display rivals to penetrate U.S. industrial and medical markets and the burgeoning growth of the laptop computer market.

Planar purchased Standish Industries Inc. of Wisconsin, manufacturer of flat-panel LCDs, in 1997, taking Planar into yet another new area—that of low-cost, low-power passive LCDs used in gas pumps and cash registers. The acquisition made Planar the largest independent domestic merchant supplier of flat-panel displays. In 1998, it began marketing its newly developed high-brightness, high-contrast, monochrome electroluminescent displays for outdoor, off-highway emergency vehicles and launched a line of medical monitors.

Revenues kept pace for a while with the company's growth. In 1996, revenues reached $80.4 million; in 1997, they were in the $90 million range. Then in 1999, with the global high-tech

Key Dates:

1983: Jim Hurd, Chris King, and John Laney acquire electroluminescent rights from Tektronix and found Planar Systems.
1986: Planar introduces the first full-color, flat-panel display.
1993: The company holds its initial public offering.
1994: Planar acquires Tektronix's avionics display unit.
1997: Planar acquires Standish Industries, adding passive liquid crystal display (LCD) capability.
1998: Planar launches a line of medical monitors.
1999: Planar's Evergreen manufacturing facility opens in Hillsboro, Oregon; Bill Walker, Planar chairman, becomes interim chief executive, followed by Balaji Krishnamurthy, who becomes chief executive and president.
2000: Jim Hurd dies; company exits the active LCD business and partners with Truly Semiconductor.
2001: The company launches a line of Planar-branded commercial desktop monitors; AllBrite Technologies is acquired; Planar exits CRT technology production.
2002: Planar acquires DOME Imaging Systems; the company closes its passive LCD manufacturing facility in Wisconsin and consolidates manufacturing in its Finland facility.

slowdown, sales began sinking, and the company experienced its first annual loss since 1993 on revenues of $123 million. Stock prices fell. Adding to the company's crisis, Hurd was diagnosed with leukemia. He underwent open-heart surgery before a scheduled bone marrow transplant and suffered a stroke. Bill Walker, Planar chairman, became interim chief as the company searched for a new leader. Balaji Krishnamurthy, a mathematician and computer scientist who had been head of Tektronix's Design, Service and Test Business Unit, became Planar's new president and chief executive officer in 1999, permanently replacing Hurd, who died in 2000.

Turnaround: 1999 Onward

Krishnamurthy inherited a company composed of near-autonomous divisions, each with separate procedures for accounting, procurement, and employee management. The company as a whole was characterized by operational inefficiencies and internal competition for business. Krishnamurthy sought to unify the company. He devoted his first quarter as chief executive to traveling to Planar's sites in Finland and Wisconsin where he held meetings with employees. The following quarter, he concentrated on focusing business units by market rather than geography and on discovering what customers needed.

The Krishnamurthy-led turnaround pushed Planar to evolve from a culture driven by engineering to one driven by marketing. Planar's new focus was fixed on its consumers rather than other manufacturers. In so doing, it left its roots as an electroluminescent manufacturer to offer finished display systems that could plug into a customer's product. Under Krishnamurthy, Planar realigned its operations, overhauled management, dropped unprofitable businesses, instituted a hiring freeze, and added new markets and technologies. It moved assembly production of its electroluminescent modules to Indonesia. It ended its six-year production of high-performance, full-color, active matrix LCD panels for military avionics and turned its attention to fast-growing commercial markets for flat display screens—medical equipment, truck instrumentation, and gas pumps. Krishnamurthy also instituted a policy of requiring executive ownership of stock beyond options and grants, wanting the company's top employees to put their own dollars into the business.

In 2000, Planar stepped further into the commercial realm and strengthened its foothold in medical monitors with an investment in Topvision Display Technologies Inc. of Taiwan, manufacturer of active matrix LCD flat-panel monitors. It also began offering desktop monitors to the commercial market via three direct retailers, TigerDirect.com, Dell Computer Corporation, and Egghead.com. ''Getting into the desktop monitor business is a statement that we're excited about going after large, high-growth commercial markets,'' Krishnamurthy was quoted as saying in a 2001 *Portland Business Journal* article. By 2001, the company's consumer products were available from nine of the top computer equipment providers. Its income for 2000 was $4 million on revenues of $169 million, a significant increase over 1999.

An economic slump hit the tech sector in 2001, but Planar continued to grow and began construction on new corporate headquarters. Its profits reached $14.5 million on sales of $208 million. The company's revenues were now almost evenly divided among its three main markets: industrial, transportation, and medical. It acquired AllBrite, a leading manufacturer of flat-panel displays for ATMs and the outdoor kiosk market. In another new initiative, the company created its photonics division to leverage its proprietary Atomic Layer Deposition technology into a variety of components, such as thin-film optical filters for fiber optic telecom systems.

In 2002, Planar continued on the path of change. It got out of the photonics components business, which it had initiated in early 2001, in the face of the telecommunications downturn. It acquired Dome Imaging Systems, maker of high-end computer displays for medical x-ray and other diagnostic images as it expanded to reach the fast-growing, profitable market. When it moved into a new 72,000-square-foot office building, it looked forward to continuing to gain ground as the leading domestic supplier of flat-panel desktop monitors and to penetrating more deeply into healthcare markets.

Principal Subsidiaries

Planar Systems Oy; Dome Imaging Systems, Inc.; Planar Taiwan LLC; Planar China LLC; Planar Systems GmbH; Planar Systems Limited; Planar Systems S.A.R.L.; Dome Imaging Systems N.V.

Principal Competitors

Hitachi, Ltd.; Matsushita Electric Industrial Co., Ltd.; Sharp Corporation; NEC Corporation; Sony Corporation.

Further Reading

Anderson, Julie, ''Spinoff Pact Sign of New Trend,'' *Portland Daily Journal of Commerce,* June 7, 1983, p. 1.

Earnshaw, Aliza, '' 'It's Not Our Fault,' '' *Portland Business Journal,* February 23, 2001, p. 17.

——, ''Planar CEO Gets the Employees Pulling Together,'' *Portland Business Journal,* February 23, 2001, p. 15.

Jenning, Steve, ''Planar Systems Launches Bold Bid for More Business,'' *Oregonian,* April 21, 1985, p. D1.

Manning, Jeff, ''Acquisition Doubles Sales, Gives Planar Top Spot in Industry,'' *Portland Business Journal,* July 23, 1990, p. 21.

——, ''Jim Hurd: Planar Exec Becomes Both Leader, Pariah Over Dumping Issue,'' *Portland Business Journal,* December 2, 1991, p. 10.

——, ''Planar Takes Off with High-Definition Work,'' *Portland Business Journal,* February 12, 1990, p. 1.

Raths, David, ''Winner, Company of the Year Larger Than $60 Million in Revenue: Planar Systems,'' *Portland Business Journal,* November 30, 2001, p. S13.

Robertson, Jack, ''Planar Plans to Pump Out AM-LCDs,'' *Electronic Buyers' News,* January 27, 1997, p. 3.

Scannell, Tim, ''Planar Punches Up Flat Panels with Enhanced, Full-Color EL Displays,'' *Mini-Micro Systems,* July 1988, p. 19.

Woodward, Steve, ''Beaverton, Oregon-Based Flat Panel Display Maker Rebounds into Record Sales,'' *Knight Ridder/Tribune Business News,* October 31, 2000.

—Carrie Rothburd

Poof-Slinky, Inc.

45400 Helm Street
Plymouth, Michigan 48170-0964
U.S.A.
Telephone: (734) 454-9552
Toll Free: (800) 329-8697
Fax: (734) 454-9540
Web site: http://www.poof-slinky.com

Private Company
Incorporated: 1945 as James Industries, Inc.
Employees: 100
Sales: $20 million (2002 est.)
NAIC: 339932 Game, Toy, and Children's Vehicle Manufacturing

Poof-Slinky, Inc. is a leading manufacturer of simple, inexpensive toys including the classic spring Slinky and various foam balls, airplanes, and rockets. The firm also produces Slinky Science educational and scientific toys and the Ideal line of tabletop games. Poof-Slinky operates manufacturing facilities in Plymouth, Michigan, and Hollidaysburg, Pennsylvania, where Slinkys are still made on machines the toy's inventor Richard James designed in the 1940s. Poof-Slinky is owned and managed by Richard Dallavecchia and Doug Ferner.

Beginnings

The origins of Poof-Slinky go back to the invention of the Slinky in the mid-1940s by Richard James, a marine engineer working for the U.S. war effort. His inspiration for the toy had come in 1943 when he saw a torsion spring, part of some test equipment he was using, fall from a shelf and then move jerkily across the floor. Struck by its potential for use as a child's toy, he began experimenting with different formulations of metal until he had perfected a rolled-steel spring that could ''walk'' down a flight of stairs. The name Slinky was supplied by his wife Betty, who had turned to the dictionary in search of a description for the spring's unique movement. Though little interest was shown in his creation at first, a Gimbel's department store in Philadelphia agreed to let James demonstrate the product just before Christmas in 1945. James sold 400 of the $1 toys in 90 minutes.

These first Slinkys were manufactured by an outside firm for the Jameses, but when sales started to take off Richard James designed machinery that could roll and coil the 80 feet of wire that each Slinky required. Calling their firm James Industries, Inc., they set up a factory in the Philadelphia suburb of Clifton Heights to produce the toy. To protect it from imitations, James patented the wire composition and manufacturing processes.

In 1948 a smaller version, Slinky Jr., was added, and it was followed in the 1950s by a Slinky Train and a Slinky Dog. The latter pair had been designed by a homemaker from Seattle named Helen Malsed, who had submitted the ideas to the firm.

The 1950s saw Richard James join a cult-like religious group that began to exert a growing influence over him, and to which he allegedly began funneling company profits. At the same time the Slinky's popularity was declining, and by the end of the decade the firm was in rough shape financially. In 1960 Richard James announced to his wife that he was planning to move to Bolivia to live with members of the group, and he gave her the choice of accompanying him, selling the company, or managing it herself. Rejecting the first option outright, she decided to stick with Slinky and run the firm on her own. Though she had always been involved with the company, she did not have full knowledge of its operations, having primarily concentrated on raising their six children, now ages 2 through 18.

In order to fully devote her energy to turning the business around, she decided to move back to her home town of Hollidaysburg, Pennsylvania, where she could rely on the assistance of family and friends to care for the children. The move necessitated a weekly commute of some 200 miles to Philadelphia, where she would stay from Sunday through Thursday. She began working on plans to relocate the company, however, and after a year and a half was able to move its operations to Hollidaysburg.

Television Ads Debuting in 1962

In 1962 James Industries began airing television commercials which featured the catchy new ''It's Slinky'' jingle. Sales

Company Perspectives:

Poof-Slinky, Inc. is a leading manufacturer of foam sport balls in North America and maker of the world famous Slinky, manufactured with pride in Hollidaysburg, PA.

shot upward, and ads using the song would continue to run for years afterwards. Richard James, meanwhile, would remain in Bolivia except for occasional visits to see his children. He died there in 1974.

Over the years the Slinky was changed very little, save for galvanizing the metal to protect it against rust and adding a crimp to the ends for safety. It continued to be produced on Richard James's original machinery, which sometimes was operated on three shifts to produce a Slinky every ten seconds around the clock. In addition to its popularity as a toy, the Slinky had been put to many other uses. In Vietnam, U.S. soldiers had employed it as an antenna, and it had also been used in light fixtures, for keeping leaves out of rain gutters, in pecan picking machines, and in any number of school science demonstrations.

In the 1970s and 1980s sales of the toy continued at a more or less steady pace, even when television advertising was not run. A survey done by a cereal manufacturer had found that 90 percent of the population knew the toy, and Betty James reasoned that ads were not necessarily vital to the still inexpensive Slinky's success. Sales were also boosted by media attention for the toy's use in experiments aboard the Space Shuttle, as well as by its appearances in television shows and movies including *Ace Ventura: Pet Detective* and Disney's *Toy Story*. For the latter, which featured a new animated version of the out-of-production Slinky Dog, James Industries had been given advance notice by Disney, and had begun work on a version that resembled the toy in the film. Unfortunately, the plastic molds were not completed in time, and the company missed the chance to sell it during *Toy Story*'s Christmas 1995 theatrical run. The Slinky Dog was finally brought to market the following February, in time for the movie's video release.

During its golden anniversary year of 1995, Slinky sales hit a peak of nearly six million, later returning to an annual average of less than four million. A total of 250 million copies of the toy had been sold in the half-century since its introduction. A colorful plastic version, which debuted in 1979, now accounted for nearly half of all Slinkys sold. Over the years James Industries had also added other products including pin wheels, plastic rings, building blocks, Pick-Up Stix, but their sales were dwarfed by those of the Slinky, which was still priced inexpensively at less than $3.

Sale to Poof Products in 1998

Though in good health and still a vital presence at the company, 80-year-old Betty James decided to sell the firm, which she co-owned with her children, so that they would not have to pay inheritance taxes. Many larger companies had tried to buy James out over the years, but her loyalty to the product and to her employees, many of whom had been with the firm for decades, had led her to turn every offer down. She finally reached an agreement in 1998 with a company called Poof Products, Inc. of Plymouth, Michigan, whose line of simple foam toys complemented the classic Slinky. Poof had also met her main requirement that Slinkys continue to be manufactured in Hollidaysburg.

Poof's origins dated to the early 1980s, when it had been started as a division of a manufacturer of foam products for the auto industry. The firm initially offered a few simple items such as footballs and soccer balls, and by the end of the decade its annual revenues had grown to approximately $2 million. In 1991 Poof was purchased by Ray Dallavecchia, Jr., and Doug Ferner, who took the positions of CEO and executive vice-president, respectively. Under their leadership the company's output was expanded, and by 1995 Poof's revenues had more than tripled, topping $6.6 million. At this time its product line included footballs, basketballs, soccer balls, puzzles, rockets, airplanes, helicopters, and other toys, most made of polyethylene or polyurethane foam.

In 1996, seeking more capital to help the firm grow, Dallavecchia had begun looking at the possibility of selling 12 percent of the company in a public stock offering. He was put off by the expenses involved, however, as the necessary legal and underwriting fees would consume as much as $700,000 of the $5 million he hoped to raise. Seeking an alternative, he discovered a software program called Capscape which created an Internet sales portal and automated the lengthy process of writing a prospectus, helping to cut the offering costs to less than $150,000. At the start of 1997 Poof began selling the stock online, requiring a minimum purchase of 150 of the $5 shares.

While the offering was getting underway the firm purchased Chasco Toy Co. of Oklahoma, another foam toy maker, and moved its jobs to Michigan. The acquisition increased the company's workforce to a total of 50. Almost half of Poof's sales at this time were to three major retailers, Wal-Mart, Kmart, and Target. Recent additions to the firm's product line included wind-up cars that could be taken apart and reassembled, and foam-tipped rockets filled with candy that could be fired as high as 30 feet in the air.

The year following the July 1998 acquisition of James Industries saw Poof sign an agreement with Chase Toys, Inc. that gave it worldwide manufacturing and distribution rights for KLIXX products. KLIXX, plastic links which could be connected to form chains or structures and made a distinctive sound when attached, were relaunched under the Slinky brand name. Poof also added new products, including a line of collectible Slinky Pets and the Slinky Jr. with Dum-Dum Pops Candy Surprise.

Poof Buys EDT in 2000

In October 2000 Poof acquired the Educational Design Toys (EDT) division of Educational Design LLC, a maker of test preparation materials. EDT, founded in 1969, made science and educational toys including the Space Theater Planetarium and Mini Lab Science Kits. Early the next year Poof bought the assets of another educational and science toy maker, Patail Enterprises, Inc. of Laguna Niguel, California. The EDT and Patail product lines were subsequently marketed under the Slinky Science brand

Key Dates:

1945: Betty and Richard James begin marketing the Slinky spring toy.
1950s: Slinky Train, Dog, and other variations are introduced.
1960: Richard James departs for Bolivia, leaving Betty to run firm.
1962: Sales are boosted by television advertising campaign with "It's Slinky" song.
1979: Plastic Slinky is introduced.
1980s: Poof Products is formed to make foam toys.
1991: Richard Dallavecchia and Doug Ferner buy Poof Products.
1995: Slinky celebrates 50th anniversary; Slinky Dog is featured in *Toy Story* film.
1997: Poof begins selling stock via online offering; acquires Chasco.
1998: James Industries, Inc. is acquired by Poof Products.
2000: Educational Design Toys is bought by Poof.
2001: Patail Enterprises, Inc. is purchased.
2003: Game maker Ideal Toy is acquired.
2004: Poof and James Industries merge to become Poof-Slinky, Inc.

name. In February 2003 the firm also bought Ideal Toy, located in Ronkonkoma, New York. Ideal made tabletop action games including Sure Shot Baseball and Rack TNU Pocket Pool.

In January 2004 Poof Products formally merged with James Industries to become Poof-Slinky, Inc. The firm would continue to make Slinkys in Hollidaysburg, Pennsylvania, and foam toys in Plymouth, Michigan, with a few other items contracted out to manufacturers overseas. Dallavecchia and Ferner had long since bought back the outstanding shares of stock sold in the 1990s to assume full ownership of the firm. Slinky matriarch Betty James was now retired, but the family connection was maintained through her eldest son Tom, who worked for the company as head of special market sales.

The year 2004 also saw production begin on a new animated film which was to feature the company's Slinky Pets line along with other Slinky spring toys. The film, tentatively entitled *The Magic Quilt,* was slated for release in the fall of 2005. Its production company, H2V Kids of Montreal, Canada, had hopes to produce a second feature film and a television series as well.

By now Poof-Slinky had reduced its product lineup to a total of 65 items, which included a variety of balls, foam rockets, and airplanes, along with the Slinky and Slinky Science lines and several Ideal games. The company's toys were available in over 20,000 stores worldwide.

With roots going back nearly 60 years, Poof-Slinky, Inc. had established a solid niche for itself in the toy marketplace. Its production of the classic Slinky, as well as a variety of foam toys, games, and educational products, gave it a proven lineup that generated steady sales.

Principal Competitors

Hasbro, Inc.; Wham-O, Inc.; JAKKS Pacific, Inc.; Toy Quest.

Further Reading

Fish, Mike, "At Danforth Awards, Everyone Knows It's Slinky," *Post-Standard* (Syracuse, N.Y.), April 28, 1995, p. B6.

Giarrusso, Michael A., "Despite Newfound Stardom, Slinky Dog Not on the Market," *Associated Press*, December 18, 1995.

Gibb, Tom, "Celebrated Slinky Toy Is 50 Years Old This Month," *Harrisburg Patriot*, March 20, 1995, p. B3.

Harvey, Robin, " 'It's Slinky, It's Slinky!' And Now It's 50," *Toronto Star*, March 30, 1995, p. D1.

"Helen Malsed, Inventor of Slinky Toys," *Associated Press Newswires*, November 17, 1998.

Nelson Jones, Diana, "Slinky Always Bounces Back," *Grand Rapids Press*, December 26, 2003, p. A11.

Palasri, Sirin, "Toy Firm Set for Offering on the Net," *Nation*, December 9, 1996.

Serwach, Joseph, "IPO Sounds Like a Soft Sell: Toy Firm to Use Internet," *Crain's Detroit Business*, July 28, 1997, p. 1.

——, "New Slinky Pets Pursue Beanie Babies' Success," *Crain's Detroit Business*, August 3, 1998, p. 1.

Shellenbarger, Pat, "That Slinking Feeling," *Grand Rapids Press*, May 23, 1995, p. C1.

"Slinky Matriarch Headed for Toy Industry Hall of Fame," *Associated Press Newswires*, January 22, 2001.

"Suburban Detroit Company Buys Maker of Slinky Toys," *Associated Press Newswires*, July 18, 1998.

"This Immortal Coil," *Express*, October 16, 1999.

Thomas, Karen, "Forever Slinky," *USA Today*, December 1, 1995, p. 1D.

Witchell, Alex, "Persevering for Family and Slinky," *New York Times*, February 21, 1996, p. C1.

—Frank Uhle

Pope & Talbot, Inc.

1500 S.W. First Avenue, Suite 200
Portland, Oregon 97201-5830
U.S.A.
Telephone: (503) 228-9161
Fax: (503) 220-2722
Web site: http://www.poptal.com

Public Company
Incorporated: 1852 as Puget Mill Company
Employees: 2,229
Sales: $546.3 million (2002)
Stock Exchanges: New York Pacific
Ticker Symbol: POP
NAIC: 321113 Sawmills; 322110 Pulp Mills

One of the oldest forest products companies in the United States, Pope & Talbot, Inc. specializes in pulp and wood products. The firm operates three pulp mills in Oregon and British Columbia that have an overall yearly capacity of 830,000 metric tons. These mills produce northern bleached softwood kraft chip and sawdust pulp for use in the production of newsprint, tissue, and coated and uncoated paper. Pope & Talbot's pulp business, which generates about 60 percent of overall revenues, distributes its products to customers in more than two dozen countries, including the United States and Canada as well as nations in South America, Europe, and the Asia-Pacific region. The company's wood products side includes three sawmills in British Columbia and one in South Dakota with a combined annual capacity of about 640 million board feet of lumber. These four sawmills produce dimension and board lumber, wood chips, and other byproducts. The primary customers of Pope & Talbot's wood products business are in the United States and Canada.

Early History: Quickly Becoming the Dominant Lumber Company on Puget Sound

Andrew Jackson Pope and Frederic Talbot, two ambitious young men from Maine, arrived in San Francisco on December 1, 1849, after a grueling 51-day journey around South America on a number of different steam ships. Although they were exhausted when they stepped ashore, the excitement of San Francisco, which had grown from a population of 6,000 to 20,000 in just six months, overwhelmed the two Easterners. Pope and Talbot immediately recognized the potential for starting a new business, and on the following day, they joined with partners Lucius Sanborn and J.P. Keller to establish a company to operate barges in San Francisco bay.

A short two months later, the partners were able not only to pay for the cost of their new barges and boats, but also to turn a profit of more than $800. After buying out Sanborn's interest, Pope, Talbot, and Keller decided to enter the lumber business. A number of disastrous fires in San Francisco had convinced the partners that demand for lumber would remain high. Soon they opened a lumberyard and began transporting consignments of the product from one area to another. A stroke of good fortune occurred when Frederic Talbot's older brother, W.C. Talbot, arrived in California with his brig, the *Oriental.* A large, seaworthy vessel, the *Oriental* provided the firm with a greater range of transport. When Frederic Talbot decided to permanently return to the East Coast and open a business in New York, his older brother replaced him as a partner in the company.

For a short time, the partners shipped lumber from Maine to California through arrangements with Pope's relatives. They found this impractical as a long-term strategy, however, especially given the enormous demand for lumber in and around the San Francisco area. They built their own mill in the Oregon Territory on Puget Sound, on a site that Native Americans called Teekalet, or ''Brightness of the Noonday Sun''; settlers renamed it Port Gamble. By 1853 the partners' mill was producing nearly 2,000 board feet of lumber per day. Four years later production had jumped to a total of eight million board feet for the year, and the company (which had been christened Puget Mill Company in 1852) was known as the largest and most successful business on Puget Sound.

The late 1850s brought an Indian war, a gold rush that destabilized the labor market, and a short period of overproduction as a result of new lumber mills established on Puget Sound. Yet the mill at Port Gamble continued to prosper. In response to a growing demand for lumber during and after the Civil War,

Company Perspectives:

Pope & Talbot's strategic focus and corporate structure encompass the complementary businesses of two forest industry groups: wood products and pulp. The Company manufactures softwood lumber and market pulp in the U.S. and Canada.

We have continually prospered in the face of cyclical markets since 1849 by planting, cultivating, and creating value for our customers, communities, and shareholders. Our achievements have created a foundation for continuing our cycle of success in the future.

the Puget Mill Company added new equipment and began to acquire smaller mills in the area, including important mills on Camano Island and Port Ludlow. By 1879 the company was producing more than 200,000 board feet per day and nearly 70 million feet per year.

As the 19th century progressed, leadership of the firm changed hands. J.P. Keller died in June 1862, and was replaced as a partner of the firm by mill superintendent Cyrus Walker. Andrew Pope died in September 1878, and Captain Talbot in August 1881. William H. Talbot, the son of Captain Talbot, had been groomed by his father in every aspect of the lumber business, and when the elder Talbot died, the son quickly became the driving force behind the company, relying heavily on Cyrus Walker's 28 years of experience in the mill. In 1882 the total capacity of all the Puget Mill operations amounted to 99 million board feet of lumber per year. In 1885 the number of cargoes of lumber shipped from the mill at Port Gamble alone reached 49; by 1888, the number had risen to 78. The company also owned one of the largest shipping fleets for the transportation of its lumber, with 14 ships carrying lumber to customers in Japan, Hawaii, Australia, South America, China, Korea, India, and South Africa. During this same period, the Puget Mill Company was also purchasing enormous tracts of timberland in order to maintain a reliable source of wood for its mills; by 1892, the firm reported ownership of 186,000 acres.

During the 1890s and the years immediately following the turn of the century, Puget Mill Company expanded its marketing operations and opened three new offices in San Francisco. The development of railroad traffic heralded even greater prosperity for the company, because it transformed the isolated state of Washington into the nation's largest distributor of lumber. As timberlands in Wisconsin, Michigan, and Minnesota were depleted, demand for Washington's lumber skyrocketed. The number of mills in Washington had grown from 46 in 1870 to 310 by 1890. By 1906 there were more than 900 lumber mills in the state producing 4.3 billion board feet of lumber.

Following Setbacks, Sale of Company in Early 20th Century

Beginning in 1907, however, the Puget Mill Company suffered a series of setbacks. When the state of Washington levied a tax increase on the acreage of timberland held by the company, Puget Mill's extensive holdings nearly became a liability. In addition, equipment used in the company's mills had become antiquated, and Puget Mill's operations were running inefficiently. In 1908 the company sold the last of its aging fleet of schooners, once the largest lumber armada on the West Coast. The company joined an organization that chartered the tonnage for shipment, thus relieving Puget Mill Company of the burden of maintaining its own fleet. By the end of World War I, the company had grown large, diverse, and somewhat cumbersome, with some 15 corporations under the direct management of Puget Mill. Labor unrest, which occurred throughout the Northwest region during this time, affected all of the company's holdings.

In July 1925, William Talbot, exhausted and in ill health, decided to sell Puget Mill Company to the Charles R. McCormick Lumber Company. McCormick, a native of Michigan, had arrived in Portland, Oregon, in 1901. He renovated a dilapidated millsite at St. Helens on the Columbia River, and from there he created a lumber empire that grew to become one of the largest on the Pacific Coast. McCormick purchased all of Puget Mill Company, including mills and timberlands, at a price of $15 million. Talbot, known as a shrewd businessman, made McCormick agree to build a new mill at Port Gamble, with Puget Mill Company holding a mortgage on all the mills, timberlands, and logging camps operated by McCormick.

From the beginning of the takeover, McCormick's management team made serious errors and miscalculations. Modernizations and improvements at Port Ludlow and St. Helens, as well as the new mill at Port Gamble, were plagued by cost overruns. McCormick soon faced rising interest rates, amortization payments, and annual taxes of more than $1 million. As his debts steadily increased, McCormick devised a strategy of expansion, hiring a larger sales staff and increasing production. Costs continued to outrun revenues, however, and by the start of the Depression in 1930 the company had posted a loss of $858,587. The company's situation only worsened with the economic problems brought on by the Depression.

Rebirth of Independent Pope & Talbot: Late 1930s

After William Talbot died, George Pope, Sr., assumed the position of president of Puget Mill Company and began to pressure McCormick to resign. When McCormick's expansion strategy failed to revitalize the company, he vacated his position in December 1931. Pope was then elected chairman of the board of Charles R. McCormick Lumber Company, with the intention of protecting the interests of the Puget Mill Company. He immediately appointed managers who exemplified his own financially conservative viewpoint, and began to reduce the debt incurred by McCormick. By 1937 all the bank loans and a significant portion of the mortgage bonds were retired. In 1938 the Puget Mill Company brought a suit of foreclosure against the Charles R. McCormick Lumber Company. Unable to pay its obligations of over $7 million, the McCormick Company was forced to cede all of its holdings to the owners of Puget Mill. The principals of the foreclosure suit, George Pope, Sr.; George Pope, Jr.; Frederic C. Talbot; and Talbot Walker, all descendants of the original owners, reacquired the company their forefathers had labored to build.

George Pope, Sr., became president of the company, which was renamed Pope & Talbot, Inc. in 1940. Before any analysis

Key Dates:

1849: Andrew Jackson Pope and Frederic Talbot, along with two other partners, establish a company to operate barges in San Francisco bay.
1852: After opening a lumberyard and beginning construction of a lumber mill at Port Gamble, Washington, the company takes the name Puget Mill Company.
1892: Firm reports owning 186,000 acres of timberland.
1925: Puget Mill Company is sold to Charles R. McCormick Lumber Company.
1938: Descendants of the original owners of Puget Mill reacquire the company.
1940: Puget Mill Company is renamed Pope & Talbot, Inc.
1963: Company ends its shipping operations, selling the last four vessels in its fleet.
1972: Pope & Talbot is listed on the New York Stock Exchange.
1978: Company expands into the pulp business with an investment in a bleached kraft pulp mill in Halsey, Oregon.
1980s: Pope & Talbot diversifies into consumer products by either acquiring or building diaper and tissue plants.
1985: Firm's real estate and timber holdings in the state of Washington are spun off to shareholders.
1992: Large sawmill in Castlegar, British Columbia, is purchased.
1995: Pope & Talbot shuts down its 142-year-old sawmill at Port Gamble.
1996: Diaper business is sold to Paragon Trade Brands, Inc.
1998: The company's private label tissue business is divested; Pope & Talbot gains 60 percent stake in Harmac Pacific Inc., operator of a pulp mill near Nanaimo, British Columbia.
1999: Company purchases full control of Harmac Pacific.
2001: Pope & Talbot buys the Mackenzie pulp mill in northern British Columbia from Norske Skog Canada.

and reorganization of the lumber operations and steamship activities could take place, however, World War II began. George Pope, Sr., became chairman of the board, allowing his son, George Pope, Jr., to assume the position of president and deal with the demands of the war years.

Pope & Talbot mills operated at full capacity during the entire war. The company produced lumber for panel bridges used in the invasion of Europe, tent poles, and Signal Corps material for communication lines. Company lumber was used for the construction of naval housing, and the company's fleet of steamships made vital contributions to the American war effort. Pope & Talbot vessels transported the supplies necessary for waging war in every area of conflict, and stopped at ports including Murmansk, Bizerte, Salerno, Guadalcanal, and Okinawa. The company also suffered casualties: four ships were sunk during the war, including the S.S. *West Ivis,* which lost its entire crew. During the height of worldwide hostilities, Pope & Talbot was responsible for more than 75 ships. The war helped improve the financial position of the company, which was one of the three largest lumber producers in the entire Northwest by the end of the war.

Developing into Fully Integrated Forest Products Company in Postwar Era

The future appeared especially promising for the company's steamship operations during the postwar years: industry along the Pacific Coast needed large quantities of bulk materials, while the East Coast needed lumber and other products from the western United States. However, volatile labor relations plagued the company. In 1948 a three-month strike by dock workers cost the firm more than $1.25 million, and a series of strikes in 1954 caused Pope & Talbot to lose a significant portion of its steamship cargoes. By 1958 the company was down to one shipping route, and another year of strikes in the maritime industry during 1959 brought its vessels to a standstill. Competition from the railroad industry also began to take business away from shipping. As a result, in 1963 Pope & Talbot decided to terminate shipping operations by selling the four remaining vessels in its once-proud fleet.

In contrast to its shipping activities, the company's lumber operations were highly successful. Having purchased a large tract of timberland near Oakridge, Oregon, in 1946, management assured itself of adequate timber holdings for the foreseeable future. By 1950 the company owned over one billion board feet of timber ready for cutting, and during the next decade it opened new mills in the United States and Canada. Pope & Talbot also implemented a diversification strategy which included building a particleboard plant, a veneer mill, and a wood treatment facility, and in 1961 the company purchased a plywood plant. These moves brought the company closer to fulfilling its goal of a fully integrated wood products program.

In 1963 George Pope, Jr., resigned as president of the company and was replaced by Cyrus T. Walker, a descendant of one of the company's early partners. In 1966 Pope & Talbot reported that its lumber division provided 61.6 percent of its revenues, plywood 13.9 percent, veneer 7.1 percent, particleboard 6.2 percent, and hardboard 6.2 percent. Net earnings increased from $717,000 in 1965 to $1.2 million in 1966. In 1968 sales increased an astronomical 73 percent over the previous year, totaling some $3 million. The company's success lay in the fact that management was moving quickly to take advantage of growing markets for new wood products. In 1969 the firm continued its expansion strategy by purchasing another mill in Canada, procuring cutting rights to more than a million acres of timberland in Canada, and constructing a new log utilization plant.

Late 1970s and 1980s: Expanding into Pulp, Tissue, and Diapers

The company changed leadership in 1971 when Cyrus Walker retired and the fourth generation of Popes and Talbots assumed control. Peter T. Pope was elected chairman of the board, and Guy B. Pope was appointed president and chief operating officer. Under their tenure, the firm continued to grow. In 1972 Pope & Talbot was listed on the New York Stock Exchange, and the following year the company surpassed $100 million in revenues. When the housing and construction industry was hit hard by a recession during the mid-1970s, Pope & Talbot made plans to enter the pulp and paper industry, which would allow the company to use all of the yield from its timberlands. Consequently, in March 1978, the firm invested $24 million in a joint venture with American Can Company to operate a bleached kraft pulp mill near Halsey, Oregon. (It took full control of this mill in 1983.)

During the 1980s, Pope & Talbot insulated itself as much as possible from the cyclical nature of the housing and construction industry. The pulp mill at Halsey took the company into an entirely new, and highly profitable, direction. Pulp is made from softwood chips, hardwood chips, and sawdust, and is used to manufacture newspaper and printing and writing grade paper. Soon the company had major contracts throughout the Pacific Northwest to sell its pulp. Not content with just pulp production, Pope & Talbot began to diversify into the consumer products market by either acquiring or building diaper and tissue plants. By the early 1990s, Pope & Talbot listed two tissue plants and six diaper plants as part of its holdings. Manufacturing an entire line of napkins, paper towels, and facial and bath tissues from 100 percent recycled paper for private label customers became highly profitable. The Ultra Thin disposable diaper developed into the company's most lucrative product. By 1993 Pope & Talbot's wood products were bringing in approximately 48 percent of revenues, while its pulp, tissue, and diaper products were generating 52 percent.

During this same period, the company gradually reduced its exposure to the timber market of the U.S. Pacific Northwest, where concerns over the environmental impact of logging was reducing logging activity and making the cost of the timber more expensive. In 1985 Pope & Talbot spun off to its shareholders its real estate and timber holdings in the state of Washington, creating a limited partnership called Pope Resources. Four years later, its sawmill in Oakridge, Oregon, was sold, and then in 1992 the company sold its remaining Oregon timberlands. Continuing to shift its wood products operations north of the border, Pope & Talbot purchased a large sawmill in Castlegar, British Columbia, from Westar Group Ltd. for $19.4 million. The shift away from the U.S. Pacific Northwest culminated on November 30, 1995, when Pope & Talbot closed its 142-year-old sawmill at Port Gamble. The company now operated three sawmills in British Columbia with total annual capacity of 465 million board feet, along with two smaller mills in the Black Hills region of the United States, in Spearfish, South Dakota; and Newcastle, Wyoming.

Late 1990s and Beyond: Focusing on Pulp and Lumber

The company moved in the late 1990s to focus on two core areas of the forest products market: lumber and pulp. In February 1996 Pope & Talbot sold its disposable diaper business to Paragon Trade Brands, Inc. for $50.5 million in cash and $14.5 million in Paragon stock. The diaper business, which had come under intense price competition from industry giants Kimberly-Clark Corporation and the Procter & Gamble Company, had generated about $157 million of revenues in 1994, or 24 percent of the total of $660 million. Then in February 1998 Pope & Talbot sold its private label tissue business to an investor group for $147 million, completing its exit from the consumer products sector. The tissue operations had generated 29 percent, or $136 million, of the 1997 revenues of $468 million.

Seeking to expand its pulp operations, Pope & Talbot gained a 60 percent stake in Harmac Pacific Inc. by the end of 1998, through a hostile takeover. Based in Vancouver, Harmac operated a pulp mill near Nanaimo, British Columbia, with an annual capacity of 370,000 tons of northern bleached softwood kraft pulp. In November 1999 Pope & Talbot purchased the remaining minority stake in Harmac, which was subsequently merged into the firm's Canadian subsidiary, Pope & Talbot Ltd. Peter T. Pope stepped down as CEO at the end of July 1999 and was succeeded by Michael Flannery, who had been president of the company since September 1995 and before that had been head of the wood products operations for several years. Flannery became chairman as well in August 2000, although Pope remained on the board of directors. Also in 2000, Pope & Talbot closed its sawmill in Newcastle, Wyoming, because of reduced availability of public timber in the Black Hills region.

Pope & Talbot further bolstered its pulp production in June 2001 when it completed a $104.4 million acquisition of the Mackenzie pulp mill in northern British Columbia from Norske Skog Canada. This mill, which used chips and sawdust to produce a fine grade of northern bleached softwood pulp, had an annual capacity of 230,000 metric tons. Unfortunately, Pope & Talbot around this time began to be buffeted by the severe economic downturn that had a particularly depressive effect on pulp prices. Concurrently, a trade dispute erupted between the United States and Canada following the April 2001 expiration of the two countries' Softwood Lumber Agreement. The United States subsequently slapped duties on Canadian lumber imports, forcing Pope & Talbot to pay $14.1 million in lumber duties during 2002. One result of these developments was that the company posted net losses of $24.9 million and $21 million for 2001 and 2002, respectively.

During the first nine months of 2003, Pope & Talbot recorded a net loss of $19.1 million. The corporation continued to be affected by the lumber trade dispute and was further hurt by an appreciating Canadian dollar, which resulted in higher manufacturing costs for the firm's Canadian operations. Some potentially positive news for the company's future came late in the year with the announcement of a proposed agreement between the United States and Canada on the lumber dispute. Nevertheless, Pope & Talbot—because it was a small player in a consolidating industry increasingly dominated by global giants—was likely to continue to be forced to ride the cyclical ups and downs of its industry without having much in the way of resources to smooth out these fluctuations.

Principal Subsidiaries

Pope & Talbot International Ltd. (Canada); Pope & Talbot Ltd. (Canada); Mackenzie Pulp Land Ltd. (Canada); Pope & Talbot Mackenzie Pulp Operations Ltd. (Canada); Pope & Talbot Wis., Inc.; Penn Timber, Inc.; Pope & Talbot Relocation Services, Inc.; P&T Power Company; Pope & Talbot Pulp Sales USA, Inc.; Pope & Talbot Pulp Sales Europe SPRL (Belgium); Pope & Talbot Lumber Sales, Inc.; Halsey Cl02 Limited Partnership; P&T Community Trust (Canada); P&T Funding Ltd. (Canada); P&T Funding Limited Partnership (Canada).

Principal Competitors

Weyerhaeuser Company; Georgia-Pacific Corporation; International Paper Company; Bowater Incorporated; Domtar Inc.

Further Reading

Coman, Edwin T., Jr., and Helen T. Gibbs, *Time, Tide & Timber: Over a Century of Pope & Talbot,* Portland, Ore.: Pope & Talbot, Inc., 1978.

Denson, Bryan, ''Historic Mill Will Pass into History,'' *Portland Oregonian,* August 22, 1995, p. A1.

Finchem, Kirk, ''Pope & Talbot: New-Sized Company Refocuses to Improve Profitability,'' *Pulp and Paper,* September 1996, pp. 46–47.

Gordon, Mitchell, ''Escape from Cyclicality: Pope & Talbot Pushes into Paper Goods,'' *Barron's,* March 2, 1987, pp. 53+.

Kadera, Jim, ''Company That Salvages Dead Timber Is in the Chips,'' *Portland Oregonian,* March 17, 1991, p. 1.

——, ''Forest Company Expands in Canada,'' *Portland Oregonian,* April 16, 1992, p. C10.

Marcial, Gene G., ''This Papermaker Could Crash Out of the Woods,'' *Business Week,* January 20, 1992, p. 80.

''Mistaken Identity?,'' *Forbes,* February 6, 1989, p. 43.

Stein, Harry H., *Old Growth, New Directions: 150 Years of Pope & Talbot,* Seattle, Wash.: Documentary Books, 2003.

—Thomas Derdak
—update: David E. Salamie

Raytech Corporation

4 Corporate Drive, Suite 295
Shelton, Connecticut 06484
U.S.A.
Telephone: (203) 925-8023
Fax: (203) 925-8088
Web site: http://www.raytech.com

Public Company
Incorporated: 1986
Employees: 1,593
Sales: $209.86 million (2002)
Stock Exchanges: New York
Ticker Symbol: RAY
NAIC: 332999 All Other Miscellaneous Fabricated Metal Products

Based in Shelton, Connecticut, Raytech Corporation and its subsidiaries manufacture and distribute engineered products for heat-resistant, inertia control, energy absorption, and transmission applications, serving both automotive original equipment manufacturers and aftermarket customers around the world. Operations are divided into three business segments. Wet Friction products, accounting for more than 60 percent of the company's revenues, are used in an oil-immersed environment found in automobiles, trucks, buses, heavy-duty equipment, farm machinery, and mining equipment. Dry Friction products are used in automobile and truck manual transmissions that do not use an oil-immersed environment. Finally, the Aftermarket segment produces wet friction products and other transmission products for automobile and light trucks, catering to warehouse distributors and aftermarket retailers. In addition to manufacturing operations in the United States, Raytech maintains facilities in Great Britain, Germany, and China. Dogged for years by asbestos-related litigation, the company finally has emerged from a 12-year period of operating under Chapter 11 protection. As a result of a 2001 agreement, Raytech has turned over 90 percent of its stock to bankruptcy court to settle current and future claims.

Founding the Company in 1902

The origins of Raytech date back to 1902 and the establishment of the A.H. Raymond Company in Bridgeport, Connecticut. The small shop served the young automotive industry, producing clutch facings, the Raymond brake, and brake linings. The company developed a new brake lining that used noncharring asbestos, which it trademarked as Raybestos and later applied to clutch facings. Asbestos, which in reality represented a range of fibrous silicate minerals, was known to the ancient Greeks and Romans and was rediscovered during the Industrial Revolution. Due to its great strength and resistance to heat, and because it was the only mineral that could be woven, asbestos began to find an increasing number of industrial applications. What the ancients also observed, and modern medicine later confirmed, was that weaving asbestos into cloth was extremely harmful to the lungs, which took in microscopic particles and fibers that often led to an early death.

A.H. Raymond Company changed its name to the Royal Equipment Company of Bridgeport, then in 1916 appropriated the Raybestos name, becoming Raybestos Company. Named president was Sumner Simpson, who proved to be the most important figure in the history of the firm, heading it for nearly four decades. The company grew as the automobile became affordable to an increasing number of people. Raybestos established a factory in Stratford, Connecticut, in 1919, and in the early 1920s completed a pair of acquisitions to maintain a reliable supply of asbestos yarns, buying United States Asbestos Company and General Asbestos and Rubber Company. A major turning point came in 1929 when Raybestos merged with competitor Manhattan Rubber Manufacturing Company, which in addition to brake and clutch products made industrial rubber products. The resulting company was Raybestos-Manhattan Friction Materials Company.

Formed only months before the stock crash that ushered in the Great Depression, Raybestos-Manhattan, nevertheless, thrived during the 1930s. Despite tough times, the United States was now very much dependent on cars and trucks, and the company enjoyed a steady demand for its products, both with automakers and the garages and service stations that repaired vehicles. Moreover, the company continued to be a pioneer in

Company Perspectives:

The Raytech of tomorrow will build on the expertise gained during the last 100 years and upon the ability to create a diverse, global, multi-market-driven company.

its field. It created a semi-metallic clutch facing, which led to the development of a friction clutch that in 1938 was used by Buick to produce an early version of automatic transmission, relying on brake pads to shift gears while the vehicle was in motion. (A clutch was still used for starting, but a year later Oldsmobile brought out the first fully automatic transmission.) Nevertheless, the company's major product continued to be asbestos brake linings, which Raybestos-Manhattan supported by launching a national advertising campaign that promoted the importance of safe brakes.

The first half of the 1940s were impacted by World War II. Raybestos-Manhattan was already supplying parts to the military, but with severe cutbacks in the manufacture of new automobiles as part of the war effort, the company greatly expanded its defense contracting. Raybestos-Manhattan brake linings were used on almost all heavy bombers, and the company's clutch plates were used on the two-speed planetary B-29 Supercharger. In addition, the company continued to produce brake and clutch parts used in almost all military vehicles. In the second half of the 1940s, Raybestos-Manhattan returned its focus to the automobile industry, which was poised to enjoy strong growth as carmakers ramped up to meet rising demand, now that the Great Depression was overcome by massive government spending on the war and an increasing number of middle class consumers were in the market for a new car. In 1948 Chevrolet introduced its Powerglide automatic transmission and Buick its Dynaflow transmission, both of which relied on Raybestos-Manhattan clutch parts. A year later, Ford and Chrysler followed suit with their own automatics, creating an even greater need for the company's automatic transmission products.

The 1950s: A Golden Era for Raybestos

The 1950s were a golden era for Raybestos-Manhattan, which diversified into new products and added manufacturing facilities. The company moved into powdered metal products, building a plant in Crawfordville, Indiana, and with the acquisition of Paramount, California-based Graf Manufacturing began producing fluorinated polymers. Automobile parts also continued to hold a significant place in the company's business mix. To meet increasing demand, Raybestos-Manhattan established factories in Neenah, Wisconsin, and Peterborough, Ontario. The Raybestos name would gain even greater credibility in automotive circles starting in 1957, when the company's disc brake pads were used by the winner of the Indianapolis 500, Sam Hanks, marking the first of 23 consecutive Indy winners relying on Raybestos products. Raybestos disc brake pads were first introduced that same year to the passenger car market, incorporated by Studebaker in its Avanti model. The later years of the 1950s also witnessed the advent of the space age, precipitated by the Soviet Union launching its Sputnik satellite, which led to a frantic race to the moon as part of a Cold War competition between the world's two superpowers. Raybestos materials would quickly find an application in the American answer to Sputnik, the U.S. Explorer I, launched early in 1958. Also of note during the decade was the 1953 death of Sumner Simpson, who was instrumental in the company's growth but whose name would gain notoriety years later in connection with asbestos litigation.

During the 1960s Raybestos-Manhattan became involved in the development of composite materials needed in the U.S. space program but that also had applications in such consumer products as fabric and hose, and even bowling balls. The company also added new hydraulic parts and smog-control devices to its line of car products. It was also during this period that the company expanded overseas, acquiring Breku Reibbelag GmbH & Co., a West German maker of clutch facings, friction washers, and disc brake pads. Domestically, Raybestos-Manhattan acquired Milford Rivet & Machine Co., a Connecticut manufacturer of rivet and rivet setting machines. Five plants were added and used in the production of rubber belts.

Raybestos-Manhattan continued its effort to expand internationally during the 1970s, moving into such countries as Australia, Ireland, and Venezuela. The company invested heavily in capital improvements and initiated a strategy to diversify into new product lines. It also discontinued the last of the products inherited from Manhattan Rubber Manufacturing Company. Furthermore, because the company no longer maintained manufacturing facilities in Manhattan, the company changed its name in 1978 to Raybestos Friction Materials Company. Of greater significance to its future, however, was a wave of lawsuits to be filed against Raybestos and other asbestos manufacturers by workers, who charged that the company knew of the hazards of asbestos yet took inadequate steps to protect them from asbestosis.

Asbestosis was coined by English physician W.E. Cook in 1924. He performed a postmortem examination on a 33-year-old woman who had worked for 20 years in an asbestos-textile factory and during the final seven years of her life endured severe coughing and poor health. Cook's autopsy revealed massive lung scarring and thick strands of abnormal fibrous tissue. His results were published in the *British Medical Journal.* For several years, American and Canadian insurance companies had already made the practical decision not to issue life insurance policies to asbestos workers, concluding without the benefit of scientific study that the asbestos industry offered working conditions injurious to health.

As early as the 1930s the largest U.S. asbestos manufacturer, Johns-Manville, and Raybestos-Manhattan, the second largest, faced the first damage suits filed by workers who suffered from asbestosis. According to investigative journalist Paul Brodeur, ''The two firms, together with other leading asbestos manufacturers, initiated a cover-up of the asbestos hazard that continued for more than forty years.'' It was not until the 1960s that the situation began to change. Sellers of dangerous products were now required by law to post adequate warnings or be held accountable, and Dr. Irving J. Selikoff at the Mount Sinai School of Medicine conducted studies that provided incontrovertible evidence about the health dangers of industrial exposure to asbestos. In 1971 the first asbestos product liability lawsuit was won, and the verdict was upheld by a federal appeals court two years later. According to Brodeur, ''During the next ten years,

Key Dates:

1902: The A.H. Raymond Company is formed in Bridgeport, Connecticut.
1916: The company changes its name to Raybestos Company.
1929: Merger with Manhattan Rubber Manufacturing Company.
1982: The company changes its name to Raymark Corp.
1986: Raytech Corporation is formed as a holding company.
1989: Due to asbestos litigation, Raytech files for Chapter 11 bankruptcy protection.
2001: Raytech emerges from bankruptcy.

Johns-Manville, Raybestos-Manhattan, and more than a dozen other manufacturers of asbestos insulation were the targets of some 15,000 lawsuits. At first, the defendant manufacturers tried to claim that they did not know about the asbestos hazard until Dr. Selikoff's pioneering studies of the early 1960s. However, plaintiff attorneys soon unearthed Sumner Simpson's correspondence.'' The so-called ''Sumner Simpson documents'' would form the basis of most asbestos lawsuits over the ensuing years. Simpson's personal papers, consisting of some 6,000 documents, came to light in the late 1970s during the course of discovery in a pending lawsuit and were used by plaintiffs to prove that Raybestos-Manhattan and other manufacturers were aware of the health hazards connected to asbestos.

Asbestos manufacturers faced millions of dollars in litigation costs and possible liabilities. In 1982 Johns-Manville filed for Chapter 11 bankruptcy protection—claiming that it was the victim of unwarranted lawsuits—as a way to shield its assets. Raybestos took a different approach, following a policy of accommodation and compromise. First, it sought to disassociate itself from asbestos. In 1982 the company changed its named to Raymark Corporation and ultimately ceased the production of asbestos products. Nevertheless, the company was forced to pay claimants millions of dollars, resulting in the sale of major assets. A new CEO, Craig R. Smith, was hired in 1985 and he launched an aggressive campaign to fight litigation, going so far as to sue lawyers representing workers, pursuing civil fraud and racketeering charges. He engineered the 1986 creation of a holding company called Raytech Corporation to protect the company's non-asbestos assets, its wet clutch, transmission, and heavy-duty brake business. Raymark shareholders became Raytech shareholders, and Raymark became a subsidiary of Raytech. According to the *Wall Street Journal,* ''The idea was to free Raytech of its costly litigation. But Mr. Smith went a step further. In January 1988, Raytech spun off Raymark entirely to distance Raytech's non-asbestos-related corporate assets from the claimants. Raytech approached seven prospective purchasers. But perhaps not surprisingly, only one submitted a bid—Asbestos Litigation Management Corp., a subsidiary of Litigation Control, formed by Mr. Smith to manage Raymark's asbestos litigation.'' Although Smith maintained that the transaction was done at arm's length and the selling price represented fair-market value, critics charged that the bid was the lowest amount that could be considered a bona fide offer. The $1 million bid, in fact, called for just $50,000 in cash and a $950,000 balloon payment at the end of six years.

Filing for Chapter 11 Bankruptcy in 1989

Because of the judgments levied against it, Raymark was soon unable to pay its bills, which allowed plaintiffs' attorneys to force the company into Chapter 7 bankruptcy, thus permitting the sale of assets to pay off Raymark's creditors. Asbestos attorneys next turned their attention to Raytech, dismissed Smith's maneuvers as little more than a corporate shell game, and began listing Raytech as a co-defendant in asbestos cases. When it became obvious that the holding company strategy was not working, Raytech followed the lead of Johns-Manville and in 1989 filed for Chapter 11 bankruptcy protection, which allowed a company to shield its assets from creditors while attempting to reorganize. Smith explained at the time, ''Because of the number of actions being initiated against our company and because we have been unable to secure a decision on successor liability that is binding across all jurisdictions, we have no recourse but to turn to the federal bankruptcy court.''

Raytech operated under Chapter 11 protection for the entire decade of the 1990s. During that time, the company reorganized its structure and expanded on a number of fronts. In 1990 it acquired Allomatic Products Co., paying nearly $2 million for the OE friction, steel, and transmission filter manufacturer. In 1992 Raytech acquired the German firm of Ferodo Beral GmbH, which made clutch facings and industrial friction products. That same year, the company formed Raybestos Aftermarket Products company and set up shop in Crawfordsville, Indiana. In 1996 Raytech bought a stake in Advanced Friction Materials Company, a Michigan maker of bands for automatic transmissions. Two years later Raytech bought the remaining interest in the business, although the deal was complicated by the eventual discovery that AFM's longtime CFO had embezzled more than $3.33 million. In addition, during the 1990s, Raytech continued to extend its global reach, opening a plant in Liverpool, England, in 1998 to produce wet clutch products, and a factory in China to manufacture dry clutch facings.

While Raytech managed to operate during the 1990s it was never free of civil litigation stemming from asbestos claims. In addition, the company faced court actions from the Environmental Protection Agency and the Connecticut Attorney General's Office regarding the cleanup costs of a 33-acre site in Stratford, Connecticut, where Raybestos had manufactured friction products for 70 years, resulting in wastes that contained asbestos, lead, PCBs, and other hazardous substances. Raytech continued to maintain that it had no successor liability, litigating the matter for eight years until finally in October 1995 the U.S. Supreme Court rejected the argument, thus forcing the company to bow to reality and begin to negotiate with the parties suing it. In October 1998 Raytech reached a tentative agreement to resolve its legal difficulties, but it was not until April 2001 that the plan was finalized and Raytech was able to emerge from Chapter 11 protection. Under terms of the settlement, Raytech turned over 90 percent of its stock to trustees appointed by bankruptcy court, as well as to state and federal government entities, in order to satisfy $7.2 million in asbestos-related claims, plus future claims. Of that $7.2 billion, $6.76 billion involved personal injury claims and $432 million was connected to cleanup costs to federal and state governments. Raytech was now completely free to plot a future course of business, which management hoped would include even more international expansion, albeit the shareholders that it now served were primarily the victims of a previous administration's earlier policy.

Principal Subsidiaries

Allomatic Products Company; Raybestos Products Company; Raybestos Powertrain, Inc.; Raytech Automotive Components Company; Raytech Systems.

Principal Competitors

Amsted Industries Incorporated; Omni U.S.A., Inc.; Twin Disc, Incorporated.

Further Reading

Breskin, Ira, ''Raytech Finally Escapes Bankruptcy,'' *Daily Deal,* April 19, 2001.

Celebrating a Century . . . and Beyond, Shelton, Conn.: Raytech Corporation, 2002.

Johnson, Reg, ''Coming to Grips with a Legacy of Asbestos,'' *New York Times,* February 28, 1999, p. 14CN.

Mastandrea, John, ''Raytech Files Chapter 11 As Asbestos Suits Mount,'' *Fairfield County Business Journal,* March 20, 1989, p. 1.

Mitchell, Cynthia F., ''Ray Tech's Assets Shuffling Misses the Mark,'' *Wall Street Journal,* March 13, 1989, p. 1.

—Ed Dinger

Rogers Corporation

1 Technology Drive
Rogers, Connecticut 06263-0188
U.S.A.
Telephone: (860) 774-9605
Fax: (860) 779-5509
Web site: http://www.rogerscorporation.com

Public Company
Founded: 1832 as Rogers Paper Manufacturing Company
Employees: 1,251
Sales: $219.4 million (2002)
Stock Exchanges: New York
Ticker Symbol: ROG
NAIC: 322130 Paperboard Mills; 325211 Plastics Material and Resins Manufacturing; 335129 Other Lighting Equipment Manufacturing; 335932 Noncurrent-Carrying Wiring Devices; 334412 Bare Printed Circuit Board Manufacturing; 334413 Semiconductor and Related Device Manufacturing; 334417 Electronic Connector Manufacturing; 334418 Printed Circuit Assembly Manufacturing

Rogers Corporation was originally founded as a paper mill in 1832 and segued from insulated paperboard into a wide range of high performance materials spanning the marketplace. Rogers Corporation's specialized products—including high-frequency and flexible circuit materials, laminates, urethane foams, liquid crystalline polymers, busbars, and electroluminescent lighting—are used in the automotive, medical, communications, electrical, military, and retail markets. From footwear to gaskets, high-speed interconnects to shock absorbers, circuit boards to digital displays, Rogers makes it all faster, clearer, and more reliable.

Pushing Paper, 1832 to the 1930s

Dutch immigrant Peter Rogers founded the Rogers Paper Manufacturing Company in 1832. Settled in a former two-story powder mill in Manchester, Connecticut, the firm was moderately successful. In 1841 Peter died and his young son Henry took control of the business. Over the next few years Henry diversified the company through experimentation and imagination. He toyed with thicker paperboard, discovered a process for bleaching colored paper, and by 1852 had invented a way to recycle the vast amounts of wastepaper that accumulated around the mill.

Henry retired in 1890 and his two children, son Knight and daughter Gertrude, began running the thriving family business. Like their father before them, Knight and Gertrude were determined to broaden the company's product and customer base beyond selling paperboard to area textiles manufacturers. In 1900 as the textiles industry suffered a downturn, Rogers began insulating its paperboard for use in the burgeoning field of electricity and electrical power.

Rogers Paper Manufacturing Company was incorporated as a public company in 1927, in the state of Massachusetts. The family-owned and operated company had grown to sales of about $1 million annually, fueled by its insulated transformer paperboard. In the early 1930s, as the nation was in the grip of the Great Depression, Rogers was forced to look into new uses for its paper-based products and find as many markets as possible to sell its goods. In 1932 the company began working with Dr. Leo Baekeland, who researched resins and plastics. To provide space for new research and development (R&D) operations as well as its paperboard products, Rogers bought a manufacturing facility in Goodyear, Connecticut, from the Goodyear Tire and Rubber Company in 1936.

A Major Departure from Paper: 1940s–50s

By the 1940s Rogers Paper Manufacturing Company had been transformed: Knight Rogers had died and Gertrude had brought in outside executives and consultants to ensure the company's survival. Paperboard was no longer the firm's primary focus; chemical engineering and the versatile applications of polymeric materials had become the future of Rogers. To reflect this new direction, the company was rechristened the ''Rogers Corporation'' in 1945.

Rogers introduced its first ''Duroid'' product line in 1949. The Duroid products were made of fiber-reinforced polymers,

Company Perspectives:

You may not know our name, but whenever you reach for your cell phone, boot up your laptop, start your car, put on your shoes, open your mail, or even look at the watch on your wrist, we're there.

had many applications for electrical insulation, and led to the first of many patents and trademarked products. Rogers Corp.'s success prompted an unusual move in 1954, when the city of Goodyear, Connecticut, changed its name to Rogers, Connecticut. The area's residents, many of whom were employed by the Rogers manufacturing plant, approved of the town's name change.

In the later 1950s Rogers poured increasing amounts of funding into R&D, blending both organic and synthetic fibers with a variety of chemicals and polymers to produce insulating devices and circuitry for the electronics and automotive industries. In 1958 sales had grown to $5 million annually and Rogers reached a major milestone with its first international partnership, granting licensing rights for some of its molding materials to Vynckier N.V. of Ghent, Belgium. A second milestone—producing circuitry in 1959 needed in a new computer built by IBM—soon propelled Rogers into the forefront of the electronics market.

Circuit Boards Take Off: 1960s–70s

In 1960 Rogers was listed on the American Stock Exchange and total sales had risen to the $10 million level by 1963. Its innovations in circuit boards made the company popular with computer makers, while its old stalwart, insulation board, remained vital to the electrical power industry. A 35,000-square-foot addition was built onto the firm's plant in Connecticut in 1963 and three years later, the company bought a new manufacturing facility in Chandler, Arizona. Rogers also bought proprietary technology from Westinghouse Electric Corporation in 1966, which turned into a goldmine. Taking sophisticated circuitry formerly used by Westinghouse and tweaking it, Rogers developed flexible circuits and busbars which then distributed voltage to the circuit boards used in the surging computer and telecommunications markets.

In 1968 the company bought another plant in Connecticut and initiated plans for a new R&D laboratory. The following year, 1969, Rogers went international in a big way by establishing Mektron N.V., a subsidiary in Ghent, Belgium; entering a partnership with Japan's Nippon Oil Seal Industry Company, Ltd. to form Nippon Mekton, Ltd. to sell computer circuitry in Asia; south of the border in the United States, Rogers Mexicana was established in Agua Prieta, Mexico.

While Rogers had experienced record sales of $28 million at the end of the previous decade, the explosion of data processing in the 1970s took the company to new heights. Electronics applications accounted for nearly a third of Rogers' sales in 1970, while sales steadily climbed to $30 million by the end of 1971. Two years later, in 1973, sales had leapt to $43 million and Rogers had seven operational manufacturing plants in the United States, as well as those in Mexico, Japan, and Belgium. It was during the middle years of the decade that a high performance urethane material was developed. Eventually named and trademarked as ''Poron,'' this moldable foam material found its way into footwear as absorbent liners and soles for athletic shoes, ski boots, and skates, and later into sports equipment such as ski racing poles and knee and elbow pads. Poron's industrial applications were also in development and uses for the urethane's cushioning and shock absorption abilities quickly found their way into the transportation and printing industries.

By the end of the 1970s it was clear Rogers had found not one but several niche markets. To keep up with demand and the continuing evolution of its products, the manufacturing facilities in Connecticut, Arizona, and Mexico were all expanded, while two new facilities in Arizona and another in Château Gontier, France, were planned for the first years of the next decade.

The Electronics Revolution: 1980s–90s

Over two-thirds of Rogers Corp.'s business was from the electronics industry in the early 1980s as computers revolutionized the workplace and then homes. Soladyne Inc., a San Diego-based microwave circuit builder, was acquired in 1980, while a new licensing partner for Nippon Mekton was established in Germany, and a sales office was opened in Japan to service the growing Asian markets. A new joint venture in 1988 with 3M Corporation, the Durel Corporation, took Rogers into electroluminescent lighting for use in the dials and display illumination of watches, clocks, medical equipment, and sporting goods.

While the 1980s had been full of heady expansion and corporate raiding for many, the early 1990s brought sobering reminders of the cyclical nature of business. To concentrate more fully on its best performing operations, Rogers divested itself of three business segments from 1992 to 1994 and its Soladyne subsidiary in 1995. Overall sales at the midpoint of the decade had reached a phenomenal $173 million.

In 1996 Rogers acquired Bisco Products from Dow Corning Corporation and the following year opened another manufacturing plant in Ghent, Belgium. The company's growing line of products, which included flexible and high-frequency circuit boards (for computers, inkjet printers, phones, radar and missile guidance systems, and air traffic control), laminates (for disk drives, video recorders, game stations, cameras, telecom cables, automotive systems, and antennas), Poron urethane foams (shock absorbers for computers, appliances, cars, and trucks, as well as footwear, sports equipment, orthotics, and prosthetic limbs), and electroluminescence (digital display and lighting for keypads, pagers, watches, radios, medical equipment, and automotive dashboards) continued to be used in an ever increasing range of applications.

By 1997 Rogers was spending around $10 million in R&D annually, which led to higher performing products, increased sales, and further expansion. In addition to enlarging its facilities in Arizona, building another plant in Belgium, and opening a sales office in Taiwan, overall sales climbed from 1997's $220.9 million to $245.3 million for 1998. The company's full-

Key Dates:

1832: Peter Rogers founds a paper mill in Manchester, Connecticut.
1841: Henry Rogers takes over his father's business.
1852: Henry invents a process to recycle waste scraps at the paper mill.
1890: Henry retires and his son and daughter take over the company.
1900: The firm begins producing insulated paperboard.
1927: Rogers Paper Manufacturing Company goes public with sales of about $1 million annually.
1932: The firm begins experimenting with resins.
1945: The company is rechristened Rogers Corporation.
1949: ''Duroid'' fiber-reinforced polymer products are introduced.
1958: The firm initiates its first international joint venture with Vynckier N.V. of Ghent, Belgium.
1967: Mektron N.V., a new subsidiary, is established in Belgium.
1980: The firm opens a manufacturing plant in France.
1981: Rogers products are licensed to a new partner in West Germany.
1984: A sales office is opened in Japan.
1988: Rogers and 3M form a joint venture called Durel Corporation.
1998: A sales office in Taiwan is opened.
2000: Rogers is listed on the New York Stock Exchange and has a phenomenal year.
2002: Rogers Technologies Suzhou Company Ltd. is established in China.
2003: The firm buys the remaining interest of its joint venture with 3M Company.

time employee roster had also grown from 993 worldwide to 1,122 in 1998.

The end of the 20th century found Rogers experiencing record sales, hitting nearly $248 million, due in large part to the thriving wireless communications industry. Rogers Corp.'s high-frequency circuit board laminates ruled the telecommunications market, while Durel Corporation—the firm's joint venture with 3M—sustained record growth in the wireless boom. Poron, the company's versatile urethane material, debuted several new products for use in the footwear and electronics markets, while another joint venture, with Mitsui Chemicals Inc., was established in 1999 as Polymide Laminate Systems LLC. Rogers finished 1999 with total sales of $285 million, up 11 percent over the previous year's figures, and net income of nearly $19 million.

The New Millennium: 2000s

In the new millennium Rogers left the American Stock Exchange and was granted listing on the New York Stock Exchange under the ticker symbol ROG. Sales and profits had been growing steadily for several years and 2000 did not disappoint. Combined sales for the company's disparate segments climbed to an all-time high of $316.8 million with net income hitting $26.7 million for the year. In 2001 Rogers formed a joint venture with Chang Chun Plastics Company, Ltd., based in Taiwan, to produce flexible circuit boards for the booming Taiwanese market, and acquired the intellectual property and foam product lines of Cellect LLC to complement its growing High Performance Foams Division. Most significant during the year was the introduction of Rogers R/flex 3600, its liquid crystalline polymer laminate with a wide range of applications for the consumer and communications industries in disk drives, high speed interconnects, handheld electronics, and inkjet printers.

The events of September 11th and the nationwide recession took their toll on Rogers in late 2001. Stock had gone from a low of $23.90 per share in the second quarter of 2001 to a high of $35.80 in the fourth, but year-end sales fell significantly to $276.2 million from 2000's high of nearly $317 million. Net income was hard hit as well at $15.7 million versus the previous year's almost $27 million. Yet Rogers was no stranger to upheaval, having survived and then thrived in the post-Depression era by doing what it did best: adapting and diversifying. In this vein, 2002 found Rogers paring noncore operations and those which had not performed as expected. The Moldable Composites Division was sold while two new manufacturing plants were opened as part of Rogers Technologies Suzhou Company Ltd. in China. The company's international partnerships continued to pay off, with three of its four joint ventures experiencing record growth (the exception was its Taiwanese upstart, which had not garnered as much of the flexible laminates market as anticipated).

The firm's ups and downs were reflected in its stock prices by topping out at $35.80 (the same as 2001's high in the fourth quarter) in the second quarter, yet falling precipitously in the fourth to a low of $20.65 per share. Combined sales for 2002, however, climbed to $286.7 million while income rose slightly to $18.6 million despite international and domestic economic pressures.

In 2003 Rogers bought the remaining interest of Durel Corporation, its joint venture with 3M. Rogers also prepared for a changing of the guard after Chairman and CEO Walter Boomer, who had been with the firm since 1997, announced his retirement from the daily responsibilities of chief executive effective the spring of 2004. Robert Wachob, who had been with Rogers since 1984 and had been serving as president and COO, succeeded Boomer as CEO in April 2004.

Rogers Corporation in the 21st century was a vastly different company than its predecessor in the 19th century, but its core remained the same: developing and manufacturing innovative, high performance products with an eye to the future. For Rogers, the future included reaching the $1 billion mark in sales before 2010 and to continue to meet the evolving needs of the markets it served.

Principal Subsidiaries

Polymide Laminate Systems LLC; Rogers Chang Chun Technology Co., Ltd.; Rogers China, Inc; Rogers Inoac Corporation; Rogers Japan, Inc.; Rogers Korea, Inc; Rogers Southeast Asia, Inc.; Rogers Taiwan, Inc.; Rogers Technologies Co., Ltd.; Rogers Technologies Singapore, Inc.

Principal Operating Units

High Performance Foams; Printed Circuit Materials; Polymer Materials and Components.

Principal Competitors

Cookson Group PLC; E.I. DuPont; Park Electrochemical Corporation.

Further Reading

Arndt, Michael, ''From Desert Storm to Gasket Foam,'' *Business Week Online,* April 11, 2003.

Lustigmann, Alyssa, ''Poron Helps Cushion Impact of Sports,'' *Sporting Goods Business,* February 1994, p. 30.

Miller, William H., ''Textbook Turnaround,'' *Industry Week,* April 20, 1992, p. 11.

''Rogers Corp. Celebrates Opening of Office in Korea, Singapore,'' *AsiaPulse News,* November 10, 2000.

''Taiwan Joint Venture: Rogers, Chan Chung,'' *Electronic Materials Update,* August 2000.

''Take a Closer Look at R/bak Cushion Mounting Products,'' *Paper, Film & Foil Converter,* October 1999, p. 138.

Thames, Cindy, ''Materials Technology Keeps Rogers in Step,'' *Electronic Business,* January 15, 1985, p. 118.

Yannity, Kathleen, ''Rogers, Conn., Electronics Company Moves Toward $1 Billion in Sales,'' *Providence Journal,* May 26, 2002.

—Nelson Rhodes

Roto-Rooter, Inc.

2600 Chemed Center
255 East Fifth Street
Cincinnati, Ohio 45202-4726
U.S.A.
Telephone: (513) 762-6900
Fax: (513) 762-6919
Web site: http://www.rotorooterinc.com

Public Company
Incorporated: 1970 as Chemed Corporation
Employees: 3,000
Sales: $314.2 million (2002)
Stock Exchanges: New York
Ticker Symbol: RRR
NAIC: 235110 Plumbing, Heating, and Air-Conditioning Contractors; 811412 Appliance Repair and Maintenance

Roto-Rooter, Inc. ranks as the leading provider of plumbing and drain-cleaning services in North America. Through company-owned outlets, independent contractors, and franchisees, Roto-Rooter serves more than 90 percent of the U.S. population and about 55 percent of the population of Canada. Franchise operations have also been established in Australia, China, Indonesia, Japan, Mexico, the Philippines, and the United Kingdom. Roto-Rooter serves residential, business, and municipal customers. While about 80 percent of the corporation's revenues in 2002 were derived from the plumbing services operations, subsidiary Service America Systems, Inc. generated the remainder. Based in Deerfield Beach, Florida, Service America offers residential and commercial customers throughout Florida and in Phoenix, Arizona, appliance and heating/air conditioning repair, maintenance, and replacement services. In addition, Roto-Rooter, Inc. reached an agreement in late 2003 to take full ownership of VITAS Healthcare Corporation, a Miami-based provider of hospice care for terminally ill patients, operating in major metropolitan areas of eight states: California, Florida, Illinois, New Jersey, Ohio, Pennsylvania, Texas, and Wisconsin. With more than 5,700 employees and fiscal 2003 revenues of $420 million, VITAS is the largest hospice provider in the United States.

The Roto-Rooter, Inc. parent company was known as Chemed Corporation until May 2003. Chemed evolved out of W.R. Grace & Company's Specialty Products Group, gaining its independence in 1982. One of Chemed's operating units was the Roto-Rooter plumbing services company, which had been acquired in 1980. Chemed took Roto-Rooter public in 1985, retaining majority ownership, but then reacquired full ownership of the subsidiary 11 years later. Service America was created as a subsidiary of Roto-Rooter in the early 1990s. Other operations of Chemed were divested between 1986 and 2002, precipitating the parent company's name change.

From DuBois Soap Company to Chemed Corporation

Chemed Corporation's history dates back to the founding of the DuBois Soap Company. In June 1920 a confident and ambitious salesman named T.V. DuBois decided to open his own business. DuBois established the DuBois Soap Company in a rented building, a small, four-story structure in Cincinnati, Ohio, adjacent to the Ohio River. The fledgling operation made soap chips and powders for the city's growing restaurant trade. Within a few short years, the firm was selling its products all over the state. As revenues increased, additional employees were added to the payroll.

DuBois Soap Company survived the bleak years of the Great Depression in good financial condition. During the late 1930s and early 1940s the company expanded its restaurant dishwashing product line to encompass a whole range of different items, including industrial cleaning and maintenance products for other industries. Soon DuBois was servicing restaurants, steel companies, heavy manufacturing firms, and food processing plants. With the rapid expansion of its product line, the company decided to increase the amount of space for its administrative and manufacturing facilities in Cincinnati. By the end of World War II, the company was producing a huge variety of cleaning and maintenance products and had developed a reputation as one of the leaders in the specialty chemical industry.

During the late 1940s and throughout the 1950s, DuBois developed its sales network and expanded its manufacturing plants. Three new facilities were built in California, New Jersey, and Texas. As DuBois's revenues increased, the company

Company Perspectives:

Our goal is to be the premier provider of a variety of repair and maintenance services to both residential and commercial accounts. As always, we'll continue to listen to our customers and to expand our service offerings to meet and exceed their changing expectations.

came to the attention of W.R. Grace & Company, a large conglomerate with holdings in the chemical, manufacturing, retail, fertilizer, food products, and restaurant industries. In 1964 Grace acquired DuBois and incorporated the company into its Specialty Products Group, renaming the firm the DuBois Chemicals Division. In 1971 Grace management transformed its specialty chemicals group, which included the DuBois Chemicals Division, into the Chemed Corporation, which had been incorporated as a Grace subsidiary the previous year. DuBois Chemicals developed and manufactured professional cleaning and maintenance chemicals, dispensing equipment, and processing compounds. It served as the single largest area of operation within Chemed. While Grace maintained ownership of the majority of Chemed stock, the company was given autonomy to develop its own products. In July 1980 Chemed acquired Roto-Rooter Corp. for $23 million in cash and stock.

Depression-Era Founding of Roto-Rooter

Roto-Rooter was founded in 1935 by Samuel Oscar Blanc in West Des Moines, Iowa. Born in Wisconsin in 1883, Blanc had been forced to quit school in the fifth grade, when his father committed suicide. He traveled throughout the Pacific Northwest working as a lumberman and telephone linesman during the first decade of the 20th century, returning to Wisconsin in 1906 to marry. Blanc had taken a variety of sales jobs over the course of the ensuing two decades, but like so many other Americans in the Depression era, was limited to odd jobs by the early 1930s. Little did he know that a backed-up toilet would lead to a permanent career.

In 1934, Blanc's son, Milton, asked for help unclogging a sewer system blocked with potato peelings. Together they used a length of flexible metal cable to free the clog, prompting the father to seek ''a better way'' to do the job. Having taken correspondence courses in electrical and mechanical engineering, S.O. Blanc spent the next few months developing an electrically powered drain cleaner that featured a rotating steel coil with blades at one end to cut through virtually any blockage, even tree roots. Blanc knew he had a great idea on his hands; the alternative was to dig a trench along the pipes, find the clog, and clear it. Before the year was out, he had started advertising his service and applied for a patent on his device. Wife Lettie came up with the name that would become the company's most valuable asset: Roto-Rooter. The firm was incorporated in 1936, the same year Blanc registered his trademark.

The foundation of the company's nationwide franchise system was laid early in 1935, when C.W. Crawford wrote asking to ''rent'' a Roto-Rooter and start his own business. That first contract, for $400, bought an exclusive, four-county territory for ''the life of the patent,'' but the agreement was soon revised to five cents per sewer in a given region. Within two years of its first lease agreement, Roto-Rooter had licensed more than 100 territories from Florida to Washington, with a concentration in the Midwest. The central organization manufactured drain-cleaning machines and replacement parts and provided a minimal amount of technical and managerial support to licensees.

But franchising fees alone were not enough to support ongoing patent and trademark registration and defense of those intellectual properties. In 1936, Blanc set up a separate operation, Roto-Rooter Service Company, with an entirely new modus operandi. Instead of licensing territories, this business essentially employed individual independent contractors in New York City, Boston, Baltimore, and other East Coast cities. Headquartered in Iowa, the central organization supervised advertising (but little else) in exchange for a percentage of each contractor's receipts.

By 1938, when Blanc received a patent on his original design, company machinists had developed an industrial-sized drain cleaner called the Royal Street Sewer Cleaning Machine as well as a kitchen-sized model dubbed the ''Niard''—drain spelled backwards.

Advertising-Fueled Growth for Roto-Rooter: 1940s–50s

Blanc realized that the Roto-Rooter concept was terribly easy to reproduce. Although he continued to defend the physical design throughout the life of the patent, he began in the early 1940s to put more support behind the Roto-Rooter trademark through advertising in such nationally circulated publications as *Better Homes and Gardens.* Up to this point, the vast majority of advertising had been underwritten by individual operators.

Although World War II's raw material shortages stunted Roto-Rooter's expansion, postwar rural electrification and water works projects furnished seemingly endless growth potential. Eric Peterson, grandson of S.O. Blanc and author of a 1988 company history, characterized this period as ''a time of unimaginable prosperity.'' By the mid-1950s, Roto-Rooter had operations in virtually every city with more than 100,000 people. The company established its first international franchise, in Mexico City, in 1945, and shipped machines to Brazil in 1952. In spite of these early efforts, international operations remained negligible until the 1970s.

Roto-Rooter reached a critical juncture in 1955, when the patent on the original device expired and the company was reorganized around the Roto-Rooter trademark. The central organization decided at this time to charge a higher franchise fee based on the number of people served in a given region. In spite of the upheaval, the firm lost less than 10 percent of its 300 franchisees. Roto-Rooter followed up the reorganization with a new national advertising campaign featuring the ditty that would help establish the brand as the country's most recognizable sewer cleaning service. Recorded by Captain Stubby and the Buccaneers, the snappy jingle, ''Roto-Rooter, that's the name, and away go troubles down the drain,'' became one of U.S. advertising's most memorable and enduring tag lines.

Notwithstanding the outward appearance of success, several endemic problems began to manifest themselves during the 1960s. Perhaps the most fundamental of these was what Eric

Key Dates:

1920: T.V. DuBois establishes the DuBois Soap Company in Cincinnati, Ohio, to make soap chips and powders.
1935: Samuel Oscar Blanc launches a drain-cleaning service in West Des Moines, Iowa; franchising begins that same year.
1936: Blanc incorporates his company as Roto-Rooter, Inc.; Roto-Rooter Service Company is set up, operating through independent contractors.
Early 1940s: National print advertising of the Roto-Rooter brand begins.
1955: Following expiration of the patent on the original Roto-Rooter drain-cleaning device, the company reorganizes around the Roto-Rooter trademark; Roto-Rooter jingle makes its debut.
1964: W.R. Grace & Company acquires DuBois Soap, incorporates it into its Specialty Products Group, and renames the firm the DuBois Chemicals Division.
1970: Grace incorporates Chemed Corporation as a subsidiary; Henry Peterson, son-in-law of Blanc, takes charge of Roto-Rooter, revitalizing and modernizing the firm.
1971: Grace's Specialty Products Group is transformed into Chemed.
1980: Chemed acquires Roto-Rooter for $23 million; the latter relocates its headquarters to Cincinnati.
1981: Roto-Rooter expands into plumbing services for the first time.
1982: Chemed gains its independence from Grace; its stock trades on the New York Stock Exchange.
1985: Chemed takes Roto-Rooter public, retaining a majority stake in the company.
1991: As part of shift to focus on marketing and service-oriented businesses, DuBois Chemicals is sold to Molson Companies, Ltd. for $243 million.
1994: Roto-Rooter combines several businesses it had recently acquired in Florida and Arizona that offer residential customers annual maintenance contracts for heating and air conditioning systems and major appliances; they begin operating under the Service America trademark.
1996: Chemed reacquires full control of Roto-Rooter in a $102.1 million deal.
2003: Chemed changes its name to Roto-Rooter, Inc.; company signs agreement to purchase the 63 percent of Miami-based hospice-care provider VITAS Healthcare Corporation it does not already own.

Peterson called a "management vacuum"; Roto-Rooter's founding executives had never really provided much guidance to franchisees or expected much more than fees from them, and, by the 1960s, many top leaders were reaching retirement age. At the same time, a growing body of antitrust law endangered the company's loose franchise system, the threat of takeover loomed large, and corruption in some operations (especially those in the Service Co. segment) endangered Roto-Rooter's future.

When founder S.O. Blanc died in 1964, his son-in-law, Russell Young, was elected to succeed him. (Blanc's own son, Milton, had not been significantly involved in the company.) The change in leadership, however, did not necessarily herald new management practices. The company moved into a new West Des Moines headquarters and built a new factory, but little else about Roto-Rooter changed in the late 1960s.

Revitalization of Roto-Rooter in the 1970s

Roto-Rooter's corporate lethargy ended in 1970, when another of S.O. Blanc's sons-in-law, Henry Peterson, advanced from secretary to president. Unlike most of the company's aging executives, Peterson brought varied outside experience in law and banking to the business. He hired new managers, instituted modern inventory controls and production schedules, automated the company's antiquated manufacturing methods, and spurred new product introductions.

Peterson also began to investigate lagging returns from the Roto-Rooter Service Company, which had been presided over (but not closely supervised) by Russ Young since its inception. The subsequent examination uncovered an organization rife with corruption; individual contractors were not reporting their gross sales accurately, sometimes keeping 90 percent of their receipts instead of the 50 percent they were contractually allowed to retain. Peterson oversaw a reorganization of the Service Company, converting it from a contractor basis to a more traditional service company with regional managers and local employees. At some point, he also changed the affiliated firm's name to Nurotoco Inc. ("new roto co"). The cleanup helped quintuple Nurotoco's profits within seven years and make it Roto-Rooter's primary revenue generator. In the meantime, the number of traditional franchisees had nearly doubled from 425 in 1969 to more than 700 by 1979.

Chemed's 1980 Acquisition of Roto-Rooter

Peterson had snatched Roto-Rooter from imminent decline, and by the end of the 1970s he was ready to retire. But no one in the next generation of the Blanc family had shown interest in accepting the mantle of leadership. Peterson had actually begun researching the sale of the company in 1975, but was impeded by litigation and reorganization concerns from concentrating on the issue. In 1980 Peterson was able to negotiate a $23 million cash/stock deal with Chemed Corporation.

Chemed moved Roto-Rooter's headquarters from West Des Moines to Cincinnati and imposed modern standards of franchise management on the corporate system. A revised franchise contract proposed by newly appointed President and CEO William Griffin opened franchisee books to corporate review, reserved right of first refusal for Roto-Rooter, and prohibited interfranchise competition. New across-the-board standards included 24-hour service, employee training in customer service, uniforms, and logo-emblazoned vehicles. Chemed also began to buy back licenses in the largest metropolitan areas, transforming them into employer–employee operations much like those of the East Coast's Nurotoco. By the end of the 1980s, Roto-Rooter, Inc. had purchased 39 such territories. Despite initial resistance from operators, these changes brought a higher level of standardization to the organization, benefiting the parent company, the franchisees, and their customers.

Chemed made a private placement of 15 percent of Roto-Rooter's stock in 1984 and raised $12.5 million in an initial public offering of another 23 percent stake the following year. The proceeds of these sales were used to expand Roto-Rooter's roster of services through internal growth as well as acquisition. Roto-Rooter had made its first reach into plumbing services in 1981; by mid-decade this sideline was contributing about 10 percent of annual sales. Chemed also expanded the subsidiary's industrial and municipal drain-cleaning services. But an initial venture into heating, ventilation, and air conditioning (HVAC) was not as successful. Roto-Rooter acquired Apollo Heating & Air Conditioning Inc., an Ohio service company, in 1986, but when the division did not pan out, it was sold to its management team.

Roto-Rooter experienced phenomenal growth under the guidance of its new parent. Sales multiplied from a mere $4.7 million in 1980 to $66.8 million by 1989, and net income grew to more than $5.5 million.

Independence for Chemed and Further Acquisitions: 1980s

The management of Chemed, meantime, armed with the thriving DuBois and Roto-Rooter businesses, decided to buy the remainder of W.R. Grace's 16.7 million shares of Chemed stock. This transaction, completed in March 1982, allowed Chemed to become a totally autonomous, independent corporation; its stock was listed on the New York Stock Exchange. Edward L. Hutton continued to serve as CEO of Chemed, having engineered the purchase of DuBois for Grace back in the early 1960s.

In October 1983 Chemed acquired National Sanitary Supply Company. Founded in 1929, National developed in much the same manner as DuBois. The company offered a variety of chemical products used to clean and maintain industrial, commercial, and institutional facilities. Goods produced by National over the years included floor finishes, trash liners, mops, buckets, brushes, paper and packaging products, and cleaning chemicals and equipment. By the time the company was purchased by Chemed, National had become the largest distributor of sanitary maintenance supplies in the United States. Just as it had with Roto-Rooter, Chemed took National public in 1986, retaining a controlling majority stake.

Even as Chemed developed into a successful independent organization, DuBois remained the cornerstone of its operations. Throughout the 1980s, Chemed grew as DuBois grew. DuBois manufactured and marketed hundreds of specialty chemical products—including paint strippers, cutting fluids, specialty lubricants, sanitation chemicals, and water treatment chemicals—for use as industrial cleaning and maintenance compounds. The company sold its product line to customers in a number of diverse industries. Public utilities, mining organizations, airlines, meat packers, breweries, dairy plants, railroads, metal finishers, publishing companies, hospitals, and retail establishments all purchased materials from DuBois. In the mid-1980s the company expanded its services to include laundry and linen supplies and uniform rentals. During this time DuBois expanded its product line to major overseas markets. By the end of the 1980s, the company had opened offices in Australia, England, France, Germany, Holland, Japan, Mexico, Saudi Arabia, Singapore, South Africa, Sweden, and Venezuela.

Chemed also established several new businesses during the 1980s. In 1981 Chemed established Omnicare, Inc., a company designed to supply pharmacy management services and distribute dental and medical supplies. Omnicare was divided into two operating divisions, the Sequoia Pharmacy Group and the Veratex Group. Sequoia provided services for more than 200 nursing homes, and by 1990 it represented over 20 percent of Omnicare revenues. The Veratex Group, a supplier of medical and dental products, grew even more rapidly. By 1990 the Veratex Group ranked third in the U.S. dressings and sponge market on the strength of its sales of over 800 different kinds of proprietary disposable paper, gauze, and cotton products to professionals working in the veterinary, medical, and dental fields.

National Sanitary Supply Company and Roto-Rooter also helped Chemed increase its revenues during the 1980s. By the early 1990s, National reported over 150,000 standing accounts across the country, with 22 distribution centers in 14 states. The performance of Roto-Rooter was even better. In 1990, a year when revenues from the company's plumbing services increased 26 percent, the firm introduced a revolutionary drain and sewer cleaning product that broke down organic waste by biological means and converted it into water and harmless carbon dioxide. Roto-Rooter also made significant inroads toward expanding its base of operations through a franchising agreement that allowed the company to distribute products in Japan.

Shifting Focus to Marketing and Service-Oriented Businesses: 1990s

In the early 1990s, management at Chemed decided to concentrate on marketing and service-oriented businesses, rather than capital or production-intensive manufacturing. Although DuBois was the largest revenue and profit-generating division within Chemed, with sales of $275 million in 1990 and 2,800 employees, management thought it best to sell its flagship operation in order to refocus the company's priorities. As a result, DuBois was sold for $243 million to Molson Companies, Ltd., the largest brewery in Canada and the sixth leading beer maker in the United States. Molson immediately combined DuBois with its Diversey Corporation subsidiary.

Chemed implemented a comprehensive restructuring program with the money garnered from the sale of DuBois. The revenue was immediately reinvested in the company's growing healthcare business. Chemed sold off Omnicare as well, but retained its highly profitable Veratex Group. Sales for Veratex amounted to over $95 million in 1994, but growing competition within the industry and significant changes in the healthcare industry forced the Veratex Group to reduce its workforce and cut operating expenses.

Money from the sale of DuBois was also funneled into the appliance repair service interests of Roto-Rooter. From 1991 to

1993, Roto-Rooter acquired three businesses in Florida and Arizona that offered residential customers annual maintenance contracts for many major repairs, ranging from heating and air conditioning systems to major appliances and plumbing. These operations were combined in 1994 under the Service America trademark.

Roto-Rooter's growth strategy in the early 1990s for its plumbing-related services included expansion of its customer base to include restaurants and motels. Roto-Rooter increased its overseas operations as well. Entering the mid-1990s the company was an industry leader in Canada and operated 17 franchises in Japan. In 1994 the company expanded the number of its service technicians by 15 percent. All this activity contributed to greater revenues for Roto-Rooter. From 1993 to 1994, the company reported a 20 percent growth in plumbing revenues. But Roto-Rooter enjoyed steady growth for a number of years. From 1984 to 1994, for instance, revenues exploded from $28.2 million to $171.9 million. By 1994, meantime, Roto-Rooter had purchased 80 of its largest franchisees. The company still had 550 independent franchisees, but these businesses contributed only $6 million of the 1994 revenues.

In January 1994 Chemed acquired Patient Care, Inc. for about $20.6 million. Founded in 1974 to provide comprehensive home-healthcare services in the New York, New Jersey, and Connecticut areas, Patient Care had a workforce that included more than 4,500 nurses, home healthcare aides, speech therapists, physical therapists, occupational therapists, medical social workers, nutritionists, and other healthcare workers. Regarded by many as one of the anticipated solutions to the ever increasing costs of in-patient health services, the $20 billion homecare industry had grown rapidly in the early 1990s. Mindful that the homecare market was extremely fragmented, Patient Care claimed that its own comprehensive line of healthcare services offered better resources and was more cost-effective than smaller home health agencies.

Continuing its shift to services, Chemed in July 1995 sold its Veratex Retail division, which sold medical products by mail order and through catalogs, to Henry Schein, Inc. The Veratex Group itself, renamed the Omnia Group, was then sold to Banta Corporation in September 1997 for $50 million in cash and $2.3 million in deferred payments. That same month, Chemed sold its majority-owned subsidiary National Sanitary Supply to Unisource Worldwide, Inc. for $138.3 million. These divestments left Chemed with three main units: Roto-Rooter, Patient Care, and Service America Systems, Inc. Another result was a large drop in revenues for Chemed, from $683.8 million in 1996 to $341.7 million in 1997.

In the meantime, Chemed in mid-1995 made an offer to buy the 42 percent of Roto-Rooter it did not already own. But the offer, which involved the swapping of Roto-Rooter stock for that of Chemed, valuing the former at $35 per share, was rejected as inadequate by a special committee of the Roto-Rooter board. Chemed abandoned this bid, only to return the following year with a tender offer of $41 in cash per share. This bid succeeded, with Chemed reacquiring full control of Roto-Rooter in September 1996 for a total price of about $102.1 million.

During the late 1990s all three of Chemed's units grew through acquisitions. For example, Patient Care acquired a number of home healthcare firms, including ones located in Stratford, Connecticut; Columbus, Ohio; Washington, D.C.; and Chicago. The bulk of the purchases, however, were made to grow the Roto-Rooter business. Franchisees continued to be bought out, and the company beefed up the plumbing-repair side of its business through acquisitions. Although Roto-Rooter's market share in the highly fragmented U.S. plumbing-repair industry was only around 2 percent—compared to about 17 percent in the much smaller drain-cleaning sector—plumbing repair by the late 1990s accounted for about 40 percent of Roto-Rooter's revenues. The plumbing business was growing smartly, its revenues jumping 20 percent per year.

Roto-Rooter at the Fore, Early 2000s and Beyond

Edward Hutton had led Chemed through its many transformations, and he finally gave up the CEO post in May 2001 at the age of 82. He remained deeply involved in the business, however, as company chairman. Kevin J. McNamara, who had served as company president since August 1994, was named president and CEO. It was McNamara, then, who oversaw the final steps in the transformation of Chemed from a conglomerate to a company focused on service businesses, principally Roto-Rooter. In October 2002 Chemed sold Patient Care to an investor group for about $70 million. As part of an overall restructuring, Service America exited from the Tucson, Arizona, market, making Phoenix its only place of business outside of Florida. The restructuring involved Roto-Rooter as well. Roto-Rooter pulled back on its move into the plumbing sector, getting rid of its non–Roto-Rooter-branded plumbing operations as well as its underperforming HVAC businesses. Plumbing services would continue to be offered through the Roto-Rooter brand operations. Chemed also stepped up efforts to buy out more Roto-Rooter franchisees. This restructuring followed a poor showing for Chemed in 2001, when sales were hurt by the economic downturn. The company reported a net loss of $10.4 million on revenues of $477.1 million.

Thanks to the divestments, revenues fell further in 2002, settling in at $314.2 million. Fully 80 percent of that figure was attributable to Roto-Rooter. During 2002 Roto-Rooter diversified by launching a branded line of drain-care products through more than 3,500 retail outlets, including grocery stores and the three main U.S. discounters, Wal-Mart Stores, Inc., Target Corporation, and Kmart Corporation. The products were not expected to provide huge revenues for the company, but were rather envisioned as advertising conduits for the Roto-Rooter brand; proceeds from the sales were to be earmarked for advertising and marketing the plumbing and drain-cleaning services of Roto-Rooter.

In May 2003 Chemed seemed to have settled on a future course as primarily a plumbing and drain-cleaning company when shareholders approved the change of the firm's name to Roto-Rooter, Inc. It came as somewhat of a surprise, then, when Roto-Rooter announced in December 2003 that it had signed an agreement to take over Miami-based VITAS Healthcare Corporation, operator of 25 hospice programs for terminally ill patients in eight states. VITAS had been founded in 1978 as the single-site Hospice of Miami and had subsequently expanded beyond Florida as Hospice Care, Inc. Chemed made its first investment in the hospice company in 1991, eventually owning a 37 percent stake in the firm, which adopted the VITAS name in 1992. By its fiscal year ending in September 2003, VITAS had more than 5,700 professionals caring for more than 7,900 terminally ill patients on a daily basis; the firm recorded revenues of $420 million. Roto-Rooter offered to pay about $410 million in cash to acquire the 63 percent of the privately owned VITAS it did not already own. Roto-Rooter officials said that a public offering of VITAS stock was ''very likely'' following the acquisition, which was expected to close by March 2004. As this latest twist in the convoluted history of Chemed/Roto-Rooter unfolded, it was certain to be interesting to see how long the company's latest foray into the healthcare field lasted.

Principal Subsidiaries

Roto-Rooter Canada, Ltd.; Roto-Rooter Corporation; Roto-Rooter Management Company; Roto-Rooter Services Company; R.R. UK, Inc.; Service America Systems, Inc.

Principal Competitors

The ServiceMaster Company; UNICCO Service Company; Lennox International Inc.

Further Reading

Bastian, Lisa, and Jeffrey Waddle, ''Corporate Profiles,'' *Cincinnati: City of Charm,* 1992, pp. 308-09.

Bounds, Wendy, ''Chemed Renews Bid to Buy Rest of Roto-Rooter,'' *Wall Street Journal,* August 9, 1996, p. B5.

——, ''It's Not That Simple Taking the Plunge to Buy Roto-Rooter: Surprisingly Independent, Two Outside Directors Block Parent Company's Plans,'' *Wall Street Journal,* August 23, 1995, p. A1.

Curtis, Richard, ''Roto-Rooter Digs into Plumbing,'' *Cincinnati Business Courier,* January 5, 1998.

Daly, Brenon, ''Roto-Rooter Grows Hospice Holdings,'' *Daily Deal,* December 22, 2003.

Driehaus, Bob, ''Course Clear for Chemed's New CEO,'' *Cincinnati Post,* May 22, 2001, p. 6B.

Frazier, Mya, ''Small-Cap Chemed Gets Little Attention from Tech-Crazy Wall Street,'' *Cincinnati Business Courier,* September 18, 2000.

Jaffe, Thomas, ''Two for the Stocking,'' *Forbes,* January 11, 1988, p. 266.

Labate, John, ''Companies to Watch: Roto-Rooter,'' *Fortune,* June 27, 1994, p. 103.

Larkin, Patrick, ''Down the Drain? Not Roto-Rooter: Plumbing Firm Awash in Growth,'' *Cincinnati Post,* April 15, 1998, p. 6B.

——, ''Roto-Rooter Jingle Returns to Television,'' *Cincinnati Post,* February 5, 1998, p. 6C.

——, ''Sanitary Supplier Sold: Pennsylvania Firm Acquires Chemed Subsidiary,'' *Cincinnati Post,* August 11, 1997, p. 7B.

Mader, Robert P., ''Roto-Rooter Quietly Continues Own Consolidation Program,'' *Contractor,* September 1998, p. 10.

Monk, Dan, ''Roto-Rooter: A Local Board in Transition,'' *Cincinnati Business Courier,* August 25, 2003.

Paton, Huntley, ''Roto-Rooter Sells Apollo to Management Group,'' *Cincinnati Business Courier,* March 13, 1989, p. 11.

Peterson, Eric Gregory, *Roto-Rooter, 1935–1988,* Michigan State University: M.A. Thesis, 1988.

Phalon, Richard, ''Roto-Rooter's New Drill,'' *Forbes,* December 11, 1989, p. 176.

''Roto-Rooter Continues Growth As Residential Service Giant,'' *Contractor,* April 1995, p. 8.

''Roto-Rooter to Sell Non-Branded Contractors,'' *Contractor,* January 2002, p. 5.

Sekhri, Rajiv, ''Roto-Rooter Growth Spurred by Acquisition Binge,'' *Cincinnati Business Courier,* July 23, 1999, p. 29.

Sword, Doug, ''Roto-Rooter Plumbing Services to Boost '86 Sales,'' *Cincinnati Business Courier,* August 18, 1986, p. 1.

Weinstein, Marc, ''Roto-Rooter Stock Flying High,'' *Cincinnati Business Courier,* June 24, 1985, p. 1.

Wood, Roy, ''Chemed to Revamp Businesses in 2002,'' *Cincinnati Post,* December 4, 2001, p. 6C.

—Thomas Derdak and April Dougal Gasbarre
—update: David E. Salamie

Sauer-Danfoss Inc.

250 Parkway Drive, Suite 270
Lincolnshire, Illinois 60069
U.S.A.
Telephone: (512) 239-6000
Fax: (515) 239-6318
Web site: http://www.sauer-danfoss.com

Public Company
Incorporated: 1986 as Sundstrand Venture Company
Employees: 7,207
Sales: $952.3 million (2002)
Stock Exchanges: New York
Ticker Symbol: SHS
NAIC: 336399 All Other Motor Vehicle Parts Manufacturing

With its headquarters located in Lincolnshire, Illinois, Sauer-Danfoss Inc. is a global leader in the manufacture of components and integrated hydraulic systems used in agricultural, construction, material handling, turf care, and road building equipment. Customers are original equipment manufacturers (OEMs), who rely on Sauer-Danfoss products to supply the necessary hydraulics to propel their equipment, transmitting power from the vehicle's engine to the wheels or tracks; to transmit power from the vehicle's engine to perform a work function; to provide an electronic control function that makes equipment much easier to use; or to supply an integrated system to govern a vehicle's propel and control function, as well as such functions as fuel management, cooling, braking, and steering. Sauer-Danfoss offers seven product lines. Hydrostatic transmissions propel a range of vehicles, from low- and medium-powered vehicles such as aerial lifts, skid steer loaders, and industrial forklift trucks, to high-powered vehicles such as combines, rollers, and forestry machinery. Open circuit products, which include gear units and axial piston pumps, perform the work function on forklifts, trucks, tractors, and road rollers. The company's orbital motors are low-speed hydraulic motors designed for moderate to heavy loads. Sauer-Danfoss also offers three categories of valves: proportional valves, directional control valves, and hydraulic integrated circuit and cartridge valves. The company offers a wide range of steering solutions for vehicles of all sizes, whether it be a normal steering wheel, a joystick, or an automatic steering mechanism controlled by sensor. Sauer-Danfoss's mobile electronic components and systems products provide advanced control systems for off-road as well as on-highway vehicles. Finally, Sauer-Danfoss's electric drives meet a wide range of needs in the forklift truck industry. Employing more than 7,000 people, Sauer-Danfoss operates 21 factories in North America, Europe, and East Asia.

Forming the Company As a Result of 1986 Joint Venture

Sauer-Danfoss was originally incorporated in Delaware in September 1986 as Sundstrand Venture Company, a joint venture between Sundstrand Corporation of Rockford, Illinois, and Sauer Getriebe AG, based in Neumuenster, West Germany. The two firms combined their hydraulic power transmission businesses, operating as Sundstrand-Sauer in the United States and Sauer-Sundstrand in Europe.

Of the two partners, Sundstrand boasted the longer history. The oldest entity connected to the company was the Rockford Tool Company, founded in 1905 in Rockford, Illinois, a community then composed predominantly of Swedish immigrants. The company focused on woodworking tools including the carving chuck and belt sander. Four years later another company, the Rockford Milling Machine Company, set up shop in the same building. It was owned by Oscar Sundstrand and his brother-in-law Edwin Cedarleaf. In 1914 Oscar's brother and an employee of the company, David Sundstrand, invented the ten-key adding machine, the first to adopt the modern arrangement of three rows of keys plus zero at the bottom. The adding machine proved to be so successful that the brothers formed a subsidiary, the Sundstrand Adding Machine Company, in 1919 to handle the business. Rockford Milling Machine and Rockford Tool Company decided in 1926 that it was in the best interests of both parties to merge, resulting in the Sundstrand Machine Tool Company. A year later the company sold the rights of the adding machine, which it could not properly market, to Underwood-Elliot Fisher Co., a typewriter and office equipment manufacturer. Sundstrand Machine Tool would now

Company Perspectives:

We offer our customers optimum solutions for their needs and develop new products and solutions in close cooperation and partnership with them.

begin to diversify into areas to which it was more suited, such as the hydraulic component business that would one day lead to the creation of Sauer-Danfoss.

During the early 1930s Sundstrand began to experiment with hydraulic tools to produce its implements, superseding its traditional handcrafted approach, which was becoming unsuited to meet the exact tolerances required in contemporary precision machine tools. Soon, all of the company's hand-cranked machinery was replaced with hydraulic devices. Sundstrand also began to produce hydraulic products, such as hydraulic pumps, fluid motors, and hydraulic transmission systems. During World War II, Sundstrand became heavily involved in aviation and the company began to apply hydraulics to aviation engineering. Sundstrand was so successful with its aviation business, supplying a variety of systems and components to commercial and military aircraft manufacturers, that it formed an aviation division that took on an increasing level of importance. To better reflect the diversity of its interests, in 1959 Sundstrand Machine Tool shortened its name to Sundstrand Corporation. Then in 1962 the company organized itself into two divisions, Industrial Products and Aerospace.

Sundstrand's Hydraulics division made great strides in the early 1960s by applying CSD technology to off-highway equipment. To better commercialize the technology, the Hydraulics and Aerospace divisions joined forces to develop yet another division, Hydro-Transmission. In 1965 Sundstrand began to supply hydrostatic transmission components to automakers. Over the next 20 years Sundstrand continued to broaden its interests and by the middle of the 1980s was generating close to $1.3 billion in annual revenues, of which just 37 percent came from industrial markets.

Founding a German Business Component in 1967

The other partner of Sauer-Danfoss, Sauer Getriebe, was founded by Dr. Klaus Murmann in 1967 and became a licensee of Sundstrand hydrostatic transmissions technology. Born in West Germany, Murmann was educated in the United States, earning an undergraduate degree from Dickinson College and later studying at Harvard Law School. He ultimately received a law degree from the University of Kiel. In 1960 he joined the family business, Sauer Group, where he gained seasoning before striking out on his own with Sauer Getriebe. With the formation of the joint venture with Sundstrand, he was named its chairman and chief executive officer, while Sundstrand's Michael J. Draper became president and chief operating officer. They presided over a company with 12 manufacturing facilities located around the world, whose combined revenues totaled in the $200 million range.

Sundstrand's involvement in the joint venture, however, was brief. Because the business failed to meet management's goals, in March 1989 Sundstrand agreed to sell its half-share to Murmann for a reported $70 million. (The Murmann family owned a 72 percent stake of Sauer Getriebe, which controlled the other half-share.) As a result, Murmann owned about 80 percent of the company. The holding company, Sundstrand Venture Company, then changed its name to Sauer, Inc. in early 1990. Also in 1990 the company made plans for an initial public offering (IPO) of four million shares of common stock, one million of which were to be offered in the United States by American underwriters and the balance to be sold in Germany through German underwriters. Due to poor conditions in world financial markets, however, Murmann decided to postpone the IPO.

Several years would pass before Murmann was ready to again attempt to take Sauer public. For five years the company enjoyed annual growth in the 12 percent to 13 percent range, so that in 1997 Sauer topped $535 million in revenues and recorded a net profit of more than $27 million. To further expand the business, and pay down some debt, Murmann looked in 1998 to tap the equity market to raise the necessary capital. To that point the company had completed a number of small acquisitions only but was interested in growing more aggressively via external means. In addition, Murmann expressed a desire to go public in order to use stock, in the form of options, as an incentive in recruiting and retaining employees. Completed in May 1998, the offering, headed by Credit Suisse First Boston, netted $48.1 million.

The price of Sauer's stock quickly dipped, due to a number of difficult business conditions. The agriculture market, accounting for a fifth of all sales, entered a difficult period, and some foreign markets also suffered—in particular Europe, which contributed about 40 percent of the company's sales. On the positive side, the company had been successful in increasing its production capacity by some 25 percent in 1997 and 1998, and also made inroads in penetrating Asian and Latin American markets. But difficult economic conditions began to be reflected on the balance sheet. Sauer only grew at a 5 percent rate in 1998, with revenues rising to $564.5 million after the company posted sales of $535.2 million in 1997. Net income also fell from $27.1 million to $26.3 million.

Even more difficult conditions were to follow in 1999. Most notably, the U.S. agriculture market continued to be mired in a slump. Sauer did, however, enjoy significant gains in construction, specialty vehicles, and the turf care market in Europe. It also invested more than $57 million in 1999 in technology, new customer programs, manufacturing efficiency, and other improvements. Also of note in 1999 was the opening of a new manufacturing plant in Lawrence, Kansas, which added $120 million of production capacity. But the financial results for the year were clearly disappointing. Net sales were off by 5.3 percent over the previous year, totaling $534.4 million, and net income fell to $18.1 million. Nevertheless, there were promising signs in 1999 that pointed to better days ahead.

Sauer-Danfoss Merger: 2000

Some acquisitions initiated in 1999 came to fruition in 2000 and would prove to have a dramatic impact on the bottom line. In January 2000 Sauer completed the $5 million acquisition of Custom Design Electronics of Sweden AB and its subsidiary

Key Dates:

1926: Sundstrand Machine Tool Company is formed.
1967: Sauer Getriebe AG is formed.
1986: Sundstrand and Sauer pool their hydraulic interests in a joint venture.
1990: Sauer buys out Sundstrand.
2000: A merger with Danfoss Fluid Power A/S results in Sauer-Danfoss Inc.

NOB Electronik AB, makers of electronic control systems, displays, and related software. But a far more significant transaction would be completed in May 2000 when Sauer acquired Danfoss Fluid Power A/S from the Denmark-based Danfoss A/S in a stock swap worth $80 million that was in effect a merger of equals. It was also part of a consolidation trend that resulted in a fourth global, full-line supplier of mobile hydraulics products. Danfoss's expertise in steering and work function products nicely complemented Sauer's propel and control functions, thereby establishing the combined company as a single-source supplier, which an increasing number of customers were seeking in order to concentrate on vehicle design rather than the development of subsystems and components.

Danfoss was founded by engineer Mads Clausen in 1933 to make automatic valves for refrigeration plants. The company diversified into a wide range of products, including hydraulics and control systems. In 1998 the Mobile Hydraulics Division was spun off as a separate company, Danfoss Fluid Power. Following the merger with Sauer Inc. the resulting entity, maintaining the Sauer corporate entity, changed its name to Sauer-Danfoss Inc. Murrmann was tabbed to serve as chairman and Sauer's David Pfeifle took over as chief executive officer. Danfoss CEO Jorgen Clausen became vice-chairman and Danfoss's Erik Hansen was named chief operating officer. Within a matter of months, however, Pfeifle would be forced to step down due to coronary artery bypass surgery necessitated by the discovery of obstruction in his major arteries. Murmann once again assumed the CEO position until Pfeifle recovered.

In December 2000 Sauer-Danfoss completed a small acquisition, paying $2.3 million for Integrated Control Technologies, a U.K.-based company that produced electronic controls and related software for mobile hydraulics. Along with the purchase of Custom Design Electronics earlier in the year, Sauer-Danfoss had greatly bolstered its European electrohydraulic operations. In addition, following the Danfoss merger, the company took steps to reorganize sales and marketing operations and to establish a training program in order to help the sales force to better understand all that the combined company now had to offer to its customers. Sauer-Danfoss also was able to realize some savings by consolidating plants, sales offices, and administrative offices. As a result of acquisitions and other organizational changes in 2000, Sauer-Danfoss saw revenues grow from $534.4 million in 1999 to more than $782.5 million, and net income improve from $18.1 million to slightly less than $27 million.

Sauer-Danfoss adopted a growth strategy that was based on two-thirds internal and one-third external, through acquisitions and joint ventures. Moreover, a major aspect of Sauer-Danfoss's acquisition strategy was as much geographic as product-related, in order to have applications resources available on a regional basis. In 2001 the company completed several key transactions. Early in the year it bought Compact Controls, Inc., located in Oregon, for $36 million in cash. CCI produced cartridge valve and hydraulic integrated circuit manifolds and bolstered Sauer-Danfoss's position in valves. Another addition in 2001 was the Italian company Italdigit s.r.l., maker of electronic controls and wiring harnesses, a deal that strengthened Sauer-Danfoss's ability to offer innovative technology for machine control systems. The acquisition of Dantal Hydraulics in India and Hidrover Valvulas S.A. in Brazil offered greater geographic reach, as did joint ventures established in Japan and China. Despite difficult world economic conditions, Sauer-Danfoss emerged in a strong position, although the results for the year proved to be disappointing. While revenues improved to nearly $855.3 million, net income declined to $7.6 million.

Working against the backdrop of a troubled worldwide economy, Sauer-Danfoss enjoyed a successful 2002 on a number of levels. It continued to manage its costs and enhanced productivity while also growing the business through strategic acquisitions. With revenues growing to more than $952 million in 2002, and net income rebounding to slightly less than $14 million, Sauer-Danfoss was positioned to become a $1 billion company. It would also have to carry on without its longtime leader on a daily basis, Klaus Murmann, who at the age of 71 retired from day-to-day involvement with the company, although he retained the chairmanship.

Principal Subsidiaries

Hydro-Gear, Inc.; TSD Integrated Controls, Inc.; Danfoss Fluid Power AB; Integrated Control Technologies Ltd.

Principal Competitors

Eaton Corporation; Parker Hannifin Corporation; Robert Bosch Corporation.

Further Reading

Brezonick, Mike, "All Part of the Plan," *Diesel Progress North American Edition,* March 1, 2002, p. 42.

Fagan, Mark, "Iowa-Based Hydraulic-System Maker Sauer to Merge with Denmark-Based Danfoss," *Journal-World,* September 16, 1999.

Osenga, Mike, "Thus Consolidation: Sauer & Danfoss to Join Forces," *Diesel Progress North American Edition,* October 1999, p. 16.

"Tales of an IPO," *Business Record,* May 17, 1999.

—Ed Dinger

Schieffelin & Somerset Co.

2 Park Avenue, Floor 17
New York, New York 10016-5701
U.S.A.
Telephone: (212) 251-8200
Fax: (212) 251-8382
Web site: http://www.schieffelin.com

Wholly Owned Subsidiary of Diageo PLC and LVMH Inc.
Incorporated: 1987
Employees: 225
NAIC: 422820 Wine and Distilled Alcoholic Beverage Wholesalers

Operating out of New York City, Schieffelin & Somerset Co. (S&S) is a major American importer of premium wines and spirits, maintaining regional centers in California, Florida, Georgia, Illinois, Massachusetts, New Jersey, and Texas. The S&S portfolio includes such prestigious brands as Hennessy, Dom Perignon, Moët & Chandon, Chandon Estates, Tanqueray, Johnnie Walker, Grand Marnier, J&B, Pinch, Buchanan's, The Classic Malts, Rufino, and Casa Lapostolle. The company is co-owned by Diageo PLC and Moët Hennessy Louis Vuitton (LVMH). S&S is one of the United States' five oldest continuously operating companies.

Tracing Company Roots Back to Colonial America

Although the Somerset portion of S&S is only 40 years old, the Schieffelin side dates back to the foundation of the United States to a man named Jacob Schieffelin, who if given the choice would not have had the republic come into existence at all. Schieffelin was born in 1857, the son of a German immigrant who settled in Philadelphia in 1745. During the Revolutionary War he remained loyal to the Crown of England and served in the loyalist army. Captured in 1779 he was imprisoned in Virginia before escaping to New York—which was held by the British—and then following the English army to Canada. In Montreal he became a merchant and importer, and after the war he returned to the States, settling in New York, where in 1894 he bought out the business of a brother-in-law, Effingham Lawrence, who had been a New York drug merchant since 1781. Schieffelin then took into partnership another brother-in-law, John B. Lawrence, and established Lawrence & Schieffelin, the distant ancestor to today's Schieffelin & Somerset. The pharmaceutical business that Schieffelin entered was in its infancy. At the time, pharmacists had no standing, and most physicians mixed their own medicines and even rolled their own pills. Lawrence & Schieffelin served as a wholesaler to druggist's shops, which did little more than supply raw materials to physicians, and also sold items such as varnish, paint ingredients, and glass. The first college of pharmacy was founded in 1821 in Philadelphia, and it was not until this period that the line between retail and wholesale druggists became blurred, as prescriptions began to be filled by trained pharmacists.

Located on Pearl Street in lower Manhattan, Lawrence & Schieffelin not only bought, sold, and imported drugs and medicines, it also traded fancy goods, perfumes, and other merchandise. Schieffelin dominated the company and was instrumental in the firm becoming involved in lucrative, yet risky, shipping ventures. His first such investment in 1795 netted a princely sum of $25,000. A few years later, as Napoleon entered the world stage and France and England were trying to deny the other's trade with the United States, the shipping business became highly dangerous. Some of Schieffelin's ships were captured, prompting Lawrence in 1799 to strike out on his own, leaving the firm to change its name to Lawrence Schieffelin. In 1805, it would become Jacob Schieffelin & Son when Henry Hamilton Schieffelin was taken into partnership. (The younger Schieffelin was a graduate of Columbia College in 1801 and then studied law with a prominent New York attorney. By all accounts he was something of a renaissance man, versed in most of the arts and sciences, regarded as a ''living encyclopedia.'') Again, Schieffelin did not limit his activities to drugs and medicines. Old newspaper advertisements indicate that the firm dealt in ''Muscovado sugars,'' ''coffee in hogsheads,'' cotton from Guadaloupe, ''double refined saltpeter,'' brimstone, and even gunpowder. The elder Schieffelin remained the head of the business through the War of 1812. Despite the loss of two ships, one seized by the French in Amsterdam and another by the English in the West Indies, the firm was able to carry on. In

Company Perspectives:

We are a passionate high performance team that thrives on challenges, drives innovation, develops the potential of our employees and maximizes the value of our brands. We respect and value every employee, encourage diversity, understand our consumers and partner with our owners and customers. We are committed to an environment that supports our core values and celebrates success. Our journey for excellence is ongoing as we become the benchmark by which all organizations are measured.

1814 Schieffelin retired (he died in 1835) and son Henry took over the business, which for the next 35 years would be called H.H. Schieffelin & Co.

The first task that Henry Hamilton Schieffelin faced in assuming leadership of the family business was to overcome the effects of a long war, which had a devastating impact on the economy of the young nation. As business conditions improved so did the firm's fortunes. The company moved from Pearl Street to larger accommodations on Maiden Lane. The panic of 1837 did little to hinder growth. In fact, in 1841 the firm moved to an even more spacious property located on John Street. In 1848 the company grew via acquisition, purchasing the stock and adding the business of Hoadley, Phelps & Co. A year later Henry Hamilton Schieffelin retired, leaving four sons—Samuel Bradhurst, Sidney Augustus, James Lawrence, and Bradhurt Schieffelin—to take control of the firm, which was now called Schieffelin Brothers & Co.

Of the four, Samuel was the dominant partner and chiefly responsible for the firm's growth during the next phase of its history. In 1854 a six-story building was constructed to house the business, an expansion that also allowed the opening of a department devoted to druggists' sundries and shop wares such as mortars, percolators, and pill machines—a major area of growth for the company for the next several decades. As had been the case from the start, however, Schieffelin was nimble enough to take advantage of opportunities that arose outside of pharmaceuticals. With the discovery of petroleum in Pennsylvania, the firm established an office in Titusville, Pennsylvania, and became the first company to ship petroleum into New York City for sale. The ability to adapt to conditions was of vital importance during the Civil War, 1861–65, when the conflict suddenly severed Schieffelin's ties to major customers in the South, many of whom had outstanding accounts that would never be paid. Nevertheless, the company was able to find new sources of income that more than made up for lost business.

Following the war, the four Schieffelin brothers retired from active participation in the company, which in 1865 was once again renamed, becoming W.H. Schieffelin & Co. Lead partner was William H. Schieffelin, son of Samuel B. Schieffelin. Other partners, nonfamily members, included William A. Gellatly, Joseph H. Westerfield, and William N. Clark. The company grew through acquisition in 1875 by purchasing A.B. Sands & Co. In 1882, Schieffelin spurred organic growth by establishing one of the finest laboratories of its kind in the United States. By the end of the 1800s, the company had sales offices located in Chicago and San Francisco, and served Europe through its operations in London, England. It also forged an important alliance with The Farbenfabriken (the Bayer Company), acting as the German drugmaker's representative in the United States.

Prohibition Leading to Shift Away from Pharmaceuticals

Schieffelin entered the 20th century as a leading pharmaceutical wholesaler. In 1906 it became the first company in the United States to file proofs of purity to federal regulators, receiving Guaranty Number One. But soon, because of Prohibition, Schieffelin's business would switch from pharmaceuticals to alcohol, albeit at first it was alcohol intended for medicinal purposes. The drive for a legal ban on alcohol grew out of the religious revivals that swept the United States in the 1820s and 1830s. Although local temperance laws were enacted, it was not until the 1900s that the drive for national prohibition gained momentum, leading to the 1917 ratification of a constitutional amendment to outlaw spirits, and the passage in 1919 of the National Prohibition Act, better known as the Volstead Act, to provide enforcement. In truth, the enforcement effort was dependent on local views regarding prohibition, so that in many areas authorities turned a blind eye to the sale and consumption of spirits. The new laws did succeed, however, in making spirits more difficult to acquire, leading to bootleggers and rum runners, who either manufactured their own beverages, sometimes in a bathtub according to popular accounts, or by smuggling through the United States' porous borders. Another way to procure spirits was the result of a loophole in the law that allowed alcohol to be purchased for medicinal purposes. As was to be expected, the number of prescriptions written for medicinal alcohol soared. Two of the most prescribed ''curatives'' were Hennessy Cognac and Moët & Chandon Champagne, both of which Schieffelin & Co., as the business was now called, imported. It was in this way that the 125-year-old drug wholesaler developed a thriving new wine and spirit business.

Bringing Schieffelin and Somerset Together in 1987 Joint Venture

The Volstead Act was repealed in 1933, ending Prohibition, but Schieffelin continued to deal in alcoholic beverages. The business grew so profitable that in 1962 the company elected to close its Pharmaceutical division in favor of becoming a pure-play wine and spirit distributor. Over the next 25 years the beer, wine, and liquor industry went through a period of intense consolidation, with storied brands changing hands and being combined together. In 1971 Moët & Chandon merged with Jas. Hennessy & Co, forming Moët-Hennessy. Then, in 1980, Moët-Hennessy acquired Schieffelin. Seven years later, in 1987, Moët-Hennessy reached an agreement to merge Schieffelin with Somerset Importers Ltd., owned by Guinness Plc, in a joint venture that brought together more than 20 premium wine and spirit brands.

Guinness had roots even deeper than those of Schieffelin, dating back to 1749 when Arthur Guinness opened a Dublin brewery. Somerset was established in 1963 as Somerset Distillers Ltd., the result of Canada Dry Corporation consolidating its Wine & Spirits Division. In 1984 Distillers Company Ltd., the

Key Dates:

1794: The predecessor to Schieffelin & Co. is established as a drug distributor.
1920: Prohibition begins, taking Schieffelin into the medicinal alcohol business.
1962: Schieffelin closes its Pharmaceutical division.
1963: Canada Dry Corporation forms Somerset Distillers.
1980: Moët-Hennessy acquires Schieffelin.
1986: Guinness acquires Somerset.
1987: Moët-Hennessy and Guinness create Schieffelin & Somerset as a joint venture.
1997: Guinness merges with Grand Metropolitan PLC, creating Diageo PLC.

world's leading Scotch whisky company, acquired Somerset, and two years later Guinness acquired Distillers. This transaction, however, led to a major scandal, the largest in the financial history of the United Kingdom. It involved acts taken by Guinness to illegally inflate the price of its stock to fend off a competing offer from Argyll Group, including the charge that Guinness bought its own stock during the offering period and indemnified other companies against loss if they purchased stock on behalf of Guinness. In the end, the chief executive of Guinness, Ernest Saunders, went to jail, and he was replaced in March 1987 by Anthony Tennant. He brought sweeping changes to Guinness, selling off peripheral assets and reorganizing the company's core businesses. One of these moves was to transfer its distribution assets, in the form of Schieffelin, to a partnership with Moët-Hennessy's Somerset.

Many of the brands that became part of the S&S portfolio also boasted a rich heritage. Dom Perignon was named for a 17th-century, blind, French monk, who developed an exceptional sense of taste and smell, which was instrumental in his rise as a wine expert. J&B Scotch Whiskies dated back to the firm of Johnson and Justerini, established to sell Scotch whiskey in 1769. In 1830 it became Justerini & Brooks after Alfred Brooks bought the business. Oban, one of the six whiskies that comprise Classic Malts of Scotland, dated back to 1794. Johnnie Walker was established in Kilmarnock, Scotland, in 1817. Tanqueray got its start in 1825 when Charles Tanqueray created his recipe for gin. In 1898 Tanqueray merged with Alexander Gordon & Co., which dated back to 1759 when Alexander Gordon launched a London gin business. Grand Marnier cognac dated back to France, 1827. The Ruffino winery was established in Italy in 1877. James Buchanan founded Buchanan's line of whiskies in 1884; and Pinch was established by John Aloysius Haig, who first offered his Pinch Blended Scotch Whisky in 1888.

S&S added Dewar's, Pinch, and The Classic Malts in 1992. In 1994 it became the exclusive agent for Grand Marnier. Dewar's was divested in 1997, and in that same year Buchanan's and J&B was added to the S&S portfolio. As they were introduced, newer products, such as Grand Marnier's Casa Lapostolle, were marketed as well. S&S endured some difficult times during the early years of the joint venture, due in large part to a drop in liquor sales throughout the 1980s. But in the 1990s, the company enjoyed notable successes, which included making Johnnie Walker Black Label the top-selling Super Premium Scotch whiskey in the United States, and establishing Moët & Chandon Nectar Imperial as the third best-selling champagne.

S&S managed to prosper despite changes to its corporate parents. Shortly after S&S was founded in 1987, Moët-Hennessy merged with Louis Vuitton to create LVMH, which soon became controlled by well-known French entrepreneur Bernard Arnault. He then proceeded to transform LVNH into an empire of luxury brands that became a dominant force in the fashion industry. But when Guinness decided to merge with Grand Metropolitan PLC in 1997, resulting in the creation of Diageo PLC, according to *Business Week,* "LVMH execs were not pleased. LVMH actively tried to block the deal, claiming it would negatively affect its joint venture with Guinness. Meanwhile, despite the bitter arguments between its parents across the Atlantic, the American joint venture was doing just fine, thank you. 'It is a good example of a joint venture network that has had the ability to ride out tension and conflict between parent companies,' says Kenneth Mildwaters, the former general counsel of Guinness' parent, Diageo PLC. Mildwaters says the reason the venture succeeded is that senior management stayed loyal to the joint venture, not to either Guinness or LVMH."

There was some concern in the summer of 2002 that Diageo, in the words of the *Financial Times,* "might break up Schieffelin & Somerset—possibly seeking to buy LVMH's Hennessy cognac in the process—rather than deepen the joint venture." Instead, Diageo decided to combine "the distribution of its brands, which includes Smirnoff vodka, with more upmarket drinks such as Dom Perignon champagne and Hennessy cognac, following an agreement with LVMH of France." In addition, Diageo announced that "it had teamed up with Schieffelin & Somerset to appoint one joint distributor in each of several key states." For the time being, at least, the corporate parents of S&S appeared to be committed to maintaining the joint venture.

Principal Competitors

Brown-Forman Corporation; Allied Domecq PLC; Remy Amerique, Inc.

Further Reading

Faith, Nicholas, "The Importance of Succeeding Ernest," *Business,* February 1988, p. 64.
Jones, Adam, "Diageo in Move to Reorganize US Distribution," *Financial Times,* July 30, 2002, p. 19.
One Hundred Years of Business Life, 1794–1894, New York: W.H. Schieffelin & Co., 1894.
Over 200 Years of Growth, New York: Schieffelin & Somerset Co., 2002.

—Ed Dinger

Signet Group PLC

Zenith House, The Hyde
London
NW9 6EW
United Kingdom
Telephone: +44 870 9090 301
Fax: +44 20 8242 8588
Web site: http://www.signetgroupplc.com

Public Company
Incorporated: 1949 as Ratners
Employees: 14,160
Sales: $2.73 billion (2003)
Stock Exchanges: London NASDAQ
Ticker Symbols: SIG; SIGY
NAIC: 448310 Jewelry Stores

Signet Group PLC is the world's leading retail jewelry specialist. The London-based company operates more than 1,600 stores in the United States and England, under the names H. Samuel, Ernest Jones, and Leslie Davis in the United Kingdom, and under the Kay and Jared names in the United States. Some 70 percent of the company's sales come from Signet's more than 1,000 U.S. stores, operated through the company's Ohio-based subsidiary, Sterling Inc.. The mall-based Kay Jewelers store chain is the group's U.S. flagship, although its self-standing Jared superstore format is its fastest growing. The company also operates a number of regional store chains in the United States, including JB Robinson and Marks & Morgan. In the United Kingdom, where the company was known as Ratners until the early 1990s, Signet's H. Samuel chain is the country's leading retail jeweler, and the Ernest Jones format, which specializes in diamonds and watches, is number two. Signet's shares are listed on both the London and NASDAQ stock exchanges. The company is led by Chairman James McAdam and CEO Terry Burman.

Building a National Jeweler in the 1940s

Leslie Ratner opened up a jewelry shop in Richmond, Surrey, England, in 1949. Ratner, later joined by son Gerald, began to expand the business, opening new branches and launching a manufacturing wing, Jadales. That operation permitted the company to produce its own branded watch line, Carronade. By the beginning of the 1970s, Ratners, as the chain was called, boasted 45 shops and sales of more than £2 million.

Ratners expanded strongly through the 1970s, and by the end of that decade the chain had grown to more than 150 stores. In 1975, Ratners made its first attempt to go international, entering the highly fragmented Dutch market. The company's expansion into the 1980s had come in large part through organic growth; in the early 1980s, however, as Ratners made a push to become a national chain, the company launched a series of acquisitions. The first of these came in 1984, with the purchase of Terry's (Jewelers) Ltd., with 26 shops based in England's southeast region.

Gerald Ratner took over the business from his father in 1985. By then, Ratners had been losing money, in part because of its expansion moves, but also because of increasing competitive pressure, particularly from a new breed of discount jewelers that had been encroaching on the company's traditionally middle to low-end market. In response, the younger Ratner moved to expand the group's offering of mid-priced jewelry, while developing an unabashed low-price advertising campaign. In 1986, Ratners sold off its Jadales manufacturing subsidiary and shut down its money-losing Netherlands stores.

Gerald Ratner then set out to build the Ratners group into one of the world's largest jewelry specialists. With less than 200 shops of its own, Ratners targeted the larger H. Samuel Plc, then the United Kingdom's largest jeweler with some 350 stores. H. Samuel was also one of the oldest jewelers in the country, with operations dating back to the early 19th century.

Ratners then began expanding its two flagship chains, Ratners and H. Samuel, opening 35 new stores in 1987, and another 50 or so the following year. Yet the company remained focused on external growth. In 1987, the group made an offer for Combined English Stores Group (CES), but was outbid by retail group Next Plc. Instead, the group picked up Ernest Jones (Jewelers) Plc, which, with 61 stores, gave Ratners an entry into the middle to high-end bracket.

Yet Ratners had already taken an even bigger step. Despite the company's failure to penetrate The Netherlands' jewelry market, it held onto its interest in foreign expansion. In 1987,

Company Perspectives:

Signet—One business, two markets. Signet Group is the world's largest speciality retail jeweler and operates in the US and UK.

the company found a new acquisition opportunity, in the form of Sterling Inc., based in Ohio, then the fourth largest specialty jeweler in the United States. That company operated nearly 120 stores, Sterling Jewelers, Shaw's Jewelers, Hudson-Goodman, and Friedlander. These stores were located mostly in the midwestern regions, although the Sterling empire stretched from coast to coast as well.

International Powerhouse in the 1980s

The United States now became Ratners' primary growth market. Soon after the Sterling acquisition, the company picked up another major jewelry group, The Westhall Company, also based in Ohio, boosting the company's U.S. holdings to more than 150 stores. Next up was another Ohio-based company, Osterman's Inc., which added 56 retail stores in ten states, helping to strengthen Sterling's geographic mix. That purchase cost the company $60 million, raising the company's U.S. total to more than 275 stores. Plans for new store openings through the end of 1988, meanwhile, were to increase the company's U.S. operation to a total of 312 stores.

Back at home, Ratners made a number of significant growth moves as well. In 1988, the company acquired Time (Jersey) Ltd., giving it 16 jewelry shops and an additional six accessories shops in Jersey, complementing the group's existing four Channel Island stores.

Ratners' U.K. expansion took off in 1988, with the purchases of the 130-store Zales chain, 73 stores operating under the Collingwood and Weir names, and Salisbury's Handbags Limited. These stores had all been part of CES, and acquired by Next, which sold them to Ratners for £135 million, as well as the repayment of nearly £16 million in debt. While the company maintained the Zales store chain, the Collingwood and Weir stores were converted to the group's H. Samuel and Ratners store formats. The addition of the Salisbury's chain meanwhile allowed the group to branch out into handbags, costume jewelry, and related accessories. During the 1980s, also, the company picked up another retailer, Watches of Switzerland. By the end of 1988, Ratners' U.K. holdings had topped 650 stores, and total group sales topped £360 million ($684 million).

The company's focus returned to the United States in 1989, when the company paid £39 million for the acquisition of Seattle's Westfield Inc. That purchase gave the company 87 new stores in nine states, including seven markets that were new to Ratners. Combined with the group's new store openings, Ratner's U.S. division topped 400 stores by the end of 1989—a figure that neared 500 stores by the middle of the next year.

Yet the company was now poised to take a leading position among the world's specialty jewelry retailers. In 1990, the company agreed to acquire Kay Jewelers Inc., one of the largest in the United States with nearly 500 stores—including 426 primarily East Coast-located Kay stores and 82 stores in the regionally operating JB Robinson chain—as well as 48 Marcus department store boutiques. Following the Kay acquisition, Ratners' U.S. store portfolio neared 1,000, making that market the company's largest for the first time.

Stumbling Through the 1990s

In just five years, Gerald Ratner had succeeded in expanding the company founded by his father into one of the world's largest jewelry retailers. Expansion came at a cost, however, and the company entered the 1990s heavily in debt—and ran headlong into an international recession. If the company's low- and mid-priced focus at first appeared to weather the initial drop in the jewelry market, it finally stumbled, in large part because of an unfortunate joke made by Ratner.

Speaking before an audience at the Institute of Directors, Ratner had been discussing the company's pricing policies. He singled out a low-priced decanter and glasses set, labeling the products as ''total crap,'' and going on to claim that even a prawn sandwich would outlast a pair of earrings carried at the company's store. Ratner went on, judging another popular product, an imitation book, as being ''in the worst possible taste.'' Ratner's comments, which might have been shrugged off in a better economic climate, raised a furor among British consumers. Almost overnight, the company's stock plummeted, losing some £500 million in value. Ratners' irate shareholders called for Gerald Ratner's head. He was forced to step down from the chairman seat, at first taking the CEO position before being ousted altogether by the end of 1992 from the company his father had founded.

Following Ratner's departure, the company changed its name, to Signet Group, and converted the Ratners store chain to the H. Samuel and Ernest Jones format. Signet was now faced with rebuilding consumer confidence, a task made all the more difficult because of the persistence of the economic slump in the United Kingdom. The company's new chairman set out to restructure the company, which had suffered from a loose organizational and logistics structure during Ratner's tenure.

The company sold off Watches of Switzerland in 1992, which was followed by the sale of the Salisbury's chain in 1994. The company also exited the Channel Islands, selling its stores there to the Asprey Group, which also had acquired Watches of Switzerland. In the meantime, Signet began slashing its retail portfolio in the United Kingdom—shutting down nearly 300 stores by the end of 1994.

The company's difficulties continued into the mid-1990s, when it faced a shareholder revolt in 1995. The company's preference shareholders, who had not received a dividend since the beginning of the decade, tried to force the company to break itself up, selling off its U.K. holdings in order to focus on its more profitable U.S. division. The company resisted this effort, winning the shareholder revolt. Nonetheless, by 1996, Signet had begun entertaining offers to buy out the U.K. branch—including interest from Gerald Ratner. Unable to find a suitable price, however, the company decided ultimately to retain control of its slimmed-down U.K. operations.

As Signet worked to dig out from the mountain of debt brought on by the group's 1980s expansion, it faced a renewed

Key Dates:

1949: Leslie Ratner opens a jewelry shop in Richmond, Surrey, England, then expands into jewelry manufacturing with subsidiary Jadales.
1975: Ratners enters the retail jewelry market in The Netherlands.
1984: Ratners acquires 26 Terry's jewelry stores.
1985: Gerald Ratner takes over the business and sells off the Jadales and Netherlands operations.
1986: The company acquires the H. Samuel jewelry store chain, then the largest in the United Kingdom.
1987: The company acquires the Ernest Jones jewelry store chain, entering the mid- to high-priced category; the company acquires Sterling and Westhall, both based in Ohio, entering the United States market.
1988: The company acquires Ostermans jewelry chain, Time (Jersey) Ltd., Zales Jewelry Ltd. (U.K.), Salisbury's, and 73 additional U.K. stores from Next.
1989: The company acquires Weisfeld's, based in Seattle.
1990: The company acquires Kay Jewelers, based in Virginia, boosting its U.S. retail operation to nearly 1,000 stores.
1992: Gerald Ratner is forced to step down from the company after making a joke about the company's products.
1993: The company name is changed to Signet Group, most Ratners stores are converted to H. Samuel signage, and the company begins restructuring, including the sale of a number of operations and the closing of some 300 stores (including all remaining Ratners stores).
1996: Signet announces its intention of selling off its U.K. holdings, but drops the plan.
1998: The Jared superstore format, originally debuted in 1993, is relaunched.
2000: After returning to profitability in 1999, Signet makes its first acquisition in ten years, buying U.S.-based Marks & Morgan.
2003: The Jared superstore format is acknowledged as the company's primary growth operation, with plans to increase the chain to 200 stores and $1 billion in sales in the early 2000s.

attempt to break up the company in 1997, as shareholders resisted the company's plans for restructuring of its capital.

Revitalized for a New Century

Signet at last returned to profitability in 1999. By then, the company's U.S. division had a new and fast-growing format: the Jared jewelry ''superstore.'' Originally launched in 1993, the superstore format took shape in the mid-1990s. The larger, self-standing stores—the company's Kay and other stores were typically located in shopping malls—featured much larger sales space and inventory, as much as five times the size of the group's other stores, as well as onsite jewelers offering jewelry repair services, and other amenities, such as children's play areas, making it a destination for wealthier jewelry shoppers.

By the end of 1999, the company had opened some 20 Jared stores—with plans to expand the chain to as many as 200 stores in the new century. The Jared format now became the company's fastest-growing segment, and Terry Burman, named as group CEO in 2000, expected the chain to be worth some $1 billion in sales.

Signet's return to health was confirmed by its first acquisition in nearly a decade, when it paid more than $161 million to acquire Marks & Morgan Jewelers Inc., the ninth largest specialty retailer in the United States with a strong presence in the southeastern region. Signet then decided to convert a little more than half of the 137-store Marks & Morgan chain to the Kay retail brand.

The Jared chain continued to grow strongly into the 2000s. By the end of 2003, the chain had grown to 70 superstores—yet already represented some 25 percent of the group's total U.S. sales surface. Helped by the growth of the superstore format, but also by strong profits at its U.K. branches, Signet once again sparkled as a leader in the world retail jewelry market.

Principal Subsidiaries

Ernest Jones Limited; H. Samuel Limited; Leslie Davis Limited; Signet Trading Limited; Sterling Inc. (U.S.A.); Signet Holdings Limited; Signet US Holdings, Inc. (U.S.A.); Checkbury Limited.

Principal Competitors

Kroger Co.; Fred Meyer Inc.; Kmart Fashions; Douglas Holding AG; Zale Corporation; Gold Meister GmbH; Tiffany and Co.; Don Quijote Company Ltd.; Nice de Mexico S.A. de C.V.; Finlay Enterprises Inc.

Further Reading

Bawden, Tom, ''Sparkling Sales for Signet,'' *Times* (London, England), February 7, 2003, p. 39.
Finch, Julia, ''Signet Saviour Makes Room for New Blood,'' *Guardian,* March 29, 2000, p. 29.
Patten, Sally, ''Signet Squires US Jewelers for $160m,'' *Times* (London, England), June 2, 2000, p. 33.
Urry, Maggie, ''Signet Enters New Century with Renewed Sparkle,'' *Financial Times,* December 29, 1999, p. 16.
Walsh, Fiona, ''Diamonds Put in the Spark As Signet's Tills Ring,'' *Evening Standard,* January 8, 2004, p. 35.

—M.L. Cohen

Solvay S.A.

Rue du Prince Albert, 33
B-1050 Brussels
Belgium
Telephone: (02) 509 6111
Fax: (02) 509 6617
Web site: http://www.solvay.com

Public Company
Incorporated: 1967 as Solvay & Cie S.A.
Employees: 30,302
Sales: EUR 7.92 billion ($8.30 billion) (2002)
Stock Exchanges: Euronext Brussels
Ticker Symbol: SOL
NAIC: 325181 Alkalies and Chlorine Manufacturing; 325188 All Other Basic Inorganic Chemical Manufacturing; 325199 All Other Basic Organic Chemical Manufacturing; 325211 Plastics Material and Resin Manufacturing; 325412 Pharmaceutical Preparation Manufacturing

The wide ranging activities of the Belgium chemical firm Solvay S.A. center on four areas: commodity and specialty chemicals, plastics, processed plastic products, and pharmaceuticals. Chemicals account for about one-third of the company's revenues. Solvay is among the world leaders in several commodity chemicals, including soda ash, hydrogen peroxide, persalts, barium and strontium carbonate, and caustic soda, as well as such specialty chemicals as fluorochemicals. In plastics, which account for about one-quarter of overall sales, Solvay produces fluorinated polymers and elastomers, as well as vinyls. About 19 percent of revenues come from plastic processing, including automobile fuel and air intake systems, various films, and swimming pool linings. Solvay's pharmaceutical operations, generating about a quarter of revenues, are relatively small on a global scale, ranking about 37th among the world players in the early 2000s. Drug development efforts focus on four main therapeutic fields: gastroenterology, hormone treatments, cardiology, and mental health. Solvay operates in 50 countries; more than 95 percent of its revenues are generated outside of Belgium, with 45 percent originating outside of the European Union.

Although Solvay was not incorporated as a public company until 1967, its roots go back to the 1860s and the discovery by its founder, Ernest Solvay, of a new industrial process for producing soda ash, an essential element in glassmaking. Under his guidance and that of four generations of Solvays, the firm became one of the largest in Belgium, combining chemical innovation with social projects and cultural programs. Although they are no longer involved in the direct management, members of the Solvay family continue to have a substantial ownership interest in the company through a 26 percent stake held by Solvac S.A., a publicly traded Belgian holding company controlled by the family.

Foundations in Soda Ash: Late 1800s

The foundations of Solvay were laid by Ernest Solvay, who was born in 1838, the son of a quarry master from Rebecq-Rognon, Belgium. In the early 1860s Solvay devised a process for the manufacture of artificial soda ash. At the time, the method in use was that discovered by the French chemist Nicolas Leblanc in 1789. Leblanc's method, while valuable as an industrial process, had serious drawbacks, most prominently its production of large amounts of alkali wastes. Although this fact called for alternative methods, none were available. In 1861 Solvay filed a patent for a method that involved the reaction of ammonium bicarbonate and salt, the product being heated to yield sodium carbonate, or soda ash. Despite his enthusiasm, his ''discovery'' met with indifferent or negative response on virtually all sides.

On the advice of an attorney, Solvay consulted patent records, only to find that the process was not original after all. It had in fact been proposed half a century earlier, in 1811, by the French physicist Augustin Fresnel. Large-scale implementation of the process, however, was made difficult by the volatility of ammonia. Over the course of those 50 years, many chemists had attempted to devise a way to make the procedure industrially viable. All had met with failure. The propositions of the young Solvay, therefore, were seen as little more than the repetition of old mistakes. While a few encouraged him, most chemists looked with disfavor on his efforts.

Company Perspectives:

Our Mission. Building on our scientific, technical and commercial expertise, we responsibly provide innovative products and services related to chemistry and human health to create ever-increasing value to our customers, shareholders and employees. Our Vision. Solvay is an independent and ethical global industrial group with a balanced portfolio of sustainable profitable and growing businesses under careful environmental management: Amongst the world leaders in selected markets and products, either alone or with sound complementary business partners. Valued by its customers as a highly competent, reliable and competitive solution provider. With a clear, motivating organization, developing and empowering people and teams through rewarding and challenging jobs. Acting as a good corporate citizen, caring for the health, safety and environment of its employees and of the community at large.

The ammonia-soda process may never have achieved its influence had Solvay been inclined to admit defeat. His character, however, had been marked since youth by intense curiosity about scientific questions and by dedicated application to whatever problem was at hand. Although illness had cut short his formal studies, he had maintained this deep-set curiosity and educated himself. The small encouragement he received, added to this dedication, was enough for him to continue his research. Not only would his process eliminate the problem of waste, but he believed that it could drastically lower the price of soda ash, reducing it by three-quarters or more.

In order to continue the work, he and his brother Alfred formed Solvay & Cie in 1863, and embarked on the difficult route to finding a workable procedure. The perfection of the process on a large scale was far more difficult than its invention had been; the setbacks faced by the young firm were enough to drive it to the brink of bankruptcy by late 1865. With their family's help and support, the brothers decided to try one last time. This time, they were successful, producing large amounts of soda ash. The key to their system and Solvay's greatest single achievement was the Solvay carbonating tower, which permitted the important but problematic reaction of carbon dioxide and ammoniacal brine to take place effectively and safely. By 1869, with the implementation of this invention, the Solvays were confident that they would become a strong presence in the market for artificial soda ash.

Having worked out the procedure, Solvay & Cie faced another difficult problem, that is, persuading others that the method was viable. The very novelty of the technique rendered it unfavorable in many eyes, and for a long while Solvay faced intense competition from adherents to the Leblanc process. Even this competition, however, had its benefits; one of its side effects was a reduction in the price of sulfuric acid, employed to treat phosphates for use in agriculture. The end result of this was increased productivity from crops treated with these products, in turn lowering the price of such staples as bread.

Agricultural benefits aside, Ernest Solvay weathered many difficult years attempting to establish his method in the industry. Eventually, however, as it became clear that the Solvay method produced soda ash at a lower cost than the Leblanc process, it became more and more widely accepted. By the turn of the century, Solvay-method production had risen from 300 tons per year in the 1860s to 900,000 tons per year, at a price around three times lower than it had been before Solvay entered the field.

The Solvay method permitted the clean production of inexpensive soda ash, with Ernest Solvay holding patents on all key phases of the process. The market share that this was to give to the company, however, was not enough for him. Ernest knew that no firm could survive by resting on one past achievement, therefore he encouraged diversification into other related areas. Most notable among these, in this phase of the company's history, was the production of chlorine and caustic soda by electrolysis. As early as 1886, Solvay wanted to proceed in the direction of chlorine manufacture. It was not until 1895, however, that the company was able to work electrolysis into its industrial scheme. The production of chlorine eventually led to one of the company's largest modern branches, chlorinated products, including plastics. Caustic soda also combined with soda ash to provide a profitable new product area.

With the success of their first factory, located in Couillet, Belgium, the Solvay brothers began to expand their firm. The initial consideration of international growth, proposed for England, came in 1872. In the following year several British plants were constructed, in addition to one in Dombasle, France. The last two decades of the century saw rapid growth of the firm. In 1881 both the United States and Russia became sites for Solvay works: in the United States the cities of Syracuse and Detroit eventually housed Solvay factories, while three Russian locales were selected. The company continued its international growth in the following years by building in Austria, Hungary, Germany, and, in the early years of the 20th century, Spain and Italy. In all, by the company's 50th anniversary in 1913, there were at least 34 Solvay plants, including an electrolytic plant in Jemeppe-sur-Sambre in Belgium.

As the 19th century progressed, Solvay & Cie was directed toward greater productivity and importance in its market. Despite such impressive growth, the management was not neglecting its workers, a fact about the company's character that should not be overlooked. In addition to his interest in natural science, Ernest Solvay had a strong interest in socioeconomic matters. A proponent of universal suffrage, his social interests led him to the senate in the 1890s; he had an idealistic view of a future when ''justice for all'' would be a reality. This vision was realized in concrete terms by the institution of many innovative workers' benefits. By the end of the 19th century, workers for Solvay & Cie were able to take advantage of sick pay, compensation for injury, and the eight-hour work day, which was a Solvay innovation at their Russian plants. His social interests also led him to various contributions to the nation during World War I, after which he was named Minister of State.

While chemical projects and social interests were part of daily business, they were not the only things surrounding Ernest Solvay's company. Since his youth, the founder had a strong interest in intellectual questions, which later led to the creation of the Solvay institutes of physiology and sociology. His self-teaching also led him to speculations on such abstract physical

Key Dates:

1861: Ernest Solvay files a patent for a method of manufacturing artificial soda ash.
1863: Solvay and his brother Alfred form Solvay & Cie to pursue this new method.
1865: After the firm is driven to the brink of bankruptcy, the brothers succeed in producing large amounts of soda ash at their first factory, in Couillet, Belgium.
1873: Several British plants are constructed, the first foreign operations.
1881: Factories open in the United States and Russia.
1895: The company is able to work electrolysis into its industrial scheme, leading to the diversification into the production of chlorine and caustic soda.
1900: Ernest Solvay continues to hold all patents related to the Solvay method of soda ash production, which has now reached 900,000 tons per year.
1922: Founder Ernest Solvay dies.
1949: Solvay & Cie diversifies into plastics when it begins producing polyvinyl chloride (PVC) at its plant in Jemeppe, Belgium.
1950s: Company moves into the life sciences field.
1959: Solvay expands further into plastics with the start of high-density polyethylene (HDPE) production.
1960s: Solvay expands into plastic processing.
1967: Company is incorporated as Solvay & Cie S.A.
1971: Solvay's shares are placed for sale on the public market for the first time; company adopts a more modern management structure, with top management positions opened up to executives from outside the founding family.
1976: Production of polypropylene begins.
1979: Company begins to make acquisitions of life sciences firms.
1980: Life sciences activities are placed within a separate Health sector.
1984: Interests in the United States are reorganized under a new holding company, Solvay America, Inc.
1992: Solvay buys Tenneco Inc.'s soda ash operations in Green River, Wyoming, gaining significant capacity in low-cost, trona-based soda ash.
1998: Aloïs Michielsen becomes the first person from outside the founding Solvay family to serve as chief executive.
1999: The European PVC business of BASF is acquired.
2001: Solvay swaps its small polypropylene business for BP's specialty polymers operations; the two companies also form HDPE joint ventures in North America and Europe.
2002: In its largest acquisition ever, Solvay buys Ausimont S.p.A., a EUR 600 million fluorinated chemicals and polymers business.

principles as mass and energy. His interest in matters such as the nature of the universe led to his initiation of the Solvay conference on physics, which drew the greatest minds of the time together: Albert Einstein, Ernest Rutherford, and Marie Curie were but a few of the names listed at the first meeting in 1911.

Surviving Two World Wars

The company's first major setback came at the end of World War I, when its Russian plants were lost in the aftermath of the revolution. Shortly thereafter, in 1922, Ernest Solvay died. His prominence was marked by a letter of condolence sent by King Albert of Belgium to their mutual friend Charles Lefébure, with whom they shared an interest for mountain climbing. The company was able to overcome these losses, however, by modernizing many of its plants in the next years and making moves into certain other areas, such as the exploitation of potassium mining. In the 1930s and 1940s, increasing efforts were directed towards electrolysis, with new plants established in Italy, Greece, and other countries.

World War II again changed the complexion of the company. Many of its important factories were damaged during the conflict; in addition, several of its plants were lost to the Soviet-dominated Eastern European countries. While rebuilding its facilities, Solvay did not neglect to make new developments, holding to its policy of careful diversification. The company first produced polyvinyl chloride in 1949, at its plant in Jemeppe, Belgium. This move into plastics was to be one of the company's most important decisions, opening up a new and very profitable field that did not diverge significantly from the company's basic product lines.

Postwar Era: New Growth Fields and More Modern Management Structure

In the 1950s and 1960s Solvay continued to grow, building and maintaining its position as a prominent manufacturer of bulk chemicals. The company also expanded the range of plastics it produced by beginning production of high-density polyethylene in 1959. Solvay's first foray into the life sciences field also occurred during the 1950s. The next major changes in the company came in the late 1960s under the direction of Baron Rene Boël. One of the most important changes made by Boël was to place Solvay's shares on the public market, in 1971, for the first time. In addition, he made major structural changes in management. Previously, Solvay & Cie had been organized by a French and Belgian managerial structure known as a ''commandité,'' in which authority was held by a group of five executives. All were required to be members of the Solvay family, into which Boël had married some time earlier. Boël abandoned this form of administration for a more modern corporate structure, paving the way for more clearly defined management responsibility and opening up top management to executives from outside the family. The initial addition of two nonfamily members was enlarged upon in subsequent years. Many European firms have been forced into similar changes by economic necessity, but Solvay managers said they chose their own time, when the changes made were able to provide significant benefits to the company.

During the same time, the company began to make record expenditures in research and development. It also began looking into new fields for growth. An example of this was its move from being a straightforward plastics manufacturer to a plastic processor as well, a development that began in the 1960s. Solvay was eventually involved in a wide range of plastic processing endeavors, including foils, automobile parts, pipes, plastic bottles, and baby seats—thereby successfully entering the consumer market as well as the industrial market. Meantime, on the plastics manufacturing side, Solvay began producing polypropylene in 1976.

The changes in Solvay's management kept the company financially healthy through the late 1970s when, under the leadership of Jacques Solvay, a great-grandson of the founder, it was acknowledged as the European leader in the manufacture of polyvinyl chloride. Production on its oldest line, soda ash and caustic soda, was reduced to approximately 20 percent of the firm's total income. Yet this reliable 20 percent was to provide the next great challenge for Solvay. In 1976 U.S. companies began manufacturing soda ash from a natural source, a rock mined in Wyoming, called trona. Suddenly a process was available that was both less expensive and cleaner than the reliable Solvay process. The situation was not helped by increasing environmental restrictions on chlorine and calcium carbonate. As a result, Solvay-method plants began to close.

In 1978 the European management felt the repercussions of this situation. In the wake of a Solvay price hike on soda ash, designed to offset losses at their oldest plants, Belgian glassmakers signed a letter of intent with the FMC Corporation in the United States. Faced with the loss of their contracts and of some 1,200 jobs, Solvay asked the Belgian government to intercede, while initiating measures to reduce their prices. Although the glassmakers seemed content to return their business to Solvay, FMC was less satisfied. The dispute led to changes in Solvay policy to suit antitrust laws, and helped support the suspicion that, sometime in the future, artificial means of production would be discontinued for this product; Solvay nevertheless remained a profitable presence in the business.

Despite such problems in the oldest branch of the firm, Solvay did not stop looking for new developments. The year 1984 saw the reorganization of its American interests under a new holding company, Solvay America, Inc., in an attempt to increase its profile in the United States. Approximately the same time, the company extended its financial outlays, marking $650 million to be dedicated to capital improvements in the period 1985–87. Another profitable move was the company's acquisition of life sciences firms, which began in 1979. The increasing importance of these life sciences endeavors was shown when the company placed them within a separate Health sector in 1980. Solvay by 1990 was producing a number of drugs and vaccines for human and animal healthcare, in plants located in Europe and in the United States.

Up to 1990 Solvay's more recent history was somewhat embattled, especially in terms of its old mainline products soda ash and caustic soda. Its newer plastics products also experienced a difficult time on the market because of a general decrease in plastics sales throughout Europe. The firm managed to maintain its financial position, however, showing higher sales in 1986 than ever before. In the 1980s Solvay management became increasingly aware of the company's vulnerability because of a reliance on bulk chemicals alone, and its diversification, more varied than ever before, showed a calculated response to this pressure.

1990s: Shedding Stodgy Reputation in a Deal-Making Decade

In 1990 Solvay's profits experienced a drop of 5 percent from the year before, and in 1993 it reported a loss—of $193 million—for the first time in 12 years and for only the second time in its long history. Moreover, throughout the 1990s observers questioned its ability to compete in the pharmaceuticals market given that its major competitors—such as Akzo and Rhône-Poulenc—were themselves pure pharmaceuticals producers. The collapse of the Berlin Wall and the Soviet Union's subsequent disintegration presented Solvay with an opportunity to recover the plants it had lost during World War II and the postwar years. In 1991 it regained ownership of its former East German soda ash and hydrogen peroxide plant, seized by the Nazis in 1939, and announced plans to invest DM 200 million in its renovation.

To improve its wavering profits, Solvay throughout the 1990s sought partnerships with global chemical and chemical end-user companies. In 1990, for example, it joined with the U.S. Dexter Corporation to form a specialty plastics joint venture and partnered with Wienerberger Canalisent L'Europe to acquire pipe manufacturers in Hungary, East Germany, and Greece. The following year it struck a deal with the U.S. pharmaceuticals giant Upjohn Company to comarket some of each other's products and entered into a joint venture with a Japanese company to produce salt in Thailand. Between 1994 and 1996, it also merged its coolant business with Germany's Hoechst, established automotive products and biosciences joint ventures in mainland China and Argentina, and formed an automotive products partnership with the O'Sullivan Corporation of the United States.

It also closed unprofitable operations and sold noncore businesses. Between 1991 and 1996, for example, it sold some of its animal health products line, its feed additive operations, its bioinsecticide business, and—in 1996—its remaining animal health units, to American Home Products. Other significant divestitures included the sale of its catalysts and sorbents businesses, its wood production and special cement operations, its industrial enzymes business, and, in 1997, its Brazilian plastics subsidiary.

Under CEO Baron Daniel Janssen, who was also related to the founding family by marriage, Solvay attempted to dispel its reputation as a stodgy industrial dinosaur by making repeated acquisitions. In 1990–91, for example, it acquired an American blow-molded plastics operation, gained a share in a Spanish polyvinylchloride producer, and broke up its hydrogen peroxide joint venture with Laporte of the United Kingdom in order to gain complete control of that important business. In June 1992 it paid Tenneco Inc. of the United States $500 million for its soda ash operations in Green River, Wyoming. This acquisition marked a historic shift as Solvay gained significant capacity in low-cost, trona-based soda ash; it also shored up the company's position as the global leader in soda ash production. In other deals, Solvay acquired a medical tubing manufacturer in 1994, bought Hoechst's fluorocarbons business and a Bulgarian soda ash plant in 1996, and acquired a Namibian fluorspar mine and a share of a Finnish hydrogen peroxide business in 1997. The company in 1997 also took full control of the U.S. plastics joint venture it had formed with Dexter Corp. Called D&S Plastics International, the Auburn Hills, Michigan-based firm had developed into a leading supplier to the North American automobile industry of polyolefin resins, principally used in the production of car bumpers.

By 1995, Solvay's sales had edged past $9.3 billion—more than a quarter of which was contributed by its U.S. subsidiaries—and in 1996 Janssen announced that Solvay would now concentrate its efforts on five principal sectors: alkalis, peroxygens, plastics, health (including pharmaceuticals), and processing (which included automotive products, industrial sheet and film, and pipes and fittings).

Early 2000s: Shifting Focus to Specialty Chemicals and Pharmaceuticals Under First Nonfamily CEO

In June 1998 Janssen succeeded Boël as chairman of Solvay's board of directors, while Aloïs Michielsen took over Janssen's position of chairman of the executive committee, a position similar to that of chief executive. In a historic development, Michielsen, a 28-year company veteran, became the first person from outside the founding Solvay family to head up the company. The new leader continued—and soon accelerated—the deal-making trend initiated by his predecessor.

During 1999 Solvay became the world's fourth largest producer of polyvinyl chloride (PVC) by acquiring the European PVC business of BASF, which was merged with Solvay's existing PVC business to create Solvin S.A., a 75–25 joint venture between Solvay and BASF headquartered in Brussels. Solvay also acquired Ellay, a leading U.S. producer of PVC films for medical applications, and entered into a joint venture with Phillips Petroleum Company to build two high-density polyethylene (HDPE) plants in North America. In 2000 Solvay and Plastic Omnium of France combined their fuel systems operations into a 50–50, Paris-based joint venture called Inergy Automotive Systems S.A., creating the world's largest manufacturer of plastic fuel tanks, with 3,300 employees and 30 facilities in 15 countries.

An important and complex deal with BP was concluded in October 2001. Solvay swapped its small, money-losing polypropylene business for BP's specialty polymers operations; at the same time, the two companies formed HDPE joint ventures in both North America and Europe. Combined, the joint ventures ranked third in the world in HDPE and had overall revenues of EUR 2 billion ($1.86 billion). The resulting Houston-based entity, BP Solvay Polyethylene North America, also took over Solvay's interest in the two HDPE plants being built with Chevron Phillips Chemical Company (Phillips Petroleum having since combined its chemicals business into a 50–50 joint venture with Chevron Corporation). As part of the deal with BP, Solvay had the right to exit from the joint ventures in late 2004, and industry observers widely expected the company to do just that.

Early in 2002 Solvay partnered with Kali und Salz to create a European salt joint venture called ESCO in which Solvay took a 38 percent stake. The big news that year, however, was Solvay's completion of its largest acquisition ever. In May 2002 Solvay acquired Ausimont S.p.A. from Montedison S.p.A. and Longside International for EUR 1.3 billion ($1.1 billion), gaining a EUR 600 million fluorinated chemicals and polymers business. Part of the funds for the deal were gained through the issuance of EUR 800 million in preferred stock to a financial investor, and Solvay was likely to use the proceeds from the sale of the BP Solvay Polyethylene joint ventures to reimburse the buyer of this stock. At the beginning of 2003, Solvay merged its existing fluoropolymers business with Ausimont to form Solvay Solexis, which was based in Bollate, Italy.

The end result of these transactions was that Solvay was much more highly focused on specialty chemicals and pharmaceuticals at the expense of the commodity chemicals business on which the firm was founded. Solvay was aiming to increase the share of group earnings before interest and tax that derived from its specialty chemical and pharmaceutical operations to 70 percent by 2006, up from 58 percent in 2001. One result of this shift in focus was that the company was better insulated from the cyclical effects of the commodity chemical sector. Overall, the various deals strengthened Solvay in another way. More of the company's businesses—80 to 90 percent of the them in 2002—had leadership positions in their specific sector, compared to less than 50 percent five years earlier.

The changes in the product portfolio also had a very positive on Solvay's bottom line. For 2002, although revenues were down 9 percent, earnings jumped 23 percent, reflecting the acquisition of more highly profitable businesses and the divestiture of less profitable ones. In fact, the company's return on equity hit 13.1 percent, a level not reached in more than ten years, though below Solvay's target rate of 15 percent.

Also boding well for the future was the rapid growth of Solvay's pharmaceutical business, where annual revenue growth was averaging 14 percent in the early 2000s. The company's focus on four main therapeutic areas—gastroenterology, hormone treatments, cardiology, and mental health—was paying off handsomely, with revenues approaching the EUR 2 billion mark. Solvay remained a small player on the global stage, ranking only in the top 40 among the world's pharmaceutical firms, and many questioned the company's continued commitment to this sector, particularly given that the trend was for major chemical groups to withdraw from drugs, as had, for example, BASF and DuPont. But Solvay had some promising products in its drug pipeline, most notably cilansetron, a treatment for irritable bowel syndrome; clinical trials for this drug were nearing completion, and Solvay hoped to launch the product in mid-2004 and was anticipating annual sales of more than EUR 250 million.

Principal Subsidiaries

Alkor Draka S.A.; Solvay BAP S.A.; Mutuelle Solvay S.C.S. (99.9%); Peptisyntha & Cie S.N.C.; Solvay Automotive Management and Research SNC; Solvay Benvic & Cie Belgium S.N.C.; Solvay Coordination Internationale des Crédits Commerciaux (CICC) S.A.; SIFMAR - Solvay Industrial Foils Management and Research S.A.; Solvay Interox S.A.; Solvay Pharma & Cie S.N.C.; Solvay Osterreich AG (Austria); Solvay do Brasil Ltda. (Brazil); Solvay Sodi AD (Bulgaria); Solvay

Deutschland GmbH (Germany); Solvay Portugal - Produtos Quimicos S.A.; Solvay Asia Pacific Pte. Ltd. (Singapore); Solvay Iberica S.L. (Spain); Solvay (Schweiz) AG (Switzerland); Solvay UK Holding Co. Ltd.; Solvay America, Inc. (U.S.A.). The company maintains 398 subsidiaries and affiliated companies in 50 countries.

Principal Competitors

FMC Corporation; The Dow Chemical Company; Occidental Chemical Corporation; Shin-Etsu Chemical Co., Ltd.; Formosa Plastics Corporation; PolyOne Corporation; GE Plastics; E.I. du Pont de Nemours and Company; Atofina; DuPont Dow Elastomers LLC; Dyneon, LLC; Ticona; Sumitomo Chemical Company, Limited; GE Specialty Materials; Novartis AG; GlaxoSmithKline plc.

Further Reading

Alperowicz, Natasha, ''Solvay Redefines Traditions for Global Growth,'' *Chemical Week,* February 8, 1995, pp. 30–32.

——, ''Solvay's Shift: A Move to Specialties; Pharma May Be Spun Off,'' *Chemical Week,* February 12, 2003, pp. 14–16.

Buckley, Neil, ''Solvay Chooses Outsider,'' *Financial Times,* August 1, 1997, p. 26.

——, ''Solvay to Sell Animal Health Businesses,'' *Financial Times,* September 21, 1996, p. 11.

Choi, Audrey, ''Solvay Tries to Drag Its Bernburg Factory 50 Years into the Present,'' *Wall Street Journal,* October 27, 1992, p. 1.

——, ''Updating East European Plants Is Taxing: Solvay's Reclaiming of Soda Ash Facility Challenges Firm,'' *Wall Street Journal,* November 20, 1992, p. B13A.

Choi, Audrey, and Bob Hagerty, ''Belgium's Solvay Moves with More Elan,'' *Wall Street Journal,* May 29, 1992, p. A5A.

——, ''Solvay Tests a Prescription for Growth,'' *Wall Street Journal Europe,* May 20, 1992, p. 9.

Hagerty, Bob, ''Belgium's Solvay to Market Certain Drugs with Upjohn,'' *Wall Street Journal,* May 22, 1991.

——, ''Solvay & Cie Announces Plan to Restructure,'' *Wall Street Journal,* November 20, 1989.

Hagerty, Bob, and Audrey Choi, ''Solvay Agrees to Acquire Soda Ash Plant of Tenneco,'' *Wall Street Journal Europe,* April 24, 1992, p. 4.

Hunter, David, ''An Ambitious Strategy Sparks New Excitement at Solvay,'' *Chemical Week,* April 19, 1989, pp. 34, 36, 38.

Luesby, Jenny, ''Solvay Keeps Its Shine,'' *Financial Times,* February 18, 1997, p. 28.

''Solvay Steps Up Its Diversification Moves,'' *Chemical Week,* January 7, 1981, p. 58.

Spielman, Adam, ''Solvay to Get Back Factory Taken by the Nazis in 1939,'' *Wall Street Journal,* August 21, 1991.

''Takeovers Bring Solvay Out of the Shadows,'' *Financial Times,* November 12, 1992, p. 27.

Westervelt, Robert, ''Solvay Swaps PP for BP's Engineering Plastics,'' *Chemical Week,* January 3, 2001, p. 9.

—updates: Paul S. Bodine, David E. Salamie

Spin Master, Ltd.

450 Front St. West
Toronto, Ontario M5V 1B6
Canada
Telephone: (416) 364-6002
Toll Free: (800) 622-8339
Fax: (416) 364-8005
Web site: http://www.spinmaster.com

Private Company
Incorporated: 1994 as Seiger Marketing, Inc.
Employees: 145
Sales: C$200 million (2003 est.)
NAIC: 339932 Game, Toy, and Children's Vehicle Manufacturing

Spin Master, Ltd. is a Canadian toy manufacturer whose string of popular, imaginative products have helped make it one of the top ten toy companies in North America. The firm's signature offerings include Air Hogs, planes that fly up to 100 yards on compressed air; Catch-A-Bubble, long-lasting soap bubbles that can be caught and stacked together; ICEE Maker, which children can use to make cold, slushy drinks; and Mighty Beanz, collectable, wobbly plastic capsules with depictions of cartoon characters on them. Spin Master also offers an updated version of the 1970s sensation Shrinky Dinks, the McDonald's-licensed McFlurry Maker, toys based on the Australian musical entertainers The Wiggles, and many more. The Toronto-based concern is owned and run by its three founders, Anton Rabie, Ronnen Harary, and Ben Varadi.

Beginnings

The origins of Spin Master date to 1994, when three young Canadians began marketing a novelty gift item called Earth Buddy. Ronnen Harary and Anton Rabie, both born in South Africa, had been friends since they attended summer camp together as children, and Rabie had gotten to know Ben Varadi while all three were students at the University of Western Ontario. Rabie and Harary had run a poster business in college, and after graduation began seeking a new type of product to sell. They found it in a gift Harary's grandmother had brought back from Israel, which consisted of a nylon stocking with a face drawn on it that was filled with sawdust and grass seed. When watered, it sprouted green ''hair'' on top. Deciding to market it in Canada, the pair took $10,000 of their savings to make 5,000 copies to sell as gifts for Mother's Day, 1994. On Rabie's suggestion, Varadi was brought in to oversee manufacturing.

The Earth Buddy was a poor cousin to the better-known Chia Pet, but it immediately caught on with the public and the partners soon found themselves expanding production to fulfill orders from such chains as Kmart. By year's end the $7.99 Earth Buddy had generated more than $1.5 million in revenues.

It was Harary, a one-time ''Deadhead'' who had traveled to follow the performances of The Grateful Dead, who came up with the firm's next product. Adapting a popular activity from the hippie-style gatherings that sprang up alongside the group's concerts, the trio began marketing ''Devil Sticks,'' a set of three rubber-covered batons which could be used to perform tricks. The company sent college students cross-country in vans to give demonstrations, and by the end of 1995 the partners had sold more than 600,000 of the $14.99 sets. Taking inspiration from this new product, the firm, which had originally used the name Seiger Marketing, Inc., became known as Spin Master, Ltd. Harary was its CEO, Rabie its president, and Varadi the executive vice-president in charge of product development.

In February 1996 they discovered another new product, one which would put the firm solidly on the map in the toy industry. While attending the annual toy fair in New York where industry buyers and sellers met to cut deals and promote new products, the partners were approached by British inventors John Dixon and Peter Manning, whose crude soda-bottle-with-Styrofoam-wings prototype airplane had been rejected by everyone they had shown it to. Impressed by the battery-less, compressed-air-powered toy's potential, Spin Master made a deal to license it and then hired two outside firms to work out the technical details. Over the next two years the partners gambled virtually every penny they had on the toy, spending $500,000 to perfect a plane that could fly up to 100 feet in height and 100 yards in distance. Its small piston engine converted 90 pounds per square inch of compressed air into 4,500 propeller revolutions per

Company Perspectives:

Despite the increasing size of the company, the spirit in which it was founded remains very much intact—a young, hip, energetic organization, willing to take risks, eager to innovate, and always looking to identify and develop new and exciting ideas.

minute, which produced a satisfyingly realistic droning sound. A bicycle pump-like ''docking station'' was supplied to give the plane its energy.

Air Hogs Sky Shark Debut in 1998; Sales Soar

In the spring of 1998 the purple and yellow Air Hogs Sky Shark began to hit the shelves of such specialty stores as Zainy Brainy. Business for the innovative new toy was brisk, and soon media attention from NBC's *Today Show,* the *Regis & Kathie Lee* program, and *Time* and *Popular Science* magazines helped boost sales through the roof. By the end of the Christmas shopping season some 400,000 of the $50 Air Hogs had been sold in Canada and the United States.

In the days following the holiday the firm was plunged into crisis, however, when thousands of customers called to complain that their plane's Styrofoam wings had broken during the first flight. Spin Master responded quickly, sending out 100,000 strengthened replacement wings and reinforcing those not yet sold with Mylar strips. The plane was later completely redesigned.

With the Sky Shark selling via such mass-marketers as Toys 'R Us, its sales topped one million units in March, and it was ranked the third best-selling toy in North America over $20 by an independent survey. Its success drove the company's annual revenues from $8 million to more than C$45 million during 1999. Other air-powered toys were soon under development, including several additional planes, a car, and a submarine, as well as the water-powered Hydro Rocket and the battery-powered E-Charger plane. Spin Master handled its own distribution in North America, and licensed its toys to companies including Japan's Bandai for foreign markets. The firm was expanding the Air Hogs line and cutting overseas deals as quickly as it could, in an effort to reduce the impact of the inevitable counterfeit and knock-off versions in the highly competitive global toy marketplace.

Gearing up for the next Christmas sales season, in the fall of 1999 Spin Master unveiled a line of collectible toys called Flick Trix Finger Bikes. The 2½ inch tall bicycles were licensed copies of popular BMX models made by such companies as Mongoose, Redline, and Huffy, and had working brakes, steering, and even tiny U-locks. The design had been licensed from a pair of Chicago inventors, who were inspired by the recent success of miniature skateboards called fingerboards. Along with the bikes, which were priced at less than $10 each, related items such as ramps and platforms were also offered. The Flick Trix line proved popular, and over the next year some six million were sold.

The year 2000 saw Spin Master address organizational inefficiencies that had arisen out of its rapid growth. Over a four-month period the company hired seven new vice-presidents to help streamline its operations, including the former head toy buyer for Wal-Mart Canada and the former vice-president in charge of Mattel's Canadian distribution system. An office was also opened in Hong Kong to oversee the firm's manufacturing, which was largely done in China. By year's end Spin Master's employment ranks had risen to more than 100, and annual revenues had grown to top C$103.5 million. The company's toys were now available in more than 25 countries.

The following year started off well for the firm, which procured exclusive rights to sell plush character toys from the Disney/Pixar movie *Monsters, Inc.* to U.S. specialty stores, and introduced a new line of toys for girls called Key Charm Cuties. However, in the spring Spin Master was sued by American Greetings Corporation of Cleveland, Ohio, over a new toy called Don't Free Freddy, which the latter firm claimed had been copied from a cartoon character it owned. Several months later the suit was settled out of court, but Don't Free Freddy, a furry talking monster doll that uttered insults when released from handcuffs, proved a dud sales-wise. The spring of 2001 also saw Spin Master voluntarily recall 108,000 Splash Blast Water Rockets, a handful of which had fired erratically and struck children. The company offered free replacements to buyers of the $30 toy.

Shrinky Dinks Revival for Christmas 2001

In August Spin Master began a major re-launch of Shrinky Dinks, a popular toy of the 1970s and 1980s that had not seen widespread distribution since 1993. The activity toy utilized a special plastic that could be drawn on and then baked until it dramatically metamorphosed and shrank. The re-issued version, which was licensed from its co-inventor Betty Morris, came complete with a new light bulb-heated oven to perform the shrinking. The revived Shrinky Dinks became a major Christmas season success story when nostalgic ''Generation X'' parents who had played with the toy as children bought it for their own offspring. By late November Spin Master had sold out of the initial run of 400,000 units and was working hard to obtain more of the toys, which retailed for under C$40. The company was now the 14th largest toy maker in North America, and it had also been designated one of the 50 best-managed companies in Canada by Deloitte & Touche.

Early 2002 saw Spin Master add more new items to its lineup. In addition to winning a license from the Jim Henson Company to make character toys based on the television program *The Hoobs,* the firm also signed a deal to market a new, longer-lasting bubble solution called ''Catch-A-Bubble'' in North America. This product, which had been developed by a Chinese inventor, had already been a runaway success in Australia, and when Spin Master brought it to the annual New York toy fair, it came away with orders for four million bottles of the inexpensive fluid. Catch-A-Bubble would go on to be a steady seller.

In May the company announced a voluntary recall of 137,000 Air Hogs planes, a few of which had burst and caused minor injuries. Free replacements were offered. August saw the introduction of a line of toys based on The Wiggles, an Australian musical group popular with small children whose act included the characters Dorothy the Dinosaur and Captain Feath-

Key Dates:

1994: Anton Rabie, Ronnen Harary, and Ben Varadi begin marketing Earth Buddy.
1995: Company has success with Devil Sticks, becomes known as Spin Master.
1998: Introduction of Air Hogs Sky Shark plane brings firm into mass-market stores.
1999: Flick Trix Finger Bikes make debut.
2000: Sales top $100 million.
2001: Spin Master re-launches 1970s sensation Shrinky Dinks to strong demand.
2002: Company finds success with Catch-A-Bubble and ICEE Maker.
2003: Firm licenses McFlurry Maker from McDonald's; Mighty Beanz prove hit.

ersword. The line, which featured a Wiggles guitar for example, was a hit with parents who saw the group as an appealing alternative to the omnipresent, Barney the Dinosaur. Other products introduced in time for the Christmas gift-giving season included the radio-controlled, battery-powered Air Hogs Helicopter and the ICEE Maker, an activity toy with which children could make slushy snow-cone drinks. Sales were strong for the latter, which vaulted to number two in the food toy category behind the venerable Easy-Bake Oven.

Shortly after Christmas Spin Master acquired the Sky Bugz line of compressed-air flying insects from cash-strapped Canadian rival Irwin Toys, and in January 2003 the firm unveiled the $25 McDonald's McFlurry Maker, which children could use to replicate an ice cream dessert found at the fast-food chain's restaurants. It was the first toy developed under a four-year licensing agreement with McDonald's, which CEO Harary hailed as the company's largest such pact to date.

New toys introduced by Spin Master in the spring of 2003 included Strobe F/X, a $10 pulsating multicolored light wand that could create patterns on a wall or ceiling, and Bounce 'Round, an eight-by-eight foot home version of the air-filled ''moon walk'' familiar from carnivals, which retailed for less than $200. The firm also launched a touring Air Hogs promotional van that would travel to air shows, festivals and shopping centers to promote its products, in conjunction with the 100th anniversary of the Wright Brothers' first flight.

In August Spin Master took on North American distribution of Stink Blasters, a collection of 24 action figures, ''each sold separately,'' which carried such names as Porta Potty Paul and Barfin' Ben. When squeezed they emitted convincing (though harmless) odors that matched their descriptive names. The firm also began to distribute an updated version of the Teenage Mutant Ninja Turtles line to capitalize on a new series of TV episodes that featured the pizza-eating, fighting martial arts characters. In the fall the company launched the Crash Zone Regenerator, a 15-inch long radio-controlled SUV that, when crashed, could sustain heavy ''damage.'' When a button was pressed on its controller, however, it was restored to normal appearance. It was priced at just under $60.

Mighty Beanz Creating Stir at End of 2003

The fall of 2003 also saw Spin Master introduce an Australian import called Mighty Beanz, small plastic capsules decorated with cartoon characters that contained ball bearings. The wobbly Beanz sold for about $8 for a pack of six, and became popular with children who sought to ''collect them all,'' as the ads implored. The toys, which were advertised on The Cartoon Network and Nickelodeon, were especially popular with preteen boys. By Christmas many stores had sold out of their stock, and Spin Master was forced to restrict distribution to the larger toy chains. At year's end more than $40 million worth had been sold, making Mighty Beanz one of the firm's best sellers ever.

The company was continuing to aggressively seek new hits, having recently moved its director of global licensing to the fertile toy-development country of Japan, and was solidifying ties to key inventors with such perks as an annual golfing, rafting, and biking trip to British Columbia. By early 2004 Spin Master was referring to itself as a ''children's entertainment consumer products company,'' rather than simply a toy maker, and was laying plans for an expanded product line that would include non-toy items for children's bedrooms, including convertible couches decorated with licensed character designs. It was now ranked the ninth largest toy maker in North America, and had annual revenues estimated at more than C$200 million.

After just a decade in business, Spin Master, Ltd. had evolved into a major player in the toy industry. Its success had come from developing innovative new product lines as well as through a series of astute licensing agreements. Under the guidance of its still young founders, the company was undoubtedly capable of reaching even greater heights in the years to come.

Principal Competitors

Hasbro, Inc.; Mattel, Inc.; JAKKS Pacific, Inc.; Wham-O, Inc.

Further Reading

Acharya, Madhavi, ''Pumped Up and Flying High,'' *Toronto Star*, December 12, 1998, p. E1.

Beck, Rachel, ''Finding Green in the Wild Blue Yonder,'' *Pittsburgh Post-Gazette*, March 23, 1999, p. F7.

Bhatia, Pooja, ''Big Hit in Toyland: Shrinky Dinks, a '70s Throwback,'' *Wall Street Journal*, November 21, 2001, p. B1.

Chmielewski, Dawn, ''Suspended Fascination—Deadhead's Devil Sticks Heat Up Toy Market,'' *Patriot Ledger*, December 5, 1995, p. 23.

Dixon, Guy, ''Firm Has High Hopes for Bubble Market,'' *Globe and Mail*, April 16, 2002, p. B11.

Flavelle, Dana, ''Toy Makers Waiting for Phone to Ring—Urgent Calls from Retailers for More Stock Is Sign of Successful Holiday Season,'' *Toronto Star*, November 16, 2002, p. D1.

Hawaleshka, Danylo, ''Young Kings of a Toy Empire,'' *Maclean's*, November 27, 2000, p. 50.

Lomartire, Paul, ''Corporate Elf Seeks Lordship over Toy Shelf,'' *Palm Beach Post*, December 17, 2003, p. 1D.

McDonnell, Colin, ''In Hot Pursuit of Cool,'' *Toronto Star*, December 6, 1999, p. 1.

McDougall, Diane, ''Putting a New Spin on Toys,'' *National Post*, December 12, 2000, p. E12.

Pereira, Joseph, ''Sales of Mighty Beanz Are Jumping, Ahead of the Holidays,'' *Wall Street Journal*, October 6, 2003, p. B1.

''Research and Development Puts Company in a Spin,'' *Globe and Mail*, October 26, 1998, p. C8.

Schneider, Richard T., ''Pneumatics Takes Flight,'' *Hydraulics & Pneumatics*, November 1, 1999, p. 14.

Schumacher, Mary Louise, ''Shrinky Dinks Resurge,'' *Milwaukee Journal-Sentinel*, December 3, 2001, p. 1A.

Silcoff, Sean, ''Out-of-Court Settlement Frees 'Lovable' Freddy,'' *National Post*, March 21, 2001, p. C6.

Steinberg, Shawna, ''Toy Maker Flies Brand Program to Combat Knockoffs,'' *Globe and Mail*, June 11, 1999, p. B9.

Won, Shirley, ''Toy Maker Plays a Different Game; Spin Master Courts Inventors and Rewards Employees Each Month for Good Ideas,'' *Globe and Mail*, January 3, 2004, p. B1.

—Frank Uhle

Ssangyong Cement Industrial Co., Ltd.

24-1, Jeo-dong 2-ga
Jung-gu, Seoul
South Korea
Telephone: (02) 2270-5114
Fax: (02) 2275-7040
Web site: http://www.ssangyongcement.co.kr

Public Company
Incorporated: 1939 as Samkong Fat Limited Co.
Employees: 1,424
Sales: W 1.17 billion (2002)
Stock Exchanges: Seoul
NAIC: 327310 Cement Manufacturing

A member of the Ssangyong conglomerate, Ssangyong Cement Industrial Co., Ltd. is South Korea's leading manufacturer of cement. It offers ready mixed concrete, ceramics, and other products. Ssangyong Cement owns and operates a number of cement plants, including the Donghae Plant, the largest single unit cement plant in the world. The company sells cement domestically and abroad.

Dynamic Leadership in the Early Years: 1930s–50s

The story of Ssangyong dates back to 1939, when the group's founder Kim Sung Kon, along with a few friends, established Samkong Fat Limited, a soap manufacturing company. In the years of great scarcity following the liberation of Korea from 35 years of Japanese administration, this soap became the leading brand. A political idealist, Kim Sung Kon joined Yo Woon-Hyong's National Reconstruction party as top financial officer at 33, thus embarking on one of the most remarkable careers in the modern history of a country known for its uniquely successful mix of government initiative and socially motivated private enterprise.

In 1947 Kim Sung Kon helped found the Koryo Fire and Marine Insurance Co., which he himself took over in 1959 and which eventually developed into a respected subsidiary with assets of US$180.3 million by the late 1980s. It had close ties with such well known insurance brokers and reinsurance companies as Munich Re in Germany and Willis Faber in the United Kingdom, and 150 domestic branches. In 1948 Kim set up the Kumsung Textile Co. with the aim of providing Korea's poverty-ridden people with cotton clothing. The company was successful, despite the scarcity of raw materials and treasury-induced inflation. Kim rebuilt the factory in 1954 after it had been burned down in the Korean War, with the help of the U.N. Korean Reconstruction Agency and turned it into the largest textile firm in the country with 30,000 looms and 250 weaving machines.

Kim's political career, always secondary to his business interests, took off with the military revolution of May 16, 1961, which led to his becoming chairman of the Financial Committee in the assembly under the Democratic Republican Party. His relationship with the military junta under President Park Chung Hee was not servile, since he opposed the latter's scheme to restrict the freedom of the press, in which he had interests, and was later fired for his part in the October 2 Revolt in which members of the cabinet sided with the opposition in order to oust the Home Affairs minister. However, he was ideally placed to implement certain aspects of President Park's first five-year plan to establish the national economy on a more sound basis and increase growth from 1.9 percent in 1953 to 7.1 percent in 1960.

Entering the Cement Market: 1960s–Mid-1970s

In 1962 Kim sold Kumsung Textiles in order to finance a venture into cement, starting with the construction of the world's largest single-unit cement plant at Donghae. Kim did this with the knowledge that two priorities of the five-year plan were production of oil, steel, and cement, in order to build up Korea's independence in strategic industries, and to launch the export drive which had characterized the Korean economy and which was directed actively by successive governments until the 1980s. During the 1980s the trade deficit was turned around, trade barriers and protectionism were dismantled slowly at the insistence of the United States, and new democratic structures were experimented with successfully in government.

Although the plant at Yongwol was dedicated in 1964, it was Donghae, first dedicated in 1968 with 1.7 million tons of pro-

Company Perspectives:

Ssangyong's corporate philosophy can be summed up as "creating one hundred years of Ssangyong's history." This means that Ssangyong will exist eternally by growing into the world's top-class enterprise and serving the society and humankind through creation. The "one hundred years of history" implies the continuity of the company and "creation" is the basis on which continuity will be secured and constantly requires inventing new products to meet the demands of the society and the times.

duction capacity and expanded to 5.6 million tons by 1974 becoming the mainstay and pride of Ssangyong Cement. Situated on limestone reserves calculated to last 200 years and serviced by the port of Pukyong nine miles away, Donghae contributed significantly to the total profits of the group. Donghae's after-tax profits in 1988 of US$54.5 million placed it seventh among Korea's leading companies.

Bolstered by Korea's growing infrastructure and its part in the first and second five-year plans representing a strategic industry, the company grew fast enough for Kim Sung Kon to expand into areas compatible with Ssangyong Cement. In 1967 he took over the Samwha Paper Co.—renamed Ssangyong Paper Co. in 1975—to produce the paper needed to package cement. He also established the Kumsung Shipping Co.—renamed Ssangyong Shipping Co. Ltd. in 1972—to transport his cement along the Korean coast. Kim's Kumsung Industry Co. Ltd., which he had founded in 1954 after the Korean War to export cotton goods, did not fare so well in the 1960s. Renamed Ssangyong Trading Co. Ltd. in 1967 the forerunner of the present Ssangyong Corporation was licensed as a general trading company in 1975 and started trading in earnest in goods unrelated to cement in the 1970s, during the "Miracle of the Han River," as Korea's period of rapid growth was termed.

Following the oil crisis of 1973, Kim established a joint venture with the shah of Iran to set up an oil refinery which would help fuel Kim's cement plants. He planned a major increase in production capacity for Donghae, took over Taehan Cement in 1975, and made moves to enter heavy industry by constructing diesel engines for vessels, generators, and rolling stock. In founding Ssangyong Cement (Singapore) in Singapore in 1973 as a joint venture with a local company, he anticipated later Korean government policy requiring *chaebols*, family-owned conglomerates, to be more competitive abroad. It was not only the first overseas capital investment by a private Korean firm at a time when foreign exchange was scarce, but it helped to reduce somewhat the reliance on domestic demand and shipments to the Middle East, both of which hit a low from 1980 to 1982. Ssangyong Cement captured a part of the competitive Japanese cartel market as its leading foreign supplier as well as expanding its distribution network there.

Having spent a year with his daughter in the United States after the collapse of his political career, Kim returned to Korea following President Park's "October revitalisation reform" in 1973, a kind of amnesty, resuming the position of chairman of Ssangyong Cement and assuming the presidency of the Korea Chamber of Commerce and Industry. He died of a stroke in 1975, at age 62.

The resulting confusion caused widespread concern, especially to President Park Chung Hee, who declared that the business ought "to be kept well maintained." Shin Hyon Hwack, then president of Ssangyong Cement, held a meeting with presidents of the group's other concerns and followed the wishes of Kim's wife when they appointed her eldest son, at that time not yet 30, as chairman.

New Leadership Bringing Diversification and Growth: Mid 1970s–80s

Kim Sung Kon and his son were opposites in management style, yet Kim Suk Won proved the equal, if not better than his father in expanding the group's fortunes. Total profit increased 26 times between 1975 and 1987, from US$164 million to US$4.2 billion.

Educated at Brandeis University, Kim Suk Won first became auditor for Ssangyong Cement and managing director at Ssangyong Shipping, but after a year of routine desk work, which he disliked, he told his father, "Please let me do anything I like; I want to learn by myself how the world goes. I assure you that I will return home when I reach 35."

He traveled throughout Korea, observing his countrymen's attempts to break away from poverty and low-tech industries. He then built the country's first ski slope at Yongpyeong, convinced that one day the middle classes would want to use it.

Kim Suk Won's first major task on becoming chairman was to complete the two projects his father had left unfinished: oil and cement expansion. The former was an uphill battle. During the 1970s, construction of the refinery proceeded at Onsan, although the National Iranian Oil Co. withdrew from the partnership in 1976, leaving a serious shortage of funds. During the second oil crisis in the early 1980s, cement was also piling up in the depots, and Kim's patience was rewarded when the Iranians supplied his crude oil at almost $3 per barrel below the OPEC price. Then equipped with the nation's largest crude-unloading facilities at Onsan, Ssangyong Oil Refining Co. Ltd. had become a major money earner for the group, with a US$824 million turnover in 1986. It was one of the country's largest oil refiners and was expanding further into petrochemicals, despite increasingly heavy competition and the problem of oversupply which faced all the *chaebols* as they ignored government warnings to specialize rather than diversify further.

During the 1970s Kim's own strategy was to lead the group away from cement, though never ceasing investment in cement. He had expanded the cement business considerably since taking over. Aware of the value of research and technology, he opened the Ssangyong Research Center in Taedok Science Town in 1975, initially to develop new types of cement and cement-related products, but also branching into ferrite magnet equipment. Most promising was its research into ceramics used in high-precision instruments and engines. It was illustrative of the way in which Ssangyong Cement stood apart from many other Korean companies, which often were plagued with the problem of production and sales outstripping technology and quality.

Key Dates:

1939: Kim Sung Kon and associates establish Samkong Fat Limited, a soap manufacturer.
1962: Ssangyong Cement Industrial Co., Ltd. is founded.
1968: Donghae Plant begins operations.
1973: Ssangyong Cement (Singapore), Ltd. is established.
1975: Ssangyong Research Center is established; founder Kim dies, and son Kim Suk Won is appointed chairman.
1987: Yongpyong Resort, a ski resort, is acquired.
1988: Ssangyong Cement (Pacific) Ltd. begins operations in the United States.
1994: Shanghai Baotailong Concrete Products Co., Ltd. and Shanghai Pulong Concrete Product Co., Ltd. are established in China.
1997: Company undergoes major restructuring.
2000: Yongpyong Resort is spun off; Japan's Taiheiyo Cement Corp. acquires a 29 percent stake in Ssangyong Cement to become the largest shareholder.
2002: Ssangyong Cement (Singapore), Ltd. is spun off.

Though production costs for ceramics were high while demand was low, Kim's refusal to hurry beyond capacity coupled with innovative research into new materials meant that with ceramics Ssangyong Cement was well prepared before the new market had even taken off.

Another example of Kim's ability to buck the trend was his longstanding independence of political connections, though with increasing deregulation and domestic unpopularity the loosening of political connections had become inevitable for most *chaebols*. Despite great pressure and the offer of heavy state subsidies, Kim refused to join the lucrative munitions industry in 1976 and 1977. Even when, as a *chaebol*, Ssangyong was pushed into concentrating on heavy industry in the same year that Ssangyong Heavy Industries Co. (SHIC) was established after the takeover of a bankrupt firm to manufacture diesel engines and other machinery, Kim managed—after 11 years of losses—to promote this branch as the center of the machine industry, providing some of the expertise needed in the construction of internal combustion engines. The latter was central to his dream of entering the car industry.

SHIC set up Ssangyong Engine Research Institute in May 1989 to develop a new model engine. Its engines were approved by the Classification Society and it was poised to take on the international competition. Other car parts and heavy-duty presses were manufactured by Ssangyong Precision Industry Co., which was equipped with the most advanced technology in Korea. Kim also took over Sunglee Machinery Works Ltd. in 1977 to further support his automobile plans, adding the manufacture of wheel discs to its specialty of weaving machines. He established Sunglee Electronics Co. Ltd. in the same year to produce radio and audio equipment. Kim never attached as much importance to the audio and radio industry as did other *chaebols*.

In 1980 Kim completed his father's projects, and it marked the end of his own five-year plan: 5.6 million tons of capacity were added to the plant at Donghae and the oil refinery started operating. He went on to expand the paper industry, producing tissue and sanitary paper in conjunction with Scott Paper Co. in the United States in 1979 and sanitary napkins in an agreement with Uni-Charm in Japan, making Ssangyong Paper the best-known paper company in Korea by the late 1980s. He also incorporated Ssangyong Construction Co. Ltd. separately in 1977, rather than firing many trained employees who had worked as an inhouse construction team—at Donghae and Onsan, for instance—as well as constructing postwar rehabilitation projects. From there, the company went on to win contracts in Southeast Asia and the Middle East, including work on a record-breaking project in 1986: the tallest hotel in Singapore, a contract it would not have obtained without Ssangyong Cement Singapore's reputation for reliability. Working closely with Ssangyong Engineering Co. Ltd. (established in 1978) and with the expertise of Namkwang Engineering & Construction Co. Ltd. (established in 1947 and taken over in 1986) Ssangyong Construction Co. continued to expand its interests overseas, notably in a joint venture with the Ralph M. Parsons Group of the United States in 1987 in high-tech construction fields, including nuclear waste plants.

Following the streamlining of Ssangyong Cement operations by emphasizing planning and the use of computers, Kim established in 1981—against the advice of his colleagues—the Ssangyong Software & Data Co., renamed Ssangyong Computer Systems Corporation in 1988, which proved its mettle in designing the management system for the Olympics in Korea in 1988. Kim said he did not want to be left behind in this field.

Kim's most obvious and profitable success story was his agreement in 1983 to buy the ailing securities firm of the Hyosung Group at a time when Korean financial services were relatively undeveloped and the Korean stockmarket rather thin. When the economy boomed in 1986 and the stockmarket was actively promoted by the economic technocrats in government, Ssangyong Investment & Securities Co. was in the right position to reap the reward: a net profit of US$6.9 million in 1986. Under Koh Byung Woo, a former assistant minister of finance, it became a co-manager of the Asian Development Equity Fund and an underwriter of Thai and Brazilian funds, establishing offices in New York, London, and Zürich. With the lifting of restrictions on direct foreign investment in 1992, the company, as one of the big five in Korea, foresaw little difficulty in consolidating its position further. It already operated a highly esteemed investment research institute.

The 1980s were a golden age for the Korean economy, bringing three blessings: cheap dollars, cheap oil, and cheap loans. There were three successive years of 12 percent economic growth starting in 1986 when wages were still low, the exchange rate was favorable, and demand was strong. Once the trade deficit had been turned to surplus, overseas investment became imperative, not least because of rising Korean labor costs and the need to get closer to overseas markets. However, between 1987 and 1990 this trend reversed as Korean exports fell because of high domestic costs, and the 25 percent appreciation of the Korean won relative to the Japanese yen. Although the *chaebols* were once more favored by the government to boost the slowing economy and credit controls were eased, the gap between price and quality of products remained a problem.

Kim was aware that the only solution lay in improved efficiency, in which his record was good (per capita sales among employees rose eight times from 1975 to 1986); in better technology, a longstanding aim of his; and in more capital intensive production, something which came naturally in his line of business. Unlike Samsung or Daewoo, in the labor-intensive electronics and textiles businesses, respectively, Ssangyong had no great need to find a cheaper source of labor in Thailand or China. At the same time, the overseas networks for most subsidiaries were already well established.

Kim's pursuit of "harmony," "reliability," and "innovation" was perhaps the key reason for the group's steady growth. Not only did he embody a successful move towards second-generation control away from the authoritarian grip of his father, something with which other *chaebols* still struggled, but the group had an outstanding record in labor disputes. Taking his cue from his stay in the United States, he delegated authority to company presidents, did not rely on elites and encouraged participation of all employees while respecting the authority of juniors, recruited employees from all regions, emphasized the public and social duties of the company, and did not favor nepotism. Only Lee Sung Won, a brother-in-law, and Kim Suk Joon, his youngest brother, were employed by the company, the former as president of Ssangyong Oil Refining Co., Ltd. and the latter as director of Ssangyong Construction. Kim made it clear that he would hand over the reins to whomever was most competent.

Kim also liked to use five-year plans, believing that without long-term planning one would only go downhill, a view borne out by analyses of *chaebols* less inclined to take a long-term view. In 1976 the group was the first in Korea to introduce a management information system, which resulted immediately in the stabilization of the quality of its cement. This was followed by the Corporate-Identity Program in 1978 and the Corporate-Culture System in 1988 after two years' research by the planning and development office. These were designed to turn Kim's systematic approach and liberal management into part of a corporate culture unique to Ssangyong. The shift in focus towards heavy machinery and high-tech industries was not made without a carefully directed change in the corporate climate to back it.

While Ssangyong continued to produce cement and oil, Kim invested massively in car production since 1986 and intended to promote it as the key business of the 1990s in line with government plans to turn Korea into a net car exporter. He took over Dong-A Motor in 1986, an ailing car manufacturing firm with a deficit of US$5.5 million. In order to produce his X-car, a four-wheel-drive wagon-style jeep, he had to start from scratch, knowing the company would be in the red for at least three years. When the initial X-car prototype was completed, Kim rejected it because its balance was faulty. The purchase of 80 percent equity in the U.K. company Panther provided the necessary technical expertise to perfect the model and also provided an opening into Europe, the intended market for the model. Through Panther, a successful high-class sports car, the Solo II, was built and marketed selectively in various countries. Furthermore, with help from Mercedes Benz and Nissan and its own diesel technology, Ssangyong Motor Company was doing well with special-purpose vehicles, including dump trucks. It had no plans to enter the extremely competitive passenger car market as Korea's fourth car producer until 1991, when the step-by-step approach would have produced the necessary consolidation of expertise, for Kim was well aware that one wrong move could spell trouble for the entire concern. Kim did not believe in grafting foreign technology nor in selling below cost to boost production and sales—illustrated by the fact that although the Ssangyong group ranked sixth in sales, it was in fourth place in terms of profits. Though his more experienced competitors had been saved recently by a surge of domestic demand, the problem of oversupply remained acute.

Major Restructuring and Renewed Focus on Cement: 1990s–2000s

Growth and expansion continued in the early 1990s, and in 1991 Ssangyong Cement built a ferrite magnet plant in Pohang. It also purchased Riverside Cement Co., Ltd. in California. In 1994 two additional Chinese subsidiaries were established: Shanghai Baotailong Concrete Products Co., Ltd. and Shanghai Pulong Concrete Product Co., Ltd. The following year Ssangyong Cement constructed a plant to manufacture fine ceramics.

In the mid-1990s Ssangyong Cement faced a stagnant South Korean economy and slow growth. Though Singapore had been a key growth market for Ssangyong, it, too, was experiencing a slowdown in the construction market, which meant lower demand for Ssangyong's products. In South Korea, the market was expected to expand only 5 percent between 1996 and 2000. In response, Ssangyong Cement aimed to expand in various regions of China, particularly Shanghai, which was undergoing modernization. The company also planned to build a cement plant in Vietnam, where demand for its products was anticipated to grow some 76 percent from 1996 to 2000.

Being involved in so many industries and businesses weighed down Ssangyong considerably, and inefficiency grew. Coupled with the sagging South Korean economy, Ssangyong's debts rose, and by 1997 Ssangyong was in serious financial trouble. The group's debts were estimated to total about W 12 trillion (US$7.5 billion), with Ssangyong Motor accounting for some W 3.4 trillion. Realizing it needed to make significant changes to remain financially viable, Ssangyong implemented a major restructuring. It planned to focus on cement and oil refining as its two main areas of operation and to shed unprofitable businesses. Ssangyong Cement became the Ssangyong Group's anchor unit.

As part of the restructuring effort, in October 1997 Ssangyong not only sold its interest in Ssangyong Paper, but it also shed its stake in a number of other companies, including Ssangyong Motor Co., Ssangyong Heavy Industries, Ssangyong Precision Industry Co., Ssangyong Engineering Co., and others in the insurance, securities, and oil refinery units. In 1998 Riverside Cement was sold to Texas Industries, Inc., and in 1999 Ssangyong Oil Refining Co. was sold to Aramco. In 2000 Ssangyong Cement spun off its resort development unit into a separate entity, Yongpyong Resort Co., then sold half of it to Pan Pacific Resort Investment II for W 100 billion (US$88.4 million).

While Ssangyong worked to right itself financially, cement production continued to grow. In 1999 Ssangyong Cement announced that its cement exports would rise 300 percent compared to 1998 to reach a total of 3.5 million tons. Exports to the United States were expected to increase to one million tons from 1999 to 2002. Ssangyong Cement also aimed to sell 1.3 million tons to Japan and southeast Asia and 1.2 million tons to Europe and Africa by generating new clients.

Despite being the backbone of the Ssangyong Group, Ssangyong Cement was not spared in the group's restructuring, and in May 1998 it was announced that Ssangyong's cement plants were for sale. Ssangyong Group hoped to raised $1 billion through foreign investments by the end of 1998. In 2000 Japan's Taiheiyo Cement Corp. bought a 29 percent stake in Ssangyong Cement, making Taiheiyo the largest shareholder. An agreement to combine forces in cement production and distribution and to share managerial powers was also made. The combined production capacity of the two companies totaled 55 million tons per year, making it the fifth largest cement manufacturer in the world.

In October 2001 the restructuring of Ssangyong Cement's debts was finalized. The company's creditors, which included Chohung Bank and Korea Development Bank, agreed to W 200 billion (US$152.9 million) in new loans and a debt to equity conversion of W 1.7 trillion. The company moved ahead cautiously and was able to make a profit in 2002. For the fiscal year ended December 2002 Ssangyong Cement reported a net profit of W 65.2 million, a significant improvement over the net losses of W 985.8 billion in 2000 and W 462.5 billion in 2001.

In 2002 Ssangyong Cement exited Singapore by selling its stake in Ssangyong Cement (Singapore) Ltd. to Afro-Asia, a shipping company. As Ssangyong Cement had anticipated, the cement market in Singapore had declined. Increasing competition also cut into the Singapore unit's profits.

Ssangyong Cement, though relieved of some financial burden with the 2001 bailout, continued to face many challenges as it journeyed into the mid-2000s. The company was still the largest producer of cement in South Korea—in 2003 it manufactured a quarter of the cement produced in the country—and its cement exports accounted for about half of South Korea's cement exports. In addition to focusing on its core materials of ready-mixed concrete, ferrite magnet, and ceramics, Ssangyong Cement planned to expand into the environmental industry with the development of wastewater disposal systems and recycling options.

Principal Subsidiaries

Shanghai Pulong Concrete Product Co., Ltd. (China); Tianjin Yanlong New Building Material Co., Ltd.; Ssangyong Materials; Shanghai Baotailong Concrete Products Co., Ltd. (China).

Principal Competitors

Hyundai Cement Co.; Asia Cement Mfg. Co.; Hanil Cement Mfg. Co.; Sung Sin Cement Ind. Co.

Further Reading

''Korea's Ssangyong Cement Lays Foundation to Normalize Operations,'' *Asia Pulse,* January 3, 2001.

Moon Ihlwan, ''So Long, Corporate Reform: Ssangyong's Bailout Shows How Seoul Has Lost Its Nerve,'' *Business Week,* January 22, 2001, p. 52.

Schuman, Michael, ''Ssangyong Ventures Outside South Korea,'' *Asian Wall Street Journal,* September 23, 1996, p. 1.

South Korea: Financial Times Supplement, May 16, 1990.

Ssangyong Business Group, Seoul: Ssangyong Cement Industrial Co., Ltd., 1990.

Ssangyong News, February 1988.

Suh Hae Sung, ''Ssangyong Creditors Approve Bailout,'' *Asian Wall Street Journal,* October 8, 2001, p. M11.

Yoo Cheong-mo, ''Ssangyong Group Reborn As Leaner, Healthier Conglomerate,'' *Korea Herald,* February 25, 1998.

——, ''Ssangyong to Raise $1 Billion Through Sales of Key Units,'' *Korea Herald,* May 13, 1998.

—Marc Du Ry
—update: Mariko Fujinaka

Statoil ASA

Forusbeen 50
N-4035 Stavanger
Norway
Telephone: (47) 51-99-00-00
Fax: (47) 51-66-00-50
Web site: http://www.statoil.com

Public Limited Company
Incorporated: 1972 as Den Norske Stats Oljeselskap AS
Employees: 17,115
Sales: $34.87 billion (2002)
Stock Exchanges: New York Oslo
Ticker Symbol: STO; STL
NAIC: 211111 Crude Petroleum and Natural Gas Extraction; 211112 Natural Gas Liquid Extraction; 213111 Drilling Oil and Gas Wells; 213112 Support Activities for Oil and Gas Operations

Formerly known as Den Norske Stats Oljeselskap AS, Statoil ASA is Norway's oil and gas powerhouse. With operations in 25 countries, Statoil is involved in all areas of the petroleum business from exploration and production to refining and distribution. The company operates about 1,500 service stations in such European countries as Ireland, Poland, Norway, Sweden, and Russia. The Norwegian government has nearly 81 percent ownership of Statoil.

Capitalizing on Large Oil and Gas Reserves: 1960s–70s

Den Norske Stats Oljeselskap AS, also known as Statoil, was established in 1972 as a state corporation able to exert what the government saw as a necessary measure of management control over the development of oil and gas exploration and production. The government decided that a state enterprise could best secure public energy supplies and ensure the nation's control over its resources and industrial development. The United Kingdom and Malaysia are examples of other countries that set up state-owned oil companies in the 1970s, responding to supply shortages in the international oil market, while the development of Norwegian policy on hydrocarbon resources has provided a framework that many other countries have attempted to emulate.

The Norwegian continental shelf contained huge oil and gas reserves, of which only a small portion had been recovered. Natural gas accounted for around 60 percent of these reserves. Oil reserves in 1991 were estimated to last 30 to 40 years and gas reserves more than 100 years. The reserves were spread over some 250 million acres, of which large parts had yet to be explored, and Norwegian oil and gas were among the most difficult in the world to extract, because of the ocean depths and climatic conditions. North Sea crude was well suited for producing motor fuels because of its low sulfur and metal content.

The oil and gas discoveries in the North Sea only began to be a significant factor in the Norwegian economy and politics after 1962, when Phillips Petroleum first applied for sole rights to explore the continental shelf. The Norwegian government refused and proclaimed sovereignty over its continental shelf in 1963, defining it, in cooperation with the British and Danish governments of the day, as the median line between Norway and those two countries, and thus gaining unquestioned access to waters beyond the Norwegian Trench. It was not until 1965 that the government began to allocate licenses permitting exploration on a ''carried-interest'' basis. This meant that the government had an option to participate on equal terms for a given percentage of a production license if a commercial find was made in the area covered by the license. The first well was drilled in 1966, and in 1968 the first find of oil occurred in the Cod field. In the early years, exploration activity, based around Stavanger, was relatively quiet, but the big Ekofisk find at the end of 1969 demonstrated the potential of Norway's oil business and prompted the government to seek to establish a consistent oil policy.

Between 1970 and 1971 the government formed committees to draw up proposals for a state corporation. The system created in 1972 consisted of the Ministry of Industry, responsible for general policy and strategy; the Norwegian Petroleum Directorate, seeing to the day-to-day control and administration, unhampered, it was hoped, by political squabbling; and Statoil. The policy reflected the view that such strategic resources as oil and

Company Perspectives:

We make a positive contribution to the development of the communities in which we work. In all our operations, we will be among the front runners with environmental protection and safety.

gas could not be left to the multinationals. The state had to have guaranteed access to these resources to formulate its fuel policies and to exert more control over the oil operations of foreign companies by way of production limits, leasing requirements, and bidding practices, as well as through taxation. The Labour Party, which governed Norway from 1964 to 1981, worked to increase Statoil's control over domestic oil production. Statoil's virtual monopoly, through its participation in every oil and gas venture, would provide for further investments in refining, transportation, and marketing. In addition the government decided to set ceilings on the production rate, not only to avoid depleting its resources but also to keep the impact of the new industry on the overall economy at a manageable level, since it recognized the potential for social and economic dislocation.

From the outset Statoil was engaged in a diverse range of oil-related activities. In 1975 Norway became a net exporter of oil. In the same year Statoil commissioned its first subsea oil pipeline, the Norpipe line from Ekofisk to Teesside in the United Kingdom, and it began exploring for oil and gas. The first two gas pipelines, Ekofisk-Emden and Frigg-St. Fergus, were commissioned in 1977 and offshore oil loading began in 1979 on Statfjord. In 1978 an ethylene plant, jointly owned by Statoil (49 percent) and Norsk Hydro, was built at Rafnes in eastern Norway. Close by were Statoil's plants that produced polyethylene and polypropylene. Polyethylene was used in the making of products such as film, packaging, and cable insulation, while polypropylene went into medical equipment, car parts, and pipes, among many other products.

During these years the Norwegian oil industry contributed to the growth of industries such as shipping and chemicals, as the leading companies in these sectors speculated in the new industry, but at the same time Norwegian manufacturing was badly affected by a slowdown in growth. Between 1975 and 1980 the Norwegian government required foreign oil companies to engage in industrial cooperative projects as a means of qualifying for license awards. Many of these projects were in non-oil sectors.

Expansion and Exploration in the 1980s and Early 1990s

The 1980s provided Norway with increased wealth from its oil revenues, but because of the growing burden of foreign loans and the inflationary effects of oil on its other industries, the economy as a whole became less competitive. The foreign loans were needed for the continuing costs of foreign technical expertise and exploration. It remained an important policy to stimulate Norwegian industry generally through subcontracts with the oil industry.

In 1981 Statoil, with its competitors Saga and Norsk Hydro as co-owners, began to operate in the Gullfaks field, the first time that a field was owned 100 percent by Norwegian interests. Production started in Gullfaks in 1987. Statoil also decided to lay a pipeline, the Statpipe, a transport and process system for gas, from the Statfjord, Gullfaks, and Heimdal fields across the Norwegian Trench to shore. The Statpipe system came onstream in 1985, with 830 kilometers of pipeline on the sea floor at depths down to 330 meters. In 1984 it was decided to lay another pipeline to land crude from the Oseberg field at Sture near Bergen.

A Conservative-led government made some important changes in Statoil's powers and conditions in 1984. It was decided that all gross income from each field would go directly into the Treasury instead of through the usual taxes and dividends. Voting procedures were to be changed in all licensee groups. Statoil lost its automatic right to veto its partners' proposals, on licenses where it held a stake of 50 percent or more. To exercise this veto it would have to obtain the consent of the Oil Ministry. It was at this time that Norway decided to aim toward bringing the management of oil production in some fields entirely under Statoil's control, rather than subcontracting to foreign companies. In late 1984 Statoil reached an agreement with Mobil under which Statoil would take over as operator of the huge Anglo-Norwegian Statfjord field by 1989 at the latest. Norway was moving away from its dependence on foreign oil. The operation of Statfjord, the largest offshore oil and gas field in the world, passed over to Statoil in 1987.

While expanding its own operations Statoil recognized the advantages of retaining a prominent position within the industry as a whole, at home and abroad. Thus in 1986 it took the lead in negotiations on behalf of a group of companies for the selling of gas from two fields, Troll and Sleipner, to other European countries. Troll, in which Statoil had a 74.6 percent share, was one of the largest offshore gas fields in the world. It was under the operatorship of Royal Dutch/Shell, which had an 8.3 percent share in it, with Statoil taking over as operator when the fields came onstream in 1996. Statoil's share in the Sleipner field was 49.6 percent and its gas was due to come onstream in 1993. A pipeline system, known as the Zeepipe, was being built from these fields to Zeebrugge in Belgium. Statoil planned to construct and operate the pipeline and the reception terminal at Zeebrugge, where any solid or liquid components would be removed from the dry gas.

By 1985 Statoil had established itself as the largest industrial company in Norway, accounting for as much as 10 percent of gross national product and a similar proportion of government revenue. As it developed it began to look abroad for acquisitions as well as markets. Its first foreign acquisition was Exxon's Swedish oil retailing and petrochemicals operation, in 1985. The petrochemicals subsidiary, renamed Statoil Petrokemi AB, used naphtha, propane, and butane as its raw materials and its main products were ethylene and propylene. Statoil Petrokemi expanded and modernized its plant, creating one of the most advanced petrochemicals facilities in Europe. In 1986 Statoil purchased Exxon's oil products marketing company in Denmark and its Kalundborg refinery. It also bought a West German factory, which produced plastic for car bumpers and cable insulation. This was seen as an important investment for Statoil because it increased its capacity to process the plastic resins made at its petrochemical plant in Rafnes, in eastern

Key Dates:

1972: Den Norske Stats Oljeselskap AS is formed as a state corporation.
1975: Statoil commissions its first subsea oil pipeline and begins exploring for oil and gas.
1981: Statoil commences operations in the Gullfaks field.
1985: Statoil makes its first foreign acquisition with the purchase of Exxon's Swedish oil retailing and petrochemicals operation; the subsidiary is renamed Statoil Petrokemi AB.
1992: Statoil enters the Irish gas market through the purchase of BP's service stations in Ireland.
1994: Statoil and Neste join forces to form Borealis, a petrochemicals company.
2001: The company changes its name to Statoil ASA and is listed on the Oslo and New York stock exchanges.
2003: Statoil's CEO and chairman both resign as a result of a corruption scandal.

Norway. Statoil was now able to offer more than 70 different grades of plastics.

Statoil experienced its worst political and financial difficulties in 1987, starting with a drastic fall in profits as a result of the worldwide collapse in the price of oil in 1986. Politicians opposed to its economic and social power began to complain about its secretiveness and its closeness to the Labour Party establishment, as symbolized by the company's president, Arve Johnsen, who had been a government minister before joining Statoil. Then an official investigation revealed that cost overruns on the Mongstad refinery project had reached about NKr 5.4 billion ($850 million) and concluded that the refinery would never be profitable. At first the oil minister rejected opponents' claims that the report showed Statoil's management was overstretched in relation to the number of projects in which the company was involved. Amid allegations that the losses had been concealed deliberately, the company's six directors resigned and Johnsen too resigned. The government appointed a new board, however, to take up the challenge of expanding and diversifying Statoil's operations further.

Statoil now had a retail distribution network in all three Scandinavian countries. The government had originally forbidden Statoil to get involved in distribution, which was thought to be better handled by the multinationals. In 1991 Statoil's Norwegian marketing affiliate, Norsk Olje AS, an oil retail firm with 650 outlets throughout Norway, was renamed Statoil Norge AS and started using Statoil livery in its marketing. By then Statoil had a total of 1,600 retail outlets in Norway, Sweden, and Denmark.

Statoil had a better year in 1988 than in 1987. Statoil became sole owner of the Norwegian petrochemical plants that it had been operating since 1984 in conjunction with Norsk Hydro. This subsidiary was renamed Statoil Bamble, in reference to its main plant at Bamble, in southern Norway, which had come into operation in 1978–79 and had become the largest center for plastics technology in Norway. In the same year the Tommeliten field began producing oil without the platforms that were the standard technology in oilfields, by using equipment placed on the seabed and connected to the Edda platform on the Ekofisk field.

The Mongstad refinery, which had been the focus of Statoil's troubles in 1987, was started up again in 1989. Two more oil platforms, Veslefrikk and Gullfaks C, came onstream. The Veslefrikk was the first floating production platform after being in the Norwegian sector of the North Sea, while the Gullfaks C platform, which stood in 220 meters of water, was the world's largest production platform. Its total height of about 380 meters made it 30 meters taller than the Eiffel Tower.

In 1990 Statoil expanded its interests into new Danish technology. Its subsidiary Dansk Bioprotein sought to use bacteria to convert natural gas into edible protein, to be used as an additive in animal and fish feeds.

As Statoil looked for new international markets, it joined forces with BP to explore for oil in West Africa, Vietnam, China, and the Soviet Union. It also held exploration and production interests in The Netherlands and a 10 percent stake in a Chinese offshore license. In 1991 it made an oil discovery in the Danish sector of the North Sea. The following year Statoil expanded into Ireland with the purchase of BP's service stations. The Sleipner field came onstream in 1993 as planned.

Continued Growth and Growing Pains: Mid- to Late 1990s

Moving into the mid-1990s Statoil remained focused on the North Sea as its primary area of exploration. Exploration of new regions off mid-Norway in the Norwegian Sea was planned as well as development of existing fields. The East Statfjord field went onstream in late 1994, and the North Statfjord subsea oilfield went onstream in early 1995. Reserves at North Statfjord were estimated at 170 million barrels of oil, and Statoil hoped to produce 300 million barrels of oil between North and East Statfjord.

Diversification was also a component of Statoil's business strategy, and in 1994 the company formed a joint venture with rival Neste of Finland to produce petrochemicals and polyolefins. The terms of the agreement called for Neste to provide its technology and chemical assets while Statoil contributed funding and ethane from its North Sea ventures. The resulting joint venture, named Borealis, was based in Copenhagen, Denmark, and became the top producer of polyolefins in Europe. With operations across Europe, Borealis was off to a promising start—after one year in operation, the company reported sales of $2.6 billion.

Many of Statoil's projects went into operation in the 1990s, including the Europipe gas trunkline to Germany, the Troll gas project in the North Sea, Lufeng off China, Azerbaijan's Azeri-Chirag, and Norne in Norway. In 1998 the Franpipe gas trunkline went onstream. Aggressive exploration continued, and Statoil made new deepwater discoveries off Angola, an area that held much promise. By the late 1990s Statoil, which originally focused efforts solely on the Norwegian shelf, had operations in eight countries including Norway.

Strategic acquisitions also carried on. In 1994 Statoil made significant headway into the U.S. energy market with the purchase of The Eastern Group, based in Virginia. This U.S. subsidiary became Statoil Energy Inc. and focused on exploration and production of natural gas. Between 1994 and 1998 the company grew rapidly through 18 acquisitions, and in 1998 Statoil Energy reported revenues of $3.6 billion. Other Statoil acquisitions included Aran Energy, which held interests in fields off Ireland and the United Kingdom, and the Blazer properties in the Appalachian basin in the United States.

Although the company's holdings grew significantly in the 1990s, its revenues did not. Low oil prices plagued the entire industry, and in 1998 Statoil reported a net income of NKr 1.64 billion on sales of NKr 114 billion, a decrease from the previous year's net income of NKr 6.5 billion on sales of NKr 134 billion. Statoil faced other hurdles as well; in 1997 BP and Amoco merged, which necessitated the severing of the partnership between Statoil and BP.

As the end of the decade approached, Statoil began oil production from Asgard in the Norwegian Sea, a subsea field. Asgard field's reserves were estimated to hold more than two billion barrels of oil equivalent (boe). The ambitious project, which had a purported budget of $3.67 billion, included the construction of a new gas pipeline, an oil transport tanker, a storage and production vessel for oil, and the development of three fields. In 2000 gas production began from Asgard B, and the Asgard gas pipeline to Karsto began operation. Upon completion, the gas pipelines would transport gas not only from Asgard but from the Norne, Heidrun, and Draugen fields as well. Statoil estimated the system would handle some 15 percent of Norway's total gas exports to Europe.

Major Changes at the Beginning of the 21st Century

Facing the new millennium, Statoil saw the need for a radical overhaul of its business strategies and implemented a major restructuring effort. Olav Fjell, who joined Statoil as CEO in 1999, explained that for the company to remain successful in an increasingly competitive and volatile climate, it needed to make significant changes. Mergers and acquisitions of major players in the oil and gas industry, deregulation of European markets, and maturation of oilfields on the Norwegian shelf were all factors Statoil needed to take into consideration. Privatization of part of Statoil, Fjell believed, was necessary for Statoil's success. Speaking at a conference of the Cambridge Energy Research Associates in 2000, Fjell noted, "Statoil has to be able to compete on equal terms with its major competitors, in Norway and in the international markets, by being more flexible and reacting faster. Therefore, we must expose Statoil fully to market challenges." On June 18, 2001, shares of Statoil were listed on the Oslo Stock Exchange and New York Stock Exchange. The company also officially changed its name to Statoil ASA.

Statoil barreled ahead with expansion and exploration, and in 2002 it commenced construction of the Snohvit project, a subsea development in the Barents Sea, located on the Norwegian shelf. The project, Statoil's most complex to date, entailed the drilling of 21 wells from the Snohvit, Askeladd, and Albatross fields. The three fields held an estimated 193 billion cubic meters of natural gas. Statoil, the development's operator, held a 22.29 percent interest in the project. Partners included Petoro AS, TotalFinaElf Exploration Norge AS, Gaz de France Norge AS, Norsk Hydro Produksjon AS, and others.

As Statoil celebrated its 30th anniversary, the company gained a stronger presence in Iran when the Iranian government agreed to allow Statoil to develop several phases of Iran's South Pars gas and condensate field. In early 2003 Statoil was named operator of gas sales for the Shah Deniz gas and condensate field in Azerbaijan. The deal also included operation of the South Caucasus pipeline system, which funneled gas to Georgia and Turkey in addition to Azerbaijan. Further, Statoil was in talks with Russian companies regarding further exploration of the Barents Sea.

Net income rose from NKr 6.4 billion ($714,301) on sales of NKr 149.6 billion ($16.67 million) in 1999 to NKr 16.15 billion ($1.8 million) on sales of NKr 229.8 billion ($35.6 million) in 2000. Oil and gas production rose 7 percent in 2002 over 2001, but Statoil reported a slightly lower net income—NKr 16.8 billion in 2002 and NKr 17.3 billion in 2001.

Statoil entered 2003 with confidence and optimism, but in September the company found itself embroiled in a major corruption scandal. Statoil was accused of paying off Iranian consultants to help secure business deals in Iran. Statoil allegedly signed an 11-year contract in 2002 with Iranian consultancy firm Horton Investments and paid the firm $15.2 million. The consultancy was said to have ties to the NIOC, the Iranian national oil group. Norwegian police raided Statoil's headquarters as part of an investigation. As a result of the scandal, both Statoil Chairman Leif Terje Loeddesoel and CEO Fjell resigned. Newly appointed Chairman Jannik Lindbaek quickly hired U.S. firm Ernst & Young to review all of Statoil's international consultancy contracts. Inge K. Hansen was named acting CEO.

Despite the scandal, Statoil forged ahead, and finances were, for the most part, unaffected. For the nine months ended September 30, 2003, the company reported sales of Nkr 183.98 billion, up 3 percent over the same period of 2002. Net income fell slightly to NKr 12.27 billion. The company entered discussions with Russian company Gazprom over the Shtokman gas field, among the world's largest fields and located in the Barents Sea. Statoil began transporting gas from the Mikkel gas and condensate field in the Norwegian Sea and the Vigdis Extension came onstream. In addition, the company signed a contract with British Gas Trading to deliver gas to the United Kingdom for three years.

At the close of 2003 Statoil announced that it would enter a joint venture to develop and operate a 740-mile pipeline from Ormen Lange, the second largest gas field in Norway, to the United Kingdom. Statoil would have a 14.95 percent stake in the joint venture, known as Langeled. The pipeline was set to begin construction in 2005 and would be the longest subsea pipeline in the world, costing an estimated $2.9 billion.

Statoil hoped to put the corruption scandal behind and move forward as a major player in the oil and gas industry. With its Norwegian Sea assets reaching a plateau, Statoil planned to strengthen and expand its foreign investments in the 2000s. The company was well on its way, having operations in 25 countries by the end of 2003.

Principal Subsidiaries

Statoil Norge AS; Statoil Danmark A/S (Denmark); Statoil AB (Sweden); Statoil (U.K.) Limited (U.K.); Statoil North America Inc. (U.S.A.); Statoil Apsheron AS; Statoil Nigeria AS; Statoil Coordination Center N.V. (Belgium); Statoil Venezuela AS; Statoil Sincor AS; Statoil Investments Ireland Ltd. (Ireland); Statoil Forsikring AS; Statoil Exploration (Ireland) Ltd.; Statoil (Orient) Inc. (Switzerland); Statoil Pernis Invest AS; Mongstad Refining DA (79%); Statoil Metanol ANS (82%); Statoil Angola Block 17AS; Statoil Dublin Bay AS.

Principal Competitors

BP p.l.c.; Royal Dutch/Shell Group of Companies; TOTAL S.A.

Further Reading

Alperowicz, Natasha, ''Borealis: Strengthening European Operations,'' *Chemical Week,* March 29, 1995, p. 17.

''Construction of Most Northerly LNG Projects Starts,'' *Oil & Gas Journal,* November 25, 2002, pp. 38–40.

Gawlicki, Scott M., ''Statoil in America,'' *Independent Energy,* September, 1999, pp. 21–23.

Larsen, Rolf Magne, ''Low Oil Prices Call for Cautious, Focused Growth,'' *World Oil,* December 1998, pp. 39–40.

Noreng, Oystein, *The Oil Industry and Government Strategy in the North Sea,* London: Croom Helm, 1980.

Klapp, Merrie G., *The Sovereign Entrepreneur,* Ithaca: Cornell University Press, 1987.

Knott, David, ''Statoil Starts Oil Production in Asgard Field,'' *Oil & Gas Journal,* May 31, 1999, pp. 32–33.

Share, Jeff, ''Energy Giant Must Change to Prosper, Statoil CEO Says,'' *Pipeline & Gas Journal,* August 2000, pp. 38–39.

''Statoil Looks to New Areas to Bolster Production,'' *Oil & Gas Journal,* February 20, 1995, p. 38.

Townsend, David, ''The Future for Statoil,'' *Petroleum Economist,* December 2000, pp. 16–17.

——, ''Statoil: Exploring New Areas,'' *Petroleum Economist,* April, 2003, pp. 16–17.

Who We Are, What We Do, Where We Are, Stavanger: Statoil, 1990.

—Monique Lamontagne
—update: Mariko Fujinaka

T · · Online ·

T-Online International AG

Waldstrasse 3
Weiterstadt
D-64331
Germany
Telephone: 49 61 51 6 80 0
Fax: 49 61 51 6 80 6 80
Web site: http://www.t-online.de

Public Company
Incorporated: 2000
Employees: 2,760
Sales: EUR 1.8 billion ($1.84 billion) (2002)
Stock Exchanges: Frankfurt
Ticker Symbol: TOIGn.DE
NAIC: 514191 On-Line Information Services

T-Online International AG is one of Europe's largest Internet service providers, with some 12.5 million subscribers—including some three million ADSL customers—in Germany, France, Spain, Portugal, Austria, and Switzerland. In addition to its T-Online brand, the company operates as Club Internet in France and Ya.com in Spain and Portugal. The bulk of the company's operations remain, however, in its German home base, where the former Deutsche Telecom spinoff is the leading ISP with more than 9.5 million customers. Fully 75 percent of T-Online's revenues, which topped EUR 1.8 billion ($1.9 billion) in 2002, come from Internet access fees. Yet the company is reducing its reliance on subscriber charges, stepping up its efforts to generate revenues from advertising and e-commerce fees and services. As such, the company has been developing its paid content services, such as fee-based newsletters, a music download service, online gaming sites, and other e-commerce sites such as online banking services and a stake in the Booxtra online shop. Many of T-Online's content ventures are developed in partnership with other groups, such as France's Lagardere, which holds a 5 percent stake of the company, and publishing group Axel Verlag. T-Online is also investing in new wireless and mobile Internet access technologies. The company is listed on the Frankfurt stock exchange.

European Online Pioneer in the 1970s

The age of online communication began in the late 1960s when Sam Fedida, an engineer at the British Post (which later became British Telecom) connected his television to a computer mainframe using a decoder to transmit via ordinary telephone lines. The Prestel system, as it was then called, debuted in 1972. Expensive to acquire and to operate, the system, later renamed as Viewdata and then Videotext, never became widely popular, attracting no more than 100,000 customers before the advent of the Internet. Nonetheless, the system garnered a great deal of interest, notably among other European countries. In 1976, Fedida brought the Viewdata system to the Bundespost, which then controlled Germany's postal and telephone monopolies, and successfully transmitted data from England to Germany.

By the end of that year, a German name for the system, Bildschirmtext, had been chosen and by 1977 Bundepost presented its own system. Field testing began in the summer of 1980, and by the end of that year, Bildschirmtext, or BTX, had been officially launched with content and services available from such sources as Quelle, Neckermann, Verbraucherbank, and Otto. Access remained restricted, however, as testing of the system continued.

In 1981, the Bundespost debuted a new service—the ability to send messages via the BTX system, foreshadowing the later email protocol. Two years later, as the full-scale rollout of the BTX network came closer, businesses were granted access to the network in order to set up their own services. At last, in September 1983, the Bundespost officially launched the BTX service nationwide.

Subscriber response was relative subdued—by 1986, only 50,000 subscribers, in a country of more than 50 million, had signed up for the BTX service. The launch of a terminal device in 1987 helped encourage consumers to join the BTX network. Patterned after the French Minitel terminal launched some years earlier, the new Multitel combined a screen, keyboard, and telephone modem, making it easier for consumers to connect to and navigate the BTX network. The launch was a success, and by the end of 1987 the BTX network counted more than 100,000 subscribers.

Company Perspectives:

Strategy. Spotlight on the customer. At the core of all our activities are our customers' needs. We bring them online to the Internet, where we collect and refine content and services from the wealth of offerings in the interactive media world. We help our customers to communicate with each other and take advantage of the Internet shopping experience via an entire range of services.

Our goal. Our goal is to extend our existing customer relations both in Germany and in the countries where we have shareholding. This includes steadily increasing the depth of use and customer profitability. To do this we follow a two-pronged approach, consisting of expanding our access business on the one hand and developing high-quality content, services and new Internet worlds on the other. Technological progress and the emergence of attractive new services allows us to offer our customers things that were previously unavailable in this form.

Innovator and integrator. As an innovator and media integrator, T-Online is present everywhere, since we offer our customers everything via all media and terminal devices in a seamlessly integrated fashion. T-Online wants to continue to be a leading player in promoting Internet growth. It is also determined however to ensure that this pure growth is accompanied by the profitability of all our services for T-Online.

At the beginning of the 1990s, the BTX services was ported for use within the new Windows 3.0 operations, as personal computer use began to take off in earnest. In 1991, also, a new "Telebrief" service debuted on the BTX network, providing the ability to send letters across the network. The need for speed drove the Bundespost to upgrade its entire telephone network to support the new higher-speed ISDN protocol in 1993. That year, the BTX was linked into similar systems in neighboring countries, giving German subscribers access to services in Austria, Switzerland, the Netherlands, and Luxembourg. By 1994, the BTX service counted more than half a million subscribers.

The breakup of Bundespost, which resulted in the creation of Deutsche Telekom, also set the stage for the creation of a dedicated online services subsidiary, called Online Pro Dienste GmbH & Co. KG, in 1996. By then, however, Germany was experiencing the first wave of the Internet revolution, stimulated by the growth of online services such as AOL and Compuserve and by the huge success of the new World Wide Web protocol which provided a graphical interface for the Internet. In 1995, Deutsche Telekom made its first demonstration of Internet access and e-mail functions at the important CeBIT trade fair. That year, also, the company introduced a nationwide access number capable of connecting 14.4K modems. By the end of the year, Deutsche Telekom had decided to phase out the BTX service, which was bundled, along with Internet access and e-mail capabilities, into a newly branded service, T-Online.

Leading the 21st-Century European Internet Market

T-Online soon shifted fully to the use of Internet protocols, a move confirmed by the launch of a new generation of its software, version 2.0, which became available in 1997. The new software signaled the start of the Internet era in Germany, and by the end of that year the company had signed up more than 1.6 million subscribers, and topped the two million mark by March of the following year. The company also began testing a new high-speed protocol, ADSL that year, while also rolling out IDSN access to T-Online customers.

T-Online now began seeking partners to help it develop its range of services. In 1999, T-Online added international dial-up access, teaming up with iPass to allow subscribers to connect to the service from more than 150 countries. Similarly, the company launched a new webmail service, enabling subscribers to consult their messages online from any computer. In another partnership, T-Online joined with three publishing groups to form the online book service, Booxtra. In 2000, the company added online banking services through a partnership with Commerzbank, then acquired a stake in online auction site Atrada.

T-Online changed its name to T-Online International AG in 2000, in part to emphasize the group's extension beyond Germany, with the launch of Internet access services in Austria at the end of 1999. France became T-Online's next target, and in February 2000 the company agreed to transfer 5 percent of its shares to Lagardere in exchange for its takeover of popular French Internet provider Club Internet.

By then, Deutsche Telekom's rapid expansion had left it heavily in debt. In an effort to pay down some of that debt, T-Online was spun off as a separate company and listed on the Frankfurt stock exchange in 2000. Following its public offering, T-Online continued its international expansion, entering Switzerland with the launch of T-Online.ch AG, and buying up Ya.com, one of the leading Internet providers in the newly developing Spanish and Portuguese Internet markets. By the end of 2000, T-Online boasted more than 4.5 million customers in Germany alone—giving it the number two rank among Internet providers worldwide.

The arrival of Thomas Holtrop as CEO announced the start of a new period of growth for T-Online, which now set out to reinvent itself as a full-fledged media content provider in addition to its Internet access operations. As part of this effort, the group adopted new access fees, lowering its off-peak access rates. At the same time, the company developed a new range of services, such as the Bilt. T-Online site developed in partnership with Axel Springer Verlag, and the launch of the T-Online Instant Messaging service. Other content-related partnerships formed that year included an online travel service, news and information sites in conjunction with the Heute newspaper, and ZDF television. The company also acquired a 50 percent stake in Interactive Media CCSP AG, Germany's largest online marketing group, previously wholly owned by Axel Springer.

The year 2001 marked the wide-scale adoption of the Internet by the German public. By the end of that year, T-Online had successfully attracted more than ten million subscribers, including roughly half of all Internet users in Germany itself, in part by offering a new unlimited access package. The company rushed to claim its status as the leading Internet provider in the world—but lost a court challenge by AOL, which pointed out that more than 90 percent of the group's subscribers were in Germany.

Key Dates:

1976: Bundespost adopts name Bildschirmtext (BTX) for Videotext technology developed by Sam Fedida in England.
1980: Bundespost begins field trials of BTX service.
1983: BTX service rolls out nationally.
1987: BTX subscribers reach 100,000.
1995: Deutsche Telekom begins offering Internet access, which is then bundled with BTX, along with e-mail services, and rebranded as T-Online.
1996: Online Pro Dienste GmbH & Co. division of Deutsche Telekom is created, takes over operation of T-Online.
1999: First international expansion occurs with creation of Austrian T-Online service.
2000: Company changes its name to T-Online International; T-Online goes public with listing on Frankfurt exchange.
2002: Launch of paid content offering is pursued as part of new strategy designed to reduce reliance on subscriber fee revenues.
2003: Company launches music download and video on demand services.

Undaunted, T-Online continued adding new subscribers, especially through its full-scale rollout of ADSL access, signing up more than two million customers to the new high-speed protocol by mid-2002. In that year, also, the company announced that it was abandoning the traditionally free concept of the Internet and would begin charging for content and other services, such as online games and information newsletters. The company also debuted its own e-commerce site, T-Online Shop, selling computers and other multimedia equipment.

T-Online's ''monetarization'' efforts continued into 2003, with the launch of Internet-based pay-television and video-on-demand services. In September of that year, the company also debuted its own music download service, initially offering some 20,000 titles. At the end of 2003, the company announced a new expansion of its content offering with the acquisition of Scout24 AG, which had developed the Scout24 brand name into a variety of segments, including AutoScout24, JobScout24, FreindScout24, and others, with operations in Switzerland, Germany and elsewhere in Europe.

T-Online efforts to develop revenue streams in addition to its subscriber access fees appeared to be paying off by the new millennium, as the group reported rising operating profits and strong sales—by the end of 2003 the company's revenues had grown by more than 21 percent over the previous year. T-Online looked forward to continued international expansion as one of the world's leading Internet access and content providers.

Principal Subsidiaries

Atrada; Bild.T-Online.de; Booxtra; comdirect bank; Day by Day; Interactive Media; T-Online Travel; T-Online Venture Fund; Club Internet SA (France); Scout24 AG; Ya.com SA (Spain); T-Online.ch AG (Switzerland); T-Online.at AG (Austria).

Principal Competitors

Time Warner Inc.; Viacom Inc.; Centrica PLC; Groupe Cegetel; Tiscali SA; Wanadoo SA; Terra Networks, S.A.

Further Reading

Ackley, Ayla Jean, ''T-Online Battles to Win over German Investors,'' *New Media Age*, April 13, 2000, p. 30.

Sullivan, Bruce, ''T-Online's Bandwidth Hog Heaven . . . and Hell,'' *ISP Business News*, February 12, 2001, p. 7.

''T-Online Charges Customers for Exclusive Content,'' *EuropeMedia*, January 17, 2002.

''T-Online Sets up Music Download Service,'' *Online Reporter*, September 6, 2003.

Warner, Bernhard, ''For T-Online, the T Stands for Turmoil,'' *Industry Standard*, October 16, 2000, p. 164.

—M.L. Cohen

Target Corporation

1000 Nicollet Mall
Minneapolis, Minnesota 55403-2467
U.S.A.
Telephone: (612) 304-6073
Fax: (612) 696-3731
Web site: http://www.target.com

Public Company
Incorporated: 1902 as Goodfellow Dry Goods
Employees: 306,000
Sales: $43.92 billion (2002)
Stock Exchanges: New York Pacific
Ticker Symbol: TGT
NAIC: 452110 Department Stores; 452910 Warehouse Clubs and Superstores; 452990 All Other General Merchandise Stores; 454110 Electronic Shopping and Mail-Order Houses

Target Corporation is the fourth largest retailer in the United States, operating 1,556 stores in 47 states. Formerly Dayton Hudson Corporation, Target has three main retail divisions: Target Stores, Mervyn's, and Marshall Field's. Target Stores is the number two discount retailer in the country, trailing only Wal-Mart Stores, Inc., and has distinguished itself from its competitors by offering upscale, fashion-conscious products at affordable prices. The 1,225 Target stores, which are located in 47 states, generated 84 percent of Target's fiscal 2002 revenues. Included in this store count are Target Greatland units, which are much larger than the typical Target store, averaging 145,000 square feet versus 126,000 square feet; as well as SuperTarget outlets, which are combined discount/grocery stores, averaging 175,000 square feet. Generating 9 percent of 2002 revenues were Mervyn's 267 stores situated in 14 states, primarily in the West, Southwest, and Midwest (specifically Minnesota and Michigan). Based in the San Francisco Bay area, Mervyn's positions itself as a chain of moderately priced, family friendly, neighborhood department stores. Target Corporation's full-service department store division, contributor of 6 percent of sales, is now consolidated under the Marshall Field's banner. The 62 Marshall Field's stores (which include locations that formerly operated under the Dayton's and J.L. Hudson's names) are located in eight states in the upper Midwest, with the majority found within three metropolitan areas: Minneapolis, Chicago, and Detroit. Target Corporation's philanthropy has been and still is legendary. In 1989 the corporation received the America's Corporate Conscience Award for its magnanimity, and Target contributes more than $2 million each week to the communities in which its stores are located.

Early Years

Target Corporation bears the strong imprint of its founder, George Draper Dayton. Dayton's father, a physician in New York state, could not afford to send him to college, in part because the doctor freely gave his services to the poor. Hence Dayton set off on his own in 1873 at age 16 to work in a coal and lumberyard. A workaholic, he undermined his health and a year later had to return to the family home to recuperate. Undeterred, he went on to become a banker. Less than ten years later, in 1883, he was rich enough to buy the Bank of Worthington in Minnesota. Meanwhile he had married and had become active in the Presbyterian Church.

Dayton's connection with the Presbyterian Church proved to be instrumental to the rise of his Dayton Company. In 1893, the year of a recession that sent local real estate prices tumbling, the Westminster Presbyterian Church in Minneapolis burned down. The insurance did not cover the cost of a new building, and the only other source of income, a corner lot next to the demolished church, was unsalable because the real estate market was doing poorly. The congregation prevailed on the Dayton family, who were faithful members of the church, to purchase it so the building of a new church could proceed. Dayton bought it and eventually erected a six-story building on the lot. Casting about for tenants, he decided to buy the nearby Goodfellow Dry Goods store and set it up in the new building. In the spring of 1902 the store was known as the Goodfellow Dry Goods store; in 1903 the corporate name was changed to Dayton Dry Goods Company, then seven years later simply Dayton Company, the forerunner of Dayton Hudson Corporation and, ultimately, Target Corporation.

Eventually the store would expand to fill the six-story edifice. Dayton, with no previous experience in the retail trade, wielded tight control of the company until his death in 1938. His

Company Perspectives:

Target Corporation is a growth company focused exclusively on general merchandise retailing. Our principal operating strategy is to provide exceptional value to American consumers through multiple retail formats ranging from upscale discount and moderate-priced to full-service department stores.

principles of thrift and sobriety and his connections as a banker enabled the company to grow. As long as he was at the helm, the store was run as a family enterprise. Every Christmas Eve he would hand out candy to each employee of the store. Obsessed with punctuality, he was known to lock the doors at the onset of a meeting, forcing latecomers to wait and apologize to him in person afterwards. The store was run on strict Presbyterian guidelines: no liquor was sold, the store was closed on Sunday, no business travel or advertising was permitted on the Sabbath, and Dayton Company refused to advertise in a newspaper that sponsored liquor ads.

This approach did not stifle business; Dayton Company became extremely successful. A multimillion-dollar business by the 1920s, Dayton Company decided it was ready to expand, purchasing J.B. Hudson & Son, a Minneapolis-based jeweler, in 1929, just two months before the historic stock market crash.

Dayton Company managed to weather the Great Depression, although its jewelry company operated in the red for its duration. Dayton's son David had died in 1923 at age 43, and George turned more and more of the company business over to another son, Nelson. George Draper Dayton died in 1938. He left only a modest personal fortune, having given away millions of dollars to charity. In 1918 the Dayton Foundation had been established with $1 million.

Nelson Dayton took over the presidency of Dayton Company in 1938, when it was already a $14 million business, and saw it grow to a $50 million enterprise. World War II did not hamper business; rather, Dayton's turned the war into an asset. Consumer goods were so scarce that it was no longer necessary to persuade shoppers to buy what merchandise was available. Sales volume increased dramatically thanks to Dayton's managers, who obtained goods to keep the store full. Nelson Dayton was scrupulous about complying with the government's wartime control of business and when, for instance, the government carried out its drive for scrap metal, he ordered the store's electric sign dismantled and added to the scrap heap. Until Nelson Dayton's death in 1950, the company was run along the strict moral lines of his father, its founder. In January 1944 Dayton's became one of the first stores in the nation to offer its workers a retirement policy, followed in 1950 by a comprehensive insurance policy.

Shedding Conservative Image, Launching Target: 1950s–60s

With Nelson Dayton's death in 1950, Dayton Company embarked on a new era. Instead of one-man rule, the company was led by a team of five Dayton cousins, although one of them, Nelson's son Donald Dayton, assumed the title of president. The prohibition of liquor in the store's dining rooms was dropped, and soon Dayton Company would be completely secularized, advertising and doing business on Sunday.

The new management of Dayton Company undertook radical and costly innovations. In 1954 the J.L. Hudson Company, which would eventually merge with Dayton's, opened the world's largest shopping mall in suburban Detroit. It was a great success, and two years later Dayton Company decided to build a mall on a 500-acre plot of land outside of Minneapolis. Horrified to learn that Minneapolis had only 113 good shopping days a year, the architect decided to build a mall under cover; Southdale, the first fully enclosed shopping mall in history, was the result, with Dayton's as one of its anchor stores.

The safe, conservative management style favored by George Draper Dayton and his son Nelson passed into history; a younger, more aggressive management pushed for radical expansion and innovation would follow in its wake. The company established the discount chain Target in 1962, opening the first unit in Roseville, Minnesota, and in 1966 decided to enter the highly competitive market of retail bookselling, opening B. Dalton Bookstores.

In 1967 the company changed its name to Dayton Corporation and made its first public stock offering. That year, it also acquired San Francisco's Shreve and Company, which merged with J.B. Hudson to form Dayton Jewelers. In 1968 it bought the Pickwick Book Shops in Los Angeles and merged them with B. Dalton. Also in 1968 the company acquired department stores in Oregon and Arizona. The following year brought the acquisition of J.E. Caldwell, a Philadelphia-based chain of jewelry stores, and Lechmere, a Boston retailer.

Acquiring Hudson's, Mervyn's, and Marshall Field's: 1969–90

The year 1969 also saw a major acquisition: the Detroit-based J.L. Hudson Company, a department store chain that had been in existence since 1881. The merger resulted in Dayton Hudson Corporation, the 14th largest retailer in the United States. Dayton Hudson stock was listed on the New York Stock Exchange.

With the merger, the Dayton Foundation changed its name to the Dayton Hudson Foundation. Since 1946, 5 percent of Dayton Company's taxable income was donated to the foundation, which continued to be the case after the merger. The foundation inspired the Minneapolis Chamber of Commerce in 1976 to establish the Minneapolis 5% Club, which eventually included 23 companies, each donating 5 percent of their respective taxable incomes to charities. By the close of 1996 the foundation had donated over $352 million to social and arts-based programs.

Dayton Hudson bought two more jewelers in 1970—C.D. Peacock, Inc., of Chicago, and J. Jessop and Sons of San Diego. Company revenues surpassed $1 billion in 1971.

California-based Mervyn's, a line of moderate-price department stores, merged with Dayton Hudson in 1978. That year Dayton Hudson became the seventh largest general merchandise retailer in the United States, its revenues by 1979 topping $3 billion. Also in 1979 the Target chain become Dayton Hudson's largest producer of revenue, eclipsing the department stores upon which the firm was founded.

Key Dates:

1902: George Draper Dayton opens the Goodfellow Dry Goods store in a six-story building in downtown Minneapolis.
1903: Corporate name is changed to Dayton Dry Goods Company.
1910: Name is shortened to Dayton Company.
1938: Dayton dies; his son Nelson takes over the $14 million business.
1956: Company builds the world's first fully enclosed shopping mall, called Southdale, located in suburban Minneapolis.
1962: The discount Target chain is launched.
1967: Company changes its name to Dayton Corporation and makes its first public stock offering.
1969: Dayton merges with the Detroit-based J.L. Hudson Company department store chain, forming Dayton Hudson Corporation.
1978: Dayton Hudson acquires the California-based Mervyn's chain of moderate-priced department stores.
1979: The Target chain becomes Dayton Hudson's largest producer of revenue.
1990: Marshall Field & Company, a Chicago-based department store operator, is acquired.
1995: The first SuperTarget combined discount/grocery store opens; the Target Guest Card, the first store credit card in the discount retail industry, makes its debut.
1998: As part of e-commerce push, Rivertown Trading Company, a Twin Cities-based mail-order firm, is acquired.
2000: Reflecting the increasing importance of its discount chain, Dayton Hudson renames itself Target Corporation; Target Direct is formed as a separate e-commerce unit.
2001: The names of the Dayton's and Hudson's department stores are changed to Marshall Field's.

Dayton Hudson bought Ayr-Way, an Indianapolis-based chain of 50 discount stores, in 1980, and converted those units to Target stores. In 1982 the company sold Dayton Hudson Jewelers to Henry Birks & Sons Ltd. of Montreal, and in 1986 it sold B. Dalton to Barnes & Noble, Inc. In 1984, meantime, the operations of the company's two full-service department stores were combined into a new unit called the Dayton Hudson Department Store Company, though the Dayton's and Hudson's units themselves retained their separate identities. Revenues topped the $10 billion mark in 1987.

The late 1980s found the company the focus of an unsolicited takeover bid by the Dart Group, which would involve lawsuits by both parties before a stock market crash in October 1987 ended the takeover attempt. A second attempt at takeover of the company would be made nine years later, when rival J.C. Penney Company, Inc. offered more than $6.5 billion for the retailer. The offer, which analysts considered an undervaluation of the company's worth, was rebuffed. Meanwhile, Dayton Hudson continued its acquisitions, purchasing Marshall Field & Company from BATUS Inc., the U.S. subsidiary of B.A.T. Industries PLC, in 1990 for about $1 billion. Venerable Marshall Field's was as much a landmark in the Chicago area as Dayton's was in Minneapolis and the Hudson's stores were in Detroit; the acquisition added 24 department stores to Dayton Hudson's Department Store division while also doubling its department store retail space.

Launching Target Greatland, SuperTargets, and the Target Guest Card: 1990–95

While the Dayton's, Hudson's, and Marshall Field's department stores offered the monied customer more costly and sophisticated merchandise, the popular Target and Mervyn's catered to the budget-conscious customer, offering apparel and recreational items on a self-service basis. With the approach of the 21st century, Target continued to be Dayton Hudson Corporation's biggest moneymaker, combining a successful business mix of clean, easy-to-navigate stores with quality, trend-responsive merchandise. The year 1990 saw the opening of the first of over 50 expanded Target Greatland stores; in 1995, following the lead of such rivals as Wal-Mart and Kmart, the company opened its first SuperTarget, which combined the chain's successful general merchandise mix with a grocery store. Along with expanding its traditional department stores along the East Coast, six new SuperTargets were planned for 1996 alone. Also introduced in 1995 was the Target Guest Card, the first store credit card in the discount retail industry. By 1998 the Guest Card had attracted nine million accounts.

The proliferation of shopping malls and the recessionary economy of the early 1990s caused sharp changes in consumer spending patterns throughout the United States. By 1996 the country could boast 4.97 billion square feet of retail space—an average of 19 square feet per person nationwide—but retailers felt the pinch caused by such a large number of stores courting increasingly spending-shy consumers. This situation most negatively affected the mid-range and upper-range sales volumes generated by stores on the level of Mervyn's, Dayton's, Marshall Field's, and Hudson's. In response, Dayton Hudson developed new merchandising, customer service, and advertising strategies in an effort to stabilize these units' falling sales volumes. Mervyn's focused greater reliance upon national brands, coupling this with the growing use of print advertising and market expansion through the acquisition of six Jordan Marsh stores and five Lord & Taylor stores in south Florida. Dayton's, Hudson's, and Marshall Field's courted the upscale consumer through an increased mix of unique, quality merchandise, an increased emphasis on customer service, and an increased sales-floor staff, all of which heralded a return to the ''old-fashioned service'' on which Dayton Hudson was founded. Meanwhile, the Department Store unit worked to reduce inventories and invest in remodeling and technologically enhancing some of its older stores.

Reaching New Heights Under Ulrich: Late 1990s and Beyond

In 1994 Target executive Robert J. Ulrich was named chairman and CEO of Dayton Hudson. In that same year the company began a new strategy: developing a ''boundaryless'' corporate structure wherein resources and marketing and management expertise could be shared by each of the three divisions to create a more efficient organization. In 1996 Ulrich launched a three-year program to cut $200 million in annual operating expenses, particularly at the underperforming Mervyn's and department store units.

By early 1997 the Dayton Hudson Corporation consisted of three major autonomously run operating units: Target, with 735 discount stores in 38 states, represented the company's primary area of growth; the moderately priced Mervyn's chain operated 300 stores in 16 states, and the upscale Department Store Company operated 22 Hudson's, 19 Dayton's, and 26 Marshall Field's stores. Such broad-based expansion from the first six-story building in which Dayton was housed no doubt would have stunned the company's founder. Capital expansion, as well as more varied retailing, had taken their place alongside the old policies of thrift and sobriety.

During 1997, as part of its drive to turn around the Mervyn's chain, Dayton Hudson sold off or closed 35 Mervyn's outlets, including all of that chain's stores in Florida and Georgia. The late 1990s also saw a retrenchment on the department store front, as Dayton Hudson sold its Marshall Field's stores in Texas and also closed its Marshall Field's store in downtown Milwaukee.

Dayton Hudson also continued its efforts to give back to the communities that it served. During 1997 the corporation and its retail divisions made grants of approximately $39 million, including $2.8 million in scholarships that were given to high school seniors who had been involved in their communities. That year, the Target chain launched its Take Charge of Education program, which quickly became one of the corporation's most popular community support efforts. The program allowed Target Guest Card holders to sign up the school of their choice to receive 1 percent of their Guest Card purchase amounts. Within two years, more than 300,000 schools were registered and more than $800,000 had been given to these schools.

Ulrich's cost-cutting efforts, the trimming of Mervyn's and Marshall Field's, and—most importantly—the juggernaut that Target had grown into combined to bring unprecedented levels of profitability to Dayton Hudson by the end of the 1990s. While revenues increased to $33.7 billion by fiscal 1999, net income passed the $1 billion mark for the first time, reaching $1.14 billion, translating into a profit margin of 3.4 percent. This represented a near tripling of the 1996 profits of $463 million and a near doubling of the profit margin that year, 1.8 percent. These results were driven primarily by the Target chain, which had become one of the hottest commodities in retailing. Ulrich had concentrated on making Target a hip chain featuring stylish products at bargain prices. For example, in early 1999 the chain began selling top-end Calphalon cookware and also launched a line of stylish small appliances and household goods designed by architect Michael Graves—the latter line becoming so popular that it quickly grew to include more than 500 items. Through such innovations Ulrich succeeded in clearly setting Target apart from its discount competitors—even leading some customers/fans to use a fancy French pronunciation of the chain's name: Tar-*zhay*. Meantime, the chain continued to grow at the rate of about 70 stores per year, expanding into the key urban areas of Chicago and New York City, as well as making a more widespread push into the Northeast. As a result, the 900-strong Target chain was generating more than three-quarters of Dayton Hudson's revenues by decade's end, compared to around half ten years earlier. The growing predominance of the discount chain led the corporation to rename itself Target Corporation in January 2000.

During this same period the corporation quietly developed an e-commerce strategy that involved managing its own online distribution. It bought Rivertown Trading Company, a Twin Cities-based mail-order firm, in 1998 for $120 million to handle fulfillment, marketing, and distribution services for the e-commerce efforts of all the corporation's retail units. Online retailing gained a larger profile in early 2000 with the formation of a separate e-commerce unit called Target Direct. New store brand web sites were launched later that year.

The Internet push also played a role in more name changes. In January 2001 the corporation announced that it would change the names of its Dayton's and Hudson's department stores to Marshall Field's. Target was planning to launch an online gift registry during 2001 and wanted to do so under a unified department store name. Marshall Field's was chosen for several reasons: it was the most widely known of the three names, its base of Chicago was bigger than both Minneapolis and Detroit and was a major travel hub, and it was the largest chain, with 24 stores, compared to 19 Dayton's and 21 Hudson's.

At Target Stores (the official name of the discount division), meantime, use of the Target Guest Card began to plateau as consumers gravitated more to third-party Visa and MasterCard cards, cutting their use of private-label cards. Testing began on a Target Visa card in the fall of 2000, and by early 2003 nearly six million Guest Card accounts had been converted to the new Visa card. The Target chain itself kept expanding in the early 2000s, adding 62 discount stores to the total as well as 32 new SuperTarget stores during fiscal 2002, bringing the overall total to nearly 1,150 and the SuperTarget count to around 100. By this time, the Target Stores division was generating 84 percent of the parent company's revenues. Profits reached $1.65 billion, despite the continuing struggles of the Mervyn's and Marshall Field's divisions, where earnings were on the decline. Rumors continued to swirl about the possible divestment of one or both of these divisions, neither one of which was adding to its store count (Marshall Field's in fact sold its two stores in Columbus, Ohio, in 2003). Ulrich consistently denied such rumors, however, and thus far the stellar success of the Target Stores division had more than made up for the disappointing performance of Target Corporation's other retail units.

Principal Subsidiaries

The Associated Merchandising Corporation; Dayton's Commercial Interiors, Inc.

Principal Divisions

Target Stores; Mervyn's; Marshall Field's; Target Financial Services; target.direct.

Principal Competitors

Wal-Mart Stores, Inc.; Kmart Corporation; J.C. Penney Corporation, Inc.; Sears, Roebuck and Co.; Federated Department Stores, Inc.; The May Department Stores Company; The TJX Companies, Inc.; Kohl's Corporation; Dillard's, Inc.; Nordstrom, Inc.; Saks Incorporated; Ross Stores, Inc.

Further Reading

Apgar, Sally, ''Dayton Hudson at Crossroads: CEO Ulrich Still Struggling to Jump-Start Mervyn's Stores,'' *Minneapolis Star-Tribune,* July 23, 1995, p. 1A.

Berner, Robert, ''Dayton Hudson's Once-Fashionable Stores Tread Water,'' *Wall Street Journal,* August 1, 1996, p. B4.

Borden, Mark, ''Shoppers Love Target, but Shareholders Are Seeing Red,'' *Fortune,* September 18, 2000, pp. 64, 68.

Branch, Shelly, ''Hot Target Got Hot,'' *Fortune,* May 24, 1999, pp. 169–70, 172, 174.

Chakravarty, Subrata N., ''Planning for the Upturn,'' *Forbes,* December 23, 1991, pp. 48+.

Chandler, Susan, '' 'Speed Is Life' at Dayton Hudson,'' *Business Week,* March 27, 1995, pp. 84–85.

——, ''Under the Gun at Dayton Hudson,'' *Business Week,* May 20, 1996, pp. 66+.

Clark, Evan, ''Is Target Cooling?: Slow Growth Feared at Hot Discounter,'' *Women's Wear Daily,* September 30, 2002, pp. 1+.

Conlin, Michelle, ''Mass with Class,'' *Forbes,* January 11, 1999, pp. 50–51.

Dayton, George Draper, II, *Our Story: With Histories of the Dayton, McDonald, and Winchell Families,* Wayzata, Minn., 1987.

Facenda, Vanessa L., ''Is Target Becoming Too Trendy?,'' *Retail Merchandiser,* December 2002, pp. 19+.

Gill, Penny, ''Macke Maps Plan for Dayton Hudson,'' *Stores,* November 1991, pp. 28+.

Halverson, Richard, ''Target Powers Dayton Hudson's Growth,'' *Discount Stores News,* June 19, 1995, pp. 21+.

Levy, Melissa, ''An Old Firm, a New Name: Target Corp.,'' *Minneapolis Star-Tribune,* January 14, 2000, p. 1A.

Moore, Janet, ''Dayton Hudson: Wall Street's Darling,'' *Minneapolis Star-Tribune,* March 15, 1998, p. 1A.

——, ''The Store Formerly Known As Dayton's: Dayton's and Hudson's Department Stores to Use Marshall Field's Name,'' *Minneapolis Star-Tribune,* January 13, 2001, p. 1A.

Rowley, Laura, *On Target: How the World's Hottest Retailer Hit a Bullseye,* Hoboken, N.J.: Wiley, 2003.

St. Anthony, Neal, ''Behind the Bull's-Eye: Bob Ulrich Transformed Target, but the Chain Still Faces Tough Competition,'' *Minneapolis Star-Tribune,* November 30, 2003, p. 1D.

Webber, Oscar, *J.L. Hudson: The Man and the Store,* New York: Newcomen Society in North America, 1954.

—Sina Dubovoj

—updates: Pamela L. Shelton, David E. Salamie

Teijin Limited

1-6-7 Minami Honmachi
Chuo-ku
Osaka 541-8587
Japan
Telephone: (06) 6268-2132
Fax: (06) 6268-3205
Web site: http://www.teijin.co.jp

Public Company
Incorporated: 1918 as Teikoku Jinzo Kenshi Co., Ltd.
Employees: 23,265
Sales: ¥890.43 billion ($7.41 billion) (2003)
Stock Exchanges: Tokyo Osaka Nagoya Fukuoka Sapporo
Ticker Symbol: 3401
NAIC: 325211 Plastics Material and Resin Manufacturing; 325222 Noncellulosic Organic Fiber Manufacturing; 325411 Medicinal and Botanical Manufacturing; 325412 Pharmaceutical Preparation Manufacturing; 333292 Textile Machinery Manufacturing; 339113 Surgical and Medical Instrument Manufacturing

Teijin Limited is one of the leading Japanese manufacturers of synthetic fibers, with fibers and textiles accounting for 55 percent of the company's total sales in fiscal 2003. Approximately 20 percent of revenues are derived from Teijin's films and plastics units, which produce such products as polyester film, polyethylene naphthalate (PEN) film and resin, and polyethylene terephthalate (PET) resin. The company's pharmaceuticals and home healthcare unit, though relatively small and limited largely to the Japanese market, is Teijin's biggest generator of earnings, accounting for more than 45 percent of 2003 operating income; about 10 percent of sales originate with this unit, which concentrates on three main therapeutic areas: respiratory, cardiovascular, and osteoporosis. More than 70 percent of Teijin's revenues are generated domestically. Sales outside Japan are made principally in Thailand, Indonesia, China, the United States, Mexico, Italy, and the Netherlands.

Leader in Rapid Development of Japanese Rayon Industry

Rayon yarn was produced commercially in Japan for the first time by Yonezawa Rayon Yarn Manufacturing Plant, a branch factory of Azuma Industries Ltd. Twenty-three years earlier, Count Chardonnet had established the first rayon manufacturing plant in France. The Japanese rayon industry developed rapidly despite its late start, and in 1936 attained the highest production level of rayon yarn in the world, only 22 years after it had begun commercial production. The rapid development of the Japanese rayon industry was led by Teikoku Jinzo Kenshi (Imperial Manmade Raw Silk) Company Ltd.

Naokichi Kaneko, head clerk of Suzuki Shoten Co., the second largest general trading company after Mitsui Bussan, played an important role in Teijin's establishment. Kaneko first became interested in rayon yarn in 1892. An English merchant showed him rayon yarn produced by Chardonnet's factory, demonstrating that an imitation raw silk could be produced. Kaneko established the Nihon Celluloid Jinzokenshi Kabushiki Kaisha (Japan Celluloid Rayon Yarn Co., Ltd.) jointly with Mitsubishi and Iwai Shoten in 1908, and planned to produce rayon yarn after the company had succeeded in producing celluloid. He instructed Hirotaro Nishida, the head of the engineering department, to explore possibilities for importing technology or to bring in engineers from foreign rayon manufacturing companies. Kaneko also delegated Taketaro Matsuda, former head of the Monopoly Department in the Formosa Government-General, to Europe to undertake research on celluloid and rayon yarn between June 1905 and October 1906, and asked an engineer of the Monopoly Department to research rayon yarn when he went to Europe a little later.

Seita Kumura, a graduate of the Department of Chemicals at the Imperial Technical University of Tokyo, had been researching leather at the Taiyo Leather Manufacturing Plant, which employed 30 to 40 employees, and acquired a patent for frosted leather. Kaneko became aware of Kumura's research and established Tokyo Leather Ltd. in partnership with the owner of Taiyo Leather and Kumura in 1907. The next year this partnership was merged with Azuma Leather Co. Ltd., a subsidiary of

Company Perspectives:

Corporate Philosophy. Enhancing the quality of life through a deep insight into human nature and needs, together with the application of our creative abilities. IN HARMONY WITH SOCIETY. Our aim is to grow and evolve in harmony with the progress of society, thus justifying the trust of our shareholders, customers and the public at large.

We place the highest priority on safety and the preservation of our natural environment. EMPOWERING OUR PEOPLE. We encourage our employees to achieve self-realization by developing and exercising their abilities to the fullest. Teijin nurtures a corporate community with a wide variety of abilities and personalities to foster creative innovation.

Suzuki Shoten. Kumura became the chief engineer of Azuma Leather Co. Ltd., and began research on rayon while he continued to research and improve artificial leather production methods. Itsuzo Hata, a friend of Kumura's, became a lecturer at Yonezawa Engineering College in 1912 and dedicated himself to research on rayon yarn in close cooperation with Kumura. In 1914 Azuma Leather Co. Ltd. gave the researchers ¥1,200 to support their project. Kaneko visited Hata's laboratory the following year, was convinced of the future potential of rayon manufacturing, and decided to continue to support the research.

In October 1915 Kaneko established the Yonezawa Jinzokenshi Seizosho (Yonezawa Rayon Yarn Manufacturing Plant) as Azuma Kogyo Bunkojo, a branch factory of Azuma Leather Co. Ltd. At the end of 1915, Azuma Leather Co. Ltd. was renamed Azuma Industries Ltd. In July 1916 the plant supplied rayon yarn to Nishida Kahei Shoten, a prominent rayon yarn dealer in Japan, for the first time. Nishida Kahei severely criticized the yarn's quality, however, saying that it was no better than the foreign yarn of ten years earlier. Kumura and Hata tried to improve their yarn's quality, and the halt of imports of rayon yarn from abroad gave them a chance to acquire market share. In April 1917 they produced 100 pounds of rayon yarn per day. This was the same level at which Count Chardonnet had begun to produce rayon yarn commercially for the first time in the world. Production of rayon yarn increased steadily during World War I, and Suzuki Shoten separated the Yonezawa Rayon Yarn Manufacturing Plant from Azuma Industries Ltd. to establish Teikoku Jinzo Kenshi (Imperial Rayon Yarn) Co., Ltd., a subsidiary of Azuma Industries Ltd., whose capital amounted to ¥1 million. The executive board members consisted of persons related to Suzuki Shoten and Azuma Industries, and included Kumura and Hata.

Mixed Fortunes in Mid-20th Century

Teikoku Jinzo Kenshi's fortunes were mixed in the early years. Many rayon yarn manufacturing companies which started up in the boom during and just after World War I went bankrupt during the Reactionary Crisis in 1920, and Teikoku Jinzo Kenshi almost went bankrupt. Its financial difficulties arose because the crisis coincided with Teikoku Jinzo Kenshi's beginning construction of a new factory in Hiroshima. Suzuki Shoten, its parent company, offered sufficient credit to enable Teikoku Jinzo Kenshi to overcome its problems and to continue the construction of the new factory. After 1923 the company entered a phase of high profits and maintained this level despite the entry into the industry of Mitsui Bussan and the three largest cotton spinning companies. Suzuki Shoten went bankrupt in the Japanese financial crisis of 1927, and Teikoku Jinzo Kenshi bore the liabilities, which amounted to ¥10 million, in place of Suzuki Shoten. Teikoku Jinzo Kenshi managed to repay the debts within four years, however, far earlier than originally scheduled, and continued to earn high profits as well. The company constructed the Iwakuni plant in 1927 and the Mihara plant in 1934. Its production volume of rayon yarn amounted to 60 million pounds in 1937, far exceeding the volume produced by Toyo Rayon Ltd., its closest competitor. By 1937, although it ranked third in the production of rayon staple, short fibers which have to be spun to make yarn, it came first in total production of rayon yarn and rayon staple. Teikoku Jinzo Kenshi was the oldest and the largest rayon producer in Japan when the Sino-Japanese War broke out.

During World War II the company's rayon production capacity decreased significantly as a result of the compulsory mergers of enterprises by the government, five of which occurred after October 1941, and the removal and destruction of equipment, the aim of which was to use scrapped iron as raw materials for weapons. Moreover, Teikoku Jinzo Kenshi was forced to convert to production of fuel for airplanes at the end of the war. Production of rayon staple ceased at the Mihara plant in March 1945 and production of rayon staple at the Iwakuni plant in April 1945. By the end of the war, the company was producing neither rayon yarn nor rayon staple. Immediately after World War II, the company experienced shortages of raw materials and chemicals. It produced a variety of goods such as salt, the sweeteners saccharin and dulcin, goggles, shoe cream, cosmetics, buckets, and handcarts in order to support its employees, and earned tens of millions of yen in cash by disposing of poison gas at an army plant. Its production of rayon increased rapidly after April 1947, however, when the GHQ agreed that Japan could return to a rayon production capacity of 150,000 tons per year. Teikoku Jinzo Kenshi's production volume increased rapidly; rayon yarn production rose from 2.02 million pounds in 1946 to 42.5 million pounds in 1955 and rayon staple from 1.3 million pounds to 37.75 million pounds during the same period. The company began to produce rayon yarn and rayon staple at the Iwakuni and Mihara plants, and constructed the Komatsu plant in 1949 and the Nagoya plant in 1951. Moreover, it earned large profits during the Korean War boom period. Its sales amounted to ¥8.1 billion, and profits before tax were ¥3.7 billion.

Moving Beyond Rayon in the Postwar Period

After World War II, however, Teikoku Jinzo Kenshi's position in the chemical fiber industry declined. Staple production in Japan rapidly increased and in 1953 its volume surpassed 1938 levels, its previous pre- and postwar peak, whereas filament production was slow to recover and failed to reach prewar peak levels. After the war, Teikoku Jinzo Kenshi ranked first in filament production but ranked between seventh and tenth in staple production. Moreover, it lagged behind other chemical-fiber companies in entering newly developing synthetic-fiber

Key Dates:

1915: Azuma Leather Co. Ltd. (later Azuma Industries Ltd.) establishes a rayon manufacturing plant.
1918: The rayon plant is separated from Azuma Industries as Teikoku Jinzo Kenshi (Imperial Rayon Yarn) Co., Ltd.
1927: Production begins at a new factory in Iwakuni.
1934: New plant in Mihara starts operation.
1945: Production of rayon temporarily ends as the company is forced to concentrate on the manufacture of military supplies.
1958: Teikoku Jinzo Kenshi begins producing polyester fiber after reaching agreement to import polyester technology from the U.K. firm Imperial Chemical Industries Ltd., jointly with Toyo Rayon.
1962: With rayon becoming less important for the company, it changes its name to Teijin Limited.
1963: Production of nylon begins.
1971: Teijin withdraws from the production of rayon yarn.
1978: Company establishes Teijin Pharmaceutical Co., Ltd.
1983: Teijin Pharmaceutical is amalgamated with the parent company, becoming an operating division.
1991: Teijin establishes joint venture companies in the United States and Europe with E.I. du Pont de Nemours and Company (duPont) for the production and sale of polyester film.
1999: As part of restructuring, the firm sets up an international advisory board.
2000: Teijin and duPont expand their polyester film alliance into a global one involving joint ventures in seven nations.
2002: Polyester apparel fiber business is spun off into a wholly owned subsidiary called Teijin Fibers Limited.
2003: Teijin adopts a holding company structure; its pharmaceutical and home healthcare unit is transferred into a wholly owned subsidiary named Teijin Pharma Limited.

industries. Toyo Rayon began to produce nylon and Kurashiki Rayon—known as Kuraray after 1970—produced vinylon, a synthetic fiber made from poly-vinyl-alcohol, in the early 1950s. Toyo Rayon, Teikoku Jinzo Kenshi's rival, earned high profits by succeeding in nylon production. Teikoku Jinzo Kenshi staked its existence upon importing polyester technology from Imperial Chemical Industries Ltd. (ICI) of the United Kingdom. Shinzo Ohya, a former leader of the company now active in the political world, returned to become Teikoku Jinzo Kenshi's president in 1956. Teijin succeeded in importing polyester technology from ICI jointly with Toyo Rayon, and began to produce polyester fiber at the Matsuyama plant in 1958. Its polyester fiber division began to produce profits in the latter half of 1959, and by the latter half of 1960 contributed 82 percent of profits. Teikoku Jinzo Kenshi monopolized the market for polyester jointly with Toyo Rayon. It started a prize-contest for product brand names with Toyo Rayon, resulting in the name "Tetoron," which it advertised actively. Teikoku Jinzo Kenshi spent more on advertising than other companies, and in the early 1960s the company's ratio of advertisement cost to sales was higher than for any other chemical fiber producing company. Teikoku Jinzo Kenshi organized a production team in the Hokuriku district, where the largest consumers of polyester fiber were located, and assisted weavers both technically and financially. These were the main reasons for its success in the polyester business.

President Ohya developed aggressive strategies, backed by the company's good business record and the rapid growth of the Japanese economy. Teikoku Jinzo Kenshi entered other fields in the synthetic fiber industry, establishing Teijin Acrylic Ltd., which produced acrylic fiber, jointly with two other chemical companies and one wool company in 1959. Teikoku Jinzo Kenshi began to produce nylon at the Mihara plant in 1963. It thus became a general synthetic-fiber-producing company, and was renamed Teijin Ltd. in 1962. However, it withdrew from rayon staple production in 1967, from strengthened rayon yarn production in 1969, and from rayon yarn production in 1971, as they were no longer profitable. The content of Teijin's business changed significantly after 1958 when it began to produce polyester fiber. By the latter half of 1959, rayon accounted for less than half of total sales, and by the first half of 1960 synthetic fiber accounted for more than half of total sales. After that, synthetic fiber's share of sales increased rapidly to reach 75.1 percent in the latter half of 1973, of which polyester represented 56.6 percent and nylon 14.1 percent.

Diversifying Widely in the 1960s and 1970s

Teijin also moved upstream to the production of raw materials for synthetic fibers. In 1963 Teijin began to produce telephtalic acid, which was necessary for polyester fiber production. In 1964 it established Teijin Hercules Ltd., which produced dimethyl-telephtalate (DMT) jointly with Hercules Inc. in the United States and in 1968 established Teijin Petro Chemicals Ltd., which produced paraxylene and orthoxylene, raw materials of polyester. In 1966 it invested in Japan Soda Ltd. and participated in its management. Nisso Petro Chemical Ltd., Japan Soda's subsidiary, produced ethylene oxide and ethylene glycol. Teijin thus became able to supply its own intermediate and raw materials for polyester fiber production. In 1963 Teijin established Japan Lactam Ltd., which produced caprolactam, jointly with Sumitomo Chemicals and Kureha Chemicals.

Teijin also began an aggressive diversification strategy, establishing a Future Business Department in 1968 and setting up many subsidiary companies in the fields of pharmaceuticals, construction materials, foods, cosmetics, and leisure. It also established an Oil Development Department in 1970 and began to develop oil resources in Iran, Nigeria, and the Straits of Malacca. Its investment in and loans to related companies increased rapidly from ¥30.6 billion at the end of March 1968 to ¥169.1 billion at the end of March 1978. On the eve of the first oil crisis in 1973, oil development and future businesses constituted two of Teijin's three main pillars—the third was textiles, its traditional business.

Under Ohya's guidance, Teijin began active expansion abroad. In 1961 it established a joint venture with a local company in Sri Lanka and subsequently entered Formosa, Korea, Thailand, Vietnam, the Philippines, Brazil, and Australia. In 1973 its foreign subsidiaries consisted of five in textiles and yarn manufacturing and 14 in spinning, weaving, dyeing, and printing. Teijin planned to increase its overseas production of polyester textiles and yarn to more than three times the level of 1973, to exceed domestic production within five years. The plan, however, was not realized.

Refocusing on Core Areas in Late 1970s and 1980s

Teijin's business performance deteriorated and its operating profits were in the red for the first time by the first half of 1977. President Ohya circulated a memorandum entitled "A State of Emergency" to all directors of departments. He ordered them to reduce manufacturing costs drastically, develop high value-added merchandise, improve non-profitable businesses, decrease administrative costs at headquarters, and develop new businesses in textiles-related fields. He emphasized the importance of adaptability if the company was to keep ahead in the 1980s. Teijin reduced its number of employees drastically, from 10,346 at the end of 1977 to 7,446 at the end of 1978, and thoroughly reexamined its related companies, including those overseas. Investment and loans in related companies decreased from ¥169 billion at the end of 1978 to ¥120 billion at the end of 1983, and its ratio to the amount of total assets decreased from 38.6 percent to 26.8 percent during this period. Teijin retreated from the oil development and polyester businesses in Spain and Brazil and from many other fields.

The liquidation of nonprofitable businesses almost came to an end in 1982 and profits before tax increased from ¥11.8 billion in 1982 to ¥37.6 billion by 1990. In 1982 polyester continued to occupy the most important position in terms of sales. Polyester film was the most profitable item among chemicals, with various uses such as photograph films; magnetic tape for VTR, audio, and computer; and wrapping materials. Especially in the field of base film for magnetic tape, Teijin shared a monopoly with Toray Industries, Inc. (the former Toyo Rayon). Its sales structure changed somewhat in 1990, and polyester's and nylon's share of sales decreased to 51.1 percent and 10.1 percent, respectively, with pharmaceuticals accounting for 12.3 percent. Chemicals' share remained almost stable, accounting for 23.3 percent of sales. Teijin established Teijin Pharmaceutical Co., Ltd. in 1978 as a 100-percent-owned subsidiary and amalgamated it in 1983. Gamma-globulin was the most successful product of its Medicine Manufacturing Department. Nonfiber products contributed more than half of Teijin's net profits as polyester film and pharmaceuticals were far more profitable than textiles. The 1980s ended with the appointment of Hiroshi Itagaki as president and CEO.

Establishing Series of Joint Ventures in the Early to Mid-1990s

One focus for Teijin in the early 1990s was returning its polyester film business to profitability. Japanese makers of polyester film, which was principally used in the production of audio- and videotape, had been hurt by shrinking demand for these products, prompting many of them to transfer production outside of Japan into markets with lower production costs. Rather than establishing its own overseas production plants, Teijin went the joint venture route. In late 1991 the company established joint venture companies in both the United States and Europe with E.I. du Pont de Nemours and Company (DuPont) for the production and sale of polyester film. Teijin subsequently closed one of its three domestic film-production plants and switched the other two plants to the production of general industry-use films. These restructuring efforts helped return Teijin's polyester film business to the black by 1995.

Teijin established several other joint ventures in the early to mid-1990s. In late 1993 the company joined with Itochu Corporation, a Japanese trading giant, and Mantero Seta S.p.A., a leading Italian silk maker, to form TMI Europe S.p.A. as a European-based manufacturer and marketer of polyester fabrics. Teijin took a 51 percent stake in the new venture, which opened a new factory in Vercelli, Italy, in June 1996. Teijin and DuPont joined forces again in September 1995, this time creating a 50–50 joint venture called Teijin DuPont Nylon Ltd. for the production and marketing of nylon fiber in Japan. Early the following year Teijin set up a polyester film joint venture in Indonesia called P.T. Indonesia Teijin Films.

Also in 1996, Teijin began independent selling of all the pharmaceutical products that it produced. This ended more than 18 years of collaboration with Fujisawa Pharmaceutical Co., a much larger Japanese drug company. Teijin no longer needed Fujisawa's assistance in marketing its products, having gradually built up its own nationwide sales network since 1988. Starting with fiscal 1997, Teijin's pharmaceutical division began consistently generating more than 50 percent of the company's total profits, while still accounting for only about 10 percent of revenues.

Late 1990s and Beyond: Restructuring for the New Century

Overall, the 1990s were a period of stagnation for Teijin as the company failed to reach the level of profits achieved in 1990. Shosaku Yasui, a one-time economist who joined the company in 1957, took over as chief executive in 1997 and concentrated on turning the firm around. Two key early initiatives of Yasui, launched in 1999, involved cutting the executive board from 24 members to 10 in order to achieve faster decision-making, and setting up an international advisory board that included John A. Krol, former chairman and CEO of DuPont, and Ronald Hampel, former chairman of ICI.

Yasui also continued to emphasize joint ventures, particularly to turn Teijin into more of a global player. In January 2000 Teijin and DuPont expanded their polyester film alliance into a worldwide one involving joint ventures in seven nations: Japan, the United States, the United Kingdom, Luxembourg, the Netherlands, Indonesia, and Hong Kong. Together, these ventures generated $1.5 billion in annual sales and commanded global market share of 25 percent, ahead of the other two major players in this field, Toray Industries and Mitsubishi Chemical Corporation. Also in 2000 Teijin gained majority control of Toho Tenax Co., Ltd. (the newly named Toho Rayon Co.), making it a consolidated subsidiary. Toho Tenax was the world's second largest producer of carbon fiber, a high-performance fiber experiencing more rapid growth than that of polyester fiber. Another growth area for Teijin was polycarbonate resin, a plastic used in production of compact discs and

DVDs. In October 1999 the company started up a large new production plant in Singapore that solidified its position as the number three polycarbonate player globally, behind GE Plastics and Bayer AG.

Teijin also gained another foothold in the North American market in 1999 by setting up a polyester filament manufacturing joint venture in Mexico with Alpek S.A. de C.V. Further foreign bases were gained in November 2000 through the acquisition of the polyester monofilament business of the U.S. firm Johns Manville Corporation, which had operations in both the United States and Germany. Polyester monofilaments were used in such applications as paper manufacturing materials, conveyor belts, and filters. In February 2001 Teijin gained its first significant wholly owned manufacturing entity in Europe by acquiring Twaron Products from the Dutch chemicals group Acordis. Twaron (renamed Teijin Twaron B.V.) was one of the world's two largest makers of para-aramid fibers, a high-performance chemical material used in the production of such products as optical fibers. Seeing the increasing importance of information technology (IT) to his business, and continuing to seek areas with greater potential for future growth, Yasui set up an IT business called Infocom Corporation that began operating as a joint venture with trading company Nissho Iwai in 2001. Infocom was involved in a wide variety of IT applications, including information services and software, working with clients both inside and outside of Teijin. Infocom went public in March 2002 with a listing on the NASDAQ.

Yasui moved into the chairmanship of Teijin in November 2001, retiring from his executive positions for health reasons. Toru Nagashima took over as president and CEO, picking up the restructuring mantle from his predecessor. Just a few months later, Teijin announced another important restructuring move: the transformation of Teijin into a holding company that would oversee eight business groups, each of which would eventually become an entirely self-contained entity. The first group to receive this treatment was the polyester apparel fiber business, which was spun off into a wholly owned subsidiary called Teijin Fibers Limited in April 2002. One year later, Teijin officially adopted the holding company system, and in October of that year the pharmaceutical and home healthcare unit was transferred into a wholly owned subsidiary named Teijin Pharma Limited. The latter move followed the collapse of a proposed merger of the pharmaceutical division with Kyorin Pharmaceutical Co., whereby Teijin would have jumped to 20th from around 40th position in the Japanese drug sector. Teijin said that it would continue to seek a merger or acquisition as it aimed to double its annual drug sales of ¥100 million.

Meantime, Teijin Seiki Co., Ltd., the company's machinery manufacturing subsidiary—producing precision equipment, aircraft and oil hydraulic equipment, and textile and industrial machinery—was merged with Nabco Ltd. to form Nabtesco Limited. Teijin held only a minority stake in the new entity. Other developments in this period included the announcement in October 2002 that Teijin and DuPont would dissolve their nylon joint venture in Japan—Teijin DuPont Nylon—having concluded that it no longer made economic sense to operate the company.

Results for fiscal 2003 of ¥890.43 billion (US$7.41 billion) represented a drop in revenues of 1.6 percent, mainly resulting from Teijin's divestment of noncore businesses, such as acetate fibers. Operating income jumped 19.7 percent, to ¥35.3 billion ($293.7 million), but Teijin suffered a net loss of ¥20.98 billion ($174.5 million), reflecting restructuring costs of ¥15.82 billion ($131.6 million) and, following stock market declines, a write-down of securities investments of ¥25.98 billion ($216.14 million). Teijin returned to profitability in the first half of fiscal 2004 as it focused on aggressively investing in the four areas of its business that were deemed to have the greatest potential for future growth: industrial fibers (aramid and carbon fibers), plastics (polycarbonate resin), pharmaceutical and home healthcare, and IT services.

Principal Subsidiaries

Infocom Corporation (50%); Teijin Solufil Limited; Teijin Advanced Films Limited (67%); Teijin Shokusan Co., Ltd.; Teijin Finance Limited; Teijin Logistics Co., Ltd.

Principal Operating Units

Textile Fibers Business Group; Industrial Fibers Business Group; Fiber Products Marketing Business Group; Films Business Group; Plastics Business Group; Medical & Pharmaceutical Business Group; Machinery & Engineering Business Group; IT Business Group.

Principal Competitors

Nan Ya Plastics Corporation; Toray Industries, Inc.; Asahi Kasei Corporation; Toyobo Co., Ltd.; Kuraray Co., Ltd.; Mitsubishi Rayon Company, Limited; Unitika Ltd.; Mitsubishi Chemical Corporation; Tuntex, Thailand Public Co. Ltd.; E.I. du Pont de Nemours and Company; KoSa B.V.; Kanebo, Ltd.; GE Plastics; Bayer AG.

Further Reading

Higuchi, Ikuko, "Teijin to Focus on Future Markets," *Daily Yomiuri,* February 18, 2002.

Hunter, David, "Teijin's Nagashima Picks His Winners," *Chemical Week,* November 20–November 27, 2002, p. 53.

——, "Teijin's Yasui Looks for Results," *Chemical Week,* October 4, 2000, pp. 39, 41.

Kurosawa, Hiroshi, "Teijin President Resists Status Quo," *Nikkei Report,* June 17, 2002.

Kurosawa, Hiroshi, and Takayuki Itagaki, "Textile Firm Beefs Up Pharmaceutical Ops," *Nikkei Report,* January 24, 2003.

Malone, Scott, "Teijin: Navigating Waters of Change," *Women's Wear Daily,* October 10, 2000, p. 18.

Marsh, Peter, "An Experiment in Restructuring," *Financial Times,* November 1, 2000, p. 16.

Mitchell, Richard H., *Justice in Japan: The Notorious Teijin Scandal,* Honolulu: University of Hawaii Press, 2002.

Smith, Charles, "Japanese Drug Companies Cancel Merger," *Daily Deal,* April 24, 2003.

Teijin Limited, *Teijin no Ayumi, vols. 1–11,* Tokyo: Teijin Ltd., 1968–1977.

Yamazaki, Hiroaki, *Nihon Kasensangyo Hattatsushi Ron,* Tokyo: University of Tokyo Press, 1975.

—Hiroaki Yamazaki
—update: David E. Salamie

Telefónica de Argentina S.A.

Tucumán 1
Buenos Aires, C.F. 1049
Argentina
Telephone: (54) (11) 4332-2066
Fax: (54) (11) 4334-1995
Web site: http://www.telefonica.com.ar

Subsidiary of Telefónica S.A.
Incorporated: 1990
Employees: 8,998
Sales: 3.04 billion pesos ($902.08 million) (2002)
Stock Exchanges: Buenos Aires New York
Ticker Symbols: TEAR; TAR
NAIC: 511140 Database and Directory Publishers; 513310 Wired Telecommunications Carriers; 518111 Internet Service Providers

Telefónica de Argentina S.A. offers local, domestic long-distance, and international fixed-line telephone services in Argentina, access to the Internet and related services, telephone accessories and equipment, and, through a subsidiary, self-published telephone guides. The company is indirectly owned by Telefónica, S.A., the Spanish-based telecommunications leader in the Spanish-speaking world; it also manages Telefónica de Argentina. Telefónica de Argentina is one of the biggest companies in Argentina and vies with Telecom Argentina Stet-France Telecom S.A. for the position of telecommunications leader in Argentina.

The Road to Privatization: 1946–90

Telephone service in Argentina began in 1881 by means of a Belgian company and a U.S. company, which were acquired by an English company the following year to form Union Telefónica del Río de la Plata, Ltd. An English rival merged with this company's successor, Compania Union Telefónica, in 1886. This became, in 1929, the Compania Union Telefónica del Río de Plata Ltd., an indirect subsidiary of the U.S.-based International Telephone & Telegraph Corporation (ITT). Union Telefónica remained by far the largest telephone company in Argentina. It was acquired by the Argentine government in 1946. Most smaller telephone companies had been added by the end of 1951, leaving only two private ones. This government quasi-monopoly was renamed Empresa Nacional de Telecomunicaciones (ENTel) in 1956.

ENTel experienced 26 changes of administration in the next 32 years. Unsatisfied demand reached such a level that people waited as long as 14 years to have a telephone line installed in their homes. Connection costs rose as high as $1,500. Of the three million lines in the late 1980s, two million were business lines. In terms of quality, over 60 percent of the network was obsolete or out of order. Each telephone was, on average, out of service and repaired several times per year. More than half of all local calls and 60 percent of international calls failed to go through. Because the cost of calls was kept low for political reasons, proper maintenance was impossible, and the company's deficit rose to $1.48 billion. In addition, ENTel was the most corrupt telephone company in the world, according to one journalist. After President Carlos Menem announced his intention in 1990 to sell 60 percent of the company to outside investors and 10 percent to its employees, a 24-hour work stoppage isolated Argentina from the rest of the world and even kept Menem from reaching his economic adviser in Washington.

For purposes of sale, ENTel was divided into two concessions, one for the northern half of Argentina and one for the southern half. The successful bid for the southern half, which included the downtown business district of Buenos Aires and more than half the surrounding province of Buenos Aires, was made by Compañia Internacional de Telecomunicaciones S.A. (Cointel), a company owned by Madrid-based Telefónica de Espana S.A., Citicorp Equity Investments S.A., and Organización Techint, a large Argentine family-controlled holding company. Cointel paid $114 million in cash and $2.7 billion in debt instruments for 60 percent of what became Telefónica de Argentina. In return, Telefónica de Argentina received a seven-year monopoly on telecommunications in the southern half of the nation, plus the right to an additional three-year concession if it fulfilled various conditions and targets intended to improve and expand service. Telefónica de Espana became the managing

Key Dates:

1990: The company is founded to provide telecommunications service in southern Argentina.
1992: The government sells its remaining 30 percent stake in Telefónica de Argentina.
1997: The company's annual revenue doubled since 1992.
1999: Telefónica de Argentina earned a double-digit profit margin in each year of the decade.
2000: Telefónica S.A. buys out its consortium partners as its subsidiary's monopoly ends.
2001: Telefónica de Argentina spins off its cellular, data transmission, and special services.
2002: Telefónica de Argentina loses almost $1 billion amid an economic crisis but avoids default.

and operating partner. To finance the acquisition, Cointel issued $588 million worth of debt and company shares to outside investors. As a result Citicorp Equity Investments (later CEI Citicorp Holdings S.A.) emerged as the main shareholder, with 20 percent, followed by Banco Río de la Plata, Telefónica de Espana (later Telefónica S.A.), Techint, the Bank of Tokyo, and the Bank of New York.

Highly Profitable in the 1990s

Telefónica de Argentina was an immediate success, earning $53.3 million on revenue of $878 million in its first 11 months of existence and paying a dividend after its first year of operation. When the government put its 30 percent stake up for sale in 1992, it collected $848.7 million for its shares—far in excess of its own expectations. The highest bidder, a Banco Río de la Plata consortium that included Merrill Lynch & Co., Inc. and CEI, took 51 percent of these shares One-quarter of the shares were reserved at a discount for small investors, and an estimated 70,000—including Menem himself—sent in bids. Telefónica de Argentina's gains were achieved although some former ENTel employees, collaborating with accomplices within Telefónica, were engaged in sabotage, ''hijacking'' lines from paying customers or putting them out of service and then demanding bribes to have them ''repaired.''

Telefónica de Argentina not only cracked down on this practice but—along with Telecom Argentina—was able to cut costs by taking a hard line with the employees retained after privatization. They lost the right to guaranteed employment, promotion by seniority, automatic wage adjustments, and special privileges like free installation of telephones and reduced rates. The workday was raised from 7 to 8¼ hours. Unions could no longer determine who would be hired, favoring the relatives and acquaintances of existing workers, and they lost a decisive say over working conditions. There was a drastic fall in employee absenteeism, to roughly one-third of the former level.

Telefónica de Argentina spent $5.4 billion between 1990 and 1996 to modernize and expand its system. The number of public phones quadrupled. The percentage of the network that was digitalized increased sixfold. The number of lines per 100 people nearly doubled, becoming the highest for a private telecommunications operator in Latin America. Telefónica earned a profit margin of at least 10 percent on sales in each year of the 1990s. Annual revenue doubled between 1992 and 1997. Between 1990 and 1996 the company paid $3.2 billion in taxes, levies, and social security contributions. These achievements did not come without social costs. Opponents of privatization felt that ENTel had been undervalued and sold at a bargain price that short-changed the public. The number of employees in Telefónica's area of operation fell from 23,000 to 11,000, of which almost 5,000 were new hires. The cost of making calls soared, far outstripping what customers in Western Europe and the United States were paying in relation to the average industrial wage.

Telefónica de Argentina, through an associated company, began offering mobile cellular service in 1993 first under the trade name Miniphone, later under the trade name Unifón. Its dial-up Internet service was later supplemented by a broadband offering named Speedy. Value-added telecommunications services included data transmission, telex, digital paging, toll-free numbers, universal numbers, shared telephone expenses, calling cards, prepaid cards, call waiting, call forwarding, voice messaging, telepolling, telemarketing, private virtual networks, point-to-point digital networks, telephone access by commercial customers to digital trunk lines, telephone access for audiotext providers, three-way conference calls, hot lines, wake-up calls, collect calls, speed dialing, and itemized billing. Competition was limited in cellular services, but any company was free to offer data-transmission and Internet services in competition with Telefónica de Argentina and Telecom Argentina. Until 1999 international telephone service was provided by Telintar S.A., a company that Telefónica de Argentina owned jointly with Telecom Argentina, but this arrangement was ended by government decree. Shortly after, Telefónica de Argentina also assumed Telintar's function of selling telephone equipment and accessories, partly through a network of retail stores.

Telefónica de Argentina became associated with the cable television network Cablevisión S.A.—ending earlier ties with Cablevision's rival Multicanal S.A. and its owner, Grupo Clarin S.A.—through the majority stake taken in this company by parent Telefónica. By the end of 1997 Techint had sold its stake in Telefónica de Argentina to Telefónica. In 2000 Telefónica purchased the shares of Telefónica de Argentina held by U.S. venture capital firm Hicks, Muse, Tate & Furst, Inc. (through CEI Citicorp Holdings) for a 30 percent premium over the market price.

Telefónica de Argentina was a member of two joint ventures of telecommunications companies that constructed in 1999 and 2000, and then continued to operate, two submarine cable systems providing new, alternative routes to the United States and other parts of the world. In 1999 the company formed E-Commerce Latina S.A. as a joint venture with Alto Palermo S.A. to sell via the Internet a variety of goods, including music compact discs, books, computer hardware and software, and electrical appliances.

Tougher Going in the Early 21st Century

Telefónica de Argentina enjoyed, in 1997, an edge over rival Telecom Argentina, with 56 percent of all basic telephone service and about 52 percent of the cellular market. However, the Telefónica-Telecom telecommunications monopoly expired in November 2000, and each began competing in the other's territory. They were joined by 24 licensed competitors vying for a portion of the market. Analysts predicted that domestic and long-distance rates would fall sharply. Telefónica ranked second in revenue among Argentine companies in 2000 but slipped behind Telecom in 2001.

The 23 percent drop in Telefónica de Argentina's 2001 revenues was the result of a company reorganization engineered by parent Telefónica. Telefónica Moviles Argentina S.A. (later Telefónica Comunicaciones Personales S.A.) was spun off as a separate company to provide cellular service and other personal communications systems. Telefónica Data Argentina S.A. was spun off to offer data transmission and Internet services, except that Telefónica de Argentina remained the Internet service provider for noncorporate customers. Like Telefónica de Argentina, the spun-off companies were listed on the Buenos Aires stock exchange but remained controlled by Telefónica.

Telefónica de Argentina was, in 2003, offering fixed-line telephone service both within Argentina and internationally. At the end of 2002, 4.89 million lines were installed, and 4.42 million were in service. About 86 percent of the lines in service were residential, and 54 percent were in the greater Buenos Aires metropolitan area. A network of access lines, exchanges, trunk lines, and long-distance transmission equipment connected telephone customers. Residential access to the Internet was being offered under the name Advance, and there were about 119,000 subscribers at the end of the year. The company was also selling telephone equipment and accessories. Telephone books were being published by a subsidiary, Telinver S.A.

The collapse of the Argentine peso at the end of 2001 worsened the existing economic crisis and resulted in a fall of about 20 percent in the nation's income in 2002. Telefónica de Argentina was affected not only by the loss in purchasing power of its customers but also by legislation barring it from raising its rates even though the consumer price index rose by 41 percent during the year. The crisis forced it to put on hold plans to expand into northern Argentina and challenge Telecom Argentina there. The value of its assets fell from $6 billion to $1.67 billion. Unlike many other Argentine enterprises, Telefónica de Argentina avoided default on its debts, but the parent company had to shoulder 81 percent of its $898 million in short-term debt as of mid-2002.

For the year 2002, Telefónica de Argentina reported revenue (in terms of constant pesos at the end of 2001) of 3.04 billion pesos ($902.08 million), with an operating loss of 53 million pesos ($15.73 million) and a net loss of 3.24 billion pesos ($961.42 million). The latter figure was due mainly to the fall of the Argentina peso from parity with the U.S. dollar to about 30 cents, which meant that the company's dollar debt more than tripled, as did the amount of its interest payments on that debt. Its long-term debt at the end of the year came to 3.26 billion pesos ($967.36 million). Of Telefónica de Argentina's revenue in 2002, basic local and domestic telephone service, including monthly basic charges, accounted for 57 percent; special services, 12 percent; Internet access, 8 percent; public telephones, 7 percent; international long-distance service, 3 percent; directory publishing, 2 percent; and installation charges and telephone equipment, 1 percent each. In terms of constant pesos, the total revenue was only a little more than half the 2001 figure.

Despite the crisis, the company announced in November 2002 a plan to invest 2 billion pesos (about $600 million) over the next four years, including some 700 million pesos for mobile cellular telephones and 400 million pesos for high-speed Internet access. Aided by an appreciation of the Argentine peso against the dollar, Telefónica de Argentina rebounded during the first half of 2003, reporting $290 million in net income.

At the end of 2002 Cointel owned 62.5 percent of the Class A shares of Telefónica de Argentina common stock. Cointel was 100 percent owned by three affiliates of Telefónica S.A. at this time. One of these affiliates, Telefónica Internacional S.A., held 32.25 percent of the Class B (publicly traded) shares.

Principal Subsidiaries

E-Commerce Latina S.A. (50%); Telinver S.A.

Principal Competitors

BellSouth Latin America Group; Telecom Argentina STET - France Telecom S.A.

Further Reading

Abeles, Martin, et al., *El oligopolio telefonico argentino frente a la liberalización del mercado,* Bernal, Argentina: Universidad Nacional de Quilmes, 2001.

"Argentina Out of the Gloom," *Euromoney,* February 1992, Argentina supplement, pp. 16, 18.

"Cambiar la cultura," *Mercado,* January 1998, pp. 31–32.

Herrera, Alejandra, "Privatization of Telecommunications: The Case of Argentina," *Columbia Journal of World Business,* Spring 1993, pp. 47–57.

Hudson, Peter, "Hicks, Muse Ends Tango," *Variety,* January 10, 2000, p. 106.

Luxner, Larry, "Argentine Telco Sale Causes Uproar," *Telephony,* April 23, 1990, pp. 9–10.

Morgan, Jeremy, "Phone Profiteers Prove to Be Thorn in Argentina's Side," *Telephony,* June 1, 1992, pp. 9, 20.

O'Brien, Maria, "A Setback for the Reconquista," *LatinFinance,* July 2002, p. 34.

"Ringing the Right Bells; Telefónica," *LatinFinance,* January/February 1992, pp. 30, 32.

Swenson, James, "Latin America Hangs Up on Monopolies," *LatinFinance,* December 2000, p. 48.

Walter, Jorge, and Cecilia Senén González, eds., *La privatización de las telecomunicaciones en America Latina,* Buenos Aires: Editorial Universitaria de Buenos Aires, 1998, pp. 37–74.

—Robert Halasz

3M Company

3M Center
St. Paul, Minnesota 55144-1000
U.S.A.
Telephone: (651) 733-1110
Toll Free: (800) 364-3577
Fax: (651) 736-2133
Web site: http://www.3M.com

Public Company
Incorporated: 1902 as Minnesota Mining and Manufacturing Company
Employees: 68,774
Sales: $16.33 billion (2002)
Stock Exchanges: New York Chicago Pacific Swiss
Ticker Symbol: MMM
NAIC: 313320 Fabric Coating Mills; 314999 All Other Miscellaneous Textile Product Mills; 321114 Wood Preservation; 322222 Coated and Laminated Paper Manufacturing; 322233 Stationery, Tablet, and Related Product Manufacturing; 325211 Plastics Material and Resin Manufacturing; 325411 Medicinal and Botanical Manufacturing; 325412 Pharmaceutical Preparation Manufacturing; 325510 Paint and Coating Manufacturing; 325520 Adhesive and Sealant Manufacturing; 325612 Polish and Other Sanitation Good Manufacturing; 325991 Custom Compounding of Purchased Resins; 325998 All Other Miscellaneous Chemical Product and Preparation Manufacturing; 326112 Unsupported Plastics Packaging Film and Sheet Manufacturing; 326113 Unsupported Plastics Film and Sheet (Except Packaging) Manufacturing; 326199 All Other Plastics Product Manufacturing; 327910 Abrasive Product Manufacturing; 332999 All Other Miscellaneous Fabricated Metal Product Manufacturing; 333314 Optical Instrument and Lens Manufacturing; 333411 Air Purification Equipment Manufacturing; 334417 Electronic Connector Manufacturing; 334510 Electromedical and Electrotherapeutic Apparatus Manufacturing; 335931 Current-Carrying Wiring Device Manufacturing; 339112 Surgical and Medical Instrument Manufacturing; 339113 Surgical Appliance and Supplies Manufacturing; 339114 Dental Equipment and Supplies Manufacturing

The largest manufacturer in Minnesota, the 110th largest U.S. company overall, and a member of the Dow Jones ''30,'' 3M Company (known officially as Minnesota Mining and Manufacturing Company from its founding in 1902 until 2002) is Wall Street's epitome of high-tech/low-tech business and solid blue-chip performance. Its daunting inventory of some 50,000 products runs the gamut from Post-it Notes and Scotch tape to transdermal patches of nitroglycerin and a prescription cream for treating genital warts. Its equally daunting global presence extends to subsidiary companies in more than 60 countries and markets in nearly 200, as well as net sales from international operations of $8.91 billion, or 55 percent of the company's total 2002 revenue. 3M owes its formidable strength to its unusual corporate culture, which comfortably fosters innovation and interdepartmental cooperation, backed by a massive research and development budget, which typically exceeds $1 billion annually. Because of this, 3M ranks as a leader in—and in many cases a founder of—a number of important technologies, including pressure-sensitive tapes, sandpaper, protective chemicals, microflex circuits, reflective materials, and premium graphics. At the beginning of 2003, the company realigned into seven major business units: Consumer and Office; Display and Graphics; Electro and Communications; Health Care; Industrial; Safety, Security, and Protection Services; and Transportation.

Rough Start As Sandpaper Maker: 1900s–10s

Minnesota Mining and Manufacturing Company (soon nicknamed 3M) was formed in 1902 in Two Harbors, Minnesota, a thriving village on the shores of Lake Superior, by five entrepreneurs—a lawyer, a doctor, two railroad executives, and a butcher—in order to mine the rare mineral corundum and market it as an abrasive. The ill-planned venture—sparked by a flurry of other forms of mining operations in northeastern Minnesota—nearly bankrupted the company, for its mineral holdings turned out to be not corundum but low-grade anorthosite, a virtually useless igneous rock. This unsettling discovery (by whom or when is unclear) was never disclosed in the company records and, for whatever reason, did not deter the owners from establishing a sandpaper factory in Duluth, another more or less ill-fated scheme that placed the company further in jeopardy (3M faced a host of abrasives competitors in the East and was soon forced to import a garnet inferior to that owned by

Company Perspectives:

In 2002, we celebrated our 100th anniversary—a century of innovation. In the years since our successful introduction of the world's first waterproof sandpaper, we've evolved into a diversified technology company with leading positions in a broad range of important markets. Today, we produce thousands of innovative products and have companies in more than 60 countries. In extending our market reach, 3M's formula for success has remained the same: first, identify customer needs, and second, use 3M technology to pioneer innovative solutions to meet these needs. We've achieved consistent, profitable growth by creating innovative products, establishing strong relationships with customers and boosting operational efficiency. At the same time, we've created a culture that promotes employee pride and well-being, fosters integrity, and supports social and environmental responsibility.

domestic manufacturers, which resulted in a lower quality product). Company headquarters were moved to Duluth in 1905.

In May 1905 a principal investor named Edgar B. Ober, determined to save the company, persuaded friend and fellow St. Paul businessman Lucius Pond Ordway to join with him in rescuing 3M from almost certain demise by paying off $13,000 in debt and pumping in an additional $12,000 in capital. Together Ordway and Ober purchased 60 percent of the company; over the next several years, Ordway, a self-made millionaire, spent an additional $250,000 on a company that had yet to produce a profit, and Ober, who proceeded to oversee 3M, went without a salary. Ordway's continued backing, despite a strong desire to cut his losses early on and his decision to move the firm to St. Paul, ensured 3M's eventual health during the boom years following World War I. A new sandpaper factory was built in St. Paul in 1910, and 3M's headquarters were shifted to that city in 1916, the same year that the firm paid its first dividend.

Legacy of Innovation: 1920s–40s

Of greatest significance to both the company's foundation and future were the hirings in 1907 and 1909 of William L. McKnight and A.G. Bush, respectively. Former farmhands trained as bookkeepers, the two worked as a team for well over 50 years and developed the system that helped make 3M a success. McKnight ran 3M between 1914 and 1966, serving as general manager from 1914 to 1929, president from 1929 to 1949, and chairman of the board from 1949 to 1966. He created the general guidelines of diversification, avoiding price cuts, increasing sales by 10 percent a year, high employee morale, and quality control that fueled the company's growth and created its unique corporate culture. In some ways, the sales system overshadowed the guidelines. McKnight and Bush designed an aggressive, customer-oriented brand of salesmanship. Sales representatives, instead of dealing with a company's purchasing agent, were encouraged to proceed directly to the shop where they could talk with the people who used the products. In so doing, 3M salesmen could discover both how products could be improved and what new products might be needed. This resulted in some of 3M's early innovations. For instance, when Henry Ford's newly motorized assembly lines created too much friction for existing sandpapers, which were designed to sand wood and static objects, a 3M salesman went back to St. Paul with the news. 3M devised a tougher sandpaper, and thus captured much of this niche market within the growing auto industry. Another salesman noticed that dust from sandpaper use made the shop environment extremely unhealthy. Around the same time, a Philadelphia ink manufacturer named Francis G. Okie wrote McKnight with a request for mineral grit samples. According to Virginia Huck, "McKnight's handling of Okie's request changed the course of 3M's history. He could have explained to Okie that 3M didn't sell bulk minerals. . . . Instead, prompted by his curiosity, McKnight instructed 3M's Eastern Division sales manager, R.H. Skillman, to get in touch with Okie to find out *why* he wanted the grit samples." The reason soon became clear: Okie had invented a waterproof, and consequently dust-free, sandpaper. In 1921, after purchasing the patent and then solving various defects, 3M came out with Wetordry sandpaper and significantly expanded its business, eventually licensing two other manufacturers, Carborundum and Behr-Manning, to keep up with demand. It also hired the inventor as its first full-time researcher. This marked the creation of one of the nation's first corporate research and development divisions.

Sending salesmen into the shops paid off a few years later in an even more significant way, by giving 3M its first non-abrasives product line. In 1923 a salesman in an auto body painting shop noticed that the process used to paint cars in two tones worked poorly. He promised the painter that 3M could develop an effective way to prevent the paints from running together. It took two years, but the research and development division invented a successful masking tape—the first in a line of pressure-sensitive tapes that now extends to more than 900 varieties. The invention of Scotch tape, as it came to be called and then trademarked, established 3M as a force for innovation in American industry. Taking a page from its sandpaper business, 3M immediately began to develop different applications of its new technology. Its most famous adaptation came in 1930, when some industrious 3M workers found a way to graft cellophane, a Du Pont invention, to adhesive, thus creating a transparent tape.

Transparent Scotch tape, now a generic commodity, provided a major windfall during the Great Depression, helping 3M to grow at a time when most businesses struggled to break even. Another salesman invented a portable tape dispenser, and 3M had its first large-scale consumer product. Consumers used Scotch tape in a variety of ways: to repair torn paper products, strengthen book bindings, mend clothes until they could be sewn, and even remove lint. By 1932 the new product was doing so well that 3M's main client base shifted from furniture and automobile factories to office supply stores. During the 1930s, 3M funneled some 45 percent of its profits into new product research; consequently, the company tripled in size during the worst decade American business had ever endured.

3M continued to grow during World War II by concentrating on understanding its markets and finding a niche to fill, rather than shifting to making military goods, as many U.S. corporations did. Nevertheless, the war left 3M with a need to restructure and modernize, and not enough cash on hand to do so. To

Key Dates:

1902: Five entrepreneurs found Minnesota Mining and Manufacturing Company (soon nicknamed 3M) in Two Harbors, Minnesota, to mine corundum and market it as an abrasive; the firm soon finds that its mineral holdings are not corundum, placing its future in jeopardy.
1905: St. Paul businessman Lucius Pond Ordway begins investing in the company, stabilizing its finances; a sandpaper factory is established in Duluth.
1910: A new factory is built in St. Paul.
1914: William L. McKnight's long reign begins with his appointment as 3M general manager.
1916: 3M headquarters are moved to St. Paul.
1921: The company introduces Wetordry sandpaper after purchasing the patent from the inventor.
1925: Scotch masking tape is introduced.
1930: Scotch cellophane tape debuts.
1946: 3M's stock is listed on the New York Stock Exchange.
1976: 3M is named one of the 30 companies comprising the Dow Jones industrial average.
1980: The company begins selling Post-it notes.
1992: Foreign sales produce more than 50 percent of total sales for the first time.
1996: The divisions responsible for making floppy disks and other data-storage media are spun off into an independent firm called Imation Corporation; audio- and videotape operations are shuttered.
2001: GE veteran W. James McNerney, Jr., takes over as chairman and CEO, becoming the first outsider at the helm in the company's history.
2002: The company changes its name to 3M Company.

meet its building needs, in 1947 3M issued its first bond offerings. Its first public stock offering, coupled with its tremendous growth rate, attracted additional attention to 3M. Among the new products debuting in the immediate postwar period was Scotch magnetic audiotape, which was introduced in 1947. In 1949, when President McKnight became chairman of the board (with A.G. Bush also moving from daily operations to the boardroom), it marked the end of a tremendous era for 3M. Under McKnight, 3M had grown almost 20-fold. By its 50th year, it had surpassed the $100 million mark and was employing some 10,000 people.

Growing Reputation: 1950s

Such growth could not be ignored. Now that 3M was publicly traded (having debuted on the New York Stock Exchange in 1946), investment bankers took to recommending it as a buy, business magazines sent reporters to write about it, and other companies tried to figure out how 3M continued to excel. McKnight's immediate successor as president, Richard Carlton, encapsulated the company's special path to prosperity with the phrase: ''We'll make any damn thing we can make money on.'' Yet the 3M method involved a great deal more than simply making and selling. Its métier had been, and would continue to be, finding uninhabited markets and then filling them relentlessly with high-quality products. Therefore, research and development received money that most companies spent elsewhere—most companies still did not have such departments by the early 1950s—and the pursuit for ideas was intense.

Carlton kept the company focused on product research (today, 3M honors its scientists through the Carlton Society), which led to further innovations in the 1950s: the first dry-printing photocopy process, ThermoFax (1951), Scotchgard fabric and upholstery protector (1956), and Scotch-Brite scouring pads (1958). 3M breezed through the 1950s in impressive fashion, with 1959 marking the company's 20th consecutive year of increased sales. Yet, for all its growth and diversity, 3M continued to produce strong profits from its established products. In a way, this was almost to be expected, given 3M's penchant for being in ''uninhabited'' markets. As noted by John Pitblado, 3M's president of U.S. Operations, ''Almost everything depends on a coated abrasive during some phase of its manufacture. Your eyeglasses, wrist watches, the printed circuit that's in a TV set, knitting needles . . . all require sandpaper.''

Skyrocketing 1960s to Earthly Ups and Downs in the 1970s and 1980s

In the 1960s 3M embarked on another growth binge, doubling in size between 1963 and 1967 and becoming a billion-dollar company in the process. Existing product lines did well, and 3M's ventures into magnetic media provided excellent returns. One venture, the backdrops used for some of the spectacular scenes from the 1968 movie *2001: A Space Odyssey,* earned an Academy Award. During the 1970s a number of obstacles interfered with 3M's seeming odyssey of growth. Among these were the resignations of several of the company's top executives when it was revealed that they had operated an illegal slush fund from company money between 1963 and 1975, which included a contribution of some $30,000 to Richard Nixon's 1972 campaign. Sales growth also slowed during the decade, particularly in the oil crunch of 1974, ending 3M's phenomenal string of averaging a 15 percent growth rate. 3M responded to its cost crunch in characteristic fashion: it turned to its employees, who devised ways for the company to cut costs at each plant.

The company also had difficulties with consumer products. Particularly galling was the loss of the cassette tape market, which two Japanese companies, TDK and Maxell, dominated by engaging in price-cutting. 3M stuck to its tradition of abandoning markets where it could not set its own prices, and backed off. Eventually, the company stopped making much of its own magnetic media, instead buying from an overseas supplier and putting the 3M label on it (3M instead focused attention on data storage media for the computer market). The loss of the cassette market was not overwhelming: revenues doubled between 1975 and 1980, and in 1976 3M was named one of the Dow Jones Industrial 30.

Unfortunately, price-cutting was not the only problem confronting 3M as it entered the 1980s. Major competitors seemed to face the company on all fronts: the niches of decades past seemed extinct. When Lewis Lehr became company president in 1981, he noted, ''There isn't a business where we don't have to come up with a new technology.'' He promptly restructured 3M from six divisions into four sectors: Industrial and Consumer, Electronic and Information Technologies, Graphic Technologies (later renamed Imaging and combined with Information and Electronic), and Life Sciences, containing a total of some 40 divisions. He also established a goal of having 25 percent of each division's earnings come from products that did not exist five years before. Lehr's concern was not to keep the company going, for 3M was still well-respected, with a less than 25 percent debt-to-equity ratio and reasonable levels of growth. Shareholders, too, had little to complain about, for 1986 marked the 18th consecutive year of increased dividends. Rather, Lehr wanted to ensure that 3M would continue to develop new ideas. The major product to come out of the 1980s was the ubiquitous Post-it, a low-tech marvel created by Art Fry.

Challenges of the 1990s

L.D. DeSimone, who joined 3M in 1958 as a manufacturing engineer and moved into management while working in international operations, was named CEO in 1991. He took the helm of a ship being buffeted by economic recession and stiff price competition: sales rose an annual average of just 2 percent from 1991 to 1993. Kevin Kelly wrote in a 1994 *Business Week* article, ''It turned out that the creative juices that had transformed 3M into a paragon of innovation and the inventor of everything from ubiquitous yellow Post-it notes to surgical staples weren't producing new products fast enough.''

DeSimone pushed research staff to work more closely with marketers and transform existing technology into commercial products. Connecting with customers' needs took on more urgency. Product turnaround time was slashed; product development rivaled basic research. Customer-driven products gleaned from the new system included the Never Rust Wool Soap Pad made from recycled plastic bottles and a laptop computer screen film that enhanced brightness without heavy battery drain.

On the international front, foreign sales produced more than 50 percent of total 3M sales for the first time in company history in 1992. The Asia-Pacific region yielded nearly 27 percent of the $7 billion foreign sales volume. A major restructuring of European operations was completed in 1993: manufacturing plants were closed and consolidated and the workforce was trimmed in response to declining operating income.

The company achieved record sales, operating income, net income, and earnings per share in 1994. More than $1 billion of the $15 billion in total sales came from first-year products. DeSimone raised the bar: at least 30 percent of future sales were to come from products introduced within the past four years.

On a more somber note, in 1994 3M took a $35 million pretax charge against probable liabilities and associated expenses related to litigation over 3M's silicone breast implant business operated through former subsidiary McGhan Medical Corporation. 3M was named in more than 5,800 lawsuits claiming injuries caused by leakage or rupture of the implants.

In 1996, 3M dismantled the Information, Imaging and Electronics sector, which accounted for a fifth of its business. It was the largest restructuring effort in company history. The divisions making floppy disks and other data-storage media, X-ray film, and specialty imaging equipment were spun off as an independent, public company (Imation Corporation), and the audio- and videotape operations shut down entirely. 3M retained the businesses making electrical tapes, connectors, insulating materials, overhead projects, and transparency films. The company cut about 5,000 jobs.

Since DeSimone took command, 3M had pumped $1.2 billion into the Information, Imaging and Electronics division, yet operating profit margins remained only a third of the Industrial and Consumer Products and Life Sciences divisions. Persistent pricing pressures from competitors such as Kodak plus rising raw material costs prompted DeSimone to pull the plug on the audio and videotape business. A smaller, leaner operation—the new $2 billion Imation—was deemed to have better prospects in the equally fierce data-storage marketplace.

Following restructuring, 3M concentrated product development efforts on about two dozen core technologies. In 1997 the company achieved one of DeSimone's goals: 30 percent of total sales were generated from products introduced within the past four years. But 3M's numbers began slipping again in 1998. Michelle Conlin wrote in an October 1998 *Forbes* article, ''Are these unavoidable downward blips on a rising curve? Or are they signs of deeper trouble? 3M has been glacially slow to respond to the economic meltdown in Asia, where it gets 23% of its business. In the U.S. a flood of cheaper products made by competitors like Korean polyester film outfits SKC and Kolon have cut into 3M's sales.'' Conlin nevertheless conceded that 3M had promising products, such as bendable fiber-optic cable and a fluid to replace ozone-depleting chlorofluorocarbons, already in the pipeline.

Declines in both revenues and profits in 1998 prompted further restructuring, including a workforce reduction of about 5,000 that was completed by the end of 1999, the closure of about 10 percent of its global factories, and the jettisoning of a number of underperforming product lines. 3M also reorganized into six business segments in 1999: Industrial Markets; Transportation, Graphics, and Safety; Health Care; Consumer and Office Products; Electro and Communications; and Specialty Material. Highlighting the company's continued commitment to innovation, nearly 35 percent of revenues in 2000 came from products that had been introduced within the previous four years. Many of these products fell within higher-technology areas—a point often ignored by Wall Street analysts critical of the company's more recent product development efforts. For example, an important new 3M product line developed in the 1990s consisted of films to enhance the brightness of electronic displays, including those found on laptop computers, cellular phones, LCD televisions, and personal digital assistants. In 2000 the company began marketing these films under the Vikuiti brand.

Early 21st Century: Outsider at the Helm for the First Time

DeSimone's stewardship of 3M ended at the end of 2000 with his retirement. At the beginning of 2001, W. James McNerney, Jr., took over as chairman and CEO, becoming the first outsider at the helm in the company's nearly 100 years of existence. McNerney was a 19-year veteran of General Electric Company (GE)—like 3M a diversified, manufacturing-oriented corporation—having most recently served as head of GE Aircraft Engines. McNerney had lost out in a three-way battle to succeed legendary GE leader John F. (Jack) Welch, Jr. One of McNerney's first initiatives was to launch Six Sigma, a quality control and improvement initiative that had been pioneered by Motorola, Inc. and AlliedSignal Inc. and then adopted by GE in the late 1990s. The aim of the statistics-driven program was to cut costs by reducing errors or defects.

McNerney's cost-cutting focus was shown in other early initiatives, and 3M during his first year saved more than half a billion dollars through various efforts, including the layoff of 6,500 of the company's 75,000 workers and a major streamlining of purchasing functions. Another initiative, dubbed 3M Acceleration, involved expending more product development funds on the most promising ideas, dropping weaker ideas earlier in the process, and in this way getting the best products to market much faster. In implementing this and other initiatives, most of which focused on making the company more efficient, McNerney had to be careful not to drive out 3M's culture of innovation on which both the company's fame and its long history of success rested. Nevertheless, one apparent victim of McNerney's efficiency drive was 3M's revered "15 Percent Rule," which had allowed its employees to spend up to 15 percent of company time on independent projects, a process called "bootlegging" or "scrounging." Although the rule still existed in theory, it was increasingly difficult to act upon it within the evolving culture at 3M, which was seemingly becoming more short-term oriented.

Early in 2002 the company finally adopted its nickname as its formal moniker, officially becoming 3M Company. Acquisitions were coming more to the fore under McNerney, and the most significant deal of the early 2000s—in fact, the most expensive acquisition in 3M history—was the December 2002 purchase of Corning Precision Lens, Inc. for $850 million. The acquired unit, which was renamed 3M Precision Optics, Inc., was the world's leading supplier of optical lenses used in projection televisions. Overall, financial results for 2002 were encouraging, particularly given the difficult economic environment. While revenues increased only marginally, net income increased by about 20 percent after excluding nonrecurring items. That year, 3M paid a dividend for the 87th straight year and increased its dividend for the 45th consecutive year.

At the beginning of 2003, 3M reorganized yet again, this time attempting to gain improved access to larger, higher-growth markets. The company's largest division—Transportation, Graphics, and Safety—was divided into three units: Display and Graphics; Safety, Security and Protection Services; and Transportation. In addition, the Specialty Material segment was split up, with the unit's consumer-related products shifted into the Consumer and Office unit and its industrial products shifted into the Industrial unit. Overall, this increased the number of business units from six to seven; it also made the Health Care unit the company's largest in terms of both revenues (22 percent of the total) and earnings (27 percent).

In October 2003, 3M implemented a major realignment of its research and development operations. Fourteen separate technology centers were closed, with the scientists at these centers shifted either to a newly formed Corporate Research Laboratory or to the company's 40 divisions, where they would be able to work closely on products within those divisions. The main goal of this R&D shakeup was to move more of 3M's R&D resources to the divisions where the products were actually developed and thereby bring the scientists closer to customers. This was the latest initiative in McNerney's attempt to, in the words of Jennifer Bjorhus, writing in the *Saint Paul Pioneer Press,* "[turn] a slightly ossified manufacturing giant into a nimbler growth machine." It was clear that 3M was changing—and in some very dramatic ways—but only the passage of time would be able to show whether the company's longstanding penchant for innovation would survive in the new environment.

Principal Subsidiaries

Dyneon LLC; 3M Financial Management Company; 3M Innovative Properties Company; 3M Investment Management Corporation; 3M Unitek Corporation; 3M Touch Systems, Inc.; 3M Precision Optics, Inc.; 3M Argentina S.A.C.I.F.I.A.; 3M Australia Pty. Limited; 3M Oesterreich GmbH (Austria); 3M Belgium S.A./N.V.; Seaside Insurance Limited (Bermuda); 3M do Brasil Limitada (Brazil); 3M Canada Company; 3M China Limited; 3M A/S (Denmark); Suomen 3M Oy (Finland); 3M France, S.A.; Dyneon GmbH (Germany); 3M Inter-Unitek GmbH (Germany); Quante AG (Germany; 99%); Quante Holding GmbH (Germany); 3M Deutschland GmbH (Germany); 3M ESPE (Germany); 3M German Holdings GmbH (Germany); 3M Hong Kong Limited; 3M Italia Finanziaria S.p.A. (Italy); Sumitomo 3M Limited (Japan; 75%); 3M Health Care Limited (Japan; 75%); 3M Korea Limited; 3M Mexico, S.A. de C.V.; Corporate Services B.V. (Netherlands); 3M Nederland B.V. (Netherlands); 3M (New Zealand) Limited; 3M Norge A/S (Norway); 3M Puerto Rico, Inc.; 3M Singapore Private Limited; 3M South Africa (Proprietary) Limited; 3M Espana, S.A. (Spain); 3M Svenska AB (Sweden); 3M (East) A.G. (Switzerland); 3M (Schweiz) A.G. (Switzerland); 3M Taiwan Limited; 3M Thailand Limited; 3M Gulf Ltd. (United Arab Emirates); 3M United Kingdom Holdings P.L.C.; 3M Venezuela, S.A.

Principal Operating Units

Consumer and Office Business; Display and Graphics Business; Electro and Communications Business; Health Care Business; Industrial Business; Safety, Security and Protection Services Business; Transportation Business.

Principal Competitors

Johnson & Johnson; Henkel KGaA; Avery Dennison Corporation; S.C. Johnson & Son, Inc.

Further Reading

"And Then There Were Two," *Economist,* November 18, 1995, pp. 74–75.

Arndt, Michael, "3M: A Lab for Growth?," *Business Week,* January 21, 2002, pp. 50–51.

Byrne, Harlan S., "A Changed Giant," *Barron's,* July 3, 2000, pp. 18, 20.

A Century of Innovation: The 3M Story, St. Paul, Minn.: 3M Company, 2002.

Conlin, Michelle, "Too Much Doodle?," *Forbes,* October 19, 1998, pp. 54–55.

DeSilver, Drew, "Aftershock Layoffs Seen for 3M's Spin-Off," *Minneapolis/St. Paul CityBusiness,* November 17, 1995, pp. 1, 45.

Dubashi, Jagannath, "Technology Transfer: Minnesota Mining & Manufacturing," *Financial World,* September 17, 1991, pp. 40–41.

Fiedler, Terry, "3M Innovation to Be Tested," *Minneapolis Star-Tribune,* December 10, 2000, p. 1D.

——, "3M Rides the Tsunami: Asia's Struggles a Big Factor in Payroll-Cut Decision," *Minneapolis Star-Tribune,* November 22, 1998, p. 1D.

Fredrickson, Tom, "3M Unifies Its Empire in Europe," *Minneapolis/St. Paul CityBusiness,* August 13–19, 1993, pp. 1, 29.

Gilyard, Burl, "Tale of the Tape," *Corporate Report Minnesota,* January 1998, pp. 35–38.

Goldman, Kevin, "Scouring-Pad Rivals Face 3M Challenge," *Wall Street Journal,* January 11, 1993, p. B5.

Houston, Patrick, "How Jake Jacobson Is Lighting a Fire Under 3M," *Business Week,* July 21, 1986, pp. 106–07.

Huck, Virginia, *Brand of the Tartan: The 3M Story,* New York: Appleton-Century-Crofts, 1955.

Kelly, Kevin, "The Drought Is Over at 3M," *Business Week,* November 7, 1994, pp. 140–41.

——, "It Really Can Pay to Clean Up Your Act," *Business Week,* November 7, 1994, p. 141.

——, "3M Run Scared? Forget About It," *Business Week,* September 16, 1991, pp. 59, 62.

Larson, Don, *Land of the Giants: A History of Minnesota Business,* Minneapolis: Dorn Books, 1979.

Lublin, Joann, Matthew Murray, and Joe Hallinan, "GE's McNerney Will Become 3M Chairman," *Wall Street Journal,* December 5, 2000, p. A3.

Lukas, Paul, "3M: A Mining Company Built on a Mistake Stuck It Out Until a Young Man Came Along with Ideas About How to Tape Those Blunders Together As Innovations—Leading to Decades of Growth," *Fortune Small Business,* April 1, 2003, pp. 36+.

Martin, Neil A., "Too Far, Too Fast: 3M Shares Have Been on a Tear That Could Be About to End," *Barron's,* September 1, 2003, pp. 17–19.

"The Mass Production of Ideas, and Other Impossibilities," *Economist,* March 18, 1995, p. 72.

McSpadden, Wyatt, "3M Fights Back," *Fortune,* February 5, 1996, pp. 94–99.

Mitchell, Russell, "Masters of Innovation: How 3M Keeps Its New Products Coming," *Business Week,* April 10, 1989, pp. 58–63.

Our Story So Far: Notes from the First 75 Years of 3M Company, St. Paul, Minn.: 3M Public Relations Department, 1977.

Peters, Thomas J., and Robert H. Waterman, Jr., *In Search of Excellence,* New York: Harper and Row, 1982.

Studt, Tim, "3M—Where Innovation Rules," *R & D,* April 2003, pp. 20+.

Tatge, Mark, "Prescription for Growth," *Forbes,* February 17, 2003, p. 64.

"3M: New Talent and Products Outweigh High Costs," *Financial World,* February 18, 1992, p. 19.

"3M: 60,000 and Counting," *Economist,* November 30, 1991, pp. 70–71.

Useem, Jerry, "[3M] + [GE] = ?," *Fortune,* August 12, 2002, pp. 127–28, 130, 132.

Weber, Joseph, "3M's Big Cleanup," *Business Week,* June 5, 2000, pp. 96–98.

Weimer, De'Ann, "3M: The Heat Is on the Boss," *Business Week,* March 15, 1999, pp. 82–84.

Weinberger, Betsy, "3M Breaking New Ground with Plan for China Plant," *Minneapolis/St. Paul CityBusiness,* April 9, 1993, pp. 1, 24.

Weiner, Steve, "A Hard Way to Make a Buck," *Forbes,* April 29, 1991, pp. 134–35, 137.

—Jay P. Pederson
—updates: Kathleen Peippo, David E. Salamie

Too, Inc.

8323 Walton Parkway
New Albany, Ohio 43954
U.S.A.
Telephone: (614) 775-3500
Fax: (614) 775-3938
Web site: http://www.limitedtoo.com

Public Company
Incorporated: 1999
Employees: 8,800
Sales: $647.5 million (2003)
Stock Exchanges: New York
Ticker Symbol: TOO
NAIC: 315212 Women's, Girls', and Infants' Cut and Sew Apparel Contractors; 315239 Women's and Girls' Cut and Sew Other Outerwear Manufacturing; 315231 Lingerie, Loungewear, and Nightwear Manufacturing; 448130 Children's & Infants' Clothing Stores; 448120 Women's Clothing Stores

Too, Inc. is a specialty retailer that sells apparel, underwear, sleepwear, swimwear, footwear, and lifestyle and personal care products for girls 7 to 14 years of age through its two chains of branded concept stores, Limited Too and Justice.

The First Decade: From Sluggish Start to Rapid Growth

Founded in 1987, adjacent to or as a department within select The Limited stores—Leslie Wexler's successful, multi-concept chain—Limited Too initially focused on offering young girls' and infants' merchandise similar to that which The Limited offered. The concept store grew moderately until 1995, and recorded somewhat inconsistent operations and financial performance during these years. In 1996, Limited Too made several management changes, and the company began to focus on more fashion-oriented offerings.

''When I got here in 1996, we were floundering,'' said Michael W. Rayden, president, chairman, and chief executive officer, in a 2000 *WWD* article. Rayden, an industry veteran, had held the top spot at Pacific Sunwear of California before coming to Limited Too. ''We were selling customers mini-versions of the clothes her mother was buying. The first thing we did was focus on the merchandise in the stores. Now we live, eat and breathe that girl.''

That girl was a '''tween,'' generally defined as a preteen aged 7 to 14. She was considered to be a sophisticated and savvy customer by merchandisers. The market segment she represented was newly lucrative and sizable. 'Tweens often made spending decisions for their parents and were up on trends. In the late 1990s, fashion magazines, such as *Cosmo Girl* and *Seventeen*, geared toward 'tweens, proliferated, and many 'tweens read them. They listened to the same music and watched the same shows as their older siblings and seemed to have an insatiable appetite for fashion, as evidenced by growing sales.

In 1997, sales of clothing for 'tween girls in the United States increased slightly less than 10 percent to $4.5 billion, according to NPD Group as cited in the *Wall Street Journal* in 1998. By 2001, 'tweens numbered about 27.6 million and influenced more than $150 million in annual family spending, according to a Roper Youth Report. According to Rayden, in *WWD* in 2000, ''Girls have always been interested in fashion and have always liked to shop. . . . Now they are more aware of what is going on around them because of the media.''

1998–2000: Expanding to Fill a Market Niche

By 1998, the 311-store Limited Too was a fast-growing division of Limited Inc., posting a 24 percent sales growth to reach revenues of $322 million. Most Limited Too stores were about 4,000 square feet and located in malls. They were brightly colored, with loud pop music and whimsically decorated with flower-shaped tables, their merchandise arranged in such a way as to encourage touching it and trying it on. Too's sales associates were a part of this distinctive atmosphere, trained to offer a high level of friendly service and to reinforce customers' fashion brand awareness by offering advice on outfits.

Striving to fill a market niche and exploit the concept of the hip, stylish, action-loving 'tween, Limited Too expanded its

Company Perspectives:

Limited Too has become the number one specialty retailer for the American 'tween girl. We have given her real fashion and cutting-edge style, in a store environment that caters to all of her senses. We mail Limited Too catazines—created specifically for her—in her name. And, Limited Too.com offers her the latest fashion on the Net. In a nutshell, we give her what she wants, when she wants it. A 360-degree brand. We've become really good at listening. Watching. Reacting. In the process, we've seen her grow up. Move on to a different stage in her life. And guess what, nobody is treating her as well as we have.

offerings and began developing its branded style in the late 1990s. It ran advertisements in teen magazines, presenting a lifestyle of ''fun, fashion, and friends,'' the total ''Too'' experience. Wanting customers to have fun while shopping and linger in its stores, it installed instant photo sticker booths and gum ball machines.

Having successfully test-marketed makeup in its stores in 1997, Too added a ''Fashion Adventure'' program to educate girls about fashion and grooming, clothing design, and retail merchandising, offering those who took part in this program a discount for shopping at Limited Too. In 1998, it began to sell home design items, such as plastic inflatable furniture and furry purple cushions. Shortly thereafter, it introduced ear-piercing services to complement its Goldmark line of gold and silver jewelry, part of a joint venture with Angus & Coote Limited. In 2000, with accessories accounting for 18 percent of sales, Limited Too extended its fashion offerings to include swimwear, robes and sleepwear, and intimate apparel. Some stores featured bath and body merchandise, such as glitter lip gloss and nail polish. There were also small umbrellas, bright notebooks, shoes, rugs and lamps, and CDs. One industry analyst described Limited Too's concept as a department store for young girls with its head-to-toe offerings.

According to J.P. Morgan analysts, Limited Too's concept was successful because it had ''mom appeal.'' In the late 1990s, the company added junior sizes up to size seven, but held to strict limits on what sort of clothes it would carry. ''Our customer may aspire to the junior look, but that clothing is not always appropriate,'' according to Rayden in *WWD* in 2000. Too's design team endeavored to stay on target with the hottest fashion trends in the junior's and women's markets, but, despite some fitted clothes and a few halter tops and low-cut items, Rayden insisted, ''[y]ou will not find a midriff top at our store.''

In 1999, The Limited spun off Limited Too, which changed its name to Too, Inc. to create more of a separate identity for itself. It began trading shares on the New York Stock Exchange under the ticker symbol TOO. During its first year of operating independently, Too, Inc. started with about 330 stores and enjoyed profits of $23.4 million, up 60.1 percent from its 1998 profits of $14.6 million. Sales for the year 1999 were up 20 percent at $452.4 million from 1998 sales of $376.9 million. However, Too, Inc., which continued to do business as Limited Too, still shared some distribution facilities with The Limited until 2002, when Too built a new distribution center, a 510,000-square-foot facility in Etna Corporate Park in Licking County, Ohio. That same year, it moved its corporate offices to New Albany, Ohio, about 20 miles away.

By 2000, Too, Inc. had a design team of nearly 40 people and used a variety of methods, such as focus groups and sponsorship of concerts and events, to stay abreast of trends in the 'tween market. Coupon programs, a frequent buyer card, and a monthly ''Wacky Wednesday'' bonus promoted sales. In late 1999, Limited Too launched a catalog to pitch its products. The ''catazine'' was mailed directly to 1.5 million preteen girls and featured, in addition to clothing and accessories for sale, plenty of articles and fashion tips, such as advice on how to mix and match colors, fashion layouts, beauty tips, a calendar of events of teen interest, and a crossword puzzle. Limited Too's web site, which debuted also in 1999, featured pages and pages of entertaining content amid items for sale. Users could view scenes of a Limited Too fashion shoot, read the latest news on current movies and popular music; take part in e-games, quizzes, and polls; follow do-it-yourself projects; or learn news about young girls around the world.

As the company continued to grow, Limited Too began to shift toward a larger store format that it called its ''Girl Power'' stores. These stores that carried a larger range of accessories and generated slightly higher sales totals per year than its other stores, $1.9 million as opposed to $1.2 million. The newer stores featured lively colors and an almost theme park atmosphere, with interactive sections such as a photo sticker booth and a makeup sampling table. Rayden described these stores as a ''theme park in the mall'' in a 1999 *Wall Street Journal* article. The company also introduced its first outlet stores in the year 2000.

2001–03: The 'Tween Market Leader

By 2001, the 'tween audience had been established as ''what's hot in the marketplace,'' according to MGM Consumer Products. ''The 'tween audience is one of the hottest, hippest, untapped markets out there,'' MGM Senior Vice-President Travis Rutherford opined in a 2001 *WWD* article. However, the market targeting preteens was getting crowded due to increased vendor interest. Manufacturers had introduced 'tween apparel; department stores had updated their girls' departments with hipper lines; and branded fashion companies had introduced fashion-forward girls' and 'tween apparel.

Too, the clear market leader in the 'tween category, began to step up its marketing with in-store promotions and events. Its ''Passion for Fashion'' six-city tour offered free concerts, sweepstakes, and contests and featured recording artists, Olympic stars, and young actors popular with 'tweens. In an effort to branch out to target teen girls 14 to 19, Too launched a second retail chain concept, its mishmash stores in 2001. In 2002, Too, Inc. marked its 15th anniversary with a foray into movie tie-ins and licensing with Universal Pictures, partnering with Disney to debut a line of clothing based on Disney's popular Lizzie McGuire character.

In 2003, Too, 500 stores strong and still growing, began branching out beyond mall locations and partnering with a

Key Dates:

1987: Limited Too is founded as a department within select Limited stores.
1999: Too, Inc. is spun off from The Limited.
2001: Too, Inc. launches a new concept store, mishmash.
2002: Too, Inc. builds a new distribution center and corporate offices in Ohio.
2003: The company replaces mishmash with its new, lower-priced concept store, Justice.

number of consumer brands popular with the 'tween age group. Nestlé's SweeTARTS became the Limited Too's ''preferred'' candy and Frito Lay its ''preferred'' salted snack. These snack foods advertised in Limited Too's catalog and sold in their stores. The company formed a licensing agreement with Build-A-Bear Workshop whereby customers could create customized plush animals at more than 100 Limited Too stores. Limited Too also began selling stuffed bear-sized styles of its popular sportswear fashions. It partnered with Mattel's My Scene brand, a fashion-based spinoff of the Barbie brand, and began to offer licensed My Scene sportswear. A marketing partnership with LEGO Systems introduced Clikits, a new designer craft system of fashion accessories, to Limited Too stores. In the spring of 2003, Too also began test marketing Reebok shoes in 51 of its stores and introduced a new book series of fiction for young girls.

As a promotional for its ''sweet 16'' year, Too sponsored ''What's Your Wish,'' a one-hour reality shoe featuring the 15 winners of its birthday wish contest who expressed wishes ranging from meeting stars to meeting ambassadors of the United Nations to being president for a day at Limited Too. The company closed its 18 underperforming mishmash stores in 2003, converting them to Justice stores, its new specialty concept that offered sportswear and accessories to value-conscious consumers in predominantly off-the-mall locations.

''We feel we have so much growth ahead of us. . . . We are the dominant brand in the marketplace. This was an underserved niche that we happened to identify,'' Rayden had said of Too, Inc. in a 2000 *WWD* article. The company's plans were to continue to grow to become a 700- to 750-store chain, offering a changing assortment of apparel and merchandise displayed in a way that encouraged touching and trying on and a fun shopping experience to match the ''energetic lifestyle'' of 'tweens. As the self-styled one-stop shop for 'tween customers and their moms, Limited Too would continue to strive to convey the essence of its brand: creativity, fashion awareness, and excitement for girls.

Principal Subsidiaries

American Factoring, Inc.; Limited Too Store Planning Inc.; Limited Too Purchasing, Inc.; Limited Too Catalog Production, Inc.; Limited Too Creative Design, Inc.; Limited Too Direct, LLC; Too Brands Investment, LLC; Too G.C., LLC; Too brands, Inc.; Too Retail & Sales Puerto Rico, Inc.

Principal Competitors

Abercrombie & Fitch Co.; dELiA*s Inc.; The Wet Seal, Inc.; The Children's Place Retail Stores, Inc.; Target Stores.

Further Reading

Kletter, Melanie, ''Junior Firms Gear Up to Claim a Piece of Growing Tween Turf,'' *WWD*, June 14, 2001, p.1.

——, ''Limited Too Claiming Territory As Pioneering New Tween Arena,'' *WWD*, August 3, 2000, p.1.

Ono, Yumiko, ''Limited Too Will Blitz Preteens with Catalogs of Their Very Own,'' *Wall Street Journal*, August 25, 1998, p.1.

—Carrie Rothburd

Traffix, Inc.

1 Blue Hill Plaza
Pearl River, New York 10965
U.S.A.
Telephone (845) 620-1212
Fax: (845) 620-1717
Web site: http://www.traffixinc.com

Public Company
Incorporated: 1993 as U.S. Teleconnect
Employees: 47
Sales: $44.04 million (2002)
Stock Exchanges: NASDAQ
Ticker Symbol: TRFX
NAIC: 517910 Other Telecommunications

Traffix, Inc. is a Pearl River, New York-based online database marketing company, operating a media network of web sites, interactive games, and e-mail marketing to generate leads, customers, and sales for both itself and clients. Traffix offers a range of online marketing solutions and possesses the ability to develop a creative program, promote it, and then capture information on participants to form a database of potential customers for corporate clients. The company's online properties include GroupLotto.com, a free daily lottery; AtlasCreditGroup.com., a sweepstakes that awards $1 million in a credit line that does not need to be repaid; AtlasAutomotiveGroup.com, a sweepstakes that gives winners $50,000 to be used in the purchase of a luxury car; PrizeAmerica.com, a ''scratch and win'' game featuring a maximum prize of $25,000; iMatchup.com, a free online dating site; TakeOneEntertainment.com, a site that offers free CDs; and prizeCade.com, a site that offers a variety of games and awards prizes to high-scoring participants. In order to use these sites, participants are required to provide demographic information and are also asked if they are interested in the products and services available from Traffix's clients. Traffix is also involved in e-mail marketing, a direct marketing effort that takes advantage of the widespread use of e-mail. Campaigns that prove to be successful may then be syndicated for use by third parties. A more recent development is the introduction of a business unit devoted to using the company's expertise to market its own proprietary products and services.

Formation of Company: 1993

Traffix's current chairman and chief executive officer, Jeffrey L. Schwartz, along with partner Jay Greenwald, founded Traffix in 1993 under the name of U.S. Teleconnect. Schwartz already had some 20 years of experience in direct marketing. In the early 1970s, after graduating from college, Schwartz became involved in the direct marketing of computer services. In 1979 he and Michael G. Miller founded Jami Marketing Services, Inc., a list brokerage and list management consulting firm. They also established Jami Data Services, Inc. to manage the resulting databases and Jami Direct to produce direct mail items. In the late 1980s Jami Marketing began to exploit the new telephone entertainment services developed by regional carriers as a way to boost phone usage. Mostly these numbers provided time and weather checks. When long-distance carriers entered the field in the late 1980s, many entrepreneurs recognized an opportunity to provide telephone entertainment via ''900'' numbers to a national, and in some cases international, audience. Jami Marketing took advantage of the trend by gathering the names of callers from such 900 phone numbers as ''Love Lines Dating and Fantasy.'' In the early 1990s, Schwartz teamed with Greenwald to launch a new business to exploit the popularity of 900 numbers. In his mid-20s, Greenwald had far less seasoning than Schwartz, but already had experience in direct-response marketing, serving in top capacities at Newald Marketing, Inc. and Newald Direct, Inc. The two men identified the ''New Age'' product market as an opportunity and in November 1993 incorporated U.S. Teleconnect, which actually began operations in August 1992.

In 1994 U.S. Teleconnect introduced its first ''club,'' the Astrological Society of America. Participants could receive a newsletter and deck of tarot cards and one month's membership for free, after which they were charged $9.95 a month on their phone bill if they wanted to join. The primary business of the Astrological Society of America, however, was the selling of live conversations with purported psychics, who acted as independent contractors. The company was careful to bill this ser-

Company Perspectives:

We are a leading on-line database marketing company that uses our on-line media network to generate leads, customers and sales for us, and our corporate clients.

vice as pure entertainment and to stay within the bounds of the law, but there was little doubt that the primary customers—mostly low income, poorly educated, and female—turned to telephone psychics in hopes of finding authentic comfort and advice. While they may have received several "free" minutes, they were billed as much as $4.99 per minute for additional time they spent on the phone with the psychic, who received a bonus for keeping callers on the line and had a vested interest in maximizing the length of the "reading." The money realized from the 900 calls were just half of the equation, of course. Before the reading took place, the psychics asked for the name, address, and telephone number of the caller. This information would then be fed into the U.S. Teleconnect databases and the resulting lists sold to outside companies, who would then inundate the callers with junk mail and telemarketing calls. Defenders of the psychic hotline concept saw the service as simply filling a need, acting in effect as "a poor man's therapist."

In 1995 U.S. Teleconnect formed a joint venture called New Lauderdale L.L.C., a successor to a joint venture created in 1994 with Psychic Readers Network Inc. (PRN), the company which provided psychics to the Astrological Society of America. PRN was founded by Steven L. Feder, his business partner Thomas Lindsey, and his cousin Peter Stolz in Fort Lauderdale, Florida. It would become better known later in the 1990s because of its popular spokeswoman, Miss Cleo, and her often parodied speaking style. Portraying herself as a Jamaican shaman, she was accused by some of employing an accent that was more in keeping with Ireland than Jamaica. In the end, she was revealed to be a Los Angeles–born actress named Youree Dell Harris, whose only career success before creating the persona of Miss Cleo was a role on the *Miami Vice* television series. In 2002 PRN and sister company Access Resource Services Inc. were fined $5 million by the Federal Trade Commission and forced to cancel $500 million in billings.) New Lauderdale created four telephone entertainment networks in 1995: a Spanish version of the Astrological Society of America called La Sociedad Astrologica de America; The Philip Michael Thomas Membership Network, a psychic telephone service that relied on infomercials hosted by Harris; The Joyce Jillson Astrology Network, which traded on the name of a former actress who was better known as Ronald Reagan's astrologer; and Psychic Enrichment Network.

Business Taken Public in 1995

U.S. Teleconnect, as well as the entire 900 telephone industry, experienced strong growth that caught the attention of investors. The company posted revenues of $8.3 million in 1993, $22.8 million in 1994, and more than $50.5 million in 1995. Net income during this period grew from $714,901 in 1993 to more than $13 million in 1995. Late in 1995 the company was reorganized with sister companies Creative Direct Marketing, Inc. and Calling Card Co. brought into the fold of what now became known as Quintel Entertainment, Inc. Quintel was then taken public in December 1995, its $15.2 million offering underwritten by Whale Securities Co. L.P. Initially priced at $5 per share, Quintel stock began trading on the NASDAQ.

Quintel bought out PRN's 50 percent interest in New Lauderdale in 1996, thus acquiring all the revenues generated by these ventures, plus gaining commercial and infomercial production capabilities and a media buying operation. Aside from income derived from telephone services and the sale of customers' names, Quintel also began to exploit its 30-million-person database to sell such merchandise as music videos, hair care products, basic voice mail services, and prepaid cellular service to people rejected for traditional cellular service. Another major development in 1996 was a deal struck with AT&T, whereby it would be paid from $50 to $70 for each person in its database that it was able to convince to use AT&T for long-distance service. For fiscal 1996 the company continued to experience strong gains in revenues, which totaled more than $86 million, along with profits of $12.2 million.

As a result of the New Lauderdale acquisition and the AT&T alliance, Quintel enjoyed record results in fiscal 1997. Revenues improved by 121 percent to $191.4 million. Of this amount nearly $95 million was attributed to New Lauderdale and $26.3 million to AT&T. Net income improved by a more modest amount, 18 percent, totaling $14.4 million. But this would prove to be the high-water mark for Quintel. Late in fiscal 1997 AT&T modified its tactics, which greatly hindered Quintel's ability to market AT&T's long-distance products. Quintel began to pull back and during the first quarter of fiscal 1998 terminated the agreement. In the meantime, the company's 900 telephone entertainment services were hit hard by significant increases in the cost to market them. Because so many customers disputed their bills, telephone carriers were charging Quintel 50 cents for every dollar the company earned in gross revenues. With margins severely eroded, Quintel began to take steps to move away from the business that had been at its core. In fiscal 1998, Quintel saw revenues drop to less than $95 million, while recording a net loss of nearly $17 million. The loss was due to special charges of $19.7 million, of which $18.5 million was a goodwill writedown connected to the New Lauderdale acquisition and another $1.2 million in asset writedowns related to the development and test marketing of an Internet telephony program.

In keeping with an effort to shift the company's focus from entertainment products to telecommunications products and services, Quintel changed its name to Quintel Communications, Inc. in August 1998. During the course of fiscal 1999, the company initiated cost-cutting measures that brought relief to the bottom line of its balance sheet. Although revenues dipped below $43 million, Quintel was able to record a profit of nearly $4 million for the year, and had some $38 million in cash and other assets at its disposal for transforming the company. As the fiscal year came to a close in November 1999, Quintel took significant steps to reposition itself, looking to take advantage of the Internet rather than the telephone. It formed a subsidiary named MultiBuyer, Inc., an Internet consumer direct marketing operation. A day after Quintel announced the creation of MultiBuyer, the new unit announced the establishment of GroupLotto.com, which initially

Key Dates:

1993: U.S. Teleconnect is incorporated.
1995: Company goes public as Quintel Entertainment, Inc.
1998: Name is changed to Quintel Communications, Inc.
2000: Traffix, Inc. is adopted as the corporate name.
2001: InfiKnowledge is acquired.

offered a daily grand prize of $1 million. Should the number of entries exceed 10,000, however, the prize automatically grew to $2 million. Participants could also earn additional entries by bringing in new players. What the free lottery was accomplishing for the Quintel operation was drumming up new entries for its direct marketing database.

Adoption of Traffix Name: 2000

To reinforce the company's change in focus, Quintel became Traffix, Inc. in October 2000. Schwartz told the *Journal News* (Westchester, New York) that the company did not use professionals in coining its new name. Rather, employees assembled a list of 50 to 100 possibilities, selecting Traffix with Alkemy coming in as the runner-up. Schwartz explained that the name referred to the company's new business of directing traffic to web sites, in keeping with a new slogan: ''Performance Marketing for the New Economy.'' Other developments in 2000 included the creation of Quintel Email Inc., the company's e-mail marketing service. While undergoing its transformation into an Internet-oriented business, Traffix continued to experience declining revenues in fiscal 2000. Although revenues fell to $26.6 million for the year, the company was able to post a net profit in excess of $5.1 million.

Over the next three years Traffix launched its current slate of web sites, intended to build the company's database of names, addresses, and telephone numbers to be exploited for direct marketing efforts. In December 2001 Traffix paid $1 million to acquire InfiKnowledge, Inc., a video game maker. In addition to an e-mail delivery system and a suite of Internet games that could be used for direct marketing purposes, Traffix received a team of some 30 video game and Web developers. In that same month, Traffix also spent approximately $675,000 acquiring ThanksMuch.Com LLC, a company that specialized in the online marketing of costume jewelry and other small gift items. Revenues improved to $32.2 million in fiscal 2001 and more than $44 million in fiscal 2002, while net income dropped to $417,500 in 2001 and rebounded to $2.74 million in 2002. Although online advertising had experienced some difficult times in the aftermath of the dotcom meltdown and poor economic conditions in general, Traffix carried on with its plans, launching iMatchup.com and other ventures, yet managing to stay profitable. While the technology platform may have changed, the company Schwartz founded remained very much a direct marketing enterprise, whose function was to gather and exploit sales leads. With some 30 years of experience in the business, Schwartz clearly knew how to make the most of the opportunities that the Internet had to offer.

Principal Subsidiaries

GroupLotto, Inc.; MultiBuyer, Inc.; Quintel E-Mail, Inc.; New Lauderdale, L.L.C.; Creative Direct Marketing, Inc.; InfiKnowledge, ULC; Atlast Sites, Inc.; iMatchup.com, Inc.

Principal Competitors

Acxiom Corporation; Alternate Marketing Networks, Inc.; Harte-Hanks, Inc.

Further Reading

Brooks, George, ''A Psychic Success,'' *Equities,* April 1997, p. 18.
Marcial, Gene G., ''More Phone Fun from Quintel,'' *Business Week,* July 7, 1997, p. 122.
McNair, James, ''Telephone Psychics Are a Gold Mine for Some, Source of Fraud for Others,'' *Miami Herald,* August 23, 1997.
''Quintel Entertainment,'' *Equities Special Situations,* May 31, 1997, p. 2.
Wordsworth, Araminta, ''She Could See Her Own Fortune: But Psychic Missed Predicting $5m Fine and Forced Refunds to TV Clients,'' *National Post,* November 16, 2002, p. A17.

—Ed Dinger

Turkiye Is Bankasi A.S.

Is Kuleleri, 34330 Levent
Istanbul
Turkey
Telephone: 90 212 316 00 00
Fax: 90 212 316 09 00
Web site: http://www.isbank.com.tr

Public Company
Incorporated: 1924
Employees: 16,135
Total Assets: $18.69 billion (2003)
Stock Exchanges: Istanbul London
Ticker Symbol: TIBD
NAIC: 522110 Commercial Banking

Few banks can be as closely identified with the development of their country as Turkiye Is Bankasi A.S. (Isbank). Created by Mustafa Kemal, the founder of modern-day Turkey, Isbank has emerged from state control in the 2000s as Turkey's largest publicly held private-sector bank, and, through its array of industrial investments, one of Turkey's top three corporations, representing more than 6 percent of the total market value of the Istanbul Stock Exchange. Isbank operates more than 830 branches throughout Turkey, and directly controls seven foreign branches. German subsidiary Isbank GmbH adds another 16 branches, serving that country's large Turkish population. In Turkey, Isbank is also present through a national network of nearly 2,300 automated teller machines, and nearly 400 Internet-connected Netmatik machines. Isbank has also been an advanced integrator of automated customer service systems, offering both telephone and online services providing access to nearly 130 types of transactions—ranging from account opening to stock brokerage services. The company, which is a main shareholder along with Italy's TIM in leading Turkish mobile telephone provider Aria, also offers banking services via WAP-capable mobile telephones. In addition to its banking services, Isbank has long played a central role as a motor for the development of Turkish industry. Isbank maintains stakes in more than 80 primarily Turkish companies, ranging from insurance provider Anadolu Anonim Türk Sigorta Şirketi, to glass manufacturer Türkiye Şişe ve Cam Fabrikaları A.Ş. (Sisecam), to oil company Petrol Ofisi A.Ş. Isbank's total assets in 2003 stood at nearly $18.7 billion. The company is led by CEO and Deputy Chairman H. Ersin Özince.

Founding a National Bank in the 1920s

Turkey's emergence from the ashes of the Ottoman empire in the years following World War I culminated in the abolition of the monarchy, the overthrow of the Allied occupation and the creation of a new, secular republic in 1923 under Mustafa Kemal—who became known as Ataturk, or "father of the Turks" a decade later when the government decreed that all of its citizens must adopt surnames. Ataturk quickly recognized the need for the creation of a national bank not only to rebuild the country's industrial infrastructure, but also to give the young republic a degree of financial stability. In a speech in July 1924 Ataturk stated: "Paramount among measures that will liberate and augment the nation is the establishment of a bank, utterly modern and national in identity, born directly out of the people's respect and confidence."

The mission for forming the bank was turned over to one of Ataturk's close aides and a minister of the new government, Celal Bayar, who became the bank's first president. Yet the financial backing for the creation of the bank came largely from Ataturk himself. During the fight for independence, Ataturk had personally been given as much as TRL 600,000 by Muslim supporters in the future Pakistan and other countries. Most of that money went to support the war effort. Following the war, some TRL 380,000 was returned to Ataturk, who then donated TRL 250,000 as the bank's starting capital. In a further show of support, Ataturk transferred the rest of his funds, some TRL 207,000, into his bank account at the new bank.

After debate in choosing a name—among the candidates was "Banque d'Affaires de Turquie"—the new Turkiye Is Bankasi was founded in August 1924. Isbank, as it came to be called, began operations in rented quarters in Ankara. The bank immediately began fulfilling its role as a venue for Turkey's economic and industrial growth. In 1925, Isbank backed the launch of Turkey's first insurance company, Anadolu Sigorta,

Company Perspectives:

Profitable growth of our business lines shall remain at the core of our business focus. Our efforts toward growth will be aided by efficient management of our operations via ongoing restructuring projects and the continued broadening of the Bank's sources of income for creating additional shareholder value. As we grow prudently, we shall continue to implement strict cost control measures to improve efficiency and capitalize on our widespread customer base, vast distribution network, and wide-ranging product and service portfolio. We shall increase our market shares further in all major areas and maximize income. One of the key pillars of our business remains our strong and growing deposit base, which speaks for the confidence that the banking public has in us.

which remained one of the country's insurance leaders into the next century. By 1925, the bank's quick growth led it to move to new, larger headquarters overlooking the city's Youth Park.

Isbank itself became closely associated with the Turkish government's economic policies, both during Ataturk's regime and following his death in 1938. The bank prospered as the government promulgated an economic system based on liberal exchange—and especially following 1929, when the government began taking an increasingly protectionist and interventionist role in the country's economic life. That year marked as well the construction of the bank's first permanent headquarters, designed by Italian architect Mongeri. The move coincided with the development of the bank's first advertising campaign—among the bank's most popular efforts was the launch of money boxes used to encourage the Turkish people to save their earnings. The campaign was later extended in 1937 when the bank gave away children's piggybanks, creating a new generation of savings-conscious Turks.

The protectionist trade policies put into place following the economic crash of 1929 led Isbank to step up its role as an industrial motor. In 1934, Ataturk turned to the bank with the request that it back the creation of a new glassmaking company, Türkiye Şişe ve Cam Fabrikaları A.Ş., or Sisecam, which later grew into one of the major European glassmakers.

From there, Isbank's investment ranged widely, and by the 1990s the bank counted more than 280 major Turkish corporations founded and developed through its financial backing. In keeping with its role as Turkey's national bank, Isbank had also begun developing an international network. In 1933, Isbank became the first Turkish bank to establish a foreign branch, in Hamburg, Germany, which was shortly followed by a branch in Alexandria, Egypt, as well. Meanwhile, at home, Isbank had been expanding its domestic branch network, and by the end of the 1930s boasted more than 50 branch offices.

Turkey maintained good relations with the Allied Forces during World War II, while its officially neutral status allowed it to escape the destruction of battle. The country therefore became an attractive investment market in the years following the war, and Isbank formed an important conduit for foreign capital investments in the country. In 1948, Isbank became the first Turkish bank to form a joint venture with a foreign company, when it joined with General Electric in establishing a light bulb factory in Istanbul, marking its first industrial presence in Turkey. Unilever became another Isbank partner in Turkey, starting in 1950.

In 1964, Isbank partnered with Bank of America in the formation of Turk Dis Ticaret Bankasi, or Disbank. The partnership remained in place until 1981, when Isbank acquired full control of Disbank, after which 15 percent of the company was sold in a public offering. Isbank later sold off its 85 percent stake to Lapis Bank in 1993, but, when Lapis stumbled financially, Isbank retook its Disbank shares. Some 65 percent of the bank was sold to the Dogan Group in 1994.

In the meantime, Isbank had continued to assert itself as Turkey's preeminent bank. By the mid-1960s, Isbank boasted nearly 300 branches throughout Turkey. The bank had also increased its international presence, opening a new representative office in Frankfurt—in support of the growing Turkish population in that country—and two branches in the recently claimed "Turkish" half of Cyprus.

During the 1970s, Isbank became the first Turkish bank to form a Securities Department. By mid-decade the group's growth led to the construction of a new headquarters, which was completed in 1976. For the time being, the bank remained in its Ankara home, despite the emergence of Istanbul—positioned closer to Western Europe—as the country's financial and political center.

Isbank maintained its position as a primary banker for the country's industrial development. Among its major investments of the period the bank included the establishment of İzmir Demir Çelik Sanayi in 1975. Construction began on a rolling mill, completed in 1983, and the site was later expanded to include a meltshop in 1987. Another important Isbank investment came in 1976, when the bank backed the launch of Antgıda Gıda Tarım Turizm Enerji ve Demir Çelik Sanayi Ticaret A.Ş., which, under the Zepa name, helped Turkey become one of the world's leading producers of olives. A more direct participation in the country's industrial development came in 1978 with the formation of engineering group Asmaş Ağır Sanayi Makinaları A.Ş.

Privatized Innovator for the 2000s

By 1983, Isbank's branch network had topped 900 branches. The bank had also continued to develop its foreign presence, opening offices in Cologne, Berlin, Munich, and Hamburg in Germany. At the same time, Isbank had crossed the channel, opening an office in London.

Through the 1980s, Isbank continued to develop new technologies, products, and services to serve its growing customer base. The bank was the first to introduce automated banking in Turkey, placing its first automated teller machine in Ankara in 1987. At the same time, Isbank launched the first debit card and then introduced credit card products as well. Isbank quickly developed a nationally operating network of ATMs, which numbered nearly 2,300 by the end of the century.

Isbank also showed an innovative streak, as it broadened the range of services available through its ATM network—by the

Key Dates:

1924: Mustafa Kemal (Ataturk) calls for the formation of a Turkish national bank, Turkiye Is Bankasi (Isbank).
1925: Isbank backs establishment of first Turkish insurance company, Anadolu Sigorta.
1933: Isbank opens foreign offices in Germany and Egypt.
1934: Isbank backs establishment of Turkish glassmaking industry, starting with Sisecam.
1948: Joint venture is formed with GE, which sets up a light bulb factory in Turkey.
1964: Joint venture is formed with Bank of America, creating Disbank.
1987: Isbank sets up first ATM in Turkey; launches first mutual fund.
1996: Interactive telephone banking service begins.
1997: Online banking service begins.
1998: Isbank is fully privatized as Turkish government sells its remaining stake in bank.
1999: Isbank moves headquarters to new office complex in Istanbul.
2000: Company acquires stake in Petrol Ofisi and joins mobile telephone joint venture with TIM.
2003: Company launches new Internet banking service for mobile telephone customers using WAP protocol.

1990s, Isbank customers were even able to conduct securities trading transactions through the bank's ATMs. In a related move, Isbank became the first in Turkey to launch a mutual fund in 1987. The success of that fund led the bank to roll out six additional mutual fund products in the 1990s and early 2000s.

Isbank's embrace of rapidly emerging technologies continued through the 1990s. In 1996, the bank became the first in the world to launch a fully automated, interactive telephone banking service. Unique to the world, the system enabled users to complete nearly 130 different financial transactions—including opening new accounts, bill-paying functions, completing loan applications and even trading stocks, currencies, and mutual funds shares—all without operator assistance.

The success of that service brought Isbank to the Internet in 1997, when it launched its online banking service. The company's web site scored a new first for the company among the Turkish banking sector, being the first to offer secure online transaction services.

Isbank had been a public company throughout its existence; yet the strong share held by the Turkish government, and the bank's role in implementing the government's industrial and economic policies, had earned it a reputation as a puppet of the government. Nonetheless, from the start, Isbank had sought to extend its shareholding, including granting stock to its employees—setting up the country's first pension fund, which grew to hold 45 percent of Isbank. By the late 1990s, the government's stake in the bank had dropped to below 13 percent.

In 1998, as part of a wider privatization of Turkey's financially troubled government-dominated industries, the Turkish government agreed to sell its stake in Isbank, which then became a fully privatized, publicly listed entity. The privatization was a success, and Isbank took its place among Turkey's top three corporations in terms of market value. Indeed, Isbank's value represented more than 6 percent of the total value of the Istanbul Stock Exchange.

Isbank had also begun preparations for another significant change. In 1996, the bank launched construction of a new headquarters—this time located in Istanbul. Completed by 2000, the new structure symbolized Isbank's historical and financial importance, becoming, at 225,000 square feet, the country's largest building complex, and, with two 27-story towers, the tallest building in Turkey. At the same time, the choice of Istanbul placed Isbank in position to benefit from Turkey's long-sought-after admittance to the European Union.

Isbank remained an important motor for Turkey's economic development in the new century. In 2000, the company joined with other investors to take a stake in the privatization of the government's oil company, Petrol Ofisi. That purchase gave Isbank access to Ofisi's some $6 billion in annual cash-based sales from the company's network of service stations—as well as the potential for placing its ATMs in the more than 6,000 stations in the Ofisi network.

Similarly, Isbank joined with Italian mobile telephone operator, TIM, to bid for one of the country's GSM-based mobile telephone licenses, launching the Aria telephone service. By 2003, Isbank had rolled out a new service for customers—banking services using the WAP Internet protocol. In the meantime, reforms of Turkey's troubled banking sector—which featured some 81 different banks, many of which were increasingly insolvent—spelled a new era of consolidation in the country. As Turkey's largest bank, Isbank was expected to play a leading role in the consolidation of the industry, continuing its role as a motor for the Turkish economy into the next century.

Principal Subsidiaries

Anadolu Anonim Türk Sigorta Şirketi; Anadolu Cam Sanayii A.Ş.; Anadolu Hayat Emeklilik A.Ş.; Antgıda Gıda Tarım Turizm Enerji ve Demir Çelik Sanayi Ticaret A.Ş.; Asmaş Ağır Sanayi Makinaları A.Ş.; Cam Pazarlama A.Ş.; Camiş Madencilik A.Ş.; Camiş Sigorta Hizmetleri A.Ş.; Camsar Sanayi Ara Malları Pazarlama A.Ş.; Camtaş Düzcam Pazarlama A.Ş.; Çayırova Cam Sanayii A.Ş.; Destek Reasürans T.A.Ş.; Ferro Döküm Sanayii ve Ticaret A.Ş.; İş Dublin Financial Services Plc.; İş Factoring Finansman Hizmetleri A.Ş.; İş Gayrimenkul Yatırım Ortaklığı A.Ş.; İş Genel Finansal Kiralama A.Ş.; İş Portföy Yönetimi A.Ş.; İş Yatırım Menkul Değerler A.Ş.; İş Yatırım Ortaklığı A.Ş.; İşbank GmbH; İstanbul Porselen Sanayii A.Ş.; İzmir Demir Çelik Sanayi A.Ş.; Mepa Merkezi Pazarlama A.Ş.; Milli Reasürans T.A.Ş.; Paşabahçe Mağazaları A.Ş.; Soda Sanayii A.Ş.; Trakya Cam Sanayii A.Ş.; Türkiye Sınai Kalkınma Bankası A.Ş.; Türkiye Şişe ve Cam Fabrikaları A.Ş. (Sisecam); Yatırım Finansman Menkul Değerler A.Ş.

Principal Competitors

Turkiye Halk Bankasi A.S.; Turkiye Cumhuriyet Merkez Bankasi A.S.; Turkiye Garanti Bankasi A.S.; Turkiye

Cumhuriyeti Ziraat Bankasi; Yapi ve Kredi Bankasi A.S.; Turkiye Imar Bankasi TAS; Turkiye Vakiflar Bankasi TAO; Turkiye Ihracat Kredi Bankasi A.S.

Further Reading

Barham, John, "Turkish Bank Sell-off Popular," *Financial Times*, May 9, 1998, p. 21.

Boulton, Leyla, "Isbank Swims Against the Tide," *Financial Times*, May 17, 2000, p. 24.

"Is Bankasi Profits Slump," *Financial Times*, August 16, 2001, p. 30.

"Isbank Meets Its New Owners," *Euromoney*, April 1998, p. 19.

Oruc, Saadet, "The History of Is Bankasi Is at the Same Time the History of the Formation of the Economy of Modern Turkey," *Turkish Daily News,* March 5, 2002.

"Turkey's Largest Ever Bank Offer," *Privatisation International*, June 1998, p. 22.

—M.L. Cohen

UNDER ARMOUR®
PERFORMANCE APPAREL

Under Armour Performance Apparel

1020 Hull Street
Baltimore, Maryland 21230-2080
U.S.A.
Toll Free: (888) 427-6687
Fax: (410) 468-2516
Web site: http://www.underarmour.com

Private Company
Founded: 1996 as Under Armour Athletic Apparel
Employees: 200
Sales: $110 million (2003 est.)
NAIC: 315999 Other Apparel Accessories and Other Apparel Manufacturing

The products of Under Armour Performance Apparel have become the top choice of athletes around the world to wear under their uniforms or during workouts. It all began with college football player Kevin Plank, who designed a T-shirt to draw sweat away from the body and into a lightweight microfiber fabric. Though moisture-wicking fabric was not a new concept, Plank's lingerie-feeling garments became a sensation when they kept football players at the University of Maryland, Georgia Tech, and Arizona State University dry and comfortable during practices and games. Under Armour has since conquered the sports world. Football, baseball, soccer, and hockey players, as well as NASCAR drivers and Olympians, wear its superior duds.

Sweat Equity: 1995–96

Kevin Plank was born in Kensington, Maryland, in August 1972. He was the youngest of five boys and like his older brothers both loved and excelled in sports. Plank attended St. John's College High School in Washington, D.C., and to further his football dreams went to Fork Union Military Academy in Virginia, where he met a number of football phenoms. After Ford Union, Plank went to the University of Maryland and began playing for the school's football team. He worked his way up to special teams captain, where his experiences on the playing field led him to a rather unusual endeavor.

As a fullback at the University of Maryland, Plank soaked through several T-shirts in the course of a routine football practice. He and the other players hated the wetness and weight of sweat-drenched shirts. Plank found it interesting, however, that the tight-fitting compression shorts he and the others wore during practice (designed to keep muscles relaxed) managed to stay dry and comfortable. As a senior, in 1995, he was determined to find a solution and visited a nearby fabric store. He found a white synthetic fabric, similar in feel to the stretchy compression shorts.

Plank had some sample tees made up and tested them on fellow Terrapin players, including pal Kip Fulks, who played lacrosse for Maryland. While it seemed like a big joke to some of the football players, who thought the lingerie-like material was too silky and smooth for macho athletes, they soon changed their tune. The undergarment not only felt good against the skin but kept players comfortable and virtually sweat-free. Plank took suggestions on how to make the tees more comfortable, from sleeve length to collar size, and continually upgraded his prototype.

While other seniors were scouting post-graduation jobs, Plank was sure his product had a future. He visited New York City's famed garment district with 500 microfiber tees. Back in his grandmother's Washington, D.C.-area rowhouse, Plank, along with fellow athlete Fulks, drew up some preliminary plans and decided how and where to market the revolutionary T-shirts. Plank graduated from the University of Maryland in May 1996. With cash advances from credit cards and his own savings from odd jobs such as cutting grass and selling roses on campus, Plank had funds totaling $40,000 and officially launched Under Armour Athletic Apparel.

Fortunately for the young entrepreneur, he had a multitude of friends and contacts throughout both the collegiate and professional sports leagues. He began to shop Under Armour to college sports teams around the country, packing samples in the trunk of his car. Georgia Tech was Under Armour's first customer and was soon followed by Arizona State University where friend Ryan Wood played. Wood, who Plank had met during his Fork Union days, went on to play for the Dallas Cowboys and later came on board as Under Armour's vice-

Company Perspectives:

Under Armour was developed by athletes for athletes. We understand their needs, and the demands of competition. What began nearly a decade ago with our superior undershirt for equipment sports has evolved into six diverse gear lines to cover all seasons, climates, and conditions. By employing only the finest microfiber fabrics, Under Armour has engineered the ultimate Moisture Transport System in garments that slide over your body like a second skin to keep you cool, dry, and light throughout the course of a game or workout. As the originator of the industry, Under Armour remains dedicated to new technology and is determined to enhance the performance of every athlete on every level. Lighter. Faster. Longer. Better. The advantage is undeniable.

president of sales. By the end of the company's first year, 500 Under Armour HeatGear (sweat-resistant) shirts had been sold in various styles (amounting to about $17,000 in sales), and Plank and Fulks (who became Under Armour's VP of production) set up offices in South Baltimore along with a manufacturing facility a few blocks away.

Under Armour Taking Off: 1997–99

In 1997 Under Armour came out with several new apparel lines, each one designed with specific needs in mind. There was ColdGear (for harsh winter weather), TurfGear (for artificial turf protection), AllseasonGear (for any season), StreetGear (hats, visors, wristbands), and increasing interest in what the industry had dubbed ''performance apparel.'' Suddenly athletes everywhere were curious about performance apparel and what it could do for them. A number of college and professional football teams jumped on the Under Armour bandwagon, since the garments seemed to give its wearers a definite edge on the playing field. By the end of 1997 over 7,500 Under Armour products had been sold.

The year 1998 proved pivotal for Under Armour; the company signed on as the official performance apparel supplier for the NFL's European teams and moved into a new 5,000-square-foot facility during the summer. Soon after, Plank sent samples of Under Armour to a Los Angeles casting director, after a friend told him about tryouts for a new football movie to be distributed by Warner Bros. The film, called *Any Given Sunday,* was being directed by Oliver Stone and starred Al Pacino, Cameron Diaz, and Jamie Fox. The company providing the wardrobe for *Any Given Sunday* was Sports Robe, which took an immediate liking to the Under Armour garments and used them in the film.

Sports Robe also signed Under Armour to supply garments for another football-themed major motion picture called *The Replacements,* starring Keanu Reeves and Gene Hackman, also produced by Warner Bros. Filming for *The Replacements* took place in Baltimore in PSINet Stadium where the Baltimore Ravens played, and it just so happened that Under Armour's headquarters was located across the street. When the movies were released, Under Armour's virtually unknown logo was prominently displayed in several scenes and immediately boosted sales. The same was true when Under Armour signed with Eastbay and became the catalogue giant's fastest selling ''soft'' goods product line.

At century's end, three-year-old Under Armour had sold more than 250,000 garments, outfitted eight Major League Baseball (MLB) teams, almost two dozen NFL teams, four National Hockey League (NHL) teams, dozens of NCAA teams, and both sponsored and outfitted the U.S. archery team at the 2000 Summer Olympic Games in Sydney, Australia. Sales had topped the $1 million mark for the first time and Plank was finally able to pay himself a regular salary.

No Chinks in the Armour: 2000–03

In 2000 Under Armour outfitted the new XFL football league and gained considerable attention during the league's debut on national television. Though the XFL later folded, the exposure helped put Under Armour gear into 1,500 retail outlets throughout the United States. To keep up with demand, the company relocated to a new 14,000-square-foot site in October and by early the next year had become the official outfitter of MLB, the NHL, and USA Baseball. Even law enforcement and military personnel were wearing Under Armour.

Under Armour earned accolades from several sources in late 2001, including being named Apparel Supplier of the Year from *Sporting Goods Business,* and a Victor Award for the best New Product Launch from the Sports Authority, the nation's largest sporting goods chain. Plank, too, was lauded for his achievements, as one of *Business Week*'s top ''under thirty'' business professionals. The company also revamped its web site, featuring three-dimensional views of some of its apparel, a more extensive product listing (including ski gear), and locations of both domestic and international dealers. Under Armour finished 2001 with sales of more than $25 million and 59 employees.

In 2002 Under Armour began testing its women's apparel line, hoping to duplicate its immense success with male athletes. The company had also become the official outfitter of Major League Soccer and the U.S. Ski Team. Under Armour's first television ad (the first print ad appeared in 1999) aired in August, during collegiate football's Kickoff Classic between Plank's alma mater, the University of Maryland, and the legendary Notre Dame. The ads ran on both ABC and ESPN for several weeks. By the end of the year, Under Armour was available in over 2,500 retail outlets and had sales of $55 million. The company had hired around 100 new employees during the year, had moved to larger headquarters on Baltimore's Inner Harbor, and added warehouse space of 65,000 square feet.

By 2003 sales for Under Armour were expected to breach $110 million and it was rumored the company had become a takeover target. New products that debuted during the year were underwear and golf apparel; Under Armour had also become a favorite among teenaged athletes and was considered ''cool'' for every day wear at middle and high schools. Even the collegiate and professional athletes who wore Under Armour in ads did it for the product, since the firm never paid endorsement fees. Under Armour got around the issue by not printing the

Key Dates:

1996: Kevin Plank develops his first microfiber T-shirt to keep athletes dry during workouts and games; he founds Under Armour Athletic Apparel.
1997: Twelve college football teams and ten National Football League (NFL) teams begin wearing Under Armour garments.
1998: Under Armour strikes a deal with Sports Robe, the wardrobe and uniform provider for the Warner Bros. film *Any Given Sunday.*
1999: The firm inks a deal with Eastbay catalogues and supplies apparel for another football-themed film, *The Replacements.*
2000: Under Armour begins national print advertising and provides apparel for the XFL football league.
2001: Supply agreements with Major League Baseball, the National Hockey League, and the NFL are signed.
2002: Under Armour gear becomes available in over 2,500 retail stores; company begins testing a women's apparel line.
2003: The Women's Performance Gear product line is officially launched in retail outlets and on the company web site.

athletes' names (figuring everybody knew anyway), and the ''models'' willingly endorsed the apparel because they truly believed in it.

Accepting No Substitutes: 2004 and Beyond

While Under Armour was a remarkable success story, perhaps there was one hiccup: Plank had been unable or unwilling to patent his performance wear. Imitators had come out in full force by 2004 and though Plank had not seemed unduly alarmed in 2001, commenting to *Sports Illustrated* that the knockoffs ''validated'' Under Armour, the imitators had begun to take their toll. Reebok International's ''Play Dry'' and Nike Inc.'s ''Pro Compression'' performance gear lines were putting chinks in Under Armour; then Reebok inked an exclusive deal with the NFL, while Nike secured the new MLB contract. While Under Armour still dominated the performance gear market, which analysts expected to top $200 million by 2005, both Reebok and Nike had considerable clout and a no-holds-barred approach to doing business. Would the Goliaths get the upper hand? Or would Kevin Plank's David still reign supreme in the performance gear industry? Only the world's athletes knew, for they held the key to Under Armour's future.

Principal Competitors

Nike Inc.; adidas-Salomon AG; Cotton Inc.; Reebok International Ltd.; Columbia Sportswear Company.

Further Reading

Durkin, Duff, ''Fitting to a T,'' *Washington Times,* Spring 2002.

Fick, Laura, ''Peeking Under Stars' Uniforms,'' *Daily Record,* July 11, 2001.

''Focus on an Industry Leader,'' *Sporting Goods Business,* January 2003, p. 26.

''40 Under 40: A Look at the Area's Emerging Leaders,'' *Baltimore Business Journal,* July 2001.

Graham, Scott, ''Young Entrepreneur of the Year,'' http://www.baltimore.tech, May 4, 2000.

Griffin, Cara, ''Battling with the Big Boys,'' *Sporting Goods Business,* December 2002, p. 32.

——, ''Focusing on Niche Market, Under Armour Gains Ground,'' *Sporting Goods Business,* August 23, 2000, p. 18.

Lloyd, Brenda, ''Armour and the Man,'' *Daily News Record,* April 14, 2003, p. 12.

——, ''Under Armour Shines at Super Show,'' *Daily News Record,* January 19, 2004, p. 16.

Olsen, Elizabeth, ''Being Chased by the Big Boys,'' *New York Times,* November 27, 2003, p. C4.

Shannon, Elaine, ''Tight Skivvies,'' *Time,* January 13, 2003, p. A1.

Thomaselli, Rich, ''Fighting in Nike's Shadow,'' *Advertising Age,* October 15, 2001, p. 10.

''Under Armour's Screenplay,'' *WWD,* August 29, 2002, p. 6.

Walker, Andrea K., ''Small Businesses Have Size Advantage,'' *Baltimore Sun,* August 12, 2001.

Wilmot-Weidman, Kimberly, ''Entrepreneur Hits Stride in World of Pro Sports,'' *Washington Business Journal,* January 28, 2000, p. 17.

—Nelson Rhodes

Webber Oil Company

700 Main Street
Bangor, Maine 04401-6800
U.S.A.
Telephone: (207) 942-5505
Toll Free: (800) 238-5505
Fax: (207) 941-9597
Web site: http://www.webenergy.com

Private Company
Incorporated: 1935
Employees: 700
Sales: $203 million (2002 est.)
NAIC: 454311 Heating Oil Dealers

Webber Oil Company, based in Bangor, Maine, is a major wholesaler of home heating fuels and gasoline in Maine and New Hampshire. In addition to providing oil and propane for home heating needs, the privately held company provides a variety of other services, including installation of heating equipment, rental of space heaters and hot water heaters, servicing of heating equipment and fuel tanks, and a remote monitoring service that ensures a home heating system is operational while the owners are away—an important consideration during frigid Maine winters. Webber also operates 16 gas stations combined with convenience stores.

Birth of Company in 1935

Webber was founded in 1935 by Bangor businessman Alburney E. ''Allie'' Webber, owner of Webber Motor Company. To run his new fuel venture he installed Frank Smart, whom he had hired three years earlier to serve as station manager for Webber Motor. At first the home fuel oil company consisted of four employees and two delivery trucks. It served as a distributor for Colonial Beacon Oil Company, owned by Standard Oil Company of New Jersey, which used it to distribute its Esso gasoline and heating oil to New England. Colonial Beacon would later become Humble Oil and eventually the Humble and Esso names were dropped in favor of Exxon. As a result of its long history with Exxon's predecessors, Webber became one of the largest Exxon distributors in the United States. In the early years, in the midst of the Great Depression, however, Webber was content to simply survive. By 1940 the company employed just 14 people to serve 20 gasoline accounts and 250 fuel oil customers. Although the economy rebounded during World War II, Webber was unable to grow because the government restricted the sale of petroleum products due to the war effort. It was not until the postwar years, and the resulting economic boom, that Webber was able to expand its fuel oil business as well as to start opening gas stations. The first major step was taken in 1948 with the company's first major acquisition, the purchase of Staples Oil Company, which not only added new fuel oil customers but also took Webber beyond Bangor into the community of Pittsfield, Maine. Another significant development during the decade was the creation of Webber Tanks, a subsidiary that in 1949 built a 32-million-gallon-deep water terminal located in Bucksport, Maine. The facility was capable of storing large amounts of heating fuel and gasoline, as well as kerosene, diesel fuel, and later jet fuel following the construction of jetports in Bangor and Portland, Maine.

In 1955 Alburney Webber died, but Smart continued to lead the company. The decade was also marked by the rise of the interstate highway system, which spread through Maine and helped to further spur Webber's gasoline business. However, it was the fuel oil business on which Smart chose to concentrate over the next decade. In 1960 the company established its first non-petroleum business, launching Webber Supply Inc., a wholesale heating supply house. In 1965 Webber's diversification efforts went even further with the acquisition of an insurance company, Sargent, Kennedy & Adams. By the middle of the decade, Webber operated in four Maine counties, with 85 gas stations, 16 heating oil trucks, 5,300 heating oil customers, and 110 employees. Expansion continued in 1968 when Webber acquired Brake Service & Parts Inc. to service its growing fleet of trucks and trailers. It was also in the 1960s, with the death of Smart in 1969, that the company underwent a change in management. Danville Webber, son of the company's founder, became chief executive officer, and a relation by marriage, Larry K. Mahaney, assumed the presidency. Of the two, Mahaney would prove to have the more lasting impact on the growth of the business.

Company Perspectives:

Whatever the future energy needs of our customers are, Webber will be there to keep them comfortable and secure.

Mahaney was born in 1930 in northern Maine's Aroostook County, and like many raised during the Depression Era grew up poor but determined to become a success. To earn money he pulled mustard weeds in potato fields, and by his own account shined shoes for 10 cents a shoe, set "bowling pins for 10 cents a string, and caddied nine holes of golf for 25 cents." Mahaney was able to attend the University of Maine, where he played basketball and graduated in 1951 with a bachelor's degree in economics. He then served a two-year stint in the Air Force before returning to school to earn a master's degree in education. For several years Mahaney taught high school and coached athletics. He became involved with Webber through his marriage to one of the founder's granddaughters, Louise "Jackie" Frost. In 1962 Mahaney joined Webber as the manager of the heating oil division and director of advertising and public relations. Mahaney's naturally ambitious nature was further sparked by a desire to prove that his position in the company was warranted by his abilities rather than simple nepotism. He quickly made his mark by taking note that all of Webber's fuel oil trucks had "Esso" stenciled on the side. Not only had Esso exited the heating oil business, Mahaney questioned why Webber trucks should promote anything but the Webber brand. He hired a public relations firm to create a logo, which he then had stenciled on the side of the delivery trucks. It was Mahaney, and his need to prove himself, that spurred Webber to the next level of growth once he assumed leadership of the family business.

Modernizing Operations: 1970s

As Mahaney had done with Webber's approach to marketing, he also introduced modern management techniques to the company and sought even further diversification. He looked to real estate investments, some of which he pursued on a private basis. In 1971 Webber tried combining its gasoline operations with a car wash, a popular concept elsewhere in the country, opening the Union Street Car Wash. It was also during the 1970s that the Exxon name replaced Esso and Humble, and Webber established an association with Sunoco. Of far more importance in the 1970s was how Webber reacted to the Arab oil embargo of the early 1970s. Out of necessity, the company secured new sources of energy and increased its storage capacity. As a result, Webber emerged from the crisis in a far stronger position and poised for even greater growth in the 1980s.

Webber expanded its operations from Bangor into southern Maine and in 1980 became involved out of state for the first time, acquiring New York-based Parish Oil, which distributed Sunoco gasoline to upstate New York communities. All told, the company completed 13 acquisitions during the 1980s, adding to all facets of its business: heating oil, gasoline, and real estate. Webber also displayed a spirit of innovation during the decade. In 1988 the company launched its Presidential Protection Plan, which for an annual fee provided heating oil customers with routine and emergency service of their heating system. It was the first service plan of its kind to be introduced in Maine. Also during the 1980s, a fight broke out over control of the family business. In 1983, according to the *Bangor Daily News,* CEO Danville Webber tried to oust Mahaney and failed when a judge ruled against him. Webber quit the company in 1984. Two years later Mahaney solidified his position when Webber and his daughters sold out to Mahaney's wife, mother-in-law, and sister-in-law.

The 1990s saw Webber continue to grow by acquisition. The largest single purchase in the company's history occurred in 1993 when Webber added six Agway oil subsidiaries. Two of the businesses were located in Maine and the other four in New Hampshire. Not only did the transaction bolster Webber's market share in Maine, it expanded the company's retail fuel business into the new market of New Hampshire. Because of stricter environmental regulations, Webber also invested in upgrading its infrastructure to provide greater environmental security. To remain competitive Webber invested in computer technology to upgrade its infrastructure. The company was also an early proponent of the Internet, launching a web page in 1996. Many of the investments Webber made during this period would be of little help in 1998 when New England suffered a severe ice storm, "The Storm of the Century," that downed power lines and, because of the lack of electricity, rendered useless all of Webber's computer technology and radio communications. Nevertheless, Webber trucks, in spite of felled trees and other damage caused by the storm, were able to deliver crucial supplies of heating oil to customers. Webber also proved to be a good neighbor, donating fuel to heat emergency shelters housing residents forced to leave their homes.

Succession Difficulties Surfacing in 1990s

In the 1990s an attempt to groom a replacement for Mahaney failed to work. James Mullen was brought in as an executive vice-president in 1991, following an 18-year career in banking. While at Key Bank of Maine, Mullen had ascended to the rank of president and chief operating officer. He succeeded Mahaney as Webber's president in February 1995 but a year later, in May 1996, Mullen announced that he was leaving the company due to philosophical differences with ownership. Both Mahaney and Mullen insisted that the break was amicable. The only explanation that Mahaney offered for the departure was related to Mullen's background with Key Bank: "Coming from a publicly owned company, the philosophy on the direction you go and the handling of people may be different than the philosophy or how you handle people in a privately owned company." After Mahaney assumed the presidency once again, his own ability to handle people came into question and would engender another unpleasant public spat.

In 1999 a former Webber manager, Hubert E. Saunders, filed a civil suit against the company because he claimed he was the victim of discrimination, fired in October 1997 after he informed Mahaney that he had prostate cancer. Saunders had come to Webber as part of the 1993 acquisition of an Agway Petroleum facility in Auburn, Maine, where he had served as a manager. He worked for over four years for Webber when in September 1997 Agway offered him a position. Webber countered with a promotion that would make Saunders a Webber vice-president. Saunders stayed. However, a short time later he

Key Dates:

1935: Company is formed.
1948: Staples Oil Company is acquired.
1955: Founder Alburney E. ''Allie'' Webber dies.
1969: Larry Mahaney becomes president.
1993: Assets of Agway Petroleum are acquired.
1999: Former Webber manager files an age discrimination lawsuit, which is eventually settled.

told Mahaney that he had been diagnosed with cancer and was hoping to take a new kind of radiation therapy. He said he would need to take some sick days for the treatment. According to Saunders's lawsuit, Mahaney told him, ''No more sick days because that's all the sick days you get.'' A week later, according to a December 1999 *Bangor Daily News* article, he was fired by a human resources executive who said, ''Mahaney wants you out of the company, no debate, no negotiation.''

The suit worked its way through the court system. In November 2000 Webber attorneys sought a summary judgment but were denied by a federal magistrate judge, who allowed the matter to go before a jury. During the course of the hearing, more facts about the relationship between Saunders and Mahaney emerged. According to the *Bangor Daily News*, ''On October 21, 1997, the two came into contact again during a meeting, and Mahaney reportedly became angered when Saunders commented about how much harder it was to manage subsidiaries and people than it was 30 years ago.'' Although Saunders said that he did not intend to insult Mahaney, he later apologized. The next day he was fired. Additional information surfaced in May 2001 when the case finally went to a jury trial. On the second day of the trial the 71-year-old Mahaney took the stand and maintained that Saunders's remark at the October meeting was an allusion to his age and questioned his ability to run Webber. After Mahaney was on the stand for some two hours, the judge called for a morning recess, but Mahaney did not retake the stand nor did the jury return. The two sides reached a settlement for an undisclosed amount.

Mahaney continued to head Webber into the early years of the new century. Although he was reported to be preparing to retire at the end of 2001, two years later he remained still very much involved in the management of the company.

Principal Competitors

Irving Oil Corporation; Yorkie Oil Company.

Further Reading

Garland, Nancy, ''Lawsuit Against Webber Oil Will Proceed,'' *Bangor Daily News*, November 21, 2000.
——, ''Oil Firm, Ex-Worker Settle Case,'' *Bangor Daily News*, May 24, 2001.
''Maine Marketer Marks 50 Years of Growth,'' *Fueloil & Oil Heat Magazine*, December 1985, p. 38.
Sund, Debra, ''Webber Chief Learned Lessons of Success in County Farm,'' *Bangor Daily News*, March 3, 1999.

—Ed Dinger

Weetabix Limited

Weetabix Mills
Burton Latimer
Kettering
Northamptonshire NN15 5JR
United Kingdom
Telephone: (+44) 1536-722-181
Fax: (+44) 1536-726-148
Web site: http://www.weetabix.co.uk

Private Company
Incorporated: 1932
Employees: 2,755
Sales: £361 million ($498.3 million) (2002)
Stock Exchanges: OFEX (non-voting shares)
NAIC: 311230 Breakfast Cereal Manufacturing; 322213 Setup Paperboard Box Manufacturing; 551112 Offices of Other Holding Companies

Privately held, family-controlled (and some say ultra-secretive) Weetabix Limited is one of the United Kingdom's leading makers of branded and private-label cereals. The company also has strong manufacturing operations in the United States and Canada and exports products to a variety of countries, including much of Europe. While slugging it out for market share against such cereal behemoths as Kellogg's and Nestlé, Weetabix has managed to thrive by establishing clear leadership in a limited number of cereal segments. Weetabix's flagship product is, of course, its renowned Weetabix branded cereal, a pressed wheat biscuit designed to turn to mush in milk—making it a favorite food choice across generations. Weetabix has also been a pioneer of the muesli market, under its popular Alpen brand, originally launched in 1971. With its Ready Brek brand, Weetabix is the market leader in the instant hot cereal category as well. Other brands in the Weetabix portfolio include Weetos and Nature's Choice granola bars. In addition to its small branded range, Weetabix has built a strong private-label operation, through subsidiaries Ryecroft Foods in the United Kingdom and Northern Golden Foods in Canada, as well as at its U.S. production facility in Clinton, Massachusetts. Weetabix also operates its own packaging subsidiary, Vibixa Limited, supporting its own products as well as its private-label production. Weetabix is led by Richard George, a member of the family that has controlled Weetabix since the 1940s. Nonvoting shares of the private company are nonetheless listed on the tiny OFEX exchange, designed to provide liquidity for small companies.

Australian Origins in the Early 20th Century

The pressed wheat product that later became world-renowned as Weetabix stemmed from recipes originally developed in Australia at the turn of the 20th century. An early version was created by a Melbourne baker, Edward Halsey, who founded the Sanitarium Health Food Company in 1898. Halsey dubbed his recipe, a biscuit made of unsweetened, pressed flaked wheat, Granose, and it became one of the first ready-to-eat breakfast cereals available in Australia.

In 1926, a new rival appeared on the market, launched by the Grain Products Company (said to be part of the Seventh Day Adventist Church). Called Weet-Bix, this cereal essentially added malt and sugar to the basic Granose formula to produce a new and quickly popular sweetened flaked biscuit. Sanitarium responded by buying up Grain Products and the Weet-Bix brand and recipe in 1928.

Weet-Bix remained one of Australia's most popular cereals into the next century, and Sanitarium also added separate operations in New Zealand. Yet the flaked wheat recipe was to find its greatest success in the United Kingdom, after a trio of Seventh Day Adventists from South Africa immigrated to England in 1932, bringing with them the Weet-Bix recipe and adding an ''a'' to set up a new company, Weetabix Limited, in Northamptonshire.

The format of the cereal changed somewhat for the new market—presenting rounded edges as opposed to Weet-Bix's square edges. Yet the product's appeal—among other features, that it dissolved almost instantly into milk—quickly enabled it to establish itself as the most-loved cereal in the United Kingdom. Indeed, Weetabix became a highly popular ''first food'' for babies—allowing the cereal to establish itself as a fixture across generations. Weetabix also was able to boast of its strong

Company Perspectives:

Today, Weetabix manufactures and markets a range of different cereals which are wholesome and energy-giving, to suit the tastes of all the family.

nutritional content—and during World War II was even touted as a viable alternative for meat, then in short supply.

Soon after its founding, Weetabix began seeking export markets, turning to the United States by the end of the decade and licensing Clinton, Massachusetts-based American Cereal Company to produce Weetabix for the U.S. market. That company changed its name to Van Brode Cereals after it was acquired by David Brody in 1941.

Weetabix too changed hands, however, in 1947, when the George family took over the business. The company then withdrew from the U.S. market. Van Brode continued to make cereals, while expanding into plastics in the 1960s—and ultimately gaining lasting notoriety as the inventor of the ''spork.'' The cereals operation later became known as Van Brode Milling Company.

Weetabix took to the airwaves in 1959, launching the first of a long and acclaimed series of television commercials. In the 1960s, the company once again eyed the North American market, which by then had become firmly dominated by the giant American cereal makers such as Kellogg's and Quaker Oats. At the same time, Weetabix appeared an unlikely candidate to win over American taste buds. Nonetheless, Weetabix's market research suggested that the Canadian market presented strong potential, and Weetabix began importing to the Canadian market in 1967.

Expanding in the 1980s

William George took over leadership of the company from his father in 1970, accompanied by son Richard, who had joined the company in 1968. The new generation of Georges led Weetabix on a slow but steady diversification drive.

In 1971 the company launched a new brand—and an entire new cereal category in the United Kingdom—Alpen, based on the Swiss cereal standard, muesli. In the meantime, the strong sales of Weetabix in Canada led the company to form a dedicated Canadian subsidiary in 1975, and to open a manufacturing facility in Cobourg, Ontario, in 1978.

In 1981, the company returned to the United States, this time to acquire Van Brode Milling Company in a bid to enter the North American private label market, as well as to re-launch its branded products in the United States. Focusing on the fast-growing private label market had enabled Van Brode to survive against the marketing might of its larger, brand-name competitors; yet its parent company's primary focus had been on its plastics products. Under Weetabix, Van Brode—renamed as The Weetabix Company, Inc.—received the capital it needed to expand production and meet the rising demand for its range of cereals.

William George retired in 1982 and Richard George took over as company chairman. Weetabix by then had grown into a profitable company with sales of some £55 million per year. Under Richard George, however, Weetabix entered a new era, boosting its sales past £360 million just 20 years later. Yet the company came under increasing pressure from its larger competitors, particularly from industry leader Kellogg's, which made steady gains in the U.K. market during the 1980s, chipping off some 2 percent of Weetabix's market share.

Weetabix had long held a rather conservative new product development schedule—for the most part, the company continued to extend its product range through introduction variations of its core products, such as fruit-flavored versions of Weetabix. In the mid-1980s, however, Weetabix began adding new products through acquisitions. Such was the case in 1986 when the company acquired California-based Barbara's Bakery. Founded in 1971 by Barbara Jaffe, then just 17 years old, that company had developed a thriving range of natural products, including its strong Nature's Choice brand of cereals, crackers, snack bars, and other baked items.

In 1990, Weetabix acquired a new and prominent cereal brand, Ready Brek, which had launched—and remained the leader of—the instant hot breakfast cereal category some decades before. At the same time, the company acquired another brand, and product category, in the form of the Applefords Cluster cereal brand. Both brands were purchased from Lyons Tetley. These moves helped the company boost its market share rating, to 20 percent in the United Kingdom, giving it a solid place in the industry's number two spot.

Yet the crushing competition among the top cereal makers continued to batter Weetabix during the 1990s. The company was particularly hurt by the entrance of Cereal Partners, a joint venture between Nestlé and General Mills, into the U.K. market. Weetabix's market share eroded steadily into mid-decade, hurt in addition by the company's somewhat phlegmatic new product development. Into the mid-1990s, Weetabix found only one new product success, a variant of the Alpen brand.

Nonetheless, the company's flagship brand remained a British institution—and even enjoyed a warrant as the official cereal of the Queen Mother—while battling with Kellogg's Corn Flakes for the position as the top-selling cereal brand in the United Kingdom. In the meantime, the company's sales topped £200 million by 1995. By then the company had placed its nonvoting shares on the OFEX board of the London Stock Exchange's new AIM market.

Weetabix expanded again in 1997, acquiring private-label supplier Ryecroft Foods, which added three manufacturing plants, in Ashton-upon-Lyne, Manchester, and Hastings. Two years later, Weetabix completed construction of a new production and warehouse facility at its home base in Burton Latimer, at a cost of some £12 million. By then, the company had added a new production line in its U.S. facility, enabling it to roll out a line of private-label ''gun-puffed'' cereals.

Weetabix hit a new high in the 2000s with the launch of its often-hilarious ''Withabix/Withoutabix'' advertising campaign. The success of the campaign, particularly in winning over young consumers, enabled Weetabix to claim—if only

Key Dates:

1898: Edward Halsey founds Sanitarium Health Food Company in Melbourne, Australia, and begins producing cereals, including flaked wheat brand Granose.
1926: The Grain Company, linked to the Seventh Day Adventist church, launches a new sweetened wheat cereal, Weet-Bix, in Australia.
1928: Sanitarium acquires Grain Company and the Weet-Bix brand.
1932: Three Seventh Day Adventists from South Africa arrive in England and form Weetabix Limited to produce and sell a U.K. version of Weet-Bix, and later enter production agreement with American Cereals Company in the United States.
1941: David Brody acquires American Cereals and changes its name to Van Brode Cereals.
1947: The George family acquires control of Weetabix Limited, and ends agreement with Van Brode.
1959: The first Weetabix television campaign is launched.
1967: Weetabix begins importing to Canada.
1971: The company launches Alpen-branded muesli cereal.
1975: A Canadian subsidiary is formed.
1978: The Canadian subsidiary builds a production facility.
1981: The company acquires the Van Brode Milling Company to enter the U.S. private label business and extend branded sales into the United States.
1986: The company acquires Barbara's Bakery in California and its Nature's Choice brand.
1990: The company acquires Ready Brek instant hot breakfast cereal.
1997: The company acquires Ryecroft Foods in England to boost private-label production.
2000: After the launch of its new advertising campaign, Weetabix becomes the top-selling cereal brand in the United Kingdom.
2003: The company launches new products including Weetabix Crrrunch, Alpen cereal bars, and Mini-Bix.

temporarily—the top spot among the United Kingdom's leading breakfast cereal brands. The ad campaign also helped the company boost its sales, which topped £300 million in 2000 and climbed past £360 million in 2002.

Yet Weetabix remained vulnerable in the highly competitive cereals market, particularly as a number of private label rivals had begun to encroach on the company's business in the early 2000s. Changing consumer trends also placed pressure on the company, particularly as the traditionally breakfast-oriented British began to skip cereals in favor of more conveniently packaged alternatives, such as cereal bars. In response the company rolled out a number of new products in 2002 and 2003, including Mini-bix and Weetabix Crrrunch. The company also launched the successful Alpen cereal bar. These moves helped the company rebound into 2003, with rising profits. All the while, Weetabix itself remained a venerable breakfast institution.

Principal Subsidiaries

Ryecroft Foods Limited; BL Marketing Limited; Vibixa Limited; Weetabix of Canada Ltd.; Northern Golden Foods (Canada); The Weetabix Company Inc. (U.S.A.); Barbara's Bakery Inc. (U.S.A.); The Cereal Manufacturing Company (Pty) Ltd. (South Africa).

Principal Competitors

Kellogg's Inc.; Nestlé S.A.; General Mills Inc.

Further Reading

Benady, Alex, "Unlocking the Secrets of Weetabix," *Marketing,* May 6, 1999, p. 20.
Bowen, David, "Square Up to the Wonderful World of Weetabix," *Independent,* June 25, 1995, p. 20.
Dignam, Conor, "Weetabix Crunched Underfoot," *Marketing,* July 13, 1995, p. 10.
"Great British Brands: Weetabix," *Marketing,* August 1, 2002, p. 46.
Newland, Francesca, "Weetabix TV Ads Aim to Reinvigorate Brand," *Campaign,* March 10, 2000, p. 4.
"Tasty Results for Weetabix," *Evening News,* April 25, 2003, p. 7.

—M.L. Cohen

Wham-O, Inc.

5903 Christie Avenue
Emeryville, California 94608
U.S.A.
Telephone: (510) 596-4202
Toll Free: (888) 942-6650
Fax: (510) 596-4292
Web site: http://www.wham-o.com

Private Company
Incorporated: 1948 as Wham-O Manufacturing Co.
Employees: 100
Sales: $50 million (2003 est.)
NAIC: 339920 Sporting and Athletic Goods Manufacturing

Wham-O, Inc. is a leading American toy manufacturer with several well-known classic products. Wham-O brought out the Frisbee flying disc in 1957, and in 1958 introduced the Hula Hoop, which became one of the world's most popular toys. Wham-O continues to hold the leading market share in flying discs, and produces other classic toys such as the Superball. The company makes more than 70 products, mostly toys designed for active, outdoor play. Wham-O manufactures a complete line of snow toys including sleds and saucers, and water toys including floating tubes, the Slip 'n Slide, and water blasters. The company makes other outdoor games such as bumper golf and croquet golf, and some tabletop action games such as Pinball Soccer. Wham-O markets the Hacky Sack, a pellet-filled ball used for a game of agility, and the Morey brand of Boogie Boards. The company was owned by giant toy firm Mattel in the 1990s, and in 1997 relaunched under a private management group. In the 2000s the company has been growing quickly and acquiring a variety of smaller manufacturers.

Making a Name in the 1950s with Fad Products

Wham-O began as a business started in the garage of two college friends, Richard Knerr and Arthur "Spuds" Melin. While attending the University of Southern California, the pair searched for some product they could easily sell through a small home business. The company name came from one of their first products, a slingshot. Melin and Knerr were fans of hunting with falcons, and they used a homemade wooden slingshot to fling bits of meat up to the birds. "Wham-O" was meant to evoke the sound of the slingshot. The two friends bought a saw from Sears on the installment plan and began making slingshots in a garage. They sold them through the mail to customers who saw their advertisements in sporting magazines such as *Field & Stream.* The company had a variety of early products, including blowguns and tomahawks. Melin and Knerr were always on the lookout for exotic new toys, and they hit it big twice in a row in the mid-1950s.

First came the Frisbee. The founding mythology of the Frisbee is contradictory. One prevailing story is that students at Yale threw pie tins from the Frisbie Baking Company for fun, as far back as the 1920s. The California version is that kids at the beach made a sport of whirling plastic coffee can lids, or that Hollywood cameramen did the same with the lids of film cans. In 1948 a California carpenter, Fred Morrison, began making plastic throwing discs, which he called Pluto Platters, and selling them on the beach and at local fairs. Morrison patented the Pluto Platter in 1955, and then sold the rights to Wham-O. Wham-O brought out the plastic Pluto Platter in 1957, and retailed it for less than a dollar. The company hired college students to hawk the Platters when it could not get distribution in regular stores. The Platters became all the rage at college campuses. Within the year, Wham-O had sold a million discs. In 1958 Wham-O enhanced the design of the disc and renamed it Frisbee. Richard Knerr claimed in an interview with the *New York Times* (July 1, 2002) that he had named the product after a cartoon character, Mr. Frisbee, and the similarity to the Frisbie Baking Co. was just a coincidence. Whatever its origin, the name Frisbee stuck, and became the generic term for plastic flying discs long after other companies began putting out their own brands.

The Frisbee proved an enduring favorite, and eventually Wham-O did much to market and promote the toy, creating Frisbee sports and then sanctioning national competitions. But this did not come until the 1960s. Wham-O was kept very busy the year the renamed Frisbee came out, because the company

Company Perspectives:

Headquartered in Emeryville, California, for more than 50 years Wham-O, Inc. has provided children and adults with innovative, imaginative toys that spark creativity, encourage social interaction and get kids playing. Founded in 1948, and inheriting its name from the sound that its flagship product, the Wham-O slingshot, made when connecting with its target, Wham-O, Inc. continually redefines the concept of fun by remaining simple, uncomplicated and without age boundaries. Led by a diverse group of multi-talented entrepreneurs, Wham-O, Inc. makes simple, fun, affordable, interactive products for all seasons.

debuted one of the hottest toys ever, the Hula Hoop. Knerr and Melin were always searching for offbeat toys, so an Australian friend introduced them to a bamboo ring kids in that country used in exercise classes. Knerr and Melin were first baffled by the hoop until they figured out that it was meant for twirling around the waist. Wham-O began making the hoops out of plastic, and introduced them to the market in the spring of 1958.

The Hula Hoop became a sudden craze, as children in southern California learned the balanced motion that kept the Hula Hoop swinging. The fad swept across the country, and Hula Hooping children were shown on television and organized into competitions. Within four months, Wham-O had sold more than 20 million hoops. Wham-O struggled to find enough manufacturers to keep stores supplied. At the peak of the craze, the company contracted with more than a hundred plastic manufacturers. As the fad went global, Wham-O also set up manufacturing outposts abroad, with factories in Tokyo, London, Frankfurt, and Toronto. In the United States, psychologists offered abstract explanations for the popularity of the Hula Hoop, explaining it as the rebellion of children against their parents (children were usually better at Hula Hooping than adults), and as a comfort that counteracted the stress of a population that frequently changed homes.

Whatever the reasons behind it, the Hula Hoop was an incredible sales phenomenon, eventually becoming the first toy ever to sell more than 100 million units. But the Hula Hoop fad disappeared as quickly as it came. By the fall of 1958, with children back in school, sales dried up completely. Although Wham-O had sold an incredible amount of hoops, the company's profit was only $10,000. Knerr later bemoaned the craziness of that year to a writer from *Forbes* (February 15, 1982): ''We completely lost control,'' he said. ''I'd rather lose money and know where I lost it than make money and not know where I made it.''

New Products and Marketing in the 1960s and 1970s

Although the Hula Hoop came and went, the Frisbee steadily gained in popularity. Wham-O promoted the Frisbee through the 1960s by developing appealing Frisbee sports. Wham-O Vice-President Ed Headrick was credited with a successful promotional campaign that spawned several official Frisbee games. The first Frisbee game (beyond simple throwing and catching) was called Guts, and it may have been played before the Frisbee era with pie tins, or even with rusty circular saws. The idea of Guts was to throw the disc at the opposing team so hard that no one could catch it. Headrick helped the burgeoning sport by introducing a Professional Model Frisbee. Headrick also modified Frisbee design with rings or grooves that made the disc fly more steadily. The rings became known as the Lines of Headrick. The game of Guts had its first officially sanctioned international tournament in 1958, and Headrick continued to organize teams and promote the sport through the late 1960s. Another Frisbee sport, Ultimate, was invented in 1969. Ultimate caught on quickly, and was an official intercollegiate college sport by 1972. By 1974, Frisbee sports had grown so popular that that year's World Frisbee Disc Championships were held in the Rose Bowl, in Pasadena, California. Spuds Melin invented Frisbee golf shortly after his company bought the rights to the Pluto Platter, and by the early 1970s, official disc golf courses were found all over the United States. Wham-O brought out many different model Frisbees for these various games. Wham-O held 90 percent of the flying disc market through the early 1980s. It had no serious competition in this market segment until that time.

Meanwhile, Melin and Knerr continued to search for other odd, engaging toys. Another big success was the Superball. Wham-O bought the rights to a bouncing ball made of a new plastic from chemical engineer Norman Stingley in the early 1960s. The Superball was a unique toy, much bouncier than anything on the market at that time, and Wham-O managed to sell some 20 million of them in the 1960s. Competitors eventually brought out similar balls, however, and Wham-O phased out its original product.

The company had scores of other products in the 1960s and 1970s. One that threatened to become another huge fad was instant fish. Melin traveled to Africa in the 1960s and was introduced to a species of fish that laid eggs in a lake bottom. The lake dried out in the dry season, becoming mud. When it rained again, the eggs hatched. Melin collected the dry mud and hawked it as just-add-water ''instant fish.'' Wham-O promoted its instant fish at a toy show and was inundated with orders. But the African fish were not happy in California, and Wham-O was simply unable to come up with enough viable fish eggs to make the product work.

Through the 1960s and 1970s Wham-O made blow guns, bubble makers, do-it-yourself bomb shelters, plastic shark teeth, and a variety of other simple toys. Most Wham-O toys were meant for outdoor play, and sold in the spring and summer months. Many competitors made most of their sales in the months and weeks before Christmas. Wham-O was able to employ seasonal workers after the Christmas rush. It contracted out most of its manufacturing and used its plant in San Gabriel, California, principally for labeling and packaging.

Under New Ownership in the 1980s and 1990s

The company's finances had been erratic at first, especially regarding the Hula Hoop. But sales grew steadily between 1977 and the early 1980s. Wham-O kept expenses down by having contractors do its manufacturing, and the company's product list was small. By 1982, the company put out only ten toy lines,

Key Dates:

1948: Arthur ''Spuds'' Melin and Richard Knerr found the business in a garage.
1957: Wham-O brings out the Pluto Platter.
1958: The company's Hula Hoop ignites a worldwide craze.
1982: The founders sell the company to Kransco.
1994: Kransco sells Wham-O to Mattel.
1997: Wham-O relaunches as a private, independent firm.
1998: The company buys Yes! Entertainment's line of girls' toys for $9.8 million.
2002: The company acquires the Sledz brand of sleds and Pro Body Boards from Earth and Ocean Sports.
2003: The company acquires Riva Sports, Inc., maker of a line of winter sports products, and Rocky Mountain, Inc., manufacturer of inflatable tubes used for snow and water play.

and these all retailed for less than $20. The company's unofficial motto was ''Keep it simple, stupid!'' Its toys did not have moving parts and they did not break easily, so the company rarely dealt with defects and returns. Wham-O kept to active, outdoor toys, and so did not worry about following trends such as licensed toys or electronic gadgets. In addition, it derived steady sales from the Frisbee. In 1982 the company decided to relaunch the Hula Hoop. This time it brought out pink-and-white-striped hoops filled with scented peppermint powder. Wham-O hoped the time was ripe for a new Hula Hoop craze. But the 1982 relaunch did not stimulate a huge revival. Several months later, Melin and Knerr decided to sell the company.

The two founders owned 52 percent of Wham-O's stock, and they had no family members following in their footsteps. Melin claimed that he was tired of the business, and he persuaded his partner to sell out. At first the company agreed to sell to Hasbro, the Pawtucket, Rhode Island company that was rapidly consolidating the toy industry. But later the company announced the deal for $16.8 million was off. One month later, in September 1982, Wham-O Manufacturing Co. was acquired for approximately $12 million by a San Francisco company called Kransco. Kransco was a private firm that made various toys and sporting goods.

Under Kransco, Wham-O made a significant acquisition in the mid-1980s. It acquired the U.S. and Canadian marketing rights to the Hacky Sack, made by Kenncorp. R. John Stalberger, Jr., invented the Hacky Sack in the early 1980s. The toy itself is a little bag filled with pellets. The game involves players standing in a circle keeping the Hacky Sack in the air using only legs and feet. Stalberger began making Hacky Sacks himself and selling them, mostly at Frisbee events. Within a few years, and with virtually no marketing beyond word of mouth, Stalberger sold more than one million Hacky Sacks. The sport seemed to appeal to the same group—mostly college kids—who made Frisbee a mainstay. Consequently, in 1984 Wham-O paid $1.5 million for the marketing rights. The company moved manufacturing to Taiwan and was able to use its clout to get the product into major chain stores. Wham-O also operated as it had with Frisbee, promoting Hacky Sack events and promulgating official rules.

Yet little else of note seemed to happen to Wham-O over the 1980s. The company came up with new toys such as bubble wands and skates, continuing its tradition of outdoor fun products. The company lost market share in the flying disc category, beginning the 1980s with 90 percent and dropping to roughly 70 percent by the early 1990s. Other companies were successful with new disc designs. Superflight Inc. made the Aerobie, a flying ring that could be thrown twice as far as the traditional Frisbee. Another competitor, Sandee Inc., made the Spinjammer, which players could easily spin on their fingers. Although games like Ultimate and disc golf continued to grow, the Frisbee brand was not always the preferred disc. The 1991 World Club Ultimate Championship, which attracted 600 players to Toronto, used the Ultra-Star, made by the Michigan company Discraft, as its official disc. This was the first time a Wham-O disc had not been used for the competition. Wham-O focused its Frisbee marketing on schools, producing a learning packet and demonstration for school physical education teachers. But it seemed unable to recapture the leading position it had long held.

In 1994 Kransco sold Wham-O to Mattel, Inc. Mattel was the nation's leading toy manufacturer. Its flagship product was the Barbie line of dolls. It also owned many smaller toy companies. Mattel was a $5 billion company by the mid-1990s, and Wham-O was just one small piece of it. Evidently, Mattel did little to promote Wham-O products. In 1997, a group of investors took Wham-O private. The company relaunched, bringing back old favorites and buying up other companies that suited its product mix.

Private Company Again in the 1990s and 2000s

In December 1997, Mattel's Wham-O division became Wham-O, Inc. The buyout was arranged by Charterhouse Group International, Inc., an investment firm that had equity in other toy companies, as well as in firms in many different industries. Charterhouse and a management group spent $20 million to take Wham-O private and to buy Mattel's sports division. This gave the new company the classic Wham-O brands Frisbee and Hula Hoop, as well as Hacky Sack and Mattel's water sport bodyboard lines Morey and Boogie, Churchill swimfins, and Aviva water toys. The company's president was Michael Cookson, who had founded Aviva and sold it to Mattel in the early 1990s. The toy industry in the late 1990s was dominated by the two giants Mattel and Hasbro, who had sales of $5 billion and $4 billion, respectively. The number three toy company had sales of $300 million, a big gap. Cookson hoped to build Wham-O into a medium-sized firm somewhere in that $300 million range, with sales coming from revived classic brands and from new lines of outdoor products. One of Wham-O's first moves as its own company again was to buy a ball company and bring back the Superball. Sales in its first full year as an independent company were estimated at $50 million.

The company moved to eliminate unprofitable product lines. This took $10 million off revenues in 1999. Wham-O also struggled to maintain a good relationship with major chain stores such as Target and Wal-Mart. These had complained that

Wham-O's shipping record was poor, and that customers returned a lot of Wham-O products. A particular disaster was the Slip 'n Slide, a plastic mat that kids used as a horizontal slide in the summer, wetting it with a hose. When a large percentage of Slip 'n Slides were returned because they were falling apart, Wham-O's COO Mojde Esfandiari went over the product on her hands and knees to figure out the problem. Esfandiari changed the manufacturing process, and her success in handling this disaster earned her the chief executive spot in 2000.

The company upped its advertising budget and also promoted sales abroad, particularly in Germany and Australia. It also moved to balance out its spring and summer product lines with new lines of snow toys. It came out with new sleds and saucers, as well as foam boards called ''Snowboogies'' built like its water bodyboards. Wham-O also began acquiring smaller companies. In 1998 it spent $9.8 million to buy Yes! Entertainment's line of girls' toys. The Yes! line included two cooking toys, the Mrs. Fields Baking Factory and the Baskin-Robbins Ice Cream Maker. The company's focus moved more to water and snow toys, and in 2002 Wham-O made another significant acquisition, buying up the Sledz brand of sleds and Pro Body Boards from Washington company Earth and Ocean Sports. In 2003 Wham-O bought another outdoor sports firm, Riva Sports, Inc. Riva, based in Maryland, made a line of winter sports products including sleds, saucers, snow boards, goggles, and snow gear. Later that year Wham-O acquired Rocky Mountain, Inc., a manufacturer of inflatable tubes used for snow and water play.

By the early 2000s, Wham-O had emerged as a company of two major complementary product lines, winter and summer. Its toys were mostly for outdoor play, from sleds to water games. The company also built on its storied past with re-releases of its classic brands. The company put out as many as 30 different Frisbee models in the 2000s. Foreign sales grew to almost 20 percent of revenue as the company made its name known again overseas. With sales in the range of $40 million to $50 million in the early 2000s, the company hoped to grow by a factor of four or five by the end of the decade.

Principal Competitors

Mattel, Inc.; Hasbro, Inc.

Further Reading

Carlsen, Clifford, ''Wham-O Makes It Pay to Play,'' *San Francisco Business Times,* May 22, 1998, p. 1.

Hansell, Saul, ''Arthur Melin, 77, a Promoter of the Hula-Hoop, Is Dead,'' *New York Times,* July 1, 2002, p. B6.

Kindel, Stephen, ''After the Frisbee,'' *Forbes,* June 4, 1984, p. 167.

Paris, Eileen, ''The KISS System,'' *Forbes,* February 15, 1982, pp. 97–100.

Raine, George, ''Fad Factory Wham-O Finds Itself Back in Style,'' *San Francisco Chronicle,* May 6, 2001, p. E1.

Schwartz, Judith, ''Frisbee Fights an Air War,'' *Adweek's Marketing Week,* September 16, 1991, p. 20.

Smillie, Dirk, ''Signs of Life,'' *Forbes,* November 11, 2002, p. 160.

''Wham-O Acquires Rocky Mountain, Inc. Inflatable Tubes,'' *Canadian Corporate News,* December 4, 2003.

''Wham-O Says Accord with Hasbro Is Over,'' *Wall Street Journal,* August 2, 1982, p. 4.

''Wham-O Signs Pact to Be Bought by Firm for About $12 Million,'' *Wall Street Journal,* September 8, 1982, p. 10.

—A. Woodward

Whittard of Chelsea Plc

Union Court, 22 Union Road
London
SW4 6JP
United Kingdom
Telephone: (+44) 20-7819-6400
Fax: (+44) 20-7627-8850
Web site: http://www.whittard.co.uk

Public Company
Incorporated: 1886
Employees: 488
Sales: £37.4 million ($59.84 million) (2003)
Stock Exchanges: London
Ticker Symbol: WOC
NAIC: 445299 All Other Specialty Food Stores

Whittard of Chelsea Plc appears finally to have found the right blend for its growing chain of tea and coffee shops. The London-based company, which originated as a tea trader in the 1880s, operates more than 100 specialty shops throughout the United Kingdom. The company also operates boutique shops in major department stores around the world, including in Japan and, in the United States, through Marshall Field's. The company's own stores, which average 100 square feet of selling space in order to preserve a feeling of intimacy and quality, stock more than 50 blended and single estate teas, as well as nearly 20 coffee varieties, and a range of hot chocolate and other drink types. The Whittard shops also sell teapots, cups and saucers, and other china and service related to tea and coffee, and most of the designs sold in the stores are exclusive to the company. In addition to its primary stores, the company operates some 20 outlet shops. Whittard also operates a small number of High Street-based "T-zone" tea bars in an attempt to recapture market share from the rising numbers of coffee shops. The company has long operated a thriving mail-order business for its teas and coffees; a rising proportion of its mail-order sales come from its Internet web site. Traded on the London Stock Exchange, the company is led by chairman and major shareholder William Hobhouse, and CEO Richard Rose.

Buying the Best in the 1880s

Whittard of Chelsea was originally founded in London in 1886 by Walter Whittard as a commodity and retail trading house for teas from the British colonies. The shop, on Mincing Lane near Fleet Street, soon established a reputation for its fine teas by adhering to Whittard's motto: "Buy the Best."

Whittard expanded his shop offerings at the dawn of the 20th century with the introduction of a selection of coffee blends as well. He also was joined by sons Richard (Dick) and Hugh Whittard, who later took over operation of the family business after their father's death in 1935. Despite the harsh economic climate of the time, Whittard managed to grow, notably by introducing a mail-order business. Orders quickly came in from all over the United Kingdom, and even from abroad, as visitors to the United Kingdom began requesting shipments of the company's teas. The company also opened its own warehouse nearby, on Mansell Street.

The years of World War II placed a new burden on the company. All supplies of tea, the British national drink, were requisitioned for the duration, and in 1940, the rationing program instituted a limit of two ounces per person per week. Yet bombing raids that same year destroyed both the shop and the warehouse. The company lost not only its entire stock, but also its brewing and blending equipment.

The Whittards quickly relocated, to Fulham Road in Chelsea, and by 1941, the company was back in business. Wartime restrictions, however, made it impossible for the brothers to obtain new equipment. Eventually the Whittards were able to locate a used coffee roaster. For its tea blending, the Whittards were forced to rely on old-fashioned methods.

In the decades following the war, the company, now known as Whittard of Chelsea, shifted the focus of its attention on its retail side. For this effort, Whittard began packaging its teas in tins designed for the company and introduced a variety of other tea- and coffee-related items, including china services and foods. Whittard also began promoting its own tea blends, including scented and fruit-based teas.

The transition to retail shops took on greater force in the early 1970s, when Richard Whittard sold his stake in the family

Company Perspectives:

Whittard of Chelsea has been specialising in the finest teas, coffees and gifts since 1886. We pride ourselves on our reputation for quality and innovation.

Walter Whittard, the firm's founder, had a philosophy to ''buy the best.'' The success of the Whittard product range lies in an uncompromising attitude towards quality of product and packaging.

store and business to David Gyle-Thompson in 1973. Thompson maintained the original store, then added two more London-area stores over the next two decades. At the end of the 1980s, however, Thompson brought in a new managing director, William Hobhouse, with the intention of developing Whittard of Chelsea into a major U.K. specialty retailer.

Just 30 years old at the time, Hobhouse already had made his fortune in the United Kingdom's retail market. After stints working for the Argyll Group and Associated British Foods, Hobhouse joined a small retail operation, Tie Rack, in the early 1980s. From just 15 stores, Hobhouse, who became managing director and a major shareholder, rapidly expanded the company using a franchise model. By the mid-1980s, there were more than 150 Tie Rack shops operating in eight countries. In 1987, after Tie Rack was listed on the London Stock Exchange, Hobhouse sold out his stake, then worth in the millions of pounds, and began looking for new challenges.

Fast Track for Growth in the Early 1990s

Whittard of Chelsea, now led by Hobhouse as managing director and Thompson as chairman, turned to venture capitalists for the funding—about £750,000—required to buy out the remainder of the company from the Whittard family and to pursue their goal of expanding it into an international retailer. In the process, Hobhouse acquired about one-third of the business with his own investment of some £100,000.

Whittard started small at first, opening two test shops in Bath and Oxford, to see if the Whittard store concept would support a national roll-out. The Whittard formula involved adapting the company's ''Buy the Best'' tradition to an extended range of high-value teas and coffee. As part of that effort, the company promoted so-called ''single estate'' teas, likened to the Bordeaux wine estates. Whittard also began selling ''vintage'' teas, which, like their wine counterparts, classified teas according to year. In keeping with its upscale market aim, the new Whittard stores were kept small, averaging 100 square feet in sales space.

The success of the new stores' first season, particularly during the winter holidays, encouraged the company to move ahead with a full roll-out of the concept. By 1990, the company had raised another £1 million from investors and began opening new stores at a rapid pace. One year later, the company already boasted more than 16 stores.

Over the next half-decade, Whittard added more than 80 stores, topping 100 in 1996. Although most of these stores were in England, with the majority in the London and southeast regions, Whittard also had gone international, adding stores in France, Poland, Iceland, and, especially, Japan, where the tea-drinking culture had rapidly abandoned traditional green teas to embrace the ''superior'' British blends. While the company maintained ownership of its stores in its U.K. expansion effort, it turned to the franchise and licensing format, as well as the placement of ''corner'' stores in department stores, for much of its overseas growth.

Whittard's sales and profits rose accordingly. After losing a bit less than £300 million in 1992, the company turned a profit of more than £230 million the following year, with sales topping £7 million. By the middle of the decade, Whittard claimed a 12 percent share of the United Kingdom's specialty market—a small segment representing less than 10 percent of a larger, billion-pound market dominated by generic store-bought teabags—against chief rival and dominant tea seller R. Twining & Co. The company also maintained a strong mail-order business, shipping more than 10,000 orders per day.

In 1996, Whittard went public, listing on the Alternative Investment Market (AIM), designed to provide liquidity to smaller companies. The successful launch enabled the company to raise more than £8 million—some £6 million of which went to buy out its initial financial backers. Hobhouse's own stake in the company had by then grown to be worth more than £6.5 million.

Buoyed by the success of the offering, Whittard then announced plans to add 10 to 15 new shops per year over the next five years, doubling its U.K. operation. The company also began expanding its original retail format to include stores featuring onsite coffee roasting, and others featuring their own espresso bars. Despite the addition of this latter format, Whittard was later to be criticized for its lack of response as a new breed of coffee bar, represented by the United States' Starbucks and Whitbread-backed Costa Coffee, had begun to capture a growing share of the British beverage budget.

Diversification at the End of the 20th Century

In 1997, Whittard's fast growth enabled it to switch its listing to the London Stock Exchange's main board. The company then announced plans to accelerate its growth, forecasting the addition of up to 20 new stores per year. A number of observers remained skeptical of the company's growth plans, however, believing that even the country's larger cities would be unable to support more than a single Whittard shop.

Nonetheless, Whittard pushed ahead with its expansion, building up its number of U.K. stores to nearly 120 by 1998. The company also had pushed into a number of new international markets, including Dubai, Abu Dhabi, Kuwait, Singapore, South Africa, and Chile. In the meantime, the company had expanded its Japanese presence with the addition of 34 in-store boutiques in many of the country's major department stores.

At the same time, Whittard began pursuing other retail opportunities. In 1997, the company launched a new retail concept, Kitchen Stores, which specialized in selling upscale kitchen equipment and products. By 1998, the company had opened six of the new city-center stores. Closer to its origins, Whittard also expanded with the launch of its own Factory Outlets stores, which opened in the growing number of shopping centers spe-

Key Dates:

1886: Walter Whittard sets up a tea commodity and retail shop in London, before expanding to include coffee sales at the turn of the century.
1935: After Whittard's death, sons Hugh and Richard take over the business and add a mail-order business.
1940: The company warehouse and shop are destroyed by bombs; the company moves to Fulham Road in Chelsea.
1973: Richard Whittard turns over the operation of business to David Gyle-Thompson, who adds two more London-area stores.
1988: Thompson hires William Hobhouse, who had successfully expanded the Tie Rack retail chain, as managing director and the pair buy out Whittard from the Whittard family.
1990: After raising venture capital to open two test stores, in Bath and Oxford, Whittard begins nationwide roll-out of tea and coffee shops, adding 80 stores by mid-decade.
1996: Whittard of Chelsea goes public on London's AIM market.
1997: Whittard switches its listing to the London main board; the company launches Kitchen and Factory Outlet retail formats.
1998: A former employee establishes an online e-commerce site for Whittard; the company unveils the "T-zone" tea bar format.
2000: Whittard takes over the e-commerce site and decides to transform itself into an Internet company, acquiring bestofbritish.com.
2001: Whittard pulls the plug on the Internet experiment; new CEO Richard Rose refocuses the company on its core tea and coffee retail offerings, and begins rolling out the packaged Whittard brand to U.K. supermarkets.
2003: The company opens its first U.S.-based in-store corner shop in the Marshall Field's department store.

cialized in factory outlet stores. Helping to orchestrate this growth was new Managing Director Richard Knight.

The company also responded to the growing presence of the new-generation coffee bars by launching its own related concept, the so-called "T-zone" tea bar. Yet by then, Whittard's fascination had been captured by a new and highly promising market: the Internet. In 1998, a member of the company's management team, Petra Schenke, had decided to move back to her native Germany in order to form her own Internet business, Dita.de. Schenke turned to Whittard for her first client, offering to set up an e-commerce site for the company. The site, Whittard .com, appeared to be an immediate success, with revenues growing by more than 300 percent in its first two years. Interestingly, more than 40 percent of the company's Internet-based sales came from the United States.

In the meantime, Whittard's retail growth appeared to have run out of steam. In 2000, the company began dismantling part of its retail network, shedding a number of stores, including its failed Kitchen concept. Instead, encouraged by the rapid growth of the Internet site, Whittard decided to base part of its future growth on reinventing itself as an online retailer. In 2000, the company took control of its site from Dita.de, and then made headlines when it paid £1.2 million to acquire an online "department store" dedicated to U.K.-made luxury goods, Bestofbritish.com.

The company's transition to the Internet initially appeared promising, especially after Bestofbritish announced that it had boosted the number of online brands to more than 70, including such prominent British names as Aston Martin, Jaguar, Duchy Originals, and Historic Royal Palaces. Yet the site remained a drain on the company's finances, costing more than £1.5 million per year—while revenues barely topped £300,000. Total com pany losses amounted to £3 million for the company's 2001 year. Nonetheless, the company's core tea and coffee sales remained healthy.

Refocused in the New Century

By September 2001, Whittard was forced to pull the plug on its Internet experiment. The company appeared uncertain as to how to proceed for the future, and announced that it had begun entertaining takeover offers, including a management buyout offer led by Richard Knight. Yet, unable to generate a suitable price, the company decided to remain independent. Following that decision, Knight left the company, replaced by Richard Rose, formerly CEO of Dutch electrical group Hagemeyer, as CEO. Hobhouse then retired to the position of company chairman.

Rose promptly began repositioning the company to focus once again on its core tea and coffee products. Among Rose's objectives was to expand the Whittard brand beyond its own retail store network and introduce its packaged products into the United Kingdom's supermarkets. By 2002, the company already had signed up two of the country's largest chains, Tesco and Sainsbury.

At the same time, the company's Internet experiment had alerted the company to its popularity in the United States, and Whittard now formed a partnership with Minneapolis-based department store group Marshall Field's to introduce Whittard corner stores. The first of these opened in Minneapolis in 2003 and proved to be a strong success, encouraging the company to expand its presence in the United States, particularly with the introduction of its own tea and coffee shops. By then, the company was buoyed by rising sales, which neared £37.5 million for the year, and a return to profit growth. Under Rose, Whittard appeared to have found the right brew to lead it into the new century.

Principal Competitors

Whitbread Plc; Starbucks Coffee Co. U.K. Ltd.; Holland and Barrett Retail Ltd.; Lyndale Foods Ltd.; Crookes Healthcare Ltd.; Bettys and Taylors Group Ltd.; Ringtons Holdings Ltd.; Longslow Dairy Ltd.

Further Reading

Aldrick, Philip, "Whittard Seeks Partner for American Tea Party," *Daily Telegraph,* January 18, 2001.

Croft, Jane, "Whittard Pays Pound 1.2m for Luxury Goods Website," *Financial Times,* July 8, 2000, p. 15.

Goff, Sharlene, "Back on Track After Turning Focus Back to Main Brews," *Financial Times,* June 28, 2003, p. 3.

Hopkins, Nic, "Whittard Profit Filters Through After Two Years," *Times,* September 13, 2002, p. 34.

Hyland, Anne, "Focus: Whittard," *Guardian,* February 2, 2000, p. 28.

Robertson, David, "Whittard to Target Starbucks with New Teashops in America," *Times,* September 6, 2003, p. 57.

—M.L. Cohen

Woodcraft Industries Inc.

525 Lincoln Avenue SE St. Cloud, MN 56304 USA *phone:* 320.252.1503 *fax:* 320.252.1504

525 Lincoln Ave. SE
St. Cloud, Minnesota, 56304
U.S.A.
Telephone: (320) 252-1503
Fax: (320) 252-1504
Web site: http://www.woodcraftind.com

Private Company
Incorporated: 1945 as Woodcraft Company
Employees: 1,300
Sales: $104.6 million (2002)
NAIC: 423310 Lumber, Plywood, Millwork and Wood Panel Merchant Wholesalers

Woodcraft Industries Inc., founded in 1945, is one of the country's premier manufacturers of hardwood volume and laminated componentry. The company designs and produces kitchen and bath cabinetry, drawers, and architectural millwork trim and molding among other wood components for residential, office, and institutional furniture. Producing products through three divisional entities—Woodcraft, PrimeWood, Inc., and Brentwood Corporation—the company maintains six production facilities in four states with over 600,000 square feet of manufacturing space and approximately 1,300 employees nationwide.

Old World Craftsmanship in the Heart of Minnesota

A wave of immigration from Germany in the late 19th and early 20th century brought many talented old world craftsmen to newly established towns on the central Minnesota frontier. As families continued to bring over relatives to established farms and businesses, the population grew and with growth came the need for more businesses, churches, schools, and homes.

Two German cabinet makers, Paul Dlugosch and Theodore Ritsche, opened a retail shop named the Woodcraft Company in St. Cloud, Minnesota, in 1945. They began with five employees and set their sights on producing cabinets and fixtures for the expanding St. Cloud neighborhood establishments.

The company began building furnishings for bars, restaurants, and retail stores. In 1947, a St. Cloud appliance manufacturer, Franklin Manufacturing, turned to the Woodcraft Company to produce its wooden shipping containers. Shipping containers remained a part of Woodcraft's product line until the 1970s.

In 1955, Woodcraft started its Builders Products business. Home cabinetry followed and the business began the slow and steady growth that marked its early years. In 1957, the company expanded its production facility, adding a finishing room and a second level shop. Two years later, fire destroyed the original plant and the company rebuilt at a secondary location. The same year Woodcraft rebuilt the shop in its original building, and increased its cabinet operation. The company employed 100 people, making it one of the largest employers in the area.

Looking for future markets, Woodcraft in 1962 began manufacturing a commercial line of cabinetry to be used in schools. The company manufactured items for use in churches as well, creating a line of church pews and church furniture in the 1960s.

Minnesota was the land of 10,000 lakes and with lakes in abundance the manufacture and use of recreational watercraft was a natural part of the regional economy. In the mid-1960s Woodcraft joined in the local boat-building trade and began creating wooden boat parts. However, the timeliness of wooden boat production was questionable. For centuries wood and steel were the only materials used for boats but with plastics and newly engineered materials being manufactured, wood lost its place in the maritime industry. Wooden boats and wooden parts were soon replaced by fiberglass and other synthetic components and Woodcraft's boat part manufacturing was short-lived.

The company also discontinued its cabinet and fixture business in 1964, and concentrated on expanding its Builders Products line. The same year, Woodcraft created a wood products line known as hardwood dimensions.

1960s and Beyond, Developing a Niche

In 1968, cofounder Theodore Ritsche's son, Tom Ritsche, bought the company and began a strategic planning process which led to a restructuring within the company. Ritsche di-

Company Perspectives:

The passing of time in the wood industry brings with it not only an increased wisdom and passion of our trade, but a further appreciation of our world's greatest natural resource—trees. Producing the broadest line of fine hardwoods and laminated componentry in the industry, Woodcraft Industries is committed to providing excellence in manufacturing and conservation of resources while supplying our customers with on-time, superior products and service.

vided the company into formal divisions, forming Builders Products and Industrial Manufacturing.

The 1970s were a time of consolidation and acquisition for the company. In 1975, Woodcraft discontinued its crating business and phased out its retail operation. The company expanded its hardwood dimensions line and its Builders Products division. At this time there were approximately 90 people working for the company.

Toward the end of the decade, Woodcraft looked for ways to expand its business through acquisition. In 1978, it purchased Weikert Brothers Millwork in Foreston, Minnesota, and in 1979 it bought D & M supply in Fargo, North Dakota.

Woodcraft continued to operate both the Fargo plant and its millwork plant in Foreston until the 1980s. In 1982, the company consolidated its operations and moved the Fargo works to St. Cloud. A 1983 merger between the Foreston Dimension Company and the Woodcraft Company resulted in the name change to Woodcraft Industries Inc.

The focus of the company had also taken a shift. Previously, Woodcraft's Builders Products division had made up a large percentage of the company's interests. In 1983, the decision was made to sell off its Builders Products division to Trimpac, Incorporated and to focus on the company's machined hardwood components.

The mid-1980s brought the company measured success in its cabinet component and product package work. Woodcraft spent its resources developing its Foreston, Minnesota operation and invested in the town of Foreston as well. The company built the city of Foreston a water tower in 1985 and officially donated it to the city the following year. In 1986, Woodcraft built an addition to its Foreston facility and streamlined production by consolidating its rough mill and machine room at the plant.

In 1989, Woodcraft Industries began expanding its markets, diversifying product lines to strongly include the furniture industry. The company also looked overseas to markets in Europe and began exporting goods to established European manufacturers.

New product development resulted in Woodcraft starting production of door assemblies. The company added on to its St. Cloud rough mill and employed approximately 340 people at its two Minnesota sites.

The 1990s brought a renewed focus on cabinet doors and in 1992 Woodcraft built a plant devoted to its cabinet works and expanded its workforce to 500 employees. The Foreston, Minnesota operation gained 50,000 board feet of drying space in 1993, increasing its production capabilities significantly. In 1994, the cabinet production plant had proved successful and a 14,000-square-foot expansion was added to the facility.

The company celebrated its 50th anniversary in 1995 and had grown substantially over the years from its meager beginning as a retail woodworking shop with five employees. The company now had over 700 workers at its two established plants and the company had just launched a third facility in Bowling Green, Kentucky. Woodcraft had been looking for a source for more timber and found it in the lush hill area of Kentucky. The Bowling Green facility was set up to process lumber that could then be shipped to Minnesota for finishing.

1990s and 2000s: Capital Investment

With a fair amount of growth already and good indicators for the future, Woodcraft was bought out by a group of Minneapolis, Minnesota-based leveraged buyout specialists, Goldner, Hawn, Johnson & Morrison Inc. Goldner, Hawn controlled seven large companies mostly within the state of Minnesota. Mike Goldner explained in a March 1996 article in the *Minneapolis Star Tribune* the company philosophy on takeovers: ''Mind you we're not talking the kind of hostile takeovers that stained the reputation of the LBO business during the 1980s. We're not in the business of taking over a company and busting it up for a quicky profit, instead the aim is to find mid-sized companies with solid market positions, experienced management and strong growth potential, then to provide the resources over a five- to seven-year period to help achieve that growth.''

In 1998, with investment capital behind it, Woodcraft Industries set its sights on PrimeWood, Incorporated. PrimeWood was founded by Ed Shorma in Wahpeton, North Dakota, in 1981. The company manufactured veneer raised panels for cabinetry and was named the fastest-growing company in its industry in 1990. With over 600 employees in 1993 and over 200,000 square feet of production space, PrimeWood had established itself as an industry leader, especially regarding its work in melamine laminating.

PrimeWood also controlled a wholly owned subsidiary by the name of Prime Wood Transportation Services, Inc. Woodcraft eventually sold off the transportation company in 1999 to Three Rivers Transport for an undisclosed amount.

PrimeWood was an industry leader in product development, and made use of an innovative technology first developed for the aerospace and automotive industry in the production of its Rigid Thermo Foil (RTF) product line. RTF used a PVC film that could be colored or pressed in unlimited designs. With extremely good durability and the possibility of countless applications, RTF production in the cabinet industry allowed the company to greatly expand its product offerings.

With the acquisition of PrimeWood, Woodcraft Industries employees now numbered 1,550. The development of its company continued throughout the late 1990s and into the next decade with a marked expansion of its facilities and the purchase of another company.

Key Dates:

1945: Woodcraft Company begins as a custom cabinet shop with five employees.
1947: Woodcraft doubles its facilities and begins manufacturing shipping crates.
1962: With over 100 employees, Woodcraft is now producing commercial cabinets for schools, and also making church pews, furniture, and boat parts.
1964: Woodcraft redirects business by expanding its Builders Products division and discontinuing its cabinet and fixtures work.
1968: Tom Ritsche buys Woodcraft.
1983: Woodcraft sells its Builders Products division to Trimpac and focuses on its machined hardwood components.
1996: Woodcraft is bought out by Goldner, Hawn, Johnson & Morrison.
1998: Woodcraft acquires North Dakota-based PrimeWood.
2002: Woodcraft acquires Brentwood Corporation.
2003: Behrman Capital purchases Woodcraft.

The company added machining capabilities to its Kentucky plant in 2002. Woodcraft also added a spray/dehumidification tunnel at its PrimeWood facility in Wahpeton. By far the biggest move in the calendar year was the purchase of Brentwood Corporation of Molalla, Oregon, in July.

Brentwood helped Woodcraft gain a foothold in the West. The company, organized in 1978 by Bud Gabriel, was initially named Homestead Cabinet and Furniture, Inc. It produced custom hardwood and rigid thermo-foil doors. Gabriel had moved his business to Molalla, Oregon, in 1994 and renamed the enterprise Brentwood Corporation.

Keeping true to its investment philosophy of buying, developing, and selling off its holdings in five to seven years, Goldner, Hawn sold off Woodcraft in 2003. In May 2003, Behrman Capital, a private investment firm headquartered in New York City and San Francisco, acquired Woodcraft and its wholly owned subsidiaries. According to an article in *Wood & Wood Products*, a trade industry publication, John Fitzpatrick, president and CEO of Woodcraft, commented on the acquisition: ''Behrman Capital has an established record of working with companies to support their growth and expansion. With Behrman's support, we will continue to expand our product development programs with the objective of further increasing our market share and pursuing opportunities for additional growth.''

With its strong production capabilities and developed market base and with the backing of Behrman Capital, Woodcraft Industries appeared well prepared for expansion in the coming years. Homebuilding and renovation were at record highs. The company was poised to capitalize on consumer trends by utilizing new technology developed for the cabinet and hardwood component industry.

Principal Divisions

Brentwood Corporation; PrimeWood, Inc.

Principal Competitors

Colonial Craft, Inc.; Cutting Edge Components; Great Lakes Wood Products; Pacific Vermillion; Northland Forest Products, Inc.; St. Croix Valley Hardwoods, Inc.; Superior Dimension & Doors, LLC.

Further Reading

''Behrman Capital Acquires Woodcraft Industries, Inc., in $145 Million Transaction,'' *Business Wire*, April 9, 2003.
Derning, Sean, ''Woodcraft Optimizes Rough Mill Productivity,'' *Wood & Wood Products*, October 1993, p. 87.
MacFadyen, Ken, ''Behrman Tackles Two Deals in One Week,'' *Buyouts*, April 28, 2003.
Pease, David A., ''Plant Tour Participants See Secondary Facilities,'' *Wood Technology*, January-February 1996, p. 21.
——, ''Rough Mill Situated in Hardwood Country,'' *Wood Technology*, May 1996, p. 20.
''Woodcraft Industries Buys Brentwood,'' *Wood and Wood Products*, October 2002, p. 16.
Youngblood, Dick, ''Goldner Hawn Helps Mid-Sized Firms Grow,'' *Star Tribune*, March 25, 1996, p. 2D.

—Susan B. Culligan

Wright Medical Group, Inc.

5677 Airline Road
Arlington, Tennessee 38002
U.S.A.
Telephone: (901) 867-9971
Toll Free: (800) 238-7117
Fax: (901) 867-9534
Web site: http://www.wmt.com

Public Company
Incorporated: 1950 as Wright Manufacturing Company
Employees: 797
Sales: $200.87 million (2002)
Stock Exchanges: NASDAQ
Ticker Symbol: WMGI
NAIC: 339113 Surgical Appliance and Supplies Manufacturing

Wright Medical Group, Inc. designs, manufactures, and markets joint and bone reconstructive devices and technology, specializing in small joint extremities, and hip and knee replacement, as well as bioorthopedic bone regeneration. Small joint orthopedic implants are available for the hand, wrist, elbow, shoulder, foot, and ankle and include the Swanson Hinge Finger, used by surgeons for more than 30 years. Hip and knee reconstructive products apply to total hip or knee replacement, surgical revision replacement implants, and limb preservation. Wright medical devices are designed to replicate the natural motion of the body and to provide stability; the company offers implant parts in a variety of shapes and sizes so that surgeons can fit the reconstructed joint to individual patient anatomy. Wright's bioorthopedic System of Choices is designed to facilitate the body's natural process of bone regeneration through the application of calcium sulfate and other biological materials to bone gaps and fractures in a variety of situations. The company offers surgical instruments for implementation of its devices and bioorthopedic products. Wright promotes worldwide sales and distribution of its products through offices in Europe, Australia, Canada, and Japan, as well as through stocking distribution partners in Europe, Asia, Africa, South America, and Australia.

Founding Innovation and First Successes

While working as a sales representative for an orthopedic products company, Frank O. Wright discovered that people in leg casts suffered from chronic back pain caused by walking on a hard steel heel in the foot of the cast. Wright conceived the idea of a rubber heel to provide a softer impact while walking, easing discomfort, and started Wright Manufacturing in 1950 to manufacture and market the "street heel." Succeeding in this endeavor, Wright expanded the company's product line to include medical soft goods, surgical instruments, and hip and knee implants.

In 1970 the company began to manufacture its most important product, the Swanson Finger. The prosthesis consisted of a one-piece silicone rubber implant with a flexible hinge. The artificial joint embedded easily because the tensile strength of tendons held the implant naturally, with only a hole bored into each end joint. Products for reconstruction of small joints in the hands, feet, and wrists followed, and the company became a world leader in small joint orthopedics.

In 1977, two years after the death of Frank Wright, Dow Corning purchased Wright Manufacturing and changed the name to Dow Corning Wright. Dow Corning's expert knowledge in silicone complemented Wright's capabilities in orthopedics as the company continued to improve and develop joint replacement products. In 1986 the company formed a plastic surgery division to produce and market a breast implant based on new technology. The Micro-Structured Implant retained its softness due to tiny pillars on the surface that prevented contracture or hardening. Questions over the safety of silicone gel breast implants led to liability lawsuits and a ban for most uses by the U.S. Food and Drug Administration, however. Dow Corning Wright halted production in 1992.

In 1990 Dow Corning Wright introduced an innovative artificial knee implant, the Whiteside Modular Knee, named for its inventor, Dr. Leo Whiteside. The product provided a finer replication of a kneecap through a system of replaceable parts that allowed orthopedic surgeons to construct the knee implant to meet the needs of individual patients. The Whiteside Modular Knee sold exceedingly well the first year and contributed signif-

Company Perspectives:

We are committed to improving the quality of life of orthopedic patients by providing our customers with the highest quality large joint, extremity, and biologic products. We will provide uncompromising service. We will foster the development of our human resources. We will operate our business ethically and in a manner beyond reproach. We will strive to benefit all who have a vested interest in our business.

icantly to a threefold increase in revenues experienced between 1985 and 1990. In addition, the Infinity hip implant, successfully introduced in 1991, worked in a manner similar to the artificial knee, in that the implant adjusted to different angles to fit the individual requirements of each patient. Dow Corning Wright expanded manufacturing facilities to meet demand for the two products.

1993: New Owners Taking the Company in New Directions

Liability related to silicone breast implants prompted Dow Corning Wright's parent to place the company up for sale. An investment group led by Herbert W. Korthoff acquired Dow Corning Wright in 1993 and gave the company a new name, Wright Medical Technology. (Liability for silicone breast implants stayed with Dow Corning.) Korthoff and Kidd Kamm Equity Partners paid $70.5 million. Korthoff, formerly executive vice-president at U.S. Surgical, Inc. during a remarkable expansion phase, became CEO and chairman of Wright Medical. He chose the company for acquisition because of the market potential of its excellent technology and management. At this time Wright Medical held 85 percent of the world market for small joint orthopedic implants and was one of the leading manufacturers of total hip and knee joint replacement. Korthoff's goals for the company involved doubling revenues to $150 million by 1998, then taking the company public.

One aspect of Korthoff's expansion plan involved strengthening international distribution, to become the only company able to offer a full line of orthopedic products to customers worldwide. The company already operated offices in Brazil, Australia, Hong Kong, and Canada and maintained distribution partnerships in 35 countries. In late 1993 Wright signed a distribution agreement with Kaneka Medix of Tokyo for the distribution of its products in Japan, and in February 1994 the company acquired Orthotechnique in Paris to strengthen distribution in France, Spain, Italy, Greece, and Portugal. The following September Korthoff diverted funds from sales and marketing toward international expansion, as well as engineering for development of spinal fixation devices. With international sales at 25 percent of revenues in 1994, Korthoff hoped to increase that amount to 40 percent by 1997.

While Korthoff envisioned Wright offering a full line of orthopedic products, this involved entering new product markets, specifically, for trauma products, spinal fixation devices, and arthroscopic imaging. The intended acquisition of Advanced Spinal Fixations Systems fell through; through an agreement with BioMed, Inc. in August 1994, however, Wright gained worldwide distribution rights for a minimally invasive spinal discectomy system. Development of the product accelerated after the agreement, putting Wright at the leading edge of that product area.

Another area of interest involved bioorthopedics, biological treatments that facilitate the body's natural healing process. A license agreement with U.S. Gypsum gave Wright worldwide distribution (except to the dental market) of a moldable bone void filler and drug delivery system called calcium sulfate hemihydrated. The product assisted in bone regeneration after part of the bone was removed due to cancer or a bone infection.

Wright expanded in the implant market through a merger with Orthomet, Inc., designer, manufacturer, and marketer of orthopedic products and reconstructive implants. The stock exchange, valued at $59.7 million, occurred through a tender offer completed in December 1994. Through the merger Wright gained rights to a license agreement for finger-joint implant development with the May Foundation for Medical Education and Research. Orthomet reported 1994 sales of $27 million and Wright reported sales of $95.8 million, a 12 percent increase over 1993. Wright recorded a net loss of $49.3 million, due to write-offs related to acquisitions.

1995–97: New Products and Product Markets

During the mid-1990s Wright expanded with a variety of new products and entered several markets for the first time. A license agreement signed in early 1995 facilitated Wright's entry into the trauma and spinal systems markets. In February the company gained the right to exclusive marketing and distribution of Medoff Sliding Plate, a new compression hip screw system used in the treatment of hip fractures. Distribution areas included the United States, Canada, and Central America, with the possibility for access to the global market. Wright added to its line of spinal systems when the company obtained distribution rights for the Single Portal Arthroscopic Lumbar Discectomy System along with an integrated video system. The system provided a minimally invasive, visual method of relieving neural compression and its painful effects, assisting healing and recovery.

Wright introduced its own spinal fixation products as well. In August the WRIGHTLOCK Spinal Fixation System received Food and Drug Administration (FDA) approval for sale of the product. WRIGHTLOCK's dual rod system featured implants and an implantation method that replaced the "nut and screw" fixation method with an easier surgical procedure. The FDA approved the product for use in cases of scoliosis, trauma, tumor, and degenerative disc disease.

Wright improved on its line of joint replacement implants with the introduction of a more durable material in the manufacture of orthopedic implant components, addressing problems of wear in polyethylene implants that began with the oxidative effects of gamma radiation sterilization. The superior quality of DURAMER Ultra High Molecular Weight Polyethylene involved sterilization with ethylene oxide (EtO) gas, which did not affect product quality. Wright improved the supply of raw material and the manufacturing process as well.

New products in the area of joint and bone replacement included the total Segmented Orthopedic System for recon-

Key Dates:

1950: Company is founded to market its rubber heel product.
1970: Wright Manufacturing begins marketing the Swanson Finger implant.
1977: Dow Corning acquires Wright Manufacturing two years after the founder's death.
1986: Dow Corning Wright forms a plastic surgery division to manufacture and market new silicone breast implant technology.
1990: A breakthrough in knee replacement, the Whiteside Modular Knee, is introduced.
1993: A group of investors acquires the company, which is renamed Wright Medical Technology.
1996: The Food and Drug Administration approves OsteoSet, a biological bone graft substitute.
1999: New owners and management focus the reincorporated Wright Medical Group on core markets.
2001: New products result in significant sales in extremity repair and bioorthopaedic markets.
2002: Wright introduces REPIPHYSIS artificial limbs that can be lengthened electromagnetically as patients grow.

struction of the femoral (thigh) system. The products applied to severe bone loss and provided more flexibility in customizing prostheses more quickly during surgery and at less cost. For instance, CONCISE Compression Hip Screw System provided a new generation of trauma-related repair of proximal femur fractures.

In November 1995 Richard D. Nikolaev, formerly president of Orthomet, became CEO and president of the company, taking over daily management while Korthoff, as chairman, focused on long-term goals. Investment funds were received from California Public Employees Retirement System, at $60 million, and Princes Gate Investors LP, at $34 million. The company's 1995 sales of $123.2 million included $1.2 million from new products in trauma, arthroscopy, and spinal fixation products. A loss of $6.4 million was within the expected range.

Wright received FDA clearance for the sale of OsteoSet Bone Graft Substitute for use in bone voids and gaps in the extremities in August 1996. Introduced to the market in late 1996, OsteoSet provided an alternative to bone grafts through implantation of medical-grade calcium sulfate pellets onto the bone. The resorbable calcium sulfate facilitates the body's natural process of bone regeneration, and the pellets disappear in four to eight weeks as the bone repairs. This system of repair posed fewer risks than artificial substitutes or bone obtained from another part of the body or a bone bank as no diseases or viruses could be transferred. OsteoSet-T Medicated Bone Graft Substitute contained the antibiotic tobramycin to prevent and heal bone infections. In October Wright acquired the patents, technology, and process of producing OsteoSet from U.S. Gypsum.

Wright continued to develop next generation versions of its reconstructive implant systems. In December 1996 the company introduced the Total Sorbie-Questor Elbow System joint replacements that replicate natural anatomy and alignment for accurate joint movement, increasing stability and reducing the possibility of dislocation. In May 1997 Wright launched VERSALOK, a low back spinal fixation system providing an adaptable system for intraoperative flexibility and reversibility without set screws or locking nuts. In late 1998 Wright introduced ADVANCE Medial Pivot Knee System, which replicated the natural motion and range of motion of the knee with a unique spherical medial component.

1998: Returning to Original Markets and Expanding on Success in Bio-orthopedics

In early 1998 Wright made executive changes to lead the company in a new direction, focusing on the company's niche markets in small joint and extremity implants and its leading position in bioorthopedics. Korthoff's broad-based strategy of product development did not lead to a substantial increase in sales. In 1997 the company generated $122 million in sales, but spinal and arthroscopy operations accounted for only $2 million and $1.5 million in sales, respectively. The small scale of Wright's operations in those areas could not compete with Sofamor Danek, the market leader, so the revenue represented only a minimal return on investment.

Thomas Patton became CEO in January, after holding the position of executive vice-president of corporate development. Patton discontinued research and development in arthroscopy. The company restructured, eliminating some executive positions and cutting 150 jobs as the company sold the spinal and trauma product businesses.

Wright intensified its focus on bio-orthopedics based on two successful products, OsteoSet and OsteoSet-T. In May 1997 the FDA cleared OsteoSet for use in the spine and pelvis and OsteoSet-T received approval for sale in Canada, Australia, and Europe in 1998, but awaited approval by the FDA. Sales for OsteoSet increased 56 percent in 1998.

In September 1999, Warburg Pincus Equity Partners L.P. and the Vertical Group, Inc. acquired a majority interest in Wright Medical Technology, involving $25 million paid to reduce debt and provide working capital. The company refinanced $60 million in debt as well. The Warburg Pincus investment supported a merger with Cremascoli Ortho Group, of Toulon, France. Cremascoli's facilities included a manufacturing facility in Toulon and a research and development laboratory in Milan, Italy. Together Cremascoli and Wright provided a wide range of reconstructive joint devices, including Cremascoli's important products in hip reconstruction. The merger improved Wright's distribution in Europe, and Wright planned to distribute Cremascoli products in the United States, Japan, and other global markets.

Wright Medical Group, formed as the parent of the two companies, hired F. Barry Bays as president and CEO. Warburg Pincus transferred Bays from Medtronic Xomed, another medical technology company owned by the investor. With a team of executives brought from Medtronic, Bays revamped distribution, increased funding for research and development, and improved the company's sales force, including initiating direct sales in Japan. The company increased funding for research and development, emphasizing innovations for niche markets, such as the Conserve-Plus metal-on-metal hip prosthesis intended for younger patients, in their 40s. The product was designed to conserve bone by replacing only the surface of the femoral head, the ball in the pelvis's socket.

Niche Market Products Leading to Profitability: Early 2000s

Bioorthopedic bone grafting substitutes contributed significantly to the company's growth. As the product line developed, Wright marketed it as the System of Choices, with different products applied to various needs. In November 1999 the company introduced a product similar to OsteoSet, the AlloMatrix Injectable Putty, a bone graft substitute composed of medical grade calcium sulfate, demineralized bone matrix (DBM) growth factors, and a biocompatible plasticizing agent. The product delivered DBM growth factors for assisting the repair of bone fracture gaps and open defects, as well as an extender in spinal fusions.

After receiving feedback from orthopedic trauma and spine surgeons, Wright developed AlloMatrix C Bone Putty, composed of DBM and cancellous bone chips carried by calcium sulfate. Introduced in early 2001, the product provided more flexible use, such as mixing in the operating room and adding bone marrow aspirate of platelet concentrate taken from the patient's own body to facilitate healing. In October 2001 OsteoSet BVF (Bone Void Filler Kit) received FDA clearance for expanded claims, specifically, the injectability of the material and hardening properties inside the bone void or fracture site. MIIG 115 Minimally Invasive Injectable Graft provided OsteoSet in powdered form.

As several successful new products increased sales and profitability, Wright Medical Group pursued public ownership through an initial stock offering in July 2001. At $12.50 per share, the company sold 7.5 million shares, raising $84.8 million for debt repayment.

Other important new products involved advancements in treating extremities. The LOCON-T system, for the repair of radial fractures, used low-profile screws to prevent complications by minimizing irritation or rupture of tendons caused by screws. EVOLVE Modular Radial Head devices provided flexibility in fitting patient body size with a variety of head and stem sizes in two pieces rather than a single piece. These products, as well as new ankle and foot products, contributed to a 21 percent increase in sales of extremity products in 2001. Along with the OLYMPIA Total Shoulder System, extremity product sales increased another 21 percent in 2002.

The AlloMatrix line and OsteoSet BVF Kits were integral to a 28 percent increase in sales of bio-orthopedic products in 2001, while AlloMatrix, MIIG, and OsteoSet Resorbable Bead Kits supported a 43 percent sales increase in 2002. OsteoSet products generated high profit margins as well.

Wright became profitable in 2002 after several years of losses. Sales of just over $200 million generated $25.1 million in net profit, after losses of $1.5 million in 2001 and $39.5 million in 2000. In 2002 revenues from state-of-the-art knee and hip reconstructive devices offset a decline in sales of older products, though sales of knee systems increased slightly.

In December 2002 Wright received FDA clearance for REPIPHYSIS Technology. Already used in Europe for six years, the technology facilitated the lengthening of limb implants through periodic treatments of electromagnetic fields. REPIPHYSIS was designed for children and teenagers who would otherwise outgrow a bone replacement implant, usually received in the treatment of bone cancers. As the child grew, no further surgery would be required to replace an implant, something that could happen on a yearly basis. Through a "compassionate use" clause in FDA regulations, the technology had already been applied successfully to 13 patients over three years at St. Jude's Children's Research Hospital in Memphis.

As technology for hip and knee reconstruction had reached the point of natural motion replication, development shifted to long-term wear and reduction of revision procedures. Toward that end Wright developed an alumina ceramic-on-ceramic bearing for total hip replacement for use in the TRANSCEND Acetabular System. In February 2003 Wright received FDA clearance to market the bearing, one of only two companies approved to produce a ceramic-on-ceramic device.

In the field of bio-orthopedics, Wright acquired ADCON Gel technology, a patented, resorbable material that provides a barrier to fibroblasts responsible for causing scarring after surgery; the scars cause postoperative pain and hinder range of motion, often resulting in revision surgery. Wright also began to market CELLPLEX TCP Synthetic Cancellous Bone, a scaffold for the application of bone marrow aspirate to bone regeneration. CELLPLEX resorbed into the body as new bone was generated.

Principal Subsidiaries

Wright Medical Technology; Cremascoli Ortho Group.

Principal Competitors

Biomet, Inc.; DePuy, Inc.; Norian Corporation; Stryker Corporation; Zimmer Holdings, Inc.

Further Reading

"Arlington, Tenn.-Based Medical Group Reports Record Jump in 2001 Sales," *Knight Ridder/Tribune Business News,* February 12, 2002.

Borowsky, Mark, "Dow Corning Wright Knee Replacement Is Best-Seller," *Memphis Business Journal,* March 4, 1991, p. 1.

Flaum, David, "Tennessee-Based Wright Medical Technology Inc. Buys Material for Bone Graft," *Knight Ridder/Tribune Business News,* October 8, 1996.

"Medical Device Maker Braves IPO Market," *Corporate Financing Week,* July 23, 2001, p. 6.

Roman, Leigh Ann, "Wright Medical Shifts Focus Under New CEO," *Memphis Business Journal,* February 25, 1998, p. 1.

——, "Wright Medical Trims Down," *Memphis Business Journal,* February 12, 1999, p. 3.

Sewel, Tim, "Dow Corning Wright's New Owner Charting Future Course for Manufacturing Firm," *Memphis Business Journal,* June 7, 1993, p. 32.

——, "Wright Medical Moves Toward International Market," *Memphis Business Journal,* September 5, 1994, p. 3.

Shepard, Scott, ''The Sky's the Limit for New Wright Medical CEO,'' *Memphis Business Journal,* July 26, 1993, p. 11.
——, ''Wright Medical May See Last Year on List As IPO Looms In,'' *Memphis Business Journal,* June 8, 2001, p. 18A.
——, ''Wright Medical Shifts Focus, Hikes Profits,'' *Memphis Business Journal,* June 23, 2000, p. 3.
Van Valkenburgh, Joan, ''Tennessee's Wright Medical Technology Inc. Releases Bone Graft Substitute,'' *Knight Ridder/Tribune Business News,* August 22, 1996.
''Wright Medical Group Inc. Arlington, Tennessee; Turnaround Effort Heals Medical Gear Maker,'' *Investor's Business Daily,* September 26, 2002, p. A7.
''Wright Offers Less-Expensive Alternative to Custom Femoral Implants,'' *Health Industry Today,* August 1995, p. 3.
''Youth's Artificial Arm Will Grow with Him,'' *Washington Post,* September 3, 2003.

—Mary Tradii

INDEX TO COMPANIES

Index to Companies

Listings in this index are arranged in alphabetical order under the company name. Company names beginning with a letter or proper name such as Eli Lilly & Co. will be found under the first letter of the company name. Definite articles (The, Le, La) are ignored for alphabetical purposes as are forms of incorporation that precede the company name (AB, NV). Company names printed in bold type have full, historical essays on the page numbers appearing in bold. Updates to entries that appeared in earlier volumes are signified by the notation **(upd.)**. Company names in light type are references within an essay to that company, not full historical essays. This index is cumulative with volume numbers printed in bold type.

INDEX TO INDUSTRIES

Index to Industries

ACCOUNTING

ADVERTISING & OTHER BUSINESS SERVICES

ADVERTISING & OTHER BUSINESS SERVICES *(continued)*

AEROSPACE

AIRLINES

AUTOMOTIVE

AUTOMOTIVE *(continued)*

BEVERAGES

BIOTECHNOLOGY

CHEMICALS

CONGLOMERATES

CONGLOMERATES *(continued)*

CONSTRUCTION

CONTAINERS

DRUGS/PHARMACEUTICALS

DRUGS/PHARMACEUTICALS *(continued)*

ELECTRICAL & ELECTRONICS

ENGINEERING & MANAGEMENT SERVICES

ENGINEERING & MANAGEMENT SERVICES *(continued)*

ENTERTAINMENT & LEISURE

FINANCIAL SERVICES: BANKS

FINANCIAL SERVICES: BANKS *(continued)*

FINANCIAL SERVICES: NON-BANKS

FOOD PRODUCTS

FOOD PRODUCTS *(continued)*

FOOD SERVICES & RETAILERS

FOOD SERVICES & RETAILERS *(continued)*

HEALTH & PERSONAL CARE PRODUCTS

INFORMATION TECHNOLOGY *(continued)*

INSURANCE

LEGAL SERVICES

MANUFACTURING

MANUFACTURING *(continued)*

MANUFACTURING *(continued)*

MANUFACTURING *(continued)*

MATERIALS

MINING & METALS

MINING & METALS *(continued)*

PAPER & FORESTRY

PERSONAL SERVICES

PETROLEUM

PUBLISHING & PRINTING

PUBLISHING & PRINTING *(continued)*

REAL ESTATE

RETAIL & WHOLESALE

RETAIL & WHOLESALE *(continued)*

RETAIL & WHOLESALE *(continued)*

RUBBER & TIRE

TELECOMMUNICATIONS

TELECOMMUNICATIONS *(continued)*

TEXTILES & APPAREL

TOBACCO

TRANSPORT SERVICES

TRANSPORT SERVICES *(continued)*

UTILITIES

WASTE SERVICES

GEOGRAPHIC INDEX

Geographic Index

Ghana

Greece

Hong Kong

Hungary

Iceland

India

Indonesia

Iran

Ireland

Israel

Italy

Jamaica

Japan

Kuwait

Libya

Liechtenstein

Luxembourg

Malaysia

Mexico

Nepal

Netherlands

New Zealand

Nigeria

Norway

Oman

Pakistan

Panama

Peru

Philippines

Poland

Portugal

Puerto Rico

Qatar

Russia

Saudi Arabia

Scotland

Singapore

South Africa

South Korea

Spain

Sweden

Switzerland

Taiwan

Thailand

Tunisia

Turkey

Ukraine

United Arab Emirates

United Kingdom

United States *(continued)*

United States *(continued)*

United States *(continued)*

United States *(continued)*

United States *(continued)*

United States *(continued)*

Venezuela

Vietnam

Virgin Islands

Wales

Zambia

NOTES ON CONTRIBUTORS

Notes on Contributors

BIANCO, David P. Writer, editor, and publishing consultant.

BROWN, Erin. Montana-based writer and researcher.

COHEN, M. L. Novelist and researcher living in Paris.

COVELL, Jeffrey L. Seattle-based writer.

CULLIGAN, Susan B. Minnesota-based writer.

DINGER, Ed. Writer and editor based in Bronx, New York.

FUJINAKA, Mariko. Writer and editor living in California.

HALASZ, Robert. Former editor in chief of *World Progress and Funk & Wagnalls New Encyclopedia Yearbook*; author, *The U.S. Marines* (Millbrook Press, 1993).

INGRAM, Frederick C. Utah-based business writer who has contributed to *GSA Business, Appalachian Trailway News,* the *Encyclopedia of Business,* the *Encyclopedia of Global Industries,* the *Encyclopedia of Consumer Brands,* and other regional and trade publications.

LORENZ, Sarah Ruth. Minnesota-based writer.

MANCINI, Candice. Researcher and writer.

PEIPPO, Kathleen. Minneapolis-based writer.

RHODES, Nelson. Editor, writer, and consultant in the Chicago area.

ROTHBURD, Carrie. Writer and editor specializing in corporate profiles, academic texts, and academic journal articles.

SALAMIE, David E. Part-owner of InfoWorks Development Group, a reference publication development and editorial services company.

TRADII, Mary. Writer based in Denver, Colorado.

UHLE, Frank. Ann-Arbor-based writer, movie projectionist, disk jockey, and staff member of *Psychotronic Video* magazine.

WOODWARD, A. Wisconsin-based writer.